Ordnance Survey

STREET ATLAS
Birmingham
and West Midlands

Contents

III *Key to map symbols*

IV-V *Key to map pages*

VI-VII *Route planning*

VIII *Administrative and post code boundaries*

1 *Street maps*

163 *Extra-large-scale maps of town centres*

> **163** *Wolverhampton*
> **164** *Birmingham*
> **165** *Coventry*

166 *Index of hospitals, railway stations, schools, shopping centres, street names and universities*

PHILIP'S

First colour edition published 1998 by

Ordnance Survey®   and George Philip Ltd
Romsey Road   an imprint of Reed Consumer Books Ltd
Maybush   Michelin House, 81 Fulham Road,
Southampton   London SW3 6RB
SO16 4GU   and Auckland and Melbourne

ISBN 0-540-07603 1 (hardback)
ISBN 0-540-07604 X (spiral)

To the best of the Publishers' knowledge, the information in this
atlas was correct at the time of going to press. No responsibility
can be accepted for any errors or their consequences.

The representation in this atlas of a road, track or path is no
evidence of the existence of a right of way.

**The mapping between pages 1 and 165 (inclusive) in this atlas
is derived from Ordnance Survey® OSCAR® and Land-Line® data
and Landranger® mapping.**

Ordnance Survey, OSCAR, Land-line and Landranger are registered
trade marks of Ordnance Survey, the national mapping agency of
Great Britain.

Printed and bound in Spain by Cayfosa

Digital Data

The exceptionally high-quality mapping
found in this book is available as digital
data in TIFF format, which is easily
convertible to other bit-mapped (raster)
image formats.

The index is also available in digital form
as a standard database table. It contains
all the details found in the printed index
together with the National Grid reference
for the map square in which each entry
is named and feature codes for places
of interest in eight categories such as
education and health.

For further information and to discuss
your requirements, please contact the
Ordnance Survey Solutions Centre on
01703 792929.

Motorway (with junction number)	(22a)
Primary route (dual carriageway and single)	
A road (dual carriageway and single)	
B road (dual carriageway and single)	
Minor road (dual carriageway and single)	
Other minor road	
Road under construction	
Pedestrianised area	
Post code boundaries	DY7
County and Unitary Authority boundaries	
Railway	
Tramway, miniature railway	
Rural track, private road or narrow road in urban area	
Gate or obstruction to traffic (restrictions may not apply at all times or to all vehicles)	
Path, bridleway, byway open to all traffic, road used as a public path	
The representation in this atlas of a road, track or path is no evidence of the existence of a right of way	

126
94
164

Adjoining page indicators

The map area within the pink band is shown at a larger scale on the page indicated by the red block and arrow

Acad	**Academy**	Meml	**Memorial**
Crem	**Crematorium**	Mon	**Monument**
Cemy	**Cemetery**	Mus	**Museum**
C Ctr	**Civic Centre**	Obsy	**Observatory**
CH	**Club House**	Pal	**Royal Palace**
Coll	**College**	PH	**Public House**
Ent	**Enterprise**	Recn Gd	**Recreation Ground**
Ex H	**Exhibition Hall**	Resr	**Reservoir**
Ind Est	**Industrial Estate**	Ret Pk	**Retail Park**
Inst	**Institute**	Sch	**School**
Ct	**Law Court**	Sh Ctr	**Shopping Centre**
L Ctr	**Leisure Centre**	TH	**Town Hall/House**
LC	**Level Crossing**	Trad Est	**Trading Estate**
Liby	**Library**	Univ	**University**
Mkt	**Market**	YH	**Youth Hostel**

British Rail station Walsall	
Midland Metro	
Metrolink station (M)	
Underground station	
Docklands Light Railway station D	
Tyne and Wear Metro M	
Private railway station	
Bus, coach station	
Ambulance station	
Coastguard station	
Fire station	
Police station	
Accident and Emergency entrance to hospital	
Hospital H	
Church, place of worship	
Information centre (open all year)	
Parking, Park and Ride P P&R	
Post Office PO PO	
Important buildings, schools, colleges, universities and hospitals Prim Sch	
Water name River Medway	
Stream	
River or canal (minor and major)	
Water	
Tidal water	
Woods	
Houses	
Non-Roman antiquity House	
Roman antiquity VILLA	

■ The dark grey border on the inside edge of some pages indicates that the mapping does not continue onto the adjacent page ■ The small numbers around the edges of the maps identify the 1 kilometre National Grid lines

The scale of the maps is 5.52 cm to 1 km (3½ inches to 1 mile)

0	¼	½	¾	1 mile
0	250m	500m	750m	1 kilometre

The scale of the map on pages numbered in red is 11.04 cm to 1 km (7 inches to 1 mile)

0	220 yards	440 yards	660 yards	½ mile
0	125m	250m	375m	½ kilometre

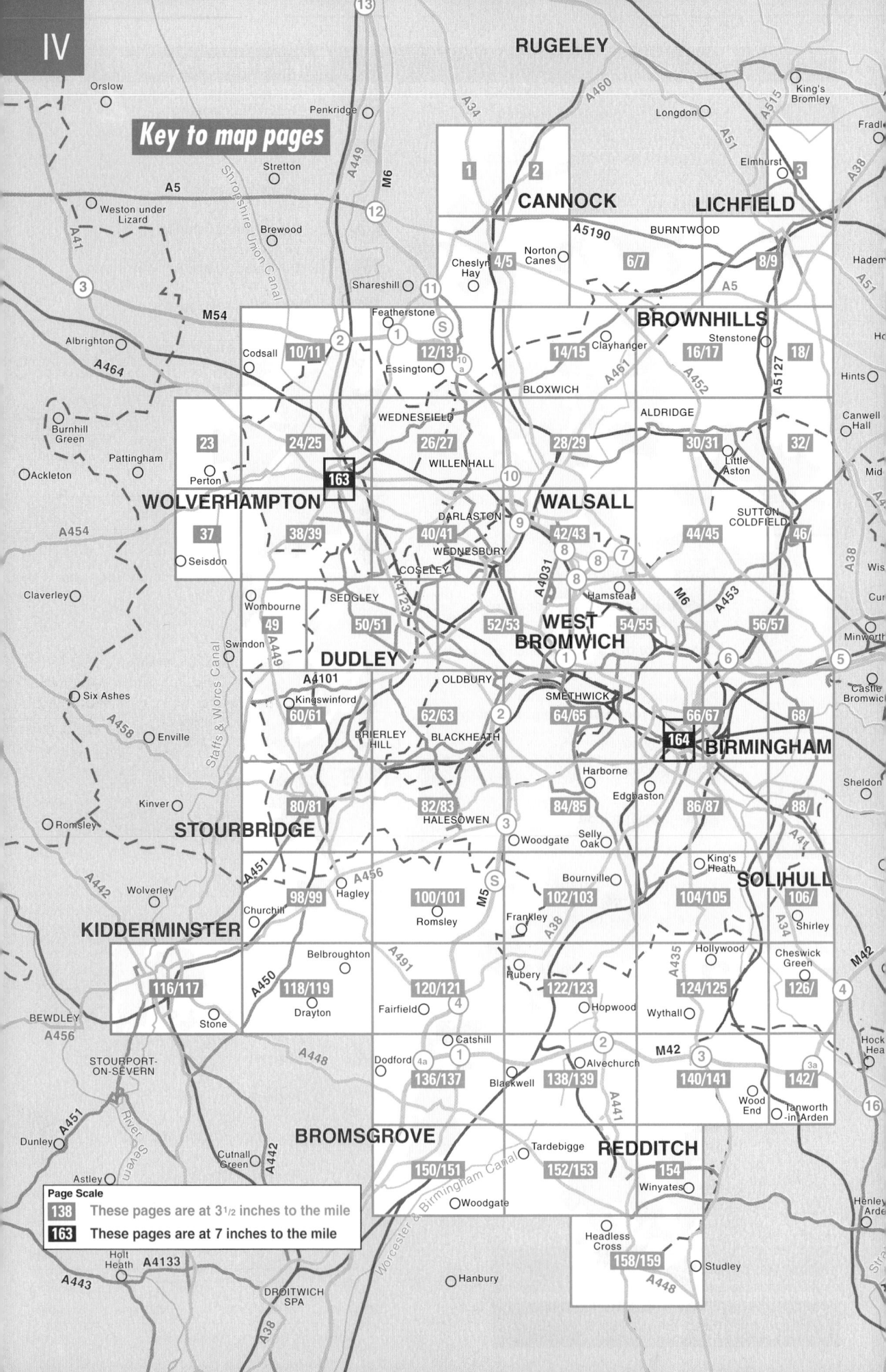

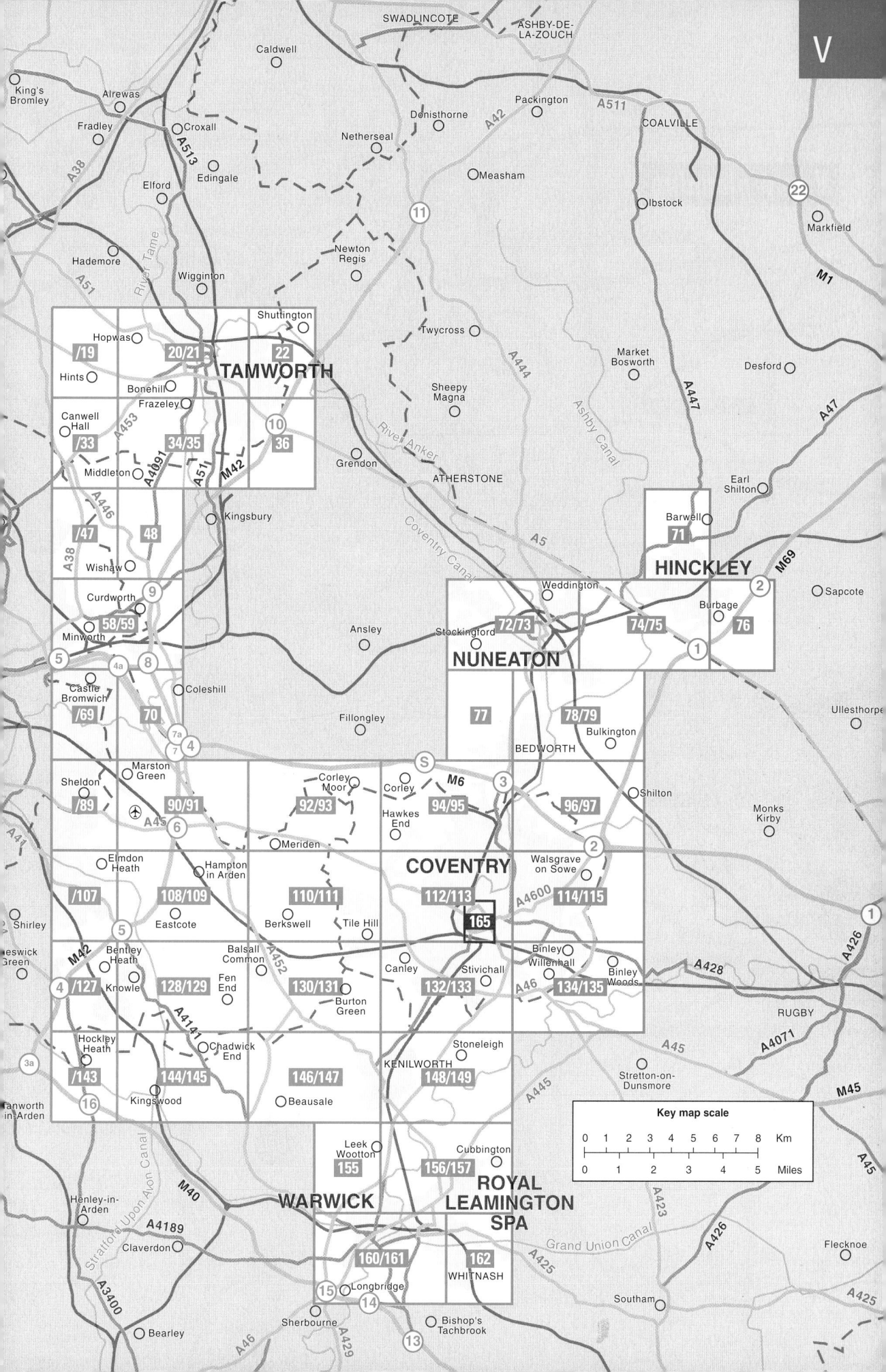

Route planning

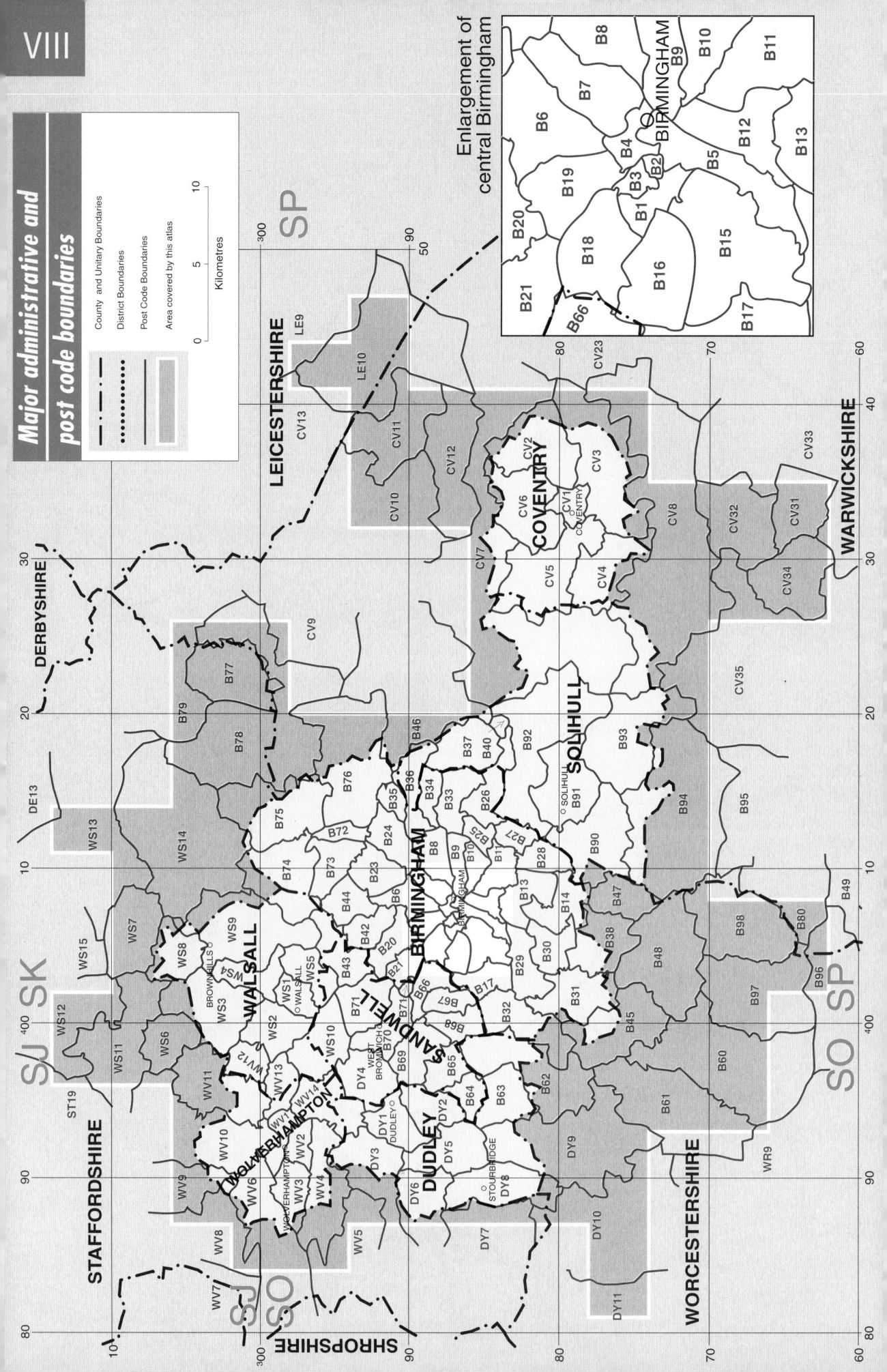

Major administrative and post code boundaries

County and Unitary Boundaries
District Boundaries
Post Code Boundaries
Area covered by this atlas

Kilometres

0   5   10

Enlargement of central Birmingham

B8
B9
B10
B11
B7
BIRMINGHAM
B6
B4
B12
B13
B2
B5
B19
B3
B1
B20
B18
B16
B15
B21
B66
B17

STAFFORDSHIRE
DERBYSHIRE
LEICESTERSHIRE
WARWICKSHIRE
WORCESTERSHIRE
SHROPSHIRE

SJ SK
SP
SO SP
SO
SJ SO

BIRMINGHAM
WOLVERHAMPTON
WALSALL
SANDWELL
DUDLEY
SOLIHULL
COVENTRY

LE9
LE10
CV13
CV11
CV12
CV10
CV9
CV7
CV6
CV1 COVENTRY
CV3
CV23
CV8
CV5
CV4
CV33
CV32
CV31
CV34
CV35
CV2

DE13
WS13
WS14
B79
B78
B77
B76
B75
B72
B74
B73
B23
B24
B35
B36
B34
B33
B46
B37
B40
B92
B93
B94
B95
B26
B25
B21
B27
B28
B90
B91
B43
B44
B42
B20
B21
B6
B9
B8
B10
B13
B14
B29
B30
B38
B47
B48
B31
B45
B60
B61
B62
B63
B64
B65
B69
B70
B71
B68
B67
B66
B17
B32
B98
B80
B96
B97
B49

WS15
WS7
WS8
WS9
WS4
WS5
WS1
WS2
WS3
WS10
WS12
WS11
WS6

ST19
WV11
WV1
WV12
WV13
WV14
WV10
WV9
WV8
WV6
WV3
WV2
WV4
WV5
WV7

DY1
DY2
DY3
DY4
DY5
DY6
DY7
DY8
DY9
DY10
DY11

WR9

BROWNHILLS
WALSALL
WEST BROMWICH
DUDLEY
STOURBRIDGE
SOLIHULL

300
90
50
80
70
60
400
10
20
30

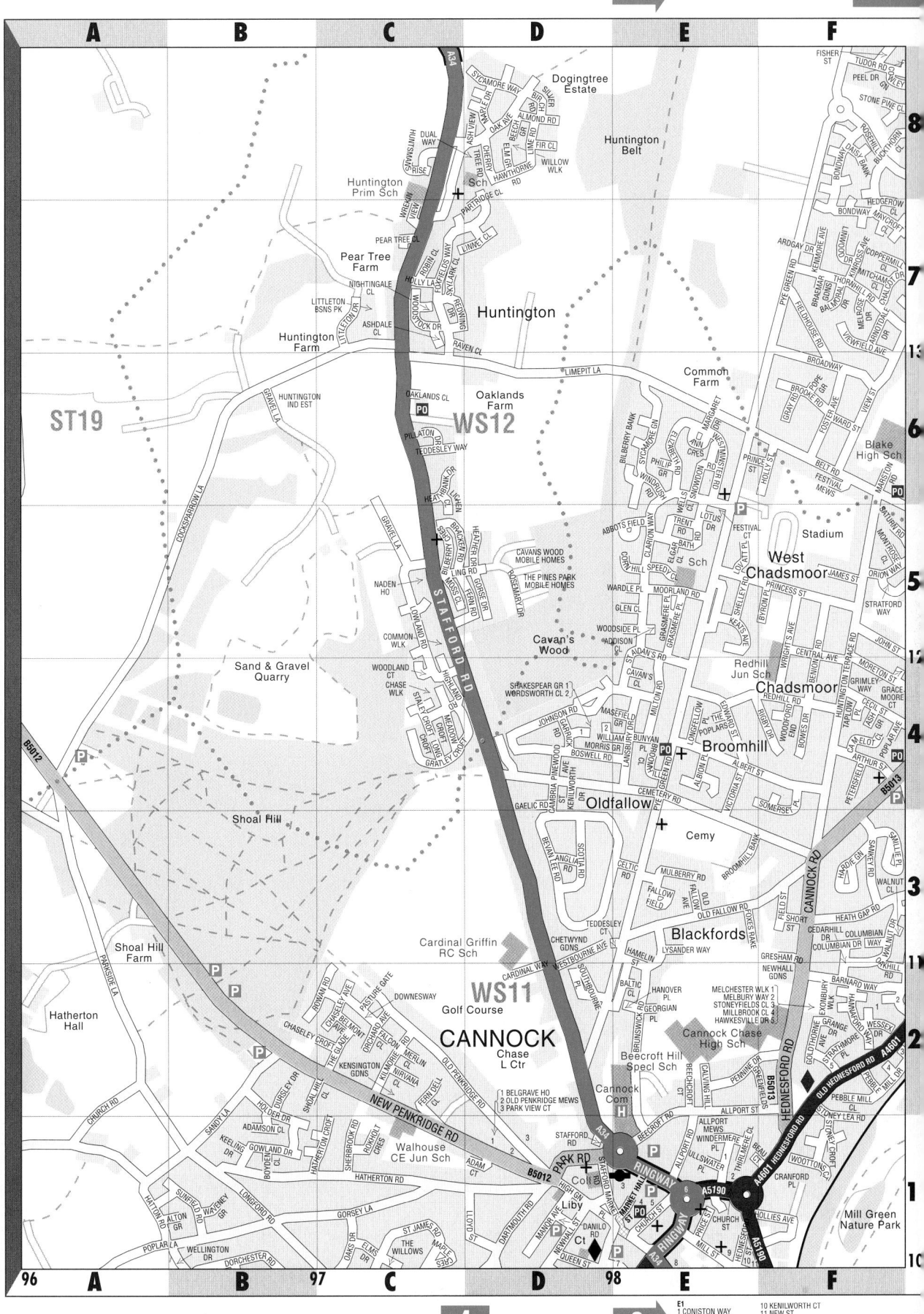

ST19

ST 19

Huntington Prim Sch

Huntington Farm

Pear Tree Farm

Dogingtree Estate

Huntington Belt

Huntington

WS12

Oaklands Farm

Common Farm

Blake High Sch

Sand & Gravel Quarry

Cavans Wood Mobile Homes

THE PINES PARK MOBILE HOMES

Cavan's Wood

West Chadsmoor

Redhill Jun Sch

Chadsmoor

Broomhill

Oldfallow

Cemy

Blackfords

Shoal Hill

Shoal Hill Farm

Hatherton Hall

Cardinal Griffin RC Sch

WS11

Golf Course

CANNOCK

Chase L Ctr

Cannock Chase High Sch

Beecroft Hill Specl Sch

Cannock Com

Mill Green Nature Park

Walhouse CE Jun Sch

NEW PENKRIDGE RD

1 BELGRAVE HO
2 OLD PENKRIDGE MEWS
3 PARK VIEW CT

STAFFORD RD

RINGWAY

RINGWAY

A5190

2

4

2

E1
1 CONISTON WAY
2 WEAVING GDNS
3 CANNOCK SH CTR
4 PEEL CT
5 PRINCE OF WALES CTR
6 QUEENS SQ
7 BACKCROFTS
8 KINGSTON ARC
9 WESLEY CT
10 KENILWORTH CT
11 NEW ST

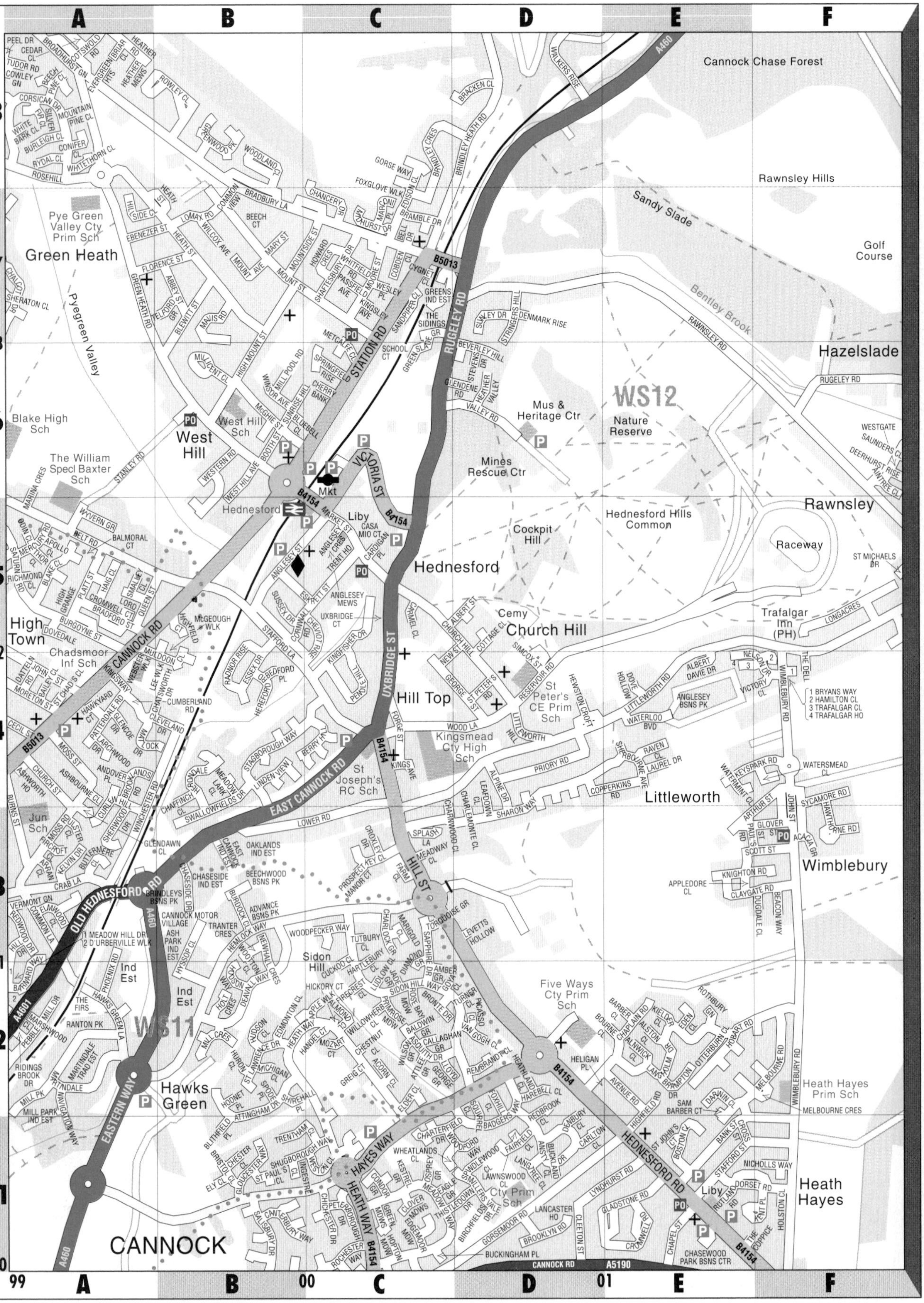

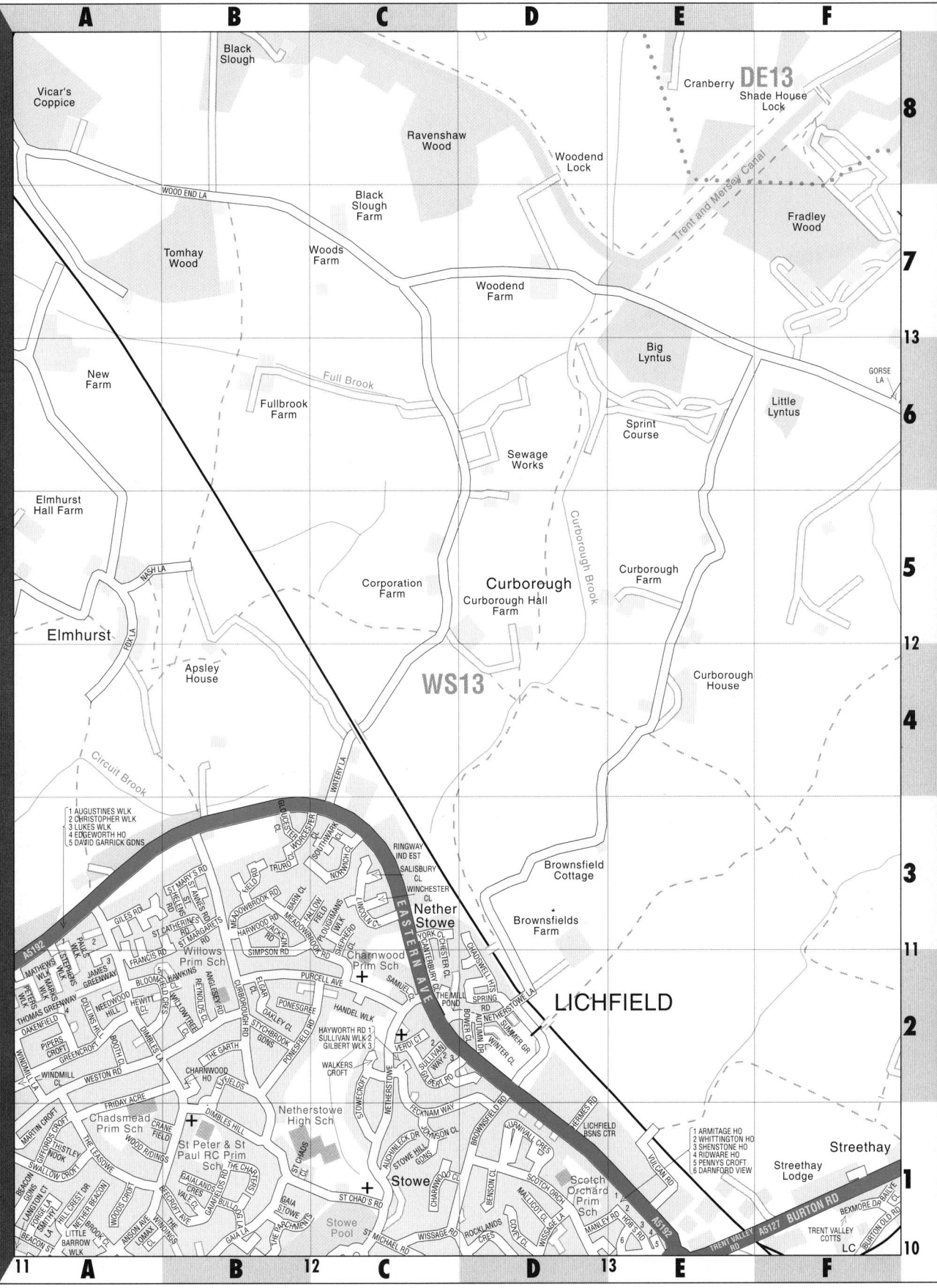

Black Slough

Vicar's Coppice

Cranberry

DE13

Shade House Lock

8

Ravenshaw Wood

Woodend Lock

Trent and Mersey Canal

Fradley Wood

WOOD END LA

Black Slough Farm

Woods Farm

Woodend Farm

7

13

Tomhay Wood

New Farm

Full Brook

Fullbrook Farm

Woodend Farm

Big Lyntus

GORSE LA

Little Lyntus

BURTON RD

6

Sprint Course

Elmhurst Hall Farm

Sewage Works

Curborough Brook

Corporation Farm

NASH LA

Curborough Hall Farm

Curborough

Curborough Farm

5

Elmhurst

FOX LA

Apsley House

WS13

Curborough House

12

Circuit Brook

WATERY LA

4

A5192

1 AUGUSTINES WLK
2 CHRISTOPHER WLK
3 LUKES WLK
4 EDGEWORTH HO
5 DAVID GARRICK GDNS

RINGWAY IND EST

SALISBURY CL
WINCHESTER CL

Brownsfield Cottage

3

GLOUCESTER CL

WORCESTER CL

SOUTHWARK CL

TRURO CL

NORWICH CL

Nether Stowe

Brownsfields Farm

ST MARY'S RD

ST ANNES RD

MEADOWBROOK RD

BARN CL

FALLOW FIELD

LINCOLN CL

YORK CL

CHESTER CL

CHADSWELL HTS

LICHFIELD

GILES RD

ST CATHERINES RD

HARWOOD RD

JACKSONS RD

MEADOWBROOK WLK

SHEPHERD WLK

CANTERBURY CL

SPRING RD

NETHERSTOWE LA

11

ST MARGARETS RD

FRANCIS RD

SIMPSON RD

Charnwood Prim Sch

PURCELL AVE

SAMUEL CL

THE MILL POND

BOWER RD

HAWKINS

MATTHEWS WLK

STEPHENS WLK

PAULS WLK

JAMES GREENWAY

BLOOMFIELD CRES

CURBOROUGH RD

Willows Prim Sch

ELGAR CL

PONESGREE

HANDEL WLK

HAYWORTH RD 1
SULLIVAN WLK 2
GILBERT WLK 3

VERDI CT

SULLIVAN WAY

WINTER CL

SUMMER GR

VULCAN RD

LICHFIELD BSNS CTR

2

PETERS WLK

THOMAS GREENWAY

COLLINS HILL

NEEDWOOD HILL

HEWITT CL

LOWLOW TREE

OAKLEY CL

STYCHBROOK GDNS

WALKERS CROFT

TECKNAM WAY

Streethay

1 ARMITAGE HO
2 WHITTINGTON HO
3 SHENSTONE HO
4 RIDWARE HO
5 PENNYS CROFT
6 DARNFORD VIEW

OAKENFIELD

DIMBLES LA

THE GARTH

CHARNWOOD HO

STOWE FIELDS

HERMES RD

Streethay Lodge

PIPERS CROFT

GREENCROFT

WESTON RD

WINDMILL

DIMBLES HILL

STOWECROFT

NETHERSTOWE

JOHNSON CL

CARNIVALL CRES

SCOTCH ORCH

Scotch Orchard Prim Sch

MANLEY RD

HOBS RD

A5192

BURTON RD

A5127

BEXMORE DRIVE

TRENT VALLEY RD

1

MARTIN CROFT

THISTLEY NOOK

THE LEASOWE

Chadsmead Prim Sch

CRANE FIELD

WOOD RIDINGS

Netherstowe High Sch

AUCHINLECK DR

STOWE HILL GDNS

CHARNWOOD CL

BENSON CL

MALLICOT CL

WISSAGE LA

CONEY CL

TRENT VALLEY COTTS

LC

10

BEACON GDNS

LANGTON CT

SMITHY

NETHER BEACON

HILL CREST DR

BROOK CL

St Peter & St Paul RC Prim Sch

THE CHASE

ST CHADS

GAIALANDS CRES

VALE CL

GAIA BULLDG

Stowe

ST CHAD'S RD

ROCKLANDS CRES

WISSAGE RD

SWALLOW CROFT

SERGE LA

BEACON ST

LITTLE BARROW WLK

WINDSOR AVE

LOMAX CL

THE PARCHMENTS

GAIA LA

Stowe Pool

ST MICHAEL RD

11 A 12 B C 13 D E F

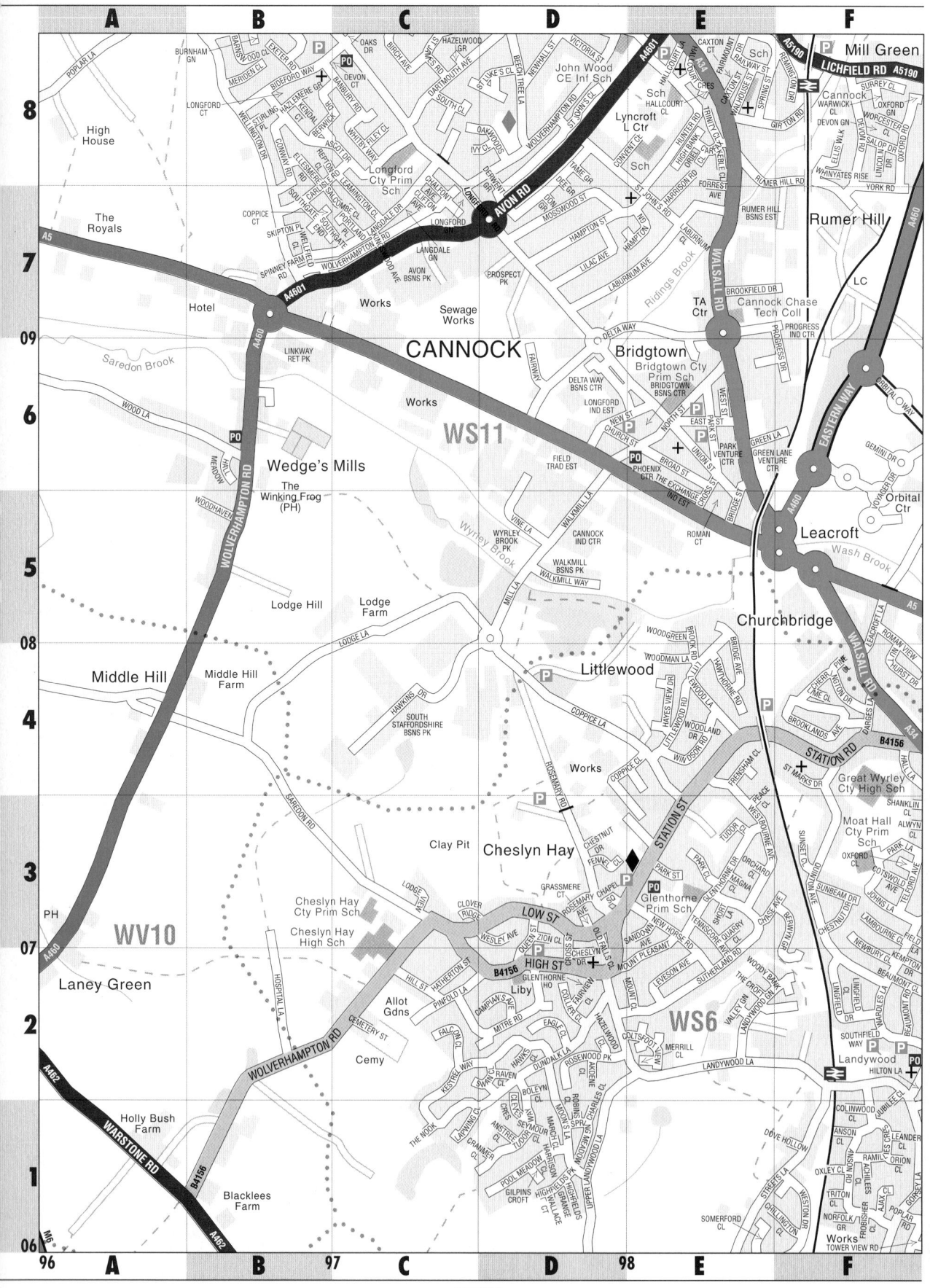

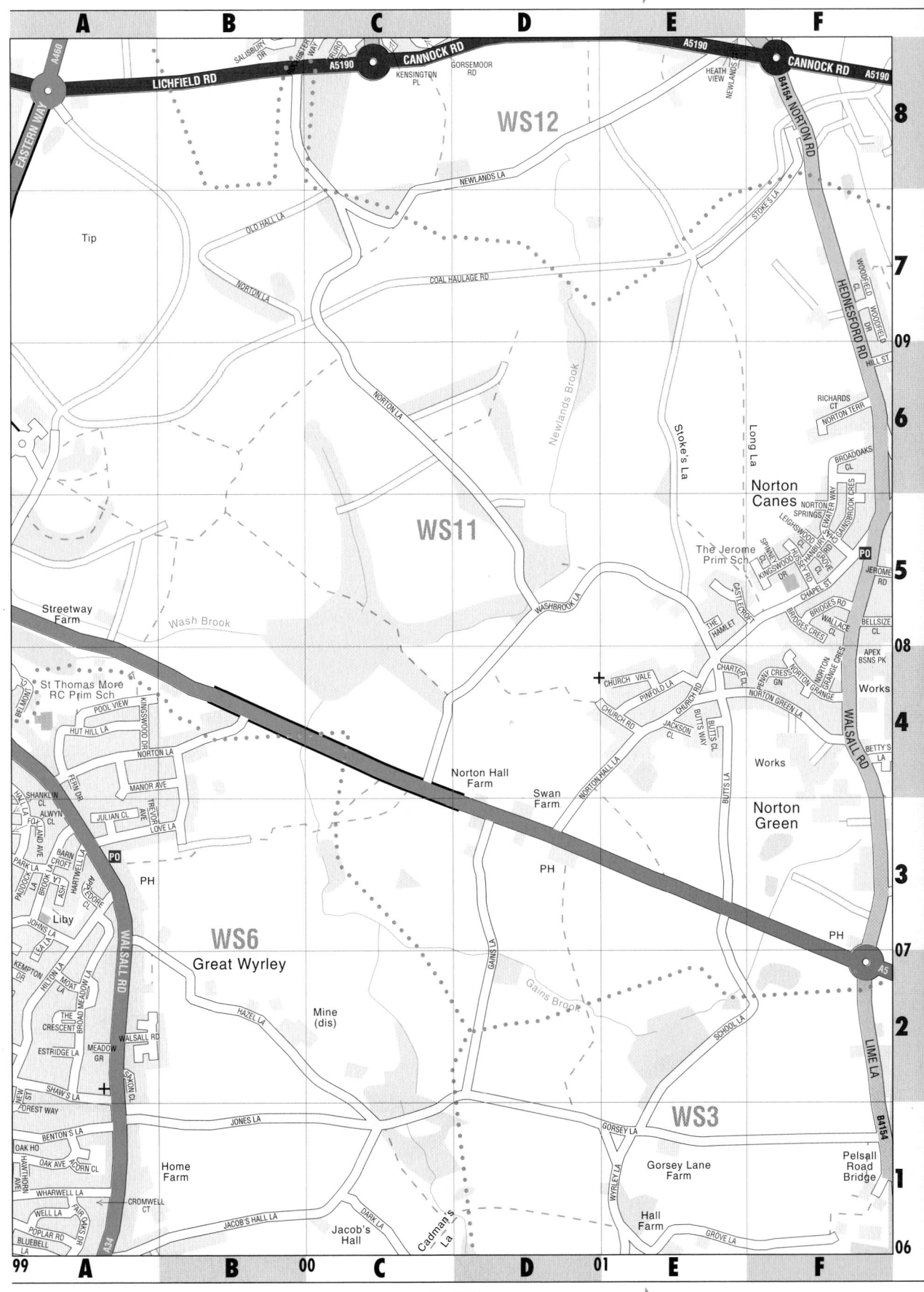

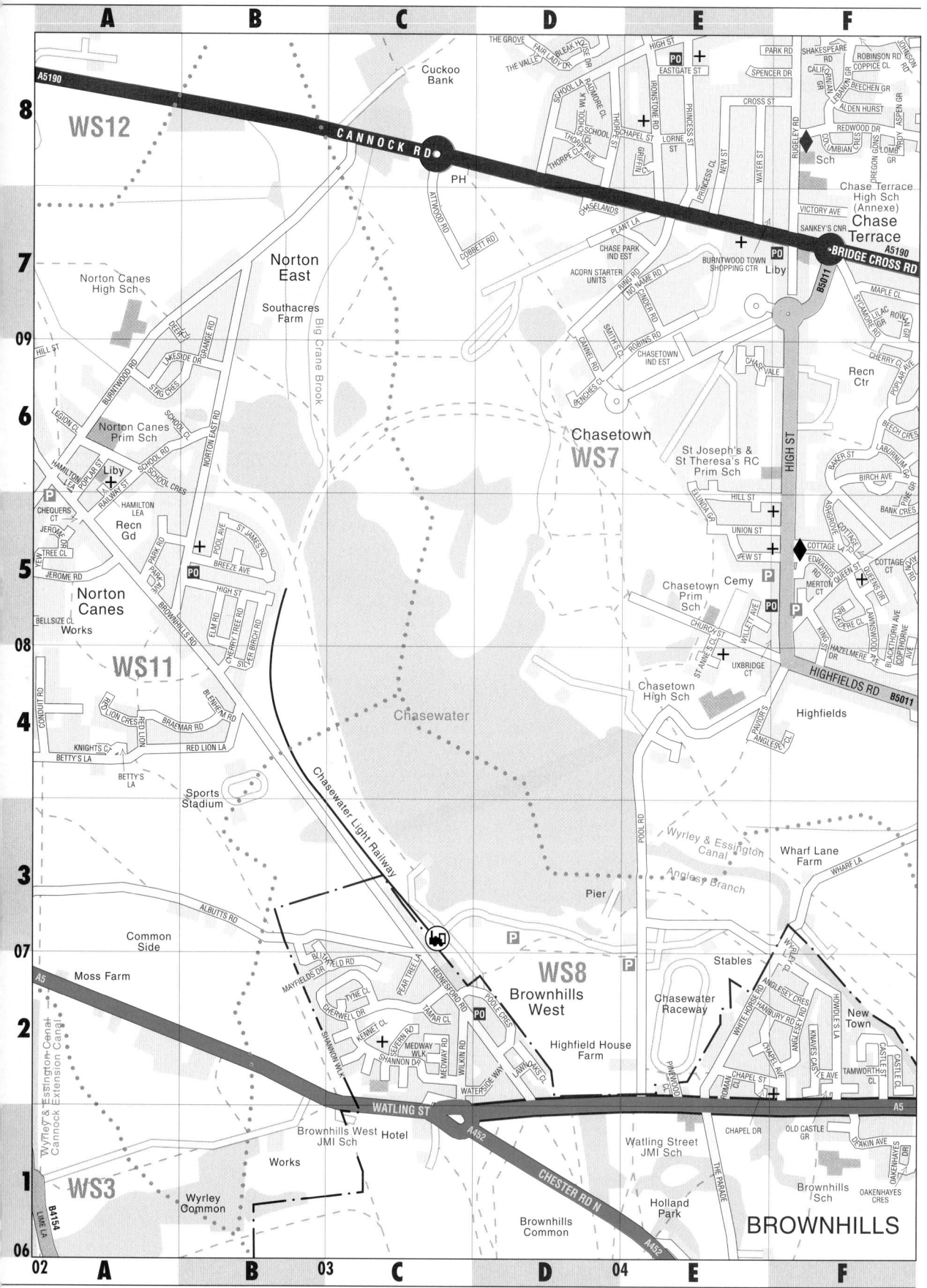

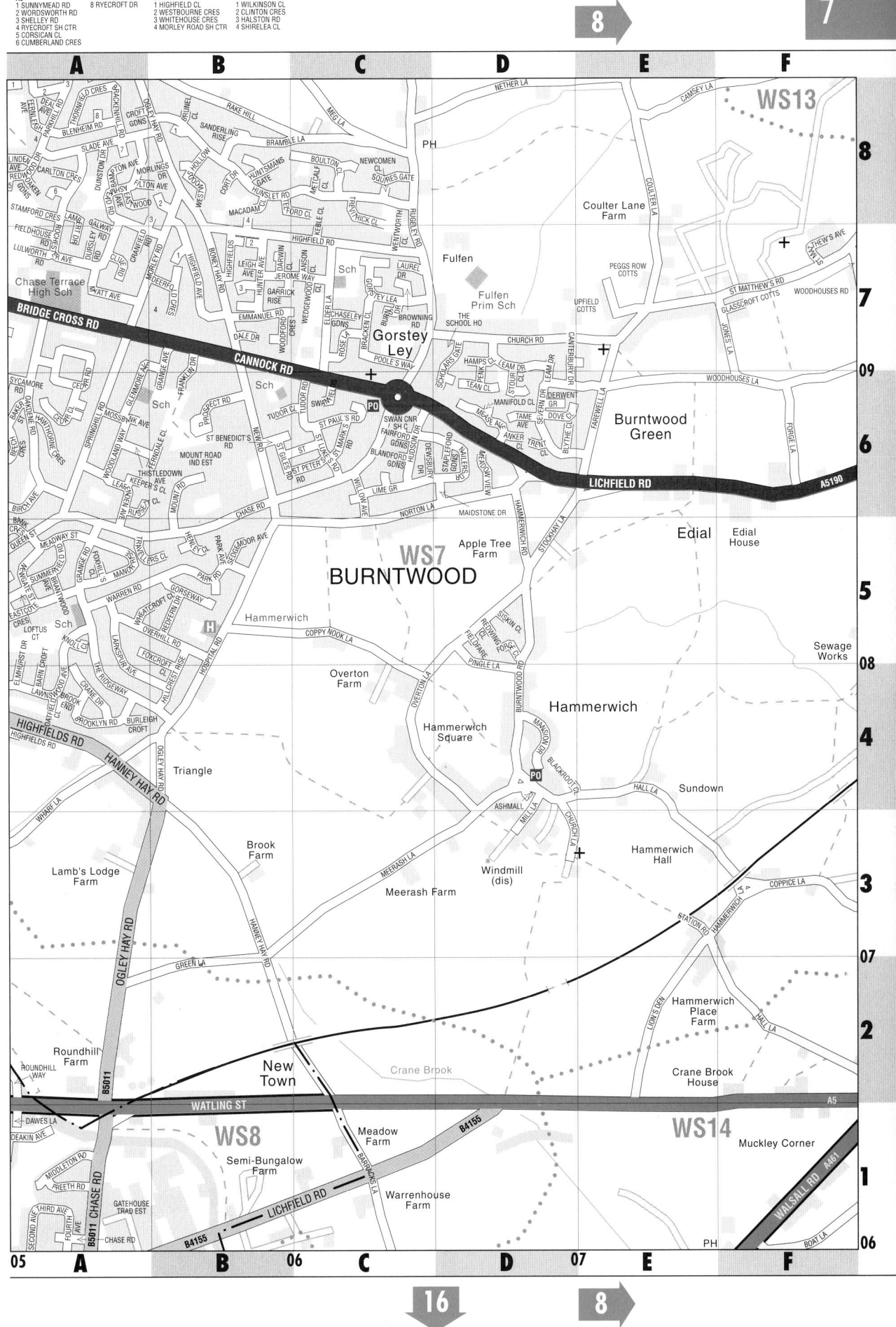

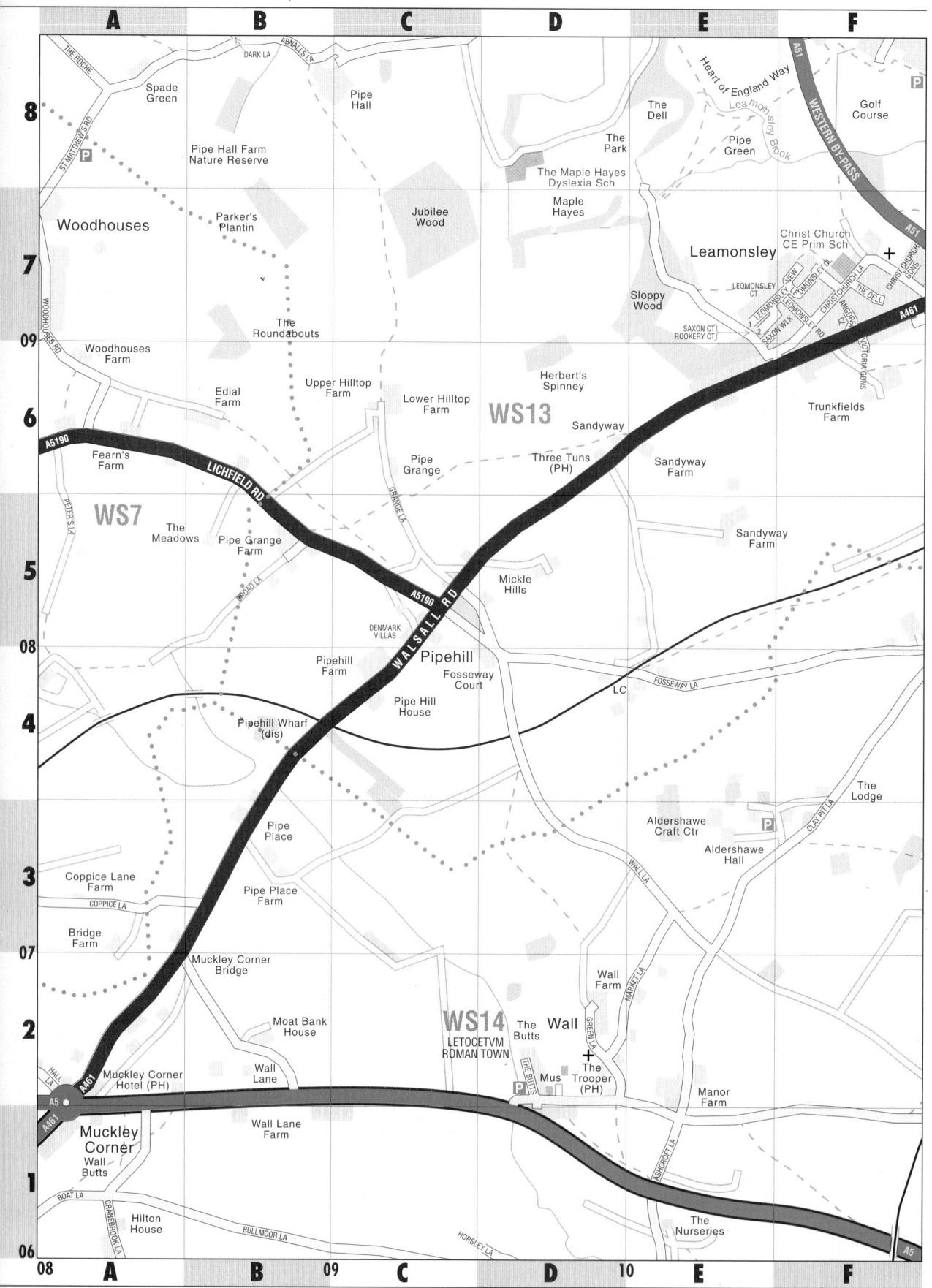

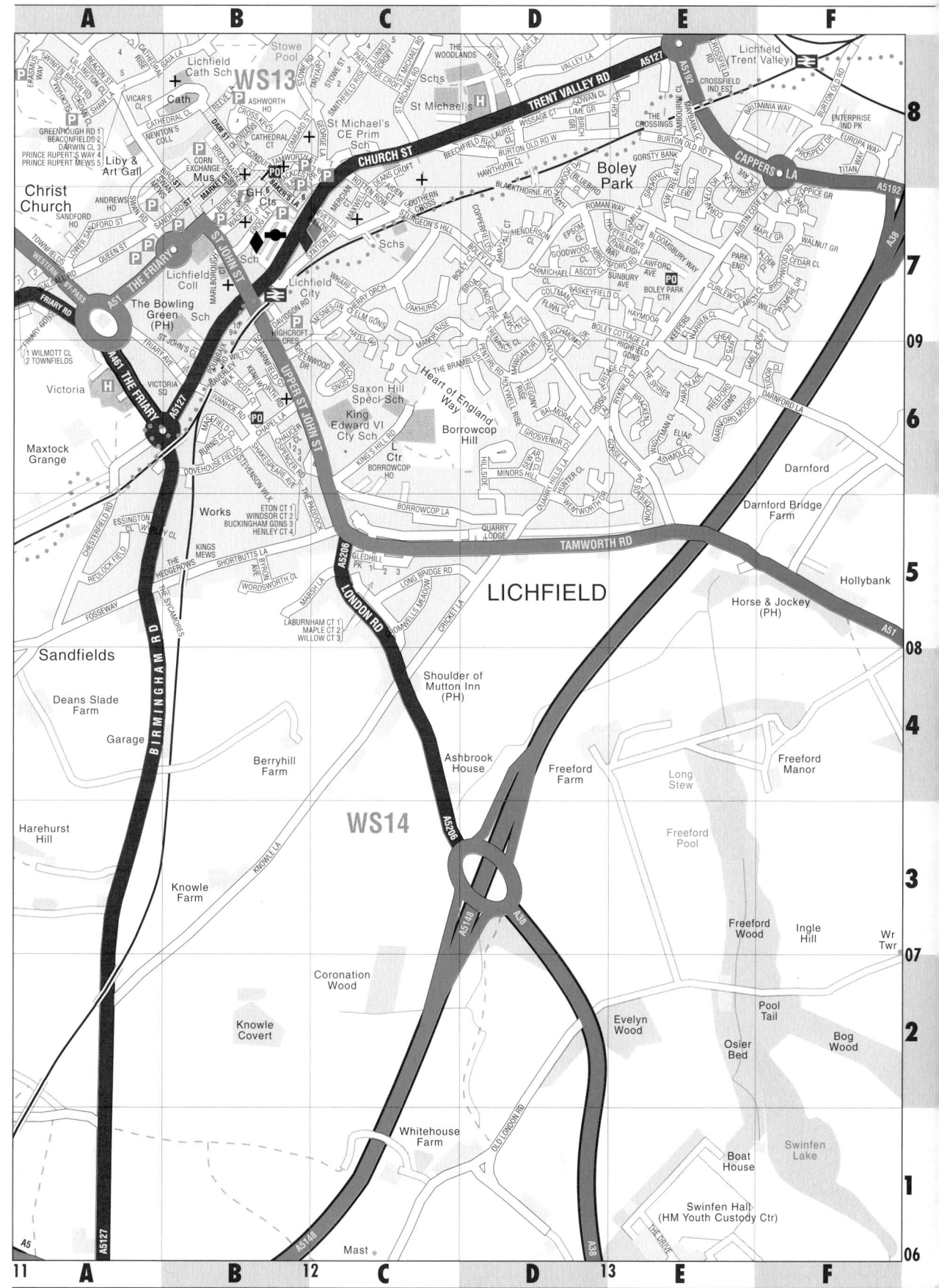

B7
1 CITY ARC
2 SARAH SIDDONS HO
3 TUDOR ROW
4 HOMELODGE HO
5 CASTLE DYKE
6 LEVETTS SQ

7 THREE SPIRES SH CTR
8 GRESLEY ROW
9 FORREST CT
10 GREEN CT

C8
1 THE CHEQUERS

2 MALLARD CROFT
3 DRAKE CROFT
4 WILLIAM LUNN'S HOMES
5 HOULBROOKE HOUSE
6 GRESLEY ROW
7 GREENHILL

3

WS13

Lichfield
(Trent Valley)

Christ
Church

Maxtock
Grange

Sandfields

Deans Slade
Farm

Garage

Harehurst
Hill

Knowle
Farm

Knowle
Covert

Coronation
Wood

Whitehouse
Farm

WS14

LICHFIELD

Boley
Park

Darnford

Darnford Bridge
Farm

Hollybank

Horse & Jockey
(PH)

Freeford
Farm

Long
Stew

Freeford
Manor

Freeford
Pool

Freeford
Wood

Ingle
Hill

Wr
Twr

Pool
Tail

Osier
Bed

Bog
Wood

Evelyn
Wood

Swinfen
Lake

Boat
House

Swinfen Hall
(HM Youth Custody Ctr)

Berryhill
Farm

Ashbrook
House

Shoulder of
Mutton Inn
(PH)

Mast

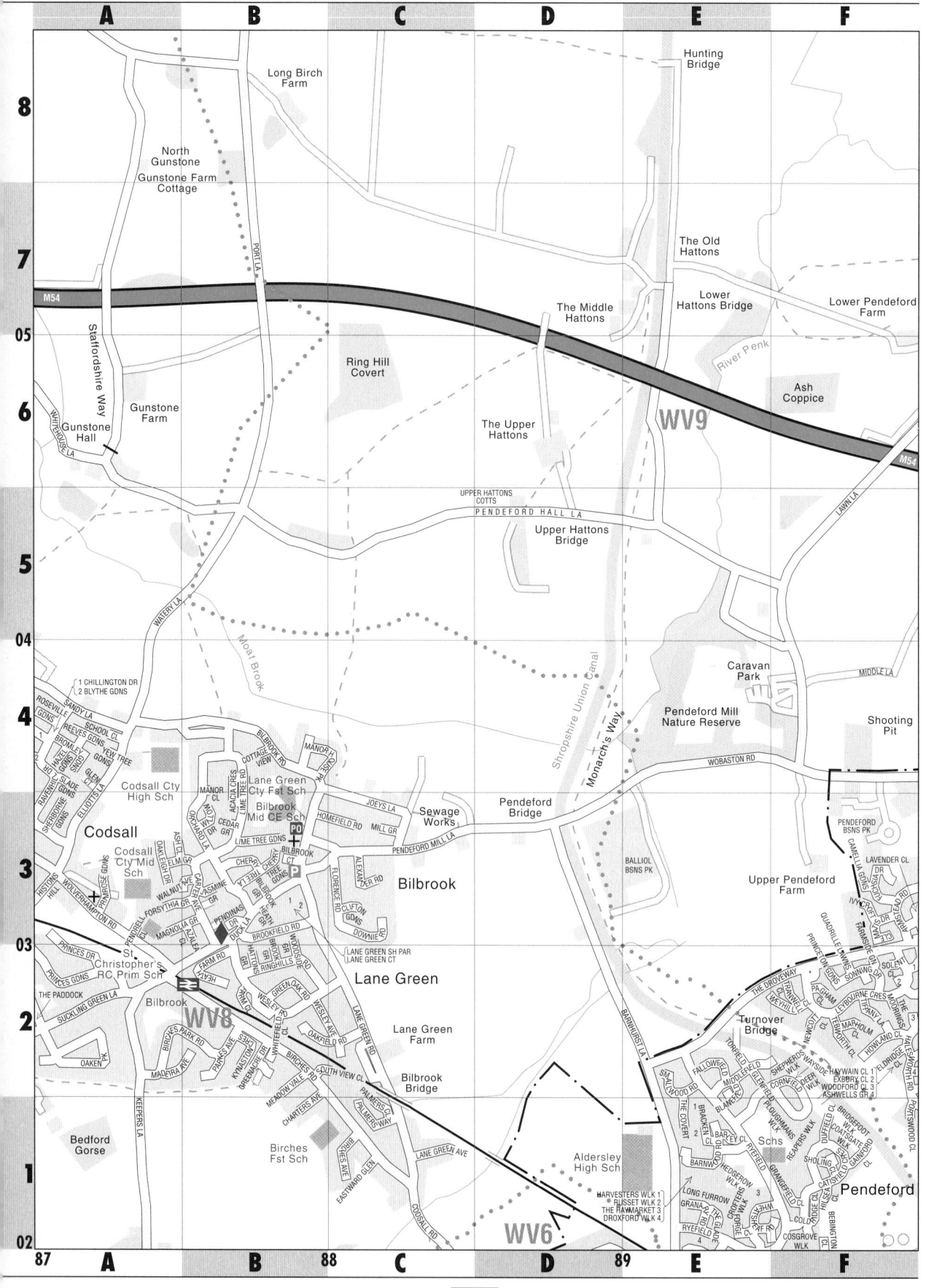

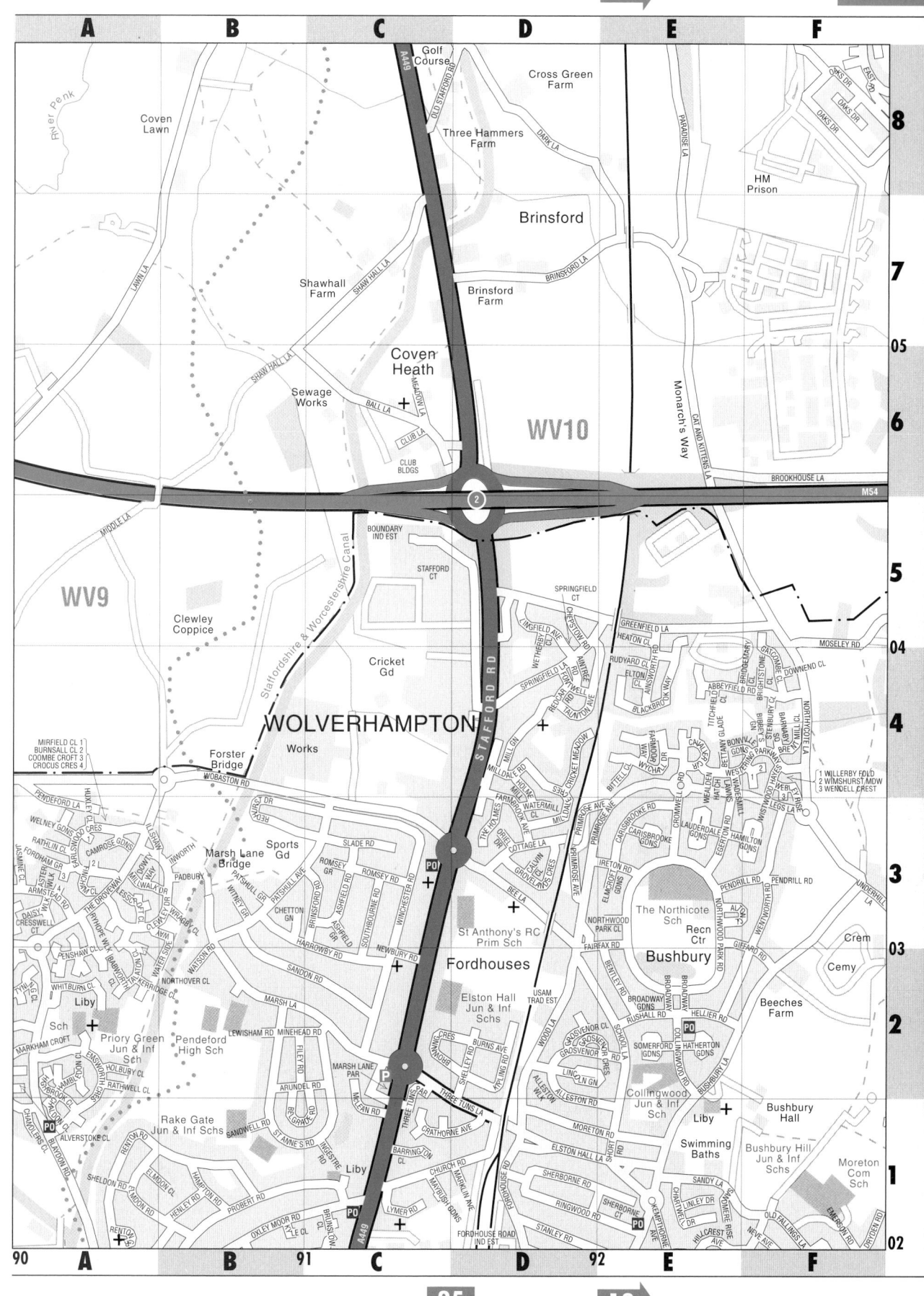

12
12

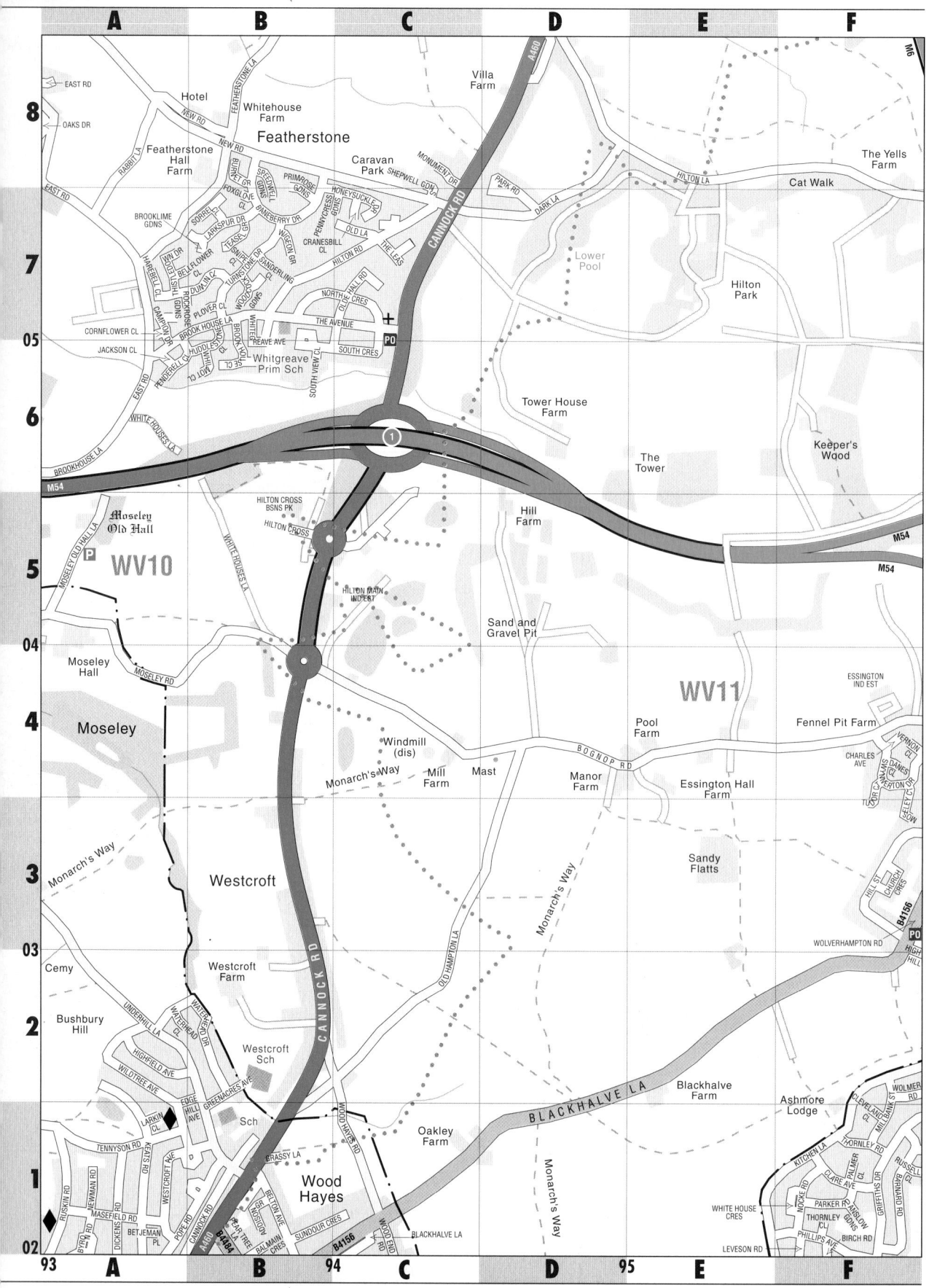

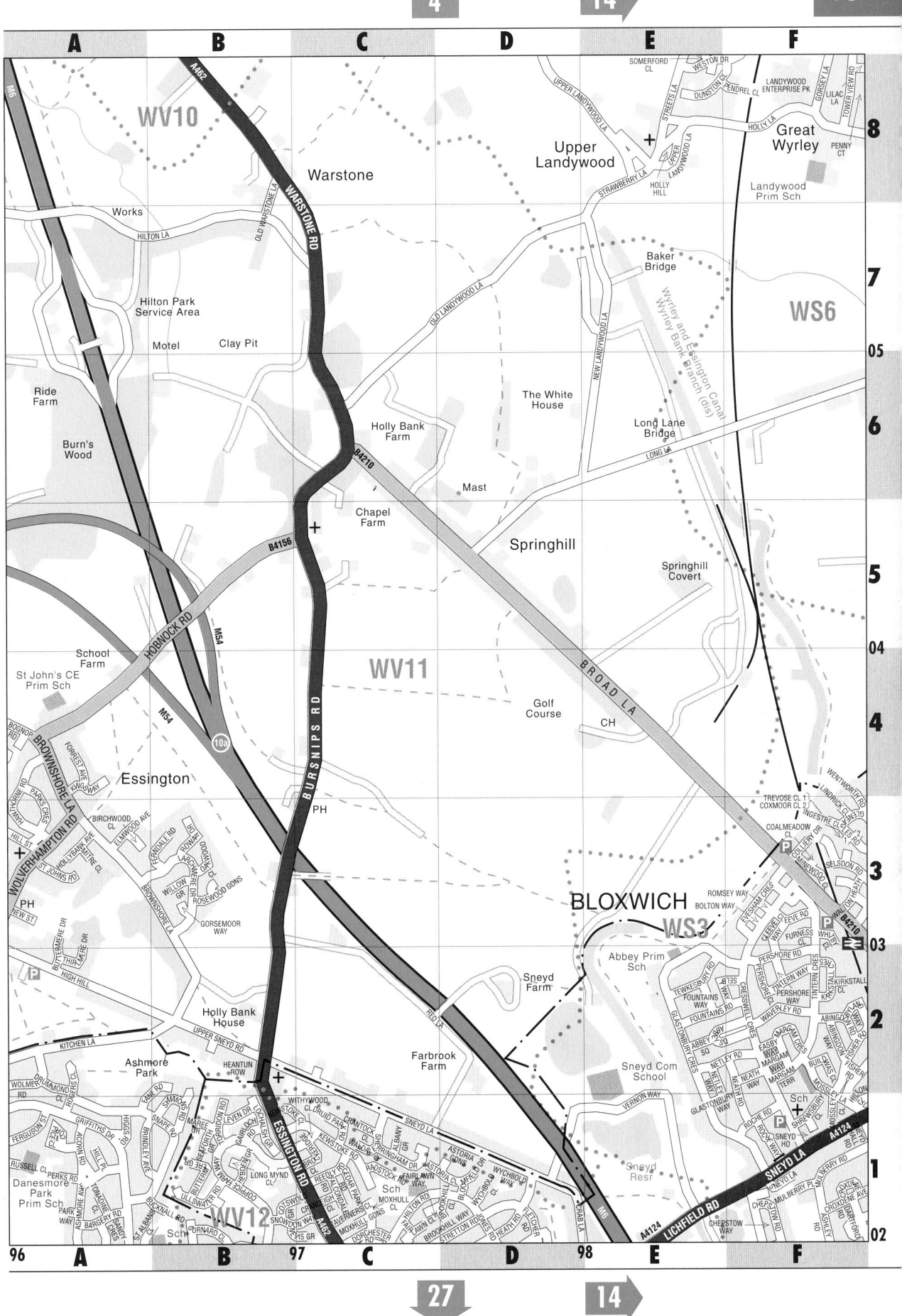

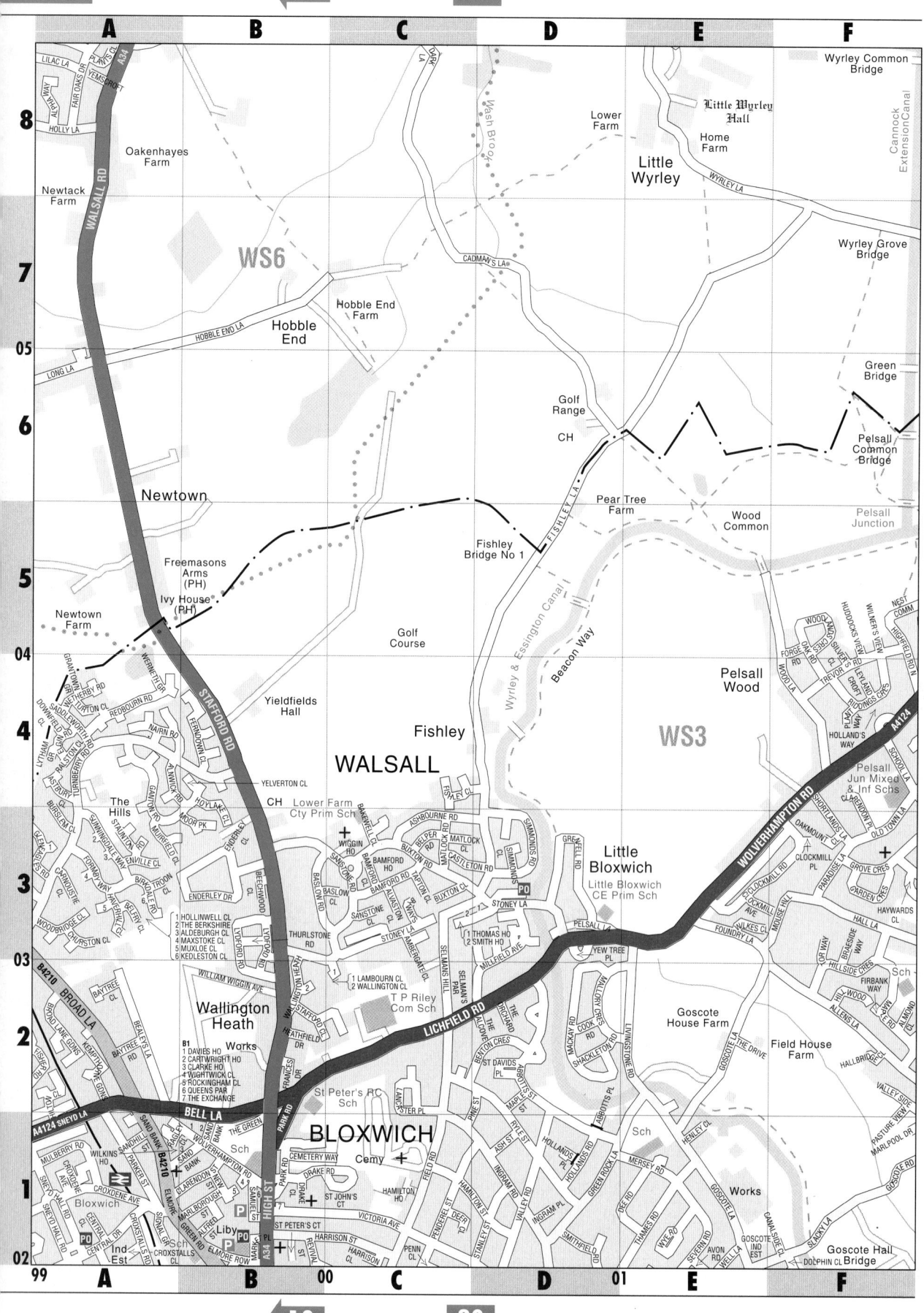

WS6

Oakenhayes Farm

Newtack Farm

WALSALL RD

Little Wyrley Hall

Lower Farm

Home Farm

Little Wyrley

Wyrley Common Bridge

Cannock Extension Canal

WYRLEY LA

Wyrley Grove Bridge

CADMAN'S LA

Hobble End Farm

Hobble End

HOBBLE END LA

LONG LA

Green Bridge

Golf Range

CH

Pelsall Common Bridge

Pear Tree Farm

Wood Common

Pelsall Junction

Newtown

Fishley Bridge No 1

FISHLEY LA

Freemasons Arms (PH)

Ivy House (PH)

Newtown Farm

Golf Course

Wyrley & Essington Canal

Beacon Way

Pelsall Wood

WS3

STAFFORD RD

Yieldfields Hall

Fishley

WALSALL

The Hills

CH Lower Farm Cty Prim Sch

YELVERTON CL

WOLVERHAMPTON RD

A4124

Pelsall Jun Mixed & Inf Schs

HOLLAND'S WAY

NEST COMM

Wiggin Ho

Bamford Ho

Ashbourne Rd

Matlock Cl

Castleton Rd

Little Bloxwich

Little Bloxwich CE Prim Sch

CLOCKMILL PL

1 HOLLINWELL CL
2 THE BERKSHIRE
3 ALDEBURGH CL
4 MAXSTOKE CL
5 MUXLOE CL
6 KEDLESTON CL

Thurlstone Rd

STONEY LA

PO

1 Thomas Ho
2 Smith Ho

PELSALL RD

Goscote House Farm

WILLIAM WIGGIN AVE

1 LAMBOURN CL
2 WALLINGTON CL

T P Riley Com Sch

YEW TREE PL

Field House Farm

B4210

BROAD LA

Wallington Heath Works

B1
1 DAVIES HO
2 CARTWRIGHT HO
3 CLARKE HO
4 WIGHTWICK CL
5 ROCKINGHAM CL
6 QUEENS PAR
7 THE EXCHANGE

LICHFIELD RD

St Peter's RC Sch

BELL LA

BLOXWICH

A4124 SNEYD LA

PARK RD

HIGH ST

Sch

CEMETERY WAY

Cemy

St John's Ct

Victoria Ave

Works

Liby

Bloxwich

Ind Est

Goscote Ind Est

Goscote Hall Bridge

DOLPHIN CL

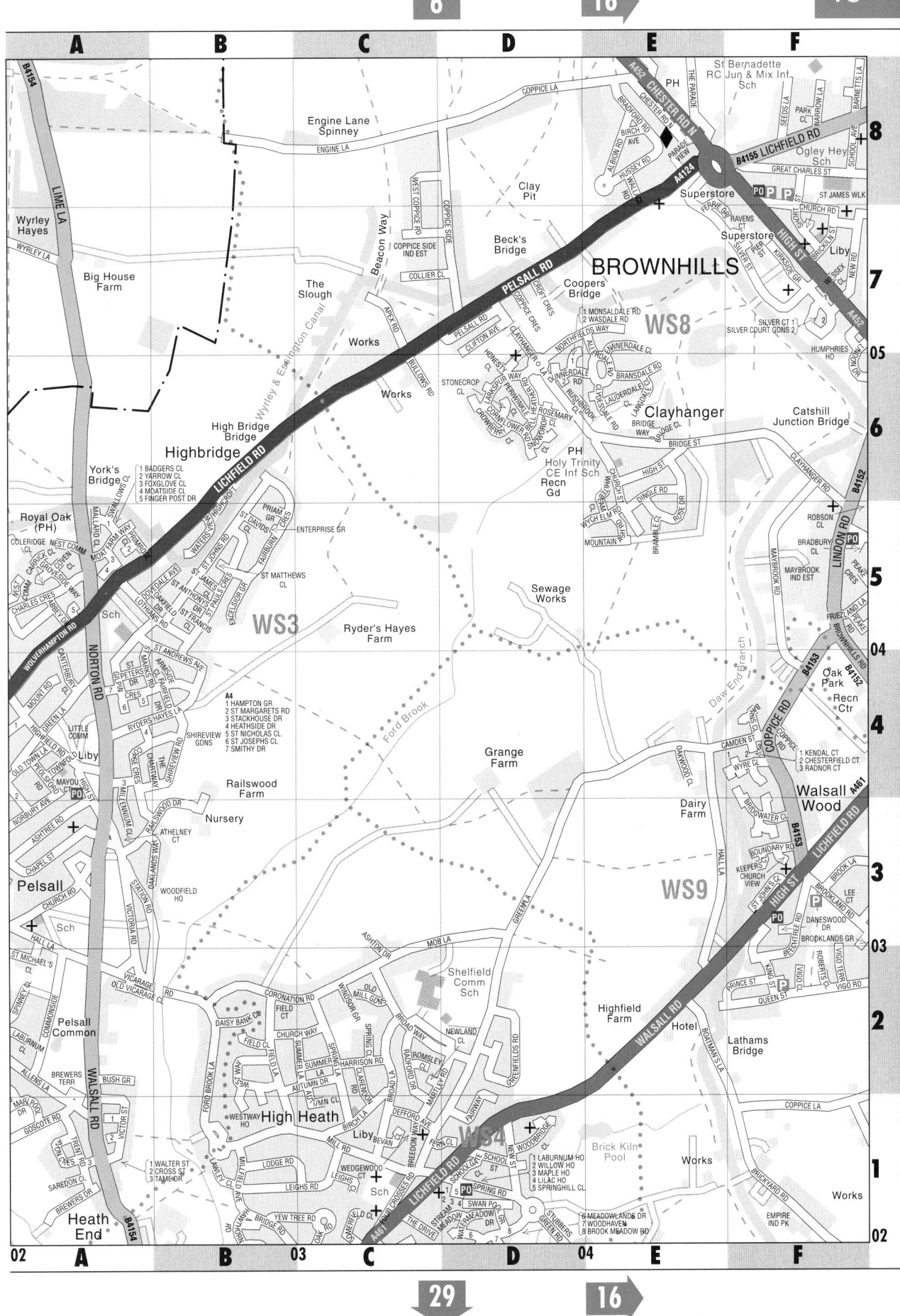

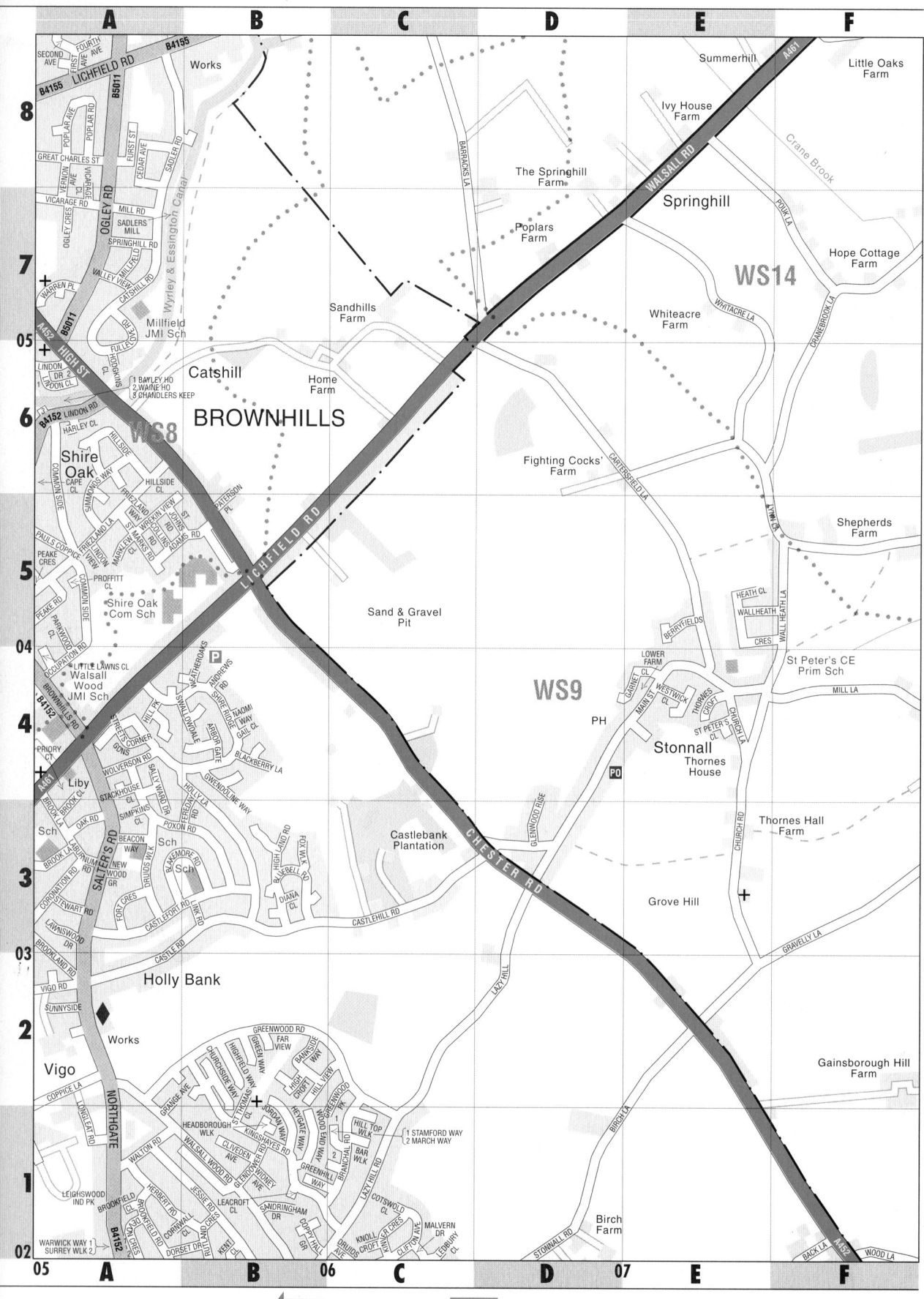

A B C D E F

8 Barn Farm
Hilton
Hilton Farm
Cranebrook Farm
CRANEBROOK LA
Bullmoor Lane Covert
Crane Brook
BULLMOOR LA
HORSLEY LA
Chesterfield Farm
Chesterfield
Lawton Grange

7 THORNYHURST LA
RAIKES LA
Poultry Houses
Gayley Cottage
Keeper's Cottage
Chesterfield Lodge
ASHCROFT LA
Ashcroft Farm

05 Malkin's Coppice
GROSVENOR CT
FODEN CLOOK DR
MILLBROOK DR
PINFOLD HILL

6 Lynn Lane House
LYNN LA
Dairy Farm
BIRCH BROOK
BIRCHBROOK LA
BIRCHBROOK IND PK
Shenstone
HOLM VIEW PL
STATION RD
PO
LINCOLN CROFT
ASTON
MAIN ST
TRINITY CL
CHURCH

5 Lynn
The Bungalow
The Nurseries
Owlett Hall Farm
WS14
Shenstone
ADMIRAL PARKER RD
RICHARD COOPER RD
NEW RD
FOOTHERLEY RD
ST JOHN'S HILL
HOLLY HILL RD
CHESTNUT DR
ST JOHN'S

04 Laurels Farm
Lower Stonnall
MILL LA
Swan Farm
Spinney Farm
Footherley Rough
Keeper's Cottage
HOLLYHILL LA
FOOTHERLEY LA
Shenstone Court
COURT DR

4 GRAVELLY LA
Footherley Hall
Home Farm
Footherley

3 WS9
New Barns Farm
NEW BARNS LA
HOOK LA
Griffin's Covert
Footherley Brook

03 WOOD LA
Footherley Farm
Croft Farm

2 Cockheath Coppice
Bagot's Barn
MOOR LA
Whites Farm

1 Biddle's Field Wood
Bosses
BACK LA

02 FORGE LA

08 A B 09 C D 10 E F

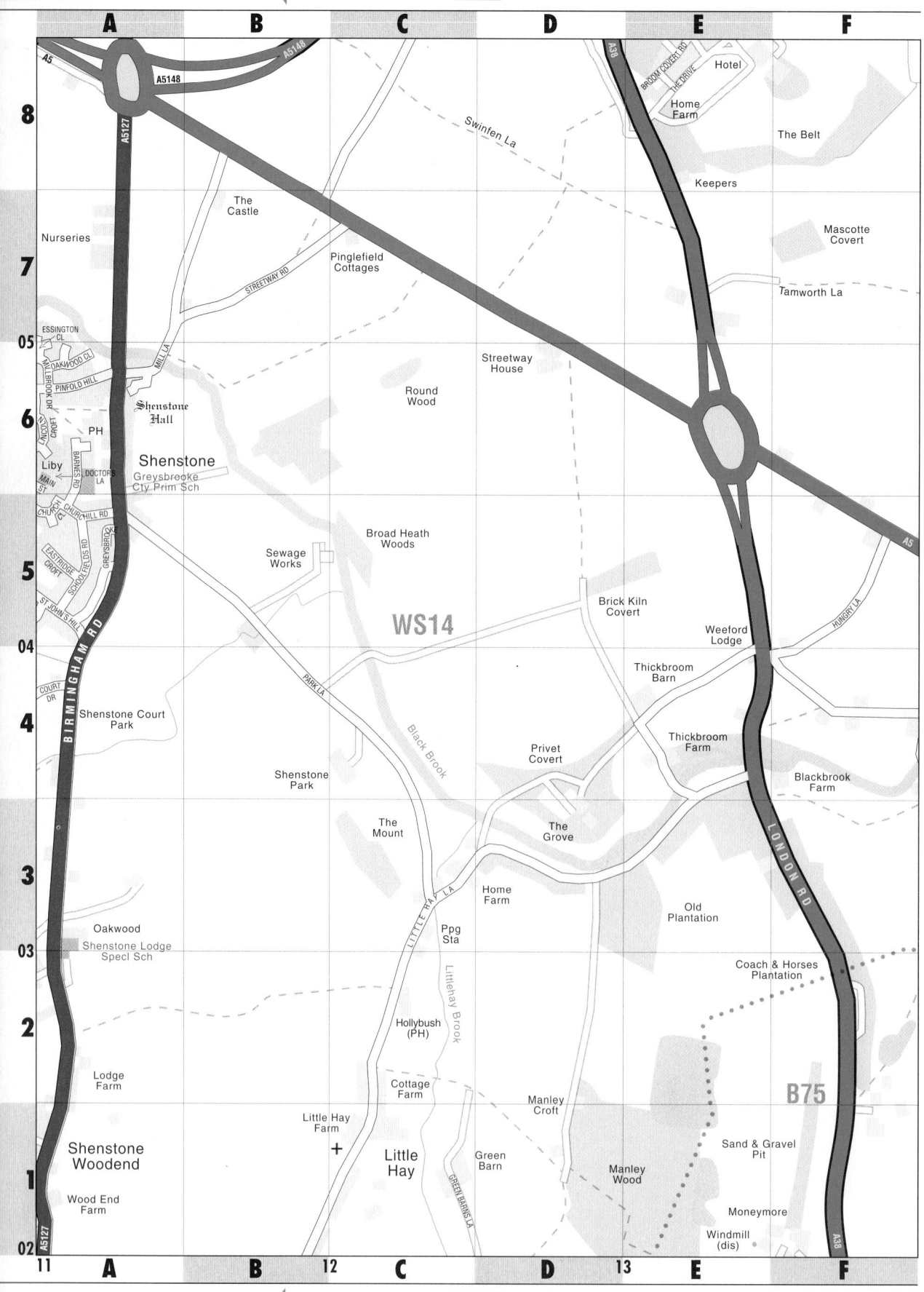

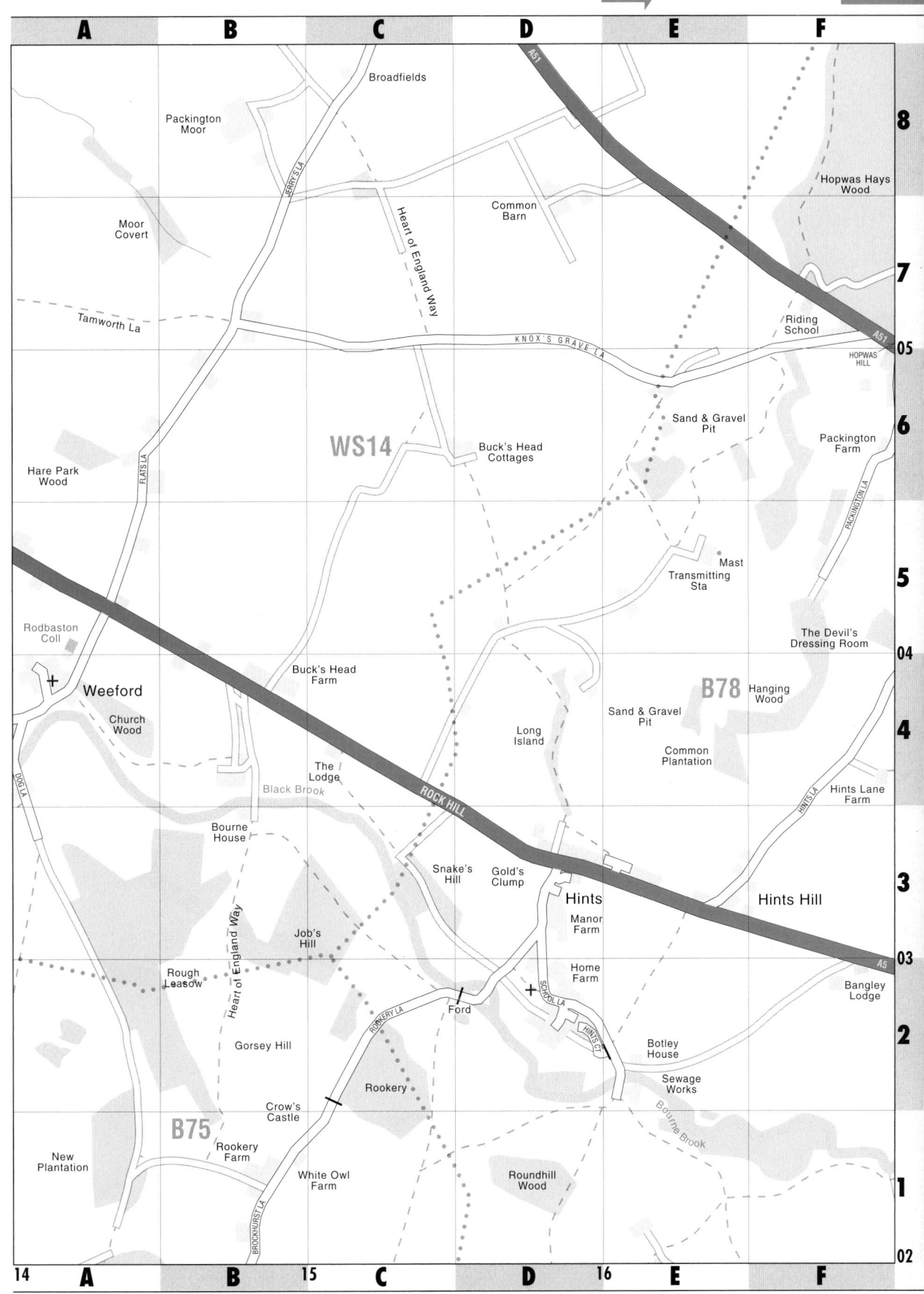

Broadfields

Packington Moor

Moor Covert

JERRY'S LA

Heart of England Way

Common Barn

Tamworth La

KNOX'S GRAVE LA

Hopwas Hays Wood

Riding School

A51

HOPWAS HILL

WS14

Buck's Head Cottages

Sand & Gravel Pit

FLATS LA

Hare Park Wood

PACKINGTON LA

Packington Farm

Mast Transmitting Sta

The Devil's Dressing Room

Rodbaston Coll

Buck's Head Farm

B78

Hanging Wood

Weeford

Church Wood

The Lodge

Black Brook

ROCK HILL

Long Island

Sand & Gravel Pit

Common Plantation

HINTS LA

Hints Lane Farm

DOG LA

Bourne House

Snake's Hill

Gold's Clump

Hints

Hints Hill

Heart of England Way

Job's Hill

Manor Farm

Rough Leasow

ROOKERY LA

Ford

SCHOOL LA

Home Farm

A5

Bangley Lodge

Gorsey Hill

HINTS CT

Botley House

Crow's Castle

Rookery

Sewage Works

Bourne Brook

B75

Rookery Farm

New Plantation

White Owl Farm

BROOKHURST LA

Roundhill Wood

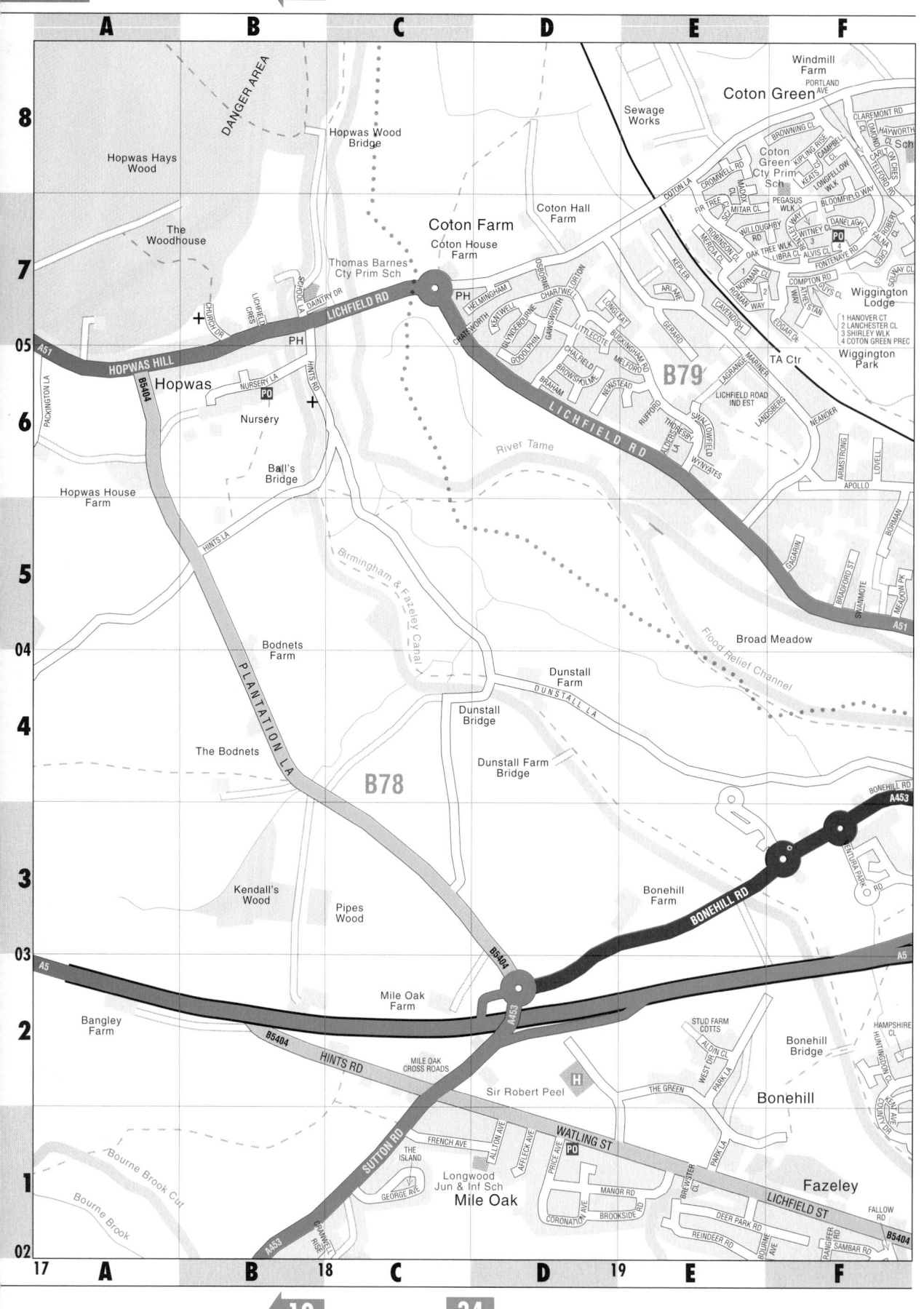

A   B   C   D   E   F

8

Coton Green

Windmill Farm

Hopwas Hays Wood

DANGER AREA

Hopwas Wood Bridge

Sewage Works

Coton Green Cty Prim Sch

Wiggington Lodge

7

The Woodhouse

Thomas Barnes Cty Prim Sch

Coton Farm

Coton House Farm

Coton Hall Farm

PH

LICHFIELD RD

05

A51

Hopwas Hill

B5404

PH

Hopwas

Nursery La

PO

Nursery

Wiggington Park

B79

Lichfield Road Ind Est

LICHFIELD RD

TA Ctr

6

Ball's Bridge

River Tame

Hopwas House Farm

Hints La

Birmingham & Fazeley Canal

5

04

Bodnets Farm

Dunstall Farm

Broad Meadow

Flood Relief Channel

A51

4

The Bodnets

PLANTATION LA

Dunstall Bridge

Dunstall La

Dunstall Farm Bridge

B78

Bonehill RD

A453

03

A5

3

Kendall's Wood

Pipes Wood

B5404

Bonehill Farm

BONEHILL RD

2

Bangley Farm

B5404

HINTS RD

Mile Oak Farm

Mile Oak Cross Roads

A453

Sir Robert Peel

H

Stud Farm Cotts

THE GREEN

Bonehill Bridge

Bonehill

1

Bourne Brook Cut

SUTTON RD

The Island

GEORGE AVE

FRENCH AVE

Longwood Jun & Inf Sch

Mile Oak

WATLING ST

PO

Fazeley

LICHFIELD ST

02

Bourne Brook

A453

GRANNELL RISE

B5404

17   A   B   18   C   D   19   E   F

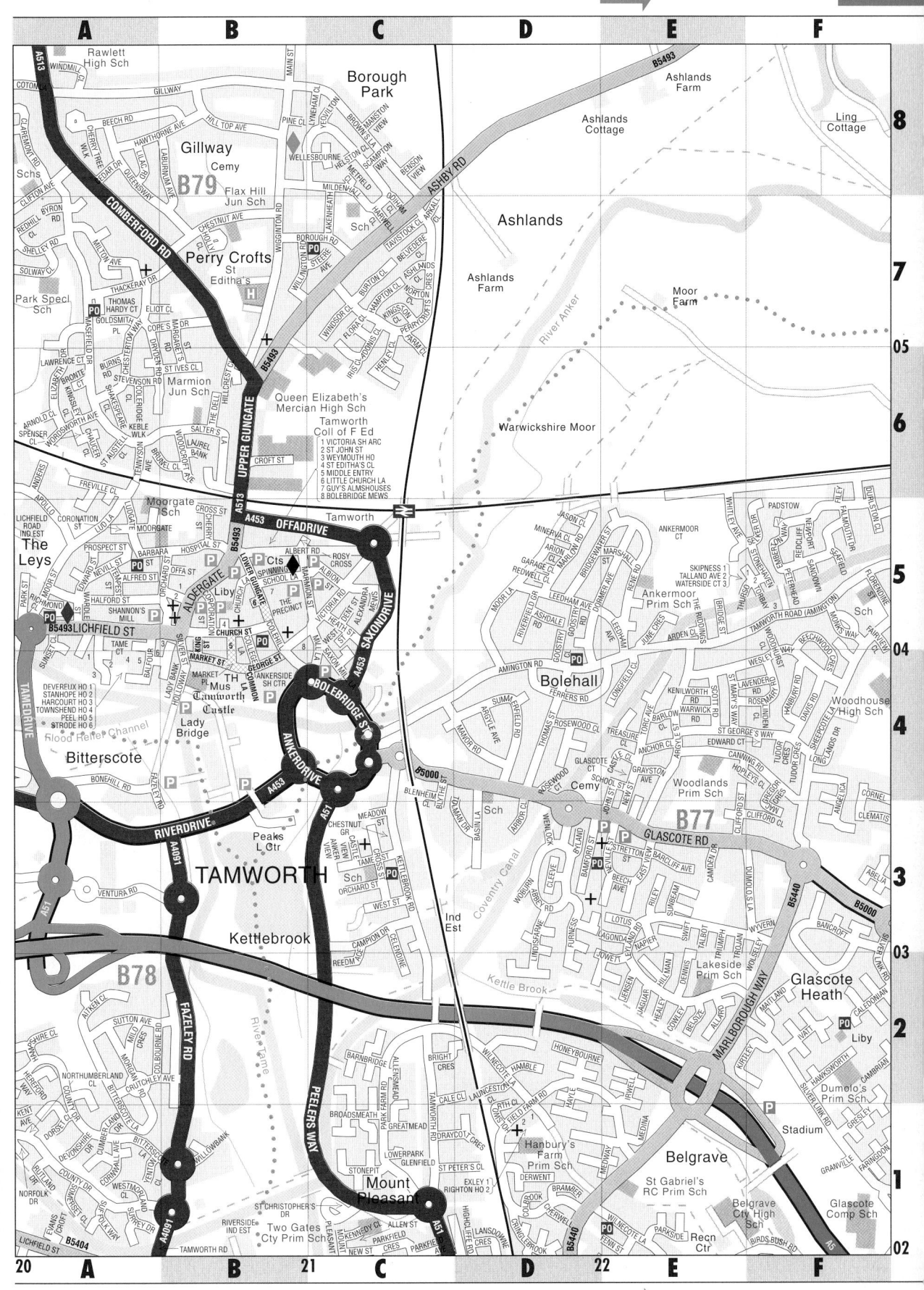

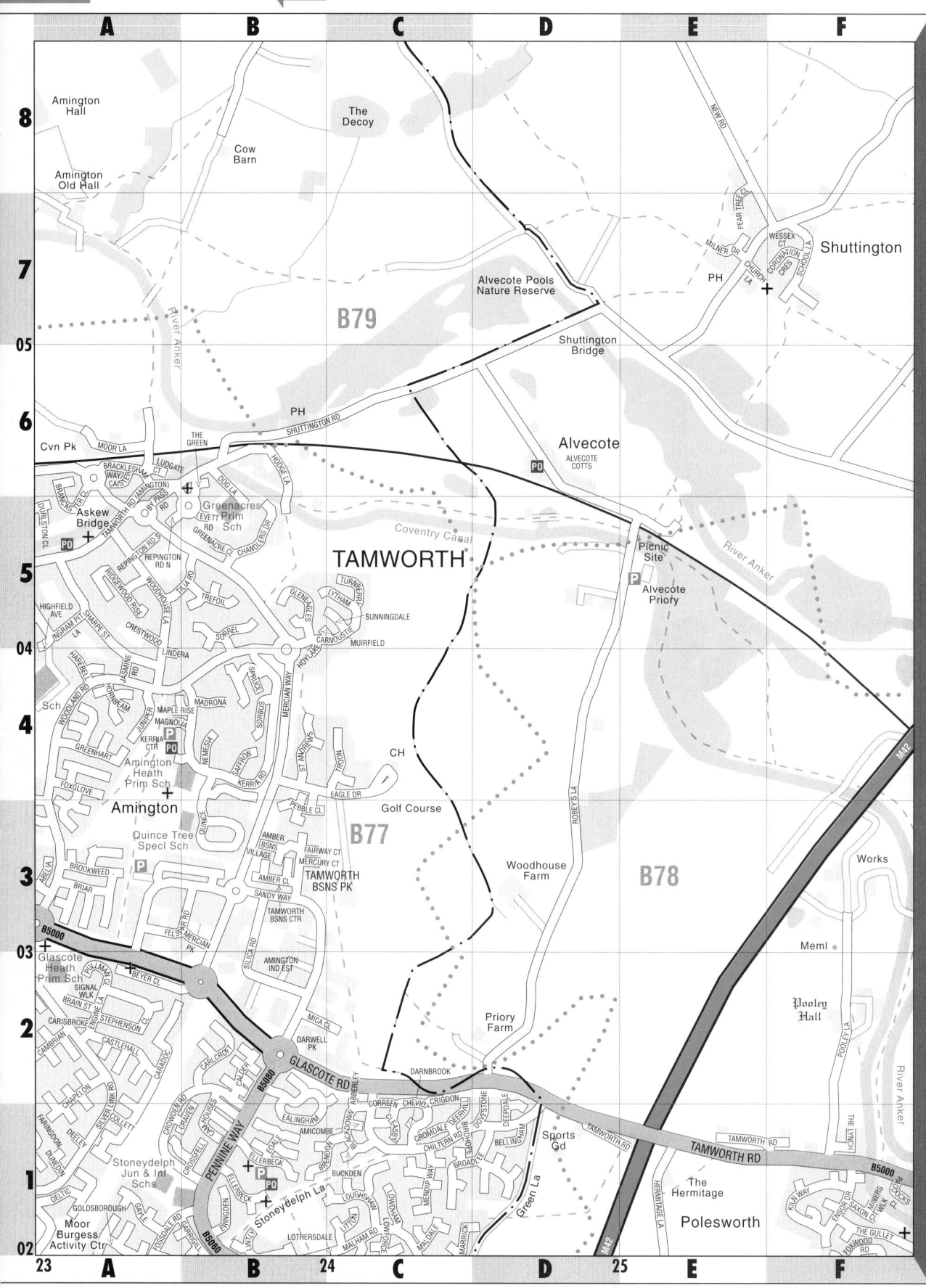

Amington Hall

The Decoy

Cow Barn

Amington Old Hall

NEW RD

Shuttington

WESSEX CT

PEAR TREE CL

MILNER DR

CHURCH LA

CORONATION CRES

SCHOOL LA

PH

B79

Alvecote Pools Nature Reserve

River Anker

Shuttington Bridge

PH

THE GREEN

SHUTTINGTON RD

Alvecote

PO

ALVECOTE COTTS

Cvn Pk

MOOR LA

LUDGATE

BRACKLESHAM WAY

FRANCIS

DURISTON CL

CL

TAMWORTH RD

BY PASS

RD

DOG LA

CAIS

Askew Bridge

PO

Greenacres

EVETT

RD

Prim Sch

GREENACRE DR

CHAMBERS DR

HODGE LA

Coventry Canal

Picnic Site

P

River Anker

TAMWORTH

REPINGTON RD S

REPINGTON RD N

ILCH RD

WOODHOUSE LA

TREFOIL

SORREL

GLENEAGLES

TURNBERRY

LYTHAM

Alvecote Priory

P

HIGHFIELD AVE

INGRAM

PIT

SHARPE ST

LA

RIDGEWOOD RISE

CRESTWOOD

LINDERA

JASMINE RD

SUNNINGDALE

CARNOUSTIE

MUIRFIELD

Sch

WOODLAND RD

HARBELL

HONEYBEAM

JUNIPER

KERRIA CTR

MADRONA

NEMESIA

SPRUCE

SORBUS

MERCIAN WAY

ST ANDREWS

NIXON

HOYLAKE

CH

Golf Course

GREENHART

FOXGLOVE

MAPLE RISE

MAGNOLIA

PO

Amington Heath Prim Sch

Amington

SAFFRON

KERRIA

PEBBLE CL

EAGLE DR

B77

ABELIA

BROOKWEED

BRIAR

Quince Tree Specl Sch

P

OLIVINE

AMBER BSNS VILLAGE

AMBER CL

FAIRWAY CT

MERCURY CT

TAMWORTH BSNS PK

Woodhouse Farm

ROBEY'S LA

B78

Works

SANDY WAY

TAMWORTH BSNS CTR

MICA CL

Meml

B5000

Glascote Heath Prim Sch

CARISBROKE

CAMBRIAN

CASTLEHALL

CARADOC

STEPHENSON

ENGINE LA

BRAIN ST

SILVER LINK RD

FELSPAR

MERCIAN

PK

BEYER CL

SILICA RD

AMINGTON IND EST

DARWELL PK

CROSSWOOD

DRANCEY

CALDER

PENNINE WAY

B5080

GLASCOTE RD

DARNBROOK

EALINGHAM

AMICOMBE

CORREEN

CHEVIOT

CRIGDON

CROMDALE

SETHILL

DEEPDALE

DOVESTONE

Priory Farm

Pooley Hall

POOLEY LA

River Anker

CHAPELON

FARRINGDON

DEELEY

DUMEDIN

DELTIC

Stoneydelph Jun & Inf Schs

CROSSFELL

DREW RD

FOSSDALE RD

GARRIGILL

LINTON

CRANBROOK

DALE

CARLCROFT

CRAWSHAW

ELLERBECK

P

PO

ELLERBECK

RINGDEN

Stoneydelph La

BIRCHLOW

BUCKDEN

LITTON

LOTHERSDALE

LOUGHSHAW

MALHAM RD

BLACKDOWN

MENDIP WAY

LOWFORCE

MALDALE

MARRICK

CASEY

CHILTERN RD

BROADLEE

BELLINGHAM

Sports Gd

Green La

M42

TAMWORTH RD

HERMITAGE LA

The Hermitage

Polesworth

TAMWORTH RD

B5000

KILN WAY

ENSOR DR

SAXON CL

KILMERS

XING

THE GULLET

FOXWOOD RD

PADDOCKS CL

THE LYNCH

Moor Burgess Activity Ctr

GOLDSBOROUGH

GAYLE

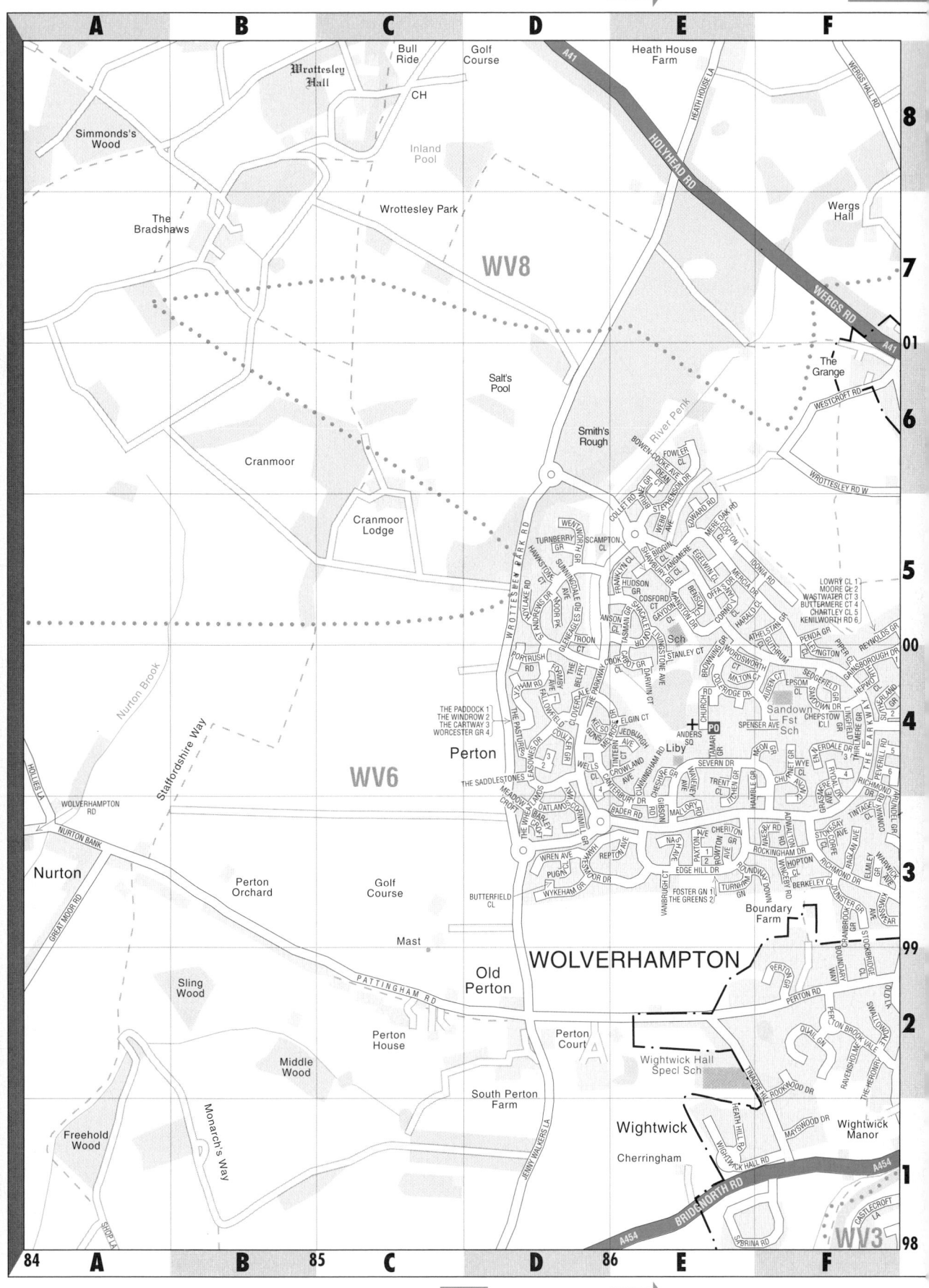

A B C D E F

8

7

01

6

5

00

4

3

99

2

1

98

Bull
Ride
Golf
Course
Wrottesley
Hall
CH
Heath House
Farm
Wergs Hall Rd
HOLYHEAD RD
A41
Heath House La

Simmonds's
Wood

Inland
Pool

Wrottesley Park

WV8

Wergs
Hall

The
Bradshaws

Wergs Rd
A41

The
Grange

Westcroft Rd

River Penk

Cranmoor

Salt's
Pool

Smith's
Rough

Wrottesley Rd W

Cranmoor
Lodge

WROTTESLEY PARK RD

Bowen-Cooke Ave
Fowler Cl
Webb
Stephenson Dr
Collet Rd
Howard Rd
Mere Oak Rd
Wentworth Gr
Turnberry Gr
Scampton Cl
Sunningdale Ave
Hawkstone
Moor Pk
Glebelands Rd
Franklyn Cl
Biggin Cl
Shawbury Gr
Langmere Gr
Edelvin Cl
Cosford Gr
Hudson Gr
Anson Ct
Shackleton Dr
Tasman Gr
Gaydon Gr
Benston
Offa's Dr
Mercia Dr
Harald Cl
Donia Rd
Athelstan Gr
Penda Gr
Reynolds Gr
Paper Gr
Gainsborough Dr
Lowry Cl 1
Moore Cl 2
Wastwater Ct 3
Buttermere Ct 4
Chartley Cl 5
Kenilworth Rd 6

Portrush Rd
Forsyth
Belfry
The Parkway
Cook Cl
Browning Gr
Wordsworth Ct
Segefield
Epsom Cl
Swadtan Dr
Sutherland Gr

Lytham Rd
Lovelace Ave
Cliveden Ave
Kelso Gr
Milton Gr
Church Rd
Coveridge Dr
Spenser Ave
Chepstow Cl

The Pastures
The Paddock 1
The Windrow 2
The Cartway 3
Worcester Gr 4
Falowfield Ave
Jedburgh Gr
Elgin Ct
Kington
Darwin Ct
Stanley Ct
Sandown Fst Sch
Chepstow Cl

Perton

The Saddlestones
Meadow Croft
Leasowes Dr
Oatlands
Barley
Cornmill Gr
Gailey Dr
Wells Cl
Canterbury Dr
Cunningham Rd
Crowland Ave
Bader Rd
Anders Sq
Liby
PO
Tamar Gr
Severn Dr
Trent Cl
Hambl Gr
Wye
Enerdale Dr
Thirlmere Gr
Richmond Gr
Arundel Gr
Peverill Rd
Conway Gr

WV6

The Wheat Lands
Paxton
Browton Gr
Cheriton Gr
Rockingham Dr
Winceby Rd
Boundary Down
Wingeor Cl
Adwalton
Raglan Ave
Stoksay
Tintagel
Elimley
Warwick
Clynster Gr

Wren Ave
Pugh
Wykeham Gr
Butterfield Cl
Repton Gr
Vanbrugh Ct
Turnway Gn
Foster Gn 1
The Greens 2
Berkeley Cl
Cranbrook Gr
Perton Rd
Boundary Way
Ravensholme
Quail Gn
Smallshire
The Hecary

Perton
Orchard

Golf
Course

Mast

Old
Perton

WOLVERHAMPTON

Boundary
Farm

Nurton

Nurton Bank
Wolverhampton Rd
Great Moor Rd
Hollies La
Side La

Sling
Wood

Pattingham Rd

Perton
House

Perton
Court

Perton Brook Vale
Tinacre Hill
Rookwood Dr
Wightwick Hall Specl Sch

Middle
Wood

Monarch's Way

South Perton
Farm

Jenny Walkers La

Wightwick
Cherringham

Heath Hill Rd
Wightwick Hall Rd
Maysnood Dr
Wightwick
Manor
The Hegory

Freehold
Wood

Bridgnorth Rd
A454

Sybrina Rd
Castlecroft La
WV3

Staffordshire Way

Nurton Brook

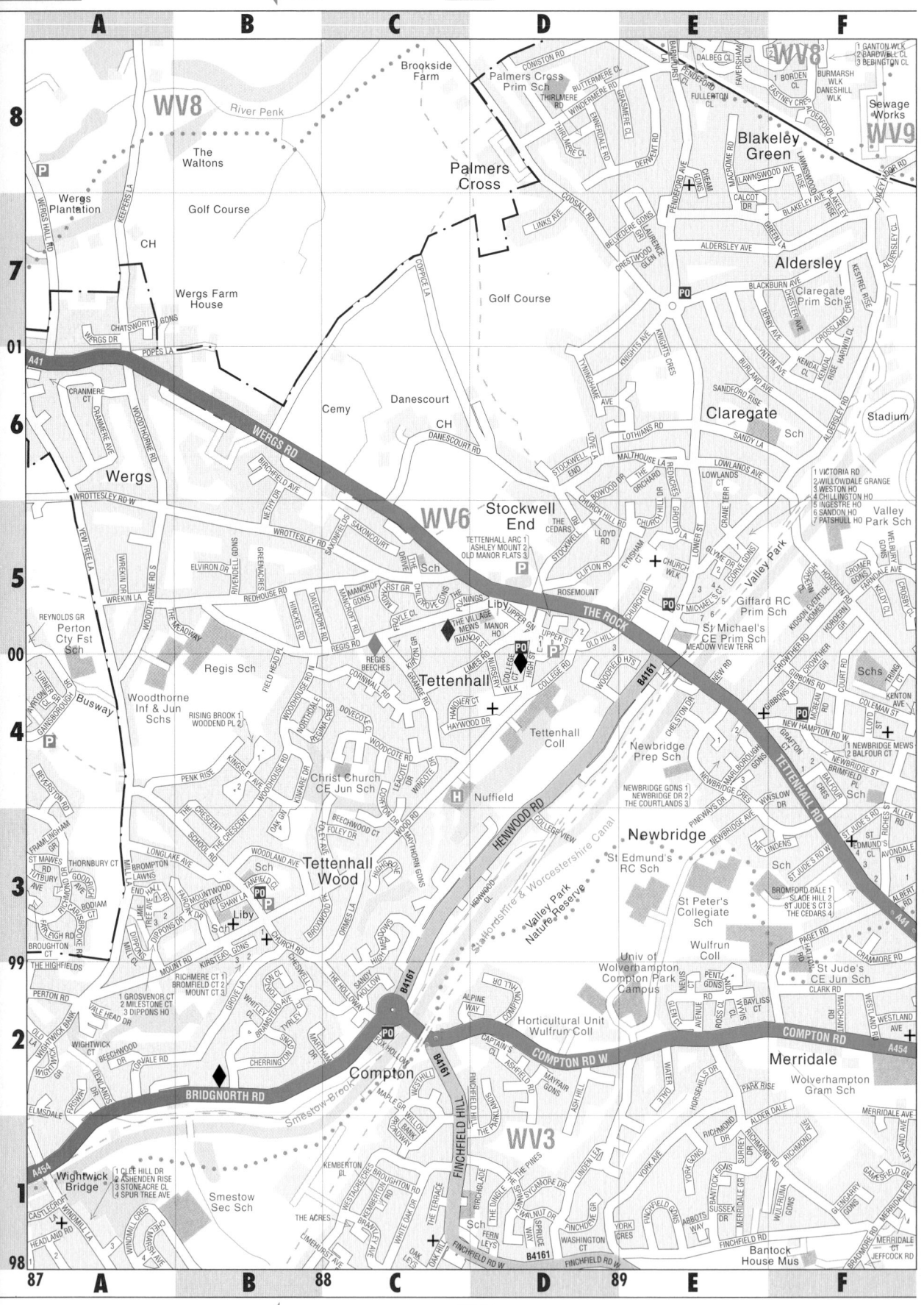

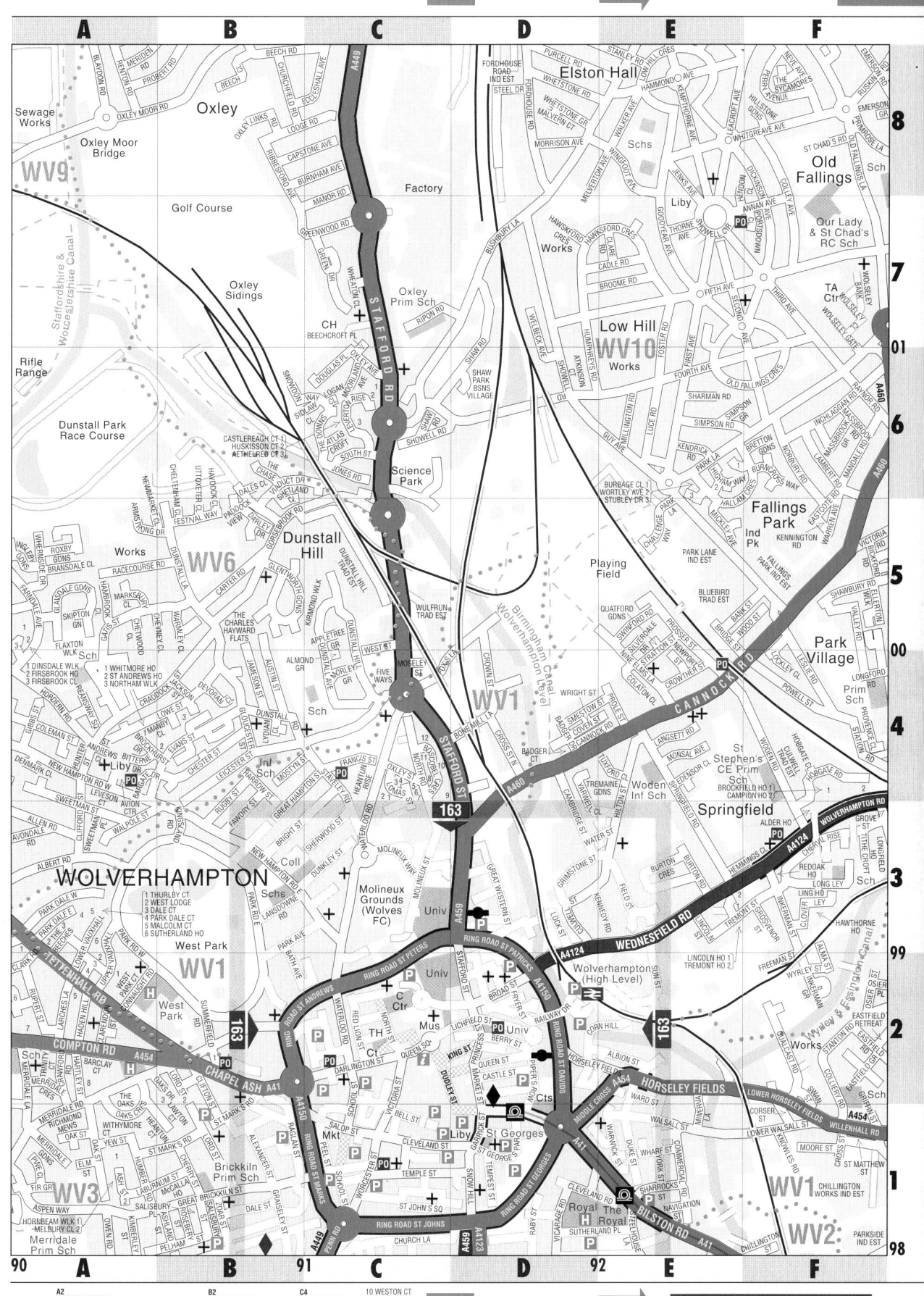

For full street detail of the highlighted area see page 163.

A2
1 CONNAUGHT HO
2 VAUXHALL HO
3 VAUXHALL AVE
4 MIDDLE VAUXHALL
5 HADEN CT
6 WESTLAND GDNS
7 COMPTON CT
8 BRIGHTON MEWS

B2
1 MEADOW ST
2 ROTARY CT
3 OAKLEIGH CT

C4
1 DURHAM HO
2 ESSEX HO
3 FLINT HO
4 GLOUCESTER HO
5 ARGYLL HO
6 BEDFORD HO
7 CUMBERLAND HO
8 LANE CT
9 TONG CT

10 WESTON CT
11 BIRCH CT
12 KILSALL CT

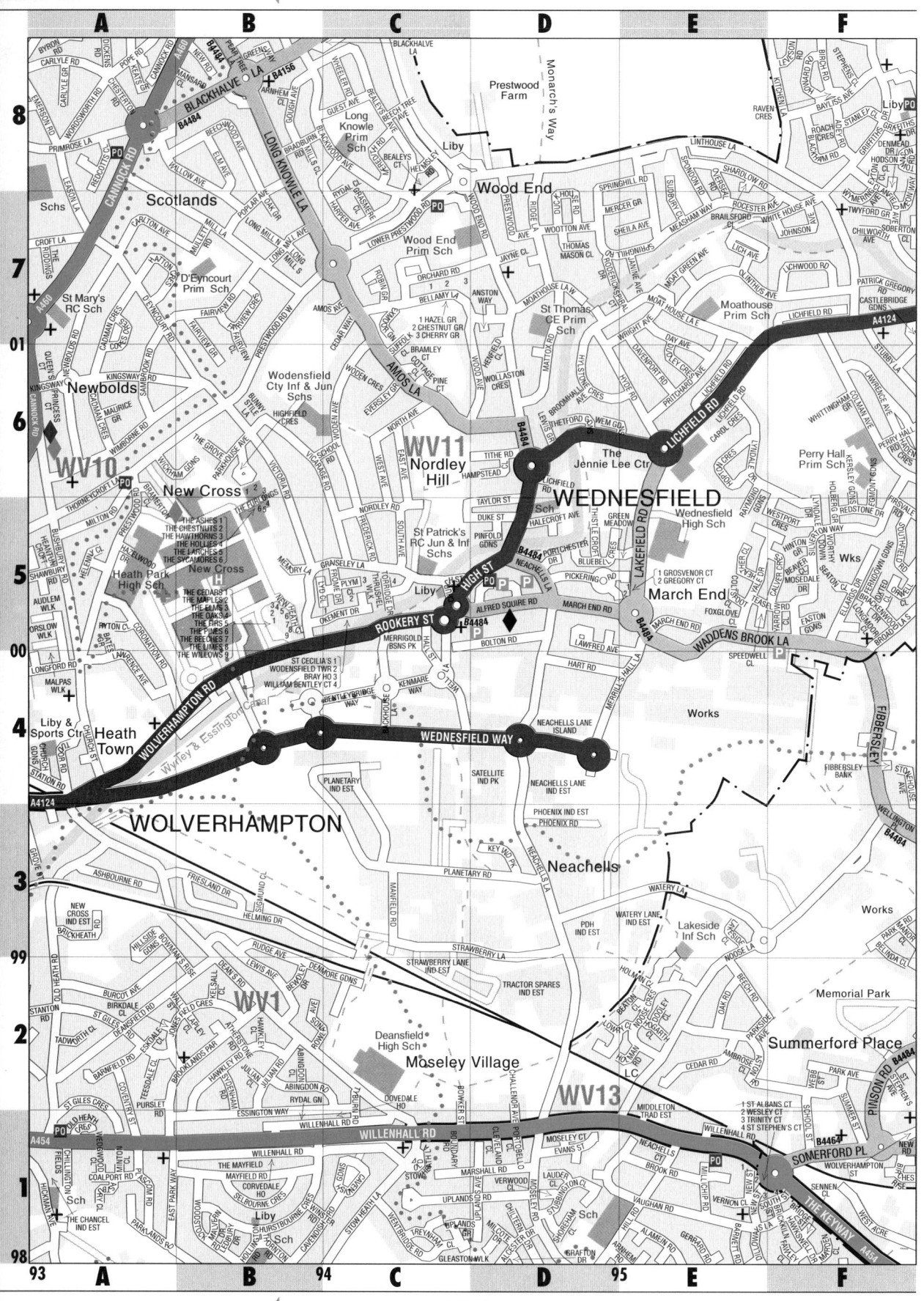

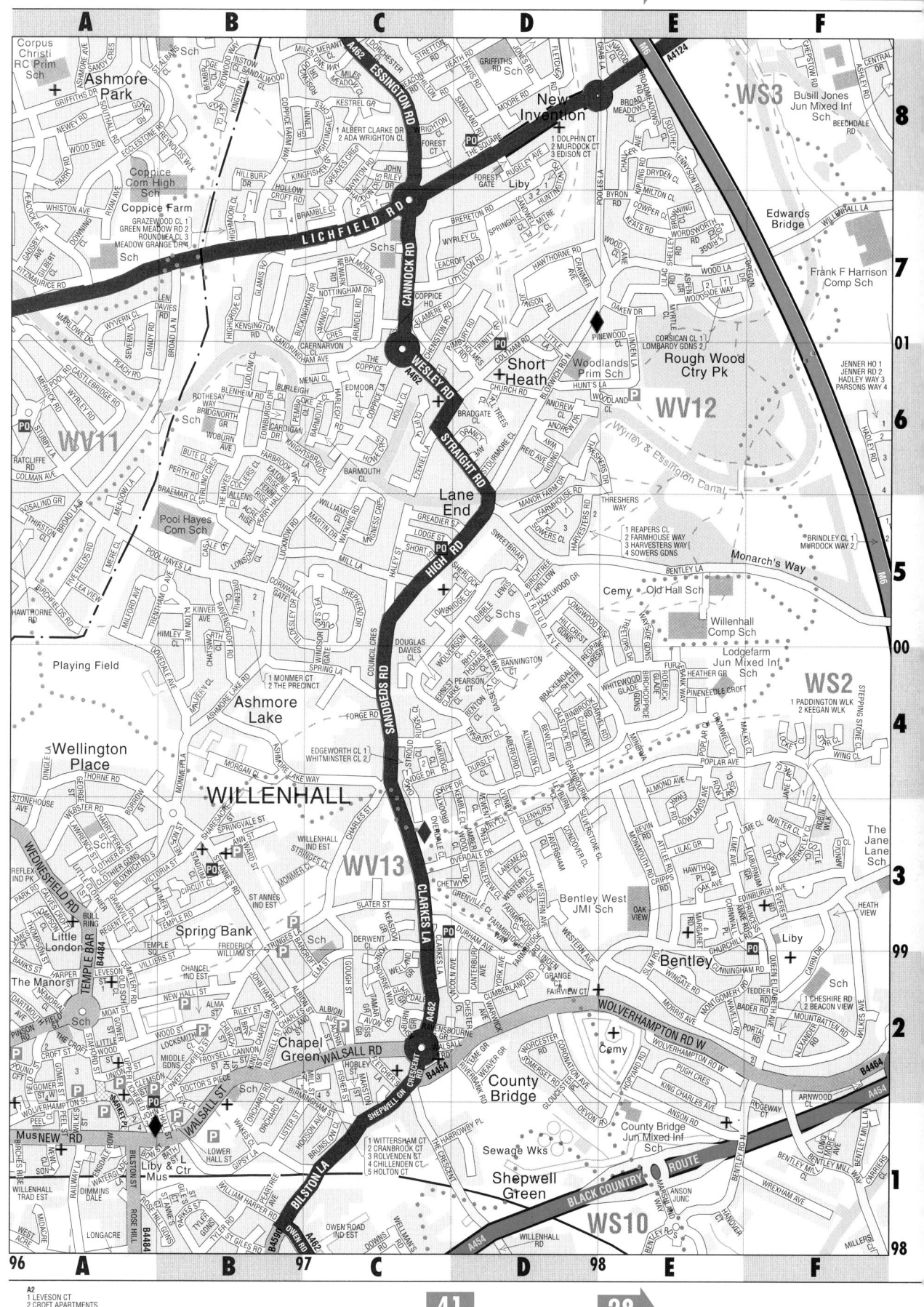

A2
1 LEVESON CT
2 CROFT APARTMENTS
3 CROFT IND EST
4 ST MARY'S CT
A1
1 ST STEPHEN'S GDNS
2 CROSS ST
3 CHEAPSIDE
4 ATLANTIC CT

28

A5
1 Murdock Way
B8
1 Church Moat Way
2 Carl Eynon Ct
3 Appledore Ct
4 The Crossings Ind Est

5 Ball Ho
6 Leadbeater Ho

C6
1 Ludlow Ho
2 Harlech Ho
3 Kenilworth Ho
4 Pembroke Ho

D8
1 Blakenall Cl
2 Victoria Ho

F6
1 Warner Pl
2 Dartmouth Ho
3 Gartbridge Wlk

27

14

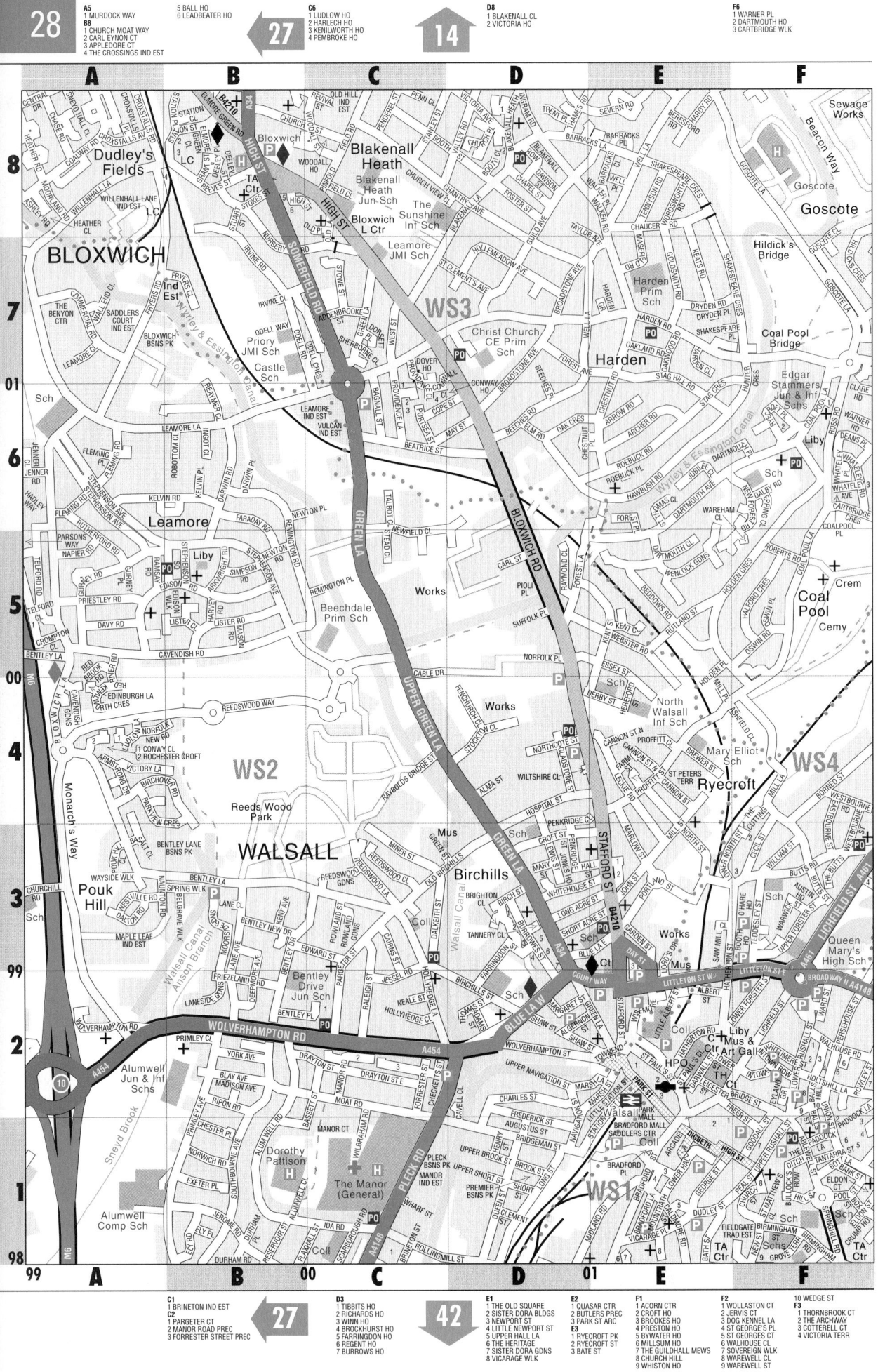

27

42

C1
1 Brineton Ind Est
C2
1 Pargeter Ct
2 Manor Road Prec
3 Forrester Street Prec

D3
1 Tibbits Ho
2 Richards Ho
3 Newport St
4 Brockhurst St
5 Upper Hall La
6 The Heritage
7 Sister Dora Gdns
8 Vicarage Wlk

E1
1 The Old Square
2 Sister Dora Bldgs
3 Newport St
4 Little Newport St
5 Upper Hall La
6 Regent Ho
7 Burrows Ho

E1
1 Ryecroft Pk
2 Ryecroft St
3 Bate St

E2
1 Quasar Ctr
2 Butlers Prec
3 Park St Arc
E3
1 Ryecroft Pk
2 Ryecroft St
3 Bate St

F1
1 Acorn Ctr
2 Croft Ho
3 Brookes Ho
4 Preston Ho
5 Bywater Ho
6 Millsum Ho
7 The Guildhall Mews
8 Church Hill
9 Whiston St

F2
1 Wollaston Ct
2 Jervis Ct
3 Dog Kennell La
4 St George's Pl
5 St Georges Ct
6 Walhouse Ct
7 Sovereign Wlk
8 Warewell Cl
9 Warewell St

10 Wedge St

F3
1 Thornbrook Ct
2 The Archway
3 Cotterell Ct
4 Victoria Terr

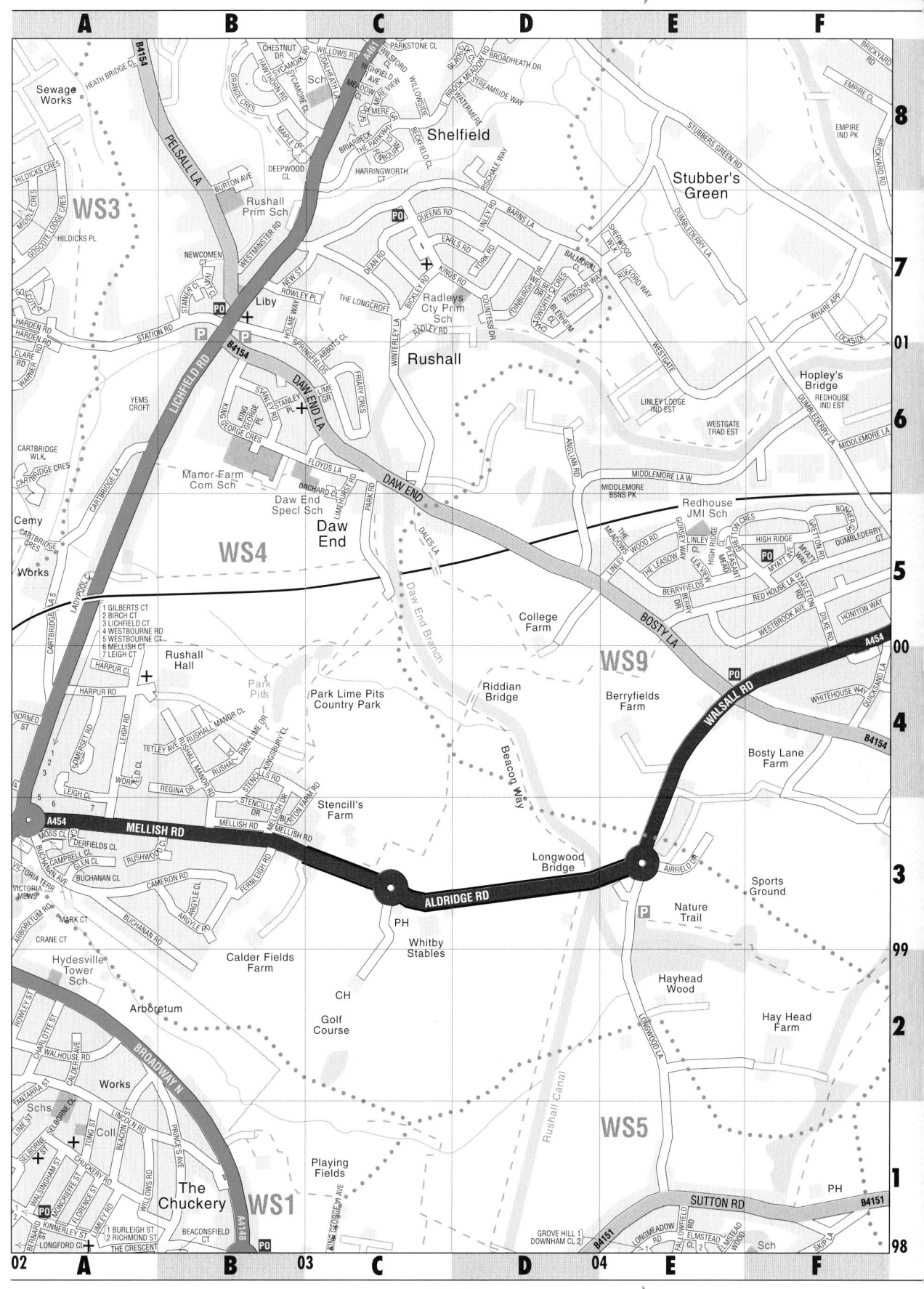

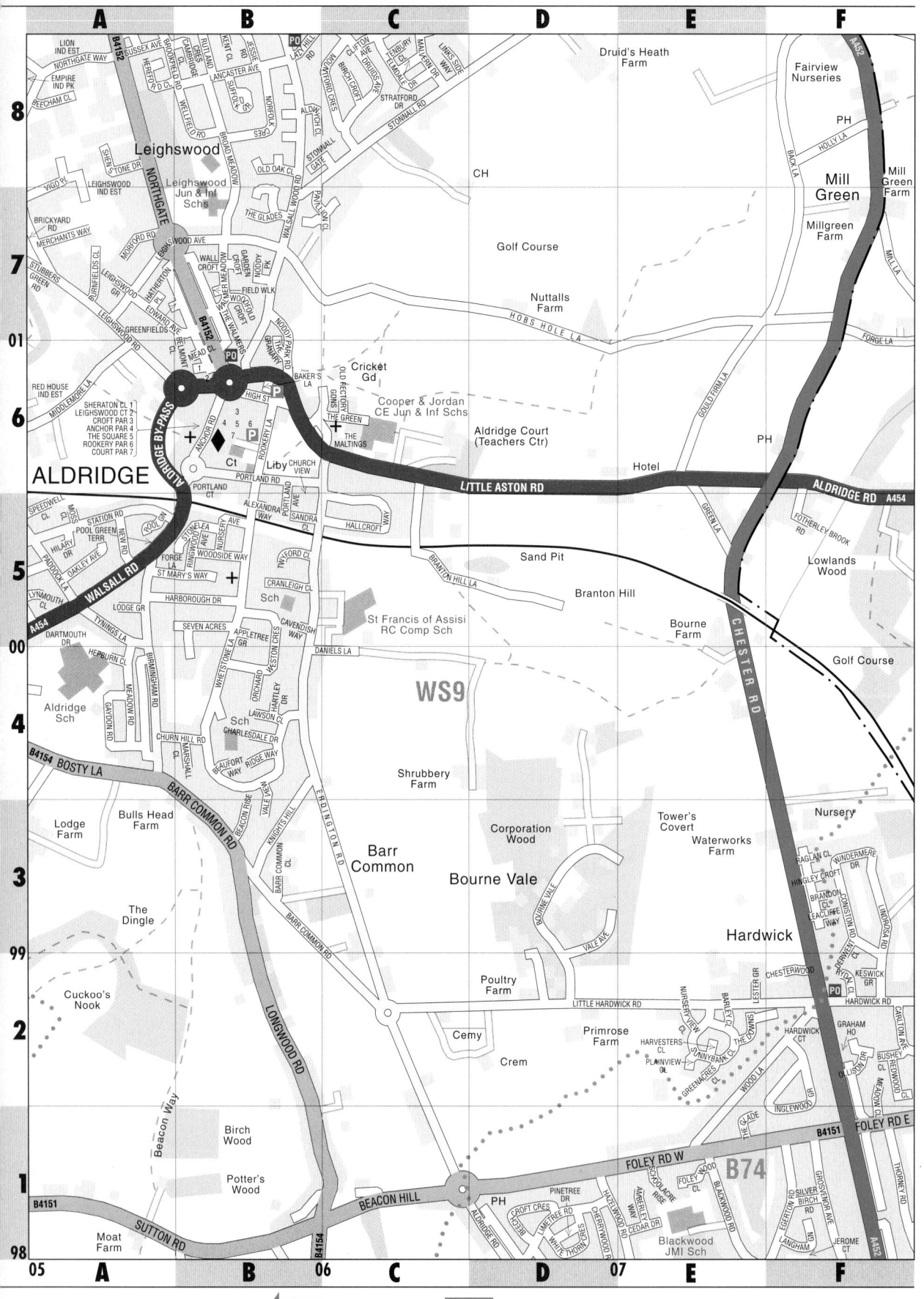

A B C D E F

8

7

WOOD LA

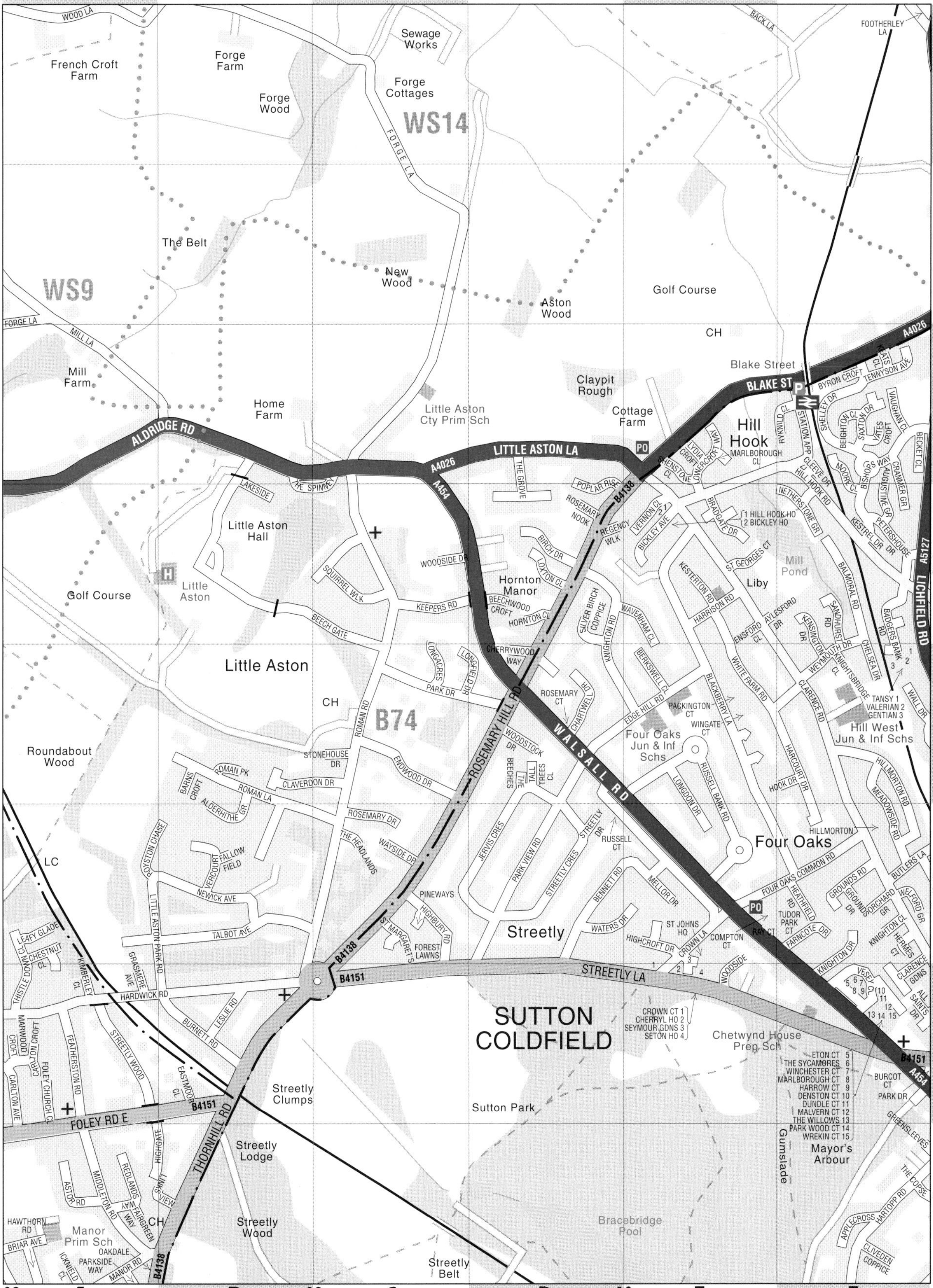

French Croft Farm

Forge Farm

Forge Wood

Sewage Works

Forge Cottages

WS14

FORGE LA

BACK LA

FOOTHERLEY LA

The Belt

New Wood

Aston Wood

Golf Course

WS9

01

A4026

FORGE LA

MILL LA

Mill Farm

Home Farm

Little Aston Cty Prim Sch

Claypit Rough

Cottage Farm

CH

Blake Street

BLAKE ST

Hill Hook

6

ALDRIDGE RD

A4026

LITTLE ASTON LA

PO

B4138

Marlborough CL

Mill Pond

LAKESIDE

THE SPINNEY

A454

THE GROVE

POPLAR RISE

ROSEMARY NOOK

REGENCY WLK

VERNON CL

BICKLEY AVE

BIRCH DR

LOXTON CL

WOODSIDE DR

1 HILL HOOK HO
2 BICKLEY HO

Liby

5

Little Aston Hall

H

Little Aston

SQUIRREL WLK

BEECH GATE

KEEPERS RD

Hornton Manor

BEECHWOOD CROFT

HORNTON CL

SILVER BIRCH COPPICE

KESTERTON RD

ST GEORGES CT

HARRISON RD

AYLESFORD DR

00

Golf Course

Little Aston

B74

CH

ROMAN PK

BARNS CROFT

ALDERHITHE

LONGCRES

PARK DR

LONGFIELD RD

ROMAN LA

CLAVERDON DR

CHERRYWOOD WAY

ROSEMARY CT

CHARTWELL

EDGE HILL RD

PACKINGTON CT

WINGATE CL

Four Oaks Jun & Inf Schs

WHITE FARM RD

Hill West Jun & Inf Schs

TANSY 1
VALERIAN 2
GENTIAN 3

4

Roundabout Wood

STONEHOUSE DR

FINWOOD DR

ROSEMARY DR

WOODSTOCK DR

THE BEECHES

THE TALL TREES CL

ROSEMARY HILL RD

WALSALL RD

RUSSELL BANK RD

HILLMORTON RD

MEADOWSIDE RD

Four Oaks

HILLMORTON RD

3

LC

KYNISTON CHASE

VERNCOURT FALLOW FIELD

NEWICK AVE

TALBOT AVE

THE HEADLANDS

WAYSIDE DR

PINEWAYS

JERVIS CRES

PARK VIEW RD

STREETLY CRES

STREETLY DR

RUSSELL CT

BENNETT RD

MELLOR DR

Four Oaks Common Rd

GROUNDS RD

HEATHFIELD

ORCHARD CROFT

BUTLERS RD

KNIGHTON CL

HELMES RD

WELFORD RD

PO

Streetly

WATERS DR

ST JOHNS RD

HIGHCROFT DR

CROWN LA

COMPTON CT

TUDOR PARK

FARNCOTE CL

KNIGHTON RD

CLARENCE GDNS

99

LEAFY GLADE

CHESTNUT CL

THISTLE DOWN RD

KIMBERLEY CL

GRASMERE AVE

HARDWICK RD

LESLIE RD

BURNETT RD

B4138

ST MARGARETS

HIGHBURY RD

FOREST LAWNS

STREETLY LA

CROWN CT 1
CHERRYL HO 2
SEYMOUR GDNS 3
SETON HO 4

ALL SAINTS DR

SUTTON COLDFIELD

ETON CT 5
THE SYCAMORES 6
WINCHESTER CT 7
MARLBOROUGH CT 8
HARROW CT 9
DENSTON CT 10
DUNDLE CT 11
MALVERN CT 12
THE WILLOWS 13
PARK WOOD CT 14
WREKIN CT 15

2

MARWOOD CROFT

FOLEY RD N

CARLTON AVE

FOLEY CHURCH CL

ASTOR RD

REDLANDS CL

MIDDLETON RD

EASTMOOR

STREETLY WOOD

B4151

THORNHILL RD

Streetly Clumps

Chetwynd House Prep Sch

Gumslade

Mayor's Arbour

BURCOT CT

PARK DR

A454

B4151

GREENSLEEVES

THE COPSE

1

HAWTHORN RD

BRIAR AVE

Manor Prim Sch

OAKDALE

PARKSIDE WAY

MANOR RD

CH

B4151

FOLEY RD E

Streetly Lodge

Streetly Wood

Sutton Park

Streetly Belt

Bracebridge Pool

APPLECROSS COPPICE

HARTOPP RD

CLIVEDEN COPPICE

98

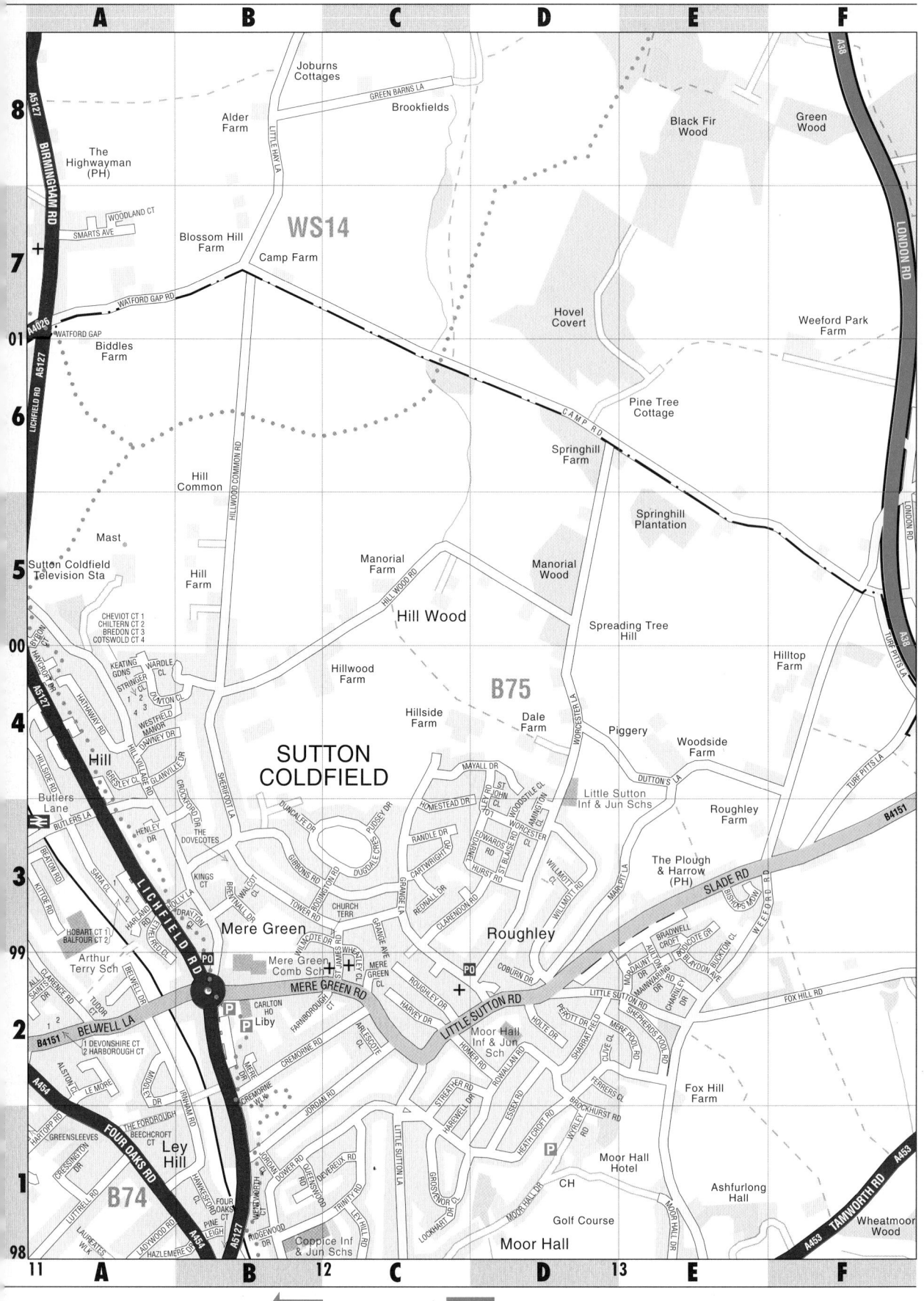

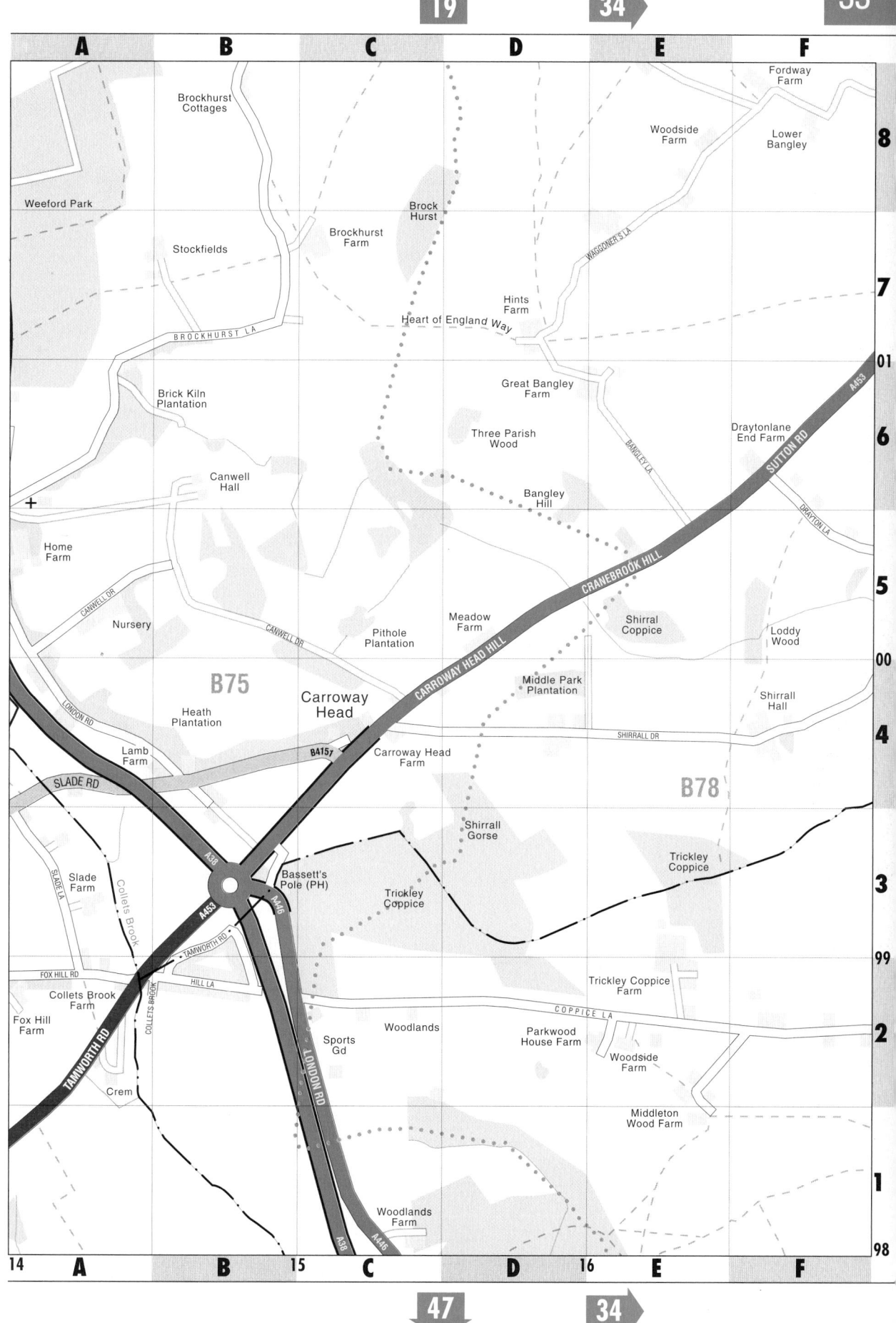

A B C D E F

Fordway Farm

Woodside Farm

Lower Bangley

Weeford Park

Brockhurst Cottages

Stockfields

Brockhurst Farm

Brock Hurst

WAGGONER'S LA

Hints Farm

Heart of England Way

BROCKHURST LA

Great Bangley Farm

Draytonlane End Farm

SUTTON RD

A453

Brick Kiln Plantation

Three Parish Wood

BANGLEY LA

DRAYTON LA

Canwell Hall

Bangley Hill

CRANEBROOK HILL

Shirral Coppice

Loddy Wood

Home Farm

CANWELL DR

Nursery

CANWELL DR

Pithole Plantation

Meadow Farm

CARROWAY HEAD HILL

Middle Park Plantation

Shirrall Hall

B75

Carroway Head

Heath Plantation

LONDON RD

Lamb Farm

B4157

Carroway Head Farm

SHIRRALL DR

B78

SLADE RD

Shirrall Gorse

Trickley Coppice

Slade Farm

SLADE LA

A38

Collets Brook

A453

Bassett's Pole (PH)

A446

Trickley Coppice

Trickley Coppice Farm

FOX HILL RD

TAMWORTH RD

COLLETS BROOK

HILL LA

COPPICE LA

Collets Brook Farm

Fox Hill Farm

Woodlands

Parkwood House Farm

Woodside Farm

Sports Gd

LONDON RD

Crem

Middleton Wood Farm

A38

A446

Woodlands Farm

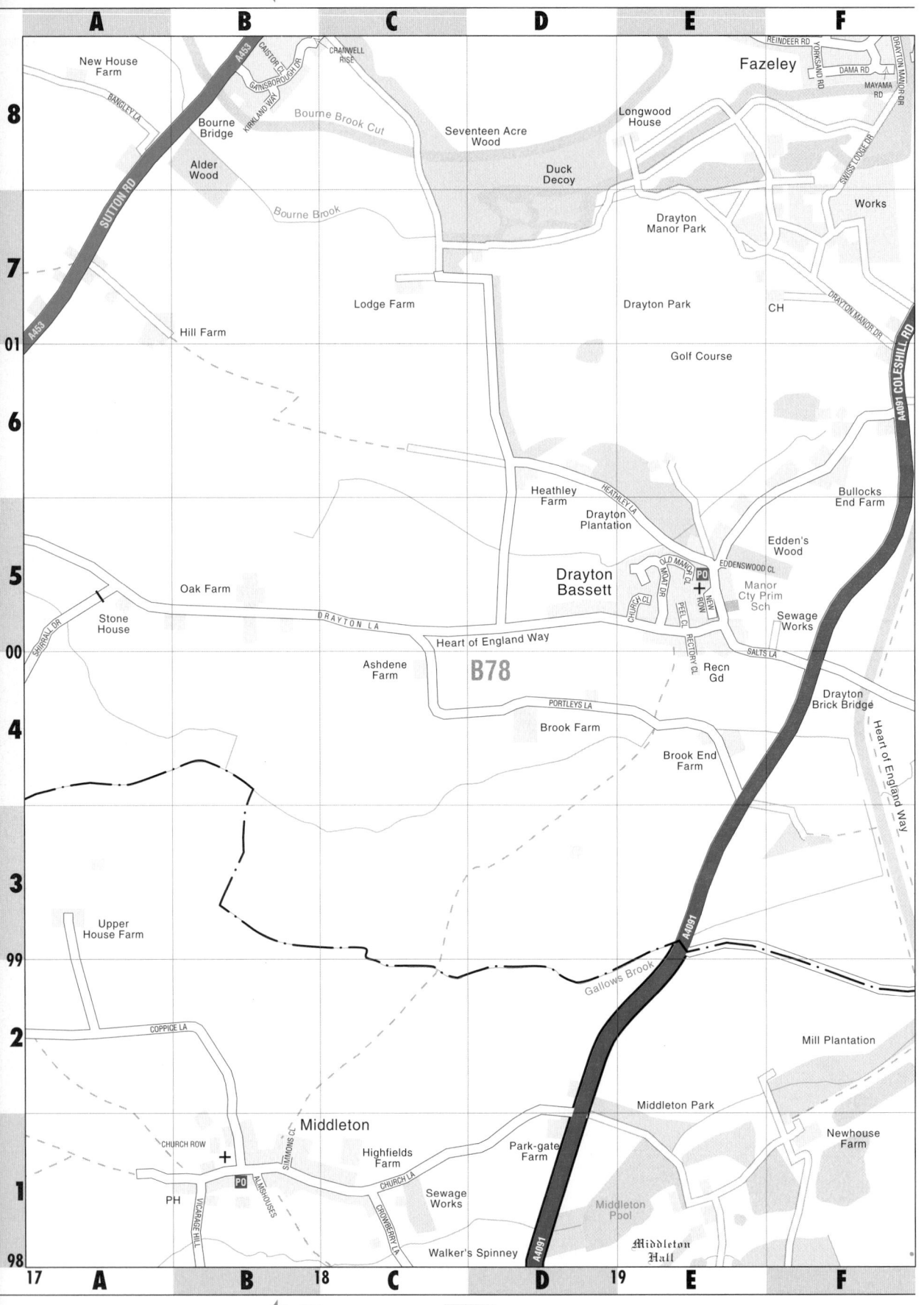

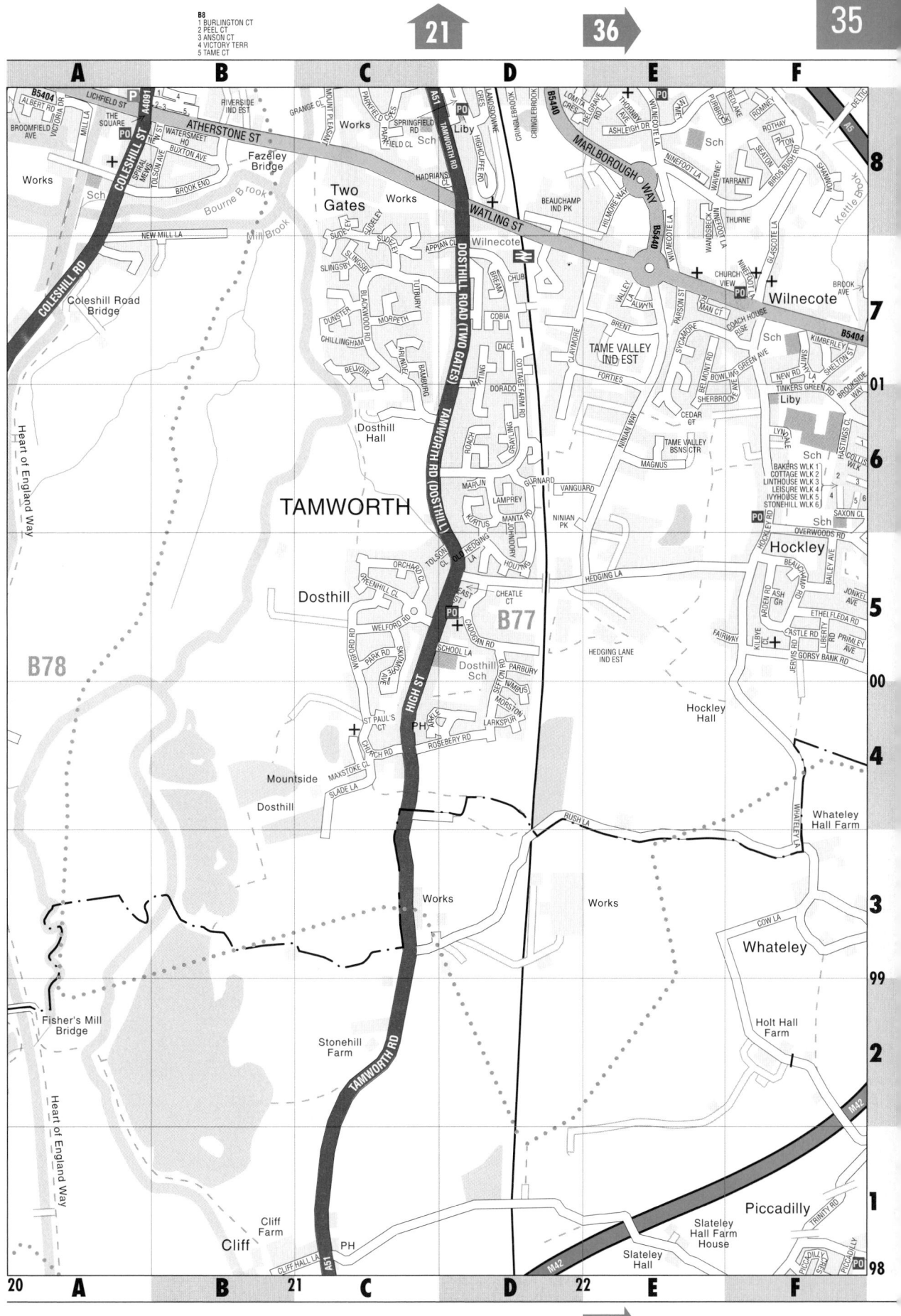

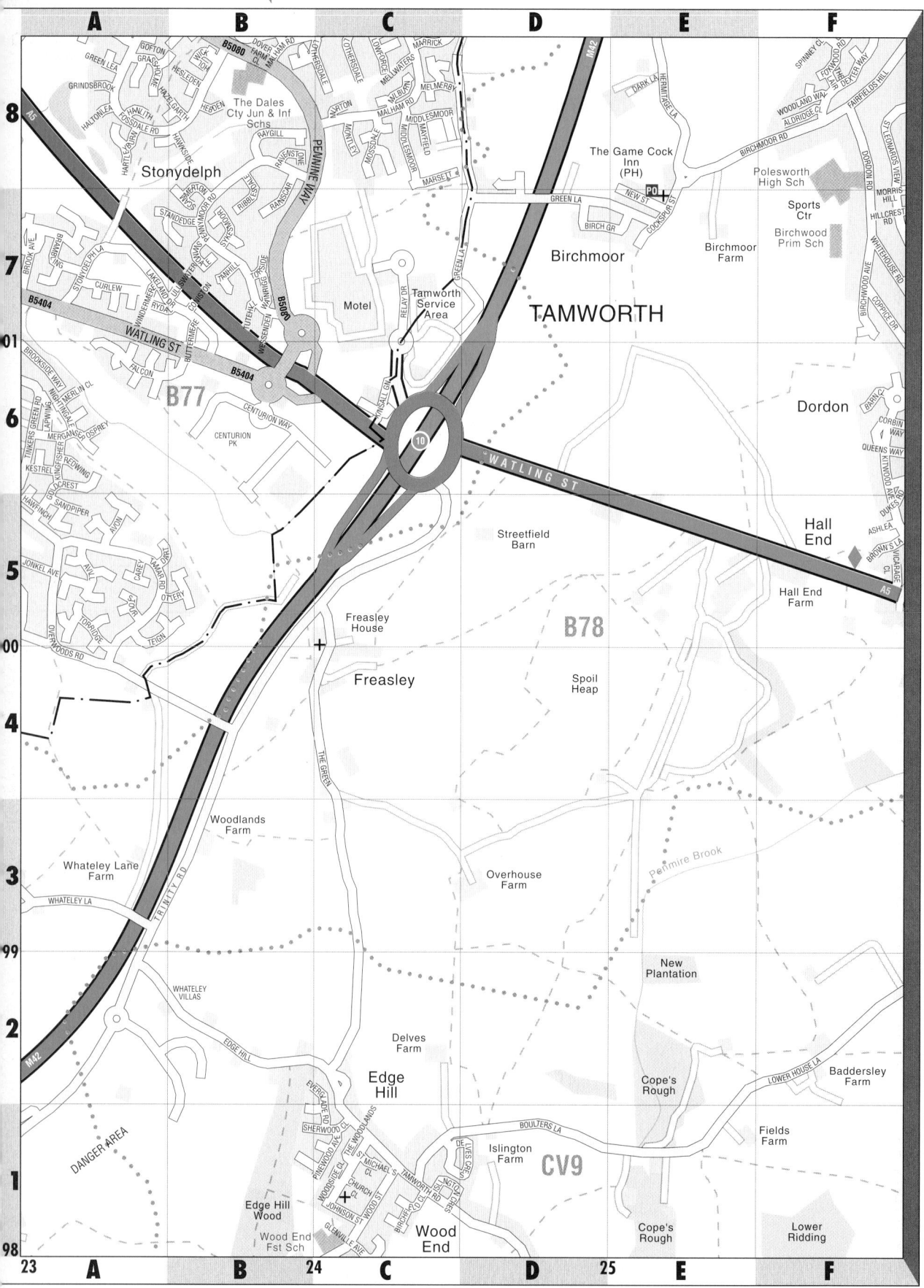

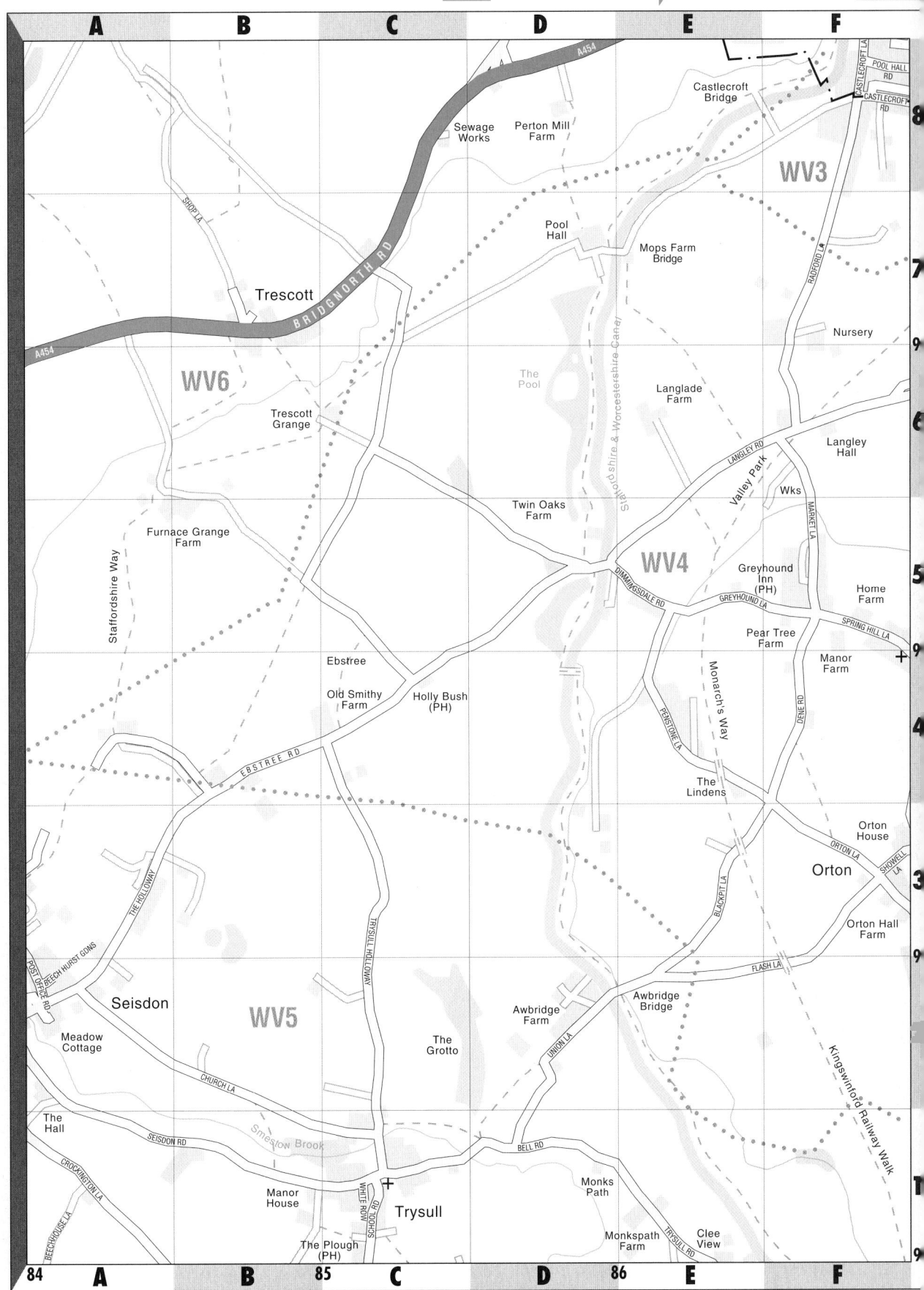

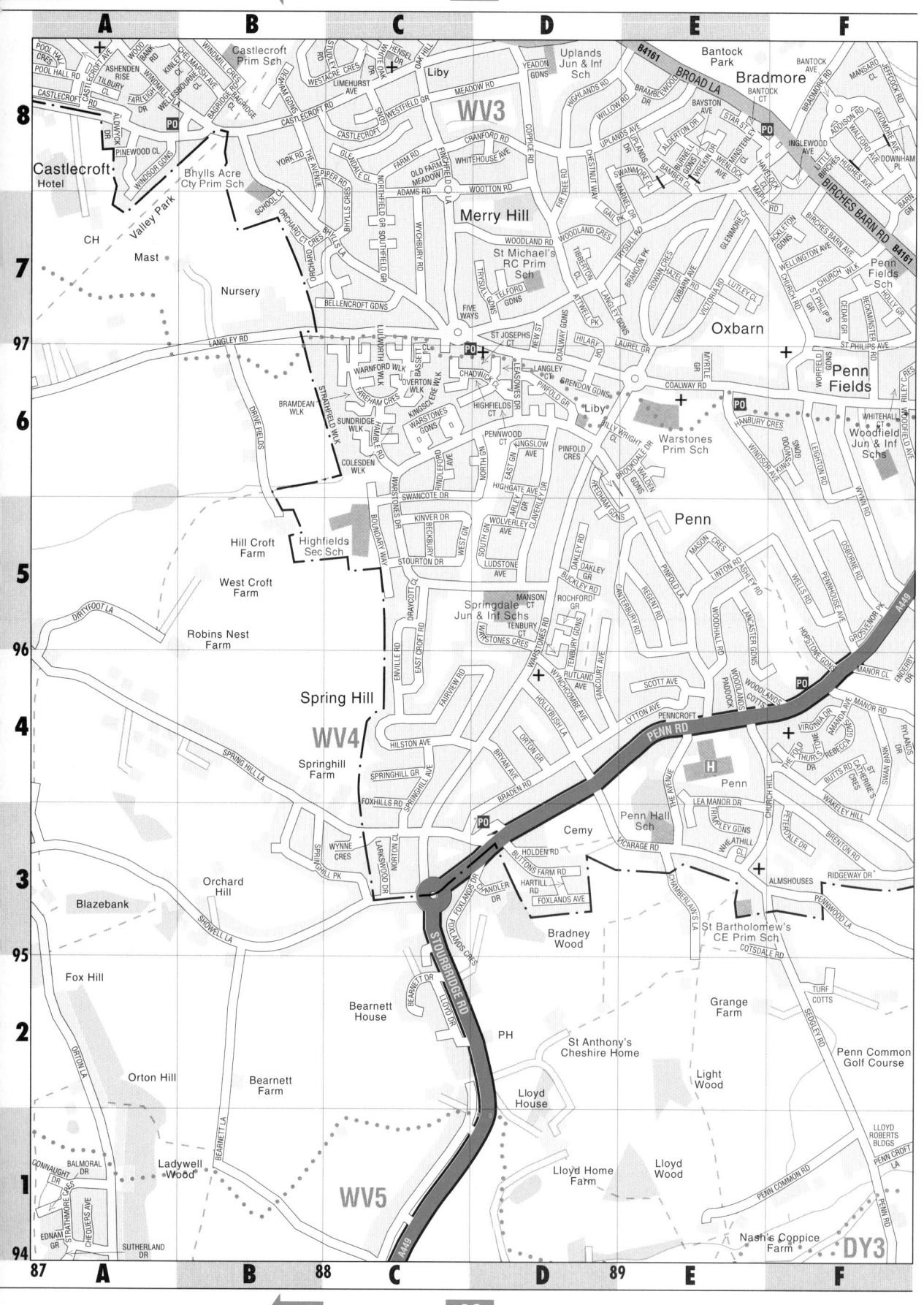

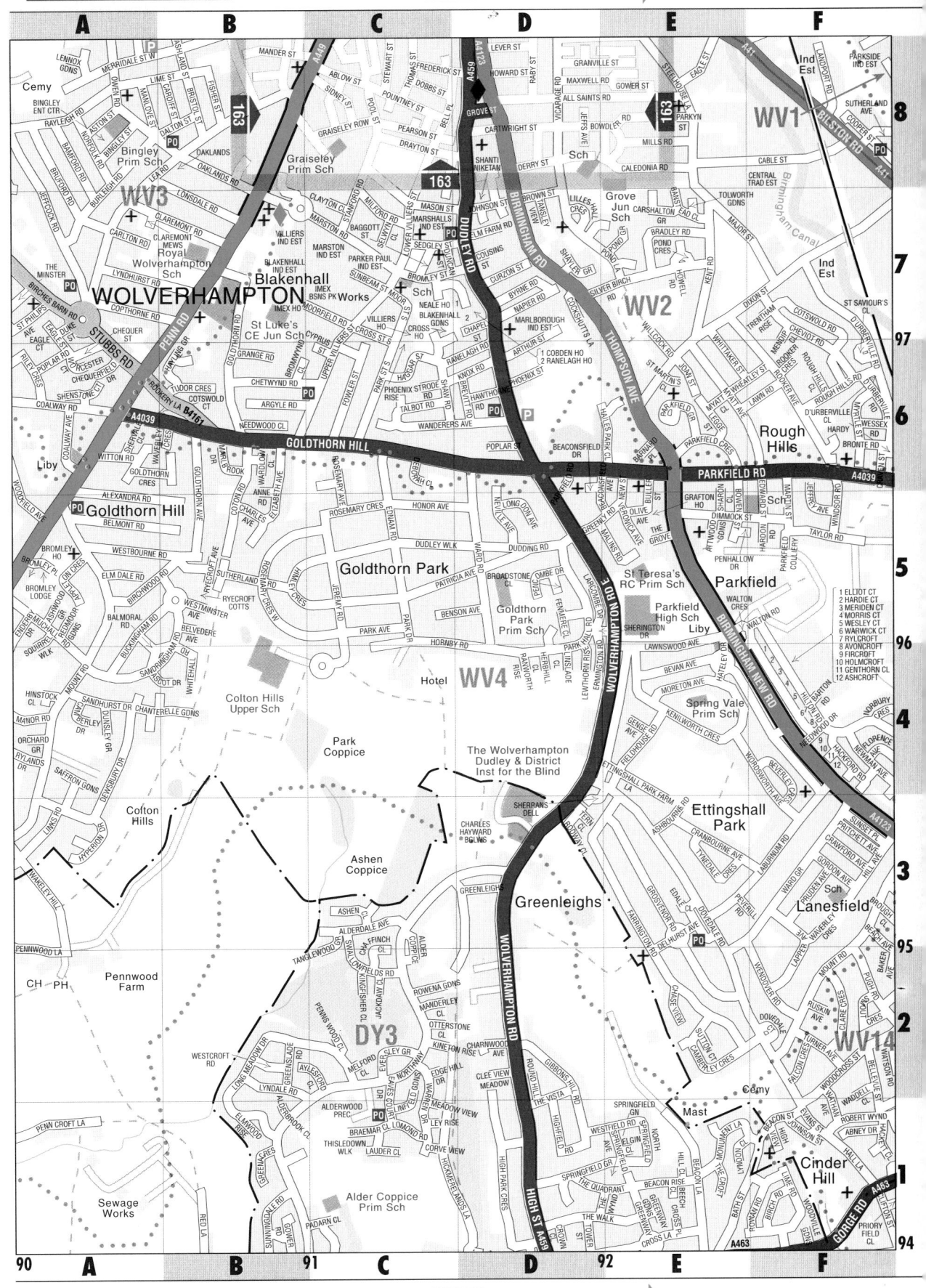

For full street detail of the highlighted area see page 163.

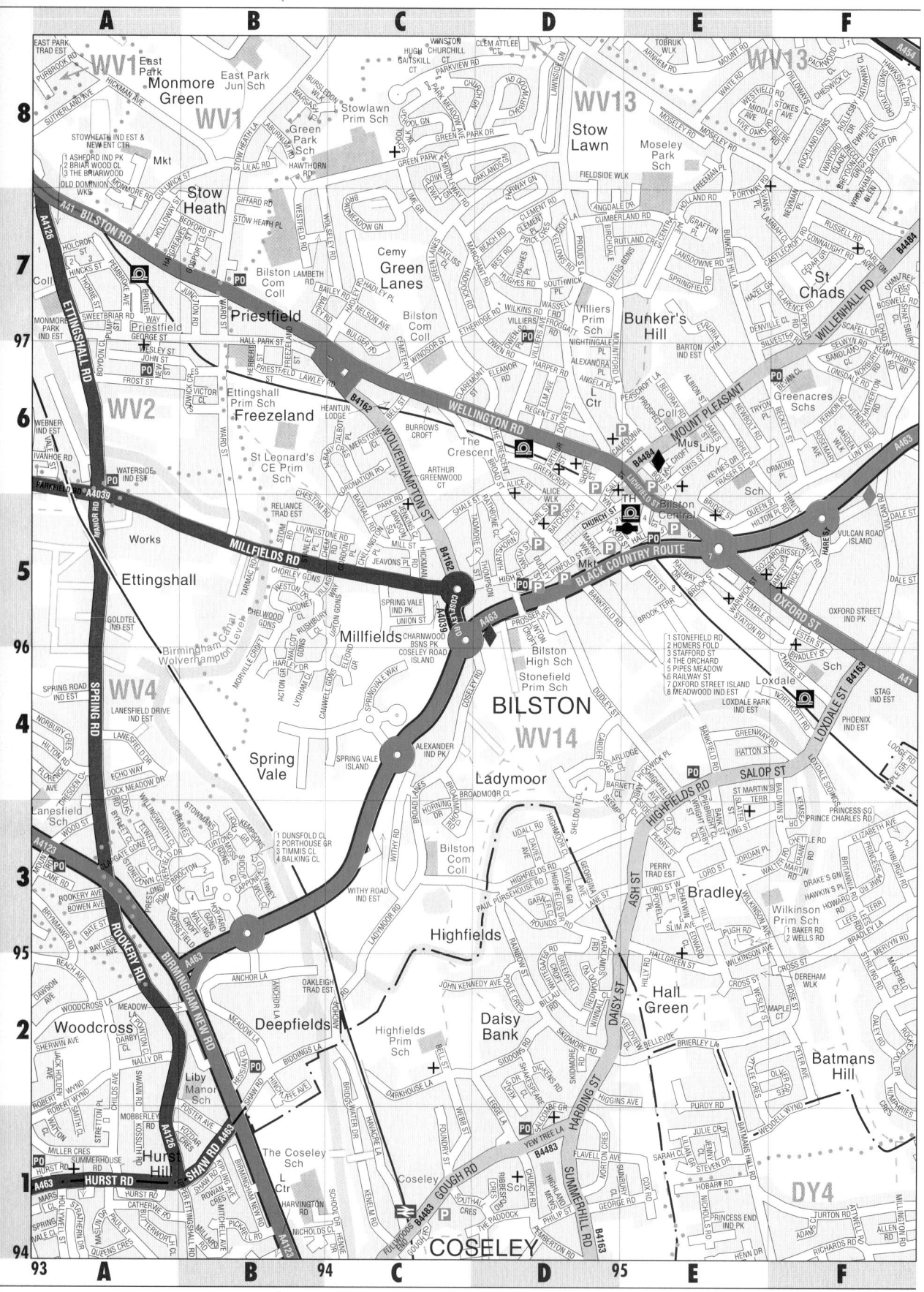

D6
1 THE LEYS
2 HIGH ST
3 GREAT CROFT HO
4 JOHN WOOTON HO
5 GREAT CROFT ST
6 PICTUREDROME WAY

27

42

41

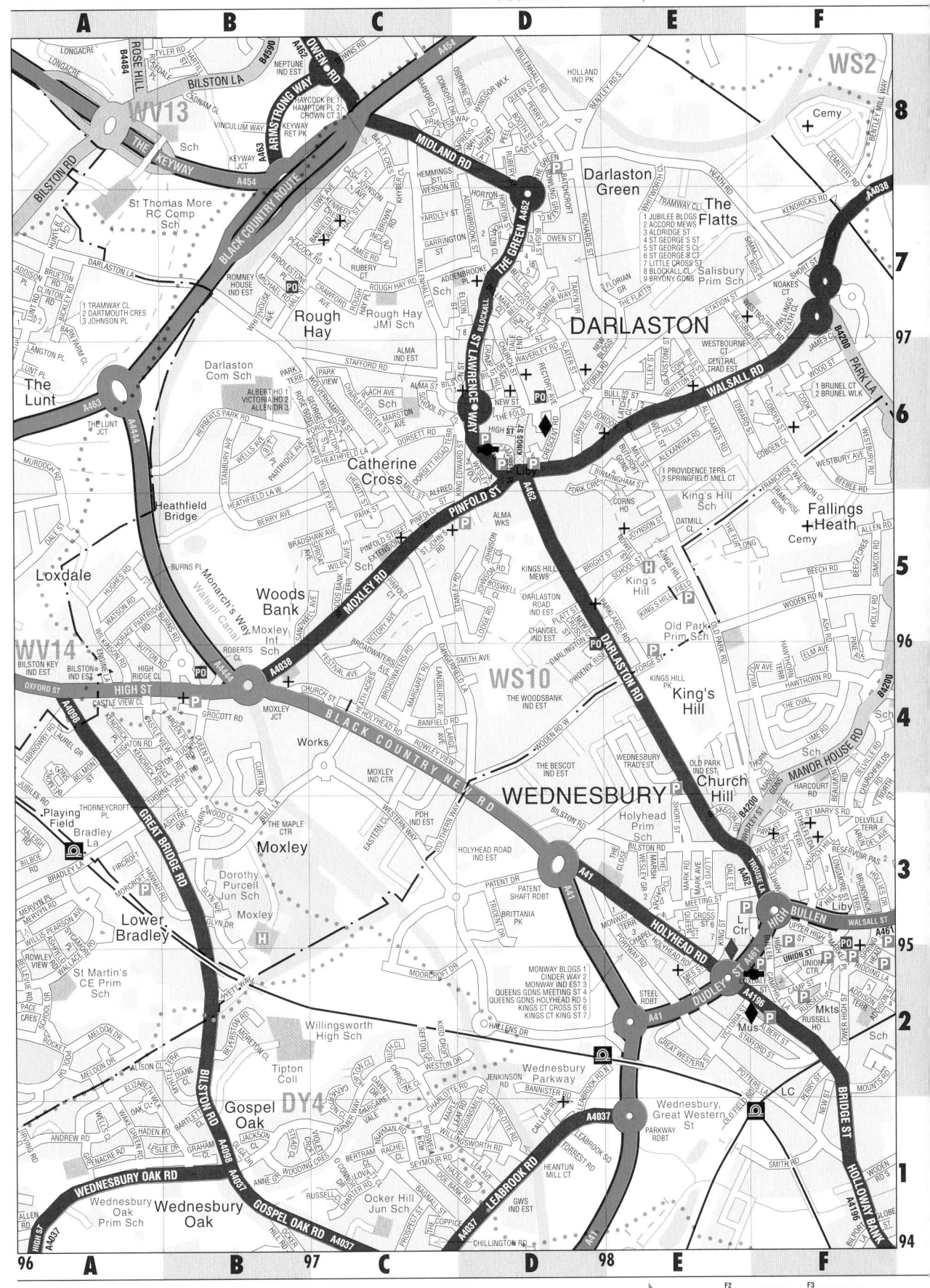

52

42

F2
1 UPPER RUSSELL ST
2 SHAMBLES
3 GREGORY CL
4 RAILWAY TERR

F3
1 CHURCH HILL CT
2 GEORGIAN GDNS
3 ST BARTHOLOMEW TERR
4 PARTRIDGE CT
5 LOVER'S WLK
6 CHURCH HILL

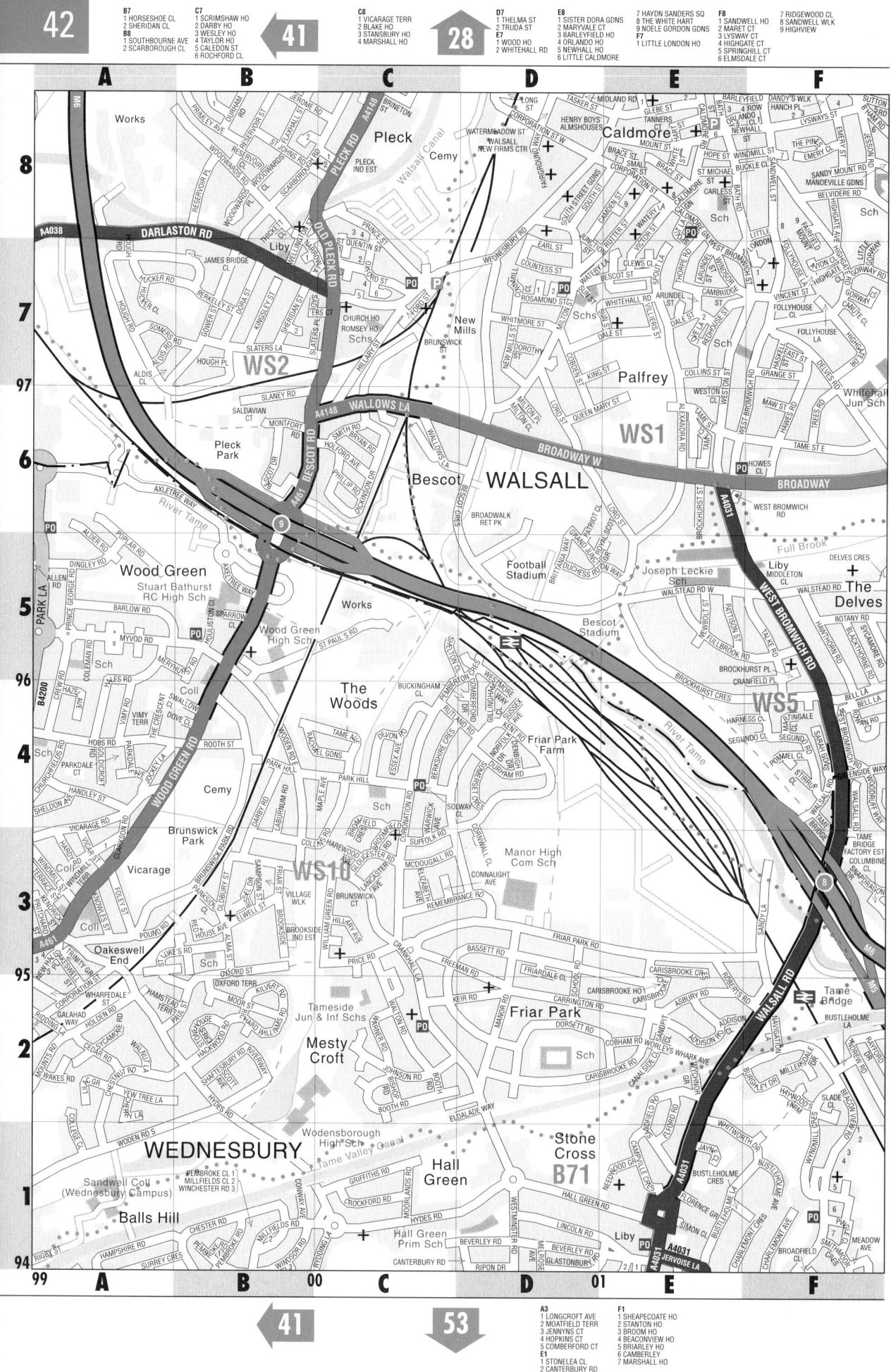

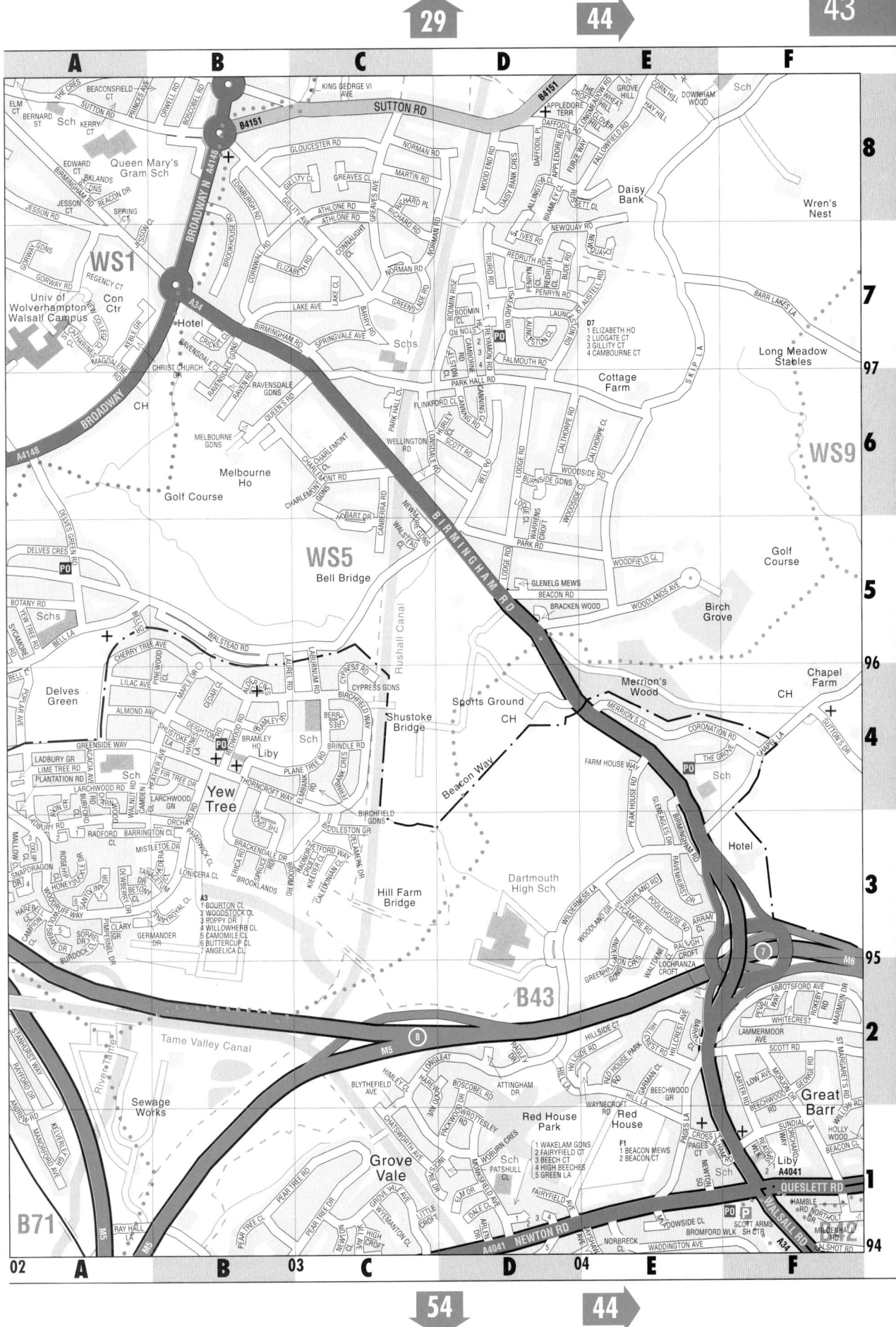

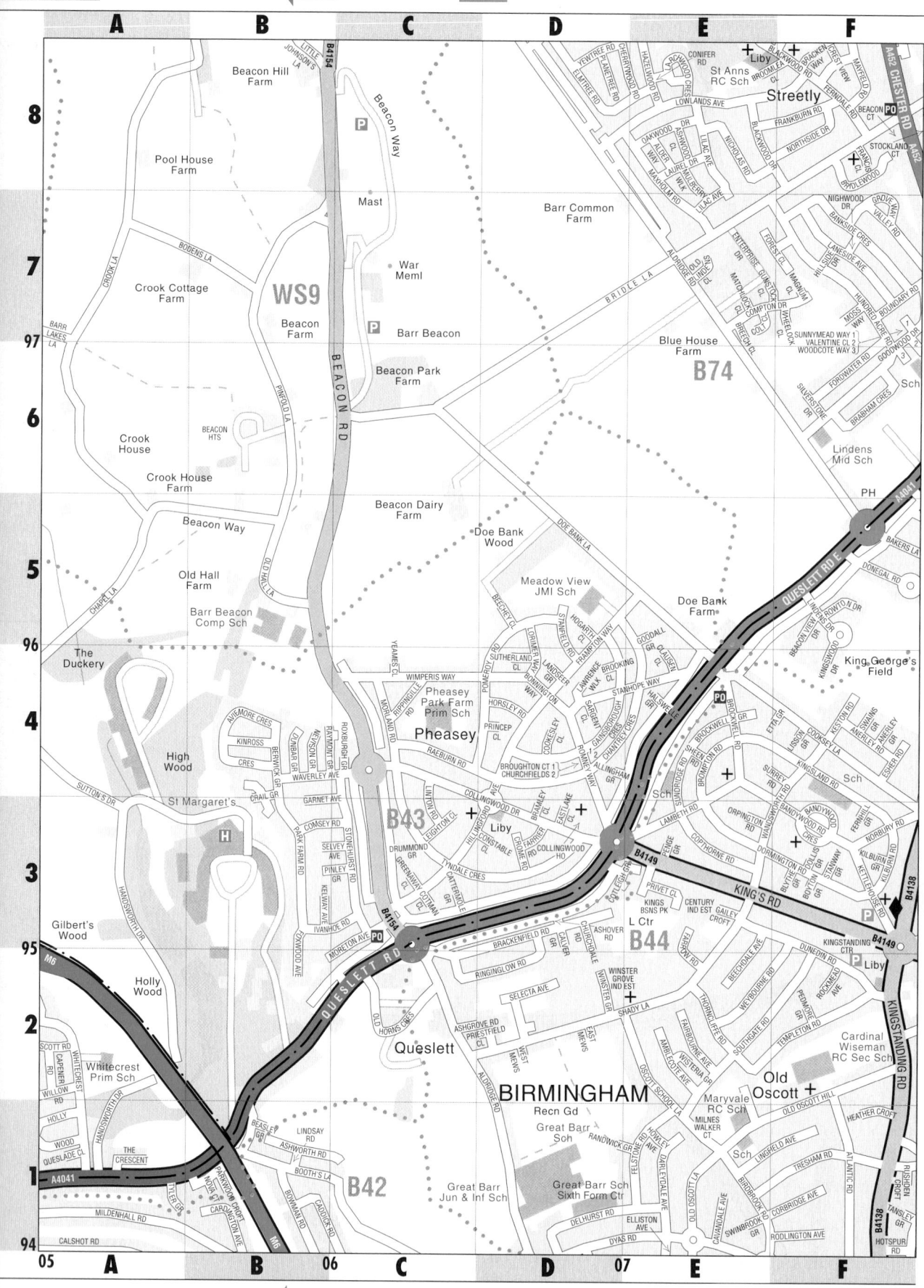

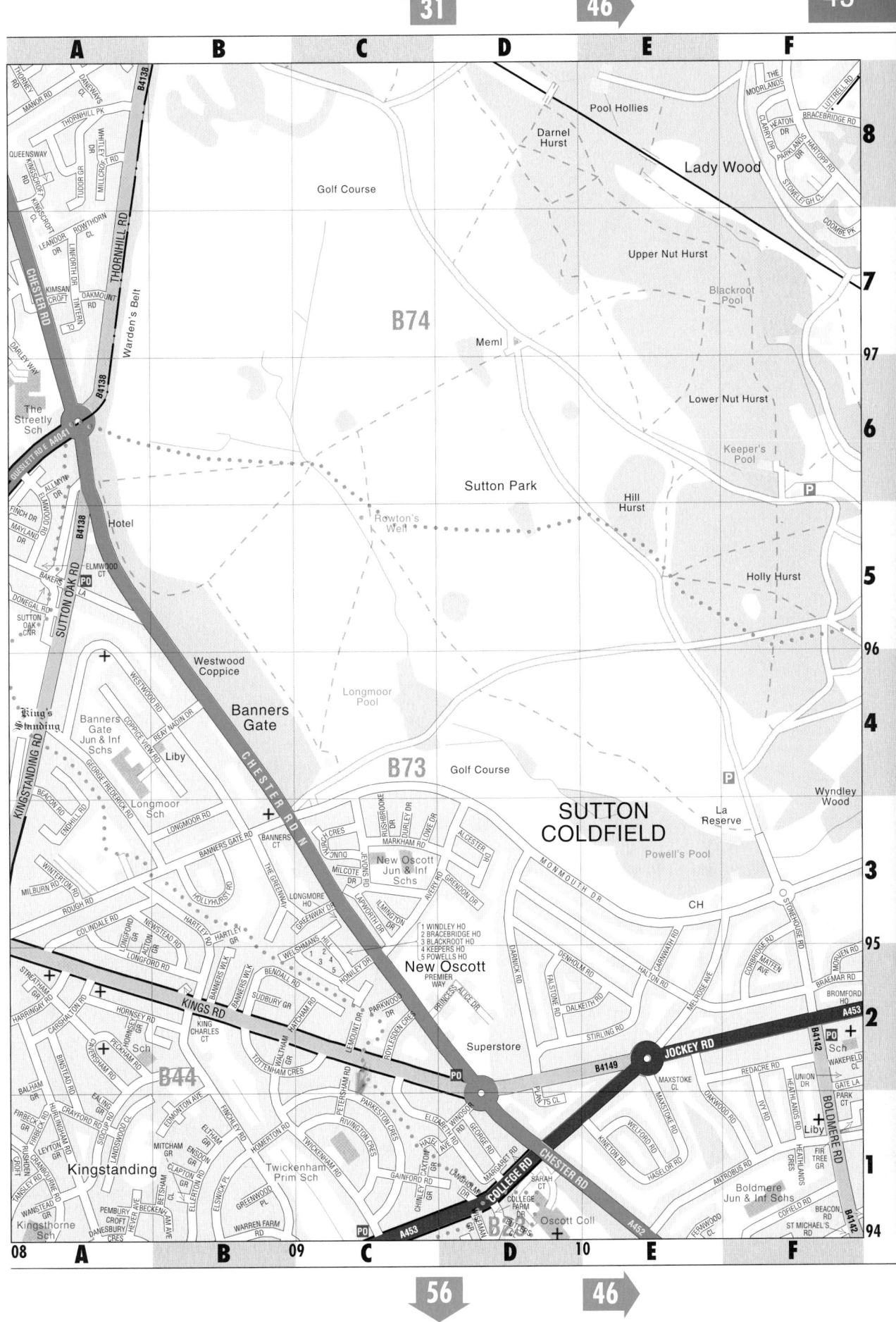

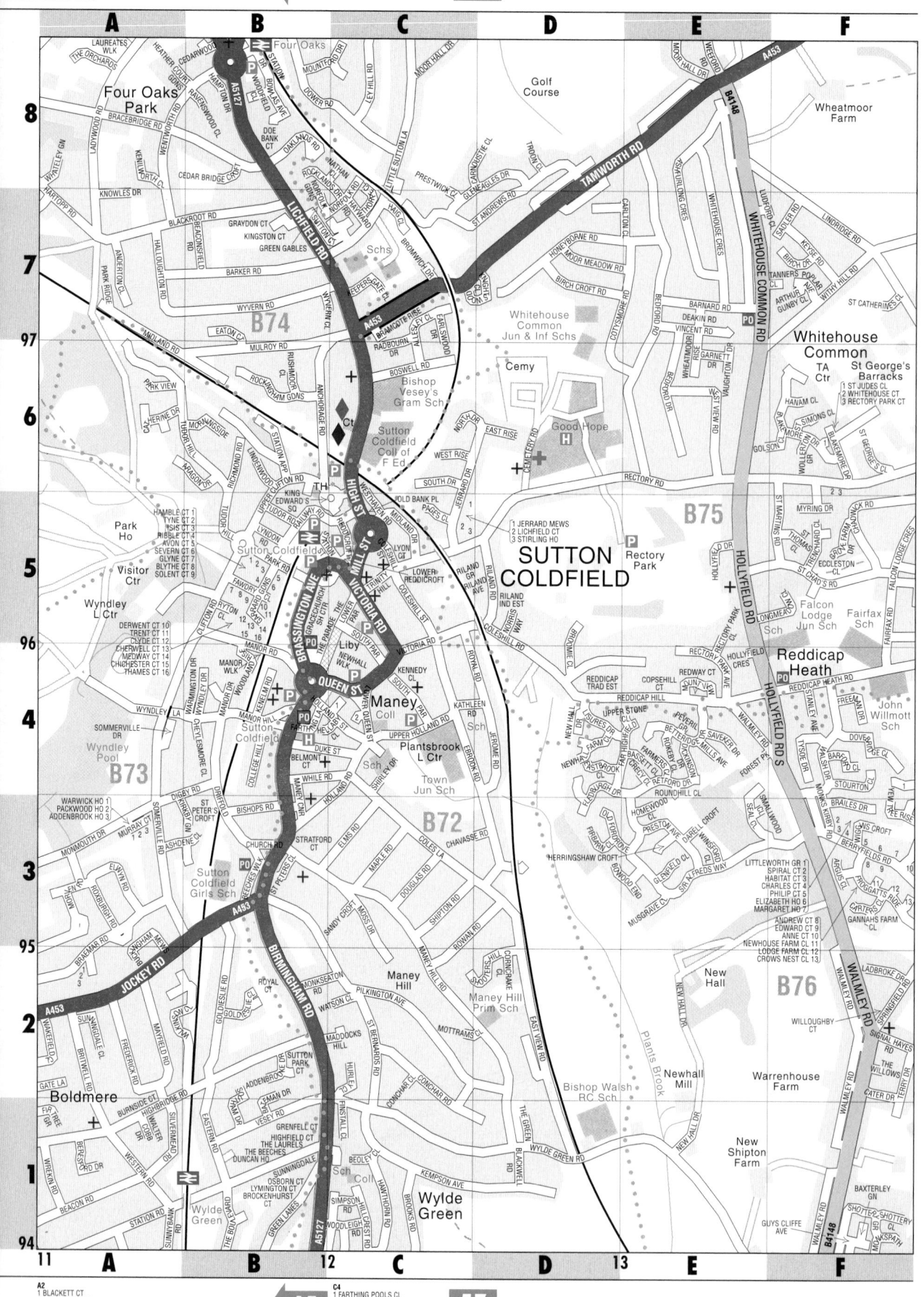

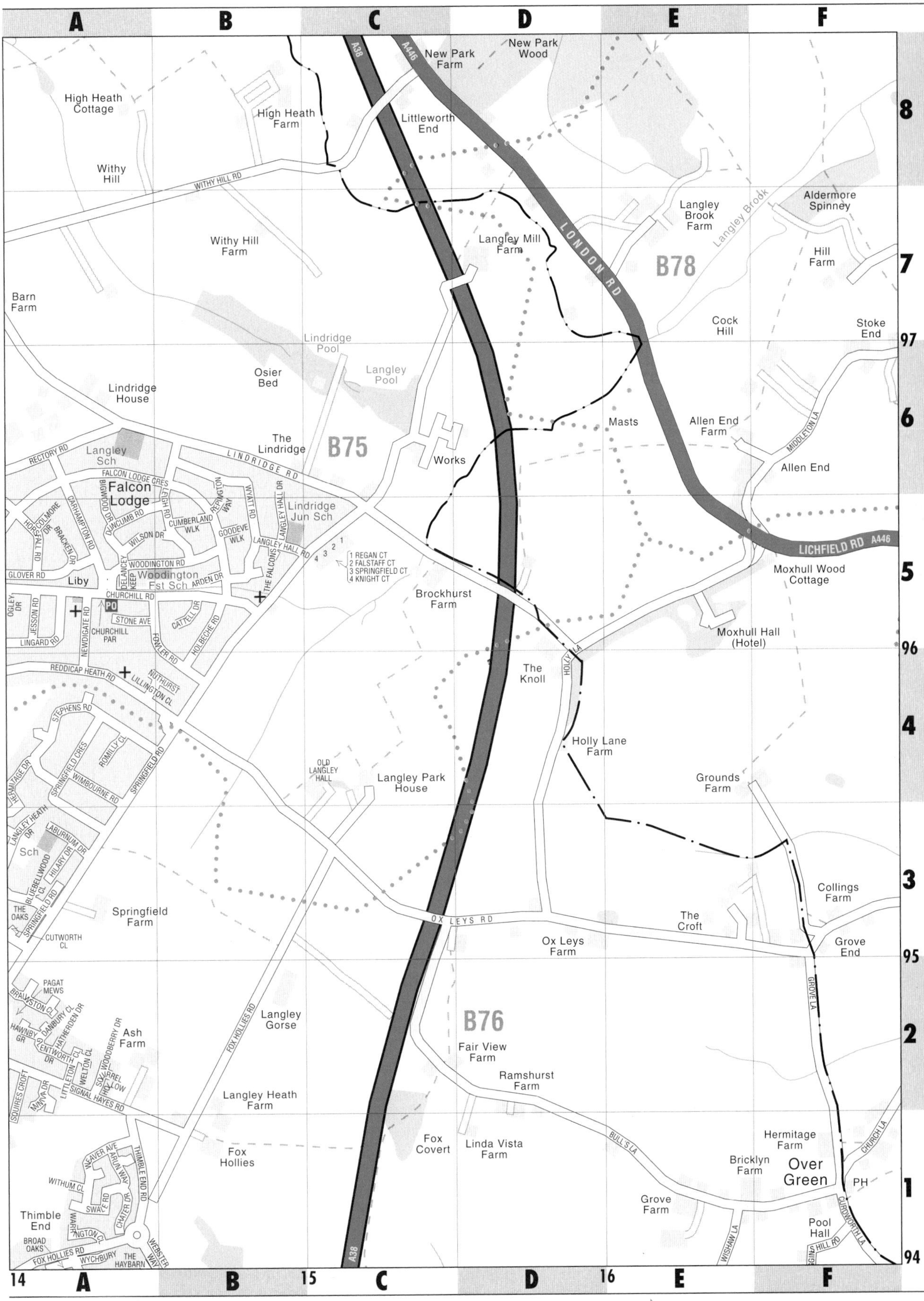

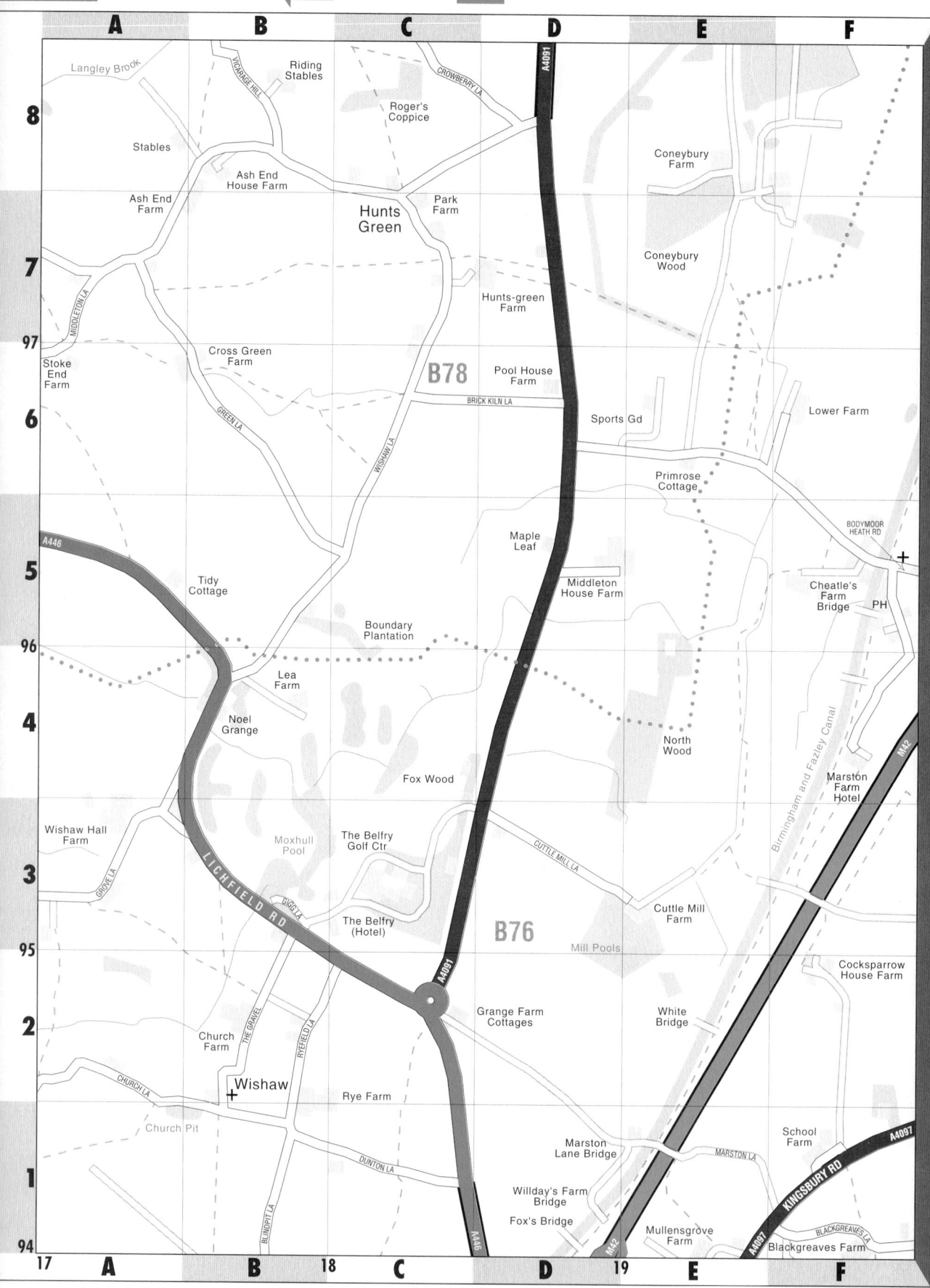

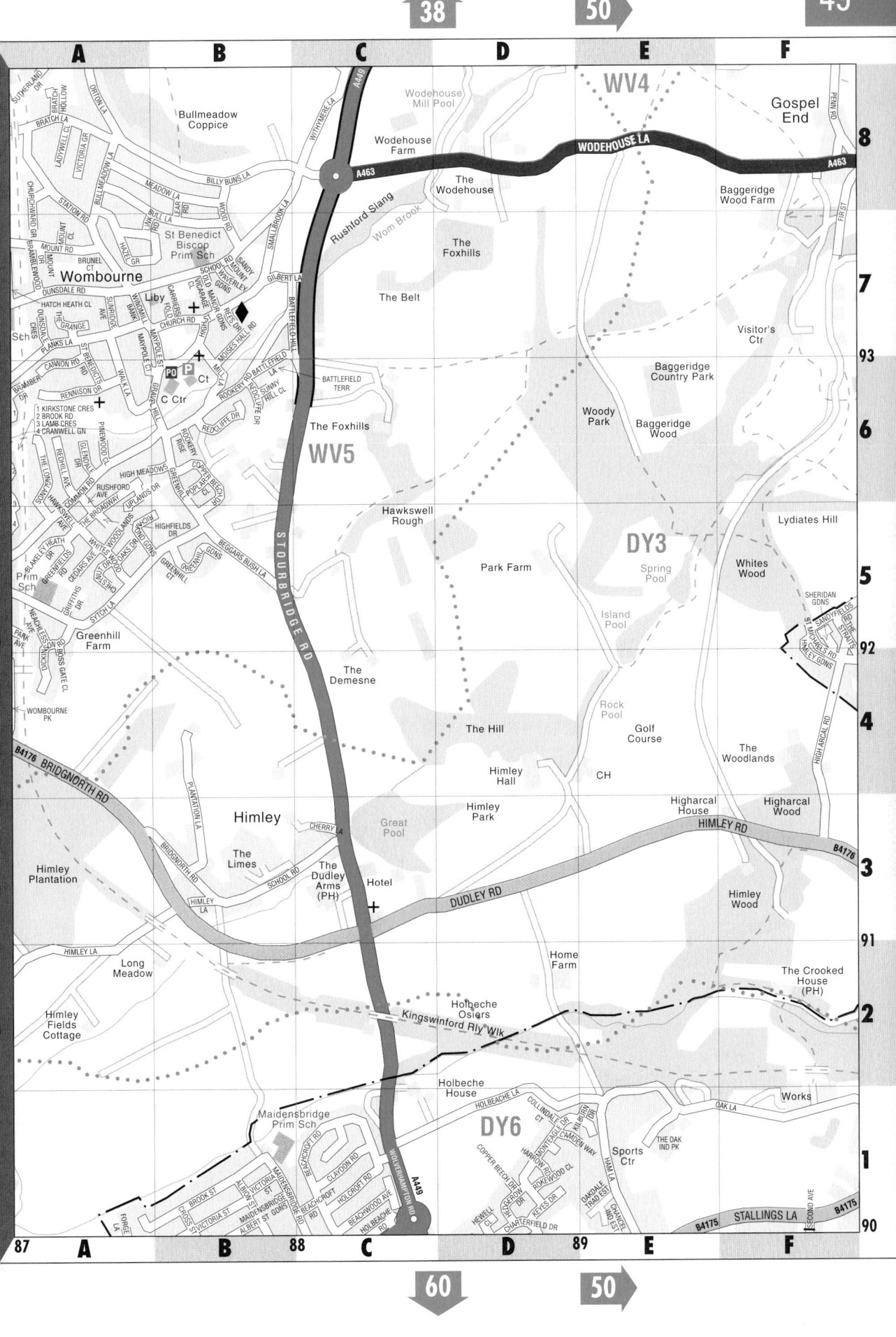

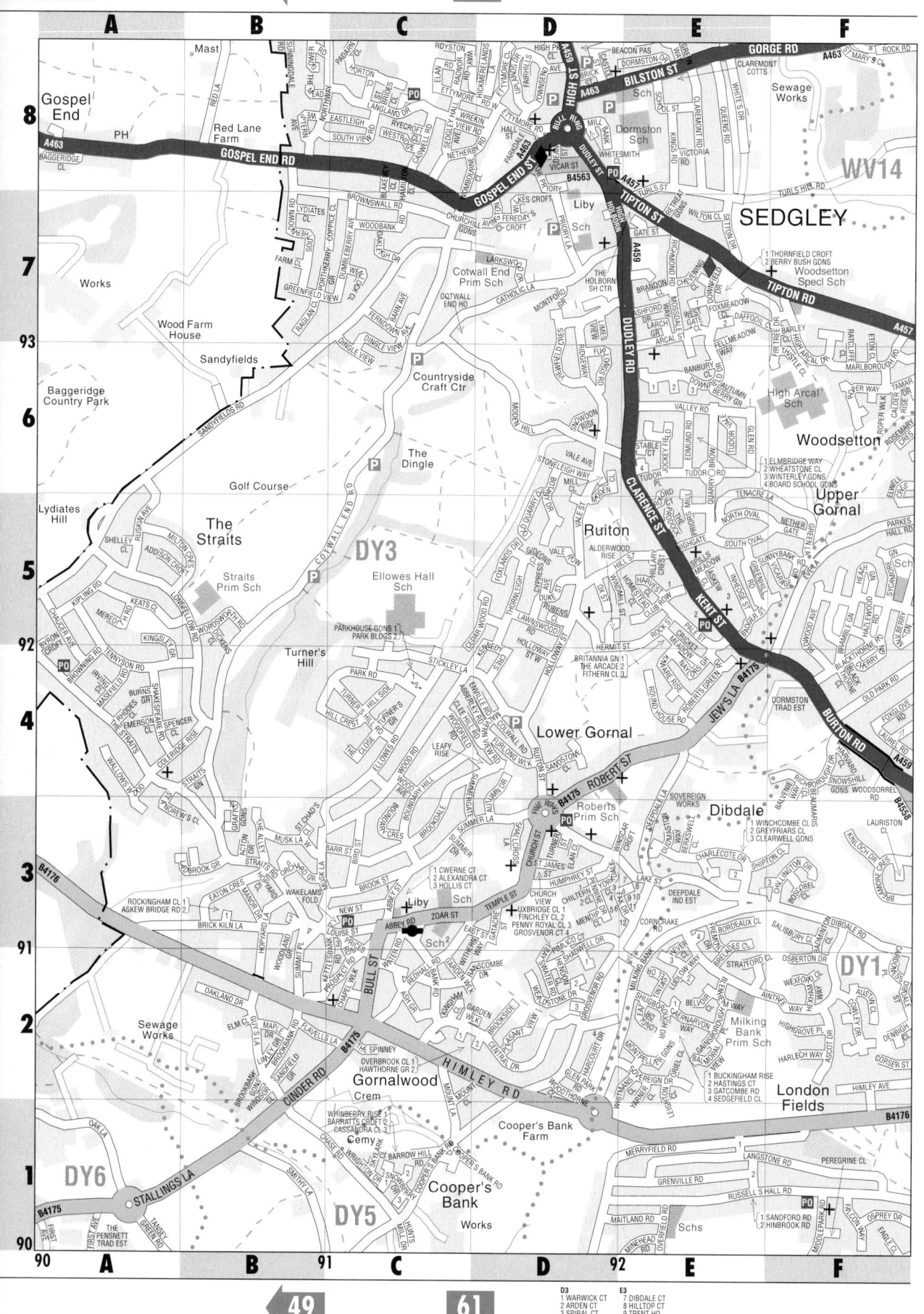

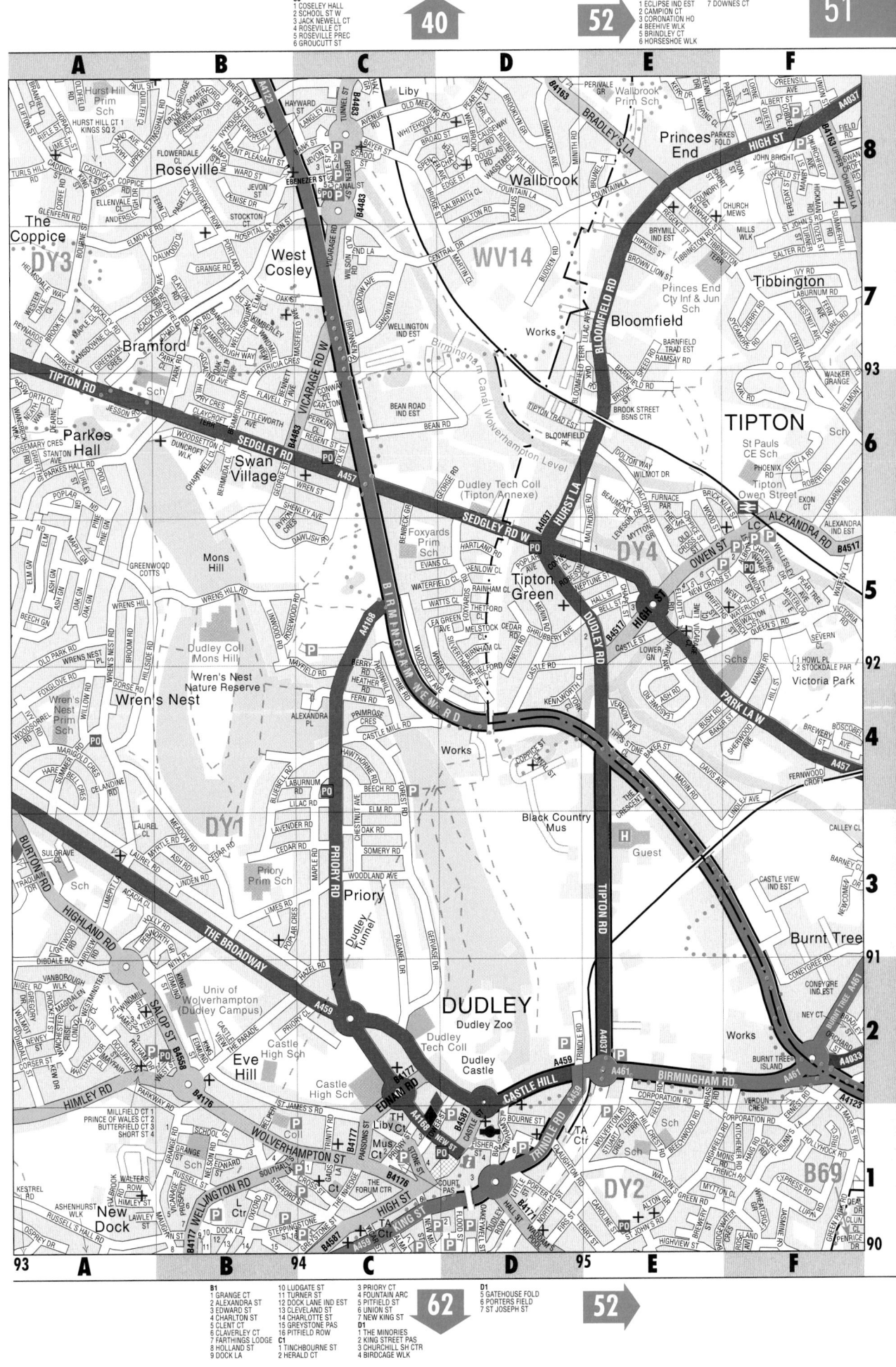

52

A8
1 RIDGEWAY RD
2 KINGSBURY RD
3 BURBERRY CT
4 JOHN F KENNEDY WLK
5 CHURCHILL WLK
6 LANSBURY WLK
7 STOKES AVE
8 KINGSWAY AVE
9 JELLICOE HO

51   **41**

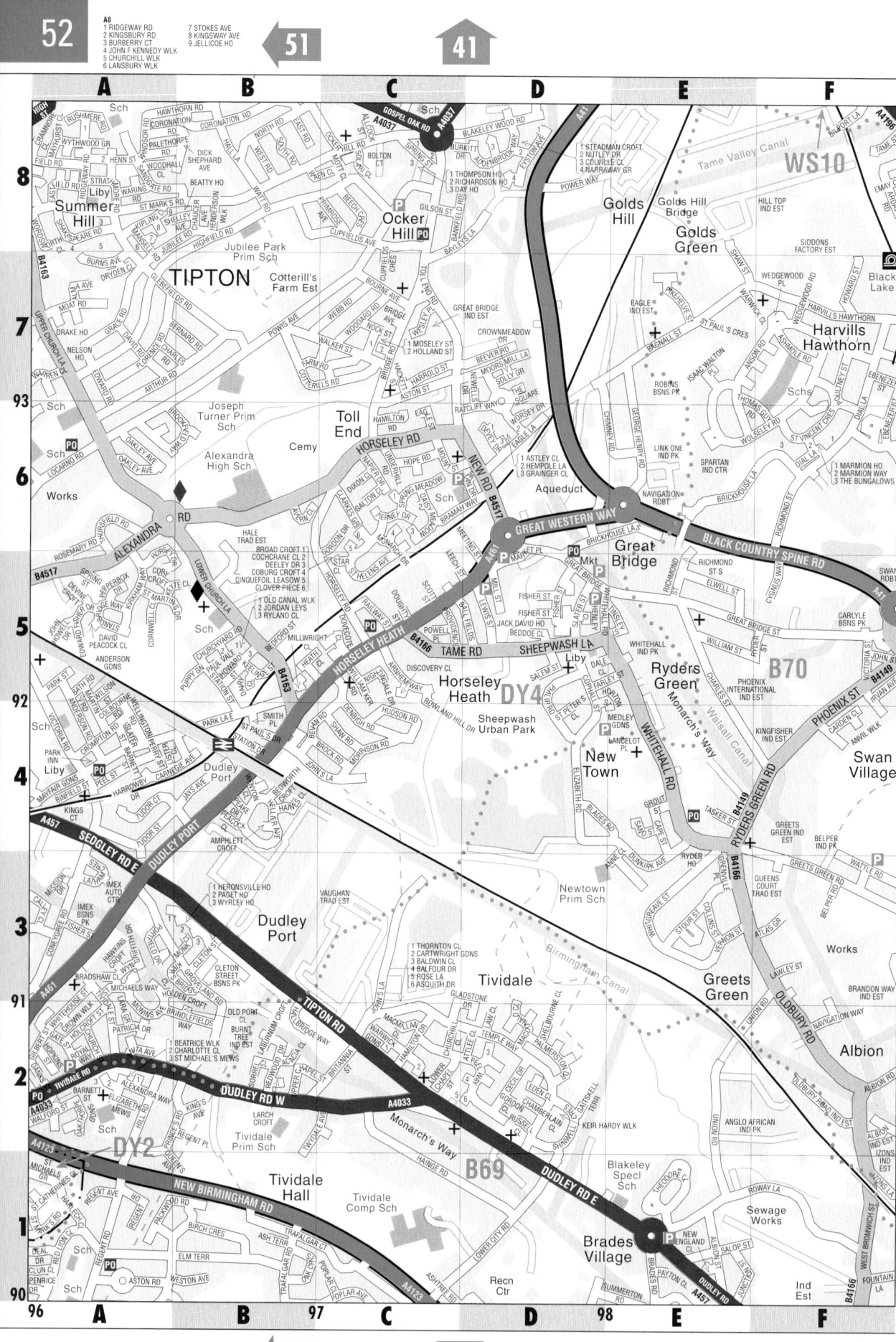

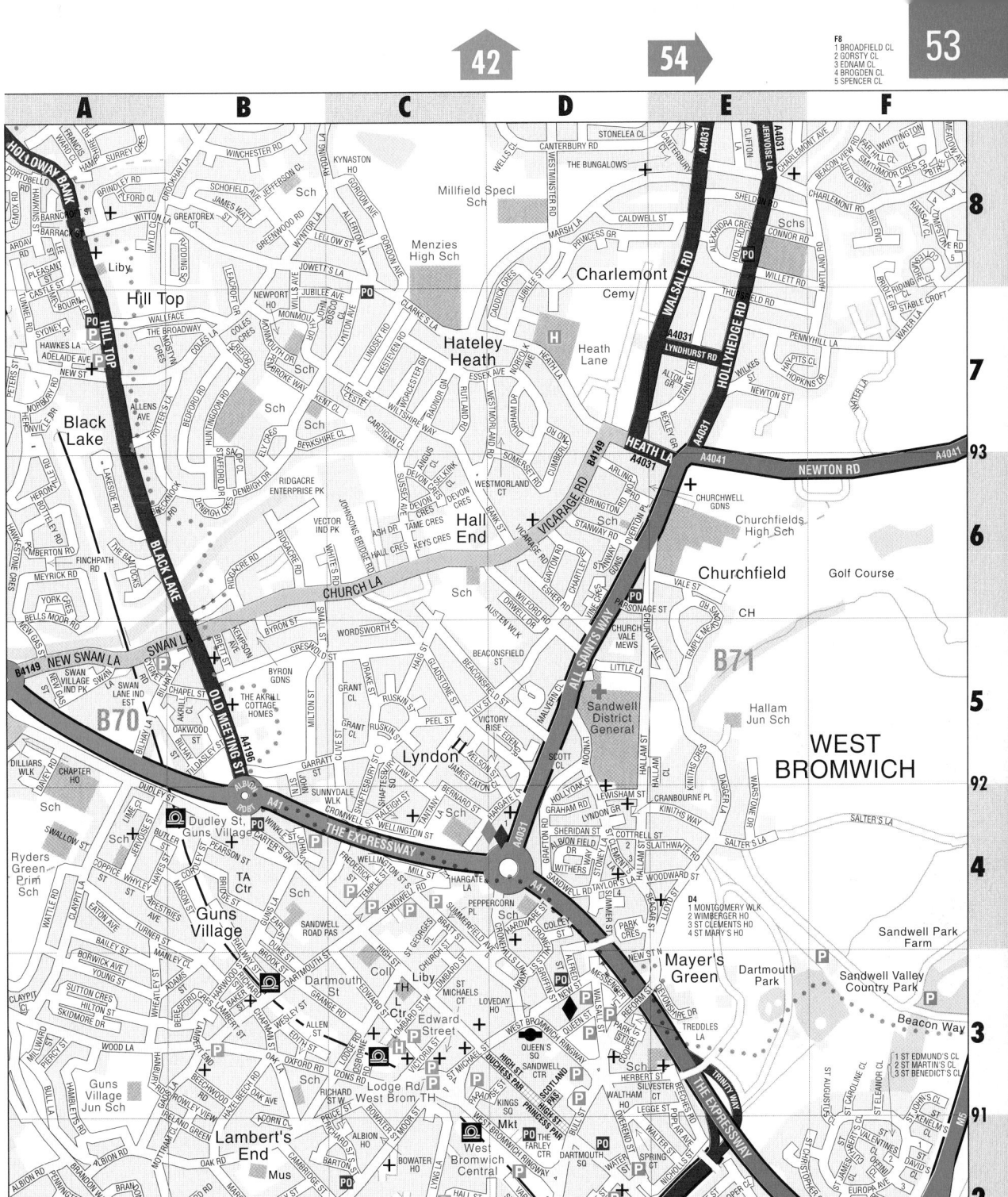

A B C D E F

8

CHARLEMONT RD
HORSECROFT DR
WIGMORE LA
LONGSTONE RD
TURNERS CROFT
WATER LA
M5

Brook Bridge

CEDAR CT
BISHOP ASBURY PEAR TREE CT
NEWTON RD
RAY HALL
BOWSTONE RD
NEWTON SNQ
STELLA GR
JOHNS GR
HOWARD RD
MARSTON RD
HEMUS GR
VALLEY RD
HEATHER RD
BROOMHILL CL
BROOMHILL RD
GREEN LA
LINDEN AV
CHUDLEIGH GR
ROUSDON GR

PO
B4167

Newton

GREEN LA
ASBURY
MANOR
AVA AV
QUINTON AV
CELBURY WAY
ABURY
CARLSTON WAY

JAYSHAW AVE
GORSTIE CROFT
CALVERTON GR
GORSE FARM RD
ALLENDALE RD
SHENSTONE RD
LANGFORD AVE
EASTWOOD RD
FARNHAM CL
B4124

A34 WALSALL RD
HOLLYWOOD CROFT
CEDARWOOD CROFT
OLD WALSALL RD

Ferndale Prim Sch

7

Crem
Haypits
A4041

Forge Farm
Forge Mill Farm
FORGE LA

Sandwell Valley Nature Ctr

REGEA RISE
BROOKE AVE
HIGHFIELD RD
TANHOUSE AVE
GREENFIELD RD
HAMSTEAD RD

LINGFIELD GR
HAMSTEAD RD

EADGAR CT
P
Hamstead Jun & Inf Sch

HAMSTEAD RD

TEMPLEMORE DR
WATERSIDE
WEST RD
ALLEN RD
STAFFORD RD
COLERIDGE RD
BANKSIDE
BRADFORD RD
GRASMERE CL
ASTON CROSS
ENNERDALE RD
KINGSTON
LANGDALE RD

B43
B42

93

6

Forge Farm
B71

FARRAN WAY
CROMANE SQ 2
FREEMOUNT SQ 3
HOLMES CL 4
LATHAM AVE 5
STAFFORD CT 6
RUSHALL CT 7
ALLEN HO 8
PEPYS CT 9
SUTTON CT 10
BOLDMERE CT 11

Hamstead
Garden Grove

HAMSTEAD HO 1
SCOTT HO 2
GROVE CT 3

WOOENED
GARDEN GROVE
GREENWAY
THE CROFTWAY
PARKSIDE

Superstore
P
RAILWAY
INTERNATIONAL
ROCKY LA

Hamstead Wks

River Tame
Beacon Way
Golf Course

Hamstead Hall Sec Sch
Golf Course
P

CHALCOT GR
ACFOLD RD
HAMSTEAD HALL AVE
CAMPLIN CRES
ELMBANK GR
CRAYTHORNE AVE
SEDGLEY GR
BEWLYS AVE
UNDERWOOD RD
GREENRIDGE RD
LEOPOLD AVE
MILLFIELD RD
DEERHURST RD
BEAUCHAMP AVE
MANWAY CL
VERNON AVE
WESTOVER RD
WEST AVE

5

Sandwell Valley Country Park
P
B71
Golf Course

Swan Pool

Park Farm

CH

MEDCROFT AVE
WEEFORD DR
PARK HILL DR
HAMSTEAD HILL
ST DAVIDS GR
ST CHRISTOPHERS
ST ANNES CL

B20
Brown's Green
Liby

92

4

CH

SILVERCROFT AVE

Sports Gd

THE SPINNEY
BROSIL AVE
MENTONE CT
WHEATLEY WRE
HAWTHORN PK
HIGH PK
FRIARY CL
WOODHAM RD
ASHCOMBE AVE
SILVERCROFT
SHIRELAND
GRESTONE AVE
WOODCROFT AVE
HANDSWORTH WOOD RD
B4124
THE SPINNEY
BROWNS GN
TAVERNER'S GN

Grestone Jun & Inf Schs

ENGLESTEDE CL
DEVONSHIRE RD
OAKLANDS
Schs

3

M5
A4041

Allot Gdns
St John Wall RC Sch

Handsworth Univ Village (Univ of Aston)
Handsworth Hall

CRADLEY CROFT
WILKS GN
POSEY CL
THE LEVERS
CORNWALL RD
STOCKWELL RD
COLLEGE RD
ROLFE ST

ROSEDENE DR
GROVE HILL RD
SOMERSET RD
CALDER DR
WILLENHALL

91

2

B70
B71
A41

Golf Course

Cemy

B21

Handsworth

St Augustine's RC Prim Sch

Recn Gd

OXHILL RD
GREENHILL RD
FARNHAM RD
UPLANDS RD
NEWCOMBE RD
MERVYN RD
FORD RD
MOUNT PLEASANT AVE
LAUREL GDNS
ELMHURST RD
ANDREW GDNS
AVENUE RD
AYLESFORD RD

CHURCH LA A4040
GROVE COT
KILBYS GR
GROVE HILL RD
PHILIP VICTOR RD
GOLDEN CROFT
HINSTOCK RD
Wilkes Green Sch
ALBERT RD

1

BIRMINGHAM RD
COLLERY LA
HALFORD'S LA
PARK LANE IND EST
MALVERN RD 1
PADDINGTON RD 2

B66
BOUNDARY
WILLOW HO
RALEIGH
FELGR
LANGDALE RD
LANCASTER RD
COPTHALL RD
CRANBROOK RD

A4040 ISLAND RD
SAMPSON
AUSTIN
HOLYHEAD RD
A41

SANDWELL RD
HOLLYCR
CLENT RD
ALBION RD
GRAFTON RD
ONIBURY RD
WESTBOURNE RD

St James CE Prim Sch
ROOKERY RD
A4040
MAPLE RD
ANTROBUS RD
BRUNSWICK RD
ELBERT RD

90

The Hawthorns
Albion Jun Sch
B71

02 A 03 B C D 04 E F

F3
1 HAWTHORN PARK DR
2 CASSOWARY RD
3 QUORN HO
4 ALBRIGHTON HO
5 MEYNELL HO
6 PYTCHLEY HO
7 COTTESMORE HO

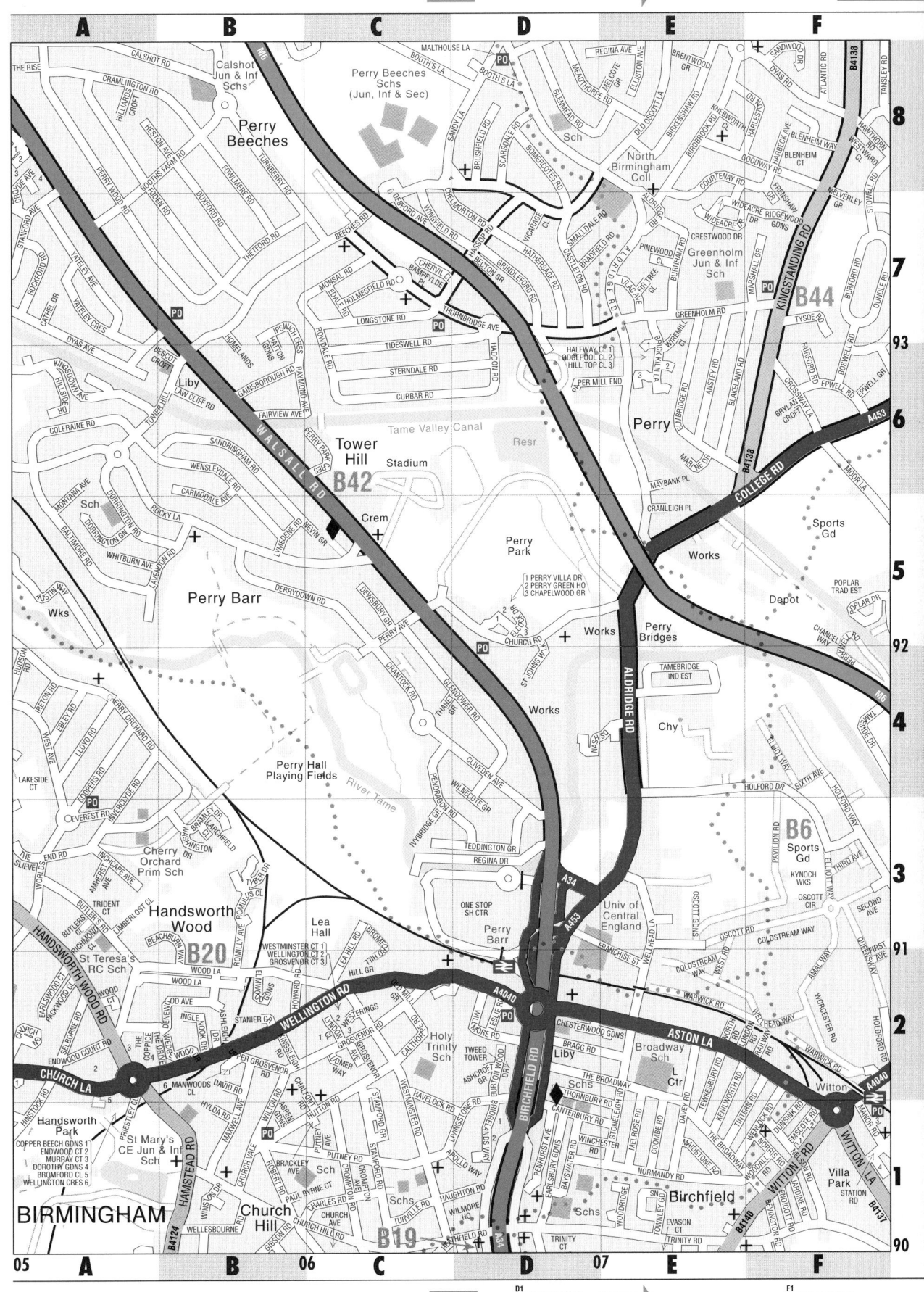

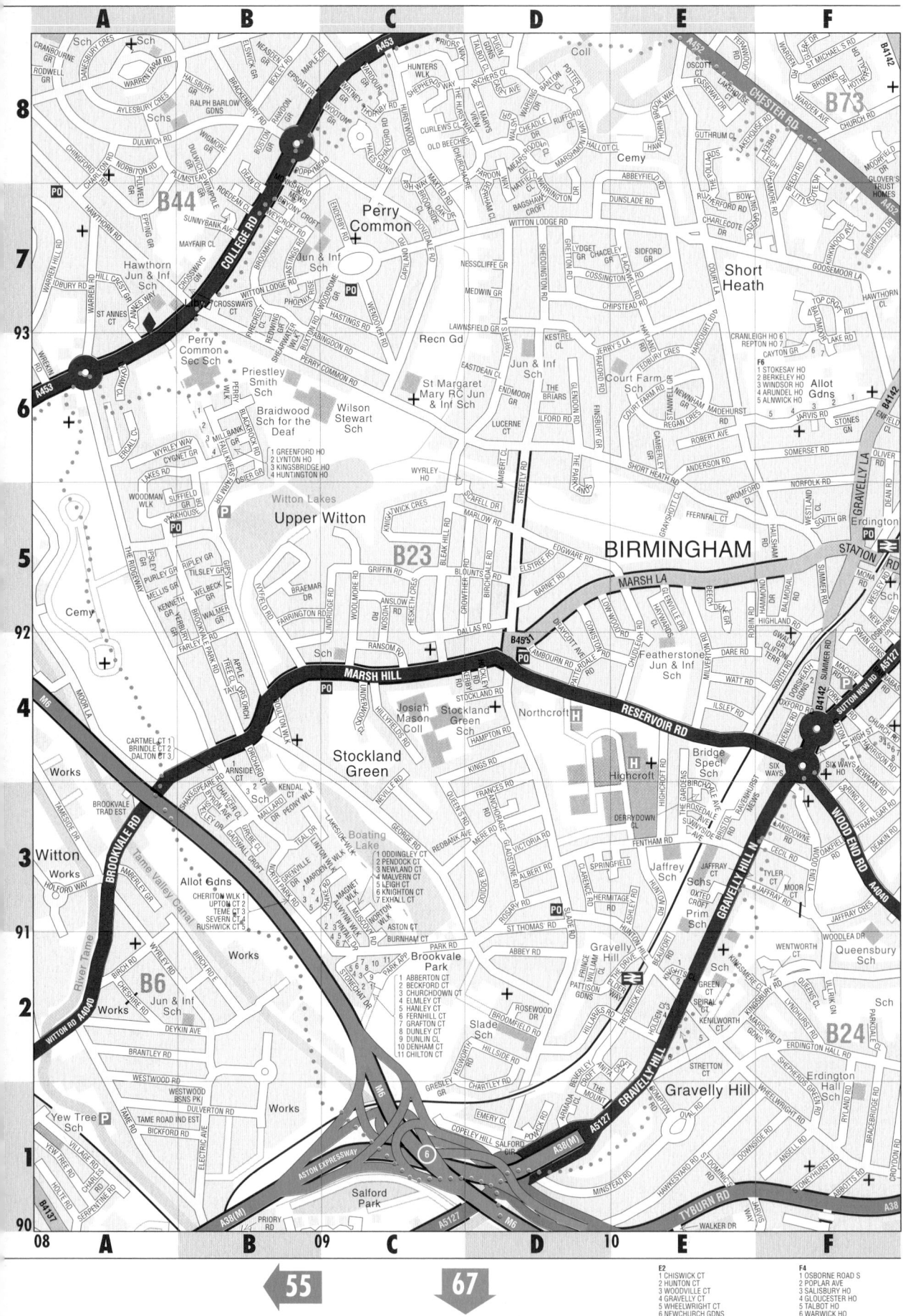

E2
1 CHISWICK CT
2 HUNTON CT
3 WOODVILLE CT
4 GRAVELLY CT
5 WHEELWRIGHT CT
6 NEWCHURCH GDNS

F4
1 OSBORNE ROAD S
2 POPLAR AVE
3 SALISBURY HO
4 GLOUCESTER HO
5 TALBOT HO
6 WARWICK HO
7 BEDFORD HO
8 EXETER HO

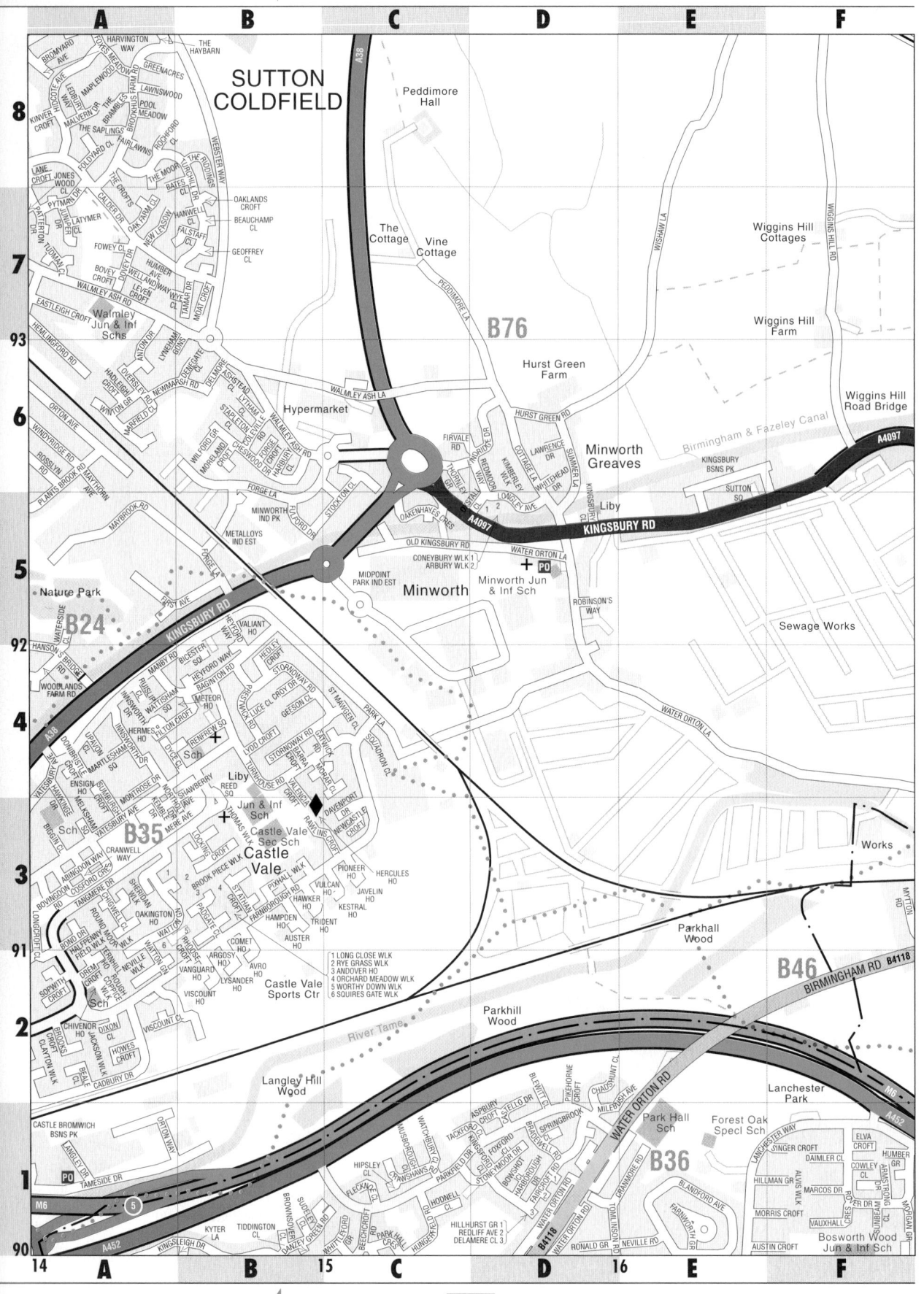

SUTTON COLDFIELD

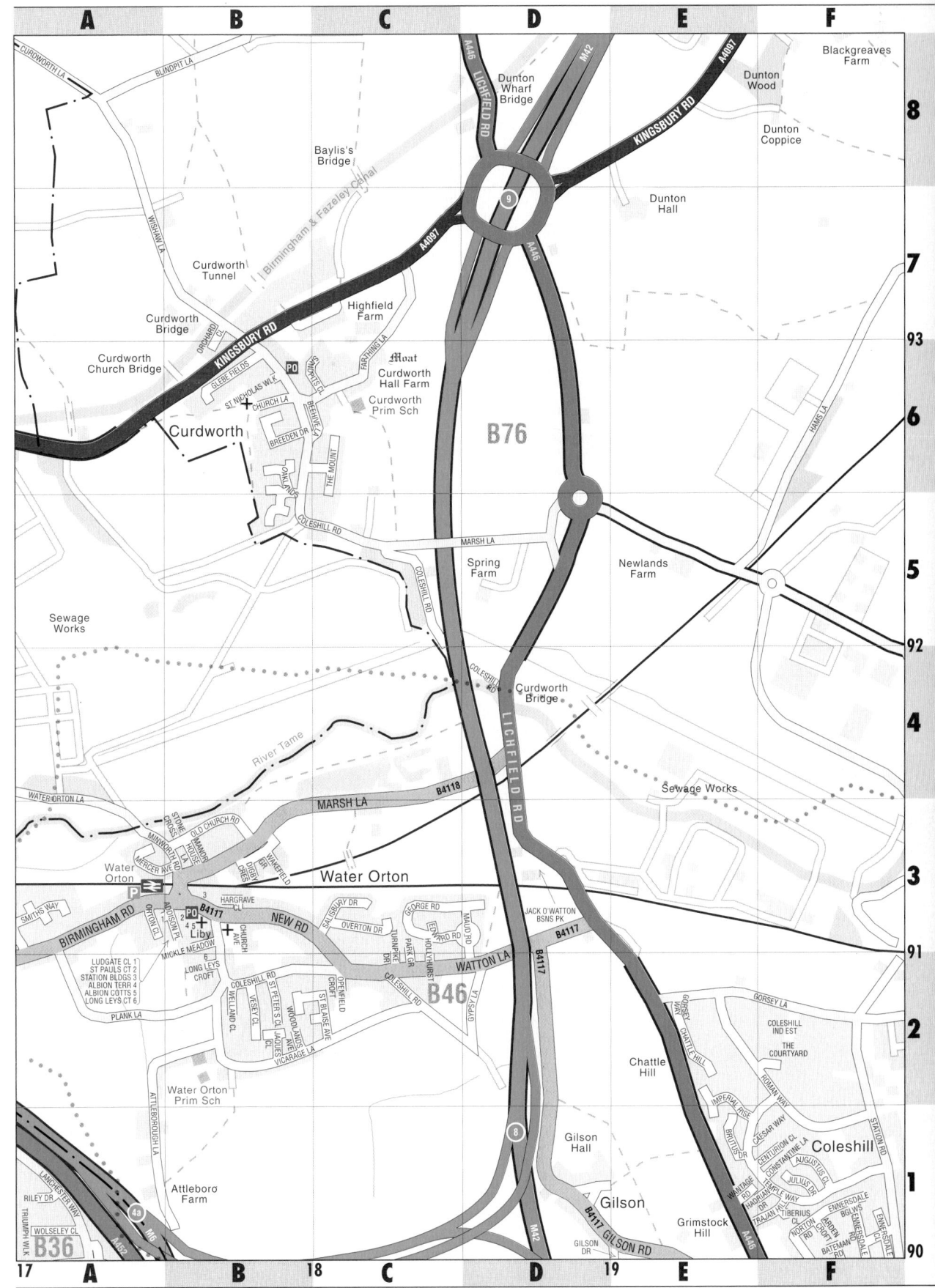

D8
1 GARRET CL
2 FLANDERS DR
3 CHARTERFIELD SH CTR

E8
1 BROADMEADOW
2 BIRCHWOOD WLK
3 OAKLEIGH WLK
4 WOODTHORNE WLK
5 ROSEDALE WLK
6 PINEWOOD WLK

7 BLOSSOMFIELD CL
8 MIMOSA WLK
9 GREENLAND CL

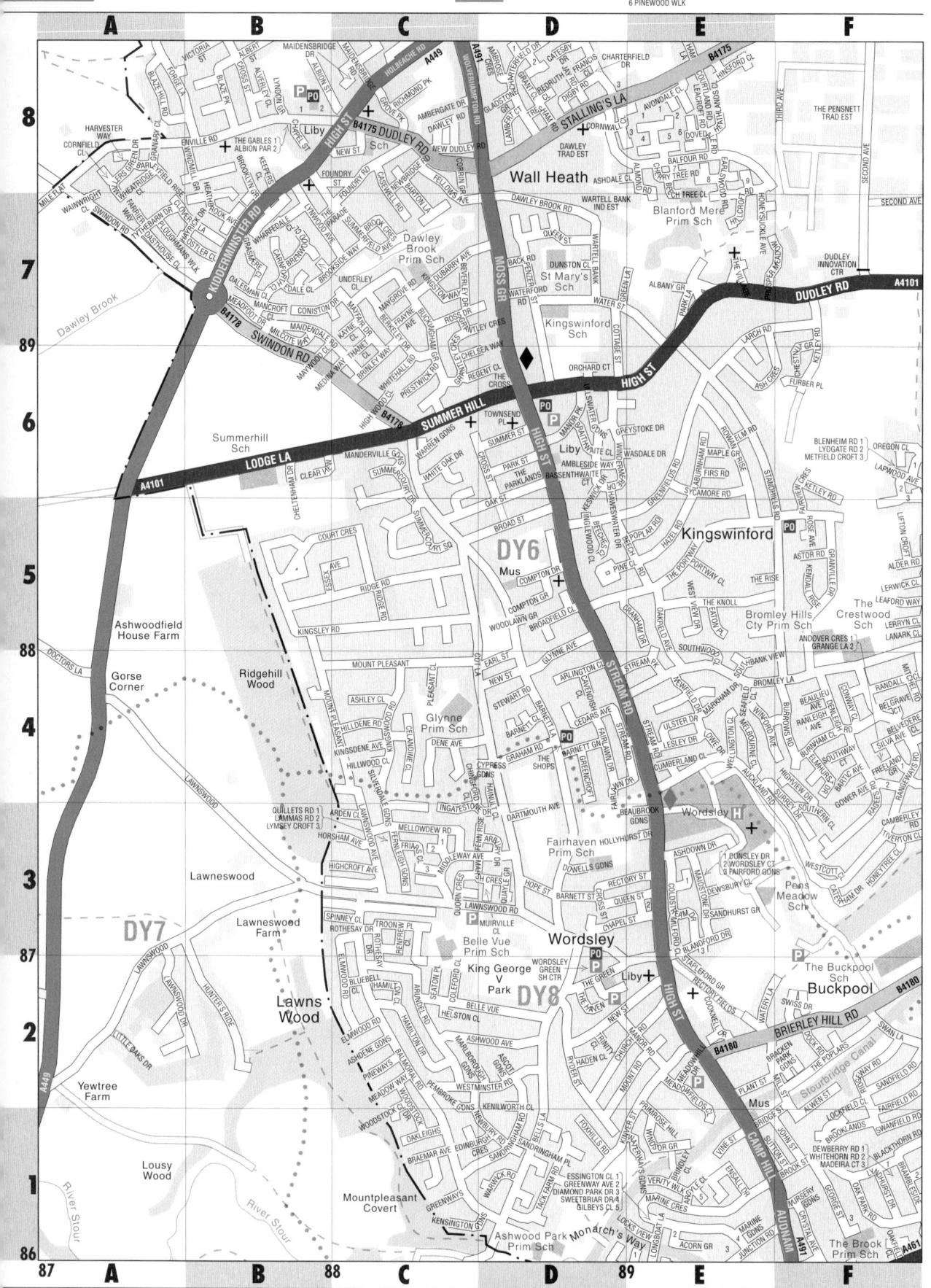

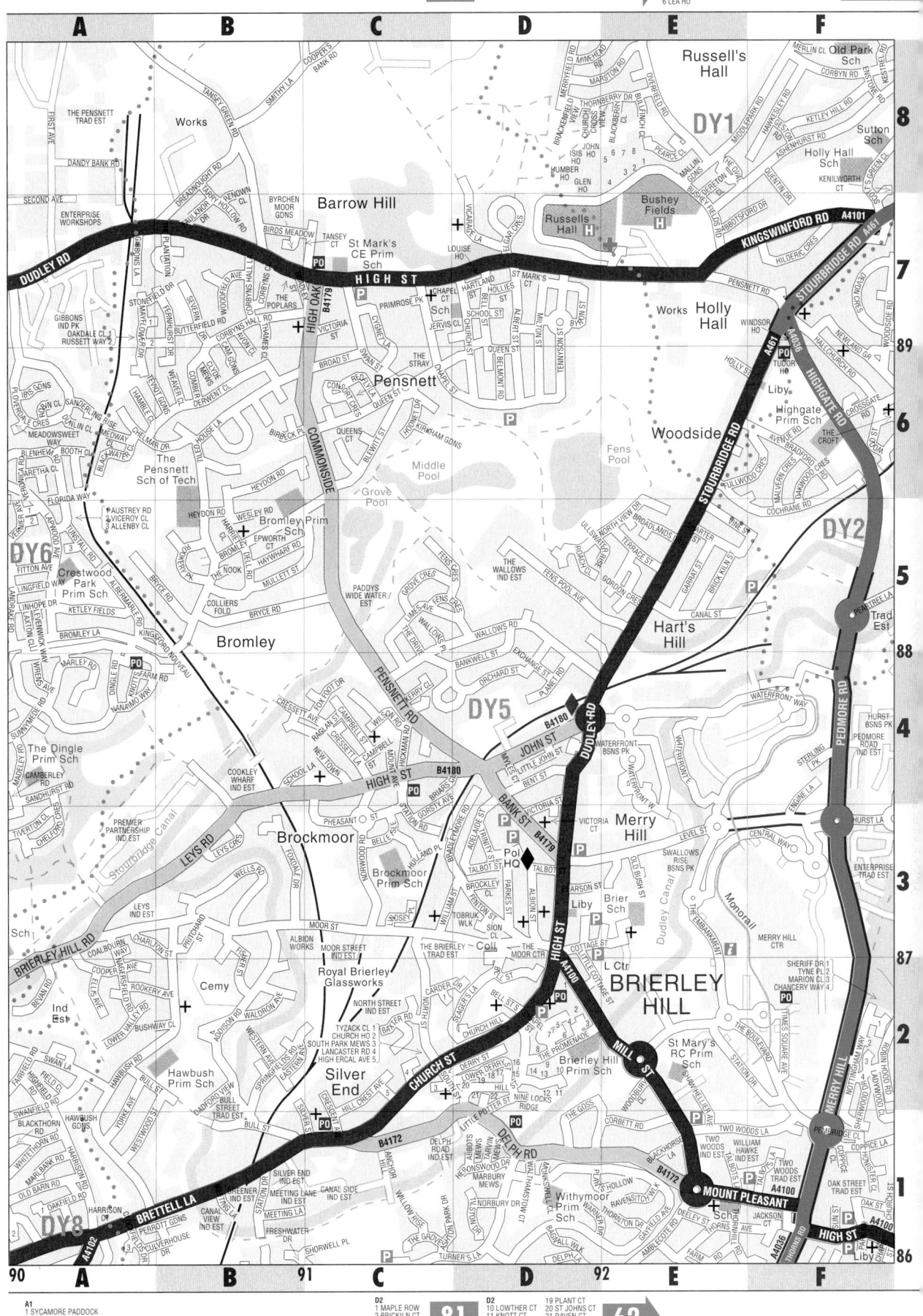

E8
1 ESK HO   7 CAM HO
2 AVON HO 8 DEE HO
3 BRENT HO
4 FROME HO
5 KENNET HO
6 LEA HO

A1
1 SYCAMORE PADDOCK
2 OAK TREE GDNS
3 AMELAS CL

D2
1 MAPLE ROW
2 BRICKILN CT
3 ADELPHI CT
4 CHAPEL CT
5 DEAN CT
6 OAKFIELD CT
7 NEW CT
8 POTTER CT
9 NORTHWOOD CT

D2
10 LOWTHER CT
11 KNOTT CT
12 ST MARYS CT
13 GIFFORD CT
14 BRIAR CT
15 YEOVIL CT
16 BODMIN CT
17 BOOTH CT
18 BURNHAM CT

19 PLANT CT
20 ST JOHNS CT
21 RAVEN CT
22 WESTBURY CT

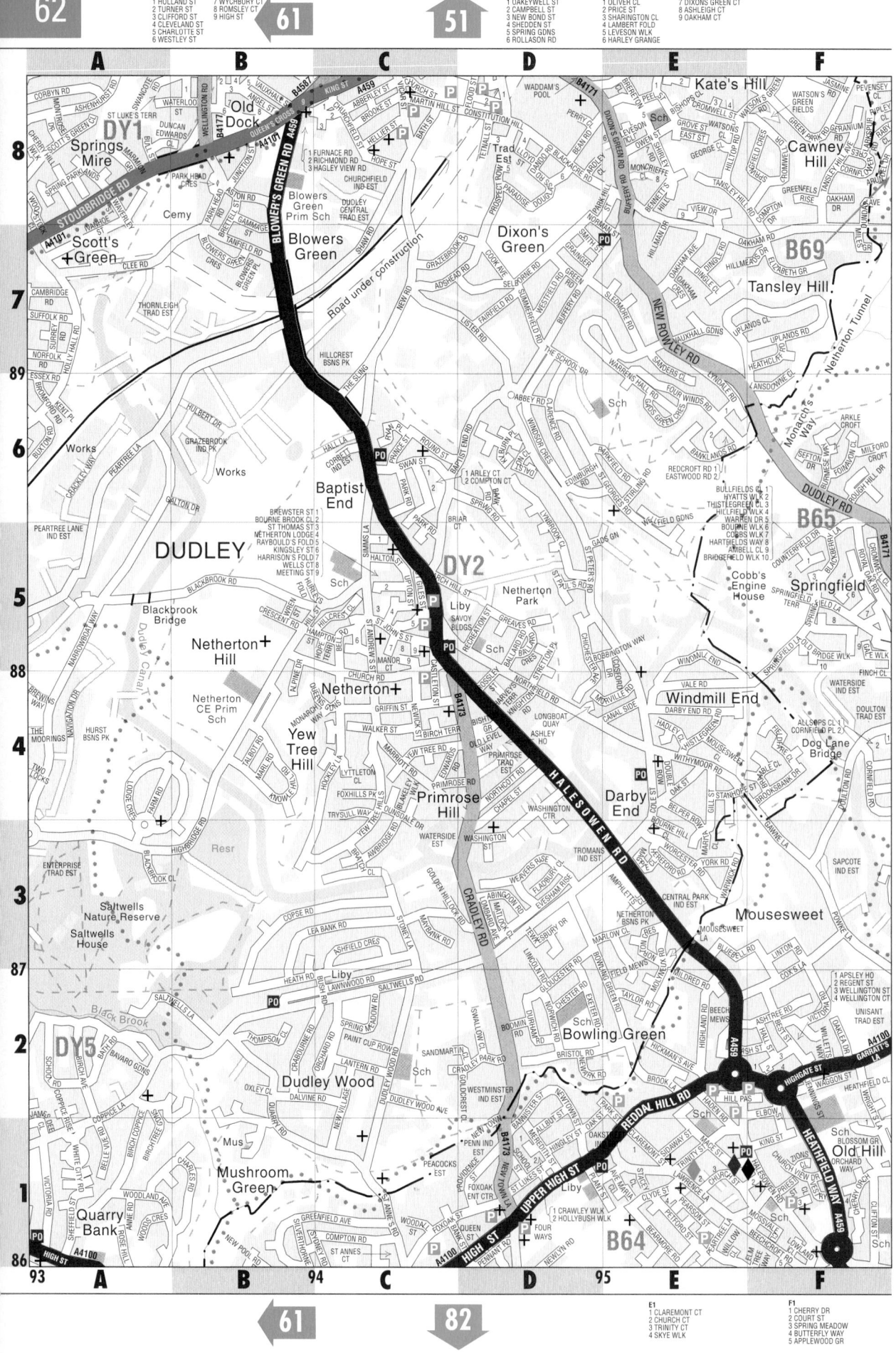

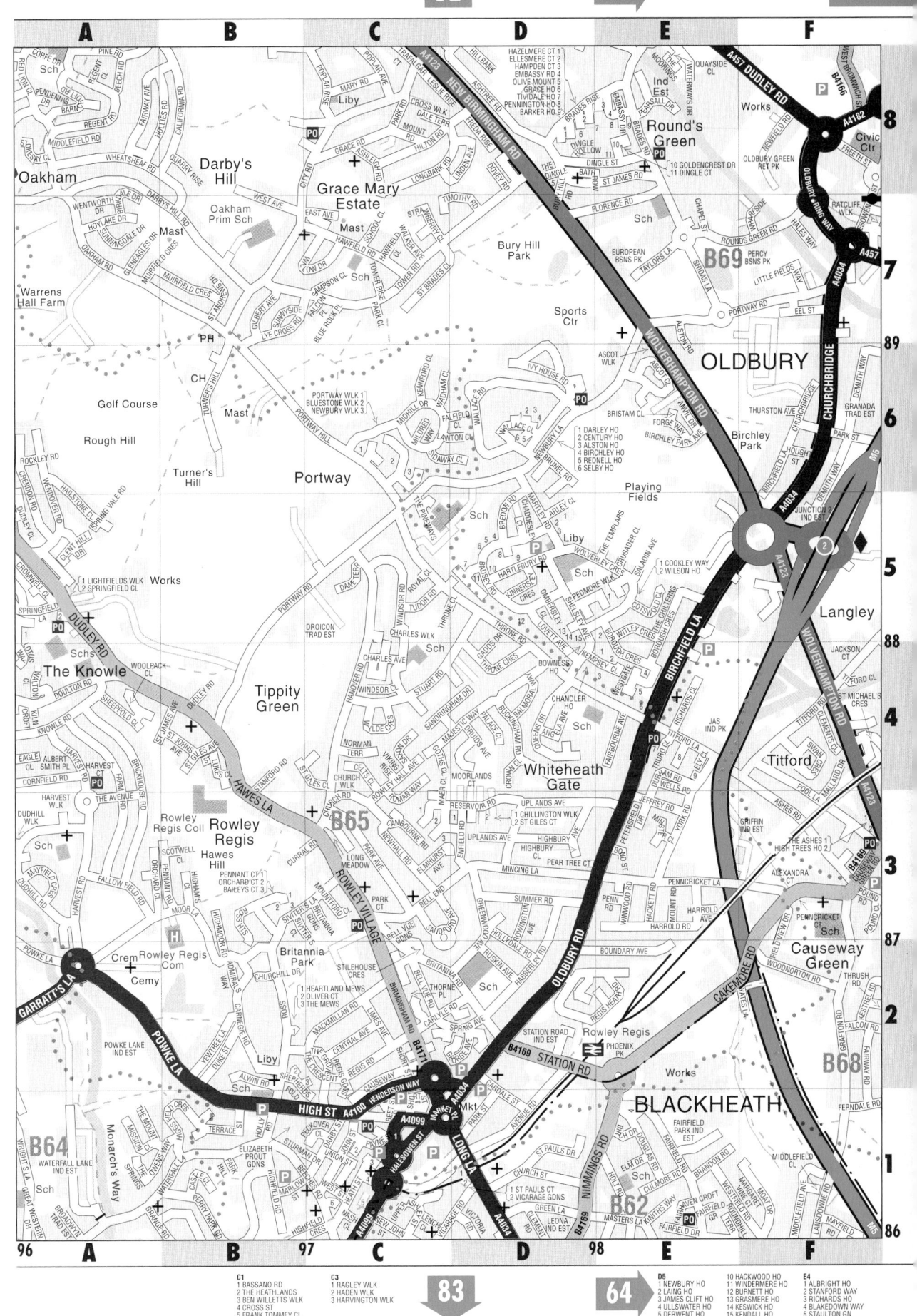

C1
1 BASSANO RD
2 THE HEATHLANDS
3 BEN WILLETTS WLK
4 CROSS ST
5 FRANK TOMMEY CL
6 DOWNING CL

C3
1 RAGLEY WLK
2 HADEN WLK
3 HARVINGTON WLK

D5
1 NEWBURY HO
2 LAING HO
3 JAMES CLIFT HO
4 ULLSWATER HO
5 DERWENT HO
6 RYDAL HO
7 CONISTON HO
8 WALLACE HO
9 HARRY PRICE HO
10 HACKWOOD HO
11 WINDERMERE HO
12 BURNETT HO
13 GRASMERE HO
14 KESWICK HO
15 KENDALL HO

E4
1 ALBRIGHT HO
2 STANFORD WAY
3 RICHARDS HO
4 BLAKEDOWN WAY
5 STAULTON GN
6 WHITEHEATH CT
7 LANCASTER HO
8 WINCHESTER CL
9 CANTERBURY CL

64

A7
1 DE SOMERLEY HO
2 HACKETT CT
3 RATCLIFF WLK
4 CHURCH SQ
5 LADY BRADES HO
6 LOW TOWN

7 DAVIES HO
8 PARKES HO
9 JACKSON HO
10 SHOWELL HO
11 JEFFRIES HO
12 WHEELER HO

E7
1 SANDFIELD
2 MALTHOUSE
3 LIZAFIELD CT

← **63**   ↑ **53**

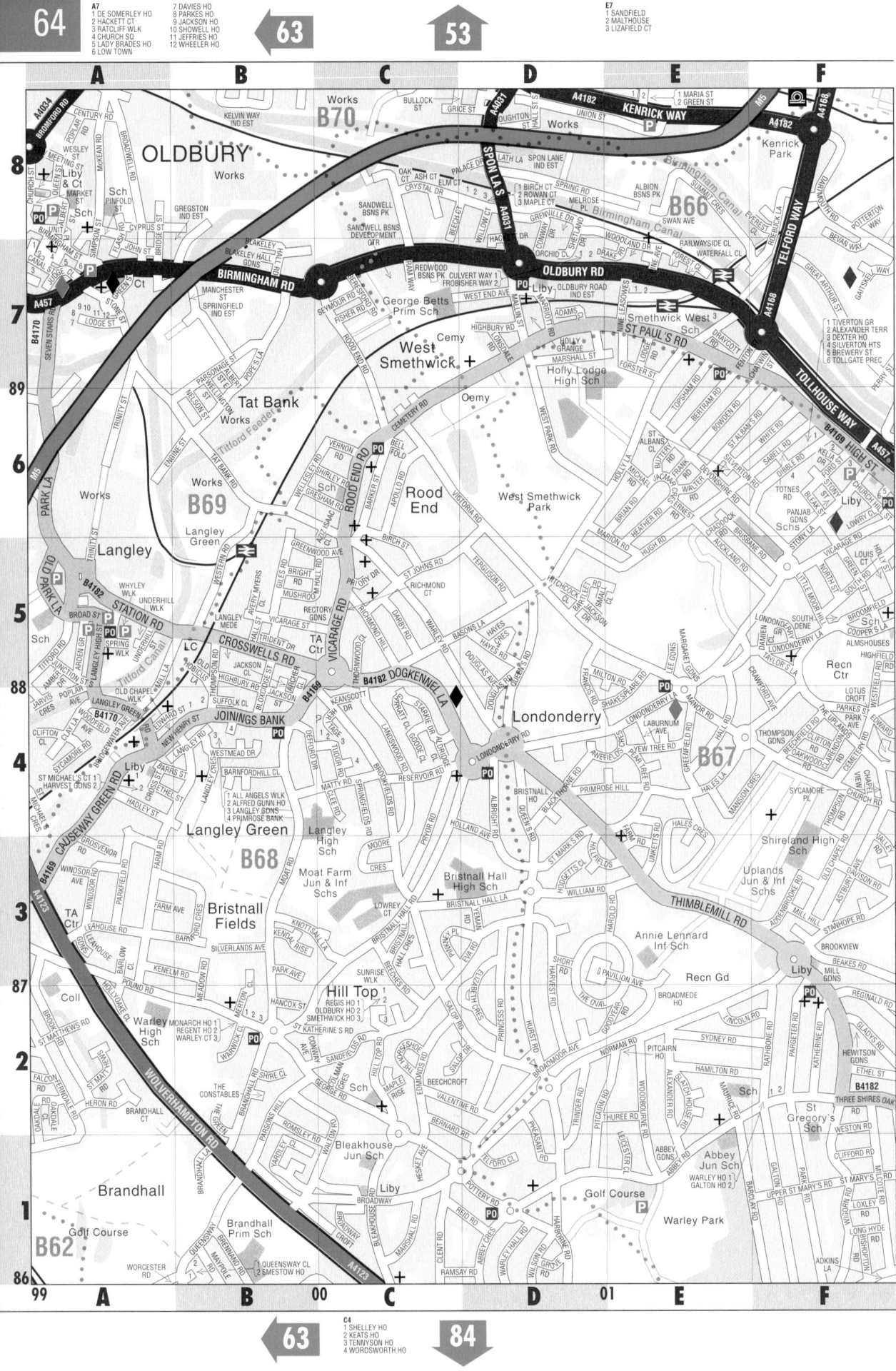

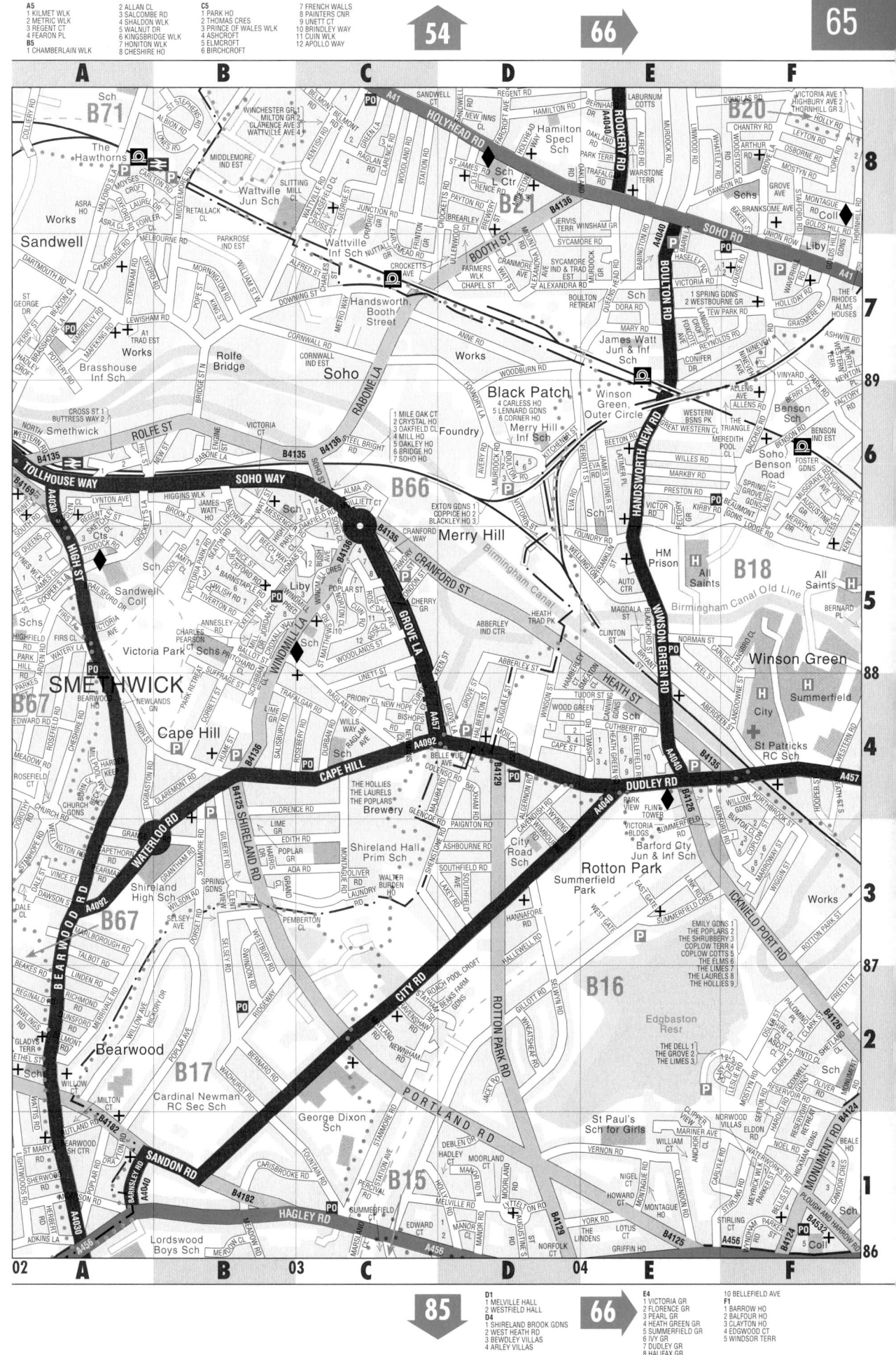

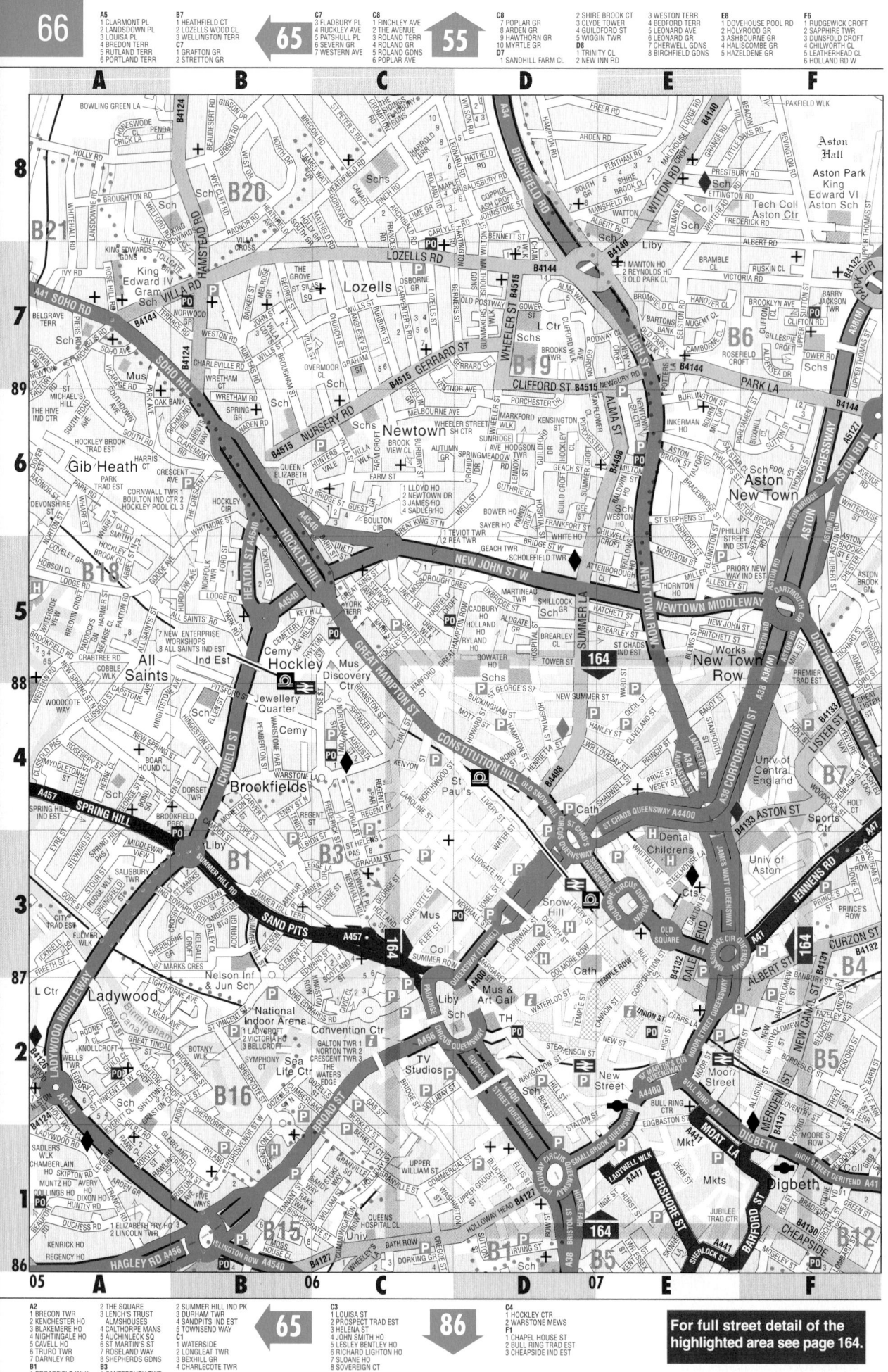

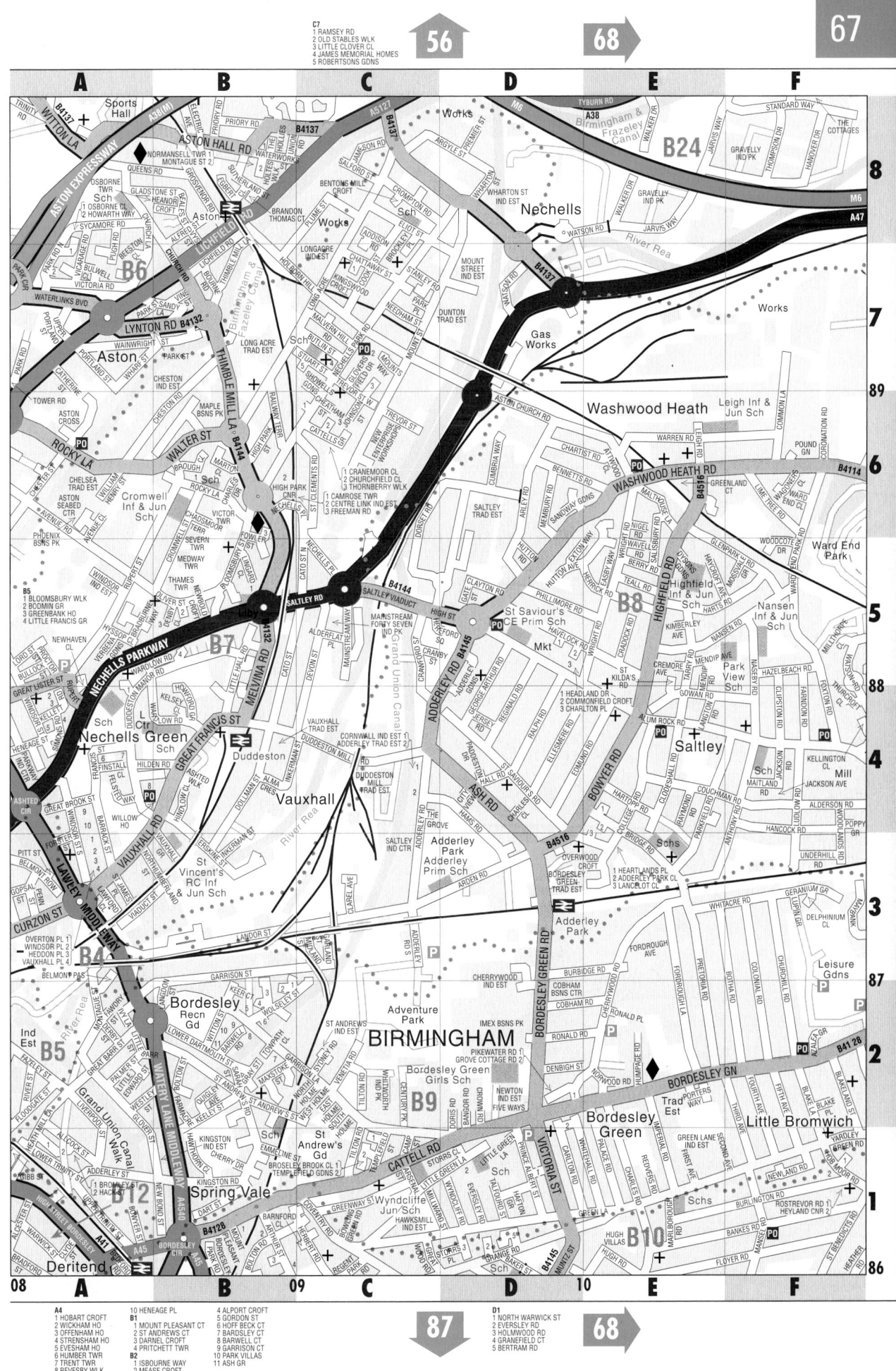

A4
1 HOBART CROFT
2 WICKHAM HO
3 OFFENHAM HO
4 STRENSHAM HO
5 EVESHAM HO
6 HUMBER TWR
7 TRENT TWR
8 REVESBY WLK
9 MOORCROFT PL

10 HENEAGE PL

B1
1 MOUNT PLEASANT CT
2 ST ANDREWS CT
3 DARNEL CROFT
4 PRITCHETT TWR

B2
1 ISBOURNE WAY
2 MEASE CROFT
3 MILL BURN WAY

4 ALPORT CROFT
5 GORDON ST
6 HOFF BECK CT
7 BARDSLEY CT
8 BARWELL CT
9 GARRISON CT
10 PARK VILLAS
11 ASH GR

D1
1 NORTH WARWICK ST
2 EVERSLEY RD
3 HOLMWOOD RD
4 GRANEFIELD CT
5 BERTRAM RD

87

68

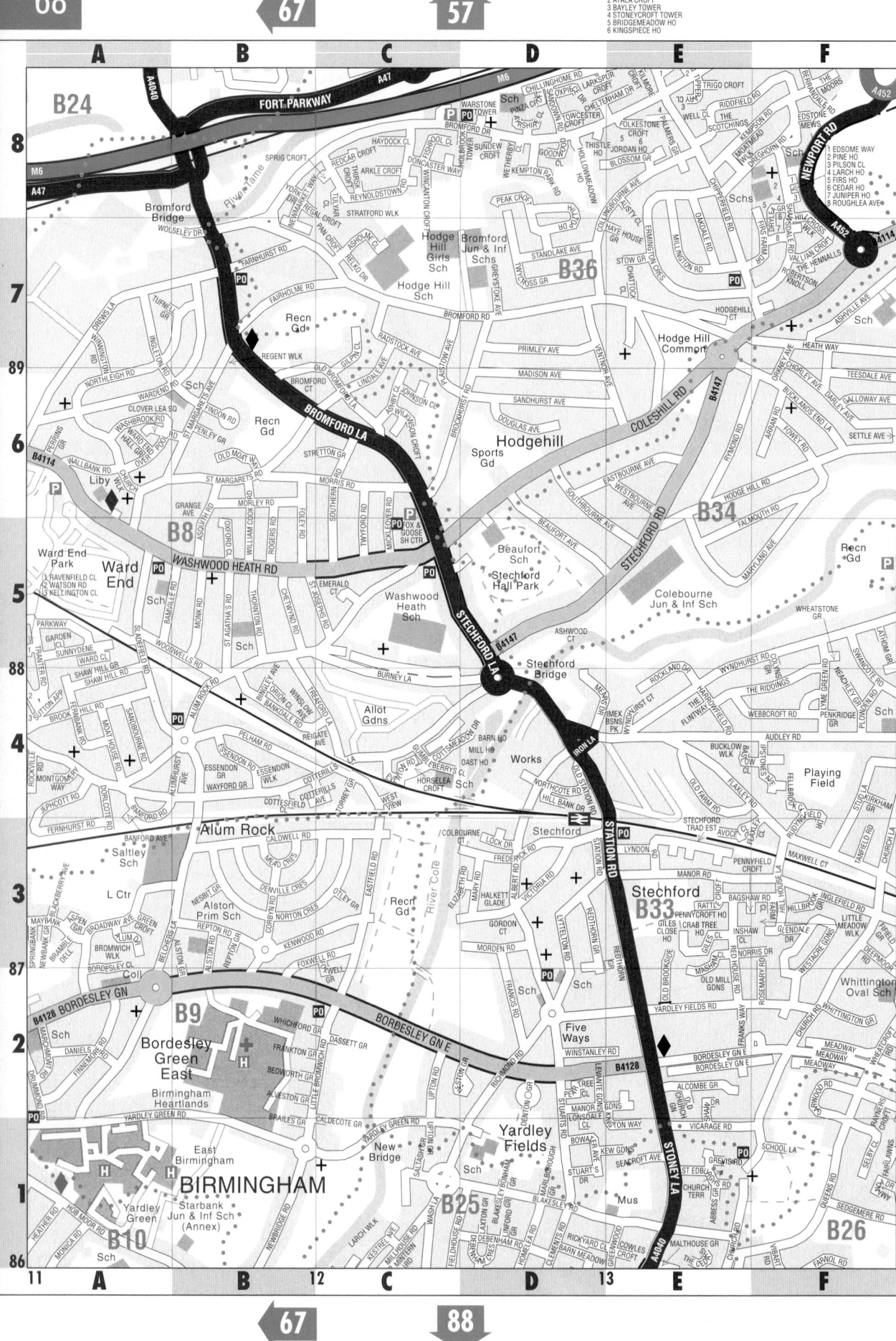

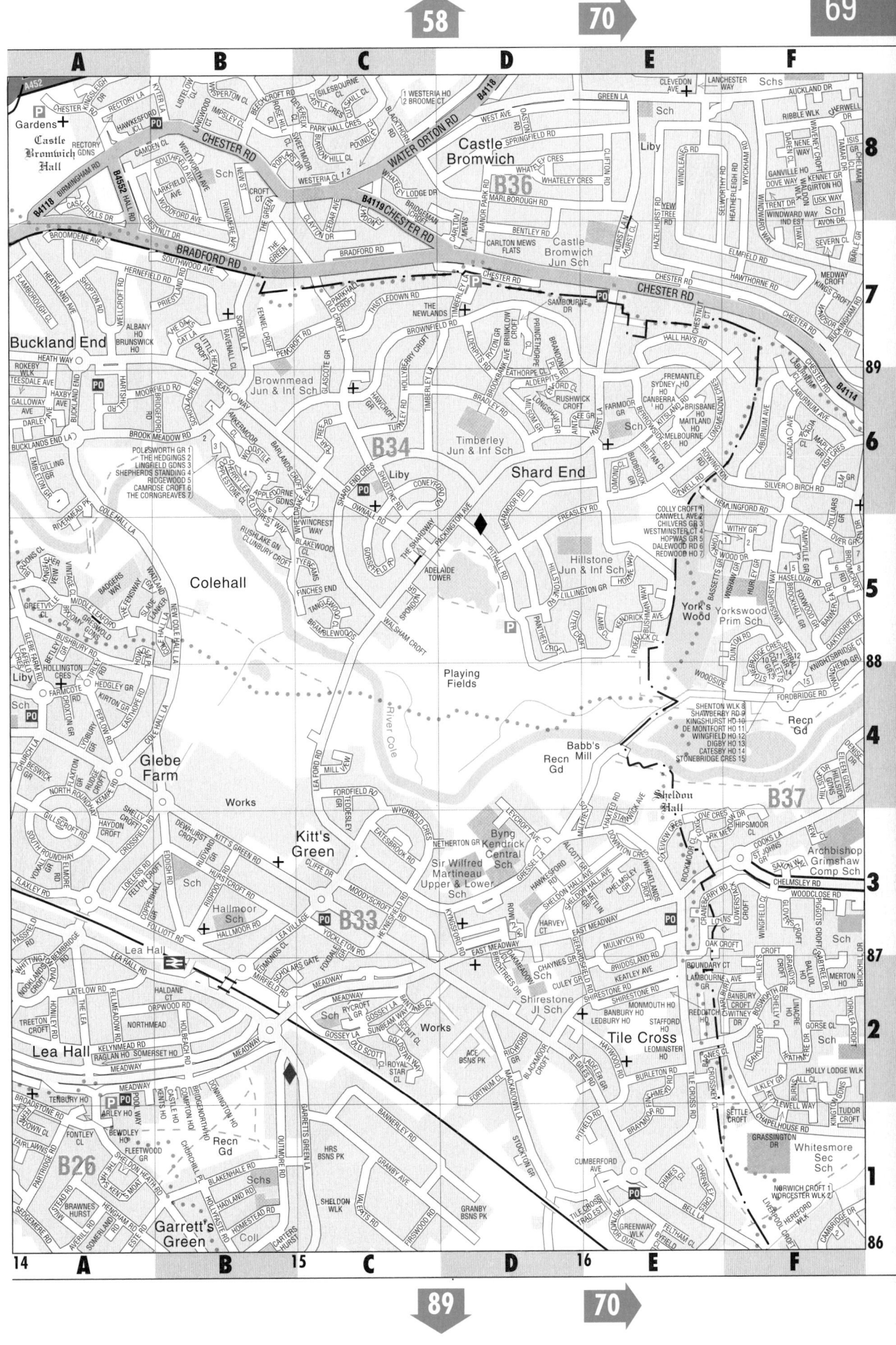

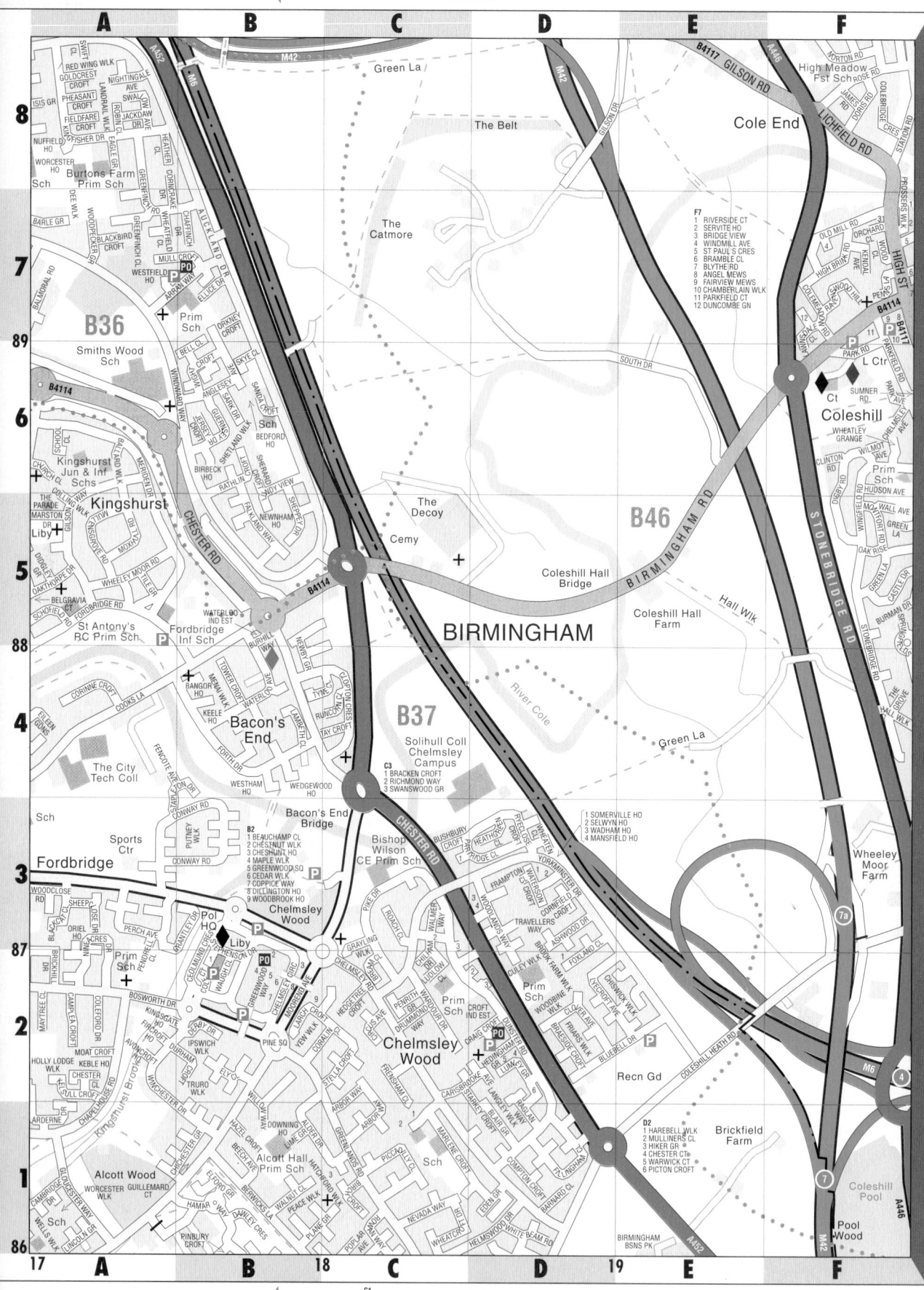

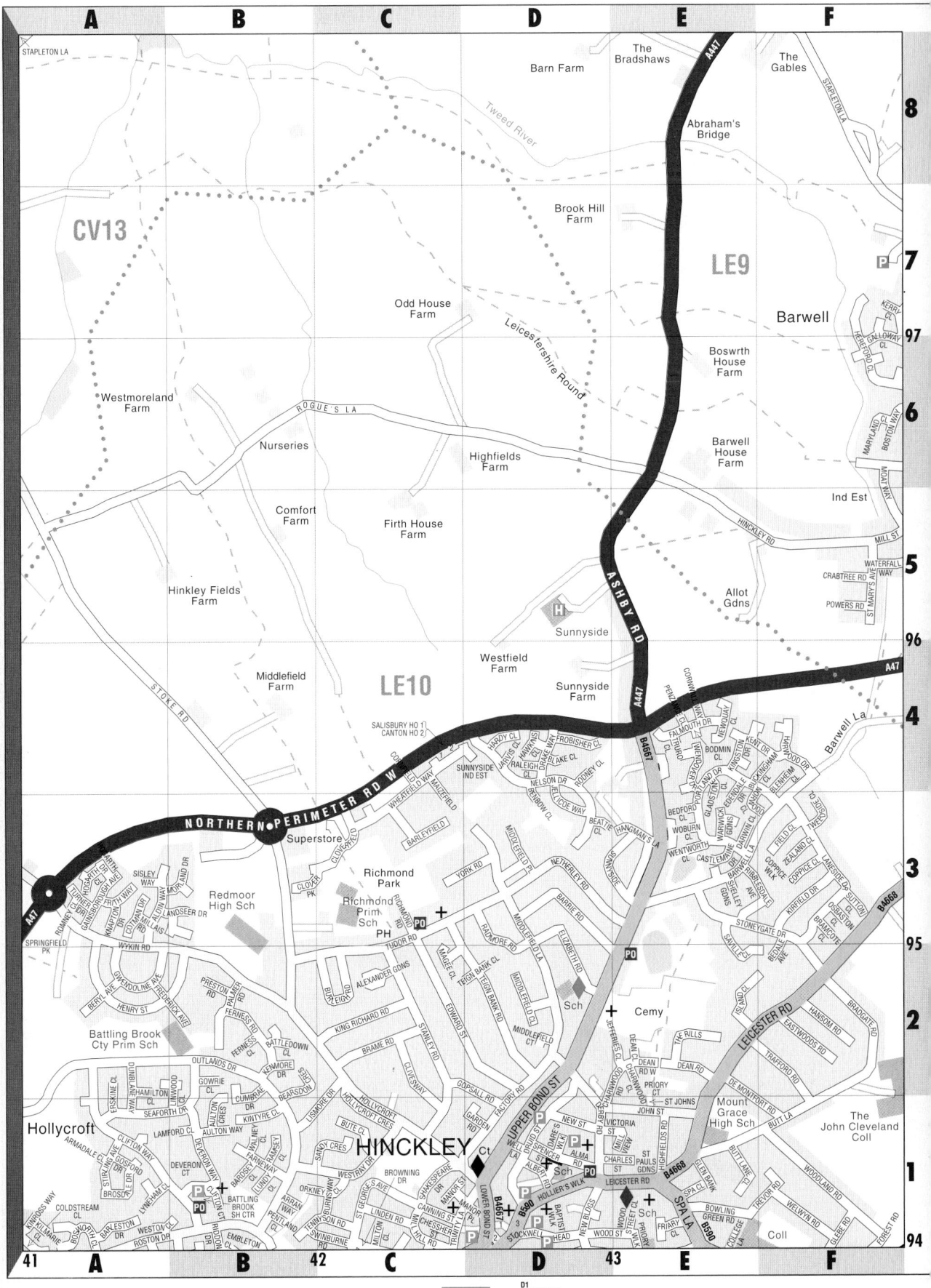

D1
1 BAINES' LA
2 KING ST
3 COUNCIL RD
4 EALES YD

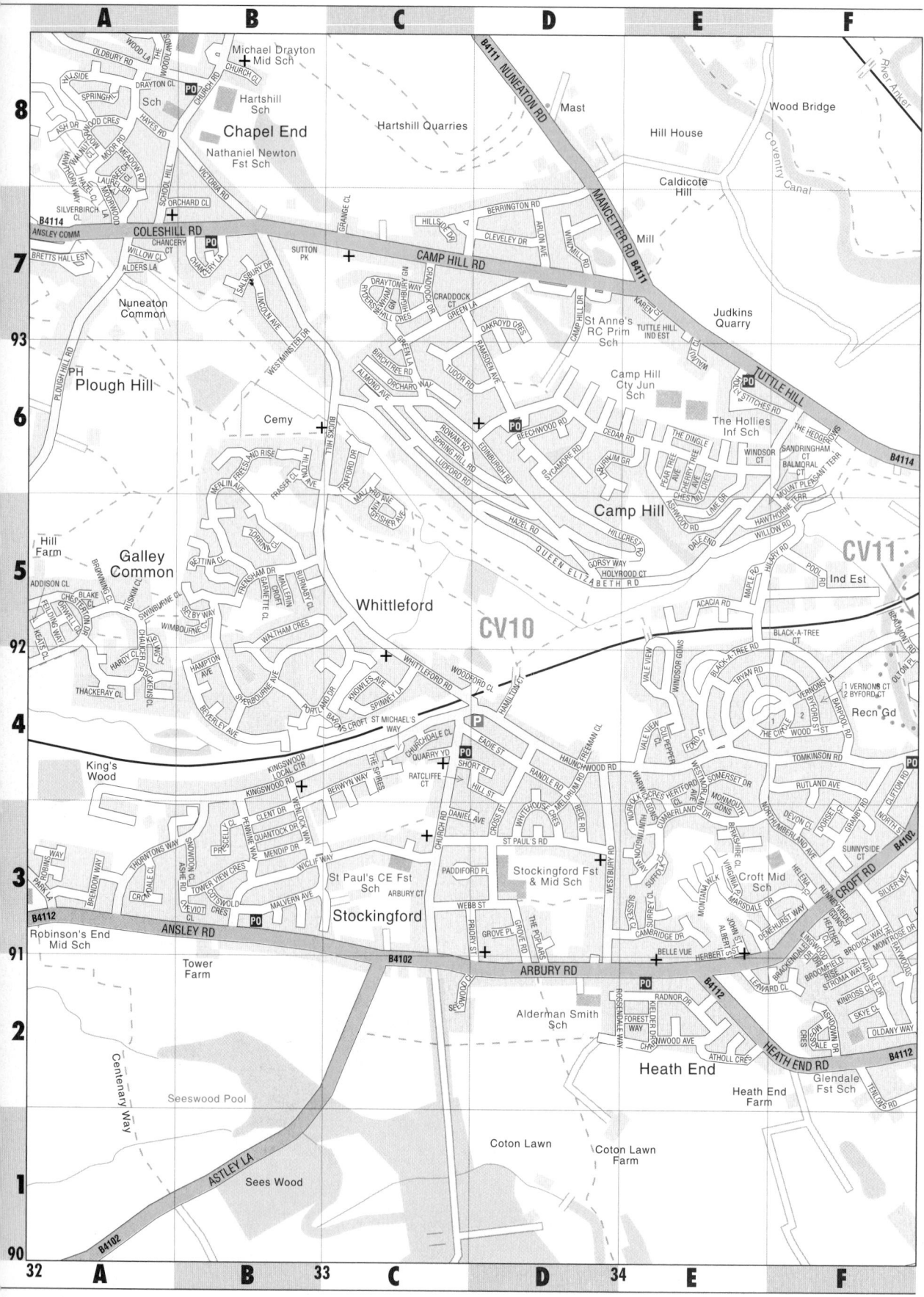

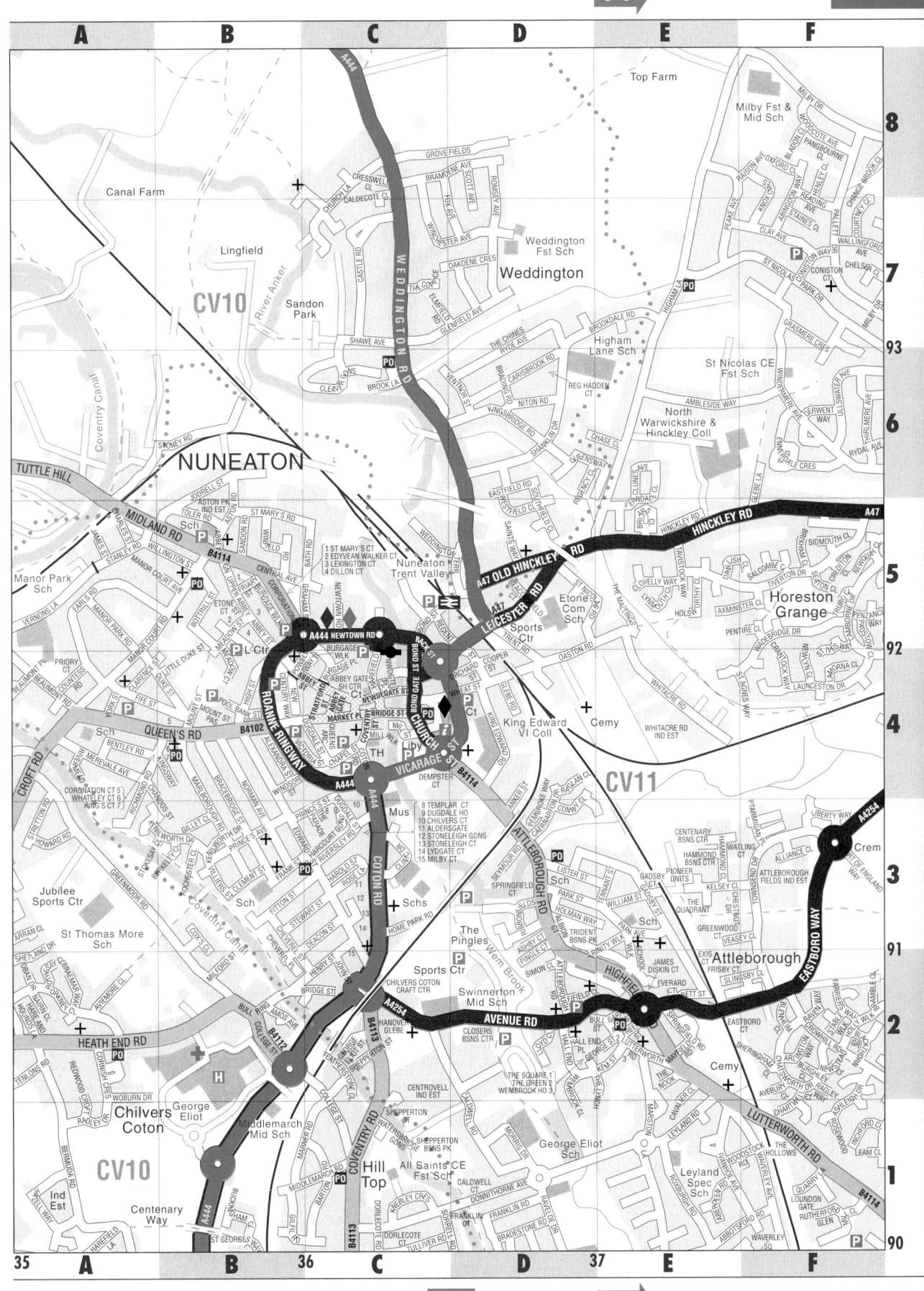

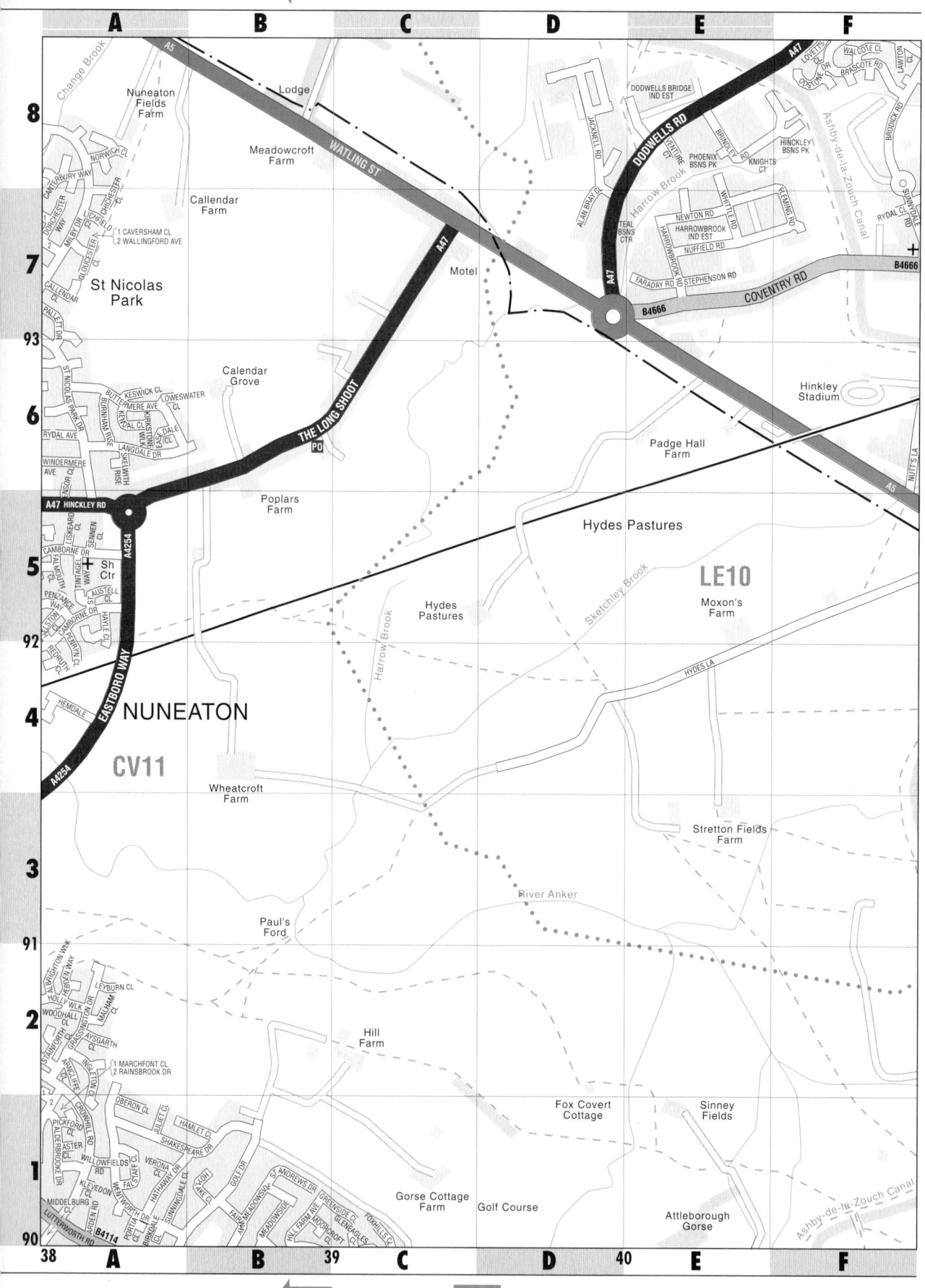

71
D8
1 MANSION ST
2 HANSON CT
3 BRITTANIA SH CTR
4 BLOCKLEY'S YD
5 REGENT CT
6 THE PARADE

76

7 EDWARDS CTR
8 THE HORSEFAIR
E8
1 THE NARROWS
2 QUEEN'S PARK FLATS
3 QUEEN'S PARK TERR
4 CLARENCE CT

75

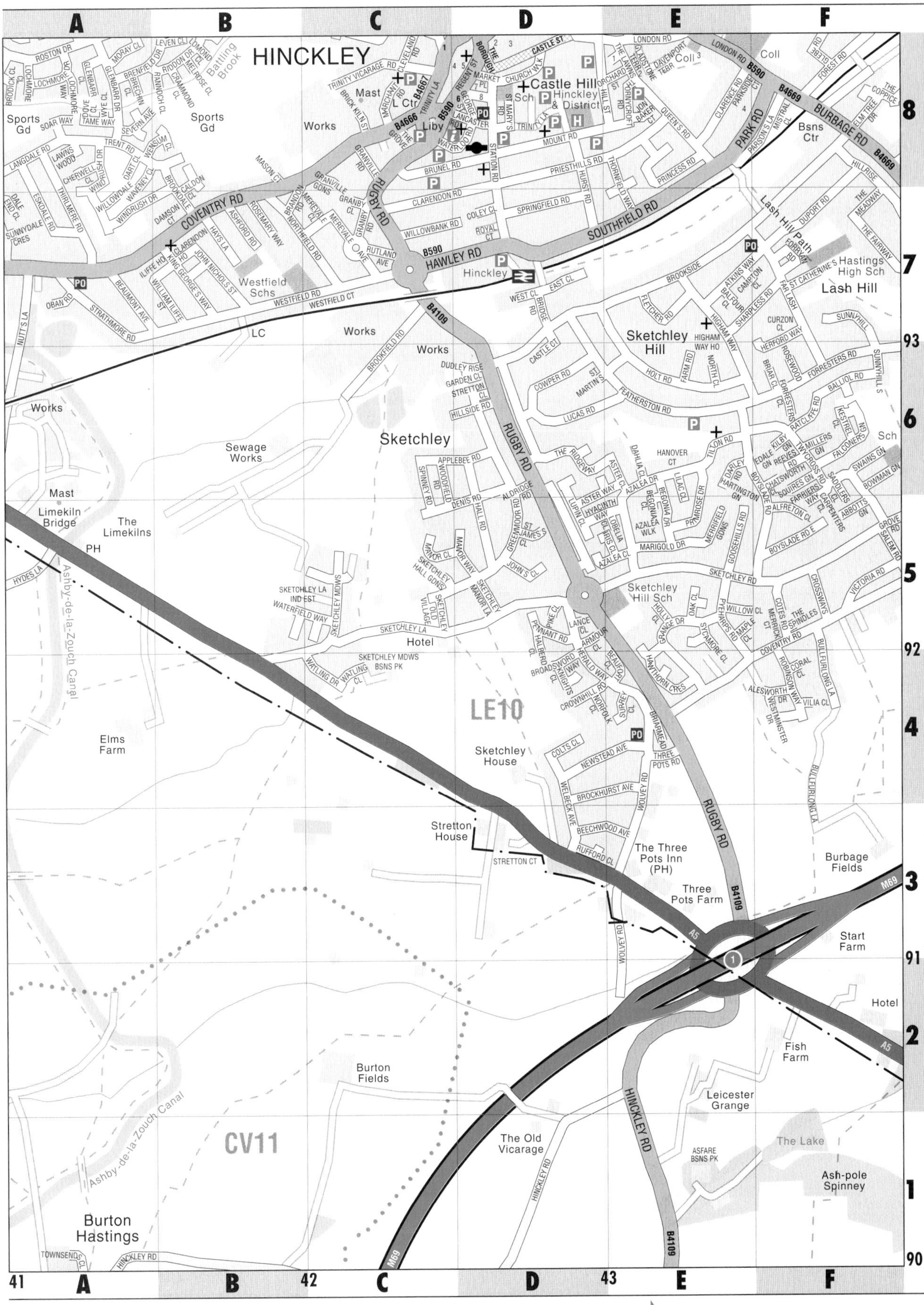

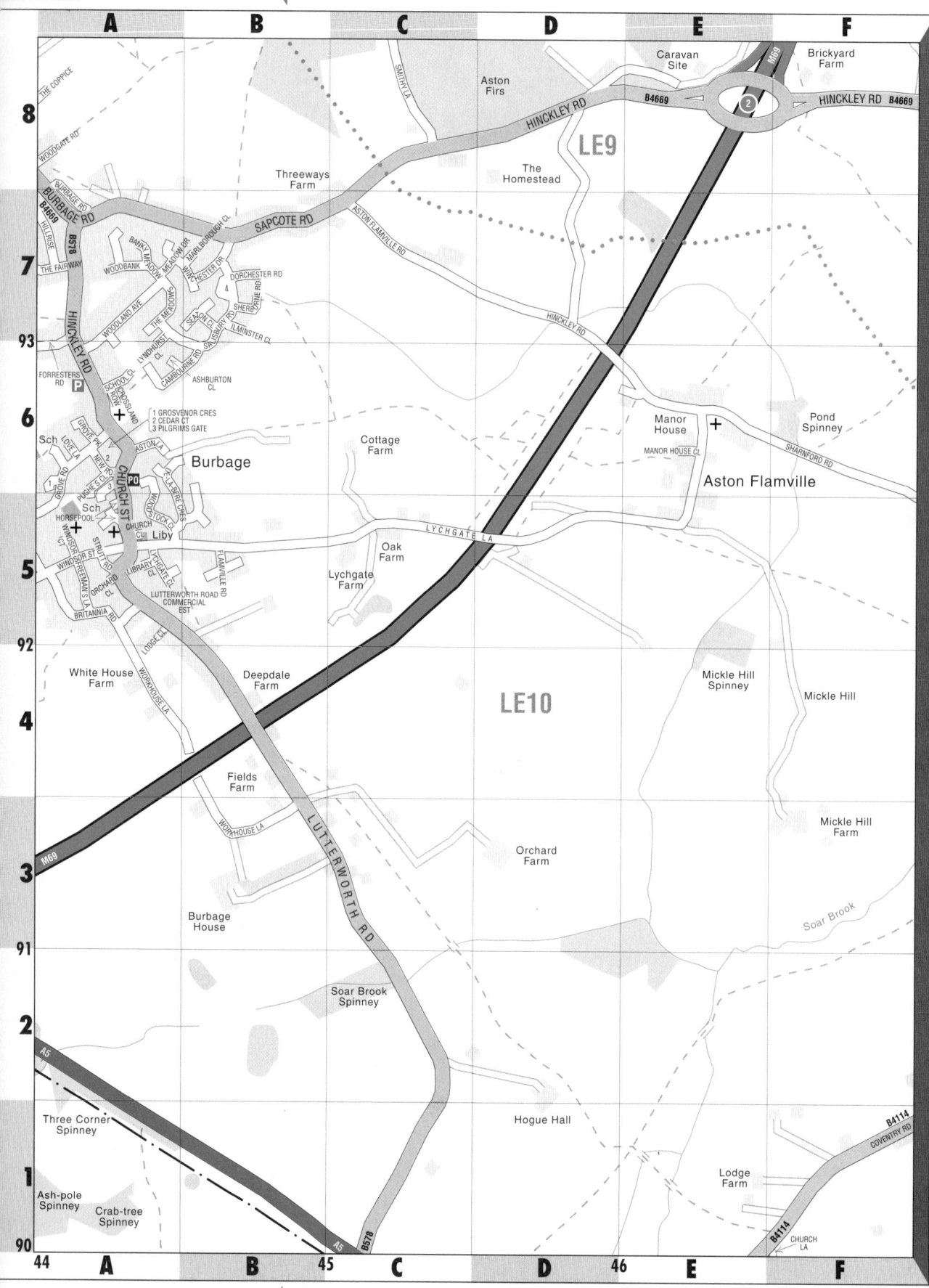

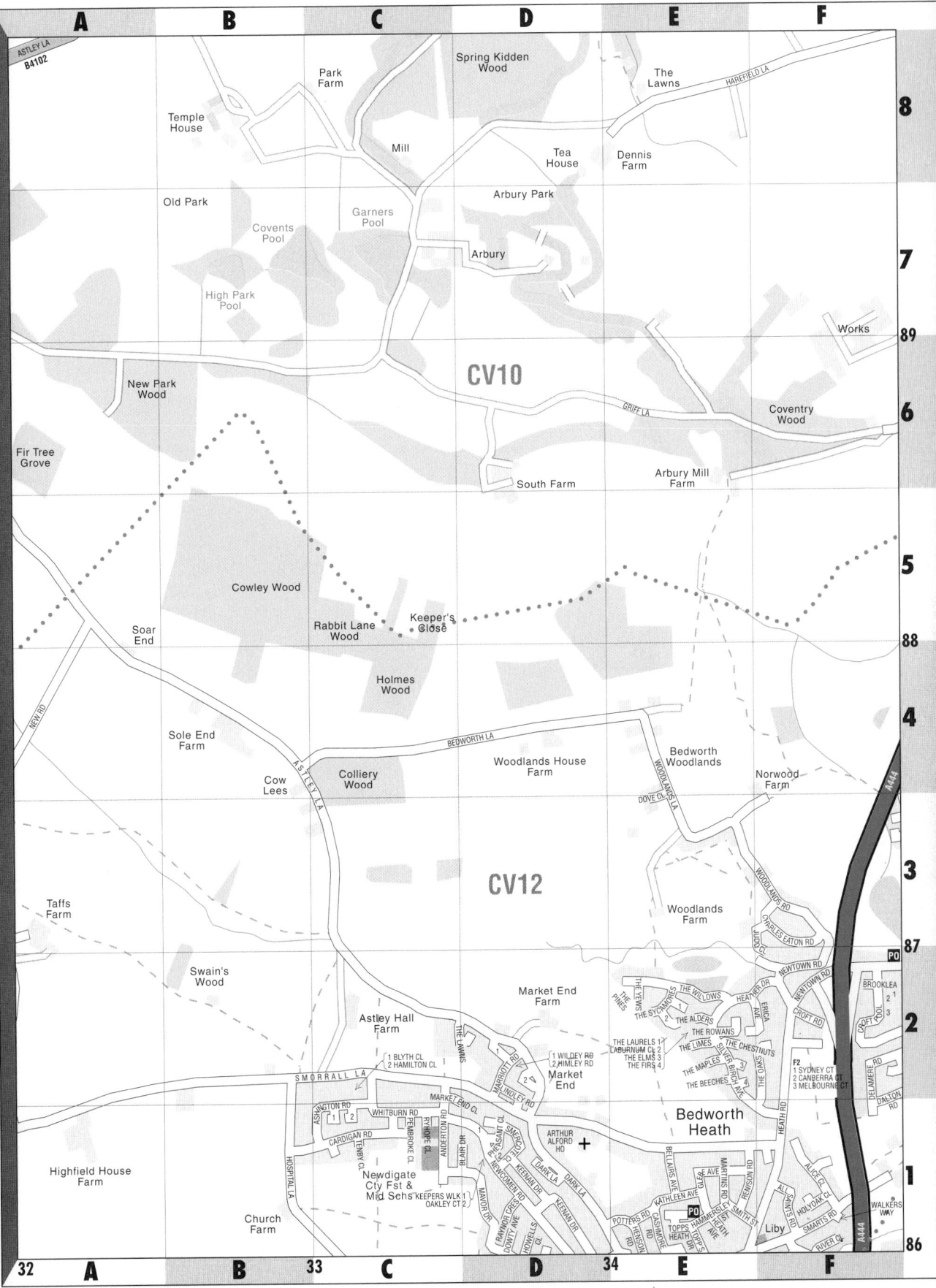

ASTLEY LA
B4102

Temple House

Park Farm

Spring Kidden Wood

The Lawns

HAREFIELD LA

8

Mill

Tea House

Dennis Farm

Old Park

Covents Pool

Garners Pool

Arbury Park

Arbury

7

High Park Pool

Works

89

CV10

New Park Wood

GRIFF LA

Coventry Wood

6

Fir Tree Grove

South Farm

Arbury Mill Farm

Cowley Wood

Keeper's Close

5

Soar End

Rabbit Lane Wood

88

NEW RD

Holmes Wood

Sole End Farm

BEDWORTH LA

Woodlands House Farm

Bedworth Woodlands

Norwood Farm

4

A444

Cow Lees

ASTLEY LA

Colliery Wood

DOVE CL

WOODLANDS LA

Taffs Farm

CV12

Woodlands Farm

3

87

PO

Swain's Wood

Market End Farm

THE PINES

THE WILLOWS

THE YEWS

THE SYCAMORES

THE ALDERS

HEATHER DR

NEWTOWN RD

WOODLANDS RD

CHARLES EATON RD

JUDD CL

Brooklea

CROFT POOL

Astley Hall Farm

THE LAWNS

MARROTT RD

LINDLEY RD

1 BLYTH CL
2 HAMILTON CL

1 WILDEY RD
2 HIMLEY RD

THE LAURELS 1
LABURNUM CL 2
THE ELMS 3
THE FIRS 4

THE ROWANS

THE LIMES

THE CHESTNUTS

THE MAPLES

THE BEECHES

ERICA AVE

SILVER BIRCH AVE

THE DANS

CROFT RD

DELAMERE RD

F2
1 SYDNEY CT
2 CANBERRA CT
3 MELBOURNE CT

SMORRALL LA

Market End

Bedworth Heath

DALTON RD

ASKINGTON RD

WHITBURN RD

CARDIGAN RD

TENBY RD

PEMBROKE CL

RY HOPE CL

MARKET END CL

ANDERTON RD

HB HIGH RD

PHEASANT CL

SMERCOTT CL

NEWCOMEN RD

KEENAN DR

PARK LA

ARTHUR ALFORD HO

BELLAIRS AVE

HEATH RD

RENSON RD

SMITH ST

HEATH ST

ALL SAINTS RD

ALICE CL

HOLYOAK CL

SMARTS RD

1

Highfield House Farm

HOSPITAL LA

Newdigate Cty Fst & Mid Schs

KEEPERS WLK 1
OAKLEY CT 2

MANOR DR

FRANMOOR CRES

DOWTY AVE

HOWELLS

KEENAN DR

KATHLEEN AVE

POTTERS RD

SE AVE

MARTINS RD

CASHMORE

PO

TOPPS HEATH

HAMMERSLEY ST

TOPPS HEATH

Liby

RIVER CL

WALKERS WAY

86

Church Farm

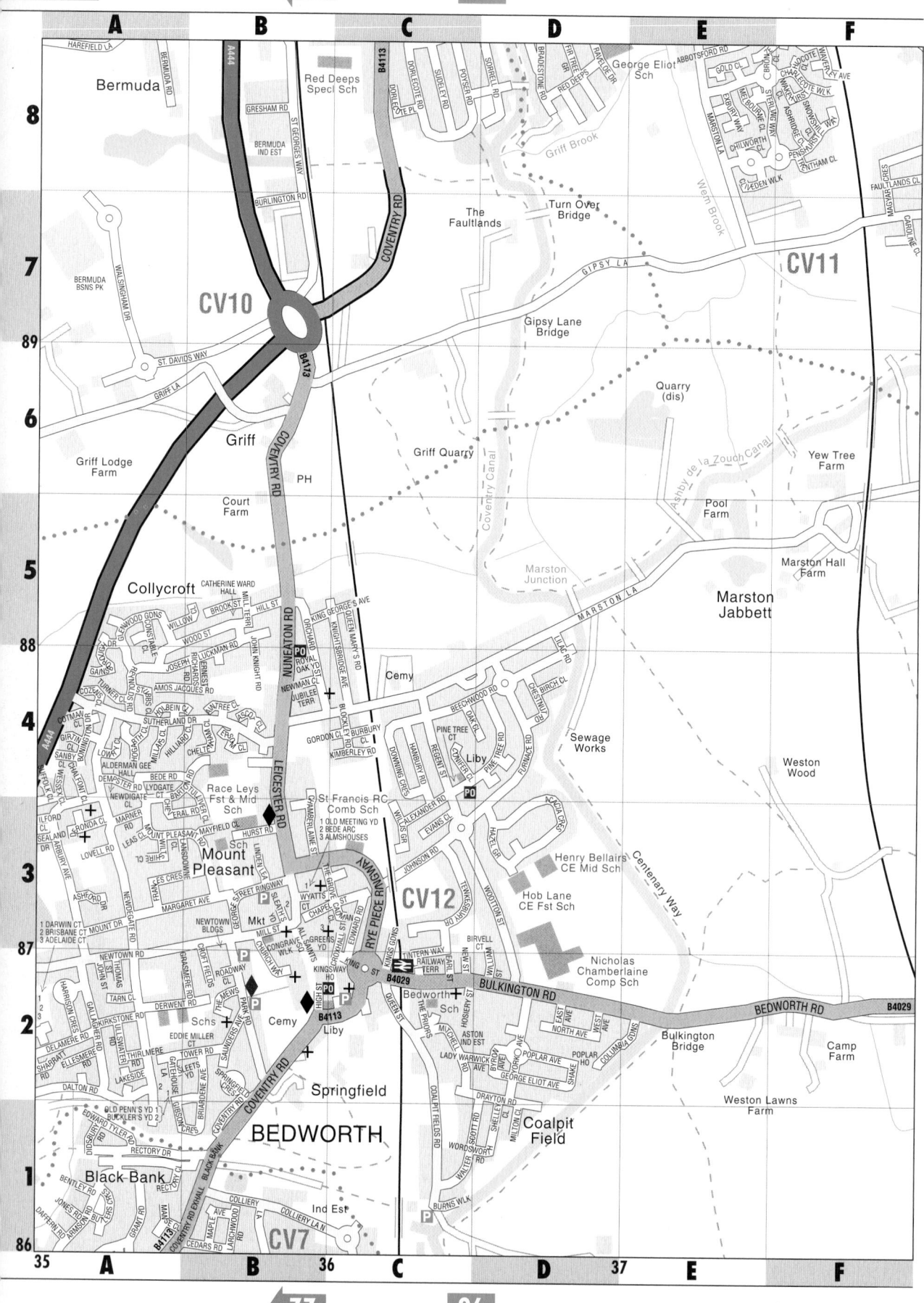

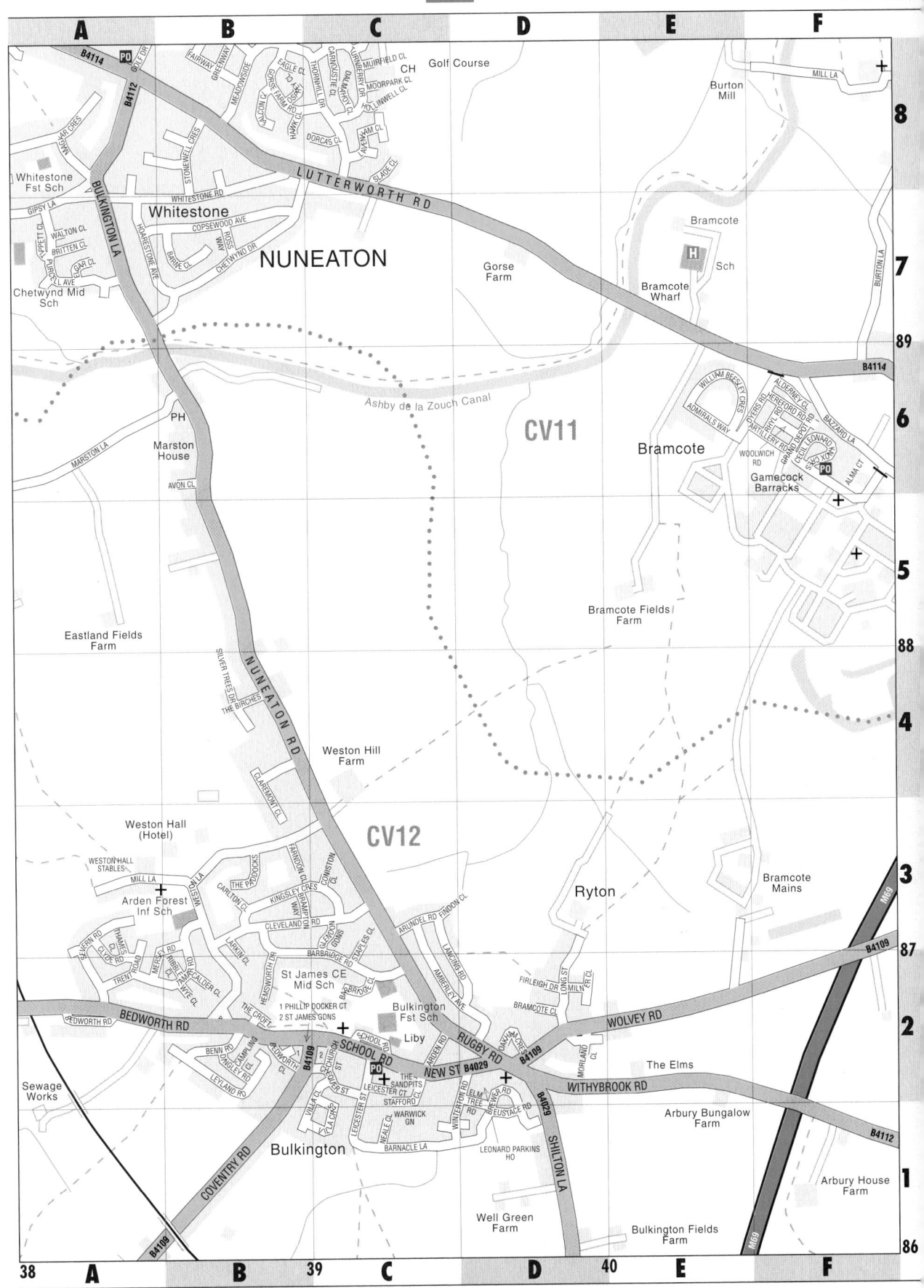

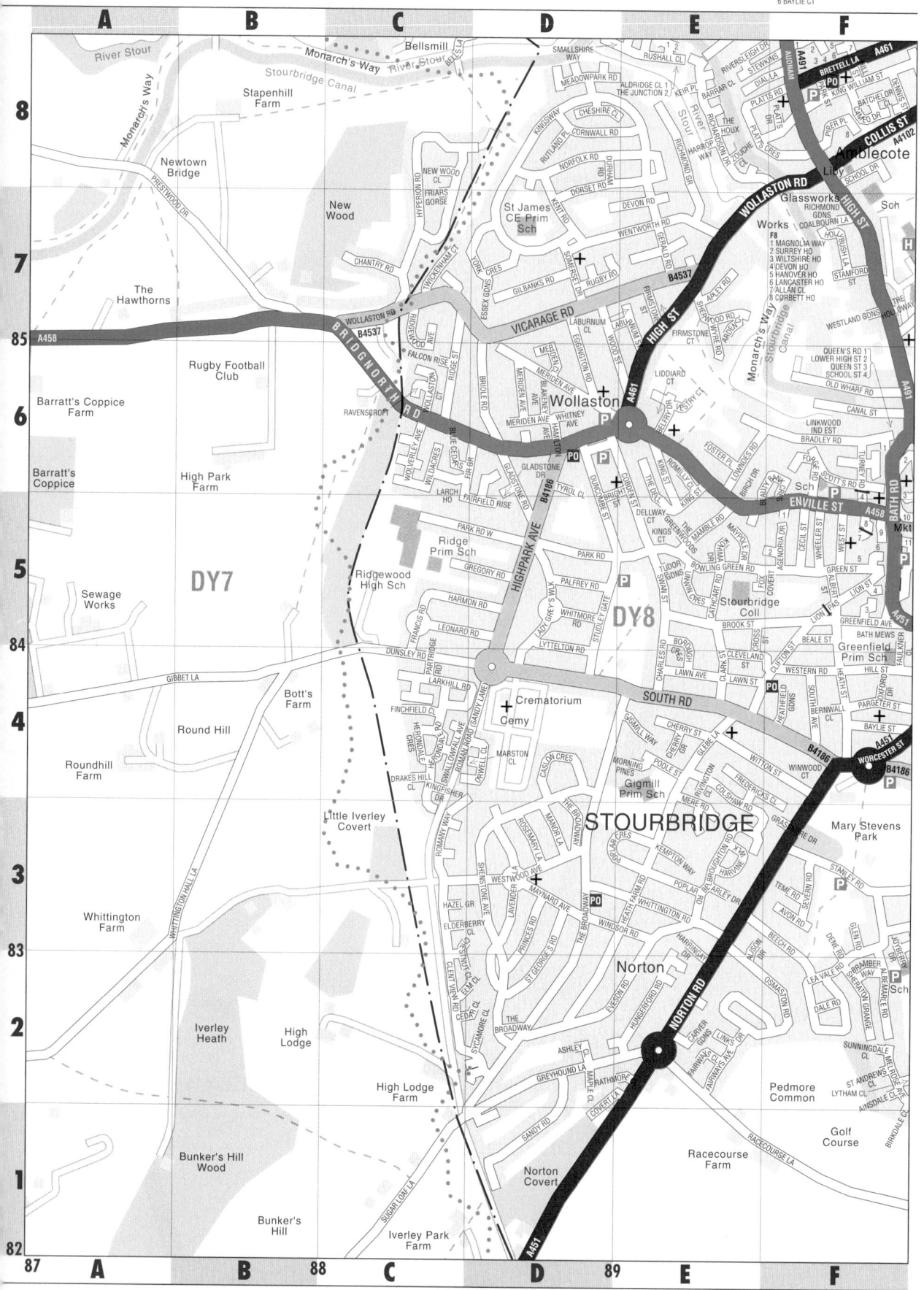

F5
1 SUMMER ST
2 HEMMINGS CL
3 BALLARAT WLK
4 HOLLY GR
5 KENNEDY CT
6 BAYLIE CT
7 ENVILLE PL
8 SHORT ST
9 HEMPLANDS RD
10 CROWN LA
11 NEW ST

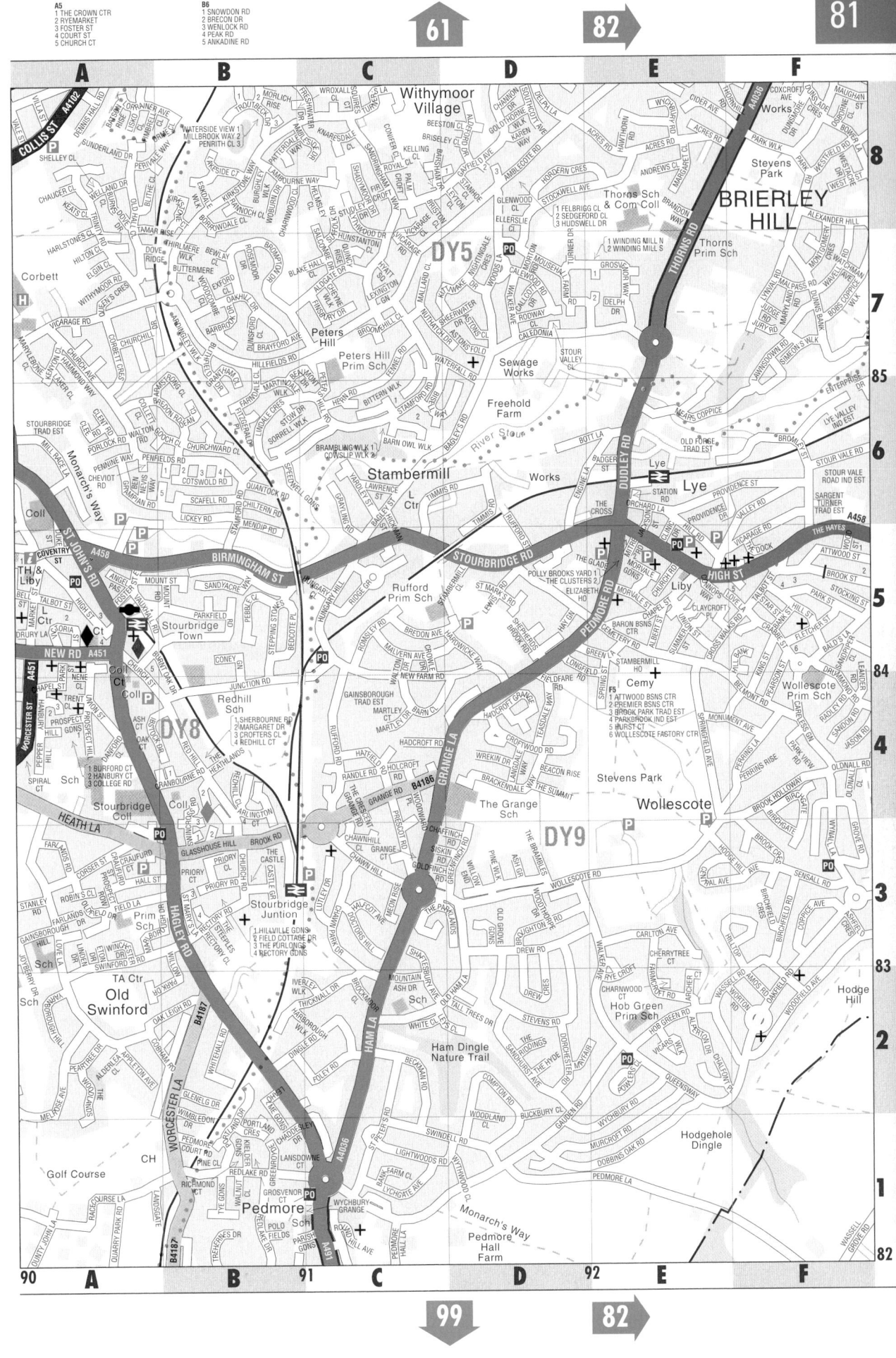

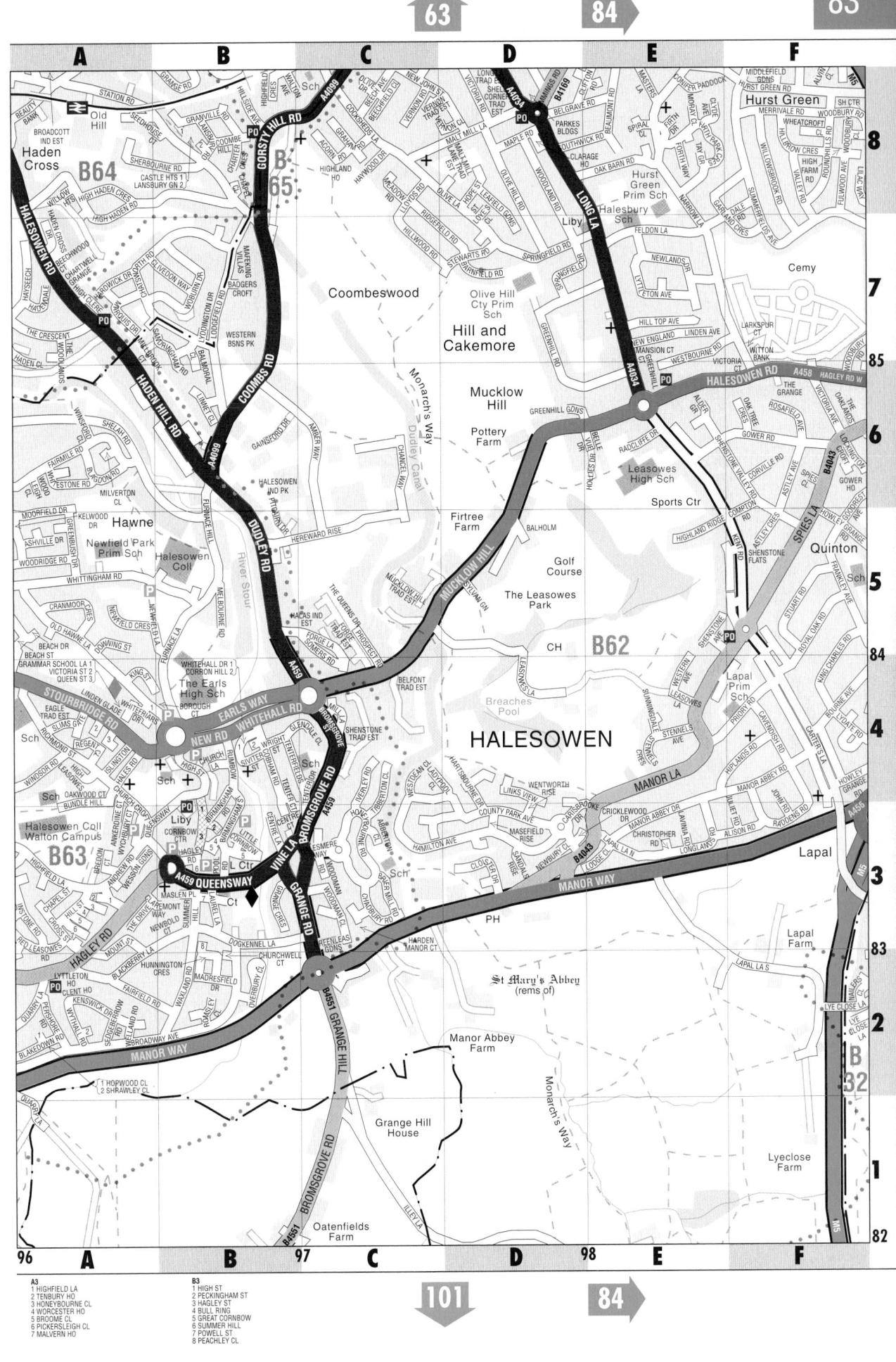

A3
1 HIGHFIELD LA
2 TENBURY HO
3 HONEYBOURNE CL
4 WORCESTER HO
5 BROOME CL
6 PICKERSLEIGH CL
7 MALVERN HO

B3
1 HIGH ST
2 PECKINGHAM ST
3 HAGLEY ST
4 BULL RING
5 GREAT CORNBOW
6 SUMMER HILL
7 POWELL ST
8 PEACHLEY CL

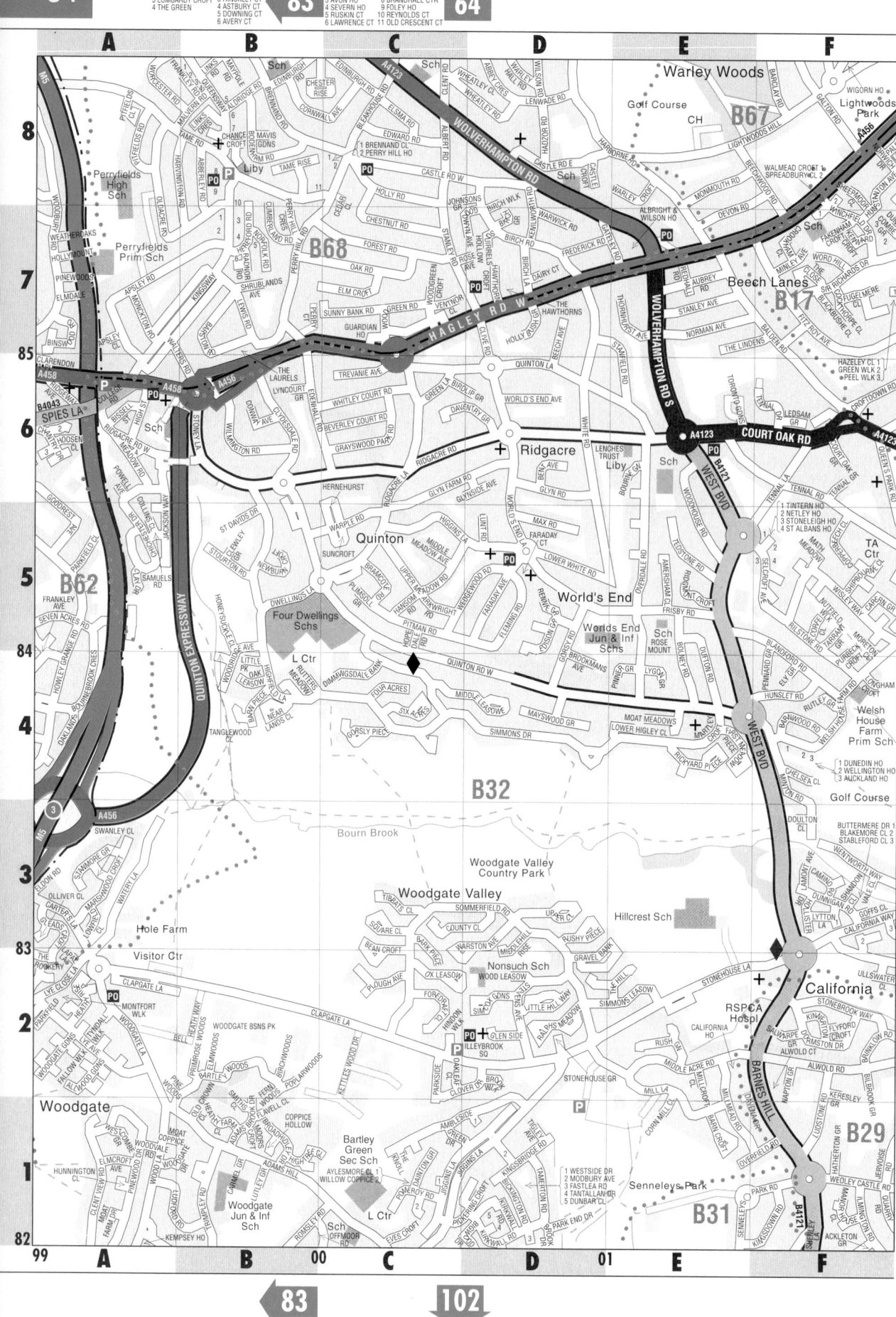

84

A6
1 BEVERLEY CT
2 HICKMANS CL
3 LOMBARDY CROFT
4 THE GREEN

B7
1 BRINDLEY CT
2 VERNON CT
3 HINCKLEY CT
4 ASTBURY CT
5 DOWNING CT
6 AVERY CT

83

B8
1 ARROW HO
2 STOUR HO
3 AVON HO
4 SEVERN HO
5 RUSKIN CT
6 LAWRENCE CT

7 HENDERSON CT
8 BRANDHALL CTR
9 FOLEY HO
10 REYNOLDS CT
11 OLD CRESCENT CT

64

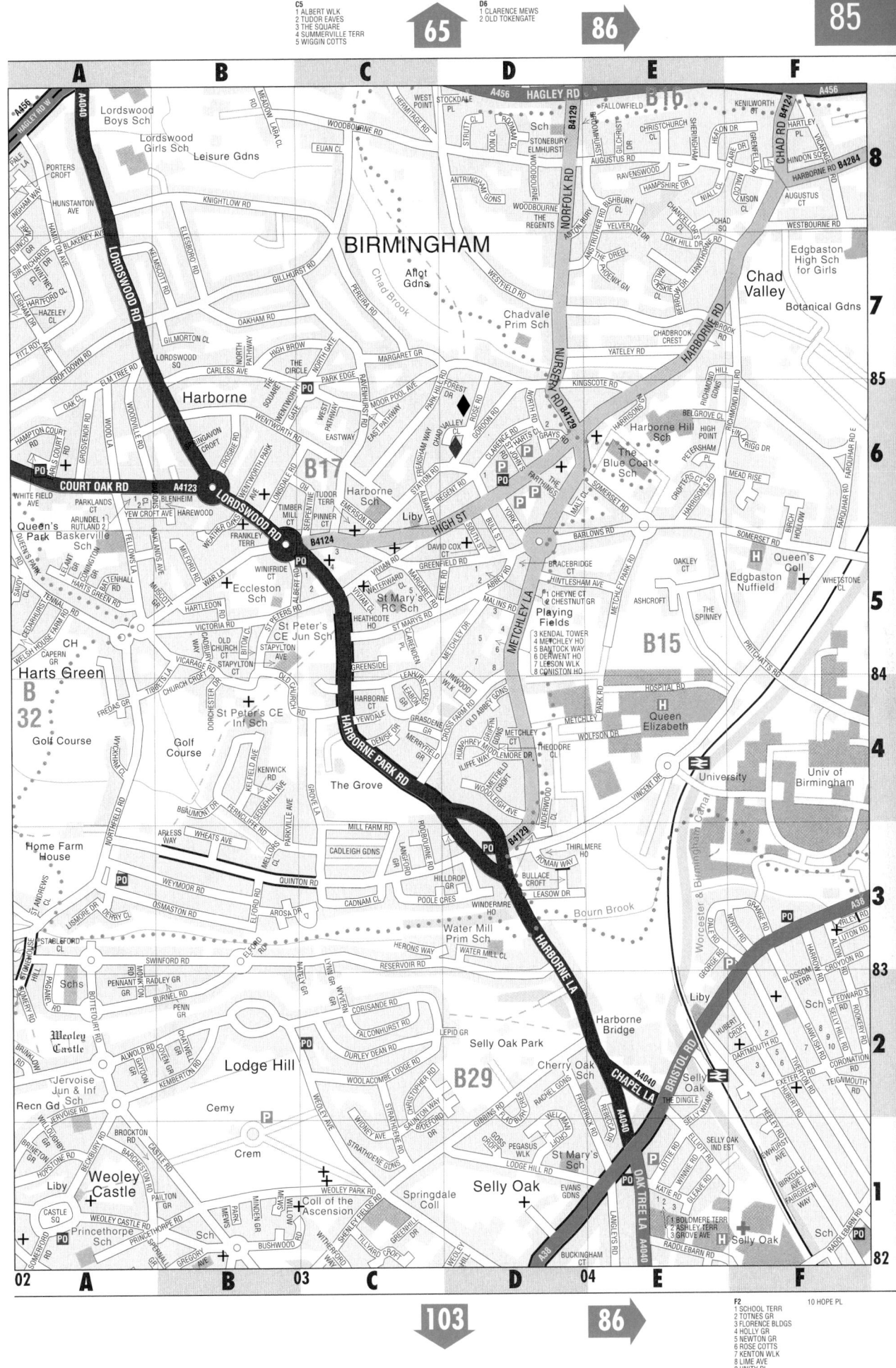

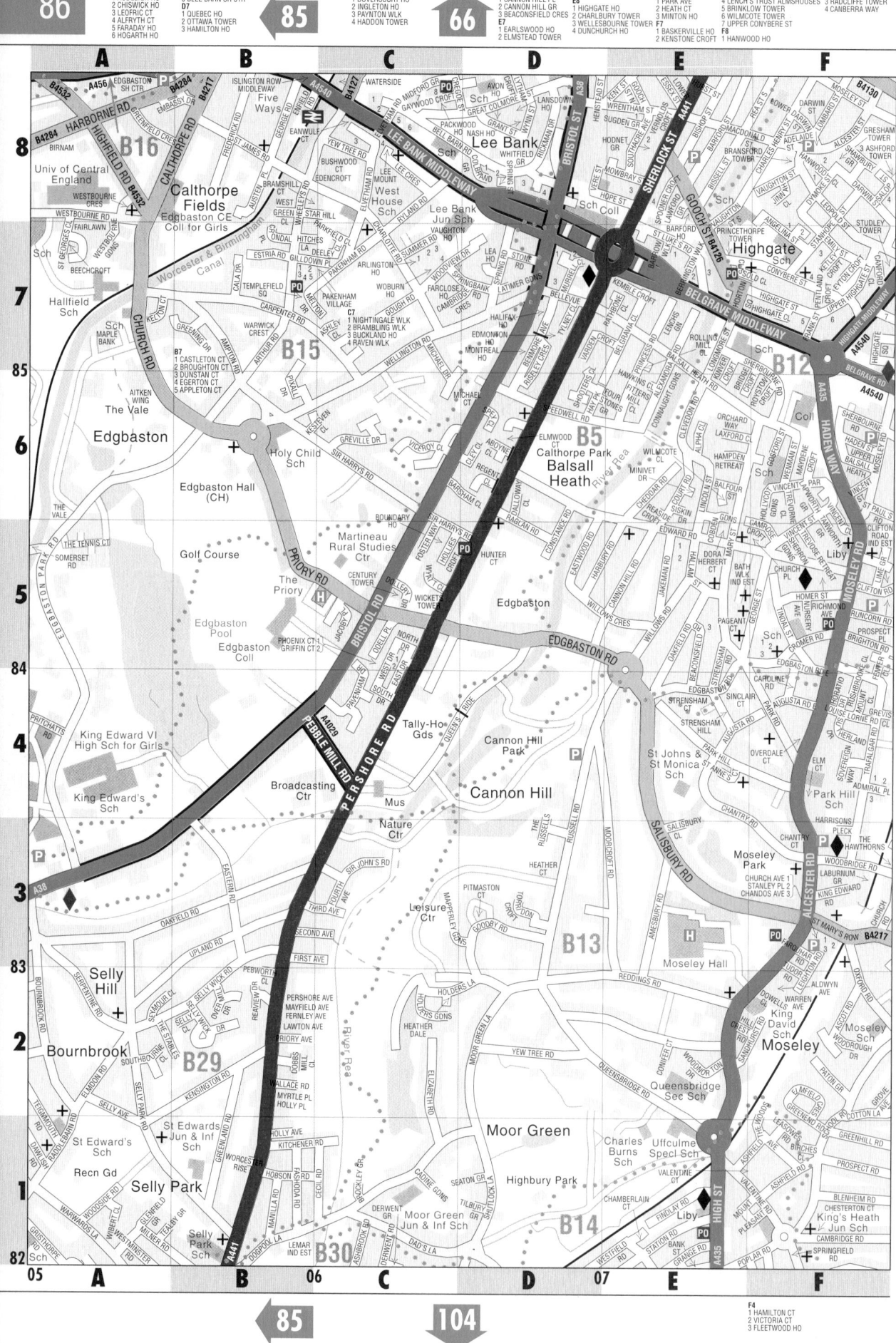

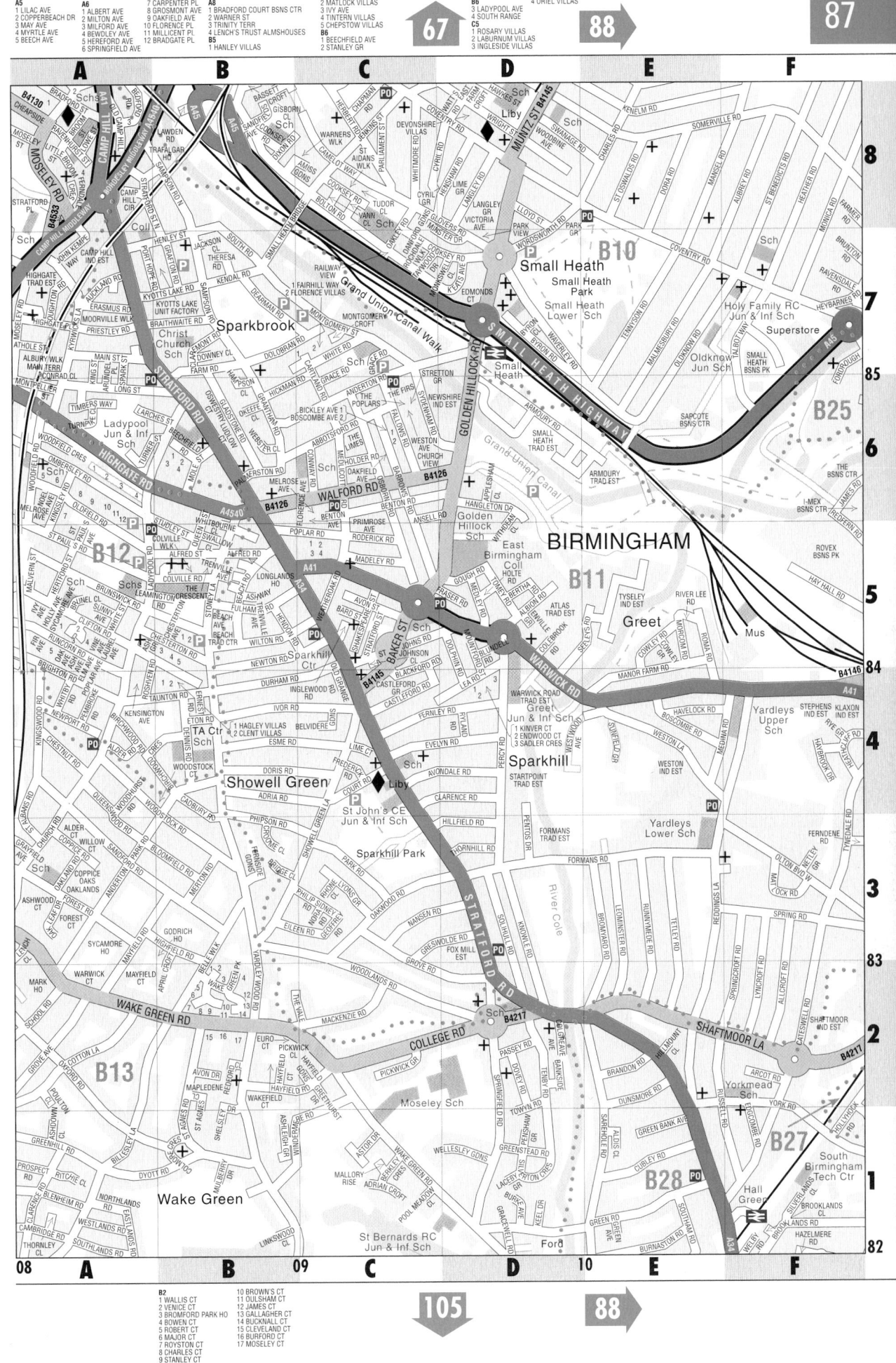

87

68

C5
1 SYCAMORE WAY
2 CYPRESS SQ
3 BRAMLEY RD
4 LAUREL GDNS
5 ASH MEWS
6 CHERRY TREE CROFT

C5
7 SNOWBERRY GDNS
8 RYE CROFT
9 HONEYSUCKLE GR
10 BLOSSOMVILLE WAY

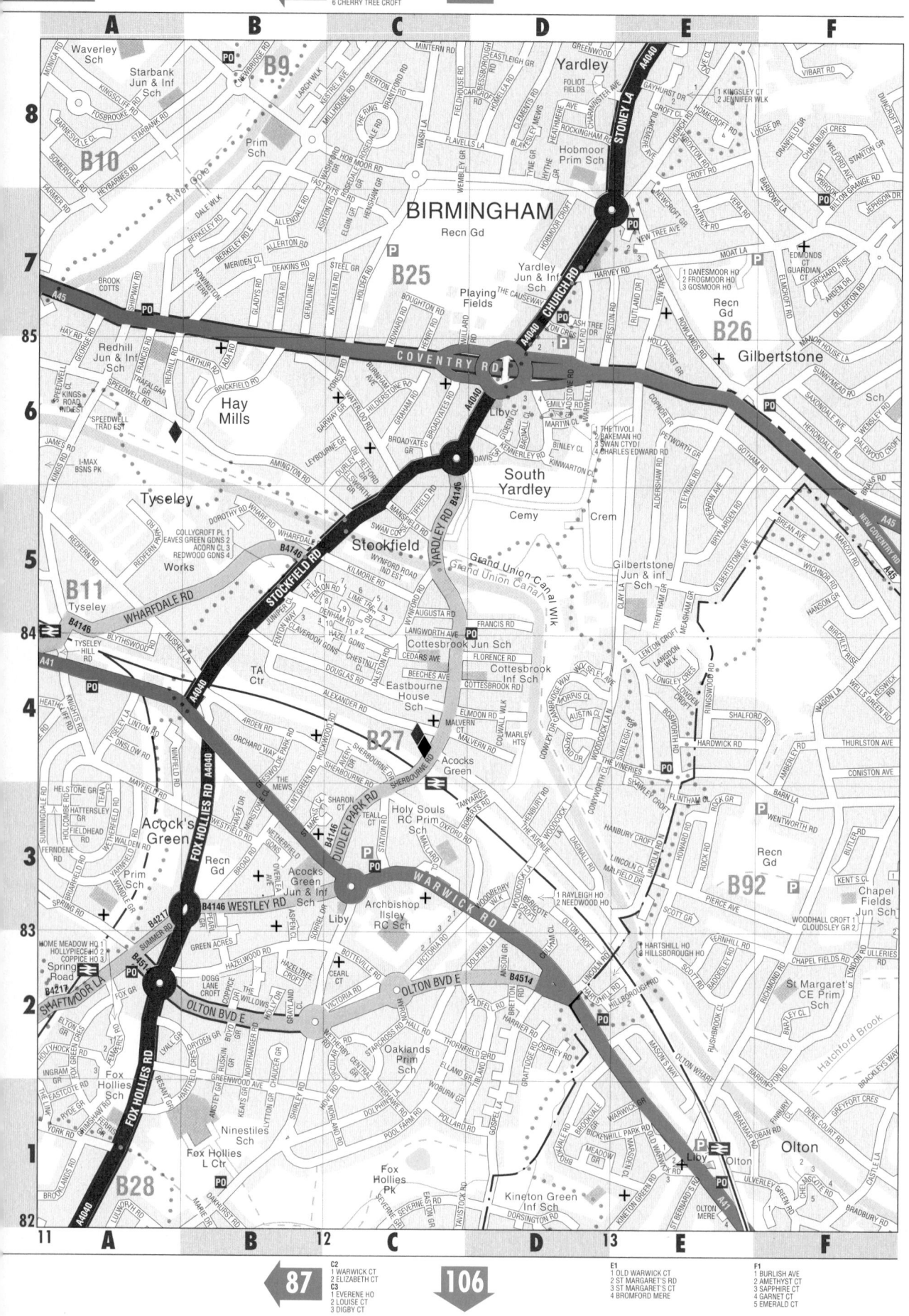

BIRMINGHAM

Yardley

Gilbertstone

Hay Mills

Tyseley

South Yardley

Stockfield

B9

B10

B25

B26

B11
Tyseley

B27

Acock's Green

B92

B28

87

106

C2
1 WARWICK CT.
2 ELIZABETH CT
C3
1 EVERENE HO
2 LOUISE CT
3 DIGBY CT

E1
1 OLD WARWICK CT
2 ST MARGARET'S RD
3 ST MARGARET'S CT
4 BROMFORD MERE

F1
1 BURLISH AVE
2 AMETHYST CT
3 SAPPHIRE CT
4 GARNET CT
5 EMERALD CT

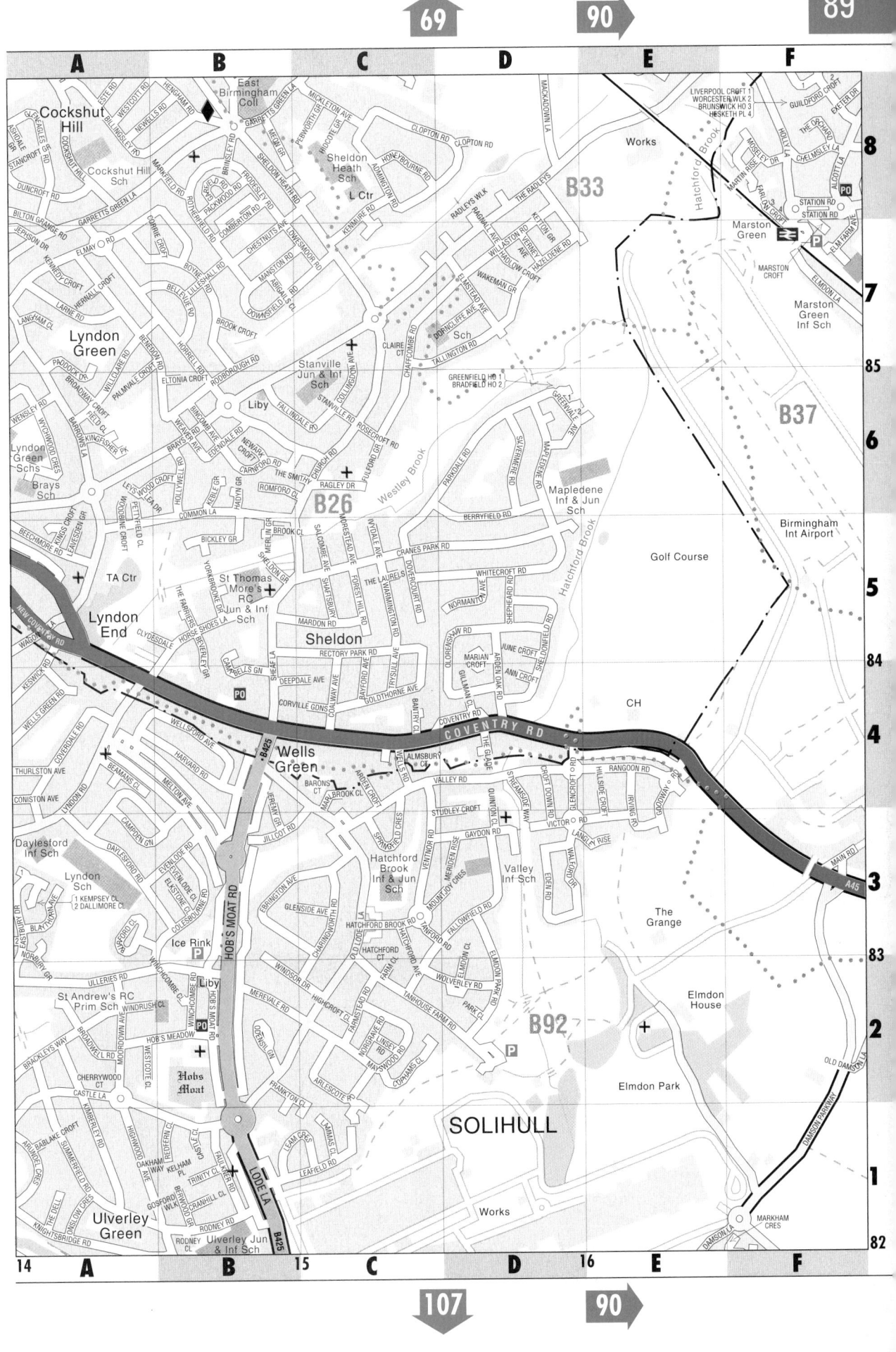

89
70

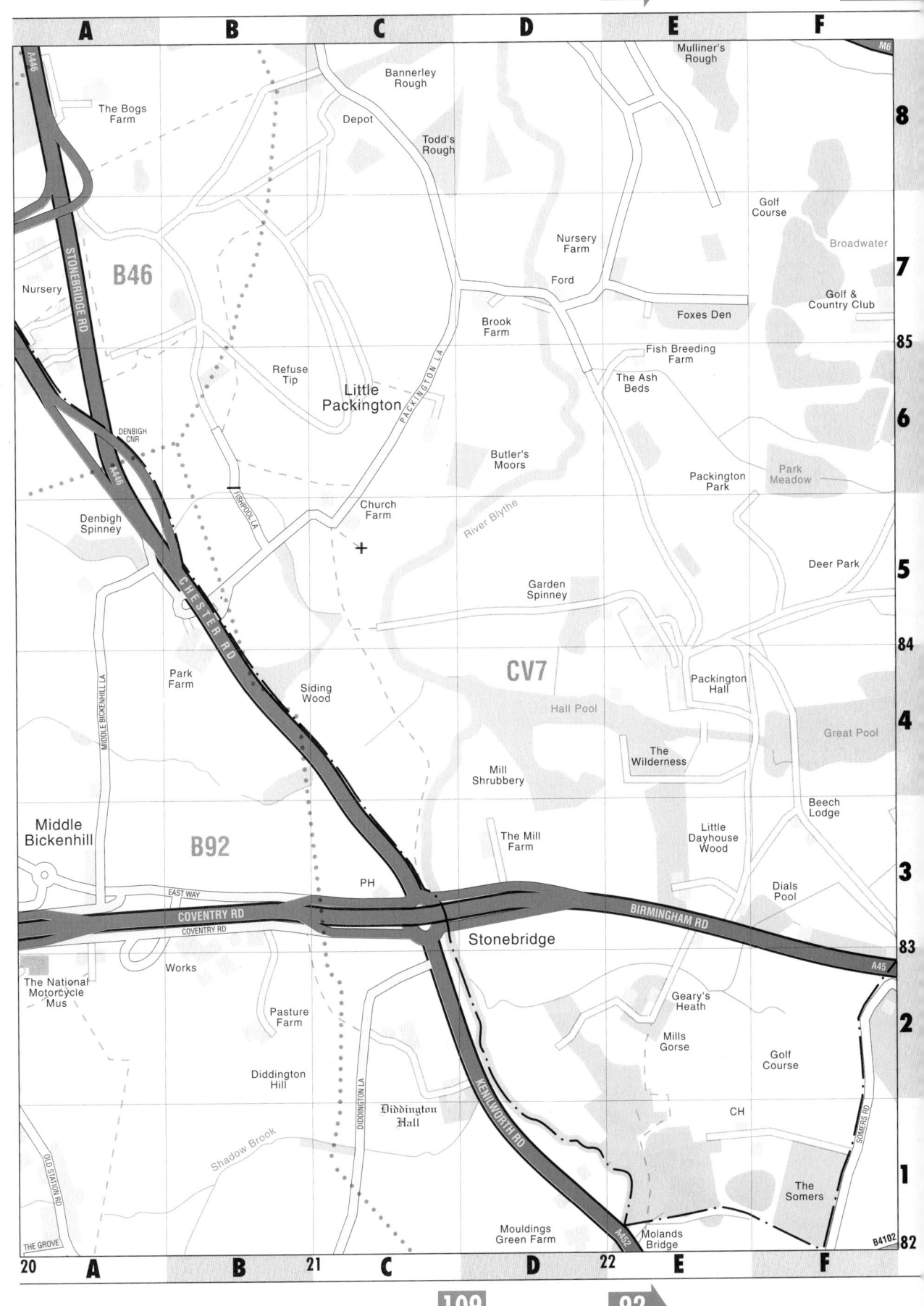

M6

The Bogs
Farm

Mulliner's
Rough

Bannerley
Rough

Depot

Todd's
Rough

Golf
Course

Broadwater

B46

Nursery
Farm

Nursery

Ford

Golf &
Country Club

STONEBRIDGE RD

Brook
Farm

Foxes Den

Fish Breeding
Farm

Refuse
Tip

Little
Packington

The Ash
Beds

DENBIGH
CNR

A46

Butler's
Moors

Packington
Park

Park
Meadow

FISHPOOL LA

PACKINGTON LA

Denbigh
Spinney

Church
Farm

River Blythe

CHESTER RD

Garden
Spinney

Deer Park

MIDDLE BICKENHILL LA

Park
Farm

Siding
Wood

CV7

Packington
Hall

Hall Pool

Great Pool

Middle
Bickenhill

B92

Mill
Shrubbery

The
Wilderness

Little
Dayhouse
Wood

Beech
Lodge

PH

The Mill
Farm

Dials
Pool

EAST WAY

COVENTRY RD

COVENTRY RD

Stonebridge

BIRMINGHAM RD

A45

The National
Motorcycle
Mus

Works

Geary's
Heath

Pasture
Farm

Mills
Gorse

Golf
Course

KENILWORTH RD

DIDDINGTON LA

Diddington
Hill

CH

SOMERS RD

OLD STATION RD

Diddington
Hall

The
Somers

Shadow Brook

A452

THE GROVE

Mouldings
Green Farm

Molands
Bridge

B4102

91

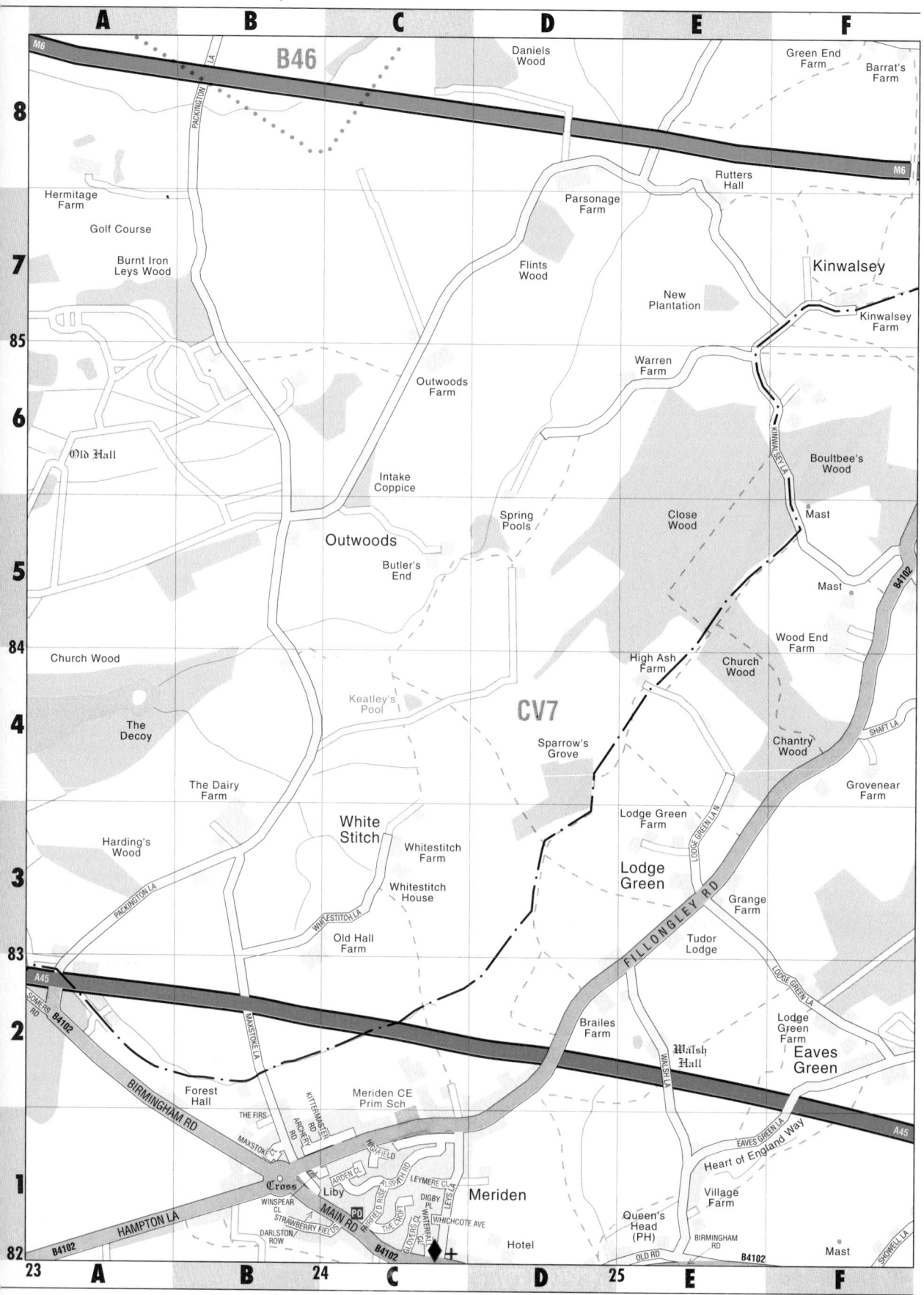

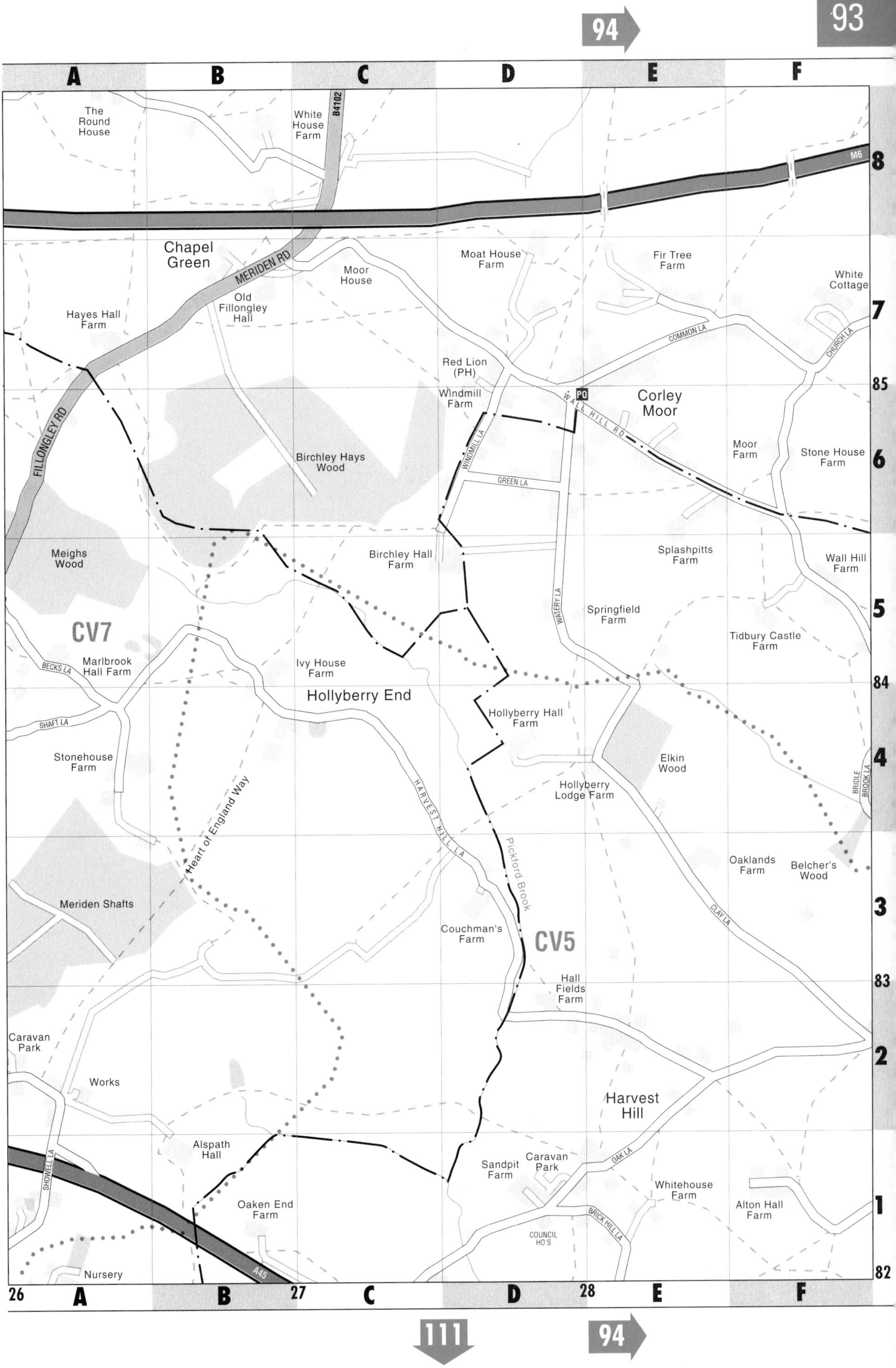
94
A
B
C
D
E
F
The Round House
White House Farm
B4102
M6
8
Chapel Green
MERIDEN RD
Moat House Farm
Fir Tree Farm
White Cottage
Moor House
Old Fillongley Hall
Hayes Hall Farm
7
COMMON LA
CHURCH LA
Red Lion (PH)
Windmill Farm
PO
Corley Moor
85
WALL HILL RD
FILLONGLEY RD
WINDMILL LA
Birchley Hays Wood
Moor Farm
Stone House Farm
6
GREEN LA
Meighs Wood
Birchley Hall Farm
Splashpitts Farm
Wall Hill Farm
WATERY LA
Springfield Farm
5
CV7
Tidbury Castle Farm
BECKS LA
Marlbrook Hall Farm
Ivy House Farm
Hollyberry End
84
SHAFT LA
Hollyberry Hall Farm
Stonehouse Farm
Elkin Wood
4
BRIDLE BROOK LA
Hollyberry Lodge Farm
HARVEST HILL LA
Heart of England Way
Pickford Brook
Oaklands Farm
Belcher's Wood
Meriden Shafts
3
CLAY LA
Couchman's Farm
CV5
83
Hall Fields Farm
Caravan Park
2
Works
Harvest Hill
Alspath Hall
OAK LA
Sandpit Farm
Caravan Park
Whitehouse Farm
SHOWELL LA
1
Oaken End Farm
BRICK HILL LA
Alton Hall Farm
COUNCIL HO'S
A45
Nursery
82
26
27
28
111
94

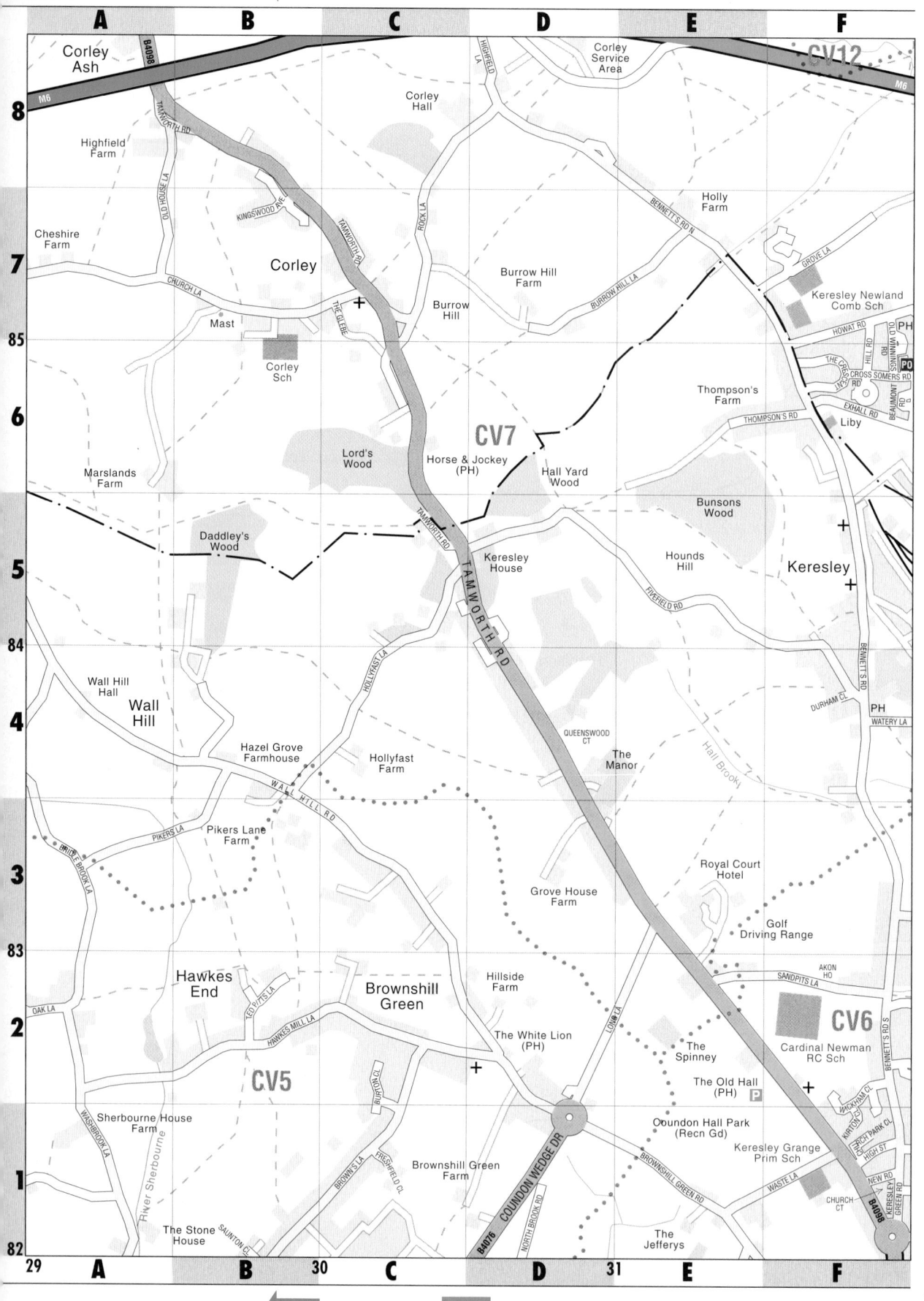

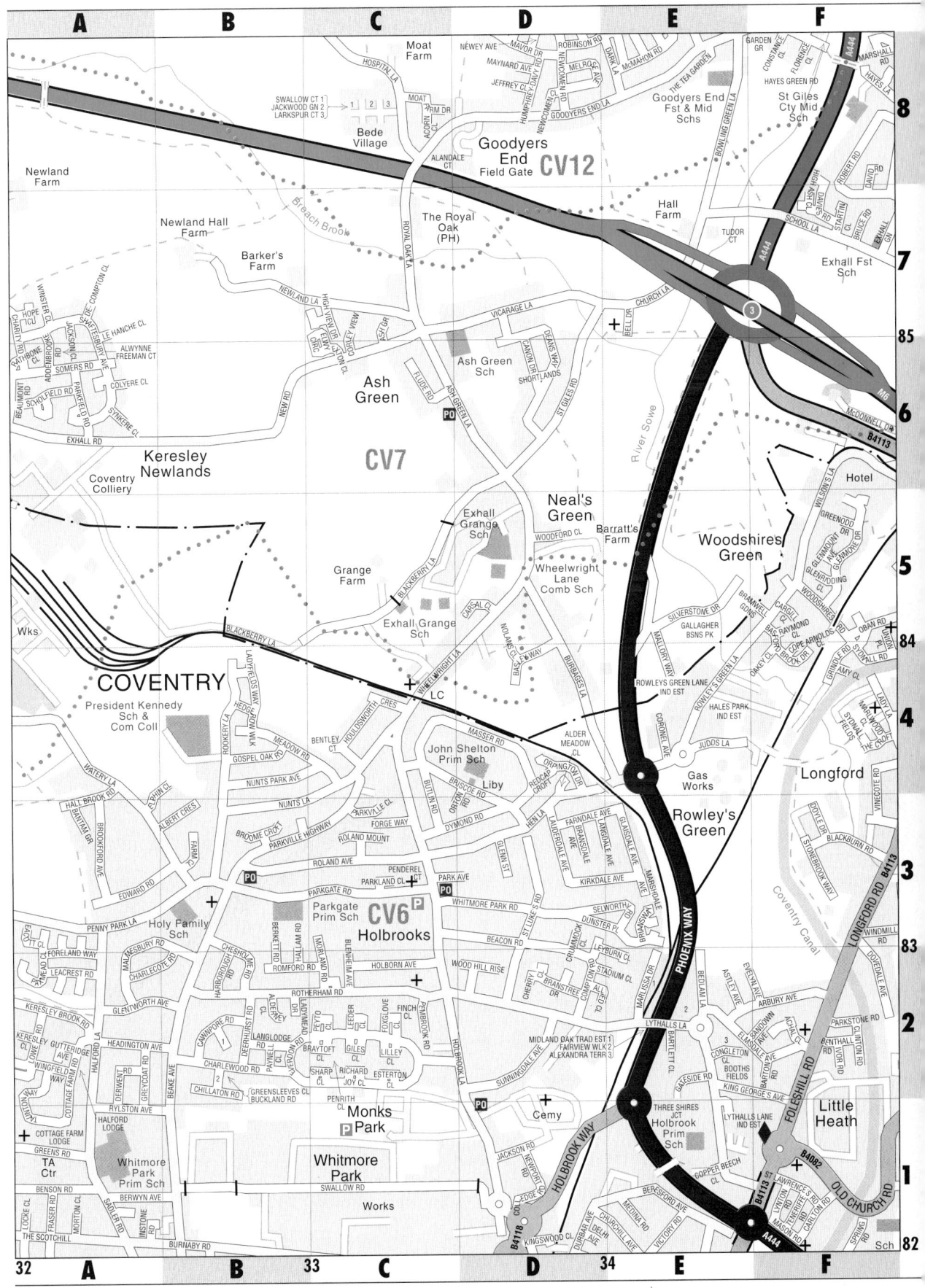

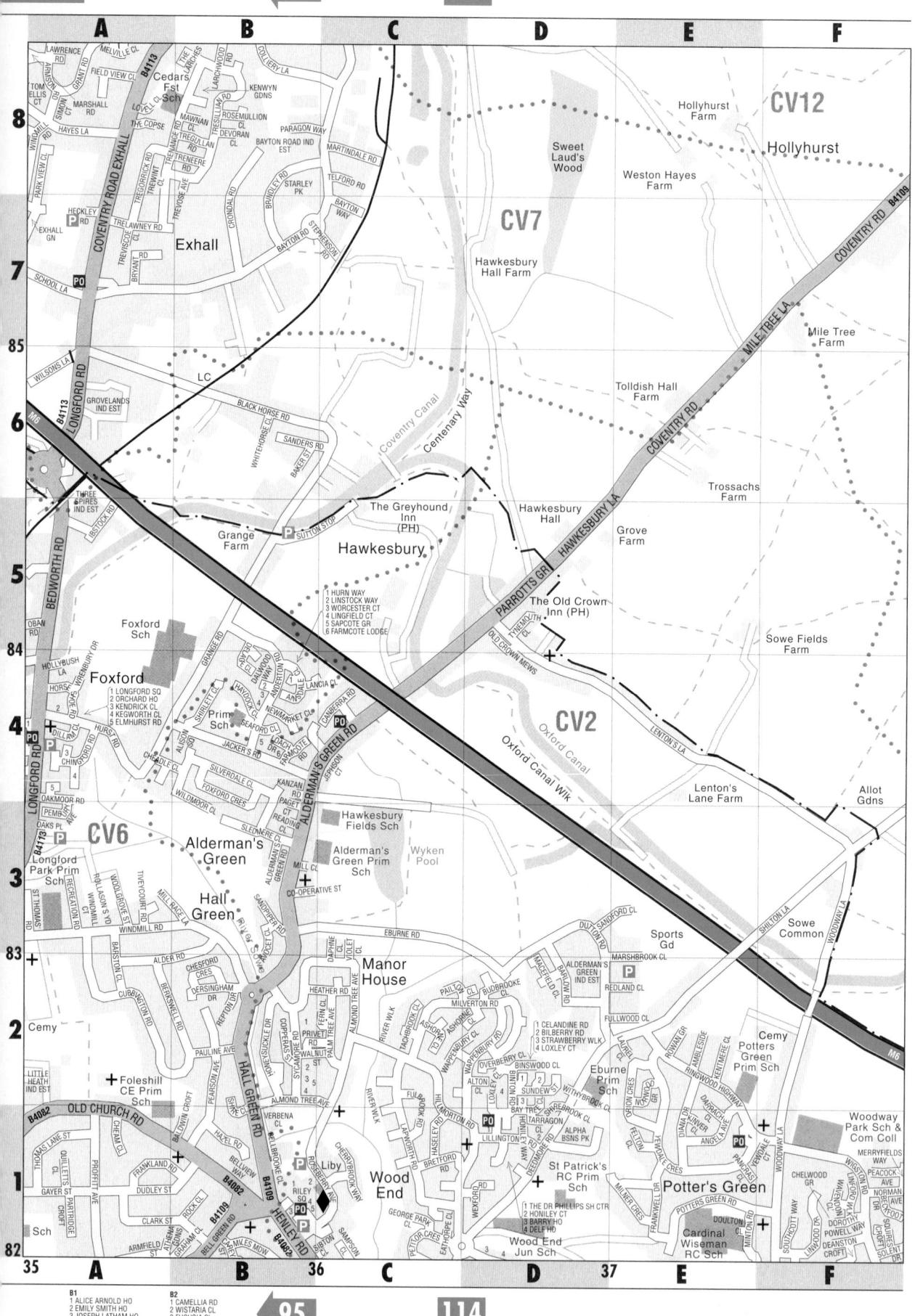

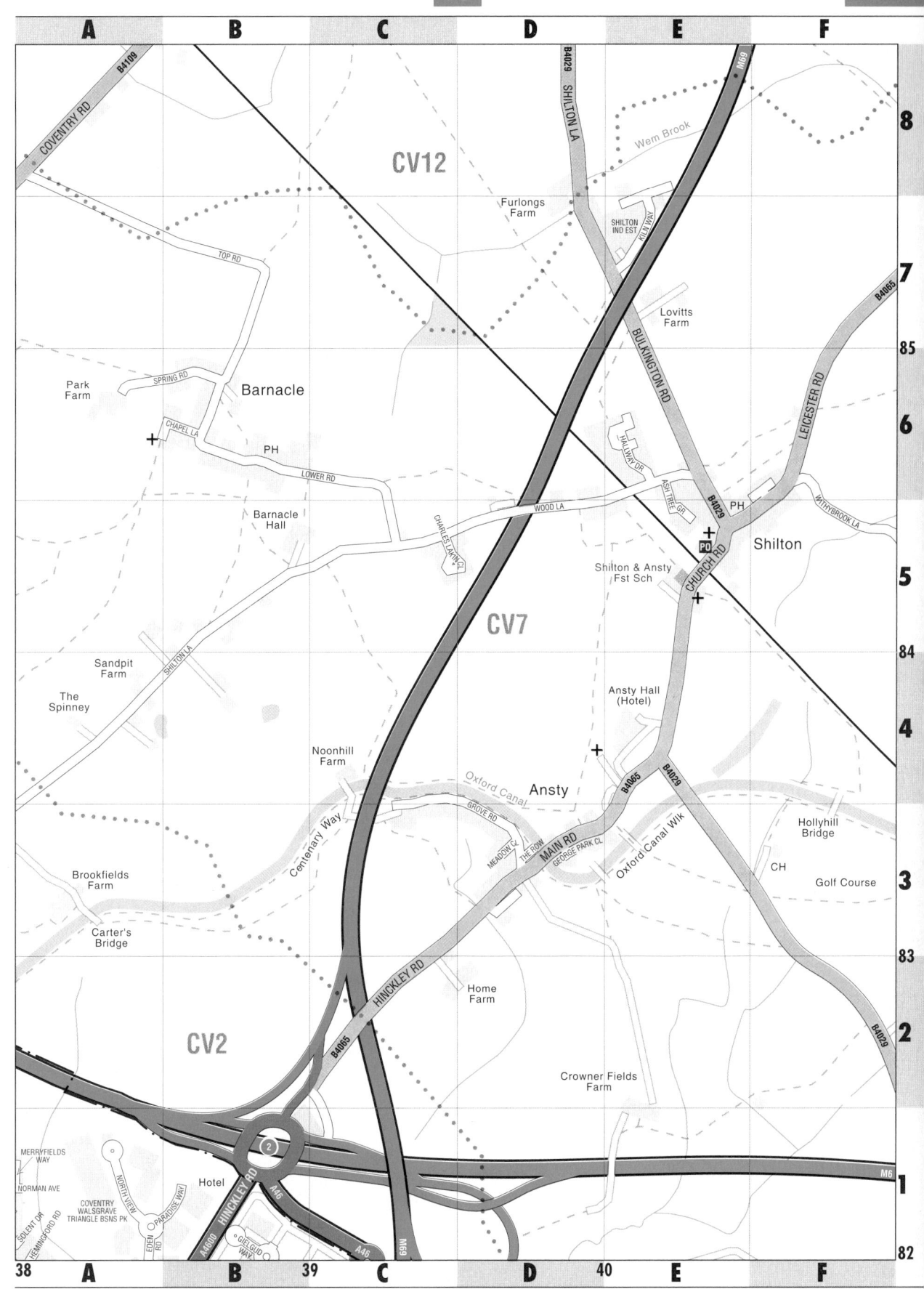

80

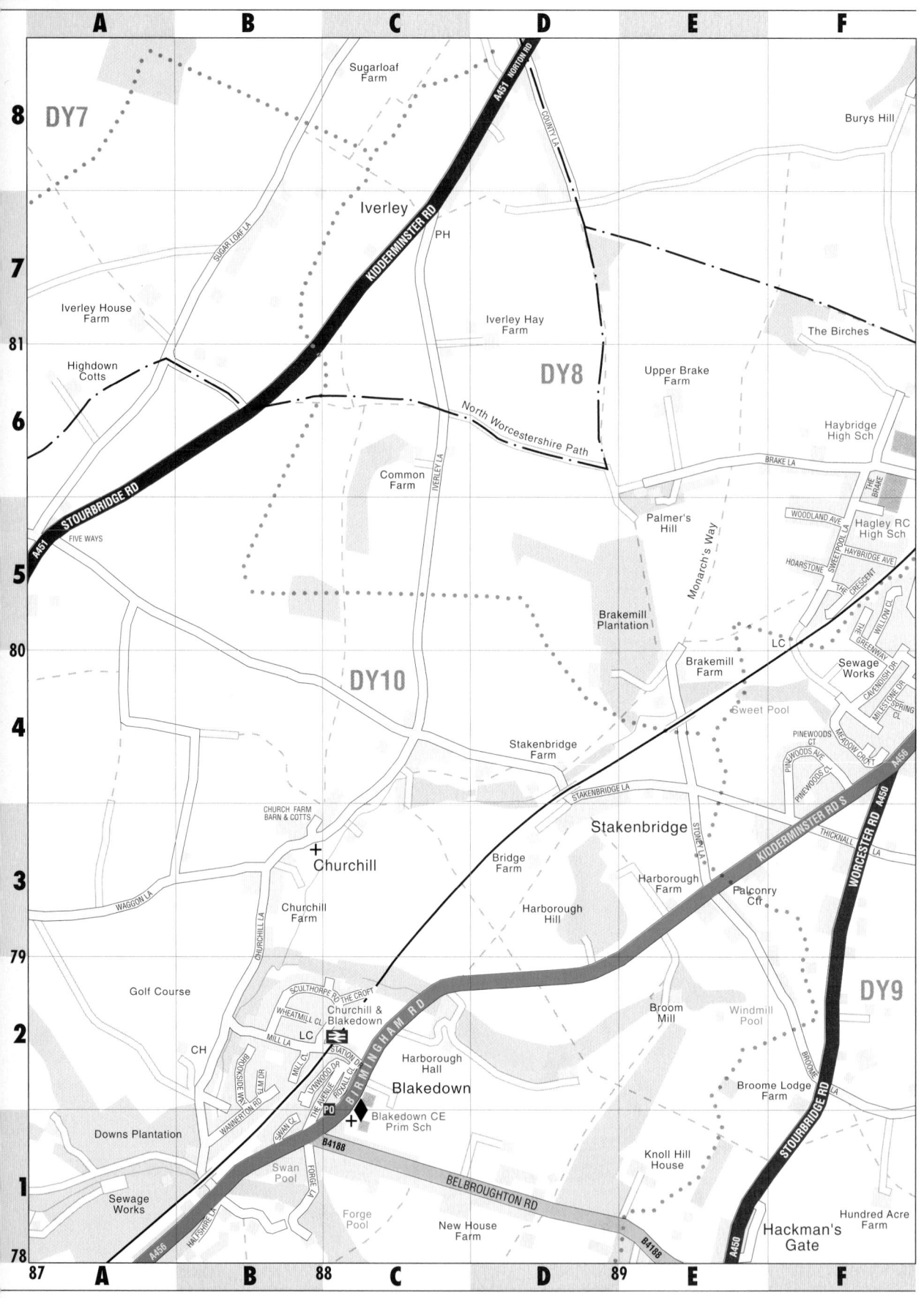

118

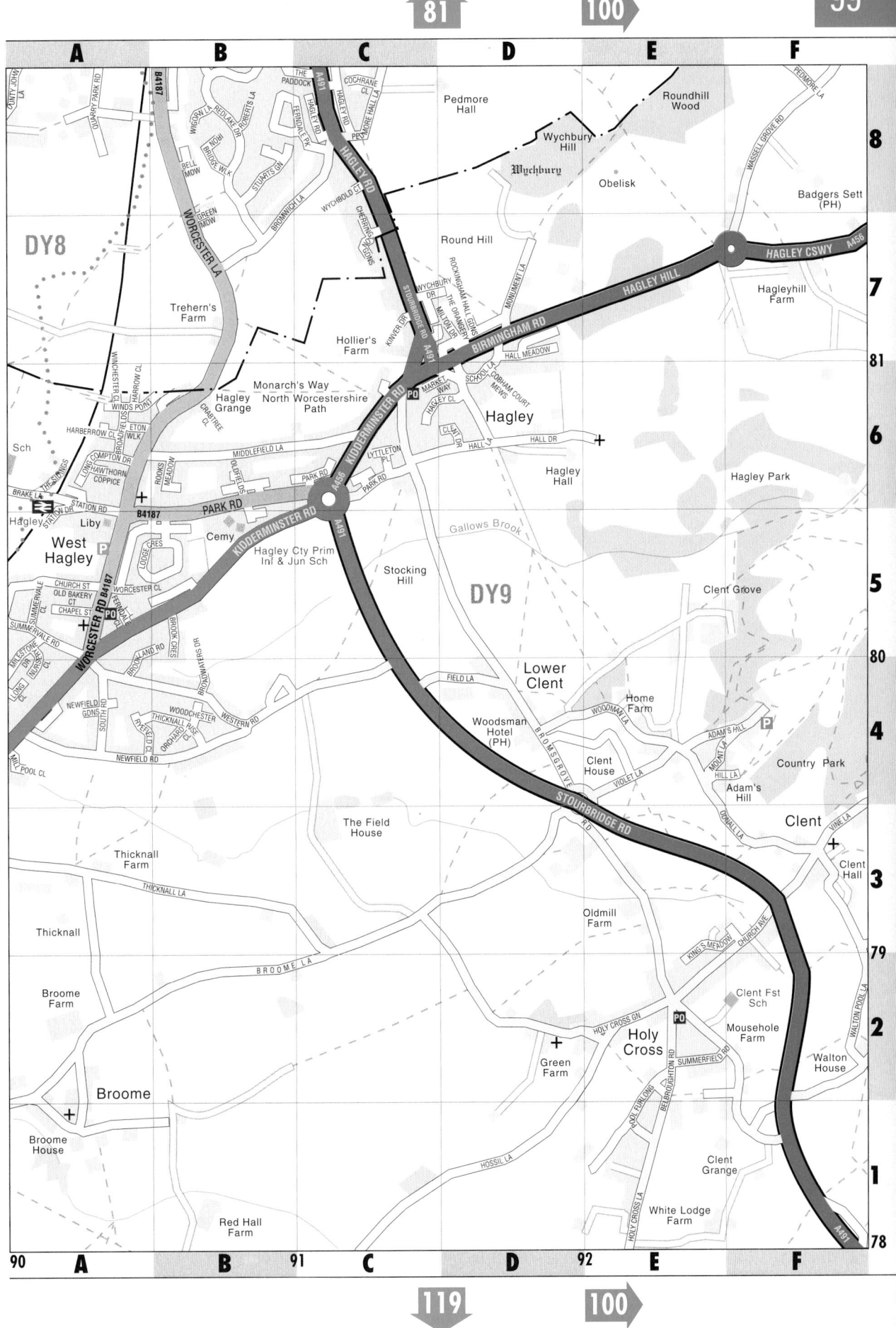

A   B   C   D   E   F

CH
Golf Course

HAGLEY RD A456

HAGLEY CSWY

A456

B63

Uffmoor Farm

LUTLEY LA

OAKLEY PARK RD

CAUSEY FARM RD

ABBOT RD

KEMELSTOWE CRES

Hagley Wood

Bogs Wood

UFFMOOR LA

HAGLEY WOOD LA

Spring Farm

Uffmoor Wood

P

Nimmings Plantation

Chapel Farm

Nimmings Visitor Ctr

Penorchard Farm

CHAPEL LA

Short Wood

North Worcestershire Path

Clent Hills

St Kenelm's Farm

Fox Farm

Four Oaks House

The Four Stones

High Harcourt Farm

P

ST KENELM'S RD

IVY ST

Clent Hills Country Park

B62

Deep Wood

Dark Pool

ST KENELM'S PASS

HOLT LA

Holt Farm

THE ALDERS

THE HEDGEROWS

WAVERLEY CRES

DARK LA

PH

VINE LA

CLATTERBACH LA

Walton Hill

SPRING LA

Oatlands

FIELDHOUSE LA

Fieldhouse Farm

Whitehall Farm

Nag Hill

Walton Hill Farm

RUMBOW LA

Caravan Site

DY9

WALTON RISE

HIGHFIELD LA

Rumbow Cottages

SHUT MILL LA

Daleswood Farm

Walton Pool

Walton Farm

Dales Wood

Squats Wood

Calcot Hill

WINNWOOD HEATH RD

North Worcestershire Path

MOOR HALL DR

Calcothill Farm

Great Farley Wood

ROMSLEY HILL GRANGE

FARLEY LA

Moor Hall

Farley Farm

8 7 81 6 5 80 4 3 79 2 1 78

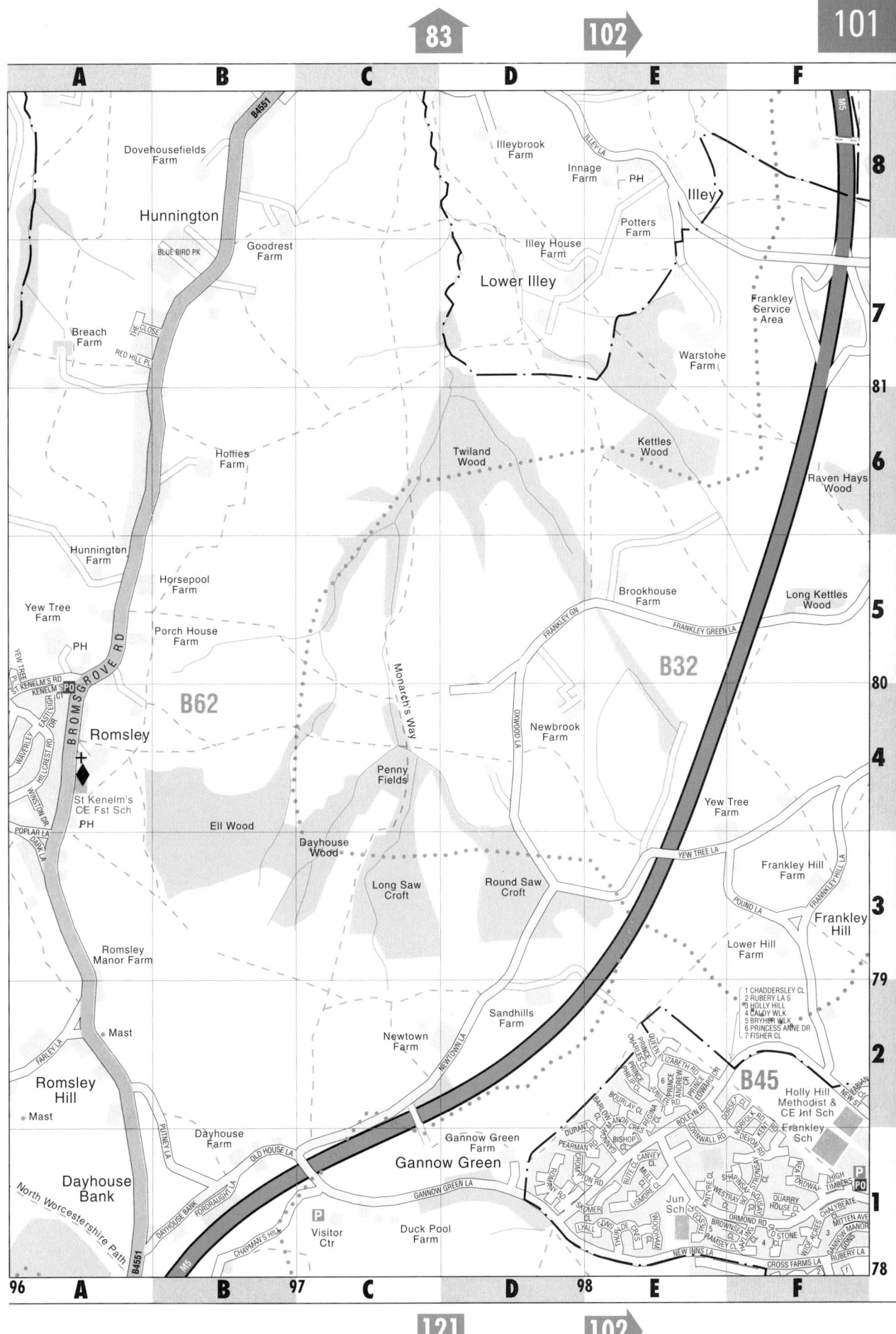

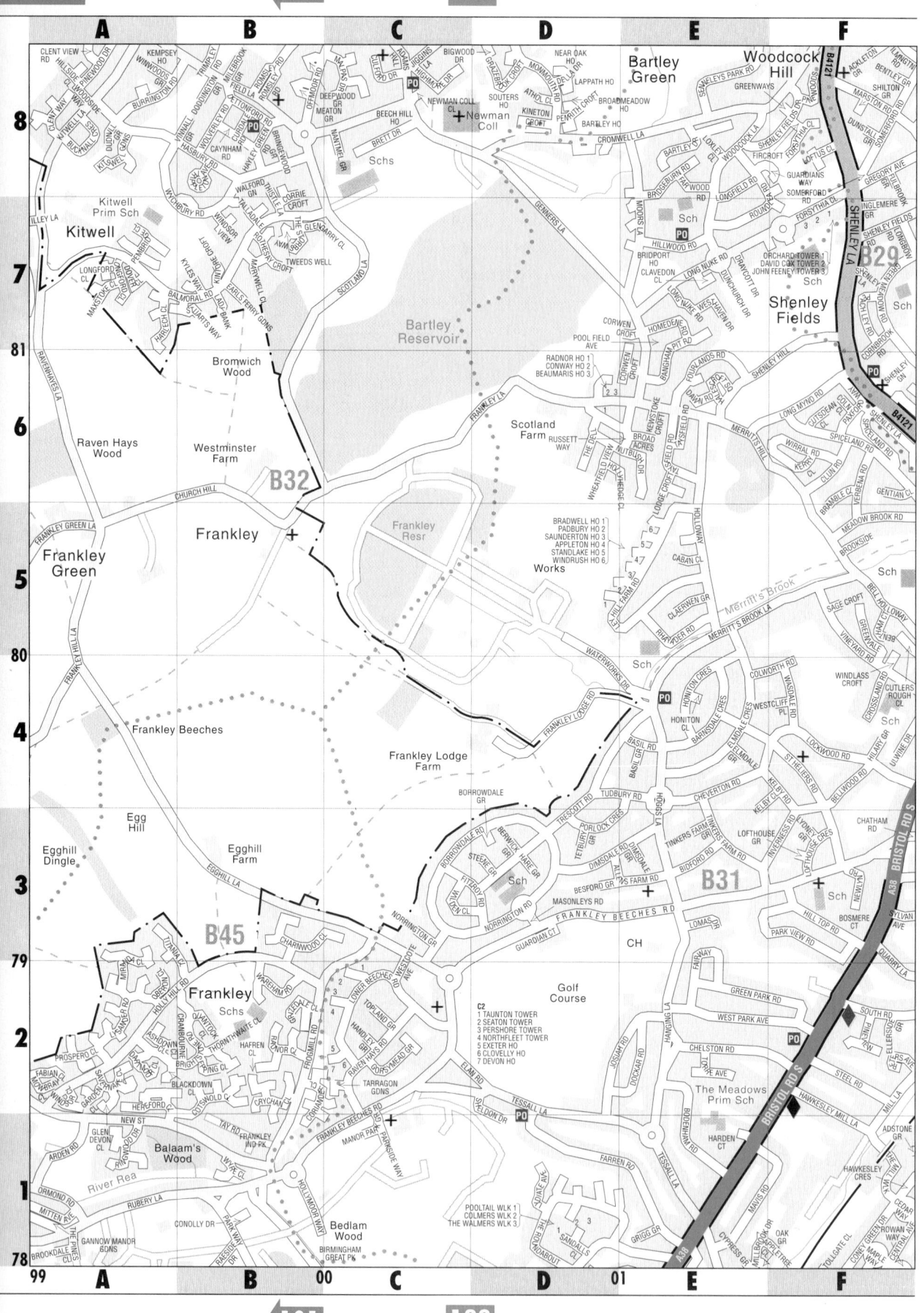

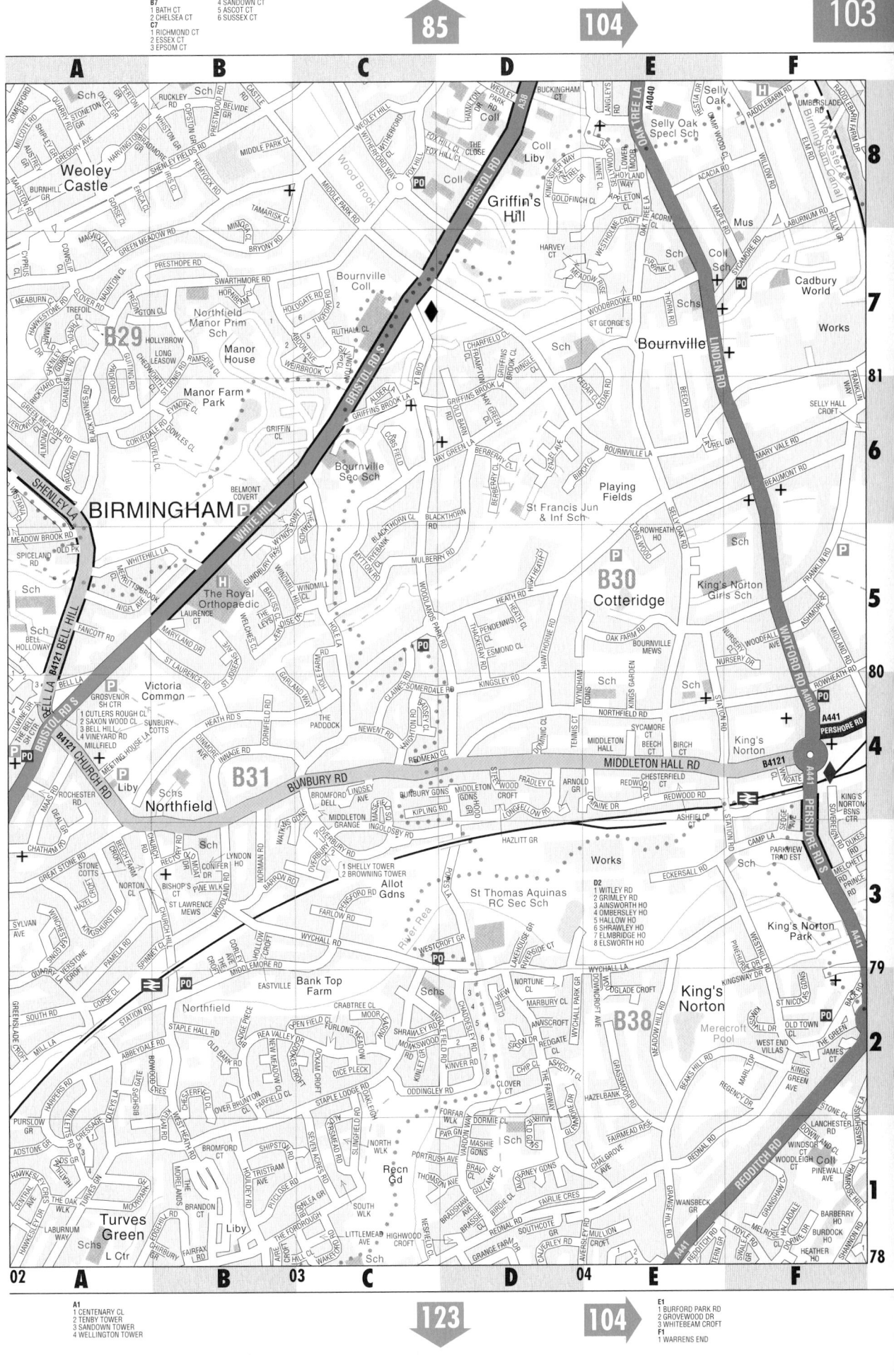

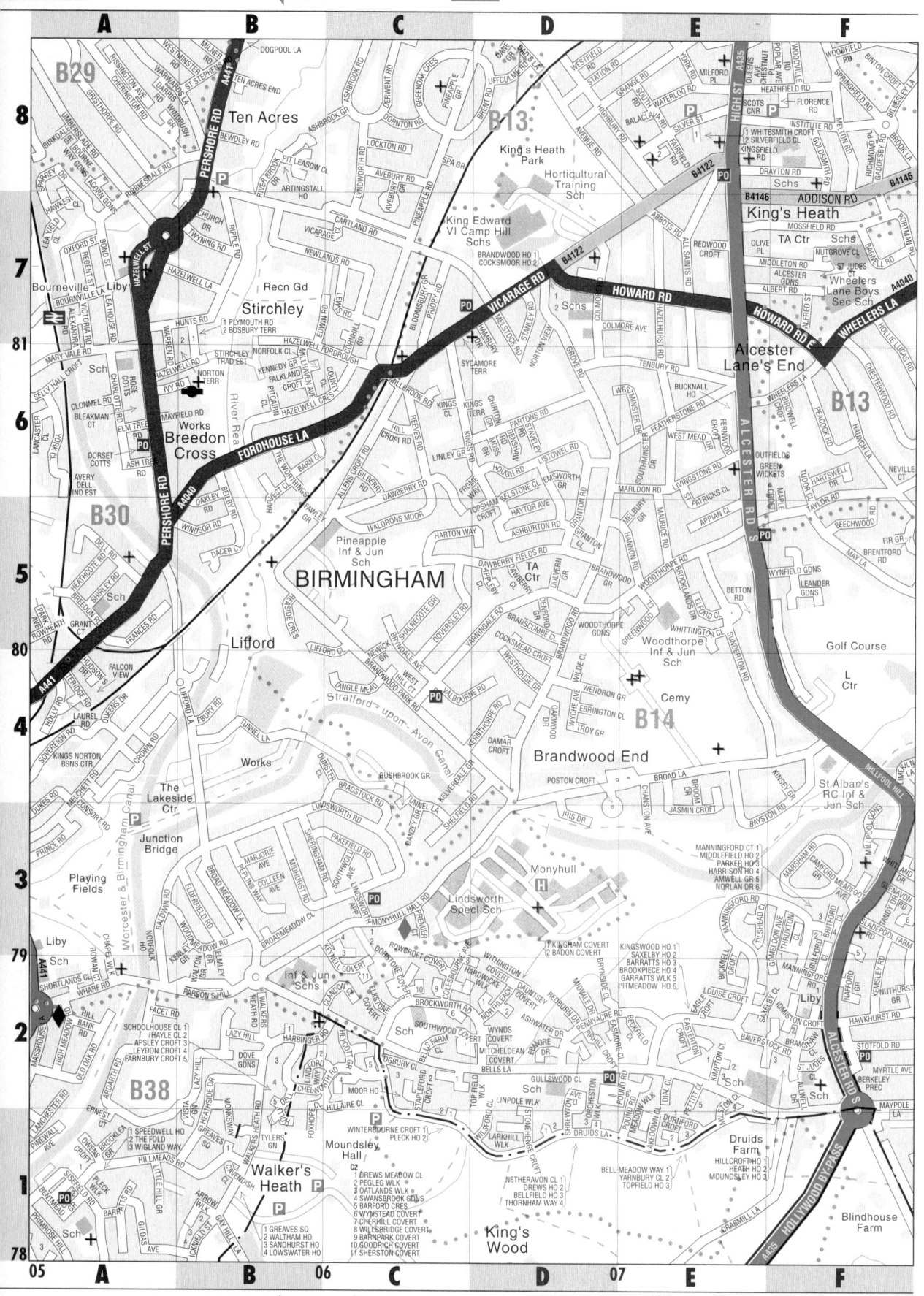

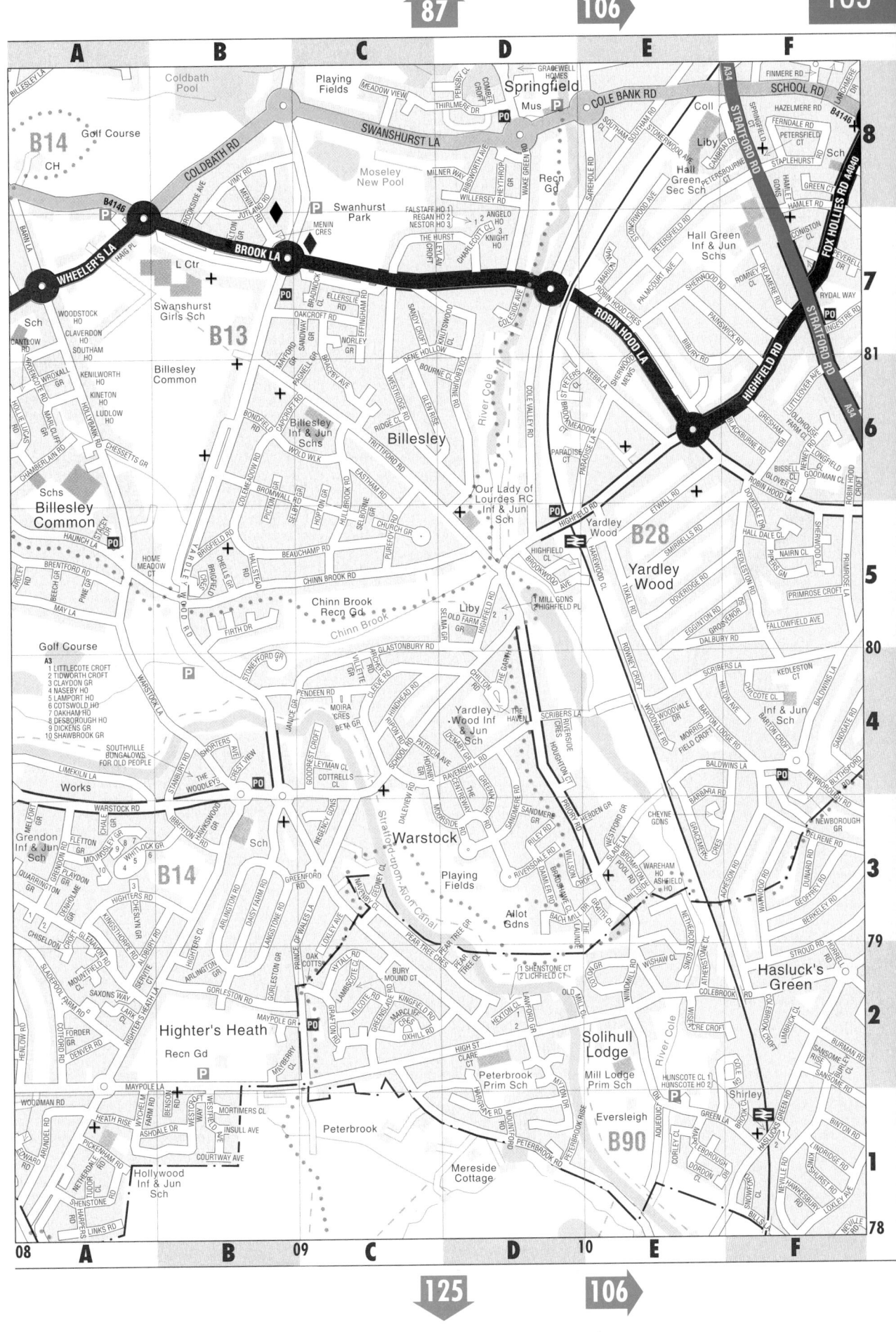

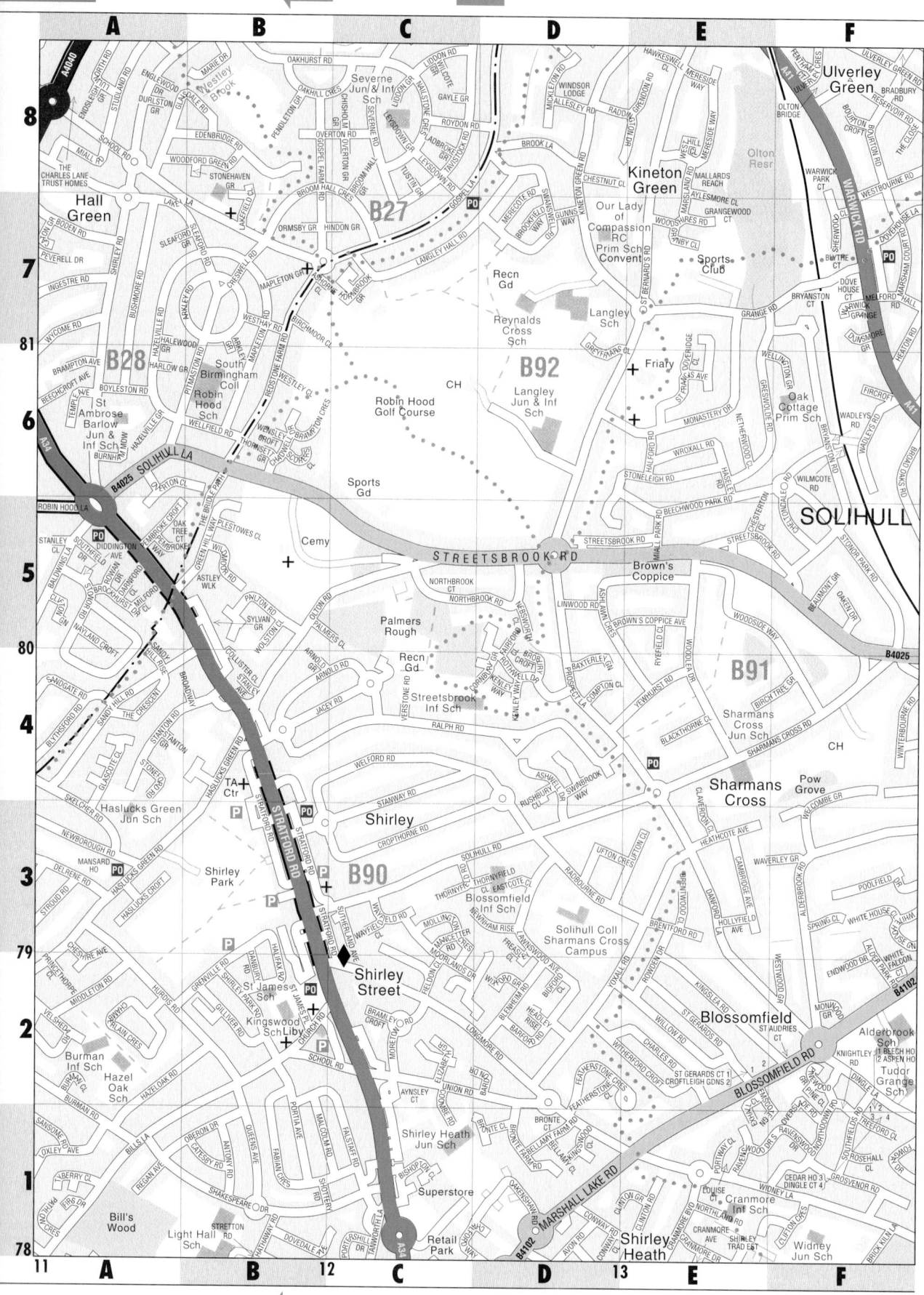

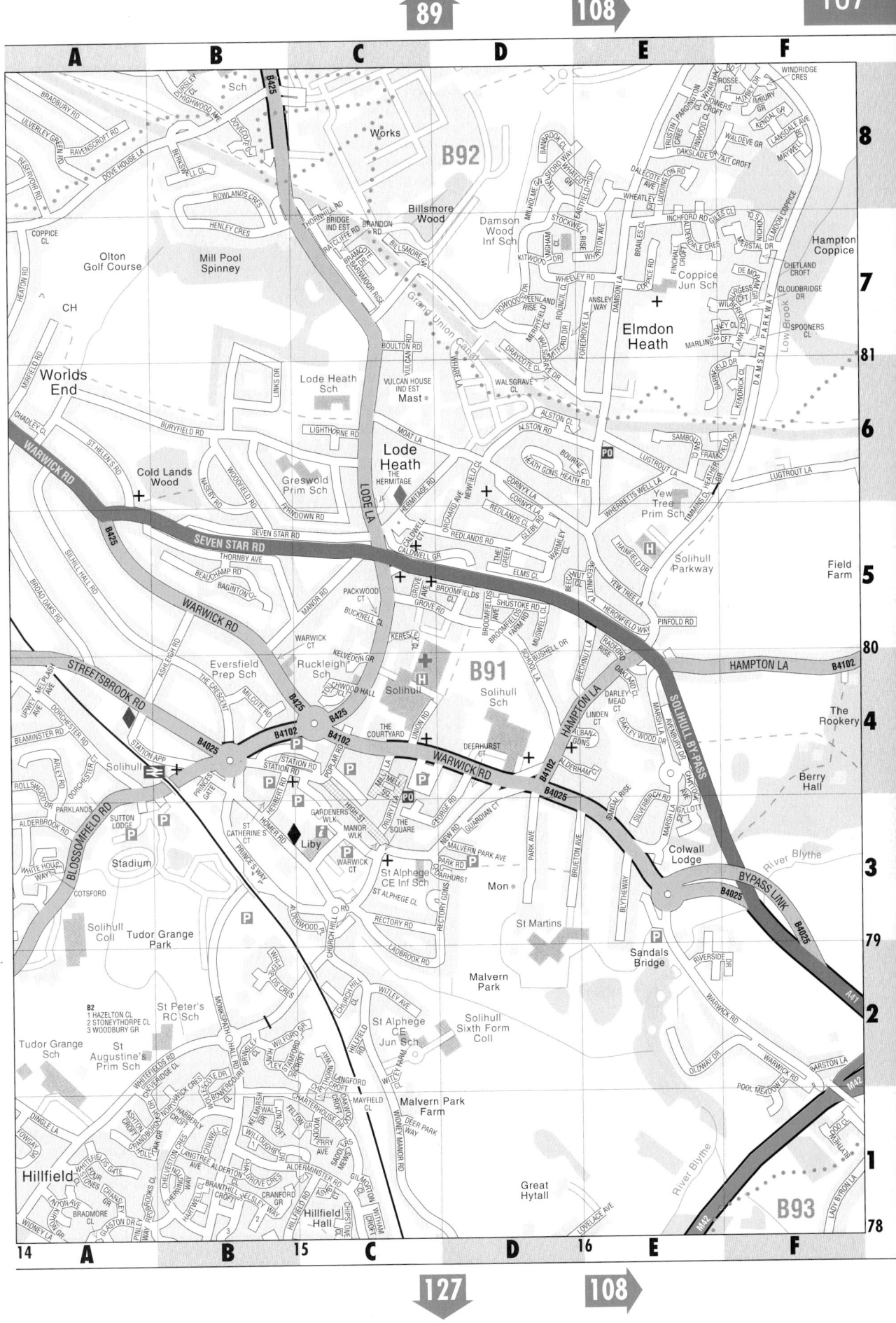

107
90

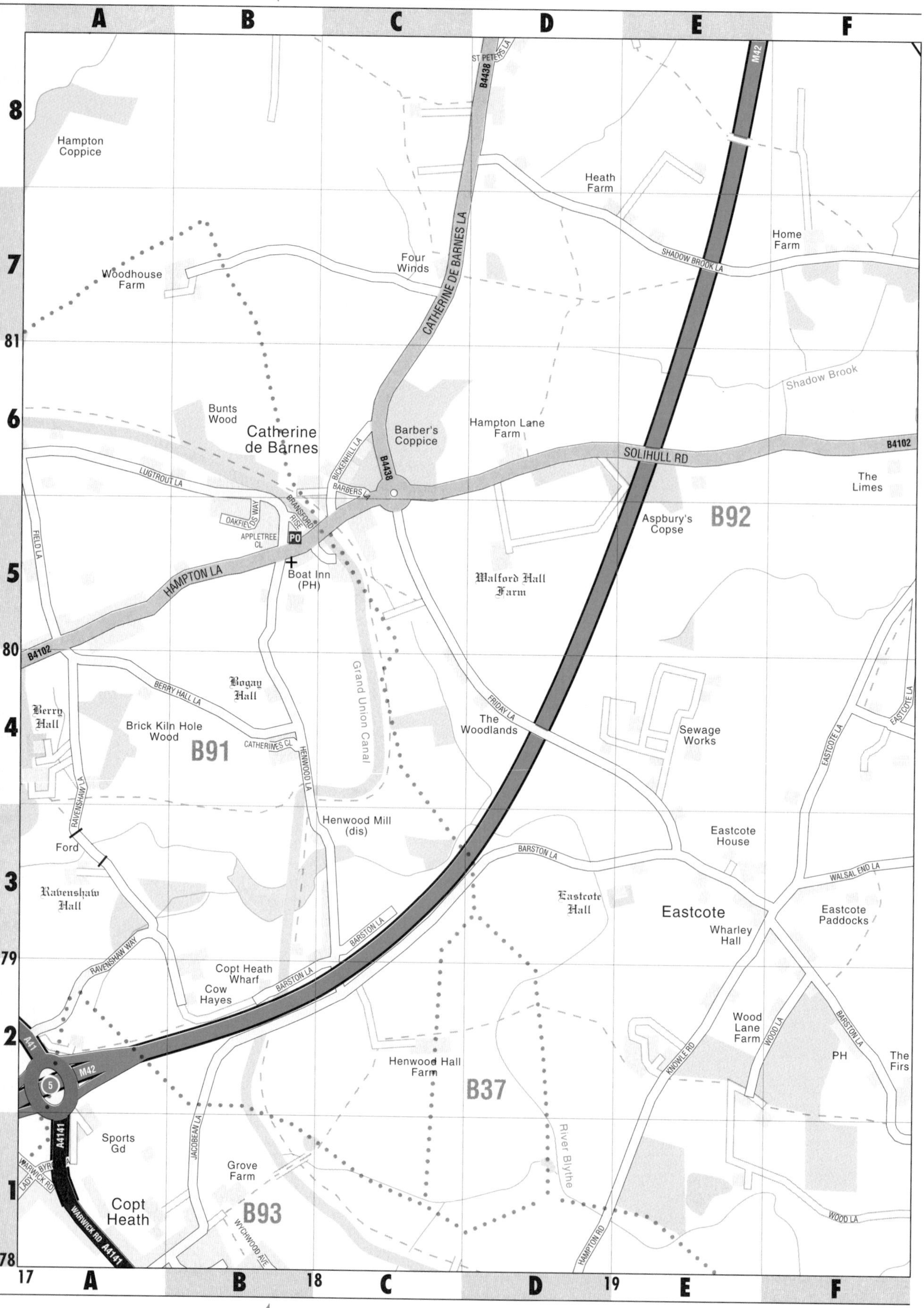

A B C D E F

8

Hampton Coppice

Heath Farm

Home Farm

7

Woodhouse Farm

Four Winds

SHADOW BROOK LA

81

Shadow Brook

6

Bunts Wood

Catherine de Barnes

Barber's Coppice

Hampton Lane Farm

SOLIHULL RD

B4102

The Limes

B4438

CATHERINE DE BARNES LA

BICKENHILL LA

BARBERS

LUGTROUT LA

OAKFIELD WAY

BRANSFORD RISE

APPLETREE CL

PO

Boat Inn (PH)

Aspbury's Copse

B92

5

HAMPTON LA

FIELD LA

Walford Hall Farm

80

B4102

Berry Hall LA

Bogay Hall

Grand Union Canal

FRIDAY LA

4

Berry Hall

Brick Kiln Hole Wood

B91

CATHERINES CL

HENWOOD LA

The Woodlands

Sewage Works

EASTCOTE LA

EASTCOTE LA

RAVENSHAW LA

Henwood Mill (dis)

Eastcote House

WALSAL END LA

3

Ford

Ravenshaw Hall

BARSTON LA

Eastcote Hall

Eastcote

Wharley Hall

Eastcote Paddocks

79

RAVENSHAW WAY

Copt Heath Wharf

BARSTON LA

BARSTON LA

Cow Hayes

KNOWLE RD

Wood Lane Farm

WOOD LA

BARSTON LA

PH

The Firs

2

A41

M42

5

JACOBEAN LA

Henwood Hall Farm

B37

River Blythe

WARWICK RD

A4141

LADY LA

A4141

Sports Gd

Grove Farm

WYCHWOOD AVE

B93

HAMPTON RD

WOOD LA

1

Copt Heath

78

107
128

ST PETERS LA

M42

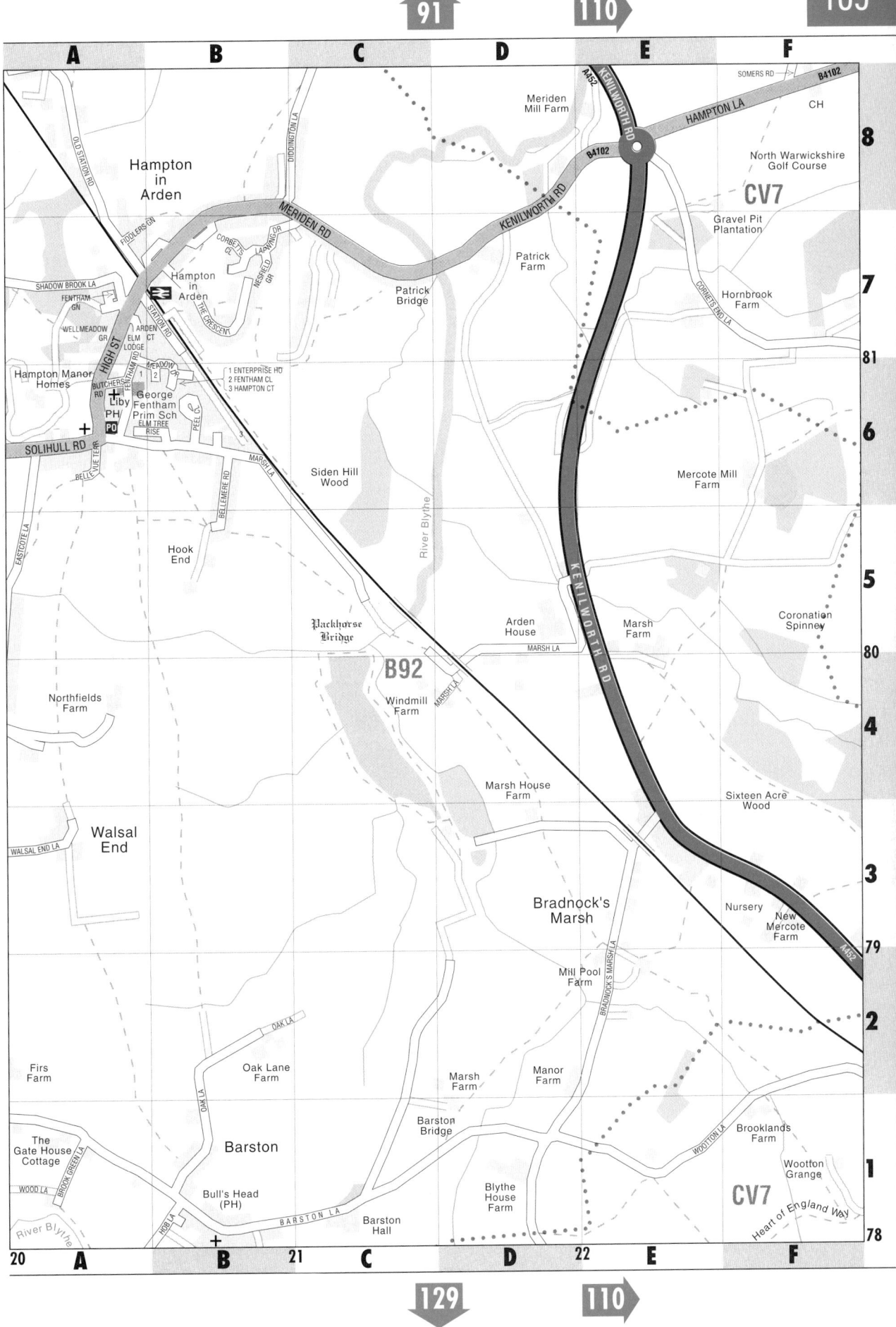

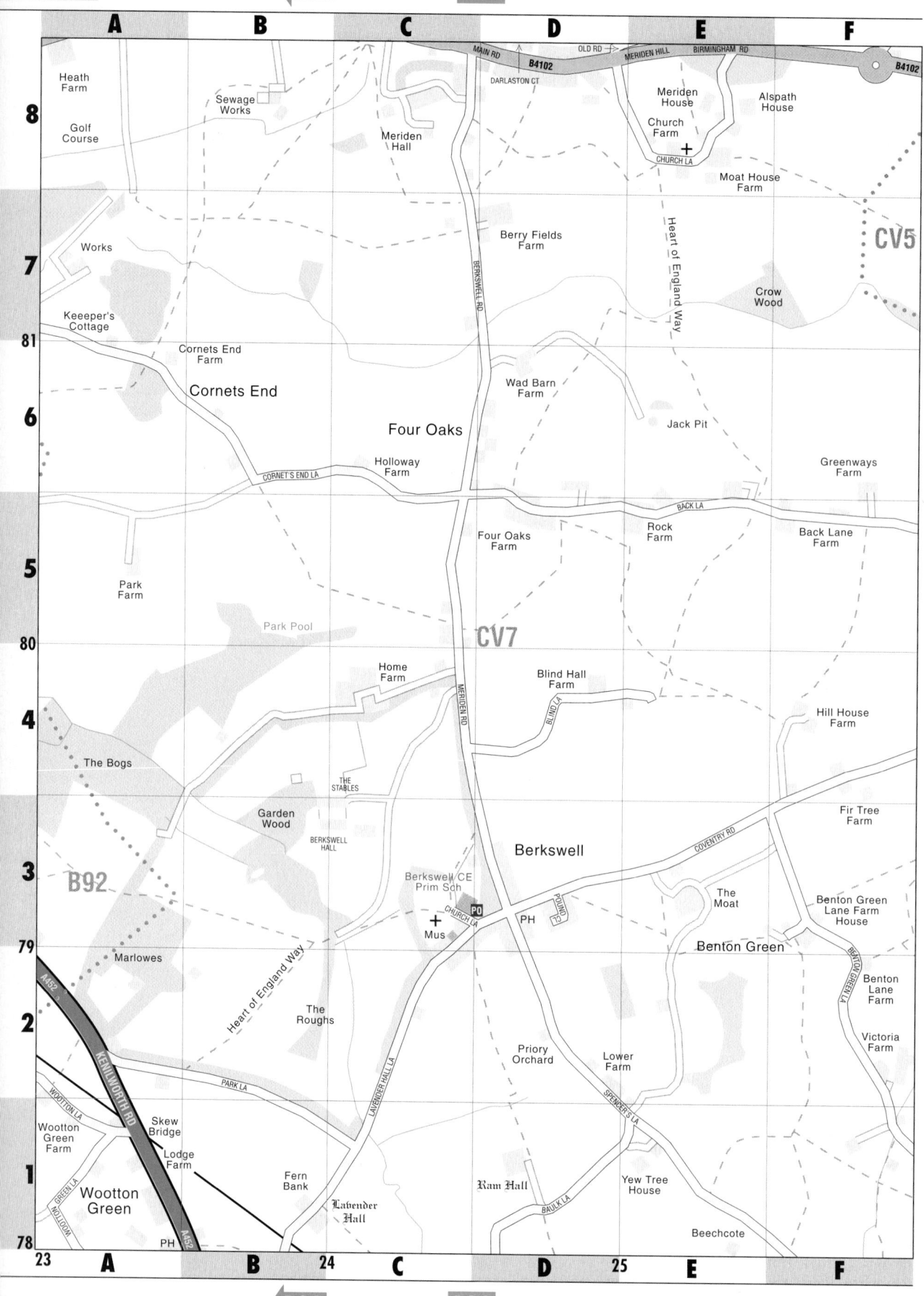

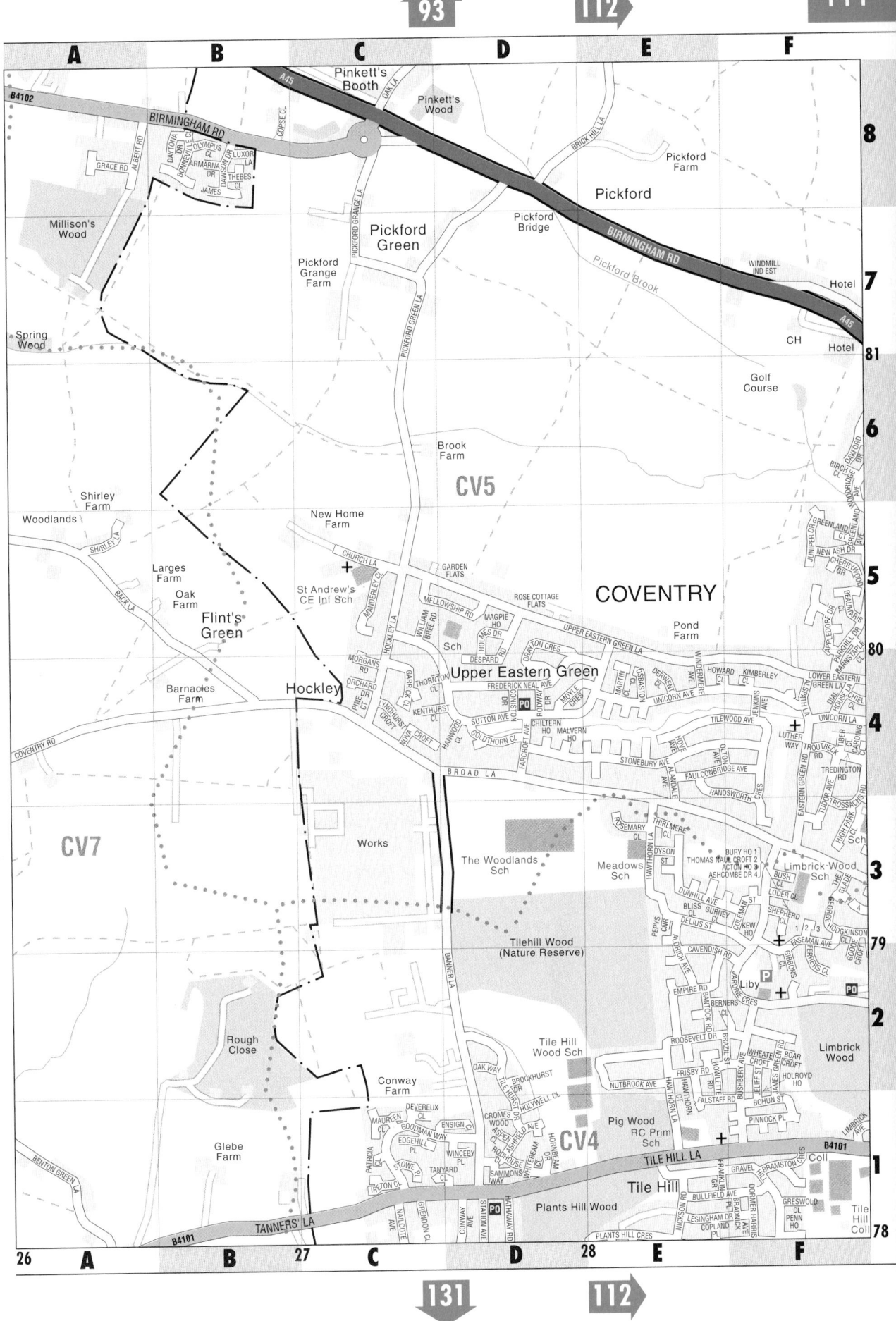

A **B** **C** **D** **E** **F**

B4102

Pinkett's Booth

A45

Pinkett's Wood

BIRMINGHAM RD

OAK LA

COPSE CL

Pickford Wood

BRICK HILL LA

8

Pickford Farm

Millison's Wood

Pickford Green

GRACE RD

ALBERT RD

DAYTONA DR

BONNEVILLE CL

OLYMPUS CL

ARMARNA DR

DAWSON DR

THEBES CL

LUXOR LA

JAMES

PICKFORD GRANGE LA

Pickford

Pickford Bridge

Pickford

BIRMINGHAM RD

Pickford Farm

WINDMILL IND EST

Hotel

7

Spring Wood

Pickford Grange Farm

Pickford Brook

CH

Hotel

81

PICKFORD GREEN LA

Golf Course

6

Shirley Farm

Woodlands

SHIRLEY LA

Brook Farm

CV5

BIRCH CL

OAKFORD CL

GREENLANDS

NEW ASH DR

CHERRYFIELD GR

5

Larges Farm

Oak Farm

BACK LA

Flint's Green

New Home Farm

CHURCH LA

MANDERLEY CL

St Andrew's CE Inf Sch

HOCKLEY LA

GARDEN FLATS

MELLOWSHIP RD

WILLIAM BREE RD

ROSE COTTAGE FLATS

Sch

MAGPIE

COVENTRY

Pond Farm

APPLEDORE DR

JUNIPER DR

BARKHILL DR

BEAUMARIS

LOWER EASTERN GREEN LA

80

Barnacles Farm

Hockley

MORGANS RD

ORCHARD DR

PINE CL

GARRICK CL

LYNDHURST CROFT

KENTHURST CL

THORNTON CL

DESPARD

JAMES HO

DAYTON CRES

UPPER EASTERN GREEN LA

FREDERICK NEAL AVE

RODWAY DR

MOYLE CRES

DERWENT AVE

WINDERMERE

MARTIN

ASBASTON

HOWARD

UNICORN AVE

KIMBERLEY

LOWER EASTERN GREEN LA

HOUSE CL

CHIEL

HESLOP CL

Upper Eastern Green

PO

UNICORN LA

4

COVENTRY RD

HAWWOOD

GOLDTHORN CL

SUTTON AVE

FANCROFT AVE

CHILTERN HO

MALVERN HO

STONEBURY AVE

HYDE RD

ARNDALE

OLD PARK AVE

TILEWOOD AVE

SUNKEL AVE

FAULCONBRIDGE AVE

HANDSWORTH CRES

EASTERN GREEN RD

TUDOR AVE

TROUSBECK RD

TIBER WAY

CROWHILL

HIGH PARK CL

LUTHER WAY

TROSSACKS RD

TREDINGTON RD

CV7

BROAD LA

Works

The Woodlands Sch

ROSEMARY CL

THIRLMERE CL

HAWTHORN LA

DYSON ST

Meadows Sch

DUNHILL AVE

BLISS CL

GURNEY CL

PEPYS CNR

DELIUS ST

KEW HO

BURY HO 1

THOMAS NAUL CROFT 2

ACTON HO 3

ASHCOMBE DR 4

LODER CL

SHEPHERD

BUSH CL

1 2 3

THE GLADE

GEORGE HODGKINSON

GOODE

ILEX CL

Limbrick Wood Sch

3

BANNER LA

Tilehill Wood (Nature Reserve)

ALTHORPE DR

CAVENDISH RD

EMPIRE RD

BANTOCK RD

JARDINE CRES

BERNERS

FERRERS CL

EASEMAN AVE

GIBBONS

Liby

P

PO

79

Rough Close

ROOSEVELT DR

BRAZIL ST

FRISBY RD

HOWLETT

Limbrick Wood

2

Conway Farm

OAK WAY

TILEHURST DR

BROCKHURST DR

HOLYWELL CL

CROMES WOOD

NUTBROOK AVE

Tile Hill Wood Sch

HAWTHORN LA

FALSTAFF RD

WHEATE CROFT

BOAR CROFT

ARLIDGE

JAMES GREEN RD

BOHUN ST

HOLROYD HO

LIMBRICK AVE

CV4

Pig Wood RC Prim Sch

PINNOCK PL

B4101

TILE HILL LA

Coll

1

Glebe Farm

DEVEREUX CL

MAUREEN CL

GOODMAN WAY

EDGEHILL PL

PATRICIA CL

TRETON CL

SOWE

TANYARD

ENSIGN

WINCEBY PL

ASHFIELD D AVE

ROW HOUSE

HORNBEAM

WHITEBEAM

SAMMONS WAY

ASPEN

CROMWELL

BENTON GREEN LA

Plants Hill Wood

Tile Hill

TILE HILL LA

FRANKLIN RD

DICKSON RD

BULLFIELD AVE

LESINGHAM DR

COPLAND

BRAMSTON GR

GRAVEL

BRAENDN CL

DORMER HARRIS AVE

HOLYOD HO

GRESWOLD CL

PENN HO

Tile Hill Coll

78

B4101

TANNERS' LA

NAILCOTE

GRENDON CL

STATION AVE

HATHAWAY RD

PO

Plants Hill Wood

PLANTS HILL CRES

A **B** **C** **D** **E** **F**

26 27 28

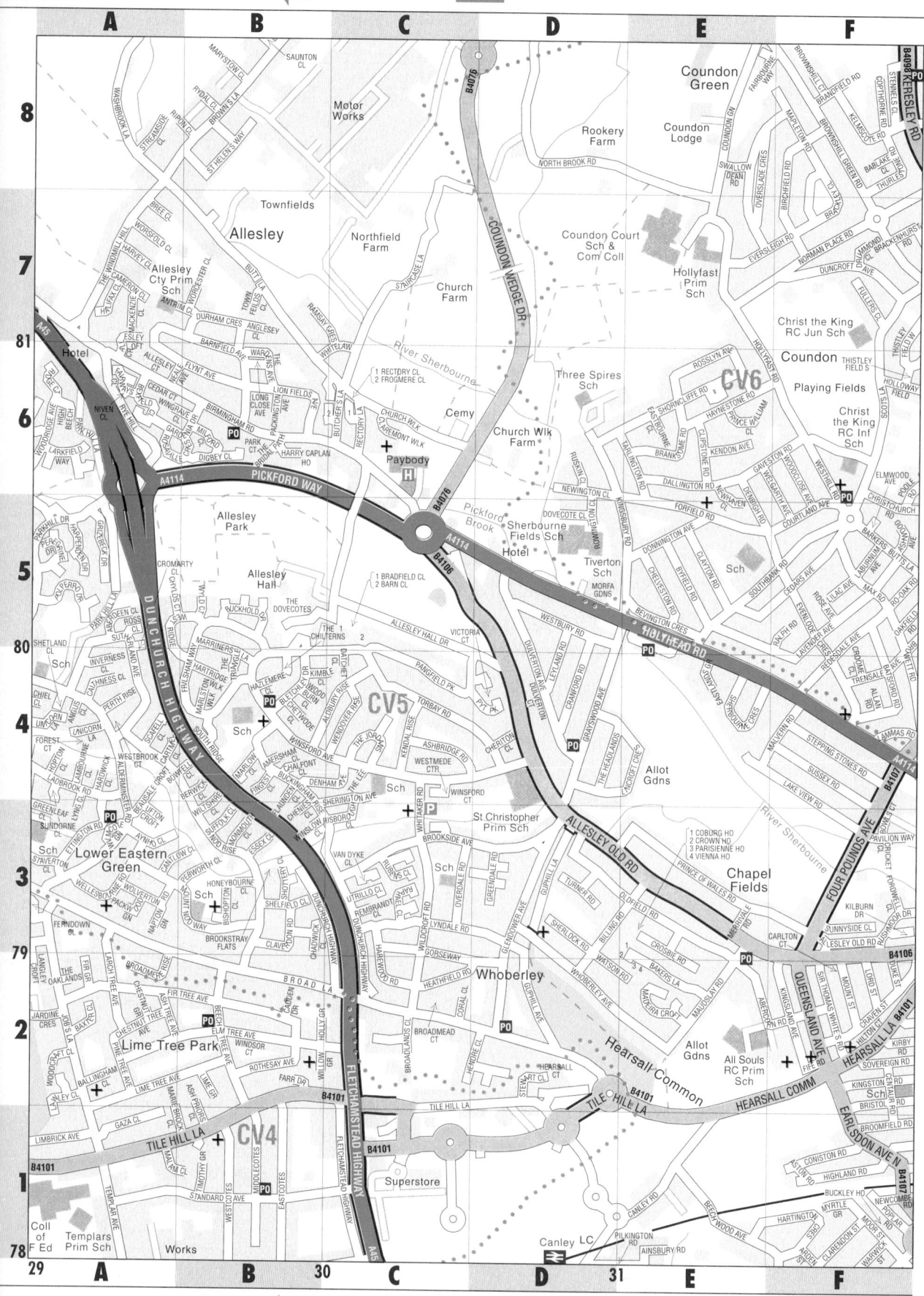

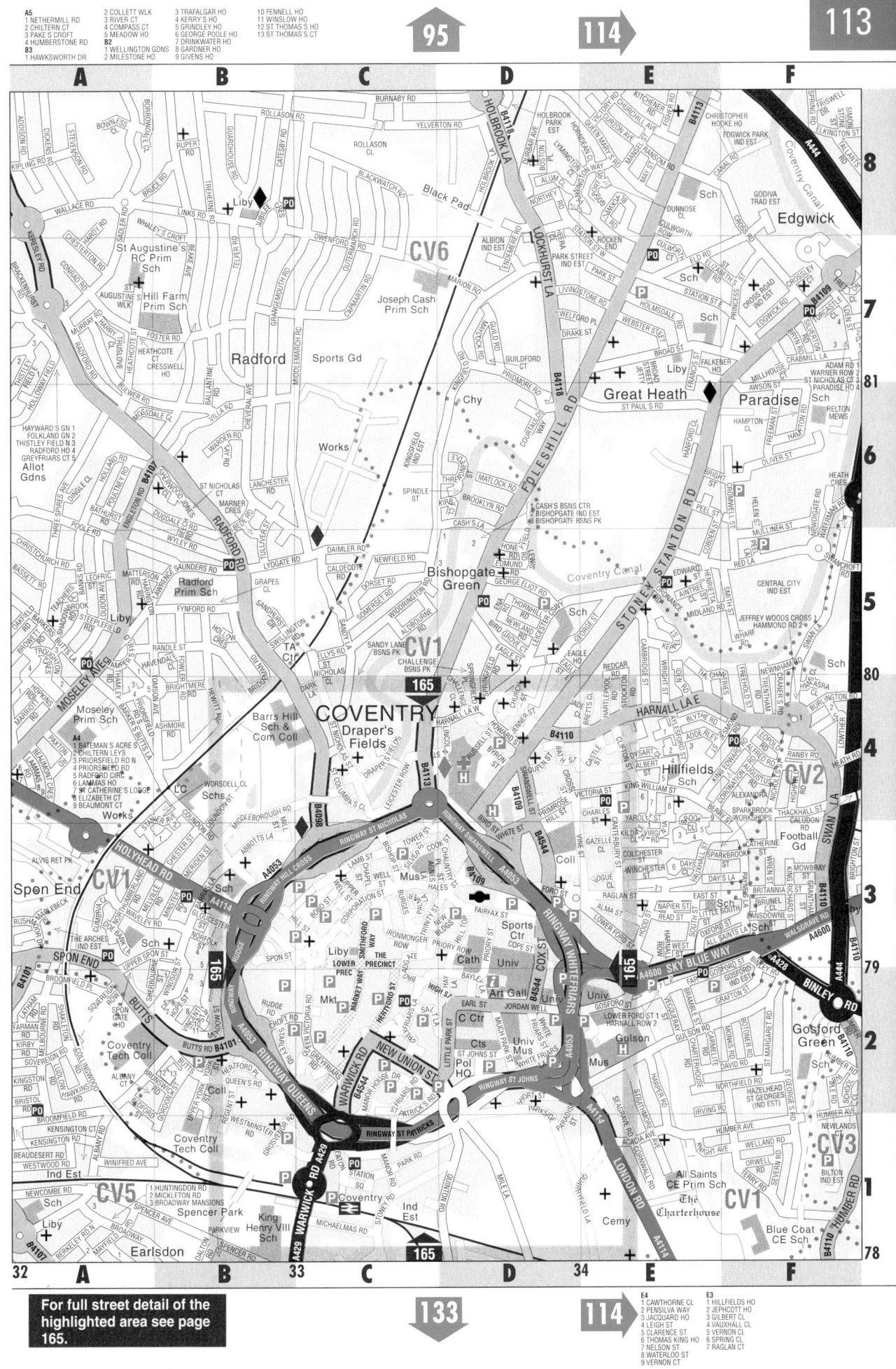

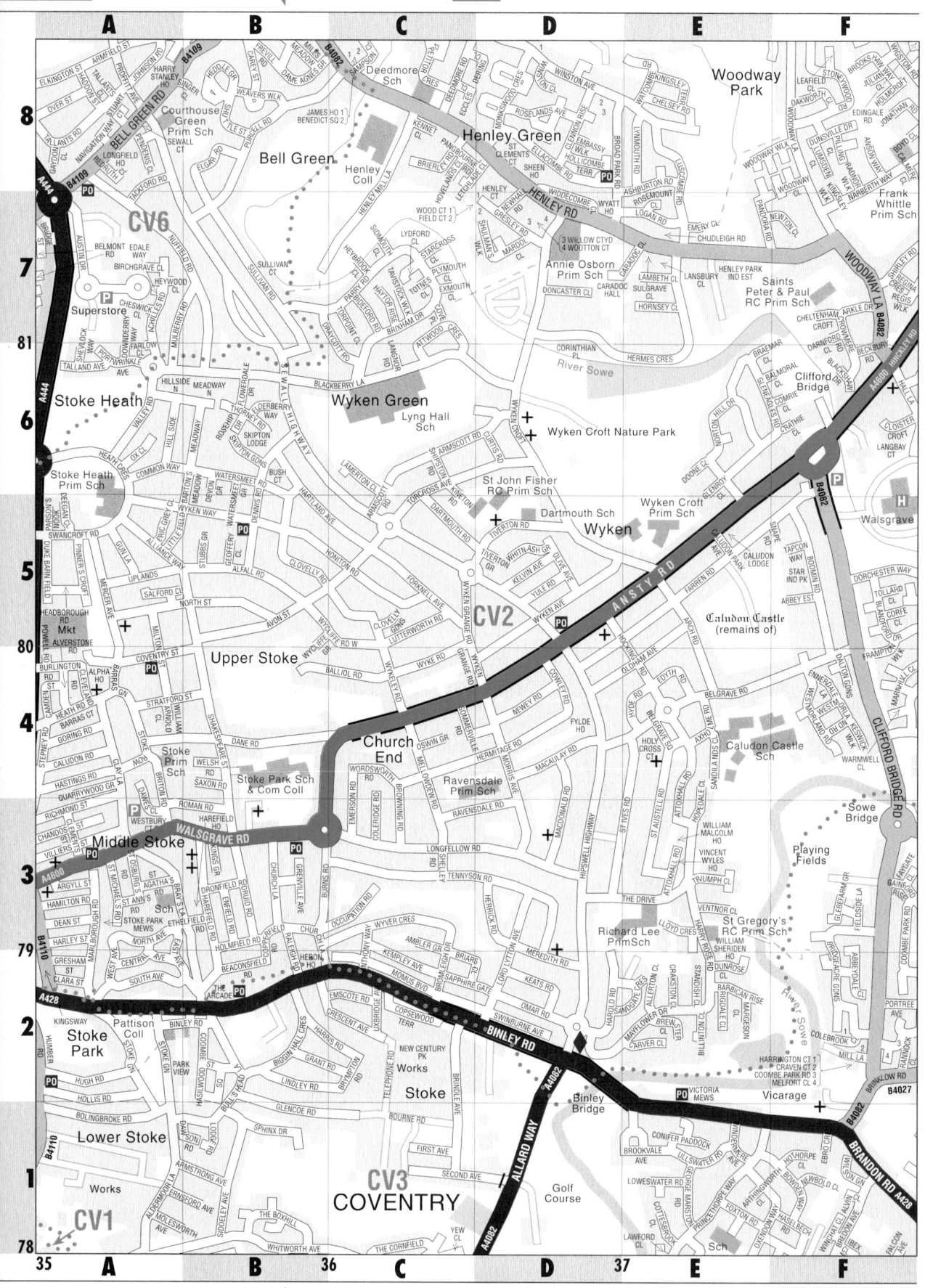

D8
1 LYNE HO
2 HARRY EDWARDS HO
3 FRISWELL HO

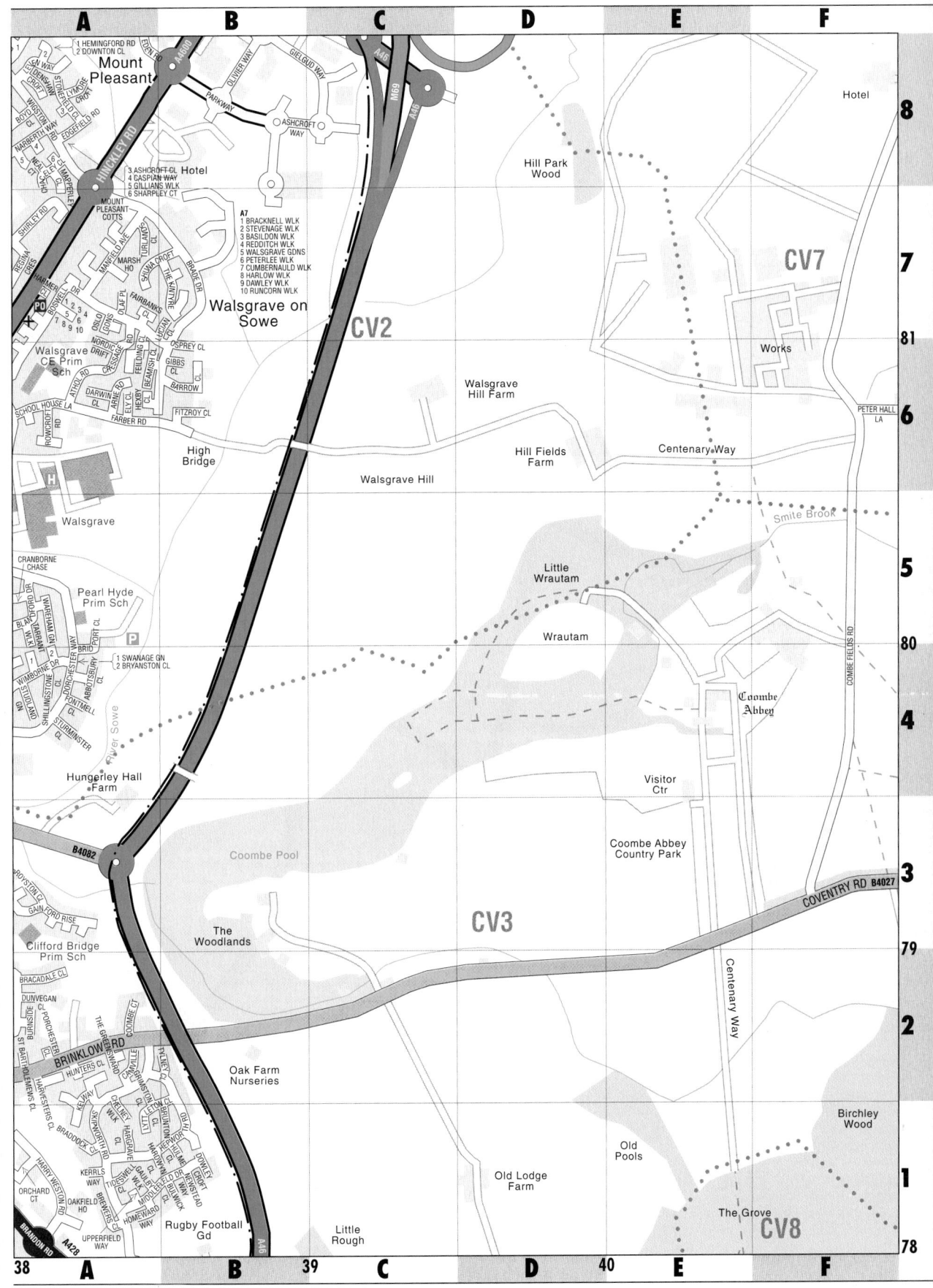

C6
1 HABBERLEY ST
2 BENNETT ST
3 ADAMS HO
4 WOODFIELD ST
5 ST JOHN'S ST
6 ST JOHN'S CL

D6
1 MILLERS CT
2 MILLFIELD GDNS
3 RUTH CHAMBERLAIN CT
4 PATERNOSTER ROW
5 PERRETT WLK
6 NEW BLDGS

7 IDEAL BLDGS
E5
1 BRIDGE ST
2 MARLBOROUGH ST
3 WORCESTER CROSS
E6
1 BLACK HORSE LA

2 CALLOWS LA
3 FREDA EDDY CT
4 KING CHARLES SQ
5 DERICK BURCHER'S MALL
6 SIR GEORGE'S MALL
7 THE SWAN CTR
8 SIR WALTER'S MALL

9 ROWLAND HILL CTR
10 SIR GEORGES CT
F6
1 TRINITY CT
2 VICTORIA CT
3 SHORT ST

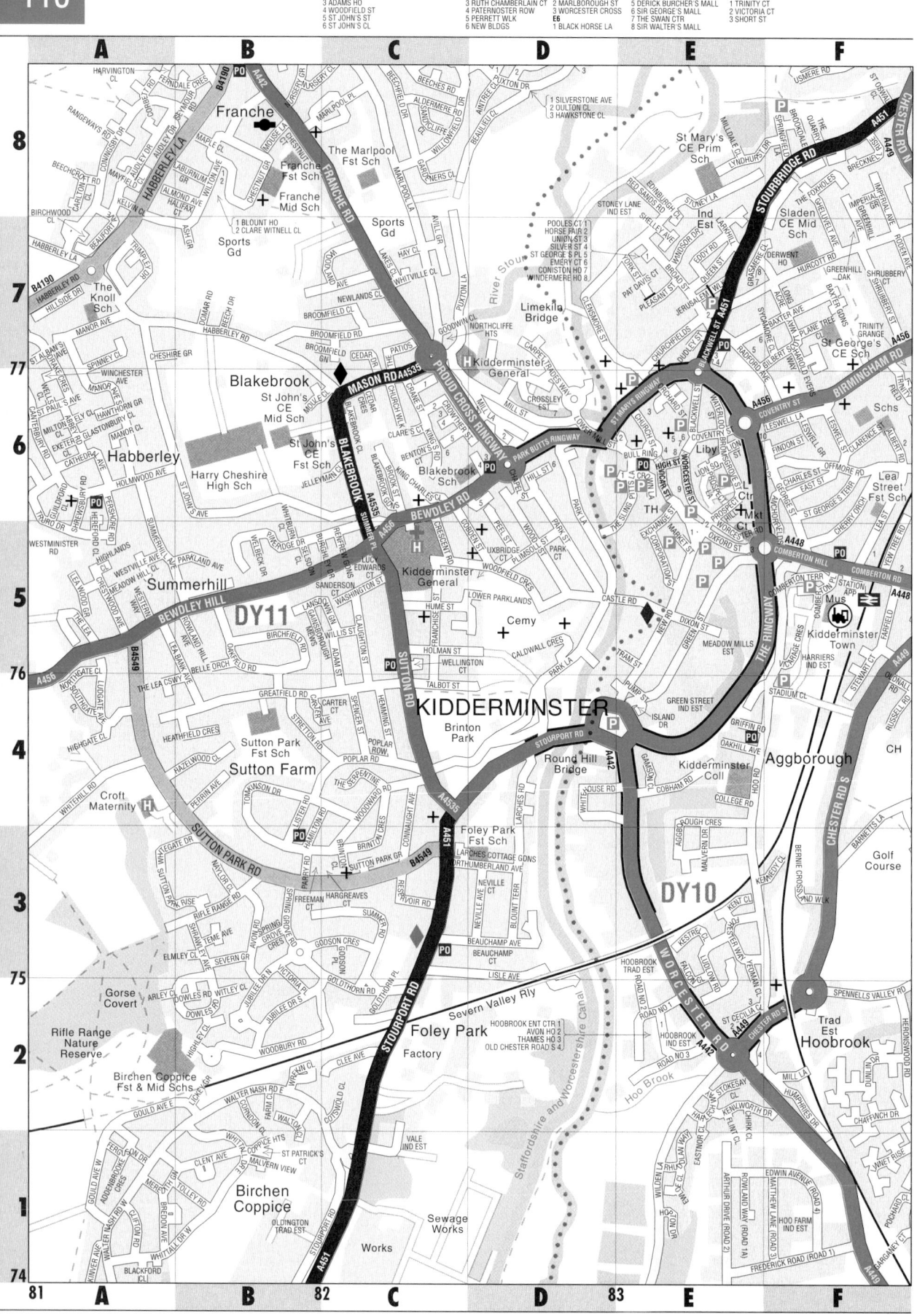

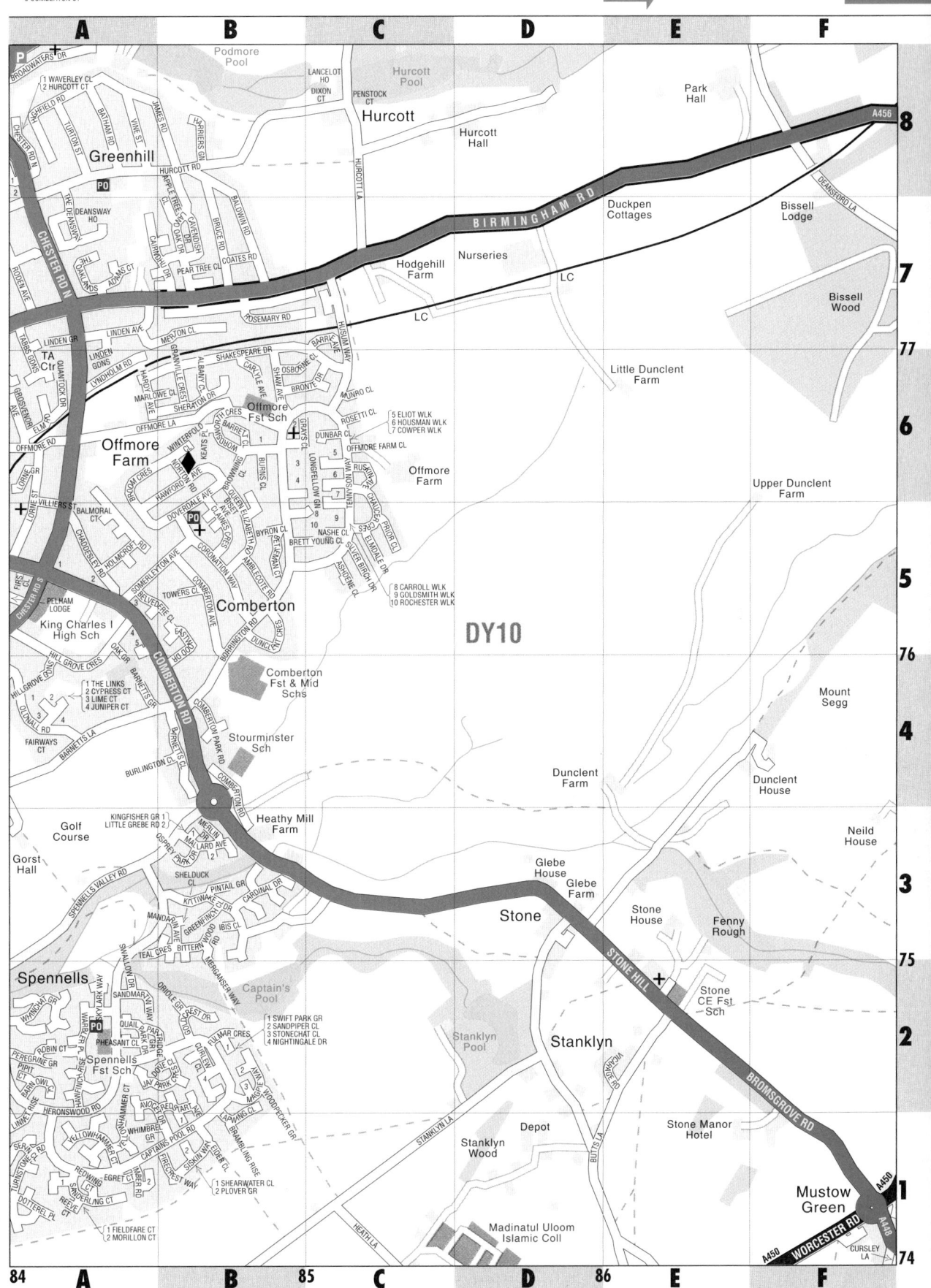

118

A5
1 THE HAWTHORNS
2 CHADDERSLEY GDNS
3 SOMERLEYTON CT
4 COMBERTON MANS
5 COMBERTON CT

B6
1 HASEFIELD GDNS
2 GEORGE DANCE CL
3 KIPLING WLK
4 CHATTERTON WLK

A B C D E F

8

BIRMINGHAM RD

A456

7

77

6

DY10

5

76

4

3

75

2

1

74

Greenhill

Podmore Pool

Hurcott

Hurcott Pool

Hurcott Hall

Park Hall

Duckpen Cottages

Bissell Lodge

Bissell Wood

Hodgehill Farm

Nurseries

LC

LC

LC

Little Dunclent Farm

Offmore Fst Sch

Offmore Farm

Offmore Farm

Upper Dunclent Farm

5 ELIOT WLK
6 HOUSMAN WLK
7 COWPER WLK

8 CARROLL WLK
9 GOLDSMITH WLK
10 ROCHESTER WLK

Comberton

King Charles I High Sch

Pelham Lodge

1 THE LINKS
2 CYPRESS CT
3 LIME CT
4 JUNIPER CT

Comberton Fst & Mid Schs

Stourminster Sch

Mount Segg

Dunclent House

Golf Course

Gorst Hall

Heathy Mill Farm

Dunclent Farm

Neild House

Glebe House

Glebe Farm

Stone

Stone House

Fenny Rough

KINGFISHER GR 1
LITTLE GREBE RD 2

Spennells

Spennells Fst Sch

Captain's Pool

1 SWIFT PARK GR
2 SANDPIPER CL
3 STONECHAT CL
4 NIGHTINGALE DR

Stanklyn Pool

Stanklyn

Stone CE Fst Sch

Stanklyn Wood

Depot

Stone Manor Hotel

1 SHEARWATER CL
2 PLOVER GR

1 FIELDFARE CT
2 MORILLON CT

Madinatul Uloom Islamic Coll

Mustow Green

WORCESTER RD

A450

A448

CURSLEY LA

CHESTER RD N

COMBERTON RD

STONE HILL

BROMSGROVE RD

A450

84 A B 85 C D 86 E F 74

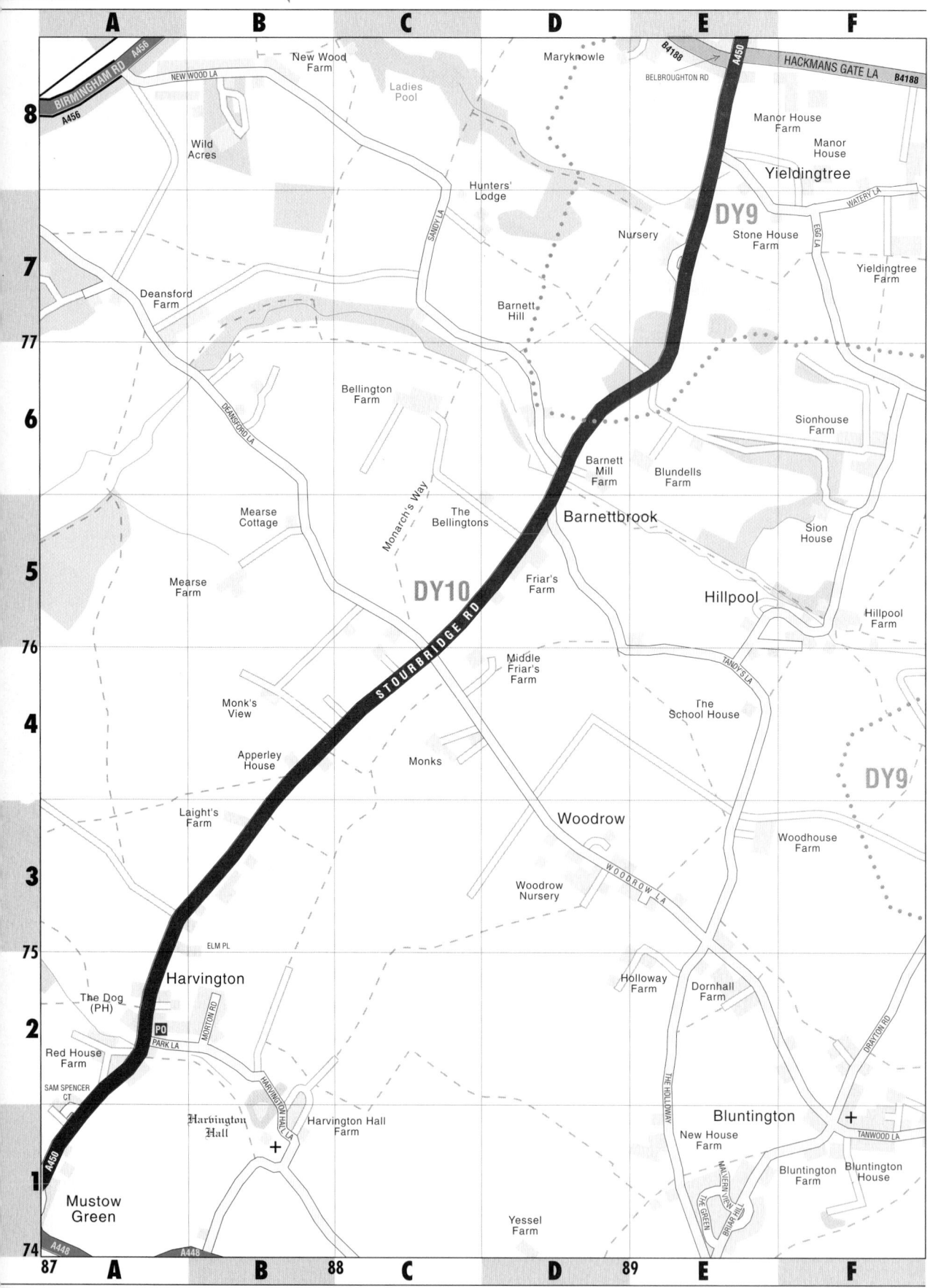

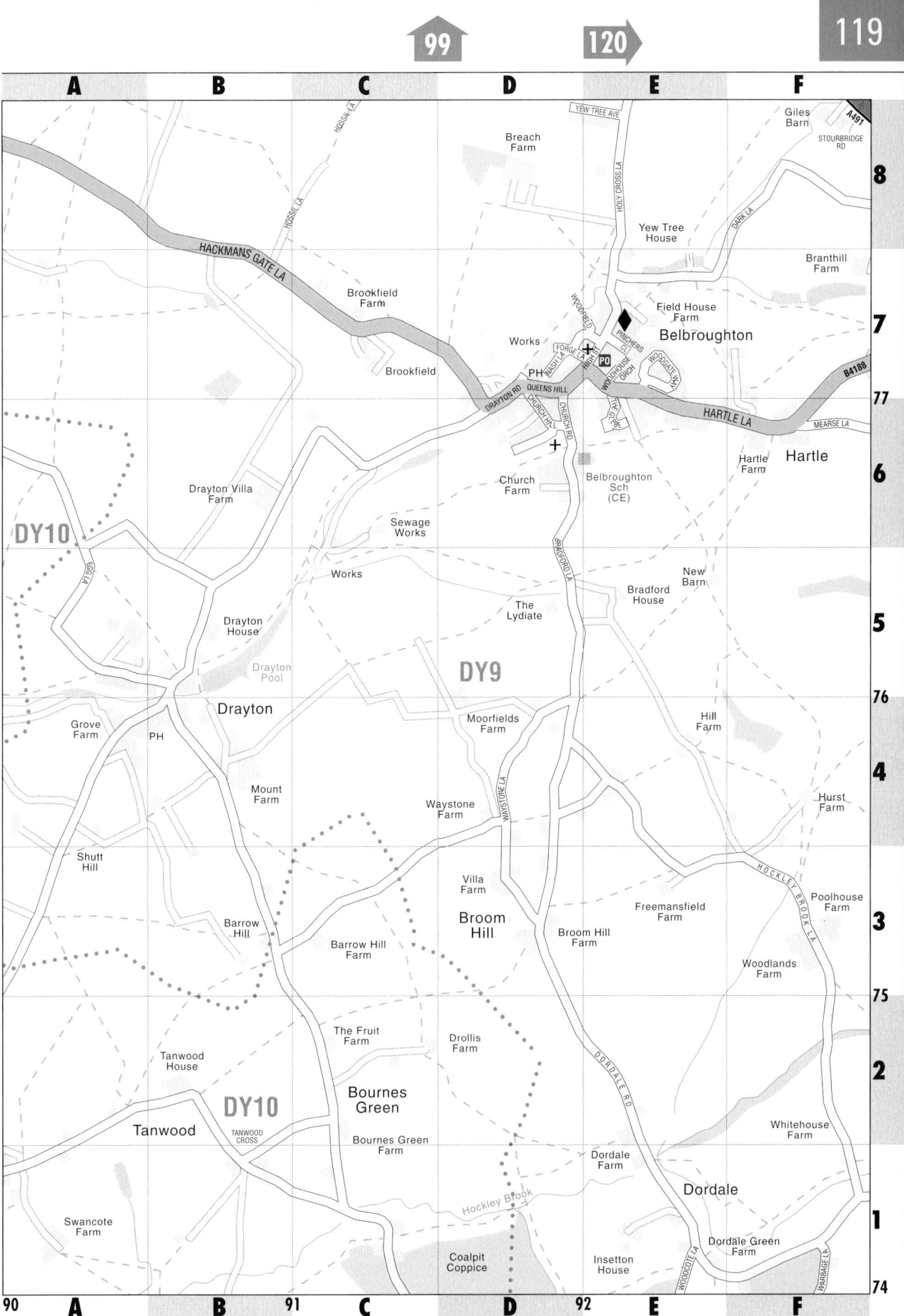

A B C D E F

8 7 77 6 5 76 4 3 75 2 1 74

B62
Chapman's Hill Farm
Chapman's Hill
Windmill Hill
Waseley Hills Country Park
Waseley Hill
Waseleyhill Farm
ROUND SAW CROFT 1
OLD QUARRY CL 2
CLENT RD
GRANGE CRES
RUBERY LA
COCK HILL LA
ROMSLEY CL
WASELEY RD
LEOMINSTER CT
WELLMEAD WLK
LEOMINSTER WLK
WINDMILL AVE
SEGBOURNE RD
LEASOWE RD
WINDMILL AVE
DELANDS RD
RUBERY FARM GR
REA AVE
BEECHES CL
HILL VIEW
CLEVES RD
CLEVES DR
WOODLANDS
Callowbrook Fst Sch
LASHBROOKE RD
CALLOWBROOK LA
BOOKEND RD
A38
DY9
Waste Site
Thistle Grove Farm
QUANTRY LA
CHADWICH LA
M 5
CHAPMAN'S HILL
B4551
MONEY LA
Barnes Close
Chadwich Grange Farm
Segbourne Coppice
North Worcestershire Path
Gannow Mid Sch
GUNNER LA
Waseley Hills High Sch
SCHOOL RD
GANNOW WLK
WHETTYBRIDGE RD
RICHMOND RD
BARRINGTON RD
KINETON RD
ROCHFORD CL
THE AVENUE
HERON WAY
LINCOLN RD
BROOK RD
LIBRARY WAY
NEW RD
PO
Liby
DODFORD CL 1
HOMEMEAD GR 2
SHRAWLEY CL 3
WHETTY LA
S CHAD'S RD
COPPICE
BIRCH RD
LEGION RD
LEACH HEATH LA
BEACON CL
Eachway
MARPLE RD
HOLMES DR
HAZEL RD
REDNAL RD
SHEARWATER CL
COTTAGE GDNS
HEATHER RD
FAIRWAY DR
STOCKWELL LA
BEACON VIEW
VALLEY FARM RD
MONUMENT LA
Golf Course
B45
Beaconside Fst & Mid Sch
Monarch's Way
Hollywell Farm
P
L Ctr
HOLYWELL LA
Chadwich Manor Estate
REDHILL LA
Redwell Farm
Chadwick Wood
Stock Hill
Heanor
Beacon Hill
Yewtree Farm
Money Lane Farm
Brookhouse Farm
SANDY LA
B4551
Chadwich Manor
Spring Pools
BIRMINGHAM RD
MADDLE LA
Keys Hill Farm
TOP RD
WILDMOOR LA
Wildmoor Oak (PH)
B61
A 491
A38
Chadwich Farm Sand Pit
4
Beaconwood
Beacon Farm
High House Farm
P
BEACON LA
HALESOWEN RD
LYDIATE ASH RD
BIRMINGHAM RD
Lydiate Ash
MILL LA
Upper Cottage Farm
The Lickey Fst & Mid Sch
HIGH HOUSE DR
ALVECHURCH HIGHWAY
B4096
LICKEY SQ
PINE GR
B60
COBNALL RD
WOODROW LA
Bellevue
Upper Marlbrook
MARLBROOK LA
MIDDLE HOUSE DR
MAYFIELD CL
MONTGOMERY CL
ALEXANDER CL
WELCOME CL
EPSOM RD
Upper Catshill
Lower Marlbrook
COTTAGE FARM LA
MERRILL GDNS
BEAUMONT LAWNS
ASHGROVE CL
Upper Marlbrook
OLD BIRMINGHAM RD
LICKEY GRANGE
Firs Farm
CHURCHILL CL
BRACES GR
PERRDALE CL
AINTREE CL
KEMPTON CT
GREEN LA
LINDFIELD WLK
PO
BIRMINGHAM RD
BROOMFIELDS
REDLAND RD
IN SLACK CRES
COTTAGE DR
FIRS CL
BEAUMONT
MIDDLE HOUSE DR
LICKEY ROCK
LINEHOUSE LA
SPRINGS AVE
GOLDEN CROSS LA
MAYFIELD CL
A38
B 4185
BELLE VUE CL
HAZELTON RD
CAVENDISH CL
B4096
FIELD AVE

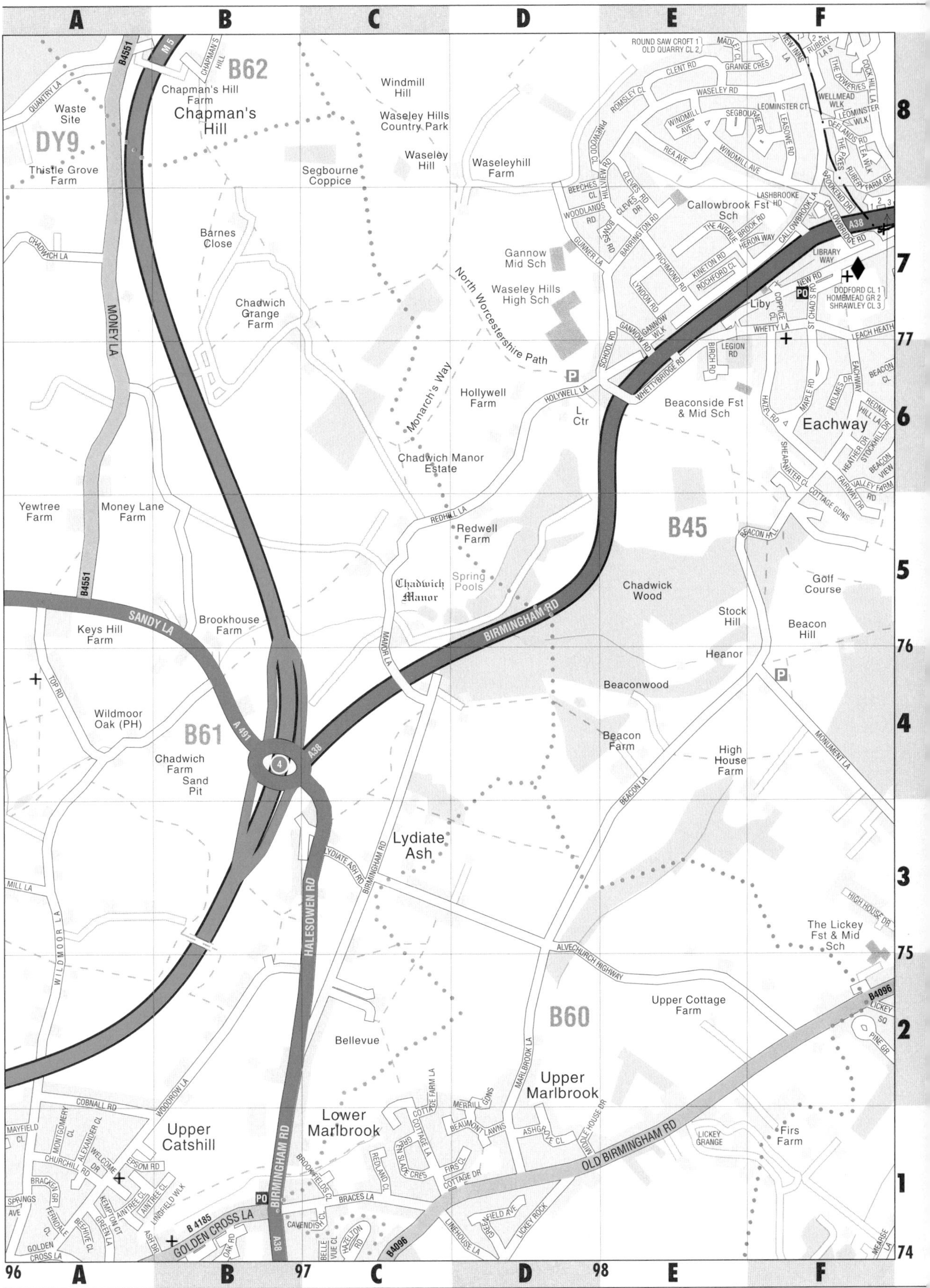

96 A B 97 C D 98 E F

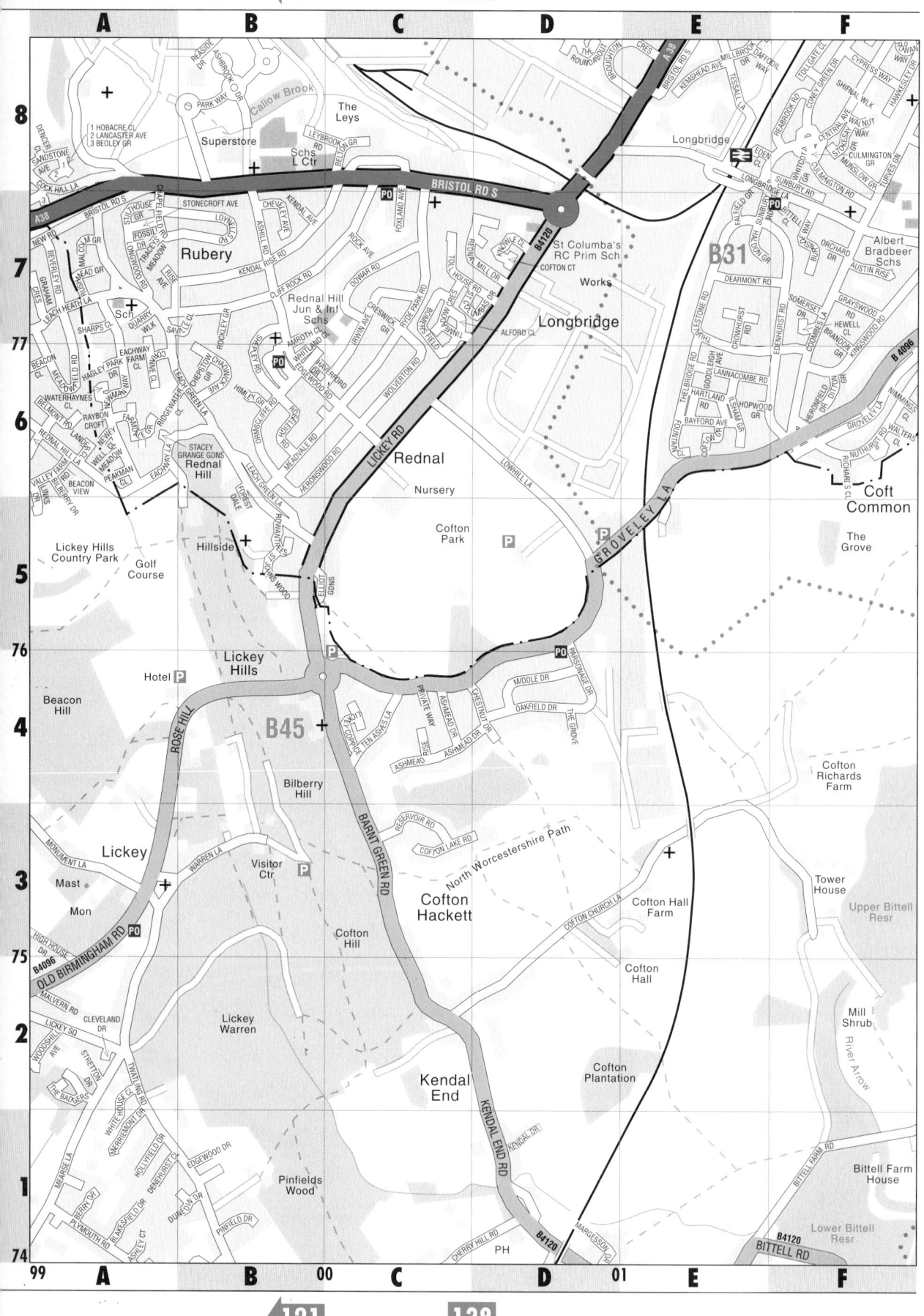

E8
1 CAMPION HO
2 SAFFRON HO
3 SEDGEBERROW COVERT
4 LYDBROOK COVERT
5 OFFENHAM COVERT
6 TARRINGTON COVERT
7 BILTON IND EST
8 REDBROOK COVERT

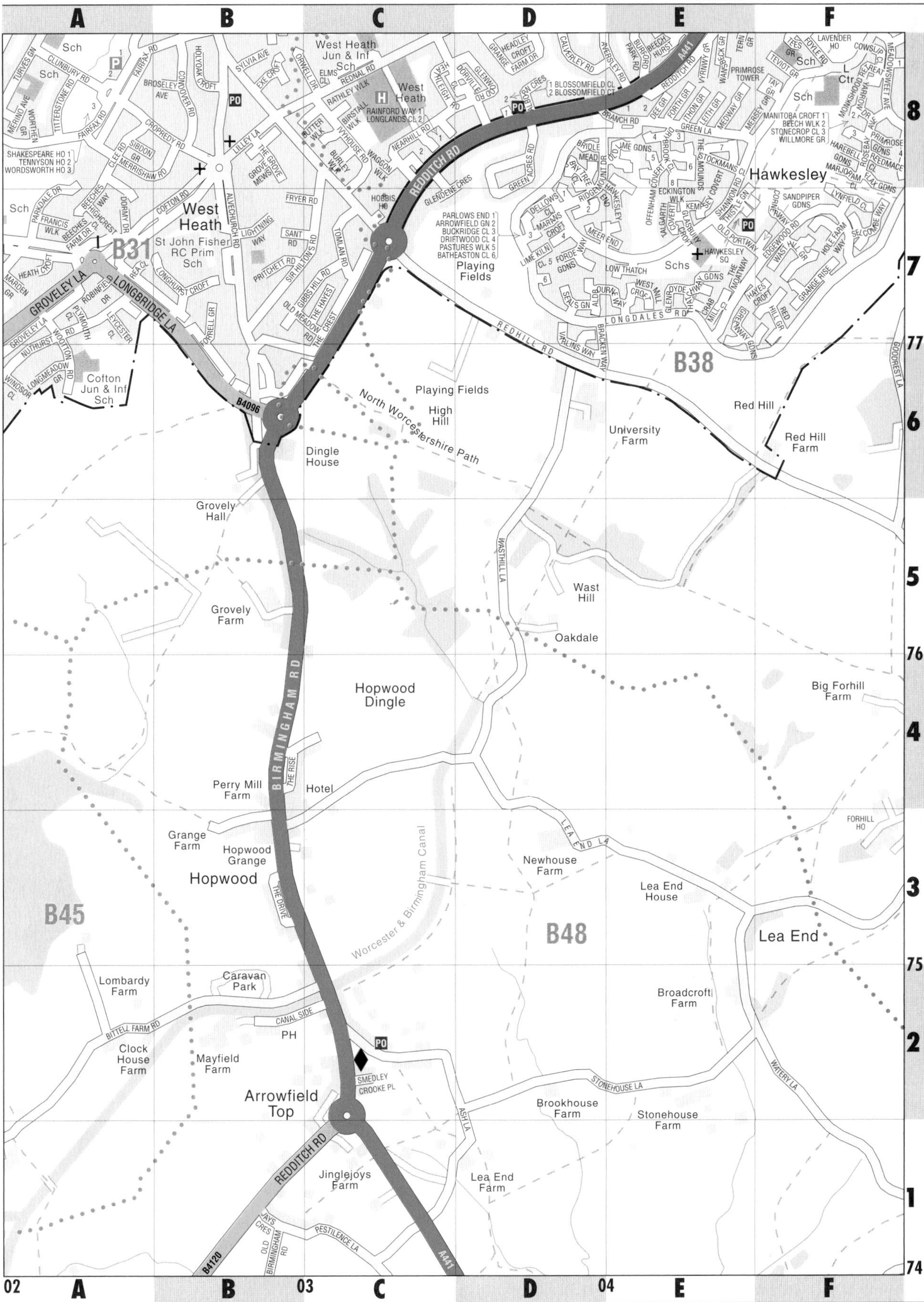

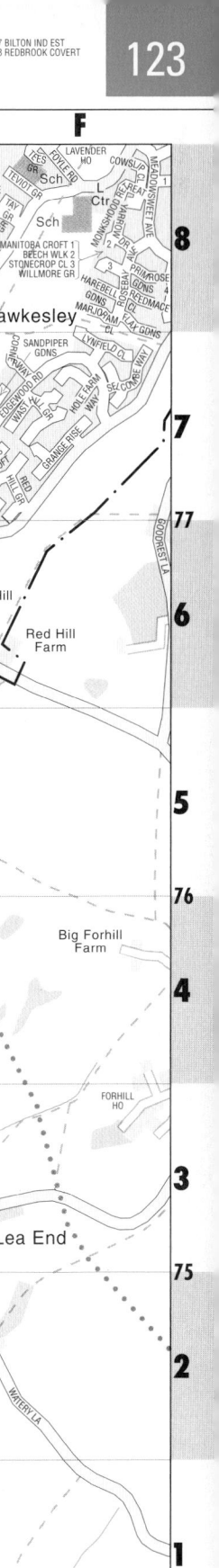

123
104

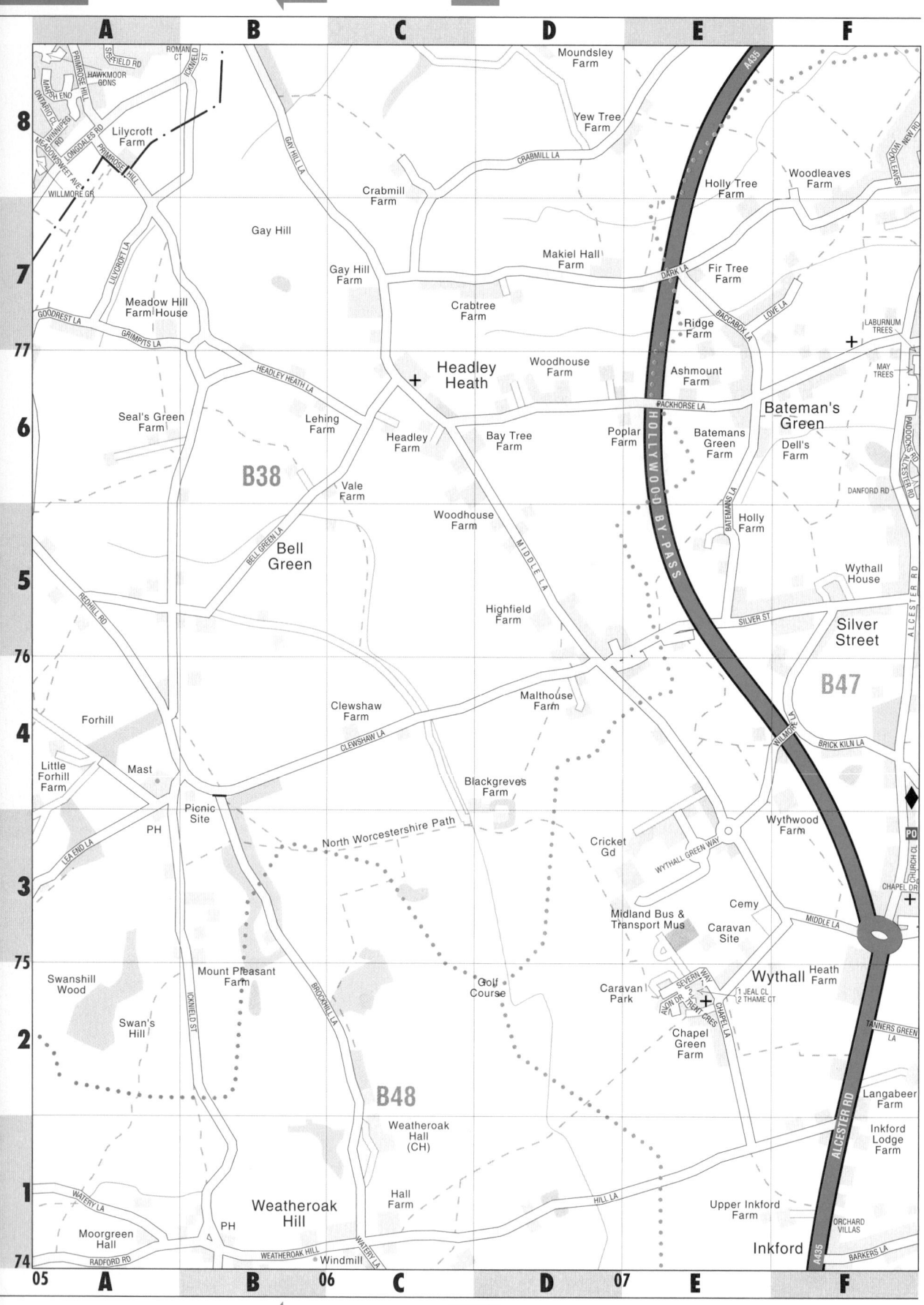

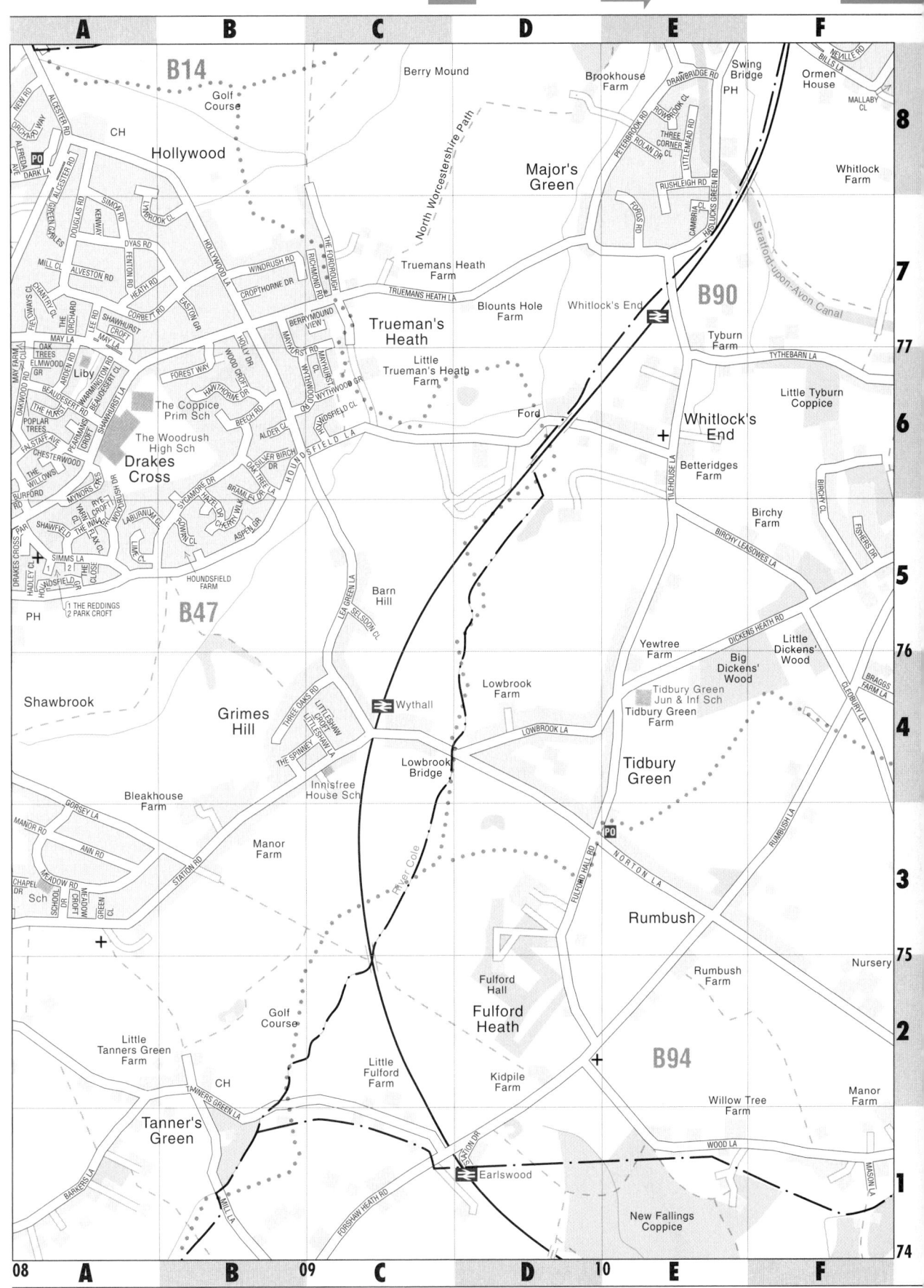

B14

Berry Mound

Golf Course

Brookhouse Farm

Swing Bridge PH

Ormen House

CH

Hollywood

Major's Green

Whitlock Farm

North Worcestershire Path

Truemans Heath Farm

Truemans Heath La

Blounts Hole Farm

Whitlock's End

B90

Trueman's Heath

Tyburn Farm

Little Trueman's Heath Farm

Tythebarn La

Little Tyburn Coppice

Ford

Whitlock's End

The Coppice Prim Sch

The Woodrush High Sch

Betteridges Farm

Drakes Cross

Birchy Farm

Houndsfield Farm

Barn Hill

Birchy Leasowes La

B47

Dickens Heath Rd

Yewtree Farm

Big Dickens' Wood

Little Dickens' Wood

Shawbrook

Grimes Hill

Wythall

Lowbrook Farm

Tidbury Green Jun & Inf Sch

Tidbury Green Farm

Braggs Farm La

Glenbury La

Lowbrook La

Tidbury Green

Bleakhouse Farm

Innisfree House Sch

Lowbrook Bridge

Manor Farm

River Cole

Fulford Hall Rd

Norton La

Rumbush

Rumbush Farm

Nursery

Sch

Fulford Hall

Fulford Heath

B94

Little Tanners Green Farm

Golf Course

Little Fulford Farm

Kidpile Farm

Willow Tree Farm

Manor Farm

CH

Tanner's Green

Tanners Green La

Forshaw Heath Rd

Station Dr

Earlswood

New Fallings Coppice

Wood La

Mill La

Stratford-upon-Avon Canal

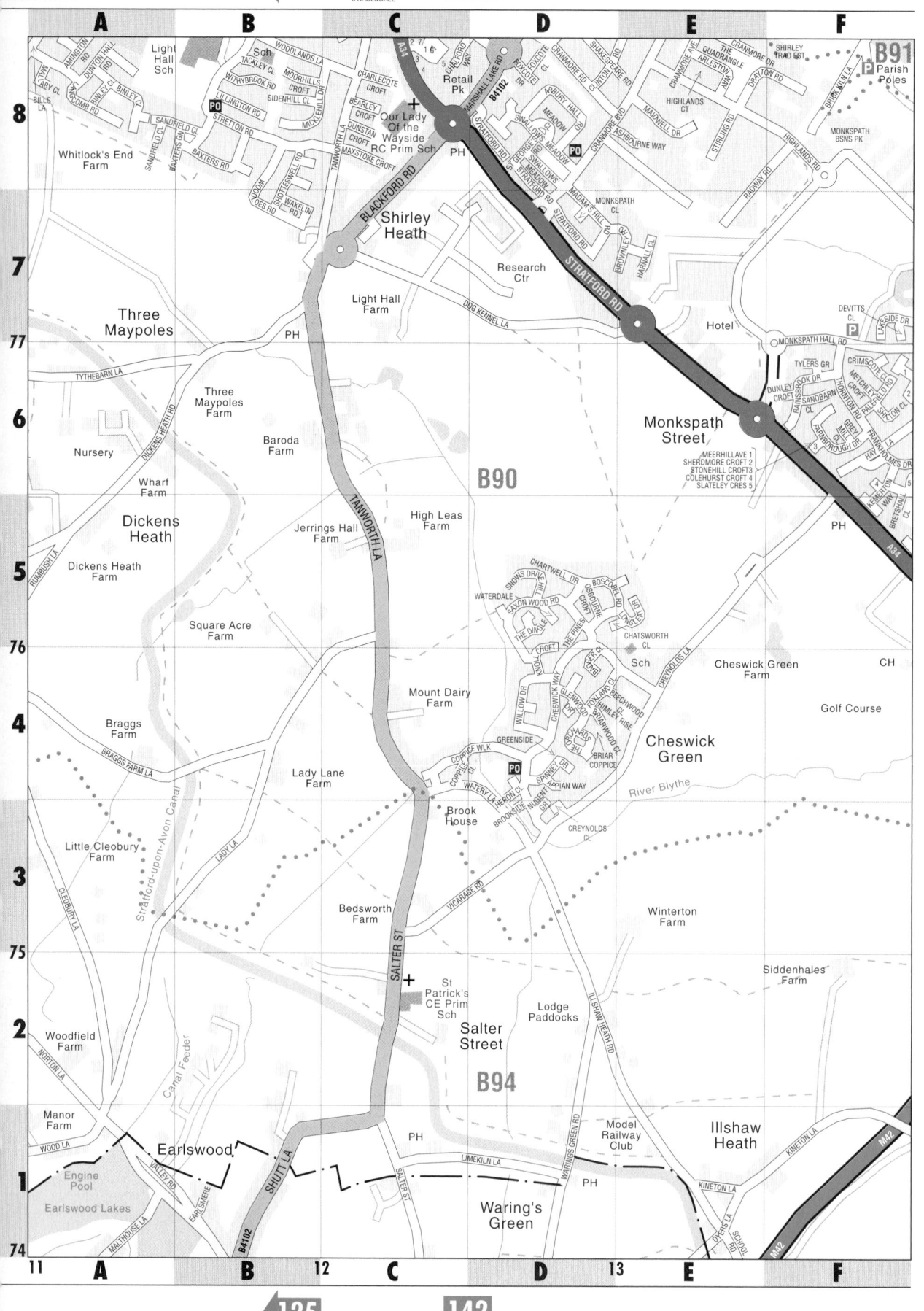

125
106

C8
1 HARWOOD GR
2 SHIRLEYDALE
3 CHELTONDALE
4 HENLEYDALE
5 QUINTONDALE
6 ARDENDALE

C8
7 YARNINGDALE

B91
P Parish
Poles

Shirley
Trad Est

Monkspath
BSNS PK

Whitlock's End
Farm

Light
Hall
Sch

WOODLANDS LA

Our Lady
Of the
Wayside
RC Prim Sch

Retail
Pk

Shirley
Heath

Research
Ctr

STRATFORD RD

Hotel

Monkspath
Street

Monkspath Hall Rd

DEVITTS
CL P

MEERHILLAVE 1
SHERDMORE CROFT 2
STONEHILL CROFT3
COLEHURST CROFT 4
SLATELEY CRES 5

Three
Maypoles

Light Hall
Farm

DOG KENNEL LA

Three
Maypoles
Farm

Baroda
Farm

Nursery

Wharf
Farm

Dickens
Heath

Dickens Heath
Farm

TANWORTH LA

Jerrings Hall
Farm

High Leas
Farm

B90

Square Acre
Farm

Mount Dairy
Farm

CHARTWELL DR

SAXON WOOD RD

WATERDALE

Chatsworth
CL

Sch

Cheswick Green
Farm

CH

Braggs
Farm

BRAGGS FARM LA

Lady Lane
Farm

GREENSIDE

BRIAR
COPPICE

Cheswick
Green

Golf Course

River Blythe

Little Cleobury
Farm

CLEOBURY LA

Brook
House

CREYNOLDS
CL

Bedsworth
Farm

VICARAGE RD

Winterton
Farm

SALTER ST

St
Patrick's
CE Prim
Sch

Siddenhales
Farm

Lodge
Paddocks

ILSHAW HEATH RD

Salter
Street

Woodfield
Farm

B94

NORTON LA

Manor
Farm

WOOD LA

Canal Feeder

Earlswood

SHUTT LA

PH

Model
Railway
Club

WARINGS GREEN RD

Illshaw
Heath

KINETON LA

M42

Engine
Pool

VALLEY RD

SALTER ST

LIMEKILN LA

PH

KINETON LA

Earlswood Lakes

MALTHOUSE LA

B4102

Waring's
Green

DYERS LA

SCHOOL

M42

125
142

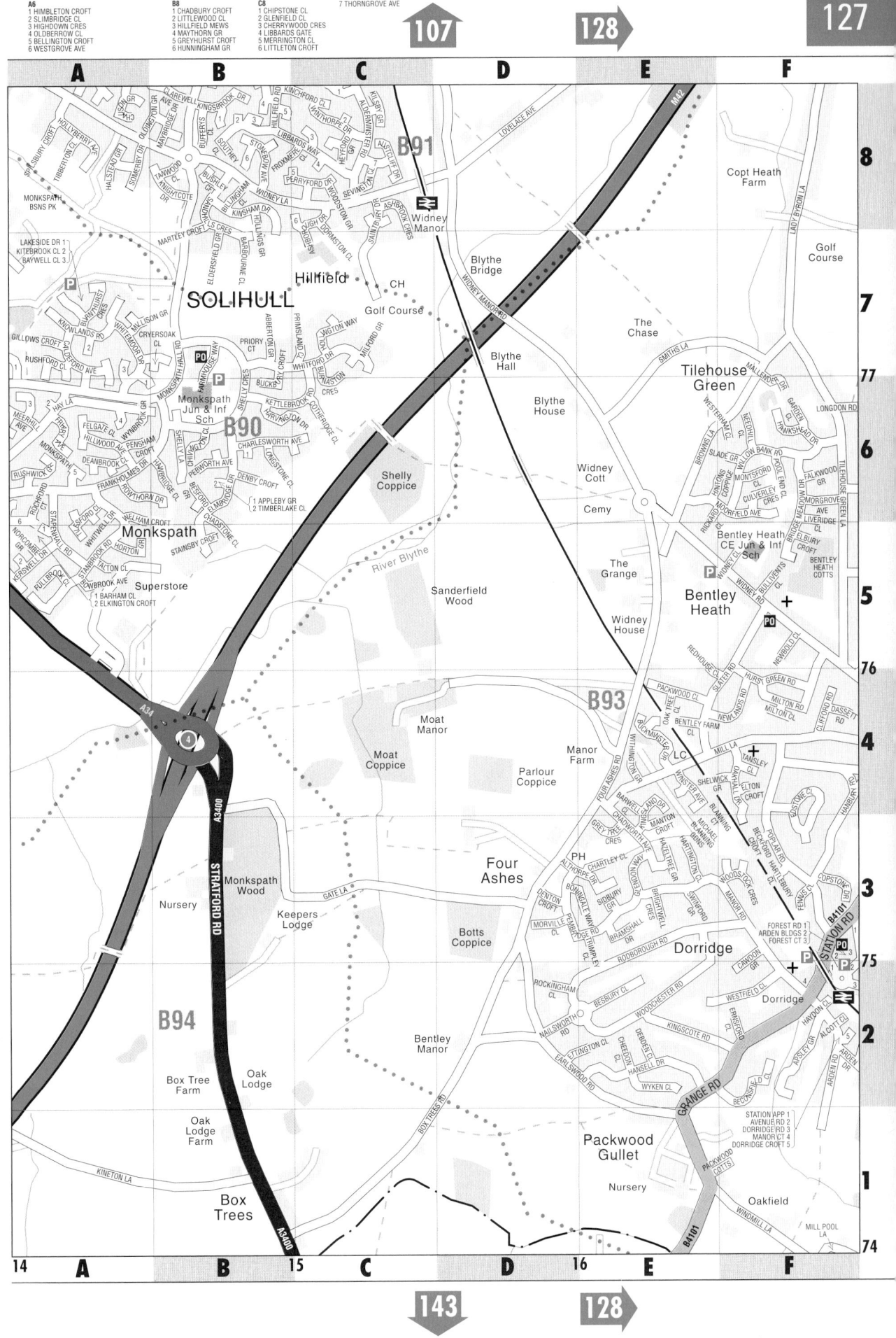

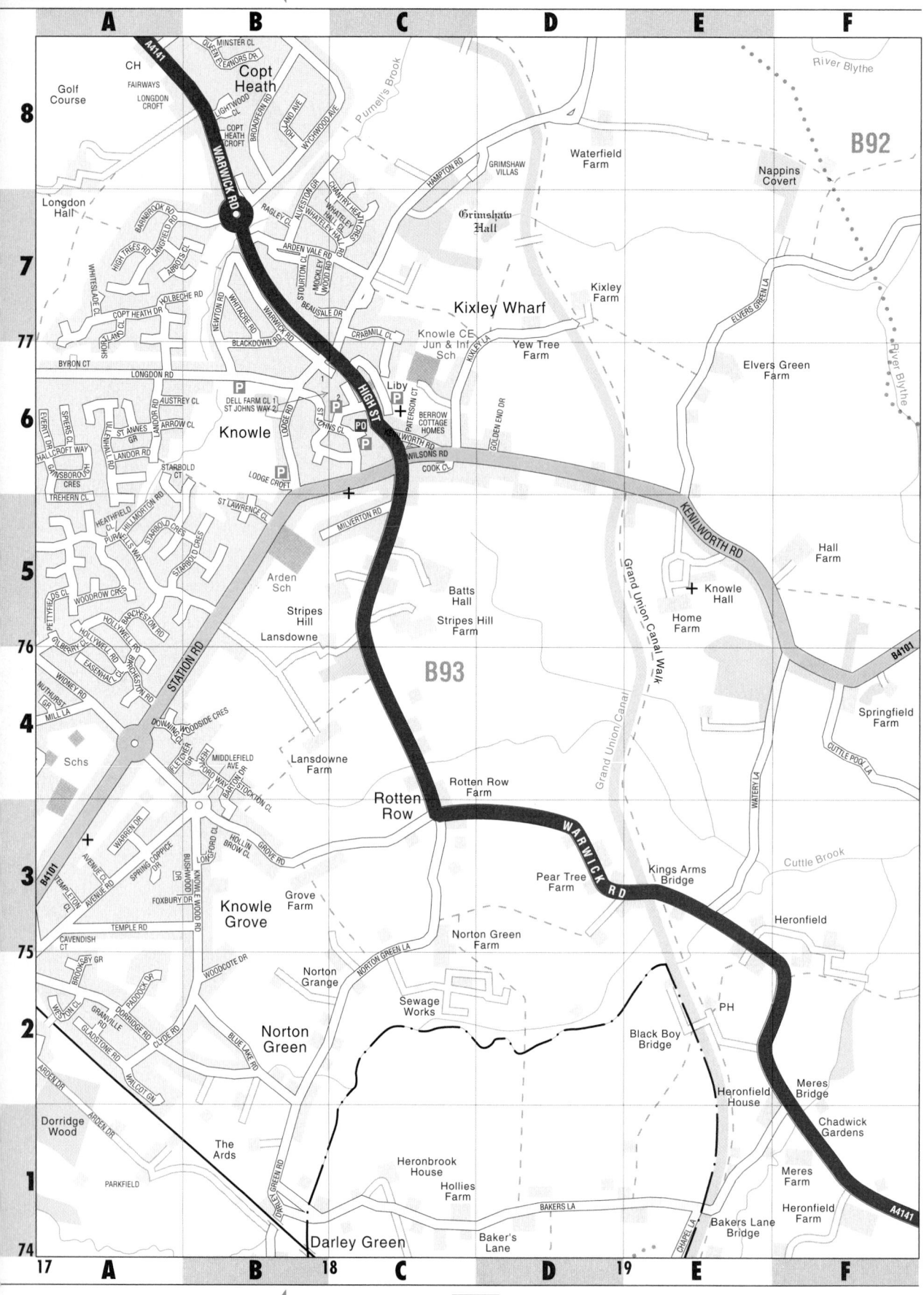

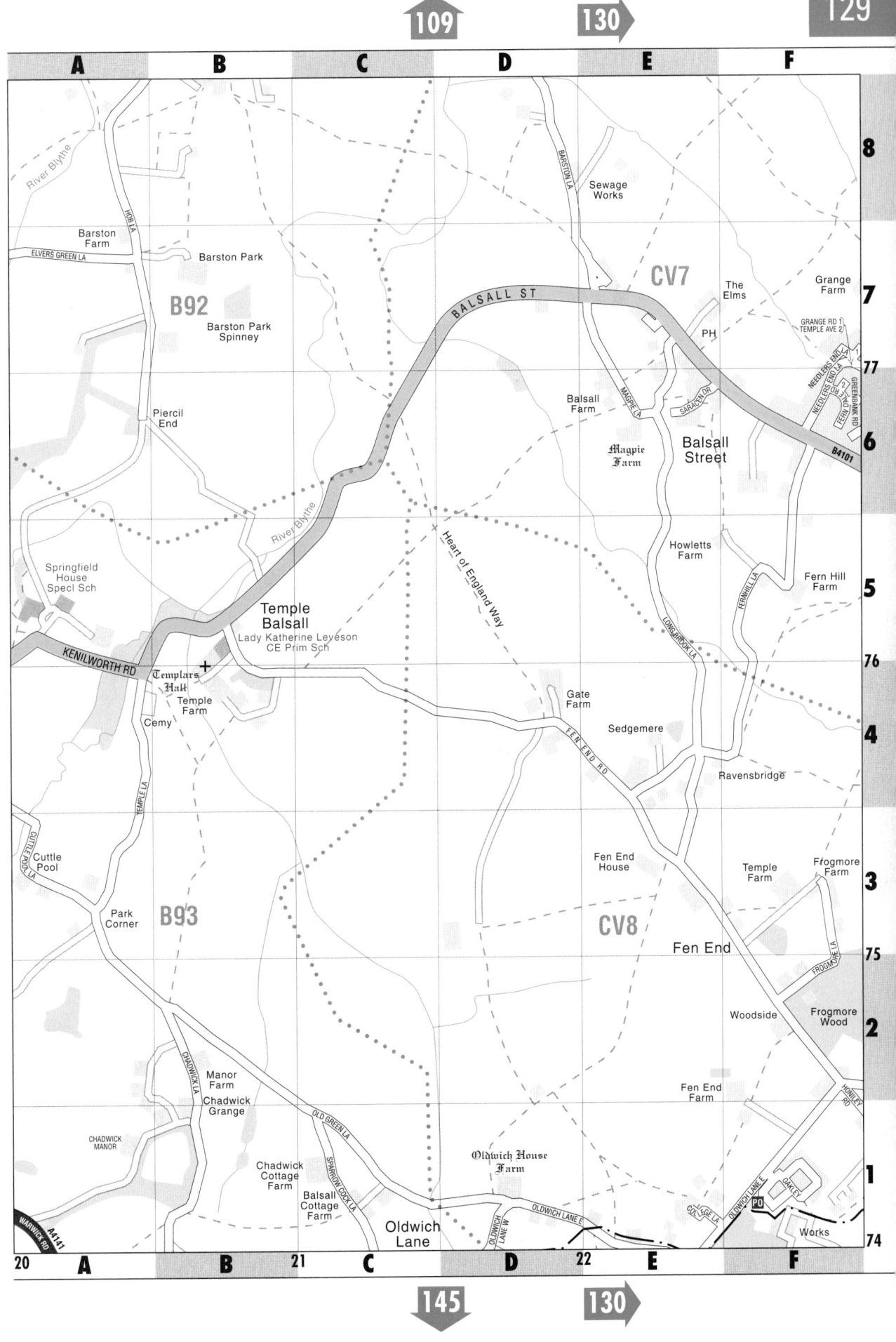

A B C D E F

8

River Blythe

Barston
Farm

ELVERS GREEN LA

Barston Park

HOB LA

B92

7

Barston Park
Spinney

Piercil
End

BALSALL ST

CV7

Sewage
Works

BARSTON LA

The
Elms

Grange
Farm

PH

GRANGE RD 1
TEMPLE AVE 2

NEEDLERS END LA

FERN RD

GREENBANK RD

77

Balsall
Farm

MAGPIE LA

SARACEN DR

B4101

6

River Blythe

Magpie
Farm

Balsall
Street

Howletts
Farm

FERN HILL LA

Fern Hill
Farm

5

Springfield
House
Specl Sch

Heart of England Way

LONGBROOK LA

76

KENILWORTH RD

Temple
Balsall

Lady Katherine Leveson
CE Prim Sch

Gate
Farm

Sedgemere

4

Templars
Hall

Temple
Farm

FEN END RD

Ravensbridge

Cemy

TEMPLE LA

CUTTLE POOL LA

Cuttle
Pool

Park
Corner

B93

Fen End
House

Temple
Farm

Frogmore
Farm

3

CV8

Fen End

FROGMORE LA

75

HORLEY RD

Woodside

Frogmore
Wood

2

CHADWICK LA

Manor
Farm

Chadwick
Grange

OLD GREEN LA

SPARROW COCK LA

Fen End
Farm

CHADWICK
MANOR

Chadwick
Cottage
Farm

Balsall
Cottage
Farm

OLDWICH LANE W

Oldwich House
Farm

OLDWICH LANE E

COLLEGE LA

OLDWICH LANE E

OAKLEY

PO

1

WARWICK RD

A4141

Oldwich
Lane

Works

74

20 A 21 B C 22 D E F

A   B   C   D   E   F

8

PH
WOOTTON GREEN LA
LAVENDER HALL LA
A452
ROSE CT
CHAPEL DR
HATHAWAY CL

Berkswell
PH P LC Berkswell House
Moat House Farm
SPENCER'S LA
BAULK LA

Carol Green
HODGETT'S LA

TRUGGIST LA

7

Balsall Common

Needlers End
GLEBE WAY OLD AV
GREENHILL RD
HAWKSMOOR
NEEDLERS END LA
WINSFORD CL
WHITINGHT
SPEEDWELL
BURBERRY GR
DUNCHURCH
STATION RD
BURLEIGH CL
P
PO
P
GREEN LA
Liby
DOCKERS CL
SUNNYSIDE CL
ASHTON
SUNNYSIDE
BEVERLEY CL

Beechwood Farm

77

Winsford CL
COALOW CL
LUDFORD
TIDMARSH CL
STONE CLS CRES
CHILDS OAK CL
FINFORD CROFT
Yew Tree
KEMPS GREEN RD
CHATTAWAY
PRIORS CL
NEWHOUSE CL
BRACEBRIDGE CL
BROOKS
BRADLEY CROFT
ASHFURLONG CL
CEDAR WOOD DR
LEVESON CRES
FOXES WAY
IDALE MEADOW
SPAR HILLS CL
LAURELS CRES
ELM WOOD
ELM GR
ROEN CL
OXHAY
AST CL
Barratt's Lane Farm
MEETING HOUSE LA
BARRATT'S LA

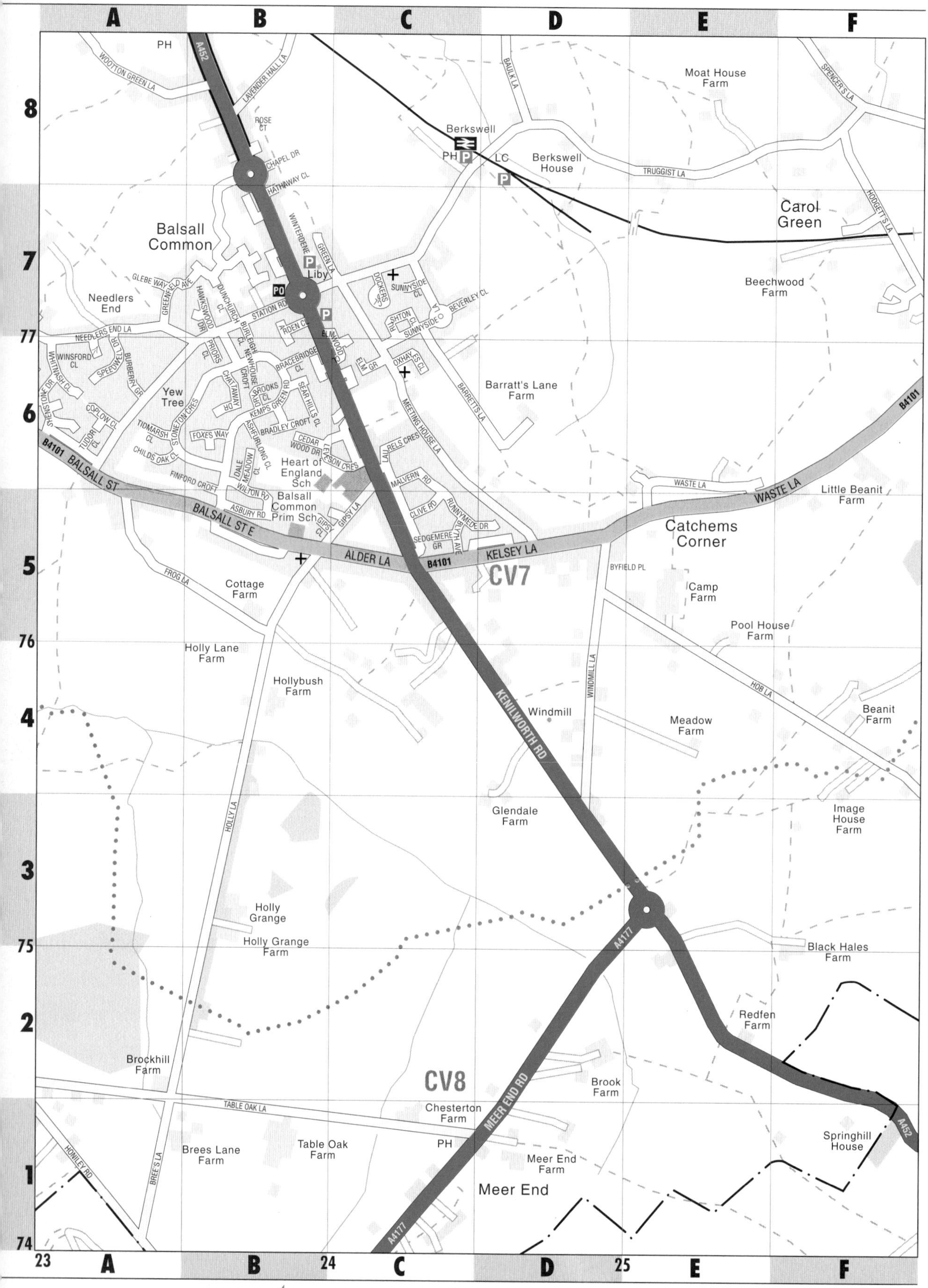

6

B4101 BALSALL ST
SPENS BR
WILTON RD
ASBURY RD
GIPSY CL
GIPSY RD
Heart of England Sch
Balsall Common Prim Sch
MALVERN RD
CLIVE RD
RUNNYMEDE DR
SEDGEMERE GR
B4101
CLINTON AVE

WASTE LA
WASTE LA
B4101
Little Beanit Farm

5

BALSALL ST E
ALDER LA
KELSEY LA
CV7
Catchems Corner
BYFIELD PL
Camp Farm

76

FROG LA
Cottage Farm
Pool House Farm

Holly Lane Farm

Hollybush Farm

Windmill
WINDMILL LA
HOB LA
Meadow Farm
Beanit Farm

4

HOLLY LA
KENILWORTH RD
Glendale Farm
Image House Farm

3

Holly Grange
A4177
Black Hales Farm

75

Holly Grange Farm
Redfen Farm

2

Brockhill Farm
CV8
MEER END RD
Brook Farm

TABLE OAK LA
Chesterton Farm
PH
A452
Springhill House

1

HONILEY RD
BREE'S LA
Brees Lane Farm
Table Oak Farm
Meer End Farm
A4177
Meer End

74

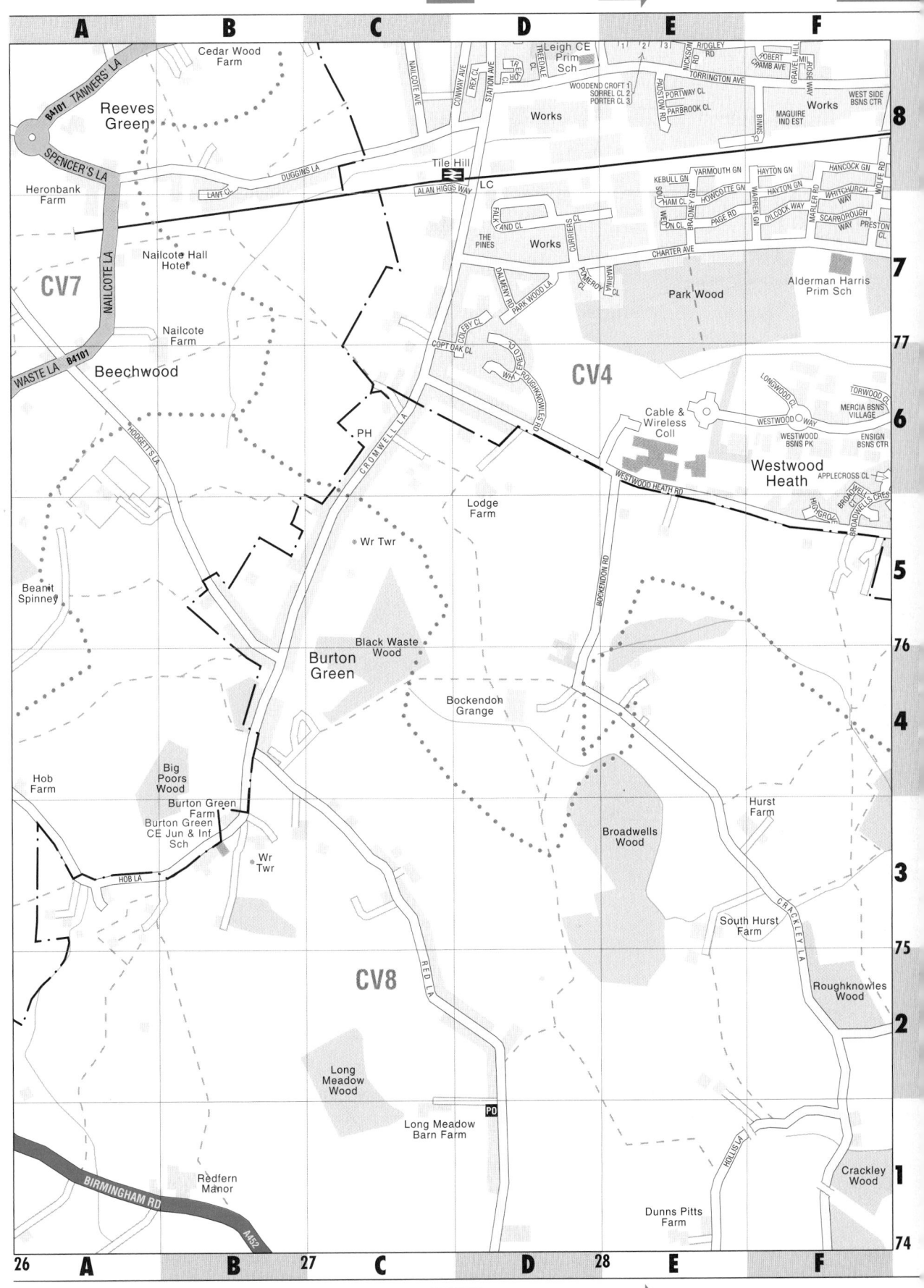

A B C D E F

8
7
77
6
5
76
4
3
75
2
1
74

A B C D E F

Tanners La
B4101
Reeves Green
Spencer's La
Heronbank Farm
CV7
Nailcote La
Cedar Wood Farm
Nailcote Ave
Conway Ave
Rex Cl
Station Ave
Duggins La
Lant Cl
Tile Hill
Alan Higgs Way
LC
Leigh CE Prim Sch
Dickson Rd
Ridgley Rd
Robert Cramb Ave
Gravel Hill
Rose Way
Wolfe Rd
Torrington Ave
Woodend Croft 1
Sorrel Cl 2
Porter Cl 3
Padstow Rd
Portway Cl
Parbrook Cl
Binns Cl
Maguire Ind Est
West Side Bsns Ctr
Works
Works
Nailcote Hall Hotel
Nailcote Farm
Beechwood
Waste La
B4101
Hodgetts La
Kebull Gn
Yarmouth Gn
Ham Cl
Howcotte Gn
Bradney Gn
Wen Cl
Page Rd
Dillock Way
Hayton Gn
Warren Gn
Hancock Gn
Marler Rd
Whitchurch Way
Scarborough Way
Preston Cl
Charter Ave
The Pines
Works
Falkland Cl
Crurers Cl
Dalmeny Rd
Park Wood La
Pomeroy
Marina
Park Wood
Alderman Harris Prim Sch
CV4
Colesby Cl
Copt Oak Cl
Wh Roughknowles Rd
Whitefield
Longwood Cl
Westwood Way
Torwood Cl
Mercia Bsns Village
Westwood Bsns Pk
Ensign Bsns Ctr
Cable & Wireless Coll
Westwood Heath
Applecross Cl
Westwood Heath Rd
Highgrove
Broadwells Crest
Broadwells Cres
PH
Cromwell La
Lodge Farm
Wr Twr
Bockendon Rd
Beanit Spinney
Black Waste Wood
Burton Green
Bockendon Grange
Hurst Farm
Hob Farm
Big Poors Wood
Burton Green Farm
Burton Green CE Jun & Inf Sch
Wr Twr
Hob La
Broadwells Wood
Crackley La
South Hurst Farm
Roughknowles Wood
CV8
Red La
Long Meadow Wood
Long Meadow Barn Farm
PO
Hollis La
Crackley Wood
Dunns Pitts Farm
Birmingham Rd
A452
Redfern Manor

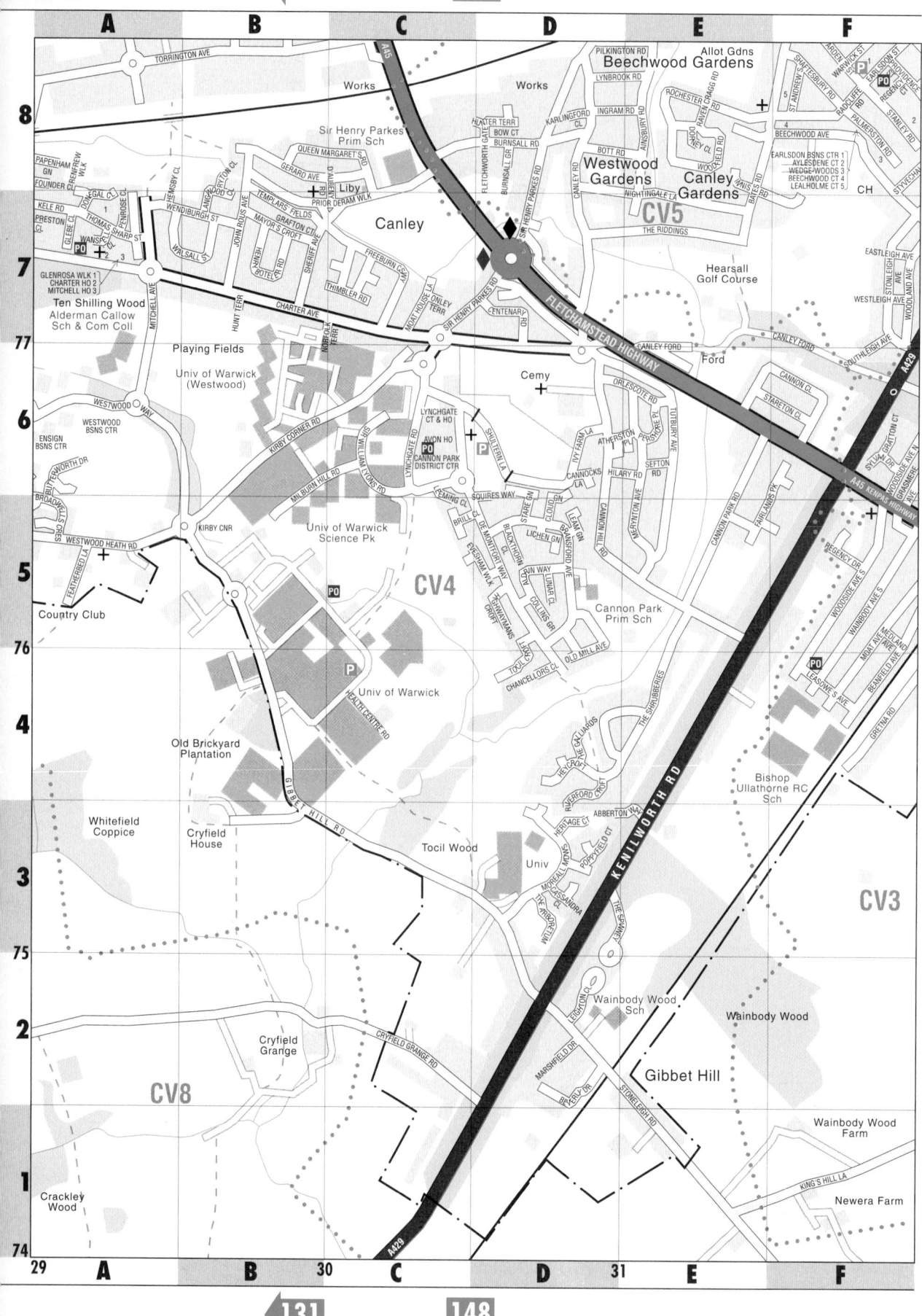

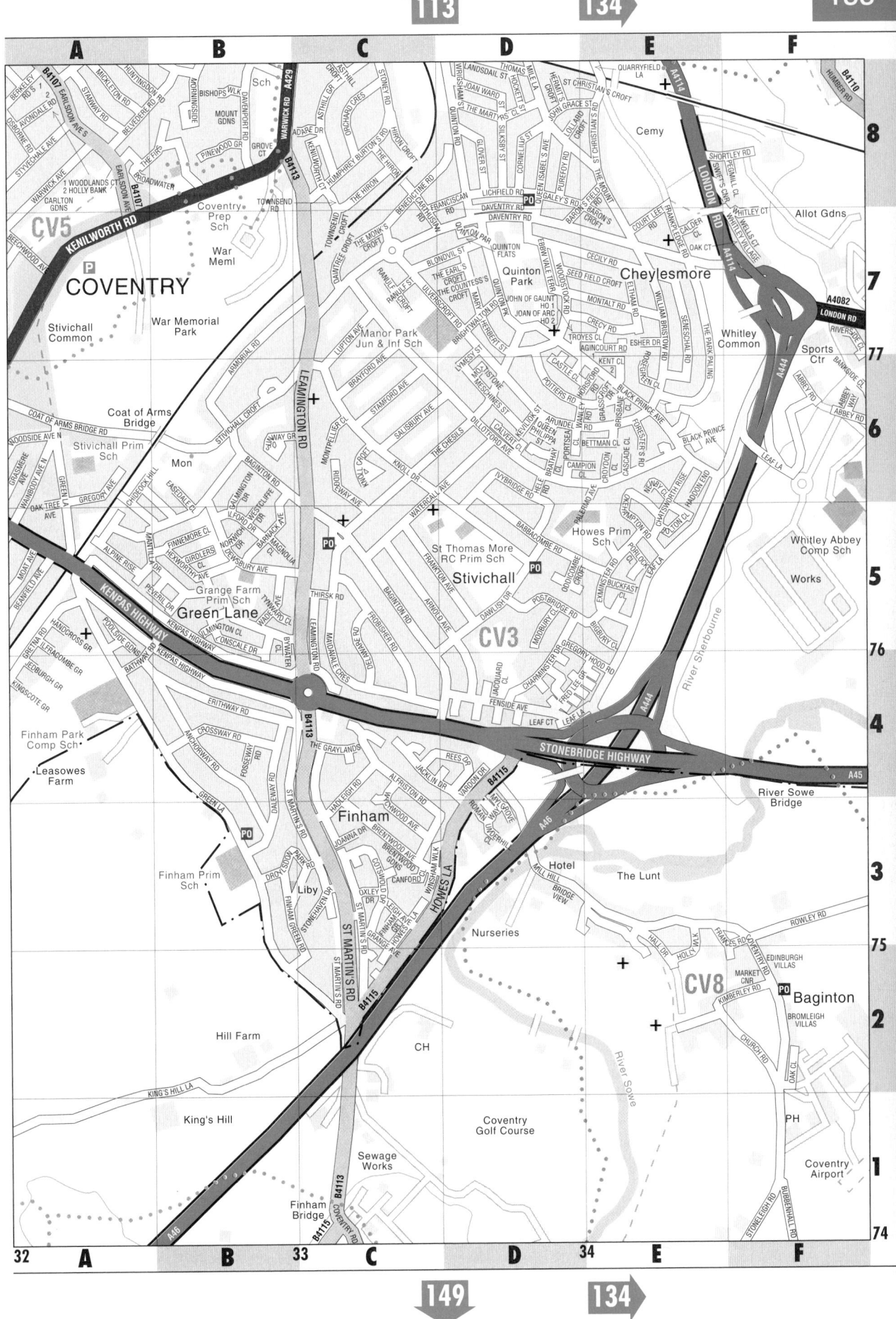

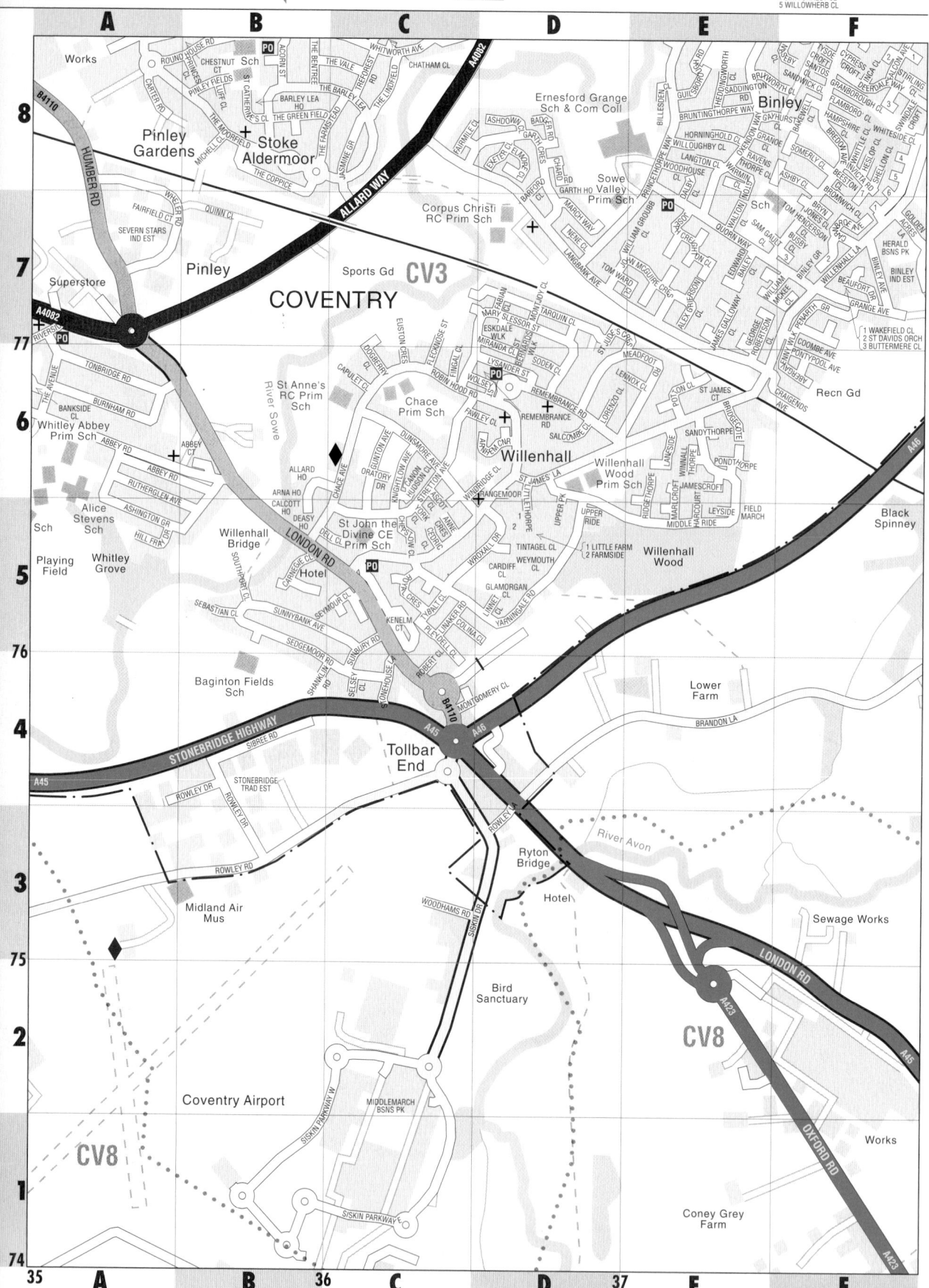

F8
1 CARDALE CROFT
2 KESTREL CROFT
3 RUTLAND CROFT
4 JIM FORREST CL
5 WILLOWHERB CL
6 WASPERTON CL
7 JOE WILLIAMS CL

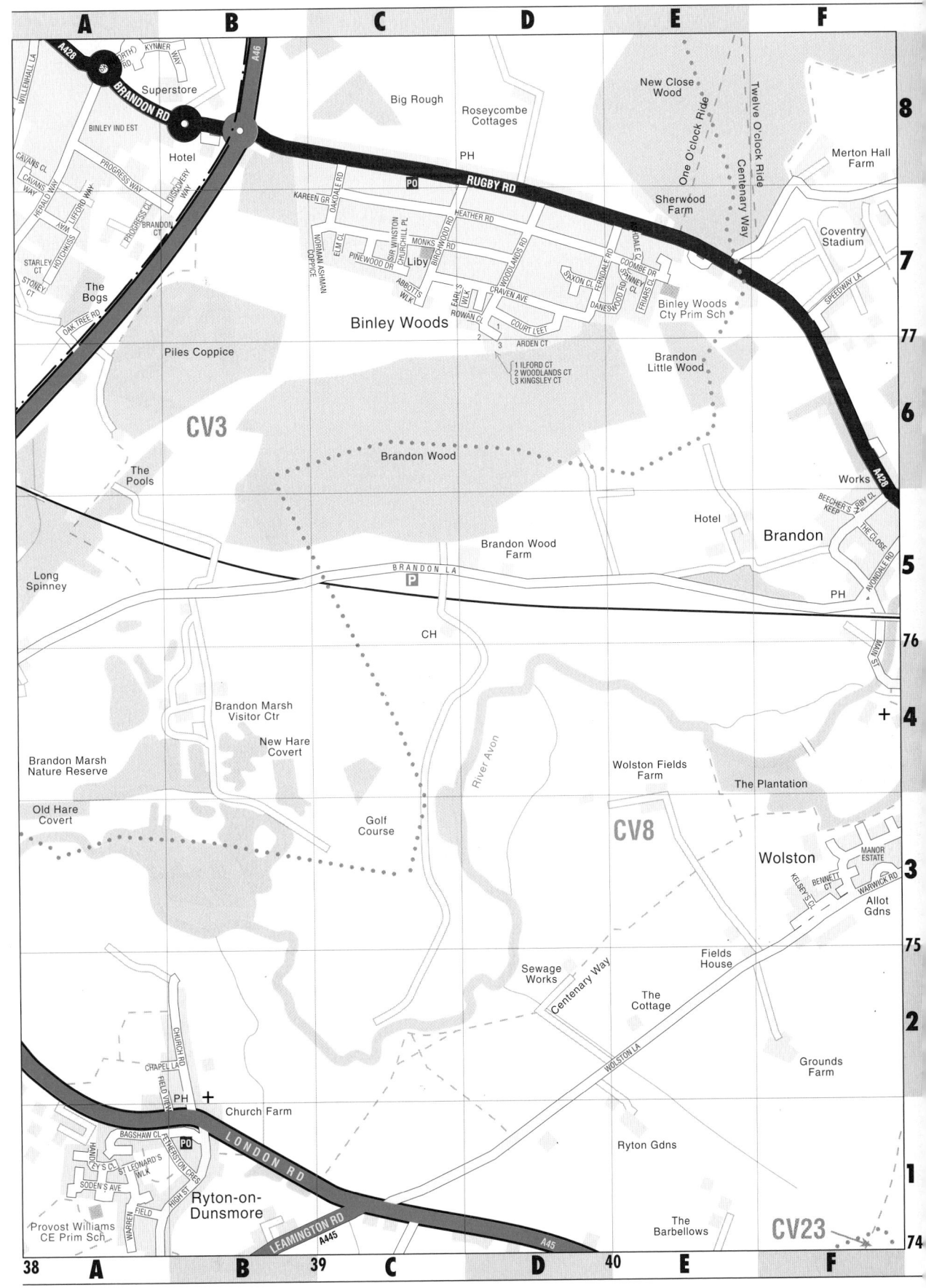

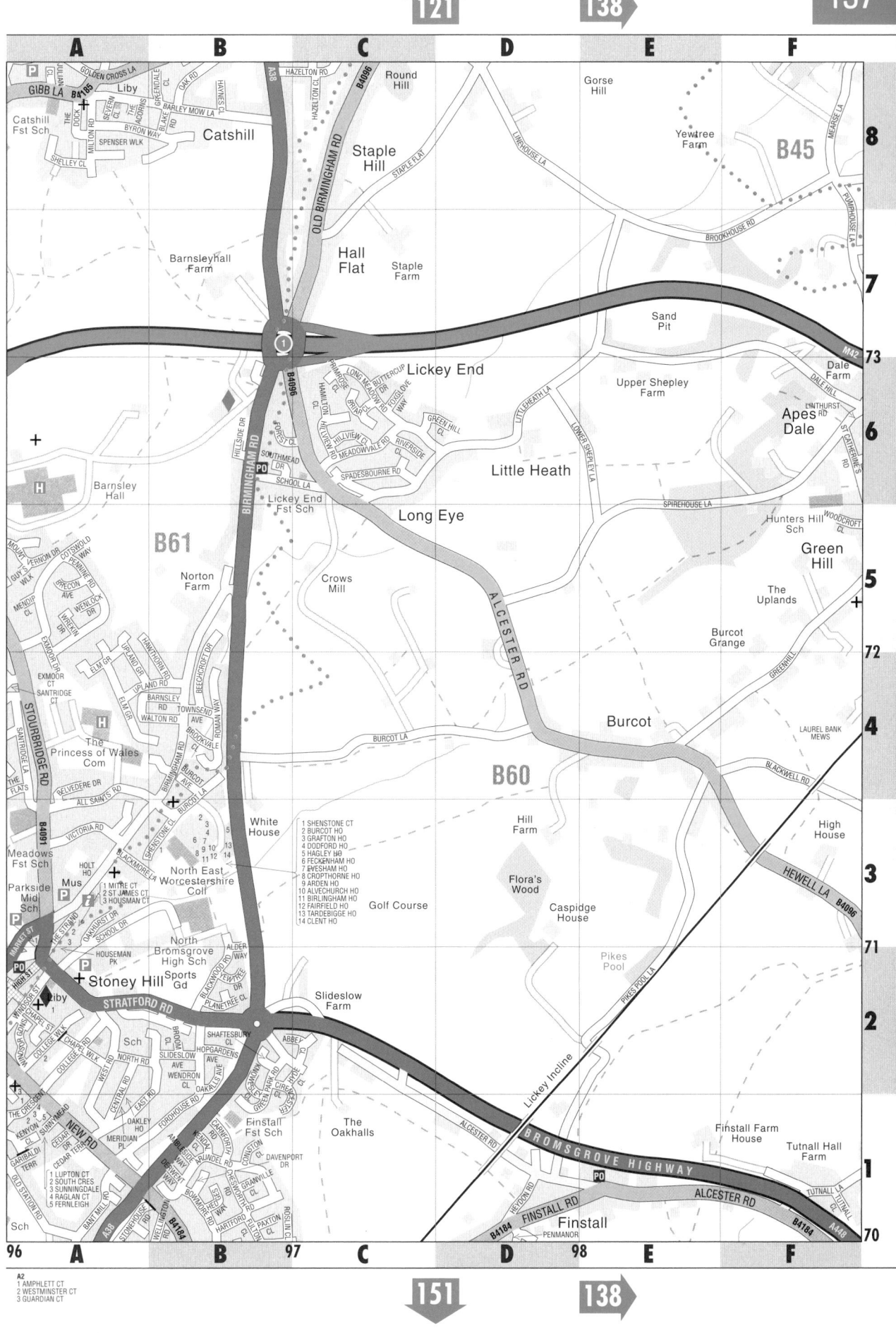

A2
1 AMPHLETT CT
2 WESTMINSTER CT
3 GUARDIAN CT

A B C D E F

8

Brook House
PLYMOUTH DR
GORSE MEADOW DR
PLYMOUTH RD
WOOD END DR
TWATLING RD
BROOKHOUSE RD
WOODSIDE DR
SHEPLEY RD
Barnt Green
BILLY LA
Fiery Hill
CHERRY HILL RD
ROSEWOOD DR
CHERRY HILL DR
CHERRY HILL AVE
FIERY HILL RD
BEECH PARK DR
OAKDENE DR
WILLOW TREE DR
HEWELL RD
STATION APP
HEWELL LA
Barnt Green
THE LONGLANDS
B4120
GREENBANK
PENCER DR
POPLAR DR
ROSE TERR
ORCHARD CROFT
St Andrew's Sch
BITTELL RD
B4120
St Andrew's Sch
BITTELL RD
B4120
PO
SANDHILLS RD
BITTELL LA
The Paddocks

7

B45
Barnt Green
SANDHILLS GM
Sandhills Farm
SANDHILLS LA
COOPERS HILL
M42
AQUEDUCT LA
M42

73
PIKE HILL
M42
Masts
Uplands
High Croft
BIRCHES LA
WITHYBED LA
FORWARD COTTS
Withybed Green
REAR COTTS
FRONT COTTS

6
THE AVENUE
Linthurst
Linthurst Prim Sch
TANGLEWOOD CT
THE GLEN
ST CATHERINES RD
FOXES CL
BROADWAY
LINTHURST NEWTOWN
Blackwell
PO
GLENEAGLES DR
BIRKDALE AV
WENTWORTH RD
FAIRWAYS DR
STATION RD
CH
Foxhill BARNS
B48
FOXHILL LA
Foxhill House
Gorsey Lane Farm
SCARFIELD HILL
Scarfields Farm

5

72
STATION COTTS
Golf Course
BLACKWELL RD
Wheeley Farm
WHEELEY RD
COBLEY HILL
Scarfields Dingle

4
Blackwell Court
AGMORE RD
B60
Mast
Cobley Hill Farm
Cobley Hill
Andrew's Coppice
GRANGE LA

3
Vigo
HOLLONTREE LA
B40496
Hollow Tree Farm
ASHGROVE LA
Cattespool
Sunny Bank Farm

71
B4096
Robin Hill Farm
STONEY LA
Stoney Lane Farm
Worcester and Birmingham Canal
Shortwood Rough Grounds

2
Stoney Lane Cottage
Tunnel
Little Shortwood

The Lower House
WHARFE LA
Bromsgrove Private
H

1
TUTNALL LA
HEWELL LA
Broad Green
Works
Oxleasows Farm
B97

70
99
A
BROCKHILL LA
B4096
00
B
C
D
01
E
F

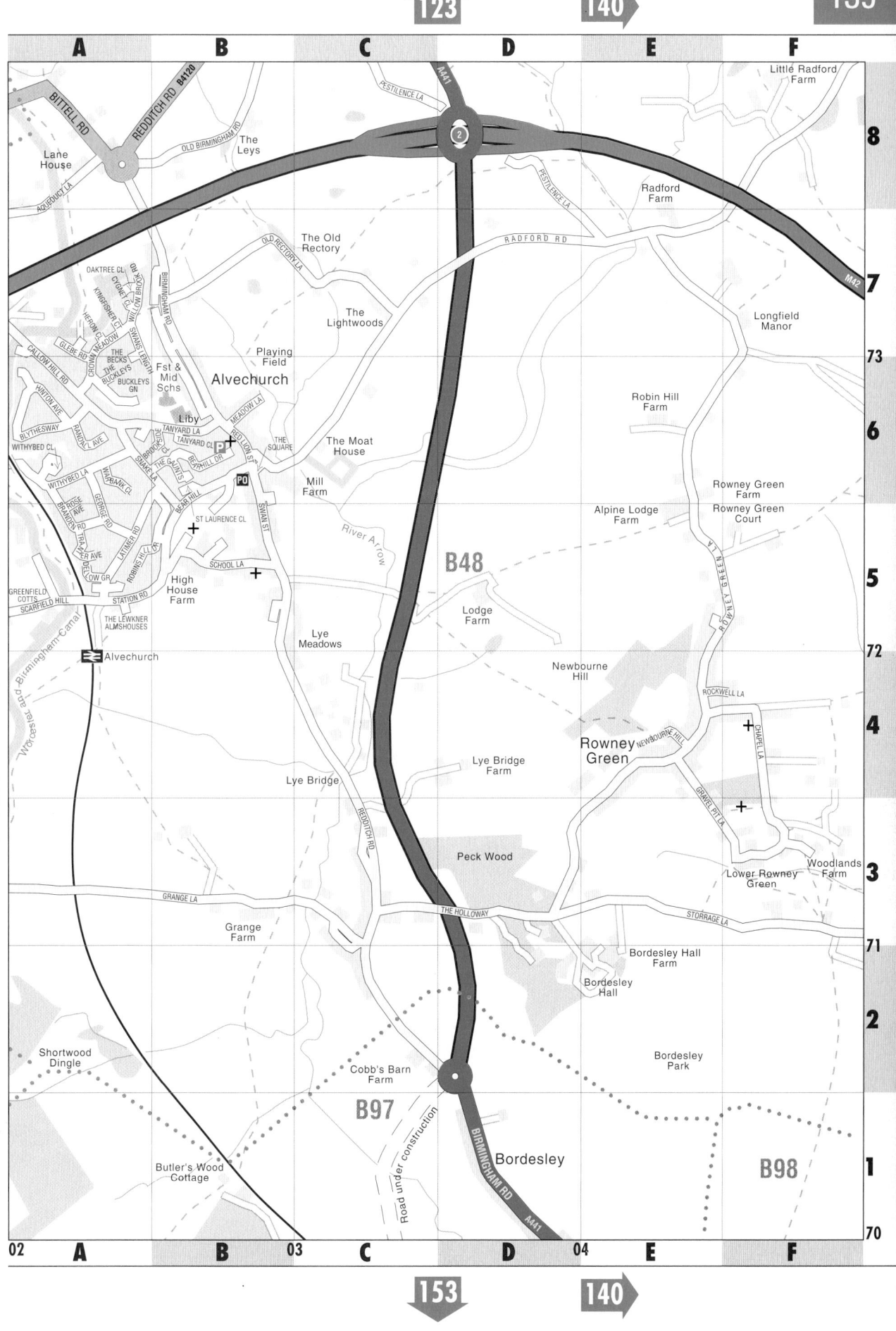

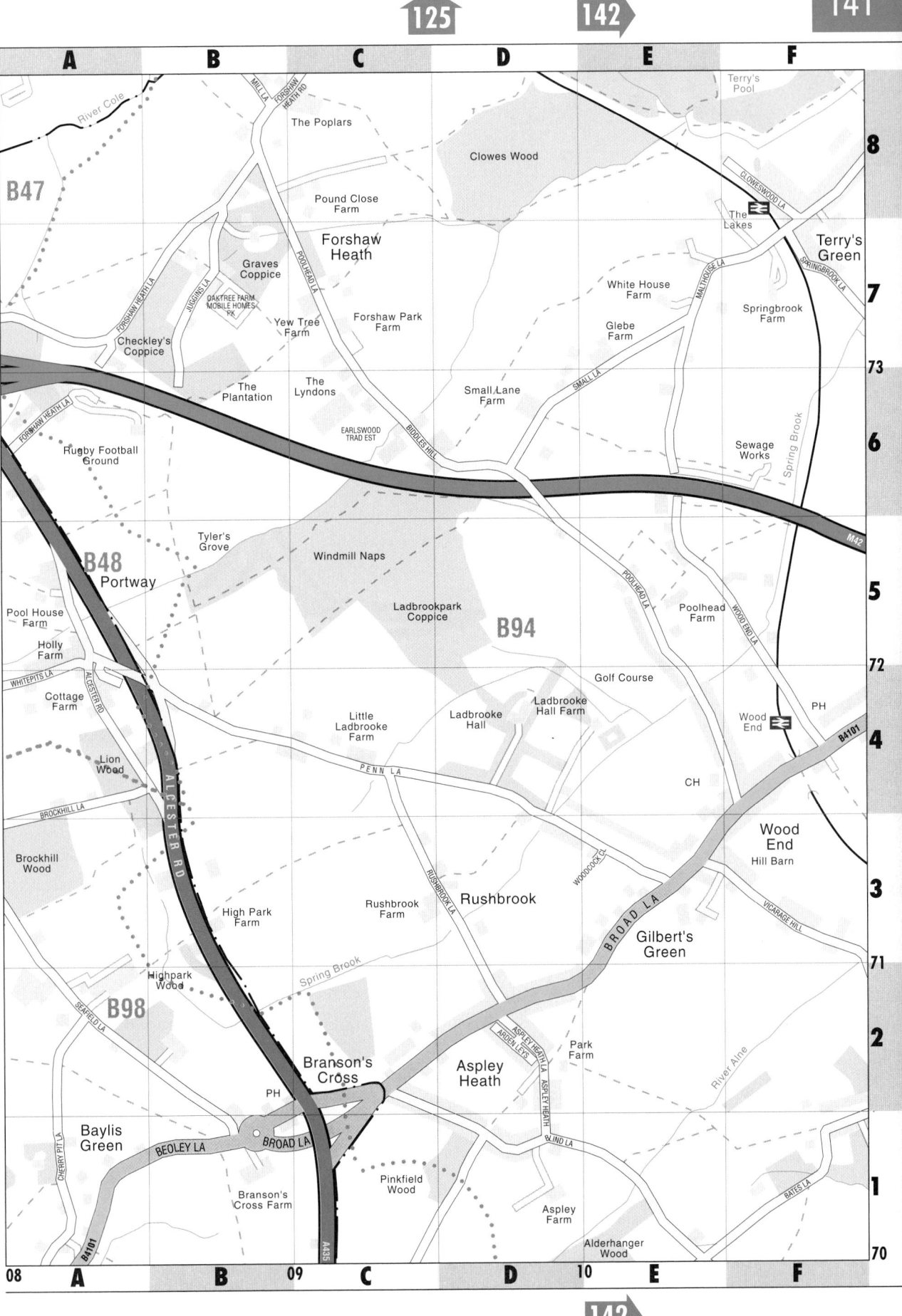

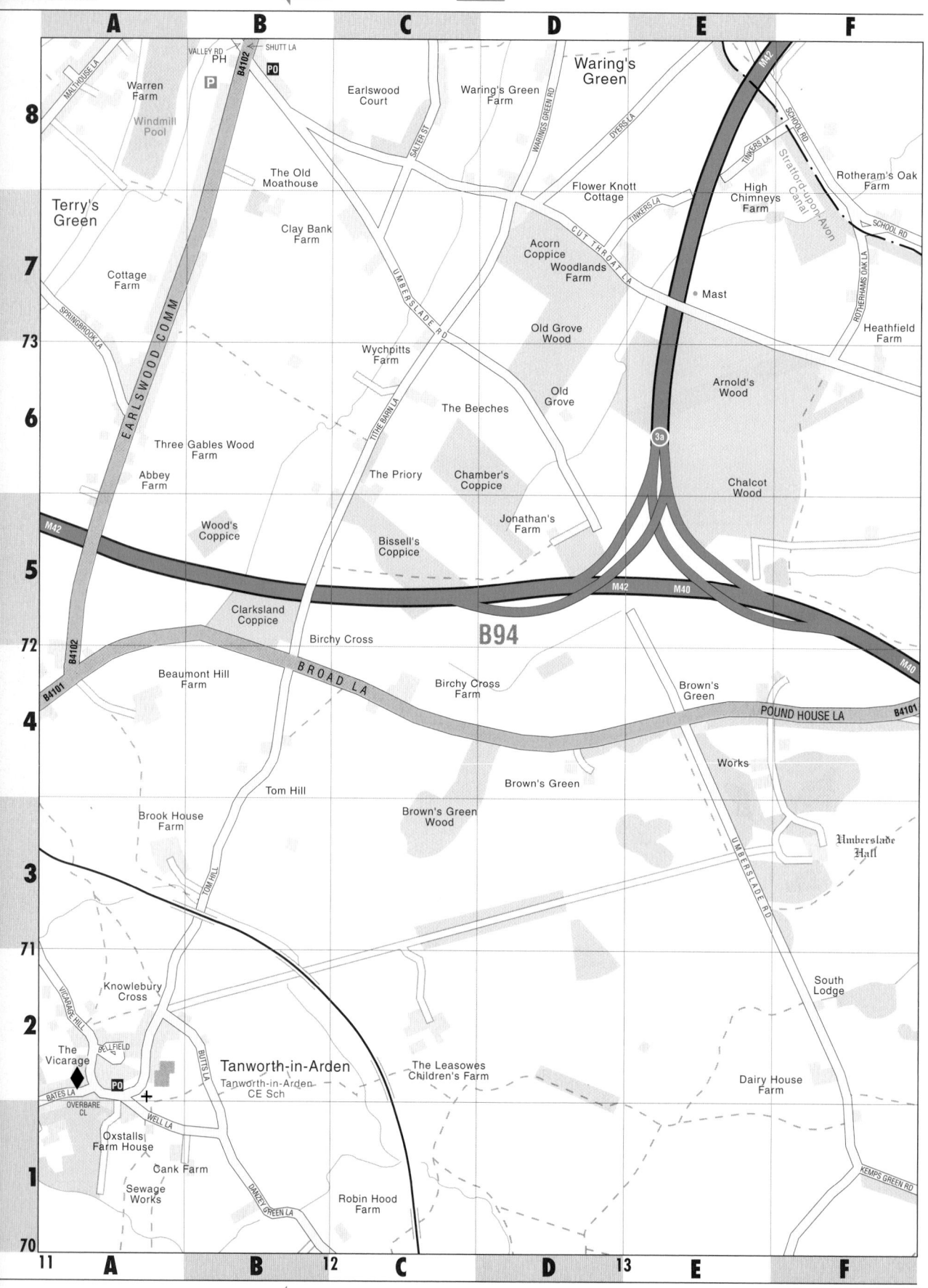

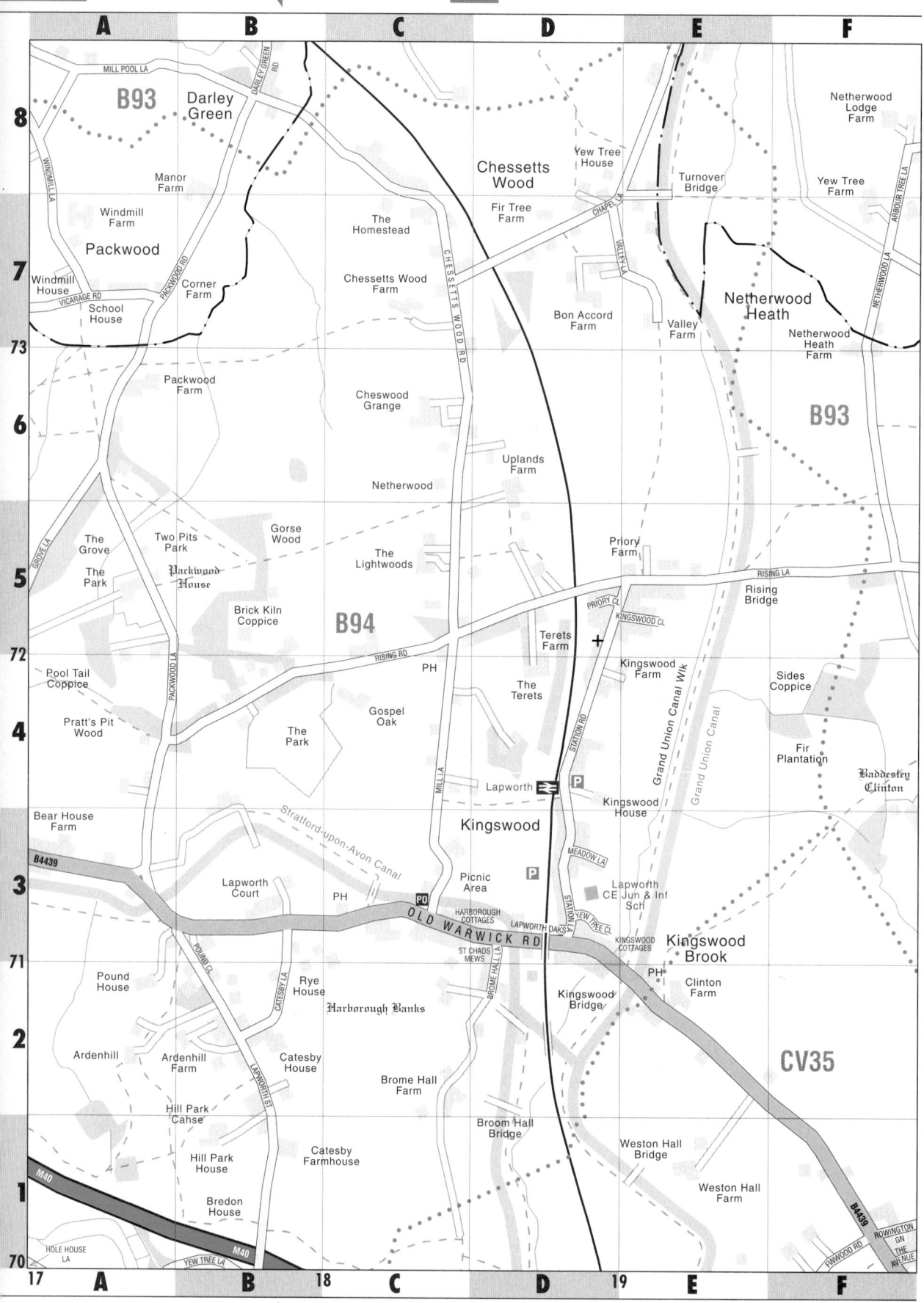

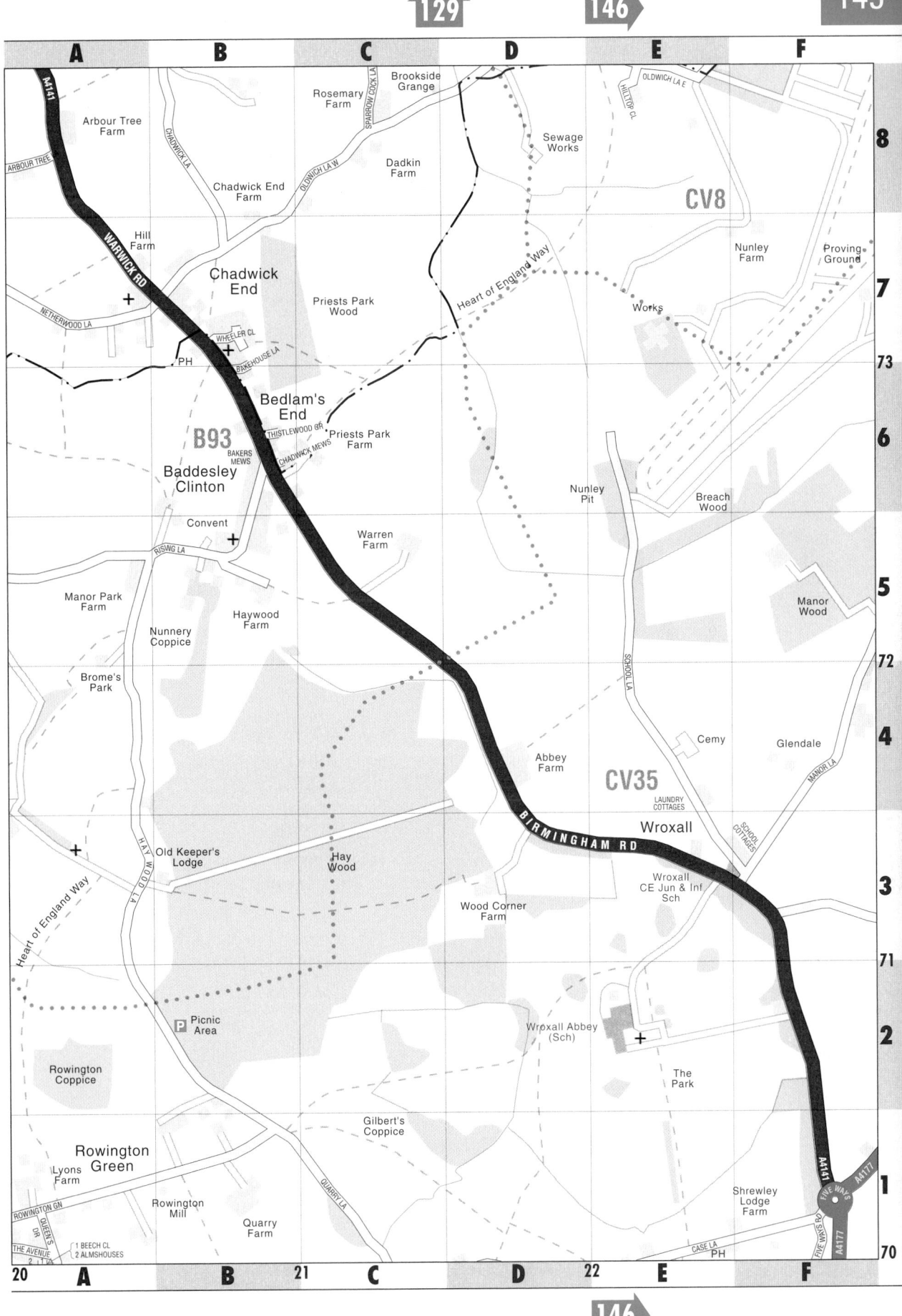

145
130

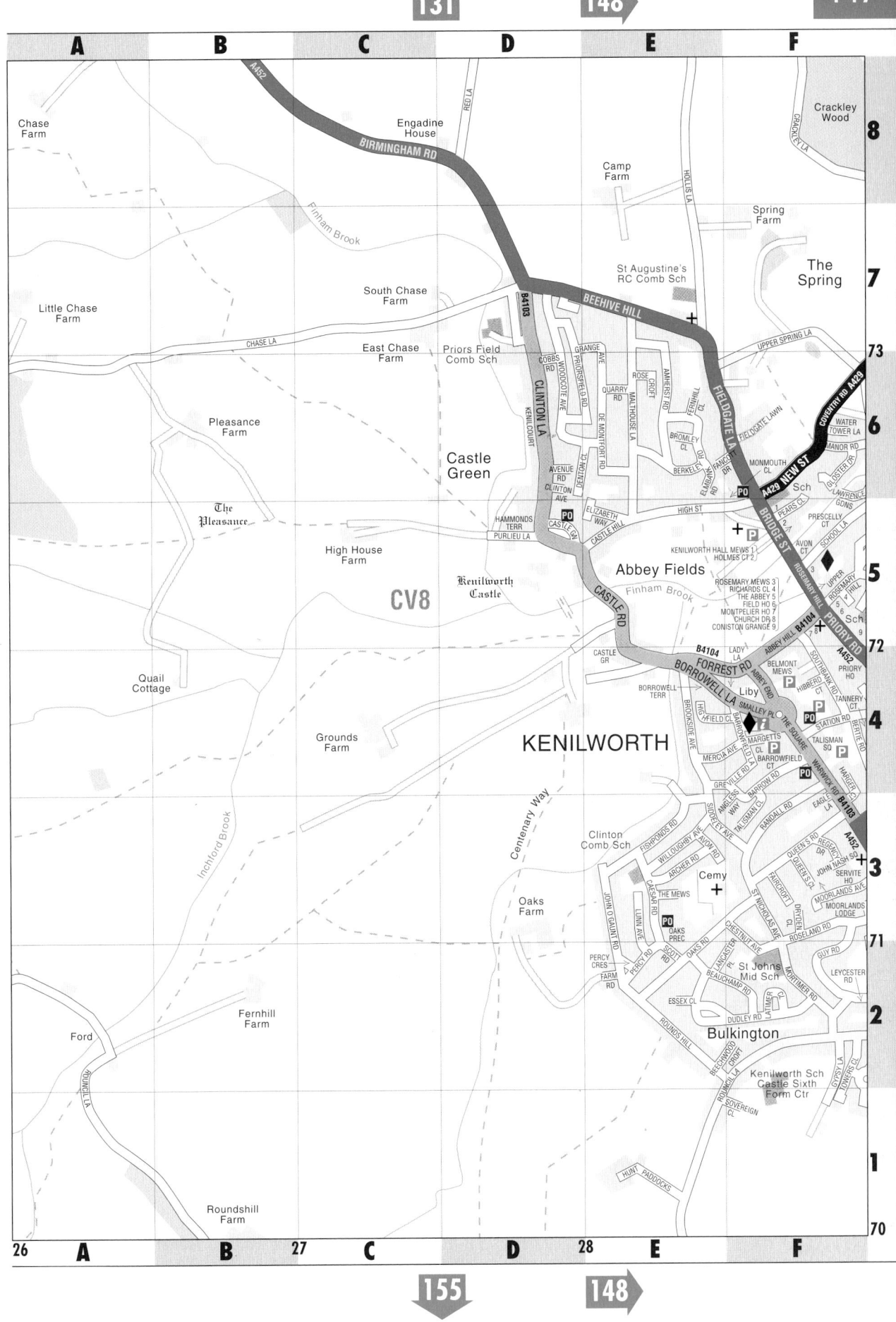

A B C D E F

Crackley Wood

Chase Farm

Engadine House

BIRMINGHAM RD

A452

Finham Brook

RED LA

Camp Farm

HOLLIS LA

Spring Farm

CRACKLEY LA

8

South Chase Farm

St Augustine's RC Comb Sch

The Spring

7

Little Chase Farm

CHASE LA

East Chase Farm

Priors Field Comb Sch

BEEHIVE HILL

B4103

Upper Spring La

UPPER SPRING LA

73

Pleasance Farm

Castle Green

COBBS RD

WOODCOTE AVE

PRIORSFIELD RD

GRANGE AVE

AMHERST RD

Rose Croft

FERNHILL

FIELDGATE LA

FIELDGATE LAWN

COVENTRY RD A429

6

CLINTON LA

KENILCOURT

QUARRY RD

MALTHOUSE LA

BROMLEY CL

DE MONTFORT RD

ELMBANK

FANCOTT DR

MONMOUTH CL

A429 NEW ST

Sch

WATER TOWER LA

MANOR RD

GLOUCESTER DR

The Pleasance

AVENUE RD

CLINTON AVE

BERKELEY

PO

LAWRENCE GDNS

72

High House Farm

HAMMONDS TERR

PURLIEU LA

PO

CASTLE GR

ELIZABETH WAY

CASTLE HILL

HIGH ST

BRIDGE ST

PEARS CL

PRESCELLY CT

AVON CT

SCHOOL LA

CV8

Kenilworth Castle

CASTLE RD

Finham Brook

Abbey Fields

KENILWORTH HALL MEWS 1
HOLMES CT 2

ROSEMARY MEWS 3
RICHARDS CL 4
THE ABBEY 5
FIELD HO 6
MONTPELIER HO 7
CHURCH DR 8
CONISTON GRANGE 9

ROSEMARY HILL

UPPER ROSEMARY HILL

Sch

5

CASTLE GR

CASTLE LA

LADY LA

B4104

ABBEY END

ABBEY HILL

B4104

PRIORY RD

A452

72

Quail Cottage

FORREST RD

BORROWELL LA

Libr

BELMONT MEWS

HIBBERD

SOUTHBANK RD

Priory Ho

PRIORY HO

TANNERY CT

4

BORROWELL TERR

BROOKSIDE AVE

HIGH FIELD CL

SMALLEY PL

THE SQUARE

BARROWELL

MERCIA AVE

MARGETTS

PO

STATION RD

BERTIE RD

Grounds Farm

KENILWORTH

ANGLESEY WAY

GREVILLE RD

BARROWFIELD

BARROW RD

TALISMAN CL

PO

WARWICK RD

TALISMAN SQ

HARGER CT

B4103

A452

Cenenary Way

Oaks Farm

Clinton Comb Sch

FISHPONDS RD

WILLOUGHBY AVE

ARCHER RD

AVON RD

SUDELEY AVE

Cemy

RANDALL RD

QUEEN S RD

QUEEN S CL

REGENT CL

DRYDEN

JOHN NASH SQ

MOORLANDS AVE

SERVITE HO

MOORLANDS LODGE

3

JOHN O GAUNT RD

CAESAR RD

LUNN AVE

THE MEWS

ST NICHOLAS AVE

ST NICHOLAS CL

FAIRCROFT

ROSELAND RD

71

PO

OAKS PREC

CHESTNUT LA

GUY RD

Ford

PERCY CRES

FARM RD

PERCY RD

SCOTT RD

OAKS RD

LANCASTER RD

BEAUCHAMP RD

LATIMER

St Johns Mid Sch

MORTIMER RD

LEYCESTER RD

2

Fernhill Farm

ROUNCIL LA

ESSEX CL

ROUNDS HILL

DUDLEY RD

Bulkington

BRECKWOOD CROFT

ROUNCIL LA

SOVEREIGN CL

Kenilworth Sch Castle Sixth Form Ctr

GYPSY LA

TOWERS CL

1

Roundshill Farm

HUNT PADDOCKS

70

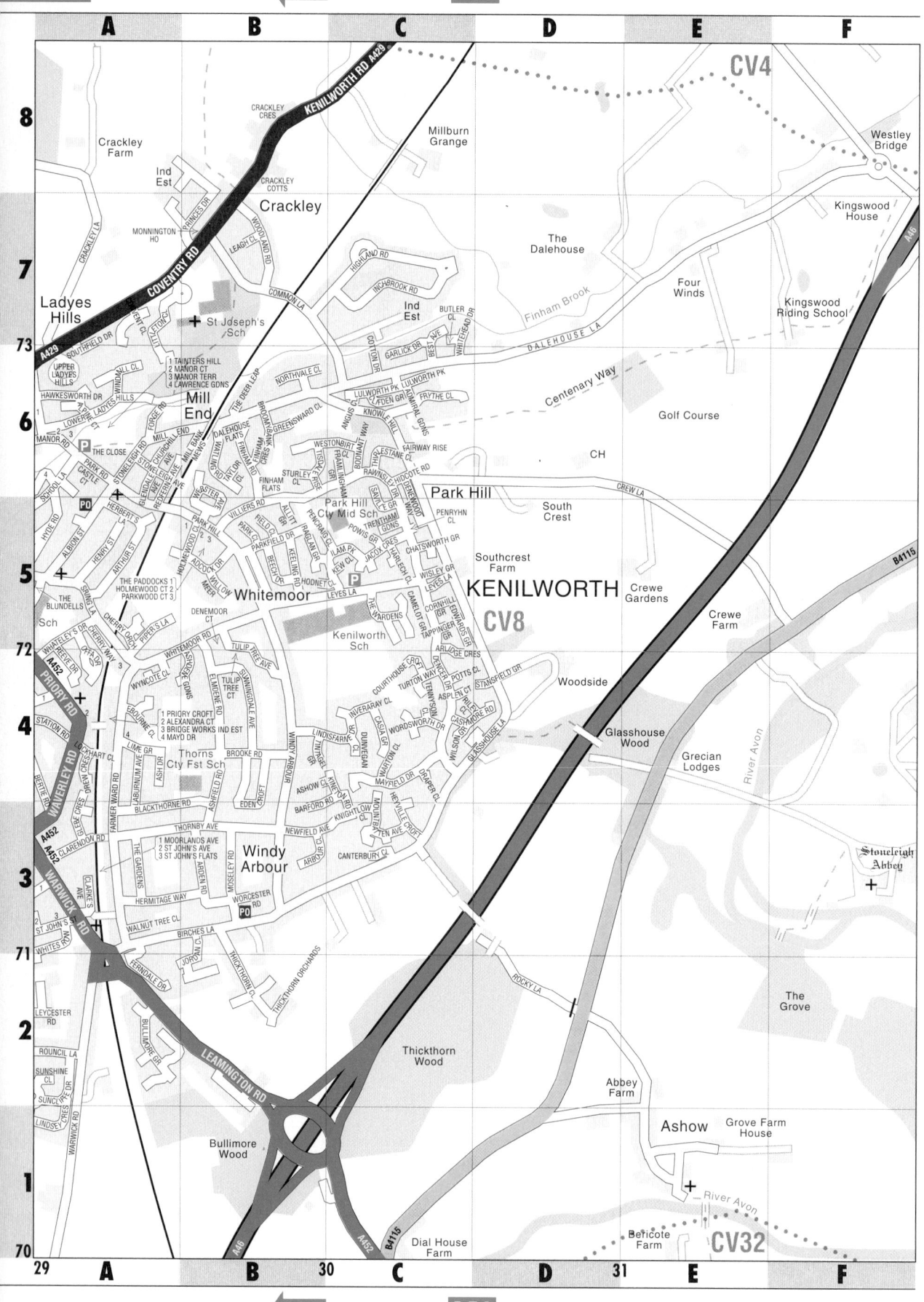

133

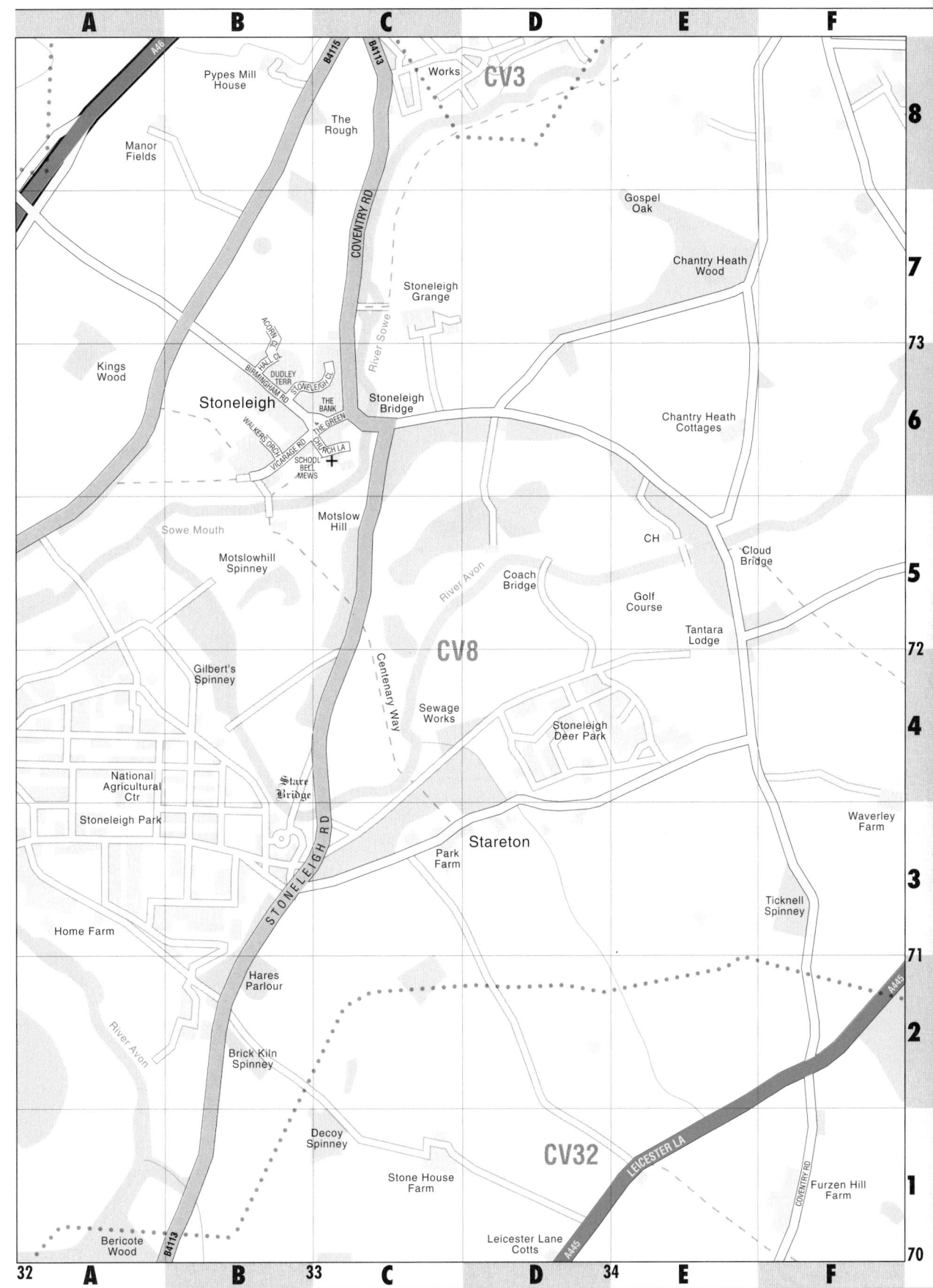

| | A | B | C | D | E | F |

157

Pypes Mill House

Works

CV3

The Rough

Manor Fields

Gospel Oak

Chantry Heath Wood

COVENTRY RD

B4115

B4113

Stoneleigh Grange

River Sowe

Kings Wood

73

Chantry Heath Cottages

ACORN CL

HALL CL

DUDLEY TERR

BIRMINGHAM RD

STONELEIGH CL

Stoneleigh

THE BANK

Stoneleigh Bridge

6

WALKERS ORCH

VICARAGE RD

THE GREEN

CHURCH LA

SCHOOL BELL MEWS

CH

Cloud Bridge

Sowe Mouth

Motslow Hill

Motslowhill Spinney

River Avon

Coach Bridge

Golf Course

5

CV8

Tantara Lodge

72

Gilbert's Spinney

Centenary Way

Sewage Works

Stoneleigh Deer Park

4

National Agricultural Ctr

Stoneleigh Park

Starr Bridge

STONELEIGH RD

Waverley Farm

3

Home Farm

Park Farm

Stareton

Ticknell Spinney

Hares Parlour

71

River Avon

A445

2

Brick Kiln Spinney

LEICESTER LA

COVENTRY RD

Decoy Spinney

CV32

Furzen Hill Farm

1

Stone House Farm

Bericote Wood

B4113

Leicester Lane Cotts

A445

70

| 32 | A | B | 33 | C | D | 34 | E | F |

136

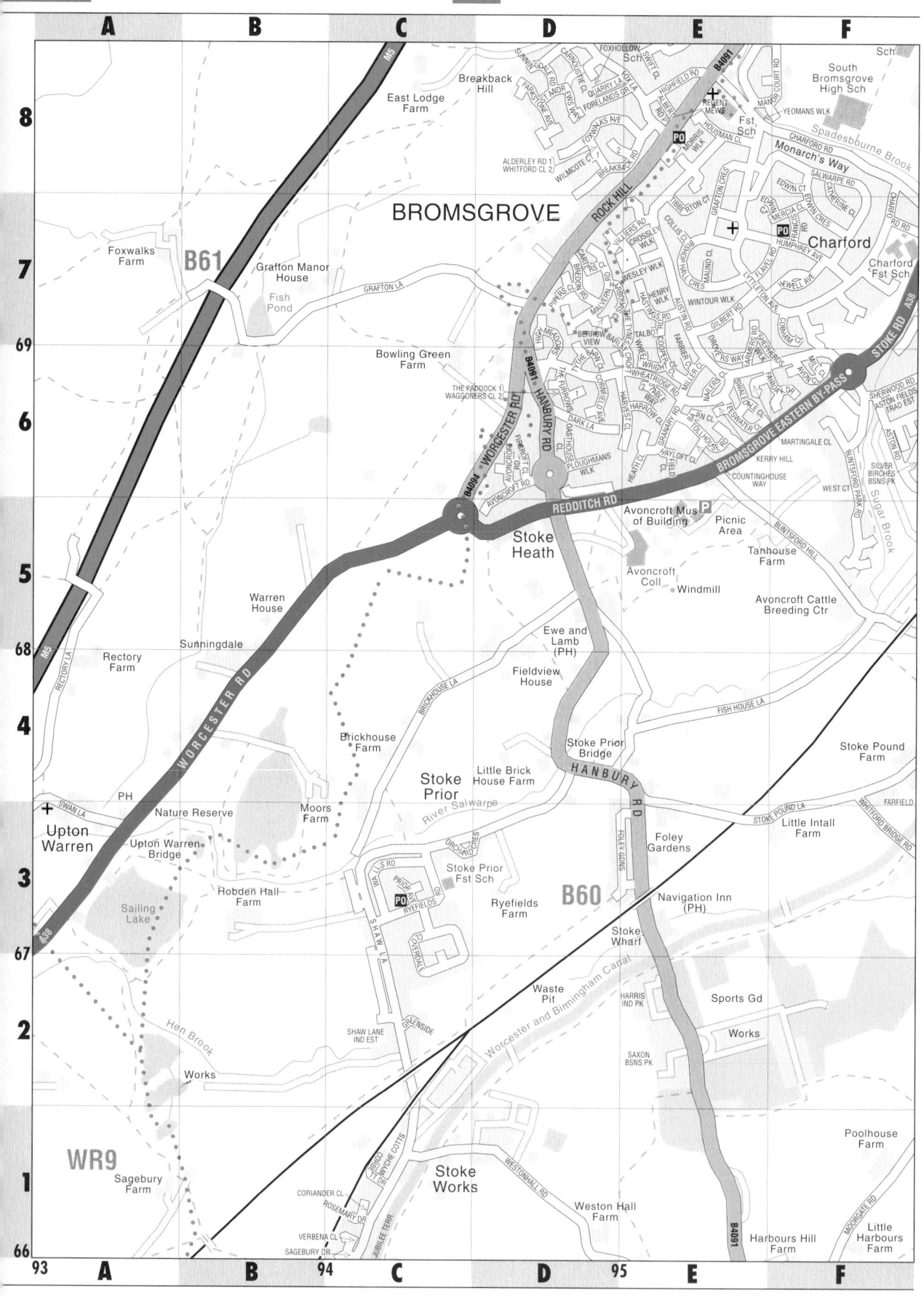

BROMSGROVE

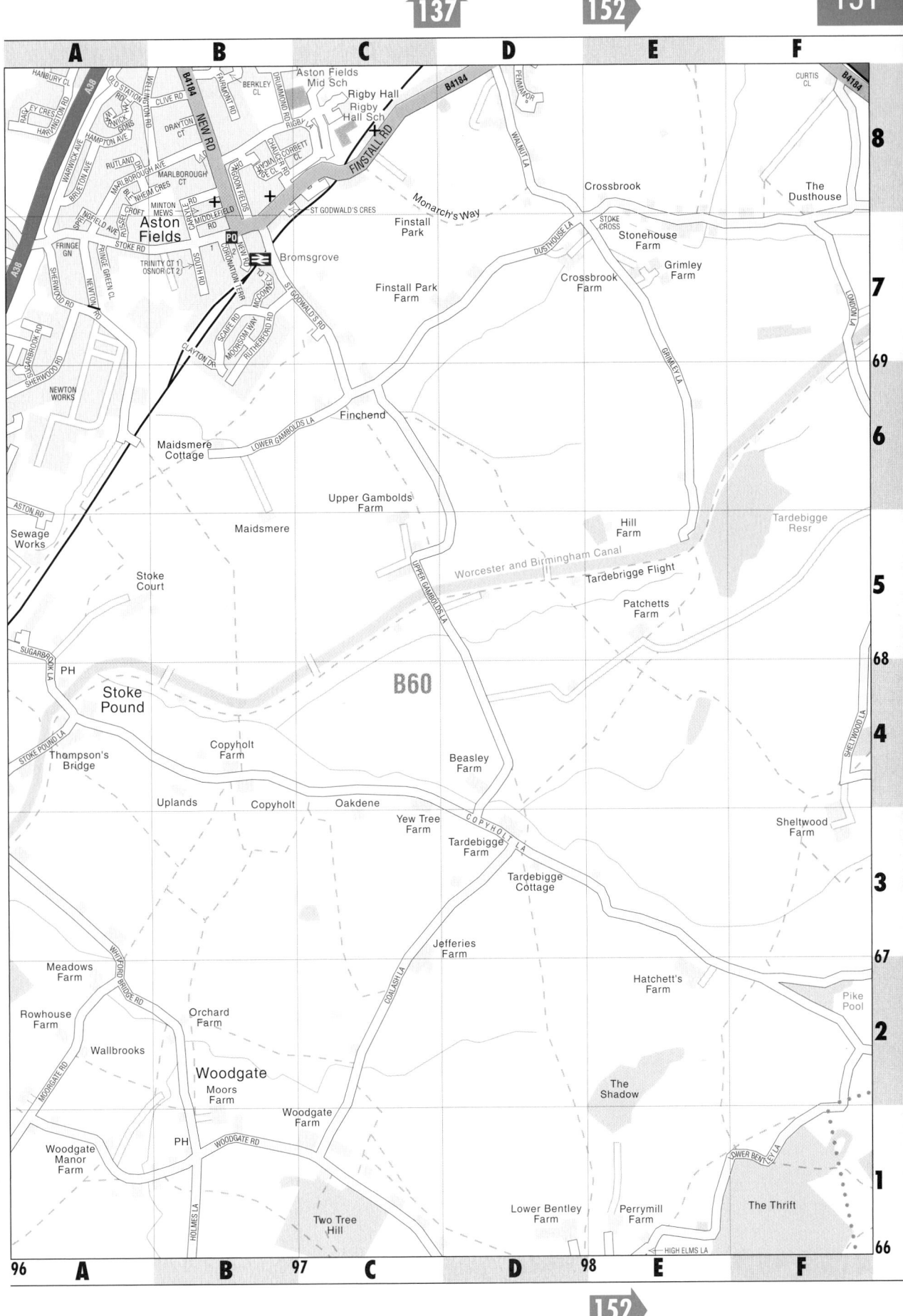

137
152
152

A B C D E F

8
7
69
6
5
68
4
3
67
2
1
66

HANBURY CL
RACEY CRES
HARRINGTON RD
OLD STATION RD
WELLINGTON RD
CLIVE RD
WICK
GDNS
HAMPTON AVE
WARWICK AVE
BRIXETON ST
RESSER
RD
RUTLAND
MARLBOROUGH AVE
NIHEIM CRES
CROFT
MINTON
CL
MIDDLEFIELD
RD
SPR
NGFIELD AVE
STOKE RD
RANGE GREEN CL
FRINGE
GN
NEWTON RD
SHERWOOD RD
SUGARBROOK RD
SHERWOOD RD
NEWTON
WORKS

A38
OLD STATION RD
B4184
NEW RD
BERKLEY
CL
FAIRMONT RD
DRUMMOND RD
RIGBY
DRAYTON
CT
MARLBOROUGH
CT
RECON FIELDS
CHALENCE RD
CORBETT
CL
CHALENCE CL
CORBETT CL
ST GODWALD'S CRES
Aston Fields
Mid Sch
Rigby Hall
Rigby
Hall Sch
FINSTALL RD
B4184
CURTIS
CL
B4184
PENNMAOR
WALNUT LA

Aston
Fields
PO
Bromsgrove
TRINITY CT 1
OSNOR CT 2
SOUTH RD
CORONATION TERR
NEWTON ST
MCCORM
SCAIFE RD
MIDROSM WAY
RUTHERFORD RD
ST GODWALD'S RD
CLAYTON DR

Monarch's Way
Finstall
Park
Finstall Park
Farm
Crossbrook
Stoke
Cross
DUSTHOUSE LA
Stonehouse
Farm
The
Dusthouse
Crossbrook
Farm
Grimley
Farm
GRIMLEY LA
LONDON LA

Finchend
LOWER GAMBOLDS LA
Maidsmere
Cottage
Upper Gambolds
Farm
Maidsmere
Hill
Farm
Tardebigge
Resr

ASTON RD
Sewage
Works
Stoke
Court
UPPER GAMBOLDS LA
Worcester and Birmingham Canal
Tardebrigge Flight
Patchetts
Farm

SUGARBRINK LA
PH
Stoke
Pound
B60
68
SHELTWOOD LA

STOKE POUND LA
Thompson's
Bridge
Copyholt
Farm
Beasley
Farm
Sheltwood
Farm

Uplands
Copyholt
Oakdene
Yew Tree
Farm
Tardebigge
Farm
COPYHOLT LA

WHITFORD BRIDGE RD
Meadows
Farm
Tardebigge
Cottage
Jefferies
Farm
COALASH LA
Hatchett's
Farm
Pike
Pool

Rowhouse
Farm
Orchard
Farm
MOORGATE RD
Wallbrooks
Woodgate
Moors
Farm
Woodgate
Farm
The
Shadow

Woodgate
Manor
Farm
PH
WOODGATE RD
HOLMES LA
Two Tree
Hill
Lower Bentley
Farm
LOWER BENTLEY LA
Perrymill
Farm
The Thrift
HIGH ELMS LA

151
138

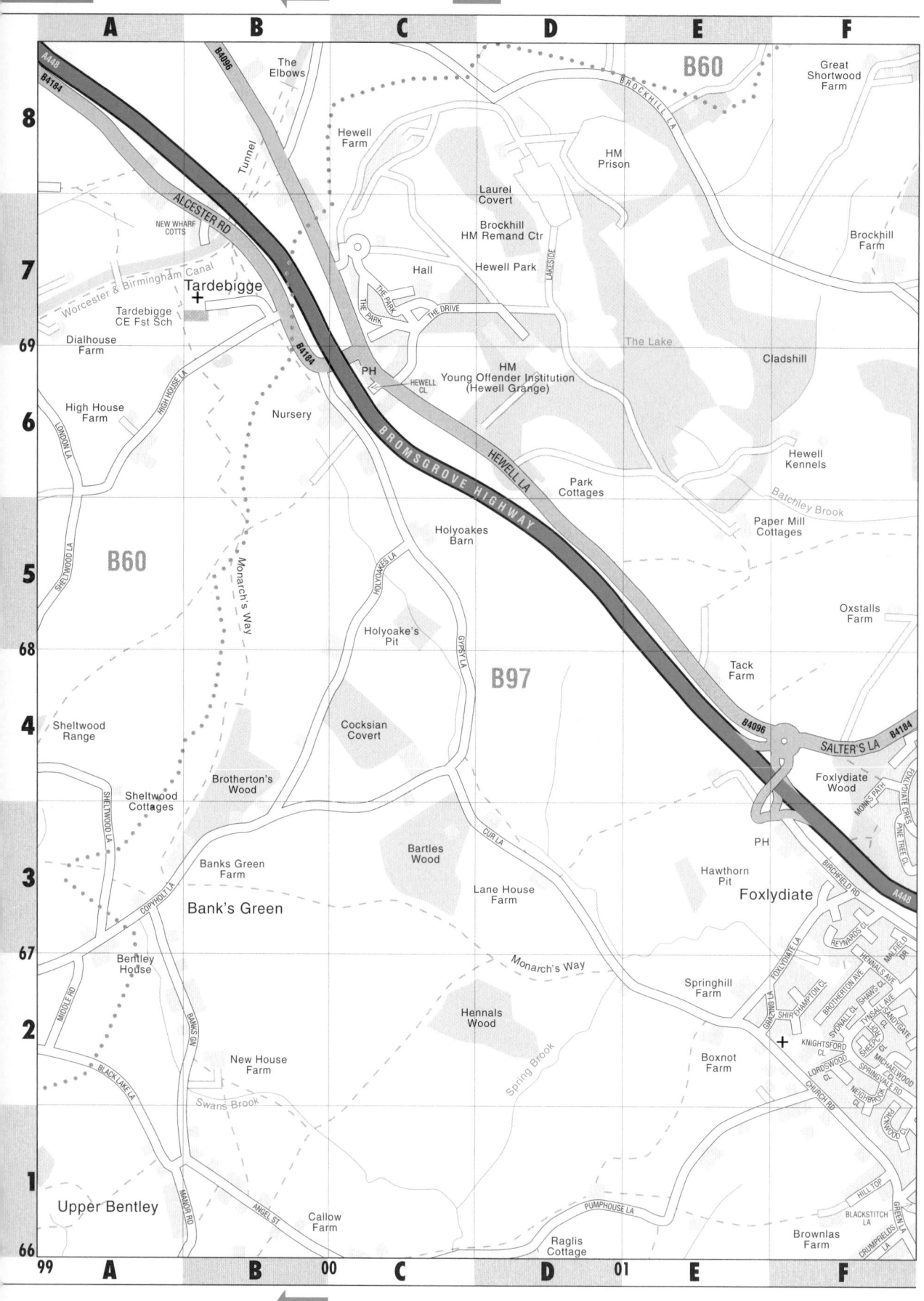

151

Column headers (top): A B C D E F

Column headers (bottom): 99 A B 00 C D 01 E F

Row labels: 8 7 69 6 5 68 4 67 3 2 66 1

B60

Great Shortwood Farm

The Elbows

Hewell Farm

HM Prison

Brockhill Farm

A448
B4184
B4096

Tunnel

ALCESTER RD

NEW WHARF COTTS

Laurel Covert

Brockhill HM Remand Ctr

Worcester & Birmingham Canal

Tardebigge
Tardebigge CE Fst Sch

Hall

Hewell Park

LAKESIDE

BROCKHILL LA

Dialhouse Farm

B4184

PH

HEWELL CL

HM Young Offender Institution (Hewell Grange)

The Lake

Cladshill

High House Farm

HIGH HOUSE LA

Nursery

Park Cottages

BROMSGROVE HIGHWAY

HEWELL LA

Hewell Kennels

Batchley Brook

Paper Mill Cottages

B60

Monarch's Way

SHELTWOOD LA
LONDON LA

HOLYOAKES LA

Holyoakes Barn

GYPSY LA

B97

Oxstalls Farm

Holyoake's Pit

Tack Farm

B4096

SALTER'S LA
B4184

Sheltwood Range

Cocksian Covert

Foxlydiate Wood

FOXLYDIATE CRES
PINE TREE CL
MOWS PATH

Brotherton's Wood

Sheltwood Cottages

SHELTWOOD LA

Banks Green Farm

Bartles Wood

CUR LA

PH

Hawthorn Pit

Foxlydiate

BIRCHFIELD RD
A448

Banks Green

COPYHOLT LA

Lane House Farm

Monarch's Way

Springhill Farm

REYNARDS CL
HENNALS LA
ANFIELD
HENNALS AVE

MIDDLE RD

Bentley House

BANKS GN

Hennals Wood

FOXLYDIATE LA
GRAFTON LA
SHIPHAMPTON CL
BROTHERTON AVE
TYNSALL AVE
SYDNALL CL
ISHAD'S CL
SANDYGATE
GREEN CL

Springhill

New House Farm

Spring Brook

Boxnot Farm

KNIGHTSFORD CL
LORDSWOOD CL
MICHAELWOOD
SPRINGVALE CL
NEIGHBROOK CL
HILL TOP

Upper Bentley

BLACK LAKE LA

MANOR RD
ANGEL ST

Swans Brook

Callow Farm

PUMPHOUSE LA

Raglis Cottage

Brownlas Farm

BLACKSTITCH LA
CRUMPFIELDS LA
CHURCH RD

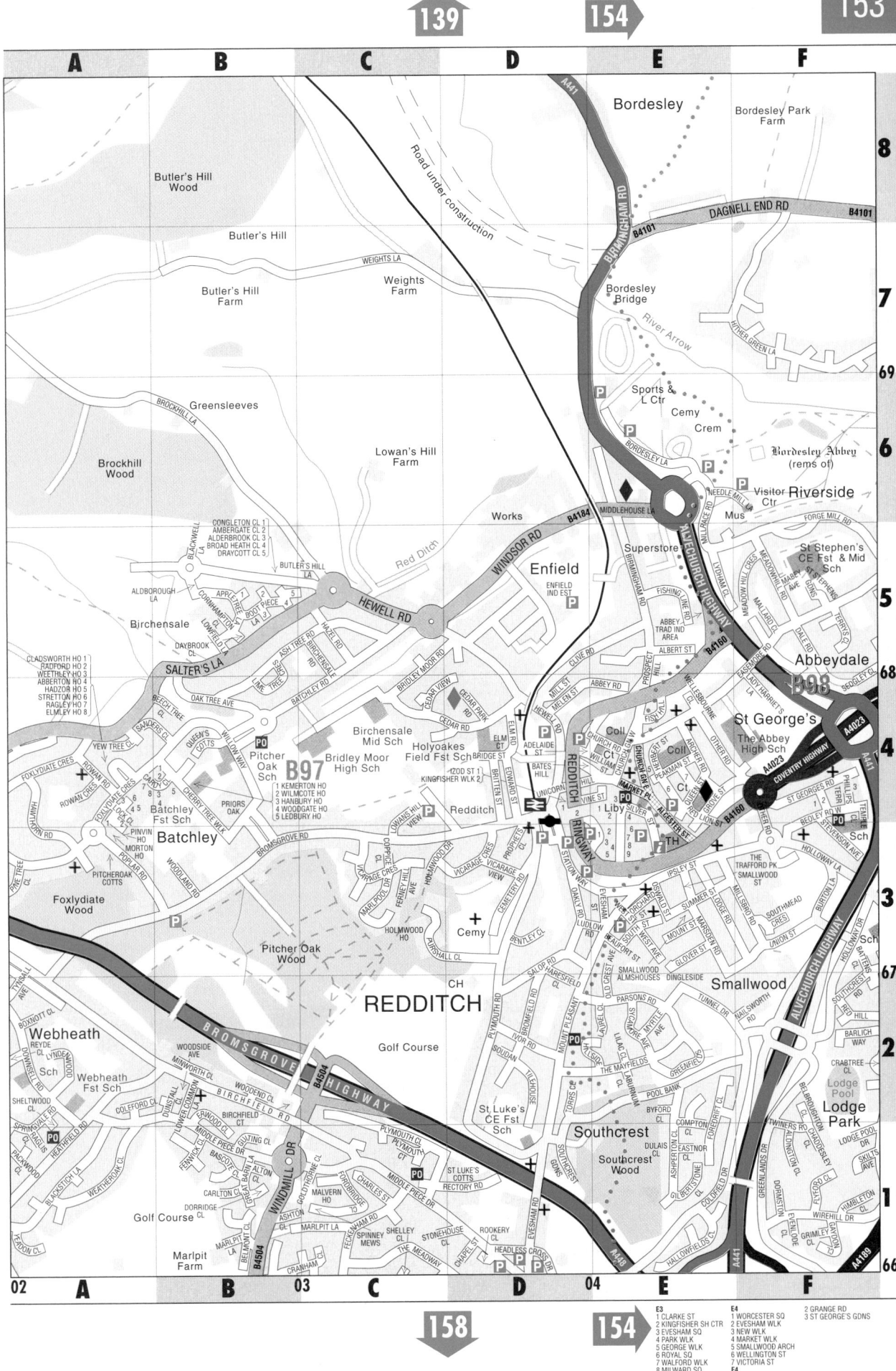

Bordesley

Bordesley Park Farm

DAGNELL END RD
B4101

B4101

Bordesley Bridge

River Arrow

HITHER GREEN LA

8

7

69

6

Butler's Hill Wood

Butler's Hill

WEIGHTS LA

Weights Farm

Greensleeves

BROCKHILL LA

Lowan's Hill Farm

Brockhill Wood

Road under construction

BIRMINGHAM RD

Sports & L Ctr

Cemy
Crem

Bordesley Abbey
(rems of)

Visitor
Ctr   Riverside

BORDESLEY LA

NEEDLE MILL LA

MIDDLEHOUSE LA

Mus

CONGLETON CL 1
AMBERGATE CL 2
ALDERBROOK CL 3
BROAD HEATH CL 4
DRAYCOTT CL 5

BLACKWELL

Works

WINDSOR RD
B4184

Red Ditch

Enfield

ENFIELD IND EST

Superstore

St Stephen's
CE Fst & Mid
Sch

5

68

ALVECHURCH HIGHWAY

Abbey
Trad Ind
Area

MILDRED RD

MEADOW RD

FORGE MILL RD

Aldborough
La

CORNHAMPTON

APPLETREE LA

BOOT PIECE

Butler's Hill
La

HEWELL RD

ALBERT ST

B4160

B98

Abbeydale

Birchensale

DAYBROOK CL

SALTER'S LA

CLADSWORTH HO 1
RADFORD HO 2
WEETHLEY HO 3
ABBERTON HO 4
HADZOR HO 5
STRETTON HO 6
RAGLEY HO 7
ELMLEY HO 8

BEECH TREE CL

OAK TREE AVE

ASH TREE RD

HAZEL RD

BIRCHENSALE RD

BATCHLEY RD

BRIDLEY MOOR RD

CEDAR VIEW

CEDAR PARK

CEDAR RD

Birchensale
Mid Sch

Holyoakes
Field Fst Sch

ELM RD

BRIDGE ST

IZOD ST 1
KINGFISHER WLK 2

MILL ST

HEWELL RD

ABBEY RD

PROSPECT HILL

Fish'g

Coll

A4023

A4041

St George's

The Abbey
High Sch

A4023

4

YEW TREE CL

FOXLYDIATE CRES

ROWAN CRES

SANDERS CL

QUEEN'S
COTTS

WILLOW WAY

Pitcher
Oak Sch

B97

1 KEMERTON HO
2 WILMCOTE HO
3 HANBURY HO
4 WOODGATE HO
5 LEDBURY HO

Bridley Moor
High Sch

LOWANS HILL VIEW

Redditch

ADELAIDE ST

BATES HILL

EDWARD ST

BRITTEN ST

UNICORN
HILL

PRIORS
OAK

CHERRY TREE WAY

Batchley
Fst Sch

Ct

CHURCH RD

PEAKMAN ST

Coll

The Trafford Pk

SMALLWOOD

COVENTRY HIGHWAY

B4160

HAWTHORN RD

PINE TREE CL

PINVIN HO
MORTON HO

Pitcheroak
Cotts

Batchley

PRIORS
OAK

WOODLAND RD

BROMSGROVE RD

COPPICE CL

VICARAGE CRES

HOMEWOOD DR

VICARAGE VIEW

STATION WAY

DAILY RD

IPSLEY ST

OSWALD ST

SMALLWOOD
CRES

MILL SBRO RD

SMITHMEAD

UNION ST

BURTON LA

Smallwood

3

67

Foxlydiate
Wood

Pitcher Oak
Wood

CH

REDDITCH

COPPICE
CL

FERNEY HILL
AVE

HOLMWOOD
HO

AUSHALL CL

Cemy

BENTLEY CL

PLYMOUTH RD

SALOP RD

HAREFIELD RD

Smallwood
Almshouses

PARSONS RD

Dingleside

TUNNEL DR

NAILSWORTH
RD

HOLLOWAY LA

STEVENSON AVE

Sch

BATENS
CL

SOUTHCREST
RD

BARLICH
WAY

CRABTREE
CL

Lodge
Pool

Lodge
Park

2

66

Webheath

REYDE
CL

DOWNSEL RD

Sch

LYNDENWOOD

Webheath
Fst Sch

MINWORTH CL

BROMSGROVE HIGHWAY

B4504

Woodside
Ave

BIRCHFIELD CL

WOODEND CL

Golf Course

St Luke's
CE Fst
Sch

Southcrest

Southcrest
Wood

POOL BANK

BYFORD
CL

COMPTON
CL

CASTNOR
CL

DULAIS
CL

ASHPERTON
CL

GILBERTSTONE
CL

COLDFIELD
CL

GREENLANDS DR

DORNASTON CL

ALDINGTON
CL

EVENLODE
CL

HIMBLETON
DR

WIREHILL DR

GRIMLEY
CL

SKILTS
AVE

LODGE POOL
DR

CHADESLEY
RD

TWINERS
RD

BELBROUGHTON
CL

A4189

SHELTWOOD
CL

SPRINGVALE RD

PACKWOOD CL

HEATHFIELD RD

COLDFORD CL

DUNSTALL
CL

BLACKSTICK CL

WEATHEROAK CL

LOWER COMMON

ELWOOD CL

FENNY CL

BASCOTE CL

GREAT BARR LA

CARLTON CL

WINDMILL DR

ALTON CL

MIDDLE PIECE DR

FOXBRIDGE

CHARLES ST

MALVERN HO

ASHTON

MARLPIT LA

PLYMOUTH CL

PLYMOUTH
CT

FECKENHAM RD

SHELLEY
CL

SPINNEY
MEWS

THE MEADWAY

STONEHOUSE
CL

ROOKERY
CL

St Luke's
Cotts

RECTORY RD

HEADLESS CROSS DR

HALLOWFIELDS CL

EVESHAM RD

A441

A448

1

Golf Course
CL

DORRIDGE
CL

Marlpit
Farm

MARLPIT
LA

BELMONT CL

B4504

CRANHAM CL

E3
1 CLARKE ST
2 KINGFISHER SH CTR
3 EVESHAM SQ
4 PARK WLK
5 GEORGE WLK
6 ROYAL SQ
7 WALFORD WLK
8 MILWARD SQ
9 EVESHAM MEWS

E4
1 WORCESTER SQ
2 EVESHAM WLK
3 NEW WLK
4 MARKET WLK
5 SMALLWOOD ARCH
6 WELLINGTON ST
7 VICTORIA ST
F4
1 GRANGE CT

2 GRANGE RD
3 ST GEORGE'S GDNS

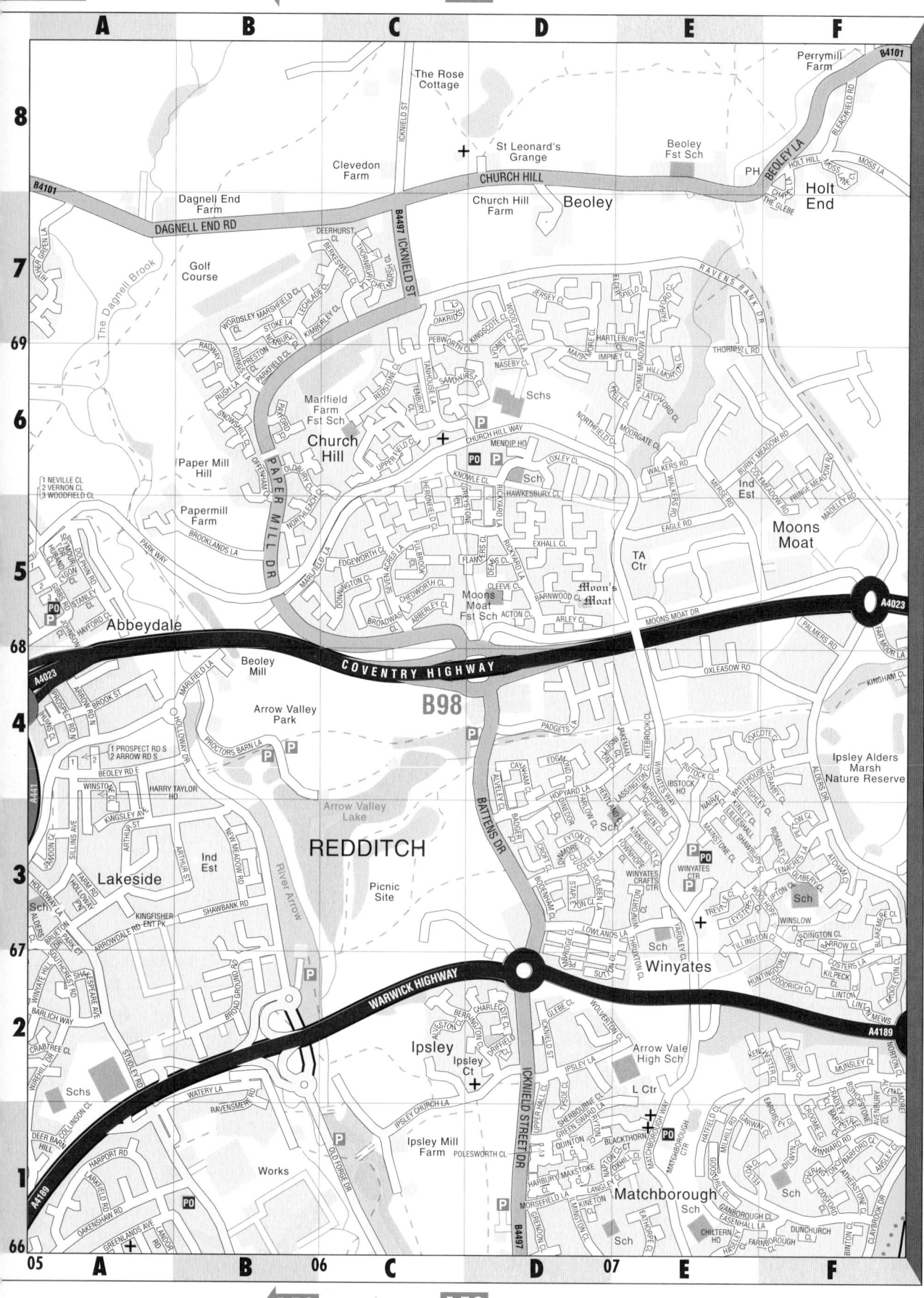

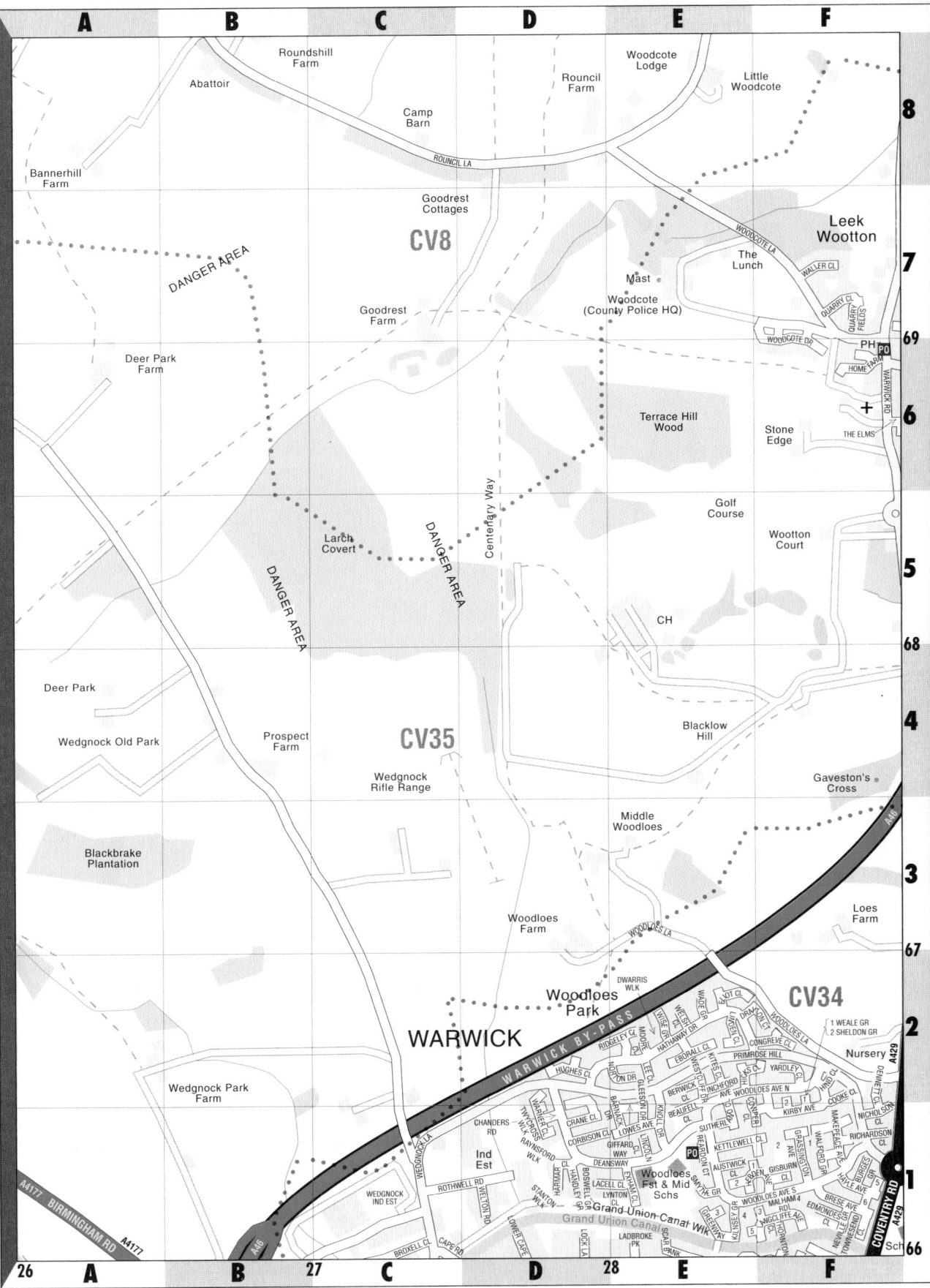

A B C D E F

8

Roundshill Farm
Abattoir
Camp Barn
Rouncil Farm
Woodcote Lodge
Little Woodcote

Bannerhill Farm
ROUNCIL LA

Leek Wootton

CV8
Goodrest Cottages

DANGER AREA

WOODCOTE LA

WALLER CL

The Lunch

7

69

Mast
Woodcote (County Police HQ)

WOODCOTE DR

QUARRY CL
QUARRY
SOUTH FIELDS

PH PO
HOME FARM
WARWICK RD

Deer Park Farm

Goodrest Farm

Terrace Hill Wood

Stone Edge

6

THE ELMS

Larch Covert

DANGER AREA

Centenary Way

DANGER AREA

Golf Course

Wootton Court

5

68

DANGER AREA

CH

Deer Park

CV35

Blacklow Hill

4

Wedgnock Old Park

Prospect Farm

Wedgnock Rifle Range

Gaveston's Cross

A46

Middle Woodloes

Blackbrake Plantation

3

Loes Farm

67

Woodloes Farm

WOODLOES LA

CV34

DWARRIS WLK

Woodloes Park

WARWICK

WARWICK BY-PASS

1 Weale Gr
2 Sheldon Gr

2

Nursery

A429

DENNETT CL

Primrose Hill
Woodloes Ave N

Woodloes Ave

Kirby Ave

Ind Est
WEDGNOCK IND EST

CHANDERS RD

ROTHWELL RD

WELTON RD

BROXELL CL

CAPE RD

LOWER CAPE

LOCK LA

Woodloes Fst & Mid Schs
PO

Woodloes Ave S

Grand Union Canal Wlk
Grand Union Canal

LADBROKE PK

SPA BANK

Coventry Rd
A429
Sch

1

66

26 A B 27 C D 28 E F

E1
1 NEWSHOLME CL
2 ADDINGHAM CL
3 WATSON CL
4 RYLSTONE WAY
5 KILDWICK WAY

F1
1 HETTON CL
2 BUCKDEN CL
3 LEYBURN CL
4 ARNCLIFFE WAY
5 HUDDISDON CL
6 PHILLIPPES RD

A4177 BIRMINGHAM RD

A46

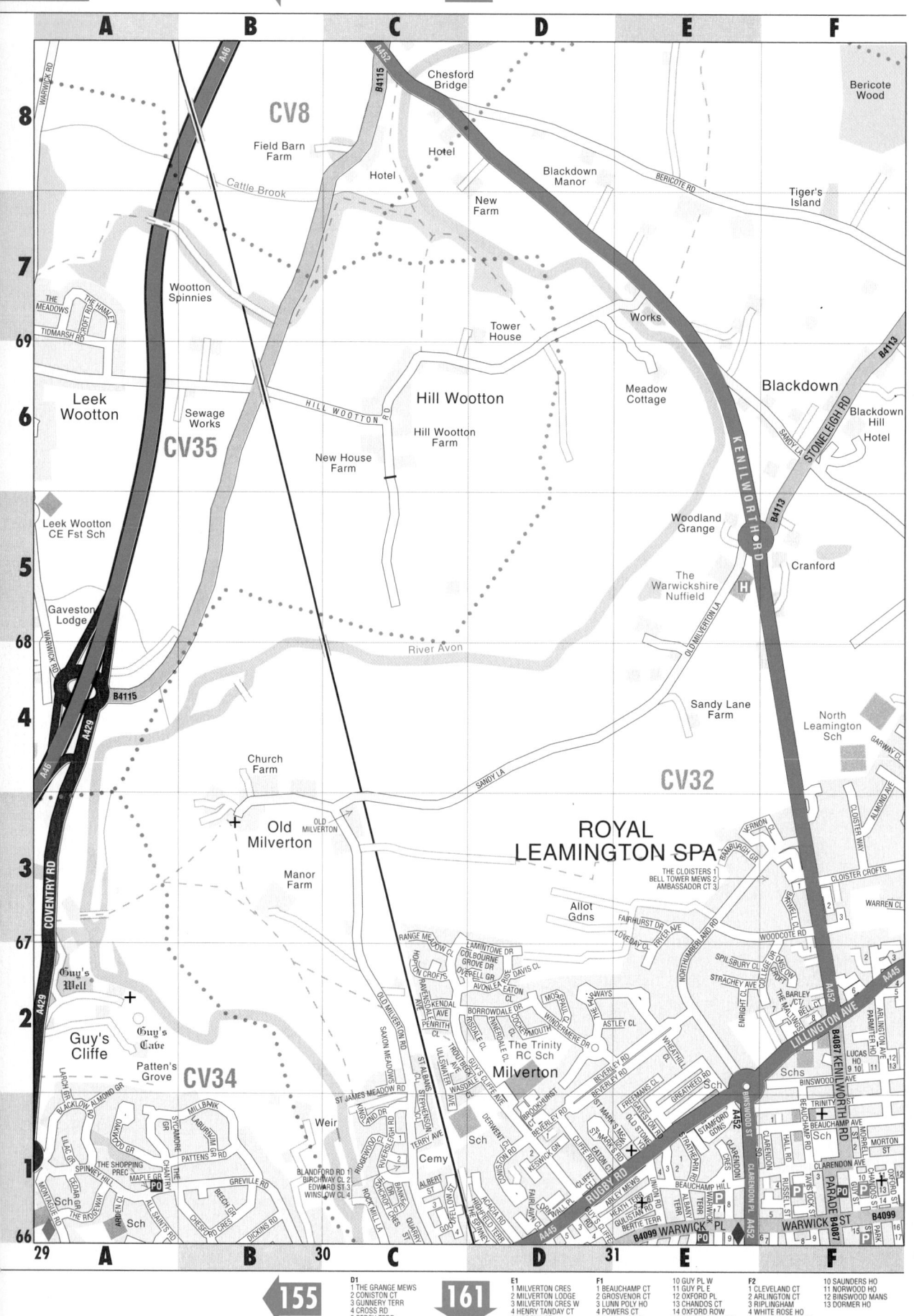

CV8

Chesford
Bridge

Field Barn
Farm

Hotel

Hotel

New
Farm

Blackdown
Manor

Bericote
Wood

Tiger's
Island

Cattle Brook

Wootton
Spinnies

Works

BERICOTE RD

The
Meadows

Tower
House

Meadow
Cottage

Blackdown

Blackdown
Hill

Hotel

HILL WOOTTON RD

Hill Wootton

Hill Wootton
Farm

Leek
Wootton

Sewage
Works

New House
Farm

STONELEIGH RD

Woodland
Grange

Cranford

CV35

KENILWORTH RD

The
Warwickshire
Nuffield

H

Leek Wootton
CE Fst Sch

Gaveston
Lodge

River Avon

Sandy Lane
Farm

North
Leamington
Sch

B4115

Church
Farm

OLD MILLERTON LA

CV32

ROYAL
LEAMINGTON SPA

Old
Milverton

OLD MILVERTON

Manor
Farm

SANDY LA

THE CLOISTERS 1
BELL TOWER MEWS 2
AMBASSADOR CT 3

Guy's
Well

Allot
Gdns

COVENTRY RD

Guy's
Cave

Guy's
Cliffe

Patten's
Grove

CV34

Weir

The Trinity
RC Sch

Milverton

RUGBY RD

Cemy

Sch

LILLINGTON AVE

KENILWORTH RD

PARADE ST

WARWICK PL

WARWICK

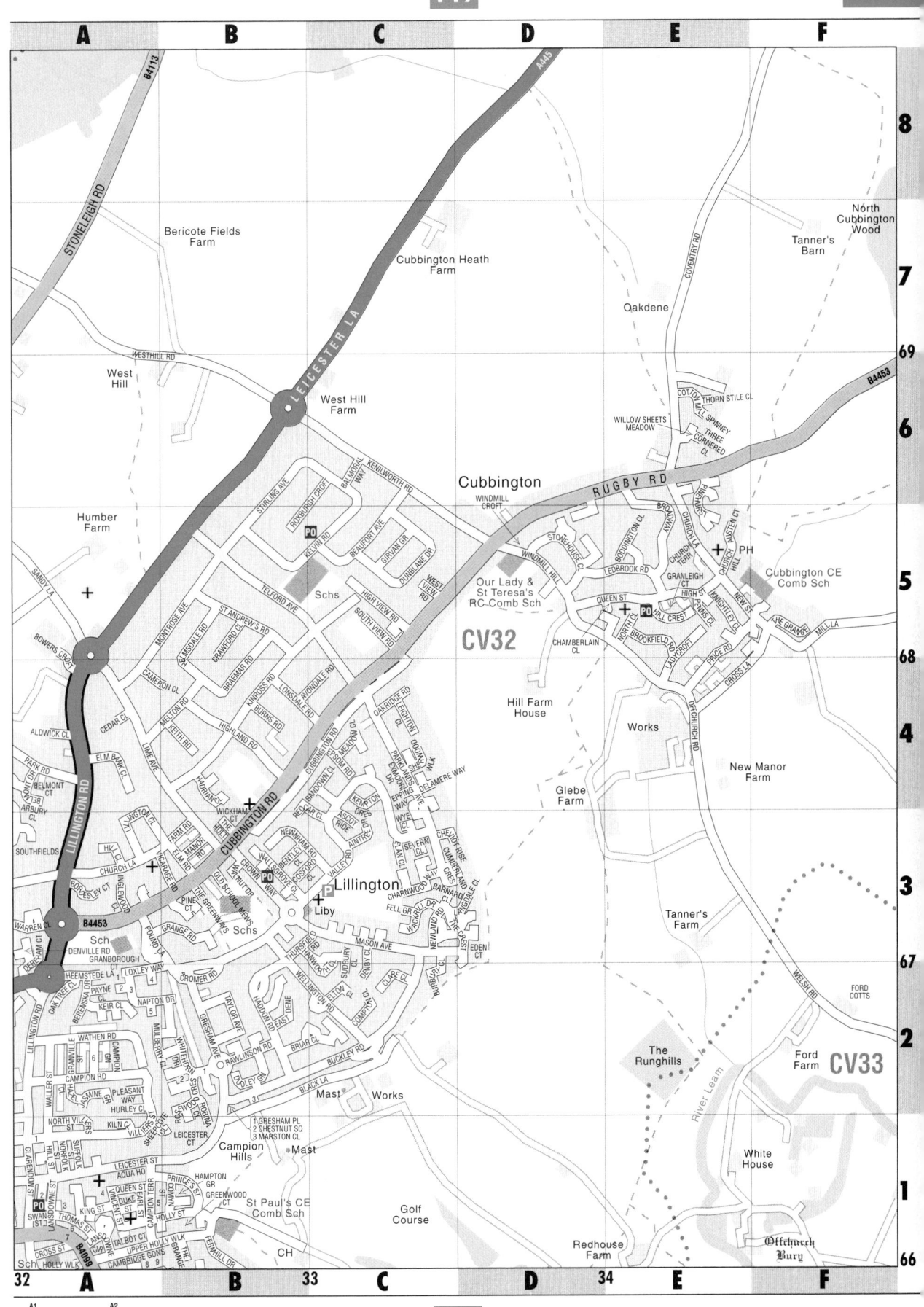

Cubbington

CV32

Lillington

CV33

A1
1 LOWER VILLIERS ST
2 LANSDOWNE RD
3 KENNEDY SQ
4 ST PAUL'S SQ
5 MERCHANTS CT
6 LANSDOWNE CRES
7 WILLES RD
8 HANOVER GDNS
9 WHITTLE CT

A2
1 ACORN CT
2 STOCKTON GR
3 WHITACRE RD
4 SHUCKBURGH GR
5 HELLIDON CL
6 BROWNLOW ST

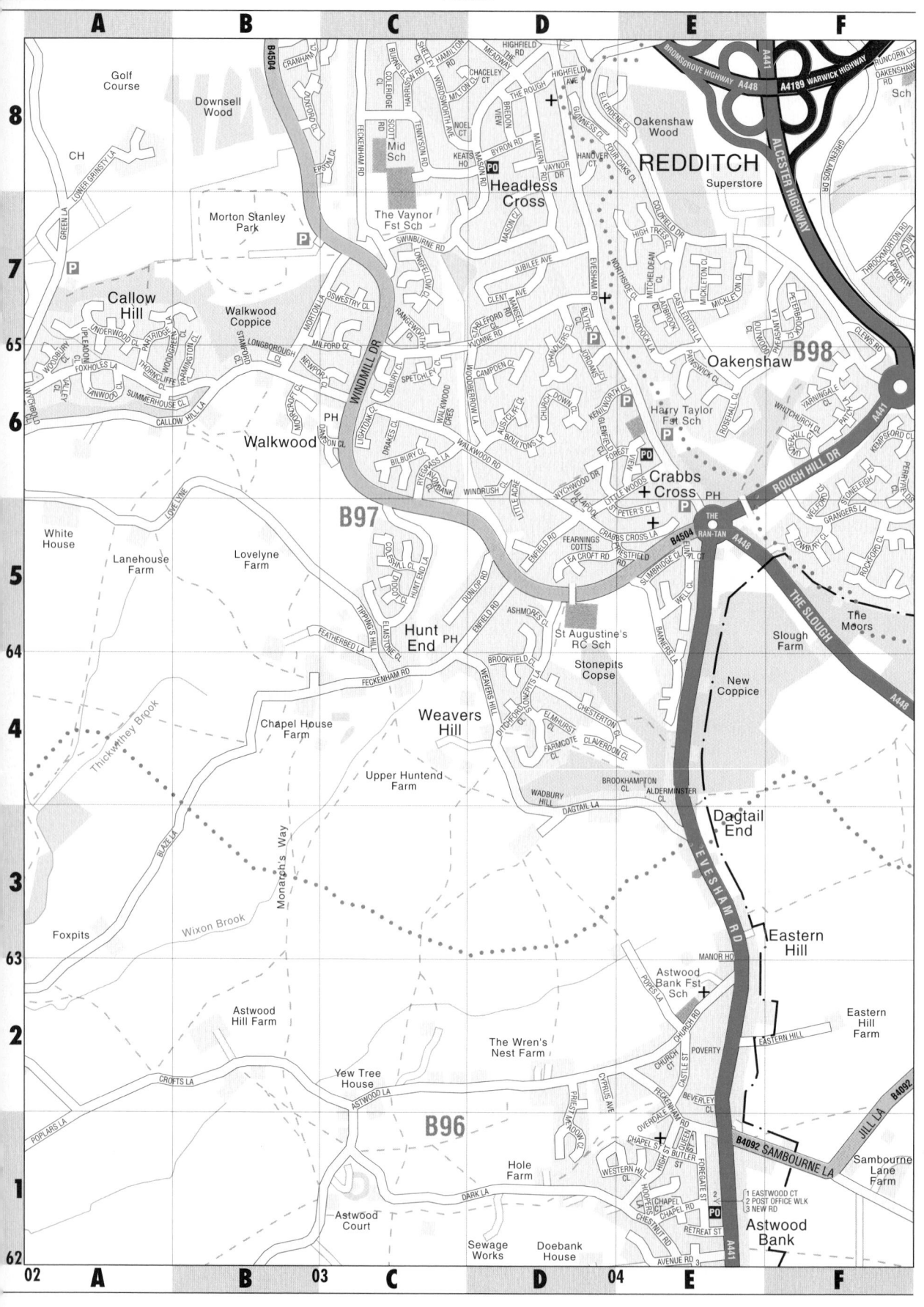

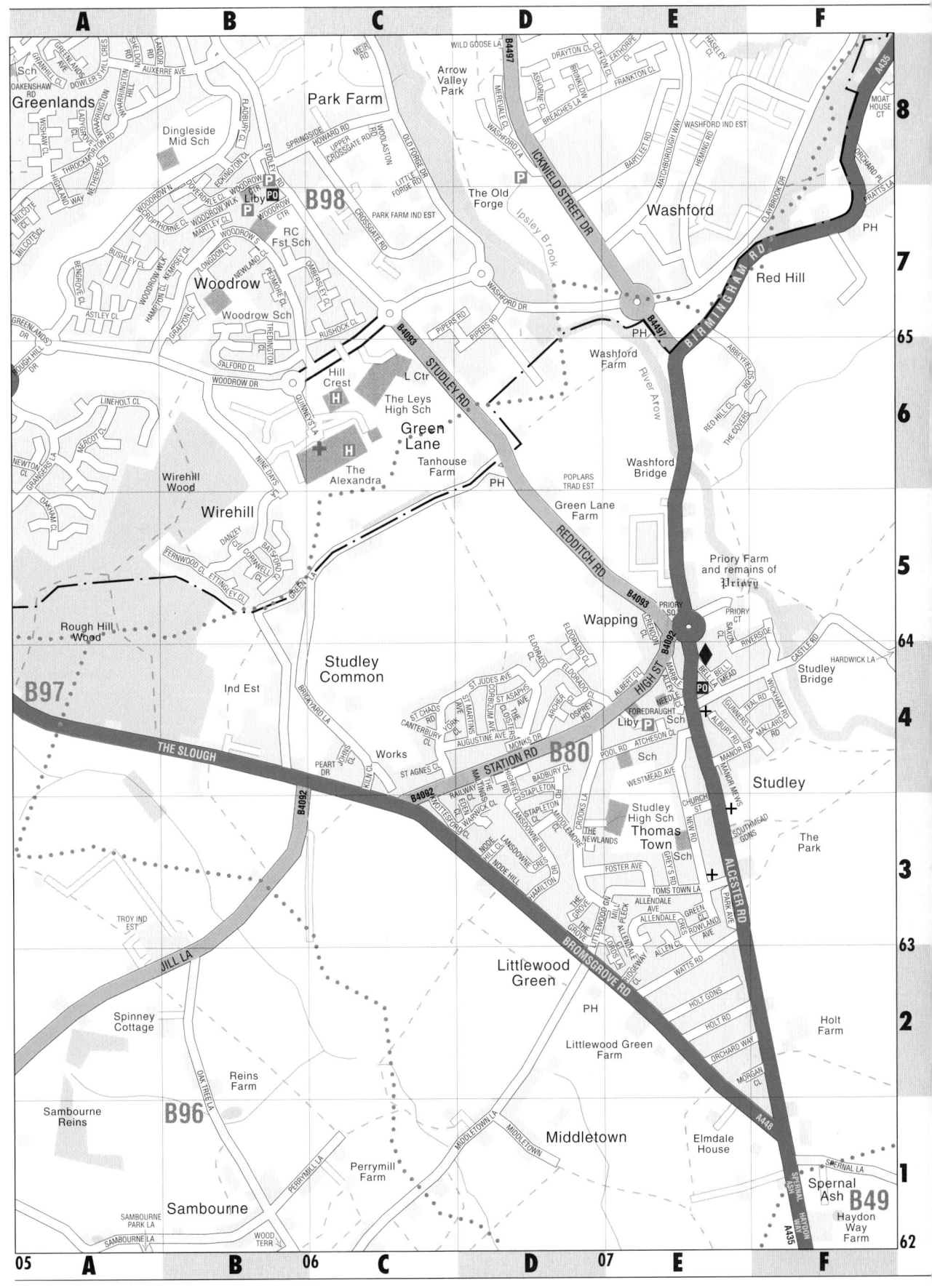

155

E6
1 OLD SQ
2 MARKET PL
3 WESTGATE HO
4 PUCKERING'S LA
5 TIBBITS CT
6 THE GUILD COTTS

7 LEYCESTER CT
8 MARKS MEWS
9 EASTGATE MEWS
10 EASTGATE HO
11 ALMSHOUSES
12 GERRARD ST

F7
1 ALEXANDER CT
2 BARTLETT CL
3 JAMES CT
4 ST JOHN'S CT
5 CASTLEGATE MEWS
6 AVERY CT

7 FAIRFAX CT
8 GOODWAY CT
9 PRIORY WLK
10 CROSS ST
11 GARDEN CT
12 YEOMANRY CL

F8
1 PEMBROKE CL
2 ARUNDEL CL
3 CORNWALL CL
4 CROSS FIELDS RD
5 MULBERRY DR
6 ROWAN DR

7 GAVESTON CL

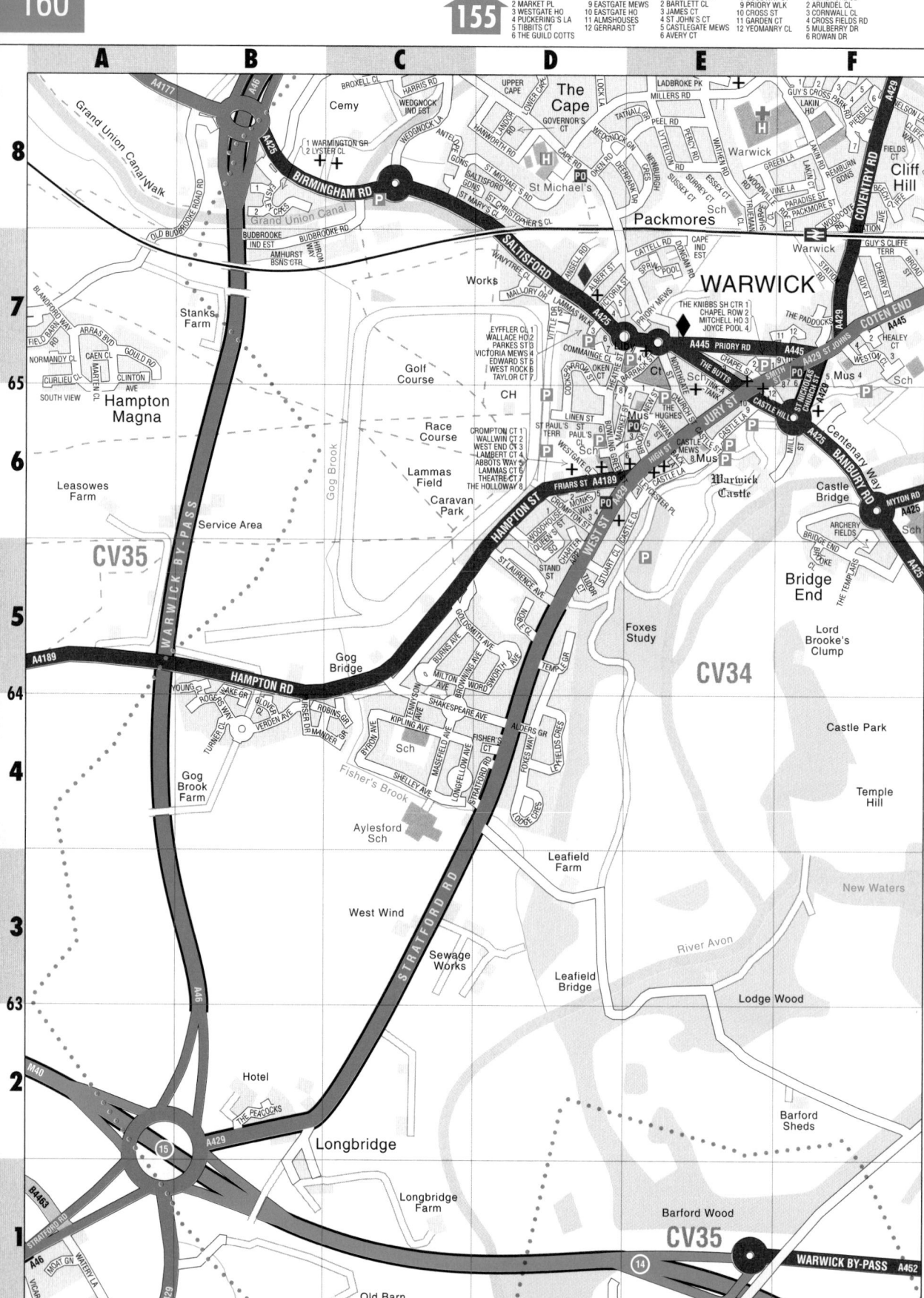

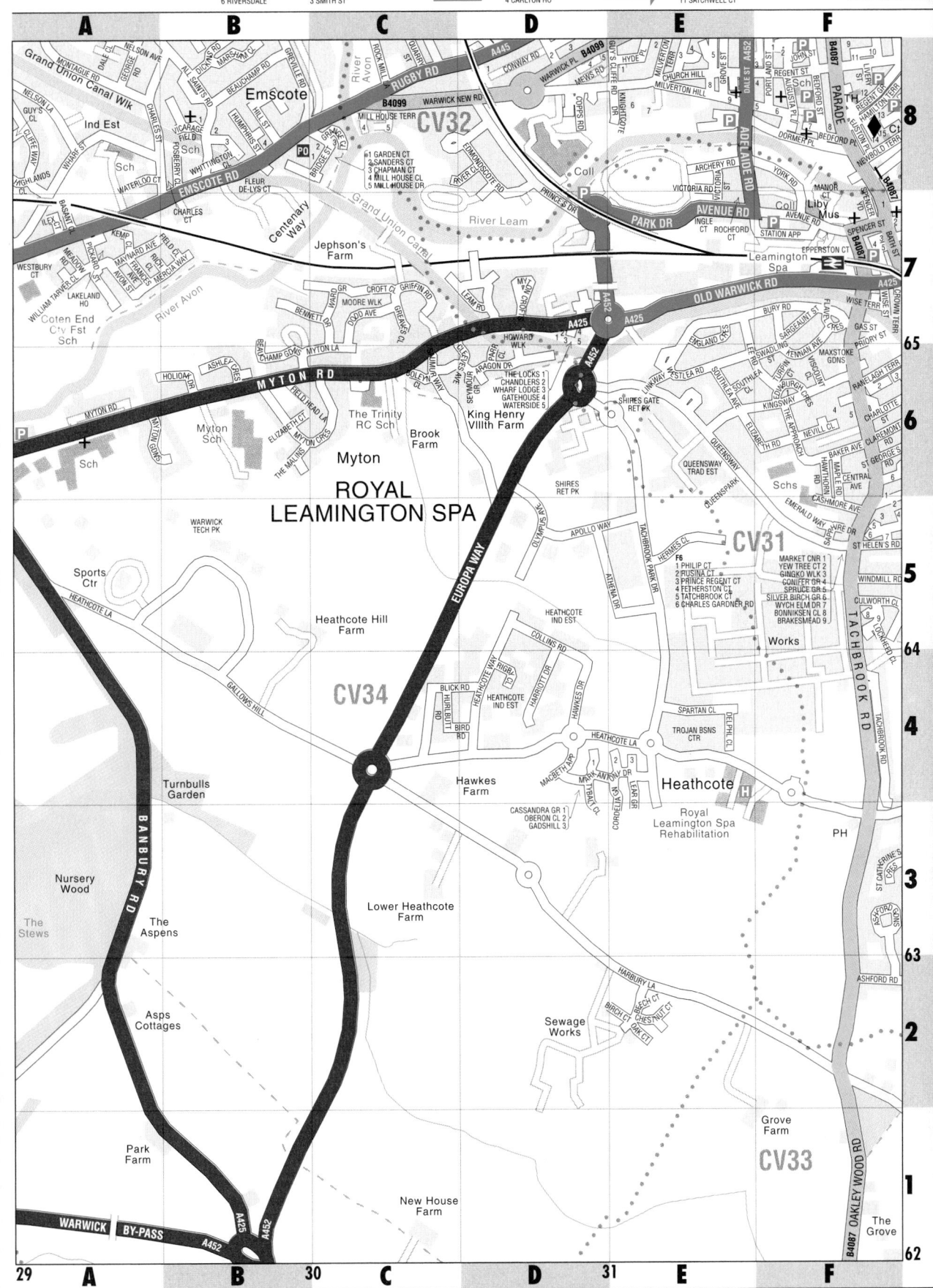

B8
1 ST EDITH'S HO
2 ST EDITH'S GN
3 AUSTIN EDWARDS DR
4 HERALDS CT

D8
1 WESTGROVE TERR
2 OSWALD RD
3 THE CEDARS MEWS
4 THE OAKS
5 PENDINE CT

E8
1 LYNDON CT
2 TENBY CT
3 WOODBINE ST
4 WOODBINE COTTS
5 NEW BROOK ST
6 RIVERSDALE

7 MILVERTON CT
8 SOMERS PL
9 PORTLAND PLACE W
F7
1 VICTORIA TERR
2 CHURCH WLK
3 SMITH ST

4 BATH PL
5 ABBOTTS ST
F8
1 PORTLAND CT
2 WINDSOR CT
3 CHURCHILL HO
4 CARLTON HO

5 PORTLAND PL E
6 PORTLAND PL
7 ST PETER'S RD
8 REGENCY ARC
9 ROYAL PRIORS
10 SATCHWELL WLK
11 SATCHWELL CT

12 DENBY BLDGS
13 ROSEFIELD WLK
14 ROSEFIELD PL
15 EUSTON SQ

156
162
162

161
157

A7
1 GLOUCESTER ST
2 REGENT PL
3 CHAPEL ST
4 PACKINGTON PL
5 TOWER ST
6 CUMMING ST
7 ALTHORPE IND EST
8 MOSS ST
9 ASH LAWN HO
10 BAXTER CT
11 VICTORIA BSNS CTR
12 RUSSELL CT
13 WARNEFORD MEWS

B7
1 SQUIRHILL PL
2 WILLES CT
3 JEPHSON PL
4 TRAFFORD LODGE
5 CLIFTON CT
6 RICHMOND CT

B7
7 NORTHCOTE ST
8 SOUTHLANDS
9 RUSHMORE TERR
A6
1 SOUTHBOROUGH TERR
2 GROVE PL

3 PRINCE REGENT CT
4 LISLE CT
5 DUGDALE CT
6 RADCLIFFE GDNS
7 AYLESFORD CT
8 BEAUMONT CT
9 CHRISTINE LEDGER SQ

10 ST JOHN'S TERR

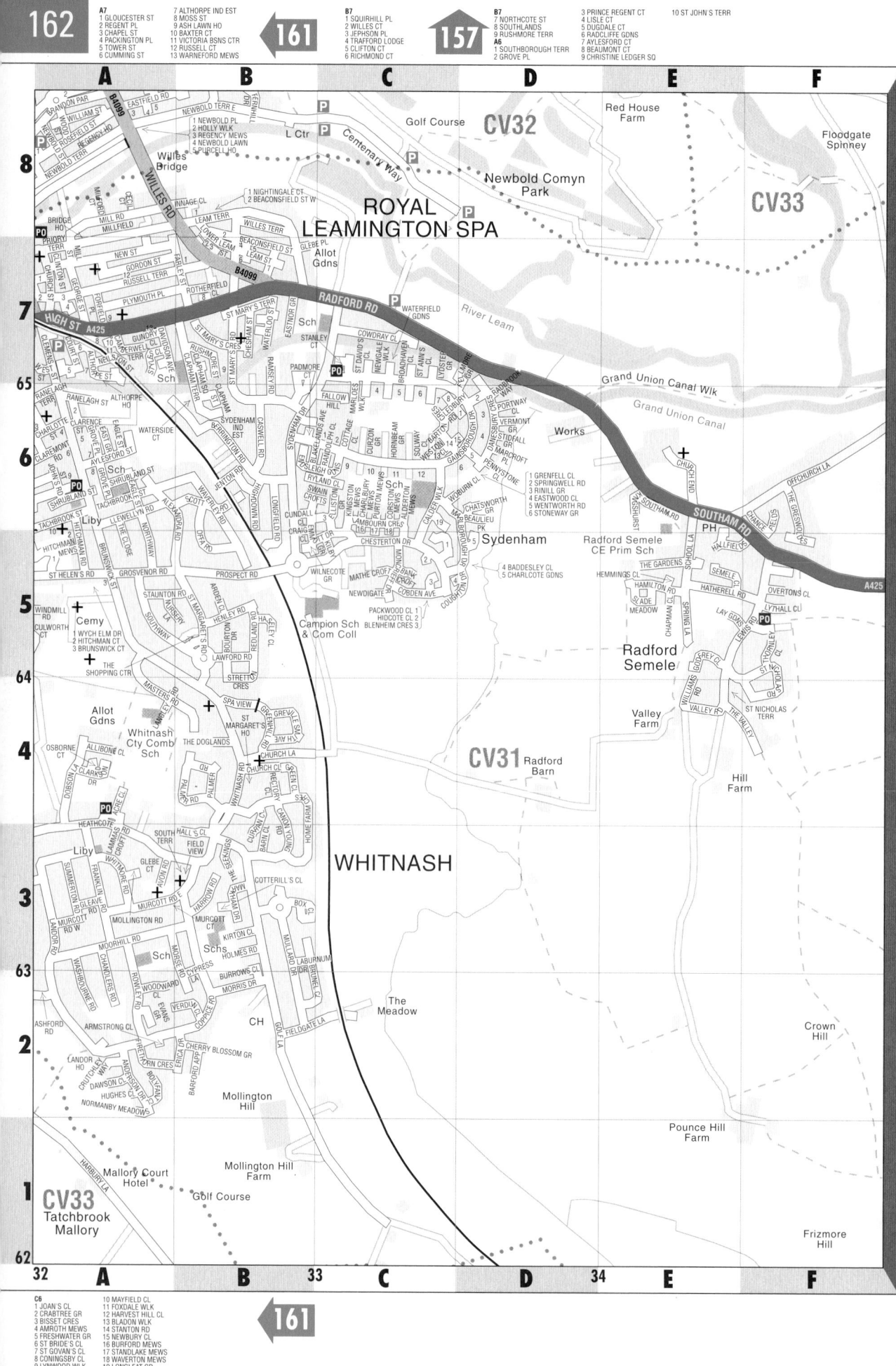

161

C6
1 JOAN'S CL
2 CRABTREE GR
3 BISSET CRES
4 AMROTH MEWS
5 FRESHWATER GR
6 ST BRIDE'S CL
7 ST GOVAN'S CL
8 CONINGSBY CL
9 LYNWOOD WLK
10 MAYFIELD CL
11 FOXDALE WLK
12 HARVEST HILL CL
13 BLADON WLK
14 STANTON RD
15 NEWBURY CL
16 BURFORD MEWS
17 STANDLAKE MEWS
18 WAVERTON MEWS
19 LONGLEAT GR

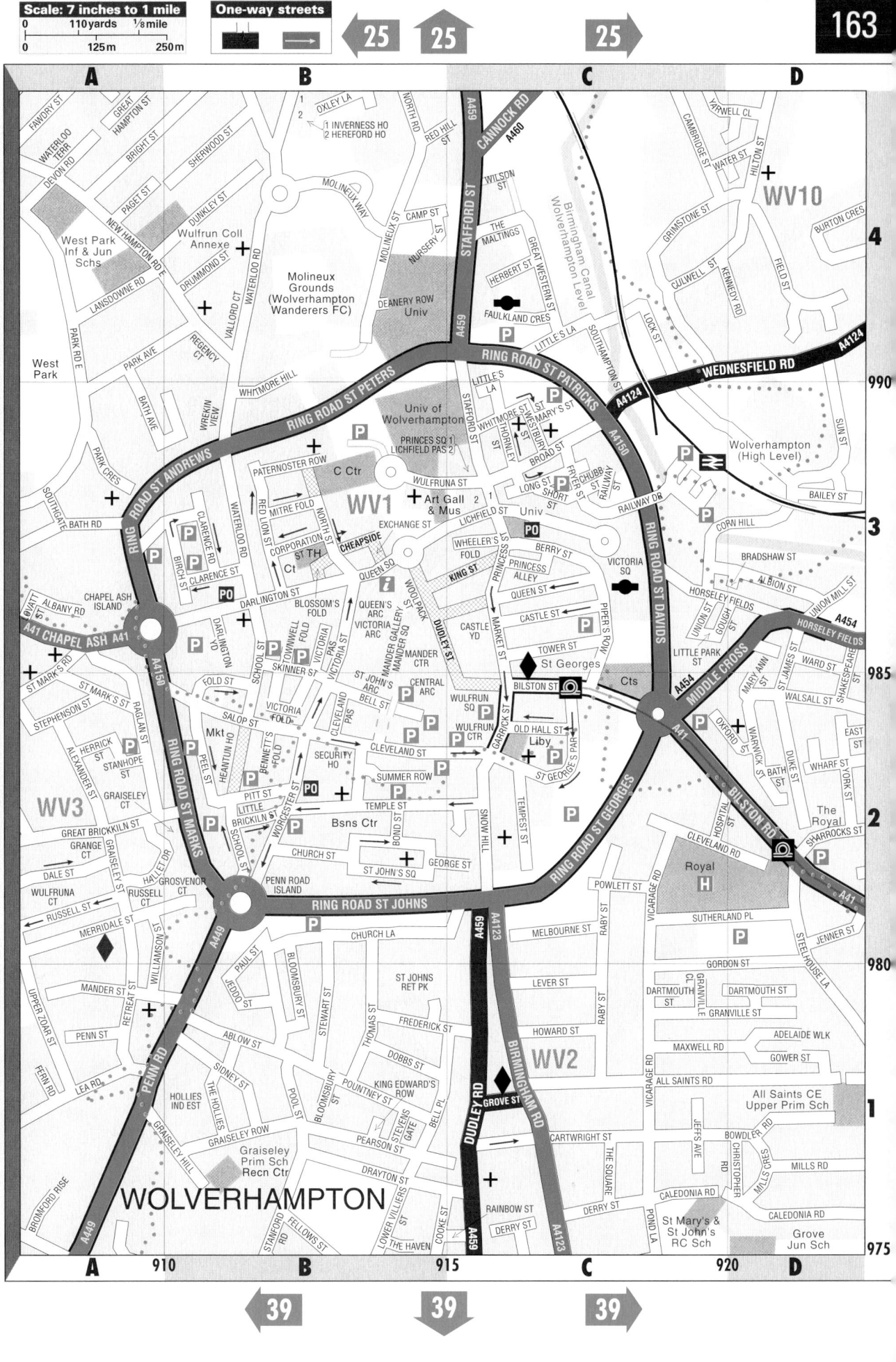

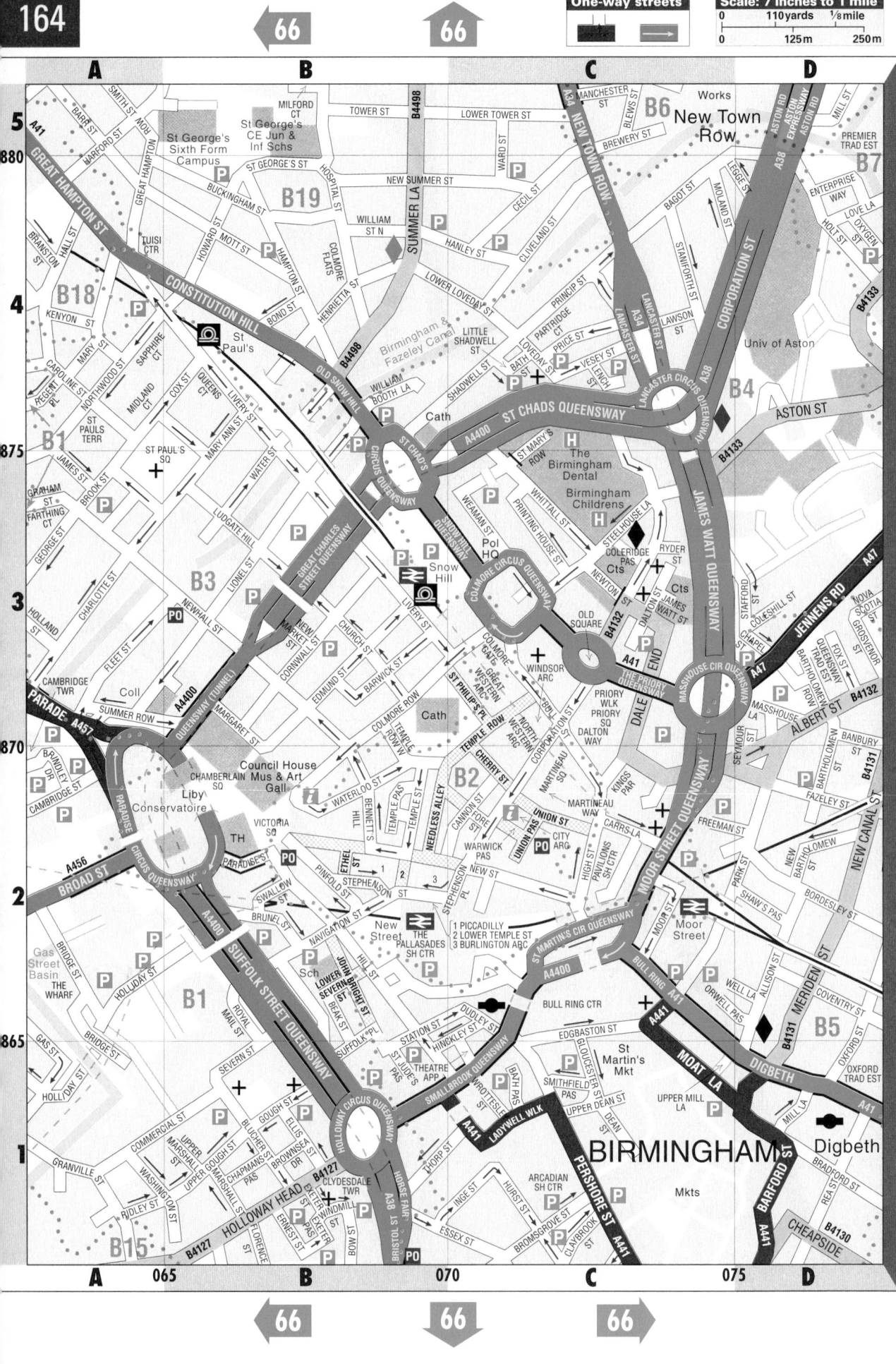

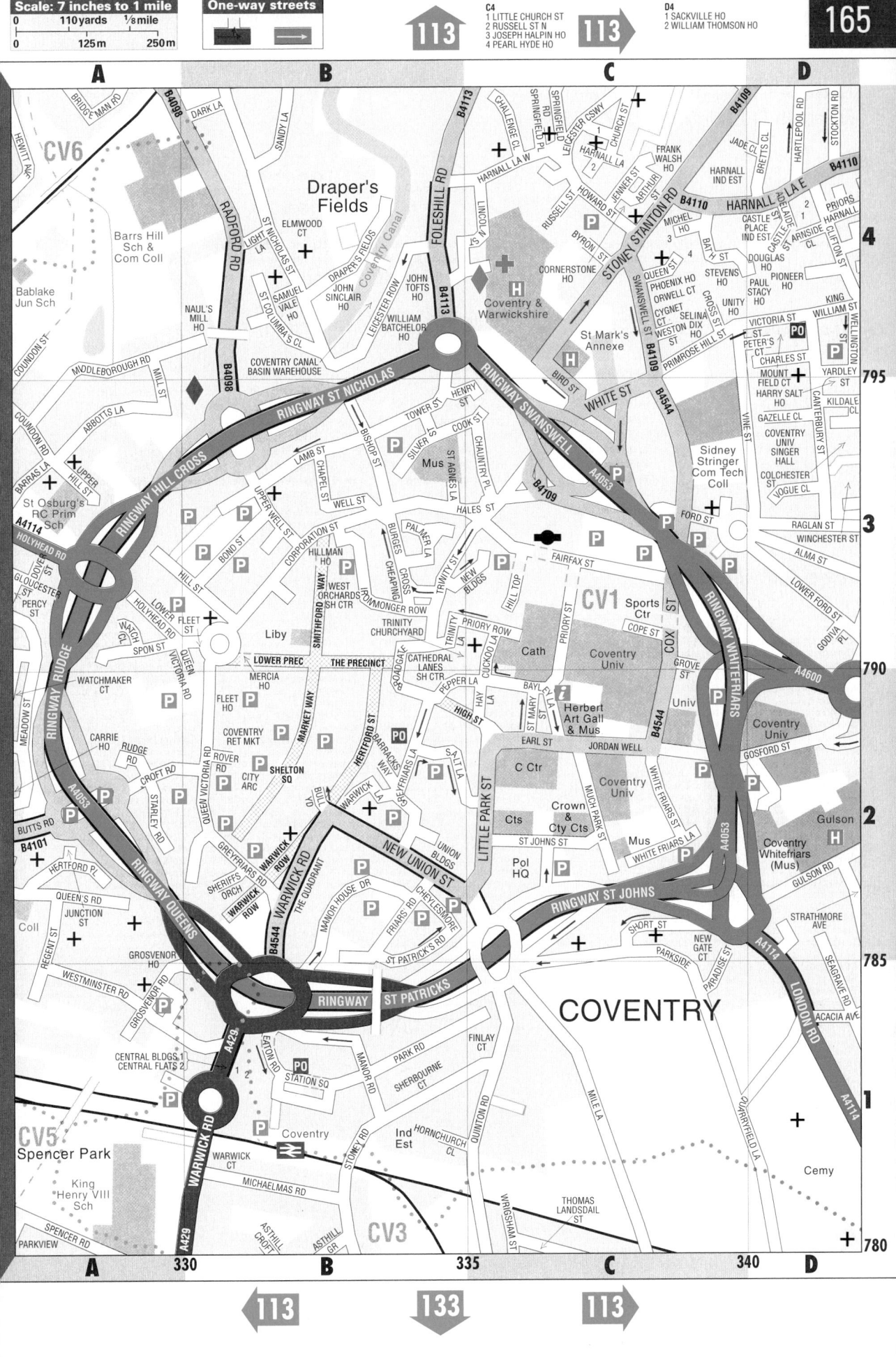

Index

Street names are listed alphabetically and show the locality, the Postcode District, the page number and a reference to the square in which the name falls on the map page

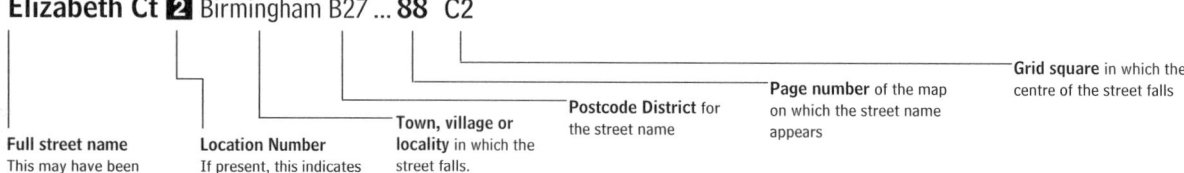

Elizabeth Ct 2 Birmingham B27 ... 88 C2

Full street name
This may have been abbreviated on the map

Location Number
If present, this indicates the street's position on a congested area of the map instead of the name

Town, village or locality in which the street falls.

Postcode District for the street name

Page number of the map on which the street name appears

Grid square in which the centre of the street falls

Schools, hospitals, sports centres, railway stations, shopping centres, industrial estates, public amenities and other places of interest are also listed. These are highlighted in magenta

Abbreviations used in the index

App **Approach**	Comm **Common**	Est **Estate**	N **North**	Sq **Square**
Arc **Arcade**	Cnr **Corner**	Gdns **Gardens**	Orch **Orchard**	Strs **Stairs**
Ave **Avenue**	Cotts **Cottages**	Gn **Green**	Par **Parade**	Stps **Steps**
Bvd **Boulevard**	Ct **Court**	Gr **Grove**	Pk **Park**	St **Street, Saint**
Bldgs **Buildings**	Ctyd **Courtyard**	Hts **Heights**	Pas **Passage**	Terr **Terrace**
Bsns Pk **Business Park**	Cres **Crescent**	Ho **House**	Pl **Place**	Trad Est **Trading Estate**
Bsns Ctr **Business Centre**	Dr **Drive**	Ind Est **Industrial Estate**	Prec **Precinct**	Wlk **Walk**
Bglws **Bungalows**	Dro **Drove**	Intc **Interchange**	Prom **Promenade**	W **West**
Cswy **Causeway**	E **East**	Junc **Junction**	Ret Pk **Retail Park**	Yd **Yard**
Ctr **Centre**	Emb **Embankment**	La **Lane**	Rd **Road**	
Cir **Circus**	Ent **Enterprise**	Mans **Mansions**	Rdbt **Roundabout**	
Cl **Close**	Espl **Esplanade**	Mdw **Meadows**	S **South**	

Town and village index

Aldridge 30 A6	Brandon 135 F5	Earlswood 126 A3	Meriden 92 C1	Stourbridge 80 F5
Allesley 112 A6	Brierley Hill 61 C2	Essington 13 A4	Middleton 34 C1	Studley 159 E6
Alvechurch 139 B6	Brinsford 11 D8	Fairfield 120 C1	Mile Oak 20 D1	Sutton Coldfield 46 A3
Alvecote 22 D6	Bromsgrove 136 E1	Fazeley 20 E2	Minworth 58 D5	Tamworth 21 D3
Ansty 97 D3	Brownhills 16 B4	Featherstone 12 C7	Mustow Green 117 F1	Tanworth-In-Arden 142 A4
Ash Green 95 C7	Bulkington 79 A2	Finstall 137 F1	Norton Canes 5 F3	Tardebigge 152 B7
Aston Flamville 76 C7	Burcot 137 D5	Great Wyrley 5 A1	Nuneaton 73 A1	Tidbury Green 125 D4
Astwood Bank 158 E2	Burntwood 7 D6	Hagley 99 C7	Nurton 23 A3	Tipton 51 F8
Baginton 133 D3	Burton Green 131 A1	Halesowen 83 C3	Oldbury 63 E4	Trescott 37 C7
Balsall Common 130 C5	Burton Hastings 75 A1	Hampton in Arden 109 A7	Outwoods 92 C5	Trysull 37 A1
Barnacle 97 B6	Cannock 4 C8	Harvington 118 B6	Perton 23 F3	Upper Bentley 152 B1
Barnt Green 138 D8	Catherine de Barnes 108 B5	Himley 49 C3	Piccadilly 35 F1	Upper Marlbrook 121 D1
Barston 109 C1	Catshill 137 A8	Hinckley 74 D7	Polesworth 22 F1	Upton Warren 150 A4
Barwell 71 F6	Chadwick End 145 B6	Hockley Heath 143 C6	Portway 141 B3	Walsall 28 F1
Beausale 146 C2	Cheslyn Hay 4 D2	Hollywood 125 B6	Radford Semele 162 F6	Warwick 160 E6
Bedworth 78 A1	Cheswick Green 126 D4	Honiley 146 B7	Redditch 153 A4	Water Orton 59 A1
Belbroughton 119 E6	Churchill 98 B3	Hopwas 20 B7	Romsley 101 A5	Wedges Mills 4 B6
Bentley Heath 127 E4	Clayhanger 15 D6	Hopwood 123 B4	Rowington Green 145 A1	Wednesbury 41 F2
Beoley 154 D7	Clent 99 F4	Hunnington 101 B7	Rowney Green 139 F4	Wednesfield 26 F8
Berkswell 110 D1	Cliff 35 C1	Huntington 1 D8	Royal Leamington Spa ... 156 D1	Weeford 19 B1
Bickenhill 90 D1	Codsall 10 C3	Iverley 98 D8	Ryton-on-Dunsmore 135 A1	West Bromwich 53 A1
Bilston 40 B4	Coleshill 70 F7	Kenilworth 148 B5	Sambourne 159 B2	Whateley 35 F3
Binley Woods 135 C7	Corley 94 B7	Keresley 94 F4	Sedgley 50 E7	White Stitch 92 C5
Birchmoor 36 F8	Coseley 40 C1	Kidderminster 116 A1	Seisdon 37 A2	Whitnash 162 A4
Birmingham 67 D5	Coven Heath 11 C6	Kingswinford 60 A4	Shenstone 18 A6	Wildmoor 120 E5
Birmingham 164 A1	Coventry 113 E1	Knowle 128 A7	Shilton 97 E5	Willenhall 27 D4
Blackdown 156 E8	Coventry 165 A3	Lapworth 143 E3	Shuttington 22 E7	Wishaw 48 F1
Blackheath 63 B3	Cubbington 157 E5	Leek Wootton 155 F6	Smethwick 65 A7	Wolston 135 F3
Blackwell 138 B3	Curdworth 59 C6	Lichfield 9 E7	Solihull 106 F2	Wolverhampton 25 A1
Blakedown 98 B2	Darlaston 41 D7	Lickey End 137 B6	Stoke Heath 150 D6	Wolverhampton 163 A1
Bloxwich 14 C1	Dodford 136 C6	Little Aston 31 B6	Stoke Pound 151 A4	Wombourne 49 C7
Bluntington 118 E1	Dordon 36 F5	Little Packington 91 C6	Stoke Prior 150 C4	Wood End 36 C1
Bournheath 136 D6	Dorridge 127 F2	Lower Marlbrook 121 D1	Stone 117 D1	Wroxall 145 D3
Bradnock's Marsh 109 E2	Drayton Bassett 34 E5	Lydiate Ash 121 D2	Stoneleigh 149 A4	Wythall 124 E2
Bramcote 79 E6	Dudley 51 A3	Meer End 130 C5	Stonnall 16 E5	

A B Row B4 .... 66 F3
A1 Trad Est B66 .... 65 A7
Abberley B77 .... 22 C2
Abberley CI Halesowen B63 . 82 F2
 Redditch B98 .... 154 C5
Abberley Ind Ctr B66 .... 65 D5
Abberley Rd Dudley DY3 ..... 50 D4
 Oldbury B68 .... 84 B8
Abberley St Dudley DY2 ...... 62 C8
 Smethwick B66 .... 65 D5
Abberton CI B63 .... 83 C3
Abberton Ct B23 .... 56 C2
Abberton Gr B90 .... 127 B7
Abberton Ho B97 .... 153 A4
Abberton Way CV4 .... 132 E3
Abbess Gr B25 .... 68 E1
Abbey CE Fst Sch CV11 ...... 73 B5
Abbey CI B60 .... 137 C2
Abbey Cres Halesowen B63 .. 82 D4
 Oldbury B68 .... 64 D1
Abbey Ct CV3 .... 134 B6
Abbey Dr WS3 .... 15 A5
Abbey End CV8 .... 147 F4
Abbey Est CV2 .... 114 F5
Abbey Gate CV11 .... 73 C4
Abbey Gate Sh Ctr CV11 .... 73 C4
Abbey Gdns B67 .... 64 E1
Abbey Gn CV11 .... 73 B5
Abbey High Sch The B98 ... 153 F4
Abbey Hill CV8 .... 147 F5
Abbey Inf Sch B67 .... 64 E2
Abbey Jun Sch B67 .... 64 E1
Abbey Mans 2 B24 .... 57 B6
Abbey Prim Sch WS3 .... 13 E2
Abbey RC Jun & Inf Sch
 B23 .... 57 A5
Abbey Rd
 Birmingham, Edgbaston B17 .. 85 D5
 Birmingham, Gravelly Hill
  B23 .... 56 D2
 Coventry CV3 .... 134 A6
 Dudley, Gornalwood DY3 .... 50 C3
 Dudley, Netherton DY2 ..... 62 D6
 Halesowen B63 .... 82 C4
 Kidderminster DY11 .... 116 A6
 Redditch B97 .... 153 F4
 Smethwick B67 .... 64 E1
 Tamworth B77 .... 21 D3
Abbey Sq WS3 .... 13 E2
Abbey St Cannock WS12 ..... 2 B7
 Dudley DY3 .... 50 C3
 Nuneaton CV11 .... 73 B5
Abbey St N B18 .... 66 A5
Abbey The CV8 .... 147 F5
Abbey Trad Ind Area B97 .. 153 E5
Abbey Way CV3 .... 133 F6
Abbeydale CI CV3 .... 114 F2
Abbeydale Rd B31 .... 103 A2
Abbeyfield Rd
 Birmingham B23 .... 56 E8
 Wolverhampton WV10 ...... 11 E4
Abbeyfields Dr B80 .... 159 E6
Abbot Rd B62 .... 100 C8
Abbots CI Knowle B93 ...... 128 A7
 Walsall WS4 .... 29 C6
Abbots Field WS11 .... 1 E5
Abbots Mews DY5 .... 61 D1
Abbots Rd B14 .... 104 E7
Abbots Way Birmingham B18 . 66 B6
 Warwick CV34 .... 160 D6
 Wolverhampton WV3 .... 24 E1
Abbotsbury CI CV2 .... 115 A4
Abbotsford Dr DY1 .... 61 E7
Abbotsford Rd
 Birmingham B11 .... 87 C6
 Lichfield WS14 .... 9 E7
 Nuneaton CV11 .... 73 E1
Abbotsford Sch CV8 .... 147 F6
Abbotts Gn LE10 .... 75 F5
Abbotts La CV1 .... 165 A3
Abbotts PI WS3 .... 14 D1
Abbotts Rd B24 .... 56 F1
Abbotts St
 5 Royal Leamington Spa
  CV31 .... 161 F7
 Walsall WS3 .... 14 D2
Abbotts Wlk CV3 .... 135 C7
Abdon Ave B29 .... 103 C7
Abelia B77 .... 21 F3
Abercorn Rd CV5 .... 112 E5
Aberdeen CI CV5 .... 112 A5
Aberdeen Rd CV11 .... 73 E1
Aberdeen St B18 .... 65 E4
Aberford CI WV12 .... 27 D4
Abergavenny Wlk CV3 .... 134 F6
Abigails CI B26 .... 89 B7
Abingdon CI WV1 .... 26 B2
Abingdon Rd
 Birmingham B23 .... 56 C6
 Dudley DY2 .... 62 D3
 Walsall WS3 .... 13 F2
 Wolverhampton WV1 .... 26 B2
Abingdon Way
 Birmingham B35 .... 58 A3
 Nuneaton CV11 .... 73 F7
 Walsall WS3 .... 13 F2
Ablewell St WS1 .... 28 F1
Ablow St WV2 .... 163 B1
Abnalls La WS13 .... 8 B8
Abney Dr WV14 .... 39 F1
Aboyne CI B5 .... 86 D6
Acacia Ave Birmingham B37 .. 69 F6
 Coventry CV1 .... 113 E1
 Walsall WS5 .... 43 A4
Acacia CI Birmingham B37 .. 69 F6
 Dudley DY1 .... 51 A3
 Tipton B69 .... 52 B2

Acacia Cres WV8 .... 10 B4
Acacia Dr WV14 .... 51 B7
Acacia Gr WS12 .... 2 C2
Acacia Rd Birmingham B30 . 103 E8
 Nuneaton CV10 .... 72 E5
 Royal Leamington Spa CV32 . 156 D1
Accord Mews WS10 .... 41 D7
Ace Bsns Pk B33 .... 69 D2
Acfold Rd B20 .... 54 E5
Achal CI CV6 .... 95 F2
Acheson Rd B28 .... 105 F3
Achilees CI WS6 .... 4 F1
Achilles Rd CV6 .... 114 A7
Ackleton Gdns WV3 .... 38 F7
Acklin Gr B23 .... 84 F1
Acklin Gr B29 .... 84 F1
Acocks Green Inf Sch B27 .. 88 B3
Acocks Green Jun Sch B27 .. 88 B3
Acocks Green Sta B27 .... 88 C4
Acorn CI 1 CV32 .... 157 A2
Acorn Ctr 1 WS1 .... 28 F1
Acorn Gdns B30 .... 104 A7
Acorn Gr Birmingham B1 ... 66 B3
 Stourbridge DY8 .... 60 E1
Acorn Rd Halesowen B62 ... 83 C8
 Wolverhampton WV11 ...... 13 A1
Acorn St Coventry CV3 .... 134 B8
 Willenhall WV13 .... 27 C2
Acorn Starter Units WS7 ... 6 D7
Acorns The B61 .... 137 A8
Acre CI B98 .... 162 A4
Acre Rise WV12 .... 27 B5
Acres The WV3 .... 24 C1
Acton CI B98 .... 154 D5
Acton Dr DY3 .... 50 B3
Acton Gr Bilston WV14 ...... 40 B4
 Birmingham B44 .... 45 A2
Acton Ho CV4 .... 111 F3
Ada Rd Birmingham B25 .... 88 B6
 Smethwick B66 .... 65 C3
Ada Wrighton CI WV12 .... 27 C7
Adam's Hill DY9 .... 99 F4
Adams Brook Dr B32 .... 84 B1
Adams CI Smethwick B66 .. 64 D7
 Tipton DY4 .... 40 F1
Adams Ct DY10 .... 117 A7
Adams Hill B32 .... 84 B1
Adams Ho 3 DY11 .... 116 C6
Adams Rd Brownhills WS8 .. 16 B5
 Wolverhampton WV3 .... 38 C8
Adams St Birmingham B7 ... 66 F5
 Walsall WS2 .... 28 D2
 West Bromwich B70 .... 53 B3
Adamson CI WS11 .... 1 B1
Adare Dr CV3 .... 133 C8
Adcock Dr CV8 .... 148 B5
Addenbrook Ho
 2 Blackheath B65 .... 82 F8
 Sutton Coldfield B73 .... 46 A3
Addenbrook Way DY4 ...... 52 D8
Addenbrooke Cres DY11 .. 116 A1
Addenbrooke Dr B73 .... 46 B2
Addenbrooke PI WS10 ..... 41 D7
Addenbrooke Rd
 Keresley CV7 .... 95 A6
 Smethwick B67 .... 64 F3
Addenbrooke St
 Darlaston WS10 .... 41 D7
 Walsall WS3 .... 28 C7
Adderley Gdns B8 .... 67 D5
Adderley Park CI B8 .... 67 E4
Adderley Park Sta B8 .... 67 D3
Adderley Prim Sch The
 B8 .... 67 D3
Adderley Rd B8 .... 67 C4
Adderley Rd S B8 .... 67 C4
Adderley St Birmingham B9 . 67 A1
 Coventry CV1 .... 113 E4
Adderley Trad Est B8 .... 67 C4
Addingham CI 2 CV34 .... 155 F1
Addison CI Cannock WS11 ... 1 E5
 Nuneaton CV10 .... 72 A5
 Wednesbury WS10 .... 42 A1
Addison Croft DY3 .... 50 A5
Addison Gr WV11 .... 12 F1
Addison PI Bilston WV14 ... 41 A7
 Water Orton B46 .... 59 B3
Addison Rd
 Birmingham, King's Heath
  B14 .... 104 F7
 Birmingham, Nechells B7 ... 67 C8
 Brierley Hill DY5 .... 61 C8
 Coventry CV6 .... 113 A8
 Wednesbury WS10 .... 42 E2
 Wolverhampton WV3 .... 38 F8
Addison St WS10 .... 41 F2
Addison Terr WS10 .... 41 F2
Adelaide Ave B70 .... 53 A7
Adelaide Ct CV12 .... 78 A2
Adelaide Rd CV31 .... 161 E8
Adelaide St Birmingham
 B12 .... 86 F8
 Brierley Hill DY5 .... 61 D3
 Coventry CV1 .... 165 D4
 Redditch B97 .... 153 D4
 Royal Leamington Spa
  CV32 .... 156 C1
 Stourbridge, Lye DY9 .... 81 E5
 Stourbridge, Wollaston DY8 . 80 F5
Adelaide Tower B34 .... 69 C5
Adelaide Wlk WV2 .... 163 D1
Adelphi Ct 3 DY5 .... 61 D2

Adey Rd WV11 .... 26 F8
Adkins La B67 .... 65 A1
Admington St B33 .... 89 C8
Admiral Gdns CV8 .... 148 C6
Admiral Parker Dr WS14 ... 17 F5
Admiral PI B13 .... 86 F4
Admirals Way Blackheath B65 63 B2
 Bramcote CV11 .... 79 E6
Adonis CI B79 .... 21 C6
Adria Rd B11 .... 87 B4
Adrian Croft B13 .... 87 C1
Adrian Ct 1 B24 .... 57 B6
Adshead Rd DY2 .... 62 C7
Adstone Gr B31 .... 103 A1
Advance Bsns Pk WS11 ...... 2 B3
Adwalton Rd WV6 .... 23 F3
Aethelred Ct WV10 .... 25 C6
Affleck Ave B78 .... 20 D1
Agenoria Dr B8 .... 80 F5
Aggborough Cres DY10 ... 116 E3
Agincourt Rd CV3 .... 133 E7
Agmore La B60 .... 138 B3
Agmore Rd B60 .... 138 B4
Aiden CI B31 .... 9 C7
Ainsbury Rd CV5 .... 132 E8
Ainsdale CI Coventry CV6 .. 96 B4
 Stourbridge DY8 .... 80 F2
Ainsdale Gdns
 Birmingham B24 .... 57 C5
 Halesowen B63 3 B38 ..... 82 D2
Ainsworth Ho 3 B38 ..... 103 D2
Ainsworth Rd WV10 .... 11 E4
Aintree CI Bedworth CV12 .. 78 B4
 Cannock WS12 .... 2 F6
 Catshill B61 .... 121 A1
 Coventry CV6 .... 113 E5
 Kidderminster DY11 ...... 116 D8
Aintree Dr CV32 .... 157 C3
Aintree Gr B34 .... 69 D6
Aintree Rd WV10 .... 11 D4
Aintree Way DY1 .... 50 F2
Aire Croft B31 .... 103 B1
Airfield Dr WS4 .... 29 E3
Airport Way B26 .... 90 C3
Aitken CI B78 .... 21 A2
Aitken Wing B15 .... 86 A6
Ajax CI WS6 .... 4 F1
Akdene CI WS6 .... 4 D2
Akon Ho CV6 .... 94 F2
Akrill CI B70 .... 53 B5
Al Hira Sch & Coll B12 ..... 87 A6
Alamein Rd WV13 .... 26 E1
Alan Bray CI LE10 .... 74 D7
Alan Higgs Way CV4 ...... 131 C8
Alandale Ave CV5 .... 111 A8
Alandale Ct CV12 .... 95 C8
Albany CI CV10 .... 117 B6
Albany Cres WV14 .... 40 C6
Albany Ct CV1 .... 113 A2
Albany Gdns B91 .... 107 E4
Albany Gr Kingswinford DY6 . 60 E7
 Willenhall WV13 .... 13 C1
Albany Ho B34 .... 69 A7
Albany Rd Birmingham B17 . 85 C6
 Coventry CV5 .... 113 A1
 Wolverhampton WV1 ...... 163 A3
Albany Terr CV32 .... 156 E1
Albemarle Rd DY8 .... 80 F2
Albermarle Rd DY6 .... 61 A5
Albert Ave 1 B12 .... 87 A6
Albert Bradbeer Inf Sch
 B31 .... 122 F7
Albert Bradbeer Jun Sch
 B31 .... 122 F7
Albert Bradford
 Specl Sch B66 .... 64 E7
Albert CI B80 .... 159 E4
Albert Clarke Dr WV12 ..... 27 C7
Albert Cres CV6 .... 95 B3
Albert Davie Dr WS12 .... 2 E4
Albert Dr B63 .... 82 F2
Albert Ho WS10 .... 41 C6
Albert Pritchard Inf Sch
 WS10 .... 42 A5
Albert Rd Allesley CV5 ..... 111 A8
 Birmingham, Aston B6 ..... 66 F8
 Birmingham, Gravelly Hill
  B23 .... 56 D3
 Birmingham, Handsworth
  B21 .... 54 E1
 Birmingham, Harborne B17 . 85 B5
 Birmingham, King's Heath
  B14 .... 104 F7
 Birmingham, Stechford B33 . 68 D3
 Bromsgrove B61 .... 150 D8
 Fazeley B78 .... 35 A8
 Halesowen B63 .... 82 F3
 Hinckley LE10 .... 71 D1
 Kidderminster DY10 ...... 116 F6
 Oldbury B68 .... 84 C8
 Tamworth B79 .... 21 B5
 Wolverhampton WV6 ...... 25 A3
Albert Smith PI B65 .... 63 A4
Albert St Birmingham B5 .. 164 D3
 Brierley Hill DY5 .... 61 D7
 Cannock, Broomhill WS11 ... 1 E4
 Cannock, Hednesford WS12 . 2 D5
 Coventry CV1 .... 113 E4
 Kingswinford DY6 .... 60 B8
 Nuneaton CV10 .... 72 E2
 Oldbury B69 .... 64 A8
 Redditch B97 .... 153 D5
 Royal Leamington Spa
  CV32 .... 156 C1
 Stourbridge, Lye DY9 .... 81 E5
 Stourbridge, Wollaston DY8 . 80 F5

Albert St continued
 Tipton DY4 .... 51 F8
 Walsall WS1 .... 28 E2
 Warwick CV34 .... 160 D7
 Wednesbury WS10 .... 41 F2
 West Bromwich B70 .... 53 C1
Albert St E B69 .... 64 B7
Albert Wlk 1 B17 .... 85 C5
Albion Ave WV13 .... 27 C2
Albion Bsns Pk B66 .... 64 E8
Albion Cotts B46 .... 59 B3
Albion CI CV11 .... 73 D3
Albion Field Dr B71 .... 53 D4
Albion Ho B70 .... 53 C2
Albion Ind Est Coventry CV6 113 C7
 West Bromwich B70 .... 52 F2
Albion Jun Sch B71 .... 54 A1
Albion Par DY6 .... 60 B8
Albion PI WS11 .... 1 E4
Albion Rd
 Birmingham, Handsworth B21 54 E1
 Birmingham, Sparkhill B11 .. 87 D5
 Brownhills WS8 .... 15 E8
 West Bromwich, Albion B70 . 53 A2
 West Bromwich, Handsworth
  B71 .... 65 B8
Albion Rdbt B70 .... 53 B4
Albion St Bilston WV14 ..... 40 E6
 Birmingham B1 .... 66 C3
 Brierley Hill DY5 .... 61 D3
 Kenilworth CV8 .... 148 A5
 Kingswinford DY6 .... 60 B8
 Oldbury B69 .... 52 E1
 Tamworth B79 .... 21 C5
 Tipton DY4 .... 51 F5
 Willenhall WV13 .... 27 B2
 Wolverhampton WV1 ...... 163 D3
Albion Terr B46 .... 59 B3
Albion Works DY5 .... 61 B3
Alborn Cres B38 .... 123 D8
Albright Ho 1 B69 .... 63 E4
Albright Rd B68 .... 64 D4
Albright & Wilson Ho B68 . 84 E7
Albrighton Ho 4 B20 ...... 54 F3
Albrighton Rd B63 .... 82 F3
Albrighton Wlk CV11 .... 74 A2
Albury Rd B80 .... 159 E4
Albury Wlk B11 .... 87 A7
Albutts Rd WS11, WS8 .... 6 B3
Alcester Dr
 Sutton Coldfield B73 .... 45 D3
 Willenhall WV13 .... 26 D1
Alcester Gdns B14 .... 104 F7
Alcester Highway B98 .... 158 F8
Alcester Rd Birmingham B13 . 86 F3
 Burcot B60 .... 137 D5
 Finstall B60 .... 137 F1
 Hollywood B47 .... 124 F5
 Portway B48 .... 140 F7
 Studley B80 .... 159 E3
 Tardebigge B60 .... 152 B7
Alcester Rd S
 Birmingham, Alcester
  Lane's End B14 .... 104 E6
 Birmingham, Higher's Heath
  B14 .... 104 F2
Alcester St Birmingham B12 . 86 F7
 Redditch B98 .... 153 E4
Alcombe Gr B33 .... 68 E2
Alcott CI B93 .... 127 F2
Alcott Gr B33 .... 69 E3
Alcott Hall Prim Sch B37 .. 70 B1
Alcott La B37 .... 89 F8
Alcove The WS3 .... 14 D2
Aldbourne La B97 .... 153 B5
Aldbourne Way B38 .... 123 E2
Aldbury Rd B14 .... 105 A3
Aldbury Rise CV5 .... 112 C4
Aldeburgh CI WS3 .... 14 A3
Aldeford Dr DY5 .... 81 D8
Alden Hurst WS7 .... 6 F8
Alder CI Hollywood B47 ... 125 B6
 Lichfield WS14 .... 9 F7
 Sutton Coldfield B76 .... 57 E7
Alder Coppice DY3 .... 39 C2
Alder Coppice Prim Sch
 DY3 .... 39 C1
Alder Cres WS5 .... 43 B4
Alder Ct B13 .... 87 A3
Alder Dale WV3 .... 24 E2
Alder Dr B37 .... 70 B1
Alder Gr B62 .... 83 E6
Alder Ho WV10 .... 25 F3
Alder La
 Balsall Common CV7 ...... 130 C5
 Birmingham B30 .... 103 C6
Alder Meadow CI CV6 ...... 95 D4
Alder Park Rd B91 .... 106 F2
Alder Rd Birmingham B12 .. 87 A4
 Coventry CV6 .... 96 A2
 Kingswinford DY6 .... 60 F5
 Wednesbury WS10 .... 42 A5
Alder Way Bromsgrove B60 . 137 B2
 Sutton Coldfield B74 .... 44 E8
Alderbrook CI Redditch B97 153 B5
 Sedgley DY3 .... 39 B1
Alderbrook Rd B91 .... 106 F3
Alderbrook Sch B91 .... 106 F2
Alderbrooke Dr CV11 .... 74 A1
Alderdale Ave DY3 .... 39 C3
Alderdale Cres B92 .... 107 E7
Alderflat PI B7 .... 67 C5
Alderford CI WV8 .... 24 F8
Aldergate B79 .... 21 C5
Alderham CI B91 .... 107 D4
Alderhithe Gr B74 .... 31 B3
Alderlea CI DY8 .... 81 A2

A B – Ale 167

Alderley Rd B61 .... 150 D8
Alderman Callow Sch &
 Com Coll CV4 .... 132 A6
Alderman Gee Hall CV12 .. 78 A4
Alderman Harris Prim
 Sch CV4 .... 131 F7
Alderman Smith Sch CV10 . 72 D2
Alderman's Green Ind Est
 CV2 .... 96 D2
Alderman's Green Prim
 Sch CV2 .... 96 C3
Alderman's Green Rd CV2 . 96 B3
Aldermere Rd DY11 .... 116 C8
Alderminster B97 .... 158 E4
Alderminster Rd
 Coventry CV5 .... 112 A4
 Solihull B91 .... 107 C1
Aldermoor Farm Prim
 Sch CV3 .... 134 B8
Alderney CI Bramcote CV11 . 79 F6
 Coventry CV6 .... 95 B2
Alderney Gdns B38 .... 103 D1
Alderpits Rd B34 .... 69 D6
Alders CI B98 .... 154 A3
Alders Dr B98 .... 154 F4
Alders Gr CV34 .... 160 D4
Alders La Nuneaton CV10 ... 72 A7
 Tamworth B79 .... 20 E6
Alders The Bedworth CV12 . 77 F2
 Romsley B62 .... 100 F4
Aldersea Dr B6 .... 66 F7
Aldersgate CV11 .... 73 C3
Aldershaw Rd B26 .... 88 E6
Aldershawe Craft Ctr WS14 . 8 E3
Aldersley Ave WV6 .... 24 F7
Aldersley CI WV6 .... 24 F7
Aldersley High Sch WV8 ... 10 E1
Aldersley Rd WV6 .... 24 F6
Aldersmead Rd B31 ...... 103 C1
Alderson Rd B8 .... 67 F4
Alderton CI B91 .... 107 B1
Alderton Dr WV3 .... 38 E8
Alderton Mews CV31 ..... 162 C6
Alderwood PI B91 .... 107 C3
Alderwood Prec DY3 .... 39 C1
Alderwood Rise DY3 .... 50 D5
Aldgate Dr DY5 .... 81 C7
Aldgate Gr B19 .... 66 D5
Aldin CI B78 .... 20 E2
Aldin Way LE10 .... 71 A3
Aldington CI B98 .... 153 F1
Aldis CI Birmingham B28 ... 87 E1
 Walsall WS2 .... 42 A7
Aldis Rd WS2 .... 42 A7
Aldrich Ave CV4 .... 111 E2
Aldridge By-Pass WS9 ...... 30 A6
Aldridge CI Birchmoor B78 .. 36 F8
 Oldbury B68 .... 64 C4
 Stourbridge DY8 .... 60 E2
Aldridge Rd Birmingham B42 55 E4
 Hinckley LE10 .... 75 D6
 Little Aston B74 .... 31 B6
 Oldbury B68 .... 84 B8
 Sutton Coldfield B74 .... 44 E7
 Walsall WS9 .... 29 C3
Aldridge Sch WS9 .... 30 A4
Aldridge St WS10 .... 41 D7
Aldrin Way CV4 .... 132 D5
Aldwick CI CV32 .... 157 A4
Aldwych CI WS9 .... 30 A8
Aldwyck Dr WV3 .... 38 A8
Aldwyn Ave B13 .... 86 F2
Alesworth Dr LE10 .... 75 F4
Alex Grierson CI CV3 ...... 134 E7
Alexander CI B61 .... 121 A1
Alexander Ct 1 CV34 .... 160 F7
Alexander Gdns LE10 ...... 71 C2
Alexander Hill DY5 .... 81 F8
Alexander Ind Pk WV14 ... 40 C4
Alexander Rd Bedworth
 CV12 .... 78 C3
 Birmingham B27 .... 88 C4
 Codsall WV8 .... 10 C3
 Smethwick B67 .... 64 E2
 Walsall WS2 .... 27 F2
Alexander St WV3 .... 163 A2
Alexander Terr B67 .... 64 F6
Alexandra Ave B21 .... 65 D7
Alexandra Cres B71 .... 53 E8
Alexandra Ct Dudley DY3 .. 50 C3
 Kenilworth CV8 .... 148 A4
 Oldbury B68 .... 64 C4
Alexandra High Sch DY4 .. 52 B6
Alexandra Hospl The B98 .. 159 F3
Alexandra Ind Est DY4 ..... 51 F5
Alexandra Mews B79 ...... 21 C5
Alexandra PI Bilston WV14 . 40 C6
 Dudley DY1 .... 51 C4
Alexandra Rd
 Birmingham, Handsworth B21 65 D7
 Birmingham, Highgate B5 .. 86 F8
 Birmingham, Stirchley B30 . 104 A7
 Coventry CV1 .... 113 F4
 Darlaston WS10 .... 41 E6
 Halesowen B63 .... 82 F4
 Royal Leamington Spa CV31 . 162 B6
 Tipton DY4 .... 52 A6
 Walsall WS1 .... 42 E6
 Wolverhampton WV4 ...... 39 A5
Alexandra St WV3 .... 163 B1
 Dudley DY1 2 .... 51 B1
 Nuneaton CV10 .... 73 B4
Alexandra Terr CV6 .... 95 E2
Alexandra Way Aldridge WS9 30 B5
 Tipton B69 .... 52 A2

Alfall Rd CV2 .... 114 B5
Alford Cl B45 .... 122 C7
Alfred Gunn Ho B68 .... 64 B4
Alfred Rd
　Birmingham, Handsworth
　B21 .... 65 E8
　Birmingham, Sparkhill B11 .. 113 F4
　Coventry CV1 .... 113 F4
Alfred Squire Rd WV11 ... 26 D5
Alfred St
　Birmingham, Aston B6 .... 67 B8
　Birmingham, King's Heath
　B14 .... 104 F7
　Birmingham, Sparkbrook
　B12 .... 87 B5
　Darlaston WS10 .... 41 C5
　Smethwick B66 .... 65 C7
　Tamworth B79 .... 21 A5
　Walsall WS3 .... 14 B1
　West Bromwich B70 .... 53 D3
Alfreda Ave B47 .... 125 A8
Alfreds Well B61 .... 136 C6
Alfreton Cl LE10 .... 75 F5
Alfriston Rd CV3 .... 133 C4
Alfryth Ct B15 .... 86 C8
Algernon Rd B16 .... 65 D4
Algernon St WS2 .... 28 D2
Alice Arnold Ho CV2 .... 77 F1
Alice Cl CV12 .... 77 F1
Alice St WV14 .... 40 D6
Alice Stevens Sch CV3 .... 134 A6
Alice Wlk WV14 .... 40 D6
Alison Cl DY4 .... 41 A2
Alison Dr DY8 .... 80 E3
Alison Rd B62 .... 83 F3
Alison Sq CV6 .... 96 B4
All Angels Wlk B68 .... 64 B4
All Saints CE Fst Sch
　Bedworth CV12 .... 78 C2
　Nuneaton CV10 .... 73 C1
All Saints CE Mid Sch
　CV34 .... 156 A1
All Saints CE Prim Sch
　Coventry CV1 .... 113 E1
　West Bromwich B71 .... 53 C6
All Saints CE Upper Prim
　Sch WV2 .... 163 D1
All Saints Dr B74 .... 32 A2
All Saints Hospl B18 .... 65 E5
All Saints Ind Est B18 ... 66 A5
All Saints La CV1 .... 113 F3
All Saints' Rd B18 .... 66 B5
All Saints Rd B14 .... 104 E7
All Saints' Rd
　Bromsgrove B61 .... 137 A3
　Darlaston WS10 .... 41 E6
All Saints Rd Warwick
　CV34 .... 161 B8
　Wolverhampton WV2 .... 163 C1
All Saints Sq CV12 .... 78 B3
All Saints' St B18 .... 66 A5
All Saints Way B71 .... 53 D5
All Souls RC Prim Sch
　CV5 .... 112 E2
Allan Cl
　Smethwick B66 .... 65 B5
　Stourbridge DY8 .... 80 F8
Allan Rd CV6 .... 112 F4
Allard B77 .... 21 E2
Allard Ho CV3 .... 134 B6
Allard Way CV3 .... 134 C7
Allbut St B64 .... 62 D1
Allcock St Birmingham B9 .. 67 A1
　Tipton DY4 .... 52 C8
Allcroft Rd B11 .... 87 F2
Allen Cl Birmingham B43 ... 54 E7
　Studley B80 .... 159 E3
Allen Dr Darlaston WS10 .. 41 C6
　West Bromwich B70 .... 53 F1
Allen Ho B43 .... 54 E7
Allen Rd Tipton DY4 .... 40 F1
　Wednesbury WS10 .... 41 F5
　Wolverhampton WV6 .... 25 A3
Allen St Tamworth B77 ..... 21 C1
　West Bromwich B70 .... 53 B3
Allen's Rough Jun Mix
　Sch WV12 .... 13 C1
Allenby Cl WV6 .... 61 A5
Allendale Ave B80 .... 159 E3
Allendale Cres B80 .... 159 E3
Allendale Ct B80 .... 159 E3
Allendale Gr B43 .... 54 E8
Allendale Rd Birmingham
　B25 .... 88 B7
　Sutton Coldfield B76 .... 57 E8
Allens Ave Birmingham B18 .. 65 F6
　West Bromwich B71 .... 53 A7
Allens Cl WV12 .... 27 B5
Allens Croft Rd B14 .... 104 C6
Allens Farm Rd B31 .... 102 E3
Allens La WS3 .... 14 F2
Allens Rd B18 .... 65 F6
Allensmead B77 .... 21 C2
Allensmore CI B98 .... 154 F2
Allerdale Rd WS8 .... 15 E6
Allerton Cl CV2 .... 114 E2
Allerton La B71 .... 53 C8
Allerton Rd B25 .... 88 B7
Allesley Cl B74 .... 46 C7
Allesley Croft CV5 .... 112 A6
Allesley Ct CV5 .... 112 A6
Allesley Cty Prim Sch
　CV5 .... 112 A7
Allesley Hall Dr CV5 .... 112 C5

Allesley Hall Prim Sch
　CV5 .... 112 B4
Allesley Old Rd CV5 .... 112 D4
Allesley Rd B92 .... 106 D8
Allesley St B6 .... 66 E5
Alleston Rd WV10 .... 11 D1
Alleston Wlk WV10 .... 11 D2
Alley The DY3 .... 50 B3
Alleyne Gr B24 .... 57 A2
Alleyne Rd B24 .... 57 A1
Alliance Cl CV11 .... 73 F3
Alliance Way CV2 .... 114 A5
Allibone Cl CV31 .... 162 A4
Allied Cl CV6 .... 95 D2
Allingham St B43 .... 44 E4
Allington Cl WS5 .... 43 D8
Allison St B5 .... 164 D2
Allitt Gr CV8 .... 148 B5
Allman Rd B24 .... 57 B4
Allmyn Dr B74 .... 45 A6
Allport Mews WS11 .... 1 E1
Allport Rd WS11 .... 1 E1
Allport St WS11 .... 1 E2
Allsops Cl B65 .... 62 F4
Allton Ave B78 .... 20 D1
Allwell Dr B14 .... 104 F2
Allwood Gdns B32 .... 84 A2
Alma Ave DY4 .... 52 A7
Alma Cres B7 .... 67 B4
Alma Ct CV11 .... 79 F6
Alma Ind Est WS10 .... 41 C6
Alma Pl DY2 .... 51 C1
Alma Rd LE10 .... 71 D1
Alma St Birmingham B19 .. 66 E6
　Coventry CV1 .... 165 D3
　Darlaston WS10 .... 41 C6
　Halesowen B63 .... 82 C5
　Smethwick B66 .... 65 C6
　Walsall WS2 .... 28 D4
　Wednesbury WS10 .... 42 B3
　Willenhall WV13 .... 27 B2
　Wolverhampton WV10 .... 25 F2
Alma Way B19 .... 66 D7
Alma Wks WS10 .... 41 D5
Almond Ave
　Kidderminster DY11 .... 116 B8
　Nuneaton CV10 .... 72 C6
　Royal Leamington Spa CV32 . 156 F3
　Walsall, Bentley WS2 .... 27 C1
　Walsall, Yew Tree WS5 .... 43 A4
Almond Cl Birmingham
　B29 .... 103 A6
　Cannock WS11 .... 2 C2
　Walsall WS3 .... 14 F2
Almond Croft B42 .... 54 F7
Almond Gr Warwick CV34 ... 156 A1
　Wolverhampton WV6 .... 25 C4
Almond Ho Huntington WS12 .. 1 D8
　Kingswinford DY6 .... 60 E8
Almond Tree Ave CV2 .... 96 C2
Almsbury Ct B26 .... 89 C4
Almshouses Bedworth CV12 .. 78 B3
　Middleton B78 .... 34 B1
　Rowington Green CV35 .... 145 A1
　Smethwick B67 .... 64 F5
　Warwick CV34 .... 160 E6
　Wolverhampton WV4 .... 38 F3
Alnwick Cl WS12 .... 2 E1
Alnwick Ho B23 .... 56 F6
Alnwick Rd WS3 .... 14 A4
Alperton Dr DY9 .... 81 E2
Alpha Bsns Pk CV2 .... 96 D1
Alpha Cl B12 .... 86 E6
Alpha Ho CV2 .... 114 A4
Alpha Way WS6 .... 14 A8
Alpine Ct CV8 .... 148 A6
Alpine Dr Cannock WS12 ... 2 D4
　Dudley DY2 .... 62 B4
Alpine Rise CV3 .... 133 A5
Alpine Way WV3 .... 24 C2
Alport Croft B9 .... 67 B2
Alspath La CV5 .... 111 F4
Alspath Rd CV7 .... 92 C1
Alston Cl Cannock WS12 ... 2 E2
　Solihull B91 .... 107 D6
　Sutton Coldfield B74 .... 32 A2
Alston Gr B9 .... 68 B2
Alston Ho B69 .... 63 D6
Alston Prim Sch B9 .... 68 B3
Alston Rd Birmingham B9 .. 68 B3
　Oldbury B69 .... 63 E7
　Solihull B91 .... 107 D6
Alston St B16 .... 66 A2
Althorpe Dr B93 .... 127 E3
Althorpe Ho CV31 .... 162 A6
Althorpe Ind Est
　CV31 .... 162 A7
Althorpe St CV31 .... 162 A7
Alton Ave WV12 .... 27 B5
Alton Cl Coventry CV2 .... 96 D2
　Redditch B97 .... 153 B1
　Wolverhampton WV10 .... 11 F3
Alton Gr Cannock WS11 ..... 1 B1
　Dudley DY2 .... 51 E1
　West Bromwich B71 .... 53 E7
Alton Rd B29 .... 85 F3
Alum Cl CV6 .... 113 D8
Alum Dr B9 .... 68 A3
Alum Rock Rd B8 .... 68 B4
Alum Well Rd WS2 .... 28 B1
Alumhurst Ave B8 .... 68 B4
Alumwell Cl WS2 .... 28 B1
Alumwell Comp Sch WS2 .. 28 A1
Alumwell Jun & Inf Schs
　WS2 .... 28 B2
Alvaston Cl WS3 .... 14 C3
Alvechurch CE Mid Sch
　B48 .... 139 B6

Alvechurch Crown
　Meadow Fst Sch B48 .... 139 B6
Alvechurch Highway
　Lydiate Ash B60 .... 121 D2
　Redditch B98 .... 153 F3
Alvechurch Ho B60 .... 137 B3
Alvechurch Rd
　Birmingham B31 .... 123 B7
　Halesowen B63 .... 82 F2
Alvechurch Sta B48 .... 139 A4
Alvecote Cotts B79 .... 22 D6
Alvecote Pools Nature
　Reserve B79 .... 22 D7
Alveley Cl B98 .... 154 D4
Alverley Cl DY6 .... 60 B8
Alverstoke Cl WV9 .... 11 A2
Alverstone Rd CV2 .... 114 A4
Alveston Cl B98 .... 154 C2
Alveston Gr Birmingham B9 .. 68 B2
　Knowle B93 .... 128 B7
Alveston Rd B47 .... 125 A7
Alvin Cl Coventry CV3 .... 114 F1
　Halesowen B62 .... 83 F8
Alvington Cl WV12 .... 27 D4
Alvis Cl B79 .... 20 F7
Alvis Ret Pk CV5 .... 113 A3
Alvis Wlk B36 .... 58 F1
Alwen St DY8 .... 60 F2
Alwin Rd B65 .... 63 B2
Alwold Ct B29 .... 84 F2
Alwold Rd B29 .... 85 A2
Alwyn B77 .... 35 E7
Alwyn Cl WS6 .... 5 A3
Alwynn Wlk B23 .... 56 C3
Alwynne Freeman Ct CV7 .. 95 A6
Amal Way B6 .... 55 F2
Amanda Ave WV4 .... 38 F4
Amanda Dr B26 .... 68 F1
Ambassador Ct CV32 .... 156 F3
Ambell Cl B65 .... 62 F5
Amber Bsns Village B77 ... 22 B3
Amber Cl B77 .... 22 B3
Amber Dr B69 .... 64 A5
Amber Gr WS11 .... 2 C2
Amber Terr DY10 .... 116 F5
Amber Way B62 .... 83 C6
Ambergate Cl Redditch
　B97 .... 153 B5
　Walsall WS3 .... 14 C3
Ambergate Dr DY6 .... 60 C8
Amberley Ave CV12 .... 79 C2
Amberley Gn B43 .... 54 E6
Amberley Gr B6 .... 56 A3
Amberley Rd B92 .... 88 F4
Amberley Way B74 .... 30 E1
Amberwood Cl WS2 .... 27 D3
Amblecote Ave B44 .... 44 E2
Amblecote Prim Sch DY8 .. 80 F7
Amblecote Rd
　Brierley Hill DY5 .... 81 D8
　Kidderminster DY10 .... 117 B5
Ambleside Birmingham B32 .. 84 C1
　Coventry CV2 .... 96 E2
Ambleside Cl WV14 .... 40 E3
Ambleside Dr DY5 .... 81 C8
Ambleside Way
　Bromsgrove B60 .... 137 B1
　Kingswinford DY6 .... 60 D6
　Nuneaton CV11 .... 73 E6
Amersham Cl
　Birmingham B32 .... 84 E5
　Coventry CV5 .... 112 B4
Ames Rd WS10 .... 41 C7
Amesbury Rd B13 .... 86 E3
Amethyst Ct B92 .... 88 F1
Amherst Ave B20 .... 55 A3
Amherst Rd CV8 .... 147 E6
Amhurst Bsns Ctr CV34 ... 160 B7
Amicombe B77 .... 22 C1
Amington Cl B75 .... 32 D3
Amington Heath Prim
　Sch B77 .... 22 B4
Amington Ind Est B77 ..... 22 B2
Amington Rd
　Birmingham B25 .... 88 B6
　Solihull B90 .... 126 A8
　Tamworth B77 .... 21 D4
Amiss Gdns B10 .... 87 C8
Amity Cl B66 .... 65 B5
Amos Ave Nuneaton CV10 .. 73 B2
　Wolverhampton WV11 .... 26 C7
Amos Jacques Rd CV12 ..... 78 A4
Amos La WV11 .... 26 C6
Amos Rd DY9 .... 81 F2
Amphlett Croft DY4 .... 52 B4
Amphlett Ct B60 .... 137 A2
Amphletts Cl DY2 .... 62 E3
Ampton Rd B15 .... 86 B7
Amroth Cl B45 .... 122 B7
Amroth Mews CV31 .... 162 C6
Amwell Gr B14 .... 104 F3
Amy Cl CV6 .... 95 F4
Anchor Cl Birmingham B16 .. 65 F1
　Tamworth B77 .... 21 E4
Anchor Hill DY5 .... 61 C1
Anchor La WV14 .... 40 B2
Anchor Par WS9 .... 30 B6
Anchor Rd Aldridge WS9 .... 30 B6
　Dudley WV14 .... 40 C2
Anchorage Rd
　Birmingham B23 .... 56 D3
　Sutton Coldfield B74 .... 46 B6
Anchorfields DY10 .... 116 F6

Anchorway Rd CV3 .... 133 B4
Anders B79 .... 21 A6
Anders Sq WV6 .... 23 E4
Andersleigh Dr WV14 .... 51 A8
Anderson Cres B43 .... 43 E2
Anderson Dr CV31 .... 162 A2
Anderson Gdns DY4 .... 52 A4
Anderson Rd Birmingham B23 .. 56 E1
　Smethwick B66 .... 65 A1
　Tipton DY4 .... 52 A4
Anderton Cl B74 .... 46 A7
Anderton Park Jun & Inf
　Sch B12 .... 87 B4
Anderton Park Rd B13 ...... 87 A3
Anderton Rd Bedworth CV12 . 77 C1
　Birmingham B11 .... 87 C6
　Coventry CV6 .... 96 B4
Anderton St B1 .... 66 B3
Andover Cres DY6 .... 60 F4
Andover Ho B35 .... 58 B3
Andover Pl WS11 .... 2 A4
Andover St B5 .... 66 F2
Andrew Cl WV12 .... 27 D6
Andrew Ct B76 .... 46 F3
Andrew Dr WV12 .... 27 D6
Andrew Gdns B21 .... 54 E1
Andrew Rd Halesowen B63 .. 83 A3
　Tipton DY4 .... 41 A1
　West Bromwich B71 .... 42 F2
Andrews Cl DY5 .... 81 E8
Andrews Ho WS13 .... 9 A7
Andrews Rd WS9 .... 16 B4
Anerley Gr B44 .... 44 F4
Anerley Rd B44 .... 44 F4
Angel Mews B46 .... 70 F7
Angel Pas B7 .... 81 A5
Angel St Dudley DY2 .... 62 B8
　Upper Bentley B97 .... 152 B1
Angela Ave Blackheath B65 . 63 D4
　Coventry CV2 .... 96 E1
Angela Pl WV14 .... 40 D6
Angelica B77 .... 21 F4
Angelica Cl WS5 .... 43 A3
Angelina St B12 .... 86 F7
Angelo Ho B13 .... 105 D7
Anglesey Ave B36 .... 70 B6
Anglesey Bsns Pk WS12 .. 2 E4
Anglesey Cl Allesley CV5 .. 112 B7
　Burntwood WS7 .... 6 F4
Anglesey Cres Brownhills WS8 .. 6 C5
　Cannock WS12 .... 2 C5
Anglesey Inf Sch B19 .... 66 C7
Anglesey Jun Sch B19 ..... 66 C6
Anglesey Mews WS12 .... 2 C5
Anglesey Rd Brownhills WS8 .. 6 F2
　Lichfield WS13 .... 3 B2
Anglesey St Birmingham B19 . 66 C7
　Cannock WS12 .... 2 B5
Angless Way CV8 .... 147 F3
Anglia Rd WS11 .... 1 D3
Anglian Rd WS9 .... 29 D6
Anglo African Ind Pk B69 .. 52 C7
Angorfa Cl WS13 .... 8 F7
Angus Cl Coventry CV5 ..... 112 A4
　Kenilworth CV8 .... 148 C6
　West Bromwich B71 .... 53 C6
Anita Ave DY4 .... 52 A2
Anita Croft B23 .... 56 E2
Ankadine Rd DY8 .... 81 B6
Anker Cl WS7 .... 7 D6
Anker St CV11 .... 73 D3
Anker View B77 .... 21 C3
Ankerdine Ct B63 .... 83 A3
Ankerdrive B77, B79 .... 21 B4
Ankermoor Cl B34 .... 69 B6
Ankermoor Prim Sch B77 .. 21 C5
Ankerside Sh Ctr B79 .... 21 B4
Ann Cres WS11 .... 1 E6
Ann Croft B26 .... 89 D4
Ann Rd B47 .... 125 A4
Ann St WV13 .... 27 B3
Annan Ave WV10 .... 25 F7
Anne Cl B70 .... 52 E3
Anne Cres CV3 .... 134 C5
Anne Ct B76 .... 46 F3
Anne Gr DY4 .... 41 B1
Anne Rd Brierley Hill DY5 ... 62 A1
　Smethwick B66 .... 65 D7
　Wolverhampton WV4 .... 39 B6
Annesley Rd B66 .... 65 B5
Annie Lennard Inf Sch B67 . 64 E3
Annie Osborn Prim Sch
　CV2 .... 114 D7
Annscroft B38 .... 103 D2
Ansbro Cl B18 .... 65 F5
Ansell Rd
　Birmingham, Gravelly Hill
　B24 .... 56 F1
　Birmingham, Sparkbrook
　B11 .... 87 C6
　Warwick CV34 .... 160 D7
Ansley Cl B98 .... 154 F1
Ansley Comm CV10 .... 72 A7
Ansley Rd CV10 .... 72 B3
Ansley Way B92 .... 107 D7
Anslow Rd B23 .... 56 C5
Anson Ave WS13 .... 3 A1
Anson Cl Burntwood WS7 .... 7 C7
　Great Wyrley WS6 .... 4 F1
　Perton WV6 .... 23 E5
Anson Ct B78 .... 35 B8
Anson Gr B27 .... 88 D2
Anson Junc WS2 .... 27 E1
Anson Rd Great Wyrley WS6 .. 4 F1
　Walsall WS2 .... 27 E1
　West Bromwich B70 .... 52 E7
Anson Way CV2 .... 114 F8

Anstey Gr B27 .... 88 B1
Anstey Rd B44 .... 55 E6
Anston Way WV11 .... 26 D7
Anstree Cl WS6 .... 4 D1
Anstruther Rd B15 .... 85 E8
Ansty Dr WS12 .... 2 D1
Ansty Rd CV2 .... 114 E5
Antelope Gdns CV34 .... 160 C8
Anthony Rd B8 .... 67 F4
Anthony Way CV2 .... 114 C2
Anton Dr B76 .... 58 A6
Antony Rd B90 .... 106 B1
Antrim Cl CV5 .... 112 B7
Antringham Gdns B15 .... 85 D8
Antrobus Rd Birmingham B21 . 54 E1
　Sutton Coldfield B73 .... 45 F1
Anvil Cl B69 .... 63 E6
Anvil Wlk B70 .... 52 F4
Apex Bsns Pk WS11 .... 5 F4
Apex Rd WS8 .... 15 C7
Apley Rd DY8 .... 80 E7
Apollo B79 .... 20 F6
Apollo Cl WS11 .... 2 A5
Apollo Croft B24 .... 57 D3
Apollo Rd Oldbury B68 ..... 64 C6
　Stourbridge DY9 .... 82 A5
Apollo Way Birmingham B20 . 55 D1
　Royal Leamington Spa CV34 .. 161 D5
　Smethwick B66 .... 65 C5
Apperley Way B63 .... 82 B7
Appian Cl Birmingham B14 .. 104 E5
　Tamworth B77 .... 35 D7
Appian Way B90 .... 126 D4
Apple Tree Cl
　Birmingham B23 .... 56 B4
　Kidderminster DY10 .... 117 B7
Apple Wlk WS11 .... 2 C2
Applebee Rd LE10 .... 75 D6
Appleby Cl B14 .... 104 D5
Appleby Gr B90 .... 127 B6
Applecross B74 .... 31 F1
Applecross Cl CV4 .... 131 F6
Appledore Cl Cannock WS12 .. 2 B3
　Great Wyrley WS6 .... 5 A3
Appledore Ct WS3 .... 28 B8
Appledore Dr CV5 .... 111 F5
Appledore Rd WS5 .... 43 D8
Appledore Terr WS5 .... 43 D8
Appledorne Gdns B34 .... 69 B6
Applesham Cl B11 .... 87 D6
Appleton Ave
　Birmingham B43 .... 54 E8
　Stourbridge DY8 .... 81 A2
Appleton Cl B30 .... 103 E8
Appleton Cres WV4 .... 39 A5
Appleton Ct B15 .... 86 B7
Appleton Rd B31 .... 102 E5
Appletree Cl
　Birmingham B31 .... 102 F1
　Catherine de B B91 .... 108 B5
Appletree Gr Aldridge WS9 .. 30 B5
　Wolverhampton WV6 .... 25 C5
Appletree La B97 .... 153 B5
Applewood Gr B64 .... 62 F1
Approach The CV31 .... 161 F6
April Croft B13 .... 87 B3
Apsley Cl B68 .... 84 A7
Apsley Croft B38 .... 104 B2
Apsley Gr Birmingham B24 .. 57 A2
　Dorridge B93 .... 127 F2
Apsley Ho B64 .... 62 F2
Apsley Rd B68 .... 84 A7
Aqua Ho CV2 .... 157 A1
Aqueduct La B48 .... 138 F7
Aqueduct Rd B90 .... 105 E1
Aragon Dr
　Royal Leamington Spa
　CV34 .... 161 D6
　Sutton Coldfield B73 .... 46 B6
Arbor Cl B77 .... 21 D3
Arbor Gate WS9 .... 16 B4
Arbor Way B37 .... 70 C1
Arboretum Rd WS1 .... 29 A3
Arboretum The CV4 .... 132 D3
Arbour Cl CV8 .... 148 B3
Arbour Tree La B93 .... 144 F2
Arbury Ave Bedworth CV12 .. 78 A3
　Coventry CV6 .... 95 F2
Arbury Cl CV32 .... 157 A4
Arbury Ct CV10 .... 72 C3
Arbury Dr DY8 .... 60 D3
Arbury Hall Rd B90 .... 126 D8
Arbury Rd CV10 .... 72 D2
Arbury Wlk B76 .... 58 D5
Arcade WS1 .... 28 E1
Arcade The CV3 .... 114 B2
Arcadian Sh Ctr B5 .... 164 C1
Arcal St DY3 .... 50 E7
Arch Hill St DY2 .... 62 C5
Arch Rd CV2 .... 114 C5
Archbishop Grimshaw
　Comp Sch B37 .... 69 F3
Archbishop Ilsley RC Sch
　B27 .... 88 C3
Archer Cl Oldbury B68 ..... 64 B4
　Studley B80 .... 159 D4
　Wednesbury WS10 .... 41 E3
Archer Ct DY9 .... 81 E2
Archer Rd Birmingham B14 . 105 A4
　Kenilworth CV8 .... 147 E3
　Redditch B98 .... 153 E4
　Walsall WS3 .... 28 E6
Archers Cl B23 .... 56 C8
Archery Fields CV34 .... 160 F6
Archery Rd Meriden CV7 .... 92 B1
　Royal Leamington Spa CV31 . 161 E3
Arches Ind Est The CV5 ... 113 A3
Archibald Rd B19 .... 66 C8

Archway The **2** WS4 .... 28 F3
Arcot Rd B28 .... 87 F2
Ardarth Rd B38 .... 104 A2
Ardav Rd B70 .... 52 F8
Arden Bldgs B93 .... 127 F3
Arden Cl
  Balsall Common CV7 .... 130 B7
  Meriden CV7 .... 92 C1
  Royal Leamington Spa CV31 .. 162 B5
  Stourbridge, Wollaston DY8 .... 80 E7
  Stourbridge, Wordsley DY8 .... 60 C3
  Tamworth B77 .... 21 E5
  Warwick CV34 .... 156 A1
Arden Croft Coleshill B46 ...... 59 F1
  Solihull B92 .... 89 C4
Arden Ct Binley Woods CV3 .. 135 D6
  2 Dudley DY3 .... 50 D3
  Hampton in A B92 .... 109 A7
  Sutton Coldfield B72 .... 57 C8
Arden Dr Birmingham B26 ...... 88 F7
  Dorridge B93 .... 128 A1
  Sutton Coldfield,
  Falcon Lodge B75 .... 47 B5
  Sutton Coldfield,
  Wylde Green B73 .... 57 B8
Arden Forest Inf Sch CV12 ... 79 B3
Arden Gr
  Birmingham, Ladywood B16 .. 66 A1
  8 Birmingham, Lozells B19 .. 66 C8
  Oldbury B69 .... 64 A5
Arden Ho B60 .... 137 B3
Arden Jun & Inf Sch B11 ...... 87 C5
Arden Leys B94 .... 141 D2
Arden Meads B94 .... 143 C6
Arden Pl WV14 .... 41 B4
Arden Rd
  Birmingham, Acock's Green
  B27 .... 88 A4
  Birmingham, Aston B6 .... 66 D8
  Birmingham, Rubery B45 .... 102 A5
  Bulkington CV12 .... 79 C2
  Dorridge B93 .... 127 F2
  Hollywood B47 .... 125 A6
  Kenilworth CV8 .... 148 B3
  Nuneaton CV11 .... 74 A1
  Smethwick B67 .... 65 A5
  Tamworth B77 .... 35 F5
Arden Sch B93 .... 128 B5
Arden Specl Sch B67 .... 65 A5
Arden St CV5 .... 132 F8
Arden Vale Rd B93 .... 128 B7
Ardencote B13 .... 105 A6
Ardendale **6** B90 .... 126 C8
Arderne Dr B37 .... 70 A1
Ardgay Dr WS12 .... 1 F7
Ardingley Wlk DY5 .... 81 B7
Ardley Cl DY2 .... 62 D8
Ardley Rd B14 .... 105 A1
Aretha Cl DY6 .... 61 A6
Argosy Ho B35 .... 58 B2
Argus Cl B76 .... 46 F3
Argyle Ave B77 .... 21 D4
Argyle Cl Stourbridge DY8 .... 60 E1
  Walsall WS4 .... 29 B3
Argyle Rd Walsall WS4 .... 29 B3
  Wolverhampton WV2 .... 39 B6
Argyle St Birmingham B7 ...... 67 D8
  Tamworth B77 .... 21 E4
Argyll Ho **5** WV3 .... 25 C4
Argyll St CV2 .... 114 A3
Ariane B79 .... 20 E7
Arion Cl B77 .... 21 D5
Arkall Cl B79 .... 21 C7
Arkle B77 .... 35 D4
Arkle Croft Birmingham B36 .. 68 C8
  Blackheath B65 .... 62 F6
Arkle Dr CV2 .... 114 F2
Arkley Gr B28 .... 106 B7
Arkley Rd B28 .... 106 B7
Arkwright Rd
  Birmingham B32 .... 84 C5
  Walsall WS2 .... 28 B5
Arlen Dr B43 .... 43 D1
Arlescote Cl B75 .... 32 C2
Arlescote Rd B92 .... 89 C2
Arless Way B17 .... 85 B3
Arleston Way B90 .... 126 E8
Arley Cl Kidderminster DY11 116 A2
  Oldbury B69 .... 63 D5
  Redditch B98 .... 154 D5
Arley Ct DY2 .... 62 C6
Arley Dr DY9 .... 80 E3
Arley Gr WV4 .... 38 D5
Arley Ho B15 .... 69 A1
Arley Mews CV32 .... 156 E1
Arley Rd Birmingham B29 ...... 85 F3
  Birmingham, Saltley B8 ...... 67 D6
  Solihull B91 .... 107 A4
Arley Villas **4** B18 .... 65 D4
Arlidge Cl WV14 .... 40 D4
Arlidge Cres CV8 .... 148 C5
Arlington Ave CV32 .... 156 F2
Arlington Cl DY6 .... 60 D4
Arlington Ct **2**
  Royal Leamington Spa CV32 . 156 F2
  Stourbridge DY8 .... 81 B4
Arlington Gr B14 .... 105 B2
Arlington Ho B15 .... 86 C7
Arlington Mews **5** CV32 .. 156 F2
Arlington Rd
  Birmingham B14 .... 105 B3
  West Bromwich B71 .... 53 D6
Arlington Way CV11 .... 73 F2
Arlon Ave CV10 .... 72 D7
Armada Cl B23 .... 56 D1
Armadale Cl LE10 .... 71 A1

Armarna Dr CV5 .... 111 B8
Armfield St CV6 .... 114 A8
Armitage Ho WS13 .... 3 E1
Armorial Rd CV3 .... 133 B7
Armour Cl LE10 .... 75 D5
Armoury Rd B11 .... 87 D6
Armoury Trad Est B11 .... 87 E6
Armscott Rd CV2 .... 114 C6
Armside Cl WS3 .... 15 B4
Armson Rd CV7 .... 78 A1
Armstead Rd WV9 .... 11 A3
Armstrong B79 .... 20 F6
Armstrong Ave CV3 .... 114 B1
Armstrong Cl
  Stourbridge DY8 .... 81 B6
  Whitnash CV31 .... 162 A2
Armstrong Dr
  Birmingham B36 .... 58 F1
  Walsall WS2 .... 28 A4
  Wolverhampton WV6 .... 25 A5
Armstrong Way WV13 .... 41 B8
Arna Ho CV3 .... 134 B6
Arncliffe Cl CV11 .... 74 A2
Arncliffe Way **4** CV34 .... 155 F1
Arne Rd CV2 .... 115 A6
Arnhem Cl WV11 .... 26 B8
Arnhem Cnr CV3 .... 134 D6
Arnhem Rd WV13 .... 40 E8
Arnhem Way **4** DY4 .... 52 C5
Arnold Ave CV3 .... 133 C5
Arnold Cl Tamworth B79 ...... 21 A6
  Walsall WS2 .... 27 F3
Arnold Gr Birmingham B30 .. 103 D4
  Solihull B90 .... 106 B4
Arnold Lodge Prep Sch
  CV32 .... 156 F2
Arnold Rd B90 .... 106 C4
Arnotdale Dr WS12 .... 1 F7
Arnside Cl CV1 .... 165 D4
Arnside Cl B23 .... 56 B4
Arnwood Cl WS2 .... 27 F2
Arosa Dr B17 .... 85 B3
Arran Cl Birmingham B43 .... 43 E3
  Cannock WS11 .... 2 A3
  Nuneaton CV10 .... 73 A3
Arran Rd B34 .... 68 F6
Arran Way Birmingham B36 .. 70 B7
  Hinckley LE10 .... 71 B1
Arras Bvd CV35 .... 160 A7
Arras Rd DY2 .... 51 E2
Arrow Cl B93 .... 128 A6
Arrow Ho **1** B68 .... 84 B8
Arrow Rd WS3 .... 28 E6
Arrow Rd N B98 .... 154 A4
Arrow S B98 .... 154 A4
Arrow Vale High Sch
  B98 .... 154 E2
Arrow Valley Park B98 .... 154 B4
Arrow Wlk B38 .... 104 B1
Arrowcrest Fst Sch B98 ...... 154 A4
Arrowdale Rd B98 .... 154 A3
Arrowfield Gn B38 .... 123 D7
Arsenal St B9 .... 67 C1
Arthingworth Cl CV3 .... 114 E1
Arthur Alford Ho CV12 ...... 77 D1
Arthur Dr (Road 2) DY10 .. 116 E1
Arthur Greenwood Ct
  WV14 .... 40 C6
Arthur Gunby Cl B75 .... 46 F7
Arthur Pl B1 .... 66 B3
Arthur Rd
  Birmingham, Edgbaston B15 ... 86 B7
  Birmingham, Erdington B24 ... 57 B4
  Birmingham, Handsworth
  B21 .... 65 F8
  Birmingham, Hay Mills B25 .... 88 B6
  Tipton DY4 .... 52 A7
Arthur St Bilston WV14 ...... 40 D6
  Birmingham B10 .... 67 B1
  Cannock, Chadsmoor WS11 .... 1 F4
  Cannock, Wimblebury WS12 ... 2 F3
  Coventry CV1 .... 165 C4
  Kenilworth CV8 .... 148 A5
  Redditch B98 .... 154 B3
  West Bromwich B70 .... 53 D1
  Wolverhampton WV2 .... 39 D6
Arthur Terry Sch B74 .... 32 A3
Artillery Rd CV11 .... 79 F6
Artingstall Ho B104 .... 104 B8
Arton Croft B24 .... 57 A2
Arun Way B76 .... 47 A1
Arundel Birmingham B17 ...... 85 A6
  Tamworth B77 .... 35 C7
Arundel Ave WS10 .... 41 F3
Arundel Cl **2** CV34 ...... 160 F8
Arundel Cres B92 .... 89 A1
Arundel Dr B69 .... 62 F8
Arundel Gr WV6 .... 23 F3
Arundel Ho **4** B23 ...... 56 F6
Arundel Pl B11 .... 87 A6
Arundel Rd Birmingham
  B14 .... 105 A1
  Bromsgrove B60 .... 137 B1
  Bulkington CV12 .... 79 C3
  Coventry CV3 .... 133 D6
  Stourbridge DY8 .... 60 C2
  Willenhall WV12 .... 27 C7
  Wolverhampton WV10 .... 11 B2
Arundel St WS1 .... 42 E7
Asbury Rd
  Balsall Common CV7 .... 130 B5
  Wednesbury WS10 .... 42 E2
Ascot Cl Bedworth CV12 ...... 78 B4
  Birmingham B16 .... 65 F2
  Coventry CV3 .... 134 C6
  Lichfield WS14 .... 9 D7
  Oldbury B69 .... 63 E6
Ascot Ct B29 .... 103 C7

Ascot Dr Cannock WS11 ...... 4 C8
  Dudley DY1 .... 50 F2
  Wolverhampton WV4 .... 39 A4
Ascot Gdns DY8 .... 60 D2
Ascot Rd B13 .... 86 F2
Ascot Ride CV32 .... 157 C3
Asfare Bsns Pk LE10 .... 75 E1
Ash Ave B12 .... 87 A5
Ash Cl WV8 .... 10 A3
Ash Cres Birmingham B37 ...... 69 E5
  Kingswinford DY6 .... 60 E6
Ash Ct Oldbury B66 .... 64 C8
  Stourbridge DY8 .... 81 A4
Ash Dr Catshill B61 .... 121 B1
  Kenilworth CV8 .... 148 A4
  Nuneaton CV10 .... 72 A8
  West Bromwich B71 .... 53 C6
Ash Gn DY1 .... 51 A5
Ash Gr Ash Green CV7 .... 95 C7
  Birmingham, Balsall Heath
  B12 .... 87 A5
  11 Birmingham, Bordesley
  B9 .... 67 B2
  Cannock WS11 .... 1 F4
  Dudley DY2 .... 50 C2
  Kidderminster DY11 .... 116 B7
  Lichfield WS13 .... 9 E8
  Stourbridge DY9 .... 81 D3
  Tamworth B77 .... 35 F5
Ash Green La CV7 .... 95 D6
Ash Green Sch CV7 .... 95 D6
Ash Hill WV3 .... 24 D2
Ash La Alvechurch B48 ...... 123 D2
  Great Wyrley WS6 .... 5 A3
Ash Lawn Ho **9** CV31 .... 162 A7
Ash Mews **5** B27 .... 88 C5
Ash Park Ind Est WS11 ...... 2 B3
Ash Priors Cl CV4 .... 112 B1
Ash Rd Birmingham B8 .... 67 D4
  Dudley B51 .... 51 B3
  Tipton DY4 .... 51 E4
  Wednesbury WS10 .... 41 F5
Ash St Bilston WV14 .... 40 E3
  Blackheath B64 .... 62 F2
  Walsall WS3 .... 14 D1
  Wolverhampton WV3 .... 25 A1
Ash Terr B69 .... 52 B1
Ash Tree Ave CV4 .... 112 A2
Ash Tree Dr B26 .... 88 D7
Ash Tree Gr CV7 .... 97 E5
Ash Tree Rd
  Birmingham B30 .... 104 A6
  Redditch B97 .... 153 B5
Ash View WS12 .... 1 D8
Ash Way B23 .... 56 C7
Ashborough Dr B91 .... 127 C8
Ashbourne Cl WS11 .... 2 A4
Ashbourne Gr **3** B6 ...... 66 E8
Ashbourne Rd
  Birmingham B16 .... 65 D3
  Walsall WS3 .... 14 C3
  Wolverhampton,
  Ettingshall Park WV4 .... 39 E3
  Wolverhampton,
  Heath Town WV1 .... 26 A3
Ashbourne Way B90 .... 126 E8
Ashbridge Rd CV5 .... 112 C4
Ashbrook Gr B30 .... 104 C8
Ashbrook Rd B30 .... 104 C8
Ashburn Gr WV13 .... 27 C2
Ashburton Cl LE10 .... 76 A6
Ashburton Rd
  Birmingham B14 .... 104 D5
  Coventry CV2 .... 114 B4
Ashbury Covert **3** B30 .... 104 C3
Ashby Cl Birmingham B8 ...... 68 C6
  Coventry CV3 .... 134 F8
Ashby Ct Nuneaton CV11 ...... 73 D3
  Solihull B91 .... 107 C1
Ashby Rd Hinckley LE9, LE10 .. 71 E5
  Tamworth B79 .... 21 C8
Ashcombe Ave B20 .... 54 E3
Ashcombe Dr CV4 .... 111 F3
Ashcombe Gdns B24 .... 57 D3
Ashcott Cl B38 .... 103 D2
Ashcroft Birmingham B15 ...... 85 E5
  4 Smethwick B66 .... 65 C5
Ashcroft Cl CV2 .... 115 A8
Ashcroft Cty Inf Sch B79 .... 21 C7
Ashcroft Gr B20 .... 55 D2
Ashcroft La Lichfield WS14 .... 8 E1
  Shenstone WS14 .... 17 E7
Ashcroft Way CV2 .... 115 B8
Ashdale Cl
  Binley Woods CV3 .... 135 E7
  Huntington WS12 .... 1 C7
  Kingswinford DY6 .... 60 E8
Ashdale Dr B14 .... 105 A1
Ashdale Gr B26 .... 89 A8
Ashdale Rd B77 .... 21 D5
Ashdene Cl
  Kidderminster DY10 .... 117 C5
  Sutton Coldfield B73 .... 46 A3
Ashdene Gdns
  Kenilworth CV8 .... 148 B4
  Stourbridge DY8 .... 60 C2
Ashdown Cl
  Birmingham, Frankley B45 .... 102 A2
  Birmingham, Highgate B13 .... 87 A1
  Coventry CV3 .... 134 D8
Ashdown Dr Nuneaton CV10 .. 72 F2
  Stourbridge DY8 .... 60 E3
Ashen Cl DY3 .... 39 C3
Ashenden Rise WV3 .... 38 A8
Ashenhurst Rd DY1 .... 61 F8

Ashenhurst Wlk DY1 .... 51 A1
Ashes Rd B69 .... 63 D3
Ashes The Oldbury B69 ...... 63 F3
  Wolverhampton WV11 .... 26 A5
Ashfern Dr B76 .... 57 F7
Ashfield Ave Birmingham
  B14 .... 86 F1
  Coventry CV4 .... 111 D1
Ashfield Cl WS3 .... 28 A4
Ashfield Cres Dudley DY2 .... 62 C3
  Stourbridge DY9 .... 82 A3
Ashfield Ct B38 .... 103 E4
Ashfield Gr Halesowen B63 .. 82 E2
  Wolverhampton WV10 .... 11 C3
Ashfield Ho B28 .... 105 E3
Ashfield Rd Bilston WV14 .... 41 A2
  Birmingham B14 .... 86 F1
  Kenilworth CV8 .... 148 B4
  Wolverhampton, Compton
  WV3 .... 24 D2
  Wolverhampton,
  Fordhouses WV10 .... 11 C3
Ashford Dr Bedworth CV12 .. 78 A3
  Sedgley DY3 .... 50 E7
  Sutton Coldfield B76 .... 57 F5
Ashford Gdns CV31 .... 161 F3
Ashford La B94 .... 143 B7
Ashford Rd Hinckley LE10 .... 75 B7
  Whitnash CV31 .... 161 F2
Ashford St B6 .... 66 E6
Ashfurlong Cl CV7 .... 130 B6
Ashfurlong Cres B75 .... 46 E8
Ashgrove WS7 .... 6 F5
Ashgrove Ct B60 .... 121 D7
Ashgrove Rd B44 .... 44 C2
Ashill Rd B45 .... 122 B7
Ashington Gr CV3 .... 134 A5
Ashington Rd CV12 .... 77 C1
Ashland St WV3 .... 25 B1
Ashlands B79 .... 21 C7
Ashlawn Cres B91 .... 106 D5
Ashlea B78 .... 36 F5
Ashleigh Ct **8** DY2 ...... 62 E8
Ashleigh Dr Birmingham B20 .. 55 B2
  Nuneaton CV11 .... 73 F1
  Tamworth B77 .... 35 E8
Ashleigh Gr B13 .... 87 B1
Ashleigh Rd Solihull B91 .... 107 B4
  Tipton B69 .... 63 C8
Ashley Cl Birmingham B15 .... 86 C7
  Kingswinford DY6 .... 60 C4
  Stourbridge DY8 .... 80 C2
Ashley Cres CV34 .... 161 B6
Ashley Ct B45 .... 122 A1
Ashley Ho DY2 .... 62 D4
Ashley Mount WV6 .... 24 D5
Ashley Rd Birmingham B23 .. 56 E3
  Walsall WS3 .... 27 F8
  Wolverhampton WV4 .... 38 E5
Ashley St WV14 .... 40 E6
Ashmall WS7 .... 7 D4
Ashmead Dr B45 .... 122 C4
Ashmead Gr B24 .... 57 A2
Ashmead Rd WS7 .... 7 A8
Ashmead Rise B45 .... 122 C4
Ashmole Cl WS14 .... 9 E6
Ashmole Rd B70 .... 52 F7
Ashmore Ave WV11 .... 13 A1
Ashmore Lake Rd WV12 .... 27 B4
Ashmore Lake Way WV12 .. 27 B4
Ashmore Rd
  Birmingham B30 .... 103 F5
  Coventry CV6 .... 113 B4
Ashmores Cl B97 .... 158 D5
Ashold Farm Rd B24 .... 57 D2
Asholme B36 .... 68 C7
Ashorne Cl Birmingham
  B28 .... 106 B7
  Coventry CV2 .... 96 C2
  Redditch B98 .... 159 D8
Ashover Gr **9** B18 ...... 65 E4
Ashover Rd B44 .... 44 D3
Ashow Cl CV8 .... 148 B4
Ashperton Cl B98 .... 153 E1
Ashridge Cl CV11 .... 78 F8
Ashstead Cl B76 .... 58 B6
Ashted Cir B7 .... 67 A4
Ashted Lock B7 .... 66 F4
Ashted Wlk B7 .... 67 B4
Ashton B97 .... 153 B1
Ashton Croft Birmingham
  B16 .... 66 A2
  Solihull B91 .... 107 A1
Ashton Dr WS4 .... 15 C2
Ashton Park Dr DY5 .... 61 C1
Ashton Rd B25 .... 88 C7
Ashtree Gr WV14 .... 41 B3
Ashtree Rd Blackheath B64 .. 62 F2
  Oldbury B69 .... 63 D8
  Tipton B69 .... 52 C1
  Walsall WS3 .... 15 A3
Ashurst Rd B76 .... 57 F7
Ashville Ave B34 .... 68 F7
Ashville Dr B63 .... 83 A5
Ashwater Dr B14 .... 104 D2
Ashway B11 .... 87 B5
Ashwell Dr B90 .... 106 B3
Ashwells Gr WV9 .... 10 F2
Ashwin Rd B21 .... 66 A7
Ashwood Ave Coventry CV6 112 F5
  Stourbridge DY8 .... 60 D6
Ashwood Cl B74 .... 44 E8
Ashwood Ct Birmingham
  B B13 .... 87 A3
  Birmingham, Stechford B34 .. 68 D5
Ashwood Dr B37 .... 70 D3
Ashwood Gr WV4 .... 39 A4

Ashwood Park Prim Sch
  DY8 .... 60 D1
Ashwood Rd CV10 .... 72 E5
Ashworth Ho Cannock WS11 .. 2 A4
  Lichfield WS13 .... 9 B8
Ashworth Rd B42 .... 44 B1
Askew Bridge Rd DY3 ...... 50 B3
Askew Cl DY3 .... 50 E5
Aspbury Croft B36 .... 58 D1
Aspen Cl Birmingham B27 .... 88 B2
  Coventry CV4 .... 111 D3
Aspen Dr B37 .... 90 C8
Aspen Gdns B20 .... 55 B1
Aspen Gr Birmingham B9 .... 68 A3
  Burntwood WS7 .... 6 F8
  Hollywood B47 .... 125 B5
  Willenhall WV12 .... 27 E7
Aspen Ho B91 .... 106 F2
Aspen Way WV3 .... 25 A1
Asplen Ct CV8 .... 148 C4
Aspley Heath B94 .... 141 D2
Aspley Heath La B94 .... 141 D2
Asquith Dr Cannock WS11 .... 2 C2
  Tipton B69 .... 52 D2
Asquith Rd B8 .... 68 B5
Asra Cl Coventry CV2 .... 113 F4
  Smethwick B66 .... 65 A8
Astbury Ave B67 .... 64 F3
Astbury Cl Walsall WS3 ...... 14 A4
  Wolverhampton WV1 .... 26 A1
Astbury Ct **7** B68 .... 84 B7
Aster Cl Hinckley LE10 ...... 75 E6
  Nuneaton CV11 .... 74 A1
Aster Way LE10 .... 75 D6
Aster Wlk WV9 .... 11 A3
Asthill Croft CV3 .... 133 C8
Asthill Gr CV3 .... 133 C8
Astley Ave Coventry CV6 .... 95 E2
  Halesowen B62 .... 83 F6
Astley Cl Redditch B98 ...... 159 A7
  Royal Leamington Spa CV32 .. 156 D2
  Tipton DY4 .... 52 D6
Astley Cres B63 .... 83 F5
Astley La Bedworth CV12 .... 77 C4
  Nuneaton CV10 .... 72 B1
Astley Rd B21 .... 54 D1
Astley Wlk B90 .... 106 B5
Aston Bridge B6 .... 66 F5
Aston Brook Gn B6 .... 66 F5
Aston Brook St B6 .... 66 F6
Aston Brook St E B6 .... 66 F5
Aston Bury B15 .... 85 D7
Aston Church Rd B7, B8 ...... 67 D6
Aston Cl Bilston WV14 ...... 41 A4
  Shenstone WS14 .... 17 F6
Aston Cross B6 .... 67 A6
Aston Ct B23 .... 56 C3
Aston Expressway B6 .... 66 F6
Aston Expressway
  (Elevated Rd) B6 .... 67 A8
Aston Fields Mid Sch
  B60 .... 151 C8
Aston Fields Trad Est
  B60 .... 150 F6
Aston Flamville Rd LE10 .... 76 C7
Aston Hall B6 .... 66 F8
Aston Hall Rd B6 .... 67 B8
Aston Ind Est CV12 .... 78 C2
Aston La Birmingham B20 .... 55 E2
  Hinckley LE10 .... 76 A6
Aston Manor Sch B6 .... 66 F6
Aston Pk Ind Est CV11 ...... 73 B5
Aston Rd Birmingham B6 ...... 66 F5
  Bromsgrove B60 .... 150 F6
  Coventry CV5 .... 112 F1
  Dudley DY2 .... 62 B8
  Nuneaton CV11 .... 73 B5
  Tipton B69 .... 52 A1
  Willenhall WV13 .... 26 E2
Aston Rd N B6 .... 66 F6
Aston Seabed Ctr B7 .... 67 A6
Aston St Birmingham B4 .... 164 D4
  Tipton DY4 .... 52 C7
  Wolverhampton WV3 .... 39 A8
Aston Sta B6 .... 67 B8
Aston Tower Inf & Jun
  Schs B6 .... 66 F7
Astons Cl DY5 .... 81 D7
Astons Fold DY5 .... 81 D7
Astor Dr B13 .... 87 C1
Astor Rd Aldridge B74 ...... 31 A1
  Kingswinford DY6 .... 60 F5
Astoria Cl WV12 .... 13 D1
Astoria Gdns WV12 .... 13 D1
Astwell Prep Sch B20 ...... 66 B8
Astwood Bank Fst Sch
  B96 .... 158 E2
Astwood La B96 .... 158 C2
Atcham Cl B98 .... 154 F3
Atcheson Cl B80 .... 159 E4
Athelney Ct WS3 .... 15 A3
Athelstan Gr WV6 .... 23 F5
Athelstan Way B79 .... 20 F7
Athena Dr CV34 .... 161 D5
Athena Gdns CV6 .... 96 A1
Atherstone Pl CV4 .... 132 C6
Atherstone Cl Redditch
  B98 .... 154 F1
  Solihull B90 .... 105 D4
Atherstone Rd WV1 .... 26 B2
Atherstone St B78 .... 35 B8
Athlone Rd WS5 .... 43 C8
Athol Cl B32 .... 102 D8
Athol Rd CV2 .... 115 A6

Athole St B12 .... 87 A7
Atholl Cres CV10 .... 72 E2
Atkins Way LE10 .... 75 E7
Atkinson Ct WV10 .... 25 D6
Atlantic Ct **4** WV13 .... 27 A1
Atlantic Rd B44 .... 44 F1
Atlas Croft WV10 .... 25 C6
Atlas Gr B70 .... 52 F3
Atlas Trad Est B11 .... 87 D5
Attenborough Cl B19 .... 66 E5
Attingham Dr
  Birmingham B43 .... 43 D2
  Cannock WS11 .... 2 B2
Attleborough Fields
  Ind Est CV11 .... 73 F3
Attleborough Fst Sch CV11 . 73 E3
Attleborough La B46 .... 59 A1
Attleborough Rd CV11 .... 73 D3
Attlee Cl B69 .... 52 D2
Attlee Cres WV14 .... 40 E2
Attlee Gr WS11 .... 2 C2
Attlee Rd WS2 .... 27 E3
Attoxhall Rd CV2 .... 114 E4
Attwell Pk WV3 .... 38 D7
Attwell Rd DY4 .... 40 F1
Attwood Bsns Ctr **1** DY9 .. 81 F5
Attwood Cl B88 .... 67 E6
Attwood Cres CV2 .... 114 C7
Attwood Gdns WV4 .... 39 E5
Attwood Rd WS7 .... 6 C7
Attwood St DY9 .... 81 F5
Aubrey Rd
  Birmingham, Beech Lanes
  B32 .... 84 E7
  Birmingham, Small Heath
  B10 .... 87 F8
Auchinleck Dr WS13 .... 3 C1
Auchinleck Sq **5** B15 ..... 66 B1
Auckland Dr B36 .... 70 B7
Auckland Ho B32 .... 84 F4
Auckland Rd Birmingham
  B11 .... 87 A7
  Kingswinford DY6 .... 60 E4
  Smethwick B67 .... 64 E5
Auden Ct WV6 .... 23 F4
Audleigh Ho **1** B15 .... 86 C8
Audlem Wlk WV10 .... 26 A5
Audley Dr DY11 .... 116 A8
Audley Jun Sch B33 .... 68 F4
Audley Rd B33 .... 68 F4
Audnam DY8 .... 60 F1
Augusta Pl CV32 .... 161 F8
Augusta Rd
  Birmingham, Acock's Green
  B27 .... 88 C5
  Birmingham, Moseley B13 .. 86 E4
Augusta Rd E B13 .... 86 F4
Augusta St B18 .... 66 C4
Augusfine Ave B80 .... 159 D4
Augustine Gr Birmingham
  B18 .... 65 F6
  Sutton Coldfield B74 .... 31 F5
Augustines Wlk WS13 .... 3 A3
Augustus Cl B46 .... 59 F1
Augustus Ct B15 .... 85 E8
Augustus Rd Birmingham
  B15 .... 85 E8
  Coventry CV1 .... 113 F4
Augustus St WS2 .... 28 D1
Ault St B70 .... 53 D1
Aulton Cres LE10 .... 71 B1
Aulton Rd B75 .... 32 E2
Aulton Way LE10 .... 71 B1
Austcliff Cl B97 .... 158 D6
Austcliff Dr B91 .... 127 C8
Austen Ct CV32 .... 157 E5
Austen Pl B15 .... 86 B8
Austen Wlk B71 .... 53 D6
Auster Ho B35 .... 58 B3
Austey Ct B73 .... 57 A7
Austin Cl Birmingham B27 .. 88 D4
  Dudley DY1 .... 50 F2
Austin Cote La WS14 .... 9 E7
Austin Croft B36 .... 58 E1
Austin Dr CV6 .... 114 A7
Austin Edwards Dr
  3 CV34 .... 161 B8
Austin Ho WS4 .... 28 F3
Austin Rd Birmingham B21 .. 54 C1
  Bromsgrove B60 .... 150 E7
Austin Rise B31 .... 122 F7
Austin St WV6 .... 25 B4
Austin Way B42 .... 55 A5
Austrey Cl B93 .... 128 A6
Austrey Gr B29 .... 103 A8
Austrey Rd DY6 .... 61 A5
Austwick Cl CV34 .... 155 C1
Austy Cl B36 .... 68 E8
Auto Ctr B18 .... 65 C5
Autumn Berry Gr DY3 .... 50 E6
Autumn Cl WS4 .... 15 C1
Autumn Dr Dudley DY3 ...... 50 D4
  Lichfield WS13 .... 3 D2
  Walsall WS4 .... 15 C2
Autumn Gr B19 .... 66 C6
Auxerre Ave B98 .... 159 B8
Avalon Cl B24 .... 57 B4
Ave Maria Cl B64 .... 62 E1
Avebury Cl CV11 .... 73 F2
Avebury Gr B30 .... 104 C2
Avebury Rd B30 .... 104 C8
Avenbury Cl B98 .... 154 F1
Avenbury Dr B91 .... 107 E4
Avenue Cl Birmingham B7 .. 67 A6
  Dorridge B93 .... 128 A3

Avenue Rd
  Astwood Bank B96 .... 158 E1
  Birmingham, Aston B7, B6 .. 67 A6
  Birmingham, Erdington B23 .. 56 F4
  Birmingham, Handsworth
  B21 .... 54 D2
  Birmingham, King's Heath
  B14 .... 104 D8
  Blackheath B65 .... 63 D1
  Cannock WS12 .... 2 E2
  Darlaston WS10 .... 41 D6
  Dorridge B93 .... 128 A3
  Dudley, Roseville WV14 .. 51 C8
  Dudley, Woodside DY2 .... 61 F6
  Kenilworth CV8 .... 147 D6
  Nuneaton CV11 .... 73 D2
  Royal Leamington Spa CV31 . 161 F7
  Wolverhampton WV3 ...... 24 E2
Avenue The
  Birmingham,
  Acock's Green B27 .... 88 D3
  Birmingham, Eachway B45 .. 121 E7
  2 Birmingham, Lozells B19 .. 66 C8
  Blackheath B65 .... 63 A3
  Blackwell B60 .... 138 A6
  Blakedown DY10 .... 98 B2
  Coventry CV3 .... 134 A6
  Featherstone WV10 .... 12 C7
  Rowington Green CV35 ... 145 A1
  Wolverhampton,
  Castlecroft WV3 .... 38 B8
  Wolverhampton, Penn WV4 .. 38 E4
Averill Rd B26 .... 69 A1
Avern Cl DY4 .... 52 B6
Aversley Rd B38 .... 123 E8
Avery Croft B35 .... 57 F2
Avery Ct **6** Oldbury B68 .. 84 B7
  6 Warwick CV34 ...... 160 F7
Avery Dell Ind Est B30 .... 104 A6
Avery Dr B27 .... 88 C4
Avery Ho B16 .... 66 A1
Avery Myers Cl B68 .... 64 B5
Avery Rd Smethwick B66 ... 65 D6
  Sutton Coldfield B73 .... 45 D3
Aviemore Cl CV10 .... 73 A2
Aviemore Cres B43 .... 44 B4
Avill B77 .... 36 A5
Avill Gr DY11 .... 116 C7
Avington Cl DY3 .... 50 D7
Avion Cl WS1 .... 42 F7
Avion Ctr W6 .... 25 A4
Avocet Cl Birmingham B33 .. 68 C3
  Coventry CV2 .... 96 B3
Avocet Dr DY10 .... 117 A2
Avon B77 .... 36 A5
Avon Bsns Pk WS11 .... 4 C7
Avon Cl Brierley Hill DY5 ... 61 B7
  Bromsgrove B60 .... 150 F6
  Bulkington CV12 .... 79 B6
  Perton WV6 .... 23 F4
Avon Cres WS3 .... 15 A1
Avon Ct Kenilworth CV8 ... 147 F5
  Sutton Coldfield B73 ...... 46 B5
Avon Dr Birmingham,
  Castle Bromwich B36 ...... 69 F7
  Birmingham, Moseley B13 .. 87 B2
  Willenhall WV13 .... 27 C2
  Wythall B47 .... 124 E2
Avon Gr WS5 .... 43 A4
Avon Ho Birmingham B15 .. 86 D8
  Coventry CV4 .... 132 C6
  1 Dudley, Dibdale DY3 .. 50 E3
  2 Dudley, Russell's Hall DY1 61 E8
  3 Oldbury B68 .... 84 B8
Avon Rd Burntwood WS7 .... 6 F5
  Cannock WS11 .... 4 D7
  Halesowen B63 .... 82 B5
  Kenilworth CV8 .... 147 E3
  Kidderminster DY11 ..... 116 B3
  Solihull B90 .... 106 D1
  Stourbridge DY8 .... 80 F3
  Walsall WS3 .... 14 E1
  Whitnash CV31 .... 162 A3
Avon St Birmingham B11 ... 87 C5
  Coventry CV2 .... 114 B5
  Warwick CV34 .... 161 A7
Avonbank Cl B97 .... 158 C6
Avoncroft WV4 .... 39 F4
Avoncroft Coll B60 .... 150 E5
Avoncroft Ho B37 .... 70 A2
Avoncroft Mus of
  Building B60 .... 150 E5
Avoncroft Rd B60 .... 150 D6
Avondale Cl DY6 .... 60 E8
Avondale Rd Birmingham
  B11 .... 87 D4
  Brandon CV8 .... 135 F5
  Coventry CV5 .... 133 A8
  Royal Leamington Spa CV32 157 C4
  Wolverhampton WV6 .... 25 A3
Avonlea Rise CV32 .... 156 D2
Avro Ho B35 .... 58 B2
Awbridge Rd DY2 .... 62 C3
Awefields Cres B67 .... 64 E4
Awson St CV6 .... 113 F6
Axholme Rd CV2 .... 114 E4
Axletree Way WS10 .... 42 B6
Axminster Cl CV11 .... 73 F5
Ayala Croft **2** B36 ...... 68 E8
Aylesbury Cl B94 .... 143 C6
Aylesbury Cres B44 .... 56 A8
Aylesbury Rd B94 .... 143 D7
Aylesdene Ct CV5 .... 132 F8
Aylesford Cl DY3 .... 39 C2
Aylesford Ct **7** CV31 .. 162 A6
Aylesford Dr Birmingham B37 90 A7
  Sutton Coldfield B74 ...... 31 E5

Aylesford Rd B21 .... 54 D1
Aylesford Sch CV34 .... 160 C4
Aylesford St Coventry CV1 . 113 E4
  Royal Leamington Spa CV31 162 A6
Aylesmore Cl
  Birmingham B32 .... 84 C1
  Solihull B92 .... 106 E8
Aynho Cl CV5 .... 112 A3
Aynsley Ct B90 .... 106 C2
Ayre Rd B24 .... 57 B4
Ayrshire Cl B36 .... 68 D8
Ayrton Cl WV6 .... 24 A4
Aysgarth Cl CV11 .... 74 A2
Azalea Cl Codsall WV8 ...... 10 B3
  Hinckley LE10 .... 75 E5
Azalea Dr LE10 .... 75 E6
Azalea Gr B9 .... 67 F2
Azalea Wlk LE10 .... 75 E5
Aziz Isaac Cl B68 .... 64 C6

Babbacombe Rd CV3 ...... 133 D5
Babington Rd B21 .... 65 E7
Bablake Cl CV6 .... 112 F8
Bablake Croft B92 .... 89 A1
Bablake Jun Sch CV1 ...... 165 A1
Bablake Sch CV1 .... 113 B4
Babors Field WV14 .... 40 A3
Babworth Cl WV9 .... 11 A2
Baccabox La B47 .... 124 E7
Bacchus Rd B18 .... 65 F6
Bach Mill Dr B28 .... 105 D3
Bache St B70 .... 53 D1
Back La Aldridge WS9 .... 30 F8
  Meriden CV7 .... 110 E5
  Shenstone WS14 .... 17 E1
  Warwick CV34 .... 160 E6
Back Rd Birmingham B38 .. 103 F2
  Kingswinford DY6 .... 60 D7
Back St CV11 .... 73 C5
Backcester La WS13 .... 9 B8
Backcrofts **7** WS11 ...... 1 E1
Backhouse La WV11 .... 26 C4
Badbury Cl B80 .... 159 D4
Baddesley Cl CV31 .... 162 D5
Baddesley Clinton B93 .... 144 F3
Baddesley Rd B92 .... 88 E2
Bader Rd Perton WV6 .... 23 E3
  Walsall WS2 .... 27 F2
Bader Wlk B35 .... 57 F2
Badger Cl
  Cheswick Green B90 ...... 126 D3
  Redditch B98 .... 154 D3
Badger Dr WV10 .... 25 D4
Badger Rd CV3 .... 134 D8
Badger St Dudley DY3 .... 50 E5
  Stourbridge DY9 .... 81 E6
Badger Way B60 .... 138 B5
Badgers Bank Rd B74 .... 31 F5
Badgers Cl WS3 .... 15 A5
Badgers Croft B62 .... 83 B7
Badgers The B45 .... 122 A2
Badgers Way
  Birmingham B34 .... 69 A5
  Cannock WS12 .... 2 D1
Badminton Cl DY1 .... 50 F3
Badon Covert B14 .... 104 D2
Badsey Cl B31 .... 103 C4
Badsey Rd B69 .... 63 D5
Baggeridge Cl DY3 .... 50 A8
Baggeridge Cty Pk DY3 ..... 49 E6
Baggott St WV2 .... 39 C7
Baginton Cl B91 .... 107 B5
Baginton Fields Sch CV3 .. 134 B4
Baginton Rd Birmingham
  B35 .... 58 B4
  Coventry CV3 .... 133 C5
Bagley Rd DY5 .... 81 D6
Bagley St DY9 .... 81 C6
Bagnall Cl B25 .... 88 D6
Bagnall Rd WV14 .... 40 C5
Bagnall St Tipton DY4 ...... 41 C1
  Walsall WS10 .... 28 C6
  West Bromwich, Golds Hill
  B70 .... 52 E7
  West Bromwich,
  Mayer's Green B70 .... 53 E2
Bagnall Wlk DY5 .... 61 D1
Bagnell Rd B13 .... 104 F7
Bagot St B4 .... 164 C4
Bagridge Cl WV3 .... 38 B8
Bagridge Rd WV3 .... 38 B8
Bagshaw Cl CV8 .... 135 A1
Bagshaw Rd B33 .... 68 E3
Bagshawe Croft B23 .... 56 D7
Bailey Ave B77 .... 35 F5
Bailey Cl WS11 .... 2 A4
Bailey Rd WV14 .... 40 B7
Bailey St West Bromwich
  B70 .... 53 A4
  Wolverhampton WV10 .... 163 D3
Baileys Ct B65 .... 63 B3
Bailye Cl WS13 .... 3 F1
Baines' La **1** LE10 .... 71 D1
Bakehouse La B93 .... 145 B6
Bakeman Ho B26 .... 88 D6
Baker Ave
  Royal Leamington Spa CV31 . 161 F6
  Wolverhampton WV14 .... 39 F2
Baker House Gr B43 .... 54 D7
Baker Rd WV14 .... 40 E3
Baker St Bedworth CV6 ..... 96 B6
  Birmingham, Handsworth B21 .. 65 F8
  Birmingham, Small Heath B10 .. 67 D1
  Birmingham, Sparkhill B11 .. 87 C5
  Burntwood WS7 .... 6 F6
  Tipton DY4 .... 51 E4
  West Bromwich B70 .... 53 B3

Baker's La Aldridge WS9 .... 30 B6
  Lichfield WS13 .... 9 B7
Bakers La Coventry CV5 ... 112 E2
  Knowle B93 .... 128 D1
  Sutton Coldfield B73, B74 .. 45 A5
Bakers Mews B93 .... 145 B6
Bakers Wlk B77 .... 35 F6
Bakewell Cl Coventry CV3 . 134 F8
  Walsall WS3 .... 14 C3
Balaclava Rd B14 .... 104 E8
Balcaskie Cl B15 .... 85 E7
Bald's La DY9 .... 81 F5
Balden Rd B32 .... 84 F7
Baldmoor Lake Rd B23 ..... 56 F6
Baldwin Cl B69 .... 52 D2
Baldwin Croft CV6 .... 96 B5
Baldwin Gr WS11 .... 2 C1
Baldwin Ho B19 .... 66 C6
Baldwin Rd Birmingham
  B30 .... 104 A3
  Kidderminster DY10 ...... 117 B7
Baldwin St Bilston WV14 ... 40 F4
  Smethwick B66 .... 65 B6
Baldwins La B28 .... 105 F4
Balfour B79 .... 21 A4
Balfour Cl LE10 .... 75 E7
Balfour Cres WV6 .... 24 F4
Balfour Ct
  Sutton Coldfield B74 .... 32 A3
  Wolverhampton WV6 .... 24 F4
Balfour Dr B69 .... 52 D2
Balfour Ho **2** B16 .... 65 F1
Balfour Rd DY6 .... 60 E8
Balfour St B12 .... 86 E6
Balham Gr B44 .... 45 A2
Balholm B62 .... 83 D5
Balking Cl WV14 .... 40 B3
Ball Fields DY4 .... 52 D5
Ball Ho **5** WS3 .... 28 B8
Ball La WV10 .... 11 C6
Ballantine Rd CV6 .... 113 B6
Ballard Cres DY2 .... 62 D5
Ballard Rd DY2 .... 62 D5
Ballard Wlk B37 .... 70 A6
Ballingham Cl CV4 .... 112 A2
Balliol Bsns Pk WV9 .... 10 E3
Balliol Ho B37 .... 69 F2
Balliol Rd Coventry CV2 .. 114 C4
  Hinckley LE10 .... 75 F6
Ballot St B66 .... 65 B5
Balls Hill WS1 .... 28 F2
Balls St WS1 .... 28 F2
Balmain Cres WV11 .... 12 B1
Balmoral Cl Coventry CV2 114 E6
  Halesowen B62 .... 83 B7
  Lichfield WS14 .... 9 D6
  Walsall WS4 .... 29 D7
Balmoral Ct Cannock WS11 .. 2 A5
  Kidderminster DY10 ...... 117 A5
  Nuneaton CV10 .... 72 E6
Balmoral Dr Cannock WS12 .. 1 F7
  Willenhall WV12 .... 27 C7
  Wombourne WV5 .... 38 A1
Balmoral Rd
  Birmingham, Erdington B23 .. 56 F5
  Birmingham, Kingshurst B36 .. 70 A7
  Birmingham, Kitwell B32 .. 102 B7
  Stourbridge DY8 .... 60 C2
  Sutton Coldfield B74 .... 31 F5
  Wolverhampton WV4 .... 39 A5
Balmoral View DY1 .... 50 E2
Balmoral Way
  Blackheath B65 .... 63 D4
  Royal Leamington Spa CV32 157 C6
Balsall Common Prim
  Sch CV7 .... 130 B5
Balsall Heath Rd B12 .... 86 E7
Balsall St B93, CV7 .... 129 D7
Balsall St E CV7 .... 130 B5
Baltic Cl WS11 .... 1 E2
Baltimore Rd B42 .... 55 A5
Balvenie Way DY1 .... 50 F4
Bamber Cl WV3 .... 38 E8
Bamburgh B77 .... 35 C7
Bamburgh Gr CV32 .... 156 E3
Bamford Cl WS3 .... 14 C3
Bamford Ho WS3 .... 14 C3
Bamford Rd Walsall WS3 ... 14 C3
  Wolverhampton WV3 .... 39 A8
Bamford St B77 .... 21 D3
Bampfylde Pl B42 .... 55 C7
Bampton Ave WS7 .... 7 A8
Bamville Rd B8 .... 68 A5
Banbrook Cl B92 .... 107 D8
Banbury Cl DY3 .... 50 E6
Banbury Croft B37 .... 69 E2
Banbury Ho B33 .... 69 E2
Banbury Rd Cannock WS11 .. 4 C8
  Warwick CV34 .... 161 A3
Banbury St B5 .... 66 F2
Bancroft B77 .... 21 F3
Bancroft St WV14 .... 51 B7
Bandywood Cres B44 .... 44 F3
Bandywood Rd B44 .... 44 F3
Baneberry Dr WV10 .... 12 B7
Banfield Ave WS10 .... 41 C7
Banford Ave B8 .... 68 A4
Banford Rd B8 .... 68 A4
Bangham Pit Rd B31 ...... 102 E6
Bangley La
  Drayton Bassett B78 ...... 35 C3
  Mile Oak B78 .... 34 A8
Bangor Ho B9 .... 67 D2
Bangor Rd B9 .... 67 D2
Bank Cres WS7 .... 6 F5
Bank Croft CV31 .... 162 C5

Bank Farm Cl DY9 .... 81 C1
Bank Rd
  Dudley, Gornalwood DY3 .. 50 C2
  Dudley, Netherton DY2 .... 62 D6
Bank St Bilston WV14 .... 40 E3
  Birmingham B14 .... 86 E1
  Blackheath B64 .... 62 C1
  Brierley Hill DY5 .... 61 D3
  Cannock WS12 .... 2 E1
  Dudley WV14 .... 51 C8
  Stourbridge DY9 .... 81 F5
  Walsall WS1 .... 28 F1
  West Bromwich B71 .... 53 D6
  Wolverhampton WV10 .... 25 E5
Bank The CV8 .... 149 C6
Bankdale Rd B8 .... 68 B4
Bankes Rd B10 .... 67 F1
Bankfield Dr CV32 .... 156 C1
Bankfield Rd Bilston WV14 . 40 D5
  Tipton DY4 .... 52 C8
Banklands Rd DY2 .... 62 E6
Banks Gn B60, B97 .... 152 B2
Banks Rd CV6 .... 113 A5
Banks St WS13 .... 82 D6
Bankside
  Birmingham, Great Barr B43 .. 54 E7
  Birmingham, Moseley B13 .. 87 D2
Bankside Cl CV3 .... 134 A6
Bankside Cres B74 .... 44 F7
Bankside Way WS9 .... 16 B2
Bankwell St DY5 .... 61 D4
Banky Mdw LE10 .... 76 A7
Banner La CV4 .... 111 D2
Bannerlea Rd B37 .... 69 F5
Bannerley Rd B33 .... 69 C1
Banners Ct B23 .... 45 B3
Banners Gate Inf Sch B73 .. 45 A4
Banners Gate Jun Sch B73 . 45 A4
Banners Gate Rd B73 .... 45 B3
Banners Gr B23 .... 57 A6
Banners La Halesowen B63 .. 82 D6
  Redditch B97 .... 158 E5
Banners St B63 .... 82 D6
Banners Wlk B44 .... 45 B2
Bannington Ct WV12 .... 27 D4
Bannister Rd WS10 .... 41 D2
Bannister St B64 .... 62 D2
Banstead Cl WV2 .... 39 E7
Bant Mill Rd B60 .... 137 A1
Bantam Gr CV6 .... 95 A3
Bantams Cl B33 .... 69 C2
Bantock Ave WV3 .... 38 F8
Bantock Ct WV3 .... 38 E8
Bantock Gdns WV3 .... 24 E1
Bantock House Mus WV3 .. 24 F1
Bantock Rd CV4 .... 111 E2
Bantock Way B17 .... 85 D5
Bantocks The B70 .... 53 A6
Banton Cl B23 .... 56 D8
Bantry Cl B26 .... 89 C4
Baptist End Rd DY2 .... 62 C6
Baptist Wlk LE10 .... 71 D1
Bar Wlk WS9 .... 16 C1
Barbara Rd B28 .... 105 E4
Barbara St B79 .... 21 A5
Barber Cl WS12 .... 2 E2
Barberry Ho B38 .... 103 F1
Barbers La B91 .... 108 C6
Barbican Rise CV2 .... 114 E2
Barbourne Cl B91 .... 127 B7
Barbridge Cl CV12 .... 79 C2
Barbridge Rd CV12 .... 79 C3
Barbrook Dr DY5 .... 81 B7
Barcheston Rd
  Birmingham B29 .... 85 A1
  Knowle B93 .... 128 A4
Barclay Ct WV3 .... 25 A3
Barclay Rd B67 .... 64 E1
Barcliff Ave B77 .... 21 E3
Barcroft WV13 .... 27 C2
Bard St B11 .... 87 C5
Bardfield Cl **1** B42 ...... 55 A8
Bardon Dr B90 .... 106 D2
Bardsey Cl LE10 .... 71 B1
Bardsley Ct **7** B9 .... 67 B2
Bardwell Cl WV8 .... 24 F8
Barford App CV31 .... 162 B2
Barford Cl Coventry CV3 .. 134 D8
  Darlaston WS10 .... 41 C8
  Redditch B98 .... 154 F1
  Sutton Coldfield B76 ...... 46 F4
Barford Cres **5** B38 ... 104 C2
Barford Cty Jun & Inf
  Sch B16 .... 65 F3
Barford Ho B5 .... 86 E8
Barford Rd Birmingham B16 .. 65 F3
  Kenilworth CV8 .... 148 B3
  Solihull B90 .... 106 D2
Barford St B5 .... 86 E8
Bargate Dr W6 .... 25 A4
Bargery Rd WV11 .... 13 A1
Barham Cl B90 .... 127 A5
Bark Piece B32 .... 84 C3
Barker Ho B69 .... 63 E8
Barker Rd B74 .... 46 B7
Barker St Birmingham B19 .. 66 B7
  Oldbury B68 .... 64 C6
Barker's Butts La CV6 .... 113 A4
Barkers' Butts La CV1 ... 113 A5
Barkers La B47 .... 125 A1
Barlands Croft B34 .... 69 C6
Barle Gr B36 .... 70 A7
Barleston Dr LE10 .... 71 A1
Barley Cl Aldridge WS9 .... 30 E2
  Dudley DY3 .... 50 F7
  Wolverhampton WV8 ...... 10 E1
Barley Croft Perton WV6 ... 23 D3
  Stoke Heath B60 .... 150 E6

Barley Ct CV32 .... 156 F2
Barley Lea Ho CV3 .... 134 B8
Barley Lea The CV3 .... 134 C8
Barley Mow La B61 .... 137 B8
Barleyfield LE10 .... 71 C3
Barleyfield Ho **3** WS1 ..... 63 F2
Barleyfield Rise DY6 .... 60 A8
Barleyfield Row WS1 ...... 42 E8
Barlich Way B98 .... 154 A2
Barlow Cl Birmingham B45 ... 101 E2
Oldbury B68 .... 64 A3
Tamworth B77 .... 21 E4
Barlow Dr B70 .... 53 F1
Barlow Rd Coventry CV2 .... 96 D2
Wednesbury WS10 .... 42 A5
Barlows Rd B15 .... 85 E5
Barmouth CV12 .... 27 C6
Barn Ave DY3 .... 50 C7
Barn Cl Birmingham B30 ... 104 B6
Blackheath B64 .... 82 E6
Coventry CV5 .... 112 C5
Dordon B78 .... 36 F6
Halesowen B63 .... 82 E2
Stoke Heath B60 .... 150 E6
Stourbridge DY8 .... 81 C4
Whitnash CV31 .... 162 B3
Wolverhampton WS13 .... 3 B3
Barn Croft Birmingham B32 .. 84 E1
Burntwood WS7 .... 7 A4
Great Wyrley WS6 .... 5 A3
Barn Farm Cl WV14 .... 41 A7
Barn Gn WV3 .... 38 F7
Barn Ho B8 .... 68 D4
Barn La
Birmingham, Handsworth B21 65 E7
Birmingham,
King's Heath B13 .... 105 A7
Solihull B92 .... 88 F3
Barn Mdw B25 .... 68 D1
Barn Owl Cl DY10 .... 117 A2
Barn Owl Wlk DY5 .... 81 C6
Barn Piece B32 .... 84 B4
Barn St B5 .... 66 F2
Barnabas Rd B23 .... 56 F4
Barnaby Sq WV10 .... 11 F4
Barnack Ave CV3 .... 133 B5
Barnack Dr CV34 .... 155 E1
Barnacle La CV12 .... 79 C1
Barnard Cl Birmingham B37 .. 70 D1
Royal Leamington Spa CV32 157 C3
Barnard Pl WV2 .... 39 E6
Barnard Rd
Sutton Coldfield B75 .... 46 E7
Wolverhampton WV11 .... 12 F1
Barnard Way WS11 .... 1 F2
Barnbridge B77 .... 21 C2
Barnbrook Rd B93 .... 128 A7
Barncroft Rd B69 .... 63 A8
Barncroft St B70 .... 53 A8
Barne Cl CV11 .... 79 B7
Barnes Cl B37 .... 69 E2
Barnes Hill B29 .... 84 F2
Barnesville Cl B10 .... 88 A8
Barnet Rd B23 .... 56 D5
Barnett Cl Bilston WV14 ..... 40 D4
Kingswinford DY6 .... 60 D4
Barnett Gn DY6 .... 60 D4
Barnett La DY6 .... 60 D4
Barnett Rd WV13 .... 26 E1
Barnett St Stourbridge DY8 ... 60 D3
Tipton, Tipton Green DY4 .... 52 A4
Tipton, Tividale B69 .... 52 A2
Barnetts Cl DY10 .... 117 B4
Barnetts Gr DY10 .... 117 A4
Barnetts La Brownhills WS8 .. 15 F8
Kidderminster DY10 .... 117 A4
Barney Cl DY4 .... 51 F3
Barnfield Ave CV5 .... 112 B6
Barnfield Cl WS14 .... 9 B6
Barnfield Dr B92 .... 107 F6
Barnfield Gr B20 .... 54 E5
Barnfield Rd
Bromsgrove B61 .... 136 E1
Halesowen B62 .... 83 D7
Tipton DY4 .... 51 E6
Wolverhampton WV1 .... 26 A2
Barnfield Trad Est DY4 ..... 51 E6
Barnford Cl B10 .... 67 C1
Barnford Cres B68 .... 64 B3
Barnfordhill Cl B68 .... 64 B4
Barnhurst La WV8 .... 10 E2
Barnmoor Rise B91 .... 107 C2
Barnpark Covert **9** B14 ... 104 C2
Barns Cl WS9 .... 15 F4
Barns Croft B74 .... 31 B4
Barns La WS4 .... 29 D7
Barnsbury Ave B72 .... 57 C6
Barnsdale Cres B31 .... 102 E4
Barnsley Hall Hospl B61 .. 137 A6
Barnsley Rd Birmingham
B17 .... 65 A1
Bromsgrove B61 .... 137 B4
Barnstaple Cl CV5 .... 111 F5
Barnstaple Rd B66 .... 65 B5
Barnswood Cl WS11 .... 4 B8
Barnt Green Junc B45 ..... 138 D8
Barnt Green Rd B45 .... 122 C3
Barnwood Cl B98 .... 154 D5
Barnwood Rd
Birmingham B32 .... 84 F4
Wolverhampton WV8 .... 10 E1
Baron Bsns Ctr DY9 .... 81 E5
Baron's Croft CV3 .... 133 E4
Baron's Field Rd CV3 ...... 133 E8
Barons Cl B17 .... 85 B6
Barons Croft CV10 .... 72 C4
Barons Ct B92 .... 89 C4

Barpool Rd CV10 .... 72 F4
Barr Beacon Comp Sch
WS9 .... 44 B5
Barr Common Cl WS9 .... 30 B3
Barr Common Rd WS9 .... 30 B3
Barr Lakes La
Birmingham WS9 .... 44 A7
Walsall WS5, WS9 .... 43 F7
Barr St Birmingham B19 .... 66 C5
Dudley DY3 .... 50 C3
Barra Croft B35 .... 58 B4
Barrack La B63 .... 82 B6
Barrack St Birmingham B7 ... 67 A3
Warwick CV34 .... 160 E7
West Bromwich B70 .... 53 A8
Barracks Cl WS3 .... 28 E8
Barracks La Beausale
CV35 .... 146 C2
Brownhills WS9 .... 16 C8
Walsall WS3 .... 28 E8
Barracks Pl WS3 .... 28 E8
Barracks Way CV1 .... 165 B2
Barrar Cl DY8 .... 80 E8
Barras Ct CV2 .... 114 A4
Barras Gn CV2 .... 114 A4
Barras La CV1 .... 113 B3
Barratts Croft DY5 .... 50 C1
Barratts Ho B14 .... 104 E2
Barratts Rd B38 .... 104 A1
Barrett Cl DY10 .... 117 B6
Barretts La CV7 .... 130 C6
Barrhill Cl B43 .... 43 E2
Barrie Ave DY10 .... 117 C2
Barrie Rd LE10 .... 71 D3
Barrington Cl Walsall WS5 .. 43 A3
Wolverhampton WV10 .... 11 C1
Barrington Rd
Birmingham B45 .... 121 E7
Solihull B92 .... 88 F1
Barron Rd B31 .... 103 B3
Barrow Cl Coventry CV2 ... 115 B6
Redditch B98 .... 154 F3
Barrow Hill Rd DY5 .... 50 C1
Barrow Ho **1** B16 .... 65 F1
Barrow Rd CV8 .... 147 F4
Barrow Wlk B5 .... 86 E7
Barrowfield Ct CV8 .... 147 F4
Barrowfield La CV8 .... 147 F4
Barrows La B26 .... 89 A6
Barrows Rd B11 .... 87 C6
Barrs Cres B64 .... 82 F8
Barrs Hill Sch &
Com Coll CV1 .... 165 A4
Barrs Rd B64 .... 82 E8
Barrs St B68 .... 64 A4
Barry Ho CV2 .... 96 D1
Barry Jackson Tower B6 ... 66 F7
Barry Rd WS5 .... 43 C7
Barsham Cl B5 .... 86 C6
Barsham Dr DY5 .... 81 C8
Barston Cl CV6 .... 96 A3
Barston La
Balsall Common CV7 ...... 129 D8
Barston B92 .... 109 C1
Cathrine de Barnes B91 ... 108 B2
Hampton in A B92 .... 108 D3
Solihull B91 .... 107 F2
Barston Rd B68 .... 84 B7
Bartestree Cl B98 .... 154 F1
Bartholomews La B61 ..... 136 F5
Bartholomew Row B5 ..... 164 D3
Bartholomew St B5 .... 164 D2
Bartic Ave DY6 .... 60 E4
Bartleet Rd Redditch B98 ... 159 E8
Smethwick B67 .... 64 D5
Bartley Cl B92 .... 88 F2
Bartley Dr B31 .... 102 E8
Bartley Green Sec Sch B32 84 C1
Bartley Ho B32 .... 102 D8
Bartley Woods B32 .... 84 B2
Barton Coll Of F Ed
Annexe WV14 .... 40 E6
Barton Cres CV31 .... 162 C6
Barton Croft B28 .... 105 F4
Barton Dr B93 .... 128 B4
Barton Ind Est WV14 .... 40 E6
Barton La DY6 .... 60 C8
Barton Lodge Rd B28 .... 105 E4
Barton Rd Bedworth CV12 .. 78 A4
Coventry CV6 .... 95 F2
Nuneaton CV10 .... 73 C1
Wolverhampton WV4 .... 39 F4
Barton St B70 .... 53 C2
Barton's Mdw CV2 .... 114 B6
Bartons Bank B6 .... 66 E7
Barwell Cl Dorridge B93 .. 127 E4
Royal Leamington Spa CV32 156 F3
Barwell Ct **8** B9 .... 67 B2
Barwell La LE10 .... 71 E3
Barwell Rd B9 .... 67 B2
Barwick St B3 .... 164 B3
Basalt Cl WS2 .... 28 A3
Basant Cl CV34 .... 161 A7
Bascote Cl B97 .... 153 B1
Basford Brook Dr CV6 ...... 95 F4
Basil Gr B31 .... 102 E4
Basil Rd B31 .... 102 E4
Basildon Wlk **3** CV2 .... 115 A7
Basin La B77 .... 21 D3
Baskerville Ho **1** B12 .... 86 F7
Baskerville Sch B17 .... 85 A5
Baskeyfield Cl WS14 .... 9 D7
Basley Way CV6 .... 95 D4
Baslow Cl Birmingham B33 .. 68 E4
Walsall WS3 .... 14 C3

Baslow Rd WS3 .... 14 B3
Basons La B68 .... 64 D5
Bassano Rd **1** B65 .... 63 C1
Bassenthwaite Ct DY6 ...... 60 B6
Bassett Cl Sutton Coldfield B76 46 E4
Willenhall WV12 .... 27 D4
Wolverhampton WV4 .... 38 C6
Bassett Croft B10 .... 87 B8
Bassett Rd Coventry CV6 ... 113 A5
Halesowen B63 .... 82 A6
Wednesbury WS10 .... 42 D3
Bassett St B29 .... 28 C2
Bassetts Gr B37 .... 69 E5
Bassnage Rd B63 .... 82 E2
Batchcroft Bilston WV14 .... 40 D5
Darlaston WS10 .... 41 D8
Batchelor Cl DY8 .... 80 F8
Batchley Fst Sch B97 ...... 153 B4
Batchley Rd B97 .... 153 C4
Bate St **3** Walsall WS2 ..... 28 E1
Wolverhampton WV4 .... 40 A3
Bateman Rd B46 .... 59 F1
Bateman's Acre S **1** CV6 . 113 A4
Batemans La B47 .... 124 E5
Bates Cl B76 .... 58 B8
Bates Gr WV10 .... 26 A4
Bates Hill B97 .... 153 D4
Bates La B94 .... 141 F1
Bates Rd CV5 .... 132 A8
Bath Ave WV1 .... 163 A3
Bath Ct **1** B29 .... 103 B7
Bath Mdw B63 .... 82 E5
Bath Mews DY8 .... 80 F5
Bath Pas B5 .... 164 C1
Bath Pl **4** CV31 .... 161 F7
Bath Rd Brierley Hill DY5 .... 62 A2
Cannock WS11 .... 1 E5
Nuneaton CV11 .... 73 C5
Stourbridge DY8 .... 80 F5
Tipton DY4 .... 52 A5
Walsall WS1 .... 42 E8
Wolverhampton WV1 ...... 163 A3
Bath Row Birmingham B15 .. 66 C1
Oldbury B69 .... 63 D8
Bath St Bilston WV14 .... 40 E5
Birmingham B4 .... 164 C4
Coventry CV1 .... 165 C4
Dudley DY2 .... 62 C8
Royal Leamington Spa
CV31 .... 161 F7
Sedgley DY3 .... 39 E1
Walsall WS1 .... 42 E8
Willenhall WV13 .... 27 B1
Wolverhampton WV1 ...... 163 D2
Bath Wlk Ind Est B12 ...... 86 E5
Batham Rd DY10 .... 117 A8
Batheaston Cl B38 .... 123 D7
Bathurst Cl CV3 .... 113 A6
Bathway Rd CV3 .... 133 A4
Batmans Hill Rd
WV14, DY4 .... 40 E1
Batsford Cl B98 .... 159 B5
Batsford Rd CV6 .... 112 F4
Batson Rise DY5 .... 81 A8
Battenhall Rd B17 .... 85 A5
Battens Cl B98 .... 153 F1
Battens Dr B98 .... 154 D3
Battledown Cl LE10 .... 71 B2
Battlefield Hill WV5 .... 49 C7
Battlefield La WV5 .... 49 B6
Battlefield Terr WV5 .... 49 B6
Battling Brook Cty
Prim Sch LE10 .... 71 B2
Battling Brook Sh Ctr
LE10 .... 71 B1
Baughan Ho B24 .... 57 D3
Baulk La CV7 .... 110 D1
Bavaro Gdns DY5 .... 62 A2
Baverstock Rd B14 .... 104 E2
Baverstock Sch B14 .... 104 E2
Baxter Ave DY10 .... 116 F7
Baxter Cl CV4 .... 112 A2
Baxter Ct **10** CV31 .... 162 A7
Baxter Gdns DY10 .... 116 F7
Baxter Rd DY5 .... 61 C2
Baxterley Gn Solihull B91 .. 106 D4
Sutton Coldfield B76 .... 46 F1
Baxters Gn B90 .... 126 B8
Baxters Rd B90 .... 126 B8
Bay Tree Cl Birmingham
B38 .... 123 D8
Coventry CV2 .... 96 D1
Bayer St WV14 .... 51 C8
Bayford Ave
Birmingham,
Coft Common B31 .... 122 C5
Birmingham, Sheldon B26 .. 89 C4
Bayley Res WS10 .... 41 C8
Bayley Ho WS8 .... 16 A6
Bayley La CV1 .... 165 C2
Bayley Tower **3** B36 ...... 68 E8
Bayleys La B33 .... 69 C2
Baylie St DY8 .... 80 F5
Baylis Ct **6** DY8 .... 80 F5
Baylie St DY8 .... 80 F4
Bayliss Ave
Wednesbury WV11 .... 26 F8
Wolverhampton WV4 .... 40 A3
Bayliss Cl Bilston WV14 .... 40 C7
Birmingham B31 .... 103 B5
Bayliss Ct WV3 .... 24 E2
Bayston Ave WV3 .... 38 E8
Bayston Rd B14 .... 104 D3
Bayswater Rd
Birmingham B20 .... 55 D1
Dudley DY3 .... 50 D2
Bayton Rd CV7 .... 96 B7

Bayton Road Ind Est CV7 .. 96 B8
Bayton Way CV7 .... 96 C7
Baytree Cl WS3 .... 14 A2
Baytree Rd WS3 .... 14 A2
Baywell Cl B90 .... 127 A7
Beach Ave Birmingham B12 .. 87 B5
Wolverhampton WV14 ...... 40 A2
Beach Dr B63 .... 83 A5
Beach Rd Bilston WV14 ..... 40 D7
Birmingham B11 .... 87 B5
Beach St B63 .... 83 A5
Beach Trad Ctr B12 .... 87 B5
Beachburn Way B20 .... 55 B3
Beachcroft Rd DY6 .... 49 C1
Beachwood Ave DY6 .... 49 C1
Beacon Cl
Birmingham, Great Barr B43 43 F1
Birmingham, Rubery B45 .. 122 A6
Smethwick B66 .... 65 A7
Beacon Ct **2** Birmingham
B43 .... 43 F1
Sutton Coldfield B74 .... 44 F8
Beacon Dr WS1 .... 43 A8
Beacon Gdns WS13 .... 3 A1
Beacon Hill Aldridge WS9 ... 30 C1
Birmingham, Aston B6 ...... 66 B3
Birmingham, Eachway B45 . 121 F5
Beacon Hts WV12 .... 44 B6
Beacon Inf & Jun Schs
WV12 .... 27 D8
Beacon La Marlbrook B45 .. 121 E4
Sedgley DY3 .... 39 E1
Beacon Mews **1** B43 ...... 43 F1
Beacon Pas DY3 .... 50 D8
Beacon Rd
Birmingham,
Kingstanding B44 .... 45 A3
Coventry CV6 .... 95 D3
Sutton Coldfield B73 .... 46 A1
Walsall WS3 .... 43 D5
Willenhall WV12 .... 27 C8
Beacon Rise Aldridge WS9 .. 30 B3
Sedgley DY3 .... 39 E1
Stourbridge DY9 .... 81 F4
Beacon St Lichfield WS13 .... 9 A8
Walsall WS1 .... 29 A1
Wolverhampton WV14 ...... 39 F1
Beacon View
Birmingham B45 .... 122 A6
Walsall WS2 .... 27 F2
Beacon View Dr B74 .... 44 F5
Beacon View Rd B71 .... 42 F2
Beacon Way Brownhills WS9 16 A3
Cannock WS11 .... 2 F3
Beaconfields WS13 .... 9 A8
Beaconsfield Ave WV4 ..... 39 D6
Beaconsfield Cres **3** B12 . 86 E5
Beaconsfield Ct
Nuneaton CV11 .... 73 D5
Walsall WS1 .... 43 B8
Beaconsfield Dr WV4 .... 39 D6
Beaconsfield Rd
Birmingham B12 .... 86 E5
Coventry CV2 .... 114 B2
Sutton Coldfield B74 .... 46 B7
Beaconsfield St
Royal Leamington Spa CV31 162 B7
West Bromwich B71 .... 53 C5
Beaconsfield St W CV31 ... 162 B8
Beaconside Fst &
Mid Sch B45 .... 121 E6
Beaconview Ho **4** B71 .... 42 F1
Beak St B1 .... 164 B2
Beake Ave CV6 .... 113 B7
Beakes Rd B67 .... 64 C5
Beaks Farm Gdns B16 ...... 65 D2
Beaks Hill Rd B38 .... 103 E2
Beale Cl B35 .... 58 A2
Beale Ho B16 .... 65 F1
Beale St DY8 .... 80 F5
Beales St B6 .... 67 B8
Bealeys Ave WV11 .... 26 C8
Bealeys Ct WV11 .... 26 C8
Bealeys La WS3 .... 14 A2
Beamans Cl B92 .... 89 A4
Beaminster Rd B91 .... 107 A4
Beamish Cl CV2 .... 115 A6
Bean Croft B32 .... 84 C2
Bean Rd
Dudley, Dixon's Green DY2 . 62 D8
Dudley, Swan Village DY1 .. 51 C4
Bean Road Ind Est DY4 .... 51 C6
Beanfield Ave CV3 .... 132 F4
Bear Hill B48 .... 139 B6
Beardmore Rd B72 .... 57 C8
Bearhill Dr B48 .... 139 B6
Bearley Croft B90 .... 126 C8
Bearmore Rd B64 .... 62 E1
Bearnett Dr WV4 .... 38 C2
Bearnett La WV4 .... 38 B1
Bearsdon Cres LE10 .... 71 B2
Bearwood Ho B66 .... 65 A4
Bearwood Jun & Inf Sch
B66 .... 65 A2
Bearwood Rd B66 .... 65 A3
Bearwood Sh Ctr B66 ...... 65 A1
Beasley Gr B43 .... 44 B1
Beaton Cl WV13 .... 26 E2
Beaton Rd B74 .... 32 A3
Beatrice St WS3 .... 28 C6
Beatrice Wlk B69 .... 52 A2
Beattie Ho LE10 .... 71 D3
Beatty Ho DY4 .... 52 B8
Beau Ct WS11 .... 1 F1
Beaubrook Gdns DY8 .... 60 E3

Beauchamp Ave
Birmingham B20 .... 54 F5
Kidderminster DY11 .... 116 D3
Royal Leamington Spa CV32 . 156 F1
Beauchamp Cl **1**
Birmingham B37 .... 70 B2
Sutton Coldfield B76 .... 58 B7
Beauchamp Ct
Kidderminster DY11 .... 116 D3
1 Royal Leamington Spa
CV32 .... 156 F1
Beauchamp Gdns CV34 .... 161 B6
Beauchamp Hill CV32 ..... 156 E1
Beauchamp Ind Pk B77 .... 35 D8
Beauchamp Rd
Birmingham B13 .... 105 C5
Kenilworth CV8 .... 147 F2
Royal Leamington Spa CV32 . 156 F1
Solihull B91 .... 107 B5
Tamworth B77 .... 35 F5
Warwick CV34 .... 161 B8
Beaudesert Cl B47 .... 125 A6
Beaudesert Rd
Birmingham B20 .... 66 B8
Coventry CV6 .... 113 A4
Hollywood B47 .... 125 A6
Beaufell Cl CV34 .... 155 E1
Beaufort Ave
Birmingham B34 .... 68 D5
Kidderminster DY11 .... 116 A4
Royal Leamington Spa
CV32 .... 157 C5
Beaufort Cl LE10 .... 75 E4
Beaufort Dr CV3 .... 134 F7
Beaufort Rd
Birmingham, Gravelly Hill
B23 .... 56 E2
Birmingham, Ladywood B16 .. 66 A1
Beaufort Sch B34 .... 68 D5
Beaufort St B98 .... 153 E3
Beaufort Way WS9 .... 30 B4
Beaulieu Ave DY6 .... 60 F4
Beaulieu Cl DY11 .... 116 D8
Beaulieu Pk CV31 .... 162 D6
Beaumaris Cl Coventry CV5 . 111 F5
Dudley DY1 .... 50 F4
Beaumaris Ho B32 .... 102 D6
Beaumont Ave LE10 .... 75 E4
Beaumont Cl
Great Wyrley WS6 .... 4 F2
Tipton DY4 .... 51 E6
Beaumont Cres CV6 .... 113 A4
Beaumont Ct
9 Coventry CV6 .... 113 A4
8 Royal Leamington Spa
CV31 .... 162 A6
Beaumont Dr
Birmingham B17 .... 85 B4
Brierley Hill DY5 .... 81 B7
Beaumont Gdns B18 .... 65 F6
Beaumont Gr B91 .... 106 F5
Beaumont Lawns B60 ..... 121 D1
Beaumont Pl CV11 .... 73 A4
Beaumont Rd
Birmingham B30 .... 103 F6
Great Wyrley WS6 .... 4 F2
Halesowen B62 .... 83 E8
Keresley CV7 .... 95 A6
Nuneaton CV11 .... 73 A4
Wednesbury WS10 .... 41 F4
Beausale Croft CV5 .... 112 A3
Beausale Dr B93 .... 128 C2
Beauty Bank B64 .... 83 A8
Beauty Bank Cres DY8 ..... 80 F6
Beauty Bank Prim Sch
DY8 .... 80 F6
Beaver Cl WV11 .... 26 E5
Beaver Pk B63 .... 82 F6
Bebington Cl WV8 .... 24 F8
Beccles Dr WV13 .... 40 F8
Beck Cl B65 .... 65 A4
Beckbury Ave WV4 .... 38 C5
Beckbury Rd Birmingham
B29 .... 85 A1
Coventry CV2 .... 114 F6
Beckenham Ave B44 .... 45 B1
Becket Cl B74 .... 31 F6
Beckett St WV14 .... 40 F6
Beckfield Cl
Birmingham B14 .... 104 D3
Walsall WS4 .... 29 C8
Beckfoot Dr CV2 .... 96 F1
Beckford Croft B93 .... 127 F3
Beckford Ct B23 .... 56 C2
Beckman Rd DY9 .... 81 C2
Beckminster Rd WV3 .... 38 F7
Becks La CV7 .... 93 A5
Becks The B48 .... 139 A7
Beconsfield Cl B93 .... 127 F2
Becton Gr B42 .... 55 D7
Bedale Ave LE10 .... 71 E2
Bedcote Pl DY8 .... 81 B5
Beddoe Cl DY4 .... 52 D5
Beddow Ave WV14 .... 51 C7
Beddows Rd WS3 .... 28 E5
Bede Arc CV12 .... 78 B3
Bede Rd Bedworth CV12 .... 78 A4
Coventry CV6 .... 113 B6
Nuneaton CV10 .... 72 D3
Bedford Cl LE10 .... 71 E3
Bedford Dr B75 .... 46 E4
Bedford Ho
7 Birmingham, Erdington B24 56 F4
Birmingham, Kingshurst B36 .. 70 B6
6 Wolverhampton WV3 .... 25 C4

Bedford Pl Cannock WS12 .... 2 B4
Royal Leamington Spa CV32 . 161 F8
Bedford Rd Birmingham B11 . 87 A8
Sutton Coldfield B75 .... 46 E7
West Bromwich B71 .... 53 B7
Bedford St Coventry CV1 ...... 113 A2
Royal Leamington Spa CV32 . 161 F8
Tipton DY4 .... 52 B5
Wolverhampton WV1 .... 40 B7
Bedford Terr **4** B19 .... 66 D8
Bedlam La CV6 .... 95 E2
Bedworth Cl CV12 .... 79 B2
Bedworth Croft DY4 .... 52 B4
Bedworth Gr B9 .... 68 B2
Bedworth La CV12 .... 77 D4
Bedworth Rd Bedworth
CV12 .... 78 F2
Bulkington CV12 .... 79 A2
Coventry CV6 .... 96 A5
Bedworth Sta CV12 .... 78 C2
Bee La WV10 .... 11 D3
Beebee Rd WS10 .... 41 F6
Beech Ave
Birmingham,
Chelmsley Wood B37 .... 70 B1
Birmingham, Quinton B32 ...... 84 D7
5 Birmingham,
Showell Green B12 .... 87 A5
Halesowen B62 .... 83 C8
Tamworth B77 .... 21 E3
Beech Cl Nuneaton CV10 .... 72 A8
Rowington Green CV35 .... 145 A1
Sedgley DY3 .... 39 E1
Wolverhampton WV10 .... 25 B8
Beech Cliffe CV34 .... 160 F8
Beech Cres Burntwood WS7 ... 6 F6
Tipton DY4 .... 52 C8
Wednesbury WS10 .... 41 F5
Beech Ct
Birmingham, Bournville B30 . 103 E4
Birmingham, Great Barr B43 .. 43 D1
Cannock WS12 .... 2 B7
Oldbury B66 .... 64 C8
Royal Leamington Spa CV34 . 161 E2
Beech Dene Gr B23 .... 56 E5
Kidderminster DY11 .... 116 B7
Beech Dr Kenilworth CV8 ... 148 B5
Kidderminster DY11 .... 116 B7
Beech Farm Croft B31 .... 103 A3
Beech Gate B74 .... 31 C5
Beech Gdns WS14 .... 9 C6
Beech Gn DY1 .... 51 A5
Beech Gr Birmingham B14 ... 105 A5
Huntington WS12 .... 1 D8
Warwick CV34 .... 156 B1
Beech Hill Ct B72 .... 57 C8
Beech Hill Ho B32 .... 102 C8
Beech Ho B91 .... 106 F2
Beech Hurst B38 .... 123 E8
Beech Hurst Gdns WV5 .... 37 A2
Beech Mews B64 .... 62 E2
Beech Park Dr B45 .... 138 C8
Beech Pine Cl WS12 .... 2 A8
Beech Rd
Birmingham, Bournville B30 . 103 E6
Birmingham, Erdington B23 .... 56 F8
Bromsgrove B61 .... 136 F4
Coventry CV6 .... 113 B5
Dudley DY1 .... 51 C4
Hollywood B47 .... 125 B6
Kingswinford DY6 .... 60 E5
Stourbridge DY8 .... 80 F3
Tamworth B79 .... 21 A8
Tipton B69 .... 63 A8
Wednesbury WS10 .... 41 F5
Willenhall WV13 .... 26 E2
Wolverhampton WV10 .... 25 B8
Beech Tree Ave
Coventry CV4 .... 112 B2
Wolverhampton WV11 .... 26 C8
Beech Tree Cl
Kingswinford DY6 .... 60 E8
Redditch B97 .... 153 B4
Beech Tree La WS11 .... 4 D8
Beech Way B65 .... 65 B5
Beech Wlk B38 .... 123 F8
Beecham Cl WS9 .... 30 A8
Beechcroft Birmingham B15 .. 86 A7
Oldbury B68 .... 64 C2
Beechcroft Ave B28 .... 106 A6
Beechcroft Cres B74 .... 30 D1
Beechcroft Ct B74 .... 32 A1
Beechcroft Dr B61 .... 137 B4
Beechcroft Est B63 .... 82 C6
Beechcroft Pl WV10 .... 25 C6
Beechcroft Rd
Birmingham B36 .... 69 B8
Blackheath B64 .... 62 F1
Kidderminster DY11 .... 116 A8
Beechdale Ave B44 .... 44 E2
Beechdale Prim Sch WS2 ... 28 C5
Beechdale Rd WS2 .... 27 F8
Beechen Gr WS7 .... 6 F8
Beecher Pl B63 .... 82 D5
Beecher Rd B63 .... 82 D5
Beecher Rd E B63 .... 82 D5
Beecher St B63 .... 82 C5
Beecher's Keep CV8 .... 135 F5
Beeches Ave B27 .... 88 C4
Beeches Cl Birmingham B45 121 D8
Kingswinford DY6 .... 60 D5
Beeches Dr B24 .... 57 C5
Beeches Farm Dr B31 .... 123 B1
Beeches Inf Sch B70 .... 53 D3
Beeches Inf Sch The B45 .. 102 B2
Beeches Pl WS3 .... 28 D6

Beeches Rd Birmingham B42 . 55 C7
Blackheath B65 .... 63 C1
Kidderminster DY11 .... 116 C8
Oldbury B68 .... 64 C3
Walsall WS3 .... 28 D6
West Bromwich B70 .... 53 C2
Beeches The Bedworth
CV12 .... 77 E2
Sutton Coldfield, Little Aston
B74 .... 31 D4
Sutton Coldfield, Wylde Green
B73 .... 46 B1
West Bromwich B70 .... 53 C2
Wolverhampton, New Cross
WV11 .... 26 B5
Wolverhampton, Newbridge
WV1 .... 25 A3
Beeches View Ave B63 .... 82 C4
Beeches Way B31 .... 123 A7
Beeches Wlk B73 .... 46 B3
Beechey Cl B43 .... 44 D5
Beechfield Dr **1** B11 .... 87 B6
Beechfield Cl B62 .... 83 C8
Beechfield Dr DY11 .... 116 C8
Beechfield Gr WV14 .... 51 B7
Beechfield Rd
Birmingham B11 .... 87 B6
Smethwick B67 .... 64 F4
Beechfield Rise WS13 .... 9 D8
Beechglade B20 .... 54 F4
Beechhouse La WV5 .... 37 A1
Beechmore Rd B26 .... 89 A5
Beechmount Dr B23 .... 57 A6
Beechnut Cl B91 .... 107 D5
Beechnut La B91 .... 107 E4
Beechtree Rd WS9 .... 15 F3
Beechwood Ave
Coventry CV5 .... 132 F8
Hinckley LE10 .... 75 D3
Wolverhampton WV11 .... 26 B8
Beechwood Bsns Pk WS11 .... 2 B3
Beechwood Cl
Cheswick Green B90 .... 126 D4
Walsall WS3 .... 14 B3
Beechwood Cres B77 .... 21 F5
Beechwood Croft
Kenilworth CV8 .... 147 F2
Little Aston B74 .... 31 D5
Beechwood Ct
1 Birmingham B30 .... 104 C3
Blackheath B64 .... 83 A7
Coventry CV5 .... 132 F8
Wolverhampton WV6 .... 24 C3
Beechwood Dr WV6 .... 24 A2
Beechwood Gr B43 .... 43 E2
Beechwood Park Rd B91 .. 106 E5
Beechwood Rd
Bedworth CV12 .... 78 D4
Birmingham, Great Barr B43 .. 43 F2
Birmingham, King's Heath
B14 .... 104 F5
Dudley DY2 .... 51 E1
Nuneaton CV10 .... 72 D6
Smethwick B67 .... 84 F8
West Bromwich B70 .... 53 B3
Beecroft Ave WS13 .... 3 B1
Beecroft Hill Specl Sch WS11 1 E2
Beecroft Rd WS11 .... 1 E1
Beehive Cl B61 .... 121 A1
Beehive Hill CV8 .... 147 E7
Beehive La B76 .... 59 C6
Beehive Wlk **4** DY4 .... 51 B5
Beeston Cl Birmingham B6 .... 67 A7
Brierley Hill DY5 .... 81 D8
Coventry CV3 .... 134 F8
Beet St B65 .... 63 C1
Beeton Rd B18 .... 65 E6
Beever Rd DY4 .... 52 D7
Beggars Bush La WV5 .... 49 B5
Begonia Cl LE10 .... 75 E5
Begonia Dr LE10 .... 75 E5
Beighton Cl B74 .... 31 F6
Beilby Rd B30 .... 104 B5
Belbroughton CE Sch DY9 119 E6
Belbroughton Cl B98 .... 153 F2
Belbroughton Rd
Blakedown DY9, DY10 .... 98 D1
Clent DY9 .... 99 E2
Halesowen B63 .... 82 F2
Stourbridge DY8 .... 80 E3
Belchers La B8 .... 68 A3
Beldray Rd WV14 .... 40 E6
Belfont Trad Est B62 .... 83 C4
Belfry Cl WS3 .... 14 A3
Belfry Dr DY8 .... 80 E6
Belfry The WV6 .... 23 D4
Belgrade Rd WV10 .... 11 B1
Belgrave Ct DY6 .... 60 F4
Belgrave Cty High Sch B77 21 E1
Belgrave Ho WS11 .... 1 D1
Belgrave Middleway
B5, B12 .... 86 E7
Belgrave Rd Birmingham
B12 .... 86 F6
Coventry CV2 .... 114 E4
Halesowen B62 .... 83 D8
Tamworth B77 .... 35 E8
Belgrave Sq CV2 .... 114 E4
Belgrave Terr B21 .... 66 A7
Belgrave Wlk WS2 .... 28 B3
Belgravia Cl B5 .... 86 E7
Belgravia Cl B37 .... 70 A5
Belgrove Cl B15 .... 85 E6
Belinda Cl WV13 .... 26 E1
Bell Barn Rd B15 .... 86 C8
Bell Barn Sh Ctr **8** B15 .. 86 C8
Bell Cl Birmingham B36 .... 70 B6
Darlaston WS10 .... 41 D7

Bell Ct CV32 .... 156 F2
Bell Dr Cannock WS12 .... 2 C7
Coventry CV7 .... 95 E7
Walsall WS5 .... 43 A5
Bell End B65 .... 63 C3
Bell Fold B68 .... 64 C6
Bell Green La B38 .... 124 B5
Bell Green Rd CV6 .... 114 A8
Bell Heath Way B32 .... 84 B2
Bell Heather Rd WS8 .... 15 D6
Bell Hill B31 .... 103 A5
Bell Holloway B31 .... 102 F5
Bell La
Birmingham, Kitt's Green B33 . 69 E1
Birmingham, Northfield B31 . 103 A4
Studley B80 .... 159 E4
Walsall, Wallington Heath
WS3 .... 14 B1
Walsall, Yew Tree WS5 .... 43 A5
Bell Mdw DY9 .... 99 B8
Bell Mead B80 .... 159 E4
Bell Meadow Way B14 .... 104 E1
Bell Pl WV2 .... 163 B1
Bell Rd Dudley DY2 .... 62 C5
Trysull WV5 .... 37 D1
Walsall WS5 .... 43 D6
Bell Sh Ctr The B31 .... 103 A4
Bell St Bilston WV14 .... 40 C6
Brierley Hill, Barrow Hill DY5 . 61 D7
Brierley Hill, Silver End DY5 .. 61 D2
Darlaston WS10 .... 41 D7
Dudley WV14 .... 40 C3
Stourbridge DY8 .... 81 A5
Tipton DY4 .... 51 E5
West Bromwich B70 .... 53 D2
Wolverhampton WV1 .... 163 B2
Bell St S DY5 .... 61 D2
Bell Tower Mews CV32 ...... 156 F3
Bell Vue Rd B65 .... 63 C2
Bellairs Ave CV12 .... 77 E1
Bellamy Cl B30 .... 106 D1
Bellamy Farm Rd B90 .... 106 D1
Bellamy La WV11 .... 26 C7
Bellbrooke Cl CV6 .... 96 B1
Bellcroft B16 .... 66 B2
Belle Cotts B94 .... 143 E5
Belle Isle DY5 .... 61 C3
Belle Orch DY11 .... 116 B5
Belle Vale B63 .... 82 E5
Belle Vue Nuneaton CV10 .... 72 E3
Stourbridge DY8 .... 60 D2
Belle Vue Ave B16 .... 65 D4
Belle Vue Cl B61 .... 121 C1
Belle Vue Dr B62 .... 83 E6
Belle Vue Gdns B65 .... 63 C3
Belle Vue Prim Sch DY8 .... 60 C3
Belle Vue Rd DY5 .... 62 A1
Belle Vue Terr B92 .... 109 A6
Belle Wlk B13 .... 87 B3
Bellefield Ave **10** B18 ..... 65 E4
Bellefield Rd B18 .... 65 E4
Bellemere Rd B92 .... 109 B6
Bellencroft Gdns WV3 .... 38 C7
Bellevue Birmingham B5 .... 86 D7
Dudley WV14 .... 40 E2
Bellevue Rd Bilston WV14 ..... 41 A2
Birmingham B26 .... 89 B7
Bellevue St WV14 .... 39 F2
Bellfield B77 .... 22 D1
Bellfield Ho B14 .... 104 D1
Bellfield Jun &
Inf Sch B31 .... 102 F4
Bellflower Cl WV10 .... 12 A7
Bellingham B77 .... 22 D1
Bellington Croft **5** B90 . 127 A6
Bellis St B16 .... 65 F1
Bellman Cl WS10 .... 41 D7
Bells Farm Cl B14 .... 104 C2
Bells Farm Inf & Jun
Sch B14 .... 104 D2
Bells La Birmingham B14 .... 104 D2
Stourbridge DY8 .... 60 D1
Bells Moor Rd B70 .... 53 A6
Bellsize Cl WS11 .... 5 F5
Bellview Way CV6 .... 96 B1
Bellwood Rd B31 .... 102 F4
Belmont Ave WS11 .... 1 C2
Belmont Cl Aldridge WS9 ...... 30 B7
Great Wyrley WS11 .... 5 A4
Redditch B97 .... 153 B1
Tipton DY4 .... 51 F6
Belmont Covert B31 .... 103 B6
Belmont Ct
Royal Leamington Spa CV32 . 157 A4
Sutton Coldfield B72 .... 46 B4
Belmont Dr CV32 .... 157 A4
Belmont Gdns WV14 .... 41 A4
Belmont Mews CV8 .... 147 F4
Belmont Pas B4 .... 67 A3
Belmont Rd
Birmingham,
Handsworth B21 .... 65 C8
Birmingham, Rubery B45 ..... 122 A6
Brierley Hill DY5 .... 61 D6
Coventry CV6 .... 114 A7
Smethwick B66 .... 65 A2
Stourbridge DY9 .... 81 F4
Tamworth B77 .... 35 E7
Wolverhampton WV4 .... 39 A5
Belmont Rd E B21 .... 65 C8
Belmont Row B4 .... 67 A3
Belmont St WV14 .... 41 A4
Belper DY1 .... 51 B1
Belper Ind Pk B70 .... 52 F4
Belper Rd Walsall WS3 .... 14 D2
West Bromwich B70 .... 52 F3
Belper Row DY2 .... 62 E4
Belsize B77 .... 21 E2

Belstone Cl B14 .... 104 D6
Belt Rd WS12 .... 2 A5
Belton Ave WV11 .... 12 B1
Belton Cl B94 .... 143 C5
Belton Gr B45 .... 122 C8
Belvedere Ave WV4 .... 39 B5
Belvedere Cl Burntwood
WS7 .... 6 F5
Kidderminster DY10 .... 117 A5
Kingswinford DY6 .... 60 F4
Tamworth B79 .... 21 C7
Belvedere Dr B61 .... 137 A4
Belvedere Gdns WV6 .... 24 E7
Belvedere Rd
Birmingham B24 .... 57 B2
Coventry CV5 .... 133 A8
Belvide Gr B29 .... 103 B8
Belvide Gdns B11 .... 87 C4
Belvidere Rd WS1 .... 42 F8
Belvoir B77 .... 35 C7
Belvoir Cl DY1 .... 50 E2
Belwell Dr B74 .... 32 A2
Belwell La B74 .... 32 A2
Bembridge Cl WV12 .... 27 B8
Bembridge Rd B33 .... 69 A3
Ben Nevis Way DY8 .... 81 A6
Ben Willetts Wlk **3** B65 .. 63 C1
Benacre Dr B5 .... 66 F2
Benbeck Gr DY4 .... 51 C6
Benbow Cl LE10 .... 71 D4
Benches WS7 .... 6 D6
Bendall Rd B44 .... 45 B2
Benedict Sq CV2 .... 114 C8
Benedictine Rd CV3 .... 133 C8
Benedon Rd B26 .... 89 B7
Bengrove Cl B98 .... 159 A7
Benion Rd WS11 .... 1 F5
Benmore Ave B5 .... 86 D7
Benn Rd CV12 .... 79 B2
Bennett Ave DY1 .... 51 B6
Bennett Ct CV8 .... 135 F3
Bennett Dr CV34 .... 161 C7
Bennett Rd B74 .... 31 A4
Bennett St Birmingham B19 .. 66 D8
2 Kidderminster DY11 ... 116 C6
Bennett's Fold WV3 .... 163 B2
Bennett's Hill
Birmingham B2 .... 164 B2
Dudley DY2 .... 62 E8
Bennett's Rd CV7 .... 94 F4
Bennett's Rd N CV7 .... 94 F4
Bennett's Rd S CV6 .... 94 F2
Bennetts Rd B8 .... 67 D6
Bennetts Well Jun &
Inf Sch B37 .... 69 F3
Bennetts Well Prim Sch
B37 .... 69 F3
Bennitt Cl B70 .... 53 C1
Benson Ave WV4 .... 39 D5
Benson Cl Lichfield WS13 .... 3 D1
Perton WV6 .... 23 E5
Benson Ind Est B18 .... 65 F6
Benson Jun & Inf Sch B18 .. 65 F6
Benson Rd
Birmingham,
Higher's Heath B14 .... 105 B1
Birmingham, Hockley B18 ..... 65 F6
Coventry CV6 .... 95 A1
Benson Rd B79 .... 21 C8
Bent Ave B32 .... 84 D6
Bent St DY5 .... 61 D4
Benthall Rd CV6 .... 95 F2
Bentham Ct B31 .... 102 F5
Bentley Cl Redditch B97 .... 153 D3
Royal Leamington Spa CV32 . 157 B3
Bentley Ct Coventry CV6 ...... 95 C4
Sutton Coldfield B76 .... 57 F8
Bentley Dr **7** WS2 .... 28 B3
Bentley Drive Jun Sch
WS2 .... 28 B2
Bentley Farm Cl B93 .... 127 E4
Bentley Gr B29 .... 102 F8
Bentley Heath CE Jun &
Inf Sch B93 .... 127 F5
Bentley Heath Cotts B93 ... 127 F5
Bentley La
Walsall, Birchills WS2 .... 28 B3
Walsall, Leamore WS2 .... 28 A5
Willenhall WV12 .... 27 E5
Bentley Lane Bsns Pk WS2 . 28 B3
Bentley Mill Cl WS2 .... 27 F1
Bentley Mill La WS2 .... 27 F1
Bentley Mill Way WS2 .... 27 F1
Bentley New Dr WS2 .... 28 B3
Bentley Pl WS2 .... 28 B2
Bentley Rd Bedworth CV7 ..... 78 A1
Birmingham B36 .... 69 D7
Nuneaton CV11 .... 73 A4
Wolverhampton WV10 .... 11 E2
Bentley Rd N WS2 .... 27 E1
Bentley Rd S Darlaston
WS10 .... 41 E8
Walsall WS10 .... 27 E1
Bentley Way B79 .... 20 F7
Bentley West JMI Sch
WS2 .... 27 E3
Bentleybridge Way WV11 .... 26 C4
Bentmead Gr B38 .... 104 A1
Benton Ave B11 .... 87 C6
Benton Cl WV12 .... 27 D7
Benton Cres WS3 .... 14 D2
Benton Green La CV7 .... 110 F2
Benton Rd B11 .... 87 C6
Benton's Ct DY11 .... 116 C6
Benton's La WS6 .... 5 A1
Bentons Mill Croft B7 .... 67 C8
Bentree The CV3 .... 134 B8
Benyon Ctr The WS2 .... 28 A7

Beoley Cl B72 .... 46 C1
Beoley Fst Sch B98 .... 154 E8
Beoley Gr B45 .... 122 A7
Beoley La Beoley B98 .... 154 F8
Portway B98 .... 141 B1
Beoley Rd E B98 .... 154 A4
Beoley Rd W B98 .... 153 F4
Berberry Cl B30 .... 103 D6
Berenska Dr CV32 .... 157 A2
Beresford Ave CV6 .... 95 E1
Beresford Cres B70 .... 53 B3
Beresford Dr B73 .... 46 A1
Beresford Rd Oldbury B69 .... 64 C7
Walsall WS3 .... 28 E8
Bericote Croft B27 .... 88 D3
Bericote Rd CV32 .... 156 E8
Berkeley Cl Nuneaton CV11 .. 73 B3
Perton WV6 .... 23 F3
Walsall WS2 .... 27 F3
Berkeley Dr DY6 .... 60 C7
Berkeley Ho **2**
Birmingham B23 .... 56 F6
Sutton Coldfield B76 .... 57 F8
Berkeley Prec B14 .... 104 C2
Berkeley Rd Birmingham
B25 .... 88 B7
Kenilworth CV8 .... 147 E6
Solihull B90 .... 105 F3
Berkeley Rd E B25 .... 88 B7
Berkeley Rd N CV5 .... 113 A1
Berkeley Rd S CV5 .... 133 A8
Berkeley St WS2 .... 42 B7
Berkeswell Cl B98 .... 154 C7
Berkett Rd CV6 .... 95 B2
Berkley Cres B13 .... 87 C1
Berkley Cres B13 .... 87 C1
Berkley Ct B1 .... 66 C1
Berkley St B1 .... 66 C1
Berkshire Cl Nuneaton CV10 . 72 E3
West Bromwich B71 .... 53 B7
Berkshire Cres WS10 .... 42 C4
Berkshire The WS3 .... 14 A3
Berkswell CE Prim Sch
CV7 .... 110 C3
Berkswell Cl Dudley DY1 ...... 50 E3
7 Solihull B91 .... 107 B8
Sutton Coldfield B74 .... 31 E4
Berkswell Hall CV7 .... 110 C3
Berkswell Rd
Birmingham B24 .... 57 B4
Coventry CV6 .... 96 B3
Meriden CV7 .... 110 C2
Berkswell Sta CV7 .... 130 C8
Bermuda Bsns Pk CV10 .... 78 A7
Bermuda Cl DY1 .... 51 B6
Bermuda Ind Est CV10 .... 78 B8
Bermuda Rd CV10 .... 73 A1
Bernard Pl B18 .... 65 F5
Bernard Rd Birmingham B17 . 65 B2
Oldbury B68 .... 64 C2
Tipton DY4 .... 52 B7
Bernard St Walsall WS1 .... 29 A1
West Bromwich B71 .... 53 C4
Berners Cl CV4 .... 111 E2
Berners St B19 .... 66 D7
Bernhard Dr B21 .... 65 E8
Bernie Crossland Wlk
DY10 .... 116 F3
Bernwall Cl DY8 .... 80 F4
Berrandale Rd B36 .... 57 F1
Berrington Cl B98 .... 154 D2
Berrington Dr WV14 .... 51 B8
Berrington Rd
Nuneaton CV10 .... 72 D7
Royal Leamington Spa CV31 . 162 B6
Berrington Wlk B5 .... 86 E7
Berrow Cottage Homes
B93 .... 128 C6
Berrow Dr B15 .... 85 E7
Berrow View B61 .... 150 D7
Berrowside Rd B34 .... 69 E6
Berry Ave WS10 .... 41 B5
Berry Cres WS5 .... 43 C4
Berry Dr Aldridge WS9 .... 29 E5
Barnt Green B45 .... 122 A1
Berry Hall La B91 .... 108 B4
Berry Hill WS12 .... 2 C4
Berry Rd Birmingham B8 .... 67 E5
Dudley DY1 .... 51 C5
Berry St Birmingham B18 ..... 65 F6
Coventry CV1 .... 113 E4
Wolverhampton WV1 .... 163 C3
Berrybush Gdns DY3 .... 50 E7
Berryfield Rd B26 .... 89 D5
Berryfields Aldridge WS9 ...... 29 E5
Stonnall WS9 .... 16 E5
Berryfields Rd B76 .... 58 A6
Berrymound View B47 .... 125 C7
Bertha Rd B11 .... 87 D5
Bertie Rd CV8 .... 148 A4
Bertie Terr CV32 .... 156 E1
Bertram Cl DY4 .... 41 C1
Bertram Rd
5 Birmingham B10 .... 67 D1
Smethwick B67 .... 64 C6
Berwick Cl Coventry CV5 ... 112 B4
Warwick CV34 .... 155 E2
Berwick Dr WS11 .... 4 C8
Berwick Gr
Birmingham, Frankley B31 .. 102 D3
Birmingham, Pheasey B43 ... 44 B4
Berwicks La B37 .... 70 B1
Berwood Farm Rd B72 .... 57 C6
Berwood Gdns B24 .... 57 C5
Berwood Gr B92 .... 89 B1
Berwood Rd B72 .... 57 D6
Berwyn Ave CV6 .... 95 A1

Berwyn Gr WS6 .... 4 F3
Berwyn Way CV10 .... 72 C4
Beryl Ave LE10 .... 71 A2
Besant Gr B27 .... 88 A1
Besbury Cl B93 .... 127 E2
Bescot Cres WS1 .... 42 D6
Bescot Croft B42 .... 55 B6
Bescot Dr WS2 .... 42 B6
Bescot Ind Est The WS10 .. 41 D4
Bescot Rd WS2 .... 42 C7
Bescot St WS1 .... 42 E7
Bescot Stadium Sta WS5 ... 42 D5
Besford Gr Birmingham B31 102 D3
Solihull B90 .... 127 B6
Bessborough Rd B25 .... 88 D8
Best Ave CV8 .... 148 C7
Best Rd WV14 .... 40 D7
Best St B64 .... 62 F2
Beswick Gr B33 .... 69 A4
Beta Gr B14 .... 105 C4
Betjeman Ct DY10 .... 117 B5
Betjeman Pl WV10 .... 12 A1
Betley Gr B33 .... 69 A5
Betony Cl WS5 .... 43 A3
Betsham Cl B44 .... 45 B1
Bett Rd B20 .... 54 F3
Bettany Glade WV10 .... 11 E4
Betteridge Dr B76 .... 46 E4
Bettina Cl CV10 .... 72 B5
Bettman Cl CV3 .... 133 E6
Betton Rd B14 .... 104 E5
Betty's La WS11 .... 6 A4
Bevan Ave WV4 .... 39 E4
Bevan Cl Bilston WV14 .... 40 F6
Walsall WS4 .... 15 C1
Bevan Lee Rd WS11 .... 1 D3
Bevan Rd Brierley Hill DY5 .. 61 A2
Tipton DY4 .... 52 B4
Bevan Way B66 .... 64 F7
Beverley Ave CV10 .... 72 B4
Beverley Cl
Astwood Bank B96 .... 158 E4
Balsall Common CV7 ...... 130 C7
Sutton Coldfield B72 .... 57 D7
Beverley Court Rd B32 ...... 84 C6
Beverley Cres WV4 .... 39 F4
Beverley Croft B23 .... 56 D2
Beverley Ct ❶ B62 .... 84 A6
Beverley Dr DY6 .... 60 C7
Beverley Gr B26 .... 89 B5
Beverley Hill WS12 .... 2 D6
Beverley Rd
Birmingham B45 .... 122 A7
Royal Leamington Spa
CV32 .... 156 D1
West Bromwich B71 .... 42 D1
Beverly Dr CV4 .... 132 D2
Beverston Rd Perton WV6 .. 24 A4
Tipton DY4 .... 41 B2
Bevin Rd WS2 .... 27 E3
Bevington Cres CV6 .... 112 E5
Bevington Rd B6 .... 66 F8
Bewdley Ave ❹ B12 .... 87 A6
Bewdley Dr WV1 .... 26 B2
Bewdley Hill DY11 .... 116 B5
Bewdley Ho B26 .... 69 A1
Bewdley Rd
Birmingham B30 .... 104 B8
Kidderminster DY11 .... 116 C6
Bewdley Villas ❸ B18 .... 65 D4
Bewell Ct B61 .... 136 F4
Bewell Head B61 .... 136 F4
Bewlay Cl DY5 .... 81 B7
Bewley Rd WV12 .... 27 D4
Bewlys Ave B20 .... 54 E4
Bexfield Cl CV5 .... 112 A6
Bexhill Gr ❸ B15 .... 66 C1
Bexley Gr B71 .... 53 E7
Bexley Rd B44 .... 56 B8
Bexmore Dr WS13 .... 3 F1
Beyer Cl B77 .... 22 A2
Bhylls Acre Cty Prim Sch
WV3 .... 38 B8
Bhylls Cres WV3 .... 38 C7
Bhylls La WV3 .... 38 C7
Bibbey's Gn WV10 .... 11 F4
Bibsworth Ave B13 .... 105 D8
Bibury Rd B28 .... 105 E7
Bicester Sq B35 .... 58 B4
Bickenhill Green Ct B92 .... 90 D1
Bickenhill La
Birmingham B37 .... 90 C6
Birmingham B40 .... 90 D4
Catherine de B B91 .... 108 C6
Bickenhill Park Rd B92 ...... 88 E1
Bickenhill Parkway B37 ..... 90 D6
Bickenhill Rd B37 .... 90 B7
Bickford Rd Birmingham B6 56 A1
Wolverhampton WV10 ...... 25 F5
Bickington Rd B32 .... 84 D1
Bickley Ave Birmingham B11 .87 C6
Sutton Coldfield B74 .... 31 E5
Bickley Gr B26 .... 89 B5
Bickley Ho B26 .... 31 E5
Bickley Rd Bilston WV14 .... 41 A7
Walsall WS4 .... 29 C7
Bicknell Croft B14 .... 104 E2
Bickton Cl B24 .... 57 C5
Biddings La WV14 .... 40 B2
Biddles Hill B94 .... 141 C6
Biddlestone Gr WS5 .... 43 C3
Biddlestone Pl WS10 .... 41 B7
Biddulph Ct B73 .... 46 A2
Bideford Dr B29 .... 85 C1
Bideford Rd Coventry CV2 114 C7
Smethwick B66 .... 65 B5
Bideford Way WS11 .... 4 B8
Bidford Cl B90 .... 106 D2

Bidford Rd B31 .... 102 E3
Bierton Rd B25 .... 88 C8
Bigbury Cl CV3 .... 133 E5
Biggin Cl Birmingham B35 .. 58 A3
Perton WV6 .... 23 E5
Biggin Hall Cres CV3 ...... 114 B2
Bigwood Dr Birmingham B32 84 D1
Sutton Coldfield B75 .... 47 A5
Bilberry Bank WS11 .... 1 E6
Bilberry Cres WS12 .... 1 C5
Bilberry Dr B45 .... 122 A6
Bilberry Rd Birmingham
B14 .... 104 C6
Coventry CV2 .... 96 D2
Bilboe Rd WV14 .... 41 A3
Bilbrook Cl WV8 .... 10 B3
Bilbrook Gr Birmingham B29 .84 F2
Codsall WV8 .... 10 B3
Bilbrook Mid CE Sch WV8 . 10 B3
Bilbrook Rd WV8 .... 10 B3
Bilbrook Sta WV8 .... 10 A2
Bilbury Cl B97 .... 158 C6
Bilhay La B70 .... 53 B5
Bilhay St B70 .... 53 B5
Billau Rd WV14 .... 40 D2
Billesden Cl CV3 .... 134 E8
Billesley Inf Sch B13 ...... 105 C6
Billesley Jun Sch B13 ..... 105 C6
Billesley La Birmingham B13 .87 A1
Portway B48 .... 140 E6
Billing Rd CV5 .... 112 D3
Billingham Cl B91 .... 127 B8
Billingsley Rd B26 .... 89 A8
Billington Cl CV2 .... 114 E2
Bills La B90 .... 106 A1
Bills St WS10 .... 41 E6
Billsmore Gn B92 .... 107 C7
Billy Buns La WV5 .... 49 B8
Billy La B45 .... 138 A7
Billy Wright Cl WV4 .... 38 D6
Bilport La WS10 .... 52 F8
Bilston Central Sta WV14 . 40 E5
Bilston Coll of F Ed
Annexe WV14 .... 40 E6
Bilston Com Coll WV14 ..... 40 B7
Bilston Com Coll
Broad Lanes Site WV14 ... 40 C3
Bilston Com Coll
Devonshire Ho WV2 .... 40 A7
Bilston Com Coll
Green Lanes WV14 .... 40 C6
Bilston High Sch WV14 ..... 40 D5
Bilston Ind Est WV14 .... 41 A4
Bilston Key Ind Est WV14 .. 41 A4
Bilston La WV14 .... 41 B8
Bilston Rd Tipton DY4 .... 41 B2
Wednesbury WS10 .... 41 E3
Willenhall WV13 .... 41 A8
Wolverhampton WV2 .... 39 F8
Bilston St Darlaston WS10 . 41 D6
Sedgley DY3 .... 50 D8
Willenhall WV13 .... 27 A1
Wolverhampton WV1 ...... 163 C2
Bilton Grange Rd B26 .... 88 F8
Bilton Ind Est
❼ Birmingham B38 .... 123 E8
Coventry CV3 .... 113 F1
Binbrook Rd WV12 .... 27 D4
Bincomb Ave B26 .... 89 B6
Binfield St DY4 .... 52 A4
Bingley Ave B8 .... 68 B4
Bingley Ent Ctr WV3 .... 39 A8
Bingley Prim Sch WV3 ...... 39 A8
Bingley St WV3 .... 39 A8
Binley Ave CV3 .... 134 F7
Binley Cl Birmingham B26 .. 88 D6
Solihull B90 .... 126 A8
Binley Gr CV3 .... 134 F7
Binley Ind Est CV3 .... 135 A8
Binley Rd CV2, CV3 .... 114 D1
Binley Woods Cty
Prim Sch CV3 .... 135 E7
Binns Cl CV4 .... 131 F8
Binstead Rd B44 .... 45 A2
Binswood Ave CV32 .... 156 F2
Binswood Cl CV2 .... 96 D2
Binswood Mans ❼ CV32 . 156 F2
Binswood Rd B62 .... 84 A7
Binswood St CV32 .... 156 E1
Binton Cl B98 .... 154 F1
Binton Croft B13 .... 104 F8
Binton Rd Coventry CV2 .... 96 D2
Solihull B90 .... 105 F1
Birbeck Ho B36 .... 70 B6
Birbeck Pl DY5 .... 61 B6
Birch Ave Brierley Hill DY5 . 62 A2
Brownhills WS8 .... 15 E8
Burntwood WS7 .... 6 F6
Cannock WS11 .... 4 C8
Birch Brook La WS14 .... 17 E6
Birch Cl Bedworth CV12 .... 78 D4
Birmingham B30 .... 103 C6
Coventry CV5 .... 111 F6
Birch Coppice DY5 .... 62 A1
Birch Cres B69 .... 52 B1
Birch Croft Aldridge WS9 .. 30 C8
Birmingham B37 .... 70 C1
Sutton Coldfield B24 .... 57 D5
Birch Croft Rd B75 .... 46 D7
Birch Ct Birmingham B30 103 E4
Oldbury B66 .... 64 D8
Royal Leamington Spa CV34 161 E2
Walsall WS4 .... 29 A4
❶ Wolverhampton WV3 .. 25 C4
Birch Dr Halesowen B62 .... 63 E1
Little Aston B74 .... 31 D5
Stourbridge DY8 .... 80 E6
Sutton Coldfield B75 .... 46 F7

Birch Gr Birchmoor B78 ..... 36 D7
Lichfield WS13 .... 9 D8
Oldbury B68 .... 84 D7
Birch Hollow B15 .... 85 F6
Birch La Aldridge WS9 .... 16 D1
Oldbury B68 .... 84 D7
Walsall WS4 .... 15 C1
Birch Rd
Birmingham, Eachway B45 121 E6
Birmingham, Witton B6 ...... 56 A4
Oldbury B68 .... 84 D7
Sedgley DY3 .... 39 F1
Wednesfield WV11 .... 26 F8
Birch Rd E B6 .... 56 B2
Birch St Oldbury B68 .... 64 C5
Tipton DY4 .... 51 F5
Walsall WS4 .... 28 D3
Wolverhampton WV1 ...... 163 B3
Birch Terr DY2 .... 62 C4
Birch Tree Gr B91 .... 106 F4
Birch Wlk B68 .... 84 D8
Birchall St B12 .... 105 F6
Birchbrook Ind Pk WS14 ... 17 E6
Birchcoppice Gdns WV12 .. 27 E4
Birchcroft ❻ B66 .... 65 C5
Birchdale WV14 .... 40 D7
Birchdale Ave B23 .... 56 E3
Birchdale Rd B23 .... 56 D5
Birchen Coppice Fst Sch
DY11 .... 116 B2
Birchen Coppice Mid Sch
DY11 .... 116 B2
Birchensale Mid Sch B97 . 153 C4
Birchensale Rd B97 .... 153 C5
Birches Ave WV8 .... 10 C1
Birches Barn Ave WV3 ...... 38 F7
Birches Barn Rd WV3 .... 38 F7
Birches Cl B13 .... 86 F1
Birches Fst Sch WV8 .... 10 B1
Birches Green Inf Sch B24 57 B2
Birches Green Jun Sch B24 57 B3
Birches Green Rd B24 .... 57 B2
Birches La Alvechurch B48 138 F6
Kenilworth CV8 .... 148 B3
Birches Park Rd WV8 .... 10 A2
Birches Rd WV8 .... 10 B2
Birches Rise WV13 .... 26 F1
Birches The CV12 .... 79 B4
Birchfield Ave WV6 .... 24 B6
Birchfield Cl Halesowen B63 .82 E2
Wood End CV9 .... 36 C1
Birchfield Cres DY9 .... 81 F3
Birchfield Ct B97 .... 153 B2
Birchfield Gdns
❽ Birmingham B6 .... 66 D8
Walsall WS5 .... 43 C4
Birchfield Jun & Inf Sch
B20 .... 55 D1
Birchfield La B69 .... 63 E4
Birchfield Rd
Birmingham B20 .... 55 D2
Coventry CV6 .... 112 F8
Kidderminster DY11 .... 116 B5
Redditch B97 .... 153 B2
Stourbridge DY9 .... 81 F3
Birchfield Tower ❶ B20 .... 55 D1
Birchfield Way WS5 .... 43 C4
Birchfields Dr WS12 .... 2 D1
Birchfields Rd WV12 .... 27 A5
Birchgate DY9 .... 81 F4
Birchglade WV3 .... 24 D1
Birchgrave Cl CV6 .... 114 A7
Birchills CE Com Prim
Sch WS2 .... 28 D2
Birchills St WS2 .... 28 D2
Birchley Ho B69 .... 63 D6
Birchley Park Ave B69 ...... 63 E6
Birchley Rise B92 .... 88 F4
Birchley Spec Sch B65 ..... 63 D4
Birchmoor Cl B28 .... 106 B7
Birchmoor Rd B78 .... 36 F8
Birchover Rd B8 .... 28 A4
Birchtree Gdns DY5 .... 62 A1
Birchtree Hollow WV12 ..... 27 D5
Birchtrees Rd CV10 .... 72 C6
Birchtrees Dr B33 .... 69 D2
Birchway Cl CV32 .... 156 C1
Birchwood Ave B78 .... 36 F7
Birchwood Cl
Essington WV11 .... 13 A3
Kidderminster DY11 .... 116 A7
Birchwood Cres B12 .... 87 A4
Birchwood Prim Sch B78 .. 36 F7
Birchwood Rd
Binley Woods CV3 .... 135 C7
Birmingham B12 .... 87 A4
Lichfield WS13 .... 9 F7
Wolverhampton WV4 .... 39 A5
Birchwood Wlk ❷ DY6 ...... 60 E8
Birchwoods B32 .... 84 B2
Birchy Cl B90 .... 125 D8
Birchy Leasowes La B90 .. 125 E5
Bird End B71 .... 53 F8
Bird Grove Ct CV1 .... 113 D5
Bird Rd CV34 .... 161 D4
Bird St Coventry CV1 ...... 165 C3
Dudley DY3 .... 50 C3
Birdbrook Rd B44 .... 55 E8
Birdcage Wlk ❹ DY2 .... 51 D1
Birdhope B77 .... 22 C1
Birdie Cl B38 .... 103 D1
Birdlip Gr B32 .... 84 C6
Birds Bush Cty Prim Sch
B77 .... 35 F8
Birds Bush Rd B77 .... 35 F8
Birds Mdw DY5 .... 61 C7
Birdwell Croft B13 .... 104 F6

Birkdale Ave Birmingham
B29 .... 85 F1
Blackwell B60 .... 138 A5
Birkdale Cl Nuneaton CV11 74 A1
Stourbridge DY8 .... 80 F2
Wolverhampton WV1 .... 26 A2
Birkdale Dr B69 .... 63 A8
Birkdale Gr B29 .... 104 A8
Birkdale Rd WS3 .... 14 A3
Birkenshaw Rd B44 .... 55 E8
Birley Gr B63 .... 82 C1
Birlingham Ho B60 .... 137 B3
Birmingham Bsns Pk B37 . 90 E8
Birmingham
Childrens Hospl B4 ...... 164 C3
Birmingham Coll of Food
Tourism &
Creative Studies B3 ...... 164 A3
Birmingham
Conservatoire B1 .... 164 B2
Birmingham Dental
Hospl The B4 .... 164 C4
Birmingham Great Pk
B31 .... 102 B1
Birmingham Heartlands
Hospl B9 .... 68 B2
Birmingham Int Airport
B40 .... 90 B4
Birmingham Int
Convention Ctr B1 .... 66 C2
Birmingham Int Sta B40 ... 90 D4
Birmingham New Rd
Dudley DY1, DY4 .... 51 C4
Wolverhampton WV4 .... 39 F4
Birmingham Rd
Aldridge WS9 .... 30 A4
Allesley CV5 .... 111 E7
Alvechurch B48 .... 139 B7
Birmingham B36 .... 69 A8
Blackheath B65 .... 63 C2
Blakedown DY10 .... 98 C2
Burton Green CV8 .... 131 A1
Coleshill B46 .... 70 E5
Dudley DY1 .... 51 E2
Hagley DY9 .... 99 D7
Halesowen B63 .... 83 B4
Hopwood B38, B48 .... 123 B4
Kenilworth CV8 .... 147 C8
Kidderminster DY10 .... 117 D7
Lichfield WS14 .... 9 A4
Lickey End B60, B61 .... 137 B6
Little Packington CV7 .... 91 E3
Lydiate Ash B45, B61 ..... 121 D5
Marlbrook B61 .... 121 B1
Oldbury B69 .... 64 B7
Redditch B97 .... 153 E8
Shenstone WS14 .... 18 A5
Stoneleigh CV8 .... 149 B6
Studley B80 .... 159 E7
Sutton Coldfield B72 .... 46 B2
Walsall WS5 .... 43 D5
Warwick CV34 .... 160 C8
Water Orton B46 .... 59 A3
West Bromwich B71 .... 54 A1
Wolverhampton WV2 .... 39 C4
Wroxall B93, CV35 .... 145 D3
Birmingham Sch of
Speech & Drama
Birmingham, Edgbaston B15 86 A1
Birmingham, Ladywood B1 164 B2
Birmingham St
Darlaston WS10 .... 41 E6
Dudley DY2 .... 51 D1
Halesowen B63 .... 83 B3
Oldbury B69 .... 64 A7
Stourbridge DY8 .... 81 B5
Walsall WS1 .... 28 F1
Willenhall WV13 .... 27 C2
Birnam B15 .... 86 A8
Birnham Cl DY4 .... 51 D5
Birstall Wlk B38 .... 123 C8
Birvell Ct CV12 .... 78 D3
Bisell Way DY5 .... 81 C6
Biset Ave DY10 .... 117 B5
Bishbury Cl B15 .... 85 E8
Bishop Asbury Cres B43 ... 54 C8
Bishop Challoner RC Sch
B14 .... 104 F8
Bishop Cl B65 .... 101 E1
Bishop Hall Cres B60 ...... 150 E7
Bishop Milner RC Sec Sch
DY1 .... 51 A3
Bishop Rd WS10 .... 42 C2
Bishop St Birmingham B5 .. 86 E8
Coventry CV1 .... 165 B3
Bishop Ullathorne RC Sch
CV3 .... 132 F2
Bishop Vesey's Gram Sch
B74 .... 46 C6
Bishop Walsh RC Sch B72 46 D1
Bishop Wilson CE Prim
Sch B37 .... 70 C3
Bishop's Cl B65 .... 103 B3
Bishopgate Bsns Pk CV1 . 113 D5
Bishopgate Ind Est CV1 .. 113 D5
Bishops Cl Dudley DY2 ..... 62 E8
Smethwick B66 .... 65 C4
Bishops Gate B31 .... 103 A2
Bishops Mdw B75 .... 32 E3
Bishops Rd B73 .... 46 B3
Bishops Way B74 .... 31 F6
Bishops Wlk CV5 .... 133 B8
Bishopsgate St B15 .... 66 B1
Bishopstone Cl B98 .... 154 F2
Bishopton Cl Coventry
CV5 .... 112 A5
Solihull B90 .... 106 C1
Bishopton Rd B67 .... 64 F1

Bishton Gr DY2 .... 62 D4
Bisley Gr B24 .... 57 B2
Bissel Dr WS10 .... 42 B3
Bissel St WV14 .... 40 F5
Bissell Cl B28 .... 105 F6
Bissell St
Birmingham, Highgate B5 .. 86 E8
Birmingham, Quinton B32 .. 84 A6
Bisset Cres ❸ CV31 .... 162 C6
Biton Cl B17 .... 85 B5
Bittell Cl Birmingham B31 122 F7
Wolverhampton WV10 ...... 11 E4
Bittell Farm Rd B48 .... 123 A2
Bittell La B45 .... 138 E8
Bittell Rd Alvechurch B48 . 139 A8
Barnt Green B45 .... 138 E8
Bittern Wlk DY5 .... 81 C6
Bittern Wood Rd DY10 .... 117 B3
Bitterne Dr W6 .... 25 A4
Bitterscote La B78 .... 21 A2
Black Bank CV7 .... 78 B1
Black Country Mus DY1 .... 51 D3
Black Country New Rd
WS10 .... 41 C4
Black Country Route
Bilston WV14 .... 40 E5
Darlaston WV13, WS10 ..... 41 B7
Walsall WS2, WV13 .... 27 E1
Black Country Spine Rd
B70 .... 52 F6
Black Haynes Rd B29 ..... 103 A6
Black Horse La ❶ DY10 .. 116 F6
Black Horse Rd CV6 .... 96 B6
Black La CV32 .... 157 C2
Black Lake B70 .... 53 A6
Black Lake Sta B70 .... 52 F7
Black Prince Ave CV3 ..... 133 E6
Black-a-Tree Ct CV10 .... 72 F5
Black-A-Tree Rd CV10 ...... 72 F5
Blackacre Rd DY2 .... 62 D8
Blackberry Ave
Birmingham B9 .... 68 A3
Tanworth-in-A B94 .... 143 C6
Blackberry Cl DY1 .... 61 E8
Blackberry La Ash Green
CV7 .... 95 C5
Blackheath B65 .... 62 F5
Brownhills WS9 .... 16 B4
Coventry CV2 .... 114 C6
Halesowen B63 .... 83 A2
Sutton Coldfield B74 .... 31 E4
Blackbird Croft B36 .... 70 A7
Blackbrook Cl DY2 .... 62 A3
Blackbrook Rd DY2 .... 62 B5
Blackbrook Way WV10 ...... 11 E4
Blackburn Ave WV6 .... 24 F7
Blackburn Rd CV6 .... 95 F3
Blackburne Rd B28 .... 105 F6
Blackbushe Cl B17 .... 84 F7
Blackcat Cl B37 .... 70 A3
Blackdown B77 .... 22 C1
Blackdown Cl B45 .... 102 A2
Blackdown Rd B93 .... 128 B6
Blackett Cl ❶ B73 .... 46 A2
Blackfirs B37, B46 .... 90 D7
Blackford Cl Halesowen
B63 .... 82 D2
Kidderminster DY11 .... 116 A1
Blackford Rd
Birmingham B11 .... 87 C4
Solihull B90 .... 126 C8
Blackford St B18 .... 65 E5
Blackgreaves La B76 .... 48 F1
Blackhalve La WV11 .... 12 D2
Blackham Dr B73 .... 57 A7
Blackham Rd WV11 .... 26 F8
Blackheath Mkt B65 .... 63 C1
Blackheath Prim Sch B65 . 63 B1
Blackhorse La DY5 .... 61 E1
Blackley Ho B66 .... 65 D6
Blackmoor Cl CV34 .... 156 A1
Blackmoor Croft B33 .... 69 D2
Blackmore La B60 .... 137 A3
Blackpit La WV4 .... 37 E3
Blackrock Rd B23 .... 56 B6
Blackroot Cl WS7 .... 7 D4
Blackroot Ho B73 .... 45 C2
Blackroot Rd B74 .... 46 B7
Blackshaw Dr CV2 .... 114 F6
Blacksmiths La B94 .... 143 C6
Blackstich La B97 .... 153 A1
Blackstitch La B97 .... 152 F1
Blackthorn Ave WS7 .... 6 F4
Blackthorn Cl
Birmingham B30 .... 103 C6
Coventry CV4 .... 132 D5
Blackthorn Ct B98 .... 154 E1
Blackthorn Gr CV11 .... 73 F2
Blackthorn Rd
Birmingham, Bournville
B30 .... 103 D6
Birmingham,
Castle Bromwich B36 .... 69 C8
Stourbridge B61 .... 61 A1
Solihull B91 .... 106 E4
Blackthorne Cl Dudley DY1 . 50 F4
Kenilworth CV8 .... 148 A3
Lichfield WS14 .... 9 D7
Smethwick B67 .... 64 D4
Walsall WS5 .... 42 F5
Blackwatch Rd CV6 .... 113 C8
Blackwater Cl DY5 .... 61 A6
Blackwell La B97 .... 153 B5

Blackwell Rd
Barnt Green B45, B60 ...... **138** B5
Coventry CV6 .... **113** E8
Sutton Coldfield B72 .... **46** D1
Blackwell St DY10 .... **116** E6
Blackwood Ave WV11 ...... **26** C8
Blackwood Dr B74 .... **44** E8
Blackwood Rd Aldridge B74 .. **30** E1
Bromsgrove B60 .... **137** B2
Tamworth B77 .... **35** C7
Blades Rd B70 .... **52** D4
Bladon Cl CV11 .... **73** F8
Bladon Wlk 13 CV31 .... **162** C6
Blaenwern Dr B63 .... **82** B7
Blagdon Rd B63 .... **83** A6
Blair Dr CV12 .... **77** D1
Blair Gr B37 .... **70** D1
Blake Cl Cannock WS11 ...... **2** A5
Hinckley LE10 .... **71** D4
Nuneaton CV10 .... **72** A5
Blake Hall DY5 .... **81** C7
Blake High Sch WS12 .... **1** F6
Blake Ho 2 WS2 .... **42** C8
Blake La B9 .... **67** F2
Blake Pl B9 .... **67** F2
Blake Rd B61 .... **137** B8
Blake St B74 .... **31** E6
Blake Street Sta B74 .... **31** F6
Blakebrook DY11 .... **116** C6
Blakebrook Cl DY11 .... **116** C6
**Blakebrook Day
Special Sch** DY11 .... **116** C6
Blakebrook Gdns DY11 .... **116** C6
Blakedon Rd WS10 .... **41** E3
Blakedown CE Prim Sch
DY10 .... **98** C1
Blakedown Rd B63 .... **82** F1
Blakedown Way 4 B69 ...... **63** E4
Blakeland Rd B44 .... **55** E6
Blakeland St B9 .... **67** F2
Blakelands Ave CV31 ...... **162** B6
Blakeley Ave WV6 .... **24** F7
Blakeley Ct B72 .... **57** C8
Blakeley Hall Gdns B69 .... **64** B7
Blakeley Hall Rd B69 .... **64** B7
**Blakeley Heath Cty Prim
Sch** WV5 .... **49** A5
Blakeley Heath Dr WV5 .... **49** A5
Blakeley Rise WV6 .... **24** F7
Blakeley Specl Sch B69 .... **52** E1
Blakeley Wood Rd DY4 ...... **52** D8
Blakemere Ave B25 .... **88** E8
Blakemere Cl B98 .... **154** F3
Blakemere Ho 3 B16 .... **66** A2
Blakemere Dr B32 .... **84** F3
Blakemore Dr B75 .... **46** F6
Blakemore Rd
Brownhills WS9 .... **16** A3
West Bromwich B70 .... **53** A1
Blakenall Cl 1 WS3 .... **28** D8
Blakenall Heath WS3 .... **28** D8
Blakenall Heath Jun Sch
WS3 .... **28** C8
Blakenall La WS3 .... **28** D8
Blakenall Row WS3 .... **28** D8
Blakeney Ave
Birmingham B17 .... **85** A7
Stourbridge DY8 .... **80** D6
Blakeney Cl DY3 .... **50** C8
Blakenhale J & I Schs
B33 .... **69** B1
Blakenhall Dr B33 .... **69** B1
Blakenhall Gdns WV2 ...... **39** C7
Blakenhall Ind Est WV2 .... **39** B7
Blakesfield Dr B45 .... **122** A1
Blakesley Cl B76 .... **57** F5
Blakesley Gr B25 .... **68** D1
**Blakesley Hall Jun &
Inf Sch** B25 .... **68** D1
Blakesley Mews B25 .... **88** D8
Blakesley Rd B25 .... **68** D1
Blakewood Cl B34 .... **69** C5
Blandford Ave B36 .... **58** E6
Blandford Dr Coventry
CV2 .... **114** F5
Stourbridge DY8 .... **60** E3
Blandford Gdns WS7 .... **7** C2
Blandford Rd
Birmingham B32 .... **84** F5
Royal Leamington Spa CV32 .. **156** C5
Blandford Way CV35 .... **160** A7
Blanefield WV8 .... **10** E2
Blanford Mere Prim Sch
DY6 .... **60** E7
Blanning Ct B93 .... **127** E3
Blay Ave WS2 .... **28** B2
Blaydon Ave B75 .... **32** E2
Blaydon Rd WV9, WV10 .... **11** A1
Blaythorn Ave B92 .... **89** A3
Blaze Hill Rd DY6 .... **60** A8
Blaze La B96, B97 .... **158** A3
Blaze Pk DY6 .... **60** B8
Bleachfield Rd B98 .... **154** F8
Bleak Hill Rd B23 .... **56** C5
Bleak House Dr WS7 .... **6** D8
Bleak St B67 .... **64** F6
Bleakhouse Jun Sch B68 .. **64** C1
Bleakhouse Rd B68 .... **64** C1
Bleakman St B30 .... **104** A6
Blenheim B17 .... **85** B6
Blenheim Ave CV6 .... **95** C2
Blenheim Cl Hinckley LE10 .. **71** F2
Nuneaton CV11 .... **73** F2
Tamworth B77 .... **21** C4
Walsall WS4 .... **29** D7

Blenheim Cres
Bromsgrove B60 .... **151** A8
Royal Leamington Spa CV31 .. **162** C5
Blenheim Ct B44 .... **55** F8
Blenheim Dr B43 .... **54** D8
Blenheim Rd Birmingham
B13 .... **86** F1
Burntwood WS7 .... **7** A8
Kingswinford DY6 .... **61** A6
Norton Canes WS11 .... **6** B8
Solihull B90 .... **106** D2
Willenhall WV12 .... **27** B6
Blenheim Way
Birmingham B44 .... **55** F8
Dudley DY1 .... **50** E2
Bletchley Dr CV5 .... **112** B4
Bletchley Rd B24 .... **57** E4
Blewitt Cl B36 .... **58** D2
Blewitt St Brierley Hill DY5 .. **61** C6
Cannock WS12 .... **2** B7
Blews St B6 .... **66** E5
Blick Rd CV34 .... **161** C4
Blind La Berkswell CV7 ...... **110** D4
Tamworth-in-A B94 .... **141** D1
Blindpit La B76 .... **59** B8
Bliss Cl CV4 .... **111** E3
Blithe Cl DY8 .... **81** A8
Blithe Ct Solihull B91 .... **106** F7
Sutton Coldfield B73 .... **46** B5
Blithe Gdns WV8 .... **10** A4
Blithe Gr B44 .... **44** F3
Blithe Rd 7 Coleshill B46 .. **70** F7
Coventry CV1 .... **113** E4
Blithe St B77 .... **21** C4
Blithefield Ave B43 .... **43** C2
Blithesway B48 .... **139** A6
Blitheway B91 .... **107** E3
Blithewood Cl B91 .... **107** F1
Blithsford Rd B28 .... **106** A4
Blithswood Rd B11 .... **88** A4
Blyton Cl B16 .... **65** F3
Boar Croft CV4 .... **111** F2
Boar Hound Cl B18 .... **66** A4
Board School Gdns DY3 .... **50** E6
Boat La Burntwood WS14 .... **7** F1
Lichfield WS14 .... **8** A1
Boatman's La WS9 .... **15** E2
Bobbington Way DY2 .... **62** E5
Bobs Coppice Wlk DY5 ...... **81** F7
Bockendon Rd CV4 .... **131** E5
Boddington Cl CV32 .... **157** E5
Boden Rd B28 .... **106** A7
Bodenham Cl B98 .... **154** D3
Bodenham Rd
Birmingham B31 .... **102** E1
Oldbury B68 .... **84** B8
Bodens La WS9 .... **44** B7
Bodiam Ct WV6 .... **24** A3
Bodicote Gr B75 .... **32** E3
Bodington Rd B75 .... **32** C3
Bodmin Cl Hinckley LE10 .... **71** E4
Walsall WS5 .... **43** D7
Bodmin Ct 15 DY5 .... **61** D2
Bodmin Gr 2 B7 .... **67** B5
Bodmin Rd Coventry CV2 .. **114** F5
Dudley DY2 .... **62** D2
Bodmin Rise WS5 .... **43** D7
Bodnant Way CV8 .... **148** C6
Bognop Rd WV11 .... **12** D4
Bohun St CV4 .... **111** F1
Boldmere Cl B73 .... **57** A7
Boldmere Ct B43 .... **54** E7
Boldmere Dr B73 .... **57** A8
Boldmere Gdns B73 .... **57** A8
Boldmere Inf Sch B73 .... **45** F1
Boldmere Jun Sch B73 ...... **45** F1
Boldmere Rd B73 .... **57** A8
Bolebridge Mews B79 ...... **21** B5
Bolebridge St B79 .... **21** C4
Boley Cl WS14 .... **9** D7
Boley Cottage La WS14 ...... **9** E7
Boley La WS14 .... **9** D7
Boley Park Terr WS14 .... **9** E7
Boleyn Cl Cheslyn Hay WS6 .. **4** D2
Warwick CV34 .... **161** C6
Boleyn Rd B45 .... **101** E2
Bolingbroke Rd CV3 .... **114** A1
Bolney Rd B32 .... **84** E4
Bolton Cl CV3 .... **133** E5
Bolton Ct DY4 .... **52** C8
Bolton Rd Birmingham B10 .. **87** C8
Wednesfield WV11 .... **26** D5
Bolton St B9 .... **67** B2
Bolton Way WS3 .... **13** F3
Bolyfant Cl CV31 .... **162** A2
Bomers Field B45 .... **122** C7
Bond Dr B35 .... **58** A3
Bond Gate CV11 .... **73** C4
Bond Sq B18 .... **66** A4
Bond St
Birmingham, Ladywood B19 .. **164** B4
Birmingham, Stirchley B30 .. **104** A7
Blackheath B65 .... **63** E3
Coventry CV1 .... **165** B3
Dudley WV14 .... **51** A8
Nuneaton CV11 .... **73** C5
West Bromwich B70 .... **53** C2
Wolverhampton WV2 .... **163** B2
Bondfield Rd B13 .... **105** B6
Bondway WS12 .... **1** F8
Bone Mill La WV1 .... **25** D4
Bonehill Rd B78 .... **20** E3
Boney Hay Rd WS7 .... **7** B7
Bonfire Hill DY9 .... **120** E6
Bonham Gr B25 .... **68** D1
Boningale Way B93 .... **127** E3
Bonner Dr B76 .... **57** F5
Bonner Gr WS9 .... **29** E5
Bonneville Cl CV5 .... **111** B8
Bonniksen Cl CV31 .... **161** F5
Bonnington Way B43 .... **44** D4
Bonsall Rd B23 .... **57** A6
Bonville Gdns WV10 .... **11** E4
Boot Piece La B97 .... **153** B5
Booth Cl Kingswinford DY6 .. **61** A6
Lichfield WS13 .... **3** A2
Walsall WS3 .... **28** D8
Booth Ct 17 DY5 .... **61** D2
Booth Ho WS4 .... **28** F3
Booth Rd WS10 .... **42** C2
Booth St Birmingham B21 .. **65** D7
Cannock WS12 .... **2** B6
Darlaston WS10 .... **41** D8
Walsall WS3 .... **28** C8
Booth's La B42 .... **44** B1
Booths Farm Rd B42 .... **55** B8
Booths Fields CV6 .... **95** E2
Bordeaux Cl DY1 .... **50** E3
Borden Cl WV8 .... **24** F8
Bordesley Abbey B98 ...... **153** F6
Bordesley Cir B10 .... **67** B1
Bordesley Cl B9 .... **68** A2
Bordesley Ct CV32 .... **157** A3

Bordesley Gn B9 .... **67** E2
Bordesley Gn E B9 .... **68** C2
Bordesley Green Girls Sch
B9 .... **67** D2
Bordesley Green Jun & Inf Sch
B9 .... **68** A2
Bordesley Green Rd B8 .... **67** D2
Bordesley Green Trad Est
B9 .... **67** D3
Bordesley La B98 .... **153** E6
Bordesley Middleway 1 B12 .. **87** A8
Bordesley Park Rd B10 ...... **67** B1
Bordesley St B5 .... **164** D2
Bordesley Sta B10 .... **67** A1
Bore St WS13 .... **9** B7
Borman B79 .... **20** F5
Borneo St WS4 .... **28** F4
Borough Cres Oldbury B69 .. **63** E5
Stourbridge DY8 .... **80** E5
Borough Rd B79 .... **21** C7
Borough The LE10 .... **75** D8
Borrington Rd DY10 .... **117** B5
Borrow St WV13 .... **27** A3
Borrowcop Ho WS14 .... **9** C6
Borrowcop La WS14 .... **9** C5
Borrowdale Cl
Brierley Hill DY5 .... **81** B8
Coventry CV6 .... **113** A8
Borrowdale Dr CV32 .... **156** D2
Borrowdale Gr B31 .... **102** D3
Borrowdale Rd B31 .... **102** C3
Borrowell La CV8 .... **147** C6
Borrowell Terr CV8 .... **147** C6
Borwick Ave B70 .... **53** A3
Bosbury Terr B30 .... **104** B7
Boscobel Ave DY4 .... **51** F4
Boscobel Cl DY1 .... **50** F3
Boscobel Cres WV1 .... **25** C4
Boscobel Rd Birmingham
B43 .... **43** D2
Cheswick Green B90 .... **126** D5
Walsall WS1 .... **43** B8
Boscombe Ave B11 .... **87** C6
Boscombe Rd B11 .... **87** E4
Bosmere Ct B31 .... **102** F3
Boss Gate Cl WV5 .... **49** A5
Boston Cl WS12 .... **2** E1
Boston Gr B44 .... **56** B8
Boston Pl CV6 .... **113** D8
Boston Way LE9 .... **71** F6
Bosty La WS9 .... **29** E5
Boswell Cl Darlaston WS10 .. **41** D5
Tipton WS10 .... **41** C1
Boswell Dr CV2 .... **115** A7
Boswell Gr CV34 .... **155** D1
Boswell Rd Bilston WV14 .... **40** F7
Birmingham B44 .... **55** F6
Cannock WS11 .... **1** D4
Sutton Coldfield B74 .... **46** C6
Bosworth Cl Dudley DY3 .... **51** A6
Hinckley LE10 .... **71** A1
Bosworth Dr B37 .... **70** A2
Bosworth Rd B26 .... **88** E4
**Bosworth Wood Jun &
Inf Sch** B36 .... **58** F1
Botany Dr DY3 .... **50** D6
Botany Rd WS5 .... **43** A5
Botany Wlk B16 .... **66** A2
Botha Rd B9 .... **67** F2
Botoner Rd CV1 .... **113** F2
Bott La Stourbridge DY9 .... **81** E6
Walsall WS1 .... **28** F1
Bott Rd CV5 .... **132** C8
Botteley Rd B70 .... **53** A6
Bottetourt Rd B29 .... **85** A2
Botteville Rd B27 .... **88** C2
Bottrill St CV11 .... **73** B5
Boughton Rd B25 .... **88** C7
Boulevard The
Brierley Hill DY5 .... **61** F2
Sutton Coldfield B73 .... **57** B8
Boultbee Rd B72 .... **57** C7
Boulters La CV9 .... **36** D1
Boulton Cir B19 .... **66** C6
Boulton Cl WS7 .... **7** C8
Boulton Ind Ctr B18 .... **66** B5
Boulton Jun & Inf Sch B21 .. **65** E7
Boulton Rd Birmingham B21 .. **65** E7
Smethwick B66 .... **65** D6
Solihull B91 .... **107** C1
West Bromwich B70 .... **53** D1
Boulton Retreat B21 .... **65** E7
Boulton Sq B70 .... **53** D1
Boulton Wlk B23 .... **56** B4
Boultons La B97 .... **158** D6
Boundary Ave B65 .... **63** E2
Boundary Cres DY3 .... **50** C3
Boundary Ct B37 .... **69** E2
Boundary Hill DY3 .... **50** C4
Boundary Ho B5 .... **86** C5
Boundary Ind Est WV10 .... **11** C5
Boundary Pl B21 .... **54** B1
Boundary Rd Brownhills
WS9 .... **15** F3
Sutton Coldfield B74 .... **44** F7
Wolverhampton WV13 .... **26** C1
Boundary Way
Wolverhampton,
Compton WV6 .... **23** F2
Wolverhampton, Penn WV4 .. **38** C5
Bourlay Cl B45 .... **101** E2
Bourn Mill Dr B6 .... **66** D6
Bournbrook Rd B29 .... **86** A2
Bourne Ave Catshill B61 .. **120** F1
Fazeley B78 .... **20** E1
Halesowen B62 .... **83** F4
Tipton DY4 .... **52** C7

Bourne Cl Birmingham B13 . **105** D6
Cannock WS12 .... **2** D2
Solihull B91 .... **107** E6
Bourne Gn B32 .... **84** E6
Bourne Hill Cl DY2 .... **62** E3
Bourne Rd Birmingham B6 .. **67** B7
Coventry CV3 .... **114** C7
Bourne St Dudley DY2 .... **51** D1
Dudley, Bramford WV14 ...... **51** A7
Bourne Vale WS9 .... **30** D3
Bourne Way Gdns B29 .... **104** A8
Bournes Cl B63 .... **82** F3
Bournes Cres B63 .... **84** A4
Bournes Hill B63 .... **82** E4
Bourneville Sta B30 .... **104** A7
Bournheath Rd B61 .... **120** D2
Bournlea Coll B31 .... **103** C7
Bournville Coll of F Ed
B30 .... **103** E7
Bournville Inf Sch B30 .... **103** E7
Bournville Jun Sch B30 .. **103** E7
Bournville La B30 .... **103** E6
Bournville Mews B30 ...... **103** E5
Bournville Sch of Art B30 . **103** E7
Bournville Sec Sch B30 .. **103** C6
Bourton Cl 1 WS5 .... **43** A3
Bourton Croft B92 .... **106** F8
Bourton Dr CV31 .... **162** B5
Bourton Rd B92 .... **106** F8
Bovey Croft B76 .... **58** A7
Bovingdon Rd B35 .... **58** A3
Bow Ct CV5 .... **132** D8
Bow St Bilston WV14 .... **40** E6
Birmingham B1 .... **164** B1
Willenhall WV13 .... **27** A1
Bowater Ave B33 .... **68** D1
Bowater Ho Birmingham B19. **66** D5
West Bromwich B70 .... **53** C2
Bowater St B70 .... **53** C2
Bowbrook Ave B90 .... **127** A5
Bowcroft Gr B24 .... **57** C6
Bowden Rd B67 .... **64** E6
Bowden Way CV3 .... **114** F1
Bowdler Rd WV2 .... **163** D1
Bowen Ave WV4 .... **40** A3
Bowen Ct 4 B13 .... **87** B2
Bowen St WV4 .... **39** E5
Bowen-Cooke Ave WV6 .... **23** E6
Bower Cl WS13 .... **3** D2
Bower Ho B19 .... **66** D6
Bower La DY5 .... **82** A8
Bowercourt Cl B91 .... **107** B2
Bowers Croft CV32 .... **157** A5
Bowes Dr WS11 .... **1** F4
Bowes Rd B45 .... **121** E7
Bowfell Cl CV5 .... **112** B4
Bowker St WV13 .... **26** C1
Bowlas Ave B74 .... **46** B8
Bowling Green Ave B77 .... **35** F7
Bowling Green Cl
Birmingham B23 .... **56** F7
Darlaston WS10 .... **41** D7
Bowling Green La
Bedworth CV7, CV12 .... **95** E8
Birmingham B20 .... **66** A8
Bowling Green Rd
Birmingham B9 .... **67** C1
Dudley DY2 .... **62** C2
Hinckley LE10 .... **71** E1
Stourbridge DY8 .... **80** E5
Bowling Green St CV34 .... **160** D6
Bowls Ct CV5 .... **112** F3
Bowman Gn LE10 .... **75** F6
Bowman Rd B42 .... **44** B1
Bowman's Rise WV1 .... **26** B3
Bowmore Rd B60 .... **137** B1
Bowness Cl CV6 .... **113** A8
Bowness Ho B65 .... **63** D4
Bowood Cres B31 .... **103** B2
Bowood Dr WV6 .... **24** D6
Bowood End B76 .... **46** E3
Bowshot Cl B36 .... **58** D1
Bowstoke Rd B43 .... **54** C8
Bowyer Rd B8 .... **67** E4
Bowyer St B10 .... **67** A1
Box Cl CV31 .... **162** B3
Box Rd B37 .... **90** C8
Box St WS1 .... **28** F1
Box Trees Rd B93 .... **127** C1
Boxhill Cl B6 .... **66** F6
Boxhill The CV3 .... **114** B1
Boxnott Cl B97 .... **153** A2
Boyd Cl CV2 .... **115** A8
Boyd Gr B27 .... **88** B2
Boyden Cl WS11 .... **1** B1
Boydon Cl WV2 .... **40** A6
Boyleston Rd B28 .... **106** A6
Boyne Rd B26 .... **89** B7
Boyslade Rd LE10 .... **75** F6
Boyslade Rd E LE10 .... **75** F5
Boyton Gr B44 .... **44** F3
Brabazon Gr B35 .... **57** F3
Brabham Cres B74 .... **44** F6
Bracadale Ave B24 .... **57** A4
Bracadale Cl CV3 .... **115** A2
Brace St WS1 .... **42** E8
Bracebridge Cl CV7 .... **130** B6
Bracebridge Dr B17 .... **85** D5
Bracebridge Ho B73 .... **45** C2
Bracebridge Rd
Birmingham B24 .... **56** F1
Sutton Coldfield B74 .... **46** A8
Bracebridge St
Birmingham B6 .... **66** E6
Nuneaton CV11 .... **73** B3

Braceby Ave B13 .... 105 C6
Braces La B60 .... 121 C1
Bracken Burntwood WS7 .. 7 C7
Cannock WS11 .... 2 D8
Lichfield WS14 .... 9 E6
Wolverhampton WV8 .... 10 E1
Bracken Croft **1** B37 ...... 70 C3
Bracken Dr B75 .... 47 A5
Bracken Gr B61 .... 121 A1
Bracken Park Gdns DY8 .. 60 F2
Bracken Rd Birmingham B24 . 57 C2
Huntington WS12 .... 1 C5
Bracken Way
Birmingham B38 .... 123 D6
Sutton Coldfield B74 ...... 44 F8
Bracken Wood WS5 .... 43 D5
Brackenbury Rd B44 .... 56 B8
Brackendale Dr
Nuneaton CV10 .... 72 F3
Walsall WS5 .... 43 B3
Brackendale Sh Ctr WV12 . 27 D4
Brackendale Way DY9 .... 81 D4
Brackenfield Rd
Birmingham B44 .... 44 D3
Halesowen B63 .... 82 E5
Brackenfield View DY1 .. 61 D8
Brackenhill Rd WS7 .... 7 A8
Brackenhurst Rd CV6 .... 113 A7
Brackenwood Dr WV11 .. 26 F5
Bracklesham Way B77 .... 22 A6
Brackley Ave B20 .... 55 C1
Brackley Cl CV6 .... 112 F7
Brackleys Way B92 .... 89 A2
Bracknell Wlk **1** CV2 .... 115 A7
Bradburn Rd WV11 .... 26 B8
Bradburne Way B7 .... 67 A5
Bradbury Cl WS8 .... 15 F5
Bradbury La WS12 .... 2 B2
Bradbury Rd B92 .... 107 A8
Braddock Cl CV3 .... 115 A1
Brade Dr CV2 .... 115 B7
Braden Rd WV4 .... 38 D4
Brades Cl B63 .... 82 B7
Brades Rd B69 .... 63 E8
Brades Rise B69 .... 63 D8
Bradestone Rd CV11 ...... 73 D1
Bradewell Rd B36 .... 58 D1
Bradfield Cl CV5 .... 112 C5
Bradfield Ho B26 .... 89 D6
Bradfield Rd B42 .... 55 D7
Bradford Cl B43 .... 54 F7
Bradford Court Bsns Ctr
1 B12 .... 87 A8
Bradford La
Belbroughton DY9 .... 119 D5
Walsall WS1 .... 28 E1
Bradford Mall WS1 .... 28 E1
Bradford Pl WS1 .... 28 E1
Bradford Rd Birmingham B36 . 69 B7
Brownhills WS8 .... 15 E8
Dudley DY2 .... 61 F6
Bradford St
Birmingham B12, B5 .... 66 F1
Cannock WS11 .... 2 A5
Tamworth B79 .... 20 F5
Walsall WS1 .... 28 E1
Bradgate Cl WV12 .... 27 C6
Bradgate Dr B74 .... 31 E5
Bradgate Pl **12** B12 ...... 87 A6
Bradgate Rd LE10 .... 71 F2
Brading Rd CV10 .... 73 D6
Bradley Croft CV7 .... 130 B6
Bradley La WV14 .... 41 A3
Bradley La Sta WV14 ..... 41 A3
Bradley Rd Birmingham B34 . 69 D6
Stourbridge DY8 .... 80 F6
Wolverhampton WV2 .... 39 E7
Bradley St Bilston WV14 . 40 F4
Brierley Hill DY5 .... 61 C7
Tipton DY4 .... 51 F2
Bradley's La WV14 .... 51 E8
Bradleymore Rd DY5 ...... 61 D3
Bradleys Cl B64 .... 82 E7
Bradmore Cl B91 .... 107 A1
Bradmore Gr B29 .... 103 A8
Bradmore Rd WV3 .... 38 F8
Bradney Gn CV4 .... 131 E7
Bradnick Pl CV4 .... 111 F1
Bradnock Cl B13 .... 105 C7
Bradnock's Marsh La
B92 .... 109 E2
Bradshaw Ave
Birmingham B38 .... 103 D1
Darlaston WS10 .... 41 C5
Bradshaw Cl DY4 .... 52 A3
Bradshaw St WV1 .... 163 D3
Bradshawe Cl B28 .... 105 D3
Bradstock Rd B30 .... 104 C4
Bradwell Croft B75 .... 32 E3
Bradwell Ho B31 .... 102 D5
Braemar Ave B20 .... 60 C1
Braemar Cl Coventry CV2 . 114 E6
Sedgley DY3 .... 39 C1
Willenhall WV12 .... 27 B5
Braemar Dr B23 .... 56 B5
Braemar Gdns WS12 .... 1 F7
Braemar Rd
Norton Canes WS11 .... 6 B4
Royal Leamington Spa CV32 . 157 B4
Solihull B92 .... 88 C1
Sutton Coldfield B73 ...... 46 A2
Braemar Way CV10 .... 73 A2
Braeside Croft B37 .... 70 C2
Braeside Way WS3 .... 14 F3
Bragg Rd B20 .... 55 D2
Braggs Farm La B90 ..... 126 A4
Braham B79 .... 20 D6
Braid Cl B38 .... 103 D1

Braidwood Sch for the Deaf
B23 .... 56 B6
Brailes Cl B92 .... 107 E7
Brailes Dr B76 .... 46 F3
Brailes Gr B9 .... 68 B1
Brailsford Cl WV11 .... 26 E8
Brailsford Dr B66 .... 65 A5
Brain St B77 .... 22 A2
Braithwaite Cl DY6 .... 60 D6
Braithwaite Rd B11 .... 87 B7
Brake La DY8 .... 98 F6
Brake The DY8 .... 98 F6
Brakesmead CV31 .... 161 F5
Bramah Way DY4 .... 52 C6
Bramber B77 .... 21 D1
Bramber Dr WV5 .... 49 A6
Bramber Way DY8 .... 80 F2
Bramble Cl
Birmingham, Aston B6 ..... 66 E7
Birmingham, Shenley Fields
B31 .... 102 F6
Blackheath B64 .... 62 F4
Clayhanger WS8 .... 15 E5
6 Coleshill B46 .... 70 F7
Nuneaton CV11 .... 73 F2
Willenhall WV12 .... 27 C7
Bramble Dell B9 .... 68 A3
Bramble Dr WS12 .... 2 C7
Bramble Gn DY1 .... 50 F5
Bramble La WS7 .... 7 B8
Bramble St CV1 .... 113 E2
Brambles The Lichfield
WS14 .... 9 D6
Stourbridge DY9 .... 81 D3
Sutton Coldfield B76 ...... 58 A8
Brambleside B60 .... 60 F1
Bramblewood WV5 .... 49 A7
Bramblewood Dr WV3 .... 38 E8
Bramblewoods B34 .... 69 C5
Brambling B77 .... 36 A7
Brambling Rise DY10 .... 117 B1
Brambling Wlk **2**
Birmingham B15 .... 86 C7
Brierley Hill DY5 .... 81 C6
Bramcote Cl Bulkington
CV12 .... 79 D2
Hinckley LE10 .... 71 F3
Bramcote Dr B91 .... 107 C7
Bramcote Hospl CV11 .... 79 E7
Bramcote Rd B32 .... 84 C5
Bramcote Rise B75 .... 46 C7
Bramdean Wlk WV4 .... 38 C6
Bramdene Ave CV10 ...... 73 D8
Brame Rd LE10 .... 71 C2
Bramerton Cl WV11 .... 26 A6
Bramford Dr DY1 .... 51 B6
Bramford Park Ind Est B70 . 53 A1
Bramford Prim Sch DY1 . 51 B6
Bramley Cl Birmingham B43 . 44 D3
Walsall WS5 .... 43 D8
Bramley Croft B90 .... 106 C2
Bramley Ct WV11 .... 26 C6
Bramley Dr Birmingham B20 . 55 B3
Hollywood B47 .... 125 B6
Bramley Ho WS5 .... 43 B4
Bramley Rd **3**
Birmingham B27 .... 88 C5
Walsall WS5 .... 43 B4
Brampton Ave B28 .... 106 A6
Brampton Cres B90 ...... 106 B6
Brampton Dr WS12 .... 2 E2
Brampton Way CV12 ...... 79 B3
Bramshall Dr B93 .... 127 E3
Bramshaw Cl B14 .... 104 F2
Bramshill Ct B15 .... 86 B8
Bramstead Ave WV6 ...... 24 B2
Bramston Cres CV4 ...... 111 F1
Bramwell Gdns CV6 .... 95 F5
Brancaster Cl B77 .... 22 A5
Branch Rd B38 .... 123 E8
Branchal Rd WS9 .... 16 C1
Branden Rd B48 .... 139 A5
Brandfield Rd CV6 .... 112 F8
Brandhall Ct B68 .... 64 A2
Brandhall Ct **8** B68 ..... 84 B8
Brandhall La B68 .... 64 B1
Brandhall Prim Sch B68 . 64 A1
Brandhall Rd B68 .... 64 B2
Brandon Cl Aldridge WS9 . 30 F3
Sedgley DY3 .... 50 E7
West Bromwich B70 .... 53 A2
Brandon Cl Birmingham B31 . 103 B1
Coventry CV3 .... 135 A7
Brandon La CV3, CV8 .... 135 C5
Brandon Marsh Nature
Reserve CV8 .... 135 A4
Brandon Marsh Visitor
Ctr CV8 .... 135 B4
Brandon Par CV32 .... 162 A8
Brandon Pk WV3 .... 38 E7
Brandon Pl B34 .... 69 D7
Brandon Rd Birmingham B28 . 87 E2
Coventry CV3 .... 135 A8
Halesowen B62 .... 63 E1
Hinckley LE10 .... 75 B7
Solihull B91 .... 107 C7
Brandon Thomas Ct B6 .. 67 B8
Brandon Way
Brierley Hill DY5, DY8 ..... 81 B1
West Bromwich B70 .... 53 A2
Brandon Way Ind Est B70 . 52 F3
Brandwood Cl B14 .... 104 D5
Brandwood Ho B14 ...... 104 D7
Brandwood Park Rd B14 . 104 C5
Branfield Cl WV14 .... 51 A8
Branksome Ave B21 ...... 65 F8

Branksome Rd CV6 ...... 112 E6
Branscombe Cl B14 ...... 104 D5
Bransdale Ave CV6 .... 95 D3
Bransdale Cl WV6 .... 25 A5
Bransdale Rd WS8 .... 15 E6
Bransford Ave CV4 .... 132 D5
Bransford Rise B91 ...... 108 B5
Branston Tower B12 ...... 86 F8
Branstree Dr CV6 .... 95 D2
Brantford Rd B25 .... 88 C8
Branthill Croft B91 ...... 107 B1
Brantley Ave WV3 .... 24 C1
Brantley Rd B6 .... 56 A2
Branton Hill La WS9 ...... 30 C5
Brantwood Ave WS7 .... 7 A5
Brascote Rd LE10 .... 74 F8
Brasshouse Inf Sch B66 . 65 A7
Brasshouse La B66 .... 65 A7
Brassie Cl B38 .... 103 D1
Brassington Ave B73 ..... 46 B5
Bratch Cl DY2 .... 62 C3
Bratch Hollow WV5 .... 49 A8
Bratch La WV5 .... 49 A8
Brathay Cl CV3 .... 133 D5
Bratt St B70 .... 53 C4
Braunston Cl B76 .... 47 A2
Brawnes Hurst B26 .... 69 A1
Bray Ho WV11 .... 26 C5
Bray St WV13 .... 27 B2
Bray's La CV2 .... 114 A3
Brayford Ave Brierley Hill
DY5 .... 81 B7
Coventry CV3 .... 133 C6
Braymoor Rd B33 .... 69 E1
Brays Rd B26 .... 89 B6
Brays Sch B26 .... 89 A6
Braytoft Cl CV6 .... 95 C2
Brazil St CV4 .... 111 E2
Breaches La B98 .... 159 D8
Breadmarket St WS13 ..... 9 B8
Breakback Rd B61 .... 150 D8
Bream B77 .... 35 D7
Bream Cl B37 .... 70 C2
Breamore Cres DY1 .... 50 F3
Brean Ave B92 .... 88 F5
Brearley Cl B19 .... 66 E5
Brearley St
Birmingham,
Handsworth B21 .... 65 D8
Birmingham, Hockley B19 . 66 E5
Brechin Cl LE10 .... 75 A8
Brecknell Rise DY10 .... 116 F8
Brecknock Rd B71 .... 53 A6
Brecon Ave B61 .... 137 A5
Brecon Dr **2** DY8 .... 81 B6
Brecon Rd B20 .... 66 B8
Brecon Tower **1** B16 .... 66 A2
Bredon Ave Coventry CV3 . 134 F8
Kidderminster DY11 ...... 116 A1
Stourbridge DY9 .... 81 C5
Bredon Croft B18 .... 66 A5
Bredon Ct Halesowen B63 . 83 A3
Sutton Coldfield B75 ...... 32 A4
Bredon Rd Bromsgrove
B61 .... 150 D7
Oldbury B69 .... 63 D5
Stourbridge DY9 .... 81 B6
Bredon Terr **4** B18 ...... 66 A5
Bredon View B97 .... 158 D8
Bree Cl CV5 .... 112 A7
Bree's La CV8 .... 130 A1
Breech Cl B74 .... 44 E7
Breeden Dr B76 .... 59 B6
Breedon Rd B30 .... 104 A5
Breedon Way WS4 .... 15 C1
Breen Rydding Dr WV14 . 51 B8
Breener Ind Est DY5 ...... 61 B1
Breeze Ave WS11 .... 6 B5
Brelades Cl DY1 .... 50 E3
Brendon B77 .... 22 B1
Brendon Way CV10 .... 72 A3
Brenfield Dr LE10 .... 75 A8
Brennand Cl B68 .... 84 C8
Brennand Rd B68 .... 84 B8
Brent B77 .... 35 E7
Brent Ho **3** DY1 .... 61 E8
Brent Rd B30 .... 104 D8
Brentford Rd
Birmingham B14 .... 105 A5
Solihull B91 .... 106 E3
Brentmill Cl WV10 .... 11 F4
Brentnall Dr B75 .... 32 B3
Brenton Rd WV4 .... 38 F3
Brentwood Ave CV3 ..... 133 C3
Brentwood Cl B91 .... 106 E3
Brentwood Gdns CV3 ... 133 C3
Brentwood Gr B44 .... 55 E8
Brenwood Cl DY6 .... 60 B7
Brereton Cl DY2 .... 62 E8
Brereton Rd WV12 .... 27 D7
Brese Ave CV34 .... 155 F1
Bretby Gr B23 .... 57 A6
Bretford Rd CV2 .... 96 C1
Bretshall Cl B90 .... 126 F5
Brett Dr B32 .... 102 C8
Brett St B71 .... 53 B5
Brett Young Cl DY10 .... 117 B5
Brettell La
Brierley Hill DY5, DY8 ..... 61 B1
Stourbridge DY8 .... 60 F1
Brettell St **5** DY2 .... 62 B8
Bretton Gdns WV10 ...... 25 F6
Bretton Rd B27 .... 88 D2
Bretts Cl CV1 .... 165 D4
Bretts Hall Est CV10 ..... 72 A7
Brevitt Rd WV2 .... 39 D6
Brewer Rd CV12 .... 79 D2

Brewer St WS2 .... 28 E4
Brewers Cl CV3 .... 115 A1
Brewers Dr WS3 .... 15 A1
Brewers Terr WS3 .... 15 A2
Brewery St
Birmingham,
Handsworth B21 .... 65 D8
Birmingham,
New Town Row B6 .... 164 C5
Dudley DY2 .... 51 E1
Smethwick B67 .... 64 F6
Tipton DY4 .... 51 F4
Brewins Way DY6 .... 62 A4
Brewster Cl Coventry CV2 . 114 E2
Fazeley B78 .... 20 E1
Brewster St DY2 .... 62 C5
Breydon Gr WV13 .... 40 F8
Brian Rd B67 .... 64 E6
Brianbourne CV6 .... 95 E3
Briansway CV6 .... 95 E3
Briar B77 .... 22 A3
Briar Ave B74 .... 31 A1
Briar Cl Birmingham B24 . 57 A4
Cannock WS12 .... 2 A8
Hinckley LE10 .... 75 F6
Lickey End B60 .... 137 C6
Royal Leamington Spa CV32 . 157 B2
Briar Coppice B90 .... 126 D4
Briar Ct **14** Brierley Hill DY5 . 61 C6
Dudley DY2 .... 62 C6
Briar Hill DY10 .... 118 E1
Briar Hill Cty Fst Sch
CV31 .... 162 B3
Briar Wood DY2 .... 40 A7
Briarbeck WS4 .... 29 C8
Briardene Ave CV12 ...... 78 B2
Briarfield Rd B11 .... 88 A3
Briarley Ho **5** B71 ...... 42 F1
Briarmead LE10 .... 75 E4
Briars Cl Brierley Hill DY5 . 61 C4
Coventry CV2 .... 114 C2
Nuneaton CV11 .... 73 E5
Briars The B23 .... 56 D6
Briarwood Cl B90 .... 126 D4
Briarwood The WV2 .... 40 A7
Brick Hill La CV5 .... 111 E8
Brick Kiln La Birmingham
B44 .... 55 C6
Dudley DY3 .... 50 B3
Middleton B78 .... 48 D6
Solihull B90 .... 126 F6
Wythall B47 .... 124 F4
Brick Kiln St
Brierley Hill, Hart's Hill DY5 . 61 E5
Brierley Hill,
Quarry Bank DY5 .... 82 A8
Hinckley LE10 .... 75 C8
Tipton DY4 .... 51 F6
Brick St DY3 .... 50 D8
Brickfield Rd B25 .... 88 B6
Brickheath Rd WV1 .... 26 A3
Brickhill Dr B37 .... 70 A2
Brickhouse La
Stoke Prior B60 .... 150 C4
West Bromwich B70 .... 52 E6
Brickhouse La S DY4 ..... 52 E6
Brickhouse Prim Sch B65 . 63 A3
Brickhouse Rd B65 .... 63 A4
Brickkiln Ct **2** DY5 ...... 61 D2
Brickkiln St WS8 .... 15 F7
Brickkiln Prim Sch WV3 . 25 B1
Brickiln St WV13 .... 26 F1
Brickyard La B80 .... 159 C4
Brickyard Rd WS9 .... 15 F1
Bridal Path The CV5 .... 112 B6
Briddsland Rd B33 .... 69 E2
Bridge Ave Cheslyn Hay WS6 . 4 E4
Tipton DY4 .... 52 C7
Bridge Cl Birmingham B11 . 87 B3
Clayhanger WS8 .... 15 E6
Bridge Croft B12 .... 86 E6
Bridge Cross Rd WS7 ..... 6 F7
Bridge End CV34 .... 160 F6
Bridge Ho
Royal Leamington Spa
CV31 .... 162 A8
Smethwick B66 .... 65 C6
Bridge Ind Est B91 .... 107 C7
Bridge Meadow Dr B93 . 127 F6
Bridge Piece B31 .... 103 B2
Bridge Rd Birmingham B8 . 67 E3
Hinckley LE10 .... 75 D7
Tipton DY4 .... 52 C7
Walsall WS4 .... 15 B1
Bridge Specl Sch B23 ... 56 E4
Bridge St Bilston WV14 .. 40 E5
Birmingham B1 .... 164 A2
Cannock WS11 .... 4 E5
Clayhanger WS8 .... 15 E6
Coventry CV6 .... 114 A7
Dudley WV14 .... 51 C8
Halesowen B63 .... 82 C7
Kenilworth CV8 .... 147 F5
1 Kidderminster DY10 . 116 E5
Nuneaton CV11 .... 73 C4
Nuneaton, Chilvers Coton
CV11 .... 73 C2
Oldbury B69 .... 64 A8
Redditch B97 .... 153 D4
Stourbridge DY8 .... 60 E1
Tamworth B77 .... 21 E5
Walsall WS1 .... 28 F2
Warwick CV34 .... 161 C8
Wednesbury WS10 .... 41 F1
West Bromwich B70 .... 53 B4
Willenhall WV13 .... 26 E1
Wolverhampton WV10 .... 25 E5
Bridge St N B66 .... 65 B7
Bridge St W B19 .... 66 D5

Bra – Bri   **175**

Bridge View Baginton CV8 . 133 D3
3 Coleshill B46 .... 70 F7
Bridge Way WS8 .... 15 E6
Bridgeacre Gdns CV3 ... 114 F2
Bridgeburn Rd B31 ...... 102 E3
Bridgecote CV3 .... 134 E6
Bridgefield Wlk B65 ...... 62 F5
Bridgefoot Wlk WV8 ...... 10 F1
Bridgeford Rd B34 .... 69 B6
Bridgelands Way B20 .... 55 D1
Bridgeman Croft B36 .... 69 C8
Bridgeman Rd CV6 ...... 113 B4
Bridgeman St WS2 .... 28 D1
Bridgemary Cl WV10 ..... 11 E4
Bridgemeadow Ho **5** B36 . 68 E8
Bridgenorth Ho B33 ...... 69 B2
Bridges Cres WS11 .... 5 F5
Bridges Rd WS11 .... 5 F5
Bridgewater Ave B69 ..... 64 A4
Bridgewater Cres DY2 ... 51 E1
Bridgewater Dr WV14 .... 40 C2
Bridgewater St B77 .... 21 D5
Bridgnorth Gr WV12 ...... 27 B6
Bridgnorth Rd Himley DY3 . 49 B3
Stourbridge DY7, DY8 ..... 80 C6
Trescott WV6 .... 37 C7
Wolverhampton WV6 ...... 24 B2
Wombourne WV5 .... 49 A4
Bridgtown Bsns Ctr WS11 . 4 E6
Bridgtown Cty Prim Sch
WS11 .... 4 E6
Bridgwater Cl WS9 .... 15 F3
Bridle Brook La CV5, CV7 . 94 A3
Bridle Gr B71 .... 53 F7
Bridle La B74 .... 44 E7
Bridle Mead B38 .... 123 D8
Bridle Path The B90 .... 106 B6
Bridle Rd DY8 .... 80 D6
Bridlewood B74 .... 44 F8
Bridley Moor High Sch
B97 .... 153 C4
Bridley Moor Rd B97 ... 153 C5
Bridport Cl CV2 .... 115 A4
Bridport Ho B31 .... 102 E7
Brier Mill Rd B62 .... 83 C3
Brier Sch DY5 .... 61 E3
Brierley Hill Prim Sch DY5 . 61 D2
Brierley Hill Rd DY8 ...... 60 F2
Brierley La WV14 .... 40 C2
Brierley Rd CV2 .... 114 C8
Brierley Trad Est The DY5 . 61 C5
Briery B64 .... 82 F7
Briery Rd B63 .... 82 E3
Brigfield Cres B13 .... 105 B5
Brigfield Rd B13 .... 105 B5
Bright Cres B77 .... 21 C2
Bright St Coventry CV6 .. 113 E6
Darlaston WS10 .... 41 D5
Stourbridge DY8 .... 80 D6
Wolverhampton WV1 ..... 163 A4
Brightmere Rd CV6 ...... 113 B4
Brighton Cl WS2 .... 28 D3
Brighton Mews **8** WV3 . 25 A2
Brighton Rd B12 .... 87 A5
Brighton St CV2 .... 113 F3
Brightstone Cl WV10 ..... 11 F4
Brightstone Rd B45 ..... 102 B2
Brightwalton Rd CV3 ... 133 D7
Brightwell Cres B93 .... 127 E3
Brill Cl CV4 .... 132 C5
Brimfield Pl WV6 .... 24 F4
Brimstone La B61 .... 136 D7
Brindle Ave CV3 .... 114 C2
Brindle Cl B26 .... 56 B3
Brindle Rd WS5 .... 43 C4
Brindlefields Way DY4 ... 52 B2
Brindley Ave WV11 .... 13 A1
Brindley Cl Stourbridge DY8 . 60 F1
Walsall WS2 .... 27 F5
Brindley Cres WS12 .... 2 F1
Brindley Ct **1** Oldbury B68 . 84 B7
5 Tipton DY4 .... 51 E5
Brindley Dr B1 .... 164 A2
Brindley Heath Rd WS12 . 2 D8
Brindley Rd Bedworth CV7 . 96 B8
Hinckley LE10 .... 74 E8
West Bromwich B71 .... 53 A8
Brindley Way **10** B66 .... 65 C5
Brindleys Bsns Pk WS11 . 2 B3
Brineton Gr B29 .... 85 A1
Brineton Ind Est **1** WS2 . 28 C1
Brineton St WS2 .... 28 C1
Bringewood Gr B32 ..... 102 B8
Brinklow Cl B98 .... 159 D8
Brinklow Croft B34 .... 69 D7
Brinklow Rd Birmingham
B29 .... 84 F2
Coventry CV3 .... 115 A2
Brinklow Tower **5** B12 . 86 F7
Brinley Way DY6 .... 60 D6
Brinsford La WV10 .... 11 D7
Brinsford Rd WV10 .... 11 C3
Brinsley Cl B91 .... 107 B2
Brinsley Rd B26 .... 89 B8
Brinton Cl DY11 .... 116 C3
Brinton Cres DY11 ...... 116 C3
Brisbane Cl CV3 .... 133 E6
Brisbane Ct CV12 .... 78 A2
Brisbane Ho B34 .... 69 E6
Brisbane Rd B67 .... 64 E5
Briscoe Rd CV6 .... 95 D4
Briseley Cl DY5 .... 81 D8
Bristam Cl B69 .... 63 E6
Bristnall Hall Cres B68 .. 64 C3

Bristnall Hall High Sch
B68 .... 64 D3
Bristnall Hall La B68 ...... 64 D3
Bristnall Hall Rd B68 ...... 64 C3
Bristnall Ho B67 .... 64 D4
Bristol Cl WS11 .... 2 B1
Bristol Rd
Birmingham,
 Balsall Heath B5 .... 86 C5
Birmingham, Gravelly Hill B23 56 E3
Coventry CV5 .... 112 F2
Dudley DY2 .... 62 D2
Bristol Rd S B31, B45 ... 102 F2
Bristol St Birmingham B15 .. 66 C2
Wolverhampton WV3 .... 39 B8
Briston Cl DY5 .... 81 C8
Britannia Gdns B65 .... 63 C3
Britannia High Sch B65 ... 63 D2
Britannia B Bilston WV14 ... 40 F3
Blackheath B65 .... 63 C2
Hinckley LE10 .... 76 A5
Britannia St Coventry CV2 .. 113 F3
Tipton B69 .... 52 C2
Britannia Way WS14 .... 9 F8
Britford Cl B14 .... 104 F3
Briton Rd CV2 .... 114 A4
Brittan Cl B34 .... 69 E6
Brittania Pk WS10 .... 41 A4
Brittania Way WS5 .... 42 D5
Britten Cl CV11 .... 79 A7
Britten St B97 .... 153 D4
Britton Dr B72 .... 57 C8
Britwell Rd B73 .... 46 A2
Brixham Cl CV11 .... 73 F5
Brixham Dr CV2 .... 114 C7
Brixham Rd B16 .... 65 D4
Brixworth Cl CV3 .... 134 E8
Broad Acres B31 .... 102 E6
Broad Croft DY4 .... 52 C6
Broad Ground Rd B98 .... 154 B2
Broad Heath Cl B97 ...... 153 B5
Broad Heath Com Prim
 Sch CV6 .... 113 E7
Broad La Birmingham B14 ... 104 E4
Coventry CV5 .... 111 D4
Lichfield WS13 .... 9 D6
Tamworth-In-A B98 ...... 141 E3
Walsall, Essington
 WV11, WS3 .... 13 E4
Walsall, Pelsall WS4 .... 15 C2
Wolverhampton, Penn WV3 .. 38 E8
Wolverhampton, Wall WS13 .. 8 B5
Broad La N WV12 .... 27 B7
Broad La S WV11 .... 27 A5
Broad Lane Gdns WS3 ..... 14 A2
Broad Lanes WV14 .... 40 C3
Broad Mdw WS9 .... 30 B8
Broad Meadow La
Birmingham B30, B38 ... 104 B3
Great Wyrley WS6 .... 5 A2
Broad Oaks B76 .... 47 A1
Broad Oaks B91 .... 107 A5
Broad Park Rd CV2 .... 114 D8
Broad Rd B27 .... 88 B3
Broad St Bilston WV14 .... 40 D6
Birmingham B15, B1 ...... 66 C2
Brierley Hill DY5 .... 61 C6
Bromsgrove B61 .... 136 F4
Cannock WS11 .... 4 E6
Coventry CV6 .... 113 E7
Dudley DY1 .... 51 C8
Kidderminster DY10 .... 116 E7
Kingswinford DY6 .... 60 D5
Oldbury B69 .... 64 A5
Warwick CV34 .... 160 F7
Wolverhampton WV1 .... 163 C3
Broad Street Jetty CV6 ... 113 E7
Broad Way WS4 .... 15 C2
Broadcott Ind Est B64 .... 83 A8
Broadfern Rd B93 .... 128 B8
Broadfield Cl
Kingswinford DY6 .... 60 D5
West Bromwich B71 .... 42 F1
Broadfield House Glass
 Mus DY6 .... 60 D5
Broadfield Wlk █1 B16 ... 66 B1
Broadfields DY9 .... 99 A6
Broadfields Rd B23 .... 57 B7
Broadgate CV1 .... 165 B3
Broadhaven Cl CV1 .... 162 C7
Broadheath Dr WS4 .... 29 D8
Broadhidley Dr B32 .... 84 B1
Broadhurst Gn WS12 .... 2 A8
Broadlands Cl CV5 ..... 112 C2
Broadlands Dr DY5 .... 61 E5
Broadlands Rise WS14 ..... 9 D7
Broadlee B77 .... 22 C1
Broadmead Ct CV4 .... 112 C2
Broadmeadow █1 DY6 ... 60 E8
Broadmeadow Cl B30 ... 104 B3
Broadmeadow Gn WV14 .. 40 C7
Broadmeadow Ho B32 ... 102 D8
Broadmeadow Inf Sch
 B30 .... 104 B2
Broadmeadow Jun Sch
 B30 .... 104 B2
Broadmeadows Cl WV12 ... 27 E8
Broadmeadows Rd WV12 .. 27 E8
Broadmede Ho B67 .... 64 E2
Broadmere Rise CV5 ..... 112 A2
Broadmoor Ave B68 ...... 64 D2
Broadmoor Cl WV14 ...... 40 C4
Broadmoor Rd WV14 ..... 40 C3
Broadoaks Cl WS11 .... 5 F6

Broadsmeath B77 .... 21 C1
Broadstone Ave
Halesowen B63 .... 82 B4
Walsall WS3 .... 28 D7
Broadstone Cl WV4 .... 39 D5
Broadstone Rd B26 .... 69 A1
Broadsword Way LE10 .... 75 D4
Broadwalk Ret Pk WS1 ... 42 C6
Broadwas Cl B98 .... 154 C5
Broadwater CV5 .... 133 A8
Broadwaters Ave WS10 ... 41 C4
Broadwaters Dr Hagley DY9 . 99 B4
Kidderminster DY10 ..... 117 A8
Broadwaters Rd WS10 .... 41 C4
Broadway Cannock WS12 ... 1 F6
Coventry CV5 .... 113 A1
Cubbington CV32 .... 157 E5
Oldbury B68 .... 64 C1
Solihull B90 .... 106 B4
Walsall WS5 .... 43 A6
Wolverhampton, Bushbury
 WV10 .... 11 E2
Wolverhampton, Compton
 WV3 .... 24 C1
Broadway Ave
Birmingham B9 .... 68 A3
Halesowen B63 .... 83 A2
Broadway Croft
Birmingham B26 .... 89 A6
Oldbury B68 .... 64 C1
Broadway Gdns WV10 ..... 11 E2
Broadway Lower Sch The
 B6 .... 66 E8
Broadway Mans CV5 ..... 113 A1
Broadway N WS1 .... 29 B2
Broadway Sch B20 .... 55 E2
Broadway Sch The B20 ... 55 D1
Broadway The
Birmingham B20 .... 55 E2
Dudley DY1 .... 51 B3
Stourbridge DY8 .... 80 D3
West Bromwich B71 .... 53 B7
Wombourne WV5 .... 49 A5
Broadway W WS1 .... 42 D6
Broadwell Ct CV4 .... 131 F6
Broadwell Ind Est B69 ... 53 A1
Broadwell Rd Oldbury B69 .. 64 A8
Solihull B92 .... 89 A2
Broadwells Cres CV4 .... 132 A5
Broadyates Gr B25 .... 88 C6
Broadyates Rd B25 .... 88 C6
Brobury Croft B91 .... 106 D4
Brock Rd DY4 .... 52 C4
Brockenhurst St B73 .... 46 B1
Brockeridge Cl WV12 ..... 13 C1
Brockhall Gr B37 .... 69 F5
Brockhill La Alvechurch
 B48 .... 124 B2
Beoley B98 .... 140 F2
Tardebigge B97 .... 152 E8
Brockhurst Ave LE10 ...... 75 D4
Brockhurst Cres WS5 ..... 42 E4
Brockhurst Dr
Birmingham B28 .... 106 A5
Coventry CV4 .... 111 D2
Wolverhampton W6 ...... 25 A4
Brockhurst Ho █4 WS2 .. 28 D3
Brockhurst La B75 .... 33 B7
Brockhurst Pl WS5 .... 42 F5
Brockhurst Rd
Birmingham B36 .... 68 D6
Sutton Coldfield B75 ..... 32 D1
Brockhurst St WS1 .... 42 E6
Brockley Cl DY5 .... 61 D3
Brockley Gr B13 .... 86 C1
Brockley Pl B7 .... 67 C7
Brockmoor Cl DY5 .... 61 C2
Brockmoor Prim Sch DY5 . 61 C3
Brockton Rd B29 .... 85 A1
Brockwell Gr B44 .... 44 E4
Brockwell Rd B44 .... 44 E4
Brockworth Rd B14 ...... 104 C2
Brocton Cl WV14 .... 40 A3
Brodick Cl LE10 .... 75 A8
Brodick Rd LE10 .... 74 F8
Brodick Way CV10 .... 72 F3
Brogden Cl █4 B71 .... 53 F8
Brome Hall La B94 .... 144 D2
Bromfield Cl B6 .... 66 E7
Bromfield Cres WS10 .... 42 C4
Bromfield Ct WV6 .... 24 B3
Bromfield Rd B97 .... 153 D2
Bromford Cl
Birmingham, Erdington B23 .. 56 E5
Birmingham,
 Handsworth B20 .... 55 A2
Bromford Ct
Birmingham,
 Turves Green B31 ..... 103 B1
Birmingham,
 Washwood Heath B8 ... 68 B6
Bromford Dale WV6 .... 24 F3
Bromford Dell B31 .... 103 C4
Bromford Dr B36 .... 68 D8
Bromford Hill B20 .... 55 C3
Bromford Ho B73 .... 45 F2
Bromford Jun & Inf Schs
 B36 .... 68 D7
Bromford La Birmingham B8 . 68 C6
West Bromwich B70 ...... 53 B2
Bromford Mere █4 B92 ... 88 E1
Bromford Park Ho █3 B37 .. 87 B2
Bromford Rd
Birmingham B36 .... 68 D2
Dudley DY2 .... 62 A6
West Bromwich B69, B70 .. 53 A1

Bromford Rise WV3 ...... 163 A1
Bromford Road Ind Est B70 53 A1
Bromford Wlk B43 .... 43 F1
Bromleigh Dr CV2 ...... 114 C2
Bromleigh Villas CV8 .... 133 F2
Bromley DY5 .... 61 B5
Bromley Gdns WV8 .... 10 A4
Bromley Cl CV8 .... 147 E6
Bromley Hills Cty Prim Sch
 DY6 .... 60 F5
Bromley Ho WV4 .... 39 A5
Bromley La DY6 .... 60 E4
Bromley Lodge WV4 .... 39 A5
Bromley Pl WV4 .... 39 A5
Bromley Prim Sch DY5 .... 61 B5
Bromley St Birmingham B9 . 67 A1
Stourbridge DY9 .... 81 F6
Wolverhampton WV2 ..... 39 C7
Brompton Dr DY5 .... 81 B7
Brompton Lawns WV6 .... 24 A3
Brompton Pool Rd B28 . 105 E3
Brompton Rd B44 .... 44 E4
Bromsgrove Eastern
 By-Pass B60 .... 150 E6
Bromsgrove Highway
Bromsgrove B60 .... 137 D1
Redditch B97 .... 153 B2
Tardebigge B97 .... 152 C6
Bromsgrove Lower Sch
 B60 .... 136 F1
Bromsgrove Pre-Prep
 Sch B60 .... 137 A2
Bromsgrove Private
 Hospl B60 .... 138 B1
Bromsgrove Rd
Bournheath B61 .... 136 D6
Clent DY9 .... 99 D4
Halesowen B63 .... 83 C4
Kidderminster DY10 .... 117 F2
Redditch B97 .... 153 B3
Romsley B62 .... 101 A5
Studley B80 .... 159 D2
Bromsgrove Sch B61 .... 136 F1
Bromsgrove St
Birmingham B5 .... 164 C1
Halesowen B63 .... 83 C4
Kidderminster DY10 .... 116 E6
Bromsgrove Sta B60 .... 151 B7
Bromwall Rd B13 .... 105 B6
Bromwich Cl CV3 .... 134 F8
Bromwich Dr B75 .... 46 C7
Bromwich La DY9 .... 99 B8
Bromwich Wlk B9 .... 68 A3
Bromwynd Cl WV2 .... 39 B6
Bromyard Ave B76 .... 58 A8
Bromyard Rd B11 .... 87 E3
Bronte Cl B90 .... 106 D1
Bronte Ct Solihull B90 .. 106 D1
Tamworth B79 .... 21 A6
Bronte Dr Cannock WS11 .. 2 C2
Kidderminster DY10 .... 117 C6
Bronte Farm Rd B90 .... 106 D1
Bronte Rd WV2 .... 39 F6
Bronwen Rd WV14 .... 51 C7
Bronze Cl CV11 .... 78 E8
Brook Ave B77 .... 36 A7
Brook Cl Birmingham B26 . 89 B5
Brownhills WS9 .... 16 A3
Coventry CV1 .... 113 E4
Lichfield WS13 .... 3 A1
Solihull B90 .... 105 F1
Brook Cotts B25 .... 88 A7
Brook Cres Hagley DY9 ... 99 B5
Kingswinford DY6 .... 60 C7
Stourbridge DY9 .... 81 F3
Brook Croft
Birmingham,
 Lyndon Green B26 ..... 89 B7
Birmingham,
 Marston Green B37 .... 90 B7
Brook Dr B32 .... 84 D1
Brook End Burntwood WS7 .. 7 A4
Fazeley B78 .... 35 B8
Brook Farm Wlk B37 ...... 70 D2
Brook Fields Cl B60 ..... 121 C1
Brook Gr WV8 .... 10 B2
Brook Green La B92 .... 109 A1
Brook Hill Rd B8 .... 68 A4
Brook Holloway DY9 ...... 81 F4
Brook House Cl WV10 ... 12 B6
Brook House La WV10 .... 12 B7
Brook La Birmingham B13 . 105 B7
Blackheath B64 .... 62 E2
Brownhills WS9 .... 15 F3
Great Wyrley WS6 .... 5 A3
Nuneaton CV10 .... 73 C6
Solihull B92 .... 106 D8
Brook Meadow Rd
Birmingham B34 .... 69 B6
Walsall WS4 .... 29 D8
Brook Park Trad Est
 █3 DY9 .... 81 F5
Brook Piece Wlk B35 ..... 58 B3
Brook Prim Sch The DY5 . 60 F1
Brook Rd
Birmingham, Chad Valley B15 . 85 E7
Birmingham, Eachway B45 . 121 E7
Bromsgrove B61 .... 136 E1
Cheslyn Hay WS6 .... 4 E4
Fairfield B61 .... 120 C2
Oldbury B68 .... 64 A2
Stourbridge DY8 .... 81 B3
Willenhall WV13 .... 26 C1
Wombourne WV5 .... 49 A6
Brook St Bedworth CV12 .. 78 A3
Bilston WV14 .... 40 E5
Birmingham B3 .... 164 A3
Brierley Hill DY5 .... 82 A8

Brook St continued
Dudley, Gornalwood DY3 .. 50 C3
Dudley, Woodsetton DY3 .. 51 A7
Kidderminster DY11 .... 116 C6
Kingswinford DY6 .... 49 B1
Redditch B98 .... 154 A4
Smethwick B66 .... 65 B6
Stourbridge, Amblecote DY8 .. 62 A7
Stourbridge, Lye DY9 .... 81 F5
Stourbridge, Wollaston DY8 .. 80 E5
Tipton DY4 .... 51 E6
Walsall WS2 .... 28 D1
Warwick CV34 .... 160 E6
West Bromwich B70 .... 53 B3
Brook Street Bsns Ctr DY4 . 51 E6
Brook Terr WV14 .... 40 E5
Brook View B19 .... 66 C6
Brook Wlk B32 .... 84 D2
Brookbank Ave B34 ..... 69 D6
Brookbank Gdns DY3 ..... 50 B2
Brookbank Rd DY3 .... 50 B2
Brookdale Dudley DY3 ... 50 C3
Hinckley LE10 .... 75 B7
Kidderminster DY10 .... 116 F8
Brookdale Cl B45 .... 102 A1
Brookdale Dr WV4 .... 38 E6
Brookdale Rd CV10 .... 73 E7
Brooke Cl CV34 .... 160 F5
Brooke Rd Cannock WS12 .. 1 A6
Kenilworth CV8 .... 148 B4
Brooke St DY2 .... 62 C8
Brookend Dr B45 .... 121 F7
Brookes Ho █3 WS1 ...... 28 F1
Brookfield Cl Aldridge WS9 .. 16 A1
Redditch B97 .... 158 D4
Brookfield Ct DY11 .... 4 E7
Brookfield Prec B18 ...... 66 B4
Brookfield Rd Aldridge WS9 . 16 A5
Birmingham B18 .... 66 A5
Codsall WV8 .... 10 B3
Cubbington CV32 .... 157 E5
Hinckley LE10 .... 75 C6
Brookfield Way Solihull
 B92 .... 106 D7
Tipton DY4 .... 52 B6
Brookfields Inf & Jun Sch
 B18 .... 66 B4
Brookfields Rd B68 .... 64 C4
Brookford Ave CV6 .... 95 A3
Brookhampton B97 ...... 158 E4
Brookhill Cl WV12 .... 13 D1
Brookhill Way WV12 ...... 13 D1
Brookhouse La WV10 ..... 11 F6
Brookhouse Rd
Barnt Green B45 .... 137 F7
Walsall WS5 .... 43 B7
Brookhurst Ct CV32 .... 156 D1
Brookhurst Cty
 Comb Sch CV32 .... 156 C1
Brookhus Farm Rd B76 .. 58 A8
Brookland Rd Brownhills
 WS9 .... 15 F3
Hagley DY9 .... 99 A5
Brooklands Stourbridge DY8 .. 60 F1
Brooklands Ave WS6 ...... 4 F4
Brooklands Cl B28 .... 87 F1
Brooklands Dr B14 ...... 104 E5
Brooklands Gr WS9 .... 15 F3
Brooklands La B98 ...... 154 B5
Brooklands Par WV1 ..... 26 B2
Brooklands Rd
Birmingham B28 .... 87 F1
Cannock WS11 .... 2 A4
Brooklea CV12 .... 77 F2
Brooklea Gr B38 .... 104 A1
Brooklime Gdns WV10 ... 12 B7
Brooklyn Ave B6 .... 66 F7
Brooklyn Gr Dudley WV14 . 51 D8
Kingswinford DY6 .... 60 B8
Brooklyn Rd Burntwood WS7 . 7 A4
Cannock WS12 .... 2 D1
Coventry CV1 .... 113 D6
Brookmans Ave B32 ...... 84 D4
Brookmeadow Ct B28 .. 105 D4
Brooks Croft B35 .... 58 A2
Brooks Rd B72 .... 57 C8
Brooks Tower B19 .... 66 D7
Brooksbank Dr B64 .... 62 F4
Brooksby Gr B93 .... 128 C2
Brookshaw Way CV2 .... 114 F8
Brookside
Birmingham, Great Barr B43 . 54 D7
Birmingham, Northfield B31 . 102 F5
Cheswick Green B90 .... 126 D3
Dudley DY3 .... 50 D2
Hinckley LE10 .... 75 E7
Brookside Ave
Birmingham B13 .... 105 B7
Coventry CV5 .... 112 C3
Kenilworth CV8 .... 147 E4
Brookside Cl
Alvechurch B48 .... 139 B6
Birmingham B23 .... 56 C7
Halesowen B63 .... 82 D3
Brookside Dr B61 .... 136 F8
Brookside Ind Est WS10 .. 42 B3
Brookside Rd B78 .... 20 E1
Brookside Way
Blakedown DY10 .... 98 B2
Kingswinford DY6 .... 60 C7
Tamworth B77 .... 36 A6
Brookstray Flats CV5 ... 112 B3
Brookthorpe Dr WV12 .... 27 C4
Brookvale Ave CV3 ...... 114 E1
Brookvale Cl B61 .... 137 B4
Brookvale Gr B92 .... 88 D3

Brookvale Jun & Inf Sch
 B23 .... 56 B3
Brookvale Park Rd B23 ... 56 B4
Brookvale Rd
Birmingham B23, B6 ..... 56 A3
Solihull B92 .... 88 D1
Brookvale Trad Est B6 ... 56 A3
Brookview B67 .... 64 F3
Brookweed B77 .... 22 A3
Brookwillow Rd B63 ...... 82 E1
Brookwood Ave B28 .... 105 D5
Broom Cl B60 .... 137 B2
Broom Covert Rd WS14 .. 18 E8
Broom Cres DY10 .... 117 A6
Broom Dr B14 .... 104 E4
Broom Hall Cres B27 ... 106 B8
Broom Hall Gr B27 ...... 106 C8
Broom Ho █3 B71 .... 42 F1
Broom Rd Dudley DY1 .... 51 A5
Walsall WS5 .... 43 B3
Broom St B12 .... 87 A8
Broomcroft B37 .... 69 F5
Broomdene Ave B34 ...... 69 A7
Broome Ave B43 .... 54 C7
Broome Cl █5 B63 .... 83 A3
Broome Croft CV6 .... 95 B3
Broome Ct B36 .... 69 D6
Broome La Blakedown DY10 . 98 F2
Hagley DY9 .... 99 B2
Broome Rd WV10 .... 25 E7
Broomehill Cl DY5 .... 81 C7
Broomfield B67 .... 64 F5
Broomfield Ave B78 ..... 35 A8
Broomfield Cl DY11 ..... 116 C7
Broomfield Gn DY11 .... 116 C7
Broomfield Pl CV5 ...... 113 A2
Broomfield Rd
Birmingham B23 .... 56 D2
Coventry CV5 .... 113 A1
Kidderminster DY11 .... 116 C7
Wednesbury WS10 .... 42 C3
Broomfield Rise CV10 ... 72 F2
Broomfields Ave B91 ... 107 D5
Broomfields Cl B91 ..... 107 D5
Broomfields Farm Rd
 B91 .... 107 D5
Broomhall Ave WV11 ..... 26 D6
Broomhill Bank WS11 ..... 1 E3
Broomhill Cl
Birmingham B43 .... 54 D8
Cannock WS11 .... 1 E4
Broomhill La B43 .... 54 D8
Broomhill Rd B23 .... 56 B7
Broomhurst B15 .... 85 E8
Broomie Cl B75 .... 46 D4
Broomlea Cl B74 .... 44 E8
Broomy Cl B34 .... 69 A5
Broomybank CV8 .... 148 B6
Brosdale Dr LE10 .... 71 A1
Broseley Ave B31 .... 123 B8
Broseley Brook Cl B9 .... 67 C1
Brosil Ave B20 .... 54 E3
Brotherton Ave B97 .... 152 F2
Brough Cl Birmingham B7 . 67 B6
Wolverhampton WV4 .... 39 F3
Brougham St B19 .... 66 B7
Broughton Cres B31 ... 122 D8
Broughton Ct
 █2 Birmingham,
 Edgbaston B15 .... 86 B7
Birmingham, Pheasey B43 . 44 D4
Perton WV6 .... 24 A3
Broughton Rd
Birmingham B20 .... 66 A8
Stourbridge DY9 .... 81 D3
Wolverhampton WV3 .... 24 C1
Browett Rd CV6 .... 113 A5
Brown Lion St DY4 .... 51 E7
Brown Rd WS10 .... 41 C7
Brown St WV2 .... 39 D7
Brown's Coppice Ave B91 . 106 E5
Brown's Ct █10 B13 ..... 87 B2
Brown's La Allesley CV5 .. 94 C1
Dordon B78 .... 36 F5
Tamworth B79 .... 21 C8
Brownfield Rd B34 .... 69 C7
Brownhills WS9 .... 16 A4
Norton Canes WS11 .... 6 A5
Brownhills Sch WS8 .... 6 F1
Brownhills West JMI Sch
 WS8 .... 6 C2
Browning Ave CV34 .... 160 C5
Browning Cl
Kidderminster DY10 .... 117 C6
Nuneaton CV10 .... 72 A5
Tamworth B79 .... 20 F8
Willenhall WV12 .... 27 E7
Browning Cres WV10 ..... 11 C2
Browning Dr LE10 .... 71 C1
Browning Gr WV6 .... 23 E4
Browning Rd Burntwood WS7 . 7 C1
Coventry CV2 .... 114 C3
Dudley DY3 .... 50 A4
Browning St B16 .... 66 B2
Browning Tower B31 .... 103 C3
Brownley Rd B90 .... 126 F3
Brownlow St █6 CV32 .. 157 A2
Brownmead Jun & Inf Sch
 B34 .... 69 B7
Browns Dr B73 .... 56 F8
Browns Gn B20 .... 54 F3
Browns La Knowle B93 . 127 E6
Tamworth B79 .... 21 C8
Brownsea Cl B45 .... 101 F1
Brownsea Dr B1 .... 164 B1
Brownsfield Rd WS13 ...... 3 D1
Brownshill Ct CV6 .... 112 F8

Brownshill Green Rd CV6 .... 94 E1
Brownshore La WV11 ..... 13 B3
Brownsover Cl B36 ..... 58 B1
Brownswall Rd DY3 ..... 50 C7
Browsholme B79 ..... 20 D6
Broxell Cl WS14 ..... 155 C1
Broxwood Pk WV6 ..... 24 C3
Bruce Rd Bedworth CV7 ..... 95 F7
  Coventry CV6 ..... 113 B8
  Kidderminster DY10 ..... 117 B7
Brueton Ave
  Bromsgrove B60 ..... 151 A8
  Solihull B91 ..... 107 D3
Brueton Dr Birmingham B24 ..... 57 A3
  Redditch B98 ..... 154 A3
Brueton Rd WV14 ..... 41 A7
Bruford Rd WV3 ..... 39 A8
Brunel Cl Birmingham B12 ..... 87 A5
  Burntwood WS7 ..... 7 B8
  Coventry CV2 ..... 113 F3
  Tamworth B79 ..... 21 B6
  Whitnash CV31 ..... 162 B2
Brunel Ct Darlaston WS10 ..... 41 F6
  Dudley WV14 ..... 51 E8
  Wombourne WV5 ..... 49 A7
Brunel Gr WV6 ..... 23 E6
Brunel Rd Hinckley LE10 ..... 75 C8
  Oldbury B69 ..... 63 D6
Brunel St B1 ..... 164 B2
Brunel Way WV2 ..... 40 A7
Brunel Wlk WS10 ..... 41 F6
Brunslow Cl Willenhall
  WV13 ..... 27 C1
  Wolverhampton WV10 ..... 11 C1
Brunswick Ct
  Royal Leamington Spa
  CV31 ..... 162 A5
  Wednesbury WS10 ..... 42 C3
Brunswick Gdns B21 ..... 54 F1
Brunswick Ho
  Birmingham,
  Buckland End B34 ..... 69 A7
  Birmingham,
  Marston Green B37 ..... 89 F8
Brunswick Park Rd WS10 ..... 42 B3
Brunswick Rd
  Birmingham,
  Handsworth B21 ..... 54 F1
  Birmingham, Sparkbrook B12 ..... 87 A5
  Cannock WS11 ..... 1 E2
  Coventry CV1 ..... 113 B2
Brunswick St
  Royal Leamington Spa
  CV31 ..... 162 A5
  Walsall WS2 ..... 42 C7
Brunswick Terr WS10 ..... 41 F3
Bruntingthorpe Way CV3 ..... 134 E8
Brunton Cl CV3 ..... 115 B1
Brunton Rd B10 ..... 87 F7
Brushfield Rd B42 ..... 55 D8
Brutus Dr B46 ..... 59 E1
Bryan Ave B14 ..... 38 D4
Bryan Rd WS2 ..... 42 C6
Bryans Way WS12 ..... 2 F4
Bryanston Cl CV2 ..... 115 A4
Bryanston Ct B92 ..... 106 F7
Bryanston Rd B91 ..... 106 F6
Bryant Rd CV7 ..... 96 A7
Bryant St B18 ..... 65 E5
Bryce Rd DY5 ..... 61 B5
Bryher Wlk B45 ..... 101 E1
Brylan Croft B44 ..... 55 F6
Brymill Ind Est DY4 ..... 51 E7
Brympton Rd CV3 ..... 114 C2
Bryn Arden Rd B26 ..... 88 E5
Bryn Jones Cl CV3 ..... 134 F7
Bryn Rd CV6 ..... 113 F7
Bryndale Ave B14 ..... 104 C4
Brynmawr Rd WV14 ..... 40 A3
Brynside Cl B14 ..... 104 D2
Bryony Croft B23 ..... 56 B7
Bryony Rd B29 ..... 103 B7
Bsns Ctr The B11 ..... 87 F6
Buchanan Ave WS4 ..... 29 A3
Buchanan Cl WS4 ..... 29 A3
Buchanan Rd WS4 ..... 29 A3
Buckbury Cl DY9 ..... 81 D2
Buckbury Croft B90 ..... 127 B6
Buckden B77 ..... 22 C1
Buckden Cl 2 CV34 ..... 155 F1
Buckfast Cl Bromsgrove
  B61 ..... 136 D1
  Coventry CV3 ..... 133 E5
Buckhold Dr CV5 ..... 112 B5
Buckingham Cl Hinckley
  LE10 ..... 71 F4
  Nuneaton CV10 ..... 73 B1
  Wednesbury WS10 ..... 42 D4
Buckingham Ct
  Birmingham,
  Griffin's Hill B29 ..... 103 D8
  Birmingham, Selly Oak B29 ..... 85 D1
Buckingham Dr WV12 ..... 27 B7
Buckingham Gdns WS13 ..... 9 B6
Buckingham Gr DY6 ..... 60 C7
Buckingham Mews B73 ..... 46 A3
Buckingham Pl WS12 ..... 2 C1
Buckingham Rd
  Birmingham B36 ..... 69 F7
  Blackheath B65 ..... 63 D4
  Tamworth B79 ..... 20 E6
  Wolverhampton WV4 ..... 39 A5
Buckingham Rise
  Coventry CV5 ..... 112 B4
  Dudley DY1 ..... 50 E2
Buckingham St B19 ..... 164 B4
Buckland Cl WS12 ..... 2 D1

Buckland End B34 ..... 69 A6
Buckland Ho 3 B15 ..... 86 C7
Buckland Rd CV6 ..... 95 B2
Bucklands End La B34 ..... 68 F6
Buckle Cl WS1 ..... 42 E8
Buckler's Yd CV12 ..... 78 A2
Buckley Ho CV5 ..... 112 F1
Buckley Rd
  Royal Leamington Spa CV32 ..... 157 C2
  Wolverhampton WV4 ..... 38 D5
Buckleys Gn B48 ..... 139 A6
Buckleys The B48 ..... 139 A6
Bucklow Wlk B33 ..... 68 E4
Buckminster Dr B93 ..... 127 E4
Bucknall Cres B32 ..... 102 A8
Bucknall Ct 14 B13 ..... 87 B2
Bucknall Ho B14 ..... 104 E6
Bucknall Rd WV11 ..... 13 B1
Bucknell Cl B91 ..... 107 C5
Buckpool Sch The DY8 ..... 60 F2
Buckridge Cl B38 ..... 123 D7
Bucks Hill CV10 ..... 72 C6
Buckthorn Cl WS12 ..... 1 F8
Buckton Cl B75 ..... 32 E2
Budbrook Gr B34 ..... 69 E6
Budbrooke Cl CV2 ..... 96 D2
Budbrooke Ind Est CV34 ..... 160 B7
Budbrooke Rd CV34 ..... 160 B7
Budden Rd WV14 ..... 51 D7
Bude Rd WS5 ..... 43 D7
Buffery Rd DY2 ..... 62 D7
Bufferys Pl B91 ..... 127 B8
Buildwas Cl WS3 ..... 13 F2
Bulford Cl B14 ..... 104 F2
Bulger Rd WV14 ..... 40 C7
Bulkington Fst Sch CV12 ..... 79 C2
Bulkington La CV11 ..... 79 A7
Bulkington Rd
  Bedworth CV12 ..... 78 D2
  Shilton CV7 ..... 97 E6
Bull La Bilston WV14, WS10 ..... 41 B3
  West Bromwich B70 ..... 53 A3
  Wombourne WV5 ..... 49 B7
Bull Ring Birmingham B5 ..... 164 C2
  4 Halesowen B63 ..... 83 B3
  Kidderminster DY10 ..... 116 E6
  Nuneaton CV10 ..... 73 B2
  Sedgley DY3 ..... 50 D8
  Willenhall WV13 ..... 27 A1
Bull Ring Ctr B5 ..... 164 C2
Bull Ring Trad Est 2 B12 ..... 66 F1
Bull St
  Birmingham, Brookfields B4 164 C3
  Birmingham, Harborne B17 ..... 85 D5
  Brierley Hill DY5 ..... 61 B1
  Darlaston WS10 ..... 41 E6
  Dudley, Gornalwood DY3 ..... 50 C2
  Dudley, Springs Mire DY1 ..... 62 A8
  Nuneaton CV11 ..... 73 D2
  West Bromwich B70 ..... 53 D3
Bull Street Trad Est DY5 ..... 61 B2
Bull Yd CV1 ..... 165 B2
Bull's Head La CV3 ..... 114 B2
Bull's La B76 ..... 47 E1
Bullace Croft B15 ..... 85 D3
Bulldog La B13 ..... 3 B1
Buller St WV4 ..... 39 E6
Bullfield Ave CV4 ..... 111 E4
Bullfields Cl B65 ..... 62 F5
Bullfinch Cl DY1 ..... 61 E8
Bullfurlong La LE10 ..... 75 F4
Bullimore Gr CV8 ..... 148 A2
Bullivents Cl B93 ..... 127 F5
Bullmeadow La WV5 ..... 49 A8
Bullmoor La WS14 ..... 8 B1
Bullock St Birmingham B7 ..... 67 A5
  West Bromwich B70 ..... 53 D1
Bullock's Row WS1 ..... 28 F1
Bullows Rd WS8 ..... 15 C6
Bulwell Cl B6 ..... 67 A7
Bulwer Rd CV6 ..... 113 A6
Bulwick Cl CV3 ..... 115 B1
Bumble Hole La B61 ..... 136 E7
Bunbury Gdns B30 ..... 103 D4
Bunbury Rd B31 ..... 103 C4
Bundle Hill B63 ..... 83 A4
Bungalows The
  West Bromwich,
  Charlemont B71 ..... 53 E8
  West Bromwich,
  Swan Village B70 ..... 52 F6
Bunker's Hill La WV14 ..... 40 E7
Bunn's La DY1, DY2 ..... 51 F1
Bunny Stile La WV11 ..... 26 B6
Buntsford Hill B60 ..... 150 F5
Buntsford Park Rd B60 ..... 150 F6
Bunyan Pl WS11 ..... 1 E4
Burbage Cty Jun Sch
  Hinckley LE10 ..... 75 F6
  Hinckley LE10 ..... 76 A5
Burbage Rd LE10 ..... 76 A7
Burbages La CV6 ..... 95 D4
Burberry Ct 3 DY4 ..... 52 A8
Burberry Gr CV7 ..... 130 A6
Burbidge Rd B9 ..... 67 B2
Burbury Cl Bedworth CV12 ..... 78 C4
Burbury St
  Birmingham, Lozells B19 ..... 66 C7
  Birmingham, Newtown B19 ..... 66 C6
Burcombe Twr B23 ..... 57 B6
Burcot Ave Bromsgrove
  B60 ..... 137 B4
  Wolverhampton WV1 ..... 26 A2
Burcot Ct B74 ..... 31 F2
Burcot Ho B60 ..... 137 B3

Burcot La
  Bromsgrove, Burcot B60 ..... 137 B3
  Bromsgrove, Stoney Hill B60 137 C4
Burcote Rd B24 ..... 57 D3
Burdock Cl Cannock WS11 ..... 2 B3
  Walsall WS5 ..... 43 A3
Burdock Ho B38 ..... 103 F1
Burdock Rd B29 ..... 103 A6
Burdons Cl B34 ..... 69 A5
Burfield Rd B63 ..... 82 C6
Burford Cl Solihull B92 ..... 89 A3
  Walsall WS5 ..... 43 A4
Burford Ct 16
  Birmingham B13 ..... 87 B2
  Stourbridge DY8 ..... 81 A4
Burford Mews 16 CV31 ..... 162 C6
Burford Park Rd B38 ..... 123 E8
Burford Rd Birmingham B44 ..... 55 F7
  Hollywood B47 ..... 125 A6
Burgage Pl CV11 ..... 73 C4
Burgage Wlk CV11 ..... 73 B5
Burges CV1 ..... 165 B3
Burgess Gr CV34 ..... 155 F1
Burgess Croft B92 ..... 107 F7
Burghley Cl CV11 ..... 73 F2
Burghley Dr
  Kidderminster DY11 ..... 116 C5
  West Bromwich B71 ..... 42 F2
Burghley Wlk DY5 ..... 81 B8
Burgoyne St CV2 ..... 2 A5
Burhill Way B37 ..... 70 B5
Burke Ave B13 ..... 87 D1
Burland Ave WV6 ..... 24 E6
Burleigh Cl
  Balsall Common CV7 ..... 130 B7
  Cannock WS12 ..... 2 B7
  Willenhall WV12 ..... 27 B6
Burleigh Croft WS7 ..... 7 A4
Burleigh Rd Hinckley LE10 ..... 71 C2
  Wolverhampton WV3 ..... 39 A8
Burleigh St WS1 ..... 29 A1
Burleton Rd B33 ..... 69 E2
Burley Cl B90 ..... 105 F2
Burley Wlk B38 ..... 123 C8
Burlington Arc B2 ..... 164 B2
Burlington Ave B70 ..... 53 E1
Burlington Cl CV10 ..... 117 B4
Burlington Ct 1 B78 ..... 35 B8
Burlington Rd
  Birmingham B10 ..... 67 F1
  Coventry CV3 ..... 113 F4
  Nuneaton CV10 ..... 78 B7
  West Bromwich B70 ..... 53 E1
Burlington St B6 ..... 66 E6
Burlish Ave 1 B92 ..... 88 F1
Burman Cl B90 ..... 106 A2
Burman Dr B46 ..... 70 F5
Burman Inf Sch B90 ..... 106 A2
Burman Rd B90 ..... 106 A2
Burmarsh Wlk WV8 ..... 24 F8
Burmese Way B65 ..... 62 F6
Burn Cl B66 ..... 65 A4
Burnaby Cl CV10 ..... 72 B5
Burnaby Rd CV6 ..... 95 B1
Burnaston Cres B90 ..... 127 C6
Burnaston Rd B28 ..... 87 E1
Burnbank Gr B24 ..... 57 B4
Burncross Way WV10 ..... 25 F6
Burnel Rd B29 ..... 85 B2
Burnell Gdns WV3 ..... 38 E8
Burnet Gr WV10 ..... 12 B8
Burnett Ho 12 B69 ..... 63 D5
Burnett Rd B74 ..... 31 B2
Burney La B8 ..... 68 C4
Burnfields Cl WS9 ..... 30 A7
Burnham Ave
  Birmingham B25 ..... 88 C6
  Wolverhampton WV10 ..... 25 C8
Burnham Cl DY6 ..... 60 F4
Burnham Ct Birmingham
  B23 ..... 56 C2
  18 Brierley Hill DY5 ..... 61 D2
Burnham Gn WS11 ..... 4 B8
Burnham Mdw B28 ..... 106 A6
Burnham Rd Birmingham
  B44 ..... 55 E7
  Coventry CV3 ..... 134 A4
Burnham Rise CV11 ..... 74 A6
Burnhill Gr B29 ..... 103 A8
Burnlea Gr B31 ..... 103 C1
Burns Ave Tipton DY4 ..... 52 A7
  Warwick CV34 ..... 160 C5
  Wolverhampton WV10 ..... 11 D2
Burns Cl Kidderminster
  DY10 ..... 117 B6
  Lichfield WS14 ..... 9 B6
  Redditch B97 ..... 158 C8
  Stourbridge DY8 ..... 81 A8
Burns Dr WS7 ..... 7 C7
Burns Gr DY3 ..... 50 A4
Burns Pl WS10 ..... 41 B5
Burns Rd Coventry CV2 ..... 114 B3
  Royal Leamington Spa CV32 ..... 157 B4
  Tamworth B79 ..... 21 A4
  Wednesbury WS10 ..... 41 B5
Burns St WS11 ..... 2 A3
Burns Wlk CV12 ..... 78 C1
Burnsall Cl Birmingham B37 ..... 69 F2
  Wolverhampton WV9 ..... 11 A3
Burnsall Gr CV5 ..... 132 D8
Burnsall Rd CV5 ..... 132 D8
Burnside CV3 ..... 115 A2
Burnside Ct B73 ..... 46 A1
Burnside Gdns WS5 ..... 43 D6
Burnside Way B31 ..... 122 F6
Burnsway LE10 ..... 71 C1
Burnt Meadow Rd B98 ..... 154 F6

Burnt Oak Dr DY8 ..... 81 B5
Burnt Tree DY4 ..... 51 F2
Burnt Tree Ind Est B69 ..... 52 B2
Burnt Tree Island DY4 ..... 51 F2
Burnt Tree Prim Sch B69 ..... 52 A2
Burnthurst Cres B90 ..... 127 A7
Burntwood Rd
  Burntwood WS7 ..... 7 D4
  Norton Canes WS11 ..... 6 A6
Burntwood Town Sh Ctr
  WS7 ..... 6 E7
Burrelton Way 1 B43 ..... 54 D8
Burrington Rd B32 ..... 102 A8
Burrow Hill Cl B36 ..... 69 C8
Burrow Hill La CV7 ..... 94 D7
Burrowes St WS2 ..... 28 D3
Burrows Cl CV31 ..... 162 B2
Burrows Croft WV14 ..... 40 C6
Burrows Ho 7 WS2 ..... 28 D3
Burrows Rd DY6 ..... 60 F4
Bursledon Wlk WV1 ..... 40 B8
Burslem Cl WS3 ..... 14 A3
Bursnips Rd WV11 ..... 13 C4
Burton Ave WS4 ..... 29 B8
Burton Cl Allesley CV5 ..... 94 C2
  Tamworth B79 ..... 21 C7
Burton Cres WV10 ..... 163 D4
Burton Farm Rd WS4 ..... 29 B3
Burton Green CE Jun &
  Inf Sch CV8 ..... 131 B3
Burton Ind Est B64 ..... 82 E8
Burton La Bramcote CV11 ..... 79 F7
  Redditch B98 ..... 153 F3
Burton Old Rd WS14 ..... 9 F8
Burton Old Rd E WS14 ..... 9 E8
Burton Old Rd W WS13 ..... 9 D8
Burton Rd Dudley DY1 ..... 50 F4
  Lichfield WS13 ..... 3 F1
  Wolverhampton WV10 ..... 25 E3
Burton Wood Dr B20 ..... 55 D2
Burtons Farm Prim Sch
  B36 ..... 70 A8
Bury Hill Rd B69 ..... 63 D8
Bury Ho CV4 ..... 111 F3
Bury Mound Ct B90 ..... 105 C2
Bury Rd CV31 ..... 161 F7
Buryfield Rd B91 ..... 107 B6
Busby Cl CV3 ..... 134 F7
Bush Ave B66 ..... 65 C5
Bush Cl CV4 ..... 111 F3
Bush Ct CV2 ..... 114 B6
Bush Gr Birmingham B21 ..... 54 C1
  Walsall WS3 ..... 15 A2
Bush Rd Dudley DY2 ..... 62 C2
  Tipton DY4 ..... 51 E4
Bush St WS10 ..... 41 D7
Bushbery Ave CV4 ..... 111 F2
Bushbury Croft B37 ..... 70 C3
Bushbury Hill Jun &
  Inf Schs WV10 ..... 11 F1
Bushbury La WV10 ..... 25 D7
Bushbury Rd Birmingham
  B33 ..... 69 A5
  Wolverhampton WV10 ..... 26 A5
Bushell Dr B91 ..... 107 D4
Bushey Cl B74 ..... 30 F2
Bushey Fields Hospl DY5 ..... 61 E7
Bushey Fields Rd DY1 ..... 61 E7
Bushley Cl B98 ..... 159 A7
Bushley Croft B91 ..... 127 B8
Bushman Way B34 ..... 69 E5
Bushmore Rd B28 ..... 106 A4
Bushway Cl DY5 ..... 61 B2
Bushwood Ct B15 ..... 86 C8
Bushwood Dr B93 ..... 128 B3
Bushwood Rd B29 ..... 85 B1
Busill Jones Jun Mixed
  Inf Sch WS3 ..... 27 F8
Bustlebolme Ave B71 ..... 42 F1
Bustlebolme Cres B71 ..... 42 E1
Bustlebolme La B71 ..... 42 E1
Butcher's La CV5 ..... 112 C6
Butchers La B63 ..... 82 C7
Butchers Rd B92 ..... 109 A6
Butcroft Gdns WS10 ..... 41 E6
Bute Cl Birmingham B45 ..... 101 E1
  Hinckley LE10 ..... 71 C1
  Willenhall WV12 ..... 27 B6
Butler Cl CV8 ..... 148 C2
Butler Rd B92 ..... 88 F3
Butler St Astwood Bank B96 ..... 158 E1
  West Bromwich B70 ..... 53 A4
Butler's Hill La B97 ..... 153 C5
Butler's Rd B20 ..... 55 A3
Butlers Cl
  Birmingham,
  Handsworth B20 ..... 55 A3
  Birmingham,
  Perry Common B73 ..... 45 D1
Butlers Cres CV7 ..... 78 A1
Butlers End CV35 ..... 146 C2
Butlers La B74 ..... 32 A3
Butlers Lane Sta B74 ..... 32 A3
Butlers Prec 2 WS1 ..... 28 E2
Butlin Cl CV6 ..... 95 C4
Butlin St B7 ..... 67 C7
Butt La Allesley CV5 ..... 112 B7
  Hinckley LE10 ..... 71 F1
Butt Lane Cl LE10 ..... 71 E1
Butter Wlk B38 ..... 123 C8
Buttercup Cl 6 WS5 ..... 43 A3
Buttercup Dr B23 ..... 137 C6
Butterfield Cl WV6 ..... 23 D5
Butterfield Rd DY5 ..... 61 B7
Butterfly Way 4 B64 ..... 62 F1
Buttermere B77 ..... 36 B7
Buttermere Ave CV11 ..... 74 A6

Buttermere Cl
  Brierley Hill DY5 ..... 81 B7
  Cannock WS11 ..... 2 A3
  Coventry CV3 ..... 134 F7
  Wolverhampton WV6 ..... 24 D8
Buttermere Ct WV6 ..... 23 F4
Buttermere Dr
  Birmingham B32 ..... 84 F3
  Essington WV11 ..... 13 A2
Buttermere Gr WV12 ..... 13 B1
Butterworth Cl WV14 ..... 40 A1
Butterworth Dr CV4 ..... 132 A6
Buttery Rd B67 ..... 64 E6
Buttons Farm Rd WV4 ..... 38 D3
Buttress Way B66 ..... 65 A6
Butts CV1 ..... 113 A2
Butts Cl WS11 ..... 5 E4
Butts JMI Sch WS4 ..... 28 F3
Butts La Norton Canes WS11 ..... 5 E4
  Stone DY10 ..... 117 D1
  Tanworth-In-A B94 ..... 142 B2
Butts Rd Coventry CV1 ..... 113 A2
  Walsall WS4 ..... 28 F3
  Wolverhampton WV4 ..... 38 F4
Butts St WS4 ..... 28 F3
Butts The Lichfield WS14 ..... 8 D2
  Walsall WS4 ..... 28 F3
  Warwick CV34 ..... 160 E2
Butts Way WS11 ..... 5 E4
Buxton Ave B78 ..... 35 B8
Buxton Cl WS3 ..... 14 C3
Buxton Rd Birmingham B23 ..... 56 B6
  Dudley DY2 ..... 62 A6
  Sutton Coldfield B73 ..... 57 A8
  Walsall WS3 ..... 14 C3
By Pass Rd B77 ..... 22 A5
Byfield Cl B33 ..... 69 E1
Byfield Pl CV7 ..... 130 D5
Byfield Rd CV6 ..... 112 E5
Byfleet Cl WV14 ..... 40 A3
Byford Cl B98 ..... 153 E2
Byford Ct CV10 ..... 72 F4
Byford St CV10 ..... 72 F4
Byland B77 ..... 21 D3
Byland Way WS3 ..... 13 F2
Bylands Cl B61 ..... 136 E1
Byng Kendrick Central
  Sch B33 ..... 69 D3
Bypass Link B33 ..... 69 E1
Byrchen Moor Gdns DY5 ..... 61 B7
Byrne Rd WV2 ..... 39 D7
Byron Ave Bedworth CV12 ..... 78 D2
  Birmingham B23 ..... 56 B3
  Lichfield WS14 ..... 9 B5
  Warwick CV34 ..... 160 C4
Byron Cl Birmingham B10 ..... 87 D7
  Kidderminster DY10 ..... 117 B5
Byron Cres DY1 ..... 51 B6
Byron Croft Dudley DY3 ..... 50 A4
  Sutton Coldfield B74 ..... 31 F6
Byron Ct Knowle B93 ..... 128 A6
  Sutton Coldfield B75 ..... 32 A5
Byron Gdns B71 ..... 53 B5
Byron Ho B63 ..... 82 B5
Byron Pl WS11 ..... 1 F5
Byron Rd Birmingham B10 ..... 87 D7
  Redditch B97 ..... 158 D8
  Tamworth B79 ..... 21 A7
  Willenhall WV12 ..... 27 E7
  Wolverhampton WV10 ..... 12 A1
Byron St Brierley Hill DY5 ..... 61 D7
  Coventry CV1 ..... 165 C4
  West Bromwich B71 ..... 53 B5
Byron Way B61 ..... 137 A8
Bywater Cl CV3 ..... 133 B5
Bywater Ho 5 WS1 ..... 28 F1
Byways WS3 ..... 14 C3

Caban Cl B31 ..... 102 E5
Cable Dr WS2 ..... 28 C5
Cable St WV2 ..... 39 F8
Cable & Wireless Coll
  CV4 ..... 131 E6
Cabot Gr WV6 ..... 23 E4
Cadbury Dr B35 ..... 58 A2
Cadbury Ho B19 ..... 66 D5
Cadbury Rd B13 ..... 87 B4
Cadbury Sixth Form Coll
  B38 ..... 103 F1
Cadbury Way B17 ..... 85 B3
Cadbury World B30 ..... 103 F7
Cadden Dr CV4 ..... 112 B2
Caddick Cres B71 ..... 53 D7
Caddick Rd B42 ..... 44 B1
Caddick St WV14 ..... 51 A8
Cadine Gdns B13 ..... 86 C1
Cadle Rd WV10 ..... 25 E7
Cadleigh Gdns B17 ..... 85 C3
Cadman Cl CV12 ..... 78 C3
Cadman Cres WV10 ..... 26 A7
Cadman's La WS6, WS3 ..... 14 D7
Cadnam Cl Birmingham B17 ..... 85 C3
  Willenhall WV13 ..... 41 B8
Cadogan Rd B77 ..... 35 D5
Caen Cl CV35 ..... 160 A4
Caernarfon Dr CV11 ..... 73 D3
Caernarvon Cl WV12 ..... 27 C7
Caernarvon Way DY1 ..... 50 E2
Caesar Rd CV8 ..... 147 E3
Caesar Way B46 ..... 59 E1
Cairn Dr WS2 ..... 27 F2
Cairndhu Dr DY10 ..... 117 B7
Cairns St WS2 ..... 28 C3
Caister B77 ..... 22 A6
Caister Dr WV13 ..... 40 F8

Caistor Cl B78 .... 34 B8
Caithness Cl CV5 .... 112 A4
Cakemore Rd B65 .... 63 F2
Cala Dr B15 .... 86 B7
Calcot Dr WV6 .... 24 E7
Calcott Ho CV3 .... 134 B5
Caldecote Cl CV10 .... 73 C8
Caldecote Gr B9 .... 68 C1
Caldecote Rd CV6 .... 113 C5
Caldeford Ave B90 .... 127 A7
Calder B77 .... 22 B2
Calder Ave WS1 .... 29 A2
Calder Cl Bulkington CV12 .... 79 B2
  Coventry CV3 .... 133 E7
Calder Dr B76 .... 58 A7
Calder Gr B20 .... 54 F2
Calder Rise DY3 .... 50 F6
Calder Tower 2 B20 .... 55 D1
Calder Wlk CV31 .... 162 C6
Calderfields Cl WS4 .... 29 A3
Caldmore Gn WS1 .... 42 E8
Caldmore Prim Sch WS1 .... 42 E8
Caldmore Rd WS1 .... 42 E8
Caldon Cl LE10 .... 75 B8
Caldwall Cres DY11 .... 116 D5
Caldwell Ct Nuneaton CV11 .... 73 D1
  Solihull B91 .... 107 C5
Caldwell Gr B91 .... 107 C5
Caldwell Ho B70 .... 53 C2
Caldwell Rd Birmingham
  B9 .... 68 B3
  Nuneaton CV11 .... 73 D1
Caldwell St B71 .... 53 D8
Caldy Wlk B45 .... 101 F1
Cale Cl B77 .... 21 C2
Caledon St 5 WS2 .... 42 C7
Caledonia DY5 .... 81 D7
Caledonia Rd WV2 .... 163 D1
Caledonia St WV14 .... 40 E6
Caledonian B77 .... 21 F2
Caledonian Cl WS5 .... 43 C3
Calewood Rd DY5 .... 81 D7
California Ho B32 .... 84 E2
California Rd B69 .... 63 B8
California Way B32 .... 84 F3
Californian Gr WS7 .... 6 F8
Callaghan Gr WS11 .... 2 C2
Callcott Dr DY5 .... 81 D7
Callear Rd WS10 .... 41 D1
Callendar Cl CV11 .... 74 A7
Calley Cl DY4 .... 52 A3
Callow Hill La B97 .... 158 B6
Callow Hill Rd B48 .... 139 A6
Callowbridge Rd B45 .... 121 F7
Callowbrook Fst Sch B45 ... 121 E7
Callowbrook La B45 .... 121 F7
Callows La 2 DY10 .... 116 E6
Calmere Cl CV2 .... 114 F8
Calshot Jun & Inf Schs
  B42 .... 55 B8
Calshot Rd B42 .... 55 A8
Calstock Rd WV12 .... 27 D4
Calthorpe Cl WS5 .... 43 E6
Calthorpe Mans 4 B15 .... 66 B1
Calthorpe Rd
  Birmingham,
  Edgbaston B15 .... 86 B8
  Birmingham
  Handsworth Wood B20 .... 55 C2
  Walsall WS5 .... 43 D6
Calthorpe Specl Sch B12 .... 87 A8
Caludon Castle Sch CV2 ... 114 E4
Caludon Lodge CV2 .... 114 E5
Caludon Park Ave CV2 .... 114 E5
Caludon Rd CV2 .... 114 A4
Calver Cres WV11 .... 26 F5
Calver Gr B44 .... 44 D3
Calverley Rd B38 .... 123 D8
Calvert Cl CV3 .... 133 D6
Calverton Gr B43 .... 54 E8
Calves Croft WV13 .... 27 A3
Calvin Cl WV10 .... 11 D3
Calving Hill WS11 .... 1 E2
Cam Gdns DY5 .... 61 B6
Cam Ho 1 DY1 .... 61 E8
Camberley 6 B71 .... 42 F1
Camberley Cres WV4 .... 39 E2
Camberley Dr WV4 .... 39 A4
Camberley Rd B23 .... 56 E6
Camberley Rd DY6 .... 61 A4
Camberwell Terr CV31 .... 162 A7
Camborne Cl B6 .... 66 E7
Camborne Dr CV11 .... 73 F5
Camborne Rd WS5 .... 43 D7
Cambourne Ct 4 WS5 .... 43 D7
Cambourne Rd
  Blackheath B65 .... 63 C3
  Hinckley LE10 .... 76 A6
Cambrai Dr B28 .... 105 F8
Cambria Cl B90 .... 125 E7
Cambria St WS11 .... 1 D4
Cambrian B77 .... 22 A2
Cambridge Ave Solihull
  B91 .... 106 E3
  Sutton Coldfield B73 .... 57 B8
Cambridge Cl WS9 .... 30 B8
Cambridge Cres B15 .... 86 D7
Cambridge Dr
  Birmingham B37 .... 69 F1
  Nuneaton CV10 .... 73 C7
Cambridge Gdns CV32 .... 157 A1
Cambridge Rd
  Birmingham B13 .... 86 F1
  Dudley DY2 .... 62 A7
  Smethwick B66 .... 65 A7

Cambridge St
  Birmingham B1 .... 164 A2
  Coventry CV1 .... 113 E5
  Walsall WS1 .... 42 E7
  West Bromwich B70 .... 53 B2
  Wolverhampton WV10 .... 163 C4
Cambridge Tower B1 .... 164 A2
Cambridge Way B27 .... 88 D4
Camden Cl Birmingham B36 .. 69 A8
  Walsall WS5 .... 43 A4
Camden Dr Birmingham B1 ... 66 C3
  Tamworth B77 .... 21 C3
Camden St
  Birmingham B18, B1 .... 66 B4
  Brownhills WS9 .... 15 F4
  Coventry CV2 .... 114 A4
  Walsall WS1 .... 42 E8
Camden Way DY6 .... 49 D1
Camellia Gdns WV9 .... 10 F3
Camellia Rd 1 CV2 .... 96 B2
Camelot Cl WS11 .... 1 F4
Camelot Gr CV8 .... 148 C5
Camelot Way B10 .... 87 C8
Cameo Dr DY8 .... 80 F8
Cameron Cl Allesley CV5 ... 112 A7
  Royal Leamington Spa
  CV32 .... 157 A4
Cameron Rd WS4 .... 29 B3
Camford Gr B14 .... 104 F3
Camhouses B77 .... 22 B1
Camino Rd B32 .... 84 F3
Camomile Cl 5 WS5 .... 43 A3
Camp Hill Birmingham B12 ... 87 A8
  Stourbridge DY8 .... 60 E1
Camp Hill Cir B12 .... 87 A8
Camp Hill Cty Jun Sch
  CV10 .... 72 E6
Camp Hill Dr CV10 .... 72 D7
Camp Hill Middleway B12 ... B7 A7 A4
Camp Hill Rd CV10 .... 72 C7
Camp La
  Birmingham,
  Handsworth B21 .... 54 C2
  Birmingham,
  King's Norton B38 .... 103 F3
Camp Rd WS14, B75 .... 32 D6
Camp St Birmingham B9 ... 67 C1
  Wednesbury WS10 .... 41 F2
  Wolverhampton WV1 .... 163 B4
Camp Wood Cl B30 .... 103 F8
Campbell Cl Tamworth B79 ... 20 F8
  Walsall WS4 .... 29 A3
Campbell Pl WS10 .... 41 D6
Campbell St Brierley Hill
  DY5 .... 61 C4
  2 Dudley DY2 .... 62 D8
Campbells Gn B26 .... 89 B4
Campden Cl B97 .... 158 C6
Campden Gn B92 .... 89 A3
Camphill La WS10 .... 41 F2
Campian's Ave WS6 .... 4 D2
Campion Cl Coventry CV3 ... 133 D6
  Walsall WS5 .... 43 A3
Campion Ct 2 DY4 .... 51 E5
Campion Dr
  Featherstone WV10 .... 12 A7
  Tamworth B77 .... 21 C3
Campion Gn CV32 .... 157 A2
Campion Gr B63 .... 82 D3
Campion Ho
  1 Birmingham B38 .... 123 E8
  Wolverhampton WV10 .... 25 F4
Campion Rd CV32 .... 157 A2
Campion Sch & Com Coll
  CV31 .... 162 C5
Campion Terr CV32 .... 157 A1
Camplea Croft B37 .... 70 A2
Camplin Cres B20 .... 54 E5
Campling Cl CV12 .... 79 B2
Campton Cl LE10 .... 75 E7
Campville Cres B71 .... 42 E1
Campville Gr B37 .... 69 F5
Camrose Croft
  Birmingham
  Balsall Heath B12 .... 86 F5
  Birmingham,
  Castle Bromwich B34 .... 69 B6
Camrose Gdns WV9 .... 11 A3
Camrose Tower B7 .... 67 B6
Camsey La WS7 .... 7 E8
Camville CV3 .... 115 A2
Canal La B24 .... 57 A1
Canal Rd CV6 .... 113 F8
Canal Side Dudley DY2 .... 62 E4
  Hopwood B48 .... 123 B2
Canal Side Ind Est DY5 .... 61 C1
Canal St Brierley Hill DY5 ... 61 C5
  Dudley, Roseville WV14 .... 51 C8
  Dudley, Tipton Green DY1 .... 51 D4
  Oldbury B69 .... 64 A7
  Stourbridge DY8 .... 80 F6
Canal View Ind Est DY5 .... 61 B1
Canalside Cl Walsall WS3 ... 14 F1
  Wednesbury WS10 .... 42 E2
Canary Gr B19 .... 66 C8
Canberra Ct 2 CV12 .... 77 F2
Canberra Ho B34 .... 69 E6
Canberra Rd Coventry CV2 ... 96 C4
  Walsall WS5 .... 43 C6
Canberra Way 4 B12 .... 86 F8
Canford Cl Birmingham B12 ... 86 F7
  Coventry CV3 .... 133 C3
Canley Ford CV5 .... 132 E2
Canley Rd CV5 .... 132 D8
Canley Sta CV5 .... 112 D1
Cannel Rd WS7 .... 6 D6
Canning Cl WS5 .... 43 D6
Canning Gdns B18 .... 65 E4

Canning Rd Tamworth B77 ... 21 F4
  Walsall WS5 .... 43 D6
Canning St LE10 .... 71 C1
Cannock Chase High Sch
  WS11 .... 1 E2
Cannock Chase Tech Coll
  Cannock, Blackfords WS11 .... 1 D1
  Cannock, Bridgtown WS11 .... 4 E7
Cannock Com Hospl WS11 ... 1 E2
Cannock Ind Ctr WS11 .... 4 D5
Cannock Motor Village
  WS11 .... 2 B3
Cannock Rd Burntwood WS7 ... 7 B7
  Cannock WS11 .... 2 B1
  Featherstone WV10 .... 12 C7
  Norton Canes WS7 .... 6 C8
  Willenhall WV12 .... 27 C7
  Wolverhampton WV10 .... 26 A8
Cannock Sh Ctr 3 WS11 .... 1 E1
Cannock Sta WS11 .... 4 F8
Cannocks La CV5 .... 132 C6
Cannon Cl CV4 .... 132 F6
Cannon Hill Gr 2 B12 .... 86 E5
Cannon Hill Pl 1 B12 .... 86 E5
Cannon Hill Rd
  Birmingham B12 .... 86 E5
  Coventry CV4 .... 132 D5
Cannon Park District Ctr
  CV4 .... 132 C6
Cannon Park Prim Sch
  CV4 .... 132 D5
Cannon Park Rd CV4 .... 132 E5
Cannon Rd WV5 .... 49 A6
Cannon St Birmingham B2 ... 164 C2
  Walsall WS2 .... 28 E4
  Willenhall WV13 .... 27 B2
Cannon St N WS2 .... 28 E4
Canon Dr CV7 .... 95 D6
Canon Evans CE Fst Sch
  CV12 .... 78 A2
Canon Hudson Cl CV3 ... 134 C6
Canon Maggs CE Mid Sch
  CV12 .... 78 B2
Canon Young Rd CV31 ... 162 B3
Canterbury Ave WV13 .... 27 D2
Canterbury Cl Blackheath
  B65 .... 63 E4
  Kenilworth CV8 .... 148 C3
  Lichfield WS13 .... 3 C3
  9 Oldbury B65 .... 63 E4
  Studley B80 .... 159 C4
  Walsall WS3 .... 15 A4
  West Bromwich B71 .... 53 E8
Canterbury Cross Prim
  Sch B20 .... 55 D1
Canterbury Dr
  Birmingham B37 .... 90 A7
  Burntwood WS7 .... 7 D7
  Perton WV6 .... 23 E4
Canterbury Rd
  Birmingham B20 .... 55 D1
  Kidderminster DY11 .... 116 A6
  West Bromwich B71 .... 53 D8
  Wolverhampton WV4 .... 38 E5
Canterbury St CV1 .... 165 D3
Canterbury Tower 1 B1 ... 66 B3
Canterbury Way
  Cannock WS12 .... 2 B1
  Nuneaton CV11 .... 74 A8
Cantlow Cl CV5 .... 112 A3
Cantlow Ho 3 B12 .... 86 F7
Cantlow Rd B13 .... 105 A6
Canton Ho LE10 .... 71 C4
Canute Cl WS1 .... 42 F7
Canvey Cl B45 .... 101 E1
Canwell Ave B37 .... 69 F5
Canwell Dr B75 .... 33 B5
Canwell Gdns WV14 .... 40 C4
Capcroft Rd B13 .... 105 B6
Cape Cl WS8 .... 16 A6
Cape Hill B66 .... 65 C4
Cape Ind Est CV34 .... 160 E7
Cape Prim Sch B66 .... 65 C4
Cape Rd CV34 .... 160 D8
Cape St Birmingham B18 ... 65 D4
  West Bromwich B70 .... 52 E4
Capener Rd B43 .... 44 A2
Capenhurst Dr WV10 .... 25 C8
Capethorn Rd B66 .... 65 A3
Capilano Rd B23 .... 56 C7
Capmartin Rd CV6 .... 113 C7
Cappers La WS13, WS14 .... 9 F8
Capponfield Cl WV14 .... 40 B3
Capstone Ave
  Birmingham B18 .... 66 A4
  Wolverhampton WV10 .... 25 C8
Captain's Cl WV3 .... 24 A1
Captain's Pool Rd DY10 ... 117 B2
Captains Pool Rd DY10 ... 117 A1
Capulet Cl CV3 .... 134 C6
Caradoc B77 .... 22 A2
Caradoc Cl CV2 .... 114 D7
Caradoc Hall CV2 .... 114 D7
Carcroft Rd B23 .... 88 D8
Cardale Croft 1 CV3 .... 134 F8
Cardale St B65 .... 63 D1
Carden Cl B70 .... 52 F4
Carder Cres WV14 .... 40 D4
Carder Dr DY5 .... 61 C2
Cardiff Cl CV3 .... 134 D5
Cardiff St WV3 .... 39 B8
Cardigan Cl B71 .... 53 C7
Cardigan Dr WV12 .... 27 B6
Cardigan Pl WS12 .... 2 C5
Cardigan Rd CV12 .... 77 C1
Cardigan St B4 .... 66 F3
Cardinal Cres B61 .... 136 D1
Cardinal Dr DY10 .... 117 B3

Cardinal Griffin RC Sch
  WS11 .... 1 D3
Cardinal Newman RC
  Sch CV6 .... 94 F2
Cardinal Newman RC
  Sec Sch B17 .... 65 A2
Cardinal Way WS11 .... 1 D2
Cardinal Wiseman RC Sch
  CV2 .... 96 E1
Cardinal Wiseman RC
  Sec Sch B44 .... 44 F2
Carding Cl CV5 .... 111 F4
Cardington Ave B42 .... 44 B1
Cardington Cl B98 .... 154 F3
Cardoness Pl DY1 .... 50 F2
Cardy Cl B97 .... 153 B4
Careless Gn DY9 .... 81 F4
Carey B77 .... 36 A5
Carey St CV6 .... 114 B8
Carfax B15 .... 4 E8
Cargill Cl CV6 .... 95 F5
Carhampton Rd B75 .... 47 A5
Carisbroke B77 .... 22 A2
Carisbrook Rd CV10 .... 73 D6
Carisbrooke Ave B37 .... 70 C2
Carisbrooke Cl WS10 .... 42 E3
Carisbrooke Cres WS10 .... 42 E3
Carisbrooke Dr B62 .... 83 D3
Carisbrooke Gdns WV10 ... 11 E3
Carisbrooke Ho WS10 .... 42 E2
Carisbrooke Rd
  Birmingham B17 .... 65 B1
  Perton WV6 .... 24 A3
  Wednesbury WS10 .... 42 E2
  Wolverhampton WV10 .... 11 E3
Carl Eynon Ct 2 WS3 .... 28 B8
Carl St WS2 .... 28 D5
Carlcroft B77 .... 22 B2
Carless Ave B17 .... 85 B7
Carless Ho B66 .... 65 D6
Carless St WS1 .... 42 E8
Carlisle Rd WS11 .... 4 B7
Carlisle St B18 .... 65 F5
Carlton Ave Aldridge B74 ... 31 A2
  Bilston WV14 .... 40 F7
  Birmingham B21 .... 54 E1
  Stourbridge DY9 .... 81 E3
  Wolverhampton WV11 .... 26 A7
Carlton Cl Bulkington CV12 ... 79 B3
  Cannock WS12 .... 2 D1
  Dudley DY2 .... 51 C6
  Kidderminster DY11 .... 116 A8
  Redditch B97 .... 153 B1
  Sutton Coldfield B75 .... 46 E7
Carlton Cres Burntwood
  WS7 .... 7 A8
  Tamworth B79 .... 20 F8
Carlton Croft B74 .... 31 A2
Carlton Ct CV5 .... 112 F2
Carlton Gdns CV5 .... 133 A8
Carlton Ho
  4 Royal Leamington Spa
  CV32 .... 161 F8
  Sutton Coldfield B75 .... 32 B2
Carlton Mews B36 .... 69 D7
Carlton Mews Flats B36 ... 69 D7
Carlton Rd Birmingham B9 ... 67 D1
  Coventry CV6 .... 95 F1
  Smethwick B66 .... 65 B8
  Wolverhampton WV3 .... 39 A7
Carlyle Ave DY10 .... 117 B6
Carlyle Bsns Pk B70 .... 52 F5
Carlyle Gr WV10 .... 26 A8
Carlyle Rd
  Birmingham, Edgbaston B16 ... 65 E1
  Birmingham, Lozells B19 ... 66 C8
  Blackheath B65 .... 63 C2
  Bromsgrove B60 .... 151 B8
  Wolverhampton WV10 .... 26 A8
Carmel Cl WS12 .... 2 C5
Carmel Gr B32 .... 84 B1
Carmelite Rd CV1 .... 113 E2
Carmichael Cl WS14 .... 9 D7
Carmodale Ave B42 .... 55 B5
Carnbroe Ave CV3 .... 134 F7
Carnegie Ave DY4 .... 52 B4
Carnegie Cl CV3 .... 134 B5
Carnegie Rd B65 .... 63 B2
Carnford Rd B26 .... 89 B6
Carnforth Cl DY6 .... 60 B7
Carnforth Rd B60 .... 137 B1
Carnoustie B77 .... 22 C5
Carnoustie Cl
  Bromsgrove B61 .... 150 D8
  Nuneaton CV11 .... 79 C8
  Sutton Coldfield B75 .... 46 C8
  Walsall WS3 .... 14 A3
Carnwath Rd B73 .... 45 E2
Carol Ave B61 .... 136 D3
Carol Cres Halesowen B63 ... 82 F5
  Wednesfield WV11 .... 26 E6
Caroline Cl CV11 .... 78 F7
Caroline Rd B13 .... 86 F4
Caroline St Birmingham
  B3 .... 164 A4
  Dudley DY2 .... 51 E1
  West Bromwich B70 .... 53 B2
Carpenter Pl 7 B12 .... 87 A6
Carpenter Rd B15 .... 86 B7
Carpenter's Rd B19 .... 66 C7
Carpenters Cl LE10 .... 75 F5
Carpet Trades Way DY11 ... 116 D7
Carrick Cl WS3 .... 15 A5
Carrie Ho CV1 .... 165 A2
Carriers Cl WS2 .... 27 F1
Carriers Fold WV5 .... 49 B7
Carrington Rd WS10 .... 42 D3
Carroll Wlk DY10 .... 117 C5

Carroway Head Hill B78 ... 33 D4
Carrs La B4 .... 164 C2
Carsal Cl CV7 .... 95 D5
Carshalton Gr WV2 .... 39 E7
Carshalton Rd B44 .... 45 A2
Cartbridge Cres WS3 .... 28 F6
Cartbridge La WS4 .... 29 A6
Cartbridge La S WS4 .... 29 A5
Cartbridge Wlk WS3 .... 29 A6
Carter Ave Codsall WV8 ... 10 B3
  Kidderminster DY11 .... 116 B4
Carter Ct DY11 .... 116 C4
Carter Rd Birmingham B43 ... 43 F2
  Coventry CV3 .... 134 A8
  Wolverhampton W6 .... 25 B5
Carter's Gn B70 .... 53 B4
Carter's La Birmingham B62 ... 84 A3
  Halesowen B62 .... 83 F4
Carters Cl Bromsgrove
  B61 .... 150 D7
  Sutton Coldfield B76 .... 46 F3
Carters Hurst B33 .... 69 B1
Cartersfield La WS9 .... 16 E6
Carthusian Rd CV3 .... 133 C7
Cartland Rd
  Birmingham,
  Sparkbrook B11 .... 87 C6
  Birmingham,
  Stirchley B14, B30 .... 104 C7
Cartmel Cl CV5 .... 112 A4
Cartmel Ct B23 .... 56 B4
Cartway The WV6 .... 23 D4
Cartwright Gdns B69 .... 52 C2
Cartwright Ho 2 WS3 .... 14 B1
Cartwright Rd B75 .... 32 C3
Cartwright St WV2 .... 163 C1
Carver Cl CV2 .... 114 E2
Carver Ct B24 .... 57 C6
Carver Gdns DY8 .... 80 E2
Carver St B1 .... 66 B4
Casa Mio Ct WS12 .... 2 C5
Cascade Cl CV3 .... 133 E6
Case La CV35 .... 145 E1
Casewell Rd DY6 .... 60 C8
Casey Ave B23 .... 56 D8
Cash Joynson Ave WS10 ... 41 C8
Cash's Bsns Ctr CV1 .... 113 D5
Cash's La CV1 .... 113 D6
Cashmore Ave CV31 .... 161 F5
Cashmore Mid Sch CV31 ... 161 F6
Cashmore Rd Bedworth
  CV12 .... 77 E1
  Kenilworth CV8 .... 148 C4
Casia Gr CV8 .... 148 C4
Caslon Cres DY8 .... 80 D4
Caslon Flats B63 .... 82 C4
Caslon Prim Sch B63 .... 82 C4
Caslon Rd B63 .... 82 C6
Caspian Way CV2 .... 115 A8
Cassandra Cl Brierley Hill
  DY5 .... 50 C1
  Coventry CV4 .... 132 D3
Cassandra Gr CV34 .... 161 D4
Cassowary Rd 2 B20 .... 54 F3
Castello Dr B36 .... 58 D1
Castle Bromwich Bsns Pk
  B35 .... 58 A1
Castle Bromwich Hall
  Gdns B36 .... 69 A8
Castle Bromwich Inf Sch
  B36 .... 69 E8
Castle Bromwich Jun Sch
  B36 .... 69 E7
Castle Cl Blackheath B64 ... 63 B1
  Brownhills WS8 .... 6 F2
  Coventry CV3 .... 133 D6
  Solihull B92 .... 89 B1
  Tamworth B77 .... 21 E4
  Warwick CV34 .... 160 E6
Castle Cres B36 .... 69 C8
Castle Croft B68 .... 84 D8
Castle Dr Coleshill B46 ... 70 F5
  Willenhall WV12 .... 27 B5
Castle Dyke 5 WS13 .... 9 B7
Castle Gr Kenilworth CV8 ... 147 E4
Castle High Sch DY1 .... 51 C2
Castle Hill Dudley DY1 ... 51 D2
  Kenilworth CV8 .... 147 E5
  Warwick CV34 .... 160 F6
Castle Ho B33 .... 69 B2
Castle Hts B64 .... 83 B8
Castle La Solihull B92 .... 89 A2
  Warwick CV34 .... 160 E6
Castle Mews CV34 .... 160 E6
Castle Mill Rd DY1 .... 51 C4
Castle Place Ind Est CV1 ... 165 D4
Castle Rd Birmingham B29 ... 85 B1
  Brownhills WS9 .... 16 A3
  Kenilworth CV8 .... 147 E5
  Kidderminster DY11 .... 116 C5
  Nuneaton CV10 .... 73 C4
  Studley B80 .... 159 F4
  Tamworth B77 .... 35 F5
  Tipton DY4 .... 51 D4
Castle Rd E B68 .... 84 D8
Castle Rd W B68 .... 84 C8
Castle Sch WS3 .... 28 B7
Castle Sq B29 .... 85 A1
Castle St Astwood Bank B96 ... 158 E2
  Brownhills WS8 .... 6 F2
  Coventry CV1 .... 165 D4
  Darlaston WS10 .... 41 D8
  Dudley DY1 .... 51 D1
  Dudley, Roseville WV14 .... 51 C8

Castle St continued
Hinckley LE10 ...... 75 D8
Sedgley DY3 ...... 50 D8
Tipton DY4 ...... 51 E5
Warwick CV34 ...... 160 E6
West Bromwich B70 ...... 53 A8
Wolverhampton WV1 ...... 163 C3
Castle The DY8 ...... 81 B3
Castle Vale Sec Sch B35 ...... 58 B3
Castle Vale Sh Ctr B35 ...... 57 F3
Castle Vale Sports Ctr
B35 ...... 58 B2
Castle View Dudley DY1 ...... 51 B2
Tamworth B77 ...... 21 C3
Castle View Cl WS10 ...... 41 A4
Castle View Ind Est DY4 ...... 51 F3
Castle View Rd WV14 ...... 41 B4
Castle Yd WV1 ...... 163 C3
Castlebridge Gdns WV11 ...... 26 F7
Castlebridge Rd WV11 ...... 27 A6
Castlecroft WS11 ...... 5 E5
Castlecroft Ave WV3 ...... 38 A8
Castlecroft Gdns WV3 ...... 38 C8
Castlecroft La WV3 ...... 23 F1
Castlecroft Prim Sch WV3 .. 38 B8
Castlecroft Rd Bilston
WV14 ...... 40 F7
Wolverhampton WV3 ...... 38 B8
Castleditch La B98 ...... 158 E7
Castleford Gr B11 ...... 87 C4
Castleford Rd B11 ...... 87 C4
Castlefort JMI Sch WS9 ...... 16 B3
Castlefort Rd WS9 ...... 16 A3
Castlegate Mews
⑤ CV34 ...... 160 F7
Castlehall B77 ...... 22 A2
Castlehill Rd WS9 ...... 16 C3
Castlehills Dr B36 ...... 69 A8
Castlemaine Dr LE10 ...... 71 E3
Castleton Ct ① B15 ...... 86 B7
Castleton Rd Birmingham
B42 ...... 55 D7
Walsall WS3 ...... 14 C3
Castleton St DY2 ...... 62 C4
Caswell Rd
Royal Leamington Spa CV31 . 162 B6
Sedgley DY3 ...... 50 C8
Cat And Kittens La WV10 ... 11 E6
Cat La B34 ...... 69 B7
Cater Dr B76 ...... 46 F2
Caterham Dr DY6 ...... 60 F3
Catesby Dr DY6 ...... 60 D8
Catesby Ho B37 ...... 69 F4
Catesby La B94 ...... 144 B2
Catesby Rd Coventry CV6 ... 113 B8
Solihull B90 ...... 106 B1
Cateswell Rd B28 ...... 87 F2
Cathcart Rd DY8 ...... 80 E5
Cathedral Ave DY11 ...... 116 A6
Cathedral Cl WS13 ...... 9 B8
Cathedral Ct WS13 ...... 9 B8
Cathedral Lanes Sh Ctr
CV1 ...... 165 B3
Cathedral Rise WS13 ...... 9 A8
Cathel Dr B42 ...... 55 A7
Catherine Cl B24 ...... 57 C4
Catherine de Barnes La
Bickenhill B92 ...... 90 D1
Catherine de B92 ...... 108 C7
Catherine Dr B73 ...... 46 A6
Catherine Rd WV14 ...... 40 A1
Catherine St Birmingham
B6 ...... 67 A7
Coventry CV2 ...... 113 F3
Catherine Ward Hall CV12 .. 78 B5
Catherines B91 ...... 108 B4
Catherton Cl DY4 ...... 41 C1
Catholic La DY3 ...... 50 D7
Catisfield Cres WV8 ...... 10 F1
Cato St B7 ...... 67 B5
Cato St N B7 ...... 67 C5
Caton Gr B28 ...... 106 A7
Catshill Fst Sch B61 ...... 137 A8
Catshill Mid Sch B61 ...... 136 F8
Catshill Rd WS8 ...... 16 A7
Cattell Dr B75 ...... 47 B5
Cattell Rd Birmingham B9 .. 67 C1
Warwick CV34 ...... 160 E7
Cattells Gr B7 ...... 67 C6
Cattermole Gr B44 ...... 44 C3
Cattock Hurst Dr B72 ...... 57 D7
Catwall End Prim Sch DY3 . 50 D7
Causeway B65 ...... 63 C2
Causeway Green Prim Sch
B68 ...... 63 F4
Causeway Green Rd B68 .... 64 A4
Causeway Rd WV14 ...... 51 D8
Causeway The B25 ...... 88 D7
Causey Farm Rd B63 ...... 100 C8
Cavalier Cir WV10 ...... 11 E4
Cavalier Cl CV11 ...... 73 E2
Cavan's Cl WS11 ...... 1 E4
Cavandale Ave B44 ...... 44 E1
Cavans Cl WS14 ...... 135 A8
Cavans Way CV3 ...... 135 A8
Cavans Wood Mobile
Homes WS12 ...... 1 D5
Cavell Cl WS2 ...... 28 D2
Cavell Ho B16 ...... 66 A2
Cavell Rd DY2 ...... 51 F1
Cavendish B77 ...... 20 E7
Cavendish Cl
Birmingham B38 ...... 104 B1
Kingswinford DY6 ...... 60 D4
Marlbrook B60 ...... 121 C1
Cavendish Ct B93 ...... 128 A3

Cavendish Dr Hagley DY9 ...... 98 F4
Kidderminster DY10 ...... 117 B7
Cavendish Gdns Walsall
WS2 ...... 28 A4
Wolverhampton WV1 ...... 26 C1
Cavendish Rd
Birmingham B16 ...... 65 D4
Coventry CV4 ...... 111 E2
Halesowen B62 ...... 83 F4
Walsall WS2 ...... 28 B5
Wolverhampton WV1 ...... 26 B1
Cavendish Way WS9 ...... 30 B5
Caversham Cl CV11 ...... 74 A7
Caversham Rd B44 ...... 45 A2
Cawdon Gr B93 ...... 127 F3
Cawdor Cres B16 ...... 65 F1
Cawnpore Rd CV6 ...... 95 B2
Cawthorne Cl ① CV1 ...... 113 E4
Caxton Ct WS11 ...... 4 E8
Caxton Gr B44 ...... 45 C1
Caxton St WS11 ...... 4 E8
Caynham Cl B98 ...... 154 D4
Caynham Rd B32 ...... 102 B8
Cayton Gr B23 ...... 56 F6
CE Prim Sch of St Edmund
& St John The DY2 ...... 51 E1
Cearl Ct B77 ...... 88 C2
Cecil Ct CV31 ...... 162 A8
Cecil Dr B69 ...... 52 D2
Cecil Rd
Birmingham,
Gravelly Hill B24 ...... 56 F3
Birmingham,
Selly Park B13 ...... 86 C1
Cecil St Birmingham B19 ...... 164 C4
Cannock WS11 ...... 1 F4
Stourbridge DY8 ...... 80 F5
Walsall WS4 ...... 28 F3
Cecily Rd CV3 ...... 133 E7
Cedar Ave Birmingham B36 ... 69 C8
Brownhills WS8 ...... 16 A8
Dudley WV14 ...... 51 B7
Cedar Bridge Croft B74 ...... 46 B8
Cedar Cl Birmingham B30 ... 103 E6
Burntwood WS7 ...... 7 A6
Cannock WS12 ...... 2 A8
Lichfield WS14 ...... 9 F7
Oldbury B68 ...... 84 C8
Royal Leamington Spa
CV32 ...... 157 A4
Stourbridge DY8 ...... 80 D2
Walsall WS5 ...... 43 B4
Cedar Cres DY11 ...... 116 C6
Cedar Ct Allesley CV5 ...... 112 A6
Birmingham B43 ...... 54 B8
Hinckley LE10 ...... 76 A6
Tamworth B77 ...... 35 E6
Cedar Dr Birmingham B74 ... 30 E1
Birmingham B24 ...... 57 C5
Bromsgrove B60 ...... 137 A1
Kidderminster DY11 ...... 116 C7
Tamworth B79 ...... 21 A8
Cedar Gr Bilston WV14 ...... 40 F7
Codsall WV8 ...... 10 B3
Warwick CV34 ...... 156 A1
Wolverhampton WV3 ...... 38 F7
Cedar Ho Birmingham B36 ... 68 F8
Solihull B91 ...... 106 F1
Cedar Park Rd
Redditch B97 ...... 153 D4
Willenhall WV12 ...... 13 C1
Cedar Rd Birmingham B30 ... 103 E6
Burntwood WS7 ...... 7 A6
Dudley DY1 ...... 51 B3
Nuneaton CV10 ...... 72 D6
Redditch B97 ...... 153 D4
Tipton DY4 ...... 51 D5
Wednesbury WS10 ...... 42 A2
Willenhall WV13 ...... 26 E2
Cedar Terr B60 ...... 137 A1
Cedar Way Birmingham
B31 ...... 102 F1
Wolverhampton WV11 ...... 26 C7
Cedar Wlk ⑥ B37 ...... 70 B2
Cedar Wood Dr CV7 ...... 130 B6
Cedar Wood Rd DY3 ...... 50 D5
Cedarhill Dr WS11 ...... 1 F3
Cedarhurst Birmingham
B32 ...... 85 A5
Solihull B91 ...... 107 C3
Cedars Ave Birmingham B27 .. 88 C4
Coventry CV6 ...... 112 F5
Kingswinford DY6 ...... 60 D4
Wombourne WV5 ...... 49 A5
Cedars Fst Sch CV7 ...... 96 A8
Cedars Mews The
⑧ CV32 ...... 161 D8
Cedars Rd CV7 ...... 78 B1
Cedars The Birmingham
B25 ...... 68 E1
Wolverhampton,
Heath Town WV11 ...... 26 B5
Wolverhampton,
Newbridge WV6 ...... 24 F3
Wolverhampton,
Tettenhall WV6 ...... 24 D5
Cedarwood B74 ...... 46 B8
Cedarwood Croft B42 ...... 54 F8
Cedric Cl CV3 ...... 134 C5
Celandine CV6 ...... 60 C4
Celandine Rd Coventry CV2 .. 96 D2
Dudley DY1 ...... 51 A4
Celbury Way B43 ...... 54 D8
Celdine Wy B77 ...... 21 C3
Celtic Rd WS11 ...... 1 E3

Celts Cl B65 ...... 63 C4
Cemetery La B18 ...... 66 B5
Cemetery Rd Cannock WS11 .. 1 E4
Darlaston WS10 ...... 41 F8
Oldbury B68 ...... 64 C6
Redditch B97 ...... 153 D3
Smethwick B67 ...... 64 F4
Stourbridge DY9 ...... 81 E5
Sutton Coldfield B75 ...... 46 D6
Willenhall WV13 ...... 27 A2
Cemetery St Bilston WV14 .... 40 C6
Cheslyn Hay WS6 ...... 4 C2
Cemetery Way WS3 ...... 14 B1
Centaur Rd CV5 ...... 112 F2
Centenary Bsns Ctr CV11 ... 73 E3
Centenary Cl ① B31 ...... 103 A1
Centenary Dr B21 ...... 54 E1
Centenary Rd CV4 ...... 132 D7
Central Arc WV1 ...... 163 B3
Central Ave Bilston WV14 ...... 40 C6
Birmingham B31 ...... 122 F8
Blackheath,
Cradley Heath B64 ...... 82 D7
Blackheath,
Rowley Regis B65 ...... 63 C2
Cannock WS11 ...... 1 F5
Coventry CV2 ...... 114 A2
Nuneaton CV11 ...... 73 B5
Royal Leamington Spa CV31 . 161 F6
Stourbridge DY9 ...... 81 E3
Tipton DY4 ...... 51 F7
Central Bldgs CV1 ...... 165 B3
Central City Ind Est CV6 ... 113 F5
Central Cl WS3 ...... 14 A1
Central Dr
Dudley, Gornalwood DY3 ...... 50 D2
Dudley, West Cosley WV14 .. 51 D7
Walsall WS3 ...... 14 A1
Central Flats CV1 ...... 165 B1
Central Gr B27 ...... 88 C2
Central Park Ind Est DY2 ... 62 E3
Central Rd B60 ...... 137 A2
Central Sq B23 ...... 57 A4
Central Trad Est
Darlaston WS10 ...... 41 E6
Wolverhampton WV2 ...... 39 F8
Central Way DY5 ...... 61 F3
Centre B63 ...... 83 B3
Centre La B63 ...... 83 B3
Centre Link Ind Est B7 ...... 67 B6
Centreway The B14 ...... 105 D4
Centrovell Ind Est CV11 .... 73 C2
Centurion Cl B46 ...... 59 F1
Centurion Pk B37 ...... 36 B6
Centurion Way B77 ...... 36 B6
Century Ho B69 ...... 63 D6
Century Ind Est B44 ...... 44 E3
Century Pk B9 ...... 67 C2
Century Rd B69 ...... 64 A8
Century Tower B5 ...... 86 C5
Ceolmund Cres B37 ...... 70 B2
Chace Ave CV3 ...... 134 C6
Chace Prim Sch CV3 ...... 134 C6
Chaceley Cl CV2 ...... 115 A8
Chaceley Ct B97 ...... 158 D8
Chaceley Gr B23 ...... 56 E7
Chad Rd Birmingham B15 .... 85 F8
Dudley WV14 ...... 51 B7
Chad Sq B15 ...... 85 E8
Chad Valley Cl B17 ...... 85 D6
Chadbrook Crest B15 ...... 85 E8
Chadbury Croft ① B91 ...... 127 B8
Chadbury Rd B63 ...... 83 C3
Chadcote Way B61 ...... 120 F1
Chaddersley Cl B45 ...... 101 F1
Chaddersley Gdns
② DY10 ...... 117 A5
Chaddesley Cl Oldbury B69 .. 63 D5
Redditch B98 ...... 153 F1
Chaddesley Dr DY9 ...... 81 B1
Chaddesley Rd
Birmingham B31 ...... 103 D2
Halesowen B63 ...... 82 F2
Kidderminster DY10 ...... 117 A5
Chadley Cl B91 ...... 107 A6
Chadsgrove Sch B61 ...... 136 F8
Chadshunt Cl B36 ...... 58 D2
Chadsmead Prim Sch
WS13 ...... 3 A1
Chadsmoor CE Jun Sch
WS11 ...... 2 A3
Chadsmoor Inf Sch WS11 ... 2 A4
Chadsmoor Terr B7 ...... 67 B6
Chadstone Cl B90 ...... 127 B6
Chadswell Hts WS13 ...... 3 D2
Chadvale Prim Sch B15 ...... 85 D7
Chadwell Dr B90 ...... 106 B6
Chadwich La DY9 ...... 120 F7
Chadwick Ave B45 ...... 122 B8
Chadwick Cl Coventry CV5 .. 112 B3
Wolverhampton WV4 ...... 38 D6
Chadwick La
Chadwick End B93 ...... 145 B8
Knowle B93 ...... 129 B2
Chadwick Manor B93 ...... 129 A1
Chadwick Mews B93 ...... 145 B6
Chadwick Rd B75 ...... 46 F5
Chadworth Ave B93 ...... 127 E3
Chaffcombe Rd B26 ...... 89 C7
Chaffinch Cl Cannock WS12 .. 2 B4
Sedgley DY3 ...... 39 C2
Chaffinch Dr Birmingham
B36 ...... 70 B7
Kidderminster DY10 ...... 116 B7
Chaffinch Rd DY9 ...... 81 D3
Chain Wlk B19 ...... 66 D7
Chainshop Mus DY2 ...... 62 B1
Chalcot Dr WS12 ...... 2 A7

Chalcot Gr B20 ...... 54 E5
Chaldon Cl WV9 ...... 11 A3
Chale Gr B14 ...... 105 A3
Chalfield Cl B79 ...... 20 D6
Chalfont Ave WS11 ...... 4 C7
Chalfont Cl Bedworth CV12 .. 78 A4
Coventry CV5 ...... 112 B4
Chalfont Pl DY9 ...... 81 E2
Chalfont Rd B20 ...... 55 C1
Chalford Rd B23 ...... 56 C8
Chalford Way B90 ...... 106 C1
Chalgrove Ave B38 ...... 103 E1
Chalgrove Cres B91 ...... 107 B1
Challenge Bsns Pk CV1 ...... 113 D5
Challenge Cl CV1 ...... 165 C4
Challenge Way WV10 ...... 25 D3
Challenor Ave WV13 ...... 26 D1
Chalybeate Cl B45 ...... 101 F1
Chamberlain Cl
Cubbington CV32 ...... 157 E5
Tipton B69 ...... 52 D2
Chamberlain Cres B90 ...... 106 A2
Chamberlain Ct B14 ...... 86 E1
Chamberlain Ho B16 ...... 66 A1
Chamberlain Rd B13 ...... 105 A6
Chamberlain Sq B3 ...... 164 B2
Chamberlain Wlk
⑩ Coleshill B46 ...... 70 F7
① Smethwick B66 ...... 65 B5
Chamberlain's La WV4 ...... 38 C3
Chamberlaine St CV12 ...... 78 B3
Chance Croft B68 ...... 84 B8
Chance Fields CV31 ...... 162 F6
Chancel Ind Est
Darlaston WS10 ...... 41 D5
Kingswinford DY6 ...... 49 E1
Willenhall WV13 ...... 27 B2
Chancel Ind Est The WV1 ... 26 A1
Chancel Way Birmingham
B6 ...... 55 F5
Halesowen B62 ...... 83 C6
Chancellor's Cl B15 ...... 85 E8
Chancellors Cl CV4 ...... 132 D4
Chancery Ct CV10 ...... 72 A7
Chancery Dr WS12 ...... 2 C1
Chancery La CV10 ...... 72 B7
Chancery Way DY5 ...... 61 F2
Chanders Rd CV34 ...... 155 D1
Chandler Dr WV4 ...... 38 D3
Chandler Ho B65 ...... 63 D4
Chandlers Cl Redditch B97 .. 158 D7
Wolverhampton WV9 ...... 11 A1
Chandlers Dr B77 ...... 22 B5
Chandlers Keep WS8 ...... 16 A6
Chandlers Rd CV31 ...... 162 A2
Chandos Ave B13 ...... 86 F3
Chandos Ct ⑬ CV32 ...... 156 F1
Chandos Jun & Inf Sch
B12 ...... 86 E8
Chandos St Coventry CV2 ... 114 A3
Nuneaton CV11 ...... 73 A4
Royal Leamington Spa CV32 . 156 F1
Change Brook Cl CV11 ...... 73 F8
Channon Dr DY5 ...... 81 D8
Chanston Ave B14 ...... 104 E4
Chanterelle Gdns WV4 ...... 39 B4
Chantrey Cres Bilston
WV14 ...... 40 F7
Birmingham B43 ...... 44 D4
Chantries The CV1 ...... 113 E5
Chantry Ave WS3 ...... 28 D8
Chantry Cl B47 ...... 125 A7
Chantry Dr B62 ...... 84 A6
Chantry Heath Cres B93 ... 128 C7
Chantry Rd
Birmingham,
Handsworth B21 ...... 65 E8
Birmingham, Moseley B13 ... 86 E4
Stourbridge DY7 ...... 80 C7
Chantry The CV34 ...... 156 A1
Chapel Ash WV3 ...... 25 B2
Chapel Ash Island WV1 ...... 163 A3
Chapel Ave WS8 ...... 6 F2
Chapel Cl B64 ...... 83 B8
Chapel Ct Astwood Bank
B96 ...... 158 E1
Brierley Hill, Barrow Hill
DY5 ...... 61 C7
④ Brierley Hill,
Silver End DY5 ...... 61 D2
Chapel Dr
Balsall Common CV7 ...... 130 B8
Brownhills WS8 ...... 6 E2
Wythall B47 ...... 124 F3
Chapel Fields Jun Sch
B92 ...... 88 F3
Chapel Fields Rd B92 ...... 88 F2
Chapel Gn WV13 ...... 27 B2
Chapel House La B62 ...... 82 C6
Chapel House St ① B12 ...... 66 F1
Chapel La Barnacle CV7 ...... 97 B6
Belbroughton DY9 ...... 120 D7
Beoley B98 ...... 154 F8
Birmingham,
Great Barr WS9 ...... 44 A5
Birmingham, Selly Oak B29 ... 85 E2
Lapworth B94 ...... 144 D7
Lichfield WS14 ...... 9 B6
Romsley B62 ...... 100 C6
Rowney Green B48 ...... 139 D4
Ryton-on-D CV8 ...... 135 B2
Walsall B43 ...... 43 F4
Wythall B47 ...... 124 F2
Chapel Rd B96 ...... 158 D1
Chapel Row CV34 ...... 160 D6
Chapel Sq WS6 ...... 4 D3

Chapel St Astwood Bank
B96 ...... 158 E1
Bedworth CV12 ...... 78 C3
Bilston WV14 ...... 40 F4
Birmingham B5 ...... 164 D3
Birmingham,
Handsworth B21 ...... 65 D7
Brierley Hill,
Barrow Hill DY5 ...... 61 C6
Brierley Hill,
Quarry Bank DY5 ...... 61 F1
Brierley Hill,
Silver End DY5 ...... 61 D2
Bromsgrove B60 ...... 137 A2
Brownhills WS8 ...... 6 E2
Burntwood WS7 ...... 6 E8
Cannock WS12 ...... 2 E1
Coventry CV1 ...... 165 B3
Dudley DY2 ...... 62 D4
Hagley DY9 ...... 99 A5
Halesowen B63 ...... 83 A3
Kidderminster DY11 ...... 116 D6
Kingswinford DY6 ...... 60 B8
Norton Canes WS11 ...... 5 F5
Nuneaton CV11 ...... 73 C4
Oldbury B69 ...... 63 F7
Redditch B97 ...... 153 D1
③ Royal Leamington Spa
CV31 ...... 162 A7
Stourbridge, Lye DY9 ...... 81 E5
Stourbridge, Wollaston DY8 .. 81 A4
Stourbridge, Wordsley DY8 .. 60 D3
Tipton DY4 ...... 51 E5
Walsall,
Blakenall Heath WS3 ...... 28 D8
Walsall, Pelsall WS3 ...... 15 A3
Warwick CV34 ...... 160 E7
Wednesbury WS10 ...... 41 E3
West Bromwich B70 ...... 53 B5
Wolverhampton WV2 ...... 39 D7
Chapel View B67 ...... 64 F4
Chapel Wlk Birmingham
B30 ...... 104 A2
Bromsgrove B60 ...... 137 A2
Dudley DY3 ...... 50 C2
Chapelfield Rd B45 ...... 122 A7
Chapelhouse Rd B37 ...... 69 F1
Chapelon B77 ...... 22 A2
Chapelwood Gr B42 ...... 55 D5
Chaplain Rd WS12 ...... 2 E2
Chapman Cl CV31 ...... 162 E5
Chapman Ct CV34 ...... 161 C8
Chapman Rd B10 ...... 87 C8
Chapman St B70 ...... 53 B3
Chapman's Hill B62 ...... 101 B1
Chapmans Pas B1 ...... 164 B1
Chapter Ho B70 ...... 53 A5
Chard Rd CV3 ...... 134 D8
Charfield Cl B30 ...... 103 D7
Charford Fst Sch B60 ...... 150 F7
Charford Rd B60 ...... 150 F8
Charingworth Rd B92 ...... 89 C3
Charity Rd CV7 ...... 95 A7
Charlbury Ave B37 ...... 69 F2
Charlbury Cres B26 ...... 88 F8
Charlbury Tower ② B5 ...... 86 E8
Charlecote Cl B98 ...... 154 D2
Charlecote Croft B90 ...... 126 C8
Charlecote Dr
Birmingham B23 ...... 56 E7
Dudley DY1 ...... 50 E3
Charlecote Gdns
Royal Leamington Spa
CV31 ...... 162 D5
Sutton Coldfield B73 ...... 57 A8
Charlecote Rd CV6 ...... 95 A2
Charlecote Rise ① WV13 .... 40 F8
Charlecote Tower ④ B15 .... 66 C1
Charlecote Wlk CV11 ...... 78 F8
Charlecott Cl B13 ...... 105 D3
Charlemont Ave B71 ...... 53 E8
Charlemont Cl WS5 ...... 43 C6
Charlemont Cres B71 ...... 42 E1
Charlemont Gdns WS5 ...... 43 C6
Charlemont Prim Sch B71 .. 53 E8
Charlemont Rd Walsall
WS5 ...... 43 C6
West Bromwich B71 ...... 53 F8
Charlemonte Cl WS12 ...... 2 D3
Charles Ave Blackheath B65 .. 63 C4
Essington WV11 ...... 12 F4
Wolverhampton WV4 ...... 39 B5
Charles Burns Rd B13 ...... 86 E1
Charles Cl Birmingham B8 ... 67 D4
Cheslyn Hay WS6 ...... 4 D1
Charles Cres WS3 ...... 15 A5
Charles Ct
⑧ Birmingham B13 ...... 87 B2
Sutton Coldfield B76 ...... 46 F3
Warwick CV34 ...... 161 B8
Charles Dr B7 ...... 67 B6
Charles Eaton Rd CV12 ...... 77 F3
Charles Edward Rd B26 ...... 88 D6
Charles Foster St WS10 ...... 41 C6
Charles Gardner Rd
⑥ CV31 ...... 161 F6
Charles Hayward Bglws
WV4 ...... 39 D3
Charles Henry St B12 ...... 86 F8
Charles Holland St WV13 ... 27 B2
Charles Lakin Cl CV7 ...... 97 C5
Charles Lane Trust Homes
The B28 ...... 106 A8
Charles Pearson Ct B66 ...... 65 B5

Charles Rd
Birmingham, Aston B6 .... 56 A1
Birmingham,
Bordesley Green B9, B10 ... 67 E1
Birmingham,
Handsworth B20 .... 55 C1
Brierley Hill DY5 .... 62 B1
Halesowen B63 .... 82 F4
Solihull B91 .... 106 E2
Stourbridge DY8 .... 80 E4
Tipton DY4 .... 52 A7
Charles St Coventry CV1 ... 165 D4
Hinckley LE10 .... 71 E1
Kidderminster DY10 .... 116 F6
Nuneaton CV11 .... 73 A5
Redditch B97 .... 153 C1
Smethwick B66 .... 65 C7
Walsall WS2 .... 28 D2
Warwick CV34 .... 161 A8
West Bromwich B70 .... 52 E5
Willenhall WV13 .... 27 C3
Charles The W6 .... 25 B5
Charles Wlk B65 .... 63 C5
Charlesdale Dr WS9 .... 30 B4
Charleville Rd B19 .... 66 B7
Charlewood Rd CV6 .... 95 B2
Charlock Gr WS11 .... 2 C3
Charlotte Cl B69 .... 52 A2
Charlotte Rd
Birmingham, Edgbaston B15 .. 86 C7
Birmingham, Stirchley B30 .. 104 A6
Tipton DY4 .... 41 C2
Charlotte St Birmingham
B3 .... 164 A3
14 Dudley DY1 .... 51 B1
Royal Leamington Spa CV31 . 161 F6
Walsall WS1 .... 29 A2
Charlton Dr B64 .... 82 D7
Charlton Pl B8 .... 67 D5
Charlton Rd B44 .... 56 A8
Charlton St Brierley Hill DY5 .. 61 A3
4 Dudley DY1 .... 51 B1
Charminster Ave B25 ...... 88 D8
Charminster Dr CV3 .... 133 D4
Charnley Dr B75 .... 32 E2
Charnwood Ave
Nuneaton CV10 .... 72 E2
Sedgley DY3 .... 39 D2
Charnwood Bsns Pk WV14 .. 40 C5
Charnwood Cl Bilston WV14 .. 41 B3
Birmingham B45 .... 102 B3
Brierley Hill DY5 .... 81 B8
Cannock WS12 .... 2 C3
Hinckley LE10 .... 71 E2
Lichfield WS13 .... 3 C1
Charnwood Ct DY9 .... 81 E2
Charnwood Ho WS13 .... 3 B2
Charnwood Prim Sch WS13 . 3 C2
Charnwood Rd
Birmingham B42 .... 54 F7
Hinckley LE10 .... 71 D2
Walsall WS5 .... 43 A4
Charnwood Way CV32 ..... 157 C3
Charter App CV34 .... 160 D5
Charter Ave CV4 .... 132 B7
Charter Cl WS11 .... 5 E4
Charter Cres B64 .... 83 B8
Charter Ho CV4 .... 132 A7
Charter House Dr B91 ..... 107 C1
Charter Rd DY4 .... 41 C1
Charter St DY5 .... 61 E5
Charterfield Dr Cannock
WS12 .... 2 C1
Kingswinford DY6 .... 60 D8
Charterfield Sh Ctr 3 DY6 . 60 D8
Charterhouse Dr B91 ...... 107 C1
Charterhouse Rd CV1 ...... 113 E2
Charters Ave WV8 .... 10 B1
Charters The WS13 .... 3 B1
Chartist Rd B8 .... 67 D6
Chartley Cl Dorridge B93 .. 127 E3
Perton WV6 .... 23 F4
Chartley Rd Birmingham B23 .. 56 D1
West Bromwich B71 .... 53 D6
Chartway The WS3 .... 15 B4
Chartwell DY3 .... 20 D7
Chartwell Cl Dudley DY1 ... 51 B6
Nuneaton CV11 .... 73 F1
Chartwell Ct B72 .... 57 C8
Chartwell Dr
Cheswick Green B90 .... 126 D5
Sutton Coldfield B74 .... 31 D4
Wolverhampton WV10 ..... 11 C1
Chartwell Grange B64 ..... 83 A7
Chase Ave WS6 .... 4 E3
Chase Cl CV11 .... 73 E6
Chase Gr B24 .... 57 D6
Chase L Ctr WS11 .... 1 D2
Chase La CV8 .... 147 B7
Chase Park Ind Est WS7 ... 6 D7
Chase Rd Brierley Hill DY5 .. 50 C1
Brownhills WS8 .... 7 A1
Burntwood WS7 .... 7 B6
Walsall WS3 .... 28 A8
Chase Terrace High Sch
WS7 .... 7 A7
**Chase Terrace HighSch
(Annexe)** WS7 .... 6 F8
Chase Terrace Prim Sch WS7 6 F8
Chase The
Sutton Coldfield B76 .... 57 D7
Wolverhampton WV6 .... 25 B6
Chase Vale WS7 .... 6 E6
Chase View WV4 .... 39 E2

Chase Wlk WS12 .... 1 C4
Chaselands WS7 .... 6 D7
Chaseley Ave WS11 .... 1 C2
Chaseley Croft WS11 .... 1 C2
Chaseley Gdns WS7 .... 7 C7
Chaseside Dr WS11 .... 2 B3
Chaseside Ind Est WS11 ... 2 B3
Chasetown High Sch WS7 . 6 E4
Chasetown Ind Est WS7 ... 6 E6
Chasetown Prim Sch WS7 . 6 E5
Chasewater Light Rlwy
WS8 .... 6 C3
Chasewater Raceway WS8 . 6 C7
Chasewater Way WS11 .... 5 F5
Chasewood Park Bsns Ctr
WS12 .... 2 E1
Chater Dr B76 .... 47 A1
Chatham Cl CV3 .... 134 C8
Chatham Rd B31 .... 103 A3
Chatsworth B79 .... 20 C7
Chatsworth Ave B43 .... 43 C1
Chatsworth Cl
Cheswick Green B90 .... 126 E5
Hinckley LE10 .... 75 F6
Sutton Coldfield B72 .... 57 D7
Willenhall WV12 .... 27 B5
Chatsworth Cres WS4 ..... 29 D7
Chatsworth Dr Cannock
WS11 .... 2 A4
Nuneaton CV11 .... 73 F2
Chatsworth Gdns WV6 ..... 24 A7
Chatsworth Gr
Kenilworth CV8 .... 148 C5
Royal Leamington Spa CV31 . 162 D6
Chatsworth Rd B62 .... 83 A7
Chatsworth Rise CV3 ...... 133 E6
Chatsworth Tower 7 B15 . 86 C8
Chattaway Dr CV7 .... 130 B6
Chattaway St B7 .... 67 C7
Chatterton Wlk 4 DY10 ... 117 B6
Chattle Hill B46 .... 59 E2
Chattock Ave B91 .... 107 E3
Chattock Cl B36 .... 68 E7
Chatwell Gr B29 .... 85 B2
Chatwin Pl WV14 .... 40 E3
Chatwin St B66 .... 64 F7
Chatwins Wharf DY4 .... 51 F5
Chaucer Ave Dudley DY3 .. 50 A5
Tipton DY4 .... 52 B8
Willenhall WV12 .... 27 E8
Chaucer Cl Birmingham B23 . 56 B3
Dudley WV14 .... 51 D8
Lichfield WS13 .... 9 B6
Stourbridge DY8 .... 81 A8
Tamworth B79 .... 21 A6
Chaucer Cres DY10 .... 117 C5
Chaucer Dr CV10 .... 72 A4
Chaucer Gr B27 .... 88 B2
Chaucer Ho B63 .... 82 B5
Chaucer Rd Bromsgrove
B60 .... 151 B8
Walsall WS3 .... 28 E8
Chauntry Pl CV1 .... 165 C3
Chauson Gr B91 .... 127 A8
Chavasse Rd B72 .... 46 D3
Chawn Hill DY9 .... 81 C3
Chawn Park Dr DY9 .... 81 C3
Chawnhill Ct DY9 .... 81 C3
Chaynes Gr B33 .... 69 D2
Cheadle Cl CV2 .... 96 A4
Cheadle Dr B23 .... 56 D8
Cheam Cl CV6 .... 96 A1
Cheam Gdns WV6 .... 24 E8
Cheapside
Birmingham B5, B12 .... 164 D1
3 Willenhall WV13 .... 27 A1
Wolverhampton WV1 .... 163 B3
Cheapside Ind Est 3 B12 . 66 F1
Cheatham St B7 .... 67 C6
Cheatle Ct B77 .... 35 D5
Checketts St WS2 .... 28 C2
Checkley Croft B76 .... 57 F8
Cheddar Rd B12 .... 86 E6
Chedworth Cl
Birmingham B29 .... 103 B6
Redditch B98 .... 154 C5
Cheedon Cl B93 .... 127 E2
Chelford Cres DY6 .... 61 A3
Chells Gr B13 .... 105 B5
Chelmar Cl B36 .... 69 F8
Chelmar Dr DY5 .... 61 A6
Chelmarsh Ave WV3 .... 38 B8
Chelmarsh Cl B98 .... 154 C7
Chelmorton Rd B42 .... 55 D7
Chelmscote Rd B92 .... 88 F1
Chelmsley Ave B46 .... 70 F6
Chelmsley Circ B37 .... 70 B3
Chelmsley Gr B33 .... 69 E3
Chelmsley La B37 .... 90 A8
Chelmsley Rd B37 .... 70 C2
Chelney Wlk CV3 .... 115 A1
Chelsea Cl Birmingham B32 . 84 F4
Nuneaton CV11 .... 73 F7
Chelsea Ct B29 .... 103 B7
Chelsea Dr B74 .... 31 F4
Chelsea Trad Est B7 .... 67 A6
Chelsea Way B74 .... 60 C6
Chelsey Rd CV2 .... 114 E8
Chelston Dr WV6 .... 24 E4
Chelston Rd B31 .... 102 E2
Cheltenham Cl
Bedworth CV12 .... 78 B4
Wolverhampton W6 .... 25 B5
Cheltenham Croft CV2 .... 114 F7
Cheltenham Dr
Birmingham B36 .... 68 D8
Kingswinford DY6 .... 60 B6
Chelthorn Way B91 .... 107 C2

Cheltondale 3 B90 .... 126 C8
Cheltondale Rd B91 .... 106 F6
Chelveston Cres B91 .... 107 B1
Chelveston Rd CV6 .... 112 E5
Chelwood Gdns WV14 ..... 40 B5
Chelwood Gr CV2 .... 96 F1
Chelworth Rd B38 .... 104 B2
Chem Rd WV14 .... 40 C5
Chenies Cl CV5 .... 112 B3
Cheniston Rd WV12 .... 27 C7
Chepstow Cl Coventry CV3 . 134 C5
Perton WV6 .... 23 F4
Chepstow Gr B45 .... 122 B6
Chepstow Rd Walsall WS3 . 13 F1
Wolverhampton WV10 ..... 11 D5
Chepstow Villas 5 B12 .... 87 B5
Chepstow Way WS3 .... 13 F1
Chequer St Bulkington CV12 . 79 C2
Wolverhampton WV3 .... 39 A6
Chequerfield Dr WV3 ...... 39 A6
Chequers Ave WV5 .... 38 A1
Chequers Ct WS11 .... 6 A5
Chequers The 1 WS13 .... 9 C8
Cherhill Covert 7 B14 ..... 104 C2
Cherington Cl B98 .... 154 F1
Cherington Rd B29 .... 104 A8
Cheriton Cl CV5 .... 112 D4
Cheriton Gr WV6 .... 23 E3
Cheriton Wlk B23 .... 56 B3
Cherrington Dr WS6 .... 4 F4
Cherrington Gdns
Stourbridge DY9 .... 99 C7
Wolverhampton WV6 .... 24 B2
Cherrington Way B91 ...... 107 B1
Cherry Bank WS12 .... 2 C6
Cherry Blossom Gr CV31 .. 162 B2
Cherry Cl Burntwood WS7 . 6 F6
Coventry CV6 .... 95 D2
Cherry Cres B61 .... 136 E2
Cherry Dr Birmingham B9 . 67 B1
1 Blackheath B64 .... 62 F1
Cherry Gn DY1 .... 50 F4
Cherry Gr Smethwick B66 . 65 C5
Stourbridge DY8 .... 80 E4
Wolverhampton WV11 ..... 26 C7
Cherry Hill Ave B45 .... 138 C8
Cherry Hill Dr B45 .... 138 C8
Cherry Hill Rd B45 .... 138 C8
Cherry Hill Wlk DY1 .... 62 A8
Cherry La Himley DY3 ..... 49 C3
Sutton Coldfield B73 .... 57 A7
Wednesbury WS10 .... 42 A2
Cherry Lea B34 .... 69 B6
Cherry Oak Sch B29 .... 85 D2
Cherry Orch Blackheath B64 . 62 F1
Kenilworth CV8 .... 148 A5
Kidderminster DY10 .... 116 F6
Lichfield WS14 .... 9 C7
Cherry Orchard Ave B63 .. 82 F5
Cherry Orchard Cres B63 . 82 F6
Cherry Orchard Dr B61 ... 136 E3
Cherry Orchard Prim Sch
B20 .... 55 A3
Cherry Orchard Rd B20 ... 55 A4
Cherry Pit La B98 .... 141 A1
Cherry Rd DY4 .... 51 F7
Cherry St Birmingham B2 . 164 C2
Halesowen B63 .... 82 F5
Stourbridge DY8 .... 80 E4
Tamworth B79 .... 21 B5
Warwick CV34 .... 160 F7
Wolverhampton WV3 .... 25 B1
Cherry Tree Ave
Nuneaton CV10 .... 72 E6
Walsall WS5 .... 43 A5
Cherry Tree Croft 6 B27 . 88 C5
Cherry Tree Gdns WV8 .... 10 B3
Cherry Tree La Codsall WV8 . 10 B3
Halesowen B63 .... 82 D1
Cherry Tree Rd
Huntington WS12 .... 1 D8
Kingswinford DY6 .... 60 E8
Norton Canes WS11 .... 6 B5
Cherry Tree Wlk
Redditch B97 .... 153 B4
Tamworth B79 .... 21 A8
Cherry Way CV8 .... 148 A5
Cherry Wlk B47 .... 125 B5
Cherrybrook Way CV2 ..... 96 C1
Cherryl Ho B74 .... 31 E2
Cherrytree Ct DY9 .... 81 E3
Cherrywood Cres 3 B91 .. 127 C8
Cherrywood Ct B92 .... 89 A2
Cherrywood Gn WV14 ..... 40 D8
Cherrywood Gr CV5 .... 111 F5
Cherrywood Ind Est B9 ... 67 D3
Cherrywood Rd
Birmingham B9 .... 67 E2
Sutton Coldfield B74 .... 44 D8
Cherrywood Way B74 ..... 31 D4
Chervil Cl B42 .... 55 C7
Chervil Rise WV10 .... 25 F3
Cherwell B77 .... 21 D1
Cherwell Cl LE10 .... 75 A8
Cherwell Ct B73 .... 46 B5
Cherwell Dr Birmingham
B36 .... 69 F8
Brownhills WS8 .... 6 C2
Cherwell Gdns 7 B6 .... 66 D6
Chesford Cres Coventry CV6 . 96 B2
Warwick CV34 .... 156 B1
Chesham St CV31 .... 162 B1
Cheshire Ave B90 .... 106 A2
Cheshire Cl DY8 .... 80 D8
Cheshire Gr
Kidderminster DY11 .... 116 A7
Perton WV6 .... 23 E4
Cheshire Ho 8 B66 .... 65 B5

Cheshire Rd Birmingham B6 . 56 A2
Smethwick B67 .... 65 A4
Walsall WS2 .... 27 F2
Chesholme Rd CV6 .... 95 B2
Cheshunt Ho 3 B37 .... 70 B2
Chesils The CV3 .... 133 D6
Cheslyn Dr WS6 .... 4 D2
Cheslyn Gr B14 .... 105 A3
Cheslyn Hay Cty Prim Sch
WS6 .... 4 C3
Cheslyn Hay High Sch WS6 . 4 C3
Chessetts Gr B13 .... 105 A6
Chessetts Wood Rd B94 .. 144 C7
Chesshyre St LE10 .... 71 C1
Chester Ave WV6 .... 24 F7
Chester Cl Birmingham B37 . 70 A2
Cannock WS11 .... 2 B1
Lichfield WS13 .... 3 C3
Willenhall WV13 .... 27 D2
Chester Ct 4 B37 .... 70 D2
Chester Hayes Ct B24 .... 57 C5
Chester Pl WS2 .... 28 B1
Chester Rd Aldridge WS9 . 30 E4
Birmingham,
Castle Bromwich B36 ...... 69 E7
Birmingham,
Chelmsley Wood B37 ...... 90 F8
Blackheath B64 .... 82 C8
Dudley DY2 .... 62 E3
Hampton In A B46, B92, CV7 . 91 B5
Stonnall WS9 .... 16 D3
Sutton Coldfield
B24, B35, B23, B73 .... 57 E4
West Bromwich B71 .... 42 B1
Chester Rd N
Birmingham B73 .... 45 B4
Brownhills WS8 .... 6 D1
Kidderminster DY10 .... 117 A7
Chester Rd S DY10 .... 116 F4
Chester Rise B68 .... 84 B8
Chester Road Sta B37 .... 57 A7
Chester St Birmingham B6 . 67 A6
Coventry CV1 .... 113 B3
Wolverhampton WV6 .... 25 B4
Chesterfield Cl B31 .... 103 B3
Chesterfield Ct B38 .... 103 E4
Chesterfield Rd WS14 ..... 9 A5
Chestergate Croft B24 .... 57 D4
Chesterton Ave B12 .... 87 B5
Chesterton Cl Redditch
B97 .... 158 D4
Solihull B91 .... 106 E5
Chesterton Ct B13 .... 86 F1
Chesterton Dr
Nuneaton CV10 .... 72 A5
Royal Leamington Spa CV31 . 162 C5
Chesterton Rd
Birmingham B12 .... 87 B5
Coventry CV6 .... 113 A7
Wolverhampton WV10 ..... 26 A8
Chesterton Way B79 ...... 21 A6
Chesterwood Aldridge WS9 . 30 F2
Hollywood B47 .... 125 A6
Chesterwood Gdns B20 ... 55 D2
Chesterwood Rd B13 ...... 104 F6
Chestnut Ave Dudley DY1 . 51 C3
Kenilworth CV8 .... 147 F3
Tamworth B79 .... 21 B7
Tipton DY4 .... 51 F7
Chestnut Cl Aldridge B74 . 31 A3
Birmingham B27 .... 88 C4
Cannock WS11 .... 2 C2
Solihull B92 .... 106 D8
Stourbridge DY8 .... 80 C3
Chestnut Cres CV10 .... 72 E5
Chestnut Ct Birmingham B36 . 69 E7
Coventry CV3 .... 134 B8
Royal Leamington Spa CV34 . 161 E2
Chestnut Dr
Birmingham,
Buckland End B36 .... 69 B7
Birmingham, Erdington B24 . 57 C4
Birmingham, Rednal B45 ... 122 D4
Cheslyn Hay WS6 .... 4 D3
Great Wyrley WS6 .... 4 F3
Nuneaton CV11 .... 73 E3
Shenstone WS14 .... 17 F5
Walsall WS4 .... 29 B8
Wombourne WV5 .... 49 A5
Chestnut Gr Birmingham
B17 .... 85 D5
Coventry CV4 .... 112 A2
Kidderminster DY11 .... 116 B8
Kingswinford DY6 .... 60 F6
Tamworth B77 .... 21 C3
Wolverhampton WV11 ..... 26 D7
Chestnut Pl Birmingham
B14 .... 104 E8
Walsall WS3 .... 28 D6
Chestnut Rd
Astwood Bank B96 .... 158 E1
Bedworth CV12 .... 78 D4
Birmingham B13 .... 87 A4
Bromsgrove B61 .... 136 F4
Oldbury B68 .... 84 C7
Walsall WS3 .... 28 E6
Wednesbury WS10 .... 42 A2
Chestnut Sq CV32 .... 157 B2
Chestnut Tree Ave CV4 ... 112 A2
Chestnut Way WV3 .... 38 D8
Chestnut Wlk 2 B37 .... 70 B2
Chestnuts Ave B26 .... 89 B7
Chestnuts The
Bedworth CV12 .... 77 C2
Wolverhampton WV11 ..... 26 B6
Chestom Rd WV14 .... 40 B5
Cheston Ind Est B7 .... 67 B7
Cheston Rd B7 .... 67 B6

Cheswell Cl WV6 .... 24 B1
Cheswick Cl Coventry CV6 . 114 A7
Willenhall WV13 .... 40 F8
**Cheswick Green Jun &
Inf Sch** B94 .... 126 E4
Cheswick Way B90 .... 126 D4
Cheswood Dr B76 .... 58 B6
Chesworth Rd B60 .... 137 B1
Chetland Croft B92 .... 107 F2
Chettle Rd WV14 .... 40 F3
Chetton Gn WV10 .... 11 B3
Chetwode Cl CV5 .... 112 B4
Chetwood Cl WV6 .... 25 A5
Chetwynd Cl WS2 .... 27 D3
Chetwynd Dr CV11 .... 79 B7
Chetwynd Gdns WS11 .... 1 D3
Chetwynd Mid Sch CV11 . 79 B8
Chetwynd Rd Birmingham
B8 .... 68 B5
Wolverhampton WV2 ...... 39 B6
Cheveley Ave B45 .... 122 B7
Chevening Cl DY3 .... 50 E7
Cheveral Ave CV6 .... 113 B6
Cheveral Rd CV12 .... 78 A3
Cheverel Pl CV11 .... 73 B2
Cheverel St CV11 .... 73 B3
Cheveridge Cl B91 .... 107 A2
Cheverton Rd B31 .... 102 F4
Cheviot B77 .... 22 C2
Cheviot Cl CV10 .... 72 B3
Cheviot Ct B75 .... 32 A4
Cheviot Rd Stourbridge DY8 . 81 A6
Wolverhampton WV2 ...... 39 F7
Cheviot Rise Cannock WS12 . 2 C5
Cheviot Rd N
Royal Leamington Spa
CV32 .... 157 C3
Cheviot Way B63 .... 82 D2
Cheylesmore CV1 .... 165 B2
Cheylesmore Cl B73 .... 46 B4
Cheyne Ct B17 .... 85 D5
Cheyne Gdns B28 .... 105 E3
Cheyne Wlk DY5 .... 81 C7
Cheyney Cl WV6 .... 25 A5
**Cheywynd House Prep
Sch** B74 .... 31 F2
Chichester Ave DY2 .... 62 D5
Chichester Cl CV11 .... 74 A7
Chichester Ct B73 .... 46 B5
Chichester Dr
Birmingham B32 .... 84 A5
Cannock WS12 .... 2 C1
Chichester Gr B37 .... 70 B1
Chideock Hill CV3 .... 133 B6
Chiel Cl CV5 .... 111 F4
Chigwell Cl B35 .... 58 A3
Chilcote Cl B28 .... 105 F4
**Chilcote Inf &
Jun Sch** B28 .... 105 F4
Childs Ave WV14 .... 40 A2
Childs Oak Cl CV7 .... 130 A6
Chilgrove Gdns WV6 ...... 24 C5
Chilham Dr B37 .... 70 C2
Chillaton Rd CV6 .... 95 B2
Chillenden Ct WV13 .... 27 C2
Chillingham B77 .... 35 C7
Chillinghome Rd B36 ...... 68 D8
**Chillinghome Tower
1** B36 .... 57 F1
Chillington Cl WS6 .... 4 F1
Chillington Dr Codsall WV8 . 10 A4
Dudley DY1 .... 50 F3
Chillington Fields WV1 .... 26 A1
Chillington Ho WV6 .... 24 E5
Chillington Pl WV14 .... 40 C5
Chillington Rd DY4 .... 41 C1
Chillington St WV1 .... 25 F1
Chillington Wlk B65 .... 63 D3
Chillington Works Ind Est
WV1 .... 25 F1
Chiltern Cl Dudley DY3 .... 50 D3
Halesowen B63 .... 82 D1
Chiltern Ct 2 Coventry
CV5 .... 113 A5
Sutton Coldfield B75 .... 32 A4
Chiltern Dr WV13 .... 26 F2
Chiltern Ho Coventry CV5 . 111 D4
Redditch B98 .... 154 E1
Chiltern Leys 2 CV6 .... 113 A4
Chiltern Rd Stourbridge DY8 . 81 B6
Tamworth B77 .... 22 C1
Chilterns The Coventry
CV5 .... 112 B4
Oldbury B69 .... 63 E5
Chilton Ct B23 .... 56 C2
Chilton Rd B14 .... 105 D4
Chilvers Coton Craft Ctr
CV11 .... 73 C2
**Chilvers Coton Fst
Sch** CV11 .... 73 B3
Chilvers Ct CV11 .... 73 C4
Chilvers Gr B37 .... 69 F5
Chilwell Cl B91 .... 107 B1
Chilwell Croft B19 .... 66 E6
Chilworth Ave WV11 ...... 26 F7
Chilworth Cl 4
Birmingham B6 .... 66 F6
Nuneaton CV11 .... 78 E8
Chimes Cl B33 .... 69 E1
Chimney Rd DY4 .... 52 D6
Chines The CV10 .... 73 D7
Chingford Cl DY8 .... 60 C4
Chingford Rd
Birmingham B44 .... 56 A8
Coventry CV6 .... 96 A4
Chinley Gr B44 .... 45 C1
Chinn Brook Rd B13 .... 105 C5
Chip Cl B38 .... 103 D2
Chipperfield Rd B36 .... 68 E8

Chipstead Rd B23 .... 56 E7
Chipstead Cl B91 .... 107 C1
Chirbury Gr B31 .... 103 B1
Chirk Cl DY10 .... 116 E2
Chiseldon Croft B14 .... 105 A3
Chisholm Gr B27 .... 106 C8
Chiswell Rd B18 .... 65 E4
Chiswick Ct 1 B23 .... 56 E2
Chiswick Ho 2 B15 .... 86 C8
Chiswick Wlk B37 .... 70 E2
Chivenor Ho B35 .... 58 A2
Chivenor Prim Sch B35 ... 58 A2
Chivington Cl B90 .... 127 B6
Chorley Ave B34 .... 68 F6
Chorley Gdns WV14 .... 40 B5
Christ Church CE Inf Sch
  Wolverhampton,
  Dunstall Hill WV6 .... 25 B4
  Wolverhampton,
  Tettenhall Wood WV6 .... 24 B3
Christ Church CE Jun Sch
  WV6 .... 24 C4
Christ Church CE Prim Sch
  Dudley WV14 .... 40 D1
  Lichfield WS13 .... 8 F7
  Oldbury B69 .... 64 A8
  Walsall WS3 .... 28 D7
Christ Church Gdns WS13 ... 8 F7
Christ Church Gr WS1 .... 43 A7
Christ Church Jun & Inf
  Sch B11 .... 87 B7
Christ the King RC Inf
  Sch CV6 .... 112 F6
Christ the King RC Jun
  Sch CV6 .... 112 F7
Christ The King RC Prim
  Sch B44 .... 56 A8
Christchurch Cl B15 .... 85 E8
Christchurch La WS13 .... 8 F7
Christchurch Rd CV6 .... 113 A5
Christine Cl DY4 .... 41 C2
Christine Ledger Sq
  9 CV31 .... 162 A6
Christopher Hooke Ho
  CV6 .... 113 E8
Christopher Rd
  Birmingham B29 .... 85 C2
  Halesowen B62 .... 83 E3
  Wolverhampton WV2 .... 163 D1
Christopher Wlk WS13 .... 3 A3
Chub B77 .... 35 D7
Chubb St WV1 .... 163 C3
Chuckery Jun & Inf Schs
  WS1 .... 29 A1
Chuckery Rd WS1 .... 29 A1
Chudleigh Gr B43 .... 54 D8
Chudleigh Rd
  Birmingham B23 .... 56 E4
  Coventry CV2 .... 114 E7
Church Ave
  Birmingham,
  Handsworth B20 .... 55 C1
  Birmingham, Moseley B13 ... 86 F3
  Clent DY9 .... 99 F3
  Stourbridge DY8 .... 81 A7
  Water Orton B46 .... 59 B3
Church Cl Birmingham B37 ... 70 A6
  Drayton Bassett B78 .... 34 E5
  Hinckley LE10 .... 76 A5
  Nuneaton CV10 .... 72 B8
  Shenstone WS14 .... 18 A5
  Whitnash CV31 .... 162 B4
  Wood End CV9 .... 36 C1
  Wythall B47 .... 124 F3
Church Cres WV11 .... 12 F3
Church Croft Birmingham
  B17 .... 85 B4
  Halesowen B63 .... 83 A4
Church Cross View DY1 ... 61 D8
Church Ct
  Astwood Bank B96 .... 158 E2
  2 Blackheath B64 .... 62 E1
  Coventry CV6 .... 94 F1
  5 Stourbridge DY8 .... 81 A5
Church Down Cl B97 .... 158 D6
Church Dr Birmingham B30 ... 104 B7
  Hopwas B78 .... 20 B7
  Kenilworth CV8 .... 147 F5
Church End CV11 .... 162 E6
Church Farm Barn & Cotts
  DY10 .... 98 B3
Church Gdns Smethwick B67 65 A4
  Wolverhampton WV10 .... 26 A4
Church Gn Bilston WV14 ... 40 D8
  Birmingham B20 .... 55 A2
Church Gn E B98 .... 153 E4
Church Gn W B97 .... 153 E4
Church Gr B13 .... 105 C5
Church Hill
  Belbroughton DY9 .... 119 D6
  Beoley B98 .... 154 D8
  Birmingham,
  Frankley Green B32 .... 102 B6
  Birmingham,
  Northfield B31 .... 103 B3
  Brierley Hill DY5 .... 61 D2
  Cannock WS12 .... 2 D5
  Cubbington CV32 .... 157 E5
  Royal Leamington Spa
  CV32 .... 161 E8
  8 Walsall WS1 .... 28 F1
  6 Wednesbury WS10 .... 41 F3
  Wolverhampton WV4 .... 38 F4
Church Hill Cl B91 .... 107 C2
Church Hill Ct 1 WS10 ... 41 F3
Church Hill Dr WV6 .... 24 E5
Church Hill Mid Sch B98 ... 154 D6

Church Hill Rd
  Birmingham B20 .... 55 C1
  Solihull B91 .... 107 C3
  Wolverhampton WV6 .... 24 D5
Church Hill St B67 .... 64 F6
Church Hill Way B98 .... 154 D6
Church Ho Brierley Hill DY5 ... 61 C2
  Walsall WS2 .... 42 C7
Church La Ash Green CV7 ... 95 E7
  Aston Flamville LE10 .... 76 F1
  Berkswell B92 .... 110 C3
  Bickenhill B92 .... 90 E2
  Birmingham, Aston B6 .... 67 A8
  Birmingham,
  Handsworth B20 .... 55 A2
  Birmingham,
  Kitt's Green B33 .... 69 A4
  Bromsgrove B61 .... 136 F2
  Burntwood WS7 .... 7 D3
  Corley CV7 .... 94 B7
  Coventry, Middle Stoke CV2 ... 114 B3
  Coventry,
  Upper Eastern Green CV5 ... 111 C5
  Cubbington CV32 .... 157 E5
  Curdworth B76 .... 59 B6
  Halesowen B63 .... 83 B4
  Lapworth B94 .... 143 E3
  Meriden CV7 .... 110 E8
  Middleton B78 .... 34 C1
  Nuneaton CV10 .... 73 C7
  Royal Leamington Spa
  CV32 .... 157 A3
  Seisdon WV5 .... 37 B2
  Shuttington B79 .... 22 E7
  Stoneleigh CV8 .... 149 C6
  Stonnall WS9 .... 16 E4
  Tamworth B79 .... 21 B5
  West Bromwich B71 .... 53 C6
  Whitnash CV31 .... 162 B4
  Wishaw B76 .... 48 A2
  Wolverhampton WV2 .... 163 B2
Church Mews DY4 .... 51 E8
Church Moat Way 1 WS3 ... 28 B8
Church of the Ascension
  CE Prim Sch DY6 .... 60 C8
Church Park Cl CV6 .... 94 F1
Church Pl Birmingham B12 ... 86 F5
  Walsall WS3 .... 28 D8
Church Rd
  Astwood Bank B96 .... 158 E2
  Baginton CV8 .... 133 F2
  Belbroughton DY9 .... 119 D6
  Birmingham, Aston B6 .... 67 B7
  Birmingham, Edgbaston B15 ... 86 A7
  Birmingham, Erdington B24 ... 57 A4
  Birmingham, Moseley B13 ... 87 A3
  Birmingham,
  Northfield B31 .... 103 A4
  Birmingham, Perry Barr B42 ... 55 D5
  Birmingham, Sheldon B26 ... 89 C6
  Birmingham,
  South Yardley B25 .... 88 E8
  Birmingham, Stechford B33 ... 68 F2
  Blackheath B65 .... 63 C3
  Bromsgrove B61 .... 136 F2
  Brownhills WS8 .... 15 F7
  Burntwood WS7 .... 7 D7
  Catshill B61 .... 136 F8
  Dodford B61 .... 136 A7
  Dudley, Daisy Bank WV14 ... 40 D1
  Dudley, Netherton DY2 .... 62 C4
  Halesowen B63 .... 82 C7
  Huntington WS11 .... 1 A2
  Norton Canes WS11 .... 5 E4
  Nuneaton, Chapel End CV10 ... 72 B8
  Nuneaton, Stockingford CV10 ... 72 C3
  Perton WV6 .... 23 E4
  Redditch, St George's B97 ... 153 E4
  Redditch, Webheath B97 ... 152 F2
  Ryton-on-D CV8 .... 135 B2
  Shenstone WS14 .... 17 F5
  Shilton CV7 .... 97 E5
  Smethwick B67 .... 65 A4
  Solihull B90 .... 106 B2
  Stonnall WS9 .... 16 E3
  Stourbridge, Lye DY9 .... 81 E5
  Stourbridge,
  Old Swinford DY8 .... 81 B3
  Stourbridge, Wordsley DY8 ... 60 D2
  Sutton Coldfield,
  Erdington B73 .... 56 F8
  Sutton Coldfield, Maney B73 ... 46 B3
  Tamworth B77 .... 35 C4
  Walsall WS3 .... 15 A3
  Willenhall WV12 .... 27 D6
  Wolverhampton, Bradmore
  WV3 .... 38 F7
  Wolverhampton, Oxley WV10 . 11 C1
  Wolverhampton,
  Tettenhall WV6 .... 24 E5
  Wolverhampton,
  Tettenhall Wood WV6 .... 24 B3
  Wombourne WV5 .... 49 B7
Church Row B78 .... 34 B1
Church Sq 4 B69 .... 64 A7
Church St Bilston WV14 ... 40 D5
  Birmingham B3 .... 164 B3
  Birmingham, Lozells B19 ... 66 C7
  Blackheath B64 .... 62 E1
  Brierley Hill, Barrow Hill DY5 . 61 D7
  Brierley Hill,
  Quarry Bank DY5 .... 61 F1
  Brierley Hill, Silver End DY5 ... 61 C2
  Bromsgrove B61 .... 136 F2
  Bulkington CV12 .... 79 C2
  Burntwood WS7 .... 6 E5
  Cannock WS11 .... 1 E1
  Cannock, Bridgtown WS11 ... 4 D6

Church St continued
  Cannock, Chadsmoor WS11 ... 2 A4
  Clayhanger WS8 .... 15 E6
  Coventry CV1 .... 165 C4
  Darlaston WS10 .... 41 D6
  Darlaston, Moxley WS10 ... 41 C4
  Dudley, Gornalwood DY3 ... 50 D3
  Dudley, Kate's Hill DY2 ... 62 C8
  Hagley DY9 .... 99 A5
  Halesowen B63 .... 63 D1
  Hinckley LE10 .... 76 A5
  Kidderminster DY10 .... 116 E6
  Lichfield WS13 .... 9 C8
  Nuneaton CV11 .... 73 D4
  Oldbury B69 .... 64 A8
  Royal Leamington Spa
  CV31 .... 162 A7
  Stourbridge DY8 .... 81 A5
  Studley B80 .... 159 E3
  Tamworth B79 .... 21 B5
  Tipton DY4 .... 52 A2
  Walsall WS1 .... 28 F1
  Walsall,
  Blakenall Green WS3 .... 28 B8
  Warwick CV34 .... 160 E6
  West Bromwich B70 .... 53 C4
  Willenhall WV13 .... 27 B2
  Wolverhampton WV2 .... 163 B2
Church Terr
  Cubbington CV32 .... 157 E5
  Royal Leamington Spa
  CV31 .... 162 A7
  Sutton Coldfield B75 .... 32 C3
Church Vale Birmingham
  B20 .... 55 B1
  Norton Canes WS11 .... 5 E4
  West Bromwich B71 .... 53 D5
Church Vale Mews B71 ... 53 D5
Church View Aldridge WS9 ... 30 B6
  Birmingham B11 .... 87 C6
  Brownhills WS9 .... 15 F3
  Dudley DY3 .... 50 D3
  Tamworth B77 .... 35 F7
Church View Cl WS3 .... 28 D8
Church View Dr B64 .... 62 F1
Church Way Bedworth CV12 ... 78 B2
  Walsall WS4 .... 15 C2
Church Wlk Allesley CV5 ... 112 C6
  Birmingham B8 .... 68 A6
  Hinckley LE10 .... 75 D8
  Kidderminster DY11 .... 116 C6
  2 Royal Leamington Spa
  CV31 .... 161 F7
  Wolverhampton, Penn WV3 ... 38 F7
  Wolverhampton,
  Tettenhall WV6 .... 24 E5
Churchacre B23 .... 56 C8
Churchbridge B69 .... 63 F6
Churchdale Cl CV10 .... 72 C4
Churchdale Rd B44 .... 44 D3
Churchdown Ct B23 .... 56 C2
Churchfield Ave DY4 .... 51 F8
Churchfield Cl B7 .... 67 C6
Churchfield Ind Est DY2 ... 62 C8
Churchfield Rd WV10 .... 25 B8
Churchfield St DY2 .... 62 C8
Churchfields Birmingham
  B43 .... 44 D4
  Bromsgrove B61 .... 136 F3
  Kidderminster DY10 .... 116 E2
Churchfields Cl B61 .... 136 F3
Churchfields Gdns B61 ... 136 F3
Churchfields High Sch
  B71 .... 53 E6
Churchfields Rd
  Bromsgrove B61 .... 136 F3
  Wednesbury WS10 .... 42 A4
Churchill Ave Coventry CV6 113 E8
  Kenilworth CV8 .... 148 A6
Churchill & Blakedown
  Sta DY10 .... 98 C2
Churchill Cl B69 .... 52 C2
Churchill Dr Blackheath B65 ... 63 B2
  Stourbridge DY8 .... 81 A7
Churchill Gdns DY3 .... 50 C7
Churchill Ho 3 CV32 ... 161 F8
Churchill La DY10 .... 98 B3
Churchill Par B75 .... 47 A5
Churchill Pl B33 .... 69 B1
Churchill Rd Birmingham B9 . 67 F3
  Catshill B61 .... 121 A1
  Halesowen B63 .... 82 F2
  Shenstone WS14 .... 18 A5
  Sutton Coldfield B75 .... 47 A5
Churchill Sh Ctr 3 DY2 ... 51 D1
Churchill Wlk 5 DY4 .... 52 A8
Churchover Cl B76 .... 57 D6
Churchside Way WS9 .... 16 B2
Churchstone Cl B61 .... 136 F8
Churchward Cl DY8 .... 81 B6
Churchward Gr WV5 .... 49 A8
Churchwell Ct B63 .... 83 B2
Churchwell Gdns B71 .... 53 E6
Churchyard Rd DY4 .... 52 B5
Churn Hill Rd WS9 .... 30 B4
Churnet Gr WV6 .... 23 F4
Churston Cl WS3 .... 14 A3
Chylds Ct CV5 .... 112 A5
Cider Ave DY5 .... 81 E8
Cinder Bank DY2 .... 62 C6
Cinder Rd Burntwood WS7 ... 6 E7
  Dudley DY3 .... 50 B2
Cinder Way WS10 .... 41 E3

Cinquefoil Leasow DY4 ... 52 C6
Circle The Birmingham
  B17 .... 85 C6
  Nuneaton CV10 .... 72 E4
Circuit Cl WV13 .... 27 B3
Circular Rd B27 .... 88 C2
Circus Ave B37 .... 70 C2
Cirencester Cl B60 .... 137 B2
City Arc Birmingham B2 ... 164 C2
  Coventry CV1 .... 165 B2
  1 Lichfield WS13 .... 9 B7
City Est B64 .... 82 D8
City Hospl B18 .... 65 F4
City Rd Birmingham B16 ... 65 C2
  Tipton B69 .... 63 C8
City Road Prim Sch B16 ... 65 D3
City Tech Coll The B37 ... 70 A4
City Trad Est B16 .... 66 A3
City View B8 .... 67 D4
Civic Cl B1 .... 66 C2
Cladsworth Ho B97 .... 153 A4
Claerwen Gr B31 .... 102 E5
Claines Cres DY10 .... 117 B5
Claines Rd Birmingham
  B31 .... 103 C4
  Halesowen B63 .... 82 D5
Claire Ct B26 .... 89 C7
Clandon Cl B14 .... 104 C2
Clanfield Ave WV11 .... 26 F7
Clapgate Gdns WV14 .... 40 A3
Clapgate La
  Birmingham, Woodgate B32 ... 84 A2
  Birmingham,
  Woodgate Valley B32 ... 84 C2
Clapham Sq CV31 .... 162 B7
Clapham St CV31 .... 162 B6
Clapham Terr CV31 .... 162 B7
Clapham Terrace Com
  Prim Sch CV31 .... 162 B7
Clapton Gr B44 .... 45 B1
Clara St CV2 .... 114 A2
Clarage Ho B62 .... 83 D8
Clare Ave WV11 .... 12 F1
Clare Cl CV32 .... 157 C2
Clare Cres WV14 .... 39 F2
Clare Ct B90 .... 105 C2
Clare Dr B15 .... 85 F8
Clare Rd Walsall WS3 .... 29 A6
  Wolverhampton WV10 .... 25 E7
Clare Witnell Cl DY11 .... 116 B8
Clare's Ct DY11 .... 116 C6
Claregate Prim Sch WV6 ... 24 F7
Clarel Ave B8 .... 67 C3
Claremont Cl CV12 .... 79 B4
  Blackheath B64 .... 62 E1
Claremont Way B63 .... 83 A3
Claremont Wlk CV5 .... 112 C6
Claremont Ct 1 B64 .... 62 E1
Claremont Mews WV3 ... 39 A7
Claremont Rd
  Birmingham, Hockley B18 ... 66 B6
  Birmingham, Sparkbrook B11 ... 87 B7
  Royal Leamington Spa CV31 ... 161 D8
  Sedgley DY3 .... 50 E8
  Smethwick B66 .... 65 B4
  Tamworth B79 .... 21 A8
  Wolverhampton WV3 .... 39 B7
Claremont St Bilston WV14 ... 40 C6
  Blackheath B64 .... 62 E1
Claremont Way B63 .... 83 A3
Claremont Wlk CV5 .... 112 C6
Clarence Ave B21 .... 65 C8
Clarence Ct 4 LE10 .... 75 E8
Clarence Gdns B74 .... 31 F2
Clarence Mans 7 CV32 ... 156 F1
Clarence Mews 1 B17 ... 85 D6
Clarence Rd Bilston WV14 ... 40 F7
  Birmingham,
  Gravelly Hill B23 .... 56 D3
  Birmingham,
  Handsworth B21 .... 65 C8
  Birmingham, Harborne B17 ... 85 D6
  Birmingham,
  King's Heath B13 .... 87 A1
  Birmingham, Sparkhill B11 ... 87 D4
  Dudley DY2 .... 62 D6
  Hinckley LE10 .... 75 E8
  Sutton Coldfield B74 .... 31 F4
  Wolverhampton WV1 .... 163 B3
Clarence St
  5 Coventry CV1 .... 113 C4
  Dudley DY3 .... 50 E5
  Kidderminster DY10 .... 116 F6
  Nuneaton CV11 .... 73 A4
  Royal Leamington Spa
  CV31 .... 162 A7
  Wolverhampton WV1 .... 163 B3
Clarence Terr 6 CV32 ... 156 F1
Clarendon Pl B17 .... 85 C5
Clarendon Ave CV32 .... 156 F1
Clarendon Cres CV32 ... 156 E1
Clarendon Ho LE10 .... 75 B7
Clarendon Pl Halesowen
  B62 .... 84 A6
  Royal Leamington Spa CV32 ... 156 F1
  Walsall WS3 .... 14 F3
Clarendon Rd
  Birmingham B16 .... 65 E1
  Hinckley LE10 .... 75 C7
  Kenilworth CV8 .... 148 A3
  Smethwick B67 .... 64 F4
  Sutton Coldfield B75 .... 32 C3
  Walsall WS4 .... 15 C2
Clarendon Sq CV32 .... 156 F1
Clarendon St Coventry CV5 . 112 F1
  Royal Leamington Spa
  CV32 .... 157 A1
  Walsall WS3 .... 14 B1
  Wolverhampton WV3 .... 25 A2
Clarewell Ave B91 .... 127 B8

Clarion Way WS11 .... 1 E5
Clark Rd WV3 .... 24 F2
Clark St Birmingham B16 ... 65 F1
  Coventry CV6 .... 96 A1
  Stourbridge DY8 .... 80 E4
Clarke Ho 3 WS3 .... 14 B1
Clarke St 1 B97 .... 153 E3
Clarke's Ave CV8 .... 148 A3
Clarke's La B71 .... 53 C7
Clarkes Gr DY4 .... 52 C6
Clarkes La WV13 .... 27 C3
Clarkson Dr CV31 .... 162 A4
Clarkson Rd WS10 .... 42 A3
Clarmont Pl 1 B18 .... 66 A5
Clarry Dr B74 .... 45 F8
Clary Gr WS5 .... 43 A3
Clatterbach La DY9 .... 100 A4
Claughton Rd DY2 .... 51 D1
Claughton St DY11 .... 116 C5
Clausen Cl B43 .... 44 E4
Clavedon Cl B31 .... 102 E7
Claverdon Cl Redditch B97 ... 158 D4
  Solihull B91 .... 106 E3
Claverdon Dr
  Birmingham B43 .... 54 D7
  Little Aston B74 .... 31 B4
Claverdon Gdns B27 .... 88 B5
Claverdon Ho B13 .... 105 A7
Claverdon Rd CV5 .... 112 B3
Claverley Ct 6 DY1 .... 51 B1
Claverley Dr WV4 .... 38 D5
Clay Ave CV11 .... 73 F7
Clay Dr B32 .... 84 A5
Clay La Allesley CV5 .... 93 A3
  Birmingham B26 .... 88 E5
  Coventry CV2 .... 114 A4
  Oldbury B69 .... 64 A4
Clay Pit La WS14 .... 8 F3
Claybrook Dr B98 .... 159 F7
Claybrook Fst Sch B98 ... 154 F1
Claybrook St B5 .... 164 C1
Claycroft Pl DY9 .... 81 E5
Claycroft Terr DY1 .... 51 B6
Claydon Gr 3 B14 .... 105 A3
Claydon Rd DY6 .... 49 C1
Claygate Rd WS12 .... 2 E3
Clayhanger La WS8 .... 15 D7
Clayhanger Rd WS8 .... 15 F6
Claymore B77 .... 35 D7
Claypit La B70 .... 53 A3
Claypit La Bournheath B61 ... 120 E1
  West Bromwich B70 .... 53 A4
Clayton Cl WV2 .... 39 C7
Clayton Dr Birmingham B36 ... 69 C7
  Bromsgrove B60 .... 151 B2
Clayton Ho 3 B16 .... 65 F1
Clayton Rd Birmingham B8 ... 67 D5
  Coventry CV6 .... 112 E5
  Dudley WV14 .... 51 B7
Clayton Wlk B35 .... 58 A2
Clear View DY6 .... 60 B6
Clearwell Gdns DY1 .... 50 F3
Cleasby B77 .... 22 C1
Cleaver Gdns CV10 .... 73 C6
Clee Ave DY11 .... 116 C2
Clee Hill Dr WV3 .... 24 A1
Clee Hill Rd DY3 .... 50 D4
Clee Rd Birmingham B31 ... 123 A8
  Dudley DY2 .... 62 A7
  Oldbury B68 .... 64 C4
  Stourbridge DY8 .... 81 A6
Clee View Mdw DY3 .... 39 D2
Cleeton St WS12 .... 2 D1
Cleeve B77 .... 21 D3
Cleeve Cl B98 .... 154 D5
Cleeve Dr B74 .... 31 F6
Cleeve Ho B24 .... 57 A2
Cleeve Rd Birmingham B14 ... 105 C4
  Walsall WS3 .... 13 F3
Cleeve Way WS3 .... 13 F3
Cleeves Ave CV34 .... 161 D6
Clem Attlee Ct WV13 .... 40 D8
Clematis B77 .... 21 F3
Clematis Dr WV9 .... 10 F3
Clemens St CV31 .... 162 A7
Clement Pl WV14 .... 40 D7
Clement Rd Bilston WV14 ... 40 D7
  Halesowen B62 .... 63 D1
Clement St Birmingham B1 ... 66 B3
  Nuneaton CV11 .... 73 B3
  Walsall WS2 .... 28 D1
Clements Cl B69 .... 63 F4
Clements Rd B25 .... 88 D8
Clements St CV2 .... 114 A3
Clemson St WV13 .... 27 A2
Clennon Rise CV2 .... 114 D8
Clensmore St DY10 .... 116 D7
Clent Ave
  Kidderminster DY11 .... 116 B1
  Redditch B97 .... 158 D7
Clent Ct 5 DY1 .... 51 B1
Clent Dr Hagley DY9 .... 99 D6
  Nuneaton CV10 .... 72 B3
Clent Fst Sch DY9 .... 99 E2
Clent Hill Dr B65 .... 63 A5
Clent Hills Ctry Pk DY9 ... 100 A4
Clent Ho Bromsgrove B60 ... 137 B3
  Halesowen B63 .... 83 A2
Clent Rd
  Birmingham,
  Handsworth B21 .... 54 D1
  Birmingham, Rubery B45 ... 121 E8
  Oldbury B68 .... 64 C1
  Stourbridge DY8 .... 81 A6
Clent View B66 .... 65 B3

Clent View Rd
Birmingham B32 ... 84 A1
Halesowen B63 ... 82 C5
Stourbridge DY8 ... 80 C2
Clent Villas B12 ... 87 B4
Clent Way B32 ... 102 A8
Cleobury La B94 ... 126 A3
Cleton St DY4 ... 52 B3
Cleton Street Bsns Pk DY4 ... 52 B3
Clevedon Ave B36 ... 69 E8
Clevedon Rd B12 ... 86 E6
Cleveland Cl Willenhall WV13 ... 26 D1
Wolverhampton WV11 ... 12 F1
Cleveland Ct
15 Birmingham B13 ... 87 B2
1 Royal Leamington Spa CV32 ... 156 F2
Cleveland Dr
Barnt Green B45 ... 122 A2
Cannock WS11 ... 2 B4
Cleveland Pas WV1 ... 163 B2
Cleveland Rd Bulkington CV12 ... 79 B3
Coventry CV2 ... 114 A4
Hinckley LE10 ... 75 C8
Wolverhampton WV2 ... 163 C2
Cleveland St
13 Dudley, New Dock DY1 ... 51 B1
3 Dudley, Old Dock DY2 ... 62 B8
Stourbridge DY8 ... 80 E4
Wolverhampton WV1 ... 163 B2
Cleveley Dr CV10 ... 72 D7
Cleves Cres WS6 ... 4 D1
Cleves Dr B45 ... 121 E7
Cleves Rd B45 ... 121 E8
Clewley Dr WV9 ... 11 B3
Clewley Gr B32 ... 84 B5
Clews Cl WS1 ... 42 E7
Clews Rd B98 ... 158 F7
Clewshaw La B38 ... 124 C4
Cley Cl B5 ... 86 D6
Clifden Gr CV8 ... 148 C6
Cliff Hall La B78 ... 35 C1
Cliff Rock Rd B45 ... 122 B7
Cliffe Ct CV32 ... 156 D1
Cliffe Dr B33 ... 69 C3
Cliffe Rd CV32 ... 156 D1
Cliffe Way CV34 ... 161 A8
Clifford Bridge Prim Sch CV3 ... 115 A3
Clifford Bridge Rd CV3 ... 114 F4
Clifford Cl B77 ... 21 F3
Clifford Rd
Bentley Heath B93 ... 127 F4
Smethwick B67 ... 64 F1
West Bromwich B70 ... 53 B2
Clifford St Birmingham B19 ... 66 D7
Dudley DY2 ... 62 B8
Tamworth B77 ... 21 E3
Wolverhampton WV6 ... 25 A3
Clifford Wlk B19 ... 66 D7
Clift Cl WV12 ... 27 C6
Clifton Ave Aldridge WS9 ... 16 C1
Cannock WS11 ... 4 C7
Clayhanger WS8 ... 15 D7
Tamworth B79 ... 21 A7
Clifton Cl Birmingham B6 ... 66 F7
Oldbury B69 ... 64 A4
Redditch B98 ... 159 E8
Clifton Cres B91 ... 106 F1
Clifton Ct Hinckley LE10 ... 71 B1
5 Royal Leamington Spa CV31 ... 162 B7
Clifton Gdns WV8 ... 10 C3
Clifton Gn B28 ... 106 A5
Clifton Inf Sch B12 ... 87 A5
Clifton Jun Sch B12 ... 87 A5
Clifton La B71 ... 53 E8
Clifton Rd
Birmingham, Aston B6 ... 66 F7
Birmingham, Balsall Heath B12 ... 87 A5
Birmingham, Castle Bromwich B36 ... 69 E8
Halesowen B62 ... 83 E8
Kidderminster DY11 ... 116 A1
Nuneaton CV10 ... 72 F4
Smethwick B67 ... 64 F4
Sutton Coldfield B73 ... 46 B5
Wolverhampton WV6 ... 24 D5
Clifton Road Ind Est B12 ... 86 F5
Clifton St Blackheath B64 ... 62 F1
Coventry CV1 ... 165 D4
Dudley WV14 ... 51 A8
Stourbridge DY8 ... 80 F4
Wolverhampton WV3 ... 25 B2
Clifton Terr B23 ... 56 F4
Clifton Way LE10 ... 71 A1
Clinic Dr Nuneaton CV11 ... 73 C3
Stourbridge DY9 ... 81 E5
Clinton Ave Kenilworth CV8 ... 147 D6
Warwick CV35 ... 160 A7
Clinton Comb Sch CV8 ... 147 E3
Clinton Cres 2 WS7 ... 7 B8
Clinton Gr B90 ... 106 E1
Clinton La CV8 ... 147 D6
Clinton Rd Bilston WV14 ... 41 A7
Coleshill B46 ... 70 F6
Coventry CV6 ... 95 F2
Solihull B90 ... 106 E1
Clinton St Birmingham B18 ... 65 E5
Royal Leamington Spa CV31 ... 162 A7
Clipper View B16 ... 65 E1
Clipston Rd B8 ... 67 F4
Clipstone Rd CV6 ... 112 E6
Clissold Cl B12 ... 86 E7
Clissold Pas B18 ... 66 A4
Clissold St B18 ... 66 A4
Clive Cl B75 ... 32 D2
Clive Rd Balsall Common CV7 ... 130 C5
Birmingham B32 ... 84 D7
Bromsgrove B60 ... 151 B8
Burntwood WS7 ... 7 A7
Redditch B97 ... 153 D5
Clive St B71 ... 53 C5
Cliveden Ave Aldridge WS9 ... 16 B1
Birmingham B42 ... 55 D4
Cliveden Coppice B74 ... 31 F1
Cliveden Wlk CV11 ... 78 E8
Clivedon Way B62 ... 83 B7
Cliveland St B19 ... 164 C4
Clivesway LE10 ... 71 C2
Clock La B92 ... 90 D2
Clockfields Dr DY5 ... 61 A1
Clockmill Ave WS3 ... 14 E3
Clockmill Pl WS3 ... 14 F3
Clockmill Rd WS3 ... 14 E3
Clodeshall Rd B8 ... 67 E4
Cloister Croft CV2 ... 114 F6
Cloister Crofts CV32 ... 156 F3
Cloister Dr B62 ... 83 D3
Cloister Way CV32 ... 156 F3
Cloisters The
Royal Leamington Spa CV32 ... 156 F3
Studley B80 ... 159 D4
Clonmel Rd B30 ... 104 A6
Clopton Cres B37 ... 70 C4
Clopton Rd B33 ... 89 C8
Close The
Birmingham, Beech Lanes B17 ... 84 F7
Birmingham, Griffin's Hill B29 ... 103 D8
Brandon CV8 ... 135 F5
Dudley DY3 ... 50 C4
Halesowen B63 ... 82 D6
Hollywood B47 ... 125 A5
Hunnington B62 ... 101 A7
Kenilworth CV8 ... 148 A6
Royal Leamington Spa CV31 ... 162 A5
Solihull B92 ... 106 F8
Wednesbury WS10 ... 41 E3
Closers Bsns Ctr CV11 ... 73 D2
Clothier Gdns WV13 ... 27 A3
Clothier St WV13 ... 27 A3
Clothier Street Prim Sch WV13 ... 27 A3
Cloud Gn CV4 ... 132 D5
Cloudbridge Dr B92 ... 107 F7
Cloudsley Gr B92 ... 88 F3
Clovelly Gdns CV2 ... 114 C5
Clovelly Ho 6 B31 ... 102 C2
Clovelly Rd CV2 ... 114 B5
Clovelly Way CV11 ... 73 E5
Clover Ave B37 ... 70 D2
Clover Ct B38 ... 103 D2
Clover Dr B32 ... 84 D2
Clover Hill WS5 ... 43 E8
Clover La DY6 ... 60 B7
Clover Lea Sq B8 ... 68 A6
Clover Ley WV10 ... 25 F3
Clover Mdws WS12 ... 2 C1
Clover Piece DY4 ... 52 C6
Clover Pk LE10 ... 71 B3
Clover Rd B29 ... 103 A7
Clover Ridge WS6 ... 4 C3
Cloverdale Perton WV6 ... 23 D4
Stoke Prior B60 ... 150 C3
Cloverfield LE10 ... 71 C3
Cloweswood La B94 ... 141 F8
Club Bldgs WV10 ... 11 C6
Club La WV10 ... 11 C6
Club Row DY3 ... 50 E5
Club View B38 ... 103 D2
Clun Cl B69 ... 52 A1
Clun Rd B31 ... 102 F6
Clunbury Croft B34 ... 69 B5
Clunbury Rd B31 ... 123 A8
Clunes Ave CV11 ... 73 E6
Clusters The DY9 ... 81 E5
Clyde Ave B62 ... 83 E8
Clyde Ct B73 ... 46 B5
Clyde Mews DY5 ... 61 B6
Clyde Rd Bulkington CV12 ... 79 A2
Dorridge B93 ... 128 A2
Clyde St Birmingham B12 ... 67 A1
Blackheath B64 ... 62 E1
Clyde Tower 3 B19 ... 66 D7
Clydesdale B26 ... 89 B5
Clydesdale Rd
Birmingham B32 ... 84 B6
Clayhanger WS8 ... 15 E6
Clydesdale Tower B1 ... 164 B1
Co-Operative St CV2 ... 96 B3
Coach House Rise B77 ... 35 F7
Coal Haulage Rd WS11 ... 5 D7
Coal Pool La
Walsall, Coal Pool WS3 ... 28 F5
Walsall, Harden WS3 ... 28 F6
Coalash La B60 ... 151 C2
Coalbourn La DY8 ... 80 F7
Coalbourn Way DY5 ... 61 A3
Coalbourne Gdns B63 ... 82 C5
Coalheath La WS4 ... 29 C8
Coalmeadow Cl WS3 ... 13 F3
Coalpit Fields Rd CV12 ... 78 C1
Coalpool Pl WS3 ... 28 F6
Coalport Rd WV1 ... 26 A1
Coalway Ave Birmingham B26 ... 89 C4
Wolverhampton WV3 ... 39 A6
Coalway Gdns WV3 ... 38 D7
Coalway Rd Walsall WS3 ... 28 A8
Wolverhampton WV3 ... 38 E6
Coat Of Arms Bridge Rd CV3 ... 133 A6
Coates Rd DY10 ... 117 B7
Coatsgate Wlk WV8 ... 10 F1
Cob La B30 ... 103 C6
Cobbett Rd WS7 ... 6 D7
Cobble Wlk B18 ... 66 A5
Cobbles The B72 ... 57 C7
Cobbs Rd CV8 ... 147 D6
Cobbs Wlk B65 ... 62 F5
Cobden Ave CV31 ... 162 C5
Cobden Cl Cannock WS12 ... 2 C7
Darlaston WS10 ... 41 F6
Tipton DY4 ... 51 F8
Cobden Gdns B12 ... 86 E6
Cobden Ho WV2 ... 39 D7
Cobden St Coventry CV6 ... 113 E5
Darlaston WS10 ... 41 F6
Kidderminster DY11 ... 116 D5
Stourbridge DY8 ... 80 E6
Walsall WS1 ... 42 D7
Cobham Bsns Ctr B9 ... 67 D2
Cobham Cl Birmingham B35 ... 57 F3
Bromsgrove B60 ... 150 F7
Cobham Court Mews DY9 ... 99 D6
Cobham Rd Birmingham B9 ... 67 D2
Halesowen B63 ... 83 B4
Kidderminster DY10 ... 116 E4
Stourbridge DY8 ... 81 B2
Wednesbury WS10 ... 42 E2
Cobia B77 ... 35 D7
Cobley Hill B48 ... 138 E4
Cobnall Rd B61 ... 121 A2
Cobs Field B30 ... 103 C6
Coburg Croft DY4 ... 52 C6
Coburg Ho CV5 ... 112 E3
Coburn Dr B75 ... 32 D2
Cochrane Cl Stourbridge DY9 ... 99 C8
Tipton DY4 ... 52 C6
Cochrane Rd DY2 ... 61 F5
Cock Hill La B45 ... 121 F8
Cockermouth Cl CV32 ... 156 D2
Cocksheds La B62 ... 83 C8
Cockshut Hill B26 ... 89 A8
Cockshut Hill Sch B26 ... 89 A8
Cockshutt La B61 ... 136 D7
Cockshutts La WV2 ... 39 D7
Cocksmead Croft B14 ... 104 D5
Cocksmoor Ho B14 ... 104 D7
Cocksparrow La ST19, WS12 ... 1 B5
Cocksparrow St CV34 ... 160 D7
Cockspur St B78 ... 36 E7
Cockthorpe Cl B17 ... 84 F7
Cocton Cl WV6 ... 23 E5
Codsall Cty High Sch WV8 ... 10 A4
Codsall Cty Mid Sch WV8 ... 10 A3
Codsall Rd Blackheath B64 ... 82 E8
Codsall WV8 ... 10 C1
Wolverhampton WV6 ... 24 D7
Cofield Rd B73 ... 45 F1
Cofton Church La B45 ... 122 D3
Cofton Ct B45 ... 122 D7
Cofton Gr B31 ... 122 E6
Cofton Jun & Inf Sch B31 ... 123 A6
Cofton Lake Rd B45 ... 122 C3
Cofton Rd B31 ... 123 B7
Cokeland Pl B64 ... 82 D8
Colaton Cl WV10 ... 25 E4
Colbourne Ct B33 ... 68 D3
Colbourne Grove Dr CV32 ... 156 D2
Colbourne Rd Tamworth B78 ... 21 A2
Tipton DY4 ... 52 A4
Colbrand Gr B15 ... 86 D8
Colbrook B77 ... 21 D1
Coldbath Rd B13 ... 105 B8
Coldfield Dr B98 ... 158 E7
Coldridge Cl WV8 ... 10 F1
Coldstream Cl LE10 ... 71 A1
Coldstream Dr DY8 ... 60 E3
Coldstream Rd B76 ... 57 E8
Coldstream Way B42, B6 ... 55 F3
Cole Bank Rd B28 ... 105 E8
Cole Ct B37 ... 70 B2
Cole Gn B90 ... 105 F2
Cole Hall La B34 ... 69 A5
Cole St DY2 ... 62 E4
Cole Valley Rd B28 ... 105 D6
Colebourne Jun & Inf Sch B33 ... 68 E5
Colebourne Rd B13 ... 105 D6
Colebridge Cres B46 ... 70 F8
Colebrook Cl CV3 ... 114 F2
Colebrook Croft B90 ... 105 F2
Colebrook Rd
Birmingham B11 ... 87 D5
Solihull B90 ... 105 F2
Coleby Cl CV4 ... 131 D7
Coleford Cl Redditch B97 ... 153 A2
Stourbridge DY8 ... 60 C2
Coleford Dr B37 ... 70 A2
Colehill B79 ... 21 B5
Colehurst Croft B90 ... 126 F6
Coleman Rd WS10 ... 42 A5
Coleman St Coventry CV4 ... 111 F3
Wolverhampton WV6 ... 24 F4
Colemeadow Rd
Birmingham B13 ... 105 B6
Coleshill B46 ... 70 F7
Redditch B98 ... 154 F6
Colenso Rd B16 ... 65 D4
Coleraine Rd B42 ... 55 A6
Coleridge Cl Redditch B97 ... 158 C8
Tamworth B79 ... 21 A6
Walsall WS3 ... 15 A5
Willenhall WV12 ... 27 E7
Coleridge Dr WV6 ... 23 E4
Coleridge Pas B4 ... 164 C3
Coleridge Rd
Birmingham B43 ... 54 E7
Coventry CV2 ... 114 C3
Coleridge Rise DY3 ... 50 A4
Coles Cres B71 ... 53 B7
Coles La Sutton Coldfield B72 ... 46 C3
West Bromwich B71 ... 53 B7
Colesbourne Ave B14 ... 104 C2
Colesbourne Rd B92 ... 89 B3
Colesden Wlk WV4 ... 38 C6
Coleshill CE Prim Sch B46 ... 70 F6
Coleshill Cl B97 ... 158 C5
Coleshill Heath Rd
Birmingham B37 ... 90 C7
Coleshill B37, B46 ... 70 E2
Coleshill Heath Sch B37 ... 70 C1
Coleshill Ind Est B46 ... 59 F2
Coleshill Rd
Birmingham, Hodgehill B36 ... 68 E6
Birmingham, Marston Green B37 ... 90 B8
Curdworth B76 ... 59 C5
Fazeley B78 ... 35 A7
Nuneaton CV10 ... 72 A7
Sutton Coldfield B75 ... 46 D5
Water Orton B46 ... 59 B2
Coleshill St Birmingham B5 ... 164 D3
Fazeley B78 ... 35 A8
Sutton Coldfield B72 ... 46 C5
Coleside Ave B13 ... 105 D7
Coleview Cres B33 ... 69 E3
Coleville Rd B76 ... 58 B6
Coley Cl LE10 ... 75 D7
Coleys La B31 ... 103 A2
Colgreave Ave B13 ... 87 D2
Colina Cl CV3 ... 134 C5
Colindale Rd B44 ... 45 A3
Colinwood Cl WS6 ... 4 F1
Coll of the Ascension B29 ... 85 C1
Colledge Rd CV6 ... 95 D1
Colleen Ave B30 ... 104 B3
College Cl WS10 ... 42 A1
College Ct WV6 ... 24 D4
College Dr Birmingham B20 ... 54 F2
Royal Leamington Spa CV32 ... 156 F2
College Farm Dr B73 ... 45 D1
College Hill B73 ... 46 B4
College La
Balsall Common CV8 ... 129 E1
Hinckley LE10 ... 71 E1
Tamworth B79 ... 21 B5
College Rd
Birmingham, Alum Rock B8 ... 67 E4
Birmingham, Handsworth B20 ... 54 E2
Birmingham, Moseley B13 ... 87 C2
Birmingham, Perry Common B44 ... 56 B7
Birmingham, Quinton B32 ... 84 A6
Bromsgrove B60 ... 137 A2
Kidderminster DY10 ... 116 E4
Stourbridge DY8 ... 81 A4
Wolverhampton WV6 ... 24 D4
College St Birmingham B18 ... 66 A4
Nuneaton CV10 ... 73 C1
College View WV6 ... 24 D3
College Wlk B60 ... 137 A2
Collet Rd WV6 ... 23 E5
Collets Brook B75 ... 33 A2
Collett B77 ... 22 A1
Collett Cl DY8 ... 81 A6
Collett Wlk 2 CV1 ... 113 B3
Colletts Gr B37 ... 69 F4
Colley Ave WV10 ... 25 F7
Colley Gate B63 ... 82 C6
Colley La B63 ... 82 C6
Colley Lane Prim Sch B63 ... 82 C6
Colley Orch B63 ... 82 C6
Colley St B70 ... 53 D4
Collier Cl Cheslyn Hay WS6 ... 4 D2
Walsall WS8 ... 15 C7
Colliers Cl WV12 ... 27 B6
Colliers Fold DY5 ... 61 B5
Colliery Dr WS3 ... 13 F3
Colliery La CV7 ... 78 B1
Colliery La N CV7 ... 78 B1
Colliery Rd Smethwick B71 ... 65 A8
West Bromwich B71 ... 54 A1
Wolverhampton WV1 ... 25 F2
Collindale Ct DY6 ... 49 D1
Colling Wlk B37 ... 70 A5
Collingbourne Ave B36 ... 68 E8
Collingdon Ave B26 ... 89 C6
Collings Ho B16 ... 66 A1
Collingwood Dr B43 ... 44 D3
Collingwood Ho B43 ... 44 D3
Collingwood Jun & Inf Sch WV10 ... 11 E2
Collingwood Rd
Coventry CV5 ... 113 A2
Wolverhampton WV10 ... 11 E2
Collins Cl B32 ... 84 A5
Collins Gr CV4 ... 132 D5
Collins Hill WS13 ... 3 A2
Collins Rd Brownhills WS8 ... 16 A5
Royal Leamington Spa CV34 ... 161 D5
Wednesbury WS10 ... 42 C3
Collins St Walsall WS1 ... 42 E7
West Bromwich B70 ... 52 E3
Collinson Cl B98 ... 154 A1
Collis Cl B60 ... 150 E7
Collis St DY8 ... 80 F8
Collister Cl B90 ... 106 B4
Collumbine Cl WS5 ... 42 F3
Colly Croft B37 ... 69 F5
Collycroft Pl B27 ... 88 B5
Colman Ave WV11 ... 26 F6
Colman Cres B68 ... 64 C2
Colman Hill B63 ... 82 D5
Colman Hill Ave B63 ... 82 D6
Colmers Farm Inf Sch B45 ... 122 B8
Colmers Farm Jun Sch B45 ... 122 B8
Colmers Farm L Ctr B45 ... 122 B8
Colmers Farm Sch B45 ... 122 B8
Colmers Wlk B31 ... 102 D1
Colmore Ave B14 ... 104 D7
Colmore Circus Queensway B4 ... 164 C3
Colmore Cres B13 ... 87 B1
Colmore Dr B75 ... 47 A5
Colmore Flats B19 ... 164 B4
Colmore Gate B2 ... 164 C3
Colmore Inf Sch B14 ... 104 D7
Colmore Jun Sch B14 ... 104 D7
Colmore Rd B14 ... 104 D7
Colmore Row B3 ... 164 B3
Coln Cl B31 ... 102 F6
Colonial Rd B9 ... 67 F2
Colshaw Rd DY8 ... 80 E4
Colston Rd B24 ... 57 B2
Colt Cl B74 ... 44 E7
Coltham Rd WV12 ... 27 D7
Coltishall Croft B35 ... 57 F2
Coltman Cl WS14 ... 9 D7
Colton Hills Upper Sch WV4 ... 39 B4
Colts Cl LE10 ... 75 D4
Colts La B98 ... 154 D3
Coltsfoot Cl WV11 ... 26 E5
Coltsfoot View WS6 ... 4 E1
Columbia Gdns CV12 ... 78 E2
Columbian Cres WS7 ... 6 F8
Columbian Dr WS11 ... 1 F3
Columbian Way WS11 ... 1 F3
Colville Cl DY4 ... 52 D8
Colville Rd B12 ... 87 B5
Colville Wlk B12 ... 87 B5
Colwall Rd DY3 ... 50 D4
Colwall Wlk B27 ... 88 D4
Colworth Rd B31 ... 102 F4
Colyere Cl CV7 ... 95 A6
Colyns Gr B33 ... 68 F5
Combe Fields Rd CV3 ... 115 F4
Comber Croft B13 ... 105 D8
Comber Dr DY5 ... 61 B6
Comberford Ct 5 WS10 ... 42 A3
Comberford Dr WS10 ... 42 D4
Comberford Rd B79 ... 21 A7
Comberton Ave DY10 ... 117 B5
Comberton Ct 3 DY10 ... 117 A5
Comberton Fst Sch DY10 ... 117 B4
Comberton Hill DY10 ... 116 F5
Comberton Mans 4 DY10 ... 117 A5
Comberton Mid Sch DY10 ... 117 B4
Comberton Park Rd DY10 ... 117 B4
Comberton Pl DY10 ... 116 F5
Comberton Rd
Birmingham B26 ... 89 B8
Kidderminster DY10 ... 117 B4
Comberton Terr DY10 ... 116 F5
Comet Ho B35 ... 58 B3
Commainge Cl CV34 ... 160 D7
Commercial Rd Walsall WS2 ... 28 A7
Wolverhampton WV1 ... 25 E1
Commercial St B1 ... 164 A1
Commissary Rd B26 ... 90 A3
Common La
Birmingham, Sheldon B26 ... 89 B6
Birmingham, Washwood Heath B8 ... 67 F6
Cannock WS11 ... 2 A3
Corley CV7 ... 93 E7
Kenilworth CV8 ... 148 B7
Tamworth B79 ... 21 B4
Common Rd WV5 ... 49 A6
Common Side WS8 ... 16 A6
Common View WS12 ... 2 B7
Common Way CV2 ... 114 A6
Common Wlk WS12 ... 1 C5
Commonfield Croft B8 ... 67 D5
Commonside
Brierley Hill DY5 ... 61 C6
Walsall WS3 ... 15 A2
Communication Row B15 ... 66 C1
Compass Ct 4 CV1 ... 113 B3
Compton Cl Redditch B98 ... 153 E2
Royal Leamington Spa CV32 ... 157 C2
Solihull B91 ... 106 D4
Compton Croft B37 ... 70 D1
Compton Ct Dudley DY2 ... 62 C6
Sutton Coldfield B74 ... 31 E3
7 Wolverhampton WV3 ... 25 A2
Compton Dr Dudley DY2 ... 62 F8
Kingswinford DY6 ... 60 D5
Sutton Coldfield B74 ... 44 E7
Compton Gr Halesowen B63 ... 82 C4
Kingswinford DY6 ... 60 D5
Compton Grange B64 ... 82 C8
Compton Hill Dr WV3 ... 24 D2
Compton Ho B33 ... 69 B2
Compton Rd Birmingham B24 ... 56 E1
Blackheath B64 ... 62 C1
Coventry CV6 ... 95 D2
Halesowen B62 ... 83 F5
Stourbridge DY9 ... 81 D2
Tamworth B79 ... 20 F7
Wolverhampton WV3 ... 24 F2

Compton Rd W WV3 .... 24 D2
Comrie CI CV2 .... 114 F6
Comsey Rd B43 .... 44 B3
Comwall CI WS3 .... 28 C6
Comyn St CV32 .... 157 B1
Conchar CI B72 .... 46 C2
Conchar Rd B72 .... 46 C2
Concorde Tower B35 .... 57 F2
Condor Gr WS12 .... 2 C1
Condover CI WS2 .... 27 D3
Condover Rd B31 .... 123 B8
Conduit Rd WS11 .... 6 A4
Conduit St WS13 .... 9 B8
Coney Gn DY8 .... 81 B5
Coney Green Dr B31 .... 122 F8
Coneybury Wlk B76 .... 58 D5
Coneyford Rd B34 .... 69 C6
Coneygre Ind Est DY4 .... 51 F2
Coneygree Rd DY4 .... 52 A3
Congleton CI Coventry CV6 .. 95 E2
Redditch B97 .... 153 B5
Congrave Wlk CV12 .... 78 B2
Congreve CI CV34 .... 155 F2
Conifer CI Bedworth CV12 .. 78 C4
Brierley Hill DY5 .... 81 C8
Cannock WS12 .... 2 A8
Conifer Ct B13 .... 86 E2
Conifer Dr
 Birmingham,
 Handsworth B21 .... 65 E7
 Birmingham, Northfield B31 .. 103 B3
Conifer Gr Bromsgrove B61 . 136 F3
Royal Leamington Spa CV31 .. 161 F5
Conifer Paddock
 Coventry CV3 .... 114 E1
 Halesowen B62 .... 83 E8
Conifer Rd B74 .... 44 E8
Coningsby CI 8 CV31 .... 162 C6
Coningsby Dr DY11 .... 116 A8
Conington Gr B17 .... 85 A5
Coniston B77 .... 36 B7
Coniston Ave B92 .... 88 F4
Coniston CI Birmingham
 B28 .... 105 F7
 Bromsgrove B60 .... 137 B1
 Bulkington CV12 .... 79 C3
Coniston Cres B43 .... 54 F7
Coniston Ct Nuneaton CV11 .. 73 F7
 2 Royal Leamington Spa
 CV32 .... 156 D1
Coniston Dr Coventry CV5 .. 111 D4
 Kingswinford DY6 .... 60 B7
Coniston Grange CV8 .... 147 F5
Coniston Ho Birmingham
 B17 .... 85 D5
 Kidderminster DY10 .... 116 E7
 7 Oldbury B69 .... 63 D5
Coniston Rd Aldridge B74 .. 30 F3
 Birmingham B23 .... 56 D4
 Coventry CV5 .... 112 F1
 Royal Leamington Spa CV32 .. 156 D1
 Wolverhampton WV6 .... 24 D8
Coniston Way
 1 Cannock WS11 .... 1 E1
 Nuneaton CV11 .... 73 F7
Connaught Ave
 Kidderminster DY11 .... 116 C4
 Wednesbury WS10 .... 42 C3
Connaught CI WS5 .... 43 C7
Connaught Dr WV5 .... 38 A1
Connaught Gdns B5 .... 86 E6
Connaught Ho 1 WV3 .... 25 A2
Connaught Rd Bilston WV14 .. 40 F7
 Wolverhampton WV1 .... 25 A2
Connops Way DY9 .... 81 E5
Connor Rd B71 .... 53 E8
Conolly Dr B45 .... 102 B1
Conrad CI B11 .... 87 A7
Conrad Rd CV6 .... 113 A7
Consort Cres DY5 .... 61 C6
Consort Dr WS10 .... 41 C8
Consort Rd B30 .... 104 A3
Constable CI Bedworth
 CV12 .... 78 A5
 Birmingham B43 .... 44 D3
Constables The B68 .... 64 B2
Constance Ave B70 .... 53 D1
Constance CI CV12 .... 95 F8
Constance Rd B5 .... 86 D5
Constantine La B46 .... 59 F1
Constitution Hill
 Birmingham B19 .... 164 B4
 Dudley DY2 .... 62 D8
Convent CI Cannock WS11 .... 4 D8
 Kenilworth CV8 .... 148 A7
Conway Ave Birmingham
 B32 .... 84 B6
 Coventry CV4 .... 131 D8
 Oldbury B68 .... 64 B2
 West Bromwich B71 .... 42 B1
Conway CI Dudley DY1 .... 51 C6
 Kingswinford DY6 .... 60 F4
 Solihull B90 .... 106 D1
Conway Cres WV12 .... 27 C7
Conway Dr B66 .... 64 D7
Conway Gr B43 .... 54 D7
Conway Ho Birmingham
 B32 .... 102 D6
 Walsall WS3 .... 28 D6
Conway Jun & Inf Sch B11 . 87 C6
Conway Rd
 Birmingham, Fordbridge B37 .. 70 B3
 Birmingham, Sparkbrook B11 . 87 C6
 Bromsgrove B60 .... 136 F1
 Cannock WS11 .... 4 B8
 Perton WV6 .... 23 F3
 Royal Leamington Spa CV32 .. 161 D8
 Solihull B90 .... 106 D1

Conwy CI Nuneaton CV11 .. 73 D3
 Walsall WS2 .... 28 A4
Conyworth CI B27 .... 88 D4
Cook Ave DY2 .... 62 D7
Cook CI Knowle B93 .... 128 C6
 Perton WV6 .... 23 E4
Cook Rd WS3 .... 14 D2
Cook St Birmingham B7 .... 67 C7
 Coventry CV1 .... 165 C3
 Darlaston WS10 .... 41 F6
Cooke CI CV34 .... 155 F2
Cooke St WV2 .... 163 B1
Cookes Croft B31 .... 103 B2
Cookesley CI B43 .... 44 D4
Cookley CI B63 .... 82 F2
Cookley Way B69 .... 63 E5
Cookley Wharf Ind Est
 DY5 .... 61 B4
Cooknell Dr DY8 .... 60 E2
Cooks La B37 .... 70 A4
Cooksey La B44 .... 44 F4
Cooksey Rd Birmingham
 B10 .... 87 B8
 Birmingham B10 .... 87 C8
 Birmingham,
 Small Heath B10 .... 87 D7
Coombe Abbey Ctry Pk
 CV3 .... 115 E4
Coombe Ave CV3 .... 134 F7
Coombe Croft WV9 .... 11 A3
Coombe Ct CV3 .... 115 A2
Coombe Dr CV3 .... 135 E7
Coombe Hill B64 .... 83 B8
Coombe Park Rd CV3 .... 114 F2
Coombe Pk B74 .... 45 F7
Coombe Rd Birmingham
 B20 .... 55 E1
 Solihull B90 .... 106 C2
Coombe St CV3 .... 114 B2
Coombes La B31 .... 122 F7
Coombes Rd B62 .... 83 B7
Coombs Rd B62 .... 83 B7
Cooper Ave DY5 .... 61 A2
Cooper CI Bromsgrove
 B60 .... 150 E6
 West Bromwich B70 .... 53 E2
Cooper & Jordan CE
 Jun & Inf Schs WS9 .... 30 C6
Cooper St Nuneaton CV11 .. 73 D4
 West Bromwich B70 .... 53 D3
 Wolverhampton WV2 .... 39 F8
Cooper's Bank Rd DY5 .. 50 C1
Cooper's La B67 .... 65 A5
Coopers Hill B48 .... 138 E6
Coopers Rd B20 .... 55 A4
Cope Arnolds CI CV6 .... 95 F4
Cope St Birmingham B18 .. 66 A3
 Coventry CV1 .... 165 C3
 Darlaston WS10 .... 41 E6
 Walsall WS3 .... 28 C6
Cope's Dr B79 .... 21 B7
Copeley Hill B23 .... 56 D1
Copes Cres WV10 .... 26 A7
Cophall St DY4 .... 52 D5
Cophams CI B92 .... 89 C2
Copland PI CV4 .... 111 E1
Coplow CI CV7 .... 130 A6
Coplow Cotts B16 .... 65 F3
Coplow St B16 .... 65 F3
Coplow Terr B16 .... 65 F3
Copnor Gr B26 .... 88 E6
Coppenhall Gr B33 .... 69 A3
Copper Beech CI CV6 .... 95 E1
Copper Beech Dr
 Kingswinford DY6 .... 49 D1
 Wombourne WV5 .... 49 B6
Copper Beech Gdns B20 .. 55 A2
Copperas St CV2 .... 96 B2
Copperbeach Dr 2 B12 .. 87 A5
Copperbeech CI B32 .... 84 F5
Copperfield Rd CV2 .... 114 B3
Copperfields WS12 .... 9 D7
Copperkins Rd WS12 .... 2 E4
Coppermill CI WS12 .... 1 C7
Coppice Ash Croft B19 .. 66 D8
Coppice Ave DY9 .... 81 F3
Coppice CI Birmingham
 B45 .... 121 F7
 Brierley Hill DY5 .... 61 F1
 Burntwood WS7 .... 6 F8
 Cheslyn Hay WS6 .... 4 D4
 Cheswick Green B90 .... 126 C4
 Hinckley LE10 .... 71 F3
 Redditch B97 .... 153 C2
 Sedgley DY3 .... 50 C7
 Solihull B92 .... 107 A7
 Wolverhampton WV11 .... 13 A1
Coppice Com High Sch
 WV11 .... 27 A8
Coppice Cres WS8 .... 15 D7
Coppice Ct WS11 .... 4 B7
Coppice Dr Birmingham
 B27 .... 88 B2
 Dordon B78 .... 36 F7
Coppice Farm Way WV12 .. 27 B8
Coppice Gr WS14 .... 9 F7
Coppice Ho
 Birmingham,
 Acock's Green B27 .... 88 A2
 Birmingham,
 Handsworth B66 .... 65 D6
 Willenhall WV12 .... 27 C7
Coppice Hollow B32 .... 84 B1
Coppice Hts DY11 .... 116 B1
Coppice Inf & Jun Schs
 B75 .... 32 B1
Coppice Jun Sch B92 .... 107 E7

Coppice La Aldridge WS9 .. 15 F1
 Brierley Hill DY5 .... 62 A1
 Brownhills WS8 .... 15 D8
 Burntwood WS7 .... 8 A3
 Cheslyn Hay WS6 .... 4 D4
 Middleton B78 .... 33 D2
 Willenhall WV12 .... 27 C6
 Wolverhampton WV6 .... 24 C7
Coppice Oaks B13 .... 87 A3
Coppice Prim Sch The B47 125 A6
Coppice Rd Birmingham B13 . 87 A3
 Blackheath B64 .... 82 E7
 Brownhills WS9 .... 15 F4
 Dudley WV14 .... 51 A8
 Solihull B92 .... 107 E7
 Whitnash CV31 .... 162 B2
 Wolverhampton WV3 .... 38 D8
Coppice Rise DY5 .... 62 A2
Coppice Side WS8 .... 15 D7
Coppice Side Ind Est WS8 . 15 C7
Coppice St Dudley DY1 .... 51 D4
 Tipton DY4 .... 51 E5
 West Bromwich B70 .... 53 A4
Coppice The Birmingham
 B20 .... 55 A2
 Cannock WS12 .... 2 E1
 Coventry CV3 .... 134 B8
 Hinckley LE10 .... 75 F8
 Nuneaton CV10 .... 73 C7
 Tipton DY4 .... 41 C1
 Willenhall WV12 .... 27 C6
Coppice View Rd B73 .... 45 A4
Coppice Way 7 B37 .... 70 B2
Coppice Wlk
 Cheswick Green B90 .... 126 D4
 Hinckley LE10 .... 71 F3
Copplestone CI B34 .... 69 B6
Copps Rd CV32 .... 161 D8
Coppy Hall Gr WS9 .... 16 B1
Coppy Nook La WS7 .... 7 C5
Copse CI Allesley CV5 .... 111 B8
 Birmingham B31 .... 103 A2
Copse Cres WS3 .... 15 A4
Copse Dr DY2 .... 62 B3
Copse The Bedworth CV7 .. 96 A8
 Sutton Coldfield B74 .... 31 F1
Copsehill Ct B75 .... 46 E4
Copsewood Ave CV11 .... 79 B7
Copsewood Terr CV3 .... 114 C2
Copston Gr B29 .... 103 B8
Copstone Dr B93 .... 127 F3
Copt Heath Croft B93 .... 128 B8
Copt Heath Dr B93 .... 128 A7
Copt Oak CI CV4 .... 131 C6
Copthall Rd B21 .... 54 C2
Copthorne Ave WS7 .... 6 F4
Copthorne Rd
 Birmingham B44 .... 44 E3
 Coventry CV6 .... 112 F8
 Wolverhampton WV3 .... 39 A7
Copyholt La Stoke Prior
 B60 .... 151 D3
 Upper Bentley B60, B97 .... 152 A3
Coral CI Coventry CV5 .... 112 C2
 Hinckley LE10 .... 75 F4
Coralin CI B37 .... 70 C2
Corbett CI B60 .... 151 B8
Corbett Cres DY3 .... 81 A7
Corbett Dr B60 .... 150 C1
Corbett Ho 8 DY8 .... 80 F8
Corbett Hospl DY8 .... 81 A7
Corbett Ind Est DY2 .... 62 C6
Corbett Inf Sch B66 .... 65 B5
Corbett Rd Brierley Hill
 DY5 .... 61 E1
 Hollywood B47 .... 125 A7
 Kidderminster DY11 .... 116 A8
Corbett St B66 .... 65 B4
Corbetts CI B92 .... 109 B7
Corbin Way B78 .... 36 F6
Corbison CI CV34 .... 155 D1
Corbizum Ave B80 .... 159 D4
Corbridge Ave B44 .... 44 F1
Corbridge Rd B73 .... 45 F2
Corbyn Rd Birmingham B9 .. 68 B3
 Dudley DY1 .... 61 F8
Corbyns CI DY5 .... 61 B7
Corbyns Hall La DY5 .... 61 B7
Corbyns Hall Rd DY5 .... 61 B7
Cordelia Gn CV34 .... 161 E4
Cordley St B70 .... 53 B4
Corfe CI Birmingham B32 .. 84 F5
 Coventry CV2 .... 114 F5
 Perton WV6 .... 23 F3
Corfe Dr B69 .... 63 A8
Corfe Rd WV14 .... 51 A8
Corfton Dr WV6 .... 24 C3
Coriander CI
 Birmingham B45 .... 102 B2
 Stoke Prior B60 .... 150 C1
Corinne CI B45 .... 122 A6
Corinne Croft B37 .... 70 A4
Corinthian PI CV2 .... 114 D6
Corisande Rd B29 .... 85 C2
Corley Ave B31 .... 103 B3
Corley CI B90 .... 105 E1
Corley Sch CV7 .... 94 B6
Corley View CV7 .... 95 C6
Corn Exchange WS13 .... 9 B8
Corn Hill Walsall WS5 .... 43 E8
 Wolverhampton WV10 .... 163 D3
Corn Mill CI B32 .... 84 E1
Cornbow Ctr B63 .... 83 B3
Cornbrook Rd B29 .... 102 F7
Cornbury Gr B91 .... 106 D4
Corncrake CI B72 .... 46 D2
Corncrake Dr B36 .... 70 A7
Corncrake Rd DY3 .... 50 E2

Corndon CI DY11 .... 116 B2
Cornel B77 .... 21 F7
Cornel CI B37 .... 90 C8
Cornelius St CV3 .... 133 D8
Corner Ho B66 .... 65 D6
Cornerstone Ho CV1 .... 165 C4
Cornerway B38 .... 123 F7
Cornet's End La CV7 .... 110 B6
Cornets End La CV7 .... 109 E7
Cornfield Hinckley LE10 .... 71 C4
 Wolverhampton WV8 .... 10 F2
Cornfield Ave B60 .... 150 D6
Cornfield CI DY6 .... 60 A8
Cornfield Croft B37 .... 70 D3
Cornfield Dr WS14 .... 9 E7
Cornfield PI B65 .... 62 F4
Cornfield Rd
 Birmingham B31 .... 103 B4
 Blackheath B65 .... 62 F4
Cornfield The CV3 .... 114 C1
Cornflower CI WV10 .... 12 A7
Cornflower Cres DY2 .... 62 F8
Cornflower Rd WS8 .... 15 D6
Corngreaves Prim Sch
 B64 .... 62 D1
Corngreaves Rd B64 .... 82 E7
Corngreaves The B34 .... 69 C6
Corngreaves Trad Est B64 . 82 D7
Corngreaves Wlk B64 .... 82 E7
Cornhampton CI B97 .... 153 B5
Cornhill WS11 .... 1 E5
Cornhill Gr Birmingham
 B30 .... 104 C7
 Kenilworth CV8 .... 148 C5
Cornish Cres CV10 .... 73 A2
Cornmill CI WS1 .... 42 D7
Cornmill Gr WV6 .... 23 D3
Cornovian CI WV6 .... 23 E5
Corns Ho WS10 .... 41 E6
Cornwall Ave Oldbury B68 .. 84 B8
 Tamworth B78 .... 21 A1
Cornwall CI Aldridge WS9 .. 16 C1
 Kingswinford DY6 .... 60 D8
 8 Warwick CV34 .... 160 F8
 Wednesbury WS10 .... 42 D3
Cornwall Gate WV12 .... 27 B5
Cornwall Ind Est
 Birmingham B8 .... 67 C4
 Smethwick B66 .... 65 C7
Cornwall PI
 Royal Leamington Spa
 CV32 .... 156 D1
 Walsall WS2 .... 27 E3
Cornwall Rd
 Birmingham,
 Handsworth B20 .... 54 F2
 Birmingham, Rubery B45 .. 101 E1
 Cannock WS12 .... 2 B5
 Coventry CV1 .... 113 E1
 Smethwick B66 .... 65 C7
 Stourbridge DY8 .... 80 D8
 Walsall WS5 .... 43 B7
 Wolverhampton WV6 .... 24 C4
Cornwall St B23 .... 164 B3
Cornwall Tower B18 .... 66 B5
Cornwall Way LE10 .... 71 E4
Cornwallis Rd B70 .... 53 A1
Cornwell CI Redditch B98 .... 159 B5
 Tipton DY4 .... 52 A5
Cornyx La B91 .... 107 D6
Coronation Ave Mile Oak
 B78 .... 20 D1
 Willenhall WV13 .... 27 D2
Coronation Cres B79 .... 22 F7
Coronation Ct CV11 .... 73 B4
Coronation Ho 3 DY4 .... 51 E5
Coronation Rd Bilston
 WV14 .... 40 C6
 Birmingham,
 Great Barr B43 .... 43 E4
 Birmingham, Selly Oak B29 .. 85 F2
 Birmingham,
 Washwood Heath B8 .... 67 F6
 Brownhills WS9 .... 16 A3
 Coventry CV1 .... 113 F4
 Tipton DY4 .... 52 B8
 Walsall WS4 .... 15 B2
 Wednesbury WS10 .... 42 C4
 Wolverhampton WV10 .... 26 A5
Coronation St B79 .... 21 A5
Coronation Terr B60 .... 151 B7
Coronation Way DY10 .... 117 B5
Coronel Ave CV6 .... 95 E4
Corporation Rd DY2 .... 51 F1
Corporation St
 Birmingham B4 .... 66 F4
 Birmingham B2 .... 164 C3
 Coventry CV1 .... 165 B3
 Kidderminster DY10 .... 116 E5
 Nuneaton CV11 .... 73 B5
 Tamworth B79 .... 21 B5
 Walsall WS1 .... 42 E8
 Wednesbury WS10 .... 42 A2
 Wolverhampton WV1 .... 163 B3
Corporation St W WS1 .. 42 D8
Corpus Christi RC Jun &
 Inf Sch B33 .... 68 D2
Corpus Christi RC Prim
 Sch Coventry CV3 .... 134 D7
 Wednesfield WV11 .... 27 A8
Correen B79 .... 22 C2
Corrie Croft
 Birmingham,
 Bartley Green B32 .... 102 B7
 Birmingham,
 Lyndon Green B26 .... 89 B7
Corrin Gr DY6 .... 60 C8
Corron Hill B63 .... 83 B4

Corser St Dudley DY1 .... 51 A2
 Stourbridge DY8 .... 81 A3
Corsican CI 5 Burntwood
 WS7 .... 7 A8
 Willenhall WV12 .... 27 E7
Corsican Dr WS12 .... 2 A8
Corston Mews CV31 .... 162 C6
Cort Dr WS7 .... 7 B8
Corve Gdns WV6 .... 24 E5
Corve View DY3 .... 39 C1
Corvedale Ho WV1 .... 26 B1
Corvedale Rd B29 .... 103 A6
Corville Gdns B26 .... 89 C4
Corville Rd B62 .... 83 F6
Corwen Croft
 Birmingham B31 .... 102 E6
 Birmingham B31 .... 102 E7
Cory Croft DY4 .... 52 A5
Coseley Hall 1 WV14 .... 51 C8
Coseley Rd WV14 .... 40 C4
Coseley Road Island WV14 . 40 C4
Coseley Sch The WV14 .... 40 B1
Coseley Sta WV14 .... 40 C1
Cosford CI Redditch B98 .... 154 F1
 Royal Leamington Spa CV32 . 157 B3
Cosford Cres B35 .... 58 A3
Cosford Ct DY2 .... 62 E5
Cosford Dr DY2 .... 62 E5
Cosgrove Wlk WV8 .... 10 F1
Cossington Rd B23 .... 56 E7
Costers La B98 .... 154 F2
Cot La DY6 .... 60 C4
Coten End CV34 .... 160 F7
Coten End Cty Fst Sch
 CV34 .... 161 A7
Coten End Prim Sch CV34 . 160 F7
Cotes Rd LE10 .... 75 F5
Cotford Rd B14 .... 105 A2
Cotheridge CI B90 .... 127 C6
Cotleigh Gr B43 .... 44 D3
Cotman CI Bedworth CV12 .. 78 A4
 Birmingham B43 .... 44 C3
Cotman Dr LE10 .... 71 A3
Coton Gr B90 .... 105 E2
Coton Green Cty Prim Sch
 B79 .... 20 F8
Coton Green Prec B79 .... 20 F7
Coton La Birmingham B23 .. 56 F4
 Tamworth B79 .... 20 E8
Coton Rd Nuneaton CV11 .. 73 C3
 Wolverhampton WV4 .... 39 B5
Cotsdale Rd WV4 .... 38 E3
Cotsford B91 .... 107 A3
Cotswold Ave WS6 .... 4 F3
Cotswold CI Aldridge WS9 .. 16 C1
 Birmingham B45 .... 102 B2
 Kidderminster DY11 .... 116 C2
 Oldbury B69 .... 63 E5
Cotswold Cres CV10 .... 72 B3
Cotswold Croft B63 .... 82 C1
Cotswold Ct
 Sutton Coldfield B75 .... 32 A4
 Wolverhampton WV2 .... 39 B6
Cotswold Dr CV3 .... 133 C3
Cotswold Gr WV12 .... 13 B1
Cotswold Ho 6 B14 .... 105 A3
Cotswold Rd Cannock WS12 .. 2 A8
 Stourbridge DY8 .... 81 B6
 Wolverhampton WV2 .... 39 F7
Cotswold Way B61 .... 137 A5
Cottage CI Burntwood WS7 .. 6 F5
 Cannock WS12 .... 2 D5
 Royal Leamington Spa CV31 . 162 C6
 Wolverhampton WV11 .... 26 C6
Cottage Ct WS7 .... 6 F5
Cottage Dr B60 .... 121 D7
Cottage Farm La B60 .... 121 C1
Cottage Farm Lodge CV6 .. 95 A1
Cottage Farm Rd
 Coventry CV6 .... 95 A2
 Tamworth B77 .... 35 D7
Cottage Gdns B45 .... 121 F6
Cottage La Burntwood WS7 .. 6 F5
 Marlbrook B60 .... 121 C1
 Minworth B76 .... 58 D6
 Wolverhampton WV10 .... 11 D3
Cottage St Brierley Hill DY5 .. 61 D3
 Kingswinford DY6 .... 60 D7
Cottage View WV8 .... 10 B4
Cottage Wlk B77 .... 35 F6
Cottages The
 Birmingham B24 .... 67 F8
 Halesowen B63 .... 82 E6
Cotteridge Inf & Jun Sch
 B30 .... 104 A5
Cotteridge Rd B30 .... 104 A4
Cotterill's CI CV31 .... 162 B3
Cotterills Ave B8 .... 68 C4
Cotterills La B8 .... 68 C4
Cotterills Rd DY4 .... 52 B7
Cottesbrook CI CV3 .... 114 E1
Cottesbrook Inf Sch B27 .. 88 D4
Cottesbrook Jun Sch B27 .. 88 D4
Cottesbrook Rd B27 .... 88 D4
Cottesfield CI B8 .... 68 B4
Cottesmore CI B71 .... 53 F8
Cottesmore Ho 7 B20 .... 54 F3
Cottle CI WS2 .... 27 F3
Cotton Dr CV8 .... 148 C6
Cotton La B13 .... 87 A2
Cotton Mill Spinney CV32 . 157 E6
Cotton Pool Rd B61 .... 136 E2
Cottrell St B71 .... 53 D4

Cottrells Cl B14 .... 105 C4
Cottsmeadow Dr B8 .... 68 C4
Cotwall End Ho DY3 .... 50 C7
Cotwall End Prim Sch
DY3 .... 50 D7
Cotwall End Rd DY3 .... 50 C5
Cotysmore Rd B75 .... 46 D7
Couchman Rd B8 .... 67 E4
Coughton Dr CV31 .... 162 D5
Coulter Gr WV6 .... 23 D4
Coulter La WS7 .... 7 E8
Council Cres WV12 .... 27 C4
Council Ho, Art Gall B3 . 164 B2
Council Ho's CV5 .... 93 D1
Council House Mus B3 ... 164 B2
Council Rd **3** LE10 .... 71 D1
Coundon Court Sch &
Com Coll CV6 .... 112 E7
Coundon Gn CV6 .... 112 E8
Coundon Prim Sch CV6 .. 112 E5
Coundon Rd CV1 .... 113 B3
Coundon St CV1 .... 165 A4
Coundon Wedge Dr CV5 .. 112 D7
Counterfield Dr B65 .... 62 F5
Countess Dr WS4 .... 29 D7
Countess Rd CV11 .... 73 A4
Countess St WS1 .... 42 D7
Countess's Croft The
CV3 .... 133 D7
Countinghouse Way
B60 .... 150 E6
County Bridge Jun Mixed
Inf Sch WS2 .... 27 E1
County Cl
Birmingham, Strchley B30 .. 104 C6
Birmingham,
Woodgate B32 .... 84 D3
County Dr B73 .... 21 A2
County La DY8 .... 98 D8
County Park Ave B62 .... 83 D3
Court Cres DY6 .... 60 C5
Court Dr WS14 .... 17 F4
Court Farm Rd B23 .... 56 E6
Court Farm Sch B23 .... 56 E6
Court La B23 .... 56 E7
Court Leet CV3 .... 135 D7
Court Leet Rd CV3 .... 133 E7
Court Oak Gr B32 .... 84 F6
Court Oak Rd B17 .... 85 A6
Court Par WS9 .... 30 B6
Court Pas DY1 .... 51 C1
Court Rd
Birmingham,
Balsall Heath B12 ...... 86 E4
Birmingham,
Sparkhill B11 .... 87 C4
Wolverhampton,
Lanesfield WV4 .... 40 A3
Wolverhampton,
Newbridge WV6 .... 24 F4
Court St **2** Blackheath B64 .. 62 F1
Royal Leamington Spa
CV31 .... 162 A7
4 Stourbridge DY8 ... 81 A5
Court Way WS2 .... 28 E2
Courtaulds Way CV6 ..... 113 D6
Courtenay Rd B44 .... 55 E8
Courthouse Croft B48 ... 148 C4
Courthouse Green Prim
Sch CV6 .... 114 A8
Courtland Ave CV6 .... 112 F5
Courtland Rd DY6 .... 60 E8
Courtlands The WV6 .... 24 E4
Courtney Cl CV11 .... 73 F7
Courtway Ave B14 .... 105 B1
Courtyard The Coleshill
B46 .... 59 F2
Solihull B91 .... 107 C4
Cousins St WV2 .... 39 D7
Cove Pl CV2 .... 114 C7
Coveley Gr B18 .... 66 A5
Coven Cl WS3 .... 15 A5
Coven Gr B29 .... 85 B2
Coven St WV10 .... 25 D4
Coventry Airport CV8 .... 134 B2
Coventry Canal Basin
Warehouse CV1 .... 165 B4
Coventry Cath Church of
St Michael CV1 .... 165 C3
Coventry City FC CV1 ... 113 F3
Coventry Golf Course
CV8 .... 133 D1
Coventry Highway B98 .... 154 C4
Coventry Prep Sch CV3 .. 133 B8
Coventry Rd Baginton CV8 .. 133 F2
Barnacle CV12 .... 97 A8
Bedworth,
Hawkesbury CV2, CV7 ... 96 E6
Bedworth, Springfield CV12 .. 78 B2
Berkswell CV7 .... 110 E3
Birmingham B10, B25, B26 .... 88 C6
Bulkington CV12 .... 79 B1
Coventry CV3 .... 115 F3
Cubbington CV32 .... 157 E7
Hampton In A B92 ...... 91 B3
Hinckley LE10 .... 75 B7
Kenilworth CV8 .... 148 A7
Nuneaton CV10 .... 78 C7
Solihull B26, B92 .... 90 C2
Stoneleigh CV8 .... 149 C7
Warwick CV34 .... 160 F8
Wigston Parva LE10 ..... 76 F1
Coventry Ret Mkt CV1 .... 165 B2
Coventry Road Exhall CV7 .. 96 A8

Coventry St Birmingham B5 .. 164 D2
Coventry CV2 .... 114 A4
Kidderminster DY10 .... 116 F6
Nuneaton CV11 .... 73 C4
Stourbridge DY8 .... 81 A5
Wolverhampton WV1 .... 26 A2
Coventry Sta CV1 .... 165 B1
Coventry Tech Coll
Coventry CV1 .... 113 A2
Coventry CV1 .... 113 B1
Coventry CV1 .... 165 A2
Coventry Univ Coventry
CV1 .... 165 C2
Coventry CV1 .... 165 C3
Coventry CV1 .... 165 D2
Coventry Univ Singer
Hall CV1 .... 165 D3
Coventry Walsgrave
Triangle Bsns Pk CV2 .. 97 A1
Coventry & Warwickshire
Hospl CV1 .... 165 C4
Coventry Whitefriars
(Mus) CV1 .... 165 D2
Coverdale Rd B92 .... 89 A4
Covers The B80 .... 159 E6
Covert La DY8 .... 80 D2
Covert The WV8 .... 10 E1
Covey Cl WS13 .... 3 D1
Cow La B78 .... 35 F3
Cowdray Cl CV31 .... 162 C7
Cowles Croft B25 .... 68 E1
Cowley B77 .... 21 E2
Cowley Cl B36 .... 58 F1
Cowley Dr Birmingham B27 .. 88 D4
Dudley DY1 .... 50 F2
Cowley Gn WS12 .... 1 F8
Cowley Gr B11 .... 87 E5
Cowley Rd Birmingham B11 .. 87 E5
Willenhall WV12 .... 13 C1
Cowper Cl Warwick CV34 .. 155 E1
Willenhall WV12 .... 27 E7
Cowper Rd LE10 .... 75 D6
Cowper Wlk DY10 .... 117 C6
Cowslip Cl
Birmingham,
King's Norton B38 ...... 123 F8
Birmingham, Selly Oak B29 .. 103 A7
Cowslip Wlk DY5 .... 81 C6
Cox Rd WV14 .... 40 E1
Cox St Birmingham B3 .... 164 B4
Coventry CV1 .... 165 C3
Cox's Cl CV10 .... 73 B3
Cox's La B64 .... 62 F1
Coxcroft Ave DY5 .... 81 F8
Coxmoor Cl WS3 .... 13 F3
Coxwell Gdns B16 .... 65 F2
Coyne Cl DY4 .... 51 D5
Coyne Rd B70 .... 53 B2
Cozens Cl CV12 .... 78 A4
Crab La Cannock WS11 ...... 2 A3
Willenhall WV12 .... 13 D1
Crab Mill Cl B38 .... 123 E7
Crab Tree Ho B33 .... 68 E3
Crabbe St DY9 .... 81 F5
Crabbs Cross La B97 .... 158 E5
Crabmill Cl B93 .... 128 C7
Crabmill La Birmingham
B38 .... 124 D8
Coventry CV6 .... 113 F7
Crabourne Rd DY2 .... 62 B2
Crabtree Cl Birmingham
B31 .... 103 C2
Hagley DY9 .... 99 B6
Redditch B98 .... 154 A2
West Bromwich B71 .... 53 F8
Crabtree Dr Birmingham
B37 .... 69 F2
Bromsgrove B61 .... 136 F3
Crabtree Gr **2** CV31 ...... 162 C6
Crabtree La B61 .... 136 E3
Crabtree Rd Barwell LE9 .. 71 F5
Birmingham B18 .... 66 A5
Crackley Cotts CV8 ...... 148 B8
Crackley Cres CV8 .... 148 B8
Crackley La Coventry CV4 .. 131 F3
Kenilworth CV8 .... 148 A7
Crackley Way DY2 .... 62 A6
Craddock Ct CV10 .... 72 C7
Craddock Dr CV10 .... 72 C7
Craddock Rd B67 .... 64 E6
Craddock St WV6 .... 25 B4
Cradley CE Prim Sch B63 .. 82 C7
Cradley Cl B98 .... 154 F2
Cradley Croft B21 .... 54 C3
Cradley Fields B63 .... 82 B5
Cradley Forge DY5 .... 82 A8
Cradley Heath Factory Ctr
B64 .... 82 B8
Cradley Heath Sta B64 .... 82 B8
Cradley High Sch B63 ..... 82 B6
Cradley Park Rd DY2 .... 62 D2
Cradley Rd Blackheath B64 .. 82 C8
Dudley DY2 .... 62 D3
Cradock Rd B8 .... 67 E5
Craig Cl CV31 .... 162 B6
Craig Croft B37 .... 70 D2
Craigends Ave CV3 .... 134 E6
Crail Gr B43 .... 44 B4
Crakston Cl CV2 .... 114 E2
Cramlington Rd B42 .... 55 A8
Crammond Cl LE10 .... 75 B8
Cramnore Cl CV4 .... 52 A8
Cramp Hill WS10 .... 41 D6
Cramper's Field CV6 ..... 113 A5
Cranborne Chase CV2 ... 115 A5
Cranbourne Ave WV4 ...... 39 E3
Cranbourne Cl B45 .... 102 B2
Cranbourne Gr B44 .... 56 A8

Cranbourne Pl B71 .... 53 D4
Cranbourne Rd
Birmingham B44 .... 45 A1
Stourbridge DY8 .... 81 B4
Cranbrook Ct WV13 .... 27 C2
Cranbrook Gr WV6 .... 23 F3
Cranbrook Rd B21 .... 54 C2
Cranby St B8 .... 67 C5
Crane Cl CV34 .... 155 D1
Crane Ct WS1 .... 29 A3
Crane Dr WS7 .... 7 A4
Crane Field WS13 .... 3 B1
Crane Rd WV14 .... 40 F3
Crane St DY11 .... 116 C6
Crane Terr WV6 .... 24 E5
Craneberry Rd B37 .... 69 E3
Cranebrook Hill B78 .... 33 E5
Cranebrook La WS14 ...... 16 F7
Cranemoor Cl B7 .... 67 C6
Craner's Rd CV1 .... 113 F4
Cranes Park Rd B26 .... 89 C5
Cranesbill Cl WV10 .... 12 C7
Cranesbill Rd B29 .... 103 A6
Cranford Gr B91 .... 107 B1
Cranford Pl WS11 .... 1 F1
Cranford Rd Coventry CV5 .. 112 D4
Wolverhampton WV3 .... 38 D8
Cranford St B66 .... 65 C5
Cranford Way B66 .... 65 C5
Cranham Cl B97 .... 153 B1
Cranham Dr DY6 .... 60 E5
Cranhill Cl B92 .... 89 B1
Crankhall La WS10 .... 42 C3
Cranleigh Cl Aldridge WS9 .. 30 B5
Willenhall WV12 .... 13 C1
Cranleigh Ho B23 .... 56 F6
Cranleigh Pl B44 .... 55 E5
Cranleigh Way WS14 .... 9 E7
Cranmer Ave WV12 .... 27 D7
Cranmer Cl WS6 .... 4 D1
Cranmer Gr B74 .... 31 F6
Cranmere Ave WV6 .... 24 A6
Cranmere Ct WV6 .... 24 A6
Cranmoor Cres B63 .... 83 A5
Cranmore Ave
Birmingham B21 .... 65 D7
Solihull B90 .... 126 E8
Cranmore Bvd B90 .... 126 D8
Cranmore Dr B90 .... 106 E1
Cranmore Inf Sch B90 ... 106 E1
Cranmore Rd
Birmingham B36 .... 58 E1
Solihull B90 .... 126 E8
Wolverhampton WV3 .... 24 F3
Cransley Gr B91 .... 107 A1
Crantock Cl WV11 .... 13 C1
Crantock Rd B42 .... 55 C4
Crantock Way CV11 .... 73 F4
Cranwell Gn WV5 .... 49 A5
Cranwell Gr B24 .... 57 D3
Cranwell Rise B78 .... 20 C1
Cranwell Way B35 .... 58 A3
Crathie Cl CV2 .... 114 F6
Crathorne Ave WV10 ...... 11 C1
Craufurd Ct DY8 .... 81 A3
Craufurd St DY8 .... 81 A3
Craven B77 .... 22 B1
Craven Ave CV3 .... 135 D7
Craven Ct CV3 .... 114 F2
Craven St Coventry CV5 .. 112 F2
Wolverhampton WV2 ..... 39 F6
Crawford Ave
Darlaston WS10 .... 41 C7
Smethwick B67 .... 64 F4
Wolverhampton WV4 ..... 39 F3
Crawford Cl CV32 .... 157 B5
Crawford Rd
Sutton Coldfield B76 ..... 57 F8
Wolverhampton WV3 ..... 25 A2
Crawford St B8 .... 67 C5
Crawley Wlk B64 .... 62 D1
Crawshaws Rd B36 .... 58 C1
Crayford Rd B44 .... 45 A1
Craythorne Ave B20 .... 54 E4
Crecy Cl B76 .... 46 E4
Crecy Rd CV3 .... 133 E7
Credenda Rd B70 .... 53 A1
Crediton Cl CV11 .... 73 F5
Cregoe St B15 .... 86 C8
Cremore Ave B7 .... 67 C5
Cremorne Rd B75 .... 32 B2
Cremorne Wlk B75 .... 32 B2
Crendon Cl B80 .... 159 E5
Crendon Rd B65 .... 63 A6
Crescent Ave
Birmingham B18 .... 66 B6
Brierley Hill DY5 .... 61 C1
Coventry CV3 .... 114 C2
Crescent Grange Rd The
DY9 .... 81 C4
Crescent Rd Darlaston WS10 .. 41 D6
Dudley DY2 .... 62 B5
Kidderminster DY11 .... 116 C5
Willenhall WV13 .... 27 C5
Crescent Sta The WV14 .. 40 D6
Crescent The Bilston WV14 .. 40 D6
Birmingham, Coleshill Heath
B37 .... 90 E8
Birmingham, Great Barr B43 .. 44 A1
Birmingham, Hockley B18 .... 66 B6
Birmingham, Sparkbrook B12 .. 87 B5
Blackheath,
Cradley Heath B64 ...... 83 A7
Blackheath,
Rowley Regis B65 ...... 63 C4

Crescent The continued
Bromsgrove B60 .... 136 F1
Dudley DY1 .... 51 E4
Great Wyrley WS6 .... 5 A2
Hagley DY8 .... 98 F5
Hampton in A B92 ...... 109 B7
Keresley CV7 .... 94 F6
Solihull, Lode Heath B91 .. 107 B4
Solihull, Shirley B90 ... 106 A4
Walsall WS1 .... 43 A8
Wednesbury WS10 .... 42 A4
Willenhall WV13 .... 27 C1
Wolverhampton WV6 .... 24 B3
Crescent Tower B1 .... 66 C2
Cressage Ave B31 .... 103 A1
Cressage Rd CV2 .... 115 A6
Cressett Ave DY5 .... 61 C4
Cressett La DY5 .... 61 C4
Cressington Dr B74 .... 32 A1
Cresswell Cl CV10 .... 73 C8
Cresswell Cres WS3 .... 13 F2
Cresswell Gr B24 .... 57 A3
Cresswell Ho CV6 .... 113 B7
Crest The Birmingham B31 .. 123 C7
Royal Leamington Spa
CV32 .... 157 D3
Crest View Birmingham
B14 .... 105 B4
Sutton Coldfield B74 ..... 44 F8
Crestwood B77 .... 22 A5
Crestwood Ave DY11 .... 116 A5
Crestwood Dr B44 .... 55 E7
Crestwood Glen WV6 ..... 24 E7
Crestwood Park Prim Sch
DY6 .... 61 A5
Crestwood Sch The DY6 .. 60 F5
Creswell Rd B28 .... 106 B7
Creswick Gr B45 .... 122 C7
Crew La CV8 .... 148 E6
Crew Rd WS10 .... 42 A4
Creynolds Cl B90 .... 126 D3
Creynolds La B90 .... 126 E4
Crick La B20 .... 66 A8
Cricket Cl Coventry CV5 .. 112 F3
Walsall WS5 .... 43 B7
Cricket La WS9 .... 9 C5
Cricket Mdw Dudley DY3 .. 50 C5
Wolverhampton WV10 .... 11 D4
Cricketers Mdw B64 .... 82 F7
Cricklewood Dr B62 .... 83 D3
Crigdon B77 .... 22 C2
Crimmond Rise B63 .... 82 E5
Crimscote Cl B90 .... 126 F6
Cringlebrook B77 .... 21 D1
Cripps Rd WS2 .... 27 E3
Crockett St DY1 .... 51 A2
Crockett's La B66 .... 65 A6
Crocketts Ave B21 .... 65 D7
Crocketts Lane Inf Sch
B66 .... 65 B5
Crockford Dr B75 .... 32 B3
Crockford Rd B71 .... 42 C1
Crockington La WV5 .... 37 A1
Crocus Cres WV9 .... 11 A3
Croft Apartments
2 WV13 .... 27 A2
Croft Cl Birmingham B25 .. 88 E3
Redditch B98 .... 154 D3
Warwick CV34 .... 161 C1
Croft Cres WS8 .... 15 D7
Croft Ct B36 .... 69 B8
Croft Down Rd B92 .... 89 D4
Croft Fields CV12 .... 78 B2
Croft Gdns WS7 .... 7 A8
Croft Ho **2** WS1 .... 28 F1
Croft Ind Est Birmingham
B37 .... 70 D2
3 Willenhall WV13 .... 27 A2
Croft La WV10 .... 26 A7
Croft Mid Sch CV10 .... 72 F3
Croft Par WS9 .... 30 B6
Croft Pool CV12 .... 77 F2
Croft Rd Bedworth CV12 .. 77 F2
Birmingham B26 .... 88 E8
Coventry CV1 .... 165 A2
Leek Wootton CV35 ..... 156 A7
Nuneaton CV10 .... 72 F3
Croft St Tamworth B79 .... 21 B6
Walsall WS2 .... 28 D3
Willenhall WV13 .... 27 A2
Croft Street JMI Sch WS2 .. 28 D3
Croft The Birmingham B31 .. 103 B2
Blakedown DY10 .... 98 C2
Bulkington CV12 .... 79 B2
Cheslyn Hay WS6 .... 4 E2
Coventry DY2 .... 61 F6
Meriden CV7 .... 92 C1
Sedgley DY3 .... 39 E1
Walsall WS5 .... 43 E8
Willenhall WV13 .... 27 A2
Croftdown Rd B17 .... 85 A4
Crofters Cl DY8 .... 81 B4
Crofters Ct B15 .... 85 E6
Crofters Wlk WV8 .... 10 E1
Croftleigh Gdns B91 ..... 106 E2
Crofts La B96 .... 158 B2
Crofts The B76 .... 58 A8
Croftway The B20 .... 54 E6
Croftwood Rd DY9 .... 81 D4
Cromane Sq B43 .... 54 E7
Cromarty Cl CV5 .... 112 A5
Cromdale B77 .... 22 C1
Cromdale Cl CV10 .... 72 A3
Cromdale Dr B63 .... 82 D3
Crome Rd B43 .... 44 D3
Cromer Gdns WV6 .... 24 F5

Cromer Rd Birmingham B12 .. 86 F5
Royal Leamington Spa CV32 .. 157 B2
Cromes Wood CV4 .... 111 D1
Crompton Ave B20 .... 55 C1
Crompton Cl WS2 .... 28 A5
Crompton Ct CV34 .... 160 D6
Crompton Rd
Birmingham,
Handsworth B20 .... 55 C1
Birmingham, Nechells B7 .. 67 C8
Birmingham, Rubery B45 .. 101 D1
Tipton DY4 .... 52 A4
Crompton St CV34 .... 160 D6
Cromwell Cl Blackheath B65 .. 63 A5
Walsall WS2 .... 27 E4
Cromwell Ct WS6 .... 5 A1
Cromwell Dr DY2 .... 62 F8
Cromwell Inf & Jun Sch B7 .. 67 B6
Cromwell La
Birmingham B31 .... 102 E8
Coventry CV4 .... 131 C6
Cromwell Rd Cannock
WS12 .... 2 E1
Tamworth B79 .... 20 E8
Wolverhampton WV10 ... 11 E4
Cromwell St Birmingham B7 .. 67 B5
Coventry CV6 .... 113 F6
Dudley DY2 .... 62 E8
West Bromwich 53 C4
Cromwells Mdw WS14 ..... 9 C5
Crondal Pl B15 .... 86 B7
Crondal Rd CV7 .... 96 B7
Cronehills Linkway B70 ... 53 D4
Cronehills Prim Sch B70 .. 53 D4
Cronehills St B70 .... 53 D4
Crook La WS9 .... 44 A7
Crookham Cl B17 .... 84 F7
Crookhay La B71 .... 53 B8
Crooks La B80 .... 159 D3
Croome Cl Birmingham B11 .. 87 B3
Coventry CV6 .... 112 F4
Redditch B98 .... 154 F1
Cropredy Rd B31 .... 123 B8
Cropthorne Cl B98 .... 159 B7
Cropthorne Dr B47 ...... 125 B7
Cropthorne Ho B60 ...... 137 B3
Cropthorne Rd B90 ...... 106 C3
Crosbie Rd Birmingham B17 .. 85 B6
Coventry CV5 .... 112 B3
Crosby Cl Birmingham B1 .. 66 B3
Wolverhampton WV6 ..... 24 F5
Cross Cheaping CV1 ..... 165 B3
Cross Ct B64 .... 62 F2
Cross Farm Rd B17 .... 85 D4
Cross Farms La B45 ..... 101 F1
Cross Fields Rd **4** CV34 .. 160 F8
Cross Ho CV2 .... 39 C7
Cross Keys WS13 .... 9 B8
Cross La Birmingham B43 .. 43 E1
Cubbington CV32 .... 157 E4
Lichfield WS14 .... 9 D6
Sedgley DY3 .... 39 E1
Cross Pl DY3 .... 39 E1
Cross Rd Coventry CV6 .. 113 F8
Keresley CV7 .... 94 F6
4 Royal Leamington Spa
CV32 .... 156 D1
Cross Road Ind Est CV6 .. 113 F7
Cross St Bilston WV14 ..... 40 F2
Birmingham B21 .... 65 C8
4 Blackheath B65 ...... 63 C1
Burntwood WS7 .... 6 E8
Cannock, Bridgtown WS11 .. 4 E5
Cannock, Heath Hayes WS12 .. 2 E1
Cheslyn Hay WS6 .... 4 D2
Coventry CV1 .... 165 C4
Dudley DY1 .... 51 C1
Halesowen B63 .... 83 A3
Kingswinford DY6 .... 60 D6
Kingswinford,
Wall Heath DY6 .... 60 B8
Nuneaton CV10 .... 72 D3
Oldbury B68 .... 64 A4
Royal Leamington Spa
CV32 .... 157 A1
Smethwick B66 .... 65 A6
Stourbridge DY8 .... 80 E5
Tamworth B79 .... 21 B5
Tamworth, Kettlebrook B77 .. 21 C3
Walsall WS3 .... 15 A1
10 Warwick CV34 .... 160 F7
Wednesbury WS10 .... 41 E3
2 Willenhall WV13 ..... 27 A1
Wolverhampton WV1 ... 25 F1
Cross St N WV1 .... 25 D4
Cross St S WV2 .... 39 C7
Cross The Kingswinford DY6 .. 60 D6
Stourbridge DY9 .... 81 E6
Cross Walks Rd DY9 .... 81 E5
Cross Wlk B69 .... 63 C8
Crossfell B77 .... 22 B1
Crossfield Rd
Birmingham B33 .... 69 A3
Lichfield WS13 .... 9 E1
Crossgate Rd Dudley DY2 .. 62 F6
Redditch B98 .... 159 C7
Crossings Ind Est The
4 WS3 .... 28 B8
Crossings The WS14 .... 9 E8
Crosskey Cl B33 .... 69 E2
Crossland Cres WV6 .... 24 F7
Crossland Row LE10 .... 76 A6
Crossley Ct CV6 .... 113 F7
Crossley Wlk B60 .... 150 E7
Crossway La B44 .... 55 F6

Crossway Rd CV3 ...... 133 B4
Crossways LE10 ...... 75 F5
Crossways Ct B44 ...... 56 B7
Crossways Gn B44 ...... 56 B7
Crosswells Rd B68 ...... 64 B5
Crowberry CI WS8 ...... 15 D6
Crowberry La B78 ...... 48 C8
Crowden Rd B77 ...... 22 A1
Crowesbridge Mews .51 B8
Crowhill Rd CV11 ...... 74 A1
Crowhurst Rd B31 ...... 122 E7
Crowland Ave WV6 ...... 23 E4
Crowle Dr DY9 ...... 81 C5
Crowmere Rd CV2 ...... 114 F3
Crown Blackheath B65 ...... 63 D4
Bromsgrove B61 ...... 136 F2
Sedgley DY3 ...... 39 D1
Crown Ct Darlaston WS10 ...... 41 C8
Sutton Coldfield B74 ...... 31 E2
Crown Ctr The 1 DY8 ...81 A5
Crown Ho 112 E3
Crown La
Kidderminster DY10 ...... 116 E6
10 Stourbridge DY8 ...... 80 F5
Sutton Coldfield B74 ...... 31 E3
Crown Mdw B48 ...... 139 A7
Crown Rd
Birmingham,
Bordesley Green B9 ...... 67 D2
Birmingham,
King's Heath B30 ...... 104 A4
Crown St WV1 ...... 25 D4
Crown Terr CV31 ...... 161 F7
Crown Way CV32 ...... 157 B3
Crown Wlk DY4 ...... 52 A2
Crownhill Rd LE10 ...... 75 D4
Crownmeadow Dr DY4 ...... 52 D7
Crows Nest B76 ...... 46 F3
Crowther Gdns B63 ...... 82 C7
Crowther Gr WV6 ...... 24 F4
Crowther Rd Birmingham
B23 ...... 56 D5
Wolverhampton WV6 ...... 24 F5
Crowther St
Kidderminster DY11 ...... 116 C6
Wolverhampton WV10 ...... 25 E4
Croxall Way B66 ...... 65 B5
Croxdene Ave WS3 ...... 14 A1
Croxhall St CV12 ...... 78 C3
Croxley Dr WV12 ...... 2 C3
Croxley Gdns WV13 ...... 40 F8
Croxstalls Ave WS3 ...... 28 A8
Croxstalls CI WS3 ...... 14 A1
Croxstalls Pl WS3 ...... 28 A8
Croxstalls Rd WS3 ...... 28 A8
Croxton Gr B33 ...... 69 A4
Croy Dr B35 ...... 58 B4
Croyde Ave B42 ...... 55 A4
Croydon CV3 ...... 133 E6
Croydon Rd
Birmingham,
Bournbrook B29 ...... 85 F3
Birmingham, Erdington B24 ...... 57 A2
Crummock CI CV6 ...... 95 D3
Crump Ho WS1 ...... 28 F1
Crumpfields La B97 ...... 152 F1
Crusader CI B69 ...... 63 E5
Crutchley Ave B78 ...... 21 A2
Crutchley Way CV31 ...... 162 A2
Crychan CI B45 ...... 102 B2
Cryersoak CI B90 ...... 127 B7
Cryfield Grange Rd CV4 ...132 C2
Crystal Ave DY8 ...... 60 F1
Crystal Dr B66 ...... 64 C8
Crystal Ho B66 ...... 65 C6
Crystal L Ctr DY8 ...... 81 A5
Cubbington CE Comb Sch
CV32 ...... 157 F5
Cubbington Rd Coventry
CV6 ...... 96 A2
Royal Leamington Spa
CV32 ...... 157 B3
Cubley Rd B28 ...... 87 E1
Cuckoo CI WS11 ...... 2 C2
Cuckoo La CV1 ...... 165 C3
Cuin Rd B66 ...... 65 C5
Cuin Wlk 11 B66 ...... 65 C5
Culey Gr B33 ...... 69 D2
Culey Wlk B37 ...... 70 D2
Culford Dr B32 ...... 102 C8
Culham CI B27 ...... 88 D2
Cullwick St WV1 ...... 40 A8
Culmington Gr B31 ...... 122 F8
Culmington Rd B31 ...... 122 F8
Culmore CI WV12 ...... 27 D4
Culmore Rd B62 ...... 63 E1
Culpepper CI CV10 ...... 72 E4
Culverhouse Dr DY5 ...... 61 A1
Culverley Cres B93 ...... 127 F6
Culvert Way B66 ...... 64 D7
Culwell St WV10 ...... 163 C4
Culwell Trad Est WV10 ...... 25 F4
Culworth CI CV31 ...... 161 F5
Culworth Ct Coventry CV6 ...113 E7
Royal Leamington Spa
CV31 ...... 162 A5
Culworth Row CV6 ...... 113 E8
Cumberland Ave B33 ...... 69 E5
Cumberland Ave 3 B5 ...86 E7
Cumberland CI DY6 ...... 60 E4
Cumberland Cres 6
Burntwood WS7 ...... 7 A8
Royal Leamington Spa
CV32 ...... 157 C3
Cumberland Dr
Nuneaton CV10 ...... 72 E3
Tamworth B78 ...... 21 A1
Cumberland Ho 7 WV3 ...25 C4

Cumberland Rd
Bilston WV14 ...... 40 D7
Cannock WS11 ...... 2 A4
Oldbury B68 ...... 84 B7
West Bromwich B71 ...... 53 D7
Willenhall WV13 ...... 27 D2
Cumberland St B1 ...... 66 B2
Cumberland Wlk B75 ...47 B5
Cumbernauld Wlk
7 ...... 115 A7
Cumbrae Dr LE10 ...... 71 B2
Cumbria CI CV1 ...... 113 A3
Cumbria Way B7 ...... 67 D6
Cumbrian Croft B63 ...... 82 D2
Cumming St 6 CV31 ...162 A7
Cundall CI CV31 ...... 162 B6
Cunningham Rd Perton
WV6 ...... 23 E4
Walsall WS2 ...... 27 E2
Cupfields Ave DY4 ...... 52 C8
Cupfields Cres DY4 ...... 52 C7
Cur La B97 ...... 152 D3
Curbar Rd B42 ...... 55 C6
Curborough Rd WS13 ...3 B2
Curdale Rd B32 ...... 102 B8
Curdworth La B76 ...... 59 A8
Curdworth Prim Sch B76 ...59 C6
Curlew B77 ...... 36 A7
Curlew CI
Kidderminster DY10 ...... 117 B2
Lichfield WS14 ...... 9 F7
Curlew Hill WS11 ...... 2 A4
Curlews CI B23 ...... 56 C8
Curlieu CI CV35 ...... 160 A7
Curral Rd B65 ...... 63 C3
Curran CI CV31 ...... 162 B4
Curriers CI CV4 ...... 131 D7
Cursley La DY10 ...... 117 F1
Curtin Dr WS10 ...... 41 B4
Curtis CI Smethwick B66 ...65 C4
Tuttnall B60 ...... 151 F8
Curtis Rd CV2 ...... 114 D6
Curzon Ave CV6 ...... 113 E8
Curzon CI LE10 ...... 75 F7
Curzon Gr CV31 ...... 162 C6
Curzon St Birmingham B4 ...67 A3
Wolverhampton WV2 ...... 39 D7
Cut Throat La B94 ...... 142 D7
Cuthbert Rd B18 ...... 65 E4
Cutler St B66 ...... 65 B6
Cutlers Rough CI B31 ...102 F5
Cutsdean CI B31 ...... 102 F6
Cutshill CI B36 ...... 69 C8
Cutting The WS4 ...... 28 F4
Cuttle Mill La B76 ...... 48 D3
Cuttle Pool La B93 ...... 128 F4
Cutworth CI B76 ...... 47 A3
Cwerne Dr DY3 ...... 50 C3
Cygnet CI Alvechurch B48 ...139 A7
Cannock WS11 ...... 2 C7
Cygnet Ct CV1 ...... 165 C4
Cygnet Gr B23 ...... 56 B6
Cygnet La DY5 ...... 61 C7
Cygnet Rd B70 ...... 53 A5
Cygnus Way B70 ...... 52 F5
Cypress Ave DY3 ...... 50 D5
Cypress Croft CV3 ...... 134 F8
Cypress Gdns
Kingswinford DY6 ...... 60 D4
Walsall WS5 ...... 43 C4
Cypress Gr B31 ...... 102 E1
Cypress La CV31 ...... 162 B2
Cypress Rd Dudley DY2 ...51 F1
Walsall WS5 ...... 43 C4
Cypress Sq 2 B27 ...... 88 C5
Cypress Way B31 ...... 122 F8
Cyprus Ave B96 ...... 158 D5
Cyprus CI B29 ...... 103 A7
Cyprus St Oldbury B69 ...64 A8
Wolverhampton WV2 ...... 39 C6
Cyril Gr B10 ...... 87 C8
Cyril Rd B10 ...... 87 D8

D'aubeny Rd CV4 ...... 132 C8
D'Eyncourt Prim Sch
WV11 ...... 26 B7
D'Eyncourt Rd WV10 ...26 A7
D'urberville Rd WV2 ...... 39 F6
D'urberville Rd WV2 ...... 39 F6
D'urberville Wlk WV11 ...2 A2
Dace B77 ...... 35 D7
Dacer CI B30 ...... 104 B5
Dad's La B13 ...... 86 C1
Dadford View DY5 ...... 61 B2
Daffern Rd CV7 ...... 78 A1
Daffodil CI DY3 ...... 50 E7
Daffodil Pl WS5 ...... 43 D8
Daffodil Rd WS5 ...... 43 D8
Daffodil Way B31 ...... 122 E8
Dagger La B71 ...... 53 E4
Dagnall Rd B27 ...... 88 D3
Dagnall End Rd B98 ...154 B7
Dagtail La B97 ...... 158 D3
Dahlia CI LE10 ...... 75 E6
Daimler CI B36 ...... 58 F1
Daimler Rd Birmingham
B14 ...... 105 D3
Coventry CV6 ...... 113 C5
Dainton Gr B32 ...... 84 C1
Daintree Croft CV3 ...... 133 C7
Daintry Dr B78 ...... 20 B7
Dairy CI DY4 ...... 52 B5
Dairy Ct B68 ...... 84 D7
Daisy Bank WS12 ...... 1 F8
Daisy Bank CI WS3 ...... 15 B2
Daisy Bank Cres WS5 ...43 D8
Daisy Farm Rd B14 ...105 B3
Daisy Mdw DY4 ...... 52 C6

Daisy Rd B16 ...... 65 F2
Daisy St Dudley DY14 ...... 40 D2
Wolverhampton W6 ...... 25 A4
Daisy Wlk WV9 ...... 11 A3
Dalbeg B77 ...... 24 E8
Dalbury Rd B28 ...... 105 E5
Dalby CI CV3 ...... 134 E8
Dalby Rd WS3 ...... 28 F6
Dale CI Birmingham B43 ...43 D1
Catshill B61 ...... 136 F7
Smethwick B66 ...... 65 A3
Tipton DY4 ...... 52 D5
Warwick CV34 ...... 161 A8
Dale Ct CV1 ...... 25 A3
Dale Dr WS7 ...... 7 B7
Dale End Birmingham B4 ...164 C3
Darlaston WS10 ...... 41 D6
Nuneaton CV10 ...... 72 E5
Dale End LE10 ...... 75 A7
Dale Hill B60 ...... 137 F6
Dale Meadow CI CV7 ...130 B6
Dale Rd Birmingham B29 ...85 E3
Halesowen B62 ...... 83 F8
Redditch B98 ...... 153 F5
Stourbridge DY8 ...... 80 F2
Dale St Bilston WV14 ...... 41 A5
Royal Leamington Spa CV32 ...161 E8
Smethwick B66 ...... 65 A3
Walsall WS1 ...... 42 E7
Wednesbury WS10 ...... 41 E3
Wolverhampton WV3 ...... 163 A2
Dale Terr B69 ...... 63 C8
Dale Wlk B25 ...... 88 B7
Dalecote Ave B92 ...... 107 E8
Dalehouse Flats CV8 ...148 B6
Dalehouse La CV8 ...... 148 D7
Dales CI WV6 ...... 25 B6
Dales Cty Jun & Inf
Schs The B77 ...... 36 B8
Dales La WS9 ...... 29 C5
Dalesman CI DY6 ...... 60 B7
Daleview Rd B14 ...... 105 C4
Daleway Rd CV3 ...... 133 B4
Dalewood Croft B26 ...88 F6
Dalewood Rd B37 ...... 69 F5
Daley CI B1 ...... 66 B3
Daley Rd WV14 ...... 40 F2
Dalkeith Rd B73 ...... 45 E2
Dalkeith St WS2 ...... 28 C3
Dallas Rd B23 ...... 56 D5
Dallimore CI B92 ...... 89 A3
Dallington Rd CV6 ...... 112 E6
Dalloway CI B5 ...... 86 D6
Dalmahoy CI CV11 ...... 79 C8
Dalmeny Rd CV4 ...... 131 D7
Dalston CI DY2 ...... 62 D6
Dalston Rd B27 ...... 88 C4
Dalton CI CV11 ...... 114 F4
Dalton Gdns CV2 ...... 114 F4
Dalton Rd Bedworth CV12 ...78 A2
Coventry CV5 ...... 113 B1
Walsall WS2 ...... 28 A3
Dalton St Birmingham B4 ...164 C3
Wolverhampton WV3 ...... 39 B8
Dalton Way B4 ...... 164 C3
Dalvine Rd DY2 ...... 62 B2
Dalwood CI WV14 ...... 51 B7
Dalwood Way CV6 ...... 96 B4
Dam St WS13 ...... 9 B8
Dama Rd B78 ...... 34 F8
Damar Croft B14 ...... 104 D4
Dame Agnes Gr CV6 ...114 B8
Dame Elizabeth Cadbury
Sec Sch B30 ...... 103 D7
Dame Ellen Pinsent Specl
Sch B13 ...... 105 A7
Damien CI B67 ...... 64 F5
Damson CI B97 ...... 158 C6
Damson Ct LE10 ...... 75 D7
Damson La B91 ...... 107 E7
Damson Parkway
B91, B92 ...... 107 D7
Damson Wood Inf
Sch B92 ...... 107 D7
Danbury CI B76 ...... 47 A2
Danbury Rd B90 ...... 106 B2
Danby Gr B24 ...... 57 B2
Dando Rd DY2 ...... 62 D8
Dandy Bank Rd DY6 ...61 A8
Dandy's Wlk WS1 ...... 42 F8
Dane Gr B13 ...... 104 D8
Dane Terr B65 ...... 63 C5
Danelagh CI B79 ...... 20 F7
Danes CI WV11 ...... 12 F4
Danesbury Cres
Birmingham B44 ...... 56 A8
Royal Leamington Spa
CV31 ...... 162 D6
Danescourt Rd WV6 ...24 C6
Daneshill Wlk WV8 ...... 25 F8
Danesmoor Ho B26 ...88 E7
Danesmore Park Prim Sch
WV11 ...... 13 A1
Daneswood Dr WS9 ...15 F3
Daneswood Rd CV3 ...135 E7
Daneways CI B74 ...... 45 A8
Danford CI DY8 ...... 81 A4
Danford Gdns B10 ...... 87 D8
Danford La B91 ...... 106 E3
Danford Rd B47 ...... 124 F6
Danford Way B43 ...... 54 D8
Dangerfield Ho B70 ...53 E1
Dangerfield La WS10 ...41 C4
Daniel Ave CV10 ...... 72 E5
Daniels La WS9 ...... 30 C4
Daniels Rd B9 ...... 68 A2
Danilo Rd WS11 ...... 1 D1

Danks St DY4 ...... 52 A2
Danzey CI B98 ...... 159 A3
Danzey Gr B14 ...... 104 C3
Danzey Green La B94 ...142 B1
Danzey Green Rd B36 ...58 B1
Daphne CI CV2 ...... 96 C3
Darby CI WV14 ...... 40 A2
Darby End Rd DY2 ...62 E4
Darby Ho 2 WS2 ...... 42 C7
Darby Rd Oldbury B68 ...64 C5
Wednesbury WS10 ...... 42 B4
Darby St B65 ...... 63 C1
Darbys Hill Rd B69 ...63 B7
Dare Rd B23 ...... 56 E4
Dare's Wlk LE10 ...... 71 D1
Darell Croft B76 ...... 46 E3
Daren CI B36 ...... 69 F8
Darfield Wlk 2 B12 ...86 F8
Darges La WS6 ...... 4 F4
Dark La Astwood Bank B96 ... 158 D1
Bedworth CV12 ...... 77 D1
Belbroughton DY9 ...... 119 F8
Birchmoor B78 ...... 36 E8
Brinsford WV10 ...... 11 D8
Coventry CV1 ...... 165 B4
Featherstone WV10 ...... 12 D7
Great Wyrley WS6 ...... 5 C1
Hollywood B47 ...... 124 E7
Lichfield WS13 ...... 8 B8
Romsley B62 ...... 100 F4
Stoke Heath B60 ...... 150 D6
Darkhouse La WV14 ...40 C2
Darlaston Com Sch WS10 ...41 B6
Darlaston CI CV7 ...... 110 D8
Darlaston La WV14 ...41 A7
Darlaston Rd Walsall WS2 ...42 B8
Wednesbury WS10 ...... 41 A4
Darlaston Road Ind Est
WS10 ...... 41 D5
Darley Ave B34 ...... 68 F6
Darley Dr W6 ...... 25 B5
Darley Green Rd B93 ...128 B1
Darley Ho DY6 ...... 63 D6
Darley Mead Ct B91 ...107 E4
Darley Rd LE10 ...... 75 E6
Darley Way B74 ...... 45 A7
Darleydale Ave B44 ...44 E1
Darlington St
Darlaston WS10 ...... 41 D5
Wolverhampton WV1 ...... 163 B3
Darlington Yd WV1 ...163 B3
Darlston Row CV7 ...... 92 B1
Darnbrook B77 ...... 22 C1
Darnel Croft 3 B10 ...67 B1
Darnel Hurst Rd B75 ...32 C3
Darnford CI
Birmingham B28 ...... 106 A5
Coventry CV2 ...... 114 F7
Sutton Coldfield B72 ...... 57 D7
Darnford La WS14 ...... 9 F6
Darnford Moors WS14 ...9 E6
Darnford View WS13 ...3 E1
Darnick Rd B73 ...... 45 D2
Darnley Rd 7 B16 ...... 66 A2
Darrach CI CV2 ...... 96 E1
Darris Rd B29 ...... 104 A8
Dart B77 ...... 36 A5
Dart CI LE10 ...... 75 A8
Dart St B9 ...... 67 B1
Dartford Rd WS3 ...... 13 F1
Dartmoor CI B45 ...... 102 A2
Dartmouth Ave Cannock
WS11 ...... 4 C8
Stourbridge DY8 ...... 60 D3
Walsall WS3 ...... 28 E6
Willenhall WV13 ...... 27 A2
Dartmouth Cir B6 ...... 66 F5
Dartmouth CI WS3 ...28 E5
Dartmouth Cres WV14 ...41 A7
Dartmouth Dr WS9 ...30 A5
Dartmouth High Sch B43 ...43 D3
Dartmouth Ho 2 WS3 ...28 F6
Dartmouth Middleway B7 ...66 F4
Dartmouth Pl WS3 ...... 28 F6
Dartmouth Rd
Birmingham B29 ...... 85 F2
Cannock WS11 ...... 1 D1
Coventry CV2 ...... 114 C5
Smethwick B66 ...... 64 F8
Dartmouth Sch CV2 ...114 D5
Dartmouth Sq B70 ...... 53 D2
Dartmouth St
West Bromwich B70 ...... 53 B3
Wolverhampton WV2 ...... 163 C1
Wolverhampton WV2 ...... 163 D1
Dartmouth Street Sta
B70 ...... 53 B3
Darvel Rd WV12 ...... 27 D4
Darwall St WS1 ...... 28 E2
Darwell Pk B77 ...... 22 B2
Darwin CI Burntwood WS7 ...7 F7
Cannock WS12 ...... 2 E2
Coventry CV2 ...... 115 A6
Hinckley LE10 ...... 71 E3
Lichfield WS13 ...... 9 A8
Darwin Ct Bedworth CV12 ...78 A2
Perton WV6 ...... 23 E4
Darwin Ho B37 ...... 70 C1
Darwin PI WS2 ...... 28 B6
Darwin Rd WS2 ...... 28 B6
Darwin St B12 ...... 86 F8
Dassett Gr B9 ...... 68 C2
Dassett Rd B93 ...... 127 F4
Datchet CI CV5 ...... 112 C4
Datteln Rd WS11 ...... 2 A4
Dauntsey Covert B14 ...104 D3
Davena Dr B29 ...... 84 E2
Davena Gr WV14 ...... 40 D3

Davenport Dr
Birmingham B35 ...... 58 C3
Bromsgrove B60 ...... 137 B1
Davenport Rd Coventry
CV5 ...... 133 D4
Wednesfield WV11 ...... 26 E6
Wolverhampton WV6 ...... 24 B5
Davenport Terr LE10 ...75 B8
Daventry Gr B32 ...... 84 D6
Daventry Rd CV3 ...... 133 D7
Davey Rd Birmingham B20 ...55 E1
West Bromwich B70 ...... 53 A5
David Cox Ct B17 ...... 85 D5
David Cox Tower B31 ...102 F7
David Garrick Gdns WS13 ...3 B2
David Peacock CI DY4 ...52 A5
David Rd Bedworth CV7 ...95 F8
Birmingham B20 ...... 55 B2
Coventry CV1 ...... 113 F2
Tipton DY4 ...... 52 A7
Davids The B31 ...... 103 C5
Davidson Ave CV31 ...162 A4
Davidson Rd WS13 ...... 9 B7
Davies Ave WV14 ...... 40 D3
Davies Ho 7 Oldbury B69 ...64 A7
1 Walsall WS3 ...... 14 B1
Davies Rd CV7 ...... 95 F7
Davis Ave DY4 ...... 51 E4
Davis CI CV32 ...... 156 D2
Davis Gr B25 ...... 88 D6
Davis Rd Tamworth B77 ...21 F4
Willenhall WV12 ...... 27 D8
Davison Rd B67 ...... 64 F3
Davy Rd WS2 ...... 28 A5
Daw End CV4 ...... 29 C6
Daw End La WS4 ...... 29 C6
Daw End Specl Sch WS4 ...29 C6
Dawberry CI B14 ...... 104 D5
Dawberry Fields Rd B14 ...104 D5
Dawberry Rd B14 ...... 104 C6
Dawes Ave B70 ...... 53 C1
Dawes CI CV2 ...... 114 A3
Dawes La WS8 ...... 7 A1
Dawley Brook Prim Sch
DY6 ...... 60 C7
Dawley Brook Rd DY6 ...60 D7
Dawley Cres B37 ...... 70 B1
Dawley Rd DY6 ...... 60 C8
Dawley Trad Est DY6 ...60 D8
Dawley Wlk 9 CV2 ...... 115 A7
Dawlish CI CV11 ...... 73 E5
Dawlish Dr CV3 ...... 133 D5
Dawlish Rd Birmingham B29 ...85 F2
Dudley DY1 ...... 51 C5
Smethwick B66 ...... 65 B5
Dawn Dr DY4 ...... 41 C2
Dawn Rd B31 ...... 102 E6
Dawney Dr B75 ...... 32 A4
Dawson Ave WV14 ...... 40 A2
Dawson CI Redditch B97 ...158 A2
Whitnash CV31 ...... 162 A2
Dawson Rd Birmingham B21 ...65 F8
Bromsgrove B61 ...... 136 E2
Coventry CV3 ...... 114 A1
Dawson Sq WV14 ...... 40 C5
Dawson St Smethwick B66 ...65 A3
Walsall WS3 ...... 28 D8
Day Ave WV11 ...... 26 E7
Day Ho DY4 ...... 52 C8
Day St WS2 ...... 28 E3
Day's La CV2 ...... 113 F3
Daybrook CI B97 ...... 153 B5
Dayhouse Bank B62 ...101 B1
Daylesford Inf Sch B92 ...89 A3
Daylesford Rd B92 ...... 89 A3
Days CI CV1 ...... 113 E3
Daytona Dr CV5 ...... 111 B8
De Marnham CI B70 ...53 E1
De Montfort Ho B37 ...69 F5
De Montfort Rd
Hinckley LE10 ...... 71 E1
Kenilworth CV8 ...... 147 F5
De Montfort Way CV4 ...132 D5
De Moram Gr B92 ...... 107 F7
De Somerley Ho 1 B69 ...64 A7
De-Compton CI CV7 ...94 B6
De-La-Bere Cres LE10 ...76 A6
Deacon St CV11 ...... 73 C3
Deakin Ave WS8 ...... 6 F1
Deakin Rd Birmingham B24 ...57 A3
Sutton Coldfield B75 ...... 46 E7
Deakins Rd B25 ...... 88 B7
Deal Ave WS7 ...... 7 A8
Deal Dr B69 ...... 52 A1
Deal Gr B31 ...... 103 A3
Dean CI Birmingham B44 ...56 B8
Hinckley LE10 ...... 71 E2
Stourbridge DY8 ...... 81 B6
Sutton Coldfield B72 ...... 57 B7
Dean Ct 5 Brierley Hill DY5 ...61 E6
Perton WV6 ...... 23 E6
Dean Rd Birmingham B23 ...56 F5
Hinckley LE10 ...... 71 E2
Walsall WS4 ...... 29 C7
Dean Rd W LE10 ...... 71 E2
Dean St Birmingham B5 ...164 C1
Coventry CV2 ...... 114 A3
Sedgley DY3 ...... 50 D8
Dean's Rd WV1 ...... 26 B2
Deanbrook CI B90 ...127 A6
Deanery Jun Sch B76 ...57 F8
Deanery Row WV1 ...163 B4
Deans CI B98 ...... 154 D5
Deans Croft WS13 ...... 9 C2
Deans Pl WS3 ...... 28 F6

Deans Way CV7 .... 95 D6
Deansfield High Sch WV1 .. 26 C2
Deansfield Rd WV1 .... 26 A2
Deansford La DY10 .... 118 B6
Deanston Croft CV2 .... 96 F1
Deansway Bromsgrove B61 .. 136 E2
Warwick CV34 .... 155 C1
Deansway Ho DY10 .... 117 A7
Deansway The DY10 .... 117 A7
Dearman Rd B11 .... 87 B7
Dearmont Rd B31 .... 122 E7
Dearne Ct DY3 .... 51 A6
Deasy Ho CV3 .... 134 B5
Deavall Way WS11 .... 2 B2
Debden Cl B93 .... 127 E2
Debenham Cres B25 .... 68 D1
Debenham Rd B25 .... 68 D1
Deblen Dr B16 .... 65 D1
Deborah Cl WV2 .... 39 C6
Dee Gr Birmingham B38 ..... 123 E8
Cannock WS11 .... 4 D8
Dee Ho **8** DY1 .... 61 E8
Dee Rd WS3 .... 14 E1
Dee Wlk B36 .... 70 A7
Deedmore Rd CV2 .... 96 D1
Deedmore Sch CV2 .... 114 C8
Deegan Cl CV2 .... 114 A5
Deelands Rd B45 .... 121 F8
Deeley B77 .... 22 A1
Deeley Cl Birmingham B15 .. 86 C7
Blackheath B64 .... 82 E7
Deeley Dr DY4 .... 52 C6
Deeley Pl WS3 .... 28 B8
Deeley St Brierley Hill DY5 .. 61 E1
Walsall WS3 .... 28 B8
Deepdale B77 .... 22 D1
Deepdale Ave B26 .... 89 B4
Deepdale Ind Est DY1 .... 50 E3
Deepdale La DY3 .... 50 E3
Deeplow Cl **2** B72 .... 46 C4
Deepmoor Rd B33 .... 68 F3
Deepmore Ave WS2 .... 28 B2
Deepwood Cl WS4 .... 29 B8
Deer Barn Hill B98 .... 154 A1
Deer Cl Norton Canes WS11 ... 6 A7
Walsall WS3 .... 14 C1
Deer Leap The CV8 .... 148 B6
Deer Park Rd B78 .... 20 E1
Deer Park Way B91 .... 107 C1
Deer Wlk WV8 .... 10 F2
Deerdale Way CV3 .... 134 F8
Deerfold Cres WS7 .... 7 B7
Deerham Cl B23 .... 56 D7
Deerhill B77 .... 22 C1
Deerhurst B98 .... 154 C7
Deerhurst Ct B91 .... 107 D4
Deerhurst Rd
  Birmingham B20 .... 54 F6
  Coventry CV6 .... 95 B2
Deerhurst Rise WS12 .... 2 F6
Deerpark Dr CV34 .... 160 E8
Defford Ave WS4 .... 15 C1
Defford Dr B68 .... 64 B4
Deighton Rd WS5 .... 43 B4
Delage Cl CV6 .... 96 B4
Delamere Cl B36 .... 58 D1
Delamere Dr WS5 .... 43 C3
Delamere Rd Bedworth
  CV12 .... 77 F2
  Birmingham B28 .... 105 F7
  Willenhall WV12 .... 27 C7
Delamere Rd CV32 .... 157 C4
Delancey Keep B75 .... 47 A5
Delaware Rd CV3 .... 133 C5
Delf Ho CV2 .... 96 D1
Delhi Ave CV6 .... 95 D1
Delhurst Ave WV4 .... 39 C5
Delhurst Rd B44 .... 44 D1
Delius St CV4 .... 111 E3
Dell Cl CV3 .... 134 C5
Dell Farm Cl B93 .... 128 B6
Dell Rd Birmingham B30 .... 104 A5
  Brierley Hill DY5 .... 61 B5
Dell The Birmingham B31 ... 102 D6
  Birmingham, Edgbaston B16 ... 65 F2
  Cannock WS12 .... 2 F4
  Lichfield WS13 .... 8 F7
  Solihull B92 .... 89 A1
  Stourbridge DY8 .... 80 E6
  Tamworth B79 .... 21 B6
Della Dr B32 .... 102 D8
Dellow Gr B48 .... 139 A5
Dellows Cl B38 .... 123 D7
Dellway Ct DY8 .... 80 E5
Delmore Way B76 .... 58 B6
Delph Dr DY5 .... 81 E7
Delph La DY5 .... 81 D8
Delph Rd DY5 .... 61 C1
Delph Road Ind Est DY5 ..... 61 C1
Delphinium Cl B9 .... 67 E3
Delphi Cl CV34 .... 161 E4
Delrene Rd B28 .... 105 F3
Delta Way WS11 .... 4 D7
Delta Way Bsns Ctr WS11 .... 4 D6
Deltic B77 .... 22 A1
Delves Cres Walsall WS5 ..... 43 A5
  Wood End CV9 .... 36 D1
Delves Green Rd WS5 .... 43 A5
Delves Inf Sch WS5 .... 43 A5
Delves Jun Mix Sch WS5 ..... 43 A5
Delves Rd WS5 .... 42 F7
Delville Rd WS10 .... 41 F4
Delville Terr WS10 .... 41 F3
Dempster Ct CV11 .... 73 C4
Dempster Rd CV12 .... 78 A4

Demuth Way B69 .... 63 F6
Denaby Gr B14 .... 105 D4
Denbigh Cl DY1 .... 50 F2
Denbigh Cnr B46 .... 91 A6
Denbigh Cres B71 .... 53 B6
Denbigh Dr
  Wednesbury WS10 .... 42 D4
  West Bromwich B71 .... 53 B6
Denbigh Rd Coventry CV6 .. 112 E5
  Tipton DY4 .... 52 C4
Denbigh St B9 .... 67 D2
Denbury Cl WS12 .... 2 D1
Denby Bldgs **12** CV32 ..... 161 F8
Denby Cl Birmingham B7 ..... 67 B5
Denby Cl
  Royal Leamington Spa
  CV32 .... 157 C3
Denby Croft B90 .... 127 B6
Dencer Cl B45 .... 122 A8
Dencer Dr CV8 .... 148 C4
Dencil Cl B63 .... 82 D5
Dene Ave DY6 .... 60 C4
Dene Court Rd B92 .... 88 F1
Dene Hollow B13 .... 105 C7
Dene Rd Stourbridge DY8 .... 80 F3
  Wombourne WV4 .... 37 F4
Denegate Cl B76 .... 58 B6
Denehurst Cl B17 .... 85 C4
Denehurst Way CV10 .... 72 F3
Denewood Ave B20 .... 55 B2
Denewood Way CV8 .... 148 C6
Denford Gr B14 .... 104 D5
Denham Ave CV5 .... 112 C4
Denham Ct B23 .... 56 C2
Denham Gdns WV3 .... 38 B8
Denham Rd B27 .... 88 C5
Denholm Rd B73 .... 45 D2
Denholme Gr B14 .... 105 A3
Denis Rd LE10 .... 75 D5
Denise Dr Birmingham B17 ... 85 C4
  Birmingham, Kingshurst B37 ... 69 F4
  Dudley WV11 .... 51 B8
Denleigh Rd DY6 .... 60 F4
Denmark Cl W6 .... 25 A4
Denmark Rise WS12 .... 2 D7
Denmark Villas WS13 .... 8 C5
Denmead Dr WV11 .... 26 F8
Denmore Gdns WV1 .... 26 C2
Dennett Cl CV34 .... 155 F2
Dennis B77 .... 21 E2
Dennis Hall Rd DY8 .... 81 A8
Dennis Rd Birmingham B12 ... 87 B8
  Coventry CV2 .... 114 B6
Dennis St DY8 .... 80 F8
Denshaw Croft CV2 .... 115 A8
Denston Ct B74 .... 31 F7
Dent St B79 .... 21 C5
Denton Cl CV8 .... 147 D6
Denton Croft B93 .... 127 D3
Denton Gr
  Birmingham, Great Barr B43 ... 54 D7
  Birmingham, Stechford B33 ... 68 D2
Denton Rd DY9 .... 82 A4
Denver Rd B14 .... 105 A2
Denville Cl WV14 .... 40 E7
Denville Cres B9 .... 68 B3
Denville Rd CV32 .... 157 A3
Depwo Gr B32 .... 102 B8
Derby Ave WV6 .... 24 F7
Derby Dr B37 .... 70 B2
Derby Rd LE10 .... 71 D1
Derby St Birmingham B9 ..... 67 A2
  Walsall WS2 .... 28 E4
Dereham Ct CV32 .... 157 A2
Dereham Wlk WV14 .... 40 E2
Dereton Cl DY1 .... 61 E8
Derick Burcher's Mall
  5 DY10 .... 116 E6
Dering Cl CV2 .... 114 D8
Deronda Cl CV12 .... 78 A3
Derron Ave B26 .... 88 E5
Derry Cl B17 .... 85 A3
Derry St Brierley Hill DY5 .... 61 D2
  Wolverhampton WV2 .... 163 B1
Derrydown Cl B23 .... 56 E3
Derrydown Rd B42 .... 55 B5
Dersingham Dr CV6 .... 96 B2
Derwent B77 .... 21 D1
Derwent Cl Aldridge B42 ..... 30 F3
  Brierley Hill DY5 .... 61 B6
  Coventry CV5 .... 111 E4
  Royal Leamington Spa
  CV32 .... 156 D1
  Willenhall WV13 .... 27 C2
Derwent Ct B73 .... 46 B5
Derwent Gr Birmingham
  B13 .... 86 C1
  Burntwood WS7 .... 7 D6
  Cannock WS11 .... 4 D7
Derwent Ho Birmingham
  B17 .... 85 D5
  Kidderminster DY10 .... 116 F7
  5 Oldbury B69 .... 63 D5
Derwent Rd Bedworth
  CV12 .... 78 A2
  Birmingham B30 .... 104 C8
  Coventry CV6 .... 95 A2
  Wolverhampton WV6 .... 24 E8
Derwent Way
  Bromsgrove B60 .... 137 B1
  Nuneaton CV11 .... 73 F6
Desborough Ho **8** B14 .... 105 A3
Desford Ave B42 .... 55 C7
Despard Rd CV5 .... 111 D4
Dettonford Rd B32 .... 102 B8
Devereux Cl Birmingham
  B36 .... 69 C8
  Coventry CV4 .... 111 C1

Devereux Ho B79 .... 21 A4
Devereux Rd
  Sutton Coldfield B75 .... 32 C1
  West Bromwich B70 .... 53 E1
Deveron Ct LE10 .... 71 B1
Deveron Way LE10 .... 71 B1
Devey Dr DY4 .... 52 D6
Devine Croft DY4 .... 52 A5
Devitts Cl B90 .... 126 F7
Devon Cl Birmingham B20 .. 54 F2
  Nuneaton CV10 .... 72 F3
Devon Cres Aldridge WS9 ... 16 A1
  Dudley DY2 .... 61 F7
  West Bromwich B71 .... 53 C6
Devon Ct WS11 .... 4 C8
Devon Gn WS11 .... 4 F8
Devon Gr CV2 .... 114 B6
Devon Ho
  7 Birmingham B31 .... 102 C2
  4 Stourbridge DY8 .... 80 F8
Devon Rd Birmingham B45 . 101 F1
  Cannock WS11 .... 4 F8
  Smethwick B67 .... 84 E7
  Stourbridge DY8 .... 80 E7
  Wednesbury WS10 .... 42 C4
  Willenhall WV13 .... 27 D1
Devon St B7 .... 67 C5
Devonshire Ave B18 .... 65 F6
Devonshire Ct B74 .... 32 A2
Devonshire Dr Tamworth
  B78 .... 21 A1
  West Bromwich B71 .... 53 E3
Devonshire Inf Sch B67 ...... 64 F5
Devonshire Jun Sch B67 ..... 64 F5
Devonshire Rd
  Birmingham B20 .... 54 F2
  Smethwick B67 .... 64 E6
Devonshire St B18 .... 66 A6
Devonshire Villas B10 .... 87 D8
Devoran Cl Bedworth CV7 ... 96 B8
  Wolverhampton WV6 .... 25 B4
Dewberry Dr WS5 .... 43 A3
Dewberry Rd DY8 .... 60 F1
Dewhurst Croft B33 .... 69 B3
Dewis Ho **4** CV2 .... 96 B1
Dewsbury Ave CV3 .... 133 B5
Dewsbury Cl DY8 .... 60 E3
Dewsbury Dr Burntwood
  WS7 .... 7 C6
  Wolverhampton WV4 .... 39 A4
Dewsbury Gr B42 .... 55 C5
Dexter Ho B67 .... 64 F6
Dexter Way B78 .... 36 F8
Deykin Ave B6 .... 56 B2
Deykin Avenue Jun & Inf
  Sch B6 .... 56 B2
Dial Cl B14 .... 104 E2
Dial House La CV5 .... 111 F4
Dial La Stourbridge DY8 ...... 80 E8
  West Bromwich B70 .... 52 F6
Diamond Gr WS11 .... 2 C2
Diamond Park Dr DY8 .... 60 E1
Diana Cl WS9 .... 16 B3
Diana Dr CV2 .... 96 E1
Diane Cl DY4 .... 41 B2
Dibble Cl WV12 .... 27 D5
Dibble Rd B67 .... 64 F6
Dibdale Ct **7** DY3 .... 50 E3
Dibdale Rd DY1 .... 50 F3
Dibdale St DY1 .... 51 A2
Dice Pleck B31 .... 103 C2
Dickens Cl Dudley DY3 .... 50 B5
  Nuneaton CV10 .... 72 A4
Dickens Gr **9** B14 .... 105 A3
Dickens Heath Rd B90 ...... 126 A6
Dickens Rd Coventry CV6 .. 113 A8
  Dudley WV14 .... 40 D2
  Wolverhampton WV10 .... 12 A1
Dickins Rd CV34 .... 156 B1
Dickinson Ave WV10 .... 25 F9
Dickinson Dr
  Sutton Coldfield B76 .... 46 E4
  Walsall WS2 .... 42 C6
Dickinson Rd WV5 .... 49 A5
Didcot Cl B97 .... 158 C5
Diddington Ave B28 .... 106 A5
Diddington La B92, CV7 ...... 91 C1
Didgley Gr B37 .... 70 A5
Didsbury Rd CV7 .... 78 A1
Digbeth Birmingham B5 .... 164 D1
  Walsall WS1 .... 28 E1
Digbey Cl CV5 .... 112 B6
Digby Cres B46 .... 59 B3
Digby Ct **3** B27 .... 88 C3
Digby Dr B37 .... 90 B6
Digby Ho B37 .... 69 F4
Digby Pl CV7 .... 92 C1
Digby Rd Coleshill B46 .... 70 F6
  Kingswinford DY6 .... 60 D8
  Sutton Coldfield B73 .... 46 B4
Dilcock Way CV4 .... 131 F7
Dilke Rd WS9 .... 29 F5
Dillam Cl CV6 .... 96 A4
Dilliars Wlk B70 .... 53 A5
Dillington Ho **8** B37 .... 70 B2
Dillon Ct CV11 .... 73 B5
Dillotford Ave CV3 .... 133 D6
Dilloways La WV13 .... 40 F8
Dilwyn Cl B98 .... 154 F1
Dimbles Hill WS13 .... 3 B1
Dimbles La WS13 .... 3 A2
Dimmingsdale Bank B32 .... 84 C4
Dimmingsdale Rd WV4 .... 37 E5
Dimmocks Ave WV14 .... 51 D8

Dimsdale Gr B31 .... 102 E3
Dimsdale Rd B31 .... 102 D3
Dinedor Cl B98 .... 154 D3
Dingle Ave B64 .... 82 E8
Dingle Cl Birmingham B30 . 103 D7
  Coventry CV6 .... 113 A6
Dingle Ct B91 .... 106 F1
Dingle Hollow B69 .... 63 D8
Dingle La Solihull B91 .... 106 F2
  Willenhall WV13 .... 27 A4
Dingle Mead B14 .... 104 C4
Dingle Prim Sch The DY6 ... 61 A4
Dingle Rd Clayhanger WS8 .. 15 E6
  Dudley DY2 .... 62 E7
  Kingswinford DY6 .... 61 A4
  Stourbridge DY9 .... 81 C2
Dingle St B69 .... 63 E8
Dingle The Birmingham B29 . 85 E2
  Cheswick Green B90 .... 126 D5
  Nuneaton CV10 .... 72 E6
  Oldbury B69 .... 63 D8
  Wolverhampton WV3 .... 24 D1
Dingle View DY3 .... 50 C6
Dingleside B98 .... 159 B8
Dingleside Mid Sch B98 .... 159 B8
Dingley Rd Bulkington CV12 . 79 B2
  Wednesbury WS10 .... 42 A5
Dinmore Ave B31 .... 103 B4
Dinmore Cl B98 .... 154 D3
Dinsdale Wlk WV6 .... 25 A5
Dippons Dr WV6 .... 24 A3
Dippons Ho WV6 .... 24 A3
Dippons Mill Cl WV6 .... 24 A3
Dirtyfoot La WV4 .... 38 A5
Discovery Cl DY4 .... 52 C5
Discovery Way CV3 .... 135 B7
Ditch The WS1 .... 28 F1
Ditchford Cl B97 .... 158 D4
Ditton Gr B31 .... 122 F6
Dixon Cl Birmingham B35 ... 58 A2
  Tipton DY4 .... 52 C6
Dixon Ct DY10 .... 117 C8
Dixon Ho B16 .... 66 A1
Dixon Rd B10 .... 87 B8
Dixon St Kidderminster
  DY10 .... 116 E5
  Wolverhampton WV2 .... 39 F7
Dixon's Green Rd DY2 .... 62 E8
Dixons Green Ct **7** DY2 ... 62 E8
Dobbins Oak Rd DY9 .... 81 E1
Dobbs Mill Cl B29 .... 86 B2
Dobbs St WV2 .... 163 B1
Dobson La CV31 .... 162 A4
Dock La Birmingham B46 .... 88 F3
Dock Lane Ind Est **12** DY1 .. 51 B1
Dock Meadow Dr WV4 .... 40 A4
Dock Rd DY8 .... 60 F2
Dock The Catshill B61 .... 137 A8
  Stourbridge DY9 .... 81 F5
Dockar Rd B31 .... 102 E2
Dockers Cl CV7 .... 130 C7
Doctor's Piece WV13 .... 27 B2
Doctors Hill
  Bournheath B61 .... 136 D8
  Stourbridge DY9 .... 81 C3
Doctors La Kingswinford
  DY6 .... 60 A4
  Shenstone WS14 .... 18 A6
Dodd Ave CV34 .... 161 C7
Doddington Gr B32 .... 102 B8
Dodford Cl B45 .... 121 F7
Dodford Fst Sch B61 .... 136 A5
Dodford Ho B60 .... 137 B3
Dodford Rd B61 .... 120 D1
Dodwells Bridge Ind Est
  LE10 .... 74 E8
Dodwells Rd LE10 .... 74 E8
Doe Bank Ct B44 .... 46 B8
Doe Bank La Birmingham
  B43 .... 44 D5
  Coventry CV1 .... 113 A3
Doe Bank Rd DY4 .... 41 C1
Dog Kennel La Solihull
  B90 .... 126 D7
  3 Walsall WS1 .... 28 F2
Dog La Tamworth B77 .... 22 B6
  Weeford WS14 .... 19 A4
Dogberry Cl CV3 .... 134 C6
Dogge Lane Croft B27 .... 88 B2
Dogkennel La Halesowen
  B63 .... 83 B3
  Oldbury B68 .... 64 C5
Doglands The CV31 .... 162 B4
Dogpool La B30 .... 86 B1
Doidge Rd B23 .... 56 D3
Dolben La B98 .... 154 D3
Doll Mus CV34 .... 160 E6
Dollery Dr B5 .... 86 C5
Dollis Gr B44 .... 44 F3
Dollman St B7 .... 67 B4
Dolman Rd B6 .... 66 E8
Dolobran Rd B11 .... 87 B7
Dolphin Cl WS3 .... 14 F1
Dolphin Ct WV12 .... 27 D8
Dolphin La B27 .... 88 C1
Dolphin Rd Birmingham
  B11 .... 87 D5
  Redditch B98 .... 154 A5
Dolton Way DY4 .... 51 E6
Domar Rd DY11 .... 116 B7
Dominic Cl B30 .... 103 D4
Don Cl B15 .... 85 D8
Don Gp CV2 .... 4 D7
Doncaster Cl CV2 .... 114 D7
Doncaster Way B36 .... 68 C8
Donegal Cl CV4 .... 132 A7
Donegal Rd B74 .... 44 F5

Dongan Rd CV34 .... 160 E7
Donibristle Croft B35 .... 58 A4
Donnington Ave CV6 .... 112 E5
Donnington Cl B98 .... 154 C5
Donnington Ho B33 .... 69 B2
Donnithorne Ave
  CV10, CV11 .... 73 D1
Dooley Cl WV13 .... 26 E2
Doone Cl CV2 .... 114 E6
Dora Herbert Ct B12 .... 86 E5
Dora Rd Birmingham B10 .... 87 E8
  Birmingham,
  Handsworth B21 .... 65 E7
  West Bromwich B70 .... 53 C1
Dora St WS2 .... 42 B7
Dorado B77 .... 35 D6
Doran Cl B63 .... 82 D1
Doranda Way B71 .... 53 F1
Dorcas Cl CV11 .... 79 C8
Dorchester Cl WV12 .... 27 C8
Dorchester Ct B91 .... 107 A4
Dorchester Dr B17 .... 85 B4
Dorchester Rd Cannock
  WS11 .... 1 B1
  Hinckley LE10 .... 76 B7
  Solihull B91 .... 107 A4
  Stourbridge DY9 .... 81 D2
  Willenhall WV12 .... 13 C1
Dorchester Way
  Coventry CV2 .... 115 A4
  Nuneaton CV11 .... 74 A7
Dordale Rd B61, DY9 .... 119 E2
Dordon Cl B90 .... 105 E1
Dordon Rd B78 .... 36 F8
Doreen Gr B24 .... 57 B2
Doris Rd Birmingham B11 .... 87 B4
  Birmingham,
  Bordesley Green B9 .... 67 D2
  Coleshill B46 .... 70 F8
Dorking Gr B15 .... 66 C1
Dorlcote Rd B8 .... 68 A4
Dorlecote Ct CV10 .... 73 C1
Dorlecote Pl CV10 .... 78 C1
Dorlecote Rd CV10 .... 78 C8
Dormer Ave B77 .... 21 E5
Dormer Harris Ave CV4 ..... 111 F1
Dormer Ho **13** CV32 ...... 156 F2
Dormer Pl CV32 .... 161 F8
Dormie Cl B38 .... 103 D1
Dormington Rd B44 .... 44 F3
Dormston Cl Redditch B98 . 153 F1
  Solihull B91 .... 127 C8
Dormston Dr Birmingham
  B29 .... 84 F2
  Sedgley DY3 .... 50 E8
Dormston Sch DY3 .... 50 E8
Dormston Trad Est DY1 .... 50 F4
Dormy B31 .... 123 A7
Dorncliffe Ave B33 .... 89 D7
Dorney Cl CV5 .... 132 E8
Dornie Dr B38 .... 103 F1
Dornton Rd B30 .... 104 C4
Dorothy Gdns B20 .... 55 A2
Dorothy Goodman Specl
  Sch The LE10 .... 71 D2
Dorothy Pattison Hospl
  WS2 .... 28 B1
Dorothy Powell Way CV2 .... 96 F1
Dorothy Purcell Jun Sch
  WV14 .... 41 B3
Dorothy Rd Birmingham
  B11 .... 88 B5
  Smethwick B67 .... 65 A4
Dorothy St WS1 .... 42 D7
Dorridge Cl B97 .... 153 B1
Dorridge Croft B93 .... 127 C8
Dorridge Jun & Inf Schs
  B93 .... 128 A8
Dorridge Rd B93 .... 128 A2
Dorridge Sta B93 .... 127 F2
Dorrington Gn B42 .... 55 A5
Dorrington Jun & Inf Sch
  B42 .... 55 A5
Dorrington Rd B42 .... 55 A5
Dorset Cl Birmingham B45 . 101 F2
  Nuneaton CV10 .... 72 F3
  Tamworth B78 .... 21 A1
Dorset Cotts B30 .... 104 A6
Dorset Dr WS9 .... 16 B1
Dorset Pl WS3 .... 28 C7
Dorset Rd Birmingham B8 ... 67 C6
  Cannock WS12 .... 2 E1
  Coventry CV1 .... 113 C5
  Smethwick B17 .... 65 B3
  Stourbridge DY8 .... 80 D8
Dorset Tower B18 .... 66 B4
Dorsett Rd Darlaston WS10 . 41 C6
  Wednesbury WS10 .... 42 D2
Dorset Road Terr WS10 ...... 41 C6
Dorsheath Gdns B23 .... 56 F4
Dorsington Rd B27 .... 88 D1
Dorstone Covert B14 .... 104 C2
Dorville Cl B38 .... 123 D8
Dosthill Rd (Two Gates)
  B77 .... 35 D7
Dosthill Sch B77 .... 35 D5
Dotterel Pl DY10 .... 117 A1
Douay Rd B24 .... 57 B6
Double Row DY2 .... 62 E4
Doughty St DY4 .... 52 C5
Douglas Ave Birmingham
  B36 .... 68 D6
  Oldbury B68 .... 64 D5
Douglas Davies Cl WV12 ... 27 C4
Douglas Ho
  5 Birmingham B36 .... 57 F1
  Coventry CV1 .... 165 D4
Douglas Pl WV10 .... 25 C6

Douglas Rd Birmingham B27 . 88 C4
Birmingham,
Handsworth B21 .... 65 F8
Dudley WV14 .... 51 D8
Halesowen B62 .... 63 E1
Hollywood B47 .... 125 A7
Oldbury B68 .... 64 D4
Sutton Coldfield B72 ...... 46 C3
Douglass Rd DY2 .... 62 D8
Doulton Cl Birmingham B32 .. 84 F3
Coventry CV2 .... 96 A5
Doulton Rd Blackheath B65 .. 63 A4
Oldbury B64, B65 .... 62 F4
Doulton Trad Est B65 ...... 62 F4
Dove Cl Bedworth CV12 .... 77 E3
Birmingham B25 .... 88 E8
Burntwood WS7 .... 7 D6
Hinckley LE10 .... 75 A8
Kidderminster DY10 ...... 117 B2
Wednesbury WS10 .... 42 B4
Dove Dr DY8 .... 81 A8
Dove Gdns B38 .... 104 B2
Dove Hollow Cannock WS12 .. 2 E4
Great Wyrley WS6 .... 4 F1
Dove House Ct B92 .... 106 F7
Dove House La B91 .... 107 A8
Dove Ridge DY8 .... 81 A7
Dove Way B36 .... 69 F8
Dovebridge Cl B46 .... 64 F4
Dovecote Cl Coventry CV6 .. 112 D5
Solihull B91 .... 107 B8
Tipton DY4 .... 52 C5
Wolverhampton WV6 .... 24 C4
Dovecote Rd B61 .... 136 E1
Dovecotes Jun & Inf Schs
WV8 .... 10 F1
Dovecotes The
Coventry CV5 .... 112 B5
Sutton Coldfield B75 .... 32 B3
Dovedale WS11 .... 2 A5
Dovedale Ave Coventry CV6 .. 95 F2
Solihull B90 .... 106 B3
Walsall WS3 .... 15 B5
Willenhall WV12 .... 27 B4
Dovedale Ct WV4 .... 39 F2
Dovedale Dr B28 .... 105 F5
Dovedale Ho WV1 .... 26 C1
Dovedale Rd Birmingham
B23 .... 56 C7
Kingswinford DY6 .... 60 E6
Wolverhampton wv4, WV14 .. 39 E3
Dovehouse Fields WS14 .... 9 B6
Dovehouse La B91 .... 106 F7
Dovehouse Pool Rd ⅰ B6 .. 66 E8
Dover Cl B32 .... 102 A7
Dover Farm Cl B77 .... 36 B8
Dover Ho WS3 .... 28 C7
Dover St Bilston WV14 ..... 40 D6
Birmingham B18 .... 66 A6
Coventry CV1 .... 165 A3
Dovercourt Ho ⅰ B15 ..... 86 D8
Dovercourt Rd B26 .... 89 C5
Doverdale Ave DY10 ...... 117 B5
Doverdale Cl Halesowen
B63 .... 82 E5
Redditch B98 .... 159 B7
Doveridge Cl B91 .... 106 E6
Doveridge Rd B28 .... 105 E5
Doversley Rd B14 .... 104 C5
Dovestone B77 .... 22 D1
Dovey Dr B76 .... 57 A8
Dovey Rd Birmingham B13 .. 87 D2
Tipton B69 .... 63 D8
Dowar Rd B45 .... 122 C7
Dowells Cl B13 .... 86 F2
Dowells Gdns DY8 .... 60 D3
Dower Rd B75 .... 32 B1
Doweries The B45 .... 121 F8
Dowler's Hill Cres B98 ... 159 A8
Dowles Cl B29 .... 103 B6
Dowles Rd DY11 .... 116 B2
Dowley Croft CV3 .... 115 B1
Downcroft Ave B38 .... 103 E2
Downderry Way CV6 ...... 114 A6
Downend Cl WV10 .... 11 F4
Downes Ct ⅰ DY4 .... 51 E5
Downesway WS11 .... 1 C2
Downey Cl B11 .... 87 B7
Downfield Cl WS3 .... 14 A4
Downfield Dr DY3 .... 50 E6
Downham Pl WV3 .... 38 F8
Downham Wood WS5 .... 43 E8
Downie Rd WV8 .... 10 C3
Downing Cl ⅰ
Blackheath B65 .... 63 C1
Knowle B93 .... 128 A4
Wednesfield WV11 .... 27 A7
Downing Cres CV12 .... 78 C4
Downing Ct ⅰ B68 .... 84 B7
Downing Ho B37 .... 70 C3
Downing St Halesowen B63 .. 83 A5
Smethwick B66 .... 65 C7
Downland B38 .... 103 F1
Downs Rd WV13 .... 41 C8
Downs The Aldridge WS9 ... 30 C2
Wolverhampton WV10 .... 25 C6
Downsell Rd B97 .... 153 A2
Downside Rd B26 .... 89 B7
Downton Cl CV2 .... 115 A8
Downton Cres B33 .... 69 E3
Dowty Ave CV12 .... 77 D1
Dowty Way WV9 .... 11 A3
Doyle Dr CV6 .... 95 F3
Dr Phillips Sh Ctr The CV2 .. 96 D1
Dragoon Fields B60 ...... 151 B8
Drake Cl WS3 .... 14 B1

Drake Cres DY11 .... 116 A7
Drake Croft ⅰ WS13 .... 9 C8
Drake Ho DY4 .... 52 A7
Drake Rd Birmingham B23 .. 56 C3
Smethwick B66 .... 64 E7
Walsall WS3 .... 14 B1
Drake St Coventry CV6 .... 113 D7
West Bromwich B71 .... 53 C5
Drake Way LE10 .... 71 D4
Drake's Gn WV14 .... 40 F3
Drakes Ct B97 .... 158 C6
Drakes Hill Cl DY8 .... 80 C4
Drancy Ave WV12 .... 27 D6
Draper Cl CV8 .... 148 C4
Draper's Fields ⅰ CV1 ... 165 B4
Drawbridge Rd B90 .... 125 E8
Draycote Cl B92 .... 107 D6
Draycott Ave B23 .... 56 D5
Draycott Cl Redditch B97 .. 153 B5
Wolverhampton WV4 .... 38 C5
Draycott Cres B77 .... 21 D1
Draycott Dr B31 .... 102 E7
Draycott Rd Coventry CV2 .. 114 C7
Smethwick B66 .... 64 E7
Drayton Cl Nuneaton CV10 .. 72 A8
Redditch B98 .... 159 D8
Sutton Coldfield B75 ...... 32 B3
Drayton Cres CV5 .... 111 D5
Drayton Ct Bromsgrove B60 . 151 B8
Warwick CV34 .... 155 E2
Drayton La B78 .... 34 C5
Drayton Manor Dr
Fazeley B78 .... 34 F7
Fazeley B78 .... 34 F8
Drayton Manor Pk B78 .... 34 E7
Drayton Rd Bedworth CV12 .. 78 D2
Belbroughton DY9 .... 119 B5
Birmingham B14 .... 104 F8
Smethwick B66 .... 65 A1
Solihull B90 .... 126 E8
Drayton St Walsall WS2 ... 28 C2
Wolverhampton WV2 .... 163 B1
Drayton St E WS2 .... 28 C2
Drayton Way CV10 .... 72 C7
Dreadnought Rd DY5 .... 61 B8
Dreel The B15 .... 85 E7
Dreghorn Rd B36 .... 68 F8
Drem Croft B35 .... 58 A2
Dresden Cl WV4 .... 40 A4
Drew Cres Kenilworth CV8 .. 148 A4
Stourbridge DY9 .... 81 D2
Drew Rd DY9 .... 81 D3
Drews Ho B14 .... 104 D1
Drews Holloway B63 .... 82 D5
Drews Holloway S B63 ..... 82 D5
Drews La B8 .... 68 A7
Drews Meadow Cl
ⅰ B14 .... 104 C2
Driffield Cl B98 .... 154 D2
Driffold B73 .... 46 B3
Driftwood Cl B38 .... 123 D7
Drinkwater Ho ⅰ CV1 .... 113 B2
Drive Fields WV4 .... 38 B6
Drive Prep Sch The WV6 .. 24 C5
Drive The
Birmingham,
Gravelly Hill B23 .... 56 C2
Birmingham,
Handsworth B20 .... 55 B2
Brierley Hill DY5 .... 61 C5
Coventry CV2 .... 114 E3
Halesowen B63 .... 83 A3
Hopwood B48 .... 123 B3
Redditch B97 .... 152 C7
Shenstone WS14 .... 18 E8
Walsall, High Heath WS4 .. 15 C1
Walsall, Pelsall WS3 ...... 14 E2
Wolverhampton WV6 .... 24 C5
Droicon Trad Est B65 ..... 63 C5
Dronfield Rd CV2 .... 114 B3
Drovers Way B60 .... 150 E6
Droveway The WV8, WV9 ... 10 F2
Droxford Wlk WV8 .... 10 E1
Droylsdon Park Rd CV3 ... 133 B3
Druid Park Rd WV12 .... 13 C1
Druid Rd CV2 .... 114 B3
Druid St LE10 .... 71 D1
Druids Ave Aldridge WS9 .. 30 C8
Blackheath B65 .... 63 D4
Druids La B14 .... 104 D1
Druids Wlk WS9 .... 16 A3
Drummond Cl Coventry
CV6 .... 112 F2
Wolverhampton WV11 ...... 13 A2
Drummond Gr B43 .... 44 C3
Drummond Rd
Birmingham B9 .... 68 A2
Bromsgrove B60 .... 151 B8
Stourbridge DY9 .... 81 F4
Drummond St WV1 .... 163 B4
Drummond Way B37 .... 70 C2
Drury La Solihull B91 .... 107 C3
Stourbridge DY8 .... 81 A5
Drybrook Cl B38 .... 123 E8
Drybrooks Cl CV7 .... 130 B6
Dryden Cl Kenilworth CV8 . 147 F3
Tipton DY4 .... 52 A7
Willenhall WV12 .... 27 E8
Dryden Gr B27 .... 88 B2
Dryden Pl WS3 .... 28 E7
Dryden Rd Tamworth B79 .. 21 A6
Walsall WS3 .... 28 E7
Wolverhampton WV10 ...... 11 F1
Drylea Gr B36 .... 68 F8
Dual Way WS11 .... 1 D8
Dubarry Ave DY6 .... 60 C7
Duchess Rd Birmingham B16 . 66 A1
Walsall WS1 .... 42 D5

Duck La WV8 .... 10 B3
Duckhouse Rd WV11 .... 26 D7
Duddeston Manor Rd B7 ... 67 A4
Duddeston Mill Rd B7, B8 .. 67 C4
Duddeston Mill Trad Est B8 67 C4
Duddeston Sta B7 .... 67 B4
Dudding Rd WV4 .... 39 D5
Dudhill Rd B65 .... 63 A3
Dudhill Wlk B65 .... 63 A4
Dudley Castle DY1 .... 51 D2
Dudley Central Trad Est
DY2 .... 62 C8
Dudley Cl B65 .... 63 A5
Dudley Coll Mons Hill DY1 . 51 B5
Dudley Coll of Tech (The
Glass Ctr Annexe) DY5 ... 61 D3
Dudley Cres WV11 .... 26 E6
Dudley Gn CV32 .... 157 B2
Dudley Gr ⅰ B18 .... 65 E4
Dudley Innovation Ctr DY6 . 60 F7
Dudley L Ctr DY1 .... 51 B1
Dudley Park Rd B27 .... 88 C3
Dudley Port DY4 .... 52 A3
Dudley Port Sta DY4 ...... 52 B4
Dudley Rd Birmingham B18 .. 65 E4
Blackheath B65 .... 63 A5
Brierley Hill DY5 .... 61 D4
Dudley DY3 .... 50 E6
Halesowen B63 .... 83 B5
Himley DY3 .... 49 D3
Kenilworth CV8 .... 147 F2
Kingswinford,
Barrow Hill DY6 .... 60 F7
Kingswinford,Wall Heath DY6 60 C8
Oldbury B69 .... 63 F8
Stourbridge DY9 .... 81 E6
Tipton DY4 .... 51 E5
Wolverhampton WV2 .... 39 D7
Dudley Rd E B69 .... 52 B3
Dudley Rd W B69 .... 52 B2
Dudley Rise LE10 .... 75 D6
Dudley Row DY2 .... 51 D1
Dudley St Bilston WV14 ... 40 D4
Birmingham B5 .... 164 C2
Coventry CV6 .... 96 A1
Kidderminster DY10 ...... 116 E7
Sedgley DY3 .... 50 D8
Walsall WS1 .... 28 E1
Wednesbury WS10 .... 41 E2
West Bromwich B70 .... 53 A5
Wolverhampton WV1 ...... 163 B3
Dudley Street, Guns
Village Sta B70 .... 53 B4
Dudley Tech Coll DY1 ..... 51 C2
Dudley Tech Coll Annexe
DY1 .... 51 B1
Dudley Tech Coll (Tipton
Annexe) DY4 .... 51 D6
Dudley Terr CV8 .... 149 B6
Dudley Wlk WV4 .... 39 C5
Dudley Wood Ave DY2 ..... 62 C2
Dudley Wood Prim Sch
DY2 .... 62 C2
Dudley Wood Rd DY2 ...... 62 C2
Dudley Zoo DY1 .... 51 D2
Dudmaston Way DY1 .... 50 E3
Dudnill Gr B32 .... 102 A8
Duffield Cl WV8 .... 10 F1
Dufton Rd B32 .... 84 E4
Dugdale Cl WS12 .... 2 F3
Dugdale Cres B75 .... 32 C3
Dugdale Ct ⅰ CV31 ...... 162 A6
Dugdale Ho CV11 .... 73 C3
Dugdale Rd CV6 .... 113 B6
Dugdale St Nuneaton CV11 .. 73 C4
Smethwick B66 .... 65 D4
Duggins La CV4, CV7 ..... 131 B8
Duke Barn Field CV2 ..... 114 A5
Duke St Blackheath B65 ... 63 B2
Coventry CV5 .... 112 F2
Dudley DY3 .... 50 D5
Nuneaton CV11 .... 73 B4
Royal Leamington Spa CV32 157 A1
Stourbridge DY8 .... 81 A6
Sutton Coldfield B72 ..... 46 C4
Wednesfield WV11 .... 26 D5
West Bromwich B70 .... 53 B4
Wolverhampton,
Penn Fields WV3 .... 39 A7
Wolverhampton,
Springfield WV1 .... 163 D2
Dukes Rd Birmingham B30 .. 104 A3
Dordon B78 .... 36 F6
Dulais Cl B98 .... 153 E1
Dulvern Gr B14 .... 104 D5
Dulverton Ave CV5 .... 112 D4
Dulverton Ct CV5 .... 112 D4
Dulverton Rd B6 .... 56 B1
Dulwich Gr B44 .... 56 B8
Dulwich Rd B44 .... 56 A8
Dumble Pit La B48 ...... 140 F7
Dumblederry Ave CV5 ..... 50 C7
Dumblederry Ct WS9 ...... 29 F5
Dumblederry La
Aldridge WS9 .... 29 F6
Walsall WS9 .... 29 E7
Dumolo's Cty Prim Sch
B77 .... 21 F3
Dumolos La B77 .... 21 F3
Dumphouse La B48 .... 140 C3
Dunard Rd B90 .... 105 C2
Dunbar Cl Birmingham B32 .. 84 D1
Kidderminster DY10 ...... 117 C6
Dunbar Gr B43 .... 44 B4
Dunblane Dr CV32 .... 157 C5
Dunblane Way LE10 .... 71 A2
Duncalfe Dr B75 .... 32 B3
Duncan Edwards Cl DY1 ... 62 A8

Duncan Ho B73 .... 46 B1
Duncan St WV2 .... 39 C7
Dunchurch Cl
Balsall Common CV7 ...... 130 B7
Redditch B98 .... 154 F1
Dunchurch Cres B73 ...... 45 C3
Dunchurch Dr B31 .... 102 E7
Dunchurch Highway CV5 . 112 A4
Dunchurch Ho ⅰ B5 ...... 86 E8
Dunclent Cres DY10 ...... 117 B5
Duncombe Gn ⅰ B46 ...... 70 F7
Duncombe Gr B17 .... 85 A7
Duncombe St DY8 .... 80 D5
Duncroft Ave CV6 .... 112 F7
Duncroft Rd B26 .... 89 A8
Duncroft Wlk DY1 .... 51 B6
Duncumb Rd B75 .... 47 A5
Dundalk La WS6 .... 4 D2
Dundas Ave DY2 .... 62 F8
Dundle Ct B74 .... 31 F2
Dunedin B77 .... 22 A1
Dunedin Dr B45 .... 122 B1
Dunedin Ho B32 .... 84 F4
Dunedin Rd B44 .... 44 F3
Dunhill Ave CV4 .... 111 E3
Dunkirk Ave B70 .... 52 E3
Dunkley St WV1 .... 163 B4
Dunley Croft B90 .... 126 F6
Dunley Ct B23 .... 56 C2
Dunlin Cl Birmingham B23 .. 56 C2
Featherstone WV10 .... 12 B7
Kingswinford DY6 .... 61 A6
Dunlin Dr DY10 .... 116 F2
Dunlop Rd B97 .... 158 D5
Dunlop Way B35 .... 57 F2
Dunnerdale Rd WS8 .... 15 D6
Dunnigan Rd B32 .... 84 F3
Dunnose Cl CV6 .... 113 E8
Dunns Bank DY5 .... 81 F7
Dunrose Cl CV2 .... 114 E2
Dunsfold Cl WV14 .... 40 A3
Dunsfold Croft ⅰ B6 ..... 66 F6
Dunsford Cl DY5 .... 81 B7
Dunsford Rd B66 .... 65 A2
Dunsink Rd B6 .... 55 F1
Dunslade Cres DY5 .... 81 F8
Dunslade Rd B23 .... 56 E7
Dunsley Dr DY8 .... 60 E3
Dunsley Gr WV4 .... 39 A4
Dunsley Rd DY8 .... 80 C4
Dunsmore Ave CV3 ...... 134 C6
Dunsmore Dr DY5 .... 81 F8
Dunsmore Gr B91 .... 106 F7
Dunsmore Rd B28 .... 87 E2
Dunstall Ave WV6 .... 25 C4
Dunstall Cl B97 .... 153 B2
Dunstall Gr B29 .... 102 F8
Dunstall Hill W6 .... 25 C5
Dunstall Hill Prim Sch
WV6 .... 25 C4
Dunstall Hill Trad Est W6 . 25 C5
Dunstall La Hopwas B78 .. 20 D4
Wolverhampton WV6 .... 25 B5
Dunstall Park Race
Course WV6 .... 25 A6
Dunstall Rd Halesowen B63 . 82 D3
Wolverhampton WV6 .... 25 B4
Dunstan Croft B90 ...... 126 C8
Dunstan Ct ⅰ B15 .... 86 B7
Dunster B77 .... 35 C7
Dunster Cl B30 .... 104 C4
Dunster Gr WV6 .... 23 F3
Dunster Pl CV6 .... 95 D3
Dunster Rd B37 .... 70 D2
Dunston Cl Great Wyrley
WS6 .... 13 E8
Kingswinford DY6 .... 60 D7
Dunston Dr WS7 .... 7 A8
Dunsville Dr CV2 .... 114 F8
Dunton Cl B75 .... 32 A4
Dunton La B76 .... 48 C1
Dunton Rd B37 .... 69 F5
Dunton Trad Est B7 ...... 67 D7
Dunvegan Cl Coventry CV3 . 115 A2
Kenilworth CV8 .... 148 C4
Dunvegan Rd B24 .... 57 A4
Duport Rd LE10 .... 75 F7
Durant Cl B45 .... 101 E1
Durban Rd B66 .... 65 C4
Durbar Ave CV6 .... 113 D8
Durham Ave WV13 .... 27 D3
Durham Cres CV5 .... 112 B7
Durham Croft B37 .... 70 B2
Durham Dr B71 .... 53 D7
Durham Ho ⅰ WV3 .... 25 C4
Durham Pl WS2 .... 28 B1
Durham Rd Birmingham B11 . 87 B4
Blackheath B65 .... 63 E4
Dudley DY2 .... 62 D2
Stourbridge DY8 .... 80 D8
Walsall WS2 .... 42 B8
Wednesbury WS10 .... 42 D4
Durham Tower ⅰ B1 ...... 66 B3
Durley Dean Rd B29 ...... 85 C2
Durley Dr B73 .... 45 C3
Durley Rd B25 .... 88 C6
Durlston Cl B77 .... 21 F5
Durlston Gr B28 .... 106 A8
Durnford Croft B14 ..... 104 E1
Dursley Cl Solihull B92 . 107 B8
Willenhall WV12 .... 27 D4
Dursley Dr WS11 .... 1 B2
Dursley Rd WS7 .... 7 A7
Dusthouse La B60 .... 151 D7

Dou – Eas 187

Dutton Rd CV2 .... 96 D3
Dutton's La B75 .... 32 E4
Duxford Cl B97 .... 158 B8
Duxford Rd B42 .... 55 B7
Dwarris Wlk CV34 .... 155 E2
Dwellings La B32 .... 84 B5
Dyas Ave B42 .... 55 A7
Dyas Rd Birmingham B44 .. 44 E1
Hollywood B47 .... 125 A7
Dyce Cl B35 .... 58 A4
Dyers La B94 .... 142 D8
Dyers Rd CV11 .... 79 F6
Dymoke St B12 .... 86 F8
Dymond Rd CV6 .... 95 D3
Dynes Wlk B67 .... 65 A5
Dyott Rd B13 .... 87 A1
Dysart Cl CV1 .... 113 E4
Dyson Cl WS2 .... 27 F3
Dyson St CV4 .... 111 E3
Dysons Gdns B8 .... 67 E5

Eachelhurst Rd B24, B76 ... 57 F5
Eachus Rd WV14 .... 51 D8
Eachway B45 .... 121 F6
Eachway Farm Cl B45 ... 122 A6
Eachway La B45 .... 122 A6
Eacott Cl CV6 .... 95 A3
Eadgar Ct B43 .... 54 D7
Eadie St CV10 .... 72 D4
Eagle Cl Blackheath B65 .. 63 A4
Cheslyn Hay WS6 .... 4 D2
Dudley DY1 .... 50 F1
Nuneaton CV11 .... 79 B8
Eagle Croft B14 .... 104 E2
Eagle Ct CV3 .... 39 A7
Eagle Dr B77 .... 22 C4
Eagle Gdns B24 .... 57 A2
Eagle Gr Birmingham B36 ... 70 A8
Cannock WS12 .... 2 C1
Eagle Ho CV1 .... 113 D5
Eagle Ind Est DY4 .... 52 E7
Eagle La Kenilworth CV8 . 147 F4
Tipton DY4 .... 52 D6
Eagle Rd B98 .... 154 E5
Eagle St Coventry CV1 ... 113 D5
Royal Leamington Spa CV31 162 A6
Tipton DY4 .... 52 C6
Wolverhampton,
Monmore Green WV2 .... 39 E8
Wolverhampton,
Penn Fields WV3 .... 39 A7
Eagle St E CV1 .... 113 D5
Eales Yd ⅰ LE10 .... 71 D1
Ealing Gr B44 .... 45 A1
Ealingham B77 .... 22 B1
Eanwulf Ct B15 .... 86 C8
Eardisley Cl B98 .... 154 F1
Earl St Bedworth CV12 ... 78 C2
Bilston WV14 .... 40 D5
Coventry CV1 .... 165 C2
Dudley WV14 .... 51 D8
Kingswinford DY6 .... 60 D4
Royal Leamington Spa CV32 157 A3
Walsall WS1 .... 42 D7
West Bromwich B70 .... 53 B4
Earl's Croft The CV3 ... 133 D7
Earl's Wlk CV3 .... 135 D7
Earls Court Rd B17 ...... 85 A6
Earls Ferry Gdns B32 ... 102 B7
Earls High Sch The B63 .. 83 B4
Earls Rd Nuneaton CV11 .. 73 A5
Walsall WS4 .... 29 D7
Earls Way B63 .... 83 B4
Earlsbury Gdns B20 ...... 55 D1
Earlsdon Ave N CV5 ..... 112 F1
Earlsdon Ave S CV5 ..... 133 A8
Earlsdon Bsns Ctr CV5 .. 132 F3
Earlsdon Prim Sch CV5 .. 113 A1
Earlsdon St CV5 .... 132 F8
Earlsmead Rd B21 .... 65 C7
Earlsmere B94 .... 126 B1
Earlston Way B43 .... 54 D8
Earlswood Comm B94 ..... 142 A6
Earlswood Cres WV9 ...... 11 A3
Earlswood Ct B20 .... 55 A2
Earlswood Dr B74 .... 46 C7
Earlswood Ho ⅰ B5 ...... 86 E7
Earlswood Rd Dorridge
B93 .... 127 D2
Kingswinford DY6 .... 60 E8
Earlswood Sta B94 ...... 125 D1
Earlswood Trad Est B94 . 141 C6
Easby Way Birmingham B8 .. 67 E5
Walsall WS3 .... 13 F2
Easedale Cl Coventry CV3 . 133 B6
Nuneaton CV11 .... 74 A6
Easemore Rd B98 .... 153 F5
Easenhall Cl B93 .... 128 A4
Easenhall La B98 .... 154 E1
Easmore Cl B14 .... 104 D2
East Ave Bedworth CV12 .. 78 D2
Coventry CV2 .... 114 A2
Tipton B69 .... 63 C7
Wolverhampton WV11 ...... 26 C6
East Birmingham Coll
Birmingham B11 .... 87 A7
Birmingham B33 .... 89 B8
Birmingham, Sparkhill B11 . 87 D5
East Birmingham Coll
Bordesley Green Campus
B9 .... 68 A2
East Birmingham Hospl
B9 .... 68 B1
East Cannock Ind Est WS12 . 2 B3

East Cannock Rd WS12 .... 2 C4
East Car Park Rd B40 .... 90 F4
East Cl LE10 .... 75 D7
East Croft Rd WV4 .... 38 C5
East Dene CV32 .... 157 B2
East Dr B5 .... 86 C4
East Farm Croft B10 .... 87 D8
East Gate B16 .... 65 E3
East Gr CV31 .... 162 A6
East Holme B9 .... 67 C2
East Meadway B33 .... 69 E3
East Mews B44 .... 44 D2
East Park Inf Sch WV1 ...... 26 B1
East Park Jun Sch WV1 ..... 40 B8
East Park Trad Est WV1 ..... 40 A8
East Park Way WV1 .... 26 A1
East Pathway B17 .... 85 C6
East Rd Bromsgrove B60 .... 137 A1
  Featherstone WV10 .... 12 A6
  Tipton DY4 .... 52 B8
East Rise B75 .... 46 D6
East St Brierley Hill DY5 .... 82 A8
  Cannock WS11 .... 4 E6
  Coventry CV1 .... 113 E3
  Dudley, Gornalwood DY3 ... 50 D3
  Dudley, Kate's Hill DY2 .... 62 E8
  Kidderminster DY10 .... 116 F6
  Tamworth B77 .... 35 D5
  Walsall WS1 .... 42 F7
  Wolverhampton WV1 .... 163 D2
East View B77 .... 21 E3
East View Rd B72 .... 46 D2
East Way B92 .... 91 B3
Eastboro Ct CV11 .... 73 E2
Eastboro Way CV11 .... 73 F2
Eastbourne Ave B34 .... 68 E6
Eastbourne CI CV6 .... 112 E6
Eastbourne House Sch
  B27 .... 88 C4
Eastbourne St WS4 .... 28 F3
Eastbrook CI B76 .... 46 D4
Eastbury Dr B92 .... 89 A3
Eastcote CI B90 .... 106 D3
Eastcote Cres WS7 .... 7 A5
Eastcote La B92 .... 108 F4
Eastcote Rd Birmingham
  B27 .... 88 A1
  Wolverhampton WV10 ...... 25 F5
Eastcotes CV4 .... 112 B1
Eastdean CI B23 .... 56 D6
Eastern Ave Brierley Hill
  DY5 .... 61 B2
  Lichfield WS13 .... 3 C3
Eastern CI WS10 .... 41 C3
Eastern Green Jun Sch
  CV5 .... 111 D5
Eastern Green Rd CV5 ...... 111 F4
Eastern Hill B96 .... 158 F2
Eastern Rd Birmingham
  B29 .... 86 B3
  Sutton Coldfield B73 .... 46 B1
Eastern Way WS11 .... 4 F6
Easterton Croft B14 .... 104 E2
Eastfield Dr B92 .... 107 E8
Eastfield Gr WV1 .... 25 F2
Eastfield Prim Sch WV1 .... 25 F2
Eastfield Rd Birmingham B9 .. 68 C3
  Nuneaton CV10 .... 73 D6
  Royal Leamington Spa
  CV32 .... 162 A8
  Tipton DY4 .... 52 A8
  Wolverhampton WV1 .... 25 F2
Eastfield Retreat WV1 .... 25 F2
Eastgate No CV34 .... 160 E6
Eastgate Mews 9 CV34 .... 160 E6
Eastgate St WS7 .... 6 E8
Eastham Rd B13 .... 105 C6
Easthope Rd B33 .... 69 A4
Eastlake CI B43 .... 44 D3
Eastlands Gr CV5 .... 112 E4
Eastlands Rd B13 .... 87 A1
Eastleigh DY3 .... 50 C8
Eastleigh Ave CV5 .... 132 F7
Eastleigh Croft B76 .... 58 A7
Eastleigh Dr B62 .... 101 A4
Eastleigh Gr B25 .... 88 D8
Eastley Cres CV34 .... 160 B8
Eastmoor CI B74 .... 31 B2
Eastney Cres WV8 .... 24 F8
Eastnor CI
  Kidderminster DY10 .... 116 E2
  Redditch B98 .... 153 E1
Eastnor Gr CV31 .... 162 B7
Easton Gdns WV11 .... 26 F5
Easton Gr Birmingham B27 ... 88 C1
  Hollywood B47 .... 125 B7
Eastridge Croft WS14 .... 18 A5
Eastville B31 .... 103 B3
Eastward Glen WV8 .... 10 C1
Eastway
  Birmingham, Bickenhill B40 .. 90 F3
  Birmingham, Harborne B17 .. 85 C6
Eastwood Ave WS7 .... 7 A8
Eastwood CI CV31 .... 162 D6
Eastwood CI B96 .... 158 E1
Eastwood Dr DY10 .... 117 B5
Eastwood Rd
  Birmingham,
  Balsall Heath B12 .... 86 D5
  Birmingham,
  Great Barr B43 .... 54 E8
  Dudley DY2 .... 62 C4
Eastwoods Rd LE10 .... 71 F2
Eatesbrook Rd B33 .... 69 C3

Eathorpe CI Birmingham
  B34 .... 69 D6
  Coventry CV2 .... 96 C1
  Redditch B98 .... 154 E1
Eaton Ave B70 .... 53 A4
Eaton CI CV32 .... 156 D2
Eaton Cres DY3 .... 50 B3
Eaton Ct
  Royal Leamington Spa
  CV32 .... 156 D1
  Sutton Coldfield B74 .... 46 B7
Eaton PI DY6 .... 60 E5
Eaton Rd CV1 .... 165 B1
Eaton Rise WV12 .... 27 B6
Eaves Court Dr DY3 .... 39 C1
Eaves Green Gdns B27 ...... 88 B5
Eaves Green La CV7 .... 92 C1
Ebbw Vale Terr CV3 .... 133 D7
Ebenezer St Cannock WS12 ... 2 A7
  Dudley WV14 .... 51 C8
  West Bromwich B70 .... 52 F6
Ebley Rd B20 .... 55 A4
Ebmore Dr B14 .... 104 D2
Eborall CI CV34 .... 155 E2
Ebourne CI CV8 .... 148 A4
Ebrington Ave B92 .... 89 B3
Ebrington CI B14 .... 104 D4
Ebrington Rd B71 .... 53 D6
Ebro Cres CV3 .... 114 F1
Ebrook Rd B72 .... 46 C4
Ebstree Rd WV4 .... 37 B4
Eburne Prim Sch CV2 .... 96 D2
Eburne Rd CV2 .... 96 C3
Ebury Rd B30 .... 104 B4
Eccles CI CV2 .... 114 C8
Eccleshall Ave WV10 .... 25 C8
Eccleston CI B75 .... 46 F5
Eccleston Sch B17 .... 85 B5
Ecclestone Rd WV11 .... 27 A8
Echells CI B61 .... 136 D2
Echo Way WV4 .... 40 A4
Eckersall Rd B38 .... 103 E3
Eckington CI B98 .... 159 B8
Eckington Wlk B38 .... 123 E7
Eclipse Ind Est 1 DY4 .... 51 E5
Edale B77 .... 22 B2
Edale CI Kingswinford DY6 ... 60 B7
  Wolverhampton WV4 .... 39 E3
Edale Gn LE10 .... 75 F6
Edale Rd B42 .... 55 C7
Edale Way CV6 .... 114 A7
Eddenswood CI B78 .... 34 E5
Eddie Miller Ct CV12 .... 78 B2
Eddish Rd B33 .... 69 B3
Eddy Rd DY10 .... 116 E7
Eden CI Birmingham B31 ... 122 E8
  Cannock WS12 .... 2 E2
  Studley B80 .... 159 D3
  Tipton B69 .... 52 D2
Eden Croft CV8 .... 148 B5
Eden Ct CV32 .... 157 D3
Eden Gr Birmingham B37 ... 70 D1
  West Bromwich B71 .... 53 D5
Eden Rd Coventry CV2 ..... 115 A8
  Solihull B92 .... 89 D3
Eden St CV6 .... 113 F7
Edenbridge Rd B28 .... 106 B8
Edencroft B15 .... 86 C8
Edendale Dr LE10 .... 71 E4
Edendale Rd B26 .... 89 B6
Edenhall Rd B32 .... 84 B6
Edenhurst Rd B31 .... 122 F7
Edensor CI WV10 .... 25 E4
Edgar CI B79 .... 20 F7
Edgar Stammers Jun &
  Inf Schs WS3 .... 28 F6
Edgbaston CE Coll for
  Girls B15 .... 86 B8
Edgbaston Coll B5 .... 86 B5
Edgbaston High Sch for
  Girls B15 .... 85 F7
Edgbaston Nuffield Hospl
  B15 .... 85 F5
Edgbaston Park Rd B15 ..... 86 A5
Edgbaston Rd
  Birmingham B12 .... 86 D5
  Smethwick B66 .... 65 A4
Edgbaston Rd E B12 .... 86 F5
Edgbaston Sh Ctr B16 .... 86 A8
Edgbaston St B5 .... 164 C2
Edgbaston (The
  Warwickshire Cty Cricket
  Club) B12 .... 86 D5
Edgcombe Rd B28 .... 87 F1
Edge Hill CV9 .... 36 B2
Edge Hill Ave WV10 .... 12 B2
Edge Hill Dr Perton WV6 .... 23 E3
  Sedgley DY3 .... 39 C2
Edge Hill Rd B74 .... 31 E4
Edge St WV14 .... 51 D8
Edgefield Rd CV2 .... 115 A8
Edgehill PI CV4 .... 111 C1
Edgehill Rd B31 .... 103 B1
Edgemond Ave B24 .... 57 F4
Edgemoor Mdw WS12 .... 2 C1
Edgewick Com Prim Sch
  CV6 .... 113 E8
Edgewood CI 1 B64 .... 82 F8
Edgewood Dr B45 .... 122 B1
Edgewood Rd
  Birmingham,
  King's Norton B38 .... 123 F7
  Birmingham, Rednall B45 .. 122 B6
Edgeworth CI Redditch
  B98 .... 154 C5
  Willenhall WV12 .... 27 C4
Edgeworth Ho WS13 .... 3 A2
Edgmond CI B98 .... 154 D4

Edgware Rd B23 .... 56 D5
Edgwick Park Ind Est CV6 .. 113 F8
Edgwick Rd CV6 .... 113 F7
Edgwood Ct 4 B16 .... 65 F1
Edinburgh Ave WS2 .... 27 F3
Edinburgh CI DY10 .... 116 E8
Edinburgh Cres
  Royal Leamington Spa CV31 .. 161 F6
  Stourbridge DY8 .... 60 C1
Edinburgh Ct B24 .... 57 D4
Edinburgh Dr Walsall WS4 ... 29 D7
  Willenhall WV12 .... 27 B6
Edinburgh La WS2 .... 28 A4
Edinburgh Rd Bilston WV14 .. 40 F3
  Dudley DY2 .... 62 D6
  Nuneaton CV10 .... 72 D6
  Oldbury B68 .... 84 B8
  Walsall WS5 .... 43 B8
Edinburgh Villas CV8 .... 133 F2
Edingale Rd CV2 .... 114 F8
Edison CI WS12 .... 2 C7
Edison Ct WV12 .... 27 D7
Edison Gr B32 .... 84 D5
Edison Rd WS2 .... 28 B5
Edison Wlk WS2 .... 28 B5
Edith Rd B66 .... 65 C3
Edith St B70 .... 53 B3
Edmondes CI CV34 .... 155 F1
Edmonds CI B33 .... 69 B2
Edmonds Ct
  Birmingham,
  Gilbertsone B26 .... 88 F7
  Birmingham,
  Small Heath B10 .... 87 D7
Edmonds Rd B68 .... 64 C2
Edmondscote Rd CV32 .... 161 D8
Edmonton Ave B44 .... 45 B1
Edmonton CI WS11 .... 2 B2
Edmonton Ho B5 .... 86 D7
Edmoor CI WV12 .... 27 C6
Edmund Rd Birmingham B8 .. 67 D4
  Coventry CV1 .... 113 D5
  Dudley DY3 .... 50 E6
Edmund St B3 .... 164 B3
Ednall La B60 .... 136 F1
Ednam CI 3 B71 .... 53 F8
Ednam Gr WV5 .... 38 A1
Ednam Rd Dudley DY1 .... 51 C2
  Wolverhampton WV4 .... 39 C5
Edsome Way B36 .... 68 F8
Edstone CI B93 .... 127 F4
Edstone Mews B36 .... 68 F8
Edward Ave WS9 .... 30 A7
Edward Bailey CI CV3 ...... 134 E7
Edward CI WV14 .... 40 E3
Edward Ct Birmingham B16 .. 65 C1
  Sutton Coldfield B76 .... 46 F3
  Tamworth B77 .... 21 F4
  Walsall WS1 .... 43 A8
Edward Fisher Dr DY4 .... 52 A5
Edward Rd Bedworth CV12 .. 78 C3
  Birmingham,
  Balsall Heath B12 .... 86 E5
  Birmingham,
  Higher's Heath B14 .... 105 A1
  Coventry CV6 .... 95 A3
  Halesowen B63 .... 82 F4
  Oldbury B68 .... 84 C8
  Perton WV6 .... 23 E5
  Smethwick B67 .... 65 A4
  Tipton DY4 .... 52 A7
  Water Orton B46 .... 59 C3
Edward St Birmingham B1 .. 66 C3
  Cannock WS11 .... 1 E4
  Coventry CV1 .... 113 E5
  Darlaston WS10 .... 41 E6
  3 Dudley DY1 .... 51 B1
  Hinckley LE10 .... 71 C2
  Nuneaton CV11 .... 73 C3
  Oldbury B68 .... 64 A4
  Redditch B97 .... 153 D4
  Royal Leamington Spa
  CV32 .... 156 C1
  Tamworth B79 .... 21 A5
  Walsall WS2 .... 28 C3
  Warwick CV34 .... 160 D7
  West Bromwich B70 .... 53 C3
  Wolverhampton WV4 .... 39 F5
Edward Street Hospl B70 .. 53 C3
Edward Tyler Rd WV11 .... 78 A1
Edwards Ctr 7 LE10 .... 75 D8
Edwards Gr CV8 .... 148 C5
Edwards Rd Birmingham
  B24 .... 57 A4
  Burntwood WS7 .... 6 F5
  Dudley DY2 .... 62 C4
  Sutton Coldfield B75 .... 32 D3
Edwin Ave (Road 4) DY10 .. 116 F1
Edwin Cres B60 .... 150 F7
Edwin Ct Bromsgrove B60 .. 150 F7
  Bromsgrove B60 .... 150 F8
Edwin Rd B30 .... 104 B7
Edyth Rd CV2 .... 114 E4
Edyvean Walker Ct CV11 ... 73 B5
Eel St B69 .... 63 F7
Effingham Rd B13 .... 105 C7
Egbert CI B6 .... 67 B8
Egelwin CI WV6 .... 23 E5
Egerton Ct 4 B15 .... 86 B7
Egerton Rd Aldridge B74 ... 30 F1
  Birmingham B24 .... 57 E3
  Wolverhampton WV10 ..... 11 E3
Egg La DY9, DY10 .... 119 A5
Egghill La B31, B45 .... 102 B3
Eggington Rd DY8 .... 80 D6
Egginton Rd B28 .... 105 E5
Egmont Gdns WV11 .... 26 F5
Egret Ct DY10 .... 117 A1

Eider CI DY10 .... 117 B1
Eileen Gdns B37 .... 69 F4
Eileen Rd B11 .... 87 C3
Elan CI Dudley DY3 .... 50 D3
  Royal Leamington Spa
  CV32 .... 157 C3
Elan Rd Birmingham B31 .. 102 D2
  Sedgley DY3 .... 50 C8
Elbow St B64 .... 62 F2
Elcock Dr B42 .... 55 D5
Eld Rd CV6 .... 113 E7
Eldalade Way WS10 .... 42 D2
Elder CI WS11 .... 2 C2
Elder La WS7 .... 7 C7
Elder Way B23 .... 56 E2
Elderberry CI DY8 .... 80 C3
Elderberry Way CV2 .... 114 B6
Elderfield Rd B30 .... 104 B3
Eldersfield CI B98 .... 154 E7
Eldersfield Gr B91 .... 127 B7
Eldon Ct WS1 .... 28 F1
Eldon Dr B76 .... 57 E7
Eldon Rd
  Birmingham, Edgbaston B16 .. 65 F2
  Birmingham, Woodgate B32 .. 84 A3
  Halesowen B62 .... 83 F3
Eldon St Darlaston WS10 ... 41 D7
  Walsall WS1 .... 28 F1
Eldorado CI B80 .... 159 D4
Eldridge CI WV9 .... 10 F2
Eleanor Rd WV14 .... 40 D6
Electric Ave B6 .... 56 B1
Elford CI B14 .... 104 E5
Elford Gr Bilston WV14 ...... 40 C4
  Birmingham B37 .... 70 B1
Elford Rd
  Birmingham B17, B29 ...... 85 B3
  West Bromwich B71 .... 42 E2
Elgar CI Cannock WS11 .... 1 E5
  Lichfield WS13 .... 3 B2
  Nuneaton CV11 .... 79 A7
Elgar Cres DY5 .... 61 D7
Elgar Mews 2 B60 .... 136 F2
Elgar Rd CV6 .... 114 B8
Elgin CI Sedgley DY3 .... 39 E1
  Stourbridge DY8 .... 81 A7
Elgin Ct WV6 .... 23 E4
Elgin Gr B25 .... 88 C7
Elgin Rd WS3 .... 14 A4
Elias CI WS14 .... 9 E6
Eliot CI Tamworth B79 .... 21 A7
  Warwick CV34 .... 155 E2
Eliot St B7 .... 67 C8
Eliot Wlk DY10 .... 117 C6
Elizabeth Ave Bilston WV14 . 40 F3
  Wednesbury WS10 .... 42 C3
  Wolverhampton WV4 .... 39 B5
Elizabeth Cres B68 .... 64 D2
Elizabeth Ct
  2 Birmingham B27 .... 88 C2
  8 Coventry CV34 .... 113 A4
  Warwick CV34 .... 161 B6
Elizabeth Dr B79 .... 21 A6
Elizabeth Fry Ho B16 .... 66 A1
Elizabeth Gr Dudley DY2 ... 62 F7
  Solihull B90 .... 106 C2
Elizabeth Ho Stourbridge
  DY9 .... 81 E5
  Sutton Coldfield B76 .... 46 F3
  1 Walsall WS5 .... 43 D7
Elizabeth Mews B69 .... 52 A2
Elizabeth Prout Gdns B65 .. 63 B1
Elizabeth Rd
  Birmingham, Moseley B13 .. 86 C2
  Birmingham,
  New Oscott B73 .... 45 D1
  Birmingham, Stechford B33 .. 68 D3
  Cannock WS11 .... 1 E6
  Halesowen B63 .... 82 F3
  Hinckley LE10 .... 71 D2
  Royal Leamington Spa CV31 .. 161 F6
  Walsall WS5 .... 43 C7
  West Bromwich B70 .... 52 D4
Elizabeth Way Coventry CV4 . 147 E5
  Hinckley LE10 .... 71 D2
Elizabeth Wlk DY4 .... 41 A2
Elkington Croft B90 .... 127 A5
Elkington St Birmingham B6 .. 66 E5
  Coventry CV6 .... 113 F8
Elkstone CI B92 .... 89 B3
Elkstone Covert B14 .... 104 C2
Ellacombe Rd CV2 .... 114 D8
Elland Gr B27 .... 88 D2
Ellards Dr WV11 .... 26 F5
Ellen St B18 .... 66 B4
Ellenvale CI WV14 .... 51 A8
Ellerbeck B77 .... 22 B2
Ellerby Gr B24 .... 57 E4
Ellerdene CI B98 .... 158 D8
Ellerside Gr B31 .... 102 F2
Ellerslie CI DY5 .... 81 D8
Ellerslie Rd B13 .... 105 C7
Ellerton Rd B44 .... 45 A1
Ellerton Wlk WV10 .... 25 F5
Ellesboro' Rd B17 .... 85 B7
Ellesmere Ct B69 .... 63 D8
Ellesmere Rd Bedworth
  CV12 .... 78 A2
  Birmingham B8 .... 67 D4
  Cannock WS11 .... 4 B8
Ellice Dr B36 .... 70 B7
Elliot CI WV4 .... 39 F4
Elliot Gdns B45 .... 122 B5
Elliot Way B6 .... 55 F4
Elliott Rd B29 .... 85 E1
Elliott Way B6 .... 55 F4
Elliott's Rd DY4 .... 51 E5
Elliotts La WV8 .... 10 A3

Ellis Ave DY5 .... 61 A2
Ellis St B1 .... 164 B1
Ellis Wlk WS11 .... 4 F8
Ellison St B70 .... 53 C1
Elliston Ave B44 .... 55 E8
Elliston Gr CV31 .... 162 C6
Ellowes Hall Sch DY3 .... 50 C5
Ellowes Rd DY3 .... 50 C4
Ellys Rd CV1 .... 113 C5
Elm Ave Bilston WV14 .... 40 D6
  Birmingham B12 .... 87 A5
  Wednesbury WS10 .... 41 F4
  Wolverhampton WV11 ...... 26 B8
Elm Bank CI CV32 .... 157 A4
Elm CI Binley Woods CV3 .. 135 C7
  Dudley DY3 .... 50 B2
  Stourbridge DY8 .... 80 C2
Elm Croft B68 .... 84 C7
Elm Ct Birmingham B13 ..... 86 F4
  Oldbury B66 .... 64 C8
  Redditch B97 .... 153 D4
  Walsall WS1 .... 43 A8
Elm Dale Rd WV4 .... 39 A5
Elm Dr Birmingham B43 ..... 43 D1
  Blakedown DY10 .... 98 B2
  Halesowen B62 .... 63 E1
Elm Farm Ave B37 .... 89 F7
Elm Farm Rd WV2 .... 39 D7
Elm Gdns WS14 .... 9 C7
Elm Gn DY1 .... 51 A5
Elm Gr Balsall Common CV7 . 130 C6
  Birmingham B37 .... 69 F6
  Bromsgrove B61 .... 137 A4
  Codsall WV8 .... 10 A3
  Huntington WS12 .... 1 D8
Elm Lodge B92 .... 109 A7
Elm PI DY10 .... 118 B3
Elm Rd Birmingham B30 ... 103 F8
  Dudley DY1 .... 51 C4
  Kidderminster DY10 .... 117 A6
  Kingswinford DY6 .... 60 E6
  Norton Canes WS11 .... 6 B5
  Redditch B97 .... 153 D4
  Royal Leamington Spa CV32 . 157 B3
  Walsall WS3 .... 28 D6
Elm St Willenhall WV13 ...... 27 C2
  Wolverhampton WV3 .... 25 A1
Elm Street Inf Sch WV13 ... 27 C2
Elm Terr B69 .... 52 B1
Elm Tree Ave CV4 .... 112 B2
Elm Tree Dr LE10 .... 75 F8
Elm Tree Gr B63 .... 82 D6
Elm Tree Rd
  Birmingham, Harborne B17 .. 85 A7
  Birmingham, Stirchley B30 .. 104 A6
  Bulkington CV12 .... 79 D2
Elm Tree Rise B92 .... 109 B6
Elm Tree Way B64 .... 62 F1
Elmay Rd B26 .... 89 A7
Elmbank Gr B20 .... 54 E5
Elmbank Rd Kenilworth
  CV8 .... 147 E6
  Walsall WS5 .... 43 C4
Elmbridge Cl B63 .... 82 D5
Elmbridge Dr B90 .... 127 B6
Elmbridge Ho 7 B38 .... 103 D2
Elmbridge Rd B44 .... 55 E6
Elmbridge Way DY3 .... 50 E6
Elmcroft 5 B66 .... 65 C5
Elmcroft Ave B32 .... 84 A1
Elmcroft Gdns WV10 .... 11 E3
Elmcroft Rd B26 .... 88 F7
Elmdale B62 .... 84 A7
Elmdale Cres B31 .... 102 E4
Elmdale Dr Aldridge WS9 ... 30 C8
  Kidderminster DY10 .... 117 C5
Elmdale Gr B31 .... 102 E4
Elmdale Rd WV14 .... 51 A7
Elmdene Rd CV8 .... 148 B4
Elmdon CI Solihull B92 ...... 89 D2
  Wolverhampton WV10 ...... 11 A1
Elmdon Coppice B92 .... 107 F7
Elmdon Ct B37 .... 90 A7
Elmdon La Birmingham B37 . 90 A6
  Solihull B26 .... 90 A3
Elmdon Park Rd B92 .... 89 D2
Elmdon Rd
  Birmingham,
  Acock's Green B27 .... 88 D4
  Birmingham,
  Marston Green B37 .... 90 A7
  Birmingham, Selly Park B29 .. 86 A2
  Wolverhampton WV10 ...... 11 A1
Elmdon Trad Est B37 .... 90 C5
Elmfield Ave B24 .... 57 F4
Elmfield Cres B13 .... 86 F2
Elmfield Rd Birmingham B36 . 69 C7
  Nuneaton CV10 .... 73 C7
Elmfield Rudolf Steiner
  Sch DY8 .... 81 A3
Elmhurst B15 .... 85 D8
Elmhurst Ave B65 .... 63 C3
Elmhurst CI B97 .... 158 D4
Elmhurst Dr Burntwood WS7 . 7 A4
  Kingswinford DY6 .... 60 F4
Elmhurst Rd Birmingham
  B21 .... 54 E1
  Coventry CV6 .... 96 A4
Elmley CI Dudley WV14 ...... 51 B7
  Kidderminster DY11 .... 116 B3
Elmley Ct B23 .... 56 C2
Elmley Gr Birmingham B30 . 104 B3
  Perton WV6 .... 23 F3
Elmley Ho B97 .... 153 A4
Elmore CI CV3 .... 134 D8
Elmore Green CI WS3 .... 28 B8
Elmore Green Cty Prim Sch
  WS3 .... 14 B1

Elmore Green Rd WS3 ...... 14 B1
Elmore Rd B33 ...... 69 A3
Elmore Row WS3 ...... 14 B1
Elms Cl Birmingham B38 ...... 107 D5
Solihull B91 ...... 107 D5
Elms Dr WS11 ...... 1 C1
Elms Farm Inf & Jun Sch
  B33 ...... 89 C7
Elms Rd B72 ...... 46 C3
Elms The Bedworth CV12 ...... 77 E2
Birmingham B16 ...... 65 F3
Leek Wootton CV35 ...... 155 F6
Wolverhampton WV11 ...... 26 B5
Elmsdale WV6 ...... 24 A2
Elmsdale Ave CV6 ...... 95 F2
Elmsdale Ct 6 WS1 ...... 42 F8
Elmstead Ave B33 ...... 89 D7
Elmstead Cl WS5 ...... 29 E1
Elmstead Tower 2 B5 ...... 86 E7
Elmstead Wood WS5 ...... 29 E1
Elmstone Cl B97 ...... 158 C5
Elmtree Rd B74 ...... 44 D8
Elmwood Ave Coventry
  CV6 ...... 112 F5
Essington WV11 ...... 13 A3
Elmwood Cl
Balsall Common CV7 ...... 130 B6
Cannock WS11 ...... 2 A3
Elmwood Ct Birmingham
  B5 ...... 86 D6
Coventry CV1 ...... 165 B4
Sutton Coldfield B74 ...... 45 A5
Elmwood Gdns B20 ...... 55 B2
Elmwood Gr B47 ...... 125 A6
Elmwood Rd Birmingham
  B24 ...... 57 C2
Stourbridge DY8 ...... 60 C2
Sutton Coldfield B74 ...... 45 A5
Elmwood Rise DY3 ...... 39 B1
Elmwoods B32 ...... 84 B2
Elphin Cl CV6 ...... 95 A4
Elphinstone End B24 ...... 57 C6
Elsma Rd B68 ...... 84 C8
Elston Hall Jun & Inf Schs
  WV10 ...... 11 C2
Elston Hall La WV10 ...... 11 D1
Elstree Rd B23 ...... 56 D5
Elswick Gr B44 ...... 56 B8
Elswick Pl B44 ...... 45 B1
Elsworth Gr B25 ...... 88 C6
Elsworth Ho 8 B38 ...... 103 D2
Eltham Gr B44 ...... 45 B1
Eltham Rd CV3 ...... 133 E7
Elton Cl
Royal Leamington Spa
  CV32 ...... 157 C2
Wolverhampton WV10 ...... 11 E4
Elton Croft B93 ...... 127 F4
Elton Gr B27 ...... 88 A2
Eltonia Croft B26 ...... 89 B6
Elunda Gr WS7 ...... 6 E5
Elva Croft B36 ...... 58 F1
Elvers Green La B93 ...... 128 E7
Elvetham Rd B15 ...... 86 C8
Elviron Dr WV6 ...... 24 B5
Elwell Cres DY1 ...... 50 F5
Elwell St Wednesbury WS10 .. 42 E3
West Bromwich B70 ...... 52 E5
Elwells CV14 ...... 40 A3
Elwy Circ CV7 ...... 95 C6
Elwyn Rd B73 ...... 46 A3
Ely Cl Birmingham B37 ...... 70 B2
Blackheath B65 ...... 63 E4
Cannock WS11 ...... 2 B1
Coventry CV2 ...... 115 A6
Kidderminster DY11 ...... 116 A6
Ely Cres B71 ...... 53 B7
Ely Gr B32 ...... 84 F4
Ely Pl WS2 ...... 28 B1
Ely Rd WS2 ...... 28 B1
Emay Cl B70 ...... 52 F8
Embankment The DY5 ...... 61 E3
Embassy Dr Birmingham
  B15 ...... 86 B8
Oldbury B69 ...... 63 E8
Embassy Rd B69 ...... 63 E8
Embassy Wlk CV2 ...... 114 D8
Emberton Way B77 ...... 21 F5
Embleton Cl LE10 ...... 71 B1
Embleton Gr B34 ...... 69 A6
Emerald Ct Birmingham B8 .. 68 C5
  5 Solihull B92 ...... 88 F1
Emerald Way CV31 ...... 161 F5
Emerson Cl DY3 ...... 50 A4
Emerson Gr WV10 ...... 25 F8
Emerson Rd Birmingham
  B17 ...... 85 C6
Coventry CV2 ...... 114 C3
Wolverhampton WV10 ...... 26 A8
Emery Cl Birmingham B23 .. 56 D1
Coventry CV2 ...... 114 E7
Walsall WS1 ...... 42 F8
Emery Ct DY10 ...... 116 E7
Emery St WS1 ...... 42 F8
Emily Gdns B16 ...... 65 F3
Emily Rd B26 ...... 88 D6
Emily Smith Ho 2 CV2 ...... 96 B1
Emily St Birmingham B12 ...... 86 F7
West Bromwich B70 ...... 53 B2
Emmanuel Rd Burntwood
  WS7 ...... 7 B7
Sutton Coldfield B73 ...... 57 B7
Emmeline St B9 ...... 67 B1
Emmott Dr CV31 ...... 162 B5
Empire Cl WS9 ...... 29 F8
Empire Ind Pk WS9 ...... 29 F8
Empire Rd CV4 ...... 111 E2
Empress Way WS10 ...... 41 D8

Emscote Cty Fst Sch
  CV34 ...... 161 B8
Emscote Dr B73 ...... 57 B7
Emscote Gn B91 ...... 106 E2
Emscote Lawn Prep Sch
  CV34 ...... 161 A8
Coventry CV3 ...... 114 C2
Warwick CV34 ...... 161 B8
Emsworth Cres WV9 ...... 11 A2
Emsworth Gr B14 ...... 104 D6
Ena Rd CV1 ...... 113 D5
End Hall Rd WV6 ...... 24 A3
Endemere Rd CV6 ...... 113 D7
Enderby Dr WV4 ...... 39 A4
Enderby Rd B23 ...... 56 C7
Enderley Cl WS3 ...... 14 B3
Enderley Dr WS3 ...... 14 B3
Endhill Rd B44 ...... 45 A3
Endicott Rd B6 ...... 55 F1
Endmoor Rd B23 ...... 56 D6
Endsleigh Gdns CV31 ...... 162 B6
Endsleigh Gr B28 ...... 106 A8
Endwood Court Rd B20 ...... 55 A2
Endwood Ct Birmingham
  B11 ...... 87 D4
Birmingham,
  Handsworth Wood B20 ...... 55 A2
Endwood Dr Little Aston
  B74 ...... 31 C4
Solihull B91 ...... 106 F2
Enfield Cl B23 ...... 56 E5
Enfield Ind Est B97 ...... 153 D5
Enfield Rd Birmingham B15 .. 86 B8
Coventry CV2 ...... 114 B3
Redditch B97 ...... 158 D5
Enford Cl B34 ...... 69 D6
Engine La Bilston WS10 ...... 41 A4
Brierley Hill DY5 ...... 61 F4
Stourbridge DY9 ...... 81 D6
Tamworth B77 ...... 22 A2
Walsall WS8 ...... 15 C4
Engine St Oldbury B69 ...... 64 B6
Smethwick B66 ...... 65 B6
England Cres CV31 ...... 161 E7
England Ho 9 CV32 ...... 156 F2
Englestede Cl B20 ...... 54 F3
Engleton Rd CV6 ...... 113 A6
Englewood Dr B28 ...... 106 A8
English Martyrs Jun &
  Inf Sch B11 ...... 87 C4
Ennerdale Cl CV32 ...... 156 D2
Ennerdale Cres CV11 ...... 73 F6
Ennerdale Dr Halesowen
  B63 ...... 82 D2
Perton WV6 ...... 23 F4
Ennerdale La CV2 ...... 114 F4
Ennerdale Rd
Birmingham B43 ...... 54 F6
Wolverhampton WV6 ...... 24 D8
Ennersdale Bglws B46 ...... 59 F1
Ennersdale Cl B46 ...... 59 F1
Ennersdale Rd B46 ...... 59 F1
Ennerdale CI WS8 ...... 15 E7
Enright Cl CV32 ...... 156 E2
Ensall Dr DY8 ...... 60 E1
Ensbury Cl WV12 ...... 27 D4
Ensdale Row WV13 ...... 27 A1
Ensdon Gr B44 ...... 45 B1
Ensford Cl B74 ...... 31 E5
Ensign Bsns Ctr CV4 ...... 131 F6
Ensign Cl CV4 ...... 111 D1
Ensign Ho B35 ...... 58 A4
Ensor Cl CV11 ...... 74 A6
Ensor Dr B78 ...... 22 F1
Enstone Rd Birmingham B23 .. 57 A7
Dudley DY1 ...... 61 F8
Enterprise Dr
Stourbridge DY9 ...... 81 F6
Sutton Coldfield B74 ...... 44 E7
Enterprise Gr WS3 ...... 15 B5
Enterprise Ho B92 ...... 109 A6
Enterprise Ind Pk WS14 ...... 9 F8
Enterprise Trad Est
Brierley Hill DY5 ...... 61 F3
Dudley DY5 ...... 62 A3
Enterprise Way B7 ...... 164 D4
Enterprise Workshops
  DY6 ...... 61 A7
Enville Cl WS3 ...... 14 A3
Enville Gr B11 ...... 87 D5
Enville Pl 7 DY8 ...... 80 F5
Enville Rd Dudley DY3 ...... 50 D4
Kingswinford DY6 ...... 60 B8
Wolverhampton WV4 ...... 38 C4
Enville St DY8 ...... 80 F5
Epperston Ct CV31 ...... 161 F7
Epping Cl Birmingham B45 .. 102 B2
Walsall WS3 ...... 28 F6
Epping Gr B44 ...... 56 A7
Epping Way CV32 ...... 157 C4
Epsom Cl Bedworth CV12 ...... 78 B4
Lichfield WS14 ...... 9 D7
Perton WV6 ...... 23 F4
Redditch B97 ...... 158 C8
Epsom Ct B29 ...... 103 C7
Epsom Gr B44 ...... 56 B8
Epsom Rd Catshill B61 ...... 121 A1
Royal Leamington Spa CV32 .. 157 C4
Epwell Gr B44 ...... 55 F6
Epwell Rd B44 ...... 55 F6
Epworth Ct DY5 ...... 61 B5
Erasmus Rd B11 ...... 87 A7
Erasmus Way WS13 ...... 9 A4
Ercall Cl B23 ...... 56 A6
Erdington Hall Jun & Inf
  Sch B24 ...... 56 F1
Erdington Hall Rd B24 ...... 56 F2

Erdington Ind Pk B24 ...... 57 F4
Erdington Rd WS9 ...... 30 C3
Erdington Sta B23 ...... 56 F5
Erdington Tech Coll B24 ...... 57 A4
Eric Grey Cl CV2 ...... 114 A5
Erica Ave CV12 ...... 77 F2
Erica Cl B29 ...... 103 A8
Erica Dr CV31 ...... 162 B2
Erica Rd WS5 ...... 43 B3
Eringden B77 ...... 22 B1
Erithway Rd CV3 ...... 133 B4
Ermington Cres B36 ...... 68 E7
Ermington Rd WV4 ...... 39 E4
Ernesford Grange Prim
  Sch CV3 ...... 114 E1
Ernesford Grange Sch &
  Com Coll CV3 ...... 134 D8
Ernest Clarke Cl WV12 ...... 27 C4
Ernest Cl B38 ...... 104 A1
Ernest Rd Birmingham B12 .. 87 B4
Dudley DY2 ...... 51 F1
Smethwick B67 ...... 64 E6
Ernest Richards Rd CV12 .. 78 B4
Ernest St B1 ...... 164 B1
Ernsford Ave CV3 ...... 114 B1
Ernsford Cl B93 ...... 127 F2
Erskine Cl LE10 ...... 71 A2
Erskine St B7 ...... 67 B3
Escott Cl B97 ...... 153 B2
Esher Dr CV3 ...... 133 E7
Esher Rd Birmingham B44 .. 44 F4
West Bromwich B71 ...... 53 D6
Esk Ho 1 DY1 ...... 61 E8
Eskdale Cl WV1 ...... 26 A2
Eskdale Rd LE10 ...... 75 A7
Eskdale Wlk Brierley Hill
  DY5 ...... 81 B8
Coventry CV3 ...... 134 D7
Eskrett St WS12 ...... 2 C5
Esme Rd B11 ...... 87 B4
Esmond Cl B30 ...... 103 D5
Essendon Gr B8 ...... 68 B4
Essendon Rd B8 ...... 68 B4
Essendon Wlk B8 ...... 68 B4
Essex Ave Kingswinford DY6 .. 60 B5
Wednesbury WS10 ...... 42 C4
West Bromwich B71 ...... 53 D7
Essex Cl Coventry CV5 ...... 112 B3
Kenilworth CV8 ...... 147 E2
Essex Ct Birmingham B29 .. 103 C7
Warwick CV34 ...... 160 E8
Essex Dr WS12 ...... 2 B4
Essex Gdns DY8 ...... 80 D7
Essex Ho 2 WV3 ...... 25 C4
Essex Rd Dudley DY2 ...... 62 A6
Sutton Coldfield B75 ...... 32 D2
Essex St Birmingham B5 ...... 164 C1
Walsall WS2 ...... 28 E5
Essington Cl Lichfield WS14 ... 9 A5
Shenstone WS14 ...... 18 A6
Stourbridge DY8 ...... 60 E1
Essington Ind Est WV11 ...... 12 F4
Essington Rd WV12 ...... 13 B1
Essington St B16 ...... 66 B1
Essington Way WV1 ...... 26 B1
Este Rd B26 ...... 69 A1
Esterton Cl CV6 ...... 95 C2
Estria Rd B15 ...... 86 B7
Estridge La WS6 ...... 5 A2
Ethel Rd B17 ...... 85 D5
Ethel St Birmingham B2 ...... 164 B2
Oldbury B68 ...... 64 A4
Smethwick B67 ...... 64 F2
Ethelfield Rd CV2 ...... 114 B3
Ethelfleda Rd B77 ...... 35 F5
Ethelfleda Terr WS10 ...... 41 F3
Ethelred Cl B74 ...... 32 A3
Etheridge Rd WV14 ...... 40 D7
Eton Cl DY3 ...... 50 F6
Eton Ct Lichfield WS14 ...... 9 B6
Sutton Coldfield B74 ...... 31 F2
Eton Dr DY8 ...... 81 A3
Eton Rd B12 ...... 87 B4
Eton Wlk DY9 ...... 99 A6
Etone Com Sch CV11 ...... 73 D5
Etone Ct CV11 ...... 73 B5
Etruria Way WV14 ...... 40 E7
Etta Gr B44 ...... 44 F4
Ettingley Cl B98 ...... 159 B5
Ettingshall Park Farm La
  WV4 ...... 39 E4
Ettingshall Prim Sch
  WV14 ...... 40 B6
Ettingshall Rd WV2 ...... 40 A7
Ettington Cl B93 ...... 127 D2
Ettington Rd Birmingham
  B6 ...... 66 E8
Coventry CV5 ...... 112 A3
Ettymore Cl DY3 ...... 50 D8
Ettymore Rd DY3 ...... 50 D8
Ettymore Rd W DY3 ...... 50 C8
Etwall Rd B28 ...... 105 E6
Euan Cl B17 ...... 85 C8
Eunal Ct B97 ...... 158 E5
Euro Ct B13 ...... 87 B2
Europa Ave B70 ...... 53 F2
Europa Way Birmingham
  B26 ...... 90 C4
Lichfield WS14 ...... 9 C7
Royal Leamington Spa
  CV34 ...... 161 D5
European Bsns Pk B69 ...... 63 E2
Eustace Rd CV12 ...... 79 D1
Euston Cres CV3 ...... 134 C6
Euston Pl CV32 ...... 161 F8
Euston Sq 15 CV32 ...... 161 F8
Eva Rd Birmingham B18 ...... 65 D6
Oldbury B68 ...... 64 D3

Evans Cl Bedworth CV12 ...... 78 C3
Dudley DY4 ...... 51 C6
Evans Croft B78 ...... 21 A1
Evans Gdns B29 ...... 85 D1
Evans Gr CV31 ...... 162 A3
Evans Pl WV14 ...... 40 E7
Evans St Willenhall WV13 ...... 26 C1
Wolverhampton,
  Cinder Hill WV14 ...... 39 F1
Wolverhampton,
  Dunstall Hill WV6 ...... 25 B4
Evason Ct B6 ...... 55 E1
Eve La DY1 ...... 50 F5
Evelyn Ave CV6 ...... 95 F2
Evelyn Croft B73 ...... 57 A8
Evelyn Rd B11 ...... 87 D4
Evenlode Cl Redditch B98 .. 153 F1
Solihull B92 ...... 89 B3
Evenlode Cres CV6 ...... 112 F5
Evenlode Rd B92 ...... 89 B3
Everard Ct CV11 ...... 73 C2
Everdon Rd CV6 ...... 95 B2
Everene Ho 1 B27 ...... 88 C3
Everest Cl B66 ...... 64 F8
Everest Rd Birmingham B20 .. 55 A3
Walsall WS2 ...... 27 F3
Everglade Rd CV9 ...... 36 C1
Evergreen Cl WV14 ...... 51 B8
Evergreen Hts WS12 ...... 2 A8
Everitt Cl B16 ...... 66 A1
Everitt Dr B93 ...... 128 A6
Evers St DY5 ...... 82 A8
Eversfield Prep Sch B91 .. 107 B4
Eversleigh Rd CV6 ...... 112 E7
Eversley Dale B24 ...... 57 A2
Eversley Gr Sedgley DY3 ...... 39 C2
Wolverhampton WV11 ...... 26 C6
Eversley Rd 2 B9 ...... 67 D1
Everton Rd B8 ...... 68 C4
Eves Croft B32 ...... 84 C1
Evesham Cres WS3 ...... 13 F3
Evesham Ho 5
Birmingham B7 ...... 67 A4
Bromsgrove B60 ...... 137 B3
Evesham Mews 9 B97 ...... 153 E3
Evesham Rd B96, B97 ...... 158 E3
Evesham Rise DY2 ...... 62 D3
Evesham Sq 3 B97 ...... 153 E3
Evesham St B97 ...... 153 E3
Evesham Wlk Coventry
  CV4 ...... 132 D5
  2 Redditch B98 ...... 153 E4
Eveson Rd DY9 ...... 80 E2
Ewart Rd WS2 ...... 27 F3
Ewell Rd B24 ...... 57 B4
Ewhurst Ave B29 ...... 85 F1
Ewhurst Cl WV13 ...... 40 F8
Ewloe Cl DY10 ...... 116 E1
Exbury Cl WV9 ...... 10 F2
Exbury Way CV11 ...... 78 E8
Excelsior Gr WS3 ...... 15 B5
Exchange Ind Est The
  WS11 ...... 4 E5
Exchange St Brierley Hill
  DY5 ...... 61 D4
Kidderminster DY10 ...... 116 E6
Wolverhampton WV1 ...... 163 B3
Exchange The 7 WS3 ...... 14 B1
Exe Croft B31 ...... 123 B8
Exeter Cl Coventry CV3 ...... 134 D8
Kidderminster DY11 ...... 116 A6
Exeter Dr B37 ...... 89 F8
Exeter Ho
  5 Birmingham B31 ...... 102 C2
  8 Birmingham, Erdington
  B24 ...... 56 F4
Exeter Pas B1 ...... 164 B1
Exeter Pl WS2 ...... 28 B1
Exeter Rd Birmingham B29 .. 85 F2
Cannock WS11 ...... 4 B8
Dudley DY2 ...... 62 D2
Smethwick B66 ...... 65 B5
Exeter St B1 ...... 164 B1
Exford Cl DY5 ...... 81 B7
Exhall Cl Redditch B98 ...... 154 D5
Solihull B91 ...... 106 E2
Exhall Ct B23 ...... 56 C2
Exhall Fst Sch CV7 ...... 95 F7
Exhall Gn CV7 ...... 95 F7
Exhall Grange Sch CV7 ...... 95 C5
Exhall Rd CV7 ...... 95 A6
Exham Cl CV34 ...... 155 E1
Exhibition Way B40 ...... 90 D4
Exis Ct CV11 ...... 73 E2
Exley DY1 ...... 21 D1
Exminster Rd CV3 ...... 133 E5
Exmoor Ct B61 ...... 137 A4
Exmoor Dr Bromsgrove B61
  137 A4
Royal Leamington Spa
  CV32 ...... 157 C2
Exmoor Gn WV11 ...... 26 C7
Exmouth Cl CV2 ...... 114 C7
Exon Ct DY4 ...... 51 F6
Exonbury Wlk WS11 ...... 1 F2
Expressway The B70 ...... 53 C4
Exton Cl Ash Green CV7 ...... 95 C6
Wednesfield WV11 ...... 26 D5
Exton Gdns B66 ...... 65 D6
Exton Way B8 ...... 67 D5
Eyffler Cl CV34 ...... 160 D7
Eyland Gr WS1 ...... 28 F2
Eymore Cl B29 ...... 103 B6
Eynsham Cl CV6 ...... 24 E5
Eyre St B18 ...... 65 F2
Eyton Cl B98 ...... 154 D3
Eyton Croft B12 ...... 86 F7

Elm – Fai 189

Ezekiel La WV12 ...... 27 C6

Fabian Cl Birmingham B45 .. 102 A2
Coventry CV3 ...... 134 D7
Fabian Cres B90 ...... 106 B1
Facet Rd B38 ...... 104 C4
Factory La B61 ...... 136 F1
Factory Rd Birmingham B18 .. 66 A6
Hinckley LE10 ...... 71 D1
Tipton DY4 ...... 51 E6
Factory St WS10 ...... 41 C6
Fair Isle Dr CV10 ...... 72 F2
Fair Lady Dr WS7 ...... 6 D8
Fair Oaks Dr WS6 ...... 14 A8
Fairbanks Cl CV2 ...... 115 A7
Fairbourne Ave
Birmingham B44 ...... 44 E2
Blackheath B65 ...... 63 E4
Fairbourne Tower 2 B23 .. 57 A6
Fairbourne Way CV6 ...... 112 E8
Fairburn Cres WS3 ...... 15 B5
Faircroft CV8 ...... 147 F3
Faircroft Ave B76 ...... 57 F6
Faircroft Rd B36 ...... 58 D1
Fairdene Way 3 B43 ...... 54 D8
Fairfax 7 CV34 ...... 160 F7
Fairfax Rd Birmingham B31 . 123 A8
Sutton Coldfield B75 ...... 46 F5
Wolverhampton WV10 ...... 11 E3
Fairfax Sch B75 ...... 46 F5
Fairfax St CV1 ...... 165 C3
Fairfield Cl WS12 ...... 2 D1
Fairfield Cty Prim Sch
  B61 ...... 120 D3
Fairfield Dr Halesowen B62 .. 63 E1
Walsall WS3 ...... 15 B4
Fairfield Gr B62 ...... 63 E1
Fairfield Ho B60 ...... 137 B3
Fairfield Mount WS1 ...... 42 F8
Fairfield Park Ind Est B62 .. 63 E1
Fairfield Rd Birmingham
  B14 ...... 104 E8
Bournheath B61 ...... 120 D1
Dudley DY2 ...... 62 D7
Halesowen B63 ...... 83 A2
Halesowen, Hurst Green B62 . 63 E1
Stourbridge DY8 ...... 60 F2
Fairfield Rise Meriden CV7 .. 92 C1
Stourbridge DY8 ...... 80 D5
Fairfield Studios DY10 ...... 116 F5
Fairfields Hill B78 ...... 36 F8
Fairford Cl Redditch B98 .. 154 E7
Solihull B91 ...... 106 D5
Fairford Gdns Burntwood
  WS7 ...... 7 C6
Stourbridge DY8 ...... 60 E3
Fairford Rd B44 ...... 55 F6
Fairgreen Way Aldridge B74 . 31 A1
Birmingham B29 ...... 85 F1
Fairground Way WS1 ...... 42 D8
Fairhaven Croft B62 ...... 63 E1
Fairhaven Prim Sch DY8 .. 60 D3
Fairhill Way B11 ...... 87 C7
Fairhills DY3 ...... 50 D8
Fairholme Rd B36 ...... 68 B7
Fairhurst Dr CV32 ...... 156 E3
Fairlands Pk CV4 ...... 132 F6
Fairlawn B15 ...... 86 A7
Fairlawn Cl
Royal Leamington Spa
  CV32 ...... 156 D1
Willenhall WV12 ...... 13 C1
Fairlawn Dr DY6 ...... 60 D4
Fairlawn Way WV12 ...... 13 C1
Fairlawns Birmingham B26 .. 69 A1
Sutton Coldfield B76 ...... 58 A8
Fairlie Cres B38 ...... 103 D1
Fairmile Cl CV3 ...... 134 C8
Fairmile Rd B63 ...... 83 A6
Fairmont Rd B60 ...... 151 B8
Fairmount Dr WS11 ...... 4 E8
Fairoak Dr Bromsgrove
  B60 ...... 150 F6
Wolverhampton WV6 ...... 24 B3
Fairview Ave B42 ...... 55 B6
Fairview Cl Cheslyn Hay
  WS6 ...... 4 D2
Tamworth B77 ...... 21 F5
Wolverhampton WV11 ...... 26 B7
Fairview Cres
Kingswinford DY6 ...... 60 F6
Wolverhampton WV11 ...... 26 B7
Fairview Ct WS2 ...... 27 D2
Fairview Gr WV11 ...... 26 B7
Fairview Mews 9 B46 ...... 70 F7
Fairview Rd Dudley DY1 ...... 51 A3
Wolverhampton, Penn WV4 .. 38 C4
Wolverhampton, Scotlands
  WV11 ...... 26 B7
Fairview Wlk CV6 ...... 95 E2
Fairway Birmingham B31 .... 102 E3
Cannock WS11 ...... 4 D6
Nuneaton CV11 ...... 79 B8
Tamworth B77 ...... 35 F5
Walsall WS4 ...... 15 D1
Fairway Ave B69 ...... 63 A8
Fairway Ct B77 ...... 22 B3
Fairway Dr B45 ...... 121 F6
Fairway Gn WV14 ...... 40 D8
Fairway Jun &Inf Sch
  B38 ...... 103 D1
Fairway Rd B68 ...... 63 F2
Fairway Rise CV8 ...... 148 C6

Fairway The
Birmingham B38 .... 103 D2
Hinckley LE10 .... 75 F7
Fairways B93 .... 128 A8
Fairways Ave DY8 .... 80 E2
Fairways Cl Coventry CV5 .. 112 A6
Stourbridge DY8 .... 80 E2
Fairways Dr B60 .... 138 B5
Fairways The CV32 ..... 156 D2
Fairyfield Ave B43 .... 43 D1
Fairyfield Ct B43 .... 43 D1
Fakenham Croft B17 ...... 84 F7
Falcon B77 .... 36 A6
Falcon Ave CV3 .... 134 F8
Falcon Cl Cannock WS11 ..... 1 C2
Cheslyn Hay WS6 .... 4 C2
Kidderminster DY10 .... 116 E2
Nuneaton CV11 .... 79 B8
Falcon Cres WV14 .... 39 F2
Falcon Lodge Cres B75 .... 47 A6
Falcon Lodge Jun Sch B75 . 46 F5
Falcon Pl B69 .... 63 C7
Falcon Rd B68 .... 63 F2
Falcon Rise DY8 .... 80 C6
Falcon View B30 .... 104 A4
Falcon Way DY1 .... 50 F1
Falcondale Rd WV12 .... 13 C1
Falconers Gn LE10 .... 75 F6
Falconhurst Rd B29 .... 85 C2
Falcons The B75 .... 47 B5
Falfield Cl B65 .... 63 D6
Falfield Gr B31 .... 122 E7
Falkener Ho CV6 .... 113 E7
Falkland Cl CV4 .... 131 D7
Falkland Croft B30 ...... 104 B6
Falkland Way B36 .... 70 B5
Falkwood Gr B93 .... 127 F6
Fallindale Rd B26 .... 89 C6
Fallings Heath Cl WS10 .... 41 F7
Fallings Park Ind Est
WV10 .... 25 F5
Lichfield WS13 .... 3 C3
Little Aston B74 .... 31 B3
Fallow Field Cannock WS11 .. 1 E3
Fallow Field Rd B65 .... 63 A3
Fallow Hill CV31 .... 162 C6
Fallow Rd B78 .... 20 F1
Fallow Wlk B32 .... 84 A2
Fallowfield Birmingham B15 . 85 E8
Perton WV6 .... 23 D4
Wolverhampton WV8 .... 10 E2
Fallowfield Ave B28 ...... 105 F5
Fallowfield Rd
Halesowen B63 .... 82 D3
Solihull B92 .... 89 D3
Walsall WS5 .... 43 E8
Fallowfields Cl B61 ..... 136 E3
Fallows Ho B19 .... 66 E5
Fallows Rd B11 .... 87 C6
Falmouth Cl CV11 .... 74 A5
Falmouth Dr Hinckley LE10 .. 71 E4
Tamworth B77 .... 21 F5
Falmouth Rd Birmingham
B34 .... 68 F6
Walsall WS5 .... 43 D7
Falna Cres B79 .... 20 F7
Falstaff Ave B47 .... 125 A6
Falstaff Cl Nuneaton CV11 .. 74 A1
Sutton Coldfield B76 .... 58 B7
Falstaff Ct B75 .... 47 C5
Falstaff Ho B13 .... 105 D7
Falstaff Rd Coventry CV4 .. 111 C1
Solihull B90 .... 106 C1
Falstone Rd B73 .... 45 D2
Fancott Dr CV8 .... 147 F6
Fancott Rd B31 .... 103 A5
Fancourt Ave WV4 .... 38 D4
Fane Rd WV11 .... 13 B2
Fanshawe Rd B27 .... 88 C1
Far Gosford St CV1 ...... 113 E2
Far Highfield B76 .... 46 E4
Far Hill Cl B71 .... 53 F8
Far Lash LE10 .... 75 F7
Far Moor La B98 .... 154 F5
Far View WS9 .... 16 B2
Far Wood Rd B31 .... 102 E8
Faraday Ave B32 .... 84 D5
Faraday Ct B32 .... 84 D5
Faraday Ho B15 .... 86 C8
Faraday Rd Hinckley LE10 .. 74 E7
Walsall WS2 .... 28 B6
Farber Rd CV2 .... 115 A6
Farbrook Way WV12 .... 27 B6
Farclose Ho B15 .... 86 C7
Farcroft Ave Birmingham
B21 .... 65 D8
Coventry CV5 .... 111 D4
Farcroft Gr B21 .... 54 D1
Farcroft Rd B21 .... 54 D1
Fardon Way B23 .... 56 D8
Fareham Cres WV4 .... 38 C6
Farewell La WS7 .... 7 E6
Farfield Kidderminster
DY10 .... 116 F5
Stoke Prior B60 .... 150 F4
Farfield Cl B31 .... 103 B2
Faringdon B77 .... 21 F1
Farlands Dr DY8 .... 81 A3
Farlands Gr B43 .... 54 F7
Farlands Rd DY8 .... 81 A3
Farleigh Dr WV3 .... 38 A8
Farleigh Rd WV6 .... 24 A3
Farley Ctr The B70 .... 53 D2
Farley La B62 .... 100 F1
Farley Rd B23 .... 56 B4

Farley St
Royal Leamington Spa CV31 . 162 B7
Tipton DY4 .... 52 D5
Farlow Cl Coventry CV6 .... 114 A6
Redditch B98 .... 154 D3
Farlow Croft B37 .... 89 F8
Farlow Rd B31 .... 103 C3
Farm Ave B68 .... 64 A3
Farm Cl Birmingham B33 ... 68 F3
Cannock WS12 .... 2 C3
Codsall WV8 .... 10 B2
Coventry CV6 .... 95 B3
Kidderminster DY11 .... 116 B2
Sedgley DY3 .... 50 B7
Solihull B92 .... 89 C2
Tamworth B79 .... 21 C7
Farm Croft B19 .... 66 C6
Farm House Way B43 ...... 43 E4
Farm Rd Birmingham B11 ... 87 B7
Blackheath B65 .... 63 A4
Brierley Hill DY5 .... 61 E1
Dudley DY2 .... 62 A4
Hinckley LE10 .... 75 E6
Kenilworth CV8 .... 147 E2
Oldbury B68 .... 64 A3
Redditch B98 .... 154 A3
Royal Leamington Spa CV32 . 157 B3
Smethwick B67 .... 64 E3
Tipton DY4 .... 52 B7
Wolverhampton WV3 .... 38 C8
Farm St Birmingham B19 ... 66 C6
Walsall WS2 .... 28 E4
West Bromwich B70 .... 53 C1
Farmacre B9 .... 67 B2
Farman Rd CV5 .... 113 A2
Farmbridge Cl WS2 .... 27 D3
Farmbridge Rd WS2 .... 27 D3
Farmbridge Way WS2 .... 27 D3
Farmbrook Ave WV10 .... 11 D3
Farmcote Cl B97 .... 158 D4
Farmcote Lodge CV6 .... 96 B4
Farmcote Rd Birmingham
B33 .... 69 A4
Coventry CV2 .... 96 B4
Farmcroft Rd DY9 .... 81 E2
Farmdale Gr B45 .... 122 A6
Farmer Rd B10 .... 88 A8
Farmer Ward Rd CV8 ...... 148 A3
Farmer Way DY4 .... 41 C1
Farmers Cl B76 .... 46 E4
Farmers Ct B63 .... 82 F4
Farmers Rd B60 .... 150 E7
Farmers Wlk B21 .... 65 D7
Farmhouse Rd WV12 .... 27 D5
Farmhouse Way
Solihull B90 .... 127 B7
Willenhall WV12 .... 27 D5
Farmoor Gr B34 .... 69 E6
Farmoor Way WV10 .... 11 E4
Farmside CV3 .... 134 D5
Farmside Gn WV9 .... 10 F2
Farmstead Rd B92 .... 89 C2
Farmstead The CV3 .... 134 B8
Farnborough Cl B98 ...... 154 F1
Farnborough Ct B75 .... 32 C2
Farnborough Dr B90 ...... 126 F6
Farnborough Rd B35 .... 58 B3
Farnbury Croft B38 ...... 104 B2
Farncote Dr B74 .... 31 F3
Farndale Ave Coventry CV6 .. 95 D3
Wolverhampton WV6 .... 25 A5
Farndale Cl DY5 .... 81 B6
Farndale Jun Sch W6 ...... 25 A4
Farndon Ave B37 .... 90 B7
Farndon Cl CV12 .... 79 B3
Farndon Rd B8 .... 67 F4
Farneway LE10 .... 71 B1
Farnham Cl B43 .... 54 F8
Farnham Rd B21 .... 54 E2
Farnhurst Rd B36 .... 68 B7
Farnol Rd B26 .... 68 F1
Farnworth Gr B36 .... 58 E1
Farquhar Rd
Birmingham, Edgbaston B15 .. 85 F6
Birmingham, Moseley B13 .... 86 F3
Farquhar Rd E B15 .... 85 F6
Farr Dr CV4 .... 112 B2
Farran Way B43 .... 54 F6
Farren Rd Birmingham B31 . 102 D1
Coventry CV2 .... 114 E5
Farrier Cl Bromsgrove B60 .. 150 E6
Sutton Coldfield B76 .... 57 F8
Farrier Rd B43 .... 44 D3
Farrier Way DY6 .... 60 A7
Farriers The B26 .... 89 B5
Farriers Way Hinckley LE10 .. 75 F6
Nuneaton CV11 .... 73 F2
Farringdon Ho [5] WS2 .... 28 D3
Farringdon St WS2 .... 28 D3
Farrington Rd
Birmingham B23 .... 56 B5
Wolverhampton WV4 .... 39 E3
Farrow Rd B44 .... 44 E3
Farthing Ct B3 .... 66 A3
Farthing La Curdworth B76 .. 59 C6
Sutton Coldfield B72 .... 46 B4
Farthing Pools Cl [1] B72 .. 46 C4
Farthings Lodge [7] DY1 ... 51 B1
Farthings The B17 .... 85 D6
Farvale Rd B76 .... 58 C6
Faseman Ave CV4 .... 111 F3
Fashoda Rd B29 .... 86 B1
Fast Pits Rd B25 .... 88 C2
Fastlea Rd B32 .... 84 D1
Fastmoor Oval B33 .... 69 E1
Fatherless Barn Cres B63 .. 82 D5
Faulconbridge Ave CV5 .... 111 E4
Faulkland Cres WV1 ...... 163 C4

Faulkner Cl DY8 .... 80 F4
Faulkner Rd B92 .... 89 B1
Faulkners Farm Dr B23 .... 56 B6
Faulknor Dr DY5 .... 61 B7
Faultlands Cl CV11 .... 78 F8
Faversham Cl Willenhall
WS2 .... 27 D3
Wolverhampton WV8 .... 24 E8
Fawdry Cl B73 .... 46 B5
Fawdry St Birmingham B9 ... 67 A2
Smethwick B66 .... 65 A5
Wolverhampton WV1 .... 163 A4
Fawley Cl Coventry CV3 ... 134 C6
Willenhall WV13 .... 26 F1
Fawley Gr B14 .... 104 B5
Faygate Cl CV3 .... 114 F3
Fazeley Cl B78 .... 21 B2
Fazeley St B5 .... 66 F2
Fearings Cotts B97 ...... 158 D5
Fearon [4] B66 .... 65 A5
Featherbed La
Coventry CV4 .... 132 A5
Redditch B97 .... 158 C5
Featherston Rd Aldridge
B74 .... 31 A2
Hinckley LE10 .... 75 E6
Featherstone Cl
Nuneaton CV10 .... 73 C2
Solihull B90 .... 106 D2
Featherstone Cres B90 ... 106 D2
Featherstone Jun & Inf
Sch B23 .... 56 E4
Featherstone La WV10 ..... 12 B8
Featherstone Rd B14 ..... 104 E6
Feckenham Ho B60 .... 137 B3
Feckenham Rd
Astwood Bank B96 .... 158 E2
Redditch,
Headless Cross B97 .... 158 C8
Redditch, Hunt End B97 .... 158 C5
Fecknam Way WS13 .... 3 C1
Feilding Cl CV2 .... 115 A6
Feilding Way CV10 .... 72 A5
Felbrigg Cl DY5 .... 81 D8
Feldings The B24 .... 57 C4
Feldon La B62 .... 83 E7
Felgate Cl B90 .... 127 A6
Fell Gr Birmingham B21 .... 54 C2
Royal Leamington Spa
CV32 .... 157 C3
Fellbrook Cl B33 .... 68 F4
Fellmeadow Rd B33 .... 69 A2
Fellmeadow Way DY3 .... 50 E2
Fellmore Gr CV31 .... 162 D7
Fellows Ave DY6 .... 60 C8
Fellows La B17 .... 85 A5
Fellows Rd WV14 .... 40 D7
Fellows St WV2 .... 163 B1
Felspar Rd B77 .... 22 B3
Felsted Way B7 .... 67 A4
Felstone Rd B44 .... 44 E1
Feltham Cl B33 .... 69 E1
Felton Cl Coventry CV2 .... 96 E1
Redditch B98 .... 154 E1
Felton Croft B33 .... 69 A3
Felton Gr B91 .... 107 C1
Fen End Rd CV8 .... 129 E4
Fenbourne Cl WS4 .... 29 C8
Fenchurch Cl WS2 .... 28 D4
Fencote Ave B37 .... 70 A4
Fenmere Cl WV4 .... 39 D5
Fenn Rise Stourbridge DY8 .. 60 D3
Willenhall WV12 .... 27 B5
Fenn St B77 .... 21 E1
Fennel Cl WS6 .... 4 D3
Fennel Croft B34 .... 69 B7
Fennel Rd DY5 .... 81 C7
Fennell Ho [10] CV1 ...... 113 B2
Fennis Cl B93 .... 127 F3
Fens Cres DY5 .... 61 C5
Fens Pool Ave DY5 .... 61 D5
Fenside Ave CV3 .... 133 D4
Fensway The B34 .... 69 A5
Fenter Cl B13 .... 86 F5
Fentham Cl B92 .... 109 B6
Fentham Ct B92 .... 106 F8
Fentham Gn B92 .... 109 A7
Fentham Rd
Birmingham, Aston B6 .... 66 E8
Birmingham,
Gravelly Hill B23 .... 56 E3
Hampton in A B92 .... 109 A6
Fenton Rd Birmingham B27 .. 88 B5
Hollywood B47 .... 125 A7
Fenton St Brierley Hill DY5 .. 61 D3
Smethwick B66 .... 64 E7
Fenton Way B27 .... 88 B5
Fenwick Cl B97 .... 153 B1
Fereday Rd WS9 .... 16 B3
Fereday St DY4 .... 51 F8
Fereday's Croft DY3 .... 50 D7
Ferguson Dr DY11 .... 116 A1
Ferguson Rd B68 .... 64 D5
Ferguson St WV11 .... 13 A1
Fern Ave DY4 .... 51 F7
Fern Cl Coventry CV2 ...... 96 C2
Dudley DY1 .... 51 B8
Walsall WS4 .... 15 D1
Fern Dale Rd CV7 .... 129 F6
Fern Dell Cl WS11 .... 1 C2
Fern Dr WS6 .... 5 A4
Fern Leys WV3 .... 24 D1
Fern Rd Birmingham B24 .... 57 A4
Dudley DY1 .... 51 C4
Huntington WS12 .... 1 D5
Wolverhampton WV3 .... 163 A1
Fernbank Cl B63 .... 82 E2
Fernbank Cres WS5 .... 43 C4

Fernbank Rd B8 .... 68 A4
Ferncliffe Rd B17 .... 85 B4
Ferndale Ave B43 .... 54 F7
Ferndale Cl Burntwood WS7 .. 7 B6
Catshill B61 .... 121 A1
Hagley DY9 .... 99 A5
Nuneaton CV11 .... 73 E5
Ferndale Cres
Birmingham B12 .... 87 A8
Kidderminster DY11 .... 116 B8
Ferndale Dr CV8 .... 148 A2
Ferndale Pk DY9 .... 99 C8
Ferndale Prim Sch B43 .... 54 E8
Ferndale Rd
Binley Woods CV3 .... 135 D7
Birmingham B28 .... 105 F8
Essington WV11 .... 13 B3
Oldbury B68 .... 64 A2
Sutton Coldfield B74 .... 44 F8
Ferndene Rd B11 .... 88 A3
Ferndown Ave DY3 .... 50 C3
Ferndown Cl Birmingham
B26 .... 69 A1
Coventry CV4 .... 112 A3
Walsall WS3 .... 14 B4
Ferndown Gdns WV11 .... 26 F5
Ferndown Rd B91 .... 107 C5
Ferness Cl LE10 .... 71 B2
Ferness Rd LE10 .... 71 B2
Ferney Hill Ave B97 ..... 153 C3
Fernhill Cl CV8 .... 147 E6
Fernhill Ct B23 .... 56 C2
Fernhill Dr CV32 .... 157 B1
Fernhill Gr B44 .... 44 F3
Fernhill La CV7 .... 129 F5
Fernhill Rd B92 .... 88 E2
Fernhurst Dr DY5 .... 61 B7
Fernhurst Rd B8 .... 68 A3
Fernleigh Rd B60 .... 137 A1
Fernleigh Ave WS7 .... 7 A8
Fernleigh Gdns DY8 .... 60 C3
Fernleigh Rd WS4 .... 29 B3
Fernley Ave B29 .... 86 B2
Fernley Rd B11 .... 87 C4
Fernside Gdns B13 .... 87 B3
Fernwood Cl Redditch B98 .. 159 B5
Sutton Coldfield B73 .... 45 E1
Fernwood Croft
Birmingham B14 .... 104 E6
Tipton DY4 .... 51 F4
Fernwood Rd B73 .... 56 E8
Fernwoods B32 .... 84 B2
Ferrers Cl Coventry CV4 ... 111 F2
Sutton Coldfield B75 .... 32 D2
Ferrers Rd B77 .... 21 D4
Ferrie Gr WS8 .... 15 E8
Ferris Gr B27 .... 88 A1
Festival Ave WS10 .... 41 C4
Festival Ct WS11 .... 1 E5
Festival Mews WS12 .... 1 F6
Festival Way W6 .... 25 B5
Fetherston Cres CV8 ..... 135 B1
Fetherston Ct [4] CV31 ... 161 F6
Ffernfail Ct B23 .... 56 E5
Fibbersley WV13, WV11 ..... 26 F4
Fibbersley Bank WV13 ...... 26 F4
Fiddlers Gn B92 .... 109 A7
Field Barn Rd CV35 ...... 160 A7
Field Cl Birmingham B26 ... 89 A6
Bromsgrove B60 .... 150 E6
Hinckley LE10 .... 71 F3
Kenilworth CV8 .... 148 B5
Stourbridge DY8 .... 61 A2
Walsall,
Blakenall Heath WS3 .... 28 C8
Walsall, Pelsall WS4 .... 15 B2
Warwick CV34 .... 161 B7
Field Cottage Dr DY8 ...... 81 B3
Field Ct Coventry CV2 .... 114 D7
Walsall WS4 .... 15 B2
Field Farm Rd B77 .... 21 D1
Field Head La CV34 ...... 161 B6
Field Head Pl WV6 .... 24 B4
Field Ho CV8 .... 147 F5
Field La Birmingham B32 .. 102 B8
Clent DY9 .... 99 D4
Great Wyrley WS6 .... 4 F3
Solihull B91 .... 108 A5
Stourbridge DY8 .... 81 A3
Walsall WS4 .... 15 B2
Field March CV3 .... 134 E5
Field Mews DY2 .... 62 E2
Field Rd Dudley DY2 .... 51 E2
Tipton DY4 .... 52 A8
Walsall WS3 .... 14 C1
Wolverhampton WS13 .... 3 B3
Field St Bilston WV14 ..... 40 E3
Cannock WS11 .... 1 F3
Willenhall WV13 .... 27 A2
Wolverhampton WV10 .... 163 D4
Field Trad Est WS11 .... 4 D6
Field View Ryton-on-D CV8 . 135 A1
Whitnash CV31 .... 162 B3
Field View Cl CV7 .... 96 A8
Field View Dr B65 .... 63 F3
Field Way B94 .... 143 C6
Field Wlk WS9 .... 30 B7
Fern Cl Coventry CV2 ...... 96 C2
Fieldfare WS7 .... 7 D5
Fieldfare Cl B64 .... 62 F4
Fieldfare Croft B36 .... 70 A8
Fieldfare Ct DY10 .... 117 A1
Fieldfare Rd DY9 .... 81 D4
Fieldgate La Kenilworth
CV8 .... 147 F6
Whitnash CV31 .... 162 B2
Fieldgate Lawn CV8 ...... 147 F6
Fieldgate Trad Est WS1 ... 28 F1
Fieldhead Rd B11 .... 88 A3

Fieldhouse La B62 .... 100 E4
Fieldhouse Rd
Birmingham B25 .... 88 C8
Burntwood WS7 .... 7 A7
Cannock WS12 .... 1 F7
Wolverhampton WV4 .... 39 E4
Fieldon Cl B90 .... 106 C2
Fields Ct CV34 .... 160 F8
Fieldside La CV3 .... 114 F3
Fieldside Wlk WV14 .... 40 D8
Fieldview Cl WV14 .... 40 E2
Fieldways Cl B47 .... 125 A7
Fiery Hill Rd B45 .... 138 C8
Fife Rd CV5 .... 112 F2
Fife St CV11 .... 73 A4
Fifield Cl CV11 .... 73 D2
Fifield Gr B33 .... 68 F3
Fifth Ave Birmingham B9 ... 67 F2
Wolverhampton WV10 .... 25 E7
Filey B77 .... 21 F6
Filey Cl WS11 .... 4 C8
Filey Rd WV10 .... 11 B2
Fillingham Cl B37 .... 70 D1
Fillongley Rd CV7 .... 92 E3
Filton Ave WS7 .... 7 A8
Filton Croft B35 .... 58 A4
Fimbrell Cl DY5 .... 81 A8
Finbury Cl B92 .... 88 F1
Finch Cl Blackheath B65 ... 62 F4
Coventry CV6 .... 95 C2
Finch Dr B74 .... 45 A6
Finch Rd B19 .... 66 C8
Finchall Croft B92 ...... 107 E7
Fincham Cl WV9 .... 11 A3
Finchdene Gr WV3 .... 24 D1
Finches End B34 .... 69 C5
Finchfield Cl DY8 .... 80 C4
Finchfield Gdns WV3 ...... 24 E1
Finchfield Hill WV3 ...... 24 C1
Finchfield La WV3 .... 38 C8
Finchfield Rd WV3 .... 24 E1
Finchfield Rd W WV3 ...... 24 D1
Finchley Ave [1] B19 ..... 66 C8
Finchley Cl DY3 .... 50 D2
Finchley Rd B44 .... 45 B1
Finchmead Rd B33 .... 69 E2
Finchpath Rd B70 .... 53 A6
Findlay Rd B14 .... 86 E1
Findon Cl CV12 .... 79 C3
Findon Rd B8 .... 68 B6
Findon St DY10 .... 116 F6
Finford Croft CV7 .... 130 B6
Fingal Cl CV3 .... 134 C6
Finger Post Dr WS3 .... 15 A5
Fingest Cl CV5 .... 112 B4
Finham Cres CV8 .... 148 B6
Finham Flats CV8 .... 148 B6
Finham Gr CV3 .... 133 C3
Finham Green Rd CV3 ..... 133 B3
Finham Park Comp Sch
CV3 .... 133 A4
Finham Prim Sch CV3 ..... 133 B3
Finham Rd CV8 .... 148 B6
Finings Ct [7] CV32 ..... 156 F2
Finlarigg Dr B15 .... 85 F6
Finlay Ct CV1 .... 165 C1
Finmere Rd B28 .... 105 F8
Finnemore Cl CV3 .... 133 B5
Finnemore Rd B9 .... 68 A2
Finney Well Cl WV14 ...... 40 B3
Finsbury Dr DY5 .... 81 C7
Finsbury Gr B23 .... 56 D6
Finstall Cl Birmingham B7 .. 67 A4
Sutton Coldfield B72 .... 46 C1
Finstall Fst Sch B60 .... 137 B1
Finstall Rd Bromsgrove
B60 .... 151 C8
Finstall B60 .... 137 D1
Finwood Cl B92 .... 107 E8
Finwood Rd CV35 .... 144 F1
Fir Ave B12 .... 87 A5
Fir Cl WS12 .... 1 D8
Fir Croft DY5 .... 81 C8
Fir Gr Birmingham B14 .... 104 F5
Coventry CV4 .... 112 A2
Stourbridge DY8 .... 80 C6
Wolverhampton WV3 .... 25 A1
Fir St DY3 .... 49 F7
Fir Tree Ave CV4 .... 112 B2
Fir Tree Cl Birmingham B44 . 55 E7
Tamworth B79 .... 20 E7
Fir Tree Dr Dudley DY3 .... 50 F7
Walsall WS5 .... 43 B4
Fir Tree Gr Nuneaton CV11 .. 78 D8
Sutton Coldfield B73 .... 45 F1
Fir Tree Prim Sch WS5 .... 43 A4
Fir Tree Rd WV3 .... 38 D8
Firbank Cl B30 .... 103 D8
Firbank Way WS3 .... 14 F2
Firbarn Cl B76 .... 46 D3
Firbeck Gr B44 .... 45 A1
Firbeck Rd B44 .... 45 A1
Fircroft Bilston WV14 ..... 41 A3
Birmingham B31 .... 102 F8
Solihull B91 .... 106 F6
Wolverhampton WV4 .... 39 F4
Fircroft Cl Cannock WS11 ... 2 A3
Stoke Heath B60 .... 150 D6
Fircroft Coll B29 .... 103 D8
Fircroft Ho B37 .... 70 A2
Fire Station Rd B26 ...... 90 C5
Firecrest Cl Birmingham B23 . 56 B7
Cannock WS11 .... 2 C2
Firecrest Way DY10 ...... 117 B1
Firethorn Cres CV31 ..... 162 D6
Firhill Croft B14 .... 104 D2
Firleigh Dr CV12 .... 79 D2
Firmstone Ct DY8 .... 80 E7

Firmstone St DY8 .... 80 E7
Firs Cl Kidderminster DY10 .. 117 A5
  Marlbrook B60 .... 121 D1
  Smethwick B67 .... 65 A5
Firs Dr B90 .... 106 A1
Firs Farm Dr B36 .... 68 F7
Firs Ho B36 .... 68 F8
Firs Inf Sch The B36 .... 68 F8
Firs La B67 .... 65 A5
Firs Rd DY6 .... 60 E6
Firs Sch The B67 .... 65 A5
Firs St DY2 .... 51 D1
Firs The Bedworth CV12 .... 77 E2
  Birmingham B11 .... 87 C6
  Cannock WS11 .... 2 A2
  Coventry CV5 .... 133 B8
  Meriden CV7 .... 92 B1
  Wolverhampton WV11 .... 26 B5
Firsbrook Cl WV6 .... 25 A5
Firsbrook Ho WV6 .... 25 A5
Firsholm Cl B73 .... 57 A7
First Ave
  Birmingham, Selly Oak B29 .. 86 B3
  Birmingham, Smallheath B9 .. 67 E1
  Birmingham, Tyburn B76 .... 58 A5
  Birmingham, Witton B6 .... 55 F2
  Brownhills WS8 .... 16 A8
  Coventry CV3 .... 114 C1
  Kingswinford DY6 .... 61 A8
  Wolverhampton WV10 .... 25 E6
First Exhibition Ave B40 .. 90 D4
First Meadow Piece B32 .. 84 E4
Firsvale Rd WV11 .... 26 F5
Firsway WV6 .... 24 A2
Firswood Rd B33 .... 69 C1
Firth Dr Birmingham B14 .. 105 B5
  Halesowen B62 .... 83 E8
Firth Park Cres B62 .... 83 E8
Firtree Rd B24 .... 57 B2
Fish Hill B98 .... 153 E4
Fish House La B60 .... 150 E4
Fisher Cl B45 .... 101 E2
Fisher Rd Coventry CV6 .. 113 E8
  Oldbury B69 .... 64 C7
  Walsall WS3 .... 13 F2
Fisher St Brierley Hill DY5 .. 61 B2
  Cannock WS12 .... 1 F8
  Dudley DY2 .... 51 D1
  Tipton, Burnt Tree DY4 .... 52 A3
  Tipton, Great Bridge DY4 .... 52 D5
  Willenhall WV13 .... 27 C2
  Wolverhampton WV3 .... 39 B8
Fisher's Ct CV34 .... 160 D4
Fishers Dr B90 .... 125 F5
Fishing Line Rd B97 .... 153 E5
Fishley Cl WS3 .... 14 C4
Fishley La WS3 .... 14 D5
Fishponds Rd CV8 .... 147 E3
Fishpool Cl B36 .... 68 C8
Fishpool La CV7 .... 91 B5
Fitters Mill Cl B5 .... 86 E6
Fitton Ave DY6 .... 61 A5
Fitton St CV11 .... 73 B3
Fitz Roy Ave B17 .... 84 F7
Fitzgerald Pl DY5 .... 81 B6
Fitzguy Cl B70 .... 53 E1
Fitzmaurice Rd WV11 .... 27 A7
Fitzroy Cl CV2 .... 115 B6
Fitzroy Rd B31 .... 102 D3
Fitzwarren Specl Sch
  DY4 .... 52 A6
Five Fields Rd WV12 .... 27 A5
Five Oaks Rd WV13 .... 40 E8
Five Ways
  Birmingham,
  Bordesley Green B9 .... 67 D2
  Birmingham, Ladywood B16 .. 66 B1
  Blackheath B64 .... 82 C8
  Churchill DY10 .... 98 A5
  Dudley DY3 .... 50 D3
  Wolverhampton,
  Dunstall Hill WV3 .... 25 C4
  Wolverhampton,
  Merry Hill WV3 .... 38 C7
  Wroxall CV35 .... 145 F1
Five Ways Cty Prim Sch
  WS12 .... 2 D2
Five Ways Rd WS12 .... 145 F1
Five Ways Sta B15 .... 86 B8
Fivefield Rd CV7 .... 94 E5
Flackwell Rd B23 .... 56 E7
Fladbury Cl Dudley DY2 .... 62 D3
  Redditch B98 .... 159 B8
Fladbury Cres B29 .... 85 D1
Fladbury Gdns B20 .... 66 C8
Fladbury Pl B19 .... 66 C7
Flamboro' Cl CV3 .... 134 F8
Flamborough Cl B34 .... 69 A7
Flamborough Way WV14 .. 51 B7
Flamville Rd LE10 .... 76 B5
Flanders Cl B98 .... 154 D5
Flanders Dr DY6 .... 60 D8
Flash La WV4 .... 37 F2
Flash Rd B69 .... 64 A7
Flats La WS14 .... 19 A6
Flats The B61 .... 136 F3
Flatts The WS10 .... 41 E7
Flaunden Cl CV5 .... 112 B4
Flavel Cres CV31 .... 161 F7
Flavel Rd B60 .... 150 E7
Flavell Ave WV14 .... 40 D1
Flavell Cl B32 .... 84 B1
Flavell St DY1 .... 51 B5
Flavells La Birmingham B25 .. 88 C8
  Dudley DY3 .... 50 B2

Flax Cl B47 .... 125 A5
Flax Gdns B38 .... 123 F8
Flax Hill Jun Sch B79 .... 21 B7

Flaxhall St WS2 .... 42 B8
Flaxley Cl B33 .... 68 F3
Flaxley Rd B33 .... 68 E4
Flaxton Gr B33 .... 69 A4
Flaxton Wlk WV6 .... 25 A5
Flecknoe Cl B36 .... 58 C1
Flecknose St CV3 .... 134 C6
Fledburgh Dr B76 .... 46 D4
Fleet Ho CV1 .... 165 B2
Fleet St Birmingham B3 .... 164 A3
  Coventry CV1 .... 165 B3
Fleetwood Gr B26 .... 69 A1
Fleetwood Ho B13 .... 86 F4
Fleming Pl WS2 .... 28 A6
Fleming Rd Birmingham B32 . 84 D5
  Hinckley LE10 .... 74 F7
  Walsall WS2 .... 28 A6
Fletchamstead Highway
  CV5 .... 132 D7
Fletcher Gr B93 .... 128 B4
Fletcher Rd Hinckley LE10 .. 75 E7
  Willenhall WV13 .... 27 D8
Fletcher St DY9 .... 81 F5
Fletcher's La WV13 .... 27 C2
Fletchworth Gate CV5 .... 132 D8
Fletton Gr B14 .... 105 A3
Fleur de-lys Ct CV34 .... 161 B8
Flinkford Cl CV5 .... 111 F8
Flinn Cl WS14 .... 9 D7
Flint Cl DY10 .... 116 E2
Flint Green Rd B27 .... 88 B3
Flint Ho WV3 .... 25 C4
Flint Tower B18 .... 65 E4
Flintham Cl B92 .... 88 E3
Flintway The B33 .... 68 E4
Flood St DY2 .... 51 D1
Floodgate St B5 .... 66 F1
Flora Cl B79 .... 21 C7
Flora Rd B25 .... 88 B7
Florence Ave
  Birmingham B11 .... 87 C5
  Sutton Coldfield B73 .... 57 B7
  Wolverhampton WV4 .... 40 A4
Florence Bldgs B29 .... 85 F2
Florence Cl CV12 .... 95 F8
Florence Dr B73 .... 57 B7
Florence Gr
  Birmingham B18 .... 65 E4
  West Bromwich B71 .... 42 E1
Florence Pl B12 .... 87 A6
Florence Rd
  Birmingham,
  Acock's Green B27 .... 88 D4
  Birmingham,
  Handsworth B21 .... 65 D8
  Birmingham,
  King's Heath B14 .... 104 F8
  Codsall WV8 .... 10 C3
  Oldbury B69 .... 63 E7
  Smethwick B66 .... 65 B4
  Sutton Coldfield B73 .... 57 B7
  Tipton DY4 .... 52 A7
  West Bromwich B70 .... 53 E1
Florence St Birmingham B1 . 164 B1
  Cannock WS12 .... 2 B7
  Walsall WS1 .... 29 A1
Florence Villas B11 .... 87 C7
Florendine Cty Prim Sch
  B77 .... 21 F5
Florendine St B77 .... 21 F5
Florian Gr WS10 .... 41 E7
Florida Way DY6 .... 61 A6
Flowerdale Cl WV14 .... 51 B8
Flowerdale Dr CV2 .... 114 B6
Floyds La WS4 .... 29 C6
Floyer Rd B10 .... 67 F1
Flude Rd CV7 .... 95 C6
Flyford Cl B16 .... 153 F1
Flyford Croft B29 .... 84 F2
Flynt Ave CV5 .... 112 B6
Fockbury Mill La B61 .... 136 E5
Fockbury Rd B61 .... 136 B5
Foden Cl WS14 .... 17 F6
Foden Rd B42 .... 55 A7
Foinavon Cl B65 .... 62 F6
Fold St WV1 .... 163 B2
Fold The Birmingham B38 .. 104 A1
  Darlaston WS10 .... 41 D6
  Wolverhampton WV4 .... 38 F4
Foldyard Cl B76 .... 58 A6
Foleshill CE Prim Sch CV6 .. 96 A1
Foleshill Rd CV1, CV6 .... 113 D6
Foley Ave WV6 .... 24 C3
Foley Church Cl B74 .... 31 A2
Foley Dr WV6 .... 24 C3
Foley Gdns B60 .... 150 E3
Foley Ho B98 .... 84 B8
Foley Park Fst Sch DY11 .. 116 D3
Foley Rd Birmingham B8 .. 68 B5
  Stourbridge DY9 .... 81 C2
Foley Rd E B74 .... 31 A2
Foley Rd W B74 .... 30 E1
Foley St WS10 .... 42 A3
Foley Wood Cl B74 .... 30 E1
Foliot Fields B25 .... 88 D8
Folkes Rd DY9 .... 82 A6
Folkestone Croft B36 .... 68 E8
Folkland Gn CV6 .... 113 A7
Folliott Rd B33 .... 69 B3
Follyhouse Cl WS1 .... 42 F7
Follyhouse La WS1 .... 42 F7
Fontenaye Rd B79 .... 20 F7
Fontley Cl B26 .... 69 A2
Fontmell Cl CV2 .... 115 A4
Fontwell Rd WV10 .... 11 D4
Footherley La WS14 .... 17 E4
Footherley Rd WS14 .... 17 F5
Ford Brook La WS4 .... 15 B2

Ford Cotts CV33 .... 157 F2
Ford Rd B61 .... 136 E1
Ford St Birmingham B18 .... 66 B5
  Coventry CV1 .... 165 C3
  Nuneaton CV10 .... 72 E4
  Smethwick B67 .... 64 F6
  Walsall WS2 .... 42 C7
Fordbridge Cl B97 .... 153 C1
Fordbridge Inf Sch B37 .. 70 A5
Fordbridge Rd B37 .... 70 A5
Forde Way Gdns B38 .... 123 D7
Forder Gr B14 .... 105 A2
Fordfield Rd B33 .... 69 C4
Fordham Gr WV9 .... 11 A3
Fordhouse La B30 .... 104 B6
Fordhouse Rd
  Bromsgrove B60 .... 137 B1
  Wolverhampton WV10 .... 11 D1
Fordhouse Road Ind Est
  WV10 .... 25 D8
Fordraught La B62 .... 101 B1
Fordrift The B37 .... 90 A6
Fordrough B25 .... 87 F7
Fordrough Ave B9 .... 67 E3
Fordrough La B9 .... 67 E2
Fordrough The
  Birmingham B31 .... 103 C1
  Hollywood B90 .... 125 C7
  Sutton Coldfield B74 .... 32 A1
Fords Rd B90 .... 125 E7
Fordwater Rd B74 .... 44 F6
Fordwell Cl CV5 .... 112 F3
Fore St B2 .... 164 C2
Foredraft Cl B32 .... 84 C2
Foredraft St B63 .... 82 D5
Foredraught B80 .... 159 E4
Foredrift Cl B98 .... 153 E2
Foredrove La B92 .... 107 E7
Foregate St B96 .... 158 E1
Foreland Way CV6 .... 95 A3
Forelands Gr B61 .... 150 D8
Forest Ave WS3 .... 28 D7
Forest Cl Lickey End B60 .. 137 B6
  Smethwick B66 .... 64 E7
  Sutton Coldfield B74 .... 44 E7
Forest Ct Birmingham B13 .. 87 A3
  Coventry CV5 .... 112 A4
  Dorridge B93 .... 127 F3
  Willenhall WV12 .... 27 C8
Forest Dale B45 .... 122 B6
Forest Dr B17 .... 85 D6
Forest Gate WV12 .... 27 D8
Forest Hill Rd B26 .... 89 C5
Forest La WS2 .... 28 D5
Forest Lawns B74 .... 31 C3
Forest Oak Specl Sch B36 .. 58 E1
Forest Pk B76 .... 46 E4
Forest Pl WS3 .... 28 E6
Forest Rd
  Birmingham, Moseley B13 .. 87 A3
  Birmingham,
  South Yardley B25 .... 88 C6
  Dorridge B93 .... 127 F3
  Dudley DY1 .... 51 B5
  Hinckley LE10 .... 75 F8
  Oldbury B68 .... 84 C7
Forest View B97 .... 158 E6
Forest Way Great Wyrley
  WS6 .... 5 A1
  Hollywood B47 .... 125 B6
  Nuneaton CV10 .... 72 E2
Forester Way DY10 .... 116 E3
Forester's Rd CV3 .... 133 E6
Forfar Wlk B38 .... 103 D2
Forfield Pl CV31 .... 162 A7
Forfield Rd CV6 .... 112 E5
Forge Cl Burntwood WS7 .... 7 D5
  Wolverhampton WV8 .... 10 E1
Forge Croft B76 .... 58 B6
Forge Dr B61 .... 136 F3
Forge La
  Aldridge, Leighswood WS9 .. 30 A5
  Aldridge, Mill Green WS9 .. 30 F7
  Belbroughton DY9 .... 119 D7
  Blackheath B64 .... 82 B8
  Blakedown DY10 .... 98 B1
  Burntwood WS7 .... 7 F6
  Halesowen B63 .... 83 C5
  Kingswinford DY6 .... 60 A8
  Lichfield WS13 .... 3 A1
  Shenstone WS14 .... 31 C8
  Sutton Coldfield B76 .... 58 B5
  West Bromwich B71 .... 54 A6
Forge Mill Farm B71 .... 54 B6
Forge Mill Rd B98 .... 153 F6
Forge Rd Darlaston WS10 .. 41 C6
  Kenilworth CV8 .... 148 A6
  Stourbridge DY8 .... 80 F6
  Walsall WS3 .... 14 F1
  Willenhall WV12 .... 27 C4
Forge St Cannock WS12 .... 2 C4
  Wednesbury WS10 .... 41 E4
Forge The B63 .... 82 B8
Forge Trad Est B62 .... 83 C5
Forge Way Coventry CV6 .. 95 C3
  Oldbury B69 .... 63 D5
Forhill Ho B38 .... 123 F3
Forknell Ave CV2 .... 114 C5
Formans Rd B11 .... 87 E3
Formans Trad Est B11 .... 87 D3
Formby Ave WV6 .... 23 D4
Formby Way WS3 .... 14 A3
Forrell Gr B31 .... 123 B7
Forrest Ave Cannock WS11 .. 4 E8
  Essington WV11 .... 13 A4
Forrest Ct WS13 .... 9 B7
Forrest's Rd Kenilworth CV8 .. 147 E4
  Wednesbury WS10 .... 41 D1

Forrester St WS2 .... 28 C2
Forrester Street Prec
  WS2 .... 28 C2
Forresters Cl LE10 .... 75 F6
Forresters Rd LE10 .... 75 F6
Forryan Rd LE10 .... 75 F7
Forshaw Heath La B94 .... 141 A7
Forshaw Heath Rd B94 .... 125 C1
Forster St Birmingham B7 .. 67 A3
  Smethwick B67 .... 64 E7
Forsythia Cl
  Birmingham,
  Shenley Fields B31 .... 102 F7
  Birmingham,
  Woodcock St B31 .... 102 F8
Forsythia Gr WV8 .... 10 A3
Fort Cres WS9 .... 16 A3
Fort Ind Pk The B35 .... 57 F1
Fort Parkway B35, B36 .... 57 D1
Fort The B24 .... 57 C1
Forth Dr B37 .... 70 B4
Forth Gr B38 .... 123 E8
Forth Way B62 .... 83 E8
Forties B77 .... 35 E7
Fortnum Cl B33 .... 69 D2
Forton Cl WV6 .... 24 B2
Forum Ctr The DY1 .... 51 C1
Forum Rd B40 .... 90 E3
Forward Cotts B48 .... 138 F6
Forward Rd B26 .... 90 A3
Fosberry Cl CV34 .... 161 B8
Fosbrooke Rd B10 .... 88 A8
Fossdale Rd B77 .... 36 A8
Fosseway WS14 .... 9 A5
Fosseway Dr B23 .... 56 E8
Fosseway La WS13 .... 8 E4
Fosseway Rd CV3 .... 133 B4
Fossil Dr B45 .... 122 A7
Foster Ave Cannock WS12 .. 1 F6
  Studley B80 .... 159 E3
  Wolverhampton WV14 .... 40 B1
Foster Gdns B18 .... 65 F6
Foster Gn WV6 .... 23 E3
Foster Pl DY8 .... 80 E6
Foster Rd Coventry CV6 .. 113 B7
  Wolverhampton WV10 .... 25 E7
Foster St Darlaston WS10 .. 41 D7
  Stourbridge DY8 .... 81 A5
  Walsall WS3 .... 28 D8
Foster St E DY8 .... 81 A5
Foster Way B5 .... 86 C5
Fotherley Brook Rd WS9 .. 30 F5
Founder Cl CV4 .... 132 A8
Foundry La Smethwick B66 .. 65 D6
  Walsall WS3 .... 14 E3
Foundry Rd Birmingham
  B18 .... 65 E5
  Kingswinford DY6 .... 60 C8
Foundry Road Prim Sch
  B18 .... 65 E6
Foundry St Dudley WV14 .. 40 C1
  Kingswinford DY6 .... 60 C8
  Tipton DY4 .... 51 E8
Fountain Arc DY1 .... 51 C1
Fountain Cl B31 .... 122 E6
Fountain La Dudley WV14 .. 51 E8
  West Bromwich B69 .... 53 A1
Fountain Rd B17 .... 65 C1
Fountains Rd WS3 .... 13 E2
Fountains Way WS3 .... 13 E2
Four Acres B32 .... 84 C4
Four Ashes Rd B93 .... 127 E4
Four Crosses Rd WS4 .... 15 C1
Four Dwellings High Sch
  B32 .... 84 B5
Four Dwellings Inf Sch
  B32 .... 84 C4
Four Dwellings Jun Sch
  B32 .... 84 B5
Four Oaks Cl B98 .... 158 D8
Four Oaks Common Rd
  B74 .... 31 F3
Four Oaks Ct B74 .... 32 B1
Four Oaks Inf Sch B74 .... 31 E4
Four Oaks Jun Sch B74 .. 31 E4
Four Oaks Rd B74 .... 32 A1
Four Oaks Sta B74 .... 46 B8
Four Pounds Ave CV5 .... 112 F3
Four Stones Cl B91 .... 107 A1
Four Stones Gr B5 .... 86 D6
Four Winds Rd DY2 .... 62 E6
Fourlands Ave B72 .... 57 D7
Fourlands Rd B31 .... 102 E6
Fourth Ave
  Birmingham,
  Bordesley Green B9 .... 67 F2
  Birmingham, Selly Oak B29 .. 86 B3
  Brownhills WS8 .... 7 A1
  Wolverhampton WV10 .... 25 E6
Fowey Cl B76 .... 58 A7
Fowey Rd B34 .... 68 F6
Fowgay Dr B91 .... 106 F1
Fowler Cl Perton WV6 .... 23 E6
  Smethwick B66 .... 65 A8
Fowler Rd Coventry CV6 .. 113 B4
  Sutton Coldfield B75 .... 47 B5
Fowler St Birmingham B7 .. 67 B6
  Wolverhampton WV2 .... 39 C6
Fowlmere Rd B42 .... 55 B8
Fownhope Cl B98 .... 154 E3
Fox Ave CV10 .... 73 D7
Fox Covert DY8 .... 80 C5
Fox Foot Dr DY5 .... 61 B1
Fox & Goose Sh Ctr B8 .. 68 C5
Fox Gr B27 .... 88 A2
Fox Green Cres B27 .... 88 A2
Fox Hill B29 .... 103 D8
Fox Hill Cl B29 .... 103 C8

Fox Hill Rd B75 .... 32 F2
Fox Hollies L Ctr B27 .... 88 B1
Fox Hollies Rd
  Birmingham B27, B28 .... 88 A1
  Sutton Coldfield B76 .... 47 B2
Fox Hollies Sch B27 .... 88 A1
Fox Hollow WV6 .... 24 C2
Fox La Bromsgrove B61 .... 150 E8
  Lichfield WS13 .... 3 A5
Fox Mill Est B11 .... 87 D3
Fox St Birmingham B5 .... 164 D3
  Dudley DY1 .... 51 C6
Fox Wlk WS9 .... 16 B3
Fox's La WV6 .... 25 C4
Foxbury Dr B93 .... 128 B3
Foxcote Ave B21 .... 65 E4
Foxcote Cl Redditch B98 .. 154 F4
  Solihull B90 .... 126 D8
Foxcote Dr B90 .... 126 D8
Foxcote La B63, DY9 .... 82 B4
Foxcroft Cl WS7 .... 7 B5
Foxdale Dr DY5 .... 61 B3
Foxdale Gr B33 .... 69 C3
Foxdale Wlk CV31 .... 162 C6
Foxes Cl B98 .... 138 B5
Foxes Mdw B76 .... 58 A8
Foxes Rake WS11 .... 1 E3
Foxes Ridge B64 .... 82 E8
Foxes Way
  Balsall Common CV7 .... 130 B6
  Warwick CV34 .... 160 D4
Foxfields Way WS12 .... 1 C7
Foxford Cl Birmingham B36 .. 58 D1
  Sutton Coldfield B72 .... 57 D7
Foxford Cres CV2 .... 96 B4
Foxford Sch CV6 .... 96 A5
Foxglove B77 .... 22 A4
Foxglove Cl Coventry CV6 .. 95 C2
  Featherstone WV10 .... 12 B7
  Walsall WS3 .... 15 A5
  Wednesfield WV11 .... 26 E5
Foxglove Cres B73 .... 69 E3
Foxglove Rd DY1 .... 51 A4
Foxglove Way B60 .... 137 C6
Foxglove Wlk WS12 .... 2 C7
Foxhill Barns B48 .... 138 E5
Foxhill Cl WS12 .... 2 D2
Foxhill La B48 .... 138 E5
Foxhill's Cl WS7 .... 7 A5
Foxhills Cl CV11 .... 74 C1
Foxhills Pk DY2 .... 62 C4
Foxhills Rd Stourbridge
  DY8 .... 60 D1
  Wolverhampton WV4 .... 38 C3
Foxholes La B97 .... 158 A6
Foxholes The DY10 .... 116 F8
Foxhollies Dr B63 .... 82 E4
Foxhollow B61 .... 150 D8
Foxhope Cl B38 .... 104 B2
Foxhunt Rd B63 .... 82 E2
Foxland Ave
  Birmingham B45 .... 122 C7
  Great Wyrley WS6 .... 5 A3
Foxland Cl Birmingham B37 .. 70 D2
  Cheswick Green B90 .... 126 D4
Foxlands Ave WV4 .... 38 D3
Foxlands Cres WV4 .... 38 C3
Foxlands Dr Dudley DY3 .. 50 D5
  Sutton Coldfield B72 .... 57 D7
  Wombourne WV4 .... 38 D3
Foxlea Rd B63 .... 82 D1
Foxlydiate Cres B97 .... 153 B2
Foxlydiate La B97 .... 152 F3
Foxmeadow Cl DY3 .... 50 E7
Foxoak Ent Ctr B64 .... 62 D1
Foxoak St B64 .... 62 C1
Foxton Rd Birmingham B8 .. 67 F4
  Coventry CV3 .... 114 C1
Foxwalks Ave B61 .... 150 D8
Foxwell Gr B9 .... 68 C3
Foxwell Rd B9 .... 68 C3
Foxwood Ave B43 .... 44 B2
Foxwood Gr B37 .... 69 F5
Foxwood Rd Birchmoor B78 .. 36 F8
  Polesworth B78 .... 22 F1
Foxyards Cl DY4 .... 51 D5
Foxyards Prim Sch DY4 .. 51 C5
Foxyards Rd DY4 .... 51 C5
Foyle Rd B38 .... 103 F1
Fozdar Cres WV14 .... 40 B1
Fradley Cl B30 .... 103 D4
Framefield Dr B91 .... 107 F6
Framlingham Gr
  Kenilworth CV8 .... 148 C6
  Perton WV6 .... 24 A3
Frampton Cl
  Birmingham,
  Bournville B30 .... 103 D7
  Birmingham,
  Chelmsley Wood B37 .... 70 D3
Frampton Way B43 .... 44 D5
Frampton Wlk CV2 .... 114 F4
Frances Ave CV34 .... 161 A7
Frances Cres CV12 .... 78 A3
Frances Dr WS3 .... 14 B2
Frances Rd Baginton CV8 .. 133 F3
  Birmingham,
  Balsall Heath B30 .... 104 A5
  Birmingham, Lozells B19 .. 66 C8
  Birmingham,
  Stockland Green B23 .... 56 D3
Franche CE Prim Sch DY11 .. 116 C6
Franche Mid Sch DY11 .. 116 C6
Franche Rd DY11 .... 116 C8
Franchise Gdns WS10 .... 41 F6

Franchise St Birmingham
B42 .... 55 E2
Darlaston WS10 .... 41 F6
Kidderminster DY11 .... 116 C5
Francis Cl Kingswinford
DY6 .... 60 D8
Sutton Coldfield B74 .... 44 F8
Francis Rd
Birmingham,
Acock's Green B27 .... 88 D5
Birmingham, Edgbaston B16 .. 66 A1
Birmingham,
South Yardley B25 .... 88 A6
Birmingham, Stechford B33 .... 68 D2
Bromsgrove B60 .... 150 F7
Lichfield WS13 .... 3 A2
Smethwick B67 .... 64 D4
Stourbridge DY8 .... 80 C5
Francis St Birmingham B7 .. 67 A4
Coventry CV6 .... 113 E7
West Bromwich B70 .... 53 D1
Wolverhampton WV1 .... 25 C4
Francis Ward Cl B71 .... 53 A8
Francis Wlk B31 .... 123 A7
Franciscan Rd CV3 .... 133 D8
Frank F Harrison Comp
Sch WS2 .... 27 F7
Frank Rd B67 .... 64 E6
Frank St Birmingham B12 .. 86 F7
Nuneaton CV11 .... 73 B3
Frank Tommey Cl [5] B65 ... 63 C2
Frank Walsh Ho CV1 .... 165 C4
Frank Whittle Prim Sch
CV2 .... 114 F8
Frankburn Rd B74 .... 44 F8
Frankfort St B19 .... 66 D6
Frankholmes Dr B90 .... 127 A6
Frankland Rd CV6 .... 96 A1
Frankley Ave B62 .... 83 F5
Frankley Beeches Rd
B31 .... 102 D3
Frankley Com Sch B45 .... 101 F1
Frankley Gn B45 .... 101 D5
Frankley Green La B45 .... 101 E5
Frankley Hill La B32 .... 102 A4
Frankley La B31, B32 .... 102 D6
Frankley Ind Pk B45 .... 102 B1
Frankley Lodge Rd B31 .. 102 D4
Frankley Rd B68 .... 84 B8
Frankley Terr B17 .... 85 B5
Franklin Ct CV11 .... 73 D1
Franklin Dr WS7 .... 7 B7
Franklin Gr CV4 .... 111 E1
Franklin Rd Birmingham
B30 .... 103 F5
Nuneaton CV11 .... 73 D1
Whitnash CV31 .... 162 A3
Franklin St B18 .... 65 E5
Franklin Way B30 .... 103 F6
Franklyn Cl WV6 .... 23 E5
Frankpledge Rd CV3 .... 133 E7
Franks Way B33 .... 68 E2
Frankton Ave CV3 .... 133 C5
Frankton Cl Redditch B98 . 159 E8
Solihull B92 .... 89 B2
Frankton Gr B9 .... 68 B2
Frankwell Dr CV2 .... 96 E1
Frannkley Hill La B45 ...... 101 F3
Fraser Cl CV10 .... 72 B6
Fraser Rd Birmingham B11 .. 87 D5
Coventry CV5 .... 95 A1
Fraser St WV14 .... 40 E6
Frayne Ave DY6 .... 60 C7
Freasley Cl B90 .... 106 D3
Freasley Rd B34 .... 69 D6
Fred Lee Gr CV3 .... 133 D4
Freda Eddy Ct [3] DY10 ... 116 E6
Freda Rd B70 .... 53 D1
Freda Rise B69 .... 63 D8
Fredas Gr B17 .... 85 A4
Frederick Ave LE10 .... 71 B2
Frederick Bird Prim Sch
CV1 .... 113 F5
Frederick Neal Ave CV5 .. 111 D4
Frederick Rd
Birmingham, Aston B6 ...... 66 F8
Birmingham, Edgbaston B15 .. 86 B8
Birmingham,
Gravelly Hill B23 .... 56 E2
Birmingham, Selly Oak B29 .. 85 D2
Birmingham, Sparkhill B11 .. 87 C4
Birmingham, Stechford B33 .. 68 D3
Oldbury B68 .... 84 D7
Sutton Coldfield B73 .... 46 A2
Wolverhampton WV11 ..... 26 C5
Frederick Rd (Road 1)
DY10 .... 116 F1
Frederick St Birmingham
B1 .... 66 C4
Walsall WS2 .... 28 D1
West Bromwich B70 .... 53 C4
Wolverhampton WV2 ...... 163 B1
Frederick William St
WV13 .... 27 B2
Fredericks Cl DY8 .... 80 E4
Freeburn Cswy CV4 .... 132 C7
Freeford Gdns WS14 .... 9 E6
Freehold St CV1 .... 113 F4
Freeland Gr DY6 .... 60 F4
Freeman Cl CV10 .... 72 D4
Freeman Ct DY11 .... 116 B3
Freeman Dr B76 .... 46 F4
Freeman Pl WV14 .... 40 E8
Freeman Rd Birmingham B7 . 67 B6
Wednesbury WS10 .... 42 D3

Freeman St Birmingham
B5 .... 164 C2
Coventry CV6 .... 113 F6
Wolverhampton WV10 ..... 25 F2
Freeman's La LE10 .... 76 A5
Freemans Cl CV32 .... 156 E2
Freemantle Ho B24 .... 57 D3
Freemount Sq B43 .... 54 E7
Freer Rd B6 .... 66 E8
Freer St Nuneaton CV11 ... 73 E2
Walsall WS1 .... 28 F2
Freesland Rise CV10 .... 72 B6
Freeth Rd WS8 .... 7 A1
Freeth St Birmingham B16 . 65 F2
Oldbury B69 .... 63 F8
Freezeland St WV14 .... 40 B6
Fremantle Ho B34 .... 69 E6
Fremont Dr DY1 .... 50 E3
French Ave B78 .... 20 C1
French Rd DY2 .... 51 F1
French Walls [7] B66 .... 65 C5
Frensham Cl Birmingham
B37 .... 70 C2
Cheslyn Hay WS6 .... 4 E4
Frensham Dr CV10 .... 72 B5
Frensham Way B17 .... 85 C6
Frenshaw Gr B44 .... 55 F7
Freshfield Cl CV5 .... 94 C1
Freshwater Dr DY5 .... 81 B8
Freshwater Gr [5] CV31 .. 162 C6
Fretton Cl CV6 .... 113 F7
Frevill Rd CV6 .... 114 B8
Freville Cl B79 .... 21 A6
Friar Park Rd WS10 .... 42 D3
Friar St WS10 .... 42 B3
Friardale Cl WS10 .... 42 D3
Friars Cl Binley Woods CV3 . 135 E7
Stourbridge DY8 .... 60 C3
Friars Gorse DY7 .... 80 C7
Friars' Rd CV1 .... 165 B2
Friars St CV34 .... 160 D6
Friars Wlk B37 .... 70 D2
Friary Ave Lichfield WS13 ... 9 A6
Solihull B90 .... 127 A6
Friary Cl Birmingham B20 .. 54 F3
Hinckley LE10 .... 71 E1
Friary Cres WS4 .... 29 C6
Friary Gdns Birmingham B21 . 54 D2
Lichfield WS13 .... 9 A7
Friary Rd Birmingham B20 . 54 E3
Lichfield WS13 .... 9 A7
Friary St CV11 .... 73 B5
Friary The WS13 .... 9 A7
Friday Acre WS13 .... 3 A2
Friday La B92 .... 108 D4
Friesland Dr WV1 .... 26 B3
Friezeland Rd WS2 .... 28 B2
Friezland La WS8 .... 16 A5
Friezland Way WS8 .... 16 A5
Frilsham Way CV5 .... 112 B4
Fringe Gn B60 .... 151 A7
Fringe Green Cl B60 .... 151 A7
Fringe Meadow Rd B98 .. 154 F6
Frinton Gr B21 .... 65 C7
Frisby Ct CV11 .... 73 E2
Frisby Rd Birmingham B32 . 84 E5
Coventry CV4 .... 111 E2
Friston Ave B16 .... 66 B1
Friswell Dr CV6 .... 113 F8
Friswell Ho [3] CV2 .... 114 D8
Frith Way LE10 .... 71 A3
Frobisher Cl Great Wyrley
WS6 .... 4 F1
Hinckley LE10 .... 71 D4
Frobisher Rd CV3 .... 133 C5
Frobisher Way B66 .... 64 D7
Frodesley Rd B26 .... 89 B8
Frog La Balsall Common
CV7 .... 130 A5
Lichfield WS13 .... 9 B7
Froggatt Rd WV14 .... 40 D7
Froggatts Ride B76 .... 46 F3
Frogmere Cl CV5 .... 112 C6
Frogmill Rd B45 .... 102 B2
Frogmoor Ho B26 .... 88 E7
Frogmore La CV8 .... 129 F2
Frome Dr WV11 .... 26 C5
Frome Ho [4] DY1 .... 61 E8
Frome Way B14 .... 104 D6
Front Cotts B48 .... 138 F6
Frost St WV2 .... 40 A6
Froxmere Cl B91 .... 127 C8
Froyle Cl WV6 .... 24 C5
Froysell St WV13 .... 27 B2
Fryer Ave CV32 .... 156 E3
Fryer Rd B31 .... 123 B7
Fryer St WV1 .... 163 C3
Fryers Cl WS3 .... 28 B7
Fryers Rd WS2 .... 28 A7
Frythe Cl CV8 .... 148 C6
Fuchsia Cl [3] CV2 .... 96 B2
Fuchsia Dr WV9 .... 10 F3
Fugelmere Cl B17 .... 84 F7
Fulbrook Cl B98 .... 154 C5
Fulbrook Gr B29 .... 102 F8
Fulbrook Rd Coventry CV2 . 96 C3
Dudley DY1 .... 51 A1
Fulfen Prim Sch WS7 .... 7 D7
Fulford Dr B76 .... 58 B5
Fulford Gr B26 .... 89 C6
Fulford Hall Rd B94 .... 125 D3
Fulham Rd B11 .... 87 B5
Fullbrook Cl B90 .... 127 A5
Fullbrook Rd WS5 .... 42 E5
Fullelove Rd WS8 .... 16 A7
Fullers Cl CV6 .... 112 F7
Fullerton Cl WV8 .... 24 E8

Fullwood CV2 .... 96 E2
Fullwood Cres DY2 .... 61 F6
Fullwoods End WV14 .... 40 C1
Fulmar Cres DY10 .... 117 B2
Fulmer Wlk B18 .... 66 A3
Fulton Cl B60 .... 137 B1
Fulwell Gr B44 .... 56 A8
Fulwood Ave B62 .... 83 F8
Furber Pl DY6 .... 60 F6
Furlong La B63 .... 82 D6
Furlong Mdw B31 .... 103 C2
Furlong The WS10 .... 41 E5
Furlong Wlk DY3 .... 50 D4
Furlongs Rd DY3 .... 50 D6
Furlongs The
Stourbridge DY8 .... 81 B3
Wolverhampton WV11 ..... 26 B5
Furnace Hill B63 .... 83 B5
Furnace La B63 .... 83 B5
Furnace Par P4 .... 51 E6
Furnace Rd Bedworth CV12 . 78 D4
Dudley DY2 .... 62 C8
Furness B77 .... 21 D3
Furness Cl WS3 .... 13 F3
Furnivall Cres WS13 .... 3 D1
Furrows The B60 .... 150 D6
Furst St B98 .... 16 A8
Furze Way WS5 .... 43 E8
Furzebank Way WV12 .... 27 E4
Fylde Ho CV2 .... 114 D4
Fynford Rd CV6 .... 113 B5

Gable Croft WS14 .... 9 F6
Gables The DY6 .... 60 B8
Gaddesby Rd B14 .... 104 F8
Gadds Dr B65 .... 63 D4
Gads Gn DY2 .... 62 D5
Gads Green Cres DY2 ...... 62 E6
Gads La Dudley DY1 .... 51 C1
West Bromwich B70 .... 53 A3
Gadsby Ave WV11 .... 27 A7
Gadshill Rd B23 .... 73 E3
Gadsby St CV11 .... 73 E3
Gadwall Croft B23 .... 56 B3
Gaelic Rd WS11 .... 1 D4
Gagarin B79 .... 20 F5
Gaia La WS13 .... 9 B8
Gaiafields Rd WS13 .... 3 B1
Gaialands Cres WS13 .... 3 B1
Gaiastowe WS13 .... 3 B1
Gail Cl WS9 .... 16 B4
Gail Pk WV3 .... 38 D7
Gailey Croft B44 .... 44 E3
Gainford Cl WV8 .... 10 F1
Gainford Rd B44 .... 45 C1
Gainford Rise CV3 .... 115 A3
Gains La WS11 .... 5 D3
Gainsborough Ave LE10 ... 71 A3
Gainsborough Cres
Birmingham B43 .... 44 D4
Knowle B93 .... 128 A6
Gainsborough Dr
Bedworth CV12 .... 78 A4
Mile Oak B78 .... 34 B8
Perton WV6 .... 24 A4
Royal Leamington Spa
CV31 .... 162 D6
Gainsborough Hill DY8 .... 81 A3
Gainsborough Mews
DY11 .... 116 B5
Gainsborough Pl DY1 ...... 50 E2
Gainsborough Rd B42 ...... 55 B6
Gainsborough Trad Est
DY9 .... 81 C4
Gainsbrook Cres WS11 ...... 5 F5
Gainsford Dr B62 .... 83 B6
Gairloch Rd WV12 .... 13 B1
Gaitskell Terr B69 .... 52 D2
Gaitskell Way B66 .... 64 F7
Galahad Way WS10 .... 42 A2
Galbraith Cl WV14 .... 51 D8
Gale Wlk B65 .... 62 F5
Galey's Rd CV3 .... 133 D8
Gallagher Bsns Pk CV6 .... 95 E5
Gallagher Ct [13] B13 .... 87 B2
Gallagher Rd CV12 .... 78 A2
Galliards The CV4 .... 132 D4
Galloway Ave B34 .... 68 F6
Galloway Cl LE10 .... 71 F7
Gallows Hill CV34 .... 161 B4
Galmington Dr CV3 .... 133 B6
Galton Cl Sutton Coldfield
B24 .... 57 F4
Tipton DY4 .... 52 C6
Galton Dr DY2 .... 62 B6
Galton Ho B67 .... 64 F2
Galton Rd B67 .... 64 F1
Galton Tower B1 .... 66 C2
Galtons La DY9 .... 120 A7
Galway Rd WS7 .... 7 A7
Gamesfield Gn WV3 .... 24 F1
Gammage St DY2 .... 62 B8
Gamson Cl DY10 .... 116 E4
Ganborough Cl B98 .... 154 E1
Gandy Rd WV12 .... 27 A4
Gannahs Farm Cl B76 ...... 46 F3
Gannow Green La B45 .... 101 D1
Gannow Manor Cres B45 . 101 E2
Gannow Manor Gdns
B45 .... 101 F1
Gannow Mid Sch B45 ..... 121 D7
Gannow Rd B45 .... 121 E7
Gannow Wlk B45 .... 121 E7
Ganton Rd WS3 .... 14 A4
Ganton Wlk WV8 .... 24 F8
Ganville Ho B36 .... 69 F8
Garage Cl B77 .... 21 D5

Garden Cl
Birmingham, Frankley B45 . 102 A2
Birmingham, Ward End B8 . 68 A5
Hinckley LE10 .... 75 D6
Knowle B93 .... 127 F6
Garden Cres WS3 .... 14 F3
Garden Croft WS9 .... 30 B7
Garden Ct
Warwick, Emscote CV34 . 161 C8
[11] Warwick, Packmores
CV34 .... 160 F7
Garden Flats CV5 .... 111 D5
Garden Gr Bedworth CV12 . 95 F8
Birmingham B20 .... 54 E6
Garden Rd LE10 .... 71 D1
Garden St WS2 .... 28 E3
Garden Wlk Bilston WV14 . 40 F6
Dudley DY3 .... 50 C2
Gardeners Cl DY11 .... 116 C8
Gardeners Wlk B91 .... 107 C3
Gardenia Dr CV5 .... 112 B6
Gardens The Birmingham
B23 .... 56 E3
Kenilworth CV8 .... 148 A3
Radford Semele CV31 .... 162 E5
Gardner Ho [8] CV1 .... 113 B2
Garfield Rd B26 .... 89 B8
Garganey Ct DY10 .... 116 F1
Garibaldi Terr B60 .... 137 A1
Garland Cres B62 .... 83 E8
Garland St B9 .... 67 C3
Garland Way B31 .... 103 C4
Garlick Dr CV8 .... 148 C6
Garman Cl B43 .... 43 E2
Garner Cl WV14 .... 40 D3
Garnet Ave B43 .... 44 B3
Garnet Cl WS9 .... 16 E4
Garnett Ct [4] B92 .... 88 F1
Garnett Dr B75 .... 46 E6
Garnette Cl CV10 .... 72 B5
Garrard Gdns B73 .... 46 B5
Garrat St DY5 .... 61 E5
Garratt Cl B68 .... 64 C4
Garratt St B71 .... 53 B5
Garratt's La B65 .... 63 A2
Garratts Wlk B14 .... 104 E2
Garret Cl [1] DY6 .... 60 D8
Garrett St CV11 .... 73 E2
Garretts Green La B26 ..... 89 A8
Garrick Cl CV5 .... 111 C4
Garrick Rise WS7 .... 7 B7
Garrick St WV1 .... 163 C2
Garrigill B77 .... 22 B1
Garrington St WS10 .... 41 C7
Garrison Ct [9] B9 .... 67 B2
Garrison La B9 .... 67 C2
Garrison St B9 .... 67 B3
Garston Way [4] B43 .... 54 D8
Garth Cres CV3 .... 134 D8
Garth Ho CV3 .... 134 D8
Garth The Birmingham B14 . 105 D4
Lichfield WS13 .... 3 B2
Garway Cl Redditch B98 . 154 E1
Royal Leamington Spa CV32 . 156 F4
Garway Gr B25 .... 88 C6
Garwood Rd B26 .... 68 F2
Gas Sq B61 .... 136 F1
Gas St Birmingham B1 ...... 66 C2
Royal Leamington Spa CV31 . 161 F7
Gas Street Basin B1 .... 164 A2
Gatacre St B73 .... 50 D3
Gatcombe Cl WV10 .... 11 F4
Gatcombe Rd DY1 .... 50 E2
Gate La Dorridge B93 ..... 127 C3
Sutton Coldfield B73 .... 45 F2
Gate St Birmingham B8 .... 67 D5
Sedgley DY3 .... 50 E7
Tipton DY4 .... 52 A2
Gatehouse Cl CV34 .... 161 D7
Gatehouse Fold [5] DY2 ... 51 D1
Gatehouse La CV12 .... 78 A2
Gatehouse Trad Est WS8 ... 7 A1
Gateley Rd B68 .... 84 D7
Gateside Rd CV6 .... 95 E2
Gatis St WV6 .... 25 A5
Gatwick Rd B35 .... 58 B4
Gauden Rd DY9 .... 81 D2
Gaulby Wlk CV3 .... 115 A3
Gaunts The B48 .... 139 B6
Gaveston Rd Coventry CV6 . 112 F6
Royal Leamington Spa CV32 . 156 E1
Gawne La B64 .... 62 F3
Gawsworth B79 .... 20 D7
Gay Hill La B38 .... 124 B8
Gaydon Cl Coventry CV6 . 114 A8
Perton WV6 .... 23 E5
Redditch B98 .... 153 F1
Gaydon Gr B29 .... 85 A2
Gaydon Rd Aldridge WS9 . 30 A4
Solihull B92 .... 89 D3
Gayer St CV6 .... 96 A1
Gayfield Ave DY5 .... 61 E1
Gayhurst Cl CV3 .... 134 E8
Gayhurst Dr B25 .... 88 E8
Gayle B77 .... 22 A1
Gayle Gr B27 .... 106 C8
Gayton Rd B71 .... 53 D6
Gaywood Croft B15 .... 86 C8
Gaza Cl CV4 .... 112 A1
Gazelle Cl CV1 .... 165 D3
Geach St B19 .... 66 D5
Geach Tower B19 .... 66 D5
Gedney Cl B90 .... 105 C3
Gee St B19 .... 66 D6
Geeson Cl B35 .... 58 B4
Gemini Dr WS11 .... 4 F6

Geneva Rd DY4 .... 51 D5
Genge Ave WV4 .... 39 E4
Genners La B32 .... 102 D7
Genthorn Cl WV4 .... 39 F4
Gentian B74 .... 31 F4
Gentian Cl B31 .... 102 F6
Geoffery Cl B74 .... 114 B5
Geoffery St B76 .... 58 B7
Geoffrey Rd Birmingham
B11 .... 87 C3
Solihull B90 .... 105 F3
George Arthur Rd B8 .... 67 D5
George Auden Specl Sch
B31 .... 102 F5
George Ave Blackheath B65 . 63 D2
Mile Oak B78 .... 20 C1
George Betts Prim Sch
B66 .... 64 C7
George Cl DY2 .... 62 E8
George Dance Cl [2] DY10 . 117 B6
George Dixon Jun & Inf
Sch B17 .... 65 C2
George Dixon Sec Sch
B17 .... 65 C2
George Eliot Ave CV12 ..... 78 D2
George Eliot Hospl CV10 . 73 B2
George Eliot Rd CV1 .... 113 D5
George Eliot Sch
Nuneaton CV11 .... 73 D1
Nuneaton CV11 .... 78 D8
George Eliot St CV11 .... 73 C2
George Fentham Prim
Sch B92 .... 109 B6
George Frederick Rd B73 . 45 A4
George Henry Rd DY4 ...... 52 E6
George Hodgkinson Cl
CV4 .... 111 F3
George La WS13 .... 9 C8
George Marston Rd CV3 . 114 E1
George Park Cl Ansty CV7 . 97 D3
Coventry CV2 .... 96 C1
George Poole Ho [6] CV1 . 113 B2
George Rd Alvechurch B48 . 139 A5
Birmingham, Edgbaston B15 . 86 B8
Birmingham, Great Barr B43 . 43 F2
Birmingham,
Perry Common B73 .... 45 D1
Birmingham, Selly Oak B29 . 85 E3
Birmingham,
South Yardley B25 .... 88 A6
Birmingham,
Stockland Green B23 .... 56 C3
Dudley, Dudley Bank WV14 . 40 D1
Dudley, Tipton Green DY4 . 51 D6
Halesowen B63 .... 82 F4
Oldbury B68 .... 64 C2
Solihull B91 .... 107 D3
Warwick CV34 .... 161 A8
Water Orton B46 .... 59 C3
George Robertson Cl CV3 . 134 E7
George Rose Gdns WS10 . 41 C6
George Salter High Sch
B70 .... 53 A4
George St
Birmingham,
Balsall Heath B12 .... 86 F5
Birmingham,
Brookfields B3 .... 164 A3
Birmingham,
Handsworth B21 .... 65 C8
Birmingham, Lozells B19 . 66 B7
[1] Bromsgrove B61 .... 136 F2
Cannock WS12 .... 2 D4
Coventry CV1 .... 113 E5
Dudley DY1 .... 51 B6
Hinckley LE10 .... 75 D8
Kidderminster DY10 .... 116 F6
Nuneaton CV11 .... 73 E2
Royal Leamington Spa
CV31 .... 162 A7
Stourbridge DY8 .... 60 F1
Tamworth B79 .... 21 B4
Walsall WS1 .... 28 E1
West Bromwich B70 .... 53 D2
Willenhall WV13 .... 27 A4
Wolverhampton WV2 ...... 163 C2
Wolverhampton,
Ettingshall WV2 .... 40 A7
George St W B18 .... 66 A4
George Street Ringway
CV12 .... 78 B3
George Wlk [3] B97 .... 153 E3
Georgian Gdns [2] WS10 . 41 F3
Georgian Pl WS11 .... 1 E2
Georgina Ave WV14 .... 40 D3
Gerald Rd DY8 .... 80 E7
Geraldine Rd B25 .... 88 B7
Geranium Gr B9 .... 67 F3
Geranium Rd DY2 .... 62 F8
Gerard B79 .... 20 E7
Gerard Ave CV4 .... 132 B8
Gerardsfield Rd B33 .... 69 E2
Gerrard Cl B19 .... 66 D7
Gerrard Rd WV13 .... 26 E1
Gerrard St Birmingham B19 . 66 C7
[12] Warwick CV34 .... 160 E6
Gervase Dr DY1 .... 51 C3
Geston Rd DY1 .... 61 F8
Gheluvelt Ave DY10 .... 116 F7
Gibb La B61 .... 137 A8
Gibb St B9 .... 66 F1
Gibbet Hill Rd CV4 .... 132 B3
Gibbet La DY7 .... 80 B4
Gibbins Rd B29 .... 85 D2
Gibbons Cl CV4 .... 111 F2
Gibbons Gr WV6 .... 24 F4
Gibbons Hill Rd DY3 .... 39 D2

Gibbons Ind Pk DY6 .... 61 A7
Gibbons La DY5 .... 61 A7
Gibbons Rd
  Sutton Coldfield B75 ...... 32 B3
  Wolverhampton WV6 ...... 24 F4
Gibbs Cl CV2 .... 115 B6
Gibbs Hill Rd B31 .... 123 C7
Gibbs Rd Redditch B98 ...... 154 A5
  Stourbridge DY9 .... 82 A5
Gibbs St W6 .... 25 A4
Gibson Cres CV12 .... 78 A1
Gibson Dr B20 .... 66 B8
Gibson Rd Birmingham B20 ... 66 B8
  Perton WV6 .... 23 E3
Gideon Cl B25 .... 88 D6
Gideons Cl DY3 .... 50 D5
Gielgud Way CV2 .... 115 B8
Giffard Rd Bilston WV1 ...... 40 B7
  Wolverhampton WV10 ...... 11 F3
Giffard Way CV34 .... 155 E1
Gifford Ct 13 DY5 .... 61 D2
Giffords Croft WS13 .... 3 A1
Gigg La B76 .... 48 B3
Gigmill Prim Sch DY8 .... 80 E4
Gigmill Way DY8 .... 80 E4
Gilbanks Rd DY8 .... 80 D7
Gilberry Cl B93 .... 128 A4
Gilbert Ave B69 .... 63 B7
Gilbert Cl 3 Coventry CV1 .. 113 E3
  Wednesfield WV11 .... 27 A7
Gilbert La WV5 .... 49 B7
Gilbert Rd Bromsgrove B60 .. 150 E7
  Lichfield WS13 .... 3 C2
  Smethwick B66 .... 65 B3
Gilbert Scott Way DY10 .... 116 F7
Gilbert St DY4 .... 52 A2
Gilbert Wlk WS13 .... 3 C2
Gilberts Ct WS4 .... 29 A4
Gilberstone Ave B26 .... 88 E5
Gilbertstone Cl B98 .... 153 E1
Gilbertstone Jun & Inf Sch
  B26 .... 88 E5
Gilbeys Cl DY8 .... 60 E1
Gilby Rd B16 .... 66 A1
Gilchrist Dr B15 .... 85 E8
Gildas Ave B38 .... 104 A1
Giles Cl Birmingham B33 .... 68 E3
  Coventry CV6 .... 95 C2
  Solihull B90 .... 107 F7
Giles Close Ho B33 .... 68 E3
Giles Rd Lichfield WS13 ...... 3 A3
  Oldbury B68 .... 64 B5
Gilfil Rd CV10 .... 73 B1
Gill St Dudley DY2 .... 62 E4
  West Bromwich B70 .... 53 C1
Gilldown Pl B15 .... 86 B7
Gillespie Croft B6 .... 66 F7
Gillet Cl CV11 .... 73 B3
Gillhurst Rd B17 .... 85 C7
Gillians Wlk CV2 .... 115 A8
Gilling Gr B34 .... 69 A6
Gillingham Cl WS10 .... 42 D4
Gillity Ave WS5 .... 43 C8
Gillity Cl WS5 .... 43 C8
Gillity Ct 3 WS5 .... 43 D7
Gilliver Rd B90 .... 106 B2
Gilman Cl B26 .... 89 D4
Gillott Cl B91 .... 107 E3
Gillott Rd B16 .... 65 D2
Gillows Croft B90 .... 127 A7
Gillscroft Rd B33 .... 69 A3
Gillway B79 .... 21 B8
Gilmorton Cl Birmingham
  B17 .... 85 B7
  Solihull B91 .... 107 C1
Gilpin Cl B8 .... 68 C7
Gilpin Cres WS3 .... 15 A4
Gilpins Croft WS6 .... 4 D1
Gilson Dr B46 .... 70 D8
Gilson Rd B46 .... 70 E8
Gilson St DY4 .... 52 C8
Gilson Way B37 .... 70 A5
Gilwell Rd B34 .... 69 E6
Gingko Wlk CV31 .... 161 F5
Gipsy Cl CV7 .... 130 B5
Gipsy La
  Balsall Common CV7 ...... 130 C5
  Birmingham B23 .... 56 B5
  Nuneaton CV10, CV11 ...... 78 D7
  Willenhall WV13 .... 27 B1
Girdlers Cl CV3 .... 133 B5
Girtin Cl CV12 .... 78 A4
Girton Ho B36 .... 69 F8
Girton Rd WS11 .... 4 F8
Girvan Gr CV32 .... 157 C5
Gisborn Cl B10 .... 87 B8
Gisburn Cl CV34 .... 155 F1
Givens Ho 9 CV1 .... 113 B2
Glade The Aldridge B74 ...... 30 E1
  Birmingham B26 .... 89 D4
  Cannock WS11 .... 1 C2
  Coventry CV5 .... 111 F3
  Stourbridge DY9 .... 81 E5
  Wolverhampton WV8 ...... 10 E1
Glades The WS9 .... 30 B7
Gladeside Cl WS4 .... 29 D8
Gladstone Cl LE10 .... 71 E4
Gladstone Dr
  Stourbridge DY8 .... 80 D6
  Tipton B69 .... 52 D3
Gladstone Gr DY6 .... 60 D8
Gladstone Rd
  Birmingham,
    Gravelly Hill B23 .... 56 D3
  Birmingham,
    South Yardley B26 .... 88 D8
  Birmingham, Sparkbrook B11 . 87 B6

Gladstone Rd continued
  Cannock WS12 .... 2 E1
  Dorridge B93 .... 128 A2
  Stourbridge DY8 .... 80 D6
Gladstone St Birmingham B6 . 67 B8
  Darlaston WS10 .... 41 E6
  Walsall WS2 .... 28 D4
  West Bromwich B71 .... 53 C5
Gladstone Terr LE10 .... 75 E8
Gladys Rd Birmingham B25 .. 88 B7
  Smethwick B67 .... 64 F2
Gladys Terr B67 .... 65 A2
Glaisdale Ave CV6 .... 95 E3
Glaisdale Gdns WV6 .... 25 A5
Glaisdale Rd B28 .... 106 B8
Glaisedale Gr WV13 .... 27 C2
Glamis Rd WV12 .... 27 B7
Glamorgan Cl CV3 .... 134 D5
Glanville Dr B75 .... 32 A4
Glasbury Croft B38 .... 123 E7
Glascote Cl B90 .... 106 A4
Glascote Ct B77 .... 21 E4
Glascote Gr B34 .... 69 C6
Glascote Heath Prim Sch
  B77 .... 22 A2
Glascote La B77 .... 35 F7
Glascote Rd B77 .... 22 B2
Glasscroft Cotts WS7 .... 7 F7
Glasshouse Hill DY8 .... 81 B3
Glasshouse La
  Kenilworth CV8 .... 148 D4
  Tanworth-in-A B94 .... 143 F6
Glaston Dr B91 .... 107 A1
Glastonbury Cl DY11 .... 116 A6
Glastonbury Cres WS3 .... 13 E2
Glastonbury Rd
  Birmingham B14 .... 105 C5
  West Bromwich B71 .... 42 D1
Glastonbury Way WS3 .... 13 E1
Gleads Croft B62 .... 84 A3
Gleason Wlk WV1 .... 26 C1
Gleave Rd Birmingham B29 .. 85 E1
  Whitnash CV31 .... 162 A3
Glebe Ave CV12 .... 77 E1
Glebe Cl Coventry CV4 ..... 132 A7
  Redditch B98 .... 154 D2
Glebe Cres CV8 .... 148 A3
Glebe Ct CV31 .... 162 A3
Glebe Dr B73 .... 56 F8
Glebe Farm Rd B33 .... 69 A5
Glebe Fields B76 .... 59 B6
Glebe La Nuneaton CV11 .... 73 F6
  Stourbridge DY8 .... 80 E4
Glebe Pl Darlaston WS10 .... 41 B6
  Royal Leamington Spa CV31 . 162 B7
Glebe Rd Alvechurch B48 ... 139 A7
  Hinckley LE10 .... 71 F1
  Nuneaton CV11 .... 73 D4
  Solihull B91 .... 107 D5
  Willenhall WV13 .... 40 F8
Glebe St WS1 .... 42 E8
Glebe The Belbroughton
  DY9 .... 119 E6
  Beoley B98 .... 154 F7
  Corley CV7 .... 94 C7
Glebe Way CV7 .... 130 A7
Glebefarm Gr CV3 .... 114 F3
Glebefields Prim Sch DY4 .. 52 A8
Glebefields Rd DY4 .... 52 A7
Glebeland Cl B16 .... 66 B1
Gledhill Pk WS14 .... 9 C5
Gleeson Dr CV34 .... 155 E1
Glen Bank LE10 .... 71 E1
Glen Cl Cannock WS11 .... 1 E5
  Walsall WS4 .... 29 A3
Glen Ct Codsall WV8 .... 10 A4
  Wolverhampton WV3 .... 24 E2
Glen Devon Cl B45 .... 102 A2
Glen Ho DY1 .... 61 D8
Glen Park Rd DY3 .... 50 D2
Glen Rd Dudley DY3 .... 50 E6
  Stourbridge DY8 .... 80 F3
Glen Rise B13 .... 105 C6
Glen Side B32 .... 84 D2
Glen The B60 .... 138 A5
Glenavon Rd B14 .... 105 A3
Glenbarr Cl LE10 .... 75 A8
Glenbarr Dr LE10 .... 75 A8
Glencoe Dr WS11 .... 2 A2
Glencoe Rd Birmingham B16 . 65 C4
  Coventry CV3 .... 114 B1
Glencroft Rd B92 .... 89 D4
Glendale Ave CV8 .... 148 A6
Glendale Cl Halesowen B63 .. 83 B4
  Wolverhampton WV3 .... 38 C8
Glendale Dr Birmingham
  B33 .... 68 F3
  Wombourne WV5 .... 49 A6
Glendale Fst Sch CV10 ...... 72 V2
Glendale Tower 5 B23 .... 57 B6
Glendawn Cl WS11 .... 2 A3
Glendene Cres B38 .... 123 C7
Glendene Dr 2 B43 .... 54 D8
Glendene Rd WS12 .... 2 D6
Glendon Gdns CV12 .... 79 C3
Glendon Rd B23 .... 56 D6
Glendon Way B93 .... 127 E3
Glendower Ave CV5 .... 112 D3
Glendower Rd Aldridge
  WS9 .... 16 B1
  Birmingham B42 .... 55 D4
Gleneagles B77 .... 22 B5
Gleneagles Cl CV11 .... 74 C1
Gleneagles Dr
  Birmingham B43 .... 43 E3
  Blackwell B60 .... 138 A5
  Sutton Coldfield B75 ...... 46 D8
  Tipton B69 .... 63 A7

Gleneagles Rd
  Birmingham B26 .... 89 A8
  Coventry CV2 .... 114 E6
  Perton WV6 .... 23 D5
  Walsall WS3 .... 13 F3
Glenelg Dr DY8 .... 81 B2
Glenelg Mews WS5 .... 43 B1
Glenfern Rd WV14 .... 51 A8
Glenfield Tamworth B77 ..... 21 C1
  Wolverhampton WV10 ...... 10 E2
Glenfield Ave CV10 .... 73 D7
Glenfield Cl Redditch B97 .. 158 D6
  2 Solihull B91 .... 127 C8
  Sutton Coldfield B76 ...... 46 E3
Glenfield Gr B29 .... 86 A1
Glengarry Cl B32 .... 102 B7
Glengarry Gdns WV3 .... 24 F1
Glenhurst Cl WS2 .... 27 D3
Glenmead Jun & Inf Sch
  B44 .... 55 D8
Glenmead Rd B44 .... 55 D8
Glenmore Ave WS7 .... 7 A6
Glenmore Cl WV3 .... 38 E7
Glenmore Dr
  Birmingham B38 .... 103 D2
  Coventry CV6 .... 95 F5
Glenmount Ave CV6 .... 95 F5
Glenn St CV6 .... 95 D3
Glenpark Rd B8 .... 67 F5
Glenridding Cl CV6 .... 95 F5
Glenrosa Wlk CV4 .... 132 A7
Glenroy Cl CV2 .... 114 E6
Glenroyde B38 .... 123 E7
Glenside Ave B92 .... 89 C3
Glenthorne Dr WS6 .... 4 E3
Glenthorne Ho WS6 .... 4 D2
Glenthorne Prim Sch WS6 .... 4 E3
Glenthorne Rd B24 .... 57 A2
Glenthorne Way B24 .... 57 A2
Glentworth Ave CV6 .... 95 A2
Glentworth Dr B76 .... 47 A2
Glentworth Gdns WV6 .... 25 B5
Glenvale Specl Sch B70 ..... 53 A4
Glenville Ave CV9 .... 36 C1
Glenville Dr B23 .... 56 E5
Glenwood Cl DY5 .... 81 D8
Glenwood Dr B90 .... 126 D4
Glenwood Gdns CV12 .... 78 A5
Glenwood Rd B38 .... 123 D8
Glenwood Rise WS9 .... 16 D3
Globe St WS10 .... 41 F1
Gloster Dr CV8 .... 147 F6
Gloucester Cl Nuneaton
  CV11 .... 74 A7
  Wolverhampton WS13 .... 3 B3
Gloucester Ho
  4 Birmingham B24 .... 56 F4
  4 Wolverhampton WV3 ..... 25 C4
Gloucester Pl WV13 .... 27 D2
Gloucester Rd Dudley DY2 .. 62 D2
  Walsall WS5 .... 43 C8
  Wednesbury WS10 .... 42 C3
Gloucester St
  Birmingham B5 .... 164 C1
  Coventry CV1 .... 113 B3
  1 Royal Leamington Spa
    CV31 .... 162 A7
  Wolverhampton WV6 .... 25 B4
Gloucester Way
  Birmingham B37 .... 70 A1
  Cannock WS11 .... 2 B1
Glover Cl Birmingham B28 .. 105 F6
  Warwick CV34 .... 160 B4
Glover Rd B75 .... 47 A5
Glover St Birmingham B9 .... 67 A2
  Cannock WS12 .... 2 F3
  Coventry CV3 .... 133 D8
  Redditch B98 .... 153 E3
  West Bromwich B70 .... 53 D1
Glover's Trust Homes B73 .. 56 F7
Glovers Cl CV7 .... 92 C1
Glovers Croft B37 .... 69 F3
Glovers Field Dr B7 .... 67 C7
Glovers Rd B10 .... 87 D8
Glyme Dr WV6 .... 24 E5
Glyn Ave WV14 .... 41 B3
Glyn Dr WV14 .... 41 B3
Glyn Farm Rd B32 .... 84 C6
Glyn Rd B32 .... 84 D6
Glyndebourne B79 .... 20 D7
Glyne Ct B73 .... 46 B5
Glynn Cres B63 .... 82 B7
Glynne Ave DY6 .... 60 D4
Glynne Prim Sch DY6 .... 60 C4
Glynside Ave B32 .... 84 D6
Godfrey Cl CV31 .... 162 E5
Godiva Pl CV1 .... 165 D3
Godiva Trad Est CV6 .... 113 F8
Godolphin B79 .... 20 D6
Godrich Ho B13 .... 87 B3
Godson Cres DY11 .... 116 C3
Godson Pl DY11 .... 116 C3
Goffs Cl B32 .... 84 F3
Gofton B77 .... 36 A8
Gold Cl CV11 .... 78 E8
Goldcrest B77 .... 36 A6
Goldcrest Cl DY2 .... 62 D2
Goldcrest Croft B36 .... 70 A8
Goldcrest Dr DY10 .... 117 B2
Golden Acres La CV3 .... 134 F1
Golden Croft B20 .... 54 F1
Golden Cross La B61 .... 121 B1
Golden End Dr B93 .... 128 D6
Golden Hillock Rd
  Birmingham B11 .... 87 B6
  Dudley DY2 .... 62 C3
Golden Hillock Sch B11 .... 87 D5
Goldencrest Dr B69 .... 63 E8

Goldfinch Cl B30 .... 103 D8
Goldfinch Rd DY9 .... 81 C3
Goldicroft Rd WS10 .... 42 A4
Goldieslie Cl B73 .... 46 B2
Goldieslie Rd B73 .... 46 B2
Golds Hill Gdns B21 .... 65 F7
Golds Hill Rd B21 .... 65 F8
Goldsborough B77 .... 22 A1
Goldsmith Ave CV34 .... 160 C5
Goldsmith Pl B79 .... 21 A7
Goldsmith Rd
  Birmingham B14 .... 104 F8
  Walsall WS3 .... 28 E7
Goldstar Way B33 .... 69 C2
Goldtel Ind Est WV4 .... 40 A5
Goldthorn Ave WV4 .... 39 B6
Goldthorn Cl CV5 .... 111 D4
Goldthorn Cres WV4 .... 39 A6
Goldthorn Hill WV2, WV4 ... 39 C6
Goldthorn Park Prim Sch
  WV4 .... 39 D5
Goldthorn Pl DY11 .... 116 C2
Goldthorn Rd
  Kidderminster DY11 ...... 116 C2
  Wolverhampton WV2 ...... 39 B6
Goldthorne Ave
  Birmingham B26 .... 89 C4
  Cannock WS11 .... 1 F2
Goldthorne Cl B97 .... 153 C1
Goldthorne Wlk DY5 .... 81 D8
Golf Dr CV11 .... 74 B1
Golf La Bilston WV14 .... 40 D7
  Whitnash CV31 .... 162 B2
Golson Cl B75 .... 46 F6
Gomeldon Ave B14 .... 104 F3
Gomer St W WV13 .... 27 A2
Gomer St WV13 .... 27 A2
Gooch Cl DY8 .... 81 B6
Gooch St B5 .... 86 E8
Gooch St N B5 .... 86 E8
Good Hope Hospl B75 .... 46 D6
Good Shepherd Prim Sch
  CV6 .... 95 F1
Goodall Gr B43 .... 44 E5
Goodall St WS1 .... 28 F1
Goodby Rd B13 .... 106 A3
Goode Ave B18 .... 66 A5
Goode Cl B68 .... 64 C4
Goode Croft CV4 .... 111 F2
Goodeve Wlk B75 .... 47 B5
Goodison Gdns B24 .... 57 B5
Goodleigh Ave B45 .... 122 E6
Goodman Cl B28 .... 105 F6
Goodman St B1 .... 66 B3
Goodman Way CV4 .... 111 C1
Goodrest Ave B62 .... 84 A5
Goodrest Croft B14 .... 105 C4
Goodrest La B38 .... 123 F6
Goodrich Ave CV6 .... 24 A3
Goodrich Cl B98 .... 154 F2
Goodrich Covert 10 B14 ... 104 C2
Goodway Ct 8 CV34 .... 160 F7
Goodway Rd Birmingham
  B44 .... 55 F8
  Solihull B92 .... 89 E4
Goodwin Cl DY11 .... 116 C7
Goodwood Cl
  Birmingham B36 .... 68 D8
  Lichfield WS14 .... 9 D7
Goodwood Dr B74 .... 44 F7
Goodwyn Ave B68 .... 84 C7
Goodyear Ave WV10 .... 25 E7
Goodyear Rd B67 .... 64 E2
Goodyers End Fst & Mid
  Schs CV12 .... 95 E8
Goodyers End La CV12 ..... 95 D8
Goosehill Cl B98 .... 154 E1
Goosehills Rd LE10 .... 75 E5
Goosemoor La B23 .... 56 F7
Goostry Cl B77 .... 21 D5
Goostry Rd B77 .... 21 D5
Gopsal St B4 .... 67 A3
Gopsall Rd LE10 .... 71 D2
Gordon Ave Birmingham B19 . 66 D7
  West Bromwich B71 .... 53 C8
  Wolverhampton WV4 ...... 39 F3
Gordon Cl Bedworth CV12 .. 78 C4
  Tipton B69 .... 52 D2
Gordon Cres DY5 .... 61 E5
Gordon Ct B33 .... 68 D3
Gordon Dr DY4 .... 52 C6
Gordon Pl WV14 .... 40 C5
Gordon Rd
  Birmingham, Harborne B17 . 85 D6
  Birmingham, Lozells B19 .. 66 C8
Gordon St
  5 Birmingham B9 .... 67 B2
  Coventry CV1 .... 113 B2
  Darlaston WS10 .... 41 E6
  Royal Leamington Spa
    CV31 .... 162 A7
  Wolverhampton WV2 ...... 163 C2
Gorey Cl WV12 .... 27 B8
Gorge Rd WV14, DY3 .... 39 F1
Goring Rd CV2 .... 114 A4
Gorleston Gr B14 .... 105 E4
Gorleston Rd B14 .... 105 B2
Gorse Cl
  Birmingham,
    Fordbridge B37 .... 69 F2
  Birmingham, Selly Oak B29 . 103 A8
  Cannock WS11 .... 1 D5
Gorse Farm Rd
  Birmingham B43 .... 54 E8
  Nuneaton CV11 .... 79 B8
Gorse Green La DY9 .... 120 C8

Gorse La Lichfield WS14 ...... 9 E6
  Lichfield, Curborough WS13 . 3 F6
Gorse Meadow Dr B45 ...... 138 B8
Gorse Rd Dudley DY1 .... 51 A4
  Wednesfield WV11 .... 27 A8
Gorse Way WS12 .... 2 C8
Gorsebrook Rd W6 .... 25 B5
Gorsefield Rd B34 .... 69 C5
Gorsemoor Cty Prim Sch
  WS12 .... 2 D1
Gorsemoor Rd WS12 .... 2 D1
Gorsemoor Way WV11 .... 13 B3
Gorseway Burntwood WS7 ... 7 B5
  Coventry CV5 .... 112 C3
Gorsey La Cannock WS11 ..... 1 C1
  Coleshill B46 .... 59 F2
  Great Wyrley WS6 .... 4 F1
  Norton Canes WS3 .... 5 E1
  Wythall B47 .... 125 A3
Gorsey Way Aldridge WS9 .. 29 E5
  Coleshill B46 .... 59 E2
Gorsly Piece B32 .... 84 C4
Gorstey Lea WS7 .... 7 C7
Gorstie Croft B43 .... 54 E8
Gorsty Ave DY5 .... 61 C3
Gorsty Cl 2 B71 .... 53 F8
Gorsty Hill Rd B65 .... 83 B8
Gorsy Bank Rd B77 .... 35 F5
Gorsy Rd B32 .... 84 D5
Gorsymead Gr B31 .... 102 C2
Gorway Cl WS1 .... 42 F7
Gorway Gdns WS1 .... 43 A7
Gorway Rd WS1 .... 43 A7
Goscote Cl WS3 .... 28 F7
Goscote Hospl WS3 .... 28 F8
Goscote Ind Est WS3 .... 14 E1
Goscote La WS3 .... 28 F8
Goscote Lodge Cres WS3 ... 29 A7
Goscote Pl WS3 .... 29 A7
Goscote Rd WS3 .... 15 A1
Gosford Dr LE10 .... 71 A1
Gosford Ind Est CV1 .... 113 F2
Gosford Park Prim Sch
  CV1 .... 113 F2
Gosford St Birmingham B12 . 86 F4
  Coventry CV1 .... 165 D2
Gosford Wlk B92 .... 89 B1
Gosmoor Ho B26 .... 88 E7
Gospel End Rd DY3 .... 50 B8
Gospel End St DY3 .... 50 D8
Gospel Farm Rd B27 .... 106 B8
Gospel La B27 .... 106 C8
Gospel Oak Rd Coventry
  CV6 .... 95 B4
  Tipton DY4 .... 41 B1
Gosport Cl WV1 .... 40 B7
Gosport Rd CV6 .... 113 E8
Goss Croft B29 .... 85 D1
Goss The DY5 .... 61 D1
Gossey La B33 .... 69 C2
Gossey Lane Jun & Inf Sch
  B33 .... 69 C2
Gotham Rd B26 .... 88 E6
Goths Cl B65 .... 63 C4
Gough Ave WV11 .... 26 B8
Gough Rd
  Birmingham, Edgbaston B15 . 86 C7
  Birmingham, Sparkhill B11 . 87 D5
  Dudley WV14 .... 40 C1
Gough St Birmingham B1 ... 164 B1
  Willenhall WV13 .... 27 C2
  Wolverhampton WV1 ...... 163 C3
Gould Ave E DY11 .... 116 A2
Gould Ave W DY11 .... 116 A1
Gould Firm La WS9 .... 30 E6
Gould Rd CV35 .... 160 A7
Governor's Ct CV34 .... 160 D8
Gowan Rd B8 .... 67 E4
Gower Ave DY6 .... 60 F4
Gower Ho B62 .... 83 F6
Gower Rd Halesowen B62 ... 83 F6
  Sedgley DY3 .... 50 B8
Gower St Birmingham B19 .. 66 D7
  Walsall WS2 .... 42 B7
  Willenhall WV13 .... 27 A2
  Wolverhampton WV2 ...... 163 C1
Gowland Dr WS11 .... 1 B1
Gowrie Cl LE10 .... 71 B2
Goya Cl WS11 .... 2 C1
Gozzard St WV14 .... 40 E5
Grace Ho B69 .... 63 D8
Grace Mary Prim Sch B69 . 63 C7
Grace Moore Ct WS11 .... 1 F4
Grace Rd Allesley CV5 .... 111 A8
  Birmingham B11 .... 87 C7
  Tipton, Summer Hill DY4 .. 52 A7
  Tipton, Tividale B69 ...... 63 C8
Gracechurch Sh Ctr B72 ... 46 B5
Gracemere Cres B28 .... 105 E3
Gracewell Homes B13 ...... 105 D8
Gracewell Rd B13 .... 87 D1
Grafton Dr B91 .... 159 B7
Grafton Cres B60 .... 150 E6
Grafton Ct Birmingham B23 . 56 C2
  Coventry CV4 .... 132 B7
  Wolverhampton WV6 ...... 24 F4
Grafton Dr WV13 .... 26 D1
Grafton Gdns DY3 .... 50 B3
Grafton Gr 1 B19 .... 66 C7
Grafton Ho Bromsgrove
  B60 .... 137 B3
  Wolverhampton WV4 ...... 39 E5
Grafton La B61 .... 150 C7

Grafton Pl WV14 .... 40 E7
Grafton Rd
  Birmingham, Handsworth B21 54 D1
  Birmingham, Sparkbrook B11 . 87 B7
  Oldbury B68 .... 63 F2
  Solihull B90 .... 105 C2
  West Bromwich B71 .... 53 D4
Grafton St CV1 .... 113 F7
Graham Cl Coventry CV6 .... 96 B1
  Tipton DY4 .... 41 B1
Graham Cres B45 .... 122 A7
Graham Ho B74 .... 30 F2
Graham Rd Birmingham B25 . 88 C6
  Halesowen B62 .... 83 C8
  Stourbridge DY8 .... 60 D4
  West Bromwich B71 .... 53 D4
Graham St
  Birmingham, Hockley B1 ...... 66 C3
  Birmingham, Lozells B19 ..... 66 C7
  Nuneaton CV11 .... 73 C5
Grainger Cl DY4 .... 52 D6
Grainger St DY2 .... 62 D7
Grainger's La B64 .... 82 D8
Graiseley Ct WV3 .... 163 B2
Graiseley Hill WV2 .... 163 B1
Graiseley La WV11 .... 26 C5
Graiseley Prim Sch WV2 ... 163 B1
Graiseley Row WV3 .... 163 B1
Graiseley St WV3 .... 163 A2
Graith Cl B91 .... 105 E3
Grammar School La B63 ... 83 A4
Grampian Rd DY8 .... 81 A6
Granada Trad Est B69 .... 63 F6
Granary Cl DY6 .... 60 A8
Granary Rd Stoke Heath
  B60 .... 150 E6
  Wolverhampton WV8 .... 10 E1
Granary The WS9 .... 30 B6
Granborough Cl CV3 .... 134 F8
Granborough Ct CV3 .... 157 A3
Granbourne Rd WS2 .... 27 D4
Granby Ave B33 .... 69 C1
Granby Bsns Pk B33 .... 69 D1
Granby Cl Hinckley LE10 .... 75 C7
  Redditch B98 .... 154 F4
  Solihull B92 .... 106 E7
Granby Rd Hinckley LE10 ... 75 C7
  Nuneaton CV10 .... 72 F3
Grand Cl B66 .... 65 B3
Grand Depot Rd CV11 .... 79 F6
Grand Junction Way WS1 .. 42 D5
Grandborough Dr B91 ...... 107 A1
Grandys Croft B37 .... 69 F2
Granefield Ct ☑ B97 .... 67 D1
Grange Ave Aldridge WS9 .. 16 A1
  Birmingham B8 .... 68 B6
  Burntwood WS7 .... 7 B7
  Coventry, Binley CV3 .... 134 F7
  Coventry, Finham CV3 ...... 133 C3
  Kenilworth CV8 .... 147 E7
  Sutton Coldfield B75 .... 32 C3
Grange Cl Nuneaton CV10 .. 72 C7
  Tamworth B77 .... 35 C8
  Warwick CV34 .... 161 C8
Grange Cres
  Birmingham B45 .... 121 F8
  Halesowen B63 .... 83 B3
  Walsall WS4 .... 29 B8
Grange Ct ☑ Dudley DY1 ... 51 B1
  ☑ Redditch B98 .... 153 F4
  Stourbridge DY9 .... 81 C3
  Willenhall WS2 .... 27 D2
  Wolverhampton WV3 .... 163 A2
Grange Dr Cannock WS11 ..... 1 F2
  Hinckley LE10 .... 75 E5
Grange Farm Dr B38 .... 123 D8
Grange Farm Prim Sch
  CV3 .... 133 B5
Grange Hill B62 .... 83 C2
Grange Hill Rd B38 .... 103 E1
Grange La Alvechurch B48 . 139 B3
  Kingswinford DY6 .... 60 F4
  Lichfield WS13 .... 8 C5
  Stourbridge DY9 .... 81 D4
  Sutton Coldfield B75 .... 32 C3
Grange Mews The
  ☑ CV32 .... 156 D1
Grange Rd
  Balsall Common CV7 .... 129 F7
  Birmingham, Aston B6 .... 66 E8
  Birmingham,
    Bordesley Green B10 .... 67 D1
  Birmingham, Erdington B24 . 57 C5
  Birmingham,
    King's Heath B14 .... 104 E8
  Birmingham, Selly Oak B29 . 85 F3
  Blackheath B64 .... 83 B8
  Burntwood WS7 .... 7 A5
  Coventry CV6 .... 96 B5
  Dorridge B93 .... 127 E2
  Dudley, New Dock DY1 .... 51 B1
  Dudley, Roseville WV14 ...... 51 B7
  Halesowen B63 .... 83 C3
  Norton Canes WS11 .... 6 B6
  ☑ Redditch B98 .... 153 F4
  Royal Leamington Spa CV32 . 157 B3
  Smethwick B66 .... 65 A3
  Solihull B91 .... 106 E7
  Stourbridge DY9 .... 81 C4
  Tanworth-in-A B94 .... 143 E8
  West Bromwich B70 .... 53 B3
  Wolverhampton,
    Blakenhall WV2 .... 39 B6
  Wolverhampton,
    Tettenhall WV6 .... 24 C4

Grange Rise B38 .... 123 F7
Grange Sch The DY9 .... 81 D4
Grange St Dudley DY1 .... 51 B1
  Walsall WS1 .... 42 F7
Grange The
  Cubbington CV32 .... 157 F5
  Halesowen B62 .... 83 F6
  Royal Leamington Spa CV32 . 157 B1
  Wombourne WV5 .... 49 A7
Grangefield Cl WV8 .... 10 F1
Grangehurst Prim Sch
  CV6 .... 96 B4
Grangemouth Rd CV6 ...... 113 B7
Grangers La B98 .... 158 F5
Grangewood Ct Solihull
  B92 .... 106 E7
  Sutton Coldfield B73 .... 57 A7
Granhill Cl B98 .... 159 A8
Granleigh Ct CV32 .... 157 E5
Granoe Cl CV3 .... 134 E8
Granshaw Cl B38 .... 103 F1
Grant Cl Kingswinford DY6 .. 60 D8
  West Bromwich B71 .... 53 C5
Grant Ct B30 .... 104 A5
Grant Rd Bedworth CV7 ...... 78 A1
  Coventry CV3 .... 114 B2
Grant St Birmingham B15 ... 86 D8
  Walsall WS3 .... 28 B8
Grantham Cl DY5 .... 81 B7
Grantham Rd
  Birmingham B11 .... 87 B6
  Smethwick B66 .... 65 B3
Grantley Cres DY6 .... 60 C6
Grantley Dr B37 .... 70 B3
Granton Cl B14 .... 104 D5
Granton Rd B14 .... 104 D5
Grantown Gr WS3 .... 14 A4
Granville B77 .... 21 F1
Granville Cl Bromsgrove
  B60 .... 137 B1
  Wolverhampton WV2 .... 163 C1
Granville Crest DY10 ...... 117 B6
Granville Dr DY6 .... 60 F5
Granville Gdns LE10 .... 75 C8
Granville Rd Blackheath B64 . 83 B8
  Dorridge B93 .... 128 A2
  Hinckley LE10 .... 75 C8
Granville Sq B1 .... 66 C1
Granville St Birmingham
  B1 .... 164 A1
  Royal Leamington Spa
    CV32 .... 157 A2
  Willenhall WV13 .... 27 A3
  Wolverhampton WV2 .... 163 C1
Grapes Cl CV6 .... 113 B5
Grasdene Gr B17 .... 85 C4
Grasmere Ave Aldridge B74 . 31 A2
  Coventry CV3 .... 132 F6
  Perton WV6 .... 23 F4
Grasmere Cl Birmingham
  B43 .... 54 F7
  Kidderminster DY10 .... 116 E7
  Kingswinford DY6 .... 60 B7
  Wolverhampton,
    Tettenhall WV6 .... 24 E8
  Wolverhampton,
    Wood End WV11 .... 26 C7
Grasmere Cres CV11 .... 73 F7
Grasmere Dr DY9 .... 80 F3
Grasmere Ho ☑ B69 .... 63 D5
Grasmere Pl WS11 .... 1 E5
Grasmere Rd Bedworth
  CV12 .... 78 B2
  Birmingham B21 .... 65 F7
Grasscroft Dr CV3 .... 133 E6
Grassholme B77 .... 36 A8
Grassington Ave CV34 ..... 155 F1
Grassington Dr
  Birmingham B37 .... 69 F1
  Nuneaton CV11 .... 74 A2
Grassmere Ct WS6 .... 4 D3
Grassmere Dr DY8 .... 80 F3
Grassmoor Rd B38 .... 103 E2
Grassy La WV11 .... 12 B1
Graston Cl B16 .... 66 A2
Gratley Croft WS12 .... 1 C4
Grattidge Rd B27 .... 88 D2
Gratton Ct CV3 .... 132 F6
Gravel Bank B32 .... 84 E3
Gravel Hill Coventry CV4 .. 111 F1
  Wombourne WV5 .... 49 B6
Gravel La Huntington WS12 .. 1 B6
  Huntington WS12 .... 1 C5
Gravel Pit La B48 .... 139 E3
Gravel The B76 .... 48 B2
Gravelly Ct ☑ B23 .... 56 E2
Gravelly Hill B23 .... 56 E2
Gravelly Hill N B23 .... 56 E3
Gravelly Hill Sta B23 .... 56 E2
Gravelly Ind Pk B24 .... 67 F8
Gravelly La Birmingham B23 . 56 F5
  Stonnall WS9 .... 16 F3
Gray Rd WS12 .... 1 F6
Gray St B9 .... 67 B2
Graydon Ct B74 .... 46 B7
Grayfield Ave B13 .... 87 A3
Grayland Cl B27 .... 88 B2
Graylands The CV3 .... 133 C4
Grayling B77 .... 35 D6
Grayling Rd DY9 .... 81 C6
Grayling Wlk B37 .... 70 C3
Grays Cl DY10 .... 117 B6
Grays Rd B17 .... 85 D6
Grayshott Cl Birmingham B23 . 56 E5
  Bromsgrove B61 .... 136 E3
Grayston Ave B77 .... 21 E4
Grayswood Ave CV5 .... 112 D4
Grayswood Park Rd B32 ... 84 C6

Grayswood Rd B31 .... 122 F7
Grazebrook Croft B32 ..... 102 D8
Grazebrook Ind Pk DY2 ..... 62 B6
Grazebrook Rd DY2 .... 62 C7
Grazewood Cl WV12 .... 27 B7
Grazing La B97 .... 152 F2
Greadier St WV12 .... 27 C5
Great Barn La B97 .... 153 B1
Great Barr Jun & Inf Sch
  B44 .... 44 D1
Great Barr Sch B44 .... 44 D1
Great Barr Sch Sixth Form
  Ctr B44 .... 44 D1
Great Barr St B9 .... 67 A2
Great Brickkiln St WV3 ..... 25 B1
Great Bridge DY4 .... 52 D5
Great Bridge Ind Est DY4 .. 52 C7
Great Bridge Prim Sch
  DY4 .... 52 C6
Great Bridge Rd WV14 ..... 41 B3
Great Bridge St B70 .... 52 E5
Great Brook St B7 .... 67 A4
Great Charles St WS8 .... 15 F8
Great Charles Street
  Queensway B3 .... 164 B3
Great Colmore St B15 ...... 86 D8
Great Cornbow ☑ B63 ..... 83 B3
Great Croft Ho ☑ WS10 ... 41 D6
Great Croft St ☑ WS10 .... 41 D6
Great Francis St B7 .... 67 A4
Great Hampton Row B19 . 164 A4
Great Hampton St
  Birmingham B18 .... 164 A4
  Wolverhampton WV1 .... 25 B4
Great King St B19 .... 66 C5
Great King St N B19 .... 66 C6
Great Lister St B7 .... 67 A4
Great Moor Rd WV6 .... 23 A3
Great Stone Rd B31 .... 103 A3
Great Tindal St B16 .... 66 A2
Great Western Arc B2 .... 164 C3
Great Western Cl B18 ...... 65 E6
Great Western Dr B64 ...... 63 A1
Great Western St
  Wednesbury WS10 .... 41 E2
  Wolverhampton WV1 .... 163 C4
Great Western Way DY4 ... 52 D6
Great Wood Rd B10 .... 67 C1
Great Wyrley Cty High Sch
  WS6 .... 4 F4
Greatfield Rd DY11 .... 116 B4
Greatheed Rd CV32 .... 156 E2
Greatmead P7 .... 21 C1
Greatorex Ct B71 .... 53 B8
Greaves Ave WS5 .... 43 C8
Greaves Cl Walsall WS5 ..... 43 A6
  Warwick CV34 .... 161 C7
Greaves Cres WV12 .... 27 C8
Greaves Rd DY2 .... 62 D5
Greaves Sq B38 .... 104 B1
Grebe Cl B23 .... 56 B3
Green Acres B27 .... 88 B2
Green Acres Rd B38 .... 123 D8
Green Ave B28 .... 87 E1
Green Bank Ave B28 .... 87 E1
Green Barns La WS14 .... 32 C8
Green Cl Studley B80 ...... 159 E3
  Whitnash CV31 .... 162 B4
  Wythall B47 .... 125 A3
Green Court B9 .... 68 A3
Green Ct
  Birmingham,
    Gravelly Hill B24 .... 56 E2
  Birmingham,
    Hall Green B28 .... 105 F8
  ☑ Lichfield WS13 .... 9 B7
Green Dr Birmingham B32 .. 84 C1
  Wolverhampton WV10 .... 25 C7
Green Field The CV3 ...... 134 B8
Green Gables
  Hollywood B47 .... 125 A7
  Sutton Coldfield B74 .... 46 B7
Green Heath Rd WS12 .... 2 A7
Green Hill Cl B60 .... 137 D6
Green Hill Way B90 .... 106 B5
Green La Aldridge WS9 ..... 30 E5
  Balsall Common CV7 .... 130 B7
  Birmingham,
    Castle Bromwich B36 .... 69 E8
  Birmingham,
    Great Barr B43 .... 43 D1
  Birmingham,
    Handsworth B21 .... 65 C8
  Birmingham,
    Hawkesley B38 .... 123 E8
  Birmingham, Newton B43 ... 54 D8
  Birmingham, Quinton B32 ... 84 C6
  Brownhills WS8 .... 7 B2
  Cannock WS11 .... 4 E6
  Catshill B61 .... 121 A1
  Coleshill B46 .... 70 F5
  Corley CV7 .... 93 D6
  Coventry CV3 .... 133 B4
  Dudley DY3 .... 50 F5
  Halesowen B63 .... 82 D2
  Kingswinford DY6 .... 60 D7
  Lichfield WS13 .... 8 D2
  Middleton B78 .... 48 B6
  Nuneaton CV10 .... 72 C7
  Redditch B97 .... 158 A2
  Solihull B90 .... 105 E1
  Stourbridge DY9 .... 81 E5
  Studley B80 .... 159 B5
  Tamworth B78 .... 36 C7
  Walsall, Birchills WS3 .... 28 C5

Green La continued
  Walsall,
    High Heath WS4, WS9 .... 15 D3
  Walsall, Pelsall WS3 .... 15 A4
  Warwick CV34 .... 160 F8
  Wolverhampton WV6 .... 24 F7
Green Lane Ind Est B9 ..... 67 E1
Green Lane Venture Ctr
  WS11 .... 4 E6
Green Lanes Bilston WV14 .. 40 C7
  Sutton Coldfield B73 .... 57 B8
Green Lanes Prim Sch
  B36 .... 69 F8
Green Lea B77 .... 36 A8
Green Leigh B23 .... 56 F8
Green Mdw Stourbridge
  DY9 .... 99 B7
  Wednesfield WV11 .... 26 E5
Green Mdws WS12 .... 2 C1
Green Meadow Prim Sch
  B29 .... 102 F7
Green Meadow Rd
  Birmingham B29 .... 103 A7
  Willenhall WV12 .... 27 B7
Green Oak Rd WV8 .... 10 B2
Green Park Ave WV14 .... 40 C8
Green Park Dr WV14 .... 40 C8
Green Park Rd
  Birmingham B31 .... 102 E2
  Bromsgrove B60 .... 137 B2
  Dudley DY2 .... 62 F8
Green Park Sch WV14 .... 40 B8
Green Rd Birmingham B28 . 87 E1
  Dudley DY2 .... 62 D7
Green Rock Jun & Mixed
  Inf Sch WS3 .... 14 E1
Green Rock La WS3 .... 14 D1
Green Slade Cres B60 ..... 121 C1
Green Slade Gr WS12 .... 2 C7
Green St Birmingham B12 .. 66 F1
  Dudley DY2 .... 51 C8
  Kidderminster DY10 .... 116 E5
  Oldbury B69 .... 64 A7
  Smethwick B67 .... 64 F5
  Stourbridge DY8 .... 80 F5
  Walsall WS2 .... 28 C3
  West Bromwich B70 .... 64 E8
Green Street Ind Est
  DY10 .... 116 E4
Green Sward La B98 .... 159 A7
Green The Aldridge WS9 ... 30 C6
  Birmingham,
    Castle Bromwich B36 .... 69 B8
  Birmingham, Erdington B23 . 57 A4
  Birmingham,
    King's Norton B38 .... 103 F2
  ☑ Birmingham, Quinton B32 . 84 A6
  Bluntington DY10 .... 118 E1
  Darlaston WS10 .... 41 D7
  Fazeley B78 .... 20 E2
  Nuneaton CV11 .... 73 E2
  Oldbury B68 .... 64 B1
  Solihull B91 .... 107 D5
  Stoneleigh CV8 .... 149 C6
  Stourbridge DY8 .... 60 D2
  Sutton Coldfield B72 .... 46 D1
  Tamworth B77 .... 22 B5
  Walsall WS3 .... 14 B1
  Wood End B78 .... 36 C4
Green Way WS9 .... 16 B2
Green Wickets B13 .... 104 E6
Green Wlk B17 .... 84 F7
Greenacre Cl B77 .... 22 B5
Greenacre Dr WV8 .... 10 B2
Greenacre Rd DY4 .... 41 A1
Greenacres
  Sedgley DY3 .... 39 B1
  Sutton Coldfield B76 .... 58 A8
  Wolverhampton WV6 .... 24 F7
Greenacres Ave WV10 ..... 12 B2
Greenacres Cl WS9 .... 30 E2
Greenacres Jun & Inf Schs
  WV14 .... 40 F6
Greenacres Prim Sch B77 . 22 B5
Greenacres Rd B61 .... 136 E3
Greenaleigh Rd B14 .... 105 D3
Greenaway Cl B43 .... 44 C3
Greenbank B45 .... 138 D8
Greenbank Ho ☑ B7 .... 67 B5
Greenbank Rd CV7 .... 129 F6
Greenbush Dr B63 .... 83 A5
Greencroft Bilston WV14 ... 40 D6
  Kingswinford DY6 .... 60 D4
  Lichfield WS13 .... 3 A2
Greendale Cl B61 .... 137 B8
Greendale Rd CV5 .... 112 D3
Greenend Rd B13 .... 86 F2
Greenfels Rise DY2 .... 62 F8
Greenfield Ave
  Balsall Common CV7 .... 130 A7
  Blackheath B64 .... 62 B1
  Marlbrook B60 .... 121 D1
  Stourbridge DY8 .... 80 F5
Greenfield Cotts B48 ...... 139 A5
Greenfield Cres B15 .... 86 A8
Greenfield Croft WV14 ..... 40 D2
Greenfield La WV10 .... 11 E5
Greenfield Prim Sch
  Stourbridge DY8 .... 80 F4
  Walsall WS4 .... 29 C8
Greenfield Rd
  Birmingham, Harborne B17 . 85 D5
  Birmingham, Newton B43 ... 54 E4
  Smethwick B67 .... 64 E4
Greenfield View DY3 .... 50 D3
Greenfields Aldridge WS9 .. 30 B7
  Cannock WS11 .... 1 E2
  Redditch B98 .... 153 E2

Greenfields Rd
  Kingswinford DY6 .... 60 E6
  Walsall WS4 .... 15 D2
  Wombourne WV5 .... 49 A5
Greenfinch Cl
  Birmingham B36 .... 70 A7
  Kidderminster DY10 .... 117 B3
Greenfinch Rd
  Birmingham B36 .... 70 A7
  Stourbridge DY9 .... 81 D3
Greenford Ho B23 .... 56 B6
Greenford Rd B14 .... 105 C3
Greenhart B77 .... 22 A4
Greenhill Blackwell B60 ... 137 F4
  ☑ Lichfield WS13 .... 9 C8
  Wombourne WV5 .... 49 B6
Greenhill Ave DY10 .... 116 F7
Greenhill Cl Tamworth B77 . 35 C5
  Willenhall WV12 .... 27 B5
Greenhill Ct Halesowen B62 . 83 C7
  Sutton Coldfield B72 .... 57 C8
Greenhill Dr B29 .... 85 C1
Greenhill Gdns
  Birmingham B43 .... 43 E2
  Halesowen B62 .... 83 D6
  Wombourne WV5 .... 49 B5
Greenhill Oak DY10 .... 116 F7
Greenhill Rd
  Birmingham,
    Handsworth B21 .... 54 E2
  Birmingham, Moseley B13 ... 87 A1
  Dudley DY3 .... 50 E5
  Halesowen B63 .... 83 D7
  Sutton Coldfield B72 .... 57 C8
  Whitnash CV31 .... 162 B4
Greenhill Way WS9 .... 16 B1
Greenholm Jun & Inf Sch
  B44 .... 55 E7
Greenholm Rd B44 .... 55 E7
Greenhough Rd WS13 .... 9 A8
Greening Dr B15 .... 86 B7
Greenland Ave CV5 .... 111 F5
Greenland Cl ☑ DY6 .... 60 E8
Greenland Ct Birmingham
  B8 .... 67 E6
  Coventry CV5 .... 111 F5
Greenland Rd B29 .... 86 B1
Greenland Rise B92 .... 107 D7
Greenlands Ave B98 ...... 154 A1
Greenlands Dr B98 .... 158 F8
Greenlands Rd B37 .... 70 C1
Greenleaf Cl CV5 .... 112 A3
Greenleas Gdns B62 .... 83 C3
Greenleighs DY3 .... 39 D3
Greenly Rd WV4 .... 39 D5
Greenmoor Rd Hinckley
  LE10 .... 75 D5
  Nuneaton CV10 .... 73 A3
Greenoak Cres
  Birmingham B30 .... 104 C8
  Dudley WV14 .... 51 A7
Greenridge Rd B20 .... 54 E5
Greenroyde DY9 .... 81 B1
Greens Ind Est WS12 .... 2 C7
Greens The CV6 .... 95 A1
Greens Yd CV12 .... 78 C3
Greenside Birmingham B17 . 85 C5
  Cheswick Green B90 .... 126 D4
  Stoke Prior B60 .... 150 C2
Greenside Cl CV11 .... 74 C1
Greenside Rd B24 .... 57 C5
Greenside Way WS5 .... 43 A4
Greensill Ave DY4 .... 51 F8
Greenslade Croft B31 .... 103 A2
Greenslade Rd Sedgley DY3 . 39 B2
  Solihull B90 .... 105 C2
  Walsall WS5 .... 43 C7
Greensleeves B74 .... 32 A1
Greensleeves Cl CV6 .... 95 B2
Greenstead Rd B13 .... 87 D1
Greensward Cl CV8 .... 148 B6
Greensward The CV3 ...... 115 A2
Greensway WV11 .... 26 B8
Greenvale B31 .... 102 F5
Greenvale Ave B26 .... 89 D6
Greenway Birmingham B20 . 54 F6
  Nuneaton CV11 .... 79 B8
  Sedgley DY3 .... 39 E1
  Warwick CV34 .... 155 E1
Greenway Ave DY8 .... 60 E1
Greenway Dr B73 .... 45 C3
Greenway Gdns
  Birmingham B38 .... 123 E7
  Sedgley DY3 .... 39 E1
Greenway Rd WV14 .... 40 E4
Greenway St B9 .... 67 C1
Greenway The
  Birmingham,
    Marston Green B37 .... 90 A6
  Birmingham,
    New Oscott B73 .... 45 B3
  Hagley DY9 .... 98 F5
Greenway Wlk B33 .... 69 E1
Greenways Birmingham
  B31 .... 102 F8
  Halesowen B63 .... 82 C6
  Stourbridge DY8 .... 60 C1
Greenways The CV32 ...... 157 B3
Greenwood B25 .... 88 D8
Greenwood Ave
  Birmingham B27 .... 88 B1
  Blackheath B65 .... 63 D3
  Oldbury B68 .... 64 C5
Greenwood Cl B14 .... 104 E5
Greenwood Cotts DY1 ..... 51 A5

Greenwood Ct
Nuneaton CV11 .... 73 E3
Royal Leamington Spa CV32 . 157 B1
Greenwood Dr WS14 .... 9 B6
Greenwood Pk Aldridge
WS9 .... 16 C2
Cannock WS12 .... 2 B8
Greenwood Pl B44 .... 45 B1
Greenwood Rd Aldridge
WS9 .... 16 B2
West Bromwich B71 .... 53 B8
Wolverhampton WV1 .... 25 C7
Greenwood Sq 5 B37 .... 70 B2
Greenwood Way B37 .... 70 B2
Greenwoods The DY8 .... 80 E5
Greet Jun & Inf Sch B11 .... 87 D4
Greethurst Dr B13 .... 87 C2
Greets Green Ind Est B70 .... 52 F4
Greets Green Rd B70 .... 52 F3
Greetville Cl B34 .... 69 A5
Gregory Ave
Birmingham B29 .... 103 A8
Coventry CV3 .... 133 A6
Gregory Cl 3 WS10 .... 41 F2
Gregory Cl WV11 .... 26 E5
Gregory Dr DY1 .... 51 A2
Gregory Hood Rd CV3 .... 133 E4
Gregory Rd DY8 .... 80 D5
Gregston Ind Est B69 .... 64 B8
Greig Ct WS11 .... 2 C2
Grendon Cl Coventry CV4 .... 111 C1
Redditch B98 .... 154 D1
Grendon Dr B73 .... 45 D3
Grendon Gdns WV3 .... 38 D6
Grendon Inf & Jun Sch
B14 .... 105 A3
Grendon Rd
Birmingham B14 .... 105 A3
Solihull B92 .... 106 E8
Grenfell Cl CV31 .... 162 D6
Grenfell Ct B73 .... 46 B1
Grenfell Dr B15 .... 85 F8
Grenfell Rd WS3 .... 14 D3
Grenville Ave CV2 .... 114 B3
Grenville Cl WS2 .... 27 D3
Grenville Dr Birmingham
B23 .... 56 B3
Smethwick B66 .... 64 D8
Grenville Pl B70 .... 52 E3
Grenville Rd Dudley DY1 .... 50 E1
Solihull B90 .... 106 B2
Gresham Ave CV32 .... 157 B2
Gresham Pl CV32 .... 157 B2
Gresham Rd
Birmingham B28 .... 105 F6
Cannock WS11 .... 1 F3
Nuneaton CV10 .... 78 B8
Oldbury B68 .... 64 C6
Gresham St CV2 .... 114 A2
Gresham Tower B12 .... 86 F8
Gresley B77 .... 21 F1
Gresley Cl B75 .... 32 A4
Gresley Gr B23 .... 56 C2
Gresley Rd CV2 .... 114 D7
Gresley Row 8 Lichfield
WS13 .... 9 B7
6 Lichfield WS13 .... 9 C8
Gressel La B33 .... 69 D3
Grestone Ave B20 .... 54 E3
Grestone Jun & Inf Schs
B20 .... 54 E4
Greswold Cl CV4 .... 111 F1
Greswold Gdns B34 .... 69 A5
Greswold Prim Sch B91 .... 107 C6
Greswold St B71 .... 53 B5
Greswolde Dr B24 .... 57 B4
Greswolde Park Rd B27 .... 88 B4
Greswolde Rd
Birmingham B11 .... 87 D3
Solihull B90 .... 106 E6
Greswoldes The CV31 .... 162 F6
Gretna Rd CV3 .... 132 F4
Gretton Cres WS9 .... 29 E5
Gretton Rd Aldridge WS9 .... 29 F5
Birmingham B23 .... 56 D7
Greville Dr B15 .... 86 C6
Greville Rd Kenilworth CV8 .... 147 F4
Warwick CV34 .... 156 B1
Greville Smith Ave CV31 .... 162 B4
Grevis Cl B13 .... 86 F4
Grevis Rd B25 .... 68 E1
Grey Mill Cl B90 .... 126 F6
Grey Tree Cres B93 .... 127 E3
Grey's Rd B80 .... 159 E3
Greycoat Rd CV6 .... 95 A2
Greyfort Cres B92 .... 88 F1
Greyfriars Cl Dudley DY1 .... 50 E3
Solihull B92 .... 106 D6
Greyfriars Ct CV6 .... 113 A7
Greyfriars La CV1 .... 165 B2
Greyfriars Rd CV1 .... 165 B2
Greyhound La
Stourbridge DY8 .... 80 D2
Wombourne WV4 .... 37 E5
Greyhurst Croft 5 B91 .... 127 B8
Greysbrooke WS9 .... 18 A5
Greysbrooke Cty Prim Sch
WS9 .... 18 A6
Greystoke Ave B36 .... 68 D2
Greystoke Dr DY6 .... 60 C6
Greystone B98 .... 154 C8
Greystone Pas 15 DY1 .... 51 B1
Grice St B70 .... 64 D8
Griff La CV10 .... 77 E6
Griffin B Birmingham B31 .... 103 B6
Burntwood WS7 .... 6 E8
Griffin Ct B5 .... 86 C5
Griffin Gdns B17 .... 85 D4

Griffin Ho B16 .... 65 E1
Griffin Ind Est B65 .... 63 F3
Griffin Rd Birmingham B23 .... 56 F5
Kidderminster DY10 .... 116 E4
Warwick CV34 .... 161 C7
Griffin St Dudley DY2 .... 62 C4
West Bromwich B70 .... 53 D3
Wolverhampton WV1 .... 25 F1
Griffins Brook Cl B30 .... 103 D7
Griffins Brook La B30 .... 103 D6
Griffiths Dr
Wolverhampton WV11 .... 13 A1
Wombourne WV5 .... 49 A1
Griffiths Rd Dudley DY1 .... 51 A6
West Bromwich B71 .... 42 C1
Willenhall WV12 .... 27 D8
Griffiths St DY4 .... 51 E5
Grigg Gr B31 .... 102 E1
Grimley Cl B98 .... 153 F1
Grimley La B60 .... 151 E6
Grimley Rd 2 B31 .... 103 D2
Grimley Way WS11 .... 1 F4
Grimpits La B38 .... 124 A7
Grimshaw Rd B27 .... 88 A1
Grimshaw Villas B93 .... 128 D8
Grimston Cl CV3 .... 115 A2
Grimstone St WV10 .... 163 C4
Grindle Rd CV6 .... 95 A4
Grindleford Rd B42 .... 55 D7
Grindley Ho 5 CV1 .... 113 B2
Grindsbrook B77 .... 36 A8
Gristhorpe Rd B29 .... 104 A8
Grizebeck Dr CV5 .... 112 A5
Grizedale Cl B45 .... 102 B2
Grocott Rd WS10 .... 41 B4
Grosmont Ave 8 B12 .... 86 E5
Grosvenor Ave Aldridge B74 .... 30 F1
Birmingham B20 .... 55 C2
Kidderminster DY10 .... 117 A6
Grosvenor Cl Lichfield WS14 .... 9 D6
Sutton Coldfield B75 .... 32 C1
Wolverhampton WV10 .... 11 D2
Grosvenor Cres
Hinckley LE10 .... 76 A6
Wolverhampton WV10 .... 11 D2
Grosvenor Ct
Birmingham, Erdington B24 .... 57 A5
Birmingham,
Handsworth B20 .... 55 C2
Birmingham,
Dudley DY3 .... 50 D2
2 Royal Leamington Spa
CV32 .... 156 F1
Shenstone WS14 .... 17 F6
Stourbridge DY9 .... 81 B1
Wednesfield WV11 .... 26 E5
Wolverhampton WV3 .... 163 B2
Wolverhampton,
Tettenhall WV6 .... 24 A3
Grosvenor Ho CV1 .... 165 A2
Grosvenor Pk WV4 .... 38 F5
Grosvenor Rd
Birmingham, Aston B6 .... 67 B8
Birmingham,
Handsworth B20 .... 55 C2
Birmingham, Harborne B17 .... 85 A6
Coventry CV1 .... 165 A1
Dudley DY3 .... 50 C2
Oldbury B68 .... 64 A3
Royal Leamington Spa
CV31 .... 162 A5
Solihull B91 .... 106 F1
Wolverhampton,
Bushbury WV10 .... 11 D2
Wolverhampton,
Ettingshall Park WV4 .... 39 E3
Grosvenor Sh Ctr B31 .... 103 A4
Grosvenor Sq B28 .... 105 F5
Grosvenor St
Birmingham B5 .... 164 D3
Wolverhampton WV10 .... 25 F3
Grosvenor St W B16 .... 66 B1
Grosvenor Way DY5 .... 81 E7
Grotto La WV6 .... 24 E5
Groucutt St 9 WV14 .... 51 C8
Grounds Dr B74 .... 31 F3
Grounds Rd B74 .... 31 F3
Grout St B70 .... 52 E4
Grove Ave
Birmingham,
Handsworth B21 .... 65 F8
Birmingham, Moseley B13 .... 87 A2
Halesowen B63 .... 82 F3
Solihull B91 .... 107 C5
Grove Cl WS11 .... 5 F5
Grove Cottage Rd B9 .... 67 D2
Grove Cres Brierley Hill DY5 .... 61 C5
Walsall WS3 .... 14 F1
Grove Ct Birmingham B43 .... 54 F5
Coventry CV5 .... 133 B8
Grove Farm Dr B75 .... 46 F5
Grove Fields CV10 .... 73 D8
Grove Gdns B20 .... 54 F2
Grove Hill WS5 .... 29 E1
Grove Hill Rd B21 .... 54 F1
Grove Jun Sch WV2 .... 163 D1
Grove La
Birmingham,
Handsworth B20 .... 54 F1
Birmingham, Harborne B17 .... 85 C4
Keresley CV7 .... 94 F7
Lapworth B94 .... 143 F4
Norton Canes WS3 .... 5 E1
Smethwick B66 .... 65 C5
Wishaw B76 .... 47 F2
Wolverhampton WV6 .... 24 B2
Grove Mews B31 .... 123 B8
Grove Pk Hinckley LE10 .... 76 A6
Kingswinford DY6 .... 60 C8

Grove Pl Nuneaton CV10 .... 72 D3
2 Royal Leamington Spa
CV31 .... 162 A6
Grove Prim Sch B21 .... 65 F8
Grove Rd Ansty CV7 .... 97 D4
Birmingham, King's Heath
B14 .... 104 D6
Birmingham, Sparkhill B11 .... 87 C2
Dorridge B93 .... 128 B3
Hinckley LE10 .... 76 A6
Nuneaton CV10 .... 72 D3
Oldbury B68 .... 64 D1
Solihull B91 .... 107 C5
Stourbridge DY9 .... 81 F3
Grove St Coventry CV1 .... 165 C3
Dudley DY2 .... 62 E8
Redditch B98 .... 153 E4
Royal Leamington Spa CV32 .... 161 E8
Smethwick B66 .... 65 D4
Wolverhampton WV2 .... 163 C1
Wolverhampton,
Springfield WV10 .... 25 F3
Grove Terr WS1 .... 28 F1
Grove The Bedworth CV12 .... 78 C3
Birmingham, Edgbaston B16 .... 65 F2
Birmingham, Great Barr B43 .... 43 E4
Birmingham, Lozells B19 .... 66 B7
Birmingham, Rednall B45 .... 122 D4
Birmingham, Saltley B8 .... 67 C4
Birmingham,
West Heath B31 .... 123 B8
Blackheath B65 .... 63 C2
Brierley Hill DY5 .... 61 C1
Burntwood WS7 .... 6 D8
Coleshill B46 .... 70 F4
Hampton In A B92 .... 91 A1
Hinckley LE10 .... 75 C8
Little Aston B74 .... 31 D5
Studley B80 .... 159 D3
Walsall WS5 .... 43 B3
Wolverhampton,
Lanesfield WV4 .... 39 E5
Wolverhampton,
New Cross WV11 .... 26 B6
Grove Vale Ave B43 .... 43 C1
Grove Vale Prim Sch B43 .... 43 D1
Grove Villas B64 .... 82 D7
Grove Way B74 .... 44 F7
Groveland Rd DY4 .... 52 B3
Grovelands Cres WV10 .... 11 D3
Grovelands Ind Est CV7 .... 96 A6
Groveley La B31, B45 .... 122 E5
Grovelley La B31, B45 .... 122 E5
Groveside Way WS15 .... 15 A5
Grovewood Dr 2 B38 .... 103 E1
Guardhouse Rd CV6 .... 113 B8
Guardian Angels RC
Jun & Inf Sch B34 .... 69 E6
Guardian Ct
Birmingham, Frankley B31 .... 102 D3
Birmingham,
Gilberstone B26 .... 88 F7
3 Bromsgrove B60 .... 137 A2
Solihull B91 .... 107 D3
Guardian Ho B68 .... 84 C7
Guardians Way B31 .... 102 E8
Guernsey Dr B36 .... 70 B6
Guest Ave WV11 .... 26 C8
Guest Gr B19 .... 66 C5
Guest Hospl DY1 .... 51 E3
Guild Ave WS3 .... 28 D8
Guild Cl B16 .... 66 A2
Guild Cotts The 6 CV34 .... 160 E6
Guild Croft B19 .... 66 C6
Guild Rd Bromsgrove B60 .... 136 F1
Coventry CV6 .... 113 D7
Guildford Cl DY11 .... 116 A6
Guildford Croft B37 .... 89 F8
Guildford Ct CV6 .... 113 D7
Guildford Dr B19 .... 66 D6
Guildford St 4 B19 .... 66 D7
Guildhall Mews The
7 WS1 .... 28 F1
Guillemard Ct B37 .... 70 B1
Guilsborough Rd CV3 .... 134 E8
Guinness Cl B98 .... 158 D8
Guiting Cl B97 .... 153 B1
Guiting Rd B29 .... 103 A7
Gulistan Ct 6 CV32 .... 156 E1
Gulistan Rd CV32 .... 156 E1
Gullane Cl B38 .... 103 D1
Gullet The B78 .... 22 F1
Gullswood Cl B14 .... 104 D2
Gulson Hospl CV1 .... 165 D2
Gulson Rd CV1 .... 113 E2
Gumbleberrys Cl B8 .... 68 C4
Gun La CV2 .... 114 A5
Gunbarrel Ind Ctr B63 .... 82 F6
Gundry Cl CV31 .... 162 A7
Gungate B79 .... 21 B5
Gunmakers Wlk B19 .... 66 D7
Gunner La B45 .... 121 D7
Gunners La B80 .... 159 E4
Gunnery Terr 3 CV32 .... 156 D1
Gunns Way B92 .... 106 D7
Guns La B70 .... 53 B4
Guns Village Inf Sch B70 .... 53 B4
Guns Village Jun Sch B70 .... 53 B4
Gunstock Cl B74 .... 44 E7
Gunter Jun & Inf Sch B24 .... 57 E3
Gunter Rd B24 .... 57 E3
Gunton Ave CV3 .... 134 C6
Guphill Ave CV5 .... 112 D2
Guphill La CV5 .... 112 D3
Gurnard B77 .... 35 D6
Gurnard Cl WV12 .... 13 B1
Gurney Cl CV4 .... 111 E3
Gurney Pl WS2 .... 28 A5

Gurney Rd WS2 .... 28 A5
Guthrie Cl B19 .... 66 D6
Guthrum Cl Birmingham B23 .... 56 E8
Perton WV6 .... 23 F5
Gutter The DY9 .... 120 E7
Gutteridge Ave CV6 .... 95 A2
Guy Ave WV10 .... 25 E6
Guy Pl E 11 CV32 .... 156 F1
Guy Pl W 10 CV32 .... 156 F1
Guy Rd CV8 .... 147 F2
Guy St
Royal Leamington Spa CV32 .... 156 F1
Warwick CV34 .... 160 F7
Guy's Almshouses B79 .... 21 B5
Guy's Cl CV34 .... 161 A8
Guy's Cliffe Ave CV32 .... 156 D2
Guy's Cliffe Rd CV32 .... 161 E8
Guy's Cliffe Terr CV34 .... 160 F8
Guy's Cross Park Rd CV34 .... 160 F8
Guy's La DY3 .... 50 B2
Guy's Wlk B61 .... 137 A5
Guys Cl B79 .... 20 F7
Guys Cliffe Ave B76 .... 46 F1
Gwalia Gr B23 .... 56 E3
Gwendoline Ave LE10 .... 71 A2
Gwendoline Way WS9 .... 16 B4
GWS Ind Est WS10 .... 41 D1
Gypsy La Kenilworth CV8 .... 147 F2
Redditch B97 .... 152 C5
Water Orton B46 .... 59 D2

Habberley La DY11 .... 116 A8
Habberley Rd Blackheath
B65 .... 63 D2
Kidderminster DY11 .... 116 B7
Habberley St 1 DY11 .... 116 C6
Habberly Croft B91 .... 107 B1
Habitat Ct B76 .... 46 F3
Hack St B9 .... 67 A1
Hackett Cl WV14 .... 39 F1
Hackett Ct 2 B69 .... 64 A7
Hackett Rd B65 .... 63 E3
Hackett St DY4 .... 52 C7
Hackford Rd WV4 .... 39 F4
Hackmans Gate La DY9 .... 119 B7
Hackwood Ho 10 B69 .... 63 D5
Hackwood Rd WS10 .... 42 B2
Hadcroft Grange DY9 .... 81 D4
Hadcroft Rd DY9 .... 81 C4
Haddock Rd WV14 .... 40 C7
Haddon Cres WV12 .... 27 C7
Haddon Croft B63 .... 82 C1
Haddon End CV3 .... 133 E6
Haddon Rd Birmingham
B42 .... 55 D6
Royal Leamington Spa CV32 .... 157 B2
Haddon St CV6 .... 114 A8
Haddon Tower 4 B15 .... 86 D8
Haden Cl Blackheath B64 .... 83 A7
Stourbridge DY8 .... 60 D2
Haden Cres WV11 .... 26 F6
Haden Cross Dr B64 .... 83 A7
Haden Ct 5 WV3 .... 25 A2
Haden Hill WV3 .... 25 A2
Haden Hill Rd B63 .... 83 B6
Haden Hill Sch B64 .... 82 F8
Haden Park Rd B64 .... 82 F7
Haden Rd Blackheath B64 .... 62 E2
Tipton DY4 .... 41 A1
Haden St B12 .... 86 F6
Haden Way B12 .... 86 F6
Haden Wlk 2 B65 .... 63 C3
Hadendale B64 .... 83 A7
Hadfield Croft B19 .... 66 C6
Hadland Rd B33 .... 69 B1
Hadleigh Croft B76 .... 58 A6
Hadleigh Rd CV3 .... 133 C4
Hadley Cl Dudley DY2 .... 62 E4
Hollywood B47 .... 125 A5
Hadley Croft B66 .... 65 A7
Hadley Pl WV14 .... 40 C7
Hadley Rd Bilston WV14 .... 40 C7
Walsall WS2 .... 27 F6
Hadley St B68 .... 64 A4
Hadley Way WS2 .... 28 A6
Hadlow Croft B33 .... 89 D7
Hadrian Cl CV32 .... 157 B4
Hadrian Dr B46 .... 59 F1
Hadrians Cl B77 .... 35 D8
Hadyn Gr B26 .... 89 B6
Hadzor Ho B97 .... 153 A4
Hadzor Rd B68 .... 84 D8
Hafren Cl B45 .... 102 B2
Hafton Gr B9 .... 67 D1
Haggar St WV2 .... 39 C6
Hagley Cl DY9 .... 99 C6
Hagley Cswy DY9 .... 100 B8
Hagley Ct DY9 .... 99 E7
Hagley Cty Prim Inf &
Jun Sch DY9 .... 99 B5
Hagley Hall DY9 .... 99 D6
Hagley Hill DY9 .... 99 E7
Hagley Ho B60 .... 137 B3
Hagley Park Dr B45 .... 122 A6
Hagley RC High Sch DY8 .... 98 F6
Hagley Rd Birmingham B16 .... 65 C1
Halesowen B63 .... 82 E2
Stourbridge DY8 .... 81 B3
Hagley Rd W B32 .... 84 D7
Hagley St 3 B63 .... 83 B3
Hagley Sta DY9 .... 99 A6
Hagley View Rd DY2 .... 62 C8
Hagley Villas 2 B12 .... 87 B4
Hagley Wood La B62 .... 100 B7
Haig Cl Cannock WS11 .... 2 A5
Sutton Coldfield B75 .... 46 C7

Haig Pl B13 .... 105 A7
Haig Rd DY2 .... 51 F1
Haig St B71 .... 53 C5
Hailes Park Cl WV4 .... 39 E6
Hailsham Rd B23 .... 56 F5
Hailstone Cl B65 .... 63 A5
Haines Cl DY4 .... 52 B4
Haines St B70 .... 53 D2
Hainfield Dr B91 .... 107 E5
Hainge Rd B69 .... 52 C1
Hainult Cl DY8 .... 60 D4
Halas Ind Est B62 .... 83 C5
Halberd Cl LE10 .... 75 D5
Halberton St B65 .... 65 D4
Haldane Ct B33 .... 69 B2
Haldon Gr B31 .... 122 E7
Hale Gr B24 .... 57 D4
Halecroft Ave WV11 .... 26 D5
Hales Cres B67 .... 64 E4
Hales Gdns B23 .... 56 C8
Hales La B62 .... 64 E4
Hales Park Ind Est CV6 .... 95 E4
Hales Rd Halesowen B63 .... 83 A4
Wednesbury WS10 .... 42 A5
Hales St CV1 .... 165 C3
Hales Way B69 .... 63 F7
Halesbury Ct B63 .... 82 F2
Halesbury Sch B62 .... 83 E7
Halescroft Sq B31 .... 102 E6
Halesmere Way B63 .... 83 C3
Halesowen CE Prim Sch
B63 .... 83 B4
Halesowen Coll B62 .... 83 B5
Halesowen Coll Walton
Campus B63 .... 83 A3
Halesowen Ind Pk B62 .... 83 B6
Halesowen Rd Dudley DY2 .... 62 D4
Halesowen B62 .... 83 F6
Lydiate Ash B61 .... 121 C3
Halesowen St Blackheath
B65 .... 63 C1
Oldbury B69 .... 63 F7
Halesworth Rd WV9 .... 10 F2
Halewood Gr B28 .... 106 A7
Haley St WV12 .... 27 C5
Halfcot Ave DY9 .... 81 C3
Halford Cres WS3 .... 28 F5
Halford Gr B24 .... 57 E4
Halford La CV6 .... 95 A2
Halford Lodge CV6 .... 95 A2
Halford Rd B91 .... 106 E6
Halford St B79 .... 21 A5
Halford's La B66 .... 65 A8
Halfpenny Field Wlk B35 .... 58 A3
Halfshire La DY10 .... 98 B1
Halfway Cl B44 .... 55 E6
Halifax Cl CV5 .... 112 A7
Halifax Gr 8 B18 .... 65 E4
Halifax Ho B5 .... 86 D7
Halifax Rd B90 .... 106 B2
Haliscombe Gr 4 B6 .... 66 E8
Halkett Glade B33 .... 68 D3
Hall Brook Rd CV6 .... 95 A4
Hall Cl CV8 .... 149 B6
Hall Cres B71 .... 53 C6
Hall Dale Cl B28 .... 105 F5
Hall Dr Baginton CV8 .... 133 E3
Birmingham B37 .... 90 A7
Hagley DY9 .... 99 D6
Hall End Nuneaton CV11 .... 73 D2
Wednesbury WS10 .... 41 F3
Hall End Pl CV11 .... 73 D2
Hall Gr WV14 .... 51 C8
Hall Green Cl B28 .... 105 F7
Hall Green Jun Sch B28 .... 105 F7
Hall Green Prim Sch B71 .... 42 D1
Hall Green Rd Coventry CV6 .... 96 B2
West Bromwich B71 .... 42 D1
Hall Green Sec Sch B28 .... 105 E8
Hall Green Sta 87 F1
Hall Hays Rd B34 .... 69 F2
Hall La Brownhills WS9 .... 15 E3
Burntwood, Hammerwich WS7 .... 7 E4
Burntwood,
Muckley Corner WS7, WS14 .... 7 F2
Coventry CV2 .... 114 F6
Dudley DY2 .... 62 C6
Great Wyrley WS6 .... 5 A3
Hagley DY9 .... 99 D6
Lichfield WS14 .... 8 A2
Tipton DY4 .... 52 B8
Walsall WS3 .... 14 F3
Wolverhampton WV11 .... 39 F1
Hall Mdw Hagley DY9 .... 99 D7
Wedges Mills WS11 .... 4 B6
Hall Park St WV14 .... 40 B7
Hall Rd
Birmingham,
Castle Bromwich B36 .... 69 A8
Birmingham,
Handsworth B20 .... 66 A8
Birmingham, Saltley B8 .... 67 D4
Hinckley LE10 .... 75 D5
Royal Leamington Spa CV32 . 156 F1
Smethwick B67 .... 64 E4
Hall St Bilston WV14 .... 40 E5
Birmingham B18 .... 164 A4
Blackheath B64 .... 62 F2
Darlaston WS10 .... 41 B7
Dudley DY2 .... 51 D1
Oldbury B68 .... 64 B5
Sedgley DY3 .... 50 D8
Stourbridge DY8 .... 81 A3
Tipton DY4 .... 51 E5
Walsall WS2 .... 28 D3

Hall St continued
West Bromwich B70 .... 53 C2
Willenhall WV13 .... 27 B1
Wolverhampton WV11 .... 26 C5
Hall St E WS10 .... 41 C7
Hall St S B70 .... 64 D8
Hall Wlk B46 .... 70 F4
Hall's Cl CV31 .... 162 B3
Halladale B38 .... 103 F1
Hallam Cl B71 .... 53 E5
Hallam Cres WV10 .... 25 E6
Hallam Jun Sch B71 .... 53 E5
Hallam Rd CV6 .... 95 B2
Hallam St Birmingham B12 ... 86 E5
West Bromwich B71 .... 53 D5
Hallbridge Cl WS3 .... 14 F2
Hallbridge Way B69 .... 52 B2
Hallchurch Rd DY2 .... 61 F6
Hallcourt Cl WS11 .... 4 E8
Hallcourt Cres WS11 .... 4 E8
Hallcourt La WS11 .... 4 E8
Hallcroft Cl B72 .... 57 C7
Hallcroft Way Aldridge WS9 .. 30 C5
Knowle B93 .... 128 A6
Hallens Dr WS10 .... 41 D2
Hallet Dr WV3 .... 163 A2
Hallewell Rd B16 .... 65 D3
Hallfield Sch B15 .... 86 A7
Hallfields CV31 .... 162 E5
Hallgreen St WV14 .... 40 E2
Hallmoor Rd WV33 .... 69 B3
Hallmoor Sch B33 .... 69 B3
Hallot Cl B23 .... 56 D8
Halloughton Rd B74 .... 46 A7
Hallow Ho **5** B38 .... 103 D2
Hallowfields Cl B98 .... 153 E1
Hallstead Rd B13 .... 105 B5
Hallway Dr CV7 .... 97 E6
Halsbury Gr B44 .... 56 B8
Halstead Gr B91 .... 127 A8
Halston Rd **3** WS7 .... 7 B8
Halswelle Gr B43 .... 44 E4
Halton Rd B73 .... 45 E2
Halton St DY2 .... 62 C5
Haltonlea B77 .... 36 A8
Ham Dingle Prim Sch DY9 .. 81 C2
Ham La Kingswinford DY6 .... 49 E1
Stourbridge DY9 .... 81 C2
Hamar Way B37 .... 70 B1
Hamberley Ct B18 .... 65 D5
Hamble B77 .... 21 D2
Hamble Cl DY5 .... 61 A6
Hamble Ct B73 .... 46 B5
Hamble Gr WV6 .... 23 F4
Hamble Rd Birmingham B42 .. 43 F1
Wolverhampton WV4 .... 38 C6
Hambledon Cl WV9 .... 11 A2
Hambleton Rd B63 .... 82 D2
Hambletts Rd B70 .... 53 A3
Hambrook Cl WV6 .... 25 A5
Hambury Dr B14 .... 104 D7
Hamelin St WS11 .... 1 E3
Hamilton Ave
Birmingham B17 .... 85 A7
Halesowen B62 .... 83 C3
Stourbridge DY8 .... 80 D6
Hamilton Cl Bedworth CV12 .. 77 C1
Cannock WS11 .... 2 F4
Hinckley LE10 .... 71 A2
Lickey End B60 .... 137 C6
Sedgley DY3 .... 50 C8
Stourbridge DY8 .... 60 C2
Hamilton Ct
1 Birmingham B13 .... 86 F4
Nuneaton CV10 .... 72 D4
Hamilton Dr
Birmingham B29 .... 103 D8
Stourbridge DY8 .... 60 C2
Studley B80 .... 159 D3
Tipton B69 .... 52 C2
Hamilton Gdns WV10 .... 11 F3
Hamilton Ho **3**
Birmingham B5 .... 86 D7
Walsall WS3 .... 14 C1
Hamilton Lea WS11 .... 6 A6
Hamilton Rd Birmingham
B21 .... 65 D8
Coventry CV2 .... 114 A4
Kidderminster DY11 .... 116 B3
Radford Semele CV31 .... 162 E5
Redditch B97 .... 158 C8
Smethwick B67 .... 64 E2
Tipton DY4 .... 52 C6
Hamilton Specl Sch B21 ..... 65 D8
Hamilton St WS3 .... 14 D1
Hamilton Terr CV32 .... 161 F8
Hamlet Cl CV11 .... 74 B1
Hamlet Gdns B28 .... 105 F8
Hamlet Rd B28 .... 105 F8
Hamlet The
Leek Wootton CV35 .... 156 A7
Norton Canes WS11 .... 5 E5
Hammer Bank DY5 .... 82 A8
Hammersley Cl B63 .... 82 C7
Hammersley St CV12 .... 77 E1
Hammerwich Hospl WS7 ...... 7 B5
Hammerwich La WS7 .... 7 F3
Hammerwich Rd WS7 .... 7 D5
Hammond Ave B18 .... 25 E8
Hammond Bsns Ctr CV11 .... 73 C3
Hammond Cl CV11 .... 73 E3
Hammond Dr B23 .... 56 F5
Hammond Rd CV2 .... 113 F4
Hammond Way DY8 .... 81 A7
Hammonds Terr CV8 .... 147 D5

Hampden Cl DY5 .... 82 A8
Hampden Ct B69 .... 63 E8
Hampden Ho B35 .... 58 B3
Hampden Retreat B12 .... 86 E6
Hamps Cl WS7 .... 7 D7
Hampshire Cl Coventry CV3 134 F8
Tamworth B78 .... 20 F2
Hampshire Dr B15 .... 85 E8
Hampshire Rd B71 .... 42 A1
Hampson Cl B11 .... 87 B6
Hampstead Cl WV11 .... 26 D6
Hampton Ave
Bromsgrove B60 .... 151 A8
Nuneaton CV10 .... 72 B4
Hampton Cl Coventry CV6 ... 113 F6
Redditch B98 .... 159 A7
Tamworth B79 .... 21 C7
Hampton Court Rd B17 .... 85 A6
Hampton Ct B92 .... 109 B6
Hampton Dr B74 .... 46 B8
Hampton Gn WS11 .... 4 E7
Hampton Gr
Royal Leamington Spa CV32 . 157 B1
1 Walsall WS3 .... 15 A4
Hampton in Arden Sta
B92 .... 109 B7
Hampton La Meriden CV7 ... 109 E8
Solihull B91 .... 108 B5
Hampton Pl WS10 .... 41 C8
Hampton Rd
Birmingham, Aston B6 .... 66 D8
Birmingham,
Stockland Green B23 .... 56 D4
Coventry CV6 .... 113 F6
Knowle B93 .... 128 C8
Warwick CV34 .... 160 B5
Wolverhampton WV10 .... 11 B1
Hampton St
Birmingham B19 .... 164 B4
Cannock WS11 .... 4 D7
Dudley, Netherton DY2 .... 62 C5
Dudley, Roseville WV14 .... 51 B8
Warwick CV34 .... 160 D6
Hams La B76 .... 59 F6
Hams Rd B8 .... 67 D4
Hamstead Hall Ave B20 .... 54 E5
Hamstead Hall Rd B20 .... 54 F4
Hamstead Hall Sec Sch
B20 .... 54 E6
Hamstead Hill B20 .... 54 F4
Hamstead Ho B43 .... 54 F7
Hamstead Jun & Inf Sch
B43 .... 54 D7
Hamstead Rd
Birmingham, Hanmstead B43 .. 54 D7
Birmingham,
Lozells B19, B20 .... 66 B7
Hamstead Sta B42 .... 54 F6
Hamstead Terr WS10 .... 42 A2
Hanam Cl B75 .... 46 F6
Hanbury Cl Bromsgrove
B60 .... 151 A8
Halesowen B63 .... 82 F1
Hanbury Cres WV4 .... 38 E6
Hanbury Croft B27 .... 88 E3
Hanbury Ct DY8 .... 81 A4
Hanbury Hill DY8 .... 81 A4
Hanbury Ho WV7 .... 153 B4
Hanbury Rd Bedworth CV12 .. 78 C4
Brownhills WS8 .... 6 F2
Dorridge B93 .... 127 F4
Norton Canes WS11 .... 5 F5
Stoke Heath B60 .... 150 D4
Tamworth B77 .... 21 F4
West Bromwich B70 .... 53 A3
Hanbury's Farm Prim Sch
B77 .... 21 D1
Hanch Pl WS1 .... 42 F8
Hancock Gn CV4 .... 131 F8
Hancock Rd B8 .... 67 F4
Hancox St B68 .... 64 B2
Handcross Gr CV3 .... 133 A5
Handel Ct WS11 .... 2 C2
Handel Wlk WS13 .... 3 C2
Handley Gr Birmingham B31 102 C2
Warwick CV34 .... 155 D1
Handley St WS10 .... 42 A4
Handley's Cl CV8 .... 135 A1
Handsworth, Booth Street
Sta B21 .... 65 C7
Handsworth Coll B21 .... 65 F8
Handsworth Coll
(Corporation)
Aston Ctr B6 .... 66 E8
Handsworth Coll F Ed B6 .... 66 E8
Handsworth Cres CV5 .... 111 E4
Handsworth Dr B43 .... 44 A3
Handsworth Gram Sch B21 65 F8
Handsworth New Rd B18 ..... 65 E6
Handsworth Univ Village
(Univ of Aston) B21 .... 54 E7
Handsworth Wood Boys' Sch
B20 .... 54 F2
Handsworth Wood Girls'
Sch B20 .... 54 F2
Handsworth Wood Rd B20 .. 55 A2
Hanford Cl CV6 .... 113 E6
Hanger Rd B26 .... 90 A3
Hanging La B31 .... 102 E2
Hangleton Dr B11 .... 87 D6
Hangman's La LE10 .... 71 E3
Hanley Cl B63 .... 82 E4
Hanley Ct B23 .... 56 C2
Hanley St B19 .... 164 C4
Hanley Villas **1** B12 .... 87 B5
Hanlith B77 .... 36 A8
Hannaford Way WS11 .... 1 F2
Hannafore Rd B16 .... 65 D3

Hannah Rd WV14 .... 41 A3
Hanney Hay Rd WS7 .... 7 B3
Hannon Rd B14 .... 104 E5
Hanover Cl B6 .... 66 E7
Hanover Ct Hinckley LE10 .... 75 E6
Redditch B98 .... 158 D8
Tamworth B79 .... 20 E7
Walsall WS2 .... 27 E1
Wolverhampton WV6 .... 24 C4
Hanover Dr B24 .... 67 F8
Hanover Gdns **8** CV32 ... 157 A1
Hanover Glebe CV11 .... 73 C2
Hanover Pl **5** B69 .... 80 F8
Hanover Pl Bromsgrove
B60 .... 136 F1
Cannock WS11 .... 1 E1
Hanover Rd B65 .... 63 C4
Hanover St B61 .... 136 F1
Hans Cl CV2 .... 113 F4
Hansell Dr B93 .... 127 E2
Hansom Rd Birmingham B32 . 84 C5
Hinckley LE10 .... 71 F2
Hanson Ct **2** LE10 .... 75 D8
Hanson Gr B92 .... 88 F5
Hanson's Bridge Rd B24 ..... 57 F5
Hanwell Cl B76 .... 58 B7
Hanwood Cl Birmingham B12 86 F8
Coventry CV5 .... 111 D4
Hanworth Cl CV32 .... 157 C2
Hanworth Rd CV34 .... 160 D8
Harald Cl WV6 .... 23 E5
Harbeck Ave B44 .... 55 F8
Harberrow Cl DY9 .... 99 A6
Harbet Dr B40 .... 90 E4
Harbinger Rd B38 .... 104 B2
Harbington Hall DY10 .... 118 B1
Harborne Ct B17 .... 85 C4
Harborne Hill Sch B15 .... 85 E6
Harborne Inf Sch B17 .... 85 C6
Harborne Jun Sch B17 .... 85 C6
Harborne La B17 .... 85 D3
Harborne Park Rd B17 .... 85 C4
Harborne Rd Birmingham
B15 .... 85 E7
Oldbury B68 .... 84 E8
Harborough Cotts B94 ...... 144 D3
Harborough Ct B74 .... 32 A2
Harborough Dr Aldridge
WS9 .... 30 B5
Birmingham B36 .... 58 D1
Harborough Rd CV6 .... 95 B2
Harborough Wlk DY9 .... 81 B2
Harbours Cl B61 .... 150 D7
Harbours Hill B60 .... 120 E6
Harbury Cl Redditch B98 ... 154 D1
Sutton Coldfield B76 .... 58 B6
Harbury La CV33, CV34 ..... 161 E2
Harbury Rd B12 .... 86 D5
Harcourt CV3 .... 134 E5
Harcourt Dr Dudley DY3 ...... 50 D2
Sutton Coldfield B74 .... 31 F4
Harcourt Gdns CV11 .... 73 C3
Harcourt Ho B79 .... 21 A4
Harcourt Rd Birmingham
B23 .... 56 E7
Blackheath B64 .... 82 F8
Wednesbury WS10 .... 41 F4
Harden Cl WS3 .... 28 E7
Harden Ct B31 .... 102 E1
Harden Gr WS3 .... 28 E7
Harden Keep B66 .... 65 A4
Harden Manor Ct B62 .... 83 C3
Harden Prim Sch WS3 .... 28 E7
Harden Rd WS3 .... 28 E7
Harden Vale B63 .... 82 E5
Hardie Ct WV4 .... 39 F4
Hardie La WS1 .... 1 F3
Harding St WV14 .... 40 D2
Hardon Rd WV4 .... 39 F5
Hardware St B70 .... 53 D4
Hardwick Cl CV5 .... 112 A4
Hardwick Ct B74 .... 30 F2
Hardwick Dr B62 .... 83 A7
Hardwick La B80 .... 159 F4
Hardwick Rd Aldridge B74 .... 31 A2
Solihull B92 .... 88 E4
Hardwicke Way DY9 .... 81 D5
Hardwick Wlk B14 .... 104 D2
Hardwyn Cl CV3 .... 115 A1
Hardy Ave DY10 .... 117 A6
Hardy Cl Hinckley LE10 .... 71 D4
Nuneaton CV10 .... 72 A4
Hardy Rd Coventry CV6 ...... 113 A8
Walsall WS3 .... 28 E8
Wednesbury WS10 .... 42 A3
Hardy Sq WV2 .... 39 F6
Hare And Hounds La CV10 .. 73 A2
Hare Gr B31 .... 102 D3
Hare St WV14 .... 40 F5
Harebell B77 .... 22 A4
Harebell Cl Cannock WS12 ... 2 D2
Featherstone WV10 .... 12 A7
Walsall WS5 .... 43 A3
Harebell Cres DY1 .... 51 A4
Harebell Gdns B38 .... 123 F8
Harebell Wlk **1** B37 .... 70 D2
Harefield Ho CV2 .... 114 B3
Harefield La CV12 .... 77 F8
Harefield Rd Coventry CV2 .. 114 B3
Nuneaton CV11 .... 73 C4
Haresfield B97 .... 153 D3
Harewell Dr B75 .... 32 C1
Harewood B17 .... 85 B6
Harewood Ave
Birmingham B43 .... 43 C2
Wednesbury WS10 .... 42 C3
Harewood Cl B28 .... 105 E5

Harewood Rd CV5 .... 112 C2
Harford St B19 .... 164 A5
Hargate La B71 .... 53 D4
Hargate Prim Sch B71 .... 53 C4
Harger Ct CV8 .... 147 F4
Hargrave Cl Coventry CV3 .. 115 A1
Water Orton B46 .... 59 B3
Hargreave Cl B76 .... 57 F8
Hargreaves Ct DY11 .... 116 C3
Hargreaves St WV1 .... 40 A7
Harington Rd CV6 .... 113 A5
Harland Rd B74 .... 32 A3
Harlech Cl Birmingham
B32 .... 102 A7
Kenilworth CV8 .... 148 C5
Tipton B69 .... 52 A1
Harlech Ho **2** WS3 .... 28 C6
Harlech Rd WV12 .... 27 C6
Harlech Tower B20 .... 55 A1
Harlech Way Dudley DY1 ..... 50 F2
Kidderminster DY10 .... 116 E2
Harleston Rd B44 .... 55 F8
Harley Cl WS8 .... 16 A6
Harley Dr WV14 .... 40 B4
Harley Grange **6** DY2 ...... 62 E8
Harley St CV2 .... 114 A3
Harlow Gr B28 .... 106 A6
Harlow Wlk **8** CV2 .... 115 A7
Harlstones Cl DY8 .... 81 A8
Harman Rd B72 .... 57 B6
Harmar Cl CV34 .... 155 D1
Harmer Cl CV2 .... 115 A7
Harmer St B18 .... 66 A5
Harmon Rd DY8 .... 80 C5
Harnall Cl B90 .... 126 E7
Harnall Ind Est CV1 .... 165 C4
Harnall La CV1 .... 165 C4
Harnall La E CV1 .... 113 E4
Harnall La W CV1 .... 165 C4
Harnall Row Coventry CV1 .. 113 E2
Coventry CV1 .... 113 E3
Harness Cl WS5 .... 42 F4
Harold Evers Way DY10 ..... 116 F7
Harold Rd Birmingham B16 .. 65 F1
Coventry CV2 .... 114 D2
Smethwick B67 .... 64 E3
Harold St CV11 .... 73 C3
Harpenden Dr CV5 .... 112 A5
Harper Ave WV11 .... 26 C7
Harper Bell Sch The B12 ... 87 A8
Harper Rd Bilston WV14 ...... 40 D6
Coventry CV1 .... 113 E2
Harper St WV13 .... 27 A2
Harpers Rd B31 .... 103 A2
Harport Rd B98 .... 154 A1
Harpur Cl WS4 .... 29 A4
Harpur Rd WS4 .... 29 A4
Harrier Rd B27 .... 88 D2
Harriers Gn DY10 .... 117 B8
Harriers Ind Est DY10 .... 116 F5
Harriet Cl DY5 .... 61 B5
Harringay Dr DY8 .... 80 E3
Harringay Rd B44 .... 45 A2
Harrington Ct CV3 .... 114 F2
Harringworth Ct WS4 .... 29 C8
Harriott Dr CV34 .... 161 D4
Harris Ct B18 .... 66 A6
Harris Dr **2** Birmingham
B42 .... 55 A8
Smethwick B66 .... 65 B3
Harris Ind Pk B60 .... 150 E2
Harris Rd Coventry CV3 ...... 114 B2
Warwick CV34 .... 160 C8
Harrison Cl Cheslyn Hay WS6 .. 4 D1
Walsall WS3 .... 14 C1
Harrison Cres CV12 .... 78 A2
Harrison Ct B79 .... 61 A1
Harrison Rd B14 .... 104 F3
Harrison Rd Birmingham B24 . 56 F4
Cannock WS11 .... 4 E7
Redditch B97 .... 158 C8
Stourbridge DY8 .... 61 A1
Sutton Coldfield B74 .... 31 E5
Walsall WS4 .... 15 C2
Harrison St WS3 .... 14 C1
Harrison's Fold DY2 .... 62 C5
Harrison's Rd B15 .... 85 E6
Harrisons Gn B15 .... 85 E6
Harrisons Pleck B13 .... 86 F3
Harrold Ave B65 .... 63 E3
Harrold Rd B65 .... 63 E3
Harrold St DY4 .... 52 C7
Harrold Terr B19 .... 66 C8
Harrop Way DY8 .... 80 E8
Harrow Cl Hagley DY9 .... 99 A6
Stoke Heath B60 .... 150 E6
Harrow Ct B74 .... 31 F2
Harrow Rd Birmingham B29 .. 85 F3
Kingswinford DY6 .... 49 D1
Whitnash CV31 .... 162 B3
Harrow St WV1 .... 25 B4
Harrowbrook Ind Est LE10 .. 74 E7
Harrowbrook Rd LE10 .... 74 E7
Harrowby Dr DY4 .... 52 A4
Harrowby Pl WV13 .... 27 C7
Harrowby Rd Bilston WV14 .. 41 A4
Wolverhampton WV10 .... 11 C2
Harrowfield Rd B33 .... 68 E4
Harry Caplan Ho CV5 .... 112 A6
Harry Cheshire High Sch
DY11 .... 116 B6
Harry Edwards Ho **2** CV2 114 D8
Harry Perks St WV13 .... 27 A3
Harry Price Ho **9** B69 ...... 63 D3
Harry Rose Rd CV2 .... 114 D5
Harry Salt Ho CV1 .... 165 D3
Harry Stanley Ho CV6 .... 114 A8

Harry Taylor Fst Sch B97 ... 158 E6
Harry Taylor Ho B98 .... 154 A4
Harry Truslove Cl CV6 .... 113 A7
Harry Weston Rd CV3 .... 115 A1
Hart Dr B73 .... 57 A8
Hart Rd Birmingham B24 ...... 57 A5
Willenhall WV11 .... 26 D4
Hart St WS1 .... 42 E8
Hartfield Cres B27 .... 88 B2
Hartfields Way B65 .... 62 F5
Hartford Cl B17 .... 85 A7
Hartford Rd B60 .... 137 B1
Hartill Rd WV4 .... 38 D3
Hartill St WV13 .... 41 B8
Hartington Cl B93 .... 127 E3
Hartington Cres CV5 .... 112 F1
Hartington Gn LE10 .... 75 E6
Hartington Rd B19 .... 66 D7
Hartland Ave Coventry
CV2 .... 114 B5
Dudley WV14 .... 51 A8
Hartland Rd
Birmingham B31 .... 122 E6
Dudley DY4 .... 51 D5
West Bromwich B71 .... 53 F8
Hartland St DY5 .... 61 D7
Hartle La DY9 .... 119 F6
Hartlebury Cl Cannock
WS11 .... 2 C2
Dorridge B93 .... 127 F3
Redditch B98 .... 154 E7
Hartlebury Rd
Halesowen B63 .... 82 F2
Oldbury B69 .... 63 D5
Hartledon Rd B17 .... 85 B5
Hartlepool Rd CV1 .... 165 D4
Hartley Dr WS9 .... 30 B4
Hartley Gr B44 .... 45 B3
Hartley Pl B15 .... 85 F8
Hartley Rd B44 .... 45 B3
Hartley St WV3 .... 25 A2
Hartleyburn B77 .... 36 A8
Harton Way B14 .... 104 C5
Hartopp Rd Birmingham B8 . 67 E4
Sutton Coldfield B74 .... 45 F8
Hartridge Wlk CV5 .... 112 B4
Harts Cl B17 .... 85 D6
Harts Green Rd B17 .... 85 A5
Harts Rd B8 .... 67 C5
Hartsbourne Dr B62 .... 83 D4
Hartshill Rd Birmingham
B34 .... 69 A6
Solihull B27 .... 88 D2
Hartshill Sch CV10 .... 72 B8
Hartshorn St WV14 .... 40 D5
Hartside Cl B63 .... 82 D2
Hartslade WS14 .... 9 E6
Hartswell Dr B13 .... 104 F6
Hartwell Cl B91 .... 107 B1
Hartwell La WS6 .... 5 A3
Hartwell Rd B24 .... 57 B2
Harvard Cl DY1 .... 50 F4
Harvard Rd B92 .... 89 B4
Harvest Cl Birmingham B30 . 104 B6
Dudley DY3 .... 50 E5
Stoke Heath B60 .... 150 E6
Harvest Ct B65 .... 63 A4
Harvest Gdns B68 .... 64 A4
Harvest Hill Cl **12** CV31 . 162 C6
Harvest Hill La CV5, CV7 .... 93 C4
Harvest Rd Blackheath B65 .. 63 A3
Smethwick B67 .... 64 D3
Harvest Wlk B65 .... 63 A4
Harvester Way DY6 .... 60 A8
Harvesters Cl Aldridge WS9 .. 30 C2
Coventry CV3 .... 115 A2
Harvesters Rd WV12 .... 27 D5
Harvesters Way WV12 .... 27 D5
Harvesters Wlk WV8 .... 10 E1
Harvey Cl CV5 .... 112 A7
Harvey Ct
Birmingham,
Bournville B30 .... 103 D7
Birmingham, Tile Cross B33 .. 69 D3
Harvey Dr B75 .... 32 C2
Harvey Rd Birmingham B26 . 88 D7
Walsall WS2 .... 28 B5
Harvey Works Ind Est B63 .. 82 F6
Harveys Terr DY2 .... 62 D4
Harvills Hawthorn B70 .... 52 F7
Harvills Hawthorn Jun &
Inf Sch B70 .... 52 F7
Harvine Wlk DY8 .... 80 E3
Harvington Cl DY11 .... 116 A8
Harvington Dr B90 .... 127 B6
Harvington Hall La DY10 .. 118 B1
Harvington Rd
Birmingham B29 .... 103 A8
Bromsgrove B60 .... 151 A8
Dudley WV14 .... 40 B1
Halesowen B63 .... 82 F1
Oldbury B68 .... 84 A8
Harvington Way B76 .... 58 A8
Harvington Wlk **3** B65 ..... 63 C3
Harwell Cl B79 .... 21 C7
Harwin Cl WV6 .... 24 F7
Harwood Dr LE10 .... 71 F4
Harwood Gr **1** B90 .... 126 C8
Harwood Rd WS13 .... 3 B3
Harwood St B70 .... 53 B3
Hasbury CE Prim Sch B63 .. 82 F2
Hasbury Cl B63 .... 82 E2
Hasbury Rd B32 .... 102 B8
Hasefield Gdns **1** DY10 .. 117 B6
Haselbech CV3 .... 114 F1
Haseley Cl Redditch B98 ... 154 E1
Royal Leamington Spa CV31 . 162 B5

Haseley Rd Birmingham B21 .. 65 E7
Coventry CV2 .... 96 C1
Solihull B91 .... 106 E6
Haselor Rd B73 .... 45 E1
Haselour Rd B37 .... 69 F5
Hasilwood Sq CV3 .... 114 B2
Haskell St WS1 .... 42 F7
Haslucks Croft B90 .... 125 C2
Haslucks Green Jun Sch
B90 .... 106 A3
Haslucks Green Rd
Hollywood B90 .... 125 C7
Solihull B90 .... 106 B4
Hassop Rd B42 .... 55 D7
Hastings B77 .... 35 F6
Hastings Ct DY1 .... 50 E2
Hastings High Sch LE10 ...... 75 F7
Hastings Rd Birmingham
B23 .... 56 B7
Bromsgrove B60 .... 150 E4
Coventry CV2 .... 114 A4
Haswell Rd B63 .... 82 D4
Hatch Heath Cl WV5 .... 49 A7
Hatcham Rd B44 .... 45 C2
Hatchett St B19 .... 66 E5
Hatchford Ave B92 .... 89 C3
Hatchford Brook Inf Sch
B92 .... 89 C3
Hatchford Brook Jun Sch
B92 .... 89 C3
Hatchford Brook Rd B92 ... 89 C3
Hatchford Ct B92 .... 89 C3
Hatchford Jun & Prim
Schs B37 .... 69 F2
Hatchford Prim Sch B37 .... 69 F2
Hatchford Wlk B37 .... 70 B1
Hateley Dr WV4 .... 39 E4
Hateley Heath Jun & Inf
Schs B71 .... 53 B7
Hately Heath Jun & Inf
Schs B71 .... 53 B7
Hatfield Cl Birmingham B23 .. 56 D8
Redditch B98 .... 154 E1
Hatfield Rd Birmingham B19 .. 66 D8
Stourbridge DY9 .... 81 C4
Hathaway Cl
Balsall Common CV7 .... 130 B7
Willenhall WV13 .... 40 F8
Hathaway Dr Nuneaton
CV11 .... 74 A1
Warwick CV34 .... 155 E2
Hathaway Rd Coventry
CV4 .... 111 D1
Solihull B90 .... 106 B1
Sutton Coldfield B75 .... 32 A4
Hatherden Dr B76 .... 47 A2
Hatherell Rd CV31 .... 162 E5
Hathersage Rd B42 .... 55 D7
Hatherton Croft WS11 .... 1 C1
Hatherton Gdns WV10 .... 11 E2
Hatherton Gr B29 .... 84 F1
Hatherton Lane JMI Sch
WS2 .... 28 A6
Hatherton Pl WS9 .... 30 A7
Hatherton Rd Bilston WV14 .. 40 F6
Cannock WS11 .... 1 C1
Walsall WS1 .... 28 E2
Hatherton St Cheslyn Hay
WS6 .... 4 C2
Walsall WS1, WS4 .... 28 E3
Hattersley Gr B11 .... 88 A3
Hatton Cres WV10 .... 26 A7
Hatton Gdns B42 .... 55 B7
Hatton Rd Cannock WS11 ..... 1 A1
Wolverhampton WV6 .... 24 F3
Hatton St WV14 .... 40 E4
Hattons Gr WV8 .... 10 B2
Haughton Rd B20 .... 55 D1
Haunch La B13 .... 105 A5
Haunchwood Dr B76 .... 57 F7
Haunchwood Rd CV10 .... 72 D4
Havacre La WV14 .... 40 C1
Havefield Ave WS14 .... 9 E7
Havelock Cl WV3 .... 38 F8
Havelock Rd
Birmingham,
Handsworth B20 .... 55 C1
Birmingham, Saltley B8 .... 67 D5
Birmingham, Sparkhill B11 ... 87 E4
Haven Croft B43 .... 54 D8
Haven Dr B27 .... 88 B3
Haven The Birmingham B14 105 D4
Stourbridge DY8 .... 60 D2
Wolverhampton WV2 .... 163 B1
Havendale Cl CV6 .... 113 B5
Haverford Dr B45 .... 122 B6
Havergal Wlk B63 .... 82 B4
Haverhill Cl WS3 .... 14 A3
Hawbridge Cl B90 .... 127 B6
Hawbush Gdns DY5 .... 61 A1
Hawbush Prim Sch DY5 ...... 61 B2
Hawbush Rd Brierley Hill DY5 61 A2
Walsall WS3 .... 28 E6
Hawcroft Gr B34 .... 69 C6
Hawes La B65 .... 63 B3
Hawes Rd WS1 .... 42 F6
Haweswater Dr DY6 .... 60 D6
Hawfield Cl B69 .... 63 C7
Hawfield Gr B72 .... 57 C7
Hawfield Rd B69 .... 63 C7
Hawfinch B77 .... 36 B5
Hawfinch Rise DY10 .... 117 A2
Hawford Ave DY10 .... 117 B6
Hawk Cl CV11 .... 79 B8
Hawker Dr B35 .... 57 F2
Hawkes Cl B30 .... 104 A7
Hawkes Dr CV34 .... 161 D4

Hawkes La B70 .... 53 A7
Hawkes Mill La CV5 .... 94 B2
Hawkes St B10 .... 87 D8
Hawkesbury Cl B98 .... 154 D5
Hawkesbury Fields Sch
CV2 .... 96 C3
Hawkesbury La CV2 .... 96 D5
Hawkesbury Rd B90 .... 105 F1
Hawkesford Cl
Birmingham B36 .... 69 A8
Sutton Coldfield B74 .... 32 B1
Hawkesford Rd B33 .... 69 D3
Hawkesley CE Inf Sch
B38 .... 123 E7
Hawkesley CE Jun Sch
B38 .... 123 E7
Hawkesley Cres B31 .... 103 A1
Hawkesley Dr B31 .... 122 F8
Hawkesley End B38 .... 123 E7
Hawkesley Mill La B31 ...... 102 F2
Hawkesley Rd DY1 .... 61 F8
Hawkesmoor Dr
Lichfield WS14 .... 9 D8
Perton WV6 .... 23 D3
Hawkestone Cres B70 .... 53 A6
Hawkestone Rd B29 .... 103 A7
Hawkesville Dr WS11 .... 1 F2
Hawkeswell Cl B92 .... 106 E8
Hawkesworth Dr CV8 .... 148 A6
Hawkesyard Rd B24 .... 56 E1
Hawkhurst Rd B14 .... 104 F2
Hawkin's Pl WV14 .... 40 F3
Hawkinge Dr B35 .... 58 A4
Hawkins Cl Birmingham B5 .. 86 E6
Hinckley LE10 .... 71 D4
Lichfield WS13 .... 3 B2
Hawkins Croft DY4 .... 52 A3
Hawkins Dr WS11 .... 4 C4
Hawkins Rd CV5 .... 113 A4
Hawkins St B70 .... 53 A8
Hawkley Cl WV1 .... 26 B2
Hawkley Rd WV1 .... 26 B2
Hawkmoor Gdns B38 .... 124 A8
Hawks Cl WS6 .... 4 D2
Hawks Green La WS11 .... 2 A2
Hawksford Cres WV10 .... 25 E7
Hawkshead Dr B93 .... 127 F6
Hawkside B77 .... 36 B8
Hawksmill Ind Est B9 .... 67 C1
Hawkstone Cl DY11 .... 116 D8
Hawkstone Ct WV6 .... 23 D5
Hawkswell Ave WV5 .... 49 A5
Hawkswell Dr WV13 .... 40 F8
Hawkswood Dr CV7 .... 130 B7
Hawkswood Gr B14 .... 105 B3
Hawksworth B77 .... 21 F2
Hawksworth Dr **1** CV1 ... 113 B3
Hawkyard Ct WS11 .... 2 A4
Hawley Rd LE10 .... 75 D7
Hawnby Gr B76 .... 47 A2
Hawne Cl B63 .... 82 E6
Hawne La B63 .... 82 F6
Hawnelands The B63 .... 82 F5
Hawsford Cres WV10 .... 25 D7
Hawthorn Ave WS6 .... 5 A1
Hawthorn Brook Way B23 .. 56 E8
Hawthorn Cl
Birmingham, Erdington B23 .. 56 F7
Birmingham, Spring Vale B9 .. 67 B1
Lichfield WS13 .... 3 B2
Hawthorn Coppice DY9 .... 99 A6
Hawthorn Cres LE10 .... 75 E4
Hawthorn Croft B68 .... 84 D7
Hawthorn Ct CV4 .... 111 E1
Hawthorn Gr **9**
Birmingham B19 .... 66 C8
Kidderminster DY11 .... 116 A6
Hawthorn Jun & Inf Sch
B44 .... 56 A7
Hawthorn La CV4 .... 111 E1
Hawthorn Park Dr **1** B20 .. 54 F3
Hawthorn Pk B20 .... 54 E3
Hawthorn Pl WS2 .... 27 E3
Hawthorn Rd Aldridge B74 .. 31 A1
Bilston WV1 .... 40 B8
Birmingham B44 .... 56 A7
Brierley Hill DY5 .... 81 E8
Bromsgrove B61 .... 137 B4
Redditch B97 .... 153 A3
Royal Leamington Spa CV31 161 F6
Tipton DY4 .... 52 B8
Walsall, Bescot WS5 .... 42 F5
Walsall, Shelfield WS4 .... 29 B8
Wednesbury WS10 .... 41 F4
Wylde Green B72 .... 46 C1
Hawthorn Terr WS10 .... 41 C6
Hawthorn Way CV10 .... 72 A8
Hawthornden Ct B72 .... 57 D7
Hawthorne Ave B79 .... 21 B8
Hawthorne Cres WS7 .... 7 A6
Hawthorne Dr B47 .... 125 B6
Hawthorne Gr DY3 .... 50 D2
Hawthorne Ho WV10 .... 25 F3
Hawthorne Rd
Birmingham,
Castle Bromwich B36 .... 69 F7
Birmingham, Edgbaston B15 .. 85 E7
Birmingham,
King's Norton B30 .... 103 D5
Cannock WS12 .... 2 F3
Cheslyn Hay WS6 .... 4 E4
Dudley DY1 .... 51 C4
Essington WV11 .... 13 A3
Halesowen B63 .... 82 D4
Huntington WS12 .... 1 D8
Wednesfield WV11 .... 27 A5
Willenhall WV12 .... 27 D7
Wolverhampton WV2 .... 39 D6

Hawthorne Terr CV10 .... 72 F5
Hawthorns Sta The B71 .... 65 B8
Hawthorns The
Birmingham B13 .... 86 F3
1 Kidderminster DY10 .... 117 A5
Oldbury B68 .... 84 D7
West Bromwich B21 .... 54 B1
Wolverhampton WV11 .... 26 B6
Haxby Ave B34 .... 69 A6
Hay Cl DY10 .... 116 C7
Hay Gn DY9 .... 81 D5
Hay Green Cl B30 .... 103 D6
Hay Green La B30 .... 103 D6
Hay Hall Rd B11 .... 87 F5
Hay Hill WS5 .... 43 E8
Hay La Coventry CV1 .... 165 C2
Solihull B90 .... 127 A6
Hay Pk B5 .... 86 D6
Hay St WV14 .... 88 A7
Hay Wood La B93, CV35 ... 145 A3
Haybarn The B76 .... 58 A8
Haybridge Ave DY8 .... 98 F5
Haybridge High Sch DY8 ... 98 F6
Haybrook Dr B11 .... 87 F4
Haycock Pl WS10 .... 41 C8
Haycroft Ave B8 .... 67 E5
Haycroft Dr B74 .... 32 A4
Haydays Rd B9 .... 67 E5
Haydn Sanders Sq **7** WS1 .. 42 E8
Haydock Cl Birmingham B36 .. 68 C8
Coventry CV6 .... 96 B4
Wolverhampton W6 .... 25 B5
Haydon Cl B93 .... 127 F2
Haydon Croft B33 .... 69 A3
Haydon Way B49 .... 159 F1
Haye House Gr B36 .... 68 E7
Hayes Cres B68 .... 64 D5
Hayes Croft B38 .... 123 F7
Hayes Gr B24 .... 57 D6
Hayes Green Rd CV12 .... 95 F8
Hayes La Bedworth CV7 ...... 96 A8
Stourbridge DY9 .... 82 A6
Hayes Mdw B72 .... 57 D7
Hayes Rd Nuneaton CV10 ... 72 A8
Oldbury B68 .... 64 D5
Hayes St B70 .... 53 A4
Hayes The Birmingham B31 123 C7
Stourbridge DY9 .... 82 A5
Willenhall WV12 .... 27 B6
Hayes Trad Est DY9 .... 82 A6
Hayes View Dr WS6 .... 4 E4
Hayes Way WS11, WS12 ...... 2 C1
Hayfield Ct B13 .... 87 B2
Hayfield Gdns B13 .... 87 C2
Hayfield Rd B13 .... 87 B2
Hayford Cl B98 .... 154 A5
Hayland Rd B23 .... 56 E6
Hayle B77 .... 21 D2
Hayle Ave CV34 .... 155 F1
Hayle Cl Birmingham B38 .. 104 B2
Nuneaton CV11 .... 74 A5
Hayley Ct B24 .... 57 C6
Hayley Green Rd B32 .... 102 B8
Hayley Park Rd B63 .... 100 C8
Hayling Cl B45 .... 101 F1
Hayling Gr WV2 .... 39 B6
Hayloft Cl B60 .... 150 E6
Haylofts The B63 .... 82 C1
Haymaker The WV8 .... 10 E1
Haymoor WS14 .... 9 E7
Haynes Cl B61 .... 137 B8
Haynes La WS5 .... 43 B4
Haynestone Rd CV6 .... 112 E6
Haypits Cl B71 .... 53 E7
Hayrick Dr DY6 .... 60 B7
Hays Kent's Moat The B26 .. 69 A1
Hays La LE10 .... 75 B7
Hayseech B64 .... 83 A7
Hayseech Rd B63 .... 82 F6
Hayton Gn CV4 .... 131 F8
Haytor Ave B14 .... 104 D5
Haytor Rise CV2 .... 114 C7
Haywain Cl WV9 .... 10 F2
Hayward Rd B75 .... 46 C7
Hayward St WV14 .... 51 B8
Hayward's Gn CV6 .... 113 A7
Haywards Cl Birmingham
B23 .... 56 E5
Walsall WS3 .... 14 F3
Haywharf Rd DY5 .... 61 B5
Haywood Dr Halesowen B62 .. 83 C8
Wolverhampton WV6 .... 24 D4
Haywood Rd B33 .... 69 C2
Haywood's Farm B71 .... 42 F2
Hayworth Cl B79 .... 20 F8
Hayworth Rd WS13 .... 3 C2
Hazel Ave Birmingham B73 .. 45 C1
Wednesbury WS10 .... 42 A4
Hazel Cl Nuneaton CV10 ..... 72 A8
Royal Leamington Spa
CV32 .... 157 A2
Hazel Croft
Birmingham,
Chelmsley Wood B37 .... 70 B1
Birmingham,
Northfield B31 .... 103 A3
Hazel Dr B47 .... 125 B5
Hazel Gdns Birmingham B27 .. 88 C5
Codsall WV8 .... 10 A4
Hazel Gr Bedworth CV12 .... 78 D3
Bilston WV14 .... 40 F7
Lichfield WS14 .... 9 C7
Stourbridge DY8 .... 80 C3
Tanworth-in-A B94 .... 143 C6
West Bromwich B70 .... 53 C1
Wolverhampton WV11 .... 26 C7
Wombourne WV5 .... 49 A7
Hazel La WS6 .... 5 B2
Hazel Oak La B90 .... 106 A2

Hazel Rd Birmingham B45 .. 121 F6
Coventry CV6 .... 96 B1
Dudley DY1 .... 51 C2
Kingswinford DY6 .... 60 E5
Nuneaton CV10 .... 72 D5
Redditch B97 .... 153 C5
Tipton DY4 .... 41 D1
Wolverhampton WV3 .... 38 E7
Hazelbank B38 .... 103 E2
Hazelbeach Rd B8 .... 67 F5
Hazelbeech Rd B70 .... 53 B3
Hazeldene Gr **5** B6 .... 66 E8
Hazeldene Rd
Birmingham B33 .... 89 D7
Halesowen B63 .... 82 E2
Hazeley Cl B17 .... 85 A7
Hazelgarth B77 .... 36 B8
Hazelhead St Georges
(Ind Est) CV1 .... 113 F2
Hazelhurst Rd
Birmingham,
Castle Bromwich B36 .... 69 E7
Birmingham,
King's Heath B14 .... 104 E7
Hazell Way CV10 .... 73 A1
Hazelmead Ct B73 .... 57 A7
Hazelmere Ct B69 .... 63 D8
Hazelmere Dr WS7 .... 6 F4
Hazelmere Rd B28 .... 105 F8
Hazeloak Rd B90 .... 106 A3
Hazelton Cl Marlbrook B61 .. 137 C8
1 Solihull B91 .... 107 B1
Hazelton Rd B61 .... 121 C1
Hazeltree Croft B27 .... 88 B2
Hazeltree Gr B93 .... 127 E3
Hazelville Gr B28 .... 106 A6
Hazelville Rd B28 .... 106 A7
Hazelwell Cres B30 .... 104 B6
Hazelwell Fordrough B30 .. 104 B6
Hazelwell La B30 .... 104 B6
Hazelwell Rd B30 .... 104 A6
Hazelwell St B30 .... 104 A7
Hazelwood Cl
Cheslyn Hay WS6 .... 4 D2
Kidderminster DY11 .... 116 B4
Hazelwood Dr WV11 .... 26 A5
Hazelwood Gr Cannock WS11 .. 4 C8
Willenhall WV12 .... 27 D5
Hazelwood Rd Aldridge B74 .. 30 D1
Birmingham B27 .... 88 B2
Hazlemere Cl CV5 .... 112 B4
Hazlemere Dr B74 .... 32 B1
Hazlemere Gr WS11 .... 4 A6
Hazlitt Gr B30 .... 103 D4
Hazlitt Gr B30 .... 103 D4
Headborough Rd CV2 .... 114 A5
Headborough Wlk WS9 ...... 16 B1
Headingley Rd B21 .... 54 E2
Headington Ave CV6 .... 95 A2
Headland Dr B8 .... 67 D5
Headland Rd WV3 .... 24 B4
Headlands The
Coventry CV5 .... 112 D4
Little Aston B74 .... 31 C3
Headless Cross Dr B97 .... 153 D1
Headley Croft B38 .... 123 D8
Headley Heath La B38 ...... 124 B6
Headley Rise B90 .... 106 D2
Heale Cl B63 .... 82 A7
Healey B77 .... 21 E2
Healey Ct CV34 .... 160 F7
Health Centre Rd CV8 .... 132 C4
Heanor Croft B6 .... 67 B8
Heantun Croft WV10 .... 26 A5
Heantun Ct WV3 .... 25 B1
Heantun Ho WV3 .... 163 B2
Heantun Lodge WV14 .... 40 D6
Heantun Mill Ct WS10 .... 41 D1
Heantun Rise WV3 .... 25 C4
Heantun Row WV11 .... 13 B2
Hearsall Com Prim Sch
CV5 .... 112 F2
Hearsall Comm CV5 .... 112 F2
Hearsall Ct CV4 .... 112 D2
Hearsall Golf Course CV5 .. 132 E7
Hearsall La CV5 .... 112 F2
Heart of England Sch CV7 130 C6
Heart of England Way
CV11 .... 73 F3
Heartland Mews B65 .... 63 B2
Heartlands High Sch B7 .... 67 B4
Heartlands Pl B8 .... 67 E4
Heath Acres WS10 .... 41 C4
Heath Ave CV12 .... 77 E1
Heath Bridge Cl WS4 .... 29 A8
Heath Cl Birmingham B30 .. 103 D5
Bromsgrove B60 .... 150 E6
Stonnall WS9 .... 16 E5
Tipton DY4 .... 52 B5
Heath Cres CV2 .... 114 A6
Heath Croft B31 .... 123 A7
Heath Croft Rd B75 .... 32 D1
Heath Ct **2** B12 .... 86 F5
Heath End Rd
Belbroughton DY9 .... 120 D7
Nuneaton CV10 .... 72 F2
Heath Farm Rd Codsall
WV8 .... 10 B2
Stourbridge DY8 .... 80 E3
Heath Gap Rd WS11 .... 1 F3
Heath Gdns B91 .... 107 D6
Heath Gn DY1 .... 50 E3
Heath Gn WV8 .... 10 B3
Heath Green Gr **4** B18 .... 65 E4
Heath Green Rd B18 .... 65 E4
Heath Hayes Cty Prim Sch
WS12 .... 2 F2
Heath Hays Prim Sch WS12 .. 2 F2

Heath Hill Rd WV6 .... 23 E1
Heath Ho B14 .... 104 F2
Heath House La WV8 .... 23 E8
Heath La
Kidderminster DY10 .... 117 C1
Stourbridge DY8 .... 81 A4
West Bromwich B71 .... 53 D7
Heath Lane Hospl B71 .... 53 D7
Heath Mill La B9 .... 67 A1
Heath Park High Sch
WV11 .... 26 A5
Heath Rd Bedworth CV12 ... 77 F1
Birmingham B30 .... 103 D5
Coventry CV2 .... 114 A4
Darlaston WS10 .... 41 E8
Dudley DY2 .... 62 C2
Hollywood B47 .... 125 A7
Solihull B91 .... 107 D6
Willenhall WV12 .... 13 D1
Heath Rd S B31 .... 103 B4
Heath Rise B14 .... 105 A1
Heath St Birmingham B18 .. 65 E4
Blackheath B65 .... 63 C1
Cannock WS12 .... 2 B7
Stourbridge DY8 .... 80 F4
Tamworth B79 .... 21 C5
Heath St S B18 .... 65 F4
Heath Terr Beausale CV35 .. 146 C2
Royal Leamington Spa CV32 .. 156 E1
Heath Trad Pk B66 .... 65 D5
Heath View Cannock WS12 .. 5 E8
Walsall WS2 .... 27 F3
Heath Way Birmingham B34 .. 69 B6
Cannock WS11 .... 2 B2
Heath-Mount Jun & Inf Sch
B12 .... 86 F6
Heathbank Dr WS12 .... 1 C6
Heathbrook Ave DY6 .... 60 B7
Heathcliff Rd Birmingham
B11 .... 87 F4
Dudley DY2 .... 62 F7
Heathcote Ave B91 .... 106 E3
Heathcote Ct CV6 .... 113 A4
Heathcote Ho B17 .... 85 C5
Heathcote Ind Est CV34 ... 161 D5
Heathcote La
Royal Leamington Spa
CV34 .... 161 E2
Warwick CV34 .... 161 A1
Heathcote Rd
Birmingham B30 .... 104 A5
Whitnash CV31 .... 162 A4
Heathcote St CV6 .... 113 A4
Heathcote Way CV34 .... 161 D4
Heather Ave WS5 .... 43 B4
Heather Cl Birmingham B36 .. 70 A8
Nuneaton CV10 .... 72 F3
Walsall WS3 .... 28 A8
Wednesfield WV11 .... 26 E5
Heather Court Gdns B74 .... 46 A8
Heather Croft B44 .... 44 F1
Heather Ct B13 .... 86 D3
Heather Dale B13 .... 86 C2
Heather Dr Bedworth CV12 .. 77 E2
Birmingham B43 .... 121 F6
Huntington WS12 .... 1 D5
Heather Gr Solihull B91 .... 107 E6
Willenhall WV12 .... 27 E4
Heather Ho B18 .... 103 F1
Heather Rd
Binley Woods CV3 .... 135 D7
Birmingham, Great Barr B43 .. 54 D8
Birmingham,
Small Heath B10 .... 87 F4
Cannock WS12 .... 2 A8
Coventry CV2 .... 96 C2
Dudley DY1 .... 51 C4
Smethwick B67 .... 64 E6
Walsall WS3 .... 28 A8
Heather Valley WS12 .... 2 C6
Heather Rd
King's Heath B14 .... 104 F8
Birmingham, Lozells B19 ..... 66 C8
Coventry CV5 .... 112 C2
Halesowen B63 .... 82 E3
Redditch B97 .... 153 A1
Sutton Coldfield B74 .... 31 F3
Heathfield Sch B64 .... 62 F2
Heathfield Way B64 .... 62 F1
Heathfields Cty Inf Sch
B77 .... 35 F6
Heathgreen Cl B37 .... 70 D3
Heathland Ave B34 .... 69 A7
Heathland Cl WS12 .... 2 D2
Heathlands Cl DY6 .... 60 D8
Heathlands Cres B73 .... 45 F1
Heathlands Gr B31 .... 103 A1
Heathlands Jun & Inf Sch
B34 .... 68 F7
Heathlands Rd B73 .... 45 F1

Heathfield Cl Blackheath
B64 .... 62 F2
Knowle B93 .... 128 A5
Heathfield Cres DY11 .... 116 B4
Heathfield Ct **1** B19 .... 66 B7
Heathfield Dr WS3 .... 14 B2
Heathfield Gdns DY8 .... 80 F4
Heathfield Inf & Jun Sch
B19 .... 66 C8
Heathfield La WS10 .... 41 C6
Heathfield La W WS10 .... 41 B6

Heathlands The
2 Blackheath B65 63 C1
Stourbridge DY8 81 B4
Heathleigh Rd B38 123 C8
Heathley La B78 34 E5
Heathmere Ave B25 88 D8
Heathmere Dr B37 69 F2
Heathside Dr
Birmingham B38 104 B2
4 Walsall WS3 15 A4
Heathy Farm Cl B32 84 B1
Heathy Rise B32 84 A2
Heaton Cl WV10 11 E5
Heaton Dr Birmingham B15 85 E8
Sutton Coldfield B73 45 F8
Heaton Rd B91 107 A7
Heaton St B18 66 B5
Hebden B77 36 B8
Hebden Ave CV34 155 F1
Hebden Gr Birmingham B28 105 E3
Willenhall WV12 13 B1
Hebden Way CV11 74 A2
Heckley Rd CV7 96 A7
Heddle Gr CV6 114 B8
Heddon Pl B7 67 A3
Hedera Cl WS5 43 B3
Hedgefield Gr B63 82 C4
Hedgerow Cl WS12 1 F7
Hedgerow Dr DY6 49 D1
Hedgerow Wlk Coventry CV6 95 B4
Wolverhampton WV8 10 E1
Hedgerows The Lichfield WS14 9 B5
Nuneaton CV10 72 F6
Romsley B62 100 F4
Hedges Way B60 137 B1
Hedgetree Croft B37 70 C2
Hedging La B77 35 E5
Hedging Lane Ind Est B77 35 E5
Hedgings The B34 69 B6
Hedgley Gr B33 69 A4
Hedingham Gr B37 70 D2
Hedley Croft B35 58 B4
Hednesford Rd
Brownhills WS8 6 C2
Cannock, Blackfords WS11 1 F2
Cannock, Heath Hayes WS12 2 E1
Norton Canes WS11 5 F7
Hednesford St WS11 1 E1
Hednesford Sta WS12 2 B5
Heeley Rd B29 85 F1
Heemstede La CV32 157 A2
Heera Cl CV6 113 D8
Hele Rd CV3 133 D6
Helen St CV6 113 F6
Helena Cl CV10 72 F3
Helena St 3 B1 66 C3
Helenny Cl WV11 26 A5
Helford Cl DY4 51 D4
Heligan Pl WS12 2 D2
Hellaby Cl B72 46 C4
Hellaby Ct B73 57 A7
Hellidon Cl 5 CV32 157 A2
Hellier Ave DY4 52 B4
Hellier Rd WV10 11 E2
Hellier St DY2 62 C8
Helming Dr WV1 26 B3
Helmingham B79 20 D7
Helmsdale Rd CV32 157 B5
Helmsdale Way DY3 51 A7
Helmsley Cl DY5 81 C8
Helmsley Rd WV11 26 C8
Helmswood Dr B37 90 C8
Helston Cl Nuneaton CV11 74 A5
Stourbridge DY8 60 C2
Tamworth B79 21 C8
Walsall WS5 43 D7
Helston Rd WS5 43 D7
Helstone Gr B11 88 A3
Hembs Cres B43 54 C8
Hemdale CV11 74 A4
Heming Rd B98 159 E8
Hemingford Rd CV2 115 A8
Hemlingford Croft B37 90 A7
Hemlingford Rd
Birmingham B37 69 F6
Sutton Coldfield B76 58 A6
Hemlock Way WS11 2 B3
Hemming St DY11 116 C4
Hemmings Cl
Radford Semele CV31 162 E5
2 Stourbridge DY8 80 F5
Wolverhampton WV10 25 E3
Hemmings St WS10 41 C8
Hemplands Rd 9 DY8 80 F5
Hempole La DY4 52 D6
Hemsby Cl CV4 132 A7
Hemsworth Dr CV12 79 B2
Hemyock Rd B29 103 B8
Hen La CV6 95 D3
Henbury Rd B27 88 D3
Henderson Cl WS14 9 D7
Henderson Ct 7 B68 84 B8
Henderson Way B65 63 C1
Henderson Wlk DY4 52 B8
Hendon Cl Dudley DY3 50 D2
Wolverhampton WV10 25 E7
Hendon Rd B11 87 B5
Hendre Cl CV5 112 D2
Heneage Pl 10 B7 67 A4
Heneage St B7 67 A4
Heneage St W B7 66 F4
Henfield Cl WV11 26 D7
Hengham Rd B26 69 A1
Henley Cl Burntwood WS7 7 B5
Nuneaton CV11 73 F8
Sutton Coldfield B73 57 B8
Tamworth B79 21 C6
Tipton DY4 52 D5
Walsall WS3 14 E1
Henley Coll CV2 114 C8
Henley Cres B91 107 B7
Henley Ct Coventry CV2 114 D7
Lichfield WS14 9 B6
Henley Dr B75 32 A3
Henley Mill La CV2 114 C7
Henley Park Ind Est CV2 114 E7
Henley Rd Coventry CV2 114 D7
Royal Leamington Spa CV31 162 B5
Wolverhampton WV10 11 B1
Henley St B11 87 B7
Henleydale 4 B90 126 C8
Henlow Cl DY4 51 D5
Henlow Rd B14 105 A2
Henn Dr DY4 40 E1
Henn St DY4 52 A8
Hennalls The B36 68 F7
Hennals Ave B97 152 F2
Henne Dr WV14 40 C1
Henrietta St
Birmingham B19 164 B4
Coventry CV6 113 E5
Henry Bellairs CE Mid Sch CV12 78 D3
Henry Boteler Rd CV4 132 B7
Henry Boys' Almshouses WS1 42 D8
Henry Rd B25 88 C7
Henry St Coventry CV1 165 B3
Hinckley LE10 71 A2
Kenilworth CV8 148 A5
Nuneaton CV11 73 C2
Walsall WS2 28 D1
Henry Tanday Ct 4 CV32 156 E1
Henry Wlk B60 150 E7
Hensel Dr WV3 38 C8
Henshaw Gr B25 88 C7
Henshaw Rd B10 87 D8
Henson Rd CV12 77 E1
Henstead St B5 86 D8
Hentland Cl B98 154 D4
Henwood Cl WV6 24 D3
Henwood La B91 108 B4
Henwood Rd WV6 24 D3
Hepburn Cl WS9 30 A4
Hepburn Edge B24 57 B4
Hepworth Cl WV6 23 F4
Hepworth Rd CV3 115 B1
Herald Bsns Pk CV3 134 F7
Herald Ct 2 DY1 51 C1
Herald Way Coventry CV3 135 A7
Hinckley LE10 75 D4
Heralds Ct 4 CV34 161 B8
Herbert Art Gall & Mus CV1 165 C2
Herbert Rd Aldridge WS9 16 A1
Birmingham, Handsworth B21 54 F1
Birmingham, Small Heath B10 87 C8
Smethwick B67 65 A1
Solihull B91 107 B4
Herbert St Bilston WV14 40 B6
Nuneaton CV10 72 E3
Redditch B98 153 E4
West Bromwich B70 53 D3
Wolverhampton WV1 163 C4
Herbert's La CV8 148 A5
Herberts Park Rd WS10 41 B6
Herbhill Cl WV4 39 D4
Hercules Ho B35 58 B3
Hereford Ave 5 B12 87 A6
Hereford Cl Aldridge WS9 30 A8
Barwell LE9 71 F6
Birmingham B45 102 A2
Kidderminster DY11 116 A5
Hereford Ho WV1 163 B4
Hereford Pl B71 53 B7
Hereford Rd Bramcote CV11 79 F6
Cannock WS12 2 B4
Dudley DY2 62 E3
Oldbury B68 84 B7
Hereford Sq B8 67 C5
Hereford St WS2 28 E4
Hereford Way B78 21 A2
Hereford Wlk B37 69 F1
Hereward Coll of FE CV4 111 F1
Hereward Rise B62 83 C5
Herford Way LE10 75 F6
Heritage Cl B68 64 C4
Heritage Ct Coventry CV4 132 D3
Lichfield WS14 9 D6
Heritage The 6 WS1 28 E1
Hermes Cl CV34 161 E5
Hermes Cres CV2 114 E6
Hermes Ct B74 31 F3
Hermes Ho B35 58 A4
Hermes Rd WS13 3 D1
Hermit St DY3 50 D5
Hermit's Croft CV3 133 D8
Hermitage Dr B76 47 A4
Hermitage La B78 22 E1
Hermitage Rd
Birmingham, Edgbaston B15 85 C8
Birmingham, Gravelly Hill B23 56 E3
Coventry CV2 114 D4
Solihull B91 107 C6
Hermitage The B91 107 C5
Hermitage Way CV8 148 A3
Hern Rd DY5 81 C6
Hernall Croft B26 89 A7
Herne Cl B18 66 A4
Hernefield Rd B34 69 A7
Hernehurst B32 84 C6
Heron Cl Alvechurch B48 139 A7
Cheswick Green B90 126 D4
Heron Ct 3 B73 57 B7
Heron Ho CV3 114 B2
Heron Rd B68 64 A2
Heron Way B45 121 F7
Herondale WS12 2 B4
Herondale Cres DY8 80 C4
Herondale Rd
Birmingham B26 88 F6
Stourbridge DY8 80 C4
Heronfield Cl B98 154 C5
Heronfield Dr B31 122 F6
Heronfield Way B91 107 E5
Heronry The WV6 23 F2
Herons Way B29 85 C3
Heronsville Ho DY4 52 B3
Heronswood Dr DY5 61 D1
Heronswood Rd
Birmingham B45 122 B6
Kidderminster DY10 117 A2
Heronville Dr B70 53 A7
Heronville Rd B70 53 A6
Herrick Rd Birmingham B8 67 E5
Coventry CV2 114 D3
Herrick St WV3 163 A2
Herringshaw Croft B76 46 E3
Hertford Cl CV10 72 E4
Hertford Pl CV1 165 A2
Hertford St Birmingham B12 87 A5
Coventry CV1 165 B2
Hertford Way B93 128 B4
Hervey Gr B24 57 D6
Hesket Ave B68 64 C1
Hesketh Cres B23 56 C5
Hesketh Pl B37 89 F8
Hesleden B77 36 B8
Heslop Cl CV3 134 F8
Hessian Cl WV14 40 B2
Hestia Dr B29 103 E8
Heston Ave B42 55 B8
Hetton Cl 1 CV34 155 F1
Hever Ave B44 45 A1
Hever Cl DY1 50 E3
Hewell Ave B60 150 F7
Hewell Cl Birmingham B31 122 F7
Kingswinford DY6 49 D1
Redditch B97 152 C6
Hewell La Barnt Green B45 138 D8
Redditch B97 152 D6
Hewell Rd Barnt Green B45 138 D8
Redditch B97 153 D4
Hewitson Gdns B67 64 F2
Hewitt Ave CV6 113 B4
Hewitt Cl WS13 3 A2
Hewitt St WS10 41 C5
Hewston Croft WS12 2 D4
Hexby Cl CV2 115 A6
Hexham Way DY1 50 F2
Hexton Cl B90 105 D2
Hexworthy Ave CV3 133 B5
Heybarnes Rd B10 88 A8
Heybrook Cl CV2 114 C7
Heycott Gr B38 104 C2
Heycroft CV4 132 D4
Heydon Rd Brierley Hill DY5 61 B6
Finstall B60 137 D1
Heyford Gr B91 127 C8
Heyford Way B35 58 B5
Heygate Way WS9 16 B1
Heyland Cnr B10 67 F1
Heynesfield Rd B33 69 C3
Heythrop Gr B13 105 D8
Heyville Croft CV8 148 C3
Heywood Cl CV6 114 A7
Hibberd Ct CV8 147 F4
Hickman Ave WV1, WV2 40 A8
Hickman Gdns B16 65 F1
Hickman Rd Bilston WV14 40 C5
Birmingham B11 87 B6
Brierley Hill DY5 61 C4
Tipton DY4 51 F8
Hickman St DY9 81 C6
Hickman's Ave B64 62 E2
Hickmans Cl 2 B62 84 A6
Hickmerelands La DY3 39 C1
Hickory Ct WS11 2 C2
Hickory Dr B17 65 A2
Hicks Cl CV34 155 E2
Hidcote Ave B76 58 A8
Hidcote Cl Nuneaton CV11 78 F8
Royal Leamington Spa CV31 162 C5
Hidcote Gr
Birmingham, Garret's Green B33 89 C8
Birmingham, Marston Green B37 90 A7
Hidcote Rd CV8 148 C6
Hidson Rd B23 56 C5
Higgins Ave WV14 40 D2
Higgins La B32 84 C5
Higgins Wlk B66 65 B6
Higgs Field Cres B64 63 B1
Higgs Rd WV11 13 A1
High Arcal Dr DY3 50 F6
High Arcal Rd DY3 49 F4
High Arcal Sch DY3 50 F6
High Ash Cl CV7 95 F7
High Ave B64 82 F8
High Bank WS11 4 E8
High Beech CV5 112 A6
High Beeches B43 43 D1
High Brink Rd B46 70 F7
High Brow B17 85 B7
High Bullen WS10 41 F3
High Clere B64 83 A7
High Croft Aldridge WS9 16 B2
Birmingham B43 43 C1
High Elms La B60 151 E1
High Ercal Ave DY5 61 C2
High Farm Rd
Halesowen, Hasbury B63 82 F3
Halesowen, Hurst Green B62 83 F8
High Gn WS11 1 D1
High Grange WS11 2 A5
High Haden Cres B64 83 A8
High Haden Rd B64 83 A8
High Heath Cl B30 103 D5
High Hill WV11 13 A2
High Holborn DY3 50 D7
High House Dr B45 121 F3
High House La B60 152 A6
High Land Rd WS9 16 B3
High Leasowes B63 83 A4
High Mdws Stoke Heath B60 150 D7
Wolverhampton WV6 24 C3
Wombourne WV5 49 B6
High Meadow Fst Sch B46 70 F8
High Meadow Rd B38 104 A2
High Mount St WS12 2 B6
High Oak DY5 61 C7
High Park Cl Coventry CV5 111 F3
Sedgley DY3 50 D8
Smethwick B66 65 B5
High Park Cnr B7 67 B6
High Park Cres DY3 39 D1
High Park Rd B63 82 C5
High Park St B7 67 B6
High Point B15 85 E6
High Rd WV12 27 C5
High Ridge WS9 29 F5
High Ridge Cl Aldridge WS9 29 E5
Bilston WS10 41 A4
High St Aldridge WS9 30 B6
Astwood Bank B96 158 E1
Bedworth CV12 78 B2
Belbroughton DY9 119 E7
Bilston WV14 40 D5
Bilston, Moxley WS10 41 A4
Birmingham B4 164 C2
Birmingham, Aston B6, B19 66 E7
Birmingham, Erdington B23 56 F4
Birmingham, Harborne B17 85 D6
Birmingham, King's Heath B14 104 E8
Birmingham, Quinton B32 84 A6
Birmingham, Saltley B8 67 D5
Blackheath, Cradley Heath B64 62 D1
Blackheath, Rowley Regis B65 63 C1
Brierley Hill, Barrow Hill DY5 61 C7
Brierley Hill, Brockmoor DY5 61 C4
Brierley Hill, Quarry Bank DY5 82 A8
Bromsgrove B61 137 A2
Brownhills WS8 15 F7
Brownhills, Walsall Wood WS9 15 F3
Burntwood, Chase Terrace WS7 6 E8
Burntwood, Chasetown WS7 6 F6
Cheslyn Hay WS6 4 D2
Clayhanger WS8 15 E6
Coleshill B46 70 F7
Coventry CV1 165 C2
Coventry, Keresley CV6 94 F1
Cubbington CV32 157 E5
2 Darlaston WS10 41 D6
Dudley DY1 51 C1
9 Dudley, Old Dock DY2 62 B8
1 Halesowen B63 83 B3
Hampton in A B92 109 A7
Kenilworth CV8 147 E5
Kidderminster DY10 116 E6
Kingswinford DY6 60 E6
Kingswinford, Wall Heath DY6 60 C8
Knowle B93 128 C6
Norton Canes WS11 6 B5
Nuneaton CV11 73 B4
Royal Leamington Spa CV31 162 A7
Ryton-on-D CV8 135 B1
Sedgley DY3 50 D8
Smethwick B66 65 A5
Solihull B91 107 C3
Solihull,Shirley B90 105 D2
Stourbridge DY8 81 A5
Stourbridge, Amblecote DY8 80 F7
Stourbridge, Lye DY9 81 E5
Stourbridge, Wordsley DY8 60 E2
Studley B80 159 E4
Sutton Coldfield B72 46 C5
Tamworth B77 35 C4
Tipton, Princes End DY4 51 F8
Tipton, Tipton Green DY4 51 E5
Walsall WS1 28 E1
Walsall, Pelsall WS3 15 A4
Walsall, Wallington Heath WS3 14 B1
Warwick CV34 160 E6
Wednesfield WV11 26 D5
West Bromwich B70 53 C3
Wolverhampton WV6 24 D4
Wombourne WV5 49 B7
High St Duchess Par B70 53 D3
High St Princess Par B70 53 D3
High Street Bordesley B12 67 A1
High Street Deritend B12 66 F1
High Timbers B45 101 F1
High Town Ragged Sch B63 82 C6
High Trees B20 54 F3
High Trees Cl B98 158 E7
High Trees Ho B69 63 F3
High Trees Rd B93 128 A7
High View WV14 39 F1
High View Dr CV7 95 C7
High View Rd CV32 157 C5
High Wood Cl DY6 60 C6
Higham La CV11 73 E7
Higham Lane Sch CV10 73 D6
Higham Way Hinckley LE10 75 E7
Wolverhampton WV10 25 E6
Higham Way Ho LE10 75 E7
Higham's Cl B65 63 B3
Highbridge Rd Dudley DY2 62 B3
Sutton Coldfield B73 46 A1
Highbrook Cl WV9 11 A2
Highbury Ave
Birmingham B21 65 F8
Blackheath B65 63 D3
Highbury Cl B65 63 D3
Highbury Gn CV10 72 C7
Highbury Rd
Birmingham B14 104 D8
Oldbury B68 64 B5
Smethwick B66 64 D7
Sutton Coldfield B74 31 C3
Highclare Sch B72 46 C1
Highcliffe Rd B77 35 D8
Highcrest Cl B31 123 A7
Highcroft WS3 15 B6
Highcroft Ave DY8 60 C3
Highcroft Cl B92 89 C2
Highcroft Cres Lichfield WS14 9 C7
Royal Leamington Spa CV32 156 C1
Highcroft Dr B74 31 E3
Highcroft Hospl B23 56 E4
Highcroft Rd B23 56 E3
Highdown Cres 3 B90 127 A6
Highdown Rd CV31 162 B6
Highfield CV7 92 C1
Highfield Ave Bilston WV14 40 E4
Burntwood WS7 7 B7
Redditch B97 158 D8
Tamworth B77 22 A5
Walsall WS4 29 C8
Wolverhampton WV10 12 A2
Highfield Cl
Birmingham B28 105 D5
1 Burntwood WS7 7 B7
Kenilworth CV8 147 E4
Highfield Cres
Blackheath B65 63 B1
Halesowen B63 82 D6
Wolverhampton WV11 26 B6
Highfield Ct Cannock WS11 2 B5
Sutton Coldfield B73 46 B1
Highfield Dr B73 56 F7
Highfield Gdns WS14 9 E6
Highfield Inf & Jun Sch B8 67 E5
Highfield La Birmingham B32 84 B4
Clent DY9 100 A3
Corley CV7 94 D8
1 Halesowen B63 83 A3
Highfield Mews B63 82 D6
Highfield Pl B14 105 D5
Highfield Rd
Birmingham, Edgbaston B15 86 A8
Birmingham, Moseley B13 87 B3
Birmingham, Newton B43 54 C7
Birmingham, Saltley B8 67 E5
Birmingham, Yardley Wood B14, B28 105 D5
Blackheath B65 63 B1
Bromsgrove B61 150 E8
Burntwood WS7 7 C7
Cannock WS12 2 E1
Coventry CV2 113 F4
Dudley DY2 51 E1
Halesowen B63 82 D5
Kidderminster DY10 117 A8
Nuneaton CV11 73 E2
Redditch B97 158 D8
Sedgley DY3 39 D1
Smethwick B67 65 A5
Stourbridge DY8 61 A2
Studley B80 159 D4
Tipton DY4 52 B8
Walsall WS3 15 A4
Highfield Rd N WS3 14 F5
Highfield Terr CV32 156 D1
Highfield Way WS9 16 B2
Highfields Bromsgrove B61 136 E1
Burntwood WS7 7 B7
Highfields Ct WV4 38 D6
Highfields Dr Dudley WV14 40 D3
Wombourne WV5 49 A5
Highfields Grange WS6 4 D1
Highfields Jun & Inf Sch B65 83 C8
Highfields Pk WS6 4 D1
Highfields Prim Sch
Burntwood WS7 7 C7
Dudley WV14 40 C2
Highfields Rd Burntwood WS7 6 F4
Dudley WV14 40 D3
Hinckley LE10 71 E1
Highfields Sec Sch WV4 38 C5
Highfields The WV6 24 A2
Highgate Aldridge B74 31 A1
Dudley DY3 50 E5
Highgate Ave Walsall WS1 42 F8
Wolverhampton WV4 38 D6

Highgate Cl Birmingham
  B12 .... 86 F7
  Kidderminster DY11 .... 116 A4
  Walsall WS1 .... 42 F7
Highgate Ct 4 WS1 .... 42 F8
Highgate Dr WS1 .... 42 F7
Highgate Ho 1 B5 .... 86 E8
Highgate Middleway B12 ..... 86 F7
Highgate Pl B12 .... 87 A7
Highgate Prim Sch DY2 .... 61 F6
Highgate Rd Birmingham
  B12 .... 87 A6
  Dudley DY2 .... 61 F6
  Walsall WS1 .... 42 F7
Highgate Sq B12 .... 86 F7
Highgate St Birmingham
  B12 .... 86 F7
  Blackheath B64 .... 62 F2
Highgate Trad Est B11 .... 87 A7
Highgrove Coventry CV4 ... 131 F5
  Wolverhampton WV6 .... 24 C3
Highgrove Cl WV12 .... 27 B7
Highgrove Pl DY1 .... 50 F2
Highland Ho B62 .... 83 C8
Highland Mews WV14 .... 40 D1
Highland Rd
  Birmingham, Erdington B23 .. 56 F5
  Birmingham, Great Barr B43 ... 43 E3
  Blackheath B64 .... 62 E2
  Cannock WS12 .... 1 C4
  Coventry CV5 .... 112 F1
  Dudley DY1 .... 51 A3
  Kenilworth CV8 .... 148 C7
  Royal Leamington Spa CV32 . 157 B4
Highland Ridge B62 .... 83 E5
Highland Way B98 .... 159 A7
Highlands Cl
  Kidderminster DY11 .... 116 A5
  Warwick CV34 .... 161 A8
Highlands Ct B90 .... 126 E8
Highlands Rd Solihull B90 .. 126 F8
  Wolverhampton WV3 .... 38 D8
Highley Cl
  Kidderminster DY11 .... 116 B2
  Redditch B98 .... 154 E4
Highmoor Cl Dudley WV14 ... 40 D3
  Willenhall WV12 .... 27 B7
Highmoor Rd B65 .... 63 B3
Highmore Dr B32 .... 102 C8
Highpark Ave DY8 .... 80 D5
Highter's Heath Inf & Jun
  Sch B14 .... 105 B3
Highter's Heath La B14 ..... 105 A3
Highters Cl B14 .... 105 B2
Highters Rd B14 .... 105 A3
Hightown B63 .... 82 C6
Hightree Cl B32 .... 84 B1
Highview 9 WS1 .... 42 F8
Highview Dr DY6 .... 60 F4
Highview St DY2 .... 51 E1
Highwaymans Croft CV4 ... 132 D5
Highwood Ave B92 .... 89 A1
Highwood Croft B38 .... 103 D1
Hiker Gr 3 B37 .... 70 D2
Hilary Cres DY1 .... 51 B6
Hilary Dr Aldridge WS9 .... 30 A1
  Sutton Coldfield B76 .... 47 A3
  Wolverhampton WV3 .... 38 D7
Hilary Gr B31 .... 102 F4
Hilary Rd Coventry CV4 ..... 132 E6
  Nuneaton CV10 .... 72 F5
Hilden Rd B7 .... 67 B4
Hilderic Cres DY1 .... 61 F7
Hilderstone Rd B25 .... 88 C6
Hildicks Cres WS3 .... 28 F7
Hildicks Pl WS3 .... 29 A7
Hill Ave WV4 .... 39 F3
Hill Avenue Cty Prim Sch
  WV4 .... 39 F3
Hill Bank DY9 .... 81 F5
Hill Bank Dr B33 .... 68 D4
Hill Bank Rd
  Birmingham B38 .... 104 A2
  Halesowen B63 .... 82 D6
Hill Cl Birmingham B31 ..... 103 C1
  Royal Leamington Spa CV32 . 157 A3
  Sedgley DY3 .... 39 E1
Hill Crest Cubbington CV32 ... 157 E5
  Dudley DY3 .... 50 C4
Hill Crest Ave DY5 .... 61 C2
Hill Crest Dr WS13 .... 3 A1
Hill Crest Gr B44 .... 56 A7
Hill Crest Hospl B98 .... 159 C6
Hill Crest Rd Birmingham
  B13 .... 86 E2
  Dudley DY2 .... 51 E1
Hill Croft Rd B14 .... 104 C6
Hill Dr WS11 .... 2 A3
Hill Farm Ave CV11 .... 74 B1
Hill Farm Prim Sch CV6 ... 113 B7
Hill Fray Dr CV3 .... 134 A5
Hill Gr B20 .... 55 C2
Hill Grove Cres DY10 .... 117 A4
Hill Hook Ho B74 .... 31 E5
Hill Hook Rd B74 .... 31 F5
Hill House La B33 .... 68 F3
Hill La Alvechurch B47, B48 .. 124 D1
  Birmingham B43 .... 43 E2
  Bromsgrove B60 .... 136 F1
  Clent DY9 .... 99 E4
  Middleton B75 .... 33 B2
Hill Pas B64 .... 62 C2
Hill Pk WS9 .... 16 A4
Hill Pl WV11 .... 13 A1
Hill Rd Keresley CV7 .... 94 F6
  Stourbridge DY9 .... 81 E5
  Tipton B69 .... 52 A2
  Willenhall WV13 .... 26 E1

Hill Side Coventry CV2 ...... 114 A6
  Dudley DY3 .... 50 C4
Hill St Bedworth CV12 .... 78 B5
  Bilston WV14 .... 40 E3
  Birmingham B5 .... 164 B2
Brierley Hill,
  Quarry Bank DY5 .... 82 A8
  Brierley Hill, Silver End DY5 ... 61 D2
  Burntwood WS7 .... 6 E5
  Cannock WS12 .... 2 C3
  Cheslyn Hay WS6 .... 4 C2
  Coventry CV1 .... 165 B3
  Darlaston DY10 .... 41 E6
  Dudley, Netherton DY2 .... 62 C5
  Dudley, Upper Gornal DY3 ... 50 E5
  Essington WV11 .... 12 F3
  Halesowen B63 .... 83 A3
  Hinckley LE10 .... 75 E8
  Kidderminster DY11 .... 116 D6
  Norton Canes WS11 .... 5 F6
  Nuneaton CV10 .... 72 E6
  Royal Leamington Spa CV32 . 157 A1
  Smethwick B66 .... 65 A6
  Stourbridge, Amblecote DY8 ... 80 F8
  Stourbridge, Lye DY9 .... 81 F5
  Stourbridge, Wollaston DY8 ... 80 F4
  Tipton DY4 .... 51 F4
  Walsall WS1 .... 28 F1
  Warwick CV34 .... 161 B8
Hill The B32 .... 84 E2
Hill Top Coventry CV1 .... 165 C3
  Redditch B97 .... 152 F1
  West Bromwich B70 .... 53 A2
Hill Top Ave Halesowen B62 .. 83 E7
  Tamworth B79 .... 21 B8
Hill Top Cl B44 .... 55 E6
Hill Top Ind Est B70 .... 52 F8
Hill Top Rd Birmingham
  B31 .... 102 F3
  Oldbury B68 .... 64 C2
Hill Top Wlk WS9 .... 16 C1
Hill View WS9 .... 16 B2
Hill Village Rd B75 .... 32 A4
Hill West Jun & Inf Schs
  B74 .... 31 F4
Hill Wood WS3 .... 14 F2
Hill Wood Rd B75 .... 32 C5
Hill Wootton Rd CV35 ...... 156 C6
Hillaire Cl B38 .... 104 C2
Hillaries Rd B23 .... 56 D2
Hillary Ave WS10 .... 42 C3
Hillary Crest DY3 .... 50 E5
Hillary Inf & Jun Schs
  WS2 .... 42 C7
Hillary St WS2 .... 42 C7
Hillbank B69 .... 63 D8
Hillborough Rd B27 .... 88 D2
Hillbrook Gr B33 .... 68 F3
Hillbrow Cres B62 .... 83 F8
Hillbury Dr WV12 .... 27 B8
Hillcrest Ave Birmingham
  B43 .... 43 E2
  Halesowen B63 .... 82 B7
  Wolverhampton WV10 .... 11 E1
Hillcrest Cl Dudley DY2 .... 62 C5
  Tamworth B79 .... 21 B6
Hillcrest Ind Est B64 .... 82 D8
Hillcrest Rd Birmingham B43 . 43 E2
  Dordon B78 .... 36 F7
  Nuneaton CV10 .... 72 E5
  Romsley B62 .... 101 A4
  Sutton Coldfield B72 .... 46 C1
Hillcrest Rise WS7 .... 7 B4
Hillcrest Sch B32 .... 84 E3
Hillcrest Sch & Com Coll
  DY2 .... 62 C5
Hillcroft Ho B14 .... 104 F2
Hillcroft Rd DY6 .... 60 E7
Hillcross Wlk B36 .... 68 F8
Hilldene Rd DY6 .... 60 C4
Hilldrop Gr B17 .... 85 D3
Hilleys Croft B37 .... 69 F2
Hillfield Mews 3 B91 .... 127 B8
Hillfield Rd Birmingham B11 .. 87 D3
  Solihull B91 .... 107 B1
  Solihull B91 .... 107 C2
Hillfield Wlk B65 .... 62 F5
Hillfields B67 .... 64 D3
Hillfields Ho 1 CV1 .... 113 E3
Hillfields Rd DY5 .... 81 B7
Hillgrove Gdns DY10 .... 117 A4
Hillhurst Gr B36 .... 58 D1
Hilliard Cl CV12 .... 78 B4
Hilliards Croft B42 .... 55 A8
Hillingford Ave B43 .... 44 D3
Hillman B77 .... 21 E2
Hillman Dr DY2 .... 62 E7
Hillman Gr B36 .... 58 F1
Hillman Ho CV1 .... 165 B3
Hillmeads Dr DY2 .... 62 F7
Hillmeads Rd B38 .... 104 A1
Hillmorton B74 .... 31 F3
Hillmorton Cl B98 .... 154 E6
Hillmorton Rd Coventry CV2 . 96 C1
  Knowle B93 .... 128 A5
  Sutton Coldfield B74 .... 31 F4
Hillmount Cl B28 .... 87 E2
Hillrise LE10 .... 75 F8
Hillsborough Ho B27 .... 88 E2
Hillside Brownhills WS8 ...... 16 A4
  Lichfield WS14 .... 9 D6
  Nuneaton CV10 .... 72 A8
  Redditch B98 .... 153 D2
Hillside Ave Blackheath B65 .. 83 B8
  Brierley Hill DY5 .... 82 B8
  Halesowen B63 .... 82 D6

Hillside Cl Birmingham B32 . 102 A8
  Brownhills WS8 .... 16 A6
  Cannock WS12 .... 2 A7
  Kidderminster DY11 .... 116 A7
Hillside Cres WS3 .... 14 F2
Hillside Croft B92 .... 89 E4
Hillside Ct B43 .... 43 E2
Hillside Dr
  Birmingham, Great Barr B42 .. 55 A6
  Birmingham, Kingshurst B37 ... 69 F4
  Kidderminster DY11 .... 116 A7
  Lickey End B61 .... 137 B6
  Nuneaton CV10 .... 72 C7
  Sutton Coldfield B74 .... 44 F7
Hillside Gdns
  Birmingham B37 .... 69 F4
  Wolverhampton WV1 .... 26 A3
Hillside N CV2 .... 114 A6
Hillside Rd
  Birmingham,
    Gravelly Hill B23 .... 56 D2
  Birmingham, Great Barr B43 .. 43 D2
  Dudley DY1 .... 51 A5
  Hinckley LE10 .... 75 D6
  Sutton Coldfield B74 .... 32 A4
Hillstone Gdns WV10 .... 25 F8
Hillstone Jun & Inf Sch
  B34 .... 69 D5
Hillstone Rd B34 .... 69 D5
Hilltop DY9 .... 81 F3
Hilltop Cl CV8 .... 145 E8
Hilltop Ct 8 DY3 .... 50 E3
Hilltop Dr B36 .... 68 D7
Hilltop Rd DY2 .... 62 E8
Hillview Halesowen B63 ...... 82 E6
  Lickey End B60 .... 137 C6
Hillview Rd Birmingham
  B45 .... 121 E8
  Lickey End B60 .... 137 C6
Hillville Gdns DY8 .... 81 B3
Hillwood Ave B90 .... 127 A6
Hillwood Cl DY6 .... 60 C4
Hillwood Common Rd
  B75 .... 32 B6
Hillwood Rd
  Birmingham B31 .... 102 E7
  Halesowen B62 .... 83 C7
Hilly Rd WV14 .... 40 E2
Hillyfields Rd B23 .... 56 C4
Hilmore Way B77 .... 35 E8
Hilsea CV WV8 .... 10 F1
Hilston Ave Halesowen B63 .. 82 F4
  Wolverhampton WV4 .... 38 C4
Hilton Ave Birmingham B28 . 105 F4
  Nuneaton CV10 .... 72 B6
Hilton Cl Stourbridge DY8 .. 81 A7
  Walsall WS3 .... 14 A2
Hilton Cross WV10 .... 12 B5
Hilton Cross Bsns Pk
  WV10 .... 12 B5
Hilton Ct Coventry CV5 ..... 112 F2
  Sutton Coldfield B72 .... 57 C8
Hilton Dr B72 .... 57 C8
Hilton La Essington WV11 ... 12 E8
  Great Wyrley WS6 .... 5 A2
Hilton Main Ind Est WV10 ... 12 C5
Hilton Pl WV14 .... 40 F5
Hilton Rd Featherstone
  WV10 .... 12 C7
  Tipton B69 .... 63 C8
  Willenhall WV12 .... 13 C1
  Wolverhampton WV4 .... 39 A8
Hilton St West Bromwich B70 . 53 A3
  Wolverhampton WV10 .... 163 D4
Himbleton Cl B98 .... 153 F1
Himbleton Croft 1 B90 ... 127 A6
Himley Ave DY1 .... 50 F2
  Willenhall WV12 .... 27 B5
Himley Cl Birmingham B43 .. 43 C2
  Willenhall WV12 .... 27 B5
Himley Cres WV4 .... 39 B5
Himley Ct 10 DY3 .... 50 E3
Himley Gdns DY3 .... 49 F4
Himley Gr B45 .... 122 B6
Himley La DY3 .... 49 A2
Himley Rd Bedworth CV12 ... 77 D2
  Dudley DY1, DY3 .... 50 D2
Himley Rise B90 .... 126 E4
Himley St DY1 .... 51 A1
Hinbrook Rd DY1 .... 50 E1
Hinchliffe Ave WV14 .... 40 B2
Hinckes Rd WV6 .... 24 B5
Hinckley Bsns Pk LE10 ...... 74 F8
Hinckley CE Jun & Inf Sch
  LE10 .... 75 D8
Hinckley Coll LE10 .... 71 F1
Hinckley Ct 3 B68 .... 84 B7
Hinckley & District Hospl
  LE10 .... 75 D8
Hinckley & North
  Warwickshire Coll LE10 ... 71 E1
Hinckley Rd Ansty CV2, CV7 .. 97 C2
  Aston Flamville LE10 .... 76 D7
  Aston Flamville LE10 .... 76 D8
  Barwell LE9 .... 71 E5
  Burton Hastings CV11 .... 75 A1
  Burton Hastings LE10 .... 75 D1
  Burton Hastings LE10 .... 75 E1
  Coventry CV2 .... 115 A8
  Hinckley LE10 .... 76 A6
  Nuneaton CV11 .... 73 E1
Hinckley St B5 .... 164 C2
Hinckley Sta LE10 .... 75 D7
Hincks St WV2 .... 40 A4
Hind Cl CV34 .... 155 F2
Hindhead Rd B14 .... 105 C4
Hindlip Cl B63 .... 82 F2
Hindlow Cl B7 .... 67 B4
Hindon Gr B27 .... 106 C7

Hindon Sq B15 .... 85 F8
Hindon Wlk B32 .... 84 C2
Hingeston St B18 .... 66 B4
Hingley Croft WS9 .... 30 F3
Hingley Rd DY9 .... 82 A6
Hingley St B64 .... 62 D1
Hinsford Cl DY5 .... 60 E8
Hinstock Cl WV4 .... 39 A4
Hinstock Rd B20 .... 54 F1
Hintlesham Ave B15 .... 85 D5
Hinton Ave B48 .... 139 A6
Hinton Fields B61 .... 136 E7
Hinton Gr WV11 .... 26 F5
Hintons Coppice B93 .... 127 E6
Hints Cl B78 .... 19 D2
Hints La Birmingham B78 ..... 20 B5
  Weeford B78 .... 19 F4
Hints Rd Hopwas B78 .... 20 B6
  Mile Oak B78 .... 20 C3
Hipkins St DY4 .... 51 E7
Hiplands Rd B62 .... 83 F4
Hipsley Cl B36 .... 58 C1
Hipsmoor Cl B37 .... 69 F3
Hipswell Highway CV2 ...... 114 D3
Hiron Croft CV3 .... 133 C8
Hiron The CV3 .... 133 C8
Hiron Way CV34 .... 160 B7
Histons Hill WV8 .... 10 A3
Hitchcock Cl B67 .... 64 D5
Hitches La B15 .... 86 B7
Hitchman Ct CV31 .... 162 A5
Hitchman Mews CV31 .... 162 A5
Hitchman Rd CV31 .... 162 A5
Hither Green La B98 .... 153 F7
Hive Ind Ctr The B18 .... 66 A6
Hoarestone Ave CV11 .... 79 A7
Hoarstone DY8 .... 98 F5
Hob Green Prim Sch DY9 .. 81 E2
Hob Green Rd DY9 .... 81 E2
Hob La Balsall Common
  CV7 .... 130 E4
  Burton Green CV8 .... 131 A3
  Knowle B92 .... 129 A8
Hob Lane CE Fst Sch CV12 . 78 D3
Hob Moor Rd B10, B25 .... 88 C8
Hob's Mdw B92 .... 89 B2
Hob's Moat Rd B92 .... 89 B3
Hob's Rd WS13 .... 3 E1
Hobacre Cl B45 .... 122 A8
Hobart Croft 1 B7 .... 67 A4
Hobart Dr WS5 .... 43 C6
Hobart Rd Cannock WS12 ...... 2 E2
  Tipton DY4 .... 40 E1
Hobbis Ho B38 .... 123 C7
Hobble End La WS6 .... 14 B7
Hobgate Rd WV10 .... 25 F4
Hobgate Rd WV10 .... 25 F4
Hobley St WV13 .... 27 C2
Hobmoor Croft B25 .... 88 D7
Hobmoor Prim Sch B25 .... 88 D8
Hobnock Rd WV11 .... 13 B5
Hobs Hole La WS9 .... 30 D7
Hobs Rd WS10 .... 42 A4
Hobson Cl B29 .... 86 B1
Hobson Rd B29 .... 86 B1
Hockett St CV3 .... 133 D8
Hocking Rd CV2 .... 114 E4
Hockley Brook Cl B18 .... 66 A5
Hockley Brook La B92 ...... 119 F3
Hockley Brook Trad Est
  B18 .... 66 A6
Hockley Cir B18 .... 66 B6
Hockley Cl B19 .... 66 D6
Hockley Cl B94 .... 143 C7
Hockley Ctr 1 B18 .... 66 C4
Hockley Heat Prim Sch
  B94 .... 143 C6
Hockley Hill B18 .... 66 C4
Hockley La Coventry CV5 ... 111 C5
  Dudley DY2 .... 62 C4
Hockley Pool Cl B18 .... 66 B5
Hockley Rd Birmingham B23 . 56 D4
  Dudley WV14 .... 51 A7
  Tamworth B77 .... 35 F6
Hockley St B19 .... 66 C4
Hodge Hill Ave DY9 .... 81 F3
Hodge Hill Girls Sch B36 ... 68 C7
Hodge Hill Rd B34 .... 68 E6
Hodge Hill Sch B36 .... 68 C7
Hodge La B77 .... 22 B6
Hodgehill Ct B36 .... 68 D7
Hodgetts La Berkswell
  CV7 .... 130 F7
  Coventry CV7 .... 131 A6
Hodgetts Cl B67 .... 64 D3
Hodgkins Cl WS8 .... 16 A6
Hodgson Tower B19 .... 66 D6
Hodnell Cl B36 .... 58 C1
Hodnet Cl Bilston WV14 ...... 40 B5
  Kenilworth CV8 .... 148 B5
Hodnet Dr DY5 .... 61 C6
Hodnet Gr B5 .... 86 E8
Hodnet Pl WS11 .... 2 B2
Hodson Ave WV13 .... 27 C1
Hodson Cl WV11 .... 26 F8
Hodson Ho 6 B15 .... 86 E8
Hoff Beck Ct 6 B9 .... 67 B2
Hogarth Cl Bedworth CV12 .. 78 A4
  Birmingham B43 .... 44 D5
Hogarth Dr LE10 .... 71 A3
Hogg's La B31 .... 102 E4
Holbeach Rd B33 .... 69 B2
Holbeache La DY6 .... 49 D1
Holbeache Rd DY6 .... 60 C8

Holbeche Rd Knowle B93 ... 128 A7
  Sutton Coldfield B75 .... 47 B5
Holbein Cl CV12 .... 78 A4
Holberg Gr WV11 .... 26 F5
Holborn Ave CV6 .... 95 C2
Holborn Hill B6, B7 .... 67 C7
Holbrook La CV6 .... 95 C2
Holbrook Park Est CV6 ..... 113 D8
Holbrook Prim Sch CV6 .... 95 E1
Holbrook Tower B36 .... 68 D8
Holbrook Way CV6 .... 95 D1
Holbury Cl WV9 .... 11 A2
Holcombe Rd B11 .... 88 A3
Holcroft Rd Halesowen B63 . 82 C5
  Kingswinford DY6 .... 49 C1
  Stourbridge DY9 .... 81 C4
Holcroft St Tipton DY4 .... 52 A2
  Wolverhampton WV2 .... 40 A7
Holden Cl B23 .... 56 E2
Holden Cres WS3 .... 28 F5
Holden Croft DY4 .... 52 A3
Holden Pl WS3 .... 28 E5
Holden Rd Wednesbury
  WS10 .... 42 A2
  Wolverhampton WV4 .... 38 D3
Holder Dr WS11 .... 1 B2
Holder Rd
  Birmingham,
    South Yardley B25 .... 88 C7
  Birmingham, Sparkbrook B11 . 87 C6
Holders Gdns B13 .... 86 C2
Holders La B13 .... 86 C2
Holdford Rd B6 .... 55 F2
Holdgate Rd B29 .... 103 C5
Hole Farm Rd B31 .... 103 C5
Hole Farm Way B38 .... 123 F7
Hole House La B94 .... 143 F1
Hole La B31 .... 103 C5
Holford Ave WS2 .... 42 C6
Holford Dr B42, B6 .... 55 F4
Holford Way B6 .... 55 F3
Holifast Rd B72 .... 57 C7
Holioak Dr CV34 .... 161 B6
Holland Ave Knowle B93 .... 128 B8
  Oldbury B68 .... 64 D4
Holland Ho B19 .... 66 D5
Holland House Inf Sch
  B72 .... 46 C4
Holland Ind Pk WS10 .... 41 D8
Holland Rd Bilston WV14 .... 40 E7
  Birmingham B43 .... 54 D7
  Coventry CV6 .... 113 A6
  Sutton Coldfield B72 .... 46 C4
Holland Rd W 6 B6 .... 66 F6
Holland St Birmingham B3 . 164 A3
  1 Dudley DY2 .... 62 B8
  Sutton Coldfield B72 .... 46 C4
  Tipton DY4 .... 52 C7
Holland's Way WS3 .... 14 F4
Hollands Pl WS3 .... 14 D1
Hollands Rd WS3 .... 14 D1
Hollaway Ct B63 .... 82 D5
Hollemeadow Ave WS3 ...... 28 D7
Holliars Gr B37 .... 69 C3
Hollicombe Terr CV2 .... 114 D8
Holliday Rd
  Birmingham, Erdington B24 .... 57 A4
  Birmingham,
    Handsworth B21 .... 65 F7
Holliday St Birmingham B1 ... 66 C1
  Birmingham B1 .... 164 A2
Hollie Lucas Rd B13 .... 104 F7
Hollier's Wlk LE10 .... 71 D1
Holliers Walk Cty Prim Sch
  LE10 .... 71 D1
Hollies Ave WS11 .... 1 F1
Hollies Croft B5 .... 86 C5
Hollies Dr Halesowen B62 ... 83 E6
  Wednesbury WS10 .... 41 F3
Hollies Inf Sch The CV10 ... 72 E6
Hollies La WV6 .... 23 A4
Hollies Rd B69 .... 63 B8
Hollies St DY5 .... 61 D7
Hollies The
  Birmingham, Aston B6 .... 67 B8
  Birmingham,
    Winson Green B16 .... 65 F3
  Smethwick B66 .... 65 C4
  Wolverhampton WV2 .... 163 B1
  Wolverhampton,
    New Cross WV11 .... 26 B5
Hollin Brow Cl B93 .... 128 B3
Hollings Gr B91 .... 127 B8
Hollington Cres B33 .... 69 A4
Hollington Rd WV1 .... 26 B1
Hollington Way B90 .... 127 C7
Hollinwell Cl Nuneaton
  CV11 .... 79 C8
  Walsall WS3 .... 14 A3
Hollis La CV8 .... 147 E8
Hollis Ct DY3 .... 50 C3
Hollis Rd CV3 .... 114 A2
Hollister Dr B32 .... 84 F3
Hollow Cres CV6 .... 113 B5
Hollow Croft B31 .... 103 B3
Hollow Croft Rd WV12 .... 27 B7
Holloway Birmingham B31 . 102 C5
  Tamworth B79 .... 21 A4
Holloway Bank
  Wednesbury WS10 .... 41 F1
  West Bromwich B70 .... 53 A8
Holloway Circus
  Queensway B1 .... 164 B1

Holloway Dr B98 .... 154 B4
Holloway Field CV6 .... 113 A6
Holloway Head B1 .... 164 B1
Holloway La B98 .... 153 F3
Holloway Pk B98 .... 154 A3
Holloway St Dudley DY3 ...... 50 D4
Wolverhampton WV1 .... 40 A7
Holloway St W DY3 .... 50 D4
Holloway The
Alvechurch B48 .... 139 D3
Bluntington DY10 .... 118 E2
Seisdon WV5 .... 37 A3
Stourbridge DY8 .... 80 F7
Warwick CV34 .... 160 D6
Wolverhampton WV6 .... 24 C2
Hollowmeadow Ho B36 ...... 68 D8
Hollows The CV11 .... 73 F1
Hollowtree La B60 .... 138 A3
Holly Ave
Birmingham,
Balsall Heath B12 .... 87 A5
Birmingham, Selly Oak B29 ..... 86 B1
Holly Bank CV5 .... 133 A8
Holly Bush Gr B32 .... 84 D7
Holly Cl Hinckley LE10 .... 75 E5
Tamworth B79 .... 21 B7
Willenhall WV12 .... 27 C6
Holly Ct B24 .... 57 A5
Holly Dell B38 .... 104 B2
Holly Dr Birmingham B27 ...... 88 B2
Hollywood B47 .... 125 B7
Holly Farm Bsns Pk CV8 .... 146 B7
Holly Gr
Birmingham, Bournville B30 . 103 F8
Birmingham, Lozells B19 ...... 66 B8
◢ Birmingham,
Selly Oak B29 .... 85 F2
Bromsgrove B61 .... 136 F3
Coventry CV4 .... 112 B2
◢ Stourbridge DY8 .... 80 F5
Wolverhampton WV3 .... 38 F7
Holly Grange B66 .... 64 D7
Holly Grove La WS7 .... 6 E8
Holly Hall Rd DY2 .... 62 A7
Holly Hall Sch DY1 .... 61 F8
Holly Hill Birmingham B45 ... 101 F1
Great Wyrley WS6 .... 13 E8
Holly Hill Meth & CE Inf
Sch B45 .... 101 F2
Holly Hill Rd
Birmingham B45 .... 102 A2
Shenstone WS14 .... 17 F5
Holly La Aldridge WS9 .... 30 F8
Balsall Common CV7 .... 130 B3
Birmingham, Erdington B24 ... 57 C4
Birmingham,
Marston Green B37 .... 89 F8
Brownhills WS9 .... 16 B4
Great Wyrley WS6 .... 13 F8
Huntington WS12 .... 1 C7
Portway B48 .... 140 F5
Smethwick B66 .... 64 E6
Sutton Coldfield B75 .... 32 B3
Wishaw B76 .... 47 D4
Holly Lodge High Sch B67 ... 64 D7
Holly Lodge Wlk B37 .... 69 F2
Holly Park Dr B24 .... 57 C4
Holly Park Ind Est B24 .... 57 C2
Holly Pl B29 .... 86 B2
Holly Rd
Birmingham, Edgbaston B16 ... 65 D1
Birmingham,
Handsworth B20 .... 66 A8
Birmingham,
King's Norton B30 .... 104 A4
Blackheath B65 .... 63 B1
Bromsgrove B61 .... 136 F4
Dudley DY1 .... 51 A3
Oldbury B68 .... 84 C8
Wednesbury WS10 .... 41 F5
West Bromwich B71 .... 53 E8
Holly St Cannock WS11 .... 1 F6
Dudley DY1 .... 61 E6
Royal Leamington Spa CV32 . 157 B1
Smethwick B67 .... 64 F5
Holly Stitches Rd CV10 .... 72 E6
Holly Wlk Baginton CV8 .... 133 E2
Nuneaton CV11 .... 73 F2
Royal Leamington Spa
CV32 .... 157 A1
Holly Wood B43 .... 44 A1
Hollybank Ave WV11 .... 13 A3
Hollybank Cl WS3 .... 14 A1
Hollybank Gr B63 .... 82 D1
Hollybank Rd B13 .... 105 A6
Hollyberry Ave B91 .... 127 A8
Hollyberry Croft B34 .... 69 C6
Hollybrow B29 .... 103 B7
Hollybush La Coventry CV6 ... 96 A4
Stourbridge DY8 .... 80 F7
Wolverhampton WV4 .... 38 D4
Hollybush Wlk B64 .... 62 D1
Hollycot Gdns B12 .... 86 F6
Hollycroft LE10 .... 71 C1
Hollycroft Cres LE10 .... 71 C1
Hollycroft Rd B21 .... 54 D1
Hollydale Rd Birmingham
B24 .... 57 C3
Blackheath B65 .... 63 D2
Hollyfast La CV7 .... 94 C4
Hollyfast Prim Sch CV6 .... 112 E2
Hollyfast Rd CV6 .... 112 E1
Hollyfaste Rd B33 .... 69 B1
Hollyfield Ave B91 .... 106 E3
Hollyfield Cres B75 .... 46 E4

Hollyfield Dr
Barnt Green B45 .... 122 A1
Sutton Coldfield B75 .... 46 E5
Hollyfield Rd B75 .... 46 E5
Hollyfield Rd S B76 .... 46 F4
Hollyhedge Cl
Birmingham B31 .... 102 D6
Walsall WS2 .... 28 C2
Hollyhedge La WS2 .... 28 C2
Hollyhedge Prim Sch
B71 .... 53 E8
Hollyhedge Rd B71 .... 53 E7
Hollyhill La WS14 .... 17 E5
Hollyhock Rd
Birmingham B27 .... 88 A2
Dudley DY2 .... 51 F1
Hollyhurst Dr DY8 .... 60 E3
Hollyhurst Gr B26 .... 88 E6
Hollyhurst Rd B73 .... 45 B3
Hollymoor Way B31 .... 102 B1
Hollymount B62 .... 84 A7
Hollyoak Gr B91 .... 107 A1
Hollyoak St B71 .... 53 D4
Hollyoake Cl B68 .... 64 A2
Hollypiece Ho B27 .... 88 A2
Hollywell Rd Birmingham
B26 .... 89 B6
Knowle B93 .... 128 A1
Hollywell St WV14 .... 40 A1
Hollywood By-Pass
Birmingham B47 .... 104 F1
Hollywood B47 .... 124 E6
Hollywood Croft B42 .... 54 F8
Hollywood Inf & Jun Sch
B14 .... 105 A1
Hollywood La B47 .... 125 B7
Holm View WS14 .... 17 F6
Holman Cl WV13 .... 26 E2
Holman Rd WV13 .... 26 E2
Holman St DY11 .... 116 C5
Holman Way WV13 .... 73 D3
Holmcroft Coventry CV2 ... 114 F8
Wolverhampton WV4 .... 39 F4
Holmcroft Rd DY10 .... 117 A5
Holme Mill WV10 .... 11 D4
Holme Way WS4 .... 29 B7
Holmes Cl B43 .... 54 E7
Holmes Ct CV8 .... 147 F5
Holmes Dr Birmingham
B45 .... 121 F6
Coventry CV5 .... 111 D5
Holmes La B60 .... 151 B1
Holmes Rd Whitnash CV31 ... 162 B3
Willenhall WV12 .... 27 D6
Holmes The WV10 .... 11 D3
Holmesfield Rd B42 .... 55 C7
Holmewood Cl CV8 .... 148 B5
Holmewood Ct CV8 .... 148 B5
Holmfield Rd CV2 .... 114 B3
Holmsdale Rd CV6 .... 113 E7
Holmwood Ave DY11 .... 116 A6
Holmwood Dr B97 .... 153 C3
Holmwood Ho B97 .... 153 C3
Holmwood Rd ◢ B10 .... 67 D1
Holroyd Ho CV4 .... 111 F2
Holston Cl WS12 .... 2 F1
Holsworth Cl B77 .... 21 D1
Holsworthy Cl CV11 .... 73 E5
Holt Cres WS11 .... 2 B2
Holt Ct B7 .... 66 F4
Holt Gdns B80 .... 159 E2
Holt Hill B98 .... 154 F8
Holt Ho B61 .... 137 A3
Holt La B62 .... 100 D4
Holt Rd Halesowen B62 ...... 63 E1
Hinckley LE10 .... 75 E6
Studley B80 .... 159 E2
Holt St B7 .... 164 D4
Holt The CV32 .... 157 B3
Holte Dr B75 .... 32 C2
Holte Rd
Birmingham, Aston B6 .... 56 A1
Birmingham, Sparkhill B11 ... 87 D5
Holte Sch B19 .... 66 D7
Holtes Wlk B6 .... 67 B8
Holton Ct WV13 .... 27 C2
Holtshill La WS1 .... 28 F2
Holwick B77 .... 36 B8
Holy Child Sch B15 .... 86 B6
Holy Cross Ct CV2 .... 114 E4
Holy Cross Gn DY9 .... 99 E2
Holy Cross La DY9 .... 119 E8
Holy Cross RC Jun & Inf
Sch B76 .... 47 A3
Holy Family RC Jun &
Inf Sch B10 .... 87 F7
Holy Family RC Prim Sch
CV6 .... 95 B3
Holy Name RC Prim Sch
B43 .... 43 E1
Holy Rosary RC Prim Sch
WV1 .... 26 A1
Holy Souls RC Prim Sch
B27 .... 88 C3
Holy Trinity CE Inf Sch
WS8 .... 15 E6
Holy Trinity CE Prim Sch
Birmingham B20 .... 55 C2
West Bromwich B70 .... 53 D1
Holy Trinity RC Prim Sch
WV14 .... 40 E6
Holy Trinity RC Sec Sch
B10 .... 87 C8
Holy Well Cl B16 .... 66 A2
Holyhead L Ctr B21 .... 65 D8
Holyhead Prim Sch WS10 ... 41 E3

Holyhead Rd Birmingham
B21 .... 65 D8
Codsall WV8 .... 23 E8
Coventry CV5 .... 112 C5
Darlaston WS10 .... 41 C4
Wednesbury WS10 .... 41 E3
Holyhead Road Ind Est
WS10 .... 41 D3
Holyhead Sch B21 .... 65 D8
Holyhead Way B21 .... 65 D8
Holyoak Cl Bedworth CV12 ... 77 F1
◢ Birmingham B6 .... 55 F1
Holyoak Croft B31 .... 123 B8
Holyoakes Field Fst Sch
B97 .... 153 D4
Holyoakes La B97 .... 152 C5
Holyrood Ct CV10 .... 72 D5
Holyrood Gr ◢ B6 .... 66 E8
Holywell Cl CV4 .... 111 D1
Holywell La B45 .... 121 D6
Holywell Rise WS14 .... 9 D6
Home Farm CV35 .... 155 F6
Home Farm Cres CV31 ..... 162 B4
Home Meadow Dr B13 ..... 105 A5
Home Meadow Ho B27 ...... 88 A2
Home Meadow La B98 ..... 154 E6
Home Park Rd CV11 .... 73 C3
Homecroft Rd B26 .... 88 E8
Homedene Rd B31 .... 102 E7
Homefield Rd WV8 .... 10 C3
Homelands B42 .... 55 B7
Homelea Rd B25 .... 88 D8
Homelodge Ho ◢ WS13 ..... 9 B7
Homemead Gr B45 .... 121 F7
Homer Hill Rd B63 .... 82 C7
Homer Rd Solihull B91 ..... 107 B3
Sutton Coldfield B75 .... 32 D2
Homer St B12 .... 86 F5
Homers Fold WV14 .... 40 D5
Homerton Rd B44 .... 45 B1
Homestead Cl DY3 .... 50 E5
Homestead Dr B75 .... 32 C3
Homestead Rd B33 .... 69 B1
Homeward Way CV3 .... 115 A1
Homewood Cl B76 .... 46 E3
Honesty Cl WS8 .... 15 D6
Honeswode Cl B20 .... 66 A8
Honeyborne Rd B75 .... 46 D7
Honeybourne B77 .... 21 D2
Honeybourne Cl
Coventry CV5 .... 112 B3
◢ Halesowen B63 .... 83 A3
Honeybourne Rd
Birmingham B33 .... 89 C8
Halesowen B63 .... 83 C3
Honeybourne Sch B28 ..... 105 F8
Honeybourne Way WV13 ... 27 C2
Honeyfield Rd CV1 .... 113 D5
Honeysuckle Ave DY6 .... 60 E7
Honeysuckle Cl B32 .... 84 B5
Honeysuckle Dr
Coventry CV2 .... 96 B2
Featherstone WV10 .... 12 C7
Walsall WS3 .... 43 A3
Honeysuckle Gr ◢ B27 ...... 88 C5
Honeytree Cl DY6 .... 60 F3
Honiley Ct CV2 .... 96 D1
Honiley Dr B73 .... 45 C2
Honiley Rd Birmingham B33 ... 69 A2
Honiley CV8 .... 146 B6
Meer End CV8 .... 130 A1
Honiley Way CV2 .... 96 D1
Honister Cl DY5 .... 61 F1
Honiton Cl B31 .... 102 E4
Honiton Cres B31 .... 102 E4
Honiton Rd CV2 .... 114 C5
Honiton Way WS9 .... 29 F5
Honiton Wlk ◢ B66 .... 65 B5
Honor Ave WV4 .... 39 C5
Hoo Farm Ind Est DY10 ... 116 F1
Hoo Rd DY10 .... 116 E4
Hoobrook Ent Ctr DY10 ... 116 E2
Hoobrook Ind Est DY10 ... 116 E2
Hoobrook Trad Est DY10 ... 116 E3
Hood Gr B30 .... 103 D4
Hood St CV1 .... 113 E3
Hook Dr B74 .... 31 F4
Hook La WS14 .... 17 C3
Hooper St B18 .... 65 F4
Hoopers La B96 .... 158 E1
Hoosen Cl B62 .... 84 A6
Hope Cl CV7 .... 95 A7
Hope Pl ◢ B29 .... 85 F2
Hope Rd DY4 .... 52 C6
Hope St Birmingham B5 ...... 86 E8
Coventry CV1 .... 113 B2
Dudley DY2 .... 62 C8
Halesowen B62 .... 83 D8
Stourbridge DY8 .... 60 D3
Walsall WS1 .... 42 E8
West Bromwich B70 .... 53 E2
Hope Terr DY2 .... 62 C5
Hopedale Cl CV2 .... 114 E3
Hopedale Rd B32 .... 84 C5
Hopgardens Ave B60 .... 137 B2
Hopkins Ct ◢ WS10 .... 42 A3
Hopkins Dr B71 .... 53 E7
Hopkins Rd CV6 .... 113 A4
Hopkins St DY4 .... 52 A2
Hopleys Cl B77 .... 21 E4
Hopstone Gdns WV4 .... 38 F4
Hopstone Rd B29 .... 85 A1
Hopton Cl Coventry CV3 ... 112 A4
Perton WV6 .... 23 F3
Tipton DY4 .... 41 C2
Hopton Cres WV11 .... 26 E6
Hopton Crofts CV32 .... 156 C2
Hopton Dr DY10 .... 116 E1

Hopton Gr B13 .... 105 C5
Hopton Mdw WS12 .... 2 C1
Hopwas Gr B37 .... 69 F5
Hopwas Hill B78 .... 20 A6
Hopwood Cl B63 .... 83 A2
Hopwood Gr B31 .... 122 E6
Hopyard Cl DY3 .... 50 B3
Hopyard La Dudley DY3 ..... 50 B2
Redditch B98 .... 159 C8
Hopyard Rd WS2 .... 27 E2
Horace Partridge Rd
WS10 .... 41 A5
Horace St WV14 .... 51 A8
Horatio Dr B13 .... 86 F4
Hordern Cl WV6 .... 24 F5
Hordern Cres DY5 .... 81 D8
Hordern Gr WV6 .... 24 F5
Hordern Rd WV6 .... 24 F5
Hornbeam B77 .... 22 A4
Hornbeam Cl B29 .... 103 B7
Hornbeam Dr CV4 .... 111 D1
Hornbeam Gr CV31 .... 162 C6
Hornbeam Wlk WV3 .... 25 A1
Hornbrook Gr B92 .... 106 C7
Hornby Gr B14 .... 105 C4
Hornby Rd WV4 .... 39 C5
Hornchurch Cl CV1 .... 165 B1
Horndean Cl CV6 .... 113 E8
Horne Way B34 .... 69 E5
Horning Dr WV14 .... 40 C3
Horninghold Cl CV3 .... 134 E8
Hornsey Cl CV2 .... 114 F7
Hornsey Gr B44 .... 45 A2
Hornsey Rd B44 .... 45 A2
Hornton Cl B74 .... 31 D5
Horrell Rd Birmingham
B26 .... 89 B7
Solihull B90 .... 105 F2
Horse Fair Birmingham B1 ... 164 B1
Kidderminster DY10 .... 116 E7
Horse Shoe Rd CV6 .... 96 A4
Horse Shoes La B26 .... 89 B5
Horsecroft Dr B71 .... 54 A8
Horsefair The ◢ LE10 .... 75 D8
Horsehills Dr WV3 .... 24 E2
Horselea Croft B8 .... 68 C4
Horselea Fields WV1 .... 163 D3
Horseley Heath DY4 .... 52 C5
Horseley Rd DY4 .... 52 C5
Horsepool LE10 .... 76 A5
Horseshoe Cl ◢ WS2 .... 42 B7
Horseshoe The B68 .... 64 C2
Horseshoe Wlk ◢ DY4 .... 51 E5
Horsfall Rd B75 .... 47 A5
Horsford Rd CV3 .... 133 E6
Horsham Ave DY8 .... 60 C3
Horsley La Lichfield WS14 .... 8 D1
Shenstone WS14 .... 17 D8
Horsley Rd B43 .... 44 D4
Horticultural Training
Sch B14 .... 104 D8
Horticultural Unit
Wulfrun Coll WV3 .... 24 D2
Horton Cl Darlaston WS10 ... 41 D7
Sedgley DY3 .... 50 C8
Horton Gr B90 .... 127 A5
Horton Pl WS10 .... 41 D7
Horton Sq B12 .... 86 E7
Horton St Darlaston WS10 ... 41 D7
Tipton DY4 .... 52 D5
West Bromwich B70 .... 53 C2
Hosiery St CV12 .... 78 C2
Hospital La Bedworth CV12 ... 77 B1
Cheslyn Hay WS6 .... 4 B2
Dudley WV14 .... 51 B7
Hospital Rd Birmingham
B15 .... 85 E4
Burntwood WS7 .... 7 B5
Hospital St Birmingham B19 ... 66 D6
Birmingham B19 .... 164 B4
Tamworth B79 .... 21 B5
Walsall WS2 .... 28 D4
Wolverhampton WV2 .... 163 C2
Hossil La Belbroughton
DY9 .... 119 C8
Clent DY9 .... 99 D1
Hotchkiss Way CV3 .... 135 A7
Hothersall Dr B73 .... 56 F8
Hothorpe Cl CV3 .... 114 F1
Hotspur Rd B44 .... 44 F1
Hough Pl WS2 .... 42 B7
Hough Rd Birmingham B14 ... 104 D6
Walsall WS2 .... 42 A7
Houghton Ct B28 .... 105 D4
Houghton St Oldbury B69 ... 63 F6
West Bromwich B70 .... 64 D8
Houlbrooke Ho ◢ WS13 ...... 9 C8
Houldey Rd B31 .... 103 B1
Houldsworth Cres CV6 ...... 95 C4
Houliston Cl WS10 .... 42 B5
Houndsfield Cl B47 .... 125 D6
Houndsfield Farm B47 ..... 125 B5
Houndsfield Gr B47 .... 125 A5
Houndsfield La B47 .... 125 C6
Houseman Pk B60 .... 137 A2
Housman Cl B60 .... 150 E8
Housman Ct B60 .... 137 A3
Housman Wlk DY10 .... 117 C6
Houting B77 .... 35 D5
Houx The DY8 .... 80 E8
Hove Ave CV5 .... 111 E4
Hove Rd B27 .... 88 C1
Hovelands Cl CV2 .... 114 C8
Howard Ave B61 .... 136 E3
Howard Cl CV5 .... 111 E4
Howard Cres WS12 .... 2 C7
Howard Ct B16 .... 65 E1

Howard Rd Bilston WV14 ...... 40 F3
Birmingham,
Handsworth B20 .... 55 B2
Birmingham,
King's Heath B14 .... 104 E1
Birmingham, Newton B43 ... 54 C8
Birmingham,
South Yardley B25 .... 88 C7
Nuneaton CV10 .... 73 A3
Redditch B98 .... 159 C8
Solihull B92 .... 88 E3
Wednesbury WS11 .... 26 F8
Howard Rd E B13 .... 104 F7
Howard St Birmingham B19 . 164 B4
Coventry CV1 .... 165 C4
Tipton DY4 .... 52 B5
West Bromwich B70 .... 52 F7
Wolverhampton WV2 .... 163 C1
Howard Wlk CV31 .... 161 D7
Howarth Way B6 .... 67 A7
Howat Rd CV7 .... 94 F7
Howcotte Gn CV4 .... 131 E8
Howden Pl B33 .... 69 A5
Howdle's La WS8 .... 6 F2
Howe Cres WV12 .... 27 C6
Howe St B4 .... 66 F3
Howell Rd WV2 .... 39 E7
Howells Cl CV12 .... 77 D1
Howes Cl WS1 .... 42 F6
Howes Croft B35 .... 58 A2
Howes La CV3 .... 133 D3
Howes Prim Sch CV3 .... 133 E5
Howford Gr B7 .... 67 B4
Howl Pl DY4 .... 51 F5
Howland Cl WV9 .... 10 F2
Howlette Rd CV1 .... 111 E2
Howley Ave B44 .... 44 E1
Howley Grange Prim Sch
B62 .... 83 F5
Howley Grange Rd B62 ...... 84 A4
Hoylake B77 .... 22 B4
Hoylake Cl Nuneaton CV11 ... 74 B1
Walsall WS3 .... 14 B4
Hoylake Dr B69 .... 63 A7
Hoylake Rd WV6 .... 23 D5
Hoyland Way B30 .... 103 E8
HRS Bsns Pk B33 .... 69 C1
Huband Cl B98 .... 154 A5
Hubert Croft B29 .... 85 F2
Hubert Rd B29 .... 85 F2
Hubert St B6 .... 66 F5
Hucker Cl WS2 .... 42 A7
Hucker Rd WS2 .... 42 A7
Huddisdon Cl ◢ CV34 ...... 155 F1
Huddlestone Cl WV10 .... 12 B6
Huddocks View WS3 .... 14 F5
Hudson Ave B46 .... 70 F6
Hudson Cl WS11 .... 2 B2
Hudson Dr WS7 .... 7 C6
Hudson Gr WV6 .... 23 E5
Hudson Rd Birmingham B20 . 55 A4
Tipton DY4 .... 52 C4
Hudson's Dr B30 .... 104 A4
Hudswell Dr DY5 .... 81 D8
Hugh Gaitskill Ct WV14 .... 40 C8
Hugh Rd Birmingham B10 ... 67 E1
Coventry CV3 .... 114 A2
Smethwick B67 .... 64 E5
Hugh Villas B10 .... 67 E1
Hughes Ave WV3 .... 38 F8
Hughes Cl Warwick CV34 ... 155 D2
Whitnash CV31 .... 162 A3
Hughes Pl WV14 .... 40 D7
Hughes Rd Bilston WV14 ... 40 D7
Wednesbury WS10 .... 41 A5
Huins Cl B98 .... 154 A4
Hulbert Dr DY2 .... 62 B6
Hulland Pl DY5 .... 61 C3
Hullbrook Rd B13 .... 105 C6
Hulme Cl CV3 .... 115 B1
Humber Ave Coventry CV1 ... 113 F1
Coventry CV3 .... 113 F2
Sutton Coldfield B76 .... 58 A7
Humber Gr B36 .... 58 F1
Humber Ho DY1 .... 61 D8
Humber Rd Coventry CV3 ... 134 A8
Wolverhampton WV3 .... 25 A1
Humber Tower ◢ B7 .... 67 A4
Humberstone Rd
◢ Coventry CV6 .... 113 A5
Sutton Coldfield B24 .... 57 E4
Hume St Kidderminster
DY11 .... 116 C5
Smethwick B66 .... 65 B4
Humpage Rd B9 .... 67 E2
Humphrey Ave B60 .... 150 F7
Humphrey Burton's Rd
CV3 .... 133 C8
Humphrey Middlemore Dr
B17 .... 85 D4
Humphrey St DY3 .... 50 D3
Humphrey-Davy Rd CV12 ... 95 D8
Humphreys Rd WV10 .... 25 D6
Humphries Cres WV14 ...... 40 F2
Humphries Dr DY10 .... 116 F2
Humphries Ho WS8 .... 15 F7
Humphris St CV34 .... 161 B8
Hundred Acre Rd B74 .... 44 F7
Hungary Cl DY9 .... 81 C5
Hungary Hill DY9 .... 81 C5
Hungerfield Rd B36 .... 58 C1
Hungerford Rd DY8 .... 80 E2
Hungry La B95 .... 18 F5
Hunningham Gr ◢ B91 ..... 127 B8
Hunnington Cl B32 .... 84 A1
Hunnington Cres B63 .... 83 B2
Hunscote Cl B90 .... 105 F1
Hunscote Ho B90 .... 105 F1

Hunslet Rd Birmingham B32 .. **84** F4
Burntwood WS7 .... **7** B8
Hunstanton Ave B17 .... **84** F8
Hunstanton CI DY5 .... **81** C7
Hunt End La B97 .... **158** C5
Hunt Paddocks CV8 .... **147** E1
Hunt Terr CV4 .... **132** B7
Hunt's La WV12 .... **27** D6
Hunter Ave WS7 .... **7** D6
Hunter CI WS14 .... **9** D6
Hunter Cres WS3 .... **28** F7
Hunter Ct B5 .... **86** D5
Hunter Rd WS11 .... **4** E8
Hunter St W6 .... **25** A4
Hunter Terr CV4 .... **132** D8
Hunter's Ride DY7 .... **60** B2
Hunters CI Bilston WV14 ...... **41** A7
Coventry CV3 .... **115** A2
Hunters Hill Sch B60 .... **137** F6
Hunters Rd B19 .... **66** B7
Hunters Rise B63 .... **82** D1
Hunters Vale B19 .... **66** C6
Hunters Wlk B23 .... **56** C8
Huntingdon CI Redditch
B98 .... **154** F2
Tamworth B78 .... **20** F2
Huntingdon Gdns B63 .... **82** C7
Huntingdon Rd
Coventry CV5 .... **133** A8
West Bromwich B71 .... **53** B7
Huntington Way CV10 .... **72** E3
Huntington Ho B23 .... **56** B6
Huntington Ind Est WS12 ...... **1** B6
Huntington Prim Sch WS12 .. **1** C8
Huntington Rd WV12 .... **27** D8
Huntington Terrace Rd
WS11 .... **1** F4
Huntingtree Prim Sch B63 .. **82** E3
Huntingtree Rd B63 .... **82** E3
Huntlands Rd B63 .... **82** F2
Huntley Dr B91 .... **107** B2
Huntly Rd B16 .... **66** A1
Hunton Ct **2** B23 .... **56** E2
Hunton Hill B23 .... **56** E2
Hunton Rd B23 .... **56** E3
Hunts Mill Dr DY5 .... **50** C1
Hunts Rd B30 .... **104** B7
Huntsmans Gate WS7 .... **7** B8
Huntsmans Rise WS12 .... **1** C8
Hurcott Ct **2** B23 .... **56** E2
Hurcott La DY10 .... **117** A8
Hurcott Rd DY10 .... **117** B8
Hurdis Rd B90 .... **106** A2
Hurdlow Ave B18 .... **66** B5
Hurlbutt Rd CV34 .... **161** C4
Hurley CI
Royal Leamington Spa CV32 **157** A2
Sutton Coldfield B72 .... **46** C2
Walsall WS5 .... **43** D6
Hurley Gr B37 .... **69** F5
Hurleys Fold DY2 .... **62** C5
Hurlingham Rd B44 .... **45** A1
Hurn Way CV6 .... **96** B4
Huron CI WS11 .... **2** B2
Hursey Dr DY4 .... **52** A6
Hurst Bsns Pk DY6 .... **61** A6
Hurst CI B36 .... **69** E7
Hurst Ct **5** B72 .... **81** F5
Hurst Green Prim Sch B62 .. **83** E8
Hurst Green Rd
Bentley Heath B93 .... **127** F4
Halesowen B62 .... **83** F8
Minworth B76 .... **58** D6
Hurst Hill Ct WV14 .... **51** A8
Hurst Hill Prim Sch WV14 .. **51** A8
Hurst La Birmingham B34 .... **69** E6
Brierley Hill DY5 .... **61** F3
Tipton DY4 .... **51** D6
Hurst La N B36 .... **69** E7
Hurst Rd Bedworth CV12 .... **78** B3
Coventry CV6 .... **96** A0
Dudley WV14 .... **40** A1
Hinckley LE10 .... **75** D8
Smethwick B67 .... **64** D2
Hurst St B5 .... **164** C1
Hurst The Birmingham B13 .. **105** D7
Hollywood B47 .... **125** A6
Hurstbourne Cres WV1 .... **26** B1
Hurstcroft Rd B33 .... **69** B3
Hurstway The B23 .... **56** C8
Hurstwood Rd B23 .... **56** C8
Huskisson Ct WV10 .... **25** C6
Hussey Rd Brownhills WS8 .. **15** E8
Norton Canes WS11 .... **5** F5
Husum Way DY10 .... **117** C7
Hut Hill La WS6 .... **5** A4
Hutton Ave B8 .... **67** D5
Hutton Rd
Birmingham,
Handsworth B20 .... **55** C1
Birmingham, Saltley B8 .... **67** D5
Huxbey Dr B92 .... **107** F8
Huxley CI WV9 .... **11** A3
Hyacinth Way LE10 .... **75** D5
Hyatt Sq DY5 .... **81** C7
Hyatts Wlk B65 .... **62** F5
Hyde CI B60 .... **137** B2
Hyde PI CV32 .... **161** E8
Hyde Rd Coventry CV2 .... **114** E4
Kenilworth CV8 .... **148** A5
Wednesfield WV11 .... **26** C6
Hyde The DY9 .... **81** D2
Hydes La LE10 .... **74** E4
Hydes Rd Wednesbury
WS10 .... **42** B2
West Bromwich B71 .... **42** C1
Hydesville Tower Sch WS1 .. **29** A2
Hyett Way WV14 .... **41** B2

Hylda Rd B20 .... **55** B1
Hylstone Cres WV11 .... **26** D6
Hylton St B18 .... **66** C5
Hyperion Dr WV4 .... **39** A3
Hyperion Rd Birmingham
B36 .... **57** F1
Stourbridge DY7 .... **80** C7
Hyron Hall Rd B27 .... **88** C2
Hyssop CI Birmingham B7 .... **67** A5
Cannock WS11 .... **2** B3
Hytall Rd B90 .... **105** C2
Hythe Gr B25 .... **88** D8

I-Max Bsns Pk B11 .... **88** A6
Ibberton Rd B14 .... **105** B3
Ibex CI CV3 .... **114** F1
Ibis CI DY1 .... **117** B3
Ibis Gdns DY6 .... **61** A6
Ibstock CI B98 .... **154** E4
Ibstock Dr DY8 .... **81** A4
Ibstock Ho B98 .... **154** E4
Ibstock Rd CV6 .... **96** A5
Icknield CI B74 .... **31** A1
Icknield Fst Sch B98 .... **154** D1
Icknield Port Rd B16 .... **65** F3
Icknield Sq B16 .... **66** A3
Icknield St Alvechurch B38 .. **124** B2
Beoley B98 .... **140** C2
Birmingham B18 .... **66** B4
Redditch, Church Hill B98 .... **154** C7
Redditch, Ipsley B98 .... **154** D2
Rowney Green B48 .... **140** B6
Icknield Street Dr B98 .... **159** D7
Ida Rd Walsall WS2 .... **28** C1
West Bromwich B70 .... **53** D1
Idbury Rd B44 .... **56** A7
Ideal Bldgs **7** DY11 .... **116** D6
Iden Rd CV1 .... **113** E4
Idmiston Croft B14 .... **104** F2
Idonia Rd WV6 .... **23** F5
Ilam Pk CV8 .... **148** C5
Ilex CI CV34 .... **161** A7
Ilford CI CV12 .... **78** A3
Ilford Ct CV3 .... **135** D7
Ilford Dr CV3 .... **133** B5
Ilford Rd B23 .... **56** D6
Ilfracombe Gr CV3 .... **133** A5
Iliffe Ho LE10 .... **75** B7
Iliffe Way B17 .... **85** D4
Ilkley Gr B37 .... **69** F2
Illey La Birmingham B32 ...... **102** A7
Halesowen B62 .... **101** E8
Illeybrook Sq B32 .... **84** D2
Illshaw WV9 .... **11** A3
Illshaw Heath Rd B94 .... **126** D2
Ilmington CI Coventry CV3 .. **133** B5
Redditch B98 .... **154** D1
Ilmington Dr B73 .... **45** C3
Ilmington Rd B29 .... **84** F1
Ilminster CI LE10 .... **76** B7
Ilsham Gr B31 .... **122** E6
Ilsley Rd B23 .... **56** E4
Imber Rd DY10 .... **117** A1
Imex Auto Ctr DY4 .... **52** A3
Imex Bsns Pk
Birmingham,
Bordesley Green B9 .... **67** D2
Birmingham, Stechford B33 .. **68** E4
Tipton DY4 .... **52** A3
Wolverhampton WV2 .... **39** C7
Imex Ho WV2 .... **39** B7
Imperial Ave DY10 .... **116** F8
Imperial Gr DY10 .... **116** F8
Imperial Rd B9 .... **67** E1
Imperial Rise B46 .... **59** E2
Impney CI B98 .... **154** E6
Impsley CI B36 .... **69** B8
Inca CI CV3 .... **134** F8
Ince Rd WS10 .... **41** C7
Incestre Dr B43 .... **43** D1
Inchbrook Rd CV8 .... **148** C7
Inchcape Ave B20 .... **55** A3
Inchford Ave CV34 .... **155** E2
Inchford CI CV11 .... **73** F1
Inchford Rd B92 .... **107** E7
Inchlaggan Rd WV10 .... **25** F6
Ingatestone Dr DY8 .... **60** C3
Inge St B5 .... **164** C1
Ingestre CI Cannock WS11 .... **2** B1
Walsall WS3 .... **13** F3
Ingestre Gr B43 .... **43** C1
Ingestre Ho WV6 .... **24** E5
Ingestre Rd Birmingham
B28 .... **106** A7
Wolverhampton WV10 .... **11** C1
Ingham Way B17 .... **85** A8
Ingle Ct CV31 .... **161** E7
Ingleby Gdns WV6 .... **25** A5
Ingledew CI WS3 .... **27** D3
Inglefield Rd B33 .... **68** F3
Inglemere Gr B29 .... **102** F7
Inglenook Dr B20 .... **55** B2
Ingleside Villas **3** B11 .... **87** C5
Ingleton CI CV11 .... **74** A3
Ingleton Ho **2** B15 .... **86** D8
Ingleton Rd B8 .... **68** A7
Inglewood Ave WV3 .... **38** F8
Inglewood CI
Kingswinford DY6 .... **60** D5
Royal Leamington Spa
CV32 .... **157** A3
Inglewood Gr B74 .... **30** F1
Inglewood Rd B11 .... **87** C5
Ingoldsby Rd B31 .... **103** C3
Ingot CI WS2 .... **28** B6
Ingram Gr B27 .... **88** A2
Ingram Pit La B77 .... **22** A5
Ingram PI WS3 .... **14** D1

Ingram Rd Coventry CV5 .... **132** D8
Walsall WS3 .... **14** D1
Inhedge St DY3 .... **50** E5
Inhedge The B1 .... **51** C1
Inkberrow Rd B63 .... **82** F2
Inkerman Gr WV10 .... **25** F2
Inkerman Ho B19 .... **66** E6
Inkerman St Birmingham B7 .. **67** B4
Wolverhampton WV10 .... **25** F3
Inland Rd B24 .... **57** B2
Innage CI CV31 .... **162** B8
Innage Rd B31 .... **103** B4
Innage The B47 .... **125** A5
Innis Rd CV5 .... **132** E8
Innisfree House Sch B47 .. **125** C4
Innsworth Dr B35 .... **58** A4
Insetton CI B98 .... **154** D4
Inshaw CI B33 .... **68** E3
Instone Rd Coventry CV6 .... **95** A1
Halesowen B63 .... **83** A3
Instow CI WV12 .... **27** B8
Insull Ave B14 .... **105** B1
Intended St B63 .... **82** C7
International Dr B26 .... **90** C4
International Ho B43 .... **54** F6
Intersection Ho B70 .... **53** E1
Intown WS1 .... **28** F2
Intown Row WS1 .... **28** F2
Inverary CI CV8 .... **148** C4
Inverclyde Rd B20 .... **55** A3
Inverness CI CV5 .... **112** A4
Inverness Ho WV1 .... **163** B4
Inverness Rd B31 .... **102** F3
Invicta Rd CV3 .... **134** F8
Inworth WV9 .... **11** B3
Ipsley Church La B98 .... **154** C1
Ipsley Fst Sch B98 .... **158** F8
Ipsley Gr B23 .... **56** A5
Ipsley La B98 .... **154** D2
Ipsley St B98 .... **153** E3
Ipstones Ave B33 .... **68** F4
Ipswich Cres B42 .... **55** B7
Ipswich Wlk B37 .... **70** B2
Ireland Green Rd B70 .... **53** B2
Ireton CI CV4 .... **111** C1
Ireton Rd Birmingham B20 .. **55** A4
Wolverhampton WV10 .... **11** E3
Iris CI Birmingham B29 ...... **103** B8
Dudley DY2 .... **51** F1
Hinckley LE10 .... **75** E5
Tamworth B79 .... **21** C6
Iris Dr B14 .... **104** D3
Irnham Rd B74 .... **32** B1
Iron Bridge Wlk DY9 .... **99** B8
Iron La B33 .... **68** D4
Ironmonger Row CV1 .... **165** B3
Ironstone Rd WS7 .... **6** E8
Irvan Ave B70 .... **52** F5
Irvine CI WS3 .... **28** B7
Irvine Rd WS3 .... **28** B7
Irving CI DY3 .... **50** A4
Irving Rd Coventry CV1 ...... **113** E4
Solihull B92 .... **89** E3
Tipton DY4 .... **41** A1
Irving St B1 .... **66** D1
Irwell B77 .... **21** E2
Irwin Ave B45 .... **122** C7
Isaac Walton PI B70 .... **52** E7
Isbourne Way **1** B9 .... **67** B2
Isis CI B73 .... **46** B5
Isis Gr Birmingham B36 ...... **69** F8
Willenhall WV13 .... **27** C2
Isis Ho DY1 .... **61** D8
Island CI LE10 .... **71** E2
Island Dr DY10 .... **116** E4
Island Rd B21 .... **54** C1
Island The B78 .... **20** C1
Islington B63 .... **83** A4
Islington Cres CV9 .... **36** C1
Islington Row B15 .... **66** B1
Islington Row Middleway
B15 .... **86** C8
Ismere Rd B24 .... **57** B2
Itchen Gr WV6 .... **23** E4
Ithon Gr B38 .... **123** E8
Ivanhoe Ave CV11 .... **73** F1
Ivanhoe Rd Birmingham B43 .. **44** C3
Lichfield WS14 .... **9** B6
Wolverhampton WV2 .... **40** A6
Ivanhoe St DY2 .... **62** A7
Ivatt B77 .... **21** F2
Ivatt CI WS4 .... **29** B7
Iverley CI DY10 .... **98** C6
Iverley Rd B63 .... **83** C4
Iverley Wlk DY9 .... **81** C2
Ivor Rd Birmingham B11 ...... **87** B4
Coventry CV6 .... **95** D2
Redditch B97 .... **153** D2
Ivy Ave Birmingham B12 ...... **87** A5
3 Birmingham B12 .... **87** B5
Ivy CI WS11 .... **4** D8
Ivy Croft WV9 .... **10** F3
Ivy Farm La CV4 .... **132** D6
Ivy Gr **6** B18 .... **65** E4
Ivy House Rd B69 .... **63** D6
Ivy La Birmingham B9 .... **67** A2
Romsley B62 .... **100** D5
Ivy Lodge CI B37 .... **90** A7
Ivy Rd
Birmingham,
Handsworth B21 .... **66** A7
Birmingham, Stirchley B30 .. **104** A6
Dudley DY1 .... **51** A4
Sutton Coldfield B73 .... **45** F1
Tipton DY4 .... **51** F7
Ivybridge Gr B42 .... **55** C3
Ivybridge Rd CV3 .... **133** D6
Ivydale Ave B26 .... **89** C5

Ivyfield Rd B23 .... **56** B5
Ivyhouse La WV14 .... **51** B8
Ivyhouse Rd B38 .... **123** C8
Ivyhouse Wlk B77 .... **35** F6
Izod St B97 .... **153** D4
Izons Ind Est B70 .... **53** A1
Izons La B70 .... **53** A1
Izons Rd B70 .... **53** C3

Jacey Rd Birmingham B16 .... **65** D2
Solihull B90 .... **106** B4
Jack David Ho DY4 .... **52** D5
Jack Holden Ave WV14 .... **40** A2
Jack Newell Ct **3** WS14 .... **51** C8
Jack O'Watton Bsns Pk
B46 .... **59** D3
Jackdaw CI DY3 .... **39** C2
Jackdaw Dr B36 .... **70** A8
Jacker's Rd CV2 .... **96** B4
Jacklin Dr CV3 .... **133** C4
Jacknell Rd LE10 .... **74** D8
Jackson Ave B8 .... **67** F4
Jackson CI Birmingham B11 .. **87** B7
Featherstone WV10 .... **12** A6
Keresley CV7 .... **95** A7
Norton Canes WS11 .... **5** E4
Oldbury B68 .... **64** B5
Tipton DY4 .... **41** B1
Jackson Ct Brierley Hill DY5 .. **61** F1
Jackson Dr B67 .... **63** F4
Jackson Ho **9** B69 .... **64** A7
Jackson Rd Birmingham B8 .. **67** F4
Coventry CV6 .... **95** D1
Wolverhampton WS13 .... **3** B3
Jackson St Oldbury B68 ...... **64** B4
Stourbridge DY9 .... **81** E6
Wolverhampton WV6 .... **25** B4
Jackson Way B32 .... **84** A5
Jackson Wlk B35 .... **58** A2
Jackwood Gn CV12 .... **95** C8
Jacmar Cres B67 .... **64** E6
Jacob's Hall La WS6 .... **5** B1
Jacobean La B93 .... **108** B1
Jacoby PI B5 .... **86** C5
Jacox Cres CV8 .... **148** C5
Jacquard CI CV3 .... **133** D4
Jacquard Ho **3** CV1 .... **113** E4
Jade CI CV1 .... **165** D4
Jade Gr WS11 .... **2** C2
Jaffray Cres B24 .... **56** F3
Jaffray Ct B23 .... **56** E3
Jaffray Rd B24 .... **56** F3
Jaffrey Jun Sch Annexe
B24 .... **56** E3
Jaffrey Sch B23 .... **56** E3
Jaguar B77 .... **21** E2
Jakeman CI B98 .... **154** E4
Jakeman Rd B12 .... **86** E5
James Bridge CI WS2 .... **42** B7
James CI Darlaston WS10 .... **41** F7
Smethwick B67 .... **65** A5
James Clift Ho **8** B69 ...... **63** D5
James Ct
Birmingham,
King's Norton B38 .... **103** F2
12 Birmingham,
Moseley B13 .... **87** B2
3 Warwick CV34 .... **160** F7
James Dawson Dr CV5 ...... **111** B8
James Dee CI DY5 .... **62** A1
James Diskin Ct CV11 .... **73** E2
James Eaton CI B71 .... **53** C5
James Galloway CI CV3 .... **134** E7
James Green Rd CV4 .... **111** E1
James Greenway WS13 .... **3** A2
James Ho Birmingham B19 .. **66** C6
Coventry CV2 .... **114** C8
James Memorial Homes
4 B7 .... **67** C7
James Rd
Birmingham, Great Barr B43 .. **54** E7
Birmingham, Tyseley B11 .... **87** F6
Coleshill B46 .... **70** F8
Kidderminster DY10 .... **117** A8
James Scott Rd B63 .... **82** A6
James St Bilston WV14 .... **40** E6
Birmingham B3 .... **164** A3
Cannock WS11 .... **1** F5
Nuneaton CV11 .... **73** A5
Willenhall WS11 .... **27** A3
James Turner St B18 .... **65** E6
James Watt Dr B19 .... **66** C8
James Watt Ho B66 .... **65** B6
James Watt Jun & Inf Sch
B21 .... **65** E7
James Watt Queensway
B4 .... **164** C3
James Watt St
Birmingham B4 .... **164** C3
West Bromwich B71 .... **53** B8
Jamescroft CV3 .... **134** E6
Jameson Rd B6 .... **67** C8
Jameson St WV6 .... **25** B4
Jane Lane CI WS2 .... **27** F4
Jane Lane Sch The WS2 ...... **27** F3
Janice Gr B14 .... **105** B4
Janine Ave WV11 .... **26** E7
Jaques CI B46 .... **59** B2
Jardine Cres CV4 .... **111** F2
Jardine Rd B6 .... **55** F1
Jarvis CI LE10 .... **71** D4
Jarvis Cres B69 .... **64** A4
Jarvis Rd B23 .... **56** F6
Jarvis Way B24 .... **67** E8
JAS Ind Pk B65 .... **63** E4
Jasmin Croft B14 .... **104** E3
Jasmine CI WV9 .... **11** A3

Jasmine Gr Bromsgrove B61 **136** F4
Codsall WV8 .... **10** B3
Coventry CV3 .... **134** C8
Royal Leamington Spa CV32 **157** A2
Jasmine Rd Dudley DY2 ...... **51** F5
Tamworth B77 .... **22** A4
Jasmine Way WS10 .... **41** D7
Jason CI B77 .... **21** D5
Jason Rd DY9 .... **81** F4
Javelin Ho B35 .... **58** C3
Jay Park Cres DY10 .... **117** B2
Jayne Ct DY6 .... **60** D8
Jayne Ct Wednesfield WV11 .. **26** D7
West Bromwich B71 .... **42** E1
Jays Ave DY4 .... **52** B4
Jays Cres B43 .... **123** B1
Jayshaw Ave B43 .... **54** E8
Jeal CI B47 .... **124** E2
Jean Dr DY4 .... **52** D6
Jeavons PI WV14 .... **40** C5
Jedburgh Ave WV6 .... **23** E4
Jedburgh Gr CV3 .... **133** A4
Jeddo St WV2 .... **163** B1
Jeffcock Rd WV3 .... **39** A7
Jefferies CI LE10 .... **71** E2
Jefferson CI B71 .... **53** B8
Jeffrey Ave WV4 .... **39** F5
Jeffrey CI CV12 .... **95** D8
Jeffrey Rd B65 .... **63** E3
Jeffrey Woods Cross CV1 .. **113** F4
Jeffries Ho **11** B69 .... **64** A7
Jeffs Ave WV2 .... **163** C1
Jeliff St CV4 .... **111** F2
Jelleyman CI DY11 .... **116** C6
Jellicoe Ho **9** DY4 .... **52** A8
Jellicoe Way LE10 .... **71** D3
Jenkins Ave CV5 .... **111** F4
Jenkins CI WV14 .... **40** C5
Jenkins St B10 .... **87** C8
Jenkinson Rd WS10 .... **41** D1
Jenks Ave WV10 .... **25** E8
Jennens Rd B4 .... **66** F3
Jenner CI WS2 .... **28** A6
Jenner Ho WS2 .... **27** F6
Jenner Rd WS2 .... **28** A6
Jenner St Coventry CV1 ...... **165** C4
Wolverhampton WV2 .... **163** D2
Jennifer Wlk B25 .... **88** E8
Jennings St B64 .... **62** F2
Jenny CI WV14 .... **40** E1
Jenny Walkers La WV6 .... **23** D1
Jennyns Ct **3** WS10 .... **42** A3
Jensen B77 .... **21** E2
Jenton Rd CV31 .... **162** B6
Jephcott Ho **2** CV1 .... **113** E3
Jephcott Rd B8 .... **68** A4
Jephson Ct CV2 .... **96** C4
Jephson Dr B26 .... **88** F7
Jephson PI **3** CV31 .... **162** B7
Jeremy Gr B92 .... **89** B3
Jeremy Rd WV4 .... **39** C5
Jerome Ct B74 .... **30** F1
Jerome Dr WS11 .... **6** A5
Jerome Prim Sch The WS11 .. **5** F5
Jerome Rd Norton Canes WS11 **6** A5
Sutton Coldfield B72 .... **46** D4
Walsall WS1 .... **28** B1
Jerome Way WS7 .... **7** C7
Jerrard Dr B75 .... **46** C6
Jerrard Mews B75 .... **46** C5
Jerry's La Birmingham B23 .. **56** E6
Weeford WS14 .... **19** B8
Jersey CI B98 .... **154** D7
Jersey Croft B36 .... **70** B6
Jersey Rd B8 .... **67** D4
Jerusalem Wlk DY10 .... **116** E7
Jervis CI DY5 .... **61** C7
Jervis Cres B74 .... **31** D3
Jervis Ct **2** WS1 .... **28** F2
Jervis Rd B77 .... **35** F5
Jervis Terr B21 .... **65** D8
Jervoise Dr B31 .... **103** B5
Jervoise Jun & Inf Sch
B29 .... **85** A1
Jervoise La B71 .... **42** E1
Jervoise Rd B29 .... **85** A2
Jervoise St B70 .... **53** A4
Jesmond Gr B24 .... **57** E4
Jesmond Rd CV1 .... **113** F4
Jessel Rd WS2 .... **28** C2
Jessie Rd WS9 .... **16** B1
Jesson CI WS1 .... **43** A7
Jesson Ct WS1 .... **43** A8
Jesson Rd Dudley DY3 .... **51** A6
Sutton Coldfield B75 .... **47** A5
Walsall WS1 .... **43** A8
Jesson St B70 .... **53** E2
Jevon St WV14 .... **51** B8
Jevons Rd B73 .... **45** C3
Jew's La DY3 .... **50** E4
Jewellery Quarter Sta B18 .. **66** B4
Jiggins La B32 .... **84** D1
Jill Ave B43 .... **43** C1
Jill La B96 .... **159** B2
Jillcot Rd B92 .... **89** B3
Jim Forrest CI **4** CV3 ...... **134** F8
Jinnah CI B12 .... **86** F8
Joan of Arc Ho CV3 .... **133** E6
Joan St WV2 .... **39** E6
Joan Ward St CV3 .... **133** D8
Joan's CI **1** CV31 .... **162** C6
Joanna Dr CV3 .... **133** C3
Job's La CV4 .... **112** A2
Jockey Field DY3 .... **50** E6

Jockey La WS10 .... 42 A4
Jockey Rd B73 .... 46 A2
Jodrell St CV11 .... 73 B6
Joe Williams Cl **7** CV3 .. 134 F8
Joeys La WV8 .... 10 C3
John Bosco Cl B71 .... 53 B7
John Bright Cl DY4 .... 51 F8
John Bright St B1 .... 164 B2
John Cleveland Coll The
LE10 .... 71 F1
John F Kennedy Wlk
4 DY4 .... 52 A8
John Feeney Tower B31 .... 102 F7
John Grace St CV3 .... 133 D8
John Gulson Prim Sch
CV1 .... 113 D5
John Harper St WV13 ...... 27 B2
John Ho DY1 .... 61 D8
John Howell Dr DY4 .... 52 A5
John Kempe Way B12 ...... 87 A7
John Kennedy Ave WV14 .. 40 D2
John Knight Rd CV12 ...... 78 B5
John McGuire Cres CV3 .. 134 E7
John Nash Sq CV8 .... 147 F3
John Nichols St LE10 ..... 75 B7
John O'Gaunt Rd CV8 ..... 147 E3
John of Gaunt Ho CV3 .... 133 L6
John Rd B62 .... 83 F3
John Riley Dr WV12 .... 27 C8
John Rous Ave CV4 .... 132 B7
John Shelton Prim Sch
CV6 .... 95 D4
John Sinclair Ho CV1 .... 165 B4
John Smith Ho **4** B1 .... 66 C3
John St Bedworth CV12 ... 78 A2
Birmingham B19 .... 66 B7
Blackheath B65 .... 63 C1
Brierley Hill DY5 .... 61 D4
Cannock, High Town WS11 .. 2 A4
Cannock, Wimblebury WS12 .. 2 F3
Hinckley LE10 .... 71 E1
Nuneaton, Coton CV11 ..... 73 C2
Nuneaton, Stockingford CV10 . 72 E3
Oldbury B69 .... 64 A7
Royal Leamington Spa CV32 . 161 D8
Stourbridge DY8 .... 60 F1
Tamworth B77 .... 21 E4
Walsall WS2 .... 28 E3
West Bromwich,
Guns Village B70 .... 53 B4
West Bromwich,
Swan Village B70 .... 52 F5
Willenhall WV13 .... 27 A1
Wolverhampton WV2 .... 40 A4
John St N B71 .... 53 B5
John Tofts Ho CV1 .... 165 B4
John Willmott Sch B76 .... 46 F4
John Wood CE Inf Sch
WS11 .... 4 D8
John Wooton Ho **4** WS10 . 41 D6
John's Cl LE10 .... 75 D5
John's La
Tipton, Dudley Port DY4 .. 52 B4
Tipton, Tividale B69 ..... 52 C3
Johndory B77 .... 35 D6
Johns Cl B80 .... 159 C4
Johns Gr B43 .... 54 C8
Johns La WS6 .... 4 F3
Johnson Ave WV11 .... 26 F7
Johnson Cl
Birmingham, Sparkhill B11 . 87 C5
Birmingham, Ward End B8 .. 68 C6
Darlaston WS10 .... 41 D5
Lichfield WS13 .... 3 C1
Redditch B98 .... 154 A5
Johnson Dr B35 .... 57 F3
Johnson Pl WV14 .... 41 A7
Johnson Rd Bedworth CV12 . 78 C3
Birmingham B23 .... 57 A6
Burntwood WS7 .... 6 F8
Cannock WS11 .... 1 D4
Coventry CV6 .... 114 A8
Darlaston WS10 .... 41 D5
Wednesbury WS10 .... 42 C2
Willenhall WV12 .... 27 D7
Johnson St Birmingham B7 . 67 C6
Wolverhampton WV2 .... 39 D7
Wolverhampton,
Cinder Hill WV14 .... 39 F1
Wood End WV9 .... 36 C1
Johnsons Bridge Rd B71 .. 53 C6
Johnsons Gr B68 .... 84 D8
Johnston St B70 .... 53 D1
Joiners Croft B92 .... 107 E8
Joinings Bank B68 .... 64 B4
Jon Baker Ct LE10 .... 75 E8
Jonathan Rd CV2 .... 114 F8
Jones Field Cres WV1 .... 26 B2
Jones Ho WS2 .... 28 D3
Jones' La WS7 .... 7 F7
Jones La WS6 .... 5 B1
Jones Rd Bedworth CV7 ... 78 A1
Willenhall WV12 .... 27 D8
Wolverhampton WV10 ...... 25 C6
Jones Wood Cl B76 .... 58 A7
Jonkel Ave B77 .... 36 A5
Jordan Cl Kenilworth CV8 . 148 B2
Lichfield WS13 .... 9 A8
Smethwick B66 .... 65 B5
Sutton Coldfield B75 ..... 32 B1
Jordan Ho B36 .... 68 E8
Jordan Leys DY4 .... 52 B5
Jordan Pl WV14 .... 40 E3
Jordan Rd B75 .... 32 B2

Jordan Way WS9 .... 16 B1
Jordan Well CV1 .... 165 C2
Jordans Cl B97 .... 158 D6
Jordans The CV5 .... 112 C4
Joseph Cash Prim Sch
CV6 .... 113 C7
Joseph Chamberlain VI
Form Coll B12 .... 86 F6
Joseph Creighton Cl CV3 . 134 E7
Joseph Halpin Ho **3** CV1 . 165 C4
Joseph Latham Ho **3** CV2 . 96 B1
Joseph Leckie Sch WS5 ... 42 E5
Joseph Luckman Rd CV12 .. 78 B4
Joseph Turner Prim Sch
DY4 .... 52 B7
Josiah Mason Coll B23 ... 56 C4
Josiah Rd B31 .... 102 D2
Jowett B77 .... 21 E2
Jowett's La B71 .... 53 B8
Joyberry Dr DY8 .... 81 A3
Joyce Pool CV34 .... 160 E7
Joynson St WS10 .... 41 E5
Jubilee Ave Redditch B97 . 158 D7
West Bromwich B71 .... 53 B7
Jubilee Bldgs WS10 ...... 41 D7
Jubilee Cl Great Wyrley
WS6 .... 4 F2
Walsall WS3 .... 28 E6
Jubilee Cres CV6 .... 113 B9
Jubilee Dr N DY11 .... 116 B2
Jubilee Dr S DY11 .... 116 B2
Jubilee Park Prim Sch
DY4 .... 52 B8
Jubilee Rd Bilston WV14 .. 41 A4
Birmingham B45 .... 101 E2
Tipton DY4 .... 52 B8
Jubilee St B31 .... 53 D8
Jubilee Terr Bedworth
CV12 .... 78 B4
Stoke Prior B60 .... 150 C1
Jubilee Trad Ctr B5 ..... 66 E1
Judd Cl CV12 .... 77 F3
Judds La CV6 .... 95 E4
Judge Cl B69 .... 64 A7
Judge Rd DY5 .... 81 F7
Juggins La B94 .... 141 B7
Julia Ave B24 .... 57 F4
Julia Gdns B71 .... 53 F8
Julian Cl Catshill B61 .. 137 A8
Coventry CV2 .... 114 F8
Great Wyrley WS6 .... 5 A3
Wolverhampton WV1 .... 26 B2
Julian Rd WV1 .... 26 B2
Julie Croft WV14 .... 40 E1
Juliet Cl CV11 .... 74 A1
Juliet Rd B62 .... 83 F3
Julius Dr B46 .... 59 F1
Junction 2 Ind Est B69 .. 63 F5
Junction Rd Birmingham
B21 .... 65 C8
Bromsgrove B61 .... 136 E3
Stourbridge DY8 .... 81 B4
Stourbridge, Amblecote DY8 . 60 E1
Wolverhampton WV2 .... 40 B1
Junction St Coventry CV1 . 165 A2
Dudley DY2 .... 62 B8
Oldbury, Brades Village B69 . 52 E1
Walsall WS1 .... 42 D7
Junction St S B69 .... 64 A5
Junction The DY8 .... 80 E8
June Cres CV32 .... 21 E5
June Croft B26 .... 89 D5
Juniper B77 .... 22 A4
Juniper Cl B27 .... 88 B5
Juniper Dr Coventry CV5 . 111 F5
Sutton Coldfield B76 .... 58 A7
Juniper Ho B36 .... 68 F7
Juniper Rise B63 .... 82 C5
Jury Rd DY5 .... 81 F7
Jury St CV34 .... 160 E6
Jutland Rd B13 .... 105 B8

Kanzan Rd CV2 .... 96 B4
Kareen Gr CV3 .... 135 C7
Karen Cl CV10 .... 72 F7
Karen Way DY5 .... 81 D8
Karlingford Cl CV5 ...... 132 D8
Kate's Hill Prim Sch DY2 . 62 E8
Katherine Rd B67 .... 64 F2
Kathleen Ave CV12 .... 77 E1
Kathleen Rd Birmingham
B25 .... 88 C7
Sutton Coldfield B72 .... 46 C4
Katie Rd B29 .... 85 E1
Kayne Cl DY6 .... 60 C7
Keanscott Dr B68 .... 64 C4
Keasdon Gr WV13 .... 27 C3
Keating Gdns B75 .... 32 A4
Keatley Ave B33 .... 69 E2
Keats Ave Birmingham B10 . 87 D7
Cannock WS11 .... 1 E5
Keats Cl Dudley DY3 ..... 50 A5
Nuneaton CV10 .... 72 A4
Stourbridge DY8 .... 81 A8
Sutton Coldfield B74 .... 31 F6
Tamworth B79 .... 20 F8
Keats Dr WV14 .... 40 D2
Keats Gr Birmingham B27 . 88 B3
Wolverhampton WV10 ...... 26 A8
Keats Ho **2** Oldbury B68 . 64 C4
Redditch B97 .... 158 C8
Keats Pl DY10 .... 117 B6
Keats Rd Coventry CV2 .. 114 D7
Walsall WS3 .... 28 E7
Willenhall WV12 .... 27 D7
Keble Cl Burntwood WS7 ... 7 C7
Cannock WS11 .... 4 E8

Keble Gr Birmingham B26 . 89 B6
Walsall WS1 .... 43 A7
Keble Ho B37 .... 70 A2
Kebull Gn CV4 .... 131 E8
Kedleston Cl WS3 .... 14 A3
Kedleston Ct B28 .... 105 F4
Kedleston Rd B28 .... 105 F5
Keegan Wlk WS2 .... 27 F4
Keel Dr B13 .... 87 D1
Keele Cl B98 .... 154 E6
Keele Ho B37 .... 70 B4
Keeley St B9 .... 67 B2
Keeling Dr WS11 .... 1 B1
Keeling Rd CV8 .... 148 B5
Keelinge St DY4 .... 52 B5
Keen St B66 .... 65 D5
Keenan Dr CV12 .... 77 D1
Keeper's Cl B17 .... 85 D5
Keeper's Cl **3** CV3 ...... 7 A6
Keepers Cl Brownhills WS9 . 15 F3
Kingswinford DY6 .... 60 B8
Lichfield WS14 .... 9 E7
Keepers Gate Cl B74 .... 46 C7
Keepers Ho B23 .... 45 C2
Keepers La Codsall WV8 .. 10 A1
Wolverhampton WV6 ...... 24 A7
Keepers Rd B74 .... 31 C5
Keepers Wlk CV12 .... 77 D1
Keer Cl B9 .... 67 B2
Kegworth Cl CV6 .... 96 A4
Kegworth Rd B23 .... 56 C2
Keir Cl CV32 .... 157 A2
Keir Hardy Wlk B69 ..... 52 D2
Keir Pl DY8 .... 80 E8
Keir Rd WS10 .... 42 D2
Keith Rd CV32 .... 157 B4
Keith Winter Cl B61 .... 136 F6
Kelby Cl B31 .... 102 E4
Kelby Rd B31 .... 102 F4
Keldy Cl WV6 .... 24 F5
Kele Rd CV4 .... 132 A4
Kelfield Ave B17 .... 85 B4
Kelham Pl B92 .... 89 B1
Kelia Dr B67 .... 64 F6
Kellett Rd B7 .... 67 A4
Kelling Cl DY5 .... 81 D8
Kellington Cl B8 .... 67 F4
Kelmarsh Dr B91 .... 107 B1
Kelmscote Rd CV6 .... 112 F8
Kelmscott Rd B17 .... 85 B7
Kelsall Cl WV1 .... 26 B2
Kelsall Croft B1 .... 66 B3
Kelsey Cl Birmingham B7 . 67 B4
Nuneaton CV11 .... 73 E3
Kelsey La CV7 .... 130 D5
Kelsey's Cl CV8 .... 135 F3
Kelso Gdns WV6 .... 23 D4
Kelsull Croft B37 .... 70 A2
Kelton Ct B15 .... 86 A7
Kelvedon Gr B91 .... 107 C4
Kelverdale Gr B14 ...... 104 C4
Kelverley Gr B71 .... 43 A1
Kelvin Ave CV2 .... 114 D5
Kelvin Cl DY11 .... 116 A4
Kelvin Dr WS11 .... 2 A3
Kelvin Pl WS2 .... 28 B6
Kelvin Rd Birmingham B31 . 103 B1
Royal Leamington Spa
CV32 .... 157 C5
Walsall WS2 .... 28 B6
Kelvin Way B70 .... 53 C1
Kelvin Way Trad Est B70 . 53 B1
Kelway CV3 .... 115 A2
Kelway Ave B43 .... 44 B3
Kelwood Dr B63 .... 83 A5
Kelynmead Rd B33 .... 69 A2
Kem St CV11 .... 73 E2
Kemberton Cl WV3 .... 24 C1
Kemberton Rd
Birmingham B29 .... 85 B2
Wolverhampton WV3 ...... 24 C1
Kemble Cl WV12 .... 27 D3
Kemble Croft B5 .... 86 E7
Kemble Dr B35 .... 58 A3
Kemelstowe Cres B63 ... 100 C8
Kemerton Ho B97 .... 153 B4
Kemerton Way B90 ...... 126 F6
Kemp Cl CV34 .... 161 A7
Kempe Rd B33 .... 69 A4
Kempley Ave CV2 .... 114 C2
Kemps Green Rd
Balsall Common CV7 ..... 130 B6
Tanworth-in-A B94 .... 143 A1
Kempsey Cl Halesowen B63 . 82 E4
Oldbury B69 .... 63 E4
Redditch B98 .... 159 B7
Solihull B92 .... 89 A3
Kempsey Covert B38 ..... 123 E7
Kempsey Ho B32 .... 102 A8
Kempsford Cl B98 ...... 158 F6
Kempson Ave
Sutton Coldfield B72 .... 46 C1
West Bromwich B71 .... 53 B5
Kempson Rd B36 .... 68 F8
Kempsons Gr WV14 .... 40 B3
Kempthorne Ave WV10 ... 25 E8
Kempthorne Gdns WS3 ... 14 A2
Kempthorne Rd WV14 .... 40 F6
Kempton Cres CV32 ..... 157 C4
Kempton Dr WS6 .... 4 F2
Kempton Park Rd B36 .... 68 D8
Kempton Way DY8 .... 80 E3
Kemsey Dr WV14 .... 40 F3
Kemshead Ave B31 ...... 122 E8
Kemsley Rd B14 .... 104 F2
Kenchester Cl B98 ..... 154 F2
Kenchester Ho **2** B16 .... 66 A2

Kendal Ave Birmingham
B45 .... 122 B7
Coleshill B46 .... 70 F7
Royal Leamington Spa
CV32 .... 156 C2
Kendal Cl Bromsgrove B60 . 137 B1
Nuneaton CV11 .... 74 A6
Wolverhampton WV6 ...... 24 F6
Kendal Ct Birmingham B23 . 56 B3
Cannock WS11 .... 4 B8
Kendal Dr B45 .... 122 D1
Kendal End Rd B45 ..... 122 D1
Kendal Gr B92 .... 107 F8
Kendal Rd B11 .... 87 B7
Kendal Rise Coventry CV5 . 112 B8
Oldbury B68 .... 64 B3
Wolverhampton WV6 ...... 24 F6
Kendal Rise Rd B45 .... 122 B7
Kendal Tower B17 .... 85 D5
Kendall Rise DY6 .... 60 F5
Kendon Ave CV6 .... 112 E6
Kendrick Ave B34 .... 69 E5
Kendrick Cl Coventry CV6 . 96 A4
Solihull B92 .... 107 F6
Kendrick Pl WV14 .... 41 A4
Kendrick Rd Bilston WV14 . 41 A4
Sutton Coldfield B76 .... 57 F5
Wolverhampton WV10 ..... 25 E6
Kendricks Rd WS10 ...... 41 F7
Kenelm Ct CV3 .... 134 C5
Kenelm Rd Birmingham B10 . 87 F5
Dudley WV14 .... 40 C1
Oldbury B68 .... 64 A3
Sutton Coldfield B73 .... 46 B4
Kenelm's Ct B62 .... 101 A4
Kenilcourt CV8 .... 147 E4
Kenilworth Castle CV8 .. 147 D5
Kenilworth Cl Redditch
B97 .... 158 D6
Stourbridge DY8 .... 60 D2
Sutton Coldfield B74 .... 46 A8
Tipton DY4 .... 51 D4
Kenilworth Cres
Walsall WS2 .... 28 A4
Wolverhampton WV4 ...... 39 E4
Kenilworth Ct
Birmingham, Edgbaston B15 . 85 F8
Birmingham,
Gravelly Hill B24 .... 56 E2
10 Coventry CV3 .... 133 C8
Dudley DY1 .... 61 F8
Kenilworth Dr Cannock WS11 . 1 D4
Kidderminster DY10 ..... 116 E2
Nuneaton CV11 .... 73 B3
Kenilworth Hall Mews
CV8 .... 147 F5
Kenilworth Ho
Birmingham B13 .... 105 A6
8 Walsall WS3 .... 28 C6
Kenilworth Rd
Balsall Common CV7, CV8 . 130 D4
Birmingham B20 .... 55 E2
Coventry CV3 .... 132 E3
Cubbington CV32 .... 157 C6
Hampton in A B92 .... 109 E5
Kenilworth CV8 .... 148 C8
Knowle B93 .... 128 E5
Lichfield WS14 .... 9 B6
Meriden CV7 .... 91 D1
Oldbury B68 .... 84 D7
Perton WV6 .... 23 F4
Royal Leamington Spa CV32 . 156 E5
Tamworth B77 .... 21 E4
Kenilworth Sch CV8 .... 148 C5
Kenilworth Sch Castle
Sixth Form Ctr CV8 .... 147 F2
Kenilworth **16** CV32 .... 156 F1
Kenley Gr B30 .... 104 B3
Kenley Way B91 .... 106 D4
Kenmare Way WV11 ...... 26 C4
Kenmore Ave WS12 .... 1 F7
Kenmore Dr LE10 .... 71 B2
Kenmure Rd B33 .... 89 C8
Kennan Ave CV31 .... 161 F6
Kennedy Cl
Kidderminster DY10 ..... 116 F3
Sutton Coldfield B72 .... 46 C4
Tamworth B77 .... 21 C7
Kennedy Cres
Darlaston WS10 .... 41 C7
Dudley DY3 .... 50 D4
Kennedy Croft B26 ...... 89 A7
Kennedy Ct **5** DY8 ..... 80 F5
Kennedy Gr B30 .... 104 B6
Kennedy Rd WV10 .... 163 D4
Kennedy Sq **3** CV32 .. 157 A1
Kennerley Rd B25 .... 88 D6
Kennet Cl Brownhills WS8 . 6 C2
Coventry CV2 .... 114 C8
Kennet Gr B36 .... 69 F8
Kennet Ho **5** DY1 ...... 61 E8
Kenneth Gr B23 .... 56 B5
Kennford Cl B65 .... 63 C6
Kennington Rd WV10 .... 25 F5
Kenpas Highway CV3 .... 133 A5
Kenrick Croft B35 ...... 57 F2
Kenrick Ho B66 .... 64 A1
Kenrick Park Sta B66 ... 64 C3
Kenrick Way B70 .... 53 E5
Kensington Ave B12 .... 87 A4
Kensington Dr B74 ...... 31 F5
Kensington Gdns
Cannock WS11 .... 1 C2
Stourbridge DY8 .... 60 C1

Kensington Pl WS12 ...... 5 C8
Kensington Rd
Birmingham B29 .... 86 B2
Coventry CV5 .... 113 A1
Willenhall WV12 .... 27 B7
Kensington St B19 ...... 66 D6
Kenstone Rd **2** B12 .... 86 F7
Kenswick Dr B63 .... 83 A2
Kent Ave Fazeley B78 .... 20 F1
Walsall WS2 .... 28 B3
Kent Cl Aldridge WS9 .... 16 B1
Coventry CV3 .... 133 E6
Kidderminster DY10 ..... 116 E3
Walsall WS2 .... 28 E5
West Bromwich B71 .... 53 C7
Kent Close Prim Sch B71 . 53 B7
Kent Dr LE10 .... 71 F4
Kent Pl Cannock WS12 .... 2 F1
Dudley DY2 .... 62 A6
Kent Rd Birmingham B45 . 101 F4
Halesowen B62 .... 83 F5
Stourbridge DY8 .... 80 D7
Wednesbury WS10 .... 42 D4
Wolverhampton WV2 ...... 39 E7
Kent St Birmingham B5 ... 66 E1
Dudley DY3 .... 50 E5
Walsall WS2 .... 28 E5
Kent St N B18 .... 65 F5
Kent's Cl B92 .... 88 F3
Kenthurst Cl CV5 .... 111 C4
Kentish Rd B21 .... 65 C8
Kentmere Cl CV2 .... 96 E3
Kentmere Tower **4** B23 . 57 B6
Kenton Ave WV6 .... 24 F4
Kenton Wlk **7** B29 ..... 85 F2
Kents Ho B33 .... 69 B2
Kentwell B79 .... 20 D7
Kenward Croft B17 ...... 84 F7
Kenway B47 .... 125 A7
Kenwick Rd B17 .... 85 B4
Kenwood Rd B9 .... 68 B3
Kenwyn Gdns CV7 .... 96 B8
Kenyon Cl Bromsgrove B60 . 137 A1
Stourbridge DY8 .... 81 A7
Kenyon St B18 .... 164 A4
Kepler B79 .... 20 E7
Keppel St CV1 .... 113 E5
Kerby Rd B23 .... 56 D4
Keresley Brook Rd CV6 .. 95 A2
Keresley Cl Coventry CV6 . 95 A2
Solihull B91 .... 107 C5
Keresley Gr B29 .... 85 A2
Keresley Grange Prim Sch
CV6 .... 94 F1
Keresley Green Rd CV6 .. 94 F1
Keresley Newland Comb
Sch CV7 .... 94 F7
Kernthorpe Rd B14 ..... 104 D4
Kerr Dr DY4 .... 51 E8
Kerria Ctr B77 .... 22 A4
Kerria Rd B77 .... 22 B4
Kerridge Cl WV9 .... 11 A2
Kerrls Way CV3 .... 115 A1
Kerry Cl Barwell LE9 .... 71 F7
Birmingham B31 .... 102 F6
Brierley Hill DY5 .... 61 C4
Kerry Ct WS1 .... 43 A8
Kerry Hill B60 .... 150 E6
Kerry's Ho **4** CV1 .... 113 B2
Kersley Gdns WV11 ...... 26 F5
Kerswell Dr B90 .... 127 A5
Kesterton Rd B74 .... 31 E5
Kesteven Cl B15 .... 86 B6
Kesteven Rd B71 .... 53 C7
Keston Rd B44 .... 44 F4
Kestral Ho B35 .... 58 C3
Kestrel B77 .... 36 A6
Kestrel Ave B25 .... 88 C8
Kestrel Cl Birmingham B23 . 56 D6
Hinckley LE10 .... 75 F6
Kidderminster DY10 ..... 116 E3
Kestrel Croft **2** CV3 . 134 F8
Kestrel Dr B74 .... 31 F5
Kestrel Gr Birmingham B30 . 103 D8
Cannock WS12 .... 2 C1
Willenhall WV12 .... 27 C8
Kestrel Rd Dudley DY1 ... 51 A1
Halesowen B63 .... 82 B7
Oldbury B68 .... 63 F2
Kestrel Rise WV6 .... 24 F7
Kestrel Way WS6 .... 4 C2
Keswick Cl CV11 .... 74 A6
Keswick Dr DY6 .... 60 D6
Keswick Gn CV32 .... 156 D1
Keswick Gr B74 .... 30 F2
Keswick Ho **14** B69 .... 63 D5
Keswick Rd B92 .... 89 A4
Keswick Wlk CV2 .... 114 F4
Ketley Croft B12 .... 86 F7
Ketley Fields DY6 ...... 61 A5
Ketley Hill Rd DY1 ..... 61 F8
Ketley Rd DY6 .... 60 F7
Kettlebrook Rd Solihull
B90 .... 127 C6
Tamworth B77 .... 21 C3
Kettlehouse Rd B44 ..... 44 F3
Kettles Wood Dr B32 ... 84 C2
Kettlesbank Rd DY3 .... 50 C2
Kettlewell Cl CV34 .... 155 E1
Kettlewell Way B37 ..... 69 F1
Ketton Gr B33 .... 89 D7
Keviliok St CV3 .... 133 C6
Kew Cl Birmingham B37 ... 69 F3
Kenilworth CV8 .... 148 C5
Kew Dr DY1 .... 51 A2
Kew Gdns B33 .... 68 E1
Kew Ho CV4 .... 111 F3

Kewstoke Cl WV12 .... 13 B1
Kewstoke Croft B31 .... 102 E6
Kewstoke Rd WV12 .... 13 C1
Key Bsns Pk B24 .... 57 E3
Key Cl WS12 .... 2 C3
Key Hill B18 .... 66 B5
Key Hill Dr B18 .... 66 B5
Key Ind Pk WV13 .... 26 D3
Keyes Dr DY6 .... 49 D1
Keynell Covert B30 .... 104 C2
Keynes Dr WV14 .... 40 E6
Keys Cres B71 .... 53 C6
Keyse Rd B75 .... 46 F7
Keyspark Rd WS12 .... 2 E4
Keyte Cl WS4 .... 52 A5
Keyway Jct WV13 .... 41 B8
Keyway Ret Pk WV13 .... 41 B8
Keyway The WV13 .... 41 A8
Khyber Cl WV10 .... 41 C8
Kidd Croft DY4 .... 41 C2
Kidderminster Coll DY10 .. 116 E4
Kidderminster General
Hospl DY11 .... 116 C5
Kidderminster General
Hospl Mill Street Branch
DY11 .... 116 C7
Kidderminster Rd
Bromsgrove B61 .... 136 C3
Hagley DY9 .... 99 B5
Iverley DY10 .... 98 C7
Kingswinford DY6 .... 60 B7
Kidderminster Rd S DY9 .. 98 F3
Kidderminster Sta DY10 .. 116 F5
Kidderminster Town Sta
DY10 .... 116 F5
Kidson Eventide Homes
WV6 .... 24 F5
Kielder Cl Cannock WS12 .... 2 E2
Walsall WS5 .... 43 C3
Kielder Dr CV10 .... 72 E2
Kielder Gdns DY9 .... 81 B1
Kier's Bridge Cl DY4 .... 52 B3
Kilburn Dr Coventry CV5 .... 112 F3
Kingswinford DY6 .... 49 E1
Kilburn Gr B44 .... 44 F3
Kilburn Pl DY2 .... 62 D6
Kilburn Rd B44 .... 44 F3
Kilby Ave B16 .... 66 A2
Kilby Gn LE10 .... 75 F6
Kilby Gr CV31 .... 162 C5
Kilbye Cl B77 .... 35 F5
Kilbys Gr B43 .... 54 F2
Kilcote Rd B90 .... 105 C2
Kildale Cl CV1 .... 165 D3
Kildwick Way ⑤ CV34 .. 155 E1
Kilmarie Cl LE10 .... 71 A1
Kilmet Wlk ❶ B67 .... 65 A5
Kilmore Croft B36 .... 68 E8
Kilmorie Rd Birmingham
B27 .... 88 C5
Cannock WS11 .... 1 C2
Kiln Cl
Royal Leamington Spa
CV32 .... 157 A1
Studley B80 .... 159 C4
Kiln Croft B65 .... 63 A4
Kiln Way Polesworth B78 .... 22 F1
Shilton CV12 .... 97 E7
Kilnsey Gr CV34 .... 155 E1
Kilpeck Cl B98 .... 154 F2
Kilsall Ct ⑫ WV3 .... 25 C4
Kilsby Gr B91 .... 127 C8
Kilvert Rd WS10 .... 42 B2
Kimberley B77 .... 35 F7
Kimberley Ave B8 .... 67 E5
Kimberley Cl Aldridge B74 .. 31 A2
Coventry CV5 .... 111 F4
Redditch B98 .... 154 B7
Kimberley Pl WV14 .... 51 B7
Kimberley Rd Baginton
CV8 .... 133 F2
Bedworth CV12 .... 78 C4
Smethwick B66 .... 65 A4
Solihull B92 .... 89 A1
Kimberley St WV3 .... 25 A1
Kimberley Wlk B76 .... 58 D6
Kimble Cl CV5 .... 112 B4
Kimble Gr B24 .... 57 D3
Kimg's Mdw DY9 .... 99 E3
Kimmond Ct ⑰ CV32 .. 156 F1
Kimpton Cl B14 .... 104 E2
Kimsan Croft B74 .... 45 A7
Kinchford Cl B91 .... 127 B8
Kineton Cl B98 .... 154 D1
Kineton Croft B32 .... 102 D8
Kineton Green Inf Sch B92 .. 88 D1
Kineton Green Rd B92 .. 106 D8
Kineton Ho B13 .... 105 A6
Kineton La B94 .... 127 A1
Kineton Rd Birmingham B45 121 E7
Coventry CV2 .... 114 C6
Kenilworth CV8 .... 148 C4
Sutton Coldfield B73 .... 45 E1
Kineton Rise DY3 .... 39 C2
Kinfare Dr WV6 .... 24 B4
Kinfare Rise DY3 .... 50 E4
King Charles Ave WS2 .... 27 E2
King Charles Cl DY11 .. 116 C6
King Charles Ct B44 .... 45 B2
King Charles Cty Prim Sch
WS2 .... 27 E2
King Charles I High Sch
DY10 .... 117 A5
King Charles Rd B62 .... 83 F4
King Charles Sq ④ B62 .. 116 C6
King David Jun & Inf Sch
B13 .... 86 F2
King Edmund St DY1 .... 51 B2

King Edward Ave B61 ..... 136 F5
King Edward IV
Handsworth Sch B21 ...... 66 A7
King Edward Rd
Birmingham B13 .... 86 F3
Bromsgrove B61 .... 136 F5
Coventry CV1 .... 113 F4
Nuneaton CV11 .... 73 D4
King Edward St WS10 .... 41 D6
King Edward VI Aston Sch
B6 .... 66 F8
King Edward VI Camp Hill
Schs B14 .... 104 D7
King Edward VI Coll
Nuneaton CV11 .... 73 D4
Stourbridge DY8 .... 81 A6
King Edward VI Cty Sch
WS14 .... 9 C6
King Edward VI Five Ways
Sch B32 .... 102 C8
King Edward VI High Sch
for Girls B15 .... 86 A4
King Edward's Row WV2 .. 163 B1
King Edward's Sch B15 ... 86 A4
King Edward's Sq B73 .... 46 B5
King Edwards Cl B20 .... 66 B8
King Edwards Gdns B20 .. 66 B7
King Edwards Rd B1 .... 66 B2
King George Ave B61 .. 136 F4
King George Cl B61 .. 136 F4
King George Cres WS4 .. 29 B6
King George Pl WS4 .... 29 B6
King George V Ave WS5 .. 29 C1
King George's Ave
Bedworth CV12 .... 78 B5
Coventry CV6 .... 95 F2
King George's Way LE10 .. 75 B7
King Henry VIII Sch CV1 .. 165 A1
King Richard Rd LE10 .... 71 C2
King Richard St CV2 .. 113 F3
King St Bedworth CV12 .. 78 C2
Bilston WV14 .... 40 E3
Birmingham B11 .... 87 A7
Blackheath B64 .... 62 F1
Brierley Hill DY5 .... 82 A8
Brownhills WS8 .... 15 F2
Burntwood WS7 .... 6 F5
Dudley DY2 .... 51 C1
Dudley, Roseville WV14 .. 51 A8
Halesowen B63 .... 83 A4
❷ Hinckley LE10 .... 71 D1
Royal Leamington Spa
CV32 .... 157 A1
Smethwick B66 .... 65 B7
Stourbridge, Lye DY9 .... 81 F5
Stourbridge, Wollaston DY8 .. 80 E6
Tamworth B79 .... 21 B5
Walsall WS1 .... 42 D7
Wednesbury WS10 .... 41 E3
Willenhall WV13 .... 27 B2
Wolverhampton WV1 .. 163 C3
King Street Pas
Brierley Hill DY5 .... 82 A8
❷ Dudley DY2 .... 51 D1
King's Ave B69 .... 52 B2
King's Ct CV11 .... 73 B4
King's Heath Boys Sch
B13 .... 105 A6
King's Heath Jun Sch B14 .. 86 F1
King's Hill Day Hospl WS10 41 E5
King's Hill Field WS10 .. 41 E5
King's Hill La CV3 .... 133 B2
King's Hill Rd WS14 .... 9 C6
King's Hill Sch WS10 .... 41 E5
King's Norton Boys Sch
B30 .... 103 E4
King's Norton Bsns Ctr
B30 .... 103 F4
King's Norton Girls Sch
B30 .... 103 F5
King's Norton Sta B38 .. 103 F4
King's Rd Birmingham B44 .. 44 E3
Kidderminster DY11 .... 116 C6
King's Rise Com Prim Sch
B44 .... 45 A2
Kingfield Rd
Coventry CV1, CV6 .... 113 D7
Solihull B90 .... 105 C2
Kingfisher B77 .... 36 A6
Kingfisher Ave CV10 .... 72 C5
Kingfisher Cl DY3 .... 39 C2
Kingfisher Ct B48 .... 139 A7
Kingfisher Dr
Birmingham B36 .... 70 A8
Cannock WS12 .... 2 C5
Stourbridge DY8 .... 80 C4
Kingfisher Gr
Kidderminster DY10 .... 117 B3
Willenhall WV12 .... 27 C8
Kingfisher Ind Est B70 .... 52 F4
Kingfisher Sh Ctr ❷ B97 .. 153 E3
Kingfisher Veiw B34 .... 69 A5
Kingfisher Way B30 .... 103 D8
Kingfisher Wlk B97 .... 153 D4
Kingham Cl Dudley DY3 .. 50 C2
Redditch B98 .... 154 F4
Kingham Covert B14 .. 104 D2
Kingland Dr CV32 .... 156 C1
Kings Ave WS12 .... 2 C4
Kings Bsns Pk B44 .... 44 E3
Kings Centre Jaffrey Sch
B23 .... 56 C1
Kings Cl B14 .... 104 C6

Kings Croft
Birmingham,
Castle Bromwich B36 ...... 69 F7
Birmingham, Sheldon B26 .. 89 A5
Kings Ct Stourbridge DY8 .. 80 E5
Sutton Coldfield B75 .... 32 B3
Tipton DY4 .... 52 A4
King Edward St WS10 .... 41 E3
Kings Ct Cross St WS10 .. 41 E3
Kings Ct King St WS10 .. 41 E3
Kings Garden B30 .... 103 E4
Kings Gdns CV12 .... 78 C2
Kings Gr CV2 .... 114 B3
Kings Green Ave B38 .. 103 F2
Kings High Sch for Girls
CV34 .... 160 E7
Kings Hill Cl WS10 .... 41 E5
Kings Hill Mews WS10 .. 41 D5
Kings Hill Pk WS10 .... 41 E4
Kings Ho B24 .... 57 A4
Kings Mews WS14 .... 9 B5
Kings Norton Bsns Ctr
B30 .... 104 A4
Kings Norton High Sch
B38 .... 123 F8
Kings Norton Inf & Jun
Sch B30 .... 104 A2
Kings Norton L Ctr B38 .. 123 F8
Kings Par B4 .... 164 C2
Kings Rd
Birmingham,
Kingstanding B44, B73 .... 45 B2
Birmingham, Stirchley B14 .. 104 C6
Birmingham,
Stockland Green B23 .... 56 D4
Birmingham, Tyseley B11 .. 88 A6
Sedgley DY3 .... 50 E8
Walsall WS4 .... 29 C7
Kings Road Ind Est B25 .. 88 A6
Kings Sq Dudley WV14 .. 51 A8
West Bromwich B70 .... 53 D3
Kings St WS10 .... 41 D6
Kings Terr B14 .... 104 C6
Kingsbridge Ho B23 .... 56 B6
Kingsbridge Rd
Birmingham B32 .... 84 D1
Nuneaton CV10 .... 73 D6
Kingsbridge Wlk ⑥ B66 .. 65 B5
Kingsbury Bsns Pk B76 .. 58 E6
Kingsbury Cl Minworth B76 .. 58 D5
Walsall WS4 .... 29 B4
Kingsbury Rd
Birmingham,
Birches Green B24 .... 57 B3
Birmingham,
Tyburn B24, B35 .... 57 E3
Coventry CV6 .... 112 E5
Curdworth B76 .... 59 B7
Minworth B76 .... 58 D5
Sutton Coldfield B35, B76 .. 58 B5
❷ Tipton DY4 .... 52 A8
Kingsbury Sch B24 .... 57 A2
Kingsclere Wlk WV4 .... 38 C6
Kingscliff Rd B10 .... 88 A8
Kingscote Cl B98 .... 154 D7
Kingscote Gr CV3 .... 133 A4
Kingscote Rd
Birmingham B15 .... 85 E6
Dorridge B93 .... 127 E6
Kingscroft Cl B74 .... 45 A8
Kingscroft Rd B74 .... 45 A8
Kingsdene Ave DY6 .... 60 C4
Kingsdown Ave B42 .... 55 A6
Kingsdown Rd B31 .... 84 F1
Kingsfield Ind Est CV1 .. 113 C6
Kingsfield Rd B14 .... 104 E8
Kingsford Cl B36 .... 58 D1
Kingsford Nouveau DY6 .. 61 A5
Kingsgate Ho B37 .... 70 A2
Kingshayes Rd WS9 .... 16 B1
Kingshill Dr B38 .... 103 F2
Kingshurst CV31 .... 162 E6
Kingshurst Ho B37 .... 69 F5
Kingshurst Inf Sch B37 .... 70 A6
Kingshurst Jun Sch B37 .... 70 A6
Kingshurst Rd
Birmingham B31 .... 103 A3
Solihull B90 .... 105 F1
Kingshurst Way B37 .... 69 F5
Kingsland Ave CV5 .... 112 F2
Kingsland Dr B93 .... 127 E4
Kingsland Jun & Inf Sch
B44 .... 44 F4
Kingsland Rd
Birmingham B44 .... 44 F4
Wolverhampton WV1 .... 25 B3
Kingslea Rd B91 .... 106 E2
Kingsleigh Dr B36 .... 69 A8
Kingsleigh Rd B20 .... 55 B2
Kingsley Ave Cannock WS12 .. 2 C7
Redditch B98 .... 154 A3
Wolverhampton WV6 .... 24 B4
Kingsley Cl B79 .... 21 A6
Kingsley Cres CV12 .... 79 B3
Kingsley Ct
Binley Woods CV3 .... 135 D6
Birmingham B25 .... 88 E8
Kingsley Gr DY3 .... 50 A5
Kingsley Prep Sch B93 .. 128 A4
Kingsley Rd
Birmingham,
Balsall Heath B12 .... 87 A6
Birmingham,
King's Norton B30 .... 103 D4
Kingswinford DY6 .... 60 B5
Kingsley Sch The CV32 .. 156 F1
Kingsley St Dudley DY2 .. 62 C5
Walsall WS2 .... 42 B7

Kingsley Terr CV2 .... 114 E8
Kingsley Wlk CV2 .... 114 F7
Kingslow Ave WV4 .... 38 D6
Kingsmead Coll B29 .. 103 D8
Kingsmead Cty High Sch
WS12 .... 2 C4
Kingsmere Cl B24 .... 56 F2
Kingspiece Ho ⑥ B36 .. 68 E8
Kingstanding Ctr B44 .... 44 F3
Kingstanding Rd B44 .... 55 F7
Kingstanding Specl Sch
B44 .... 44 E1
Kingsthorne Jun & Inf Sch
B44 .... 45 A1
Kingsthorpe Rd B14 .. 105 A3
Kingston Arc ⑧ WS11 .... 1 E1
Kingston Cl B79 .... 21 C7
Kingston Ct B74 .... 46 B7
Kingston Dr LE10 .... 71 E4
Kingston Ind Est B9 .... 67 B1
Kingston Mews CV31 .... 162 C6
Kingston Rd Birmingham B9 .. 67 B1
Coventry CV5 .... 112 F2
Kingston Row B1 .... 66 C2
Kingston Way DY6 .... 60 C7
Kingsway Cannock WS11 .... 2 A3
Coventry CV2 .... 114 A3
Essington WV11 .... 13 A4
Nuneaton CV11 .... 73 B4
Oldbury B68 .... 84 B7
Royal Leamington Spa CV31 . 161 F6
Stourbridge DY8 .... 80 D8
Wolverhampton WV6 .... 26 A6
Kingsway Ave ⑧ DY4 .. 52 A8
Kingsway Dr B38 .... 103 F2
Kingsway Ho CV12 .... 78 C2
Kingsway Rd WV10 .... 26 A6
Kingswear Ave WV6 .... 23 F3
Kingswinford Rd DY1 .... 61 F7
Kingswinford Sch DY6 .... 60 D7
Kingswood Ave Cannock
WS11 .... 4 C7
Corley CV7 .... 94 B8
Kingswood Cl Coventry CV6 .. 95 D1
Lapworth B94 .... 144 E5
Solihull B90 .... 106 D1
Kingswood Cotts B94 .. 144 D3
Kingswood Croft B7 .... 67 C7
Kingswood Dr
Great Wyrley WS6 .... 5 A4
Norton Canes WS11 .... 5 F5
Sutton Coldfield B44 .... 44 F5
Kingswood Gdns WV4 .. 38 F6
Kingswood Ho B14 .. 104 C3
Kingswood Local Ctr CV10 . 72 B4
Kingswood Rd
Birmingham,
Coft Common B31 .... 122 F7
Birmingham, Moseley B13 .. 87 A4
Kingswinford DY6 .... 60 C4
Nuneaton CV10 .... 72 B4
Kingswood Sch B90 .. 106 B2
Kington Cl WV12 .... 27 B8
Kington Gdns B37 .... 69 F2
Kington Way B33 .... 68 E1
Kiniths Cres B71 .... 53 E5
Kiniths Way Halesowen B62 .. 63 E1
West Bromwich B71 .... 53 E4
Kinlet Cl Redditch B98 .. 154 E3
Wolverhampton WV3 .... 38 A8
Kinlet Gr B31 .... 103 C2
Kinloch Dr DY1 .... 50 F3
Kinnerley St WS1 .... 29 A1
Kinnerley St WS1 .... 29 A1
Kinnersley B98 .... 154 E3
Kinnersley Cres B69 .... 63 D5
Kinnerton Cres B29 .... 84 F2
Kinross Ave WS12 .... 1 F7
Kinross Cl CV10 .... 72 C2
Kinross Cres B43 .... 44 B4
Kinross Rd CV32 .... 157 B4
Kinross Way LE10 .... 71 A1
Kinsall Gn B77 .... 36 C6
Kinsey Gr B14 .... 104 F4
Kinsham Dr B91 .... 127 B8
Kintore Croft B32 .... 102 B7
Kintyre Cl B Birmingham B45 .. 101 E1
Hinckley LE10 .... 71 B1
Kintyre The CV2 .... 115 B7
Kinver Ave
Kidderminster DY11 .... 116 A1
Willenhall WV12 .... 27 B5
Kinver Cl CV2 .... 96 C1
Kinver Cres WS9 .... 16 C1
Kinver Croft Birmingham
B12 .... 86 E7
Sutton Coldfield B76 .... 58 A8
Kinver Ct B11 .... 87 D4
Kinver Dr Hagley DY9 .... 99 C7
Wolverhampton WV4 .... 38 C5
Kinver Rd B31 .... 103 D2
Kinver St DY8 .... 60 E1
Kinwalsey La CV7 .... 92 F6
Kinwarton Cl B26 .... 88 D6
Kipling Ave Burntwood WS7 .. 7 A8
Dudley WV14 .... 40 B1
Warwick CV34 .... 160 C4
Kipling Cl Nuneaton CV10 .. 72 A5
Tipton DY4 .... 52 A8
Kipling Ho B63 .... 82 B5
Kipling Rd Birmingham
B30 .... 103 C4
Coventry CV6 .... 113 A8
Dudley DY3 .... 50 A5
Willenhall WV12 .... 27 C5
Wolverhampton WV10 .... 11 D2
Kipling Rise B79 .... 20 F8
Kipling Wlk ❸ DY10 .. 117 B6
Kirby Ave CV34 .... 155 F1

Kirby Cl Bilston WV14 .... 40 E3
Brandon CV8 .... 135 F5
Coventry CV1 .... 113 D6
Kirby Cnr CV4 .... 132 B5
Kirby Corner Rd CV4 .. 132 B6
Kirby Rd Birmingham B18 .. 65 E6
Coventry CV5 .... 112 F2
Kirfield Dr LE10 .... 71 F3
Kirkby Gn B73 .... 46 B3
Kirkdale Ave CV6 .... 95 D3
Kirkham Gdns DY5 .... 61 C6
Kirkham Gr B33 .... 68 F4
Kirkham Way DY4 .... 52 A5
Kirkland Way B78 .... 34 B8
Kirkside Gr WS8 .... 15 F7
Kirkstall Cl WS3 .... 13 F2
Kirkstall Cres WS3 .... 13 F2
Kirkstone Cres
Birmingham B43 .... 54 F6
Wombourne WV5 .... 49 A6
Kirkstone Ct DY5 .... 81 B8
Kirkstone Rd CV12 .... 78 A2
Kirkstone Way DY5 .... 81 B8
Kirkstone Wlk CV11 .... 74 A6
Kirkwall Rd B32 .... 84 D1
Kirkwood Ave B23 .... 56 F7
Kirmond Wlk WV6 .... 25 C5
Kirstead Gdns WV6 .... 24 B3
Kirtley B77 .... 21 E2
Kirton Cl Coventry CV6 .. 94 F1
Whitnash CV31 .... 162 B3
Kirton Gr Birmingham B33 .. 69 A4
Solihull B91 .... 107 A1
Wolverhampton WV6 .... 24 C4
Kitchen La Wednesfield
WV11 .... 26 F8
Wolverhampton WV11 .... 12 F1
Kitchener Rd
Birmingham B29 .... 86 B1
Coventry CV6 .... 113 E8
Dudley DY2 .... 51 F1
Kitchener St B66 .... 65 D6
Kitebrook Cl Redditch B98 .. 154 E4
Solihull B90 .... 127 A4
Kites Cl CV34 .... 155 E2
Kites Nest La CV35 .... 146 C1
Kitsland Rd B34 .... 69 E6
Kitswell Gdns B32 .... 102 A8
Kitt's Green Rd B33 .... 69 B3
Kittermaster Rd CV7 .... 92 C1
Kittiwake Dr Brierley Hill
DY5 .... 81 D7
Kidderminster DY10 .... 117 B3
Kittoe Rd B74 .... 32 A3
Kitwell La B32 .... 102 A8
Kitwell Prim Sch B32 .. 102 A7
Kitwood Ave B78 .... 36 F6
Kitwood Dr B92 .... 107 D7
Kixley La B93 .... 128 C6
Klaxon Ind Est B11 .... 87 F4
Klevedon Cl CV11 .... 74 A1
Knapton Dr LE10 .... 71 A3
Knaresdale Cl DY5 .... 81 C8
Knaves Castle Ave WS8 .. 6 F2
Knebley Cres CV10 .... 73 C1
Knebworth Cl B44 .... 55 E8
Knibbs Sh Ctr The CV34 .. 160 E7
Knight Ave CV1 .... 113 E4
Knight Ct B75 .... 47 C5
Knight Ho B13 .... 105 D7
Knightcote Dr
Royal Leamington Spa
CV32 .... 161 E8
Solihull B91 .... 127 B8
Knightley Cl CV32 .... 157 E5
Knightley Rd B91 .... 106 F2
Knightlow Ave CV3 .... 134 C6
Knightlow Cl CV8 .... 148 C3
Knightlow Rd B17 .... 85 B8
Knighton Cl B74 .... 31 F3
Knighton Ct B23 .... 56 C2
Knighton Dr B74 .... 31 F3
Knighton Rd
Birmingham B31 .... 103 C4
Cannock WS12 .... 2 E3
Dudley DY2 .... 62 D4
Sutton Coldfield B74 .... 31 D5
Knights Ave WV6 .... 24 E6
Knights Cl Birmingham B23 .. 56 E2
Hinckley LE10 .... 75 D4
Knights Cres WV6 .... 24 E6
Knights Hill Hinckley LE10 .. 74 E8
Norton Canes WS11 .... 6 A4
Knights Hill WS9 .... 30 B3
Knights Rd B11 .... 88 A4
Knights Wood Cl B75 .... 46 D7
Knightsbridge Ave CV12 .. 78 C4
Knightsbridge Cl B74 .... 31 F4
Knightsbridge Ct B37 .... 69 F5
Knightsbridge La WV12 .. 27 C6
Knightsbridge Rd B92 .. 89 A1
Knightsford Cl B97 .. 152 F2
Knightstone Ave B18 .... 66 A4
Knightwick Cres B23 .... 56 C5
Knipersley Rd B73 .... 57 A7
Knoll Cl WS7 .... 7 A5
Knoll Croft Aldridge WS9 .. 16 C1
Cheswick Green B90 .. 126 D4
Coventry CV3 .... 133 C6
Knoll Dr Coventry CV3 .. 133 C6
Warwick CV34 .... 155 E1
Knoll Sch The DY11 .. 116 A7
Knoll The Birmingham B32 .. 84 C1
Kingswinford DY6 .... 60 E5
Knollcroft B16 .... 66 A2

Knott Ct **11** DY5 .... 61 D2
Knottesford Cl B80 .... 159 C3
Knotts Farm Rd DY6 .... 61 A4
Knottsall La B68 .... 64 B3
Knowesley Cl B60 .... 137 B2
Knowlands Rd B90 .... 127 A7
Knowle CE Jun & Inf Sch
B93 .... 128 C6
Knowle Cl Birmingham B45 .. 122 D7
Redditch B98 .... 154 C6
Knowle Hill CV8 .... 148 C6
Knowle Hill Rd DY2 .... 62 B4
Knowle La WS14 .... 9 B3
Knowle Rd Birmingham B11 ... 87 D3
Blackheath B65 .... 63 A4
Hampton in A B92 .... 108 E2
Knowle Sch The B65 .... 63 A4
Knowle Wood Rd B93 .... 128 B3
Knowles Ave CV10 .... 72 C4
Knowles Dr B74 .... 46 A7
Knowles Rd WV1 .... 25 F1
Knowles St WS10 .... 42 A3
Knox Cres CV11 .... 73 F8
Knox Rd WV2 .... 39 D6
Knox's Grave La WS14 ...... 19 D7
Knutswood Cl B13 .... 105 D7
Kohima Dr DY8 .... 80 E5
Kossuth Rd WV14 .... 40 A1
Kurtus B77 .... 35 D6
Kyle Cl WV10 .... 11 B1
Kyles Way B32 .... 102 B7
Kynaston Cres WV8 .... 10 B2
Kynaston Ho B71 .... 53 C8
Kyngsford Rd B33 .... 69 D3
Kynner Way CV3 .... 135 B8
Kyotts Lake Rd B11 .... 87 B7
Kynoch Wks B6 .... 55 F3
Kyotts Lake Unit Factory
B11 .... 87 B7
Kyrwicks La B11 .... 87 A7
Kyter La B36 .... 69 B8

Laburnham Ct WS14 .... 9 C5
Laburnham Rd DY6 .... 60 E6
Laburnum Ave
Birmingham B37 .... 69 F6
Cannock WS11 .... 4 E7
Coventry CV6 .... 112 F5
Kenilworth CV8 .... 148 A4
Smethwick B67 .... 64 E4
Tamworth B79 .... 21 B8
Laburnum Cl Bedworth
CV12 .... 77 E2
Birmingham B37 .... 69 F6
Cannock WS11 .... 4 E7
Hollywood B47 .... 125 A5
Redditch B98 .... 153 E2
Stourbridge DY8 .... 80 E7
Walsall WS3 .... 15 A2
Laburnum Cotts B21 .... 65 E8
Laburnum Croft B69 .... 52 B2
Laburnum Dr
Sutton Coldfield B76 .... 47 A3
Whitnash CV31 .... 162 B3
Laburnum Gr
Birmingham B13 .... 86 F3
Bromsgrove B61 .... 136 F4
Burntwood WS7 .... 6 F6
Kidderminster DY11 .... 116 B8
Nuneaton CV10 .... 72 D6
Walsall WS3 .... 27 F3
Warwick CV34 .... 156 B1
Laburnum Ho WS4 .... 15 D1
Laburnum Rd Bilston WV1 .. 40 B8
Birmingham B30 .... 103 F8
Brownhills WS9 .... 16 A3
Dudley DY1 .... 51 C4
Tipton DY4 .... 51 F7
Walsall WS3 .... 43 C4
Wednesbury WS10 .... 42 B4
Wolverhampton WV4 .... 39 F3
Laburnum St Stourbridge
DY8 .... 80 E7
Wolverhampton WV3 .... 25 B1
Laburnum Trees B47 .... 124 F6
Laburnum Villas **2** B11 ... 87 C5
Laburnum Way B31 .... 103 A1
Laceby Gr B13 .... 87 D1
Lacell Cl CV34 .... 155 E1
Ladbroke Dr B76 .... 46 F2
Ladbroke Gr B27 .... 106 C8
Ladbroke Pk CV34 .... 155 E1
Ladbrook Cl B98 .... 158 E2
Ladbrook Gr DY3 .... 50 B3
Ladbrook Rd Coventry CV5 .. 112 A4
Solihull B91 .... 107 C2
Ladbury Gr WS5 .... 43 A4
Ladbury Rd WS5 .... 43 A3
Ladeler Gr B33 .... 69 E2
Lady Bank Birmingham B32 .. 102 B7
Tamworth B79 .... 21 B4
Lady Brades Ho **5** B69 .. 64 A7
Lady Byron La B93 .... 127 F8
Lady Grey's Wlk DY8 .... 80 D5
Lady Harriet's La B98 ...... 153 F4
Lady Katherine Leveson
CE Prim Sch B93 .... 129 B5
Lady La Coventry CV6 .... 95 F4
Earlswood B90, B94 .... 126 B3
Kenilworth CV8 .... 147 F4
Lady Warwick Ave CV12 .... 78 D2
Ladycroft Birmingham B16 .. 66 B2
Cubbington CV32 .... 157 E5
Ladyfields Way CV6 .... 95 B4
Ladygrove B98 .... 159 A8

Ladymead Dr CV6 .... 95 B2
Ladymoor Rd WV14 .... 40 C3
Ladypool Ave **3** B11 .... 87 B6
Ladypool Cl Halesowen B62 .. 83 C4
Walsall WS4 .... 29 A5
Ladypool Jun & Inf Sch
B11 .... 87 B6
Ladypool Rd B11, B12 .... 87 A5
Ladysmith Rd B63 .... 82 C6
Ladywell Cl WV5 .... 49 A8
Ladywell Wlk B5 .... 164 C1
Ladywood Cl DY5 .... 61 F2
Ladywood Middleway B16 .. 66 A2
Ladywood Rd
Birmingham B16 .... 66 A1
Sutton Coldfield B74 .... 46 A8
Lagonda B77 .... 21 E3
Lagrange B79 .... 20 E6
Laing Ho **2** B69 .... 63 D5
Lair The B78 .... 36 F8
Lake Ave WS5 .... 43 C7
Lake Cl WS5 .... 43 C7
Lake St DY3, DY1 .... 50 E3
Lake View Rd CV5 .... 112 F4
Lakedown Cl B14 .... 104 E1
Lakefield Cl B28 .... 106 B7
Lakefield Rd WV11 .... 26 E5
Lakehouse Ct B23 .... 56 E8
Lakehouse Gr B38 .... 103 D3
Lakehouse Rd B73 .... 56 F8
Lakeland Dr WV14 .... 40 D6
Lakeland Ho CV34 .... 161 A7
Lakenheath B79 .... 21 C7
Laker Cl DY8 .... 81 A7
Lakes Cl DY11 .... 116 C7
Lakes Rd B23 .... 56 A6
Lakes Sta The B94 .... 141 F8
Lakeside Bedworth CV12 ... 78 A2
Little Aston B74 .... 31 B5
Redditch B97 .... 152 D7
Lakeside Cl WV13 .... 26 E3
Lakeside Ct Birmingham B20 .. 55 A4
Brierley Hill DY5 .... 81 B8
Lakeside Dr
Norton Canes WS11 .... 6 B6
Solihull B90 .... 126 F7
Lakeside Inf Sch WV13 ...... 26 E3
Lakeside Prim Sch B77 ...... 21 E2
Lakeside Rd B70 .... 53 A6
Lakeside Wlk B23 .... 56 C3
Lakey La B28 .... 106 A7
Lakey Lane Prim Sch B28 .. 106 B7
Lakin Ct CV34 .... 160 E8
Lakin Ho CV34 .... 160 F8
Lakin Rd CV34 .... 160 F8
Lamb Cl B34 .... 69 E5
Lamb Cres WV5 .... 49 A5
Lamb St CV1 .... 165 B3
Lambah Cl WV14 .... 40 F7
Lambert Cl B23 .... 56 D6
Lambert Ct Kingswinford
DY6 .... 60 D8
Warwick CV34 .... 160 D6
Lambert Dr WS7 .... 7 A8
Lambert End B70 .... 53 B3
Lambert Fold **4** DY2 ...... 62 E8
Lambert Rd WV11 .... 25 F6
Lambert St B70 .... 53 B3
Lambeth Cl Birmingham B37 .. 70 B4
Coventry CV2 .... 114 E7
Lambeth Rd Bilston WV14 .. 40 B7
Birmingham B44 .... 44 E3
Lambourn Cl WS3 .... 14 C2
Lambourn Cres CV31 .... 162 C6
Lambourn Rd B23 .... 56 D4
Lambourne Cl Coventry
CV5 .... 112 A4
Great Wyrley WS6 .... 4 F3
Lichfield WS14 .... 9 E8
Lambourne Gr B37 .... 69 E2
Lambourne Way DY5 .... 81 B8
Lambscote Cl B90 .... 105 C2
Lamerton Cl CV2 .... 114 C6
Lamford Cl LE10 .... 71 B1
Lamintone Dr CV32 .... 156 D2
Lammas Cl B92 .... 89 C1
Lammas Croft CV31 .... 162 A3
Lammas Ct CV34 .... 160 D6
Lammas Ho **6** CV6 .... 113 A4
Lammas Rd Coventry CV6 .. 112 F4
Stourbridge DY8 .... 60 C3
Lammas Wlk CV34 .... 160 D7
Lammermoor Ave B43 .... 43 F2
Lamont Ave B32 .... 84 F3
Lamorna Cl CV11 .... 73 F4
Lamport Ho **5** B14 .... 105 A3
Lamprey B77 .... 35 D6
Lanark Cl DY6 .... 60 F5
Lanark Croft B35 .... 57 F3
Lancaster Ave Aldridge WS9 .. 30 B8
Birmingham B45 .... 122 A8
Wednesbury WS10 .... 42 C3
Lancaster Circus
Queensway B4 .... 164 C4
Lancaster Cl B30 .... 104 A6
Lancaster Gdns WV4 .... 38 E5
Lancaster Ho Cannock WS12 .. 2 D1
7 Oldbury B65 .... 63 E4
6 Stourbridge DY8 .... 80 F8
Lancaster Pl Kenilworth
CV8 .... 147 E2
Walsall WS3 .... 14 C1
Lancaster Rd
Brierley Hill DY5 .... 61 C2
Hinckley LE10 .... 75 D8
Lancaster St B4 .... 164 C4
Lance Cl LE10 .... 75 D5
Lancelot Cl B8 .... 67 E3

Lancelot Ho DY10 .... 117 C8
Lancelot Pl B70 .... 52 E4
Lanchester Cl B79 .... 20 E7
Lanchester Rd
Birmingham B38 .... 104 A1
Coventry CV6 .... 113 B6
Lanchester Way B36 .... 58 F1
Lancia Cl CV6 .... 96 B4
Lancing Rd CV12 .... 79 C2
Land La B37 .... 90 A7
Land Oak Dr DY10 .... 117 B7
Lander Cl B45 .... 122 A6
Landgate Rd B21 .... 54 C2
Landor Ho CV31 .... 162 A2
Landor Rd Knowle B93 ..... 128 A6
Redditch B98 .... 154 A1
Warwick CV34 .... 160 D8
Whitnash CV31 .... 162 A3
Landor St B8 .... 67 B3
Landport Rd WV2 .... 39 F8
Landrail Wlk B36 .... 70 A8
Landrake Rd DY6 .... 61 A5
Landsberg B79 .... 20 F6
Landsdown Pl **2** B18 ..... 66 A5
Landseer Dr LE10 .... 71 B3
Landseer Gr B43 .... 44 D4
Landsgate DY8 .... 81 A1
Landswood Cl B44 .... 45 A1
Landswood Rd B68 .... 64 C4
Landywood Ent Pk WS6 .... 13 F8
Landywood Gn WS6 .... 4 E2
Landywood La WS6 .... 4 E2
Landywood Prim Sch WS6 .. 13 F8
Landywood Sta WS6 .... 4 F2
Lane Ave WS2 .... 28 B3
Lane Cl WS2 .... 28 B3
Lane Croft B76 .... 58 A8
Lane Ct **8** WV3 .... 25 C4
Lane Green Ave WV8 .... 10 C4
Lane Green St WV8 .... 10 B3
Lane Green Fst Sch WV8 .. 10 B4
Lane Green Rd WV8 .... 10 C2
Lane Green Sh Par WV8 .... 10 B3
Lane Rd WV4 .... 40 A3
Lane St WV14 .... 40 D3
Lanes Sh Ctr The **1** B73 .. 57 B7
Lanesfield Dr WV4 .... 40 A4
Lanesfield Drive Ind Est
WV4 .... 40 A4
Lanesfield Prim Sch WV4 .. 40 A4
Laneside CV3 .... 134 E6
Laneside Ave B74 .... 44 F7
Laneside Dr LE10 .... 71 F3
Laneside Gdns WS2 .... 28 B2
Langbank Ave CV3 .... 134 D7
Langbay Ct CV2 .... 114 F6
Langcliffe Ave CV34 .... 155 F1
Langcomb Rd B90 .... 126 A8
Langdale Ave CV6 .... 95 D3
Langdale Cl Clayhanger
WS8 .... 15 E6
Royal Leamington Spa
CV32 .... 157 D3
Langdale Croft B21 .... 65 E7
Langdale Dr Bilston WV14 .. 40 D7
Cannock WS11 .... 4 C7
Nuneaton CV11 .... 74 A6
Langdale Gn WS11 .... 4 C7
Langdale Rd Birmingham
B43 .... 54 F7
Hinckley LE10 .... 75 A8
Langdale Way DY9 .... 81 D4
Langdon St B9 .... 67 B2
Langdon Wlk B27 .... 88 E4
Langfield Rd B93 .... 128 A3
Langford Ave B43 .... 54 E8
Langford Croft B91 .... 107 C2
Langford Gr B17 .... 85 C3
Langham Cl B26 .... 89 A7
Langham Gn B74 .... 30 F1
Langholm Dr
Birmingham B44 .... 45 D1
Cannock WS12 .... 2 E2
Langland Dr DY3 .... 50 C8
Langley Ave WV14 .... 51 C8
Langley Cl B98 .... 154 D1
Langley Cres B68 .... 64 B4
Langley Croft CV4 .... 112 A2
Langley Ct WV4 .... 38 D6
Langley Dr B35 .... 58 A1
Langley Gdns Oldbury B68 .. 64 B4
Wolverhampton WV3 .... 38 D7
Langley Green Rd B69 .... 64 A4
Langley Green Sta B68 ...... 64 B5
Langley Hall Dr B75 .... 47 B5
Langley Hall Rd
Solihull B92 .... 106 C7
Sutton Coldfield B75 .... 47 B5
Langley Heath Dr B76 .... 47 A3
Langley High Sch B68 .... 64 A5
Langley High St B69 .... 64 A5
Langley Jun & Inf Sch
B92 .... 106 D6
Langley Mede B68 .... 64 B5
Langley Prim Sch B69 .... 64 A5
Langley Rd Birmingham
B10 .... 87 D8
Oldbury B68 .... 64 B4
Whitnash CV31 .... 162 A4
Wolverhampton WV3, WV4 .. 38 B7
Langley Rise B92 .... 89 E3
Langley Sch Solihull B92 .. 106 D7
Sutton Coldfield B75 .... 47 A6
Langley Wlk B37 .... 70 D2
Langleys Rd B29 .... 85 E1
Langlodge Rd CV6 .... 95 B2
Langmead Cl WS2 .... 27 D3
Langnor Rd CV2 .... 114 C6
Langsett Rd WV10 .... 25 E4

Langstone Rd
Birmingham B14 .... 105 B3
Dudley DY1 .... 50 F1
Langton Cl CV3 .... 134 E8
Langton Cl WS13 .... 3 A1
Langton Pl WV14 .... 41 A6
Langton Rd B8 .... 67 E4
Langtree Ave B91 .... 107 B1
Langtree Cl WS12 .... 2 D1
Langwood Cl CV4 .... 132 B8
Langwood Ct B36 .... 69 B8
Langworth Ave B27 .... 88 C5
Lannacombe Rd B31 .... 122 E6
Lansbury Ave WS10 .... 41 C4
Lansbury Dr WS11 .... 1 E4
Lansbury Gn B64 .... 83 B8
Lansbury Rd B64 .... 83 B8
Lansbury Wlk **6** DY4 ...... 52 A8
Lansdale Ave B92 .... 107 F8
Lansdown Gn DY11 .... 116 C5
Lansdowne Cir CV32 .... 157 A1
Lansdowne Cl
Bedworth CV12 .... 78 A3
Dudley, Tansley Hill DY2 .. 62 F6
Dudley, West Coseley WV14 .. 51 A7
Lansdowne Cres
6 Royal Leamington Spa
CV32 .... 157 A1
Studley B80 .... 159 D3
Tamworth B77 .... 35 D8
Lansdowne Ct DY9 .... 81 C1
Lansdowne Rd Bilston
WV14 .... 40 E7
Birmingham, Erdington B24 .. 56 F3
Birmingham,
Handsworth B21 .... 66 A8
Halesowen, Hasbury B63 .. 82 D2
Halesowen, Hurst Green B62 .. 63 F1
2 Royal Leamington Spa
CV32 .... 157 A1
Studley B80 .... 159 D3
Wolverhampton WV1 .... 163 A4
Lansdowne St
Birmingham B18 .... 65 F4
Coventry CV2 .... 113 F3
Royal Leamington Spa CV32 .. 157 A1
Lant Cl CV7 .... 131 B7
Lantern Rd DY2 .... 62 C2
Lapal La B68 .... 84 A2
Lapal La N B62 .... 83 E3
Lapal La S B62 .... 83 F2
Lapal Prim Sch B62 .... 83 F4
Lapley Cl WV1 .... 26 B2
Lapper Ave WV4 .... 39 F2
Lapwing B77 .... 36 A6
Lapwing Cl Cheslyn Hay
WS6 .... 4 C1
Kidderminster DY10 .... 117 B1
Lapwing Dr B92 .... 109 B7
Lapwood Ave DY6 .... 61 A5
Lapworth CE Jun &
Inf Sch B94 .... 144 D3
Lapworth Cl B98 .... 158 F7
Lapworth Dr B73 .... 45 C3
Lapworth Gr B12 .... 86 F6
Lapworth Oaks B94 .... 144 D3
Lapworth Rd CV2 .... 96 C1
Lapworth St B94 .... 144 B2
Lapworth Sta B94 .... 144 D4
Lara Cl B17 .... 85 B8
Lara Gr DY4 .... 52 A2
Larch Ave B21 .... 54 D2
Larch Cl WS14 .... 9 E7
Larch Croft Birmingham B37 .. 70 B2
Tipton B69 .... 52 B2
Larch Gr Sedgley DY3 .... 50 E7
Warwick CV34 .... 156 A1
Larch Ho Birmingham B36 .. 68 F8
Stourbridge B80 .... 80 C6
Larch Rd DY6 .... 60 E7
Larch Tree Ave CV4 .... 112 A2
Larch Wlk B25 .... 88 B8
Larches Cottage Gdns
DY11 .... 116 C3
Larches La WV3 .... 25 A2
Larches Rd DY11 .... 116 D4
Larches St B11 .... 87 B6
Larches The Bedworth CV7 .. 96 B8
Wolverhampton WV11 .... 26 B5
Larchfield Cl B20 .... 55 B3
Larchmere Dr
Birmingham B28 .... 105 F8
Bromsgrove B61 .... 136 E3
Essington WV11 .... 13 B3
Larchwood Cres B74 .... 44 E8
Larchwood Dr WS11 .... 2 A4
Larchwood Gn WS5 .... 43 B4
Larchwood Rd Bedworth
CV7 .... 78 B1
Walsall WS5 .... 43 A4
Larcombe Dr WV4 .... 39 E5
Large Ave WS10 .... 41 C4
Lark Cl B14 .... 104 E4
Lark Hall Cty Inf Sch B79 .. 21 A8
Lark Meadow Dr B37 .... 69 F8
Larkfield Ave B36 .... 69 B8
Larkfield Rd B98 .... 154 A1
Larkfield Way CV5 .... 112 A6
Larkhill DY10 .... 116 E7
Larkhill Rd DY8 .... 80 D4
Larkhill Wlk B14 .... 104 D1
Larkin Cl Bulkington CV12 .. 79 B3
Wolverhampton WV10 .... 12 A1
Larkspur B77 .... 35 D4
Larkspur Ave WS7 .... 7 A5

Larkspur Croft B36 .... 68 D8
Larkspur Ct Bedworth CV12 .. 95 C8
Halesowen B62 .... 83 F7
Larkspur Dr WV10 .... 12 B7
Larkspur Rd DY2 .... 62 F8
Larkspur Wlk WS8 .... 15 D6
Larkswood Dr Sedgley DY3 .. 50 D7
Wolverhampton WV4 .... 38 C3
Larne Rd B26 .... 89 A7
Lashbrooke Ho B45 .... 121 F7
Lassington Cl B98 .... 154 E4
Latches Cl WS10 .... 41 E6
Latchford Cl B98 .... 154 E6
Latelow Rd B33 .... 69 A2
Lath La B66 .... 64 D8
Latham Ave B43 .... 54 E7
Latham Cres B31 .... 52 A3
Latham Rd CV5 .... 113 A2
Lathom Gr B33 .... 68 F5
Latimer Cl CV8 .... 147 F2
Latimer Gdns B15 .... 86 D7
Latimer Pl B18 .... 65 E6
Latimer Rd B48 .... 139 A5
Latimer St WV13 .... 27 B3
Latymer Cl B76 .... 58 A7
Lauder Cl Sedgley DY3 ...... 39 C1
Willenhall WS13 .... 26 D1
Lauderdale Ave CV6 .... 95 D3
Lauderdale Cl WS8 .... 15 E6
Lauderdale Gdns WV10 ..... 11 E3
Launceston Cl Tamworth
B77 .... 21 D2
Walsall WS5 .... 43 D7
Launceston Rd CV11 .... 73 F4
Launceston Rd WS5 .... 43 D7
Launde The B28 .... 105 E3
Laundry Cotts CV35 .... 145 E4
Laundry Rd B66 .... 65 C3
Laureates Wlk B74 .... 46 A8
Laurel Ave B12 .... 87 A5
Laurel Bank B79 .... 21 B6
Laurel Bank Mews B60 .... 137 F4
Laurel Cl Coventry CV2 ...... 96 E2
Dudley DY1 .... 51 A3
Lichfield WS13 .... 9 D8
Redditch B98 .... 153 E2
Laurel Dr Burntwood WS7 .. 7 C7
Cannock WS12 .... 2 E4
Nuneaton CV10 .... 72 A7
Smethwick B66 .... 65 A8
Sutton Coldfield B74 .... 44 E8
Laurel Gdns Birmingham
B21 .... 54 E1
4 Birmingham, Stockfield
B27 .... 88 C5
Laurel Gr Bilston WV14 ...... 41 A4
Birmingham B30 .... 103 E6
Bromsgrove B61 .... 136 F4
Wolverhampton WV3 .... 38 E6
Laurel La B63 .... 83 B3
Laurel Rd
Birmingham,
Handsworth B21 .... 54 F1
Birmingham, King's Norton
B30 .... 104 A4
Dudley DY1 .... 51 A3
Tipton DY4 .... 51 F7
Walsall WS3 .... 43 B4
Laurels Cres CV7 .... 130 C6
Laurels The Bedworth CV12 .. 77 E2
Birmingham, Ladywood B16 .. 65 F3
Birmingham, Sheldon B26 .. 89 C5
Oldbury B68 .... 84 B6
Smethwick B66 .... 65 C4
Sutton Coldfield B73 .... 46 B1
Laurence Ct B31 .... 103 B5
Laurence Gr WV6 .... 24 E7
Lauriston Cl DY1 .... 50 F3
Lavender Ave CV6 .... 112 F5
Lavender Cl WV9 .... 10 F3
Lavender Gr WV14 .... 40 F6
Lavender Hall La CV7 .... 110 C2
Lavender Ho B38 .... 123 F6
Lavender La DY8 .... 80 D3
Lavender Rd Dudley DY1 ... 51 B3
Tamworth B77 .... 21 F4
Lavendon Rd B42 .... 55 B5
Lavenham Cl CV11 .... 79 C8
Lavinia Rd B62 .... 83 E3
Law Cl B69 .... 52 D2
Law Cliff Rd B42 .... 55 B6
Law St B71 .... 53 C5
Lawden Rd B10 .... 87 B8
Lawford Ave WS14 .... 9 E7
Lawford Cl Birmingham B7 .. 67 A3
Coventry CV3 .... 114 C1
Lawford Gr Birmingham B5 .. 86 E8
Solihull B90 .... 105 D2
Lawford Rd CV31 .... 162 B5
Lawfred Ave WV11 .... 26 D5
Lawley Cl Coventry CV4 ... 112 A2
Walsall WS4 .... 15 B1
Lawley Middleway B4 .... 67 A3
Lawley Rd WV14 .... 40 B6
Lawley St Dudley DY1 .... 51 A1
West Bromwich B70 .... 52 F3
Lawley The B63 .... 82 D1
Lawn Ave DY8 .... 80 E4
Lawn La Coven Heath WV9 .. 11 A7
Wolverhampton WV9 .... 10 F5
Lawn Rd WV2 .... 39 F6
Lawn St DY8 .... 80 E4
Lawnoaks Cl WS8 .... 6 D2
Lawns The Bedworth CV12 .. 77 C2
Hinckley LE10 .... 75 E8
Lawnsdale Cl B46 .... 70 F7
Lawnsdown Rd DY5 .... 81 F6
Lawnsfield Gr B23 .... 56 D7

Lawnside Gn WV14 .... 40 D8
Lawnswood Hinckley LE10 .. 75 A8
Stourbridge DY7 .... 60 A2
Sutton Coldfield B76 .... 58 A8
Lawnswood Ave
　Burntwood WS7 .... 6 F5
　Solihull B90 .... 106 D3
　Stourbridge DY8 .... 60 C3
　Wolverhampton,
　Parkfields WV4 .... 39 E4
　Wolverhampton,
　Tettenhall WV6 .... 24 E8
Lawnswood Cl WS12 .... 2 D1
Lawnswood Dr
　Brownhills WS9 .... 16 A3
　Stourbridge DY7 .... 60 A2
Lawnswood Gr B21 .... 54 C1
Stourbridge DY8 .... 60 D3
Lawnswood Rd Dudley DY3 .. 50 D5
　Stourbridge DY8 .... 60 D3
Lawnswood Rise WV6 .... 24 F8
Lawnwood Rd DY2 .... 62 C2
Lawrence Ave
　Wednesfield WV11 .... 26 F6
　Wolverhampton WV10 .... 26 A4
Lawrence Ct 6 Oldbury B68 .. 84 B8
　Tamworth B79 .... 21 A6
Lawrence Dr B76 .... 58 D6
Lawrence Gdns CV8 .... 148 A6
Lawrence La B62 .... 62 E1
Lawrence Rd CV7 .... 96 A8
Lawrence Saunders Rd
　CV6 .... 113 B5
Lawrence St Stourbridge
　DY9 .... 81 C6
　Willenhall WV13 .... 27 A3
Lawrence Wlk B43 .... 44 D4
Lawson Cl WS9 .... 30 B4
Lawson St B4 .... 164 C4
Lawton Ave B29 .... 86 B2
Lawton Blackheath B65 ...... 63 D6
　Hinckley LE10 .... 74 F8
Lawton Ct WV3 .... 25 B1
Laxey Rd B16 .... 65 D3
Laxford Cl B12 .... 86 E6
Laxton Cl DY6 .... 61 A5
Laxton Gr B25 .... 68 D1
Lay Gdns CV31 .... 162 E5
Lazy Hill Birmingham B38 .. 104 B2
　Stonnall WS9 .... 16 D2
Lazy Hill Rd WS9 .... 16 C1
Le Hanche Cl CV7 .... 95 A7
Le More B74 .... 32 A2
Lea Ave WS10 .... 41 D1
Lea Bank Ave DY11 .... 116 B5
Lea Bank Rd DY3 .... 62 C3
Lea Cswy The DY11 .... 116 A4
Lea Dr B26 .... 89 A6
Lea End La B38, B48 .... 123 D3
Lea Ford Rd B33 .... 69 C4
Lea Green Ave DY4 .... 51 D5
Lea Green La B47 .... 125 C5
Lea Hall Rd B33 .... 69 A2
Lea Hall Sta B33 .... 69 A2
Lea Hill Rd B20 .... 55 C2
Lea Ho Birmingham B15 ...... 86 D7
　6 Dudley DY1 .... 61 E8
Lea House Rd B30 .... 104 A7
Lea La WS6 .... 5 A3
Lea Manor Dr WV4 .... 38 E4
Lea Park Rise B61 .... 136 F5
Lea Rd Birmingham B11 ...... 87 D4
　Wolverhampton WV3 .... 39 B8
Lea St DY10 .... 116 F6
Lea Street Fst Sch DY10 .. 116 F6
Lea The Birmingham B33 .... 69 A2
　Kidderminster DY11 .... 116 A5
Lea Vale Rd DY8 .... 80 F2
Lea View Aldridge WS9 ...... 29 E5
　Wednesfield WV12 .... 27 A5
Lea Village B33 .... 69 B3
Lea Wlk B45 .... 121 F8
Lea Wood Gr DY11 .... 116 A5
Lea Yield Cl B30 .... 104 A7
Leabon Gr B17 .... 85 C4
Leabrook B26 .... 88 F8
Leabrook Rd DY4, WS14 ..... 41 D1
Leabrook Rd N WS10 .... 41 D2
Leabrook Sq WS10 .... 41 D1
Leach Green La B45 .... 122 B6
Leach Heath La B45 .... 122 A7
Leacliffe Way WS9 .... 30 F3
Leacote Dr WV6 .... 24 C4
Leacrest Rd CV6 .... 95 A2
Leacroft WV12 .... 27 C7
Leacroft Ave WV10 .... 25 E8
Leacroft Cl WS9 .... 16 B1
Leacroft Gr B71 .... 53 B7
Leacroft La WS11 .... 4 F5
Leacroft Rd DY6 .... 60 E8
Leadbeater Ho 4 WS3 ...... 28 B8
Leadbetter Dr B61 .... 136 D2
Leaf Ct CV3 .... 133 D4
Leaf La Coventry CV3 ...... 133 D5
　Coventry CV3 .... 133 F6
Leafdown Cl WS12 .... 2 D1
Leafenden Ave WS7 .... 7 A6
Leafield Cl CV2 .... 114 F8
Leafield Cres B33 .... 69 A5
Leafield Gdns B62 .... 83 D8
Leafield Rd B92 .... 89 C1
Leaford Way DY6 .... 60 F5
Leafy Glade B74 .... 31 A3
Leafy Rise DY3 .... 50 D4
Leagh Cl CV8 .... 148 B7
Leaholme Gdns DY9 .... 81 B2
Leahouse Gdns B68 .... 64 A3

Leahouse Rd B68 .... 64 A3
Leahurst Cres B17 .... 85 C4
Lealholme Cl CV5 .... 132 F8
Leam Cl CV11 .... 73 F1
Leam Cres B92 .... 89 B1
Leam Dr WS7 .... 7 D7
Leam Gn CV4 .... 132 D5
Leam Rd CV31 .... 161 D7
Leam St CV31 .... 162 B7
Leam Terr CV31 .... 162 B8
Leamington Cl WS11 .... 4 C7
Leamington Rd
　Birmingham B12 .... 87 B5
　Coventry CV3 .... 133 C6
　Kenilworth CV8 .... 148 B2
　Ryton-on-D CV8 .... 135 B1
Leamington Spa Sta CV31 . 161 F7
Leamore Cl WS2 .... 28 A7
Leamore Ind Est WS2 .... 28 C6
Leamore La WS3 .... 28 C7
Leamore JMI Sch WS3 .... 28 B6
Leander Cl WS6 .... 4 F1
Leander Gdns B14 .... 104 F5
Leander Rd DY9 .... 81 F4
Leandor Dr B74 .... 45 A7
Lear Gr CV34 .... 161 E4
Lear Rd WV5 .... 49 B8
Leas Cl CV12 .... 78 A3
Leas The WV10 .... 12 C7
Leason La WV10 .... 26 A7
Leasow Dr B15 .... 85 D3
Leasow The WS9 .... 29 E5
Leasowe Rd
　Birmingham B45 .... 121 F8
　Tipton DY4 .... 51 E4
Leasowe The WS13 .... 3 A1
Leasowe's Ave CV3 .... 132 F4
Leasowes Children's
　Farm The B94 .... 142 D4
Leasowes Ct B63 .... 82 F3
Leasowes Dr Perton WV6 ... 23 D4
　Wolverhampton WV4 .... 38 D6
Leasowes High Sch B62 .... 83 E6
Leasowes La B62 .... 83 D4
Leasowes Rd B14 .... 86 F1
Leasowes Rd B14 .... 86 F1
Leaton Gr B13 .... 87 A3
Leavesden Gr B26 .... 89 A5
Leaward Cl CV10 .... 72 E2
Lebanon Gr WS7 .... 6 F8
Lebanon Ho 6 B36 .... 57 F1
Lechlade Cl B98 .... 154 B7
Lechlade Rd B43 .... 54 E8
Leckie Rd WS2 .... 28 E4
Ledbrook Rd CV32 .... 157 E5
Ledbury Cl Aldridge WS9 ... 16 C1
　Birmingham B16 .... 66 A2
　Redditch B98 .... 154 F2
Ledbury Dr WV1 .... 26 B1
Ledbury Ho Birmingham B33 . 69 E2
　Redditch B97 .... 153 B4
Ledbury Rd CV31 .... 162 C6
Ledbury Way B76 .... 58 A8
Ledsam Gr B32 .... 84 F6
Ledsam St B16 .... 66 A2
Lee Bank Jun Sch B15 ...... 86 C7
Lee Bank Middleway B15 ... 86 C8
Lee Cl CV34 .... 155 E2
Lee Cres B15 .... 86 C8
Lee Ct WS9 .... 15 F3
Lee Gdns B67 .... 64 E5
Lee Mount B15 .... 86 C8
Lee Rd Blackheath B64 ...... 82 F8
　Hollywood B47 .... 125 A7
　Royal Leamington Spa CV31 . 161 E6
Lee St DY4 .... 53 A8
Lee The CV5 .... 112 C4
Lee Wlk WS11 .... 2 B4
Leebank Rd B63 .... 82 E2
Leech St DY4 .... 52 C5
Leeder Cl CV6 .... 95 C2
Leedham Ave B77 .... 21 D5
Leek Wootton CE Fst Sch
　CV35 .... 156 A5
Leeming Cl CV4 .... 132 C6
Lees Rd WV14 .... 40 F3
Lees St B18 .... 65 F6
Lees Terr WV14 .... 40 F3
Leeson Wlk B17 .... 85 D5
Legge La Birmingham B1 ..... 66 C3
　Dudley WV14 .... 40 D1
Legge St Birmingham B4 ... 164 F4
　West Bromwich B70 .... 53 B4
　Wolverhampton WV2 .... 39 E6
Legion Cl WS11 .... 6 A6
Legion Rd B45 .... 121 E7
Legs La WV10 .... 11 F3
Leicester Cl B67 .... 64 E1
Leicester Cswy CV1 .... 113 D5
Leicester Ct CV12 .... 79 C2
Leicester La
　Cubbington CV32 .... 149 E1
　Royal Leamington Spa
　CV32 .... 157 C6
Leicester Pl B71 .... 53 C7
Leicester Rd Bedworth CV12 . 78 B4
　Hinckley LE10 .... 71 F2
　Nuneaton CV11 .... 73 D5
　Shilton CV7 .... 97 F6
Leicester Row CV1 .... 165 B4
Leicester Sq 8 Birmingham
　B29 .... 85 F4
Leicester St Bedworth CV12 . 78 B3
　Bulkington CV12 .... 79 C2
　Royal Leamington Spa CV32 . 157 A1
　Walsall WS1 .... 28 E2
　Wolverhampton WV6 .... 25 B4
Leigh Ave Burntwood WS7 .... 7 B7
　Coventry CV3 .... 133 C3
Leigh CE Prim Sch CV4 .... 131 D8
Leigh Cl WS4 .... 29 A4

Leigh Ct Birmingham B23 .... 56 C2
　Walsall WS4 .... 29 A3
Leigh Inf & Jun Sch B8 .... 67 E6
Leigh Rd Birmingham B8 .... 67 E6
　Sutton Coldfield B75 ...... 47 B5
　Walsall WS4 .... 29 A4
Leigh St 4 CV1 .... 113 E4
Leigham Dr B17 .... 85 A7
Leighs Cl WS4 .... 15 C1
Leighs Rd WS4 .... 15 C1
Leighswood Ave WS9 .... 30 B7
Leighswood Cl WS11 .... 5 F5
Leighswood Gr WS9 .... 30 B6
Leighswood Gr WS9 .... 30 A7
Leighswood Ind Est WS9 ... 30 A8
Leighswood Inf Sch WS9 ... 30 B8
Leighswood Jun Sch WS9 .. 30 B7
Leighswood Rd WS9 .... 30 A7
Leighton Cl Birmingham B43 . 44 C3
　Coventry CV4 .... 132 D2
　Dudley DY1 .... 50 E2
　Royal Leamington Spa
　CV32 .... 157 C4
Leighton Rd Bilston WV14 ... 41 A4
　Birmingham B13 .... 86 F2
　Wolverhampton WV4 .... 38 F6
Leisure Wlk B77 .... 35 F6
Leith Gr B38 .... 123 E8
Lelant Gr B17 .... 85 A5
Lellow St B71 .... 53 C8
Lemar Ind Est B30 .... 86 B1
Lemount Dr B44 .... 45 C2
Lemox Rd B70 .... 53 A8
Len Davies Rd WV12 .... 27 B7
Lench Cl Birmingham B13 .... 87 A3
　Halesowen B62 .... 63 C1
Lench St B4 .... 164 C4
Lench's Trust Almshouses
　4 Birmingham,
　Edgbaston B12 .... 87 A8
　4 Birmingham,
　Highgate B12 .... 86 F7
　3 Birmingham,
　Ladywood B16 .... 86 F7
Lenches Trust B32 .... 84 E6
Lenchs Gn B5 .... 86 E7
Lennard Gdns B66 .... 65 B5
Lennox Cl CV3 .... 134 E6
Lennox Gdns WV3 .... 39 A8
Lennox Gr B73 .... 57 A7
Lennox St B19 .... 66 D6
Lenton Croft B26 .... 88 E4
Lenton's La CV2 .... 96 E4
Lenwade Rd B68 .... 84 D8
Leofric Ct 3 B15 .... 86 C8
Leofric St CV6 .... 113 A5
Leominster Ct B45 .... 121 F8
Leominster Ho B33 .... 69 E2
Leominster Rd B11 .... 87 E3
Leominster Wlk B45 .... 121 F8
Leomonsley Cl WS13 .... 8 F7
Leomonsley Ct WS13 .... 8 E7
Leomonsley Rd WS13 .... 8 F7
Leomonsley View WS13 .... 8 F7
Leona Ind Est B62 .... 63 D1
Leonard Ave 5 B19 .... 66 D8
Leonard Gr 6 B19 .... 66 D8
Leonard Parkins Ho CV12 .. 79 D2
Leonard Rd Birmingham B19 . 66 D8
　Stourbridge DY8 .... 80 C5
Leopold Ave B20 .... 54 F5
Leopold Rd CV1 .... 113 F4
Leopold St B12 .... 86 F8
Lepid Gr B29 .... 85 D2
Lerryn Cl DY6 .... 60 F5
Lerwick Cl DY6 .... 60 F5
Lesingham Dr CV4 .... 111 E1
Lesley Bentley Ho 5 B1 ... 66 C3
Lesley Dr DY6 .... 60 E4
Leslie Dr DY4 .... 41 B1
Leslie Rd
　Birmingham, Edgbaston B16 ... 65 F2
　Birmingham,
　Handsworth B20 .... 55 D2
　Little Aston B74 .... 31 B2
　Wolverhampton WV10 .... 25 F4
Leslie Rise B69 .... 63 C8
Lesscroft Cl WV9 .... 11 A3
Lester Gr WS9 .... 30 E2
Lester St WV14 .... 40 F5
Leswell Gr DY10 .... 116 F6
Leswell La DY10 .... 116 F6
Leswell St DY10 .... 116 F6
Letchlade Cl CV2 .... 114 C8
Levante Gdns B33 .... 68 D2
Leve La WV13 .... 27 B1
Level St DY5 .... 61 E3
Leven Cl LE10 .... 75 B8
Leven Croft B76 .... 58 A7
Leven Dr WV12 .... 13 B1
Leven Way CV2 .... 115 A8
Lever St WV2 .... 163 C1
Leverretts The B21 .... 54 C3
Leverton Rise WV10 .... 25 C6
Leveson Ave WS6 .... 4 E2
Leveson Cl DY2 .... 62 E8
Leveson Cres CV7 .... 130 B6
Leveson Ct
　1 Willenhall WV13 .... 27 A2
　Wolverhampton W6 .... 25 A4
Leveson Dr DY4 .... 51 E6
Leveson Rd WV11 .... 26 F8
Leveson St WV13 .... 27 A2
Leveson Wlk 5 DY2 .... 62 E8
Levett Rd B77 .... 22 B5
Levetts Fields WS13 .... 9 C7
Levetts Hollow WS12 .... 2 D3

Levetts Sq 6 WS13 .... 9 B7
Levington Cl WV6 .... 23 F4
Lewis Ave WV1 .... 26 B2
Lewis Cl Lichfield WS14 ...... 9 F7
　Willenhall WV12 .... 27 D5
Lewis Gr WV11 .... 26 D6
Lewis Rd Birmingham B30 .. 104 C7
　Coventry CV1 .... 113 D5
　Oldbury B68 .... 84 B7
　Radford Semele CV31 ...... 162 F1
　Stourbridge DY9 .... 81 D5
Lewis St Bilston WV14 ...... 40 E6
　Tipton DY4 .... 52 D5
　Walsall WS2 .... 28 D3
Lewisham Rd Smethwick
　B66 .... 65 A7
　Wolverhampton WV10 .... 11 B2
Lewisham St B71 .... 53 D4
Lewkner Almshouses The
　B48 .... 139 A5
Lewthorn Rise WV4 .... 39 D4
Lexington Ct CV11 .... 73 B5
Lexington Gn DY5 .... 81 C7
Ley Hill Farm Rd B31 ...... 102 E5
Ley Hill Prim Sch B31 ..... 102 E5
Ley Hill Rd B75 .... 46 C8
Ley Rise DY3 .... 39 C1
Leybourne Cres WV9 .... 10 F2
Leybourne Gr B25 .... 88 C6
Leybrook Rd B45 .... 122 B8
Leyburn Cl Coventry CV6 .... 95 E2
　Nuneaton CV11 .... 74 A2
　3 Warwick CV34 .... 155 F1
　Willenhall WS2 .... 27 D3
Leyburn Rd B16 .... 66 A1
Leycester Cl B31 .... 123 A7
Leycester Ct 7 CV34 ...... 160 E6
Leycester Pl CV34 .... 160 E6
Leycester Rd CV8 .... 148 A2
Leycroft Ave B33 .... 69 D3
Leyes La CV8 .... 148 C5
Leyfields WS13 .... 3 B2
Leyfields Cres CV34 .... 160 D4
Leylan Croft B13 .... 105 D7
Leyland Ave WV3 .... 24 F1
Leyland Croft WS3 .... 14 F4
Leyland Rd Bulkington CV12 .. 79 B2
　Coventry CV5 .... 112 D4
　Nuneaton CV11 .... 73 E1
　Tamworth B77 .... 21 E3
Leyland Spec Sch CV11 .... 73 E1
Leyman Cl B14 .... 105 C4
Leymere Cl CV7 .... 92 C1
Leys Cl DY9 .... 81 C2
Leys Cres DY5 .... 61 B3
Leys High Sch The B98 .... 159 C6
Leys Ind Est DY5 .... 61 A3
Leys La CV7 .... 92 C1
Leys Rd DY5 .... 61 B3
Leys The Birmingham B31 .. 103 B5
　1 Darlaston WS10 .... 41 D6
Leys Wood Croft B26 .... 89 B6
Leysdown Gr B27 .... 106 C8
Leysdown Rd B27 .... 106 C8
Leyside CV3 .... 134 E5
Leysters Cl B98 .... 154 E3
Leyton Cl DY5 .... 81 D8
Leyton Gr B44 .... 45 A1
Leyton Rd B21 .... 65 F8
Libbards Gate 4 B91 ...... 127 C8
Libbards Way B91 .... 127 B8
Liberty Rd B77 .... 35 F5
Liberty Way CV11 .... 73 F3
Libra Cl B79 .... 20 F7
Library Cl LE10 .... 76 A5
Library Way B45 .... 121 F7
Lich Ave WV11 .... 26 E7
Lichen Cl WS12 .... 1 C6
Lichen Gn CV4 .... 132 D5
Lichfield Bsns Ctr WS13 ..... 3 D1
Lichfield Cl WS13 .... 9 B8
Lichfield Cath Sch
　(St Chads) WS13 .... 9 B8
Lichfield City Sta WS13 ..... 9 B7
Lichfield Cl CV11 .... 74 A7
Lichfield Coll WS13 .... 9 B7
Lichfield Cres B78 .... 20 B7
Lichfield Rd Solihull B90 .. 105 D2
　Sutton Coldfield B75 ...... 46 C5
　Walsall WS4 .... 29 A4
Lichfield Pas WV1 .... 163 C3
Lichfield Rd Birmingham B6 .. 67 B8
　Brownhills, New Town WS8 ... 7 C1
　Brownhills,
　Shire Oak WS8, WS9 .... 16 B5
　Burntwood WS7 .... 7 E6
　Cannock WS11 .... 5 B8
　Coventry CV3 .... 133 D8
　Hopwas B78 .... 20 B7
　Sutton Coldfield B74 ...... 32 A3
　Tamworth B79 .... 20 D6
　Walsall, Highbridge WS3 .. 14 C2
　Walsall, Rushall WS4 ...... 29 B6
　Walsall,
　Wallington Heath WS3 ..... 15 B6
　Water Orton B46, B76 ...... 59 D4
　Wednesfield WV11 .... 26 E6
　Willenhall WV12 .... 27 D8
　Wishaw B76 .... 48 B3
Lichfield Road Ind Est
　B79 .... 20 E6
Lichfield St Bilston WV14 ... 40 E5
　Fazeley B78 .... 20 F1
　Tamworth B79 .... 21 A5
　Tipton DY4 .... 51 F8
　Walsall WS1 .... 28 F2
　Wolverhampton WV1 .... 163 C3

Lichwood Rd WV11 .... 26 F7
Lickey Coppice B45 .... 122 C4
Lickey End Fst Sch B60 ... 137 C6
Lickey Fst & Mid Sch The
　B45 .... 121 F3
Lickey Gr DY11 .... 116 B2
Lickey Grange B45 .... 121 E1
Lickey Hills Ctry Pk B45 . 122 A5
Lickey Rd Birmingham B45 .. 122 C6
　Stourbridge DY8 .... 81 B6
Lickey Rock B60 .... 121 D1
Lickey Sq B45 .... 122 A2
Liddiard Ct DY8 .... 80 E6
Liddon Gr B27 .... 106 C8
Liddon Rd B27 .... 106 C8
Lifford Cl B14 .... 104 C4
Lifford Way CV3 .... 135 A7
Lifton Croft DY6 .... 60 F5
Light Hall Sch B90 .... 126 B8
Light La CV1 .... 165 B4
Lightfields Wlk B65 .... 63 A5
Lighthorne Ave B16 .... 66 B2
Lighthorne Rd B91 .... 107 C6
Lightning Way B31 .... 123 B7
Lightoak Cl B97 .... 158 C6
Lightwood Cl B93 .... 128 B8
Lightwood Rd DY1 .... 51 A3
Lightwoods Hill B67 .... 84 E8
Lightwoods Jun & Inf Sch
　B68 .... 84 D8
Lightwoods Prim Sch B68 .. 84 D8
Lightwoods Rd
　Smethwick B67 .... 65 A1
　Stourbridge DY9 .... 81 C1
Lilac Ave
　1 Birmingham,
　Balsall Heath B12 .... 87 A5
　Birmingham, Perry B44 ..... 55 E7
　Cannock WS11 .... 4 D7
　Coventry CV6 .... 112 F5
　Sutton Coldfield B74 ...... 44 E8
　Tipton DY4 .... 51 E7
　Walsall WS5 .... 43 A4
Lilac Cl Hinckley LE10 ..... 75 E6
　Redditch B98 .... 153 E2
Lilac Gr Burntwood WS7 ...... 6 F3
　Walsall WS2 .... 27 E3
　Warwick CV34 .... 156 A1
　Wednesbury WS10 .... 42 A2
Lilac Ho WS4 .... 15 C1
Lilac La WS6 .... 14 A8
Lilac Rd Bedworth CV12 .... 78 D5
　Bilston WV14 .... 40 B8
　Dudley DY1 .... 51 C4
　Tamworth B79 .... 21 A8
　Willenhall WV12 .... 27 E7
Lilac Way B62 .... 83 F8
Lilian Gr WV14 .... 40 E1
Lilleshall Cl B98 .... 154 E3
Lilleshall Cres WV2 .... 39 D7
Lilleshall Rd B26 .... 89 B7
Lilley Cl CV6 .... 95 C2
Lilley Green Rd B48 ...... 140 D5
Lilley La B31 .... 123 B8
Lillington Ave CV32 .... 156 F2
Lillington CE Fst Sch
　CV32 .... 157 A3
Lillington Cl Lichfield WS13 . 9 A8
　Royal Leamington Spa
　CV32 .... 157 A3
　Sutton Coldfield B75 ...... 47 A4
Lillington Gr B34 .... 69 D5
Lillington Prim Sch
　CV32 .... 157 B3
Lillington Rd Coventry CV2 .. 96 D1
　Royal Leamington Spa
　CV32 .... 157 A3
　Solihull B90 .... 126 B8
Lily Rd B26 .... 88 D7
Lily St B71 .... 53 C5
Lilycroft La B38 .... 124 A7
Limberlost Cl B20 .... 55 A3
Limbrick Ave CV4 .... 112 A1
Limbrick Cl B90 .... 105 F2
Limbrick Wood Prim Sch
　CV4 .... 111 F3
Limbury Gr B92 .... 107 C6
Lime Ave 8 Birmingham
　B29 .... 85 F4
　Royal Leamington Spa
　CV32 .... 157 A4
　Walsall WS2 .... 27 E3
Lime Cl Great Wyrley WS6 .... 4 F4
　Hollywood B47 .... 125 A5
　Tipton DY4 .... 51 E5
　Walsall WS2 .... 27 E3
　West Bromwich B70 .... 53 A4
Lime Ct B11 .... 87 C4
Lime Gr Bilston WV14 .... 40 C7
　Birmingham,
　Balsall Heath B12 .... 86 F5
　Birmingham,
　Chemsley Wood B37 .... 70 B3
　Birmingham, Lozells B19 .. 66 C8
　Birmingham,
　Small Heath B10 .... 87 D8
　Bromsgrove B61 .... 136 F4
　Burntwood WS7 .... 7 C6
　Coventry CV4 .... 112 B2
　Kenilworth CV8 .... 148 A4
　Lichfield WS13 .... 9 D8
　Nuneaton CV10 .... 72 E5

Lime Gr continued
Smethwick B66 .... **65** B3
Smethwick B66 .... **65** B4
Sutton Coldfield B73 ...... **57** B7
Walsall WS4 .... **29** C6
Lime Kiln Cl B38 .... **123** D7
Lime La Norton Canes WS3 ...... **6** A1
Walsall WS3 .... **15** A8
Lime Rd Huntington WS12 ...... **1** D8
Sedgley DY3 .... **39** F1
Wednesbury WS10 .... **41** F4
Lime St Dudley WV14 ...... **51** A8
Walsall WS1 .... **29** A1
Wolverhampton WV3 ...... **39** B8
Lime Tree Ave
Coventry CV4 .... **112** A2
Wolverhampton WV6 ...... **24** A3
Lime Tree Cres B97 ...... **153** B4
Lime Tree Gdns WV8 ...... **10** B3
Lime Tree Rd
Birmingham,
Acock's Green B27 ...... **88** C5
Birmingham, Saltley B8 ...... **67** F6
Codsall WV8 .... **10** B4
Walsall WS5 .... **43** A4
Limehurst Ave WV3 ...... **38** C8
Limehurst Rd WS4 ...... **29** C6
Limekiln La Birmingham
B14 .... **105** A4
Tanworth-in-A B94 ...... **126** D1
Limepit La Dudley DY1 ...... **51** A3
Huntington WS11, WS12 ...... **1** D6
Limes Ave Blackheath B65 ...... **63** C2
Brierley Hill DY5 .... **61** C5
Limes Rd Dudley DY1 ...... **51** B3
Wolverhampton WV6 ...... **24** D4
Limes The Bedworth CV12 ...... **77** E2
Birmingham, Ladywood B16 ...... **65** F2
Birmingham,
Rotton Park B16 .... **65** F3
Birmingham, Sparkbrook B11 ...... **87** C6
Wolverhampton WV11 ...... **26** B5
Limes View DY3 .... **50** D7
Limetree Rd B74 .... **30** D1
Linacre Ho B37 .... **69** F2
Linaker Rd CV34 ...... **134** C5
Linchmere Rd B21 ...... **54** C2
Lincoln Ave Nuneaton CV10 ...... **72** B7
Willenhall WV13 .... **27** D2
Lincoln Cl Birmingham B27 ...... **88** E3
Lichfield WS13 .... **3** C3
Warwick CV34 .... **155** E1
Lincoln Croft WS14 ...... **17** F6
Lincoln Dr WS11 .... **4** F8
Lincoln Gn WV10 ...... **11** D2
Lincoln Gr B37 .... **70** A1
Lincoln Ho WV10 ...... **25** D3
Lincoln Rd Birmingham B27 ...... **88** D2
Bromsgrove B61 .... **136** E4
Dudley DY2 .... **62** D2
Smethwick B67 .... **64** E2
Walsall WS1 .... **29** A1
West Bromwich B71 ...... **42** D1
Lincoln Rd N B27 ...... **88** E3
Lincoln St Birmingham B12 ...... **86** E6
Coventry CV1 .... **165** C4
Wolverhampton WV10 ...... **25** E3
Lincoln Tower B16 ...... **66** A1
Lincroft Cres CV5 ...... **112** E4
Lindale Ave B36 .... **68** C6
Lindale Cres DY5 ...... **81** B6
Linden Ave Birmingham B43 ...... **54** D8
Burntwood WS7 .... **7** A8
Halesowen B62 .... **83** E7
Kidderminster DY10 ...... **117** A4
Tipton B69 .... **63** D8
Linden Cl Tamworth B77 ...... **21** F4
Warwick CV34 .... **155** E2
Willenhall WS2 .... **27** D2
Linden Ct B91 .... **107** E4
Linden Dr DY8 .... **81** A3
Linden Gdns DY10 ...... **117** A6
Linden Glade B63 ...... **83** A4
Linden Gr DY10 .... **117** A7
Linden La WV12 .... **27** E6
Linden Lea Bedworth CV12 ...... **78** B3
Wolverhampton WV3 ...... **24** D1
Linden Rd Birmingham B30 ...... **103** E7
Dudley DY1 .... **51** B3
Hinckley LE10 .... **71** C1
Smethwick B66 .... **65** A2
Linden View WS12 ...... **2** B4
Lindens Dr B74 .... **44** F5
Lindens Mid Sch B74 ...... **44** F6
Lindens The
Birmingham,
Beech Lanes B32 ...... **84** E7
Birmingham, Edgbaston B16 ...... **65** D1
Wolverhampton WV6 ...... **24** E3
Lindenwood B73 .... **46** B6
Lindera B77 .... **22** A4
Lindfield The CV3 ...... **134** C8
Lindford Way B38 ...... **104** B2
Lindhurst Dr B94 ...... **143** C6
Lindisfarne B77 .... **21** D3
Lindisfarne Dr CV8 ...... **148** C4
Lindley Ave DY4 .... **51** F4
Lindley Rd Bedworth CV12 ...... **77** D2
Coventry CV3 .... **114** B2
Lindon Cl WS8 .... **16** A6
Lindon Dr WS8 .... **15** F6
Lindon Rd WS8 .... **15** F5
Lindon View WS8 ...... **16** A5
Lindrick Cl WS3 .... **13** F3
Lindridge Dr B76 ...... **58** D6

Lindridge Jun Sch B75 ...... **47** B5
Lindridge Rd Birmingham
B23 .... **56** C5
Solihull B90 .... **105** F1
Sutton Coldfield B75 ...... **47** B6
Lindsay Rd B42 .... **44** B1
Lindsey Ave B31 .... **103** C4
Lindsey Cres CV8 ...... **148** A1
Lindsey Pl DY5 .... **61** C3
Lindsey Rd B71 .... **53** C7
Lindsworth App B30 ...... **104** C3
Lindsworth Ct B30 ...... **104** C3
Lindsworth Rd B30 ...... **104** C3
Lindsworth Specl Sch
B30 .... **104** C3
Lineholt Cl B98 .... **159** A6
Linehouse La
Lickey End B60 .... **137** D8
Marlbrook B60 .... **121** D1
Linen St CV34 .... **160** D6
Linfield Gdns DY3 ...... **39** C1
Linford Gr B25 .... **68** D1
Linford Wlk CV2 .... **96** F1
Linforth Dr B74 .... **45** A7
Ling Ho WV10 .... **25** F3
Ling Rd WS12 .... **1** C5
Lingard Cl B7 .... **67** B5
Lingard Ho B76 .... **57** F8
Lingard Rd B75 .... **47** A5
Lingen Cl B98 .... **154** E3
Lingfield Ave Birmingham
B44 .... **44** F1
Wolverhampton WV10 ...... **11** D5
Lingfield Cl WS6 .... **4** F2
Lingfield Ct Birmingham
B43 .... **54** D7
Coventry CV6 .... **96** B4
Lingfield Dr WS6 .... **4** F2
Lingfield Gdns B34 ...... **69** B6
Lingfield Gr WV6 .... **23** F4
Lingfield Way DY6 ...... **61** A5
Lingfield Wlk B61 ...... **121** B1
Lingham Cl B92 .... **107** D7
Lingwood Dr CV10 ...... **72** F3
Linhope Dr DY6 .... **61** A5
Link One Ind Pk DY4 ...... **52** E6
Link Rd Birmingham B16 ...... **65** E3
Brownhills WS9 .... **16** B3
Wombourne WV5 .... **49** A7
Link The B27 .... **88** A1
Links Ave WV6 .... **24** D7
Links Cres B68 .... **84** B8
Links Dr Birmingham B45 ...... **122** A5
Solihull B91 .... **107** B6
Stourbridge DY8 .... **80** E2
Links Rd Birmingham B14 ...... **105** A1
Coventry CV6 .... **113** B8
Oldbury B68 .... **84** B8
Wolverhampton WV4 ...... **39** A3
Links Side Way WS9 ...... **30** C8
Links View Aldridge B74 ...... **31** B1
Halesowen B62 .... **83** D4
Linkswood Cl B13 ...... **87** B1
Linkway CV31 .... **161** E6
Linkway Ret Pk WS11 ...... **4** B6
Linkwood Ind Est DY8 ...... **80** F6
Linley Cl WS9 .... **29** E5
Linley Dr WV10 .... **11** E1
Linley Gr Birmingham B14 ...... **104** C6
Dudley DY3 .... **50** B2
Linley Lodge Ind Est WS9 ...... **29** E6
Linley Rd WS4 .... **29** D7
Linley Wood Rd WS9 ...... **29** E5
Linnet Cl Birmingham B30 ...... **103** E8
Coventry CV3 .... **134** D5
Halesowen B62 .... **83** B6
Huntington WS12 .... **1** D7
Linnet Gr WV12 .... **27** C8
Linnet Rise DY10 ...... **116** F1
Linpole Wlk B14 .... **104** D1
Linsey Rd B92 .... **89** C2
Linslade Cl WV4 .... **39** D4
Linstock Way CV6 ...... **96** B4
Linthouse La WV11 ...... **26** E8
Linthouse Wlk B77 ...... **35** F6
Linthurst Newtown B60 ...... **138** B5
Linthurst Prim Sch B60 ...... **138** A6
Linthurst Rd B45, B60 ...... **138** A7
Lintly B77 .... **22** B1
Linton Ave B91 .... **107** A1
Linton Cl Halesowen B63 ...... **82** D5
Redditch B98 .... **154** F2
Linton Croft WV14 ...... **40** D5
Linton Mews B98 ...... **154** F2
Linton Rd
Birmingham,
Acock's Green B11 ...... **88** A4
Birmingham, Great Barr B43 ...... **44** C3
Blackheath B64 .... **62** F3
Wolverhampton WV4 ...... **38** E5
Linton Wlk B23 .... **56** C3
Linwood Cl LE10 ...... **71** B2
Linwood Dr Cannock WS12 ...... **1** F7
Coventry CV2 .... **96** F1
Linwood Rd Birmingham
B21 .... **65** E8
Dudley DY1 .... **51** B5
Solihull B91 .... **106** D5
Linwood Wlk B17 ...... **85** D4
Lion Fields Ave CV5 ...... **112** B6
Lion Ind Est WS9 ...... **30** A8
Lion Pas DY8 .... **80** F5
Lion Sq DY10 .... **116** E6
Lion St Kidderminster DY10 ...... **116** E6
Stourbridge DY8 .... **80** F5
Lion's Den WS14 ...... **7** E2
Lionel St B3 .... **164** B3

Liskeard Cl CV11 ...... **74** A5
Liskeard Rd WS5 ...... **43** D7
Lisko Cl DY5 .... **81** A8
Lisle Ave DY11 .... **116** D3
Lisle Ct CV31 .... **162** A6
Lismore Cl B45 .... **101** E1
Hinckley LE10 .... **71** C1
Lisson Gr B44 .... **44** F4
Listelow Cl B36 .... **69** B8
Lister Cl Tipton DY4 ...... **52** A4
Walsall WS2 .... **28** B5
Lister Rd Dudley DY2 ...... **62** D7
Kidderminster DY11 ...... **116** B4
Walsall WS2 .... **28** B5
Lister St Birmingham B7 ...... **66** F4
Nuneaton CV11 .... **73** D3
Willenhall WV13 .... **27** B1
Listowel Rd B14 ...... **104** D6
Lisures Dr B76 .... **46** D4
Little Acre B97 .... **158** D6
Little Albert St WS2 ...... **28** E2
Little Ann St B5 .... **66** F2
Little Aston Cty Prim Sch
B74 .... **31** C6
Little Aston Hospl B74 ...... **31** B5
Little Aston La B74 ...... **31** D6
Little Aston Park Rd B74 ...... **31** A3
Little Aston Rd WS9 ...... **30** D6
Little Barr St B9 .... **67** A2
Little Birches WV3 ...... **38** F8
Little Bloxwich CE Prim
Sch WS3 .... **14** D3
Little Brickiln St WV3 ...... **163** B2
Little Bromwich Rd B9 ...... **68** C2
Little Broom St B12 ...... **87** A8
Little Caldmore B6 ...... **42** E8
Little Church La B79 ...... **21** B5
Little Church St CV1 ...... **165** C4
Little Clothier St WV13 ...... **27** A3
Little Clover Cl B7 ...... **67** C7
Little Comm WS3 ...... **15** A4
Little Cornbow B63 ...... **83** B3
Little Cottage St DY5 ...... **61** D2
Little Croft B43 .... **43** C1
Little Cross St WS10 ...... **41** D7
Little Duke St CV11 ...... **73** B4
Little Edward St B9 ...... **67** A2
Little Farm CV3 .... **134** D5
Little Field CV2 .... **114** A5
Little Fields Way B69 ...... **63** F7
Little Forge Rd B98 ...... **159** C8
Little Francis Gr B7 ...... **67** B5
Little Gorway WS1 ...... **42** F7
Little Grebe Rd DY10 ...... **117** B3
Little Green La B9 ...... **67** C1
Little Green Lanes B73 ...... **57** B7
Little Hall Rd B7 ...... **67** B5
Little Hardwick Rd WS9 ...... **30** D2
Little Heath Croft B34 ...... **69** B7
Little Heath Ind Est CV6 ...... **96** A2
Little Hill WS10 .... **41** F3
Little Hill Gr B38 ...... **104** A1
Little Hill Way B32 ...... **84** D2
Little John St DY5 ...... **61** D4
Little La West Bromwich B71 ...... **53** D5
Willenhall WV12 .... **27** D7
Little Lawns Cl WS8 ...... **16** A4
Little London WS1 ...... **42** E8
Little London Ho WS1 ...... **42** F7
Little London Jun Mixed
Inf Sch WV13 ...... **27** A2
Little Meadow Wlk B33 ...... **68** D3
Little Moor Hill B67 ...... **64** F5
Little Newport St WS1 ...... **28** E1
Little Oaks Dr DY7 ...... **60** A2
Little Oaks Rd B6 ...... **66** E8
Little Park St Coventry CV1 ...... **165** C2
Wolverhampton WV1 ...... **163** C3
Little Pitts Cl B24 ...... **57** D5
Little Pk B32 .... **84** B4
Little Potter St DY5 ...... **61** D2
Little Pountney St WV2 ...... **163** B1
Little Shadwell St B4 ...... **164** C4
Little South St CV1 ...... **113** E3
Little St DY2 .... **51** D1
Little Station St WS2 ...... **28** E2
Little Sutton Fst, Jun &
Mid Schs B75 ...... **32** D4
Little Sutton La B75 ...... **46** C8
Little Sutton Rd B75 ...... **32** D2
Little Wood St WV13 ...... **27** A2
Little Woods B97 ...... **158** E6
Little's La
Wolverhampton WV1 ...... **163** C3
Wolverhampton WV1 ...... **163** C3
Littlecote B79 .... **20** D7
Littlecote Croft B14 ...... **105** A3
Littlecote Dr B23 ...... **56** F7
Littleheath La B60 ...... **137** D6
Littlemead Ave B31 ...... **103** C1
Littlemead Rd B90 ...... **125** E8
Littleover Ave B28 ...... **105** F6
Littleshaw Croft B47 ...... **125** D4
Littleshaw La B47 ...... **125** C4
Littlethorpe CV3 ...... **134** D6
Littleton Bsns Pk WS12 ...... **1** C7
Littleton Cl Kenilworth
CV8 .... **148** A1
Sutton Coldfield B76 ...... **47** A2
Littleton Croft B91 ...... **127** C8
Littleton Dr WS12 ...... **1** C7
Littleton Rd WV12 ...... **27** D7
Littleton St E WS1 ...... **28** F3
Littleton St W WS2 ...... **28** E2

Littlewood Cl B91 ...... **127** B8
Littlewood Gn B80 ...... **159** D3
Littlewood La WS6 ...... **4** E4
Littlewood Rd WS6 ...... **4** E4
Littleworth Gr B76 ...... **46** F4
Littleworth Hill WS12 ...... **2** D4
Littleworth Rd WS12 ...... **2** D4
Litton B77 .... **22** C1
Liveridge Cl B93 ...... **127** F6
Liverpool Croft B37 ...... **89** F8
Liverpool St B9 .... **67** A2
Livery St Birmingham B3 ...... **164** B3
Birmingham B3 .... **164** B4
Royal Leamington Spa CV32 ...... **161** F8
Livingstone Ave WV6 ...... **23** E5
Livingstone Rd Bilston
WV14 .... **40** B5
Birmingham,
Handsworth B20 ...... **55** D1
Birmingham,
King's Heath B14 ...... **104** E6
Coventry CV6 .... **113** E7
Walsall WS3 .... **14** C2
West Bromwich B70 ...... **53** B1
Lizafield Ct B66 .... **64** E7
Llewellyn Rd CV31 ...... **162** A6
Lloyd Cl CV11 .... **73** D2
Lloyd Cres CV2 .... **114** E3
Lloyd Dr WV4 .... **38** C2
Lloyd George Gr WS11 ...... **2** C2
Lloyd Ho B19 .... **66** C6
Lloyd Rd Birmingham B20 ...... **55** A4
Wolverhampton WV6 ...... **24** D5
Lloyd Roberts Bldgs WV4 ...... **38** F1
Lloyd St Birmingham B10 ...... **87** D8
Cannock WS11 .... **1** D1
Dudley DY2 .... **62** C4
Wednesbury WS10 ...... **41** E3
West Bromwich B71 ...... **53** E4
Wolverhampton WV6 ...... **24** F4
Lloyds Rd B62 .... **83** C8
Loach Dr CV2 .... **96** B4
Lobelia Cl LE10 .... **75** E5
Locarno Jun & Inf Schs
DY4 .... **52** A6
Locarno Rd DY4 ...... **52** A6
Lochalsh Gr WV12 ...... **13** B1
Lochmore Cl LE10 ...... **75** A8
Lochmore Dr LE10 ...... **75** A8
Lochmore Way LE10 ...... **75** A8
Lochranza Croft B43 ...... **43** E2
Lock Cl B97 .... **153** A4
Lock Dr B33 .... **68** D3
Lock La CV34 .... **160** D8
Lock St WV1 .... **163** C4
Locke Cl CV34 .... **95** A1
Locket Cl WS2 .... **27** F4
Lockfield Cl DY8 ...... **60** F2
Lockhart Cl CV8 ...... **148** A4
Lockhart Dr B75 ...... **32** C1
Lockheed Cl CV31 ...... **161** F5
Lockhurst La CV6 ...... **113** D7
Locking Croft B35 ...... **58** B3
Lockington Croft B62 ...... **83** F6
Lockley Cl WV10 ...... **25** F4
Locks View DY8 ...... **60** E1
Locks The CV31 .... **161** D7
Lockside WS9 .... **29** F7
Locksmith Cl WV13 ...... **27** B2
Lockton Rd B30 ...... **104** C8
Lockwood Rd B31 ...... **102** F4
Lode Heath B91 ...... **107** C6
Lode La B91, B92 ...... **107** C6
Loder Cl CV4 .... **111** F3
Lodge Cl Halesowen B62 ...... **83** E3
Hinckley LE10 .... **76** A5
Walsall WS5 .... **43** D6
Lodge Cres Dudley DY2 ...... **62** A4
Hagley DY9 .... **99** B5
Warwick CV34 .... **160** D4
Lodge Croft
Birmingham B31 .... **102** E6
Knowle B93 .... **128** B6
Lodge Dr B26 .... **88** F8
Lodge Farm B76 ...... **46** F3
Lodge Farm Mid Sch
B98 .... **154** A2
Lodge Forge Trad Est B64 ...... **62** C7
Lodge Gr WS9 .... **30** A5
Lodge Green La CV7 ...... **92** F2
Lodge Green La N CV7 ...... **92** E3
Lodge Hill Rd B29 ...... **85** D1
Lodge La Cheslyn Hay WS11 ...... **4** F5
Kingswinford DY6 ...... **60** B6
Lodge Pool Dr B98 ...... **153** F1
Lodge Prim Sch B70 ...... **53** B3
Lodge Rd Bilston WV14 ...... **40** F4
Birmingham B18 .... **65** F5
Coventry CV3 .... **114** B1
Darlaston WS10 .... **41** D5
Knowle B93 .... **128** B6
Redditch B98 .... **153** E3
Smethwick B67 .... **64** E7
Walsall, Pelsall WS4 ...... **15** B1
Walsall, THe Chuckery WS5 ...... **42** F6
West Bromwich B70 ...... **53** C3
Wolverhampton WV10 ...... **25** B8
Lodge Rd/ West Bromwich
TH Sta B70 .... **53** C3
Lodge St Oldbury B69 ...... **64** A7
Willenhall WV12 .... **27** C5
Lodge View WS6 ...... **4** C3
Lodgefarm Jun Mixed Inf
Sch WV12 .... **27** C5
Lodgefield Rd B62 ...... **83** B7
Lodgepool Cl B44 ...... **55** E6
Loeless Rd B33 .... **69** A3

Lofthouse Cres B31 ...... **102** F3
Lofthouse Gr B31 ...... **102** F3
Lofthouse Rd B20 ...... **54** F3
Loftus Cl B29 .... **102** F8
Loftus Ct WS7 .... **7** A5
Logan Cl WV10 .... **25** C6
Logan Rd CV2 .... **114** E7
Lollard Croft CV3 ...... **133** D8
Lomaine Dr B30 ...... **103** E4
Lomas Dr B31 .... **102** E3
Lomas St WV1 .... **25** C4
Lomax Cl WS13 .... **3** A1
Lomax Rd WS12 ...... **2** B7
Lombard Ave DY2 ...... **62** D3
Lombard St Birmingham B12 ...... **86** F8
Lichfield WS13 .... **9** B8
West Bromwich B70 ...... **53** C3
Lombard St W B70 ...... **53** C3
Lombardy Croft B62 ...... **84** A6
Lombardy Gdns WV12 ...... **27** E7
Lombardy Gr WS7 ...... **6** F8
Lomita Cres B77 ...... **35** D8
Lomond Cl Birmingham B34 ...... **69** E6
Hinckley LE10 .... **75** B8
Tamworth B79 .... **20** F8
Lomond Rd DY3 ...... **39** C1
London Hts DY1 ...... **51** A2
London La Bromsgrove B60 ...... **151** F7
Tardebigge B60 .... **152** A6
London Rd Birmingham B20 ...... **55** E2
Coventry, Cheylesmore CV3 ...... **133** E7
Coventry, Willenhall CV3 ...... **134** B5
Hinckley LE10 .... **75** F8
Lichfield WS14 .... **9** C5
Middleton B75, B78 ...... **47** D7
Ryton-on-D CV8 .... **135** B1
Shenstone B75, WS14 ...... **32** F7
London St B66 .... **65** C5
Londonderry Gr B67 ...... **64** F5
Londonderry La B67 ...... **64** E4
Londonderry Rd B68 ...... **64** D4
Lones Rd B71 .... **65** B8
Long Acre Birmingham B7 ...... **67** C2
Kidderminster DY10 ...... **116** F7
Long Acre St WS2 ...... **28** D3
Long Acre Trad Est B7 ...... **67** B7
Long Cl DY9 .... **99** A4
Long Close Ave CV5 ...... **112** B6
Long Close Wlk B35 ...... **58** A3
Long Compton Dr DY9 ...... **99** A6
Long Croft WS12 ...... **1** C4
Long Furrow WV8 ...... **10** E1
Long Hyde Rd B67 ...... **64** F1
Long Innage B63 ...... **82** B6
Long Knowle La WV11 ...... **26** B8
Long Knowle Prim Sch
WV11 .... **26** C8
Long La Allesley CV5, CV7 ...... **94** D2
Great Wyrley WV11, WS6 ...... **13** E6
Halesowen B62 .... **83** E8
Long La Trad Est B62 ...... **83** D8
Long Leasow B29 ...... **103** B7
Long Ley WV10 .... **25** F3
Long Ley Prim Sch WV10 ...... **25** F3
Long Leys Croft B46 ...... **59** B2
Long Leys Ct B46 ...... **59** B2
Long Mdw B65 .... **63** C3
Long Meadow Dr DY3 ...... **39** B2
Long Meadow Rd B60 ...... **137** C6
Long Mill Ave WV11 ...... **26** B7
Long Mill N WV11 ...... **26** B7
Long Mill S WV11 ...... **26** B7
Long Mynd B63 .... **82** D1
Long Mynd Cl WV12 ...... **13** B1
Long Mynd Rd B31 ...... **102** F6
Long Nuke Rd B31 ...... **102** E7
Long Shoot The CV11 ...... **74** C6
Long St Birmingham B11 ...... **87** A6
Bulkington CV12 .... **79** D2
Walsall WS2 .... **28** D1
Wolverhampton WV1 ...... **163** C3
Long Wood B30 .... **103** E5
Longacre WS10 .... **41** A8
Longacre Ind Est B7 ...... **67** C7
Longacres Cannock WS12 ...... **2** F5
Little Aston B74 .... **31** C4
Longbank Rd B69 ...... **63** C8
Longboat La DY8 ...... **60** E1
Longboat Quay DY2 ...... **62** D4
Longborough Cl B97 ...... **158** B6
Longbow Rd B29 ...... **102** F7
Longbridge La B31 ...... **122** E8
Longbridge Sta B31 ...... **122** E8
Longcroft Ave WS10 ...... **42** A3
Longcroft Cl B35 ...... **58** A2
Longcroft The
Halesowen B63 .... **82** E4
Walsall WS4 .... **29** C7
Longdales Rd B38 ...... **123** E7
Longdon Ave WV4 ...... **39** D5
Longdon Cl B98 .... **159** B7
Longdon Croft B93 ...... **128** A8
Longdon Dr B74 ...... **31** E3
Longdon Rd B93 ...... **128** A6
Longfellow Ave CV34 ...... **160** C4
Longfellow Cl B97 ...... **158** C7
Longfellow Pl WS11 ...... **1** E4
Longfellow Rd
Birmingham B30 .... **103** D4
Coventry CV2 .... **114** C2
Dudley DY3 .... **50** B5
Longfellow Wlk B79 ...... **20** F8
Longfield Cl
Birmingham B28 .... **105** F6
Tamworth B77 .... **21** E4
Longfield Dr B74 ...... **31** D4

Longfield Ho Coventry
　CV6 .... 114 A8
　Wolverhampton WV10 ...... 25 F3
Longfield Rd
　Birmingham B31 .... 102 E8
　Royal Leamington Spa CV31 . 162 B6
　Stourbridge DY9 .... 81 D5
Longford Cl
　Birmingham B32 .... 102 A7
　Dorridge B93 .... 128 B3
　Walsall WS1 .... 29 A1
Longford Ct WS11 .... 4 B8
Longford Cty Prim Sch
　WS11 .... 4 C8
Longford Gn WS11 .... 4 C7
Longford Gr B44 .... 45 A3
Longford Ind Est WS11 .... 4 D6
Longford Park Prim Sch
　CV6 .... 96 A3
Longford Rd Bedworth CV7 .. 96 A6
　Birmingham B44 .... 45 A2
　Cannock WS11 .... 4 D7
　Coventry CV6 .... 96 A4
　Wolverhampton WV10 ...... 26 A4
Longford Sq CV6 .... 96 A4
Longham Croft B32 .... 84 F4
Longhurst Croft B31 .... 123 B7
Longlake Ave WV6 .... 24 B3
Longlands Cl B38 .... 123 C8
Longlands Dr B77 .... 21 F4
Longlands Ho B11 .... 87 B5
Longlands Rd B62 .... 83 E3
Longlands The
　Barnt Green B45 .... 138 D7
　Wombourne WV5 .... 49 A6
Longleat Birmingham B43 .. 43 C2
　Tamworth B79 .... 20 D7
Longleat Dr
　Cheswick Green B90 ...... 126 E5
　Dudley DY1 .... 50 E2
Longleat Gr 19 CV31 .... 162 C6
Longleat Rd WS9 .... 16 A1
Longleat Tower 2 B15 ...... 66 C1
Longley Ave B76 .... 58 D5
Longley Cres B26 .... 88 E4
Longmeadow Cl B75 .... 46 F5
Longmeadow Cres B34 ...... 69 E6
Longmeadow Gr B31 .... 123 A6
Longmoor Cl WV11 .... 26 F5
Longmoor Rd
　Birmingham B73 .... 45 B3
　Halesowen B63 .... 82 E3
Longmoor Specl Sch B73 ... 45 A4
Longmore Ave WS2 .... 27 F1
Longmore Ho B73 .... 45 C3
Longmore Rd B90 .... 106 D2
Longmore St Birmingham
　B12 .... 86 E7
　Wednesbury WS10 .... 41 F3
Longshaw Gr B34 .... 69 D6
Longstone Cl B90 .... 127 B6
Longstone Rd B42 .... 55 C7
Longwill Specl Sch B31 .... 103 A5
Longwood Cl CV4 .... 131 F6
Longwood Jun & Inf Sch
　B78 .... 20 D1
Longwood La WS5, WS4 .... 29 E2
Longwood Rd Aldridge WS9 . 30 B2
　Birmingham B45 .... 122 A7
Longwood Rise WV12 .... 27 D5
Lonicera Cl WS5 .... 43 B3
Lonscale Dr CV3 .... 133 B5
Lonsdale Cl Birmingham B33 . 68 D2
　Willenhall WV12 .... 27 B5
Lonsdale Rd Bilston WV14 .. 40 F6
　Birmingham B17 .... 85 B6
　Royal Leamington Spa CV32 . 157 B4
　Smethwick B66 .... 64 D7
　Walsall WS5 .... 43 C6
　Wolverhampton WV3 .... 39 B7
Lord Cromwell Ct WS11 ..... 2 A5
Lord Lytton Ave CV2 .... 114 D2
Lord St Bilston WV14 .... 40 E3
　Birmingham B7 .... 66 F5
　Coventry CV5 .... 112 F2
　Walsall WS1 .... 42 E6
　Wolverhampton WV3 .... 25 B1
Lord St W WV14 .... 40 E3
Lord's Dr WS2 .... 28 E3
Lords La B80 .... 159 E2
Lordswood Boys Sch B17 .. 65 A1
Lordswood Cl B97 .... 152 F2
Lordswood Girls Sch B17 .. 85 A8
Lordswood Rd B17 .... 85 A7
Lordswood Sq B17 .... 85 B7
Lorenzo Cl CV3 .... 134 D6
Lorimer Way B43 .... 44 D4
Lorne Gr DY10 .... 117 A6
Lorne St Burntwood WS7 .... 6 E4
　Kidderminster DY10 ...... 117 A5
　Tipton DY4 .... 51 F8
Lorrainer Ave DY5 .... 81 A8
Lorton B79 .... 20 D7
Lothersdale B77 .... 36 C8
Lothians Rd Walsall WS3 .. 15 A5
　Wolverhampton WV6 .... 24 E6
Lottie Rd B29 .... 85 E1
Lotus B77 .... 21 E3
Lotus Croft B67 .... 64 F4
Lotus Ct B16 .... 65 E1
Lotus Dr WS11 .... 1 E5
Lotus Way B65 .... 63 A4
Loudon Ave CV6 .... 113 A6
Loughshaw B77 .... 22 C1
Loughton Gr B63 .... 82 F4
Louis Ct B67 .... 64 F5
Louisa Pl 3 B18 .... 66 A5

Louisa St 1 B1 .... 66 C3
Louise Croft B14 .... 104 E2
Louise Ct 2 Birmingham
　B27 .... 88 C3
　Solihull B91 .... 106 E1
Louise Ho DY5 .... 61 D7
Louise Lorne Rd B13 .... 86 F4
Louise Rd B21 .... 65 F7
Louise St DY3 .... 50 C3
Loundon Gate CV11 .... 73 F1
Lovatt Cl DY4 .... 41 C1
Lovatt Pl WS11 .... 1 E5
Lovatt St WV1 .... 163 A3
Love La Birmingham B7 .... 66 F4
　Great Wyrley WS6 .... 5 B3
　Hinckley LE10 .... 76 A6
　Hollywood B47 .... 124 F7
　Stourbridge, Lye DY9 ..... 81 F5
　Stourbridge, Old Swinford
　DY8 .... 81 A3
　Walsall WS1 .... 42 E7
　Wolverhampton WV6 .... 24 D6
Love Lyne B97 .... 158 B5
Loveday Cl CV32 .... 156 E2
Loveday Ho B70 .... 53 D3
Loveday St B4 .... 164 C4
Lovelace Ave B91 .... 127 D8
Lovell B79 .... 20 F6
Lovell Cl Bedworth CV7 .... 96 A8
　Birmingham B29 .... 103 B6
Lovell Rd CV12 .... 78 A3
Lover's Wlk 5 WS10 .... 41 F3
Lovett Ave B69 .... 63 D5
Lovetts Cl LE10 .... 74 F8
Low Ave B43 .... 43 F2
Low Hill Cres WV10 .... 25 E8
Low St WS6 .... 4 D3
Low Thatch B38 .... 123 E7
Low Town 6 B69 .... 64 A7
Low Wood Rd B23 .... 56 E5
Lowans Hill View B97 .... 153 C4
Lowbridge Cl WV12 .... 27 C5
Lowbrook La B90 .... 125 D4
Lowden Croft B26 .... 88 E4
Lowdham B77 .... 22 C1
Lowe Ave WS10 .... 41 C7
Lowe Dr Kingswinford DY6 .. 60 E4
　Sutton Coldfield B73 ...... 45 C3
Lowe Rd CV6 .... 95 A2
Lowe St Birmingham B12 .. 87 A8
　Wolverhampton WV6 .... 25 B4
Lower Ave CV31 .... 161 F7
Lower Beeches Rd B31 .. 102 C2
Lower Bentley La B60 .... 151 F1
Lower Bond St LE10 .... 71 D1
Lower Cape CV34 .... 160 D8
Lower Chapel St B69 .... 52 C2
Lower Church La DY4 ...... 52 B5
Lower City Rd B65 .... 52 D1
Lower Common La B97 ... 153 B2
Lower Dartmouth St B9 ... 67 B2
Lower Darwin St B12 ...... 86 F8
Lower Derry St DY5 .... 61 D7
Lower Eastern Green La
　CV5 .... 111 F4
Lower Essex St B5 .... 66 E1
Lower Farm WS9 .... 16 E4
Lower Farm Cty Prim Sch
　WS3 .... 14 C3
Lower Ford St CV1 .... 165 D3
Lower Forster St WS1 ..... 28 F3
Lower Gambolds La B60 .. 151 B6
Lower Gn DY4 .... 51 E5
Lower Grinsty La B97 .... 158 A8
Lower Ground Cl 1 B6 .... 55 F1
Lower Hall La WS1 .... 28 E1
Lower Hall St WV13 .... 27 B1
Lower High St
　Blackheath B64 .... 82 C8
　Stourbridge DY8 .... 80 F6
　Wednesbury WS10 .... 41 F2
Lower Higley Cl B32 .... 84 E4
Lower Holyhead Rd CV1 .. 165 A3
Lower Horseley Fields
　WV1 .... 25 F2
Lower House La CV9 .... 36 F2
Lower Ladies Hills CV8 ... 148 A6
Lower Leam St CV31 ...... 162 B7
Lower Lichfield St WV13 ... 27 B2
Lower Loveday St B19 .... 164 C4
Lower Mill St DY11 .... 116 D6
Lower Moor B30 .... 103 E8
Lower North St WS4 .... 28 E3
Lower Par The B72 .... 46 C5
Lower Parklands DY11 ... 116 C5
Lower Prec CV1 .... 165 B3
Lower Prestwood Rd
　WV11 .... 26 C7
Lower Queen St B72 .... 46 C4
Lower Rd Barnacle CV7 ... 97 C6
　Cannock WS11 .... 2 C3
Lower Reddicroft B73 ..... 46 C5
Lower Rushall St WS1 ..... 28 F2
Lower Sandford St WS13 ... 9 A7
Lower Severn St B1 .... 164 B2
Lower Shepley La B60 .... 137 E6
Lower St WV6 .... 24 E5
Lower Temple St B2 .... 164 B2
Lower Tower St B19 ...... 164 C5
Lower Trinity St B9 .... 67 A1
Lower Valley Rd DY5 .... 61 A2
Lower Vauxhall WV1 .... 25 A3
Lower Villiers St
　1 Royal Leamington Spa
　CV32 .... 157 A1
　Wolverhampton WV2 .... 39 C7
Lower Walsall St WV1 ...... 25 F1
Lower White Rd B32 .... 84 D5

Lowercroft Way B74 .... 31 E6
Lowerpark B77 .... 21 C1
Lowerstack Croft B37 ..... 69 F3
Lowes Ave CV34 .... 155 E1
Lowesmoor Rd B26 .... 89 C7
Loweswater Cl CV11 .... 74 A6
Loweswater Rd CV3 ...... 114 E1
Lowfield Cl B62 .... 84 A3
Lowfield La B97 .... 153 B5
Lowforce B77 .... 36 C8
Lowhill La B45 .... 122 D6
Lowland Rd B45 .... 62 F1
Lowland Rd WS12 .... 1 C4
Lowlands Ave
　Sutton Coldfield B74 .... 44 E8
　Wolverhampton WV6 .... 24 E6
Lowlands La B98 .... 154 D3
Lowndes Rd DY8 .... 80 E6
Lowrey Rd B68 .... 64 C3
Lowry Cl Bedworth CV12 .. 78 A4
　Perton WV6 .... 23 F4
　Smethwick B67 .... 64 F6
Lowry Ct CV34 .... 26 E2
Lowswater Ho B38 .... 104 B1
Lowther Ct 10 DY5 .... 61 D2
Lowther St CV2 .... 113 F4
Loxdale Park Ind Est
　WV14 .... 40 E4
Loxdale Prim Sch WV14 ... 40 F4
Loxdale Sidings WV14 ..... 40 F4
Loxdale St Bilston WV14 .. 40 F4
　Wednesbury WS10 .... 41 E2
Loxdale Sta WV14 .... 40 F4
Loxley Ave Birmingham
　B14 .... 105 C3
　Solihull B90 .... 105 F1
Loxley Cl Birmingham B31 . 102 E8
　Coventry CV2 .... 96 D2
　Redditch B98 .... 154 D6
Loxley Ct CV2 .... 96 D2
Loxley Rd Smethwick B67 . 64 F1
　Sutton Coldfield B75 ...... 32 D3
Loxley Way CV32 .... 157 A2
Loxton Cl B74 .... 31 D5
Loynells Rd B45 .... 122 B7
Loyns Cl B37 .... 69 E3
Lozells Inf & Jun Sch B19 . 66 D7
Lozells Rd B19 .... 66 C7
Lozells St B19 .... 66 C7
Lozells Wood Cl 2 B19 ... 66 B7
Lucas Ho CV32 .... 156 F2
Lucas Rd LE10 .... 75 D6
Luce Cl B35 .... 58 B4
Luce Rd WV10 .... 25 E6
Lucerne Ct B23 .... 56 D6
Lucian Cl CV2 .... 115 B7
Lucknow Rd WV12 .... 27 B5
Lucy Edwards Ct DY11 ... 116 C5
Lud La B79 .... 21 A5
Luddington Rd B92 .... 107 E8
Ludford Cl B75 .... 46 F7
Ludford Rd Birmingham B32 . 84 A1
　Nuneaton CV10 .... 72 C6
Ludgate B79 .... 21 A5
Ludgate Ave DY11 .... 116 A4
Ludgate Cl B46 .... 59 B3
Ludgate Ct Tamworth B77 ... 22 A6
　2 Walsall WS5 .... 43 D7
Ludgate Hill B3 .... 164 B3
Ludgate St 10 DY1 .... 51 B1
Ludlow Cl Birmingham B37 . 70 C2
　Cannock WS11 .... 2 C2
　Willenhall WV12 .... 27 B6
Ludlow Ct B11 .... 87 B6
Ludlow Ho Birmingham B13 . 105 A6
　1 Walsall WS3 .... 28 C6
Ludlow La WS2 .... 28 A4
Ludlow Rd Birmingham B8 ... 67 F4
　Coventry CV5 .... 113 A2
　Kidderminster DY10 ...... 116 E3
　Redditch B97 .... 153 E3
Ludlow Way DY1 .... 50 E2
Ludmer Way B20 .... 55 C2
Ludstone Ave WV4 .... 38 D5
Ludstone Rd B29 .... 84 F1
Luff Cl CV3 .... 134 B8
Lugtrout La
　Catherine de B B91 ...... 108 A6
　Solihull B91 .... 107 F6
Lukes Wlk WS13 .... 3 A2
Lulworth Cl B63 .... 82 C6
Lulworth Pk CV8 .... 148 C6
Lulworth Rd Birmingham
　B28 .... 88 A1
　Burntwood WS7 .... 7 A7
Lulworth Wlk WV4 .... 38 C6
Lumley Gr B37 .... 70 D2
Lumley Rd WS1 .... 29 A1
Lumsden Cl CV2 .... 114 F8
Lunar Cl CV4 .... 132 D5
Lundy Cl LE10 .... 71 B1
Lundy View B36 .... 70 B6
Lunn Ave CV8 .... 147 E3
Lunn Poly Ho 3 CV32 .... 156 F1
Lunns Croft WS13 .... 9 C8
Lunt Jct The WV14 .... 41 A6
Lunt Pl WV14 .... 41 A6
Lunt Rd Bilston WV14 ...... 40 F6
　Birmingham B32 .... 84 D5
Lupin Cl LE10 .... 75 D5
Lupin Gr B9 .... 67 F3
Lupin Rd DY2 .... 51 F1
Lupton Ave CV3 .... 133 C7
Lupton Ct B60 .... 137 A1
Lusbridge Cl B63 .... 82 B4
Luscombe Rd CV2 .... 114 E8
Luther Way CV5 .... 111 F4

Lutley Ave B63 .... 82 E4
Lutley Cl WV3 .... 38 E7
Lutley Dr DY9 .... 81 C3
Lutley Gr B32 .... 84 B1
Lutley La B63 .... 82 C2
Lutley Mill Rd B63 .... 82 E4
Lutley Prim Sch B63 .... 82 D1
Luton Rd B29 .... 85 F3
Lutterworth Rd
　Coventry CV2 .... 114 C5
　Hinckley LE10 .... 76 C3
　Nuneaton CV11 .... 79 C8
Lutterworth Road
　Commercial Est LE10 .... 76 A5
Luttrell Rd B74 .... 32 A1
Luxor La CV5 .... 111 E8
Lyall Gdns B45 .... 101 E1
Lyall Gr B27 .... 88 A2
Lychgate Ave DY9 .... 81 C1
Lychgate Cl LE10 .... 76 A5
Lychgate La LE10 .... 76 C5
Lyd Cl WV11 .... 26 B5
Lydate Rd B62 .... 83 F4
Lydbrook Covert 4 B38 .. 123 E8
Lydbury Gr B33 .... 69 A4
Lydd Croft B35 .... 58 B4
Lyddington Dr B62 .... 83 B7
Lyde Gn B62 .... 82 B7
Lydford Cl CV2 .... 114 C7
Lydford Gr B24 .... 57 A1
Lydford Rd WS3 .... 14 B3
Lydgate Ct Bedworth CV12 . 78 A4
　Nuneaton CV11 .... 73 C3
Lydgate Rd Coventry CV6 . 113 B5
　Kingswinford DY6 .... 60 F6
Lydget Gr B23 .... 56 D7
Lydham Cl Bilston WV14 .. 40 B4
　Birmingham B44 .... 56 A6
　Redditch B98 .... 153 E5
Lydia Croft B74 .... 31 E6
Lydian Cl WV6 .... 25 B4
Lydiate Ash Rd B60 .... 121 C3
Lydiate Ave B31 .... 102 D1
Lydiates Cl DY3 .... 50 B7
Lydney Cl Redditch B98 .. 154 D7
　Willenhall WV12 .... 27 D4
Lydney Gr B31 .... 102 F3
Lydstep Gr CV31 .... 162 C7
Lye Ave B32 .... 84 A2
Lye Bsns Ctr DY9 .... 82 A6
Lye Cl B32 .... 84 A2
Lye Cl La B32 .... 84 A2
Lye Cross Rd B69 .... 63 B7
Lye Sta DY9 .... 81 E6
Lye Valley Ind Est DY9 .... 81 F6
Lyecroft Ave B37 .... 70 D2
Lygon Cl B98 .... 154 A5
Lygon Gr B32 .... 84 E4
Lyme Green Rd B33 .... 68 F4
Lymedene Rd B42 .... 55 B5
Lymer Rd WV10 .... 11 C1
Lymesy St CV3 .... 133 D7
Lymington Cl CV6 .... 113 D8
　Nuneaton CV10 .... 72 A3
Lymington Rd WV13 .... 27 D2
Lymore Croft CV2 .... 115 A8
Lymsey Croft DY8 .... 60 C3
Lynbrook Cl Dudley DY2 .. 62 D5
　Hollywood B47 .... 125 A7
Lynbrook Rd CV5 .... 132 D8
Lynch The Nuneaton CV11 . 73 D2
　Polesworth B78 .... 22 F1
Lynchgate Ct CV4 .... 132 C6
Lynchgate Ho CV4 .... 132 C6
Lynchgate Rd CV4 .... 132 C6
Lyncourt Gr B32 .... 84 B6
Lyncroft House Sch WS11 ... 4 E8
Lyncroft L Ctr WS11 .... 4 E8
Lyncroft Rd B11 .... 87 F2
Lyndale B77 .... 35 F6
Lyndale Dr WV11 .... 26 B6
Lyndale Rd Coventry CV5 . 112 C3
　Dudley DY2 .... 62 E6
　Sedgley DY3 .... 39 B2
Lynden Cl B61 .... 136 E3
Lyndenwood B97 .... 153 A2
Lyndholm Rd DY10 .... 117 A6
Lyndhurst Cl LE10 .... 76 A7
Lyndhurst Croft CV5 ...... 111 C4
Lyndhurst Dr
　Kidderminster DY10 ...... 116 E8
　Stourbridge DY8 .... 60 F1
Lyndhurst Rd
　Birmingham B24 .... 56 F2
　Cannock WS12 .... 2 E1
　West Bromwich B71 .... 53 E7
　Wolverhampton WV3 .... 39 A7
Lyndon B71 .... 53 D5
Lyndon Cl
　Birmingham,
　Castle Bromwich B36 ...... 69 C8
　Birmingham,
　Handsworth B20 .... 55 C2
　Halesowen B63 .... 82 F4
　Sedgley DY3 .... 39 E1
Lyndon Croft B37 .... 90 B7
Lyndon Ct 1 CV32 .... 161 E8
Lyndon Gr Kingswinford DY6 . 60 B8
　West Bromwich B71 .... 53 D4
Lyndon Green Inf Sch B26 . 89 A6
Lyndon Green Jun Sch
　B26 .... 89 A6
Lyndon Ho B31 .... 103 B3
Lyndon Rd Birmingham B33 . 68 E3
　Birmingham, Eachway B45 . 121 E7
　Solihull B92 .... 88 F2
　Sutton Coldfield B73 ...... 46 B5
Lyndon Sch B92 .... 89 A3
Lyndworth Rd B30 .... 104 C8
Lyne Ho 1 CV2 .... 114 D8

Lyneham Cl Hinckley LE10 . 71 A1
　Tamworth B79 .... 21 C8
Lyneham Gdns B76 .... 58 B6
Lyneham Way B35 .... 57 F3
Lynfield Cl B38 .... 123 F7
Lyng Hall Sch CV2 .... 114 C6
Lyng La B70 .... 53 C2
Lyng Prim Sch B70 .... 53 C1
Lynmouth Cl Aldridge WS9 . 30 A5
　Nuneaton CV11 .... 73 E5
Lynmouth Rd CV2 .... 114 E8
Lynn Gr B29 .... 85 C3
Lynn La WS14 .... 17 C6
Lynton Ave Smethwick B66 . 65 A6
　West Bromwich B71 .... 53 C7
　Wolverhampton WV6 .... 24 F6
Lynton Cl CV34 .... 155 E1
Lynton Ho B23 .... 56 B6
Lynton Rd Birmingham B6 . 67 B7
　Coventry CV6 .... 95 F1
Lynval Rd DY5 .... 81 F7
Lynwood Ave DY6 .... 60 B7
Lynwood Cl WV12 .... 27 E8
Lynwood Dr DY10 .... 98 C2
Lynwood Wlk 9 CV31 .... 162 C6
Lyon Ct B72 .... 46 C5
Lysander Ho B35 .... 58 B2
Lysander Rd B45 .... 102 A2
Lysander St CV3 .... 134 D6
Lysander Way WS11 .... 1 E3
Lyster Cl CV34 .... 160 B8
Lysway Ct 3 WS1 .... 42 F8
Lysways St WS1 .... 42 F8
Lythall Cl CV31 .... 162 F5
Lythalls La CV6 .... 95 E2
Lythalls Lane Ind Est CV6 . 95 E1
Lytham B77 .... 22 C5
Lytham Cl Stourbridge DY8 . 80 F2
　Sutton Coldfield B76 ...... 58 B6
Lytham Croft B15 .... 86 D8
Lytham Gr WS3 .... 14 A4
Lytham Rd WV6 .... 23 D4
Lythwood Dr DY5 .... 81 C8
Lyttelton
　Birmingham, Edgbaston B16 . 65 D1
　Birmingham, Stechford B33 . 68 D3
　Stourbridge DY8 .... 80 C5
　Warwick CV34 .... 160 E8
Lyttelton Ave
　Bromsgrove B60 .... 150 E7
　Halesowen B63 .... 82 E7
Lyttelton Cl Coventry CV3 . 115 A1
　Dudley DY2 .... 62 C4
Lyttelton Ho B63 .... 83 A2
Lyttelton Pl DY9 .... 99 C6
Lyttelton St B70 .... 53 C2
Lytton Ave WV4 .... 38 E4
Lytton Gr B27 .... 88 B1
Lytton La B32 .... 84 F3

Maas Rd B31 .... 103 A4
Mabey Ave B98 .... 153 F5
Mac Gregor Cres B77 ...... 21 F3
Macadam Cl WS7 .... 7 B8
Macarthur Rd B64 .... 82 C8
Macaulay Ho B70 .... 53 D1
Macaulay Rd CV2 .... 114 D4
Macbeth App CV34 .... 161 E4
Macdonald Cl B69 .... 52 D2
Macdonald Rd CV2 .... 114 D3
Macdonald St B5 .... 86 E8
Mace St B64 .... 62 E1
Macefield Cl CV2 .... 96 D2
Machin Rd B23 .... 56 F4
Mackadown La B33 .... 69 D2
Mackay Rd WS3 .... 14 D2
Mackenzie Cl CV5 .... 112 A7
Mackenzie Rd B11 .... 87 C2
Mackmillan Rd B65 .... 63 C2
Macmillan Rd B69 .... 52 C2
Macrome Rd WV6 .... 24 E8
Madam's Hill Rd B90 .... 126 D7
Maddocks Hill B72 .... 46 C2
Madehurst Rd B23 .... 56 E6
Madeira Ave WV8 .... 10 A2
Madeira Croft CV5 .... 112 E2
Madeira Ct DY8 .... 60 F1
Madeley Rd
　Belbroughton DY9 .... 120 D6
　Birmingham B11 .... 87 C5
　Kingswinford DY6 .... 61 A4
　Redditch B98 .... 154 F5
Madin Rd DY4 .... 51 E4
Madinatul Uloom Islamic
　Coll DY10 .... 117 D1
Madison Ave Birmingham
　B36 .... 68 D4
　Walsall WS2 .... 28 B2
Madley Cl B45 .... 121 E8
Madox Cl B79 .... 20 E7
Madresfield Dr B63 .... 83 B2
Madrona B77 .... 22 B4
Maer Cl B65 .... 63 C3
Mafeking Rd B66 .... 65 A7
Mafeking Villas B62 .... 83 B7
Magdala St B18 .... 65 E5
Magdalen Cl DY1 .... 51 A4
Magdalene Rd WS1 .... 43 A7
Magee Cl LE10 .... 71 C2
Magna Cl WS6 .... 4 E3
Magness Cres WV12 .... 27 C5
Magnet Wlk B23 .... 56 C3
Magnolia B77 .... 22 A4

Magnolia Cl
Birmingham B29 .... **103** A7
Coventry CV3 .... **133** B5
Magnolia Gr WV8 .... **10** B3
Magnolia Way 🏠 DY8 .... **80** F8
Magnum Cl B74 .... **44** F7
Magnus B77 .... **35** E6
Magpie Cl DY2 .... **62** E3
Magpie Ho CV5 .... **111** D5
Magpie La CV7 .... **129** E6
Magpie Way DY10 .... **117** B2
Maguire Ind Est CV4 .... **131** F8
Magyar Cres CV11 .... **79** A8
Maidavale Cres CV3 .... **133** C4
Maidendale Rd DY6 .... **60** B7
Maidenbridge Dr DY6 .... **60** C8
Maidensbridge Gdns DY6 .. **49** B1
Maidensbridge Prim Sch
DY6 .... **49** B1
Maidensbridge Rd DY6 .... **49** B1
Maidstone Dr Burntwood
WS7 .... **7** D6
Stourbridge DY8 .... **60** E3
Maidstone Rd B20 .... **55** E1
Maidwell Dr B90 .... **126** E8
Main Ave B26 .... **90** C4
Main Rd Ansty CV7 .... **97** D3
Birmingham B26 .... **89** F3
Meriden CV7 .... **110** D8
Main St Birmingham B11 .. **87** A7
Brandon CV8 .... **135** F4
Shenstone WS14 .... **17** F6
Stonnall WS9 .... **16** E4
Tamworth B79 .... **21** B8
Main Terr B11 .... **87** A7
Mainstone Cl B98 .... **154** E3
Mainstream Forty Seven
Ind Pk B7 .... **67** C5
Mainstream Way B7 .... **67** C5
Mainwaring Dr B75 .... **32** E2
Maisemore Cl B98 .... **154** D6
Maitland B77 .... **21** F2
Maitland Ho B34 .... **69** E6
Maitland Rd Birmingham B8 .. **67** F4
Dudley DY1 .... **50** E1
Maizefield LE10 .... **71** C4
Majestic Way B65 .... **63** D4
Major Ct 🏠 B13 .... **87** B2
Major St WV2 .... **39** E7
Majuba Rd B16 .... **65** C4
Makepeace Ave CV34 .... **155** F1
Malam Cl CV4 .... **112** A1
Malcolm Ave Birmingham
B24 .... **57** C5
Bromsgrove B61 .... **136** E3
Malcolm Ct WV1 .... **25** A3
Malcolm Gr B45 .... **122** A7
Malcolm Rd B90 .... **106** B1
Malcolmson Cl B15 .... **85** F8
Maldale B77 .... **22** C1
Malfield Dr Birmingham B27 .. **88** E3
Redditch B97 .... **152** F3
Malham Cl CV11 .... **74** A2
Malham Rd Tamworth B77 .. **36** C8
Warwick CV34 .... **155** F1
Malins Rd Birmingham B17 .. **85** D5
Wolverhampton WV4 .... **39** E5
Malins The CV34 .... **161** B6
Malkit Cl WS2 .... **27** F4
Mallaby Cl B90 .... **126** A8
Mallard Ave
Kidderminster DY10 .... **117** B3
Nuneaton CV10 .... **72** C6
Mallard Cl Birmingham B27 .. **88** C3
Brierley Hill DY5 .... **81** C7
Redditch B98 .... **153** F5
Walsall WS3 .... **15** A5
Mallard Croft 🏠 WS13 .... **9** C8
Mallard Dr Birmingham B23 .. **56** B3
Oldbury B69 .... **63** F4
Mallard Rd B80 .... **159** F4
Mallards Reach B92 .... **106** E8
Mallender Dr B93 .... **127** F6
Mallerin Croft CV10 .... **72** B5
Mallicot Cl WS13 .... **3** D1
Mallin Gdns DY1 .... **61** E8
Mallin St B66 .... **64** D7
Mallory Cres WS3 .... **14** D2
Mallory Dr
Kidderminster DY11 .... **116** D8
Warwick CV34 .... **160** D7
Mallory Rd WV6 .... **23** E3
Mallory Rise B13 .... **87** C1
Mallory Way CV6 .... **95** E4
Mallow Cl WS5 .... **43** A3
Malmesbury Rd
Birmingham B10 .... **87** E7
Coventry CV6 .... **95** A3
Malpas Dr B32 .... **102** C8
Malpas Wlk WV10 .... **26** A4
Malpass Rd DY5 .... **81** F7
Malt Cl B17 .... **85** D6
Malt Mill La B62 .... **83** D8
Malt Mill Lane Trad Est
B62 .... **83** D8
Malthouse 🏠 B66 .... **64** E7
Malthouse Croft B6 .... **66** E8
Malthouse Gdns B19 .... **66** D7
Malthouse Gr B25 .... **68** E1
Malthouse La
Birmingham B8 .... **67** E6
Birmingham, Great Barr B42 .. **55** D8
Earlswood B94 .... **141** E7
Kenilworth CV8 .... **147** E6
Wolverhampton WV6 .... **24** E6

Malthouse Rd DY4 .... **51** E5
Malthouse Row B37 .... **90** A8
Maltings The Aldridge WS9 .. **30** C6
Nuneaton CV11 .... **73** E5
Royal Leamington Spa CV32 .. **156** F2
Studley B80 .... **159** D4
Wolverhampton WV1 .... **163** C4
Malton Gr B13 .... **105** B7
Malvern Ave Nuneaton CV10 .. **72** B3
Stourbridge DY9 .... **81** C5
Malvern Cl
West Bromwich B71 .... **53** D5
Willenhall WV12 .... **27** B4
Malvern Cres DY2 .... **61** F6
Malvern Ct
Birmingham,
Acock's Green B27 .... **88** C4
Birmingham,
Stockland Green B23 .... **56** C3
Sutton Coldfield B74 .... **31** F2
Wolverhampton WV10 .... **25** D8
Malvern Dr Aldridge WS9 .. **30** C8
Kidderminster DY10 .... **116** E3
Sutton Coldfield B76 .... **58** A8
Wolverhampton WV1 .... **26** B1
Malvern Hill Rd B7 .... **67** C7
Malvern Ho Coventry CV5 .. **111** D4
🏠 Halesowen B63 .... **83** A3
Redditch B97 .... **153** C1
Malvern Park Ave B91 .... **107** D3
Malvern Rd
Balsall Common CV7 .... **130** C6
Barnt Green B45 .... **122** A2
Birmingham,
Acock's Green B27 .... **88** D4
Birmingham,
Handsworth B21 .... **54** C1
Bromsgrove B61 .... **150** D7
Coventry CV5 .... **112** F4
Oldbury B68 .... **84** B8
Redditch B97 .... **158** D8
Malvern St B12 .... **87** A5
Malvern View
Bluntington DY10 .... **118** E1
Kidderminster DY11 .... **116** B1
Malvern View Rd DY3 .... **50** D4
Mamble Rd DY8 .... **80** E5
Manby Cl W6 .... **25** A4
Manby Rd B35 .... **58** A4
Manby St DY4 .... **51** F8
Mancetter Rd Nuneaton
CV10 .... **72** D7
Solihull B90 .... **106** C3
Manchester St
Birmingham B6 .... **164** C5
Oldbury B69 .... **64** B7
Mancroft Cl DY6 .... **60** B7
Mancroft Gdns WV6 .... **24** C5
Mancroft Rd WV6 .... **24** C5
Mandale Rd WV10 .... **25** F6
Mandarin Dr DY10 .... **117** B3
Mander Ctr WV1 .... **163** B3
Mander Gallery WV1 .... **163** B3
Mander Gr CV34 .... **160** C4
Mander Sq WV1 .... **163** B3
Mander St WV3 .... **39** C2
Manderley Cl Coventry CV5 .. **111** C5
Sedgley DY3 .... **39** C2
Manderville Gdns DY6 .... **60** C6
Mandeville Gdns WS1 .... **42** F8
Mandeville Way B61 .... **136** F5
Maney Cnr B72 .... **46** B4
Maney Hill Prim Sch B72 .... **46** D2
Maney Hill Rd B72 .... **46** C2
Manfield Ave CV2 .... **115** A7
Manfield Rd WV13 .... **26** C3
Manifold Cl WS7 .... **7** D6
Manifoldia Grange B70 .... **53** B2
Manilla Rd B29 .... **86** B1
Manitoba Croft B38 .... **123** F8
Manley Cl B70 .... **53** A3
Manley Rd WS13 .... **3** D1
Manlove St WV3 .... **39** A8
Manningford Ct B14 .... **104** F3
Manningford Rd B14 .... **104** E3
Manor Abbey Dr B62 .... **83** E3
Manor Abbey Rd B62 .... **83** F4
Manor Ave Cannock WS11 .... **1** D1
Great Wyrley WS6 .... **5** A4
Kidderminster DY11 .... **116** A7
Manor Ave S DY11 .... **116** A6
Manor Cl Birmingham B16 .. **65** D1
Codsall WV8 .... **10** B4
Hinckley LE10 .... **75** C5
Kidderminster DY11 .... **116** A6
Willenhall WV13 .... **26** F3
Wolverhampton WV4 .... **38** F4
Manor Court Ave CV11 .... **73** B5
Manor Court Rd
Bromsgrove B60 .... **150** F8
Nuneaton CV11 .... **73** A5
Manor Ct Dorridge B93 .... **127** F2
Dudley DY2 .... **62** C5
Kenilworth CV8 .... **148** A6
Royal Leamington Spa CV31 .. **161** F7
Walsall WS2 .... **28** D2
Manor Cty Prim Sch B78 ..... **34** E5
Manor Dr Dudley DY3 .... **50** B3
Sutton Coldfield B73 .... **46** B4
Manor Est CV8 .... **135** F3
Manor Farm Com Sch
WS4 .... **29** B6
Manor Farm Dr WV12 .... **27** D5
Manor Farm Rd B11 .... **87** E4
Manor Gdns Birmingham
B33 .... **68** D2
Wednesbury WS10 .... **41** F4
Wombourne WV5 .... **49** B7

Manor (General) Hospl The
WS2 .... **28** C1
Manor High Com Sch WS10 .. **42** D3
Manor Hill B73 .... **46** B4
Manor Ho Astwood Bank B96 .. **158** E3
Wolverhampton WV6 .... **24** D5
Manor House Cl
Aston Flamville LE10 .... **76** E6
Birmingham B29 .... **84** F1
Manor House Dr CV1 .... **165** B2
Manor House La
Birmingham B26 .... **88** F7
Water Orton B46 .... **59** B3
Manor House Pk WV8 .... **10** C4
Manor House Rd WS10 .... **41** F4
Manor Ind Est WS2 .... **28** C1
Manor La Halesowen B62 ... **83** E4
Honiley CV8 .... **146** A5
Lydiate Ash B61 .... **121** C4
Stourbridge DY8 .... **80** D3
Wroxall CV35 .... **145** F4
Manor Mews B80 .... **159** E4
Manor Park Gr B31 .... **102** C1
Manor Park Jun & Inf
Sch CV3 .... **133** D7
Manor Park Prim Sch B6 .... **67** A8
Manor Park Rd
Birmingham B36 .... **69** D8
Nuneaton CV11 .... **73** A5
Manor Park Sch CV11 .... **73** A5
Manor Pk DY6 .... **60** D6
Manor Pl LE10 .... **71** D1
Manor Prim Sch
Aldridge B74 .... **31** A1
Wolverhampton WV14 .... **40** B2
Manor Rd
Birmingham, Birchfield B6 .. **55** F1
Birmingham, Edgbaston B16 .. **65** D1
Birmingham, Stechford B33 .. **68** E3
Coventry CV1 .... **165** B1
Dorridge B93 .... **127** F3
Kenilworth CV8 .... **147** F6
Mile Oak B78 .... **20** D1
Royal Leamington Spa CV32 .. **157** B3
Smethwick B67 .... **64** E4
Solihull B91 .... **107** C5
Stourbridge B60 .... **60** E2
Studley B80 .... **159** E4
Sutton Coldfield, Maney B73 ... **46** B4
Sutton Coldfield, Streetly B74 .. **45** A8
Tamworth B77 .... **21** D4
Tipton DY4 .... **51** F4
Upper Bentley B60, B97 .... **152** B1
Walsall WS2 .... **28** C2
Wednesbury WS10 .... **42** D2
Wolverhampton,
Ettingshall WV4 .... **40** A5
Wolverhampton, Oxley WV10 .. **25** C7
Wolverhampton, Penn WV4 .. **38** F4
Wythall B47 .... **125** A3
Manor Rd N B16 .... **65** D1
Manor Rise Burntwood WS7 .. **7** A5
Lichfield WS14 .... **9** C7
Manor Road Prec 🏠 WS2 .. **28** C2
Manor St Hinckley LE10 ..... **71** C1
Wolverhampton WV6 .... **24** D5
Manor Terr CV8 .... **148** A6
Manor Way Birmingham B62 .. **84** A3
Halesowen B62 .... **83** D3
Hinckley LE10 .... **75** D5
Manor Way Prim Sch B62 ... **83** C3
Manor Wlk Solihull B91 ..... **107** C3
Sutton Coldfield B73 .... **46** B4
Manorford Ave B71 .... **43** A4
Mansard Cl
Wolverhampton,
Bradmore WV3 .... **38** F8
Wolverhampton,
Scotland WV10 .... **26** B8
Mansard Ho B90 .... **106** A3
Manse Cl CV7 .... **78** A1
Mansel Rd B10 .... **87** E8
Mansel St CV6 .... **113** E6
Mansell Cl B63 .... **82** B7
Mansell Rd Redditch B97 .. **158** D7
Tipton DY4 .... **52** A8
Mansfield Green Inf &
Jun Sch B6 .... **66** E8
Mansfield Ho B37 .... **70** D3
Mansfield Rd
Birmingham, Aston B6 .... **66** E8
Birmingham,
South Yardley B25 .... **88** C5
Mansion Cres B67 .... **64** E4
Mansion Ct B62 .... **83** E7
Mansion Dr WS7 .... **7** D4
Mansion St 🏠 LE10 .... **75** D8
Manson Ct WV4 .... **38** D5
Manston Dr WV6 .... **23** E5
Manston Rd B26 .... **89** B7
Manston View B79 .... **21** C8
Manta Rd B77 .... **35** D6
Mantilla Dr CV3 .... **133** B5
Manton Croft B93 .... **127** E3
Manton Ho B19 .... **66** E7
Manway CT B20 .... **54** F4
Manwoods Cl B20 .... **55** B2
Maple Ave Bedworth CV7 .... **78** B1
Wednesbury WS10 .... **42** C4
Maple Bank B15 .... **86** A7
Maple Cl Birmingham B21 .. **54** E1
Burntwood WS7 .... **6** F7
Dudley WV14 .... **51** A7
Hinckley LE10 .... **75** E5
Kidderminster DY11 .... **116** B8
Stourbridge DY8 .... **80** D2
Maple Cres WS11 .... **1** C1

Maple Croft B13 .... **104** F5
Maple Ct Bilston WV14 .... **40** F2
Lichfield WS14 .... **9** C5
Oldbury B66 .... **64** D8
Maple Ctr The WS10 .... **41** B3
Maple Dr Birmingham B44 .. **56** C8
Dudley DY3 .... **50** B2
Huntington WS12 .... **1** D8
Walsall, Shelfield WS4 .... **29** B8
Walsall, Yew Tree WS5 .... **43** B4
Maple Gn DY1 .... **51** A5
Maple Gr Bilston WV14 .... **40** F4
Birmingham, Aston B19 ...... **66** D8
Birmingham, Kingshurst B37 .. **69** F6
Kingswinford DY6 .... **60** E6
Lichfield WS14 .... **9** F7
Warwick CV34 .... **156** A1
Wolverhampton WV3 .... **24** C2
Maple Hayes Dyslexia Sch
The WS13 .... **8** D8
Maple Ho WS4 .... **15** D1
Maple Leaf Dr B37 .... **90** C8
Maple Leaf Ind Est WS2 ..... **28** A3
Maple Leaf Rd WS10 .... **41** C1
Maple Rd
Birmingham, Eachway B45 .. **121** F6
Birmingham, Selly Oak B30 .. **103** E8
Dudley DY1 .... **51** C3
Halesowen B62 .... **83** D8
Nuneaton CV10 .... **72** E5
Royal Leamington Spa CV31 .. **161** F6
Sutton Coldfield B72 .... **46** C3
Walsall WS3 .... **14** F2
Wolverhampton WV3 .... **38** E7
Maple Rise Oldbury B68 ..... **64** C2
Tamworth B77 .... **22** A4
Maple Row 🏠 DY5 .... **61** D2
Maple St WS3 .... **14** D2
Maple Tree La B63 .... **82** C6
Maple Way B31 .... **102** F1
Maple Wlk 🏠 B37 .... **70** B2
Mapledene 🏠 B13 .... **87** B2
Mapledene Inf Sch B26 ..... **89** D6
Mapledene Jun Sch B26 .... **89** D6
Mapledene Rd B26 .... **89** D6
Maples The Bedworth CV12 .. **77** E2
Wolverhampton WV11 .... **26** B5
Mapleton Gr B28 .... **106** B7
Mapleton Rd
Birmingham B28 .... **106** B7
Coventry CV6 .... **112** F8
Maplewood B76 .... **58** A8
Mapperley Cl CV2 .... **115** A8
Mapperley Gdns B13 .... **86** C3
Mappleborough Rd B90 .... **105** E1
Marans Croft B38 .... **123** D7
Marble Alley B80 .... **159** E4
Marbury Cl B38 .... **103** D2
Marbury Mews DY5 .... **61** D1
March Cl WS6 .... **4** D1
March End Rd WV11 .... **26** D5
March Way Aldridge WS9 ... **16** C1
Coventry CV3 .... **134** D7
Marchant Rd Bilston WV14 .. **40** D7
Hinckley LE10 .... **75** C8
Wolverhampton WV3 .... **24** F2
Marchfont Cl CV11 .... **74** A1
Marchmont Rd B9 .... **68** A2
Marchmount Rd B72 .... **57** C8
Marcliff Cres B90 .... **105** C2
Marconi Pl WS12 .... **2** C7
Marcos Dr B36 .... **58** F1
Marcot Rd B92 .... **88** F5
Marcroft Pl CV31 .... **162** D6
Marden Cl WV13 .... **26** F1
Marden Gr B31 .... **123** A7
Marden Wlk B23 .... **56** C3
Mardol Cl CV2 .... **114** D7
Mardon Rd B26 .... **89** C5
Maree Gr WV12 .... **13** B1
Maret Ct 🏠 WS1 .... **42** F8
Marfield Cl B76 .... **58** A6
Margam Cres WS3 .... **13** F2
Margam Terr WS3 .... **13** F2
Margam Way WS3 .... **13** F2
Margaret Ave Bedworth
CV12 .... **78** B3
Halesowen B63 .... **82** F4
Margaret Cl DY5 .... **81** E8
Margaret Dr Cannock WS11 ... **1** E6
Stourbridge DY8 .... **81** B4
Margaret Gdns B67 .... **64** E5
Margaret Gr B17 .... **85** C7
Margaret Ho B76 .... **46** F3
Margaret Rd Birmingham
B73 .... **45** D1
Birmingham, Harborne B17 .. **85** C3
Darlaston DY10 .... **41** C4
Walsall WS2 .... **27** E3
Margaret St Birmingham
B3 .... **164** B3
Walsall WS2 .... **28** D2
West Bromwich B70 .... **53** B2
Margaret Vale DY4 .... **41** C1
Margaret Vine Ct B62 .... **63** F1
Margeson Cl CV2 .... **114** C2
Margesson Dr B45 .... **122** D1
Margetts Cl CV8 .... **147** F4
Marholm Cl WV9 .... **10** F2
Maria St B70 .... **64** B8
Marian Croft B26 .... **89** D4
Marie Brock Cl CV4 .... **112** B1
Marie Dr B27 .... **106** B8
Marigold Cl WS11 .... **2** C3
Marigold Cres DY1 .... **51** A4
Marigold Dr LE10 .... **75** E5
Marina Cl CV4 .... **131** E7

Marina Cres WS12 .... **2** A5
Marine Cres DY8 .... **60** E1
Marine Dr B44 .... **55** E6
Marine Gdns DY8 .... **60** E1
Mariner B79 .... **20** E6
Mariner Ave B16 .... **65** E1
Marion Cl DY5 .... **61** F2
Marion Rd Coventry CV6 .. **113** D7
Smethwick B67 .... **64** E5
Marion Way B28 .... **105** E7
Marita Cl DY2 .... **62** E3
Marjoram Cl B38 .... **123** F8
Marjorie Ave B30 .... **104** B3
Mark Antony Dr CV34 ...... **161** D4
Mark Ave WS10 .... **41** E3
Mark Ct WS1 .... **29** A3
Mark Ho B13 .... **87** A2
Mark Rd WS10 .... **41** E3
Markby Rd B18 .... **65** E6
Market Cnr Baginton CV8 .. **133** F2
Royal Leamington Spa CV31 .. **161** F5
Market End Cl CV12 .... **77** C2
Market Hall St WS11 .... **1** E1
Market La Lichfield WS14 ..... **8** E2
Wombourne WV4 .... **37** F5
Market Pl Blackheath B65 ... **63** C1
Bromsgrove B61 .... **136** F2
Cannock WS11 .... **1** D1
Hinckley LE10 .... **75** D8
Nuneaton CV11 .... **73** C4
Redditch B98 .... **153** E4
Tamworth B79 .... **21** B4
Tipton DY4 .... **52** D5
Walsall WS3 .... **14** B1
🏠 Warwick CV34 .... **160** E6
Wednesbury WS10 .... **41** F2
Willenhall WV13 .... **27** A1
Market Sq B64 .... **82** C8
Market St Bromsgrove B61 .. **136** F2
Cannock WS12 .... **2** C5
Kidderminster DY10 .... **116** E5
Lichfield WS13 .... **9** B8
Oldbury B69 .... **64** A8
Stourbridge DY8 .... **81** A5
Tamworth B79 .... **21** B4
Warwick CV34 .... **160** D6
Wolverhampton WV1 .... **163** C3
Market Way Bilston WV14 ... **40** D5
Coventry CV1 .... **165** B2
Hagley DY9 .... **99** C6
Market Wlk 🏠 B98 .... **153** E4
Markfield Rd B26 .... **89** B8
Markford Wlk B19 .... **66** D6
Markham Cres B92 .... **89** F1
Markham Croft WV9 .... **11** A2
Markham Dr
Kingswinford DY6 .... **60** E4
Whitnash CV31 .... **162** B3
Markham Rd B73 .... **45** C3
Marklew Cl WS8 .... **16** A5
Marklin Ave WV10 .... **11** D1
Marks Mews 🏠 CV34 .... **160** E6
Marks Wlk B79 .... **3** A2
Marksbury Cl WV6 .... **25** A5
Marl Rd DY2 .... **62** B4
Marl Top B38 .... **103** F2
Marlbank Rd DY8 .... **61** A1
Marlborough Ave B60 ...... **151** A8
Marlborough Cl
Hinckley LE10 .... **76** B7
Sutton Coldfield B74 .... **31** E6
Marlborough Ct
Bromsgrove B60 .... **151** B8
Lichfield WS13 .... **9** B7
Sutton Coldfield B74 .... **31** F2
Marlborough Dr
Royal Leamington Spa
CV31 .... **162** D3
Stourbridge DY8 .... **81** A3
Marlborough Gdns
Stourbridge DY8 .... **60** D2
Wolverhampton WV6 .... **24** E4
Marlborough Gr B25 .... **68** D1
Marlborough Ind Est WV2 .. **39** D7
Marlborough Inf Sch B10 ... **67** E1
Marlborough Jun Sch
B10 .... **67** E1
Marlborough Rd
Birmingham,
Castle Bromwich B36 .... **69** D8
Birmingham,
Small Heath B10 .... **67** E1
Coventry CV2 .... **114** A3
Dudley DY3 .... **50** F6
Nuneaton CV11 .... **73** B3
Smethwick B66 .... **65** A3
Marlborough St
🏠 Kidderminster DY10 ..... **116** E5
Walsall WS3 .... **14** B1
Marlborough Way B77 .... **21** F4
Marlbrook Cl B92 .... **89** C4
Marlbrook Dr WV4 .... **39** B6
Marlbrook La B60 .... **121** D2
Marlcliff Gr B13 .... **105** A6
Marlcroft CV3 .... **134** C5
Marldon Rd B14 .... **104** E6
Marlene Croft B37 .... **70** C1
Marler Rd CV4 .... **131** F7
Marley Hts B27 .... **88** D4
Marley Rd DY6 .... **61** A4
Marlfield Farm Fst Sch
B98 .... **154** C6
Marlfield La Redditch B98 .. **154** B4
Redditch B98 .... **154** B5
Marlin B77 .... **35** D6
Marling Croft B92 .... **107** F3
Marlissa Dr CV6 .... **95** E2
Marloes Wlk CV31 .... **162** C6

Marlow Cl Coventry CV5 .... 112 B4
Dudley DY1 .... 62 E3
Marlow Rd Birmingham B23 .. 56 D5
Tamworth B77 .... 21 D5
Marlow St Blackheath B65 .... 63 B1
Walsall WS2 .... 28 E3
Marlowe Cl DY10 .... 117 B6
Marlowe Dr WV12 .... 27 A7
Marlpit La Redditch B97 .... 153 C1
Sutton Coldfield B75 .... 32 E3
Marlpool Fst Sch The
DY11 .... 116 C8
Marlpool Fst Sch The DY11 .. 116 C8
Marlpool Pl DY11 .... 116 C8
Marlston Wlk CV5 .... 112 B4
Marlwood Cl CV6 .... 95 F4
Marmion B43 .... 43 F2
Marmion Gr DY1 .... 62 A8
Marmion Ho B70 .... 52 F6
Marmion Jun Sch B79 ...... 21 B6
Marmion St B79 .... 21 B5
Marmion Way B70 .... 52 F6
Marnel Dr WV3 .... 38 E7
Marner Cres CV6 .... 113 B5
Marner Rd Bedworth CV12 .. 78 A3
Nuneaton CV10 .... 73 B1
Marnhull Cl CV2 .... 114 F4
Marquis Dr B62 .... 83 A7
Marrick B77 .... 22 C1
Marriners La CV5 .... 112 B6
Marriott Rd Bedworth CV12 .. 77 D2
Coventry CV6 .... 113 A4
Dudley DY2 .... 62 C4
Smethwick B66 .... 64 D7
Marroway St B16 .... 65 F3
Mars Cl WV14 .... 40 A1
Marsdale Dr CV10 .... 72 E3
Marsden Cl B92 .... 88 E1
Marsden Rd B98 .... 153 E3
Marsett B77 .... 36 C8
Marsh Cres CV9 .... 60 D3
Marsh End B38 .... 124 A8
Marsh Hill B23 .... 56 C4
Marsh Hill Jun & Inf Sch
B23 .... 56 C4
Marsh Ho CV2 .... 115 A7
Marsh La Birmingham B23 .. 56 E5
Bradnock's Marsh B92 ...... 109 D5
Curdworth B76 .... 59 D5
Hampton in A B92 .... 109 B6
Lichfield WS14 .... 9 C5
Solihull B91 .... 107 E3
Walsall WS2 .... 28 E2
Water Orton B46 .... 59 C3
West Bromwich B71 .... 53 D8
Wolverhampton WV10 .... 11 B2
Marsh Lane Par WV10 .... 11 C2
Marsh St WS2 .... 28 E2
Marsh The WS10 .... 41 E3
Marshall Cl WS9 .... 30 B4
Marshall Gr B44 .... 55 F7
Marshall Ho 4 Walsall WS2 42 C8
7 West Bromwich B71 .... 42 F1
Marshall Lake Rd B90 ...... 106 D1
Marshall Rd Bedworth CV7 .. 95 F8
Oldbury B68 .... 64 C1
Willenhall WV13 .... 26 D1
Marshall St Birmingham
B1 .... 164 B1
Smethwick B67 .... 64 D7
Tamworth B77 .... 21 E5
Marshalls Ind Est WV2 ...... 39 C7
Marsham Cl CV34 .... 161 B8
Marsham Court Rd B91 .... 106 F7
Marsham Rd B14 .... 104 F3
Marshbrook Cl CV2 .... 96 E3
Marshbrook Rd B24 .... 57 D4
Marshdale Ave CV6 .... 95 E3
Marshfield B74 .... 154 B7
Marshfield Dr CV4 .... 132 D2
Marshfield Gdns B24 .... 56 F2
Marshland Way WS2 .... 27 E1
Marshmont Way B23 .... 56 D8
Marshwood Cl WS11 .... 2 A2
Marshwood Croft B62 .... 84 A3
Marsland Cl B17 .... 65 C1
Marsland Rd B92 .... 106 E8
Marston Ave WS10 .... 41 C6
Marston Cl
Royal Leamington Spa CV32 157 B2
Stourbridge DY8 .... 80 D4
Marston Croft B37 .... 89 F7
Marston Dr B37 .... 70 A5
Marston Gr B43 .... 54 C8
Marston Green Inf Sch
B37 .... 89 F7
Marston Green Jun Sch
B37 .... 90 A7
Marston Green Sta B37 ..... 89 F7
Marston Ind Est WV2 .... 39 C7
Marston La Bedworth CV12 .. 78 D5
Nuneaton CV11 .... 78 E8
Wishaw B76 .... 48 E1
Marston Rd Birmingham
B29 .... 102 F8
Cannock WS12 .... 1 F6
Dudley DY1 .... 61 E8
Sutton Coldfield B73 .... 57 A7
Wolverhampton WV2 .... 39 C7
Marston St WV13 .... 27 C2
Marten Cl CV35 .... 160 A7
Martham Dr WV6 .... 24 B2
Martin Cl Birmingham B26 .. 88 D6
Bromsgrove B61 .... 136 E1
Coventry CV5 .... 111 E4
Dudley WV14 .... 51 D7

Martin Croft WS13 .... 3 A1
Martin Dr WV12 .... 27 C5
Martin Hill St DY2 .... 62 C8
Martin Rd Bilston WV14 ...... 40 F3
Tipton DY4 .... 52 A4
Walsall WS5 .... 43 C8
Martin Rise B37 .... 89 F8
Martin St WV4 .... 39 F5
Martindale WS11 .... 2 A2
Martindale Rd CV7 .... 96 C8
Martindale Trad Est WS11 .... 2 A2
Martindale Wlk DY5 .... 81 B6
Martineau Rural Studies
Ctr B5 .... 86 C5
Martineau Sq B2 .... 164 C2
Martineau Tower B19 .... 66 D5
Martineau Way B2 .... 164 C2
Martingale Cl
Bromsgrove B60 .... 150 E6
Walsall WS5 .... 42 F4
Martins Rd CV12 .... 77 E1
Martlesham Sq B35 .... 58 A4
Martley Cl B98 .... 159 B7
Martley Croft
Birmingham B32 .... 84 E4
Solihull B91 .... 127 B8
Martley Ct DY9 .... 81 C4
Martley Dr DY9 .... 81 C4
Martley Rd Oldbury B69 ..... 63 D5
Walsall WS4 .... 15 C2
Marton Ave 7 WS7 .... 7 A8
Marton Cl B7 .... 67 B6
Martyrs' Cl The CV3 .... 133 D8
Marwood Croft B74 .... 31 A2
Mary Ann St Birmingham
B3 .... 164 B4
Wolverhampton WV1 .... 163 D2
Mary Elliot Sch WS2 .... 28 E4
Mary Herbert St CV3 .... 133 D7
Mary Rd
Birmingham,
Handsworth B21 .... 65 E7
Birmingham, Stechford B33 .. 68 D3
Tipton B69 .... 63 C8
West Bromwich B70 .... 53 D1
Mary Slessor St CV3 .... 134 D7
Mary St
Birmingham,
Balsall Heath B12 .... 86 E5
Birmingham, Brookfields B1 164 A4
Cannock WS12 .... 2 B7
Walsall WS2 .... 28 D3
Mary Vale Rd B30 .... 103 F6
Maryland Ave B34 .... 68 F5
Maryland Cl LE9 .... 71 F6
Maryland Dr B31 .... 103 B5
Maryland Rd DY5 .... 81 F7
Marylebone Cl DY8 .... 81 A7
Marystow Cl CV5 .... 112 B8
Maryvale Ct Lichfield WS14 ... 9 D7
2 Walsall WS1 .... 42 E8
Maryvale RC Jun & Inf Sch
B44 .... 44 E1
Marywell Cl B32 .... 102 B7
Masefield Ave Dudley DY1 .. 51 C7
Warwick CV34 .... 160 C4
Masefield Cl Bilston WV14 ... 40 F2
Lichfield WS14 .... 9 B6
Masefield Dr B79 .... 21 A7
Masefield Gr WS11 .... 1 E4
Masefield Rd Dudley DY3 .... 50 A4
Walsall WS3 .... 28 E7
Wolverhampton WV10 .... 12 A1
Masefield Rise B62 .... 83 D3
Masefield Sq B31 .... 103 C4
Masham Cl B33 .... 68 E3
Mashie Gdns B38 .... 103 D1
Maslen Pl B63 .... 83 B3
Maslin Dr WV14 .... 40 A1
Mason Ave CV32 .... 157 C3
Mason Cl B97 .... 158 D7
Mason Cotts B24 .... 57 B5
Mason Cres WV4 .... 38 E5
Mason Ct LE10 .... 75 B8
Mason La B94 .... 125 F1
Mason Rd Birmingham B24 .. 57 A4
Coventry CV6 .... 95 F1
Kidderminster DY11 .... 116 C6
Redditch B97 .... 158 D8
Walsall WS3 .... 28 B5
Mason St Dudley WV14 ...... 51 B7
West Bromwich B70 .... 53 B4
Wolverhampton WV2 .... 39 C7
Mason's Way B92 .... 88 E2
Masonleys Rd B31 .... 102 D3
Masons Cl B63 .... 82 C6
Masons Way B92 .... 88 E2
Massbrook Gr WV10 .... 25 F6
Massbrook Rd WV10 .... 25 F6
Masser Rd CV6 .... 95 D4
Masshouse Circus
Queensway B4 .... 164 C3
Masshouse La
Birmingham, Digbeth B5 ... 164 D3
Birmingham,
King's Norton B38 .... 103 F1
Masters La B62 .... 63 E1
Masters Rd CV31 .... 162 A4
Matchborough Ctr B98 .... 154 E1
Matchborough Way B98 .... 154 E1
Matchlock Cl B74 .... 44 E7
Matfen Ave B73 .... 45 F2
Math Mdw B32 .... 84 F5
Mathe Croft CV31 .... 162 C5
Mathews Wlk WS13 .... 3 A2
Matlock Cl Dudley DY2 ...... 62 D3
Walsall WS3 .... 14 C3
Matlock Dr WS11 .... 2 A4

Matlock Rd Birmingham B11 . 87 F3
Coventry CV1 .... 113 D6
Walsall WS3 .... 14 C3
Matlock Villas 2 B12 .... 87 B5
Matterson Rd CV6 .... 113 A5
Matthew Boulton Coll B15 . 86 D8
Matthew La (Road 3)
DY10 .... 116 F1
Mattox Rd WV11 .... 26 D6
Matty Rd B68 .... 64 C4
Maud Rd Water Orton B46 ... 59 D3
West Bromwich B70 .... 53 C1
Maudslay Rd CV5 .... 112 E2
Maughan St Brierley Hill
DY5 .... 82 A8
Dudley DY1 .... 51 B1
Maund Cl B60 .... 150 E7
Maureen Cl CV4 .... 111 C1
Maurice Gr WV10 .... 26 A6
Maurice Rd Birmingham
B14 .... 104 E5
Smethwick B67 .... 64 E2
Mavis Gdns B68 .... 84 B8
Mavis Rd Birmingham B31 . 102 E1
Mavor Dr CV12 .... 77 D1
Maw St WV1 .... 42 F6
Mawgan Dr WS14 .... 9 D6
Mawnan Cl CV7 .... 96 B8
Max Rd Birmingham B32 ..... 84 D5
Coventry CV6 .... 112 F5
Maxholm Rd B74 .... 44 E8
Maxstoke Cl
Birmingham B32 .... 102 A7
Meriden CV7 .... 92 B1
Redditch B98 .... 154 D1
Sutton Coldfield B73 .... 45 E2
Tamworth B77 .... 35 C4
Walsall WS3 .... 14 A3
Maxstoke Croft B90 .... 126 C8
Maxstoke Gdns CV31 ...... 161 F6
Maxstoke La CV7 .... 92 B2
Maxstoke Rd B73 .... 45 E1
Maxstoke St B9 .... 67 B2
Maxted Rd B23 .... 56 C7
Maxwell Ave B20 .... 55 B1
Maxwell Cl WS13 .... 9 C7
Maxwell Rd WV2 .... 163 C1
May Ave 3 B12 .... 87 A5
May Farm Cl B47 .... 125 A6
May La Birmingham B14 ... 104 F5
Hollywood B47 .... 125 A7
May St Coventry CV6 .... 113 E8
Walsall WS3 .... 28 D6
May Tree Gr B20 .... 54 F3
May Trees B47 .... 124 F5
Mayall Dr B75 .... 32 D4
Mayama Rd B78 .... 34 F8
Maybank B9 .... 67 F3
Maybank Cl WS14 .... 9 E8
Maybank Pl B44 .... 55 E6
Maybank Rd DY2 .... 62 C3
Mayberry Cl B14 .... 105 B2
Maybridge Dr B91 .... 127 B8
Maybrook Ind Est WS8 ...... 15 F5
Maybrook Rd Brownhills
WS8 .... 15 F5
Sutton Coldfield B76 .... 58 A5
Maybush Gdns WV10 .... 11 C1
Maycock Rd CV6 .... 113 D7
Maycroft WS12 .... 1 F7
Maydene Croft B12 .... 86 F6
Mayfair DY9 .... 81 D2
Mayfair Cl Birmingham B44 .. 56 B7
Dudley DY1 .... 51 A2
Mayfair Dr DY6 .... 60 C7
Mayfair Gdns Tipton DY4 .... 52 A4
Wolverhampton WV3 .... 24 D2
Mayfield B77 .... 36 C8
Mayfield Ave B29 .... 86 B2
Mayfield Cl Bedworth CV12 .. 78 B3
Catshill B61 .... 120 F1
Kidderminster DY11 .... 116 A8
10 Royal Leamington Spa
CV31 .... 162 C6
Solihull B91 .... 107 C1
Mayfield Cres B65 .... 63 A3
Mayfield Ct B13 .... 87 A2
Mayfield Prep Sch WS1 ..... 43 A8
Mayfield Rd
Birmingham,
Acock's Green B11 .... 88 A3
Birmingham, Lozells B19 .... 66 C8
Birmingham, Moseley B13 ... 87 A3
Birmingham, Stirchley B30 .. 104 A6
Coventry CV5 .... 113 A1
Dudley DY1 .... 51 C4
Halesowen B62 .... 63 F1
Halesowen, Hasbury B63 ... 82 E2
Nuneaton CV11 .... 73 E2
Sutton Coldfield,
Boldmere B73 .... 46 A2
Sutton Coldfield, Streetly B74 44 F8
Wolverhampton WV1 .... 26 B1
Mayfield Sch
Birmingham B19 .... 66 C6
Birmingham B19 .... 66 C6
Mayfield The WV1 .... 26 B1
Mayfields Dr WS8 .... 6 B2
Mayfields The B98 .... 153 E2
Mayflower Cl B19 .... 66 D6
Mayflower Dr
Brierley Hill DY5 .... 61 A7
Coventry CV2 .... 114 E2
Mayford Gr B13 .... 105 B6
Maygrove Rd DY6 .... 60 C7

Mayhurst Cl Hollywood
B47 .... 125 C6
Tipton DY4 .... 52 A8
Mayhurst Rd B47 .... 125 B6
Mayland Dr B74 .... 45 A5
Mayland Rd B16 .... 65 C2
Maynard Ave Bedworth CV12 95 D8
Stourbridge DY8 .... 80 D3
Warwick CV34 .... 161 A7
Mayo Dr CV3 .... 148 A4
Mayor's Croft CV4 .... 132 B7
Mayou Ct WS3 .... 15 A4
Maypole Cl B64 .... 82 B8
Maypole Ct WV5 .... 49 A6
Maypole Dr DY8 .... 80 E5
Maypole Fields B63 .... 82 A7
Maypole Gr B14 .... 105 B2
Maypole Hill B63 .... 82 A7
Maypole La B14 .... 105 A2
Maypole Rd B68 .... 64 B1
Maypole St WV5 .... 49 B7
Mayswood Dr WV6 .... 23 F1
Mayswood Gr B32 .... 84 D4
Mayswood Rd B92 .... 89 C2
Maythorn Ave B76 .... 58 A6
Maythorn Gdns WV6 .... 24 C3
Maythorn Gr 4 B91 .... 127 B8
Maytree Cl B37 .... 70 A2
Maywell Dr B92 .... 107 F8
Maywood Cl DY6 .... 60 B6
McKean Cl B70 .... 53 C1
McKean Rd Oldbury B69 ..... 64 A8
West Bromwich B70 .... 53 C1
McBean Rd WV6 .... 24 F4
McCalla Ho WV3 .... 25 B1
McConnell Cl B60 .... 151 B7
McDonnell Dr CV6 .... 95 F6
McDougall Rd WS10 .... 42 C3
McGeough Wlk WS11 .... 2 B5
McGhie St WS12 .... 2 B6
McGregor Cl 4 B6 .... 55 F1
McLean Rd WV10 .... 11 C1
McMahon Rd CV12 .... 95 E8
Meaburn Cl B29 .... 103 A7
Mead Cl WS9 .... 30 B6
Mead Cres B9 .... 68 B3
Mead Rise B15 .... 85 F6
Mead The DY3 .... 50 B8
Meadfoot Ave B14 .... 104 F3
Meadfoot Dr DY6 .... 60 B7
Meadfoot Rd CV3 .... 134 C6
Meadow Ave B71 .... 53 F8
Meadow Brook Rd B31 .... 102 F5
Meadow Cl Aldridge B74 .... 30 F2
Ansty CV7 .... 97 D3
Birmingham B17 .... 65 B1
Royal Leamington Spa
CV32 .... 157 C4
Tanworth-in-A B94 .... 143 C6
Walsall WS3 .... 29 C8
Meadow Croft Cannock WS12 1 C4
Hagley DY9 .... 98 F4
Perton WV6 .... 23 D3
Wythall B47 .... 125 A3
Meadow Ct CV11 .... 73 B4
Meadow Dr
Hampton in A B92 .... 109 B7
Hinckley LE10 .... 76 A7
Meadow Gr Great Wyrley
WS6 .... 5 A2
Solihull B92 .... 88 D1
Meadow Grange Dr WV12 ... 27 B7
Meadow Green Prim Sch
B47 .... 125 A3
Meadow Hill Cl DY11 ...... 116 A5
Meadow Hill Cres B98 .... 153 F5
Meadow Hill Dr WS11 .... 2 A2
Meadow Hill Rd B38 .... 103 E2
Meadow Ho 5 CV1 .... 113 B3
Meadow La Alvechurch B48 139 B6
Coven Heath WV10 .... 11 C6
Lapworth B94 .... 144 D3
Wednesfield WV12 .... 27 A5
Wolverhampton WV14 .... 40 D2
Wombourne WV5 .... 49 B8
Meadow Lark Cl WS12 .... 2 B4
Meadow Mills Est DY10 ... 116 E5
Meadow Pk B79 .... 20 F5
Meadow Rd Aldridge WS9 ... 30 A4
Birmingham, Harborne B17 .. 65 B1
Birmingham, Quinton B32 ... 84 A6
Catshill B61 .... 136 F8
Coventry CV6 .... 95 A4
Dudley DY1 .... 51 B3
Halesowen B62 .... 83 C8
Nuneaton CV10 .... 72 A8
Oldbury B68 .... 64 B3
Smethwick B67 .... 65 A4
Warwick CV34 .... 161 A7
Wolverhampton WV3 .... 38 D8
Wythall B47 .... 125 A3
Meadow Rise B30 .... 103 E7
Meadow St Blackheath B64 .. 82 F8
Coventry CV1 .... 165 A2
Nuneaton CV11 .... 73 B5
Tamworth B77 .... 21 C3
Walsall WS1 .... 42 D8
1 Wolverhampton WV1 ...... 25 B2
Meadow Vale WV8 .... 10 B2
Meadow View
Birmingham B13 .... 105 C8
Burntwood WS7 .... 7 D1
Sedgley DY3 .... 39 C1
Meadow View JMI Sch
B43 .... 44 D5
Meadow View Terr WV6 ..... 24 F4
Meadow Way Cannock WS12 .. 2 C1
Stourbridge DY8 .... 60 C2

Meadow Wlk
Birmingham B14 .... 104 E1
Blackheath B64 .... 82 D8
Meadowbrook Rd
Halesowen B63 .... 82 E3
Wolverhampton WS13 .... 3 B3
Meadowfield Rd B45 .... 122 A6
Meadowfields Cl DY8 .... 60 E2
Meadowhill Dr DY8 .... 60 E2
Meadowhill Rd B98 .... 153 F5
Meadowlands Dr WS4 .... 15 D1
Meadowpark Rd DY8 .... 80 D8
Meadows Fst Sch B61 .... 137 A3
Meadows Prim Sch The
B31 .... 102 E1
Meadows Sch CV4 .... 111 E3
Meadows The Aldridge WS9 . 29 E5
Hinckley LE10 .... 76 A7
Leek Wootton CV35 .... 156 A7
Meadowside CV11 .... 79 B8
Meadowside Cl B43 .... 43 E1
Meadowside Rd B74 .... 31 F3
Meadowsweet Ave B38 .... 123 F8
Meadowsweet Way DY6 ..... 61 A6
Meadowvale Rd B60 .... 137 C6
Meadthorpe Rd B44 .... 55 D8
Meadvale Rd B45 .... 122 B6
Meadway Birmingham B33 .. 69 B2
Coventry CV2 .... 114 B6
Meadway Cl WS12 .... 2 C3
Meadway N CV2 .... 114 B6
Meadway St WS7 .... 7 A5
Meadway The Hinckley LE10 . 75 F7
Redditch B97 .... 153 C1
Wolverhampton WV6 .... 24 A5
Meadwood Ind Est WV14 .... 40 E5
Mears Cl B23 .... 56 D8
Mears Coppice DY5 .... 81 E6
Mears Dr B33 .... 68 D4
Mearse La Barnt Green B45 122 A1
Belbroughton DY9 .... 120 B6
Mease Ave WS7 .... 7 D6
Mease Croft 2 B9 .... 67 B2
Measham Gr B26 .... 88 E5
Measham Way WV11 .... 26 E7
Meaton Gr B32 .... 102 B8
Medcroft Ave B20 .... 54 E4
Medina B77 .... 21 E1
Medina Rd Birmingham B11 . 87 E4
Coventry CV6 .... 95 E1
Medina Way DY6 .... 60 C6
Medland Ave CV3 .... 132 F5
Medley Gdns DY4 .... 52 E4
Medley Rd B11 .... 87 D5
Medlicott Rd B11 .... 87 C6
Medway B77 .... 21 E1
Medway Cl DY5 .... 61 A6
Medway Croft B36 .... 69 F7
Medway Gr B73 .... 46 B5
Medway Gr B38 .... 123 E8
Medway Rd WS8 .... 6 C2
Medway Tower B7 .... 67 B5
Medway Wlk WS8 .... 6 C2
Medwin Gr B23 .... 56 D7
Meer End B38 .... 123 D7
Meer End Rd CV8 .... 130 D1
Meerash La WS7 .... 7 C3
Meerhill Ave B90 .... 127 A6
Meeting House La
Balsall Common CV7 .... 130 C6
Birmingham B31 .... 103 A4
Meeting La DY5 .... 61 B1
Meeting Lane Ind Est DY5 .. 61 B1
Meeting St Dudley DY2 ...... 52 D5
Tipton DY4 .... 52 D5
Wednesbury WS10 .... 41 E3
Meg La WS7 .... 7 C8
Meir Rd B98 .... 159 C8
Melbourne Ave
Birmingham B19 .... 66 C6
Bromsgrove B61 .... 136 E4
Melbourne Cl
Bromsgrove B61 .... 136 E3
Kingswinford DY6 .... 60 E4
Nuneaton CV11 .... 78 E8
West Bromwich B70 .... 53 A7
Melbourne Cres WS12 .... 2 F1
Melbourne Ct 3 CV12 .... 77 F2
Melbourne Gdns WS5 .... 43 B6
Melbourne Ho B34 .... 69 E6
Melbourne Rd
Bromsgrove B61 .... 136 E3
Cannock WS12 .... 2 F2
Coventry CV5 .... 113 A2
Halesowen B63 .... 83 B5
Smethwick B66 .... 65 B7
Melbourne St WV2 .... 163 C2
Melbury Cl WV3 .... 25 A1
Melbury Gr B14 .... 104 E5
Melbury Way WS11 .... 1 F2
Melchester Wlk WS11 .... 1 F2
Melchett Rd B30 .... 104 A4
Melcote Gr B44 .... 55 E8
Meldon Dr WV14 .... 41 A2
Meldrum Rd CV10 .... 72 D4
Melen St B97 .... 153 D4
Melford B79 .... 20 E6
Melford Cl DY3 .... 39 C2
Melford Hall Rd B91 .... 106 F7
Melfort Cl CV3 .... 114 F2
Melfort Gr B14 .... 105 A3
Melksham Sq B35 .... 58 A3
Mell Sq B91 .... 107 C4
Mellis Gr B23 .... 56 A5

Mellish Ct WS4 .... 29 A3
Mellish Dr WS4 .... 29 B3
Mellish Rd WS4 .... 29 A3
Mellor Dr B74 .... 31 E3
Mellors Cl B17 .... 85 B3
Mellowdew Rd
  Coventry CV2 .... 114 C4
  Stourbridge DY8 .... 60 C3
Mellowship Rd CV5 .... 111 D5
Mellwaters B77 .... 36 C8
Melmerby B77 .... 36 C8
Melplash Ave B91 .... 107 A4
Melrose Ave Bedworth
  CV12 .... 95 D8
  Birmingham,
    Sparkbrook B12 .... 87 A6
  Birmingham, Sparkhill B11 .. 87 C6
  Stourbridge DY8 .... 81 A2
  Sutton Coldfield B73 .... 45 E2
  West Bromwich B71 .... 42 D1
Melrose Cl Birmingham
  B38 .... 103 F1
  Hinckley LE10 .... 75 B8
Melrose Dr Cannock WS12 .. 1 F7
  Perton WV6 .... 23 E4
Melrose Gr B19 .... 66 B7
Melrose Pl B66 .... 64 D8
Melrose Rd B20 .... 55 E1
Melstock Cl DY4 .... 51 D5
Melstock Rd B14 .... 104 D7
Melton Ave B92 .... 89 A4
Melton Dr B15 .... 86 B7
Melton Rd Birmingham
  B14 .... 104 F8
  Royal Leamington Spa
  CV32 .... 157 B4
Melverley Gr B44 .... 55 F7
Melverton Ave WV10 .... 25 E8
Melville Cl CV7 .... 96 A8
Melville Hall ■ B16 .... 65 D1
Melville Rd Birmingham B16 .. 65 D1
  Coventry CV1 .... 113 A3
Melvina Rd B7 .... 66 E4
Membury Rd B8 .... 67 D6
Memorial Cl WV13 .... 27 A2
Memory La Darlaston WS10 .. 41 D8
  Wolverhampton WV11 .... 26 B5
Menai Cl WV12 .... 27 C6
Menai Wlk B37 .... 70 B4
Mendip Ave B8 .... 67 E5
Mendip Cl Bromsgrove B61 .. 137 A5
  Dudley DY3 .... 50 D3
  Wolverhampton WV2 .... 39 F7
Mendip Dr CV10 .... 72 B3
Mendip Ho B98 .... 154 D6
Mendip Rd Birmingham B8 .. 67 E5
  Halesowen B63 .... 82 D1
  Stourbridge DY8 .... 81 B6
Mendip Way B77 .... 22 C1
Menin Cres B13 .... 105 B7
Menin Rd Birmingham B13 .. 105 B8
  Tipton DY4 .... 51 D5
Mentone Ct 54 E3
Menzies High Sch B71 .... 53 C8
Meon Gr Birmingham B33 .. 89 B8
  Perton WV6 .... 23 F4
Meon Rise DY9 .... 81 C3
Meon Way WV11 .... 26 F7
Meranti Cl WV12 .... 27 C8
Mercer Ave Coventry CV2 .. 114 A5
  Water Orton B46 .... 59 A3
Mercer Gr WV11 .... 26 D7
Merchants Ct ■ CV32 .... 157 A1
Merchants Way WS9 .... 30 A7
Mercia Ave CV7 .... 147 F4
Mercia Bsns Village CV4 . 131 F6
Mercia Cl Bromsgrove B60 .. 150 F7
  Tamworth B79 .... 20 E7
Mercia Dr WV6 .... 23 E5
Mercia Ho CV1 .... 165 B3
Mercia Way CV34 .... 161 B7
Mercian Ct WS13 .... 9 C7
Mercian Pk B77 .... 22 B3
Mercian Way B77 .... 22 B4
Mercot Cl B98 .... 159 A6
Mercury Ct B77 .... 22 B3
Mercury Rd WS11 .... 2 A5
Mere Ave B35 .... 58 B3
Mere Cl WV12 .... 27 A5
Mere Dr B75 .... 32 B2
Mere Green Cl B75 .... 32 C2
Mere Green Comb Sch
  B75 .... 32 B2
Mere Green Rd B75 .... 32 C2
Mere Oak Rd WV6 .... 23 E5
Mere Pool Rd B75 .... 32 E2
Mere Rd Birmingham B23 .. 56 D3
  Stourbridge DY8 .... 80 E3
Mere View WS4 .... 29 C8
Merecote Rd B92 .... 106 D7
Meredith B92 .... 89 A4
Meredith Pool Cl B18 .... 65 F6
Meredith Rd Coventry CV2 . 114 D2
  Dudley DY3 .... 50 A5
  Wolverhampton WV11 .... 26 C8
Meredith St B64 .... 62 D1
Meres Rd B63 .... 82 C5
Mereside Way B92 .... 106 E8
Merevale Ave Hinckley LE10 . 75 C7
  Nuneaton CV11 .... 73 A4
Merevale Cl Hinckley LE10 .. 75 C7
  Redditch B98 .... 159 D8
Merevale Rd B92 .... 89 B2
Merganser B77 .... 36 A6
Merganser Way DY10 .... 117 B3

Meriden Ave DY8 .... 80 D6
Meriden CE Prim Sch CV7 .. 92 C1
Meriden Cl Birmingham B25 .. 88 B7
  Cannock WS11 .... 4 B8
  Stourbridge DY8 .... 80 D6
Meriden Ct WV4 .... 39 F4
Meriden Dr B37 .... 70 A6
Meriden Hill CV7 .... 110 E8
Meriden Rd Berkswell CV7 . 110 C4
  Corley CV7 .... 93 B7
  Hampton in a B92 .... 109 B8
  Wolverhampton WV10 .... 25 A8
Meriden Rise B92 .... 89 D3
Meriden St Birmingham B5 . 164 D1
  Coventry CV1 .... 113 B3
Meridian Pl B60 .... 137 A1
Merino Ave B31 .... 123 A8
Merlin Ave CV10 .... 72 B6
Merlin Cl Cannock WS11 .... 1 C2
  Dudley DY1 .... 61 F8
  Tamworth B77 .... 36 A6
Merlin Dr DY10 .... 117 B3
Merlin Gr B26 .... 89 B5
Merrick Cl B63 .... 82 D2
Merrick Ct LE10 .... 75 F5
Merrick Rd WV11 .... 27 A6
Merridale Ave WV3 .... 24 F2
Merridale Cres WV3 .... 25 A2
Merridale Gdns WV3 .... 24 F1
Merridale Gr WV3 .... 24 E1
Merridale La WV3 .... 25 A1
Merridale Prim Sch WV3 .. 25 A1
Merridale Rd WV3 .... 25 A1
Merridale St WV3 .... 163 A1
Merridale St W WV3 .... 39 A8
Merriemont Dr B45 .... 122 A4
Merrifield Gdns LE10 .... 75 E5
Merrigold Bsns Pk WV11 .. 26 C5
Merrill Cl WS6 .... 4 E1
Merrill Gdns B60 .... 121 D2
Merrill's Hall La WV11 .... 26 E1
Merrington Cl ■ B91 .... 127 C8
Merrion's Cl B43 .... 43 E4
Merrishaw Rd B31 .... 123 A8
Merritt's Brook La B31 .... 102 E5
Merritts Brook Cl B29 .... 103 A5
Merritts Hill B31 .... 102 E6
Merrivale Rd Coventry CV5 . 112 E3
  Halesowen B62 .... 83 F8
  Smethwick B66 .... 65 A2
Merry Hill DY5 .... 61 F2
Merry Hill Ctr DY5 .... 61 F3
Merry Hill Inf Sch B66 .... 65 D6
Merryfield Cl B92 .... 107 D7
Merryfield Gr B17 .... 85 C4
Merryfield Rd DY1 .... 50 E1
Merryfields Way CV2 .... 96 F1
Merryhill Dr B18 .... 65 F6
Merse B98 .... 154 E6
Mersey Gr B38 .... 123 E8
Mersey Rd Bulkington CV12 .. 79 A3
  Walsall WS3 .... 14 E1
Merstal Dr B92 .... 107 F7
Merstone Cl WV14 .... 40 C6
Merstone Sch B37 .... 70 A1
Merstowe Cl B27 .... 88 B3
Merton Cl
  Kidderminster DY10 .... 117 B7
  Oldbury B68 .... 64 B2
Merton Ct WS7 .... 6 F5
Merton Ho B37 .... 69 F2
Merton Rd B13 .... 87 B3
Mervyn Pl WV14 .... 41 A3
Mervyn Rd Bilston WV14 .... 41 A3
  Birmingham B21 .... 54 E1
Meryhurst Rd WS10 .... 42 B5
Merynton Ave CV4 .... 132 E5
Meschines St CV3 .... 133 D6
Mesnes Gn WS14 .... 9 C7
Messenger La B70 .... 53 D3
Messenger Rd B66 .... 65 B6
Mesty Croft Prim Sch
  WS10 .... 42 B3
Metalloys Ind Est B76 .... 58 B5
Metcalf Cl WS7 .... 7 C8
Metcalfe Cl WS12 .... 2 C6
Metchley Croft B90 .... 126 F6
Metchley Ct B17 .... 85 D4
Metchley Dr B17 .... 85 D5
Metchley Ho B17 .... 85 D5
Metchley La B17 .... 85 D5
Metchley Park Rd B15 .... 85 E4
Meteor Ho B35 .... 58 B4
Metfield Cl B79 .... 21 C8
Metfield Croft
  Birmingham B17 .... 85 C4
  Kingswinford DY6 .... 60 F6
Metlin Gr B33 .... 69 E3
Metric Wlk ■ B67 .... 65 A5
Metro Way B66 .... 65 C7
Mews Rd CV32 .... 161 D8
Mews The Bedworth CV12 .. 78 B2
  Birmingham B27 .... 88 B3
  Blackheath B65 .... 63 B2
  Kenilworth CV8 .... 147 E3
Meynell Ho ■ B20 .... 54 F3
Meyrick Rd B70 .... 53 A6
Meyrick Wlk B16 .... 65 F1
Miall Park Rd B91 .... 106 E5
Miall Rd B28 .... 106 A8
Mica Cl B77 .... 22 B2
Michael Blanning Gdns
  B93 .... 127 E3
Michael Ct B5 .... 86 D6
Michael Dr B15 .... 86 C6
Michael Drayton Mid Sch
  CV10 .... 72 A8

Michael Rd Darlaston WS10 .. 41 B7
  Smethwick B67 .... 64 E6
Michaelmas Rd CV3 .... 165 B1
Michaelwood Cl B97 .... 152 F2
Michel Ho CV1 .... 165 C4
Michell Cl CV3 .... 134 B8
Michigan Cl WS11 .... 2 B2
Mickle Mdw B46 .... 59 B3
Micklehill Dr B90 .... 126 B8
Mickleover Rd B8 .... 68 C5
Mickleton Ave B33 .... 89 C8
Mickleton Cl B98 .... 158 E7
Mickleton Rd Coventry
  CV5 .... 133 A8
  Solihull B92 .... 106 D8
Mickley Ave WV10 .... 25 E5
Midacre WV13 .... 27 A1
Middleburg Cl WV11 .... 74 A1
Middle Acre Rd B32 .... 84 E2
Middle Ave WV13 .... 40 E8
Middle Bickenhill La B92 .. 91 A4
Middle Cres WS3 .... 29 A7
Middle Cross WV1 .... 163 D3
Middle Entry B79 .... 21 B5
Middle Field Rd B31 .... 103 D2
Middle Gdns WV13 .... 27 B2
Middle House Dr B60 .... 121 D1
Middle La
  Wolverhampton WV9 .... 11 A5
  Wythall B38 .... 124 D5
Middle Leaford B34 .... 69 A5
Middle Leasowe B32 .... 84 D4
Middle Meadow Ave B32 .. 84 C5
Middle Park Cl B29 .... 103 B8
Middle Park Rd B29 .... 103 C8
Middle Piece Dr B97 .... 153 B1
Middle Rd
  Upper Bentley B60 .... 152 A2
  Wildmoor B61 .... 120 F4
Middle Ride CV3 .... 134 E5
Middle Vauxhall ■ WV1 .. 25 A2
Middleborough Rd CV1 .... 165 A4
Middlecotes CV4 .... 112 B1
Middlefield WV8 .... 10 E2
Middlefield Ave
  Halesowen B62 .... 63 F1
  Knowle B93 .... 128 B4
Middlefield Cl
  Halesowen B62 .... 63 F1
  Hinckley LE10 .... 71 D2
Middlefield Ct LE10 .... 71 D2
Middlefield Dr CV3 .... 115 A1
Middlefield Gdns B62 .... 83 F8
Middlefield Ho B14 .... 104 F3
  Hinckley LE10 .... 71 D3
Middlefield Pl LE10 .... 71 D3
Middlefield Rd
  Bromsgrove B60 .... 151 B7
  Tipton B69 .... 63 B4
Middlefield Dr CV3 .... 115 A1
Middlehill Rise B32 .... 84 D3
Middlehouse La B98 .... 153 E6
Middlemarch Bsns Pk
  CV3 .... 134 C2
Middlemarch Mid Sch
  CV10 .... 73 B1
Middlemarch Rd
  Coventry CV6 .... 113 C7
  Nuneaton CV10 .... 73 C1
Middlemist Gr B43 .... 54 E7
Middlemore Cl B80 .... 159 D3
Middlemore Bsns Pk WS9 .. 29 E6
Middlemore Ind Est B66 .. 65 B8
Middlemore La WS9 .... 30 A6
Middlemore La W WS9 .... 29 E6
Middlemore Rd
  Birmingham B31 .... 103 B3
  Smethwick B66 .... 65 B8
Middlepark Rd DY1 .... 61 F8
Middlesmoor B77 .... 36 C8
Middleton Cl Redditch B98 .. 154 F2
  Walsall WS5 .... 42 F5
Middleton Fst Sch B78 .... 34 B1
Middleton Gdns B30 .... 103 D4
Middleton Grange B31 .... 103 C4
Middleton Hall
  Birmingham B30 .... 103 E4
  Middleton B78 .... 34 E1
Middleton Hall Rd B30 .... 103 E4
Middleton La B78 .... 47 F6
Middleton Rd Aldridge B74 .. 31 A1
  Birmingham B14 .... 104 F7
  Bromsgrove B61 .... 136 F4
  Brownhills WS8 .... 7 A1
  Solihull B90 .... 106 A2
Middleton Trad Est WV13 .. 26 E1
Middletown B80 .... 159 D1
Middletown La B96 .... 159 D1
Middletree Rd B63 .... 82 C7
Middleway Ave DY8 .... 60 C3
Middleway Gn WV14 .... 40 C8
Middleway Rd WV14 .... 40 C7
Middleway View B18 .... 66 A3
Midford Gr B15 .... 86 C8
Midgley Dr B74 .... 32 A2
Midhill Dr B65 .... 63 C6
Midhurst Dr WS12 .... 2 C7
Midhurst Gr WV6 .... 24 C5
Midhurst Rd B30 .... 104 B3
Midland Air Mus CV3 .... 134 B3
Midland Bus & Transport
  Mus B47 .... 124 E3
Midland Cl B21 .... 65 F7
Midland Ct B3 .... 164 A4
Midland Dr B72 .... 46 C5
Midland Oak Trad Est CV6 . 95 E2

Midland Rd Birmingham
  B30 .... 103 F5
  Coventry CV6 .... 113 E5
  Darlaston WS10 .... 41 C8
  Nuneaton CV11 .... 73 A5
  Sutton Coldfield B74 .... 46 A6
  Walsall WS1 .... 28 E1
Midland St B9 .... 67 C3
Midpoint Park Ind Est B76 .. 58 C5
Midvale Dr B14 .... 104 D2
Milburn B77 .... 36 C8
Milburn Hill Rd CV4 .... 132 B6
Milburn Rd B44 .... 45 A3
Milby Ct CV11 .... 73 C3
Milby Dr CV11 .... 74 A7
Milby Fst & Mid Sch CV11 .. 73 C3
Milcote Cl B98 .... 159 A7
Milcote Dr
  Sutton Coldfield B73 .... 45 C3
  Willenhall WV13 .... 26 D1
Milcote Rd Birmingham
  B29 .... 103 A8
  Smethwick B67 .... 64 F1
  Solihull B91 .... 107 B4
Milcote Way DY6 .... 60 B6
Mildenhall B79 .... 21 C8
Mildenhall Rd B42 .... 44 A1
Mildred Rd B64 .... 62 E2
Mildred Way B65 .... 63 C6
Mile Flat DY6 .... 60 A7
Mile La CV1 .... 165 C2
Mile Oak Cross Rds B78 .. 20 C2
Mile Oak Ct B66 .... 65 C6
Mile Tree La CV2 .... 96 F7
Milebrook Gr B32 .... 102 B8
Milebush Ave B36 .... 58 D1
Miles Gr DY2 .... 62 F7
Miles Mdw CV6 .... 96 B1
Miles Meadow Cl WV12 .. 27 C6
Milestone Ct WV6 .... 24 A3
Milestone Dr WV6 .... 98 F4
Milestone Ho ■ CV1 .... 113 B2
Milestone La B21 .... 65 D8
Milestone Way WV12 .... 27 C8
Milford Ave
  ■ Birmingham B12 .... 87 A6
  Willenhall WV12 .... 27 A5
Milford Cl Allesley CV5 .... 112 B6
  Birmingham B28 .... 106 A5
  Redditch B97 .... 158 C6
  Stourbridge DY8 .... 60 E3
Milford Croft B65 .... 62 F6
  Royal Leamington Spa
  CV31 .... 162 A8
Milford Gr B90 .... 127 C7
Milford Pl B14 .... 104 E8
Milford Rd Birmingham B17 .. 85 B5
  Wolverhampton WV2 .... 39 C7
Milford St CV10 .... 73 B2
Milhill Rd B98 .... 154 E1
Milholme Gn B92 .... 107 D8
Milk St B5 .... 66 F1
Milking Bank DY1 .... 50 E2
Milking Bank Prim Sch
  DY1 .... 50 E2
Mill Bank DY3 .... 50 D8
Mill Bank Mews CV8 .... 148 B6
Mill Burn Way ■ B9 .... 67 B2
Mill Cl Blakedown DY10 .... 98 B2
  Bromsgrove B60 .... 150 F6
  Coventry CV6 .... 96 B3
  Dudley DY3 .... 50 D6
  Hollywood B47 .... 125 A7
  Nuneaton CV11 .... 73 F1
Mill Cres WS11 .... 2 B2
Mill Croft WV14 .... 40 E6
Mill Dr B66 .... 65 B5
Mill End CV8 .... 148 A6
Mill Farm Rd B17 .... 85 C3
Mill Gdns Birmingham B14 .. 105 D5
  Smethwick B67 .... 64 F3
Mill Gn WV10 .... 11 D4
Mill Gr WV8 .... 10 C3
Mill Green Nature Pk WS11 .. 1 F1
Mill Hill Baginton CV8 .... 133 D3
  Smethwick B67 .... 64 F3
Mill Hill Rd LE10 .... 71 C1
Mill Ho Birmingham B8 .... 68 D4
  Smethwick B66 .... 65 C6
Mill House Cl CV32 .... 161 C8
Mill House Dr CV32 .... 161 C8
Mill House Terr CV32 .... 161 C8
Mill La Aldridge WS9 .... 30 F7
  Bentley Heath B93 .... 127 F4
  Birmingham, Digbeth B5 .. 164 D1
  Birmingham,
    Northfield B31 .... 103 A2
  Birmingham,
    Woodgate Valley B32 .... 84 E2
  Blakedown DY10 .... 98 B2
  Bramcote CV11 .... 79 F8
  Bromsgrove B61 .... 136 F2
  Bulkington CV12 .... 79 A3
  Burntwood WS7 .... 7 D3
  Cheslyn Hay WS11 .... 4 D5
  Coventry CV3 .... 114 F2
  Cubbington CV32 .... 157 F5
  Earlswood B94 .... 141 B8
  Fazeley B78 .... 35 A8
  Halesowen B63 .... 83 C4
  Kidderminster,
    Blakebrook DY11 .... 116 D6
  Kidderminster,
    Hoobrook DY10 .... 116 F2
  Lapworth B94 .... 144 C4
  Little Aston WS9 .... 31 A6
  Oldbury B69 .... 64 A5

Mill La continued
  Shenstone WS14 .... 18 A6
  Solihull B91 .... 107 C4
  Stonnall WS9 .... 17 A4
  Tamworth B79 .... 21 C5
  Tettenhall Wood WV6 .... 24 A3
  Walsall WS4 .... 28 F4
  Wildmoor B61 .... 120 F3
  Willenhall WV12 .... 27 C5
  Wolverhampton WV11 .... 26 B7
  Wombourne WV5 .... 49 B6
  Wythall B47 .... 125 B1
Mill Lodge Prim Sch B90 .. 105 E2
Mill Park Ind Est WS11 .... 2 A2
Mill Pk WS11 .... 2 A2
Mill Pl WS3 .... 28 E4
Mill Pleck B80 .... 159 E3
Mill Pond The WS13 .... 3 C2
Mill Pool Cl DY9 .... 99 A4
Mill Pool La Dorridge B93 .. 144 A8
  Tanworth-in-A B94 .... 143 F8
Mill Pool Rd WS12 .... 2 B6
Mill Race La Coventry CV6 .. 96 B3
  Stourbridge DY8 .... 81 A6
Mill Rd Blackheath B64 .... 82 E7
  Brownhills WS8 .... 16 A7
  Royal Leamington Spa
  CV31 .... 162 A8
  Walsall WS4 .... 15 C1
Mill St Barwell LE9 .... 71 F5
  Bedworth CV12 .... 78 B3
  Bilston WV14 .... 40 C5
  Birmingham B6 .... 164 C5
  Brierley Hill DY5 .... 61 E2
  Cannock WS11 .... 1 E1
  Coventry CV1 .... 165 A3
  Darlaston,
    Cathrine Cross WS10 .. 41 C6
  Darlaston, King's Hill WS10 .. 41 E6
  Halesowen B63 .... 82 C7
  Kidderminster DY11 .... 116 D6
  Nuneaton CV11 .... 73 C4
  Redditch B97 .... 153 D4
  Royal Leamington Spa
  CV31 .... 162 A7
  Stourbridge DY8 .... 60 F2
  Sutton Coldfield B72 .... 46 C5
  Walsall WS2 .... 28 E3
  Warwick CV34 .... 160 F6
  West Bromwich B70 .... 53 C4
  Willenhall WV13 .... 27 C2
Mill Terr CV12 .... 78 B5
Mill View Birmingham B33 .. 69 C4
  Hinckley LE10 .... 71 E1
Mill Wlk CV11 .... 73 C4
Mill Wlk The B31 .... 102 F1
Millais Cl CV12 .... 78 A4
Millais Rd LE10 .... 71 A3
Millard Rd WV14 .... 40 B1
Millbank CV34 .... 156 B1
Millbank Gr B23 .... 56 B6
Millbank St WV11 .... 12 F1
Millbrook Cl WS11 .... 1 F2
Millbrook Ct B62 .... 83 A7
Millbrook Dr
  Birmingham B31 .... 122 E8
  Shenstone WS14 .... 17 F6
Millbrook Rd B14 .... 104 C6
Millbrook Way DY5 .... 81 B8
Millcroft Cl B32 .... 84 E2
Millcroft Rd B74 .... 45 A8
Milldale Cl DY10 .... 116 E8
Milldale Cres WV10 .... 11 D3
Milldale Rd WV10 .... 11 D4
Millennium Cl WS3 .... 15 A3
Miller Cl B60 .... 150 E6
Miller Cres WV14 .... 40 A1
Miller St B6 .... 66 E6
Millers Cl WS2 .... 27 F1
Millers Cl ■ DY11 .... 116 D6
Millers Gn LE10 .... 75 F6
Millers Green Dr DY6 .... 60 A8
Millers Rd CV34 .... 160 E6
Millers Vale WS12 .... 2 D1
Millersdale Dr B71 .... 42 F2
Millfield Birmingham B31 .. 103 A4
  Royal Leamington Spa CV31 .. 162 A8
Millfield Ave
  Walsall, High Heath WS4 .. 15 B1
  Walsall, Little Bloxwich WS3 .. 14 D3
Millfield Ct DY1 .... 51 B2
Millfield Gdns ■ DY11 .. 116 D6
Millfield JMI Sch WS8 .... 16 A7
Millfield Prim Sch B78 .... 35 A8
Millfield Rd Birmingham B20 .. 54 F5
  Bromsgrove B61 .... 136 E1
  Brownhills WS8 .... 16 A7
Millfield Specl Sch B71 .. 53 D8
Millfield View B63 .... 82 E4
Millfields B33 .... 69 E3
Millfields Cl B71 .... 42 B1
Millfields Fst Sch B61 .... 136 E1
Millfields Rd
  Bilston WV14, WV4 .... 40 B5
  West Bromwich B71 .... 42 B1
Millhaven Ave B30 .... 104 B6
Millhouse Ct CV6 .... 113 F7
Millhouse Rd B25 .... 88 C8
Millicent Cl WS12 .... 2 B6
Millicent Pl ■ B12 .... 87 A6
Millichip Rd WV13 .... 26 E1
Millington Rd
  Birmingham B36 .... 68 C2
  Tipton DY4 .... 40 F1
  Wolverhampton WV10 .... 25 A7
Millison Gr B90 .... 127 A7
Millmead Rd B32 .... 84 E1

Millpool Gdns B14 .... 104 F3
Millpool Hill Alcester
  Rd S B14 .... 104 F4
Millpool Way B66 .... 65 A4
Millrace Rd B98 .... 153 E5
Mills Ave B76 .... 46 E4
Mills Cl WV11 .... 26 B8
Mills Cres WV2 .... 163 D1
Mills Rd WV2 .... 163 D1
Mills Wlk DY4 .... 51 F7
Millsbro Rd B98 .... 153 F3
Millside B28 .... 105 E3
Millsum Ho 6 WS1 .... 28 F1
Millthorpe Cl B8 .... 67 F5
Millwalk Dr WV9 .... 11 A3
Millward St Birmingham B9 .. 67 C1
  West Bromwich B70 .... 53 A3
Millwright Cl DY4 .... 52 B5
Milner Cl CV12 .... 79 D2
Milner Cres CV2 .... 96 E1
Milner Dr B79 .... 22 E7
Milner Rd B29 .... 86 A1
Milner Way B13 .... 105 D8
Milnes Walker Ct B44 .... 44 E1
Milo Cres B78 .... 21 A2
Milrose Way CV4 .... 131 F8
Milsom Gr B34 .... 69 D6
Milstead Rd B26 .... 69 A1
Milston Cl B14 .... 104 E1
Milton Ave
  2 Birmingham B12 .... 87 A6
  Tamworth B79 .... 21 A7
  Warwick CV34 .... 160 C5
Milton Cl Bedworth CV12 .... 78 D1
  Bentley Heath B93 .... 127 F4
  Hinckley LE10 .... 71 C1
  Kidderminster DY11 .... 116 A6
  Redditch B97 .... 158 C8
  Walsall WS1 .... 42 D6
  Willenhall WV12 .... 27 E7
Milton Cres Birmingham B25 .. 88 D7
  Dudley DY3 .... 50 B5
Milton Ct Perton WV6 .... 23 E4
  Smethwick B66 .... 65 A1
Milton Dr DY9 .... 99 C8
Milton Gr B21 .... 65 C8
Milton Ho B63 .... 82 B5
Milton Pl WS1 .... 42 D6
Milton Rd Bentley Heath
  B93 .... 127 F4
  Cannock WS11 .... 1 E4
  Catshill B61 .... 137 A8
  Dudley WV14 .... 51 D8
  Smethwick B67 .... 64 E5
  Wolverhampton WV10 .... 26 A5
Milton St Birmingham B19 .. 66 E6
  Brierley Hill DY5 .... 61 D7
  Coventry CV2 .... 114 A4
  Walsall WS1 .... 42 D7
  West Bromwich B71 .... 53 B5
Milverton Cl Halesowen B63 .. 83 A6
  Sutton Coldfield B76 .... 57 F7
Milverton Comb Sch
  CV32 .... 156 E1
Milverton Cres 1 CV32 .. 156 E1
Milverton Cres W 3 CV32 156 E1
Milverton Ct 7 CV32 .... 161 E8
Milverton Hill CV32 .... 161 E8
Milverton House Prep Sch
  CV11 .... 73 D3
Milverton Lodge 2 CV32 .. 156 E1
Milverton Rd Birmingham
  B23 .... 56 E4
  Coventry CV2 .... 96 D2
  Knowle B93 .... 128 C5
Milverton Terr CV32 .... 161 E8
Milward Sq 8 B97 .... 153 E3
Mimosa Cl B29 .... 103 B7
Mimosa Wlk 8 DY6 .... 60 E8
Mincing La B65 .... 63 D3
Minden Gr B29 .... 85 B1
Minehead Rd Dudley DY1 .. 61 D8
  Wolverhampton WV10 .... 11 B2
Miner St WS2 .... 28 C3
Miners Wlk B78 .... 22 F1
Minerva Cl Tamworth B77 .. 21 D5
  Willenhall WV12 .... 27 E4
Minerva La WV1 .... 25 E1
Minewood Cl WS3 .... 13 F3
Minith Rd WV14 .... 51 D8
Miniva Dr B76 .... 47 A2
Minivet Dr B12 .... 86 E6
Minley Ave B17 .... 84 F7
Minories The 1 DY2 .... 51 D1
Minors Hill WS14 .... 9 D6
Minstead Rd B24 .... 56 D1
Minster Cl Blackheath B65 .. 63 E3
  Knowle B93 .... 128 B8
Minster Dr B10 .... 87 D7
Minster Rd CV1 .... 113 B3
Minster The WV3 .... 39 A7
Minster Wlk B61 .... 136 F8
Minsterley Cl WV3 .... 38 E8
Mintern Rd B25 .... 88 C8
Minton Cl WV1 .... 26 A1
Minton Ho 3 B12 .... 86 F5
Minton Mews B60 .... 151 B8
Minton Rd Birmingham B32 .. 84 F4
  Coventry CV2 .... 96 E1
Minworth Cl B97 .... 153 B2
Minworth Ind Pk B76 .. 58 B5
Minworth Jun & Inf Sch
  B76 .... 58 D5
Minworth Rd B46 .... 59 A3
Miranda Cl Birmingham
  B45 .... 102 A3
  Coventry CV3 .... 134 D7
Mirfield Cl WV9 .... 11 A3

Mirfield Rd Birmingham B33 .. 69 B2
  Solihull B91 .... 107 A6
Mission Cl B64 .... 63 A1
Mission Dr DY4 .... 52 A3
Mistletoe Dr WS5 .... 43 B3
Mistral Cl LE10 .... 75 F8
Mitcham Cl WS12 .... 1 F7
Mitcham Gr B44 .... 45 B1
Mitchel Rd DY6 .... 60 F4
Mitcheldean Cl B98 .... 158 E7
Mitcheldean Covert B14 .. 104 D2
Mitchell Ave Coventry CV4 . 132 A7
  Dudley WV14 .... 40 B1
Mitchell Ho Coventry CV4 .. 132 A7
  Warwick CV34 .... 160 E7
Mitchell Rd CV12 .... 78 C2
Mitford Dr B92 .... 107 D7
Mitre Cl Essington WV11 .. 13 A3
  Willenhall WV12 .... 27 D7
Mitre Ct B61 .... 137 A3
Mitre Fold WV1 .... 163 B3
Mitre Rd Cheslyn Hay WS6 .. 4 D2
  Stourbridge DY9 .... 81 E5
Mitten Ave B45 .... 102 A1
Mitton Rd B20 .... 54 E2
Moat Ave CV3 .... 132 F5
Moat Coppice B62 .... 84 A1
Moat Croft Birmingham B37 .. 70 A2
  Sutton Coldfield B76 .... 58 B7
Moat Dr Drayton Bassett B78 .. 34 E5
  Halesowen B62 .... 63 F1
Moat Farm Dr
  Bedworth CV12 .... 95 C8
  Birmingham B32 .... 84 A1
Moat Farm Inf Sch B68 .. 64 C3
Moat Farm Jun Sch B68 .. 64 C3
Moat Farm Way WS3 .... 15 A5
Moat Gn B35 .... 160 A1
Moat Green Ave WV11 .. 26 E7
Moat Hall Cty Prim Sch
  WS6 .... 4 F3
Moat House Ct B80 .... 159 F8
Moat House La E WV11 .. 26 E7
Moat House La E WV11 .. 26 E7
Moat House Rd B8 .... 68 A4
Moat La
  Birmingham, Digbeth B5 .. 164 C1
  Birmingham,
    South Yardley B26 .... 88 B5
  Great Wyrley WS6 .... 5 A2
  Solihull B91 .... 107 C6
Moat Mdws B32 .... 84 E4
Moat Rd Oldbury B68 .... 64 B3
  Tipton DY4 .... 52 A7
  Walsall WS2 .... 28 C2
Moat St WV13 .... 27 A2
Moat Way LE9 .... 71 F6
Moatfield Mid Sch B98 .. 154 E1
Moatfield Terr 2 WS10 .. 42 A3
Moathouse La W WV11 .. 26 D7
Moathouse Prim Sch
  WV11 .... 26 E7
Moatmead Wlk B36 .... 68 E8
Moatside Cl WS3 .... 15 A5
Mob La WS4 .... 15 C3
Mobberley Rd WV14 .... 40 A1
Mockley Wood Rd B93 .. 128 B7
Modbury Ave B32 .... 84 D1
Modbury Cl CV3 .... 133 D5
Moden Cl DY3 .... 50 D6
Moden Hill DY3 .... 50 D6
Mogul La B63 .... 82 A7
Moillett St B18 .... 65 D4
Moilliett Ct B66 .... 65 C6
Moira Cres B14 .... 105 C4
Moises Hall Rd WV5 .... 49 B7
Moland St B4 .... 164 C4
Mole St B11 .... 87 B6
Molesworth Ave CV3 .... 114 A1
Molhay Gdns 4 B42 .... 55 A8
Molineux Gds
  (Wolverhampton
  Wanderers FC) WV1 .. 163 B4
Molineux St WV1 .... 163 B4
Molineux Way WV1 .... 163 B4
Mollington Cres B90 .... 106 C3
Mollington Rd CV31 .... 162 A3
Molyneux Rd DY2 .... 62 E2
Momus Bvd CV2 .... 114 C2
Mona Rd B23 .... 56 F5
Monarch Dr DY4 .... 52 C6
Monarch Ho B68 .... 64 B2
Monarch Way DY2 .... 62 C4
Monastery Dr B91 .... 106 E6
Monckton Rd B68 .... 84 A7
Moncrieff Dr CV31 .... 162 C5
Moncrieffe Cl DY2 .... 62 E8
Moncrieffe St WS1 .... 29 A1
Money La B61 .... 121 A7
Monica Rd B10 .... 87 F8
Monins Ave DY4 .... 52 A2
Monk Cl DY4 .... 52 B3
Monk Rd B8 .... 68 B5
Monk's Croft The CV3 .. 133 C7
Monks Dr B80 .... 159 D4
Monks Kirby Rd B76 .... 46 F3
Monks Path B97 .... 152 F4
Monks Rd Binley Woods
  CV3 .... 135 C7
  Coventry CV1 .... 113 F2
Monks Way Tamworth B77 .... 21 F5
  Warwick CV34 .... 160 D6
Monkseaton Rd B72 .... 46 B2
Monksfield Ave B43 .... 43 D1
Monkshood Mews B38 .. 56 B7
Monkshood Retreat B38 .. 123 F8
Monkspath Solihull B90 .. 127 A6
  Sutton Coldfield B76 .... 46 F1

Monkspath Bsns Pk B90 .. 126 F8
Monkspath Cl B90 .... 126 D7
Monkspath Hall Rd B90 .. 127 B7
Monkspath Jun & Inf Sch
  B90 .... 127 B6
Monksway B38 .... 104 B1
Monkswell Cl
  Birmingham B10 .... 87 D7
  Brierley Hill DY5 .... 61 D1
Monkswood Cres CV2 .. 114 D8
Monkswood Rd B31 .... 103 C2
Monkton Rd B29 .... 85 A2
Monmer Cl WV13 .... 27 B3
Monmer Ct WV12 .... 27 B5
Monmer La WV13 .... 27 B4
Monmore Park Ind Est
  WV2 .... 40 A7
Monmore Rd WV1 .... 40 A7
Monmouth Cl Coventry
  CV5 .... 112 B3
  Kenilworth CV8 .... 147 F6
Monmouth Dr
  Sutton Coldfield B73 .... 45 D3
  West Bromwich B71 .... 53 B7
Monmouth Gdns CV10 .. 72 E3
Monmouth Ho B33 .... 69 E2
Monmouth Rd
  Birmingham B32 .... 102 D8
  Smethwick B67 .... 84 E8
  Walsall WS2 .... 27 E3
Monnington Ho CV8 .... 148 B7
Mons Rd DY2 .... 51 F1
Monsal Ave WV10 .... 25 E4
Monsal Rd B42 .... 55 C7
Monsaldale Rd WS8 .... 15 D6
Monsieurs Hall La B61 .. 136 B3
Montague Ho B16 .... 65 E1
Montague Rd
  Birmingham,
    Birches Green B24 .... 57 A1
  Birmingham, Edgbaston B16 .. 65 E1
  Birmingham,
    Handsworth B21 .... 65 F8
  Smethwick B66 .... 65 C3
  Warwick CV34 .... 161 A8
Montague St
  Birmingham, Aston B6 .... 67 B8
  Birmingham, Bordesley B9 .. 67 A2
Montalt Rd CV3 .... 133 E7
Montana Ave B44 .... 55 A5
Montana Wlk CV10 .... 72 E3
Monteagle Dr DY6 .... 49 D1
Montford Gr DY3 .... 50 D7
Montfort Rd Coleshill B46 .. 70 F5
  Walsall WS2 .... 42 B6
Montfort Wlk B32 .... 84 A2
Montgomery Cl
  Catshill B61 .... 121 A1
  Coventry CV3 .... 134 C4
Montgomery Cres DY5 .. 81 F7
Montgomery Croft B11 .. 87 C7
Montgomery Jun & Inf Sch
  B11 .... 87 C7
Montgomery Rd WS2 .... 27 E2
Montgomery St B11 .... 87 C7
Montgomery Way B8 .... 68 A4
Montgomery Wlk 1 B71 .. 53 D4
Montjoy Cl CV3 .... 134 D7
Montley B77 .... 36 C8
Montpelier Ho CV8 .... 147 F5
Montpelier Rd B24 .... 57 A1
Montpellier Cl CV3 .... 133 C6
Montpellier Gdns DY1 .. 50 E2
Montpellier St B12 .... 87 A6
Montreal Ho B5 .... 86 D7
Montrose Ave CV32 .... 157 B5
Montrose Cl WS11 .... 1 F5
Montrose Dr Birmingham
  B35 .... 58 A4
  Dudley DY1 .... 62 A8
  Nuneaton CV10 .... 72 F3
Montsford Cl B93 .... 127 F6
Monument Ave DY9 .... 81 E4
Monument Dr WV10 .... 12 C8
Monument La
  Barnt Green B45 .... 121 F4
  Hagley DY9 .... 99 D7
  Sedgley DY3 .... 39 E1
Monument Rd B16 .... 65 F1
Monway Bldgs WS10 .... 41 E3
Monway Ind Est WS10 .... 41 E3
Monway Terr WS10 .... 41 E3
Monwood Gr B91 .... 106 F2
Monyhull Hall Rd B30 .. 104 C3
Monyhull Hospl B14 .... 104 D3
Moon's La WS6 .... 4 D1
Moodyscroft Rd B33 .... 69 C3
Moons Moat Dr B98 .... 154 E5
Moons Moat Fst Sch B98 .. 154 D5
Moor Burgess Activity Ctr
  B77 .... 22 A1
Moor Ct B24 .... 56 F3
Moor Ctr The DY5 .... 61 D3
Moor End Ct B24 .... 57 B4
Moor End La B24 .... 57 B4
Moor Green Jun & Inf Sch
  B13 .... 86 C1
Moor Green La B13 .... 86 D2
Moor Hall Dr Clent DY9 .. 100 A1
  Sutton Coldfield B75 .... 32 D1
Moor Hall Inf & Jun Sch
  B75 .... 32 D2
Moor Ho B14 .... 104 C2
Moor La Birmingham B6 .. 56 A4
  Blackheath B65 .... 63 C3
  Shenstone WS14 .... 17 E2
  Tamworth, Amington B77 .. 22 A6
  Tamworth, Bolehill B77 .. 21 D5

Moor Leasow B31 .... 103 C2
Moor Meadow Rd B75 .. 46 D3
Moor Pk Perton WV6 .... 23 D5
  Walsall WS3 .... 14 B3
Moor Pool Ave B17 .... 85 C6
Moor Rd CV10 .... 72 A8
Moor St Birmingham B5 .. 164 C2
  Brierley Hill DY5 .... 61 C3
  Coventry CV5 .... 112 F1
  Tamworth B79 .... 21 A5
  Wednesbury WS10 .... 42 B2
  West Bromwich B70 .... 53 C2
Moor St WV13 .... 39 C7
Moor Street Ind Est DY5 .. 61 C3
Moor Street Queensway
  B5 .... 164 C2
Moor Street Ringway B5 .. 164 C2
Moor Street Sta B5 .... 164 C2
Moor The B76 .... 58 A8
Moorcroft Cl Nuneaton
  CV11 .... 74 B1
  Redditch B97 .... 158 B6
Moorcroft Dr DY4 .... 41 C2
Moorcroft Pl 9 B7 .... 67 A4
Moorcroft Rd B13 .... 86 E3
Moordown Ave B92 .... 89 A2
Moore Cl Perton WV6 .... 23 F4
  Sutton Coldfield B74 .... 31 F6
  Warwick CV34 .... 155 E2
Moore Cres B68 .... 64 C3
Moore Rd WV12 .... 27 D8
Moore St Cannock WS12 .. 2 C7
  Wolverhampton WV1 .... 25 F1
Moore Wlk CV34 .... 161 C7
Moore's Row B5 .... 66 F1
Moorend Ave B37 .... 70 B2
Moorfield Ave B93 .... 127 F6
Moorfield Dr
  Bromsgrove B61 .... 136 F3
  Halesowen B63 .... 83 A5
  Sutton Coldfield B73 .... 57 A8
Moorfield Rd
  Birmingham B34 .... 69 B6
  Wolverhampton WV2 .... 39 C7
Moorfield The CV3 .... 134 B8
Moorfoot Ave B63 .... 82 C1
Moorgate B79 .... 21 A5
Moorgate B98 .... 154 E6
Moorgate Cty Prim Sch
  B79 .... 21 B5
Moorgate Rd B60 .... 151 A2
Moorhill Cty Prim Sch
  WS11 .... 1 E5
Moorhill Rd CV31 .... 162 A3
Moorhills Croft B90 .... 126 B8
Moorings The
  Brierley Hill DY5 .... 62 A4
  Oldbury B69 .... 63 E8
  Wolverhampton WV9 .... 10 F2
Moorland Ave WV10 .... 25 C6
Moorland Ct B16 .... 65 D1
Moorland Rd
  Birmingham B16 .... 65 D1
  Cannock WS11 .... 1 E5
  Walsall WS3 .... 28 A8
Moorlands Ave CV8 .... 147 F3
Moorlands Ct B65 .... 63 D4
Moorlands Dr B90 .... 106 C2
Moorlands Lodge CV8 .. 147 F3
Moorlands Prim Sch B71 .. 53 B8
Moorlands Rd B71 .... 42 C1
Moorlands The B74 .... 45 F8
Moorpark Cl CV11 .... 79 C8
Moorpark Rd B31 .... 103 A1
Moors Croft B32 .... 84 B1
Moors La B31 .... 102 E7
Moors Mill La DY4 .... 52 D7
Moors The B36 .... 68 F8
Moorside Gdns WS2 .... 28 B3
Moorside Rd B14 .... 105 D3
Moorsom St B6 .... 66 E5
Moorville Wlk B11 .... 87 A7
Moorwood Cres CV10 .. 72 A8
Moorwood La CV10 .... 72 A7
Morar Cl B35 .... 58 C4
Moray Cl Halesowen B62 .. 83 E8
  Hinckley LE10 .... 75 A4
Morcom Rd B11 .... 87 E5
Morcroft WV14 .... 41 A3
Mordaunt Dr B75 .... 32 E2
Morden Rd B33 .... 68 D3
Mordiford Cl B98 .... 154 E4
Moreall Mdws CV4 .... 132 D3
Moreland Croft B76 .... 58 B6
Morelands The B31 .... 103 B1
Morestead Ave B26 .... 89 C5
Moreton Ave Birmingham
  B43 .... 44 C3
  Wolverhampton WV4 .... 39 E4
Moreton Cl Birmingham B32 .. 84 F5
  Tipton DY4 .... 41 B2
Moreton Com Sch WV10 .. 11 F1
Moreton Rd Solihull B90 .. 106 C2
  Wolverhampton WV10 .... 11 D1
Moreton St Birmingham B1 .. 66 B4
  Cannock WS11 .... 1 F4
Morfa Gdns CV6 .... 112 D5
Morford Rd WS9 .... 30 A7
Morgan Cl Studley B80 .. 159 F2
  Willenhall WV13 .... 27 B4
Morgan Ct B24 .... 57 C6
Morgan Gr B36 .... 58 F1
Morgan Rd B78 .... 21 A2
Morgans Rd CV5 .... 111 C4
Morgrove Ave B93 .... 127 F6
Morillon Ct DY10 .... 117 A1
Morjon Dr B43 .... 43 F2

Morland Cl CV12 .... 79 D2
Morland Dr LE10 .... 71 B3
Morland Rd Birmingham
  B43 .... 44 C4
  Coventry CV6 .... 95 C2
Morley Gr WV6 .... 25 C4
Morley Rd Birmingham B8 .. 68 B6
  Burntwood WS7 .... 7 B7
Morley Road Sh Ctr 4 WS7 .. 7 B7
Morlich Rise DY5 .... 81 B8
Morlings Dr WS7 .... 7 B8
Morning Pines DY8 .... 80 E4
Morningside Coventry CV5 .. 133 B8
  Sutton Coldfield B73 .... 46 B6
Mornington Rd B66 .... 65 B7
Morpeth B77 .... 35 C7
Morrell St CV32 .... 156 F1
Morris Ave Coventry CV2 .. 114 D4
  Walsall WS2 .... 27 E2
Morris Cl B27 .... 88 D4
Morris Croft B36 .... 58 F1
Morris Ct WV4 .... 39 F4
Morris Dr Nuneaton CV11 .. 73 D1
  Whitnash CV31 .... 162 B2
Morris Field Croft B28 .. 105 E4
Morris Hill B78 .... 36 F7
Morris Rd B8 .... 68 C6
Morris St B70 .... 53 C1
Morris Wlk B60 .... 150 E8
Morrison Ave WV10 .... 25 D8
Morrison Rd DY4 .... 52 C4
Morse Rd CV31 .... 162 B3
Morsefield La B98 .... 154 D1
Morston B77 .... 35 D4
Mortimer Rd CV8 .... 147 F2
Mortimers Cl B14 .... 105 B1
Morton Cl CV6 .... 95 A1
Morton Ho B97 .... 153 A3
Morton La B97 .... 158 B7
Morton Rd Brierley Hill DY5 .. 81 F7
  Harvington B50 .... 118 B2
Morton St CV32 .... 156 F1
Morvale Gdns DY9 .... 81 E5
Morvale St DY9 .... 81 E5
Morven Rd B73 .... 46 A3
Morville Cl B93 .... 127 D3
Morville Croft WV14 .... 40 B5
Morville Rd DY2 .... 62 E4
Morville St B16 .... 66 B1
Mosborough Cres B19 .. 66 C5
Mosedale Dr WV11 .... 26 F5
Moseley Ave CV6 .... 113 A4
Moseley CE Prim Sch B13 .. 86 F2
Moseley Ct 17
  Birmingham B13 .... 87 B2
  Essington WV11 .... 12 F3
  Willenhall WV13 .... 26 D1
Moseley Dr B37 .... 89 F8
Moseley Hall Hospl B13 .. 86 E3
Moseley Old Hall WV10 .. 12 A5
Moseley Old Hall La WV10 .. 12 A5
Moseley Park Sch WV14 .. 40 E8
Moseley Prim Sch CV6 .. 113 A4
Moseley Rd Bilston WV14 .. 40 E8
  Birmingham B12 .... 86 F6
  Kenilworth CV8 .... 148 B3
  Willenhall WV14, WV13 .. 26 D1
  Wolverhampton WV10 .... 12 A4
Moseley Sch B13 .... 87 C2
Moseley St Birmingham B12 .. 86 F8
  Tipton DY4 .... 52 C7
  Wolverhampton WV6 .... 25 C4
Moss Cl Aldridge WS9 .... 30 A5
  Huntington WS12 .... 1 C5
  Walsall WS4 .... 29 A3
Moss Dr B72 .... 46 C3
Moss Gdns WV14 .... 40 B5
Moss Gr Birmingham B14 .. 104 D6
  Kingswinford DY6 .... 60 D7
Moss House Cl B15 .... 66 B1
Moss La B98 .... 154 F8
Moss Lane Cl B98 .... 154 F8
Moss Rd WS11 .... 2 A3
Moss St Cannock WS11 .. 2 A4
  8 Royal Leamington Spa
    CV31 .... 162 A7
Moss Way B74 .... 44 F7
Mossbank Ave WS7 .... 7 A6
Mossdale B77 .... 36 C8
Mossdale Cl CV6 .... 113 B6
Mossdale Cres CV10 .... 72 F2
Mossdale Way DY3 .... 50 E2
Mossfield Rd B14 .... 104 F7
Mossley Cl WS3 .... 13 F1
Mossley La WS3 .... 13 F2
Mossley Prim Sch WS3 .. 13 F2
Mosspaul Cl CV32 .... 156 D2
Mossvale Cl B64 .... 62 F1
Mossvale Gr B8 .... 67 F5
Mosswood Rd WS11 .... 4 D7
Mostyn Cres B71 .... 53 A7
Mostyn Rd
  Birmingham, Edgbaston B16 .. 65 F2
  Birmingham,
    Handsworth B21 .... 65 E8
Mostyn St WV1 .... 25 B4
Mott Cl DY4 .... 52 C8
Mott St B19 .... 164 B4
Mottistone Cl CV3 .... 133 C6
Mottram Cl B70 .... 53 B2
Mottrams Cl B72 .... 46 C2
Moule Cl DY11 .... 116 C6
Mounds The B38 .... 123 E8
Moundsley Gr B14 .... 105 A3
Moundsley Ho B14 .... 104 F2

Mount Ave Brierley Hill DY5 .. **61** C4
Cannock WS12 .... **2** B7
Mount Carmel RC Fst Sch
B97 .... **153** A2
Mount Cl Birmingham B13 .. **86** F4
Cheslyn Hay WS6 .... **4** E2
Dudley DY3 .... **50** C2
Wombourne WV5 .... **49** A7
Mount Ct WV6 .... **24** B3
Mount Dr Bedworth CV12 ..... **78** A3
Wombourne WV5 .... **49** A7
Mount Field Ct CV1 .... **165** D4
Mount Gdns CV5 .... **133** B8
Mount Grace High Sch
LE10 .... **71** E1
Mount La Clent DY9 .... **99** A4
Dudley DY3 .... **50** C2
Mount Nod Prim Sch
CV5 .... **112** A3
Mount Nod Way CV5 .... **112** B3
Mount Pleasant
Bilston WV14 .... **40** E6
Birmingham,
King's Heath B14 .... **86** F1
Birmingham,
Small Heath B10 .... **67** B1
Brierley Hill DY5 .... **61** C4
Cheslyn Hay WS6 .... **4** E2
Kingswinford DY6 .... **60** C4
Redditch B97 .... **153** D2
Tamworth B77 .... **35** C8
Mount Pleasant Ave B21 ..... **54** E1
Mount Pleasant Cotts
CV2 .... **115** A7
Mount Pleasant Ct **1** B10 .. **67** B1
Mount Pleasant Prim Sch
DY5 .... **61** C1
Mount Pleasant Rd CV12 ..... **78** A3
Mount Pleasant St
Dudley WV14 .... **51** B8
West Bromwich B70 .... **53** C2
Mount Pleasant Terr CV10 .. **72** F6
Mount Rd Birmingham B21 ... **65** D7
Blackheath B65 .... **63** E3
Burntwood WS7 .... **7** B6
Fairfield B61 .... **120** C2
Hinckley LE10 .... **75** D8
Stourbridge, Stambermill
DY8 .... **81** B5
Stourbridge, Wordsley DY8 ... **60** E2
Tipton B69 .... **63** C8
Walsall WS3 .... **15** A4
Willenhall WV13 .... **40** E8
Wolverhampton,
Lanesfield WV4 .... **39** F2
Wolverhampton, Penn WV4 ... **39** A4
Wolverhampton,
Tettenhall WV6 .... **24** B2
Wombourne WV5 .... **49** A7
Mount Road Ind Est WS7 ...... **7** B6
Mount St Birmingham B7 ...... **67** C7
Cannock WS12 .... **2** B7
Coventry CV5 .... **112** F2
Halesowen B63 .... **83** A3
Nuneaton CV11 .... **73** B4
Redditch B98 .... **153** E3
Stourbridge DY8 .... **81** B5
Tipton DY4 .... **52** C6
Walsall WS1 .... **42** E8
Mount Street Ind Est B7 ...... **67** D7
Mount Street Pas CV11 .... **73** B4
Mount The Birmingham B23 .. **56** D1
Blackheath B64 .... **63** A1
Coventry CV5 .... **133** E8
Curdworth B76 .... **59** C6
Mount Vernon Dr B61 .... **137** A5
Mount View B75 .... **46** E4
Mountain Ash Dr DY9 .... **81** C2
Mountain Ash Rd WS8 .... **15** E5
Mountain Pine Cl WS12 .... **2** A8
Mountbatten Ave CV8 .... **148** C3
Mountbatten Cl B70 .... **53** F2
Mountbatten Rd WS2 .... **27** F2
Mountfield Cl B14 .... **105** A2
Mountford Cl B65 .... **63** C3
Mountford Cres WS9 .... **30** C8
Mountford Dr B75 .... **46** A3
Mountford La WV14 .... **40** D6
Mountford Rd B90 .... **105** D1
Mountford St B11 .... **87** D5
Mountjoy Cres B92 .... **89** C3
Mountrath St WS1 .... **28** E1
Mounts Rd WS10 .... **41** F2
Mounts Way B7 .... **67** C2
Mountside St WS12 .... **2** C7
Mountwood Covert WV6 ...... **24** B3
Mouse Hill WS3 .... **14** F3
Mouse La DY11 .... **116** B8
Mousehall Farm Rd DY5 ...... **81** D7
Mousesweet Cl DY2 .... **62** E4
Mousesweet La DY2 .... **62** E3
Mousesweet Wlk B64 .... **82** B8
Mowbray Cl B45 .... **102** A2
Mowbray St Birmingham B5 .. **86** E8
Coventry CV2 .... **113** F3
Mowe Croft B37 .... **90** B7
Mows Hill Rd B94 .... **143** A1
Moxhull Cl WV12 .... **13** C1
Moxhull Dr B76 .... **57** E7
Moxhull Gdns WV12 .... **13** C1
Moxhull Rd B37 .... **70** A5
Moxley Ct WV14 .... **41** B3
Moxley Ind Ctr WS10 .... **41** C4
Moxley Inf Sch WS10 .... **41** B4
Moxley Jct WS10 .... **41** B4

Moxley Rd WS10 .... **41** C5
Moyle Cres CV5 .... **111** D4
Moyle Dr B63 .... **82** B7
Moyses Croft B66 .... **65** A8
Mozart Ct CV1 .... **165** C2
Much Park St CV1 .... **165** C2
Muchall Rd WV4 .... **39** A5
Mucklow Hill B62 .... **83** D5
Mucklow Hill Trad Est B62 . **83** C5
Muirfield B77 .... **22** B5
Muirfield Cl Nuneaton CV11 .. **79** C8
Walsall WS3 .... **14** A3
Muirfield Cres B63 .... **63** B7
Muirfield Gdns B38 .... **103** D1
Muirville Cl DY8 .... **60** D3
Mulberry Cl CV32 .... **157** A2
Mulberry Dr Birmingham
B13 .... **87** B1
5 Warwick CV34 .... **160** F8
Mulberry Gn DY1 .... **50** F5
Mulberry Pl WS3 .... **13** F1
Mulberry Rd
Birmingham B30 .... **103** C5
Cannock WS11 .... **1** E3
Coventry CV6 .... **114** A7
Walsall WS3 .... **14** A1
Mulberry Wlk B74 .... **44** E8
Muldoon Cl WS11 .... **2** B4
Mull Cl B45 .... **101** E1
Mull Croft B36 .... **70** B7
Mullard Dr CV31 .... **162** B3
Mullensgrove Rd B37 .... **70** A5
Mullett Rd WV11 .... **26** B8
Mullett St B65 .... **61** B5
Mulliner St CV6 .... **113** F5
Mulliners Cl **2** B37 .... **70** D2
Mullion Croft B38 .... **103** E1
Mulroy Rd B74 .... **46** B6
Mulwych Rd B33 .... **69** E3
Munches La DY9 .... **120** C8
Munro Cl DY10 .... **117** C6
Munsley Cl B98 .... **154** F1
Munslow Gr B31 .... **122** F8
Muntz Cres B94 .... **143** C6
Muntz Ho B16 .... **66** A1
Muntz St B10 .... **87** D8
Murcott Ct CV31 .... **162** A3
Murcott Rd CV31 .... **162** A3
Murcott Rd E CV31 .... **162** A3
Murcroft Rd DY9 .... **81** E1
Murdoch Rd WV14 .... **41** A6
Murdock Ct WV12 .... **27** D7
Murdock Gr B21 .... **65** E7
Murdock Rd Birmingham
B21 .... **65** E8
Smethwick B66 .... **65** D6
Murdock Way **1** WS2 .... **28** A5
Murray Ct Birmingham B20 .. **55** A2
Sutton Coldfield B73 .... **46** A3
Murray Rd CV6 .... **113** A7
Murrell Cl B5 .... **86** D7
Murton B77 .... **36** C8
Musborough Cl B36 .... **58** C1
Muscott Gr B17 .... **85** B5
Muscovy Rd B23 .... **56** C3
Musgrave Cl B76 .... **46** E3
Musgrave Rd B18 .... **65** F6
Mushroom Hall Rd B68 .... **64** B5
Musk La DY3 .... **50** B3
Musk La W DY3 .... **50** B3
Muxloe Cl WS3 .... **14** A3
Myatt Ave Aldridge WS9 ...... **29** F5
Burntwood WS7 .... **7** A7
Wolverhampton WV2 .... **39** E6
Myatt Cl WV2 .... **39** E6
Myatt Way WS9 .... **29** F5
Myddleton St B18 .... **66** A4
Myles Ct DY5 .... **61** D4
Mylgrove CV3 .... **133** D3
Mynors Cres B47 .... **125** A6
Myring Dr B75 .... **46** F5
Myrtle Ave
4 Birmingham,
Balsall Heath B12 .... **87** A5
Birmingham,
Highter's Heath B14 .... **104** F2
Redditch B98 .... **153** E2
Myrtle Cl WV12 .... **27** E7
Myrtle Gr
10 Birmingham B19 .... **66** C8
Coventry CV5 .... **112** F1
Wolverhampton WV3 .... **38** E6
Myrtle Pl B29 .... **86** B2
Myrtle Rd DY1 .... **51** B3
Myrtle St WV2 .... **39** F6
Myrtle Terr DY4 .... **41** B2
Myton Cres CV34 .... **161** C6
Myton Crofts CV31 .... **161** D7
Myton Dr B90 .... **105** D1
Myton Gdns CV34 .... **161** A6
Myton La CV34 .... **161** C6
Myton Rd CV31, CV34 .... **161** B6
Myton Sch CV34 .... **161** B6
Mytton Cl DY2 .... **51** E1
Mytton Gr DY4 .... **51** E5
Mytton Rd Birmingham B30 . **103** C5
Water Orton B46 .... **58** F3
Myvod Rd WS10 .... **42** A5

Naden Ho WS12 .... **1** C5
Naden Rd B19 .... **66** B6
Nadin Rd B73 .... **57** A8
Naesby Rd WV6 .... **23** F3
Nafford Gr B14 .... **104** F2
Nagersfield Rd DY5 .... **61** A2
Nailcote Ave CV4 .... **131** C8
Nailcote La CV7 .... **131** A7

Nailers Cl Birmingham B32 .. **83** F2
Stoke Heath B60 .... **150** E6
Nailers Cl **3** B60 .... **136** F2
Nailers Dr WS7 .... **7** D6
Nailstone Cres B27 .... **106** C8
Nailsworth Rd Dorridge
B93 .... **127** D2
Redditch B98 .... **153** F2
Nairn Cl Birmingham B28 .. **105** F5
Nuneaton CV10 .... **73** A2
Redditch B98 .... **154** E4
Nairn Rd WS3 .... **14** A4
Nally Dr WV14 .... **40** A2
Nanaimo Way DY6 .... **61** A4
Nansen Inf & Jun Sch B8 ... **67** F5
Nansen Rd Birmingham B8 ... **67** F5
Birmingham, Sparkhill B11 ... **87** C3
Nantmel Gr B32 .... **102** C8
Naomi Way WS9 .... **16** B4
Napier B77 .... **21** E3
Napier Dr DY4 .... **52** C6
Napier Rd Walsall WS2 .... **28** A5
Wolverhampton WV2 .... **39** D7
Napier St CV1 .... **113** E3
Napton Cl B98 .... **154** D1
Napton Dr CV32 .... **157** A2
Napton Gn CV5 .... **112** A3
Napton Gr B29 .... **84** F2
Narberth Way CV2 .... **114** F8
Narraway Dr DY5 .... **52** D8
Narrow La Brownhills WS8 ... **15** F8
Halesowen B62 .... **83** E8
Walsall WS2 .... **42** B7
Narrowboat Way DY2, DY5 .. **62** A5
Narrows The **1** LE10 .... **75** E8
Naseby Cl Coventry CV3 .... **134** F8
Redditch B98 .... **154** D6
Naseby Dr B63 .... **82** D2
Naseby Ho **4** B14 .... **105** A3
Naseby Rd Birmingham B8 ... **67** F5
Solihull B91 .... **107** B6
Nash Ave WV6 .... **23** E3
Nash Cl B65 .... **63** C1
Nash Ho B15 .... **86** D8
Nash La Belbroughton DY9 . **119** D7
Lichfield WS13 .... **3** A5
Nash Sq B42 .... **55** D4
Nashe Cl DY10 .... **117** C5
Nately Gr B29 .... **85** C3
Nathan Cl B75 .... **46** C8
Nathaniel Newton Fst Sch
CV10 .... **72** B8
National Ag Ctr CV8 .... **149** A4
National Ex Ctr B40 .... **90** E4
National Indoor Arena B1 ... **66** B2
National Lock Mus WV13 .... **27** A1
National Motorcycle Mus
The B92 .... **91** A2
National Needle Mus B98 . **153** F6
National Sea Life Ctr B1 .... **66** B2
Naul's Mill Ho CV1 .... **165** B4
Naunton Cl B29 .... **103** A7
Naunton Rd WS2 .... **28** A3
Navenby Cl B90 .... **105** C3
Navigation Dr DY5 .... **62** A4
Navigation La WS10 .... **42** F2
Navigation Rdbt DY4 .... **52** E6
Navigation St
Birmingham B2 .... **164** B2
Walsall WS2 .... **28** D1
Wolverhampton WV1 .... **25** E1
Navigation Way
Cannock WS11 .... **2** A2
Coventry CV6 .... **114** A8
West Bromwich B70 .... **52** F2
Nayland Croft B28 .... **106** A5
Naylor Cl DY11 .... **116** B3
Naylors Gr DY3 .... **50** E4
Neachells Cl WS11 .... **26** E1
Neachells La
Wednesfield WV11 .... **26** D5
Willenhall WV13 .... **26** D5
Neachells Lane Ind Est
WV11 .... **26** D4
Neachells Lane Island
WV11 .... **26** D4
Neachless Ave WV5 .... **49** A5
Neachley Gr B33 .... **68** F4
Neal Ct CV2 .... **115** A8
Neale Ave CV5 .... **112** A6
Neale Cl CV12 .... **79** C1
Neale Ho West Bromwich
B70 .... **53** D1
Wolverhampton WV2 .... **39** C7
Neale St WS2 .... **28** C2
Neander B79 .... **20** F6
Near Lands Cl B32 .... **84** B4
Near Oak Ho B32 .... **102** D8
Nearhill Rd B38 .... **123** C8
Nearmoor Rd B34 .... **69** D6
Neath Rd WS3 .... **13** F2
Neath Way Dudley DY3 .... **51** A6
Walsall WS3 .... **13** F2
Nebsworth Cl B90 .... **106** D5
Nechells Inf & Jun Sch B7 . **67** C8
Nechells Park Rd B7 .... **67** C7
Nechells Parkway B7 .... **67** C7
Nechells Pl B7 .... **67** C5
Needham St B7 .... **67** C7
Needhill Cl B93 .... **127** F6
Needle Cl B80 .... **159** E4
Needle Mill La B98 .... **153** E6
Needlers End La CV7 .... **130** A7
Needless Alley B2 .... **164** B2
Needwood Cl CV6 .... **95** C3
Needwood Dr WV4 .... **39** F4
Needwood Gr B71 .... **42** E1

Needwood Hill WS13 .... **3** A2
Needwood Ho B27 .... **88** D3
Neighbrook Cl B97 .... **152** F2
Neilston St CV31 .... **162** A7
Nelson Ave Bilston WV14 ... **40** C7
Warwick CV34 .... **161** A8
Nelson Dr Cannock WS12 ..... **2** F4
Hinckley LE10 .... **71** D4
Nelson Ho B7 .... **52** A7
Nelson Inf & Jun Sch B1 ..... **66** B3
Nelson Mandela Com Prim
Sch B12 .... **87** B5
Nelson Rd Birmingham B6 .. **55** F1
Dudley DY1 .... **51** B1
7 Coventry CV1 .... **113** E4
Oldbury B69 .... **64** B6
West Bromwich B71 .... **53** C5
Willenhall WV13 .... **27** B3
Nemesia B77 .... **22** B4
Nene Cl Coventry CV3 .... **134** D7
Stourbridge DY8 .... **81** A5
Nene Way B36 .... **69** F8
Neptune Ind Est WV13 .... **41** B8
Neptune St DY4 .... **51** E5
Nesbit Gr B9 .... **68** B3
Nesfield Cl B38 .... **103** C1
Nesfield Gr B92 .... **109** B7
Nesscliffe Gr B23 .... **56** D7
Neston Gr B33 .... **68** C2
Nestor Ho B13 .... **105** D7
Nether Beacon WS13 .... **3** A1
Nether La WS7 .... **7** D8
Netheravon Cl B14 .... **104** D1
Netherbrook Prim Sch
DY2 .... **62** D2
Netherby Rd DY3 .... **50** C8
Nethercote Gdns B90 .... **105** E3
Nethercott Cl B72 .... **57** D7
Netherdale Rd B14 .... **105** A1
Netherend Cl B63 .... **82** A7
Netherend La B63 .... **82** B7
Netherend Sq B63 .... **82** A7
Netherfield B98 .... **159** A8
Netherfield Gdns B27 .... **88** B3
Nethergate DY3 .... **50** F5
Netherley Rd LE10 .... **71** D3
Nethermill Rd **1** CV6 .... **113** A5
Netherstone Gr B74 .... **31** F5
Netherstowe WS13 .... **3** C2
Netherstowe High Sch
WS13 .... **3** B1
Netherstowe La WS13 .... **3** D2
Netherton Bsns Pk DY2 ...... **62** E3
Netherton CE Prim Sch
DY2 .... **62** B4
Netherton Gr B33 .... **69** C3
Netherwood Cl B91 .... **106** E6
Netherwood La B93 .... **145** A4
Nethy Dr WV6 .... **24** B5
Netley Gr B11 .... **87** F3
Netley Ho B32 .... **84** F5
Netley Rd WS3 .... **13** E2
Netley Way WS3 .... **13** E2
Nevada Way B37 .... **70** C1
Neve Ave WV10 .... **25** F8
Nevill Cl CV31 .... **161** F6
Nevill St B79 .... **21** A5
Neville Ave
Kidderminster DY11 .... **116** D3
Wolverhampton WV4 .... **39** D5
Neville Cl B98 .... **154** A5
Neville Ct Birmingham B13 . **104** F6
Kidderminster DY11 .... **116** D3
Neville Gr CV34 .... **155** F1
Neville Rd
Birmingham,
Castle Bromwich B36 .... **58** E1
Birmingham,
Stockland Green B23 .... **56** C3
Solihull B90 .... **105** F1
Neville St B77 .... **21** E3
Neville Wlk B35 .... **58** A2
Nevin Gr B42 .... **55** C5
Nevis Ct WV3 .... **24** E2
Nevis Gr WV12 .... **13** B1
Nevison Gr B43 .... **44** B4
New Ash Dr CV5 .... **111** F5
New Barns La WS14 .... **17** B3
New Bartholomew St B5 .. **164** D2
New Bldgs Coventry CV1 .. **165** C3
Darlaston WS10 .... **41** E6
Halesowen B63 .... **82** A7
Hinckley LE10 .... **71** D1
6 Kidderminster DY11 .. **116** D6
New Bond St Birmingham B9 **67** B1
3 Dudley DY2 .... **62** D8
New Brook St **5** CV32 .... **161** E8
New Canal St B5 .... **164** D2
New Century Pk CV3 .... **114** C2
New Century Way CV11 ..... **73** B4
New Church Rd B73 .... **57** A8
New Cole Hall La B33, B34 .. **69** B5
New College Cl WS1 .... **43** A7
New Coventry Rd B26 .... **89** A5
New Croft B19 .... **66** E7
New Cross Hospl WV11 ...... **26** B5
New Cross Ind Est WV1 ...... **26** A3
New Cross St
Darlaston WS10 .... **41** E6
Tipton DY4 .... **51** E5
New Ct **7** DY5 .... **61** D2

Needwood Hill WS13 .... **3** A2
New England B62 .... **83** E7
New England Cl B69 .... **52** E1
New Ent Workshops
Birmingham B7 .... **67** C6
Birmingham, All Saints B18 .. **66** A5
New Farm Rd DY9 .... **81** C4
New Forest Rd WS3 .... **28** F6
New Gas St B70 .... **53** A5
New Gate Ct CV1 .... **165** C2
New Hall Dr
Sutton Coldfield, Maney B75 . **46** D4
Sutton Coldfield,
Wylde Green B76 .... **46** E2
New Hall Pl WS10 .... **42** A3
New Hall St WV13 .... **41** A8
New Hampton Rd E WV1 .. **163** A4
New Hampton Rd W W6 ..... **25** A4
New Heath Cl WV11 .... **26** B5
New Henry St B68 .... **64** B4
New Hope Rd B66 .... **65** C4
New Horse Rd WS6 .... **4** E3
New Inn Rd **2** B19 .... **66** D8
New Inns Cl B21 .... **65** D8
New Inns La B45 .... **101** E1
New Invention Inf & Jun
Schs WV12 .... **27** C7
New John St Birmingham B6 . **66** E5
Halesowen B62 .... **83** C8
New John St W B19 .... **66** D5
New King St **7** DY1 .... **51** C1
New Landywood La WV11 ... **13** E7
New Leasow B76 .... **58** A7
New Market St B3 .... **164** B3
New Meadow Cl B31 .... **103** B2
New Meadow Rd B98 .... **154** B3
New Meeting St B69 .... **64** A8
New Mill La B78 .... **35** B8
New Mills St WS1 .... **42** D7
New Oscott Inf Sch B73 ...... **45** C3
New Oscott Jun Sch B73 .... **45** C3
New Penkridge Rd WS11 ..... **1** C1
New Pool Rd B64 .... **82** B8
New Rd Aldridge WS9 .... **30** A5
Ash Green CV7 .... **95** B6
Astwood Bank B96 .... **158** E1
Bedworth CV12 .... **77** A4
Birmingham B45 .... **121** F7
Bromsgrove B60 .... **137** A1
Bromsgrove, Sidemoor B61 . **136** E3
Brownhills WS8 .... **15** F7
Burntwood WS7 .... **7** B6
Coventry CV6 .... **94** F1
Dudley DY2 .... **62** C7
Fairfield B61 .... **120** E2
Featherstone WV10 .... **12** B8
Halesowen B63 .... **83** B4
Hinckley LE10 .... **76** A6
Hollywood B47 .... **125** A8
Kidderminster DY10 .... **116** E5
Shenstone WS14 .... **17** F6
Shuttington B79 .... **22** E8
Solihull B91 .... **107** D3
Stourbridge DY8 .... **81** A5
Studley B80 .... **159** E3
Tamworth B77 .... **35** F7
Tipton DY4 .... **52** D6
Water Orton B46 .... **59** B3
Willenhall WV13 .... **27** A1
Wolverhampton,
Newbridge WV6 .... **24** E4
Wolverhampton,
Scotlands WV10 .... **26** B8
New Row B78 .... **34** E5
New Rowley Rd DY2 .... **62** E7
New Spring St B18 .... **66** A4
New Spring St N B18 .... **66** A4
New St Bedworth CV12 .... **78** C2
Birchmoor B78 .... **36** E7
Birmingham,
Castle Bromwich B36 .... **69** B8
Birmingham, Digbeth B2 .. **164** C2
Birmingham, Erdington B23 . **56** F5
Birmingham, Frankley B45 .. **102** A1
Brierley Hill DY5 .... **82** A8
Bulkington CV12 .... **79** D2
Burntwood,
Chase Terrace WS7 .... **6** E8
Burntwood, Chasetown WS7 .. **6** E5
11 Cannock, Blackfords WS11 .. **1** E1
Cannock, Bridgtown WS11 .... **4** D6
Cannock, Hednesford WS12 .. **2** C4
Cubbington CV32 .... **157** E5
Darlaston WS10 .... **41** D6
Dudley, Eve Hill DY1 .... **51** D1
Dudley, Gornalwood DY3 ... **50** C3
Essington WV11 .... **13** A3
Fazeley B78 .... **35** B8
Great Wyrley WS6 .... **5** A1
Hinckley LE10 .... **71** D1
Kenilworth CV8 .... **147** F6
Kingswinford,
Wall Heath DY6 .... **60** C8
Kingswinford,
Wordsley DY6 .... **60** D4
Royal Leamington Spa CV31 **162** A7
Smethwick B66 .... **65** B6
Stourbridge DY8 .... **60** D2
11 Stourbridge,
Wollaston DY8 .... **80** F5
Tamworth, Bolehill B77 ...... **21** E4
Tamworth,
Mount Pleasant B77 .... **21** C1
Tipton DY4 .... **51** F5
Walsall, High Heath WS4 .... **15** D1
Walsall, Rushall WS4 .... **29** B7
Walsall, The Chuckery WS1 . **28** F1

New St continued
Walsall,
Wallington Heath WS3 .... **14** B1
Warwick CV34 .... **160** E6
Wednesbury WS10 .... **41** F1
West Bromwich,
Hill Top B70 .... **53** A7
West Bromwich,
Mayer's Green B70 .... **53** D3
Willenhall WV13 .... **26** E1
Wolverhampton,
Ettingshall WV2 .... **40** A6
Wolverhampton,
Merry Hill WV3 .... **38** D7
Wolverhampton,
Parkfields WV4 .... **39** E6
New St N B71 .... **53** D3
New Street Sta B2 .... **164** B2
New Summer St B19 .... **164** B4
New Swan La B70 .... **53** B5
New Town Brierley Hill DY5 .. **61** C4
Dudley DY2 .... **62** D1
New Town La B64 .... **62** D1
New Town Row B6 .... **66** E5
New Union St CV1 .... **165** B2
New Village DY2 .... **62** C2
New Wharf Cotts B60 .... **152** B7
New Wlk 3 B98 .... **153** E4
New Wood Cl DY7 .... **80** C8
New Wood Gr WS9 .... **16** A3
New Wood La DY10 .... **118** B8
Newark Croft B26 .... **89** B6
Newark Rd Dudley DY2 .... **62** D2
Willenhall WV12 .... **27** C7
Newbank Gr B9 .... **68** A3
Newbold Cl
Bentley Heath B93 .... **127** F5
Coventry CV3 .... **114** F1
Newbold Comyn Pk
CV32 .... **162** D8
Newbold Croft B7 .... **67** B5
Newbold Ct B63 .... **83** B3
Newbold Lawn CV32 .... **162** A8
Newbold Pl CV32 .... **162** A8
Newbold St CV32 .... **162** A8
Newbold Terr CV32 .... **162** A8
Newbold Terr E CV32 .... **162** B8
Newbolds Rd WV10 .... **26** A6
Newbolt Rd WV14 .... **40** E6
Newbolt St WS5 .... **42** E5
Newborough Gr B28 .... **105** F3
Newborough Rd
Birmingham B28 .... **105** F4
Solihull B90 .... **106** A3
Newbourne Hill B48 .... **139** E4
Newbridge Ave WV6 .... **24** E3
Newbridge Cres WV6 .... **24** E4
Newbridge Dr WV6 .... **24** E4
Newbridge Gdns WV6 .... **24** E4
Newbridge Mews WV6 .... **24** E4
Newbridge Prep Sch WV6 .. **24** E4
Newbridge Rd
Birmingham B9 .... **68** B1
Kingswinford DY6 .... **60** C8
Newbridge St WV6 .... **24** F4
Newburgh Cres CV34 .... **160** E8
Newburn Prim Sch
CV34 .... **160** C4
Newburn Croft B32 .... **84** B5
Newbury Cl Great Wyrley WS6 . **4** F2
Halesowen B62 .... **83** D3
15 Royal Leamington Spa
CV31 .... **162** C6
Newbury Ho 1 B69 .... **63** D5
Newbury La B69 .... **63** D6
Newbury Rd Birmingham
B19 .... **66** E7
Stourbridge DY8 .... **60** D1
Wolverhampton WV10 .... **11** C2
Newbury Wlk B65 .... **63** C6
Newby Cl CV3 .... **133** E6
Newby Gr B37 .... **70** B4
Newcastle Croft B35 .... **58** C3
Newchurch Gdns 6 B24 ..... **56** E2
Newcombe Rd
Birmingham B21 .... **54** D2
Coventry CV5 .... **113** A1
Newcomen Cl
Bedworth CV12 .... **95** D8
Burntwood WS7 .... **7** C8
Newcomen Ct WS4 .... **29** B7
Newcomen Dr DY4 .... **51** F3
Newcomen Rd CV12 .... **77** D1
Newcott Cl WV9 .... **10** F2
Newcroft Gr B26 .... **88** E7
Newdegate Pl CV11 .... **73** C4
Newdegate Rd CV12 .... **78** A3
Newdegate St CV11 .... **73** C4
Newdigate CV31 .... **162** C5
Newdigate Cl CV12 .... **78** A4
Newdigate Cty Fst Sch
CV12 .... **77** C1
Newdigate Cty Mid Sch
CV12 .... **77** C1
Newdigate Rd Coventry
CV6 .... **113** F6
Sutton Coldfield B75 .... **47** A5
Newells Dr DY4 .... **52** D7
Newells Rd B26 .... **89** B8
Newent Cl WV12 .... **27** D3
Newent Rd B31 .... **103** C4
Newey Ave CV12 .... **95** D8
Newey Cl B45 .... **122** A6
Newey Rd Birmingham B28 .. **105** F6
Coventry CV2 .... **114** D4
Wednesfield WV11 .... **27** A8
Newey St DY1 .... **51** A2
Newfield Ave CV8 .... **148** B3

Newfield Cl Solihull B91 ...... **107** D6
Walsall WS2 .... **28** C5
Newfield Cres B63 .... **83** A5
Newfield Dr DY6 .... **60** E4
Newfield Gdns DY9 .... **99** A4
Newfield La B63 .... **83** B5
Newfield Park Prim Sch
B62 .... **83** A5
Newfield Rd Coventry CV1 .. **113** C5
Hagley DY9 .... **99** A4
Oldbury B69 .... **63** F8
Newgale Wlk CV31 .... **162** C7
Newgate St WS7 .... **7** A5
Newhall Cres WS11 .... **2** B3
Newhall Farm Cl B76 .... **46** D4
Newhall Gdns WS11 .... **1** F2
Newhall Hill B1 .... **66** C3
Newhall Ho 5 WS1 .... **42** E8
Newhall Pl B1 .... **66** C3
Newhall Rd Blackheath B65 ... **63** C3
Coventry CV2 .... **114** D7
Newhall St Birmingham B3 .. **164** B3
Cannock WS11 .... **1** D1
Tipton DY4 .... **51** E8
Walsall WS1 .... **42** E8
West Bromwich B70 .... **53** C2
Newhall Wlk 6 B72 .... **46** C4
Newham Gn CV10 .... **72** C7
Newhaven Cl Birmingham
B7 .... **67** A5
Coventry CV6 .... **112** E6
Newhouse Cl CV7 .... **130** B6
Newhouse Farm Cl B76 .... **46** F3
Newick Ave B74 .... **31** B3
Newick Gr B14 .... **104** C4
Newick St DY2 .... **62** C4
Newington Cl CV6 .... **112** D6
Newington Rd B37 .... **90** B8
Newland Cl Redditch B98 .... **159** B7
Walsall WS4 .... **15** C2
Newland Ct B23 .... **56** C3
Newland Gdns B64 .... **82** E7
Newland Gr DY2 .... **61** F7
Newland La CV7 .... **95** B7
Newland Rd Birmingham B9 .. **67** F1
Coventry CV1 .... **113** D5
Royal Leamington Spa
CV32 .... **157** C3
Newlands Cl
Kidderminster DY11 .... **116** C7
Willenhall WV13 .... **27** A1
Newlands Ct Cannock WS11 .... **5** E8
Coventry CV3 .... **113** C2
Newlands Dr B62 .... **83** E7
Newlands Gn B66 .... **65** A4
Newlands La Birmingham
B37 .... **90** A6
Norton Canes WS11 .... **5** D8
Newlands Rd
Bentley Heath B93 .... **127** F4
Birmingham B30 .... **104** C7
Newlands The
Birmingham B34 .... **69** C7
Studley B80 .... **159** D3
Newlyn Cl Lichfield WS14 .... **9** D7
Nuneaton CV11 .... **73** F4
Newlyn Rd Birmingham B31 .. **102** F3
Blackheath B64 .... **82** D8
Newman Ave WV4 .... **39** F4
Newman Cl CV12 .... **78** B4
Newman Coll B32 .... **102** C8
Newman College Cl B32 .... **102** C8
Newman Pl WV14 .... **40** F7
Newman Rd Birmingham B24 . **56** F4
Tipton DY4 .... **41** C1
Wolverhampton WV10 .... **12** A1
Newman Way B45 .... **122** A6
Newmans Cl B66 .... **65** D8
Newmarket Cl Coventry CV6 . **96** B3
Wolverhampton WV6 .... **25** A5
Newmarket Way B36 .... **68** B7
Newmarsh Rd B76 .... **58** B6
Newmore Gdns WS5 .... **43** C5
Newnham Gr B23 .... **56** E6
Newnham Ho B36 .... **70** B5
Newnham Rd
Birmingham B16 .... **65** C2
Coventry CV1 .... **113** F5
Royal Leamington Spa
CV32 .... **157** B3
Newnham Rise B90 .... **106** D3
Newport Cl B77 .... **21** F5
Newport Cl B97 .... **158** B6
Newport Ho B71 .... **53** B7
Newport Rd
Birmingham,
Balsall Heath B12 .... **87** A4
Birmingham,
Buckland End B36 .... **68** F8
Coventry CV6 .... **95** D1
Newport St 3 Walsall WS1 ... **28** E1
Wolverhampton WV10 .... **25** E4
Newquay Cl Hinckley LE10 ..... **71** E4
Nuneaton CV11 .... **73** F5
Walsall WS5 .... **43** E7
Newquay Rd WS5 .... **43** D7
Newshire Ind Est B11 .... **87** D6
Newsholme Cl 1 CV34 .... **155** E1
Newstead B79 .... **20** D6
Newstead Ave LE10 .... **75** D4
Newstead Cl CV11 .... **73** F2
Newstead Rd B44 .... **45** B3
Newstead Way CV3 .... **115** B1
Newton Cl Birmingham B43 ... **43** C1
Coventry CV2 .... **114** F7
Redditch B98 .... **159** A6
Newton Gdns B43 .... **54** B8
Newton Gr 5 B29 .... **85** F2

Newton Ind Est B9 .... **67** D2
Newton Manor Cl B43 .... **54** D8
Newton Pl Birmingham B18 ... **66** A7
Walsall WS2 .... **28** B6
Newton Rd
Birmingham,
Balsall Heath B11 .... **87** B5
Birmingham, Newton B43 ..... **54** B8
Bromsgrove B60 .... **151** A7
Hinckley LE10 .... **74** E7
Knowle B93 .... **128** B7
Walsall WS2 .... **28** B5
West Bromwich B71 .... **53** F6
Newton Sq B43 .... **43** E1
Newton St Birmingham B4 .. **164** C3
West Bromwich B71 .... **53** E7
Newton Works B60 .... **151** A6
Newton's Coll WS13 .... **9** A8
Newtown Bldgs CV12 .... **78** B3
Newtown Dr B19 .... **66** C6
Newtown La Romsley B62 ... **101** D2
Wildmoor B62 .... **120** D8
Newtown Middleway B6 .... **66** E5
Newtown Prim Sch B70 ...... **52** D3
Newtown Rd Bedworth
CV12 .... **78** A2
Nuneaton CV11 .... **73** C5
Nuneaton Sh Ctr B19 .... **66** E6
Newtown St B64 .... **62** D2
Ney Ct DY4 .... **51** F2
Niall Cl B15 .... **85** E8
Nibletts Hill B61 .... **136** B7
Nicholas Chamberlaine
Comp Sch CV12 .... **78** D3
Nicholas Rd B74 .... **44** E8
Nicholds Cl WV14 .... **40** B1
Nicholls Rd DY4 .... **40** E1
Nicholls St Coventry CV2 .... **113** F4
West Bromwich B70 .... **53** E2
Nicholls Way WS12 .... **2** F1
Nichols Cl B92 .... **107** F7
Nicholson Cl CV34 .... **155** F1
Nickson Rd CV4 .... **111** E1
Nigel Ave B31 .... **103** A5
Nigel Cl B16 .... **65** E1
Nigel Rd Birmingham B8 .... **67** E6
Dudley DY1 .... **51** A2
Nightingale B77 .... **36** A6
Nightingale Ave B36 .... **70** A8
Nightingale Cl WS12 .... **1** C7
Nightingale Cres
Brierley Hill DY5 .... **81** D7
Willenhall WV12 .... **27** C8
Nightingale Ct CV31 .... **162** B8
Nightingale Dr
Kidderminster DY10 .... **117** B2
Tipton DY4 .... **52** C5
Nightingale Ho 4 B16 .... **66** A2
Nightingale La CV5 .... **132** E7
Nightingale Pl WV14 .... **40** D7
Nightingale Wlk 1 B15 .... **86** C7
Nighwood Dr B74 .... **44** F7
Nijon Cl B21 .... **54** D1
Nimbus B77 .... **35** D4
Nimmings Cl B31 .... **122** F6
Nimmings Rd B62 .... **63** D1
Nimmings Visitor Ctr
DY9 .... **100** B6
Nine Days La B98 .... **159** B6
Nine Elms La WV10 .... **25** E4
Nine Leasowes B66 .... **64** E7
Nine Locks Ridge DY5 .... **61** D2
Nine Pails Wlk B70 .... **53** D1
Nineacres Dr B37 .... **70** A3
Ninefoot La Tamworth B77 .... **35** E8
Tamworth B77 .... **35** F7
Ninestiles Sch B27 .... **88** B1
Nineveh Ave B21 .... **65** F7
Nineveh Rd B21 .... **65** F7
Ninfield Rd B27 .... **88** A4
Ninian Pk B77 .... **35** D6
Ninian Way B77 .... **35** E6
Nirvana Cl WS11 .... **1** C2
Nith Pl DY1 .... **51** B3
Niton Rd CV10 .... **73** D6
Niven Cl CV5 .... **112** A6
No Name Rd WS7 .... **6** F7
Noakes Ct WS10 .... **41** F7
Noble Cl CV34 .... **160** D5
Nock St DY4 .... **52** C7
Nocke Rd WV11 .... **12** F1
Nod Rise CV5 .... **112** B3
Noddy Park Rd WS9 .... **30** B6
Noddy Pk WS9 .... **30** B7
Node Hill B80 .... **159** D3
Node Hill Cl B80 .... **159** D3
Noel Ave B12 .... **87** A6
Noel Ct B97 .... **158** C8
Noel Rd B16 .... **65** F1
Noele Gordon Gdns WS1 ..... **42** E8
Nolans Cl CV6 .... **95** D4
Nolton Cl B43 .... **54** D8
Nonsuch Jun & Inf Sch
B32 .... **84** D2
Nook The Brierley Hill DY5 ... **61** B5
Cheslyn Hay WS6 .... **4** C1
Nuneaton CV11 .... **73** E2
Nooklands Croft B33 .... **69** A2
Noose Cres WV13 .... **26** E2
Noose La WV13 .... **26** E3
Nora Rd B11 .... **87** C3
Norbiton Rd B44 .... **56** A8
Norbreck Cl B43 .... **43** D1
Norbury Ave WS3 .... **15** A3
Norbury Cl B98 .... **154** B7
Norbury Cres WV4 .... **40** A4
Norbury Dr DY5 .... **61** D1
Norbury Gr B92 .... **89** A3

Norbury Rd Bilston WV14 ..... **40** F6
Birmingham B44 .... **44** F3
West Bromwich B70 .... **53** A7
Wolverhampton WV10 .... **25** F7
Norcombe Gr B90 .... **127** A5
Nordic Drift CV2 .... **115** A6
Nordley Rd WV11 .... **26** C5
Norfolk Ave B71 .... **53** D7
Norfolk Cl Birmingham B30 .. **104** B6
Hinckley LE10 .... **75** D4
Norfolk Cres Aldridge WS9 .... **30** B8
Nuneaton CV10 .... **72** E4
Norfolk Ct B16 .... **65** D1
Norfolk Dr Tamworth B78 ...... **21** A1
Wednesbury WS10 .... **42** D4
Norfolk Gdns B75 .... **46** B7
Norfolk Gr WS9 .... **4** F1
Norfolk Ho B30 .... **104** A3
Norfolk House Sch B15 .... **85** D8
Norfolk New Rd WS2 .... **28** A4
Norfolk Pl WS2 .... **28** D5
Norfolk Rd Birmingham
B45 .... **101** F2
Birmingham, Edgbaston B15 .. **85** D8
Birmingham, Erdington B23 .... **56** F5
Dudley DY2 .... **62** A7
Oldbury B68 .... **84** B7
Stourbridge DY8 .... **80** D8
Sutton Coldfield B75 .... **46** C7
Wolverhampton WV3 .... **39** A8
Norfolk St Coventry CV1 .... **113** B3
Royal Leamington Spa
CV32 .... **157** A1
Norfolk Terr CV4 .... **132** B7
Norfolk Tower B18 .... **66** B5
Norgrave Rd B92 .... **89** C2
Norlan Dr B14 .... **104** F3
Norland Rd B27 .... **88** C1
Norley Gr B13 .... **105** C7
Norman Ashman Coppice
CV3 .... **135** C7
Norman Ave Birmingham
B32 .... **84** E7
Coventry CV2 .... **96** F1
Nuneaton CV11 .... **73** B4
Norman Cl B79 .... **20** C7
Norman Place Rd CV6 .... **112** F7
Norman Rd Birmingham
B31 .... **103** B3
Smethwick B67 .... **64** E2
Walsall WS5 .... **43** D7
Norman St Birmingham B18 ... **65** E5
Dudley DY2 .... **62** E7
Norman Terr B65 .... **63** C4
Normanby Mdws CV31 .... **162** A2
Normandy Cl CV35 .... **160** A7
Normandy Rd B20 .... **55** E1
Normansell Tower B6 .... **67** B8
Normanton Ave B26 .... **89** D5
Normanton Tower 1 B23 ..... **57** A6
Norrington Gr B31 .... **102** C3
Norrington Rd B31 .... **102** C3
Norris Dr B33 .... **68** E3
Norris Rd B6 .... **55** F1
Norris Way B75 .... **46** D5
North Ave Bedworth CV12 ..... **78** D2
Birmingham B40 .... **90** F5
Coventry CV2 .... **114** A3
Wolverhampton WV11 .... **26** C6
North Birmingham Coll
B44 .... **55** E7
North Bromsgrove High
Sch B60 .... **137** B3
North Brook Rd CV5 .... **112** D8
North Cl Cubbington CV32 ... **157** E5
Hinckley LE10 .... **75** E6
North Cres WV10 .... **12** C7
North Dr
Birmingham,
Balsall Heath B5 .... **86** C5
Birmingham, Lozells B20 .... **66** B8
Sutton Coldfield B75 .... **46** C6
North East
Worcestershire Coll
B98 .... **153** E4
North East
Worcestershire Coll
(Annexe) B98 .... **153** E4
North East
Worcestershire Coll
Bromsgrove Campus
B60 .... **137** B3
North Gate B17 .... **85** C7
North Gn WV4 .... **38** D6
North Holme B9 .... **67** C2
North Leamington Sch
CV32 .... **156** F4
North Leamington Sch
(Binswood Hall)
CV32 .... **156** F2
North Oval DY3 .... **50** E5
North Park Rd B23 .... **56** B3
North Pathway B17 .... **85** B7
North Rd
Birmingham,
Handsworth B20 .... **55** E2
Birmingham, Harborne B17 ... **85** D6
Birmingham, Selly Oak B29 ... **85** F3
Bromsgrove B60 .... **137** A2
Tipton DY4 .... **52** B8
Wolverhampton WV1 .... **25** C4
North Roundhay B33 .... **69** A4
North Springfield DY3 .... **39** E1
North St Brierley Hill DY5 ..... **61** C2
Cannock WS11 .... **4** E6
Coventry CV2 .... **114** B5
Dudley DY2 .... **51** D1
Nuneaton CV10 .... **72** F3

New – Nor 213

North St continued
Smethwick B67 .... **64** F5
Walsall WS2 .... **28** E4
Wednesbury WS10 .... **41** F3
Wolverhampton WV1 .... **163** B3
North View CV7 .... **97** A1
North View Dr DY5 .... **61** E5
North Villiers St CV32 .... **157** A1
North Walsall Inf Sch
WS2 .... **28** E4
North Walsall Jun Sch
WS2 .... **28** E4
North Warwick St 1 B9 .... **67** D1
North Warwickshire &
Hinkley Coll
Hinkley LE10 .... **75** F8
Nuneaton CV11 .... **73** E6
North Western Arc B2 .... **164** C2
North Western Rd B66 .... **65** A6
North Western Terr B18 .... **65** F7
North Wlk B31 .... **103** C1
Northam Wlk WV6 .... **25** B4
Northampton St B18 .... **66** C4
Northanger Rd B27 .... **88** B2
Northbrook Ct B90 .... **106** C5
Northbrook Rd B90 .... **106** D5
Northbrook St B16 .... **65** F4
Northcliffe Hts DY11 .... **116** C4
Northcote Rd B33 .... **68** D4
Northcote St
7 Royal Leamington Spa
CV31 .... **162** B7
Walsall WS2 .... **28** D4
Northcott Rd Bilston WV14 ... **40** F4
Dudley DY2 .... **62** D4
Northdale WV6 .... **24** B4
Northdown Rd B91 .... **106** F1
Northern Perimeter Rd W
LE10 .... **71** B3
Northey Rd CV6 .... **113** D6
Northfield Cl B98 .... **154** D6
Northfield Gr WV3 .... **38** C7
Northfield Manor Prim
Sch B29 .... **103** B7
Northfield Rd
Birmingham,
Harborne B17, B32 .... **85** A3
Birmingham,
King's Norton B30 .... **103** E4
Coventry CV1 .... **113** F2
Dudley DY2 .... **62** D4
Hinckley LE10 .... **75** C7
Northfield Road Prim Sch
DY2 .... **62** D5
Northfield Sta B31 .... **103** D4
Northfields Way WS8 .... **15** D7
Northfleet Tower 4 B31 ...... **102** C2
Northgate Aldridge WS9 .... **30** A7
Blackheath B64 .... **82** D8
Northgate Cl DY11 .... **116** A4
Northgate St CV34 .... **160** E7
Northgate Way WS9 .... **30** A8
Northicote Sch The
WV10 .... **11** E3
Northland Rd B90 .... **106** E1
Northlands Rd B13 .... **87** A1
Northleach Ave B14 .... **104** D2
Northleach Cl B98 .... **154** B5
Northleigh Rd B8 .... **68** A6
Northmead B33 .... **69** A2
Northolt Dr B35 .... **58** B3
Northolt Gr B42 .... **43** F1
Northover Cl WV9 .... **11** A2
Northside Cl B98 .... **158** E7
Northside Dr B74 .... **44** F8
Northumberland Ave
Kidderminster DY11 .... **116** D3
Nuneaton CV10 .... **72** F3
Northumberland Cl B78 .... **21** A1
Northumberland Rd
Coventry CV1 .... **113** A3
Royal Leamington Spa
CV32 .... **156** E2
Northumberland St B7 .... **67** A3
Northvale Cl CV8 .... **148** B6
Northway Birmingham
B40 .... **90** F5
Royal Leamington Spa
CV31 .... **162** A3
Sedgley DY3 .... **39** C2
Northwick Cres B91 .... **107** B1
Northwood Ct 9 DY5 .... **61** D2
Northwood Park Cl WV10 ..... **11** E3
Northwood Park Rd
WV10 .... **11** E3
Northwood St B3 .... **164** A4
Northycote La WV10 .... **11** F4
Norton Canes High Sch
WS11 .... **6** A5
Norton Canes Prim Sch
WS11 .... **6** A6
Norton Cl Birmingham B31 .. **103** A3
Redditch B98 .... **154** F2
Smethwick B66 .... **65** C5
Tamworth B79 .... **21** C7
Wolverhampton WV4 .... **38** C5
Norton Cres Bilston WV14 ... **40** D1
Birmingham B9 .... **68** B3
Dudley DY2 .... **62** E3
Norton Dr CV34 .... **155** E2
Norton East Rd WS11 .... **6** B6
Norton Grange WS11 .... **5** F4
Norton Grange Cres WS11 ..... **5** F4

Norton Green La
Knowle B93 .... **128** C2
Norton Canes WS11 .... **5** F4
Norton Hall La WS11 .... **5** D4
Norton Hill Dr CV2 .... **114** E6
Norton La Burntwood WS7 ... **7** C6
Great Wyrley WS6 .... **5** A4
Norton Canes WS11 .... **5** C6
Tidbury Green B47, B94 .... **125** E3
Norton Rd Coleshill B46 ..... **70** F8
Iverley DY8 .... **98** D8
Kidderminster DY10 .... **117** B6
Norton Canes WS12 .... **5** F8
Stourbridge DY8 .... **80** E2
Walsall WS3 .... **15** A4
Norton Springs WS11 .... **5** F5
Norton St B18 .... **66** A6
Norton Terr
Birmingham B30 .... **104** B6
Norton Canes WS11 .... **5** F6
Norton Tower B1 .... **66** C2
Norton View B14 .... **104** D7
Norton Wlk B23 .... **56** C3
Nortune Cl B38 .... **103** D2
Norwich Cl Lichfield WS13 .... **3** C3
Nuneaton CV11 .... **74** A8
Norwich Croft B37 .... **69** F1
Norwich Dr Birmingham
B17 .... **84** F8
Coventry CV3 .... **133** B5
Norwood Ave B64 .... **82** E7
Norwood Cl LE10 .... **71** E3
Norwood Gr Birmingham
B19 .... **66** B7
Coventry CV2 .... **96** E2
Norwood Ho 11 CV32 ..... **156** F2
Norwood Rd Birmingham
B9 .... **67** E2
Brierley Hill DY5 .... **61** C3
Norwood Villas B16 .... **65** F1
Nottingham Dr WV12 .... **27** C7
Nottingham Way DY5 .... **61** F2
Nova Croft CV5 .... **111** C4
Nova Ct B43 .... **44** B1
Nova Scotia St B4 .... **164** D3
Novotel Way B26 .... **90** C4
Nowell St WS10 .... **41** E5
Nuffield Ho B36 .... **70** A8
Nuffield Hospl WV4 .... **24** C4
Nuffield Rd Coventry CV6 ... **114** A7
Hinckley LE10 .... **74** E7
Nugent Cl B6 .... **66** E7
Nugent Gr B90 .... **126** D3
Nuneaton Rd Bedworth
CV12 .... **78** B4
Bulkington CV12 .... **79** B4
Nuneaton CV10 .... **72** D8
Nuneaton Trent Valley Sta
CV11 .... **73** C5
Nunts La CV6 .... **95** B3
Nunts Park Ave CV6 .... **95** B4
Nursery Ave Aldridge WS9 ... **30** B5
Birmingham B12 .... **86** F5
Nursery Cl Birmingham B30 . **103** B3
Hagley DY9 .... **99** A4
Kidderminster DY11 .... **116** B8
Nursery Dr B30 .... **103** F5
Nursery Gdns DY8 .... **60** F1
Nursery Gr DY11 .... **116** B8
Nursery La Hopwas B78 .... **20** B6
Royal Leamington Spa
CV31 .... **162** A5
Nursery Rd
Birmingham, Harborne B15 .. **85** D7
Birmingham, Lozells B19 .... **66** C6
Walsall WS3 .... **28** B7
Nursery St WS1 .... **163** B4
Nursery View Cl WS9 .... **30** E2
Nursery Wlk WV6 .... **24** D4
Nurton Bank WV6 .... **23** A3
Nutbrook Ave CV4 .... **111** E2
Nutbush Dr B31 .... **102** E6
Nutfield Wlk B32 .... **84** F5
Nutgrove Cl B14 .... **104** F7
Nuthatch Dr DY5 .... **81** C7
Nuthurst B75 .... **47** B4
Nuthurst Dr WS11 .... **4** F4
Nuthurst Gr
Bentley Heath B93 .... **128** A4
Birmingham B14 .... **104** F2
Nuthurst Grange Rd B94 .. **143** C4
Nuthurst Rd
Birmingham B31 .... **122** F6
Lapworth B94 .... **143** B2
Nutley Dr DY4 .... **52** D8
Nutt's La LE10 .... **75** A7
Nuttall Gr B21 .... **65** C7
Nymet B77 .... **35** E8

O'Connor Dr DY4 .... **41** C1
O'Hare Ho WS4 .... **28** F3
Oak Ave Birmingham B12 ... **87** A5
Great Wyrley WS6 .... **5** A1
Huntington WS12 .... **1** D8
Walsall WS2 .... **27** E3
West Bromwich B70 .... **53** B3
Oak Bank B18 .... **66** A6
Oak Barn Rd B62 .... **83** E8
Oak Cottage Baginton CV8 . **133** F2
Bedworth CV12 .... **78** C4
Birmingham B17 .... **85** A6
Hinckley LE10 .... **75** E5
Tipton DY4 .... **41** A1

Oak Cottage Prim Sch
B91 .... **106** F6
Oak Cotts B14 .... **105** C2
Oak Cres Tipton B69 .... **52** B1
Walsall WS3 .... **28** D6
Oak Croft B37 .... **69** E3
Oak Ct Coventry CV3 ...... **133** F7
Halesowen B63 .... **82** F2
Oldbury B66 .... **64** C8
Royal Leamington Spa
CV34 .... **161** E2
Stourbridge DY8 .... **81** A4
Oak Dr B23 .... **56** C7
Oak Farm Cl B76 .... **58** A7
Oak Farm Rd B30 .... **103** E5
Oak Gn Dudley DY1 .... **51** A5
Wolverhampton WV6 .... **24** B3
Oak Gr Birmingham B31 ... **102** E1
Kidderminster DY10 .... **117** A5
Wolverhampton WV11 .... **26** B7
Oak Hill DY8 .... **24** C1
Oak Hill Dr B15 .... **85** E7
Oak Ho WS6 .... **5** A1
Oak House (Mus) B70 ...... **53** B2
Oak Ind Pk The DY6 .... **49** E1
Oak La Allesley CV5 .... **93** E1
Barston B92 .... **109** B1
Kingswinford DY6 .... **49** F1
West Bromwich B70 .... **53** B3
Oak Leaf Dr B13 .... **87** A3
Oak Leasow B32 .... **84** B4
Oak Leigh Rd DY8 .... **81** B2
Oak Leys WV3 .... **24** C1
Oak Meadow Prim Sch
WV11 .... **27** A7
Oak Park Rd DY8 .... **60** F1
Oak Rd Brownhills WS9 .... **16** A3
Catshill B61 .... **137** B8
Dudley DY1 .... **51** C3
Oldbury B68 .... **84** C7
Tipton DY4 .... **51** E6
Walsall, High Heath WS4 ... **15** C1
Walsall, Pelsall Wood WS3 .. **14** F5
West Bromwich B70 .... **53** B2
Willenhall WV13 .... **26** E2
Oak Rise B46 .... **70** F5
Oak St Blackheath B64 ..... **62** D1
Brierley Hill DY5 .... **61** F1
Dudley, Darby End DY2 ...... **62** E4
Dudley, West Coseley WV14 .. **51** B7
Kingswinford DY6 .... **60** D5
Wolverhampton WV3 .... **25** A3
Oak Street Trad Est DY5 ... **61** F1
Oak Tree Ave Coventry CV3 . **133** A6
Redditch B97 .... **153** B4
Oak Tree Cl
Bentley Heath B93 .... **127** E4
Royal Leamington Spa CV32 . **157** A2
Oak Tree Cres B62 .... **83** F6
Oak Tree Ct B28 .... **106** A5
Oak Tree Gdns 2 DY8 ..... **61** A1
Oak Tree La Birmingham
B29 .... **85** E1
Hollywood B47 .... **125** B6
Sambourne B96 .... **159** B2
Oak Tree Rd CV3 .... **135** A7
Oak Tree Wlk B79 .... **20** F7
Oak Trees B47 .... **125** A4
Oak View WS2 .... **27** E3
Oak Wlk The B31 .... **103** A1
Oakalls Ave B60 .... **137** B2
Oakcroft Rd B13 .... **105** C7
Oakdale B74 .... **31** A1
Oakdale Cl Brierley Hill DY5 . **61** A7
Oldbury B68 .... **64** A2
Oakdale Rd
Binley Woods CV3 .... **135** C7
Birmingham B36 .... **68** E7
Oldbury B68 .... **64** A2
Oakdale Trad Est DY6 ..... **49** E1
Oakdene Cres CV10 .... **73** D7
Oakdene Dr B45 .... **138** C8
Oakdene Rd WS7 .... **7** A6
Oaken Dr Solihull B91 .... **106** F5
Willenhall WV12 .... **27** E7
Oaken Gdns WS7 .... **7** A8
Oaken Pk WV8 .... **10** A2
Oakenfield WS13 .... **3** A2
Oakenhayes Cres
Brownhills WS8 .... **6** F1
Sutton Coldfield B76 .... **58** C5
Oakenhayes Dr WS8 .... **6** F1
Oakenshaw Rd
Redditch B98 .... **154** A1
Solihull B90 .... **106** D1
Oakeswell St WS10 .... **42** A3
Oakey Cl CV6 .... **95** F4
Oakeywell St 1 DY2 ...... **62** D8
Oakfield Ave
9 Birmingham,
Balsall Heath B12 .... **87** A6
Birmingham, Sparkbrook B11 . **87** C6
Dudley DY1 .... **51** B6
Kingswinford DY6 .... **60** E5
Oakfield Cl Smethwick B66 .. **65** C6
Stourbridge DY8 .... **60** F1
Oakfield Ct 6 DY5 .... **61** D2
Oakfield Dr Birmingham
B45 .... **122** D4
Walsall WS3 .... **15** B5
Oakfield Ho CV3 .... **115** A1
Oakfield Rd
Birmingham,
Balsall Heath B12 .... **86** E5
Birmingham, Erdington B24 .. **56** F3
Birmingham, Selly Oak B29 .. **86** B3
Codsall WV8 .... **10** C2

Oakfield Rd continued
Coventry CV6 .... **112** F5
Kidderminster DY11 .... **116** B5
Smethwick B66 .... **65** C6
Stourbridge DY8 .... **61** A1
Stourbridge, Wollaston DY9 .. **81** F2
Oakfield Trad Est B64 ...... **82** D8
Oakfields Way B91 .... **108** B5
Oakford Dr CV5 .... **111** F6
Oakhall Dr B93 .... **127** F4
Oakham Ave DY2 .... **62** E7
Oakham Cl B98 .... **159** A5
Oakham Cres
Bulkington CV12 .... **79** D2
Dudley DY2 .... **62** E7
Oakham Ct 9 DY2 .... **62** E8
Oakham Dr DY2 .... **62** E8
Oakham Ho 7 B14 .... **105** A3
Oakham Prim Sch B69 ..... **63** A7
Oakham Rd Birmingham B17 . **85** B7
Dudley DY2 .... **62** F7
Tipton B69 .... **63** A7
Oakham Way B92 .... **89** B1
Oakhill Ave DY10 .... **116** E4
Oakhill Cres B27 .... **106** B8
Oakhill Dr DY5 .... **81** B7
Oakhill Rd WS11 .... **1** F2
Oakhurst WS14 .... **9** C7
Oakhurst Ct B72 .... **57** C8
Oakhurst Dr B60 .... **137** A3
Oakhurst Rd
Birmingham B27 .... **106** B8
Sutton Coldfield B72 .... **57** C8
Oakington Ho B35 .... **58** A3
Oakland Cl B91 .... **107** E4
Oakland Dr DY3 .... **50** B2
Oakland Rd
Birmingham,
Handsworth B21 .... **65** E8
Birmingham,
Moseley B13 .... **87** A3
Walsall WS3 .... **28** E7
Oaklands Birmingham B13 .. **87** A3
Curdworth B76 .... **59** B5
Halesowen B62 .... **84** A4
Wolverhampton WV3 .... **39** B8
Oaklands Ave B17 .... **85** B5
Oaklands Cl WS12 .... **1** C6
Oaklands Croft B76 .... **58** B7
Oaklands Dr B20 .... **54** F2
Oaklands Gn WV14 .... **40** D8
Oaklands Ind Est WS12 ..... **2** B3
Oaklands Prim Sch B27 .... **88** C2
Oaklands Rd
Sutton Coldfield B74 .... **46** B8
Wolverhampton WV3 .... **39** B8
Oaklands The
Birmingham B37 .... **90** A7
Coventry CV4 .... **112** A2
Halesowen B62 .... **83** F6
Kidderminster DY10 .... **117** A7
Oaklands Way WS3 .... **15** B3
Oaklea Dr B64 .... **62** F2
Oakleaf Cl B32 .... **84** C2
Oakleigh B31 .... **103** C2
Oakleigh Ct 3 WS3 .... **25** B2
Oakleigh Dr Codsall WV8 ... **10** A3
Sedgley DY3 .... **50** C7
Oakleigh Wlk 3 DY6 .... **60** E8
Oakleighs DY8 .... **60** C1
Oakley CV8 .... **129** F1
Oakley Ave Aldridge WS9 ... **30** A5
Tipton DY4 .... **52** A6
Oakley Cl WS13 .... **3** B2
Oakley Ct Bedworth CV12 .. **77** D1
Birmingham B15 .... **85** E5
Oakley Gr WV4 .... **38** D5
Oakley Ho Bromsgrove B60 . **137** A1
Smethwick B66 .... **65** C6
Oakley Rd
Birmingham, Sparkbrook B10 . **87** C2
Birmingham, Stirchley B30 .. **104** B5
Wolverhampton WV4 .... **38** D5
Oakley Wood Dr B91 ...... **107** E4
Oakley Wood Rd CV33 ..... **161** F1
Oakly Rd B97 .... **153** D3
Oakmeadow Cl B33 .... **69** D3
Oakmeadow Way B24 .... **57** D3
Oakmoor Rd CV6 .... **96** A4
Oakmount Cl WS3 .... **14** F3
Oakmount Rd B74 .... **45** A7
Oakridge Cl Redditch B98 .. **154** C7
Willenhall WV12 .... **27** C4
Oakridge Dr WV12 .... **27** C4
Oakridge Rd CV32 .... **157** C4
Oakroyd Cres CV10 .... **72** D7
Oaks Cres WS3 .... **25** A1
Oaks Dr Cannock WS11 ...... **1** C1
Featherstone WV10 .... **11** F8
Wolverhampton WV3 .... **25** B2
Wombourne WV5 .... **49** A5
Oaks Pl CV6 .... **96** A3
Oaks Prec CV8 .... **147** E3
Oaks Rd CV8 .... **147** E2
Oaks The Bedworth CV12 ... **77** F2
Birmingham B34 .... **69** B7
4 Royal Leamington Spa
CV32 .... **161** D8
Sutton Coldfield B76 .... **47** A3
Wolverhampton,
Merridale WV3 .... **25** A2
Wolverhampton,
New Cross WV11 .... **26** B5
Oakslade Dr B92 .... **107** E8
Oakthorpe Dr B37 .... **69** F5
Oakthorpe Gdns B69 .... **52** A2
Oaktree Cl B48 .... **139** A7

Oaktree Farm Mobile
Homes Pk B94 .... **141** B7
Oakwood Cl Brownhills WS9 . **15** E4
Essington WV11 .... **13** B3
Shenstone WS14 .... **18** A6
Oakwood Cres DY2 .... **61** F6
Oakwood Ct B63 .... **83** A4
Oakwood Dr
Birmingham B14 .... **104** D4
Sutton Coldfield B74 .... **44** E8
Oakwood Gr CV34 .... **156** A1
Oakwood Rd Birmingham
B11 .... **87** C3
Hollywood B47 .... **125** A6
Smethwick B67 .... **64** F4
Sutton Coldfield B73 .... **45** E1
Walsall WS3 .... **28** E7
Oakwood Specl Sch WS9 ... **16** A3
Oakwood St B70 .... **53** B5
Oakwoods WS11 .... **4** D8
Oakworth Cl CV2 .... **114** F8
Oast Ho B8 .... **68** D4
Oasthouse Cl
Kingswinford DY6 .... **60** A7
Stoke Heath B60 .... **150** D6
Oaston Rd Birmingham B36 .. **69** D8
Nuneaton CV11 .... **73** D4
Oatfield Cl WS7 .... **7** A4
Oatlands Way WV6 .... **23** D3
Oatlands Wlk 3 B14 ...... **104** C2
Oatmill Cl WS10 .... **41** E5
Oban Dr CV10 .... **73** A2
Oban Rd Coventry CV6 ...... **95** F5
Hinckley LE10 .... **75** A7
Solihull B92 .... **88** F1
Oberon Cl Birmingham B45 .. **102** A2
Nuneaton CV11 .... **74** A1
Royal Leamington Spa CV34 . **161** E4
Oberon Dr B90 .... **106** B1
Occupation Rd
Brownhills WS8 .... **16** A4
Coventry CV2 .... **114** C3
Occupation St DY1 .... **51** A2
Ockam Croft B31 .... **103** C2
Ocker Hill Inf Sch DY4 ...... **52** C8
Ocker Hill Jun Sch DY4 ..... **41** C1
Ocker Hill Rd DY4 .... **52** C8
Oddicombe Croft CV3 ..... **133** D5
Oddingley Ct B23 .... **56** C3
Oddingley Rd B31 .... **103** C2
Odell Cres WS3 .... **28** C7
Odell Pl B5 .... **86** C5
Odell Rd WS3 .... **28** B7
Odell Way WS3 .... **28** B7
Odensil Gn B92 .... **89** B2
Odiham Cl B79 .... **21** C7
Odin Cl WS11 .... **2** A5
Odnall La DY9 .... **99** F3
Odstone Dr LE10 .... **74** F8
Offa Dr CV8 .... **148** A4
Offa Rd CV31 .... **162** B5
Offa St B79 .... **21** B5
Offa's Dr WV6 .... **23** E5
Offadrive CV31 .... **21** C5
Offchurch La CV31 .... **162** F6
Offchurch Rd CV32 .... **157** E4
Offenham Cl B98 .... **154** B6
Offenham Covert 5 B38 .. **123** E8
Offenham Ho 3 B7 .... **67** A4
Offini Cl B70 .... **53** F2
Offmoor Rd B32 .... **102** B8
Offmore Farm Cl DY10 .... **117** C6
Offmore Fst Sch DY10 .... **117** B6
Offmore La DY10 .... **117** A6
Offmore Rd DY10 .... **116** F6
Ogbury Cl B14 .... **104** C2
Ogley Cres WS8 .... **16** A7
Ogley Dr B75 .... **47** A5
Ogley Hay Rd
Burntwood,
Chase Terrace WS7 .... **7** B8
Burntwood,
New Town WS7, WS8 .... **7** A3
Ogley Hey Jun Mixed Sch
WS8 .... **15** F8
Ogley Rd WS8 .... **16** A7
Okeefe Cl B11 .... **87** B6
Okehampton Rd CV3 ...... **133** E5
Okement Dr WV11 .... **26** C5
Oken Ct CV35 .... **160** D8
Oken Rd CV34 .... **160** D8
Olaf Pl CV2 .... **115** A7
Old Abbey Gdns B17 .... **85** D4
Old Acre Cl B76 .... **57** D6
Old Bakery Ct DY9 .... **99** A5
Old Bank Pl B72 .... **46** C5
Old Bank Rd B31 .... **103** B2
Old Barn Rd
Birmingham B30 .... **103** D6
Stourbridge DY8 .... **61** A1
Old Beeches B23 .... **56** C8
Old Bell Rd B23 .... **57** B6
Old Birchills WS2 .... **28** C3
Old Birmingham Rd
Alvechurch B48 .... **139** B8
Catshill B60 .... **137** C8
Marlbrook B45 .... **121** E1
Old Bridge St B19 .... **66** C6
Old Bridge Wlk B65 .... **62** F5
Old Bromford La B8 .... **68** C6
Old Brookside B33 .... **68** E2
Old Budbrooke Rd CV35 .. **160** A7
Old Bush St DY5 .... **61** E3
Old Camp Hill B12 .... **87** A8
Old Canal Wlk DY4 .... **52** B5
Old Castle Gr WS8 .... **6** F2
Old Chapel Rd B67 .... **64** F3

Old Chapel Wlk B68 .... **64** A3
Old Chester Rd S DY10 .... **116** E2
Old Church CE Prim Sch
WS3 .... **41** C6
Old Church Ct B17 .... **85** B5
Old Church Gn B33 .... **68** E2
Old Church Rd
Birmingham B17 .... **85** B4
Coventry CV6 .... **96** A1
Water Orton B46 .... **59** B3
Old Crescent Ct 11 B68 ... **84** B8
Old Crest Ave B98 .... **153** E2
Old Croft La B34 .... **69** C7
Old Cross St DY4 .... **51** E5
Old Crown Cl B32 .... **84** B1
Old Crown Mews CV2 .... **96** D5
Old Damson La B92 .... **90** A2
Old Dominion Wks WV1 .... **40** A7
Old End La WV14 .... **51** C7
Old Fallings Cres WV10 .... **25** F6
Old Fallings La WV10 ...... **25** F8
Old Fallow Ave WS11 .... **1** E3
Old Fallow Rd WS11 .... **1** E3
Old Falls Cl WS6 .... **4** D3
Old Farm Gr B14 .... **105** D5
Old Farm Mdw WV3 .... **38** C8
Old Farm Rd B33 .... **68** E4
Old Field Rd WS10 .... **41** E1
Old Fordrove B76 .... **46** D3
Old Forest Way B34 .... **69** B6
Old Forge Dr B98 .... **159** C8
Old Forge Trad Est DY9 .... **81** E6
Old Grange Rd B11 .... **87** C4
Old Green La CV8 .... **129** C1
Old Grove Gdns DY9 .... **81** D3
Old Hall Cl DY8 .... **81** A8
Old Hall La Norton Canes
WS11 .... **5** B7
Walsall WS9 .... **44** B8
Old Hall Sch WS2 .... **27** E5
Old Hall St WV1 .... **163** C2
Old Ham La DY9 .... **81** D2
Old Hampton La WV10 ...... **12** C2
Old Hawne La B63 .... **83** A5
Old Heath Cres WV1 .... **26** A1
Old Heath Rd WV1 .... **26** A2
Old Hedging La B77 .... **35** D5
Old Hednesford Rd WS11 ... **2** E2
Old Hill WV6 .... **24** D5
Old Hill Ind Est WS3 .... **28** C8
Old Hill Prim Sch B64 ...... **62** F1
Old Hill Sta B64 .... **83** A8
Old Hinckley Rd CV10 ...... **73** D5
Old Hobicus La B68 .... **64** B5
Old Horns Cres B44 .... **44** C2
Old House La Corley CV7 ... **94** A7
Romsley B62 .... **101** B1
Old Kingsbury Rd B76 ...... **58** C5
Old La Featherstone WV10 .. **12** C7
Rowney Green B48 .... **140** D4
Walsall WS3 .... **28** C8
Wolverhampton WV6 .... **23** F2
Old Landywood La WV11 .... **13** D7
Old Langley Hall B75 .... **47** C4
Old Level Way DY2 .... **62** D4
Old Lime Gdns B38 .... **123** E8
Old Lindens Cl B74 .... **44** E7
Old Lode La B92 .... **89** C3
Old London Rd WS14 .... **9** D1
Old Manor Cl B78 .... **34** E5
Old Manor Flats WV6 .... **24** D5
Old Meadow Rd B31 ...... **123** C7
Old Meeting Rd WV14 ...... **51** C8
Old Meeting St B70 .... **53** B5
Old Meeting Yd CV12 .... **78** B3
Old Mill Ave CV4 .... **132** D5
Old Mill Cl B90 .... **105** D2
Old Mill Gdns
Birmingham B33 .... **68** E2
Walsall WS4 .... **15** C2
Old Mill Gr B20 .... **55** C2
Old Mill Rd B46 .... **70** F7
Old Milverton CV32 .... **156** C3
Old Milverton La CV32 .... **156** E5
Old Milverton Rd CV32 .... **156** C2
Old Moat Dr B31 .... **103** B3
Old Moat Way B8 .... **68** B6
Old Oak Cl WS9 .... **30** B8
Old Oak Rd B38 .... **104** A2
Old Oscott Hill B44 .... **44** F2
Old Oscott La B44 .... **55** E8
Old Park Cl B6 .... **66** E7
Old Park Ind Est WS10 ..... **41** E4
Old Park La B69 .... **64** A5
Old Park Prim Sch WS10 ... **41** E5
Old Park Rd Dudley DY1 .... **51** A5
Wednesbury WS10 .... **41** F4
Old Park Special Sch DY1 .. **61** F8
Old Park Wlk B6 .... **66** E7
Old Penkridge Mews WS11 .. **1** D1
Old Penkridge Rd WS11 ..... **1** C2
Old Penn's Yd CV12 .... **78** A2
Old Pk B29 .... **103** A5
Old Pl WS3 .... **28** C8
Old Pleck Rd WS2 .... **42** C7
Old Port Cl DY4 .... **52** B2
Old Portway B38 .... **123** E7
Old Postway B19 .... **66** D7
Old Quarry Cl B45 .... **121** F8
Old Quarry Dr DY3 .... **50** D5
Old Rd CV7 .... **92** E1
Old Rectory Gdns WS9 ..... **30** C6
Old Rectory La B48 ...... **139** B7
Old School Cl WV13 .... **27** A1
Old School Mews CV32 .... **157** B3
Old Scott Cl B33 .... **69** C2
Old Smithy Pl B18 .... **66** A5
Old Snow Hill B3, B4,B19 . **164** B4

Old Sq **1** CV34 ...... 160 E6
Old Sq The **1** WS1 ...... 28 E1
Old Square B4 ...... 164 C3
Old Stables Wlk **2** B7 ... 67 C7
Old Stafford Rd WV10 ...... 11 C8
Old Station Rd
  Birmingham B33 ...... 68 D4
  Bromsgrove B60 ...... 137 A1
  Hampton in A B92 ...... 109 A8
Old Stone Cl B45 ...... 101 F1
Old Stone Yd CV32 ...... 156 E1
Old Stowheath La WV1 ...... 26 C1
Old Swinford Hospital Sch
  DY8 ...... 81 A4
Old Tokengate **2** B17 ... 85 D6
Old Town Cl B38 ...... 103 F2
Old Town La WS3 ...... 14 F3
Old Vicarage Cl Walsall
  WS3 ...... 15 A2
  Wombourne WV5 ...... 49 B7
Old Walsall Rd B42 ...... 54 F7
Old Warstone La WV13 ... 38 B6
Old Warwick Rd **1** B92 ... 88 E1
Old Warwick Rd
  Lapworth B94, CV35 ...... 144 D3
  Royal Leamington Spa CV31 . 161 E7
  Solihull B92 ...... 88 E1
Old Wharf Rd DY8 ...... 80 F6
Old Winnings Rd CV7 ... 94 F6
Oldacre Rd B68 ...... 84 A7
Oldany Way CV10 ...... 72 F2
Oldberrow Cl **4** B90 ... 127 A6
Oldbury Cl B98 ...... 154 B6
Oldbury Green Ret Pk B69 . 63 F7
Oldbury Ho B68 ...... 64 C2
Oldbury Rd Blackheath B65 .. 63 D2
  Nuneaton CV10 ...... 72 A8
  Smethwick B66 ...... 64 D7
  West Bromwich B70 ...... 52 F2
Oldbury Ring Way B69 ... 63 F8
Oldbury Road Ind Est
  Smethwick B66 ...... 64 D7
  West Bromwich B70 ...... 52 F2
Oldbury St WS10 ...... 42 B3
Olde Hall Rd WV10 ...... 12 C7
Oldfallings Inf & Jun Schs
  WV10 ...... 26 A8
Oldfield Dr DY8 ...... 81 A2
Oldfield Rd Birmingham B12 .. 87 A6
  Coventry CV5 ...... 112 C3
  Dudley WV14 ...... 51 A8
Oldfields Blackheath B64 ... 82 D8
  Hagley DY9 ...... 99 B6
Oldham Ave CV2 ...... 114 E4
Oldhouse Farm Cl B28 ... 105 F6
Oldington Gr B91 ...... 127 B8
Oldington Trad Est DY11 ... 116 B1
Oldknow Jun Sch B10 ... 87 E7
Oldknow Rd B10 ...... 87 E7
Oldnall Cl DY9 ...... 81 F4
Oldnall Rd
  Kidderminster DY10 ...... 117 A4
  Stourbridge B63, DY9 ...... 82 A4
Oldswinford Prim Sch DY8 .. 81 A3
Oldway Dr B91 ...... 107 E2
Oldwich La E Honiley CV8 ... 145 E8
  Knowle CV8 ...... 129 D1
Oldwich La W B93 ...... 145 C8
Olga Dr DY4 ...... 41 B1
Olinthus Ave WV11 ...... 26 E7
Olive Ave Coventry CV2 ... 114 D5
  Wolverhampton WV4 ...... 39 E5
Olive Dr B62 ...... 83 C8
Olive Hill Prim Sch B62 ... 83 D7
Olive Hill Rd B62 ...... 83 D8
Olive La B62 ...... 83 D8
Olive Mount B69 ...... 63 D8
Olive Pl B14 ...... 104 E7
Oliver Cl **1** DY2 ...... 62 E8
Oliver Cres WV14 ...... 40 F2
Oliver Ct B65 ...... 63 B2
Oliver Rd
  Birmingham, Erdington B23 ... 56 F6
  Birmingham, Ladywood B16 ... 65 F2
  Smethwick B66 ...... 65 C3
Oliver St Birmingham B7 ... 67 B5
  Coventry CV6 ...... 113 F6
Olivier Way CV2 ...... 115 B8
Ollerton Rd B26 ...... 88 F7
Ollison Dr B74 ...... 30 F2
Olliver Cl B62 ...... 84 A3
Olorenshaw Rd B26 ...... 89 D5
Olton Ave CV5 ...... 111 E4
Olton Bridge B92 ...... 106 F8
Olton Bvd E B27 ...... 88 C2
Olton Bvd W B11 ...... 87 F3
Olton Croft B27 ...... 88 D2
Olton Mere B92 ...... 88 E1
Olton Pl CV11 ...... 72 F4
Olton Rd B90 ...... 106 B5
Olton Sta B92 ...... 88 E1
Olton Wharf B92 ...... 88 E2
Olympus Ave CV34 ...... 161 D5
Olympus Cl CV5 ...... 111 B8
Omar Rd CV2 ...... 114 D2
Ombersley Cl Oldbury B69 ... 63 F5
  Redditch B98 ...... 159 C7
Ombersley Ho **4** B38 ... 103 D2
Ombersley Rd
  Birmingham B12 ...... 87 A6
  Halesowen B63 ...... 82 F2
One Stop Sh Ctr B42 ...... 55 D3
Onibury Rd B21 ...... 54 D1
Onley Terr CV4 ...... 132 C7
Onslow Cres B92 ...... 89 A1
Onslow Croft CV32 ...... 156 F2
Onslow Rd B11 ...... 88 A4
Ontario Cl B38 ...... 124 A8

Oozells St B1 ...... 66 C2
Oozells St N B16 ...... 66 B2
Open Field Cl B31 ...... 103 C2
Openfield Croft B46 ...... 59 C2
Orangery The DY9 ...... 99 D7
Oratory Dr CV3 ...... 134 C6
Oratory Prim Sch B16 ... 65 F2
Orchard Ave Cannock WS11 ... 1 C1
  Solihull B91 ...... 107 D5
Orchard Cl Birmingham B21 .. 54 F1
  Blackheath B65 ...... 63 A3
  Cheslyn Hay WS6 ...... 4 E3
  Coleshill B46 ...... 70 F7
  Curdworth B76 ...... 59 B7
  Hagley DY9 ...... 99 B4
  Halesowen B63 ...... 82 C6
  Hinckley LE10 ...... 76 A5
  Nuneaton CV10 ...... 72 B7
  Sutton Coldfield B73 ...... 57 A8
  Tamworth B77 ...... 35 C5
  Walsall WS4 ...... 29 C5
  Willenhall WV13 ...... 27 B1
Orchard Cres Coventry CV3 133 C8
  Stoke Prior B60 ...... 150 C3
  Wolverhampton WV3 ...... 38 B7
Orchard Croft B45 ...... 138 D8
Orchard Ct
  Birmingham, Erdington B24 ... 57 A5
  Birmingham,
    Stockland Green B23 ...... 56 B4
  Blackheath B65 ...... 63 B3
  Coventry CV3 ...... 115 A1
  Kingswinford DY6 ...... 60 D6
  Wolverhampton WV3 ...... 38 B7
Orchard Dr Birmingham
  B31 ...... 122 F7
  Coventry CV5 ...... 111 C4
  Dudley DY3 ...... 50 B3
  Sutton Coldfield B73 ...... 31 F3
  Wolverhampton WV4 ...... 39 A4
Orchard Ho CV6 ...... 96 A4
Orchard La Codsall WV8 ... 10 B3
  Stourbridge DY9 ...... 81 E6
Orchard Meadow Wlk B35 .. 58 B3
Orchard Pl B80 ...... 159 F8
Orchard Rd Birmingham B24 . 57 B5
  Bromsgrove B61 ...... 136 F4
  Dudley DY2 ...... 62 C2
  Tanworth-in-A B94 ...... 143 C6
  Walsall WS5 ...... 43 B3
  Willenhall WV13 ...... 27 B1
  Wolverhampton WV11 ...... 26 C7
Orchard Rise B26 ...... 88 F7
Orchard St Bedworth CV12 .. 78 B4
  Brierley Hill DY5 ...... 61 D4
  Hinckley LE10 ...... 75 B8
  Kidderminster DY10 ...... 116 E6
  Nuneaton CV11 ...... 73 D4
  Redditch B98 ...... 153 E3
  Tamworth, Kettlebrook B77 ... 21 C3
  Tamworth, The Leys B79 ... 21 B5
  Tipton DY4 ...... 51 F2
Orchard The Bilston WV14 .. 40 E5
  Birmingham B37 ...... 89 F8
  Walsall WS3 ...... 14 D2
  Wolverhampton WV6 ...... 24 E6
Orchard Tower B1 ...... 102 F7
Orchard Villas Fairfield
  B61 ...... 120 D2
  Wythall B47 ...... 124 F1
Orchard Way
  Birmingham,
    Acock's Green B27 ...... 88 B4
  Birmingham,
    Balsall Heath B12 ...... 86 E6
  Birmingham,
    Great Barr B43 ...... 43 F1
  Hollywood B47 ...... 125 A8
  Nuneaton CV10 ...... 72 C6
  Studley B80 ...... 159 E2
Orchards The
  Cheswick Green B90 ...... 126 D4
  Hollywood B47 ...... 125 A7
  Sutton Coldfield B74 ...... 46 A8
Orcheston Wlk B14 ...... 104 D2
Orchid Cl B66 ...... 64 D7
Orchid Dr B19 ...... 66 D6
Ordnance Rd CV6 ...... 113 E5
Oregon Cl DY6 ...... 60 F6
Oregon Dr WV12 ...... 27 E7
Oregon Gdns WS7 ...... 6 F8
Oregon Ho **3** B36 ...... 57 F1
Orford Gr B21 ...... 65 C8
Oriel Cl Cannock WS11 ...... 4 E8
  Dudley DY1 ...... 50 E2
Oriel Dr WV10 ...... 11 D3
Oriel Ho B37 ...... 70 A3
Oriel Villas **4** B11 ...... 87 C5
Oriole Gr DY10 ...... 117 B2
Orion Cl Birmingham B8 ... 68 B4
  Great Wyrley WS6 ...... 4 F1
Orion Cres CV2 ...... 96 E2
Orion Way WS11 ...... 1 F5
Orkney Ave B34 ...... 68 F7
Orkney Cl Hinckley LE10 ... 71 C1
  Nuneaton CV10 ...... 73 A2
Orkney Croft B36 ...... 70 B7
Orlando Cl WS1 ...... 42 E8
Orlando Ho **4** WS1 ...... 42 E8
Orlescote Rd CV4 ...... 132 C6
Ormande Cl B63 ...... 82 B7
Orme Cl DY5 ...... 81 B8
Ormes La WV6 ...... 24 C3
Ormond Pl WV14 ...... 40 F6
Ormond Rd B45 ...... 101 F1
Ormonde Cl B63 ...... 82 D6
Ormsby Gr B27 ...... 106 A2

Ormscliffe Rd B45 ...... 122 B6
Orphanage Rd B24 ...... 57 B6
Orpington Dr CV6 ...... 95 D4
Orpington Rd B44 ...... 44 E3
Orpwood Rd B33 ...... 69 B2
Orslow Wlk WV10 ...... 26 A5
Orton Ave B76 ...... 58 A6
Orton Gr WV4 ...... 38 D4
Orton La WV4, WV5 ...... 38 A2
Orton Rd CV6 ...... 95 D4
Orton Way B35 ...... 58 A1
Orwell Cl Nuneaton CV10 .. 72 A5
  Stourbridge DY8 ...... 80 D4
  Wednesfield WV11 ...... 26 F5
Orwell Ct CV1 ...... 165 C4
Orwell Dr Birmingham B38 .. 123 C8
  West Bromwich B71 ...... 53 D6
Orwell Pas B5 ...... 164 C2
Orwell Rd Coventry CV1 ... 113 F1
  Walsall WS1 ...... 43 B8
Osbaston Cl Coventry CV5 .. 111 E4
  Hinckley LE10 ...... 71 F3
Osberton Dr DY1 ...... 50 F2
Osborn Ct B73 ...... 46 B1
Osborn Rd B11 ...... 87 C6
Osborne B79 ...... 20 D7
Osborne Cl Birmingham B6 ... 67 A7
  Brierley Hill DY5 ...... 81 F8
  Kidderminster DY10 ...... 117 B6
Osborne Ct CV31 ...... 162 A4
Osborne Dr WS10 ...... 41 D8
Osborne Gr B19 ...... 66 C7
Osborne Jun & Inf Sch
  B23 ...... 57 A5
Osborne Rd
  Birmingham, Erdington B23 ... 56 F5
  Birmingham,
    Handsworth B21 ...... 65 F8
  Coventry CV5 ...... 133 A8
  West Bromwich B70 ...... 53 C3
  Wolverhampton WV4 ...... 38 F5
Osborne Rd S **1** B23 ...... 56 F4
Osborne Tower B6 ...... 67 A8
Osbourne Croft B90 ...... 126 D5
Oscott Cir B6 ...... 56 F3
Oscott Coll B73 ...... 45 D1
Oscott Ct B23 ...... 56 E3
Oscott Gdns B42 ...... 55 E3
Oscott Rd B42 ...... 55 F5
Oscott School La B44 ...... 44 E2
Osier Gr B23 ...... 56 B6
Osier Pl WV1 ...... 25 F2
Osier St WV1 ...... 25 F2
Osler St B16 ...... 65 F2
Oslo Gdns CV2 ...... 115 A7
Osmaston Rd
  Birmingham B17 ...... 85 B3
  Stourbridge DY8 ...... 80 F2
Osmington Cl B63 ...... 82 D6
Osnor Ct B60 ...... 151 B7
Osprey B77 ...... 36 A6
Osprey Cl Coventry CV2 ... 115 B6
  Nuneaton CV11 ...... 73 B4
Osprey Dr DY1 ...... 51 A1
Osprey Ho B80 ...... 159 D4
Osprey Park Dr DY10 ...... 117 B3
Osprey Rd B27 ...... 88 D2
Ostler Cl DY6 ...... 60 B7
Oswald Rd **2** CV32 ...... 161 D8
Oswald St B98 ...... 153 E3
Oswestry Cl B97 ...... 158 C7
Oswestry Ct B11 ...... 87 B6
Other Rd B98 ...... 153 E4
Otley Gr B9 ...... 68 C3
Ottawa Tower **2** B5 ...... 86 D7
Otter Croft B34 ...... 69 D5
Otterburn Cl WS12 ...... 2 E2
Otterstone Cl DY3 ...... 39 C2
Ottery B77 ...... 36 B5
Oughton Rd B12 ...... 87 A7
Oulsham Ct **11** B13 ...... 87 B2
Oulton Cl DY11 ...... 116 D8
Oundle Rd B44 ...... 55 F7
Ounsdale Cres WV5 ...... 49 A7
Ounsdale Dr DY2 ...... 62 C4
Ounsdale Rd WV5 ...... 49 A7
Ounty John La DY8 ...... 81 A1
Our Lady & Kenelms RC
  Sch B63 ...... 83 A4
Our Lady of Compassion
  RC Prim Sch B92 ...... 106 D7
Our Lady of Fatima RC
  Sch B17 ...... 84 F7
Our Lady of Lourdes RC
  Inf & Jun Sch B13 ...... 105 D5
Our Lady of the Angels
  RC Fst Sch CV11 ...... 73 C3
Our Lady of the
  Assumption RC Prim Sch
  CV4 ...... 111 E1
Our Lady Of the Wayside
  RC Prim Sch B90 ...... 126 C8
Our Lady & St Chad's RC
  Sch WV10 ...... 25 F7
Our Lady & St Rose of
  Lima RC Jun &Inf Sch
  B29 ...... 103 B8
Our Lady & St Rose of
  Lima Sch B29 ...... 85 B1
Our Lady & St Rose RC
  Prim Sch B29 ...... 103 A8
Our Lady & St Teresa's
  RC Comb Sch CV32 ...... 157 D1

Our Lady's RC Jun & Inf
  Sch B33 ...... 69 D2
Outermarch Rd CV6 ...... 113 C7
Outfields B13 ...... 104 E6
Outlands Dr LE10 ...... 71 B2
Outmore Rd B33 ...... 69 B1
Outwood Cl B98 ...... 158 E7
Oval Rd Birmingham B24 ... 56 E1
  Tipton DY4 ...... 51 F6
Oval The Dudley DY1 ...... 61 E8
  Smethwick B67 ...... 64 D2
  Wednesbury WS10 ...... 41 F4
Over Brunton Cl B31 ...... 103 B2
Over Green Dr B37 ...... 69 F5
Over Mill Dr B29 ...... 86 B2
Over Pool Rd B8 ...... 68 A6
Over St CV6 ...... 114 A8
Overbare Cl B94 ...... 142 A1
Overberry Cl CV2 ...... 96 D2
Overbrook Cl DY3 ...... 50 C2
Overbury Cl
  Birmingham B31 ...... 103 C3
  Halesowen B63 ...... 83 B2
Overbury Rd B31 ...... 103 C3
Overdale B96 ...... 158 E1
Overdale Ave B76 ...... 57 F6
Overdale Cl WS2 ...... 27 C3
Overdale Ct B13 ...... 86 F4
Overdale Dr WS2 ...... 27 D3
Overdale Rd Birmingham
  B32 ...... 84 E5
  Coventry CV5 ...... 112 C3
Overell Gr CV32 ...... 156 D2
Overend Rd B63, B64 ...... 82 D7
Overend St B70 ...... 53 D2
Overfield Dr WV14 ...... 40 A3
Overfield Rd Birmingham
  B32 ...... 84 F1
  Dudley DY1 ...... 61 E8
Overhill Rd WS7 ...... 7 B5
Overlea Ave B27 ...... 88 B3
Overmoor Cl B19 ...... 66 C7
Overseal Rd WV11 ...... 26 E8
Overslade Cres CV6 ...... 112 E8
Overslade Rd B91 ...... 106 F2
Oversley Rd B76 ...... 58 A6
Overton Cl B28 ...... 106 A6
Overton Dr B46 ...... 59 C3
Overton Gr B27 ...... 106 C8
Overton La WS7 ...... 7 C4
Overton Pl Birmingham B7 ... 67 A3
  West Bromwich B71 ...... 53 D6
Overton Rd B27 ...... 106 C8
Overton Wlk WV4 ...... 38 C6
Overtons Cl CV31 ...... 162 F5
Overwood Croft B8 ...... 67 E3
Overwoods Rd B77 ...... 36 A4
Owen Pl WV14 ...... 40 D6
Owen Rd Bilston WV14 ...... 40 D6
  Willenhall WV13 ...... 41 C8
  Wolverhampton WV3 ...... 39 A8
Owen Road Ind Est WV13 ... 27 C1
Owen St Darlaston WS10 ... 41 D7
  Dudley DY2 ...... 62 E8
  Tipton DY4 ...... 51 E5
Owenford Rd CV6 ...... 113 C7
Owens Croft B38 ...... 104 A1
Owens Way B64 ...... 63 A1
Ownall Rd B34 ...... 69 C6
Ox Cl CV2 ...... 114 A6
Ox Leasow B32 ...... 84 C2
Ox Leys Rd B75, B76 ...... 47 D3
Ox St DY3 ...... 50 D5
Oxbarn Ave WV3 ...... 38 E7
Oxendon Way CV3 ...... 134 E8
Oxenton Croft B63 ...... 82 D2
Oxford Cl Birmingham B8 ... 68 B5
  Great Wyrley WS6 ...... 4 F3
  Nuneaton CV11 ...... 73 B8
Oxford Dr Birmingham B27 .. 88 D4
  Stourbridge DY8 ...... 80 F4
Oxford Gn WS11 ...... 4 F8
Oxford Pl **12** CV32 ...... 156 F1
Oxford Rd
  Birmingham,
    Acock's Green B27 ...... 88 C3
  Birmingham, Erdington B23 ... 56 F4
  Birmingham, Moseley B13 ... 87 A2
  Cannock WS11 ...... 4 F8
  Ryton-on-D CV8 ...... 134 F1
  Smethwick B66 ...... 65 A7
  West Bromwich B70 ...... 53 B3
Oxford Row **14** CV32 ...... 156 F1
Oxford St Bilston WV14 ... 40 F5
  Birmingham, Digbeth B5 ... 164 C2
  Birmingham, Stirchley B30 .. 104 A7
  Coventry CV1 ...... 113 E3
  Dudley DY1 ...... 51 B1
  Kidderminster DY10 ...... 116 E5
  Royal Leamington Spa CV32 . 156 F1
  Walsall WS2 ...... 42 C7
  Wednesbury WS10 ...... 42 B3
  Wolverhampton WV1 ...... 163 D2
Oxford Street Ind Pk
  WV14 ...... 40 F5
Oxford Street Island WV14 . 40 F5
Oxford Terr WS10 ...... 42 B2
Oxford Trad Est B5 ...... 164 D2
Oxhayes Cl CV7 ...... 130 C6
Oxhill Cl B98 ...... 154 A1
Oxhill Rd Birmingham B21 ... 54 E2
  Solihull B90 ...... 105 C2
Oxleasow Rd B98 ...... 154 E4
Oxley Ave WV10 ...... 25 C6
Oxley Cl Dudley DY2 ...... 62 B2
  Great Wyrley WS6 ...... 4 F1
Oxley Dr CV3 ...... 133 C2
Oxley Gr B29 ...... 103 A8

Oxley La WV1 ...... 163 B4
Oxley Links Rd WV10 ...... 25 B8
Oxley Moor Rd WV10 ...... 25 A8
Oxley Prim Sch WV10 ...... 25 C7
Oxley St WV1 ...... 25 C4
Oxlip Cl WS5 ...... 43 A3
Oxpiece Dr B36 ...... 68 D8
Oxstall Cl B76 ...... 58 D5
Oxted Cl WV11 ...... 26 F5
Oxted Croft B23 ...... 56 E3
Oxwood La B32 ...... 101 D4
Oxygen St B7 ...... 164 D4
Pace Cres WV14 ...... 41 A2
Packhorse La B47 ...... 124 E6
Packington Ave
  Allesley CV5 ...... 112 B6
  Birmingham B34 ...... 69 D5
Packington Ct B74 ...... 31 E4
Packington La
  Little Packington CV7 ...... 91 C6
  Outwoods B46, CV7 ...... 92 B8
  Weeford B78 ...... 19 F5
  White Stitch CV7 ...... 92 A3
Packington Pl **4** CV31 ... 162 A7
Packmore St CV34 ...... 160 F8
Packwood Cl
  Bentley Heath B93 ...... 127 E4
  Birmingham B20 ...... 55 A2
  Redditch B97 ...... 152 F1
  Royal Leamington Spa
    CV31 ...... 162 C5
  Willenhall WV13 ...... 40 F8
Packwood Cotts B93 ...... 127 C5
Packwood Ct B91 ...... 107 C5
Packwood Dr B43 ...... 43 D1
Packwood Gn CV5 ...... 112 A3
Packwood Ho
  Birmingham B15 ...... 86 C8
  Sutton Coldfield B73 ...... 46 A3
Packwood House B94 ...... 144 A5
Packwood La B94 ...... 144 A4
Packwood Rd
  Birmingham B26 ...... 89 B8
  Lapworth B94 ...... 144 A4
  Tipton B69 ...... 52 A1
Padarn Cl DY3 ...... 39 C1
Padbury WV9 ...... 11 B3
Padbury Ho B31 ...... 102 E5
Paddester Dr B8 ...... 67 D4
Paddiford Pl CV10 ...... 72 C3
Paddington Rd B21 ...... 54 C1
Paddington Wlk WS2 ...... 27 C1
Paddock Dr Birmingham B26 . 89 A7
  Dorridge B93 ...... 128 A2
Paddock La Aldridge WS9 ... 30 A5
  Great Wyrley WS6 ...... 5 A3
  Redditch B98 ...... 158 E7
  Walsall WS1 ...... 28 F1
Paddock The Bilston WV14 .. 40 E1
  Birmingham B31 ...... 103 C4
  Codsall WV8 ...... 10 A2
  Dudley DY3 ...... 50 E5
  Lichfield WS14 ...... 9 C5
  Perton WV6 ...... 23 D4
  Stoke Heath B60 ...... 150 D6
  Stourbridge DY9 ...... 99 B8
Paddock View WV6 ...... 25 B5
Paddocks Cl B78 ...... 22 F1
Paddocks Gn B18 ...... 66 A5
Paddocks Rd B47 ...... 124 F6
Paddocks The
  Bulkington CV12 ...... 79 B3
  Kenilworth CV8 ...... 148 B5
  Warwick CV34 ...... 160 F7
Paddys Wide Water Est
  DY5 ...... 61 C5
Padgate Cl B35 ...... 58 B3
Padgets La B98 ...... 154 D4
Padmore Ct CV31 ...... 162 B6
Padstow B77 ...... 21 F5
Padstow Cl CV11 ...... 73 F5
Padstow Rd Birmingham
  B24 ...... 57 D4
  Coventry CV4 ...... 131 C3
Paganal Dr B70 ...... 53 E1
Paganel Dr DY1 ...... 51 C3
Paganel Inf Sch B29 ...... 85 A2
Paganel Jun Sch B29 ...... 85 A2
Paganel Rd B29 ...... 85 A2
Pagat Mews B76 ...... 47 A2
Page Rd CV4 ...... 131 E7
Pageant Ct B12 ...... 86 E5
Pages Cl B75 ...... 46 C5
Pages Ct B43 ...... 43 E1
Pages La B43 ...... 43 E1
Paget Cl Bromsgrove B61 ... 136 E2
  Dudley WV14 ...... 51 B8
Paget Ct CV2 ...... 96 B3
Paget Ho DY4 ...... 52 B3
Paget Jun & Inf Sch B24 ... 57 C4
Paget Rd Birmingham B24 ... 57 D4
  Wolverhampton WV6 ...... 24 E4
Paget St WV1 ...... 163 A4
Pagham Cl WV9 ...... 10 F2
Pagnell Gr B13 ...... 105 C6
Paignton Rd B16 ...... 65 D3
Pailton Cl CV2 ...... 96 C2
Pailton Gr B29 ...... 85 B1
Pailton Rd B90 ...... 106 B5
Painswick Cl Redditch B98 .. 158 E6
  Walsall WS5 ...... 43 B3
Painswick Rd B28 ...... 105 F7
Paint Cup Row DY2 ...... 62 C2
Painters Cnr **8** B66 ...... 65 C5

Pake's Croft 🖪 CV6 .... 113 A5
Pakefield Rd B30 .... 104 C3
Pakenham Cl B76 .... 57 F8
Pakenham Ho B76 .... 57 F8
Pakenham Rd B15 .... 86 C7
Pakenham Village B15 .... 86 C7
Pakfield Wlk B6 .... 66 F8
Palace Cl B65 .... 63 D4
Palace Dr B66 .... 64 D8
Palace Rd B9 .... 67 E1
Pale La B17 .... 84 F8
Pale St DY3 .... 50 E5
Palefield Rd B90 .... 126 F6
Palermo Ave CV3 .... 133 E6
Palethorpe Rd DY4 .... 52 A8
Palfrey Jun & Inf Schs
  WS1 .... 42 D7
Palfrey Rd DY8 .... 80 D5
Pallasades Sh Ctr The
  B2 .... 164 B2
Pallett Dr CV11 .... 73 F7
Palm Croft DY5 .... 81 C8
Palm Tree Ave CV2 .... 96 C2
Palmcourt Ave B28 .... 105 E7
Palmer Cl WV11 .... 12 F1
Palmer La CV1 .... 165 B3
Palmer Rd Hinckley LE10 ... 71 B2
  Whitnash V31 .... 162 B4
Palmer St B9 .... 67 A2
Palmers Cl Codsall WV8 ..... 10 C1
  Solihull B90 .... 106 B5
Palmers Cross Prim Sch
  WV6 .... 24 D8
Palmers Gr B36 .... 68 E8
Palmers Rd B98 .... 154 F5
Palmers Way WV8 .... 10 C1
Palmerston Dr B69 .... 52 D2
Palmerston Rd
  Birmingham B11 .... 87 B6
  Coventry CV5 .... 132 F8
Palmvale Croft B26 .... 89 A7
Palomino Pl B16 .... 65 F2
Pamela Rd B31 .... 103 A3
Pan Croft B36 .... 68 C7
Pancras Cl CV2 .... 96 E1
Pandora Rd CV2 .... 114 E7
Pangbourne Cl CV11 .... 73 F8
Pangbourne Rd CV2 .... 114 C8
Pangfield Pk CV5 .... 112 C4
Panjab Gdns B67 .... 64 F6
Pannel Croft B19 .... 66 D6
Panther Croft B34 .... 69 D5
Papenham Gn CV4 .... 132 A8
Paper Mill Dr B98 .... 154 B5
Paper Mill End B44 .... 55 D6
Papworth Dr B61 .... 136 F5
Papyrus Way B36 .... 57 F1
Par Gn B38 .... 103 D1
Parade Birmingham B1 ..... 164 A3
  Royal Leamington Spa
  CV32 .... 161 F8
Parade The Birmingham B37 . 70 A5
  Blackheath B64 .... 82 E8
  Brownhills WS8 .... 6 E1
  Dudley DY1 .... 51 B2
  🖪 Hinckley LE10 .... 75 D8
  Kingswinford DY6 .... 60 B7
  Nuneaton CV11 .... 73 C3
  Sutton Coldfield B72 .... 46 B5
Parade View WS8 .... 15 E8
Paradise DY2 .... 62 D8
Paradise Circus
  Queensway B1, B3 .... 164 A2
Paradise Ct B28 .... 105 D6
Paradise Ho CV6 .... 113 F7
Paradise La Birmingham
  B28 .... 105 E6
  Walsall WS3 .... 14 F3
  Wolverhampton WV10 ..... 11 E8
Paradise Row B60 .... 136 F2
Paradise St Birmingham B3 . 164 B2
  Coventry CV1 .... 165 C1
  Warwick CV34 .... 160 F8
  West Bromwich B70 .... 53 C3
Paradise CV7 .... 97 B1
Paragon Way CV7 .... 96 B8
Parbrook Cl CV4 .... 131 E8
Parbury B77 .... 35 D5
Parchments The WS13 .... 3 B1
Pardington Cl B92 .... 107 E8
Pargeter Ct 🖪 WS2 .... 28 C2
Pargeter Rd B67 .... 64 F2
Pargeter St Stourbridge
  DY8 .... 80 F4
  Walsall WS2 .... 28 C3
Parish Gdns DY9 .... 81 C1
Parish Hill B61 .... 120 D1
Parisienne Ho CV5 .... 112 E2
Park App B23 .... 56 C2
Park Ave
  🖪 Birmingham,
  Balsall Heath B12 .... 86 F5
  Birmingham, Hockley B18 . 66 A6
  Birmingham,
  King's Norton B30 .... 104 A5
  Blackheath B65 .... 63 C3
  Burntwood WS7 .... 7 B5
  Coleshill B46 .... 70 F6
  Coventry CV6 .... 95 C3
  Norton Canes WS11 .... 6 A5
  Nuneaton CV11 .... 73 E3
  Oldbury B68 .... 64 A4
  Smethwick B67 .... 64 F4
  Solihull B91 .... 107 D3
  Studley B80 .... 159 E3

Park Ave continued
  Tipton DY4 .... 51 E5
  Willenhall WV13 .... 26 F2
  Wolverhampton WV1 ...... 163 A4
Wolverhampton,
  Goldthorn Park WV4 .... 39 C5
  Wombourne WV5 .... 49 A5
Park Bldgs DY3 .... 50 C4
Park Butts Ringway DY11 . 116 D6
Park Cir B6 .... 66 F7
Park Cl Brownhills WS8 ...... 15 F8
  Cheslyn Hay WS6 .... 4 E3
  Dudley DY1 .... 51 B7
  Kenilworth CV8 .... 148 B5
  Solihull B92 .... 89 D2
  Sutton Coldfield B24 .... 57 D5
  Tipton B69 .... 63 C7
Park Cres
  West Bromwich B71 .... 53 D4
  Wolverhampton WV1 ...... 163 A3
Park Croft B47 .... 125 A5
Park Ct Allesley CV5 .... 112 B6
  Blackheath B65 .... 63 C3
  Kidderminster DY11 .... 116 D5
  Redditch B98 .... 154 A3
  Sutton Coldfield B73 .... 45 F1
Park Dale Ct WV1 .... 25 A3
Park Dale E WV1 .... 25 A3
Park Dale W WV1 .... 25 A3
Park Dr Little Aston B74 .... 31 C4
  Royal Leamington Spa CV31 . 161 E7
  Sutton Coldfield B74 .... 31 F2
  Wolverhampton WV4 .... 39 C5
Park Edge B17 .... 85 C7
Park End WS14 .... 9 E7
Park End Dr B32 .... 84 D1
Park Farm Ind Est B98 ..... 159 C7
Park Farm Rd
  Birmingham B43 .... 44 B3
  Tamworth B77 .... 21 C1
Park Gr Birmingham B10 .... 87 D8
  Water Orton B46 .... 59 C2
Park Hall Cl WS5 .... 43 C6
Park Hall Cres B36 .... 69 C8
Park Hall Inf Sch WS5 ...... 43 C7
Park Hall Jun Sch WS5 ..... 43 C7
Park Hall Rd Walsall WS5 .. 43 D6
  Wolverhampton WV4 .... 39 D5
Park Hall Sch B36 .... 58 E1
Park Head Cres DY2 .... 62 B8
Park Head Rd DY2 .... 62 B8
Park Hill Birmingham B13 .. 86 E4
  Blackheath B65 .... 63 B1
  Kenilworth CV8 .... 148 B5
  Wednesbury WS10 .... 42 C4
Park Hill Cty Mid Sch
  CV8 .... 148 C5
Park Hill Dr B20 .... 54 F4
Park Hill Jun & Inf Sch
  B13 .... 86 F4
Park Hill La Allesley CV5 .. 112 A6
  Coventry CV5 .... 112 A5
Park Hill Prim Sch
  Coventry CV5 .... 112 A4
  Wednesbury WS10 .... 42 C4
Park Hill Rd Birmingham
  B17 .... 85 C6
  Smethwick B67 .... 65 A5
Park Hill St DY2 .... 62 B8
Park Ho 🖪 B66 .... 65 C5
Park Inn DY4 .... 52 A4
Park La Berkswell CV7 ...... 110 B2
  Birmingham B26 .... 90 C4
  Birmingham, Aston B6 ..... 66 F7
  Birmingham, Castle Vale B35 . 58 C4
  Birmingham,
  Handsworth B21 .... 54 B3
  Fazeley B78 .... 20 E2
  Great Wyrley WS6 .... 4 F3
  Halesowen B63 .... 82 B6
  Harvington DY10 .... 118 A2
  Kidderminster DY11 .... 116 D6
  Kingswinford DY6 .... 60 E7
  Nuneaton CV10 .... 72 A3
  Oldbury B69 .... 64 A6
  Shenstone WS14 .... 18 B4
  Wednesbury WS10 .... 42 A5
  Wolverhampton WV10 ..... 25 E6
Park La E DY4 .... 52 B4
Park La W DY4 .... 51 F4
Park Lane Ind Est
  West Bromwich B71 .... 54 B1
  Wolverhampton WV10 ..... 25 E5
Park Lime Dr WS4 .... 29 B4
Park Lime Pits Ctry Pk
  WS4 .... 29 C4
Park Mall WS1 .... 28 E2
Park Meadow Ave WV14 ... 40 C8
Park Mews B79 .... 85 B1
Park Paling The CV3 .... 133 E7
Park Pl B7 .... 67 C7
Park Prim Sch WS7 .... 7 B6
Park Rd Bedworth CV12 .... 78 B2
  Bilston WV14 .... 40 C5
  Birmingham, Aston B6 ..... 67 A7
  Birmingham, Hockley B18 . 66 A6
  Birmingham, Moseley B13 . 86 F4
  Birmingham, Sparkhill B11 . 87 C3
Birmingham,
  Stockland Green B23 ...... 56 C2
  Brierley Hill DY5 .... 81 F8
Burntwood,
  Chase Terrace WS7 .... 6 F8
  Burntwood, Chasetown WS7 . 7 B5
  Cannock WS11 .... 1 D1
  Coleshill B46 .... 70 F6
  Coventry CV1 .... 165 B1
  Darlaston WS10 .... 41 C6

Park Rd continued
  Dudley, Lower Gornal DY3 . 50 C4
  Dudley, Netherton DY2 ..... 62 C6
  Dudley, West Coseley DY1 . 51 B7
  Featherstone WV10 .... 12 D8
  Hagley DY9 .... 99 B6
  Halesowen B63 .... 82 B5
  Hinckley LE10 .... 75 E8
  Kenilworth CV8 .... 148 A6
  Norton Canes WS11 .... 6 A5
  Royal Leamington Spa CV32 . 157 A4
  Smethwick B67 .... 64 F1
  Solihull B91 .... 107 D3
  Stourbridge DY8 .... 80 D5
  Sutton Coldfield B73 .... 46 B5
  Tamworth B77 .... 35 C5
  Tipton B69 .... 63 C8
  Walsall, Daw End WS4 ..... 29 C5
  Walsall, The Chuckery WS5 . 43 D5
Walsall,
  Wallington Heath WS3 .... 14 B1
  Willenhall WV13 .... 26 F3
Park Rd E WV1 .... 163 A4
Park Rd N B6 .... 67 A7
Park Rd S B18 .... 66 B5
Park Rd W Stourbridge DY8 . 80 D5
  Wolverhampton WV1 ...... 25 A3
Park Retreat B66 .... 65 B5
Park Ridge B74 .... 46 A7
Park Ridge Dr B63 .... 82 B6
Park Rise WV3 .... 24 E2
Park Specl Sch B79 .... 21 A7
Park Sq B37 .... 90 D8
Park St B Birmingham,
  Aston B6 .... 67 A7
  Birmingham, Digbeth B5 . 164 D2
Blackheath,
  Cradley Heath B64 .... 62 E2
Blackheath,
  Rowley Regis B65 .... 63 D1
  Cannock WS11 .... 4 E6
  Cheslyn Hay WS6 .... 4 E3
  Coventry CV6 .... 113 E7
  Darlaston WS10 .... 41 C5
  Kidderminster DY11 .... 116 D5
  Kingswinford DY6 .... 60 D6
  Nuneaton CV11 .... 73 D3
  Oldbury B69 .... 63 F6
  Royal Leamington Spa
  CV32 .... 156 F1
  Stourbridge, Amblecote DY8 . 80 F8
  Stourbridge, Lye DY9 ...... 81 F5
Stourbridge,
  Stambermill DY8 .... 81 A5
  Tamworth B79 .... 21 A5
  Tipton DY4 .... 52 A5
  Walsall WS1 .... 28 E2
  Wednesbury WS10 .... 41 F3
  West Bromwich B70 .... 53 D3
Park St Arc 🖪 WS1 .... 28 E2
Park St S WV2 .... 39 C6
Park Street Ind Est CV6 ... 113 D7
Park Terr Birmingham B21 . 65 E8
  Darlaston WS10 .... 41 B6
Park The B97 .... 152 C7
Park Trad Est B18 .... 66 A6
Park Venture Ctr WS11 ...... 4 E6
Park View
Birmingham,
  Rotton Park B18 .... 65 E4
Birmingham,
  Small Heath B10 .... 87 D7
  Coventry CV3 .... 114 A2
  Darlaston WS10 .... 41 C6
  Sutton Coldfield B73 .... 46 A6
  Tamworth-in-A B94 .... 143 C6
Park View Cl CV7 .... 96 A8
Park View Ct WS11 .... 1 D1
Park View Rd
  Birmingham B31 .... 102 F3
  Stourbridge DY9 .... 81 F4
  Sutton Coldfield B74 .... 31 D3
  Park View Sch B8 .... 67 F5
Park Villas 🔟 B9 .... 67 B2
Park Way Birmingham B45 . 102 B1
  Redditch B98 .... 154 A5
Park Wlk Brierley Hill DY5 . 81 F8
  🖪 Redditch B97 .... 153 E3
Park Wood Ct B74 .... 31 F2
Park Wood La CV4 .... 131 D7
Parkbrook Ind Est
  🖪 DY9 .... 81 F5
Parkdale DY3 .... 50 D8
Parkdale Ave WS10 .... 42 A4
Parkdale Cl B24 .... 56 F2
Parkdale Cl WS10 .... 42 A4
Parkdale Dr B31 .... 123 A7
Parkdale Rd B26 .... 89 D6
Parker Ho B14 .... 104 F3
Parker Paul Ind Est WV2 ... 39 C7
Parker Rd WV11 .... 12 F1
Parker St Birmingham B16 . 65 F1
  Walsall WS3 .... 14 A1
Parkes Ave WV8 .... 10 B2
Parkes Bldgs B62 .... 83 D8
Parkes Fold DY4 .... 51 F8
Parkes Hall Rd DY1 .... 51 A6
Parkes Ho 🖪 B69 .... 64 A7
Parkes La Dudley DY3 .... 51 A7
  Tipton DY4 .... 51 F8
Parkes St Brierley Hill DY5 . 61 D3
  Smethwick B67 .... 64 F4
  Warwick CV34 .... 160 D7
  Willenhall WV13 .... 27 B1
Parkeston Cres B44 .... 45 C1
Parkfield Birmingham B32 . 84 A2
  Dorridge B93 .... 128 A1

Parkfield Ave B77 .... 21 C1
Parkfield Cl Birmingham
  B15 .... 86 C7
  Halesowen B62 .... 84 A5
  Redditch B98 .... 154 B6
  Tamworth B77 .... 35 C8
Parkfield Colliery WV4 ..... 39 F5
Parkfield Cres Tamworth
  B77 .... 35 C8
  Wolverhampton WV2 .... 39 E6
Parkfield Ct 🔟 B46 .... 70 F7
Parkfield Dr Birmingham
  B36 .... 58 C1
  Kenilworth CV8 .... 148 B5
Parkfield Gr WV2 .... 39 E6
Parkfield High Sch WV4 .... 39 E5
Parkfield Inf & Jun Sch
  B8 .... 67 E3
Parkfield Prim Sch
  Tamworth B77 .... 35 C8
  Wolverhampton WV4 .... 39 F5
Parkfield Rd Birmingham B8 . 67 E4
  Coleshill B46 .... 70 F6
  Dudley DY2 .... 62 E6
  Keresley CV7 .... 95 A6
  Oldbury B68 .... 64 A3
  Stourbridge DY8 .... 81 B5
  Wolverhampton WV4 .... 39 E6
Parkgate Prim Sch CV6 .... 95 B3
Parkgate Rd CV6 .... 95 C3
Parkhall Croft B34 .... 69 C7
Parkhill Dr CV5 .... 112 A5
Parkhill Rd Burntwood WS7 . 7 A8
  Sutton Coldfield B76 .... 57 F6
Parkhouse Ave WV11 .... 26 B6
Parkhouse Dr B23 .... 56 B5
Parkhouse Gdns DY3 .... 50 C4
Parkland Ave DY11 .... 116 B5
Parkland Cl CV6 .... 95 C3
Parklands B91 .... 107 A3
Parklands Ave CV32 .... 157 C4
Parklands Ct B17 .... 85 A6
Parklands Dr B74 .... 45 F8
Parklands Gdns WS1 .... 43 A8
Parklands Rd Darlaston
  WS10 .... 41 E5
  Wolverhampton WV1 ...... 26 A1
Parklands The
  Birmingham B23 .... 56 D5
  Kingswinford DY6 .... 60 D6
  Stourbridge DY9 .... 81 D3
  Wolverhampton WV3 .... 24 D1
Parkrose Ind Est B66 .... 65 B7
Parks Cres WV11 .... 13 A3
Parkside Birmingham B32 . 84 C2
  Coventry CV1 .... 165 C2
  Tamworth B77 .... 21 E1
Parkside Ave WV13 .... 26 E2
Parkside Cl WS10 .... 42 B3
Parkside Ct LE10 .... 75 E8
Parkside Ind Est WV1 .... 25 F1
Parkside Jun Sch B66 .... 65 B5
Parkside La WS11 .... 1 A2
Parkside Mid Sch B61 ..... 137 A3
Parkside Rd Birmingham
  B20 .... 54 E6
  Halesowen B63 .... 82 D5
Parkside Way Aldridge B74 . 31 A1
  Birmingham B31 .... 102 C1
Parkstone Ave B61 .... 150 D8
Parkstone Cl WS4 .... 29 C8
Parkstone Rd CV6 .... 95 F2
Parkview CV3 .... 165 A1
Parkview Cres WS2 .... 28 A4
Parkview Rd WV14 .... 40 C8
Parkview Trad Est B38 .... 103 F3
Parkville Ave B17 .... 85 B3
Parkville Cl CV6 .... 95 C3
Parkville Highway CV6 ..... 95 B3
Parkway Birmingham B8 ... 68 A5
  Coventry CV2 .... 115 B8
Parkway Ind Ctr B7 .... 67 A4
Parkway Rd DY1 .... 51 A2
Parkway Rdbt WS10 .... 41 E1
Parkway The Perton WV6 .. 23 F1
  Walsall WS4 .... 29 C8
Parkwood Cl WS8 .... 16 A5
Parkwood Croft B43 .... 44 B1
Parkwood Ct CV8 .... 148 B5
Parkwood Dr B73 .... 45 C2
Parkwood Rd B61 .... 136 E3
Parkyn St WV2 .... 39 E8
Parliament St
  Birmingham, Aston B6 ..... 66 F6
Birmingham,
  Small Heath B10 .... 87 C8
  West Bromwich B70 .... 53 D1
Parlows End B38 .... 123 D7
Parmington Cl B97 .... 158 B6
Parmiter Ho CV32 .... 156 F2
Parr Cl CV34 .... 161 D6
Parrotts Gr CV2 .... 96 D5
Parry Rd Coventry CV2 .... 114 C7
  Kidderminster DY11 .... 116 B3
  Wednesfield WV11 .... 27 A8
Parson St B77 .... 35 E7
Parson's Hill B38 .... 104 B2
Parson's La LE10 .... 75 F8
Parson's Nook CV2 .... 114 A5
Parsonage Dr
  Birmingham B45 .... 122 D4
  Halesowen B63 .... 82 A7
Parsonage St Oldbury B69 . 64 A7
  West Bromwich B71 .... 53 D6
Parsons Hill B68 .... 64 B2
Parsons Rd B98 .... 153 E2
Parsons St DY1 .... 51 C1
Parsons Way WS2 .... 27 F6

Partons Rd B14 .... 104 D6
Partridge Ave WS10 .... 41 B6
Partridge Cl Birmingham B37 . 70 D3
  Huntington WS12 .... 1 D7
Partridge Ct Birmingham
  B4 .... 164 C4
  🖪 Wednesbury WS10 ...... 41 F3
Partridge Gr DY10 .... 117 A2
Partridge Rd B97 .... 158 A7
Partridge Rd Birmingham
  B26 .... 69 A1
  Stourbridge DY8 .... 80 C4
Passey Rd B13 .... 87 D2
Passfield Ave WS12 .... 2 C7
Passfield Rd B33 .... 69 A3
Pasture Gate WS11 .... 1 C2
Pasture View WS3 .... 14 F2
Pastures The WV6 .... 23 D4
Pastures Wlk B38 .... 123 D7
Pat Davis Ct DY10 .... 116 E7
Patch La B98 .... 158 F6
Patent Dr WS10 .... 41 D3
Patent Shaft Rdbt WS10 ... 41 D3
Paternoster Row
  Birmingham B5 .... 66 F2
  🖪 Kidderminster DY11 ... 116 D6
  Wolverhampton WV1 ...... 163 B3
Paterson Ct B93 .... 128 C6
Paterson Pl WS8 .... 16 B5
Pathlow Cres B90 .... 106 A1
Patios The DY11 .... 116 C7
Paton Gr B13 .... 86 F2
Patricia Cl CV4 .... 111 C1
Patricia Ave
  Birmingham B14 .... 105 C4
  Wolverhampton WV4 .... 39 D5
Patricia Cres DY1 .... 51 B7
Patricia Dr DY4 .... 52 A2
Patrick Gregory Rd WV11 . 26 F7
Patrick Rd B26 .... 88 E7
Patriot Cl WS1 .... 42 D5
Patshull Ave WV10 .... 11 B3
Patshull Cl B43 .... 43 D1
Patshull Gr WV10 .... 11 B3
Patshull Ho WV6 .... 24 E5
Patshull Pl 🖪 B19 .... 66 C7
Pattens Rd CV34 .... 156 B1
Patterdale Rd
  Birmingham B23 .... 56 D4
  Cannock WS11 .... 2 A4
Patterdale Way DY5 .... 81 B8
Patterton Dr B76 .... 58 A7
Pattingham Rd WV6 .... 23 C2
Pattison Coll CV3 .... 114 A2
Pattison Gdns B23 .... 56 D2
Pattison St WS5 .... 42 E5
Paul Byrne Ct B20 .... 55 B1
Paul Pursehouse Rd WV14 . 40 D3
Paul St Dudley WV14 .... 40 A1
  Wednesbury WS10 .... 42 B2
  Wolverhampton WV2 ...... 163 B2
Paul Stacy Ho CV1 .... 165 D4
Paul Vale DY4 .... 52 B5
Pauline Ave CV6 .... 96 B2
Pauls Coppice WS8 .... 16 A5
Pauls Wlk WS13 .... 3 A2
Pavenham Dr B5 .... 86 C4
Pavilion Ave B67 .... 64 D3
Pavilion Dr B6 .... 55 F3
Pavilion Way CV5 .... 112 F3
Pavilions Sh Ctr B4 .... 164 C2
Pavillion Cl WS9 .... 30 B7
Pavior's Rd WS7 .... 6 E4
Paxford Cl B98 .... 154 B6
Paxford Way B31 .... 102 F6
Paxmead Cl CV6 .... 95 A2
Paxton Ave WV6 .... 23 E3
Paxton Cl B60 .... 137 B1
Paxton Rd Birmingham B18 . 66 A5
  Coventry CV6 .... 113 A4
  Stourbridge DY9 .... 82 A4
Paybody Hospl CV5 .... 112 C6
Payne Cl CV32 .... 157 A2
Payne St B65 .... 63 C1
Payne's La CV1 .... 113 F3
Paynell Cl CV6 .... 95 B2
Paynton Wlk 🖪 B15 .... 86 D8
Payton Cl B69 .... 52 E1
Payton Rd B21 .... 65 D8
PDH Ind Est
  Wednesbury WS10 .... 41 C3
  Willenhall WV13 .... 26 D3
Peace Cl WS6 .... 4 E3
Peace Wlk B37 .... 70 B1
Peach Ave WS10 .... 41 C6
Peach Ley Rd B31 .... 102 F7
Peach Rd WV12 .... 27 A6
Peachley Cl B63 .... 83 B3
Peacock Ave Coventry CV2 . 96 F1
  Wednesfield WV11 .... 27 A7
Peacock Cl DY4 .... 52 B5
Peacock Rd Birmingham B13 . 104 F6
  Darlaston WS10 .... 41 B7
Peacocks Est B64 .... 62 C1
Peacocks The CV34 .... 160 B2
Peak Croft B36 .... 68 D8
Peak Dr DY3 .... 50 E3
Peak House Rd B43 .... 43 E4
Peak Rd 🖪 DY8 .... 81 B6
Peake Ave CV11 .... 73 E7
Peake Dr DY4 .... 52 B4
Peake Rd WS8 .... 16 A5
Peakman Cl B45 .... 122 A6
Peakman St B98 .... 153 E4

Peaks L Ctr B79 ...... 21 B3
Peal St WS1 ...... 28 F1
Pear Tree Ave
Nuneaton CV10 ...... 72 E6
Tipton DY4 ...... 51 F5
Pear Tree Cl
Birmingham, Grove Vale B43 ...... 43 B1
Birmingham, Stechford B33 ...... 68 D2
4 Coventry CV2 ...... 96 B2
Huntington WS12 ...... 1 C7
Kidderminster DY10 ...... 117 B7
Shuttington B79 ...... 22 E8
Solihull B90 ...... 105 D2
Pear Tree Cres B90 ...... 105 C2
Pear Tree Ct Birmingham
B43 ...... 54 C8
Blackheath B65 ...... 63 D3
Pear Tree Dr B43 ...... 43 C1
Pear Tree Gr B90 ...... 105 C2
Pear Tree La Brownhills WS8 ...... 6 C2
Dudley WV14 ...... 51 D8
Wolverhampton WV11 ...... 26 B8
Pear Tree Rd
Birmingham B34 ...... 69 C6
Birmingham, Grove Vale B43 ...... 43 B1
Smethwick B67 ...... 64 E4
Pearce Cl DY1 ...... 61 E8
Pearl Gr
Birmingham,
Acock's Green B27 ...... 88 B3
3 Birmingham,
Rotton Park B18 ...... 65 E4
Pearl Hyde Ho 4 CV1 ...... 165 C4
Pearl Hyde Prim Sch CV2 ...... 115 A5
Pearman Rd
Birmingham B45 ...... 101 E1
Smethwick B66 ...... 65 A3
Pearmans Croft B47 ...... 125 A6
Pears Cl CV8 ...... 147 F5
Pearson Ave CV6 ...... 96 B2
Pearson Ct WV12 ...... 27 D4
Pearson St Blackheath B64 ...... 62 E1
Brierley Hill DY5 ...... 61 D3
Stourbridge DY9 ...... 81 F4
West Bromwich B70 ...... 53 B4
Wolverhampton WV2 ...... 163 B1
Peart Dr B80 ...... 159 C4
Peartree Ave WV13 ...... 27 B1
Peartree Dr B79 ...... 81 A2
Peartree La Blackheath B64 ...... 62 E1
Dudley DY2 ...... 62 A6
Peartree Lane Ind Est DY2 ...... 62 A6
Peascroft La WV14 ...... 40 E6
Peasefield Cl B21 ...... 65 C8
Pebble Cl Stourbridge DY8 ...... 81 B5
Tamworth B77 ...... 22 B3
Pebble Mill Cl WS11 ...... 1 F2
Pebble Mill Dr WS11 ...... 2 A2
Pebble Mill Rd B5 ...... 86 C4
Pebworth Ave B90 ...... 127 B6
Pebworth Cl Birmingham
B29 ...... 86 B2
Coventry CV5 ...... 112 B3
Redditch B98 ...... 154 C7
Pebworth Gr Birmingham
B33 ...... 89 C8
Dudley DY1 ...... 51 B3
Peckham Rd B44 ...... 45 A2
Peckingham St 2 B63 ...... 83 B3
Peckover Cl B65 ...... 63 C1
Peddimore La B76 ...... 58 C7
Pedmore CE Prim Sch
DY9 ...... 81 C1
Pedmore Cl B98 ...... 159 B7
Pedmore Court Rd DY8 ...... 81 B1
Pedmore Gr B44 ...... 44 F2
Pedmore Hall La DY9 ...... 99 C8
Pedmore La Hagley DY9 ...... 99 F8
Stourbridge DY9 ...... 81 E1
Pedmore Rd
Brierley Hill DY5, DY2 ...... 61 F4
Stourbridge DY9 ...... 81 E1
Pedmore Road Ind Est
DY5 ...... 61 F4
Pedmore Wlk B69 ...... 63 D5
Peel Cl Coventry CV6 ...... 113 E6
Darlaston WS10 ...... 41 D8
Drayton Bassett B78 ...... 34 E5
Hampton in A B92 ...... 109 B6
Willenhall WV13 ...... 27 A1
Peel Ct 1 Cannock WS11 ...... 1 E1
2 Fazeley B78 ...... 35 B8
Peel Dr WS12 ...... 1 F4
Peel Ho B79 ...... 21 A4
Peel La CV6 ...... 113 F5
Peel Rd CV34 ...... 160 E8
Peel St Birmingham B18 ...... 65 E5
Coventry CV6 ...... 113 E6
Dudley DY2 ...... 62 E8
Kidderminster DY11 ...... 116 D5
Tipton DY4 ...... 52 A4
West Bromwich B71 ...... 53 C5
Willenhall WV13 ...... 27 A1
Wolverhampton WV3 ...... 163 B2
Peel Way B69 ...... 52 D2
Peel Wlk B17 ...... 84 F7
Peelers Way B77 ...... 21 C1
Pegasus Jun & Inf Sch B35 ...... 58 B3
Pegasus Wlk Birmingham B29 ...... 85 D1
Tamworth B79 ...... 20 F7
Peggs Row Cotts WS7 ...... 7 E7
Pegleg Wlk 2 B14 ...... 104 C2
Pegmill Cl CV3 ...... 133 F8
Pelham Dr DY1 ...... 51 A2
Pelham Lodge DY10 ...... 117 A5
Pelham Rd B8 ...... 68 B4
Pelham St WV3 ...... 25 B1

Pelsall La
Walsall, Little Bloxwich WS3 ...... 14 D3
Walsall, Shelfield WS4 ...... 29 B8
Pelsall Rd WS8 ...... 15 D7
Pelsall Village Jun
Mixed & Inf Schs WS3 ...... 14 F4
Pemberly Rd B27 ...... 88 A2
Pemberton Cl B66 ...... 65 B3
Pemberton Cres WS10 ...... 42 D5
Pemberton Rd Dudley
WV14 ...... 40 D1
West Bromwich B70 ...... 53 A6
Pemberton St B18 ...... 66 B4
Pembridge Cl
Birmingham B32 ...... 102 A2
Brierley Hill DY5 ...... 61 F1
Redditch B98 ...... 154 D2
Pembridge Rd B93 ...... 127 E3
Pembroke Ave WV2 ...... 40 A7
Pembroke Cl Bedworth
CV12 ...... 77 C1
1 Warwick CV34 ...... 160 F8
West Bromwich B71 ...... 42 B1
Willenhall WV12 ...... 27 B6
Pembroke Croft B28 ...... 106 A5
Pembroke Ct 8 CV32 ...... 156 F2
Pembroke Gdns DY8 ...... 60 C2
Pembroke Ho 4 WS3 ...... 28 C6
Pembroke Rd
Birmingham B12 ...... 87 A4
West Bromwich B71 ...... 42 B1
Pembroke Way
Birmingham B28 ...... 106 A5
Nuneaton CV11 ...... 73 D3
West Bromwich B71 ...... 53 B7
Pembrook Rd CV6 ...... 95 C2
Pembury Ave CV6 ...... 96 A3
Pembury Croft B44 ...... 45 A1
Penarth Gr CV3 ...... 134 F7
Pencombe Dr WV4 ...... 39 D5
Pencraig Cl CV8 ...... 148 C5
Pencroft Rd B34 ...... 69 C7
Penda Ct B20 ...... 66 A8
Pendeen Rd B14 ...... 105 C4
Pendeford Ave WV6 ...... 24 E8
Pendeford Bsns Pk WV9 ...... 10 F3
Pendeford Cl WV6 ...... 24 E8
Pendeford Hall La WV9 ...... 10 D5
Pendeford High Sch
WV10 ...... 11 B2
Pendeford La WV9 ...... 11 A3
Pendeford Mill La WV8 ...... 10 C3
Pendenis Cl CV6 ...... 114 A8
Pendennis Cl B30 ...... 103 C5
Pendennis Dr B69 ...... 63 A8
Penderel Ct CV6 ...... 95 C3
Penderel St WS3 ...... 14 C1
Penderell Cl WV10 ...... 12 A6
Pendigo Way
Birmingham B40 ...... 90 E3
Birmingham B40 ...... 90 F4
Pendinas Dr WV8 ...... 10 B3
Pendine Ct 5 CV32 ...... 161 D8
Pendle Hill WS12 ...... 2 C4
Pendleton Gr B27 ...... 106 B8
Pendock Ct B23 ...... 56 C3
Pendragon Rd B42 ...... 55 C4
Pendrel Cl WS6 ...... 13 F8
Pendrell Cl Birmingham B37 ...... 70 A3
Codsall WV8 ...... 10 A3
Pendrill Rd WV10 ...... 11 E3
Penfields Rd DY8 ...... 81 B6
Penge Gr B44 ...... 44 E3
Penhallow Dr WV4 ...... 39 E5
Penhurst Ave B20 ...... 55 D1
Penk Dr WS7 ...... 7 D6
Penk Rise WV6 ...... 24 B4
Penkridge Cl WS2 ...... 28 D3
Penkridge Gr B33 ...... 68 F4
Penkridge St WS2 ...... 28 D3
Penley Gr B8 ...... 68 B6
Penmanor B60 ...... 151 D8
Penn Cl WS3 ...... 28 C8
Penn Common Golf
Course WV4 ...... 38 F2
Penn Common Rd WV4 ...... 38 F1
Penn Croft La WV4 ...... 39 A1
Penn Fields Sch WV3 ...... 38 F7
Penn Gr B29 ...... 85 B2
Penn Hall Sch WV4 ...... 38 E3
Penn Ho CV4 ...... 111 F1
Penn Hospl WV4 ...... 38 E4
Penn Ind Est B64 ...... 62 D1
Penn La B94 ...... 141 C4
Penn Rd Blackheath B65 ...... 63 E3
Sedgley DY3 ...... 49 F8
Wolverhampton WV3, WV4 ...... 39 B7
Penn Road Island WV2 ...... 163 B2
Penn St Birmingham B4 ...... 67 A3
Blackheath B64 ...... 82 F8
Wolverhampton WV3 ...... 163 A1
Pennant Ct B65 ...... 63 B3
Pennant Gr B29 ...... 85 A2
Pennant Rd
Blackheath,
Cradley Heath B64 ...... 62 D1
Blackheath,
Rowley Regis B65 ...... 63 B3
Hinckley LE10 ...... 75 D5
Pennard Gr B32 ...... 84 F4
Penncricket Ct B68 ...... 63 F3
Penncricket La B65, B68 ...... 63 F3
Penncroft WV4 ...... 38 E4
Pennhouse Ave WV4 ...... 38 F5
Pennine Dr Cannock WS11 ...... 1 E2
Dudley DY3 ...... 50 D3
Pennine Rd B61 ...... 137 A5

Pennine Way Nuneaton CV10 ...... 72 B3
Stourbridge DY8 ...... 81 A6
Tamworth B77 ...... 36 B8
Willenhall WV12 ...... 27 D4
Pennington Cl B70 ...... 53 A2
Pennington Ho B69 ...... 63 E8
Pennington Way CV6 ...... 113 E8
Penns Cl CV32 ...... 157 E5
Penns Ct B76 ...... 57 F7
Penns La Coleshill B46 ...... 70 F7
Sutton Coldfield B72 ...... 57 D7
Penns Lake Rd B76 ...... 57 E7
Penns Prim Sch B72 ...... 57 D6
Penns Wood Cl DY3 ...... 39 C2
Penns Wood Dr B76 ...... 57 F7
Pennwood Cl WV4 ...... 38 C6
Pennwood La WV4 ...... 38 F3
Penny Cress Gn WS11 ...... 5 F4
Penny Ct WS6 ...... 13 F8
Penny Park La CV6 ...... 95 A3
Penny Royal Cl DY3 ...... 50 D2
Pennyacre Rd B14 ...... 104 D2
Pennycress Gdns WV10 ...... 12 C7
Pennycroft Ho B33 ...... 68 E3
Pennyfield Croft B33 ...... 68 E3
Pennyhill La B71 ...... 53 F7
Pennymoor Rd B77 ...... 36 B7
Pennyroyal Cl WS5 ...... 43 B3
Pennys Croft WS3 ...... 3 E1
Pennystone Cl CV31 ...... 162 D6
Penrice Dr B69 ...... 52 A1
Penrith Cl Brierley Hill DY5 ...... 81 B8
Coventry CV6 ...... 95 C2
Royal Leamington Spa CV32 ...... 156 C2
Penrith Croft B32 ...... 102 D8
Penrith Gr B37 ...... 70 C2
Penrose Cl CV4 ...... 132 A7
Penrhyn Cl CV8 ...... 148 C5
Penryn Cl Nuneaton CV11 ...... 74 A4
Walsall WS5 ...... 43 D7
Penryn Rd WS5 ...... 43 D7
Pens Meadow Sch DY8 ...... 60 E3
Pensby Cl B13 ...... 105 D8
Pensford Rd B31 ...... 103 C3
Pensham Croft B90 ...... 127 A6
Penshaw Cl WV9 ...... 11 A3
Penshaw Gr B13 ...... 87 D1
Penshurst Way CV11 ...... 78 F8
Pensilva Way 2 CV1 ...... 113 E4
Pensnett Rd Brierley Hill
DY5 ...... 61 C4
Dudley DY1 ...... 61 F7
Pensnett Sch of Tech The
DY5 ...... 61 B6
Pensnett Trad Est The
DY6 ...... 60 F8
Penstock Ct DY10 ...... 117 C8
Penstone La WV4 ...... 37 E4
Pentire Cl CV11 ...... 73 F5
Pentland Cl LE10 ...... 71 B1
Pentland Croft B12 ...... 86 F7
Pentlands Gdns WV3 ...... 24 E2
Pentos Dr B11 ...... 87 D3
Pentridge Cl B76 ...... 57 F5
Penzance Cl LE10 ...... 71 E4
Penzance Way CV11 ...... 74 A5
Penzer Dr B45 ...... 138 D8
Penzer St DY6 ...... 60 D7
Peolsford Rd WS3 ...... 15 A4
Peony Wlk B23 ...... 56 B3
Peplins Way B30 ...... 104 B3
Peplow Rd B33 ...... 69 A4
Pepper Hill DY8 ...... 81 A4
Pepper La CV1 ...... 165 B2
Pepperbox Dr DY4 ...... 52 A5
Pepperwood Cl B61 ...... 120 C3
Pepys Cnr CV4 ...... 111 E3
Pepys Ct B43 ...... 54 E7
Perch Ave B37 ...... 70 A3
Percival Rd B16 ...... 65 C1
Percy Bsns Pk B69 ...... 63 F7
Percy Cres CV8 ...... 147 E2
Percy Rd Birmingham B11 ...... 87 D4
Kenilworth CV8 ...... 147 E2
Warwick CV34 ...... 160 E8
Percy Shurmer Jun &
Inf Sch B12 ...... 86 E7
Percy St CV1 ...... 165 A3
Percy Terr 5 CV32 ...... 156 D1
Peregrine Cl DY1 ...... 50 F1
Peregrine Dr CV5 ...... 112 A5
Peregrine Gr DY10 ...... 117 A2
Pereira Rd B17 ...... 85 C7
Perimeter Rd
Birmingham B40 ...... 90 D4
Birmingham B40 ...... 90 E4
Perivale Gr WV14 ...... 51 D8
Perivale Way DY8 ...... 81 A8
Periwinkle Cl WS8 ...... 15 D6
Perkins Cl DY1 ...... 51 C6
Perks Rd WV11 ...... 13 A1
Perott Dr B75 ...... 32 D2
Perrett Wlk 5 DY11 ...... 116 D6
Perrin Ave DY11 ...... 116 B4
Perrins Gr B8 ...... 68 A6
Perrins La DY9 ...... 81 F4
Perrins Rise DY9 ...... 81 F4
Perrott Gdns DY5 ...... 61 B1
Perrott St B18 ...... 65 E6
Perry Ave B42 ...... 55 C5
Perry Barr Sta B20 ...... 55 D7
Perry Common Jun & Inf Sch
B23 ...... 56 B7
Perry Common Rd B23 ...... 56 C6

Perry Common Sec Sch
B44 ...... 56 B6
Perry Ct B44 ...... 84 B7
Perry Green Ho B42 ...... 55 D5
Perry Hall Dr WV12 ...... 27 B5
Perry Hall Prim Sch WV11 ...... 26 F6
Perry Hall Rd WV11 ...... 26 F5
Perry Hill Cres B68 ...... 84 B7
Perry Hill Ho B68 ...... 84 C8
Perry Hill La B32 ...... 84 B7
Perry Hill Rd B68 ...... 84 B7
Perry La B61 ...... 136 F2
Perry Park Cres B42 ...... 55 C6
Perry Park Rd B64 ...... 63 B1
Perry St Bilston WV14 ...... 40 E3
Darlaston WS10 ...... 41 D8
Smethwick B66 ...... 65 A7
Tipton DY4 ...... 52 A4
Wednesbury WS10 ...... 41 F2
Perry Trad Est WV14 ...... 40 E3
Perry Villa Dr B42 ...... 55 D5
Perry Wlk B23 ...... 56 D6
Perry Wood Rd B42 ...... 55 A8
Perrycrofts Cres B79 ...... 21 C7
Perryfields Cl B98 ...... 158 F6
Perryfields Cres B61 ...... 136 F5
Perryfields High Sch B68 ...... 84 A8
Perryfields Prim Sch B68 ...... 84 A7
Perryfields Rd B61 ...... 136 D4
Perryford Dr B91 ...... 127 C8
Perrymill La B96 ...... 159 B1
Perrywell Rd B6 ...... 55 F4
Persehouse St WS1 ...... 28 F2
Pershore Ave B29 ...... 86 B2
Pershore Cl WS3 ...... 13 F2
Pershore Pl CV4 ...... 132 E5
Pershore Rd
Birmingham,
Balsall Heath B5 ...... 86 C4
Birmingham,
Breedon Cross B30 ...... 104 A5
Birmingham, Ten Acres B30 ...... 104 B8
Halesowen B63 ...... 83 A2
Kidderminster DY11 ...... 116 A6
Walsall WS3 ...... 13 F2
Pershore Rd S B30 ...... 103 F3
Pershore St B5 ...... 164 C2
Pershore Tower 3 B31 ...... 102 C2
Pershore Way WS3 ...... 13 F2
Perth Rd WV12 ...... 27 B6
Perth Rise CV5 ...... 112 A4
Perton Brook Vale WV6 ...... 23 F4
Perton Cty Fst Sch WV6 ...... 24 A4
Perton Fst Sch WV6 ...... 23 F5
Perton Gr Birmingham B29 ...... 103 A8
Wolverhampton WV6 ...... 23 F2
Perton Rd WV6 ...... 23 F2
Pestilence La
Alvechurch B48 ...... 139 C8
Alvechurch B48 ...... 139 D8
Peter Ave WV14 ...... 40 F2
Peter Hall La CV7 ...... 115 F6
Peter's Finger B60 ...... 136 F1
Peter's Hill Rd DY5 ...... 81 C6
Peter's La WS7 ...... 8 A5
Peterborough Dr WS12 ...... 2 C1
Peterbrook Cl B98 ...... 158 F7
Peterbrook Prim
Sch B90 ...... 105 D2
Peterbrook Rd B90 ...... 105 D1
Peterbrook Rise B90 ...... 105 D1
Peterdale Dr WV4 ...... 38 F3
Peterhead 7 ...... 21 F5
Peterlee Wlk 6 CV2 ...... 115 A7
Peters Ave B31 ...... 102 F2
Peters Hill Prim Sch DY5 ...... 81 C7
Peters St B70 ...... 53 A7
Peters Wlk WS13 ...... 3 A2
Petersbourne Ct B28 ...... 105 F8
Petersfield WS11 ...... 1 F4
Petersfield Ct B28 ...... 105 F8
Petersfield Dr B65 ...... 63 E3
Petersfield Rd B28 ...... 105 E7
Petersham Pl B15 ...... 85 E6
Petersham Rd B44 ...... 45 C1
Petershouse Dr B74 ...... 31 F5
Petford St B64 ...... 62 E1
Petitor Cres CV2 ...... 96 C1
Pettitt Cl B14 ...... 104 E2
Petton Cl B98 ...... 154 F3
Pettyfield Cl B26 ...... 89 A6
Pettyfields Cl B93 ...... 128 A5
Petworth Cl 3 WV13 ...... 40 F8
Petworth Gr B26 ...... 88 E6
Pevensey Cl B69 ...... 62 F8
Peverell Dr B28 ...... 105 F7
Peveril Dr CV3 ...... 133 B5
Peveril Gr B76 ...... 46 E4
Peverill Rd Perton WV6 ...... 23 F4
Wolverhampton WV4 ...... 39 E3
Pevril Way B43 ...... 43 F2
Peyto Cl CV6 ...... 95 C2
Pheasant Cl Bedworth CV12 ...... 77 D1
Kidderminster DY10 ...... 117 A2
Pheasant Croft B36 ...... 70 A8
Pheasant La B98 ...... 158 F7
Pheasant Rd B67 ...... 64 D1
Pheasant St DY5 ...... 61 C3
Pheasey Park Farm Prim
Sch B43 ...... 44 C4
Philip Ct
1 Royal Leamington Spa
CV31 ...... 161 F6
Sutton Coldfield B76 ...... 46 F3
Philip Dr WS11 ...... 1 E6
Philip Rd Halesowen B63 ...... 82 F3
Tipton DY4 ...... 52 D5
Philip Sidney Rd B11 ...... 87 C3

Philip St WV14 ...... 40 D1
Philip Victor Rd B20 ...... 54 F1
Phillimore Rd B8 ...... 67 D5
Phillip Docker Ct CV12 ...... 79 B2
Phillip Rd WS2 ...... 42 C6
Phillippes Rd 6 CV34 ...... 155 F1
Phillips Ave WV11 ...... 12 F1
Phillips St B6 ...... 66 E6
Phillips Street Ind Est B6 ...... 66 F6
Phillips Terr B98 ...... 153 F4
Phipson Rd B11 ...... 87 B3
Phoenix Bsns Pk
Birmingham B7 ...... 67 A6
Hinckley LE10 ...... 74 E8
Phoenix Cl B5 ...... 86 C5
Phoenix Ctr WS11 ...... 4 E6
Phoenix Gn B15 ...... 85 E7
Phoenix Ho CV1 ...... 165 C4
Phoenix Ind Est Bilston
WV14 ...... 40 F4
Willenhall WV11 ...... 26 D3
Phoenix Int Ind Est B70 ...... 52 E5
Phoenix Pk B62 ...... 63 E1
Phoenix Rd Cannock WS11 ...... 2 A2
Tipton DY4 ...... 51 F6
Willenhall WV11 ...... 26 D3
Phoenix Rise Birmingham
B23 ...... 56 B7
Wednesbury WS10 ...... 41 E4
Wolverhampton WV2 ...... 39 C6
Phoenix St
West Bromwich WV70 ...... 52 F4
Wolverhampton WV2 ...... 39 D6
Phoenix Way CV6 ...... 95 E3
Picasso Cl WS11 ...... 2 D2
Piccadilly Birmingham B2 ...... 164 B2
Piccadilly B78 ...... 35 F1
Piccadilly Cl B37 ...... 70 C1
Piccadilly Cres B78 ...... 35 F1
Pickard St CV34 ...... 161 A7
Pickenham Rd B14 ...... 105 A1
Pickering Croft B32 ...... 84 D1
Pickering Rd WV11 ...... 26 D5
Pickersleigh Ct 6 B63 ...... 83 A3
Pickford Cl CV11 ...... 74 A1
Pickford Grange La CV5 ...... 111 C7
Pickford Green La CV5 ...... 111 C7
Pickford St B5 ...... 66 F2
Pickford Way CV5 ...... 112 B6
Pickrell Rd WV14 ...... 40 B1
Pickwick Cl B13 ...... 87 B2
Pickwick Gr B13 ...... 87 C2
Pickwick Pl WV14 ...... 40 E4
Picton Croft 8 B37 ...... 70 D2
Picton Gr B13 ...... 105 B6
Picturedrome Way
6 WS10 ...... 41 D6
Piddock Rd B66 ...... 65 A5
Pier St WS8 ...... 15 F7
Pierce Ave B92 ...... 88 E3
Piercy St B70 ...... 53 A3
Piers Cl CV34 ...... 160 F8
Piers Rd B21 ...... 66 A7
Piggots Croft B37 ...... 69 F3
Pike Cl LE10 ...... 75 D5
Pike Dr B37 ...... 70 C3
Pike Hill B60 ...... 138 A7
Pikehelve St B70 ...... 52 E7
Pikehorne Croft B36 ...... 58 D2
Pikers La CV7 ...... 94 A3
Pikes Pool La B60 ...... 137 E5
Pikes The B45 ...... 121 F8
Pikewater Rd B9 ...... 67 D2
Pilgrims Gate LE10 ...... 76 A6
Pilkington Ave B72 ...... 46 C2
Pilkington Rd CV5 ...... 132 D8
Pillaton Dr WS12 ...... 1 C6
Pilling Cl CV2 ...... 114 F8
Pilson Cl B36 ...... 68 F8
Pimbury Rd WV12 ...... 27 D7
Pimlico Ct DY3 ...... 50 D3
Pimpernel Dr WS5 ...... 43 A3
Pinbury Croft B37 ...... 70 B1
Pinchers Cl DY9 ...... 119 E7
Pine Ave Smethwick B66 ...... 64 E7
Wednesbury WS10 ...... 41 F4
Pine Cl Great Wyrley WS6 ...... 4 F4
Kingswinford DY6 ...... 60 D5
Solihull B91 ...... 106 F2
Stourbridge DY9 ...... 81 B1
Tamworth B79 ...... 21 A5
Wolverhampton WV3 ...... 25 A1
Pine Ct Coventry CV5 ...... 111 C4
Royal Leamington Spa CV32 ...... 157 B3
Wolverhampton WV11 ...... 26 C6
Pine Gn DY1 ...... 51 A5
Pine Gr Barnt Green B45 ...... 121 F2
Birmingham B45 ...... 105 A5
Burntwood WS7 ...... 6 F5
Pine Ho B36 ...... 68 F8
Pine Leigh B74 ...... 32 B1
Pine Rd Dudley DY1 ...... 51 C4
Tipton B69 ...... 63 A8
Pine Sq B37 ...... 70 B2
Pine St WS3 ...... 14 D2
Pine Tree Ave CV4 ...... 112 A2
Pine Tree Cl B97 ...... 152 F3
Pine Tree Ct CV12 ...... 78 C4
Pine Tree Rd CV12 ...... 78 D4
Pine Wlk Birmingham B31 ...... 103 B3
Stourbridge DY9 ...... 81 D3
Pine Woods B32 ...... 84 A4
Pineapple Gr B30 ...... 104 C8
Pineapple Inf & Jun Sch
B14 ...... 104 C5

Pineapple Rd B30 .... 104 C7
Pinehurst CV32 .... 157 E6
Pinehurst Dr B38 .... 103 F3
Pineneedle Croft WV12 ...... 27 E4
Pineridge Dr DY11 .... 116 B5
Pines Mobile Homes The
WS12 .... 1 D5
Pines Sch The B36 .... 68 F8
Pines The Bedworth CV12 .... 77 E2
  Birmingham B45 .... 102 A1
  Cheswick Green B90 .... 126 D5
  Coventry CV4 .... 131 D7
  Lichfield WS14 .... 9 F7
  Walsall WS1 .... 42 F8
  Wolverhampton,
  Compton WV3 .... 24 D1
  Wolverhampton,
  New Cross WV11 .... 26 B5
Pinetree Dr B74 .... 30 D1
Pineview B31 .... 102 F2
Pinewall Ave B38 .... 104 A1
Pineways Stourbridge DY8 ... 60 C2
  Sutton Coldfield B74 .... 31 C3
Pineways Dr WV6 .... 24 E4
Pineways The B69 .... 63 D5
Pinewood Ave Cannock WS11 . 1 D4
  Wood End CV9 .... 36 C1
Pinewood Cl
  Birmingham, Eachway B45 .. 121 D8
  Birmingham, Great Barr B44 . 55 E7
  Brownhills WS8 .... 6 E2
  Walsall WS5 .... 43 B4
  Willenhall WV12 .... 27 E7
  Wolverhampton WV3 .... 38 A8
  Wombourne WV5 .... 49 A6
Pinewood Dr
  Binley Woods CV3 .... 135 C7
  Birmingham B32 .... 84 A1
Pinewood Gr Coventry
  CV5 .... 133 B8
  Solihull B91 .... 106 F2
Pinewood Wlk 6 DY6 .... 60 E8
Pinewoods Birmingham
  B31 .... 102 F8
  Halesowen B62 .... 84 A7
Pinewoods Ave DY9 .... 98 F4
Pinewoods Cl DY9 .... 98 F4
Pinewoods Ct DY9 .... 98 F4
Pinfield Dr B45 .... 122 B1
Pinfold WS3 .... 28 C8
Pinfold Cres WV4 .... 38 D6
Pinfold Ct WS10 .... 41 C5
Pinfold Gdns WV11 .... 26 D5
Pinfold Gr WV4 .... 38 D6
Pinfold Hill WS14 .... 18 A6
Pinfold La Cheslyn Hay WS6 .. 4 C2
  Norton Canes WS11 .... 5 E4
  Walsall WS9 .... 44 B6
  Wolverhampton WV4 .... 38 E5
Pinfold Rd B91 .... 107 E5
Pinfold St Bilston WV14 ...... 40 D5
  Birmingham B2 .... 164 B2
  Darlaston WS10 .... 41 C5
  Oldbury B69 .... 64 A8
Pinfold Street Extension
  WS10 .... 41 C5
Pinfold Street JMI Sch
  WS10 .... 41 C5
Pingle Cl B71 .... 42 F1
Pingle Ct CV11 .... 73 D2
Pingle La WS7 .... 7 D5
Pinkney Pl B69 .... 64 C3
Pinley Fields CV3 .... 134 B8
Pinley Gr B43 .... 44 C3
Pinley Way B91 .... 107 A1
Pinner Ct B17 .... 85 C6
Pinner Gr B32 .... 84 E4
Pinner's Croft CV2 .... 114 A5
Pinnock Pl CV4 .... 111 F1
Pinson Rd WV13 .... 26 F2
Pintail Dr B23 .... 56 C2
Pintail Gr DY10 .... 117 B3
Pinto Cl B16 .... 65 F2
Pinvin Ho B97 .... 153 A3
Pinza Croft B36 .... 68 D8
Pioli Pl WS2 .... 28 D5
Pioneer Ho Birmingham
  B35 .... 58 C3
  Coventry CV1 .... 165 D4
Pioneer Units CV11 .... 73 E3
Pipe Hall Farm Nature
  Reserve WS13 .... 8 B8
Piper Cl WV6 .... 23 F4
Piper Pl DY8 .... 80 F8
Piper Rd WV3 .... 38 C8
Piper's La CV8 .... 148 A5
Piper's Row WV1 .... 163 C3
Pipers Cl B61 .... 150 D7
Pipers Croft WS13 .... 3 A2
Pipers Gn B28 .... 105 F5
Pipers Rd B98 .... 159 D7
Pipes Mdw WV14 .... 40 E5
Pipit Ct DY10 .... 117 A2
Pippin Ave B63 .... 82 B7
Pirbright Cl WV14 .... 40 E3
Pit Leasow Cl B30 .... 104 B8
Pitcairn Cl B30 .... 104 B6
Pitcairn Dr B62 .... 83 B5
Pitcairn Ho B67 .... 64 E2
Pitcairn Rd B67 .... 64 D2
Pitcher Oak Sch B97 .... 153 B4
Pitcheroak Cotts B97 .... 153 A3
Pitclose Rd B31 .... 103 B1
Pitfield Rd B33 .... 69 E1
Pitfield Row 16 DY1 .... 51 B1

Pitfield St 5 DY1 .... 51 C1
Pitfields Cl B68 .... 84 A8
Pitfields Rd B68 .... 84 A8
Pithall Rd B34 .... 69 D5
Pitman Rd B32 .... 84 C5
Pitmaston Ct B13 .... 86 D3
Pitmaston Rd B28 .... 106 B6
Pitmeadow Ho B14 .... 104 E2
Pitsford St B18 .... 66 B4
Pitt La B92 .... 90 D2
Pitt St Birmingham B4 .... 67 A3
  Wolverhampton WV3 .... 163 B2
Pitts Farm Rd B24 .... 57 C6
Pitts La DY10 .... 116 E6
Pixall Dr B15 .... 86 B6
Pixhall Wlk B35 .... 58 B3
Plainview CV9 .... 30 E2
Plaistow Ave B36 .... 68 C7
Plane Gr B37 .... 70 B1
Plane Tree Cl DY10 .... 116 F7
Plane Tree Rd WS5 .... 43 C4
Planet Rd DY5 .... 61 D4
Planetary Ind Est WV13 .... 26 C4
Planetary Rd WV13 .... 26 C3
Planetree Cl B60 .... 137 B2
Planetree Rd B74 .... 44 D8
Plank La B46 .... 59 A2
Plank La WV5 .... 49 A7
Plant Ct 19 DY5 .... 61 D2
Plant La B92 .... 89 D7
Plant St Blackheath B64 .... 62 D1
  Stourbridge DY8 .... 60 E2
Plant Way WS3 .... 14 F4
Plantation La Himley DY3 ... 49 B3
  Hopwas B78 .... 20 B4
Plantation Rd WS5 .... 43 A4
Plantation The DY5 .... 61 B7
Plants Brook Rd B76 .... 57 F6
Plants Cl Great Wyrley WS6 .. 14 A8
  Sutton Coldfield B73 .... 45 D1
Plants Gr B24 .... 57 D6
Plants Hill Cres CV4 .... 111 E1
Plants Hollow DY5 .... 61 D1
Plascom Rd WV1 .... 26 A1
Platt St Cannock WS11 ...... 2 A5
  Darlaston WS10 .... 41 D5
Platts Cres DY8 .... 80 E8
Platts Dr DY8 .... 80 F8
Platts Rd DY8 .... 80 E8
Playdon Gr B14 .... 105 A3
Pleasant Cl DY6 .... 60 C4
Pleasant Mead WS9 .... 29 E5
Pleasant St
  Kidderminster DY10 .... 116 E7
  West Bromwich,
  Hill Top B70 .... 53 A8
  West Bromwich,
  Lambert's End B70 .... 53 C2
Pleasant View DY3 .... 50 D2
Pleasant Way CV32 .... 157 A2
Pleck Bsns Pk WS2 .... 28 C1
Pleck Ho B14 .... 104 C1
Pleck Ind Est WS2 .... 42 C8
Pleck Rd WS2 .... 28 C1
Pleck Wlk B38 .... 104 A1
Plestowes Cl B90 .... 106 B5
Pleydell Cl CV3 .... 134 C5
Plimsoll Gr B32 .... 84 C5
Plimsoll St DY11 .... 116 D5
Plough And Harrow Rd
  B16 .... 65 F1
Plough Ave B32 .... 84 C2
Plough Hill Rd CV10 .... 72 A6
Ploughmans Wlk
  Kingswinford DY6 .... 60 A7
  Lichfield WS13 .... 3 C3
  Stoke Heath B60 .... 150 D6
  Wolverhampton WV8 .... 10 F1
Plover Cl WV10 .... 12 B7
Plover Dr DY10 .... 117 B1
Ploverdale Cres DY6 .... 61 A6
Plowden Rd B33 .... 68 F4
Plume St B6 .... 67 C8
Plumstead Rd B44 .... 56 B8
Plym Pl WV11 .... 26 C5
Plymouth Cl
  Birmingham B31 .... 123 A7
  Coventry CV2 .... 114 C7
  Redditch B97 .... 153 C1
Plymouth Ct B97 .... 153 C1
Plymouth Dr B45 .... 138 A8
Plymouth Pl CV31 .... 162 A7
Plymouth Rd
  Barnt Green B45 .... 138 A8
  Birmingham B30 .... 104 B7
  Redditch B97 .... 153 D2
Pochard Cl DY10 .... 116 F1
Pointon Cl WV14 .... 40 A2
Poitiers Rd CV3 .... 133 D6
Polden Cl B63 .... 82 C1
Polesworth Cl B98 .... 154 D1
Polesworth Gr B34 .... 69 B6
Polesworth High Sch B78 .. 36 F8
Pollard Rd B27 .... 88 C1
Pollards The B23 .... 56 E8
Polly Brooks Yd DY9 .... 81 E5
Polo Fields DY9 .... 81 B1
Polperro Dr CV5 .... 112 A5
Pomeroy Cl CV4 .... 131 D7
Pomeroy Rd
  Birmingham, Pheasey B43 . 44 D4
  Birmingham, Woodgate B32 . 84 C1
Pommel Cl WS5 .... 42 F4
Pond Cres WV2 .... 39 E7
Pond Gr WV2 .... 39 E7
Pond La WV2 .... 39 E7

Pondthorpe CV3 .... 134 E6
Ponesfield Rd WS13 .... 3 B2
Ponesgreen WS13 .... 3 B2
Pontypool Ave CV3 .... 134 F6
Pool Ave WS11 .... 6 B5
Pool Bank B98 .... 153 B2
Pool Bank St CV11 .... 73 B4
Pool End Cl B93 .... 127 F6
Pool Farm Rd B27 .... 88 C1
Pool Field Ave B31 .... 102 E7
Pool Furlong DY9 .... 99 E1
Pool Gn WS9 .... 30 A5
Pool Green Terr WS9 .... 30 A5
Pool Hall Cres WV3 .... 38 A8
Pool Hall Rd WV3 .... 38 A8
Pool Hayes Com Sch
  WV12 .... 27 B5
Pool Hayes Cty Prim Sch
  WV12 .... 27 B6
Pool Hayes La WV12 .... 27 B5
Pool Mdw Cheslyn Hay WS6 .. 4 D1
  Sutton Coldfield B76 .... 58 A8
Pool Meadow Cl
  Birmingham B13 .... 87 C1
  Solihull B91 .... 107 C2
Pool Rd Burntwood WS7 ...... 6 E3
  Halesowen B63 .... 83 B3
  Nuneaton CV10 .... 72 F5
  Smethwick B66 .... 65 B5
  Studley B80 .... 159 E4
  Wednesfield WV11 .... 27 A6
Pool St Birmingham B6 ...... 66 F6
  Dudley DY1 .... 51 A6
  Walsall WS1 .... 28 F1
  Wolverhampton WV2 ...... 163 B1
Pool View WS6 .... 5 A4
Pool Way B33 .... 69 A2
Poole Cres Birmingham B17 . 85 C3
  Brownhills WS8 .... 6 D2
  Dudley WV14 .... 40 D2
Poole Rd CV6 .... 113 A6
Poole St DY8 .... 80 E4
Poole's Way S7 .... 7 C7
Poolehouse Rd B43 .... 43 E3
Pooles Ct DY10 .... 116 E7
Pooles La WV12 .... 27 D8
Pooley La B78 .... 22 F2
Poolfield Dr B91 .... 106 F3
Poolhead La Earlswood
  B94 .... 141 C7
  Tanworth-In-A B94 .... 141 E5
Poolside Gdns CV3 .... 133 A5
Pooltail Wlk B31 .... 102 D1
Pope Gr WS12 .... 1 F6
Pope Rd WV10 .... 12 A1
Pope St Birmingham B1 ...... 66 B3
  Smethwick B66 .... 65 B7
Pope's La B69 .... 64 B7
Popes La Astwood Bank
  B96 .... 158 C2
  Birmingham B30 .... 103 D3
  Wolverhampton WV6 .... 24 A6
Poplar Ave Bedworth CV12 .. 78 D2
  Birmingham,
  Balsall Heath B12 .... 87 A5
  Birmingham,
  Coleshill Heath B37 .... 90 C8
  Birmingham, Edgbaston B17 . 65 B2
  2 Birmingham,
  Erdington B23 .... 56 F4
  Birmingham,
  King's Heath B14 .... 104 F8
  6 Birmingham, Lozells B19 . 66 C8
  Brownhills WS8 .... 16 A8
  Burntwood WS7 .... 6 F6
  Cannock WS11 .... 1 F4
  Oldbury B69 .... 64 A4
  Sutton Coldfield B75 .... 46 F7
  Tipton, Tipton Green DY4 ... 51 D5
  Tipton, Tividale B69 .... 63 C8
  Walsall, Bentley WS2 .... 27 E4
  Walsall, Yew Tree WS5 ...... 43 A4
  West Bromwich B70 .... 53 E2
  Wolverhampton WV11 ...... 26 B7
Poplar Cl Catshill B61 ..... 136 F8
  Tipton B69 .... 52 C1
  Walsall WS2 .... 27 E4
  Wombourne WV5 .... 49 B6
Poplar Cres Dudley DY1 ..... 51 B3
  Stourbridge DY8 .... 80 D3
Poplar Dr Barnt Green
  B45 .... 138 D8
  Birmingham B6 .... 55 F5
Poplar Gn DY1 .... 51 A6
Poplar Gr 7 Birmingham
  B19 .... 66 C8
  Smethwick B66 .... 65 B3
  West Bromwich B70 .... 53 E1
Poplar Ho CV12 .... 78 D2
Poplar La Cannock WS11 ..... 1 A1
  Romsley B62 .... 101 A4
Poplar Rd Bilston WV14 ..... 40 F7
  Birmingham, Moseley B14 .. 86 E1
  Birmingham, Sparkhill B11 . 87 C5
  Brownhills WS8 .... 16 A8
  Coventry CV5 .... 112 F1
  Dorridge B93 .... 127 F3
  Great Wyrley WS6 .... 5 A1
  Kidderminster DY11 .... 116 C4
  Kingswinford DY6 .... 60 E5
  Oldbury B69 .... 64 A8
  Redditch B97 .... 153 A3
  Smethwick B66 .... 65 A1
  Solihull B91 .... 107 C4
  Stourbridge DY8 .... 80 E3
  Wednesbury WS10 .... 42 A5
  Wolverhampton WV3 .... 39 A6

Poplar Rise
  Sutton Coldfield B74 .... 31 D5
  Tipton B69 .... 63 C8
Poplar Row Norton Canes
  WS11 .... 6 A6
  Smethwick B66 .... 65 C5
  Wolverhampton WV10 .... 39 D6
Poplar Trad Est B6 .... 55 F5
Poplar Trees B47 .... 125 A7
Poplars Dr B36 .... 69 B8
Poplars La B96 .... 158 A1
Poplars The
  Birmingham,
  Rotton Park B16 .... 65 F3
  Birmingham, Sparkhill B11 . 87 C6
  Brierley Hill DY5 .... 61 B7
  Cannock WS11 .... 1 E4
  Nuneaton CV10 .... 72 D3
  Smethwick B66 .... 65 C4
  Stourbridge DY8 .... 60 F2
Poplars Trad Est B80 ...... 159 D6
Poplarwoods B32 .... 84 B2
Poppy Dr 3 WS5 .... 43 A3
Poppy Gr B8 .... 67 F4
Poppy La B24 .... 57 C5
Poppyfield Ct CV4 .... 132 D3
Poppymead B23 .... 56 B8
Porchester Cl CV3 .... 115 A2
Porchester Dr B19 .... 66 D6
Porchester St B19 .... 66 D6
Porlock Cl CV3 .... 133 E5
Porlock Cres B31 .... 102 D3
Porlock Rd DY8 .... 81 A6
Port Hope Rd B11 .... 87 A7
Port La WV8, WV9 .... 10 B7
Portal Rd WS2 .... 27 F2
Portchester Dr WV11 .... 26 D5
Porter Cl Coventry CV4 ... 131 E8
  Sutton Coldfield B72 .... 57 B7
Porter St DY2 .... 51 D1
Porters Croft B17 .... 85 A8
Porters Field 6 DY2 .... 51 D1
Porters Way B9 .... 67 E2
Portersfield Ind Est B64 .... 82 C8
Portersfield Rd B64 .... 82 C8
Portershill Dr B90 .... 106 C1
Portfield Dr DY4 .... 52 A3
Portfield Gr B23 .... 57 A6
Porthkerry Gr DY3 .... 50 B7
Porthouse Gr WV14 .... 40 B3
Portia Ave B90 .... 106 B1
Portia Cl CV11 .... 74 A1
Portland Ave Aldridge WS9 . 30 B5
  Tamworth B79 .... 20 F8
Portland Cres DY9 .... 81 B5
Portland Ct Aldridge WS9 ... 30 B6
  1 Royal Leamington Spa
  CV32 .... 161 F8
Portland Dr Hinckley LE10 .. 71 E4
  Nuneaton CV10 .... 72 C4
  Stourbridge DY9 .... 81 B5
Portland Pl Cannock WS11 .. 4 C7
  Dudley WV14 .... 51 B7
  6 Royal Leamington Spa
  CV32 .... 161 F8
Portland Pl E 5 CV32 ...... 161 F8
Portland Pl W 9 CV32 ..... 161 F8
Portland Rd Aldridge WS9 ... 30 B5
  Birmingham B16 .... 65 D1
Portland St Birmingham B6 . 67 A7
  Royal Leamington Spa CV32 . 161 F8
  Walsall WS2 .... 28 E3
Portland Terr 6 B18 .... 66 A5
Portleys La B78 .... 34 D4
Portman Rd B13 .... 104 F7
Portobello Cl WV13 .... 26 D1
Portobello Rd B70 .... 53 A8
Portree Ave CV3 .... 114 F2
Portrush Ave B38 .... 103 D1
Portrush Rd WV6 .... 23 D4
Portsdown Cl WV10 .... 25 F7
Portsdown Rd B63 .... 82 D2
Portsea Cl CV3 .... 133 D6
Portsea St WS3 .... 28 C6
Portswood Cl WV9 .... 10 F1
Portway Cl Coventry CV4 . 131 E8
  Kingswinford DY6 .... 60 E5
  Royal Leamington Spa
  CV31 .... 162 D6
  Solihull B91 .... 106 E1
Portway Hill B65 .... 63 C6
Portway Rd Bilston WV14 ... 40 E7
  Blackheath B65 .... 63 B5
  Oldbury B69 .... 63 E7
  Wednesbury WS10 .... 41 E2
Portway The B65 .... 60 E5
Portway Wlk B65 .... 63 C6
Portwrinkle Ave CV6 .... 114 A6
Posey Cl B21 .... 54 C3
Post Office Rd WS5 .... 37 A2
Post Office Wlk B96 .... 158 E1
Postbridge Rd CV3 .... 133 D5
Poston Croft B14 .... 104 D3
Potter Cl B23 .... 56 D8
Potter Ct 8 DY5 .... 61 D2
Potters Green Prim Sch
  CV2 .... 96 E2
Potters Green Rd CV2 ...... 96 E1
Potters La Birmingham B6 .. 66 E2
  Wednesbury WS10 .... 41 F2
Potters Rd CV12 .... 77 E1
Potterton Way B66 .... 64 F8
Pottery Rd Oldbury B68 ..... 64 D1
  Smethwick B66 .... 65 A7
Potton Cl CV3 .... 134 E6
Potts Cl CV8 .... 148 C4
Pouk Hill Cl WS2 .... 28 A3

Pouk La WS14 .... 16 F7
Poultney Rd CV6 .... 113 A6
Poultney St B70 .... 52 F7
Poulton Cl B13 .... 87 A2
Pound Cl Berkswell CV7 ... 110 D3
  Lapworth B94 .... 144 B3
  Oldbury B68 .... 63 F3
Pound Gn B8 .... 67 F6
Pound House La
  Tanworth-in-A B94 .... 142 F4
  Tanworth-in-A B94 .... 143 A4
Pound La Birmingham B32 . 101 F3
  Royal Leamington Spa
  CV32 .... 157 A3
Pound Rd Birmingham B14 . 104 E2
  Oldbury B68 .... 64 A2
  Wednesbury WS10 .... 42 A3
Poundley Cl B36 .... 69 C8
Pountney St WV2 .... 163 B1
Pourbaix Cl WS13 .... 9 B6
Poverty B96 .... 158 E2
Powell Ave B32 .... 84 A6
Powell Pl Bilston WV14 ..... 40 E3
  Tipton DY4 .... 52 C5
Powell Rd CV2 .... 114 A4
Powell St Birmingham B1 ... 66 B3
  7 Halesowen B63 .... 83 B3
  Wolverhampton WV10 ...... 25 F4
Powell Way CV11 .... 73 C4
Powells Ho B73 .... 45 C2
Power Way DY4 .... 52 D8
Powers Ct 4 CV32 .... 156 F1
Powers Rd LE9 .... 71 F5
Powick Rd B23 .... 56 D1
Powis Ave CV8 .... 148 C5
Powis Gr CV8 .... 148 C5
Powke La B65 .... 63 A2
Powke Lane Ind Est B65 .... 63 A2
Powlers Cl DY9 .... 81 E2
Powlett St WV2 .... 163 C2
Poxon Rd WS9 .... 16 A3
Poynings The WV6 .... 24 C5
Poyser Rd CV10 .... 78 C8
Pratts La B80 .... 159 F7
Precinct The Coventry
  CV1 .... 165 B3
  Tamworth B79 .... 21 B5
  Willenhall WV12 .... 27 B5
Premier Bsns Ctr 2 B9 ..... 81 F5
Premier Bsns Pk WS2 .... 28 C1
Premier Ct B30 .... 104 C3
Premier Partnership
  Ind Est DY5 .... 61 A3
Premier St B7 .... 67 D8
Premier Trad Est B7 .... 66 F5
Premier Way B73 .... 45 D2
Prescelly Cl CV10 .... 72 B3
Prescelly Ct CV8 .... 147 F5
Prescot Rd DY9 .... 81 C3
President Kennedy Sch &
  Com Coll CV6 .... 95 B4
Prestbury Rd B6 .... 66 E8
Presthope Rd B29 .... 103 B7
Preston Ave B76 .... 46 E3
Preston Cl Coventry CV4 ... 131 F7
  Redditch B98 .... 154 B6
Preston Ho 4 WS1 .... 28 F1
Preston Rd
  Birmingham, Hockley B18 .. 65 E6
  Birmingham,
  South Yardley B26 .... 88 D7
  Hinckley LE10 .... 71 B2
Prestons Row WV14 .... 40 A3
Prestwick Cl B75 .... 46 C7
Prestwick Rd
  Birmingham B35 .... 58 B4
  Kingswinford DY6 .... 60 C6
Prestwood Dr DY7 .... 80 A7
Prestwood Rd
  Birmingham B29 .... 103 B8
  Wolverhampton WV11 ...... 26 A5
Prestwood Rd W WV11 ..... 26 B7
Pretoria Rd B9 .... 67 E3
Priam Gr WS3 .... 15 B5
Price Ave B78 .... 20 D1
Price Cres WV14 .... 40 D7
Price Rd Cubbington CV32 . 157 E5
  Stourbridge DY9 .... 82 A6
  Wednesbury WS10 .... 42 C3
Price St Bilston WV14 .... 40 F5
  Birmingham B4 .... 164 C4
  Cannock WS11 .... 1 E1
  2 Dudley DY2 .... 62 E8
  Smethwick B66 .... 65 B5
  West Bromwich B70 .... 53 C3
Prices Rd DY3 .... 50 C3
Pridmore Rd CV6 .... 113 D7
Priest Meadow Cl B96 .... 158 D1
Priest St B64 .... 62 F1
Priestfield Cl B44 .... 44 D2
Priestfield Rd B97 .... 158 E5
Priestfield Sta WV14 .... 40 B6
Priestfield Sta WV2 .... 40 A7
Priesthills Rd LE10 .... 75 D8
Priestland Rd B34 .... 69 B7
Priestley Cl Birmingham
  B20 .... 55 A2
  Halesowen B63 .... 82 B6
Priestley Rd Birmingham
  B11 .... 87 A7
  Walsall WS2 .... 28 A5
Priestley Smith Sch B23 ... 56 B6
Primley Ave Birmingham
  B36 .... 68 D7
  Tamworth B77 .... 35 F5
  Walsall WS2 .... 28 B2
Primley Cl WS2 .... 28 B2

Primrose Ave
Birmingham B11 .... 87 C5
Tipton DY4 .... 52 C8
Wolverhampton WV10 ...... 11 E3
Primrose Bank B68 .... 64 B4
Primrose Cl Blackheath B64 .. 82 B8
Lickey End B60 .... 137 C6
Walsall WS3 .... 15 A5
Primrose Cres DY1 .... 51 C4
Primrose Croft B28 ...... 105 F5
Primrose Dr LE10 .... 75 E5
Primrose Gdns
Birmingham B38 .... 123 F8
Codsall WV8 .... 10 A3
Featherstone WV10 .... 12 B7
Primrose Hill
Birmingham B38 .... 124 A8
Smethwick B67 .... 64 D4
Stourbridge DY8 .... 60 E1
Warwick CV34 .... 155 E2
Primrose Hill Jun &
Inf Sch B38 .... 123 F8
Primrose Hill St CV1 ...... 165 C4
Primrose La
Birmingham B28 .... 105 F5
Wolverhampton WV10 ...... 26 A8
Primrose Mdw WS11 .... 2 C1
Primrose Pk DY5 .... 61 C7
Primrose Rd DY2 .... 62 C4
Primrose Tower B38 ...... 123 E8
Primrose Trad Est DY2 .. 62 D4
Primrose Woods B32 ...... 84 B2
Primsland Cl B90 .... 127 C7
Prince Albert Inf & Jun Sch
B6 .... 66 E8
Prince Albert St B9 ...... 67 D1
Prince Andrew Cres B45 .. 101 E2
Prince Charles Cl B45 .... 101 E2
Prince Charles Rd WV14 .... 40 F3
Prince Edward Dr B45 .... 101 E2
Prince George Rd WS10 .... 42 A5
Prince of Wales Ct DY1 .. 51 A2
Prince of Wales Ctr
5 WS11 .... 1 E1
Prince Of Wales La B14 .. 105 C3
Prince Of Wales Rd CV5 .. 112 E3
Prince of Wales Wlk
3 B66 .... 65 C5
Prince Philip Cl B45 ...... 101 E2
Prince Rd B30 .... 104 A3
Prince Regent Ct 3 CV31 .. 161 F6
Prince Rupert Mews WS13 .. 9 A8
Prince Rupert's Way WS13 .. 9 A8
Prince St Blackheath B64 .. 82 D8
Brownhills WS9 .... 15 F2
Cannock WS11 .... 1 E6
Dudley DY2 .... 62 C6
Walsall WS2 .... 42 C8
Prince William Cl
Birmingham B23 .... 56 D2
Coventry CV6 .... 112 E6
Prince's Ave Nuneaton CV11 .. 73 B3
Walsall WS4 .... 29 B1
Prince's Dr CV31 .... 161 D7
Prince's Rd B69 .... 52 B2
Prince's Row B4 .... 66 F3
Prince's St Birmingham B4 .. 66 F3
Nuneaton CV11 .... 73 C3
Royal Leamington Spa CV32 .. 157 B1
Prince's Way B91 .... 107 B3
Princep Cl B43 .... 44 D4
Princes Ave WS1 .... 43 A8
Princes Cl CV3 .... 134 B8
Princes Dr Codsall WV8 .. 10 A2
Kenilworth CV8 .... 148 B7
Princes End Inf &
Jun Sch DY4 .... 51 E7
Princes Gate B91 .... 107 B4
Princes Gdns WV8 .... 10 A2
Princes Rd DY8 .... 80 D3
Princes Sq WV1 .... 163 C3
Princess Alice Dr B73 .... 45 D2
Princess Alley WV1 ...... 163 C3
Princess Anne Dr B45 .... 101 E2
Princess Anne Rd
Bilston WV14 .... 40 F3
Walsall WS10 .... 27 F3
Princess Cl WS7 .... 6 E7
Princess Cres B63 .... 82 E6
Princess Ct WV10 .... 26 A6
Princess End Ind Pk DY4 .. 40 E1
Princess Gr B71 .... 53 D8
Princess of Wales Com
Hospl The B61 .... 137 A4
Princess Rd Birmingham B5 .. 86 E7
Hinckley LE10 .... 75 E8
Oldbury B68 .... 64 D2
Princess Sq WV14 .... 40 F3
Princess St Burntwood WS7 .. 6 E8
Cannock WS11 .... 1 F5
Coventry CV6 .... 113 F7
Wolverhampton WV1 ...... 163 C3
Princess Way WS10 .... 41 C8
Princethorpe Cl
Birmingham B34 .... 69 D7
Solihull B90 .... 106 A2
Princethorpe Inf Sch B29 .. 85 A1
Princethorpe Jun Sch B29 .. 85 A1
Princethorpe Rd B29 ...... 85 A1
Princethorpe Tower B12 .... 86 E7
Princethorpe Way CV3 .. 134 E8
Princeton Gdns WV9 .... 10 F2
Princip St B4 .... 164 C4
Printing House St B4 .... 164 C3
Prior Ave WS10 .... 150 C3
Prior Cl DY10 .... 117 C5
Prior Deram Wlk CV4 ...... 132 C7
Priors Cl CV7 .... 130 B6

Priors Field Comb Sch
CV8 .... 147 D7
Priors Harnall CV1 .... 165 D4
Priors Mill DY3 .... 50 E5
Priors Oak B97 .... 153 B4
Priors The CV12 .... 78 C2
Priors Way B23 .... 56 C8
Priorsfield Cl 4
Coventry CV6 .... 113 A4
Kenilworth CV8 .... 147 D6
Priorsfield Rd N 3 CV6 .. 113 A4
Priorsfield Rd S CV6 ...... 113 A4
Priory Ave B29 .... 86 B2
Priory Cl Dudley DY1 ...... 51 B2
Lapworth B94 .... 144 D5
Smethwick B66 .... 65 C4
Stourbridge DY8 .... 81 B3
West Bromwich B70 ...... 53 F2
Priory Croft CV8 .... 148 A4
Priory Ct Brownhills WS9 .. 16 A4
3 Dudley DY1 .... 51 C1
Hinckley LE10 .... 71 E2
Nuneaton CV11 .... 73 A4
Solihull B91 .... 127 B7
Stourbridge DY8 .... 81 B3
Studley B80 .... 159 E5
Priory Dr B68 .... 64 C5
Priory Field Cl WV14 ...... 39 F1
Priory Green Jun & Inf Sch
WV9 .... 11 A2
Priory Ho Halesowen B63 .. 82 F5
Kenilworth CV8 .... 147 F4
Priory Hospl The B5 ...... 86 C5
Priory JMI Sch WS3 ...... 28 B7
Priory La DY3 .... 50 D7
Priory Mews CV34 .... 160 E7
Priory New Way Ind Est
B6 .... 66 F5
Priory Prim Sch DY1 ...... 51 B3
Priory Prim Sch The B71 .. 42 D2
Priory Queensway The
B4 .... 164 C3
Priory Rd
Birmingham, Aston B6 .... 67 B8
Birmingham,
Edgbaston B5, B15 ...... 86 B5
Birmingham, Stirchley B14 .. 104 C7
Birmingham, Warstock B28 .. 105 D3
Cannock WS12 .... 2 D4
Dodford B61 .... 136 A6
Dudley DY1 .... 51 C3
Halesowen B62 .... 83 F4
Kenilworth CV8 .... 148 A4
Stourbridge DY8 .... 81 B3
Warwick CV34 .... 160 E7
Priory Row CV1 .... 165 C3
Priory Sq Birmingham B4 .. 164 C3
Studley B80 .... 159 E5
Priory St Coventry CV1 .. 165 C3
Dudley DY1 .... 51 C1
Nuneaton CV10 .... 72 D3
Royal Leamington Spa CV31 .. 161 F6
Priory Terr CV31 .... 162 A7
Priory The DY3 .... 50 D8
Priory Wlk Birmingham B4 .. 164 C3
Hinckley LE10 .... 71 E1
Sutton Coldfield B72 ...... 57 C7
9 Warwick CV34 .... 160 F7
Pritchard Ave WV11 ...... 26 E6
Pritchard Cl B66 .... 65 B5
Pritchard St Brierley Hill
DY5 .... 61 B3
Wednesbury WS10 .... 42 A3
Pritchatts Rd B15 .... 85 F5
Pritchett Ave WV4 .... 39 F3
Pritchett Rd B31 .... 123 B7
Pritchett St B6 .... 66 E5
Pritchett Tower 4 B10 .. 67 B1
Private Way B45 .... 122 C4
Privet Cl B44 .... 44 E3
Privet Rd CV2 .... 96 B2
Probert Rd WV10 .... 11 B1
Proctor St B7 .... 67 A5
Proctors Barn La B98 ...... 154 B4
Proffitt Ave CV6 .... 96 A1
Proffitt Cl Brownhills WS8 .. 16 A5
Walsall WS2 .... 28 E4
Proffitt St WS2 .... 28 E4
Progress Cl CV3 .... 135 A7
Progress Dr WS11 .... 4 F6
Progress Ind Ctr WS11 ...... 4 F7
Progress Way CV3 .... 135 A8
Prole St WV10 .... 25 E4
Promenade The DY5 ...... 61 D2
Prophets Cl B97 .... 153 D3
Prospect Dr WS14 .... 9 F8
Prospect Gdns B21 .... 81 A4
Prospect Hill
Kidderminster DY10 ...... 116 E6
Redditch B97 .... 153 E4
Stourbridge DY8 .... 81 A4
Prospect La
Kidderminster DY10 ...... 116 E6
Solihull B91 .... 106 D4
Prospect Manor Ct WS12 .. 2 C3
Prospect Pk WS11 .... 4 D7
Prospect Pl B12 .... 86 F5
Prospect Rd Birmingham
B13 .... 86 F1
Burntwood WS7 .... 7 B6
Dudley DY3 .... 50 C2
Halesowen B62 .... 83 C5
Royal Leamington Spa
CV31 .... 162 B5
Prospect Rd N B98 ...... 154 A4
Prospect Rd S B98 ...... 154 A4
Prospect Row Dudley DY2 .. 62 D8
Stourbridge DY8 .... 81 A3

Prospect St Bilston WV14 .. 40 E6
Tamworth B79 .... 21 A5
Tipton DY4 .... 41 C1
Prospect Trad Est 2 B1 .. 66 C3
Prosper Mdw DY6 .... 60 F7
Prospero Cl B45 .... 102 A2
Prosser St Bilston WV14 .. 40 D5
Wolverhampton WV10 ...... 25 E5
Prossers Wlk B46 .... 70 F7
Proud Cross Ringway
DY11 .... 116 C6
Proud's La WV14 .... 40 D7
Provence Cl WV10 .... 25 F4
Providence Cl WS3 .... 28 C7
Providence Dr DY9 .... 81 E6
Providence La WS3 .... 28 C6
Providence Rd B61 ...... 136 F3
Providence Row WV14 .... 51 B8
Providence St
Blackheath B64 .... 62 D1
Coventry CV5 .... 132 F8
Stourbridge DY9 .... 81 F6
Tipton DY4 .... 52 C5
Providence Terr WV11 .... 41 E6
Provost Williams CE Prim
Sch CV8 .... 135 A1
Pruden Ave WV4 .... 39 F3
Pryor Rd B68 .... 64 C4
Ptarmigan Pl CV11 .... 73 F3
Puckering's La 4 CV34 .. 160 E6
Pudsey Dr B75 .... 32 C3
Pugh Cres WS2 .... 27 E2
Pugh Rd Bilston WV14 .... 40 E3
Birmingham B6 .... 67 A8
Wolverhampton WV14 .... 39 F2
Pughe's Cl LE10 .... 76 A6
Pugin Cl WV6 .... 23 D3
Pugin Gdns B23 .... 56 D8
Pullman Cl B77 .... 22 A2
Pump St Kidderminster
DY10 .... 116 E4
Wolverhampton WV2 ...... 40 A7
Pumphouse La
Blackwell B45, B60 ...... 137 F7
Redditch B97 .... 152 D1
Puppy Gn DY4 .... 52 B5
Purbeck Cl B63 .... 82 D1
Purbeck Croft B32 .... 84 F4
Purbrook Rd WV1 .... 40 A8
Purcell Ave Lichfield WS13 .. 3 C2
Nuneaton CV11 .... 79 A7
Purcell Cl CV32 .... 162 A8
Purcell Rd Coventry CV6 .. 114 B8
Wolverhampton WV10 .... 25 D1
Purdy Rd WV14 .... 40 E2
Purefoy Rd Birmingham
B13 .... 105 C5
Coventry CV3 .... 133 D8
Purley Gr B23 .... 56 A5
Purlieu La CV8 .... 147 D5
Purnells Way B93 .... 128 A5
Purser Dr CV34 .... 160 B4
Purshall Cl B97 .... 153 C3
Purslet Rd WV1 .... 26 A2
Purslow Gr B31 .... 103 A1
Purton Mews CV31 .... 162 C6
Putney Ave B20 .... 55 C1
Putney La B62 .... 101 B1
Putney Rd B20 .... 55 C1
Putney Wlk B37 .... 70 B3
Puxton Dr DY11 .... 116 D8
Puxton La DY11 .... 116 C7
Pye Green Rd WS11 .... 1 E4
Pye Green Valley Cty
Prim Sch WS12 .... 2 A7
Pyeharps Rd LE10 .... 75 E5
Pype Hayes Rd B24 ...... 57 D4
Pyt Pk CV5 .... 112 D4
Pytchley Ho B20 .... 54 F3
Pytman Dr B76 .... 58 A7

Quadrangle The B90 ...... 126 E8
Quadrant The Coventry
CV1 .... 165 B2
Nuneaton CV11 .... 73 E3
Sedgley DY3 .... 39 D1
Quadrille Lawns WV9 ...... 10 F2
Quail Gn WV6 .... 23 F2
Quail Park Dr DY10 ...... 117 A2
Qualcast Rd WV1, WV10 .... 25 F2
Quale Gr DY3 .... 60 D3
Quantock Cl
Birmingham B45 .... 102 B2
Halesowen B63 .... 82 D2
Quantock Dr
Kidderminster DY10 ...... 117 A6
Nuneaton CV10 .... 72 B3
Quantock Rd DY8 .... 81 B6
Quantry La DY9 .... 120 F8
Quarrington Gr B14 ...... 105 A3
Quarry Brow DY3 .... 50 E6
Quarry Cl Cheslyn Hay WS6 .... 4 F3
Leek Wootton CV35 ...... 155 F7
Quarry Fields CV35 ...... 155 F7
Quarry Hill B63 .... 82 F2
Quarry Hills La WS14 ...... 9 D6
Quarry House Cl B45 .... 101 F1
Quarry La Birmingham B31 .. 103 A2
Bromsgrove B60 .... 150 D8
Chadwick End CV35 ...... 145 C1
Halesowen B63 .... 83 A2
Nuneaton CV11 .... 73 F1
Quarry Lodge WS14 .... 9 D5
Quarry Rd Birmingham B29 .. 103 A8
Dudley DY2 .... 62 B1
Kenilworth CV8 .... 147 E6

Quarry Rise B69 .... 63 B8
Quarry St CV32 .... 161 E2
Quarry The DY10 .... 116 F8
Quarry Wlk B45 .... 122 A7
Quarry Yd CV10 .... 72 C4
Quarryfield La CV1 ...... 165 C1
Quarrywood Gr CV2 ...... 114 A4
Quasar Ctr 1 WS1 .... 28 E2
Quatford Gdns WV10 ...... 25 E5
Quayle Gr DY8 .... 60 D3
Quayside Cl B69 .... 63 E8
Quebec Ho 1 B5 .... 86 D7
Queen Eleanors Dr B93 .. 128 B8
Queen Elizabeth Ave WS2 .. 27 F2
Queen Elizabeth Cl B19 .. 66 B6
Queen Elizabeth Hospl
B15 .... 85 E4
Queen Elizabeth Rd
Birmingham B45 .... 101 E2
Kidderminster DY10 ...... 117 B5
Nuneaton CV10 .... 72 D5
Queen Elizabeth's Mercian
High Sch B79 .... 21 B6
Queen Isabel's Ave CV3 .. 133 D8
Queen Margaret's Rd CV4 .. 132 C8
Queen Mary St WS1 ...... 42 D6
Queen Mary's Gram Sch
WS1 .... 43 A8
Queen Mary's High Sch
WS4 .... 28 F3
Queen Philippa St CV3 .. 133 D6
Queen Sq WV1 .... 163 B3
Queen St Astwood Bank
B96 .... 158 E1
Bedworth CV12 .... 78 C2
Bilston, Bunker's Hill WV14 .. 40 E5
Bilston, Moxley WS10 .... 41 B4
Birmingham B12 .... 87 B5
Blackheath B64 .... 62 D1
Brierley Hill, Pensnett DY5 .. 61 C6
Brierley Hill,
Quarry Bank DY5 .... 82 A8
Brownhills WS9 .... 15 F2
Burntwood WS7 .... 6 F5
Cannock, Blackfords WS11 .. 1 D1
Cannock, High Town WS11 .. 2 A5
Cheslyn Hay WS6 .... 4 D3
Coventry CV1 .... 165 C4
Cubbington CV32 .... 157 E5
Darlaston WS10 .... 41 D8
Halesowen B63 .... 83 A4
Kidderminster DY10 ...... 116 E7
Kingswinford DY6 .... 60 D7
Lichfield WS13 .... 9 A7
Oldbury B69 .... 64 A8
Redditch B98 .... 153 E4
Royal Leamington Spa CV32 .. 157 A1
Stourbridge, Wollaston DY8 .. 80 F6
Stourbridge, Wordsley DY8 .. 60 E3
Sutton Coldfield B72 ...... 46 C4
Tipton DY4 .... 51 F8
Walsall WS2 .... 28 D1
Wednesbury WS10 .... 41 E3
West Bromwich B70 ...... 53 D3
Wolverhampton WV1 ...... 163 C3
Queen Street Pas DY5 .... 82 A8
Queen Victoria Rd
Coventry CV1 .... 165 B2
Coventry CV1 .... 165 B3
Queen Victoria Sch DY3 .. 50 D8
Queen's Arc WV1 .... 163 B3
Queen's Ave B69 .... 52 A1
Queen's Cl CV8 .... 147 F3
Queen's Coll B15 .... 85 F5
Queen's Cotts B97 .... 153 B4
Queen's Cres DY8 .... 81 A7
Queen's Croft Specl Sch
WS13 .... 9 B7
Queen's Cross DY2 .... 62 B8
Queen's Ct WV10 .... 26 A6
Queen's Dr CV35 .... 145 A1
Queen's Lea WV12 .... 27 C5
Queen's Park Flats
2 LE10 .... 75 E8
Queen's Park Rd B32 ...... 84 F6
Queen's Park Terr 3 LE10 .. 75 E8
Queen's Rd Birmingham B23 .. 56 C3
Coventry CV1 .... 165 A2
Hinckley LE10 .... 75 E8
Kenilworth CV8 .... 147 F3
Nuneaton CV11 .... 73 B4
Oldbury B68 .... 64 D5
Smethwick B67 .... 64 D4
Stourbridge DY8 .... 80 F6
Tipton DY4 .... 51 F5
Walsall WS5 .... 43 B6
Queen's Ride B12 .... 86 D4
Queen's Sq Warwick CV34 .. 160 F5
West Bromwich B70 ...... 53 D3
Queens Ave
Birmingham B14 .... 104 E8
Solihull B90 .... 106 B1
Queens CE Mid Sch CV11 .. 73 A4
Queens Cl Birmingham B24 .. 56 F2
Smethwick B67 .... 65 A5
Queens Court Trad Est
B70 .... 52 F3
Queens Cres WV14 .... 40 A1
Queens Ct Birmingham B3 .. 164 B4
Brierley Hill DY5 .... 61 C6
Blackheath B65 .... 63 D4
Burntwood WS7 .... 6 F5
Queens Dr Birmingham B30 .. 104 A4
Queens Dr The B62 ...... 83 C5

Queens Gdns Bilston WV14 .. 40 D7
Dudley DY2 .... 62 C4
Queens Gdns Holyhead Rd
WS10 .... 41 E3
Queens Gdns Meeting St
WS10 .... 41 E3
Queens Head Rd B21 ...... 65 E7
Queens Hill DY9 .... 119 D7
Queens Hospital Cl B15 .. 66 C1
Queens Par 6 WS3 .... 14 B1
Queens Rd
Birmingham, Aston B6 .... 67 A8
Birmingham, Yardley B26 .. 68 F1
Sedgley DY3 .... 50 E8
Walsall WS4 .... 29 C7
Queens Sq 6 WS11 .... 1 E1
Queens Way B78 .... 36 F6
Queensbridge Rd B13 ...... 86 E2
Queensbridge Sec Sch
B13 .... 86 E2
Queensbury Sch B24 ...... 56 F2
Queensland Ave CV5 ...... 112 F2
Queenspark CV31 .... 161 E6
Queensway Birmingham B6 .. 55 E5
Halesowen B63 .... 83 B3
Nuneaton CV10 .... 73 D6
Oldbury B68 .... 64 B1
Royal Leamington Spa CV31 .. 161 E6
Stourbridge DY9 .... 81 E2
Sutton Coldfield B74 ...... 45 A8
Tamworth B79 .... 21 A3
Queensway Ct B68 .... 64 B1
Queensway Trad Est
Birmingham B5 .... 164 D3
Royal Leamington Spa
CV31 .... 161 E6
Queensway (Tunnel) B3 .. 164 B3
Queenswood Ct CV7 ...... 94 D4
Queenswood Rd
Birmingham B13 .... 87 A4
Sutton Coldfield B75 ...... 32 B1
Quentin Dr DY1 .... 61 F8
Queslade Cl B43 .... 44 A1
Queslett Rd B43 .... 44 C2
Queslett Rd E B74, B43 .... 44 F5
Quibery Cl B98 .... 154 F3
Quicksand La WS9 .... 29 F4
Quigley Ave B9 .... 67 B2
Quillets Rd DY8 .... 60 C3
Quilletts Cl CV6 .... 96 A1
Quilter Cl Dudley WV14 .... 51 A8
Walsall WS2 .... 27 F3
Quilter Rd B24 .... 57 B2
Quince B77 .... 22 B3
Quince Tree Specl Sch
B77 .... 22 B3
Quincey Dr B24 .... 57 C3
Quincy Rise DY5 .... 81 C7
Quinn Cl CV3 .... 134 B7
Quinneys La B98 .... 159 B6
Quinton Ave WS6 .... 4 F3
Quinton CE Jun & Inf Sch
B32 .... 84 A6
Quinton Cl Redditch B98 .. 154 D1
Solihull B92 .... 89 D3
Quinton Expressway B32 .. 84 B4
Quinton Flats CV3 .... 133 D7
Quinton La B32 .... 84 D6
Quinton Par CV3 .... 133 D7
Quinton Pk CV3 .... 133 D7
Quinton Rd Birmingham
B17 .... 85 C3
Coventry CV1 .... 165 C1
Quinton Rd W B32 .... 84 D4
Quintondale 5 B90 ...... 126 C8
Quonians La WS13 .... 9 B8
Quorn Cres DY8 .... 60 C3
Quorn Gr B24 .... 57 C2
Quorn Ho 3 B20 .... 54 F3
Quorn Way CV3 .... 134 C7

Rabbit La WV10 .... 12 A8
Rabone La B66 .... 65 C6
Raby Cl B69 .... 62 F8
Raby St WV2 .... 163 C2
Race Leys Fst Sch CV12 .. 78 B3
Race Leys Mid Sch CV12 .. 78 B4
Racecourse La DY8 .... 80 F1
Racecourse Rd WV6 ...... 25 A5
Rachael Gdns WS10 ...... 42 C4
Rachel Cl DY4 .... 41 C1
Rachel Gdns B29 .... 85 D2
Radbourn Dr B74 .... 46 C6
Radbourne Dr B63 .... 82 A7
Radbourne Rd B90 ...... 106 D3
Radbrook Way CV31 ...... 162 D6
Radcliffe Dr B62 .... 83 E6
Radcliffe Gdns 6 CV31 .. 162 A6
Radcliffe Rd CV5 .... 132 F8
Radcliffe Tower 3 B12 .... 86 F8
Raddens Rd B62 .... 83 F7
Raddington Dr B92 ...... 106 D8
Raddlebarn Farm Dr
B29 .... 103 F8
Raddlebarn Jun & Inf Sch
B29 .... 85 F1
Raddlebarn Rd B29 ...... 103 F8
Radford Ave DY10 .... 116 E7
Radford Circ 5 CV6 ...... 113 A4
Radford Cl WS5 .... 43 A3
Radford Dr WS4 .... 15 C2
Radford Ho Coventry CV6 .. 113 A4
Redditch B97 .... 153 A4
Radford La WV3 .... 37 F7
Radford Prim Sch CV6 .. 113 B5

Radford Rd Alvechurch
B48 .... **139** D7
Birmingham B29 .... **103** A6
Coventry CV1 .... **113** B5
Royal Leamington Spa
CV31 .... **162** C7
Radford Rise B91 .... **107** E5
Radford Semele CE
Prim Sch CV31 .... **162** E5
Radley Dr CV10 .... **73** A1
Radley Gr B29 .... **85** A2
Radley Rd Stourbridge DY9 .... **81** F4
Walsall WS4 .... **29** C7
Radleys Cty Prim Sch WS4 .. **29** D7
Radleys The B33 .... **89** D8
Radleys Wlk B33 .... **89** D8
Radmore Cl WS7 .... **6** D8
Radmore Rd LE10 .... **71** D3
Radnor Cl B45 .... **102** B2
Radnor Croft WS5 .... **43** C3
Radnor Dr CV10 .... **72** C2
Radnor Gn B71 .... **53** C7
Radnor Ho B32 .... **102** D6
Radnor Rd Birmingham B20 .... **66** B8
Oldbury B68 .... **84** B7
Sedgley DY3 .... **50** C8
Radnor Rise WS12 .... **2** B4
Radnor St B18 .... **66** A6
Radnor Wlk CV2 .... **114** F8
Radstock Ave B36 .... **68** C7
Radstock Rd WV12 .... **13** C1
Radway Cl B98 .... **154** B6
Radway Rd B90 .... **126** E8
Raeburn Rd B43 .... **44** C4
Raeside Dr B45 .... **102** B1
RAF Cotts B35 .... **57** F2
Raford Rd B23 .... **56** D6
Ragees Rd DY6 .... **60** F4
Raglan Ave Perton WV6 ... **23** F3
Smethwick B66 .... **65** C4
Raglan Cl Aldridge WS9 ... **30** F3
Nuneaton CV11 .... **73** D4
Sedgley DY3 .... **50** B7
Raglan Ct Bromsgrove B60 . **137** A1
7 Coventry CV1 .... **113** E3
Raglan Gr CV8 .... **148** B5
Raglan Ho B33 .... **69** A2
Raglan Rd Birmingham B21 .. **65** C8
Birmingham,
Balsall Heath B5 .... **86** D5
Smethwick B66 .... **65** C4
Raglan St Brierley Hill DY5 .. **61** C4
Coventry CV1 .... **165** D3
Wolverhampton WV3 ...... **163** A2
Raglan Way B37 .... **70** D1
Ragley Cl Knowle B93 .... **128** B7
Walsall WS3 .... **14** A1
Ragley Cres B60 .... **151** A8
Ragley Dr
Birmingham, Grove Vale B43 .. **43** D2
Birmingham, Sheldon B26 .... **89** C6
2 Willenhall WV13 .... **40** F8
Ragley Ho B97 .... **153** A4
Ragley Way CV11 .... **73** F2
Ragley Wlk **1** B65 .... **63** C3
Raglis Cl B97 .... **153** A2
Raikes La WS14 .... **17** C7
Rail Bridge Est B70 .... **53** A1
Railswood Rd WS3 .... **15** B3
Railway Cl B80 .... **159** D4
Railway Dr Bilston WV14 .... **40** E5
Wolverhampton WV1 ...... **163** C3
Railway La WV13 .... **27** A1
Railway Rd Birmingham B20 .. **55** F2
Sutton Coldfield B73 .... **46** B5
Railway St Bilston WV14 .... **40** E5
Cannock WS11 .... **4** E1
Norton Canes WS11 .... **6** A5
Tipton DY4 .... **52** C5
West Bromwich B70 .... **53** B4
Wolverhampton WV1 ...... **163** C3
Railway Terr Bedworth CV12 .. **78** C2
Birmingham, Aston B7 .... **67** B6
Birmingham, Hamstead B42 .. **54** F6
4 Wednesbury WS10 ..... **41** F2
Railway View B10 .... **87** C7
Railwayside Cl B66 .... **64** F2
Rainbow St Dudley WV14 ... **40** D2
Wolverhampton WV2 ...... **163** C1
Rainford Way B38 .... **123** C8
Rainham Cl DY4 .... **51** D5
Rainsbrook Dr
Nuneaton CV11 .... **74** A1
Solihull B90 .... **126** F6
Rainscar B77 .... **36** B7
Raison Ave CV11 .... **73** E4
Rake Gate Jun & Inf Schs
WV10 .... **11** B1
Rake Hill WS7 .... **7** B8
Rake Way B15 .... **66** B1
Raleigh Cl Birmingham B21 .. **54** B1
Hinckley LE10 .... **71** D4
Raleigh Croft B43 .... **43** E3
Raleigh Ind Est B21 .... **54** B1
Raleigh Rd Bilston WV14 ... **41** A3
Coventry CV2 .... **114** B2
Raleigh St Walsall WS2 .... **28** C2
West Bromwich B71 .... **53** C4
Ralph Barlow Gdns B44 .... **56** B8
Ralph Rd Birmingham B8 ... **67** D4
Coventry CV6 .... **112** F5
Solihull B90 .... **106** C4
Ralphs Mdw B32 .... **84** D2
Ralston Cl WS3 .... **14** A4

Ramillies Cres WS6 .... **4** F1
Ramp Rd B26 .... **90** C5
Ramsay Cl B71 .... **53** F8
Ramsay Cres CV5 .... **112** B7
Ramsay Rd Oldbury B68 .... **64** C1
Tipton DY4 .... **51** E7
Walsall WS2 .... **28** A5
Ramsden Ave CV10 .... **72** D6
Ramsden Cl B29 .... **103** B7
Ramsey Cl Birmingham B45 .. **101** F1
Hinckley LE10 .... **71** B1
Ramsey Rd **1** Birmingham
B7 .... **67** C7
Royal Leamington Spa CV31 . **162** B7
Ran-tan The B97 .... **158** E5
Ranby Rd CV2 .... **113** F4
Randall Ave B48 .... **139** A6
Randall Cl DY6 .... **60** F4
Randall Rd CV8 .... **147** F3
Randle Dr B75 .... **32** C3
Randle Rd Nuneaton CV10 .. **72** D4
Stourbridge DY9 .... **81** C4
Randle St CV6 .... **113** B5
Randolph Cl CV31 .... **162** C6
Randwick Gr B44 .... **44** E1
Ranelagh Ho WV2 .... **39** D7
Ranelagh Rd WV2 .... **39** D6
Ranelagh St CV31 .... **162** A6
Ranelagh Terr CV31 .... **162** A6
Range Meadow Cl CV32 ... **156** C3
Rangemoor CV3 .... **134** D6
Rangeways Rd
Kidderminster DY11 .... **116** A8
Kingswinford DY6 .... **60** F4
Rangeworthy Cl B97 .... **158** C2
Rangifer Rd B78 .... **20** F1
Rangoon Rd B92 .... **89** E4
Ranleigh Ave DY6 .... **60** F4
Rann Cl B16 .... **66** A1
Rannoch Cl Brierley Hill DY5 . **81** B8
Hinckley LE10 .... **75** B8
Rannock Cl CV3 .... **114** F2
Ranscombe Dr DY3 .... **50** D2
Ransom Rd Birmingham B23 . **56** C4
Coventry CV6 .... **113** E8
Ranton Pk WS11 .... **2** A2
Ranulf Croft CV3 .... **133** C7
Ranulf St CV3 .... **133** C7
Ranworth Rise WV4 .... **39** D4
Raphael Cl CV5 .... **112** C3
Ratcliff Way DY4 .... **52** D6
Ratcliff Wlk **3** B69 .... **64** A7
Ratcliffe Ct CV10 .... **72** C4
Ratcliffe Rd Hinckley LE10 .. **75** F6
Solihull B91 .... **107** C7
Wednesfield WV11 .... **27** A8
Rathbone Cl Bilston WV14 .. **40** D5
Birmingham B5 .... **86** E7
Keresley CV7 .... **95** A6
Rathbone Rd B67 .... **64** F2
Rathlev Wlk B38 .... **123** C8
Rathlin Cl WV9 .... **11** A3
Rathlin Croft B36 .... **70** B6
Rathmore Cl DY8 .... **80** E2
Rathvilly Ish B31 .... **103** B3
Rathwell Cl WV9 .... **11** A2
Rattle Croft B33 .... **68** E3
Raveloe Dr CV11 .... **73** D1
Raven Cl Cannock WS12 .... **2** E4
Cheslyn Hay WS6 .... **4** D2
Huntington WS12 .... **1** C7
Raven Cragg Rd CV5 ...... **132** E8
Raven Cres WV11 .... **26** F8
Raven Ct **21** DY5 .... **61** D2
Raven Hays Rd B31 .... **102** C2
Raven Rd WS5 .... **43** B6
Raven Way CV11 .... **73** F2
Raven Wlk **4** B15 .... **86** C7
Ravenall Cl B34 .... **69** B7
Ravenfield Cl B8 .... **68** A5
Ravenhill Dr WV8 .... **10** A4
Ravenhurst Dr B43 .... **43** E3
Ravenhurst Mews B23 ..... **56** E3
Ravenhurst Rd B17 .... **85** C6
Ravenhurst St B12 .... **87** A8
Ravens Bank Dr B98 ...... **154** E7
Ravens Bank Fst Sch
B98 .... **154** D6
Ravens Ct WS8 .... **15** F7
Ravensbourne Gr WV13 .... **27** C2
Ravenscroft DY8 .... **80** C6
Ravenscroft Rd Solihull
B92 .... **107** A8
Willenhall WV12 .... **27** B5
Ravensdale Ave CV32 ..... **156** C2
Ravensdale Cl WS5 .... **43** B7
Ravensdale Gdns WS5 ...... **43** B7
Ravensdale Prim Sch
CV2 .... **114** D4
Ravensdale Rd
Birmingham B10 .... **87** F7
Coventry CV2 .... **114** D3
Ravenshaw La B91 .... **108** A4
Ravenshaw Rd B16 .... **65** C2
Ravenshaw Way B91 ...... **108** A3
Ravenshill Rd B14 .... **105** D4
Ravensholme WV6 .... **23** F2
Ravensitch Wlk DY5 .... **61** E1
Ravensmere Rd B98 .... **154** B1
Ravensthorpe Cl CV3 ..... **134** E8
Ravenstone B77 .... **36** B8
Ravenswood B15 .... **85** E8
Ravenswood Cl B74 .... **46** B8
Ravenswood Dr B91 .... **106** F1
Ravenswood Dr S B91 .... **106** E1
Ravenswood Hill B46 .... **70** F7

Rawdon Gr B44 .... **56** B8
Rawlett High Sch B79 ..... **21** A8
Rawlings Rd B67 .... **65** A2
Rawlins Croft B35 .... **58** C3
Rawlins St B16 .... **66** A1
Rawlinson Rd CV32 .... **157** B2
Rawnsley Dr CV8 .... **148** C6
Rawnsley Rd WS12 .... **2** E7
Ray Ct B74 .... **31** E3
Ray Hall La Birmingham B43 .. **54** B8
West Bromwich B71 .... **43** A1
Raybolds Bridge St WS2 ... **28** C4
Raybon Croft B45 .... **122** A6
Raybould's Fold DY2 .... **62** C5
Rayford Dr B71 .... **43** A2
Raygill B77 .... **36** B8
Rayleigh Ho B27 .... **88** D3
Rayleigh Rd WV3 .... **39** A8
Raymond Ave B42 .... **55** B6
Raymond Cl Coventry CV6 ... **95** F5
Walsall WS2 .... **28** D5
Raymond Gdns WV11 .... **26** E6
Raymond Rd B8 .... **67** E4
Raymont Gr B43 .... **44** B4
Rayners Croft B26 .... **68** F2
Raynor Cres CV12 .... **77** D1
Raynor Rd WV10 .... **25** F6
Raynsford Wlk CV34 ...... **155** D1
Raywoods The CV10 .... **72** F3
Rea Ave B45 .... **121** E8
Rea Cl B31 .... **123** A7
Rea Fordway B45 .... **101** F1
Rea St B5 .... **164** D1
Rea St S B5 .... **86** F8
Rea Terr B5 .... **66** F2
Rea Tower B19 .... **66** C5
Rea Valley Dr B31 .... **103** B2
Reabrook Rd B31 .... **122** F8
Read St CV1 .... **113** E3
Readers Wlk B43 .... **43** F1
Reading Ave CV11 .... **73** F7
Reading Cl CV2 .... **96** B3
Reansway Sq W6 .... **25** A4
Reapers Cl WV12 .... **27** D5
Reapers Wlk WV8 .... **10** F1
Rear Cotts B48 .... **138** F6
Reardon Ct CV34 .... **155** E1
Reaside Cres B14 .... **104** B5
Reaside Croft B12 .... **86** E6
Reaside Jun Sch B45 ..... **101** E1
Reaview Dr B29 .... **86** B2
Reay Nadin Dr B73 .... **45** B4
Reaymer Cl WS2 .... **28** B6
Rebecca Dr B29 .... **85** E2
Rebecca Gdns WV4 .... **38** F4
Recreation Rd
Bromsgrove B61 .... **136** F3
Coventry CV6 .... **96** A3
Recreation St DY2 .... **62** D5
Rectory Ave WS10 .... **41** D6
Rectory Cl Allesley CV5 ... **112** C6
Bedworth CV7 .... **78** A1
Drayton Bassett B78 .... **34** E5
Stourbridge DY8 .... **81** B3
Whitnash CV31 .... **162** B4
Rectory Dr CV7 .... **78** A1
Rectory Fields DY8 .... **60** E2
Rectory Gdns
Birmingham B36 .... **69** A8
Oldbury B68 .... **64** C5
Solihull B91 .... **107** C3
Stourbridge DY8 .... **81** B3
Rectory Gr B18 .... **65** E6
Rectory La Allesley CV5 ... **112** C6
Birmingham B36 .... **69** A8
Upton Warren B61 .... **150** A4
Rectory Park Ave B75 ...... **46** E4
Rectory Park Cl B75 .... **46** E4
Rectory Park Ct B75 .... **46** F6
Rectory Park Rd B26 .... **89** C5
Rectory Rd Birmingham
B31 .... **103** B3
Redditch B97 .... **153** D1
Solihull B91 .... **107** C3
Stourbridge B93 .... **81** B3
Sutton Coldfield B75 .... **46** E6
Rectory St DY8 .... **60** E3
Red Brick Cl B64 .... **82** D7
Red Brook Rd WS2 .... **28** A5
Red Deeps CV11 .... **78** D8
Red Deeps Specl Sch
CV10 .... **78** B8
Red Hall Prim Sch DY3 .... **50** C3
Red Hill Redditch B98 ..... **153** F2
Stourbridge DY8 .... **81** B4
Red Hill Cl B80 .... **159** E6
Red Hill Gr B38 .... **123** F7
Red Hill Pl B62 .... **101** A7
Red Hill St WV1 .... **163** B4
Red House Ave WS10 .... **42** B3
Red House La WS9 .... **29** F5
Red House Park Rd B43 .... **43** E2
Red House Rd B33 .... **68** E2
Red La Burton Green CV8 ... **131** C2
Coventry CV6 .... **113** F5
Essington WV11 .... **13** C2
Kenilworth CV8 .... **147** D8
Sedgley DY3 .... **50** B8
Red Leasowes Rd B63 ...... **83** A3
Red Lion Ave WS11 .... **6** A4
Red Lion Cl DY2 .... **62** A1
Red Lion Cres WS11 .... **6** A4
Red Lion La WS11 .... **6** B4
Red Lion St Alvechurch B48 . **139** B6
Redditch B98 .... **153** E4
Wolverhampton WV1 ...... **163** B3
Red River Rd WS2 .... **28** A5
Red Sands Rd DY10 .... **116** E8

Red Wing Wlk B36 .... **70** A8
Redacre Rd B73 .... **45** F2
Redacres WV6 .... **24** E6
Redbank Ave B23 .... **56** C3
Redbourn Rd WS3 .... **14** A4
Redbrook Cl B91 .... **107** A1
Redbrook Covert **8** B38 . **123** E8
Redbrooks Cl B91 .... **107** A1
Redburn Dr B14 .... **104** D2
Redcap Croft CV6 .... **95** D4
Redcar Cl CV32 .... **157** C4
Redcar Croft B36 .... **68** C8
Redcar Rd Coventry CV1 ... **113** E5
Wolverhampton WV10 .... **11** D4
Redcliff B77 .... **21** F5
Redcliffe Dr WV5 .... **49** B6
Redcotts Cl WV10 .... **26** A8
Redcroft Dr B24 .... **57** C5
Redcroft Rd DY2 .... **62** E6
Reddal Hill Rd B64 .... **62** E2
Reddicap Heath Inf Sch
B75 .... **46** F5
Reddicap Heath Rd B75 ... **46** F4
Reddicap Hill B75 .... **46** E4
Reddicap Trad Est B76 ..... **46** D4
Reddicroft B73 .... **46** C5
Reddings La B28 .... **87** E3
Reddings Rd B13 .... **86** E2
Reddings The B47 .... **125** A5
Redditch Ho B33 .... **69** E2
Redditch Rd
Alvechurch,
Arrowfield Top B48 .... **139** B8
Alvechurch,
Rowney Green B48 .... **139** C3
Birmingham B38 .... **123** C8
Hopwood B48 .... **123** B1
Stoke Heath B60 .... **150** D5
Studley B80 .... **159** D5
Redditch Ringway B97 ..... **153** D4
Redditch Sta B97 .... **153** D4
Redditch Wlk **4** CV2 ..... **115** A7
Redesdale Ave CV6 .... **112** F5
Redfern Ave CV8 .... **148** A6
Redfern Cl B92 .... **89** B1
Redfern Dr WS7 .... **7** B5
Redfern Park Rd B11 .... **88** A5
Redfern Rd B11 .... **88** A5
Redfly La DY5 .... **61** C6
Redford Cl B13 .... **87** B2
Redgate Cl B38 .... **103** D2
Redhall Rd Birmingham
B32 .... **84** E7
Dudley DY3 .... **50** C2
Redhill Ave WV5 .... **49** A6
Redhill Cl Stourbridge DY8 ... **81** B4
Tamworth B79 .... **21** A7
Redhill Ct DY8 .... **81** B4
Redhill Jun & Inf Sch B25 .. **88** A6
Redhill Jun Sch WS11 .... **1** F4
Redhill Rd
Birmingham,
King's Norton B38 .... **123** D7
Birmingham, Tyseley B25 ... **88** A6
Cannock WS11 .... **1** F4
Redhill Sch DY8 .... **81** B4
Redhouse Cl B93 .... **127** E4
Redhouse Ind Est WS9 ..... **29** E6
Redhouse JMI Sch WS9 .... **29** E7
Redhouse Rd WV6 .... **24** B5
Redhouse St WS1 .... **42** E7
Redhurst Dr WV10 .... **11** B3
Redlake B77 .... **35** F8
Redlake Dr DY9 .... **99** B8
Redlake Rd DY9 .... **81** B1
Redland Cl Coventry CV2 .... **96** E2
Marlbrook B60 .... **121** C1
Redland Rd CV31 .... **162** B5
Redlands Cl B91 .... **107** D5
Redlands Rd B91 .... **107** D5
Redlands Way B74 .... **31** A1
Redliff Ave B36 .... **58** D1
Redlock Field WS14 .... **9** A5
Redmead Cl B30 .... **103** C4
Redmoor Gdns WV4 .... **39** A5
Redmoor High Sch LE10 ... **71** B3
Redmoor Way B76 .... **58** D6
Rednal Hill Inf Sch B45 ... **122** C7
Rednal Hill Jun Sch B45 .. **122** C7
Rednal Hill La B45 .... **122** A6
Rednal Mill Dr B45 .... **122** C7
Rednal Rd B38 .... **103** E1
Rednall Dr B75 .... **32** C3
Rednell Ho B69 .... **63** D6
Redoak Ho WV10 .... **25** F3
Redruth Cl Coventry CV6 .. **114** A8
Kingswinford DY6 .... **60** D8
Nuneaton CV11 .... **74** A4
Walsall WS5 .... **43** D7
Redruth Rd WS5 .... **43** D7
Redstart Ave DY10 .... **117** B2
Redstone Cl B98 .... **154** C6
Redstone Dr WV11 .... **26** F5
Redstone Farm Rd B28 ... **106** B6
Redthorn Gr B33 .... **68** F3
Redvers Rd B9 .... **67** E1
Redway Ct B75 .... **46** E4
Redwell Cl B77 .... **21** D5
Redwing B77 .... **36** A6
Redwing Cl DY10 .... **117** A1
Redwing Ct WS12 .... **1** C7
Redwing Gr B23 .... **56** B7
Redwood Ave DY1 .... **50** F5
Redwood Bsns Pk B66 ..... **64** C7

Redwood Cl Aldridge B74 .... **30** F2
Birmingham B30 .... **103** E4
Redwood Croft
Birmingham B14 .... **104** E7
Nuneaton CV10 .... **73** A1
Redwood Dr Burntwood WS7 ... **6** F8
Cannock WS11 .... **2** A3
Tipton B69 .... **52** B2
Redwood Gdns B27 .... **88** B5
Redwood Ho B37 .... **69** F5
Redwood Rd
Birmingham B30 .... **103** E4
Dudley WV14 .... **40** D2
Walsall WS5 .... **43** B4
Redwood Way WV12 .... **27** B8
Reed Sq B35 .... **58** B4
Reedham Gdns WV4 .... **38** D5
Reedly Rd WV12 .... **13** C1
Reedmace B77 .... **21** C2
Reedmace Cl B38 .... **123** F8
Reedswood Cl WS2 .... **28** C3
Reedswood Gdns WS2 ...... **28** C3
Reedswood La WS2 .... **28** C3
Reedswood Way WS2 .... **28** B4
Rees Dr Coventry CV3 ...... **133** D4
Wombourne WV5 .... **49** B7
Reeve Cl CV10 .... **117** A1
Reeve Dr CV8 .... **148** A4
Reeve La WS13 .... **9** B8
Reeves Gdns WV8 .... **10** A4
Reeves Rd Birmingham
B14 .... **104** C6
Hinckley LE10 .... **75** F6
Reeves St WS3 .... **28** B8
Reflex Ind Pk WV13 .... **27** A3
Reform St B70 .... **53** D3
Reg Hadden Ct CV10 .... **73** D6
Regal Croft B36 .... **68** B8
Regan Ave B90 .... **106** A1
Regan Cres B23 .... **56** E6
Regan Ct B75 .... **47** C5
Regan Ho B13 .... **105** D7
Regency Arc **8** CV32 .... **161** E8
Regency Cl CV10 .... **73** D6
Regency Ct Coventry CV5 .. **132** F5
Walsall WS1 .... **43** A7
Wolverhampton WV1 ...... **163** B4
Regency Dr Birmingham
B38 .... **103** F2
Coventry CV3 .... **132** F5
Kenilworth CV8 .... **147** F3
Regency Gdns B14 .... **105** C3
Regency Ho Birmingham
B16 .... **66** A1
Royal Leamington Spa
CV32 .... **162** A8
Regency Mews CV32 .... **162** A8
Regency Wlk B74 .... **31** D5
Regent Ave B69 .... **52** A1
Regent Cl Birmingham B5 ... **86** D6
Halesowen B63 .... **83** A4
Kingswinford DY6 .... **60** C6
Tipton B69 .... **63** A8
Regent Ct **5** Hinckley LE10 ... **75** D8
3 Smethwick B66 .... **65** A5
Regent Dr B69 .... **52** A1
Regent Gr CV32 .... **161** F8
6 Oldbury B68 .... **64** B2
Regent Mews B60 .... **150** E8
Regent Par B1 .... **66** C4
Regent Park Rd B10 .... **67** C1
Regent Pl Birmingham B1 .. **66** C4
2 Royal Leamington Spa
CV31 .... **162** A7
Tipton B69 .... **52** B2
Regent Rd
Birmingham,
Handsworth B21 .... **65** D8
Birmingham, Harborne B17 ... **85** D6
Tipton B69 .... **63** A8
Wolverhampton WV4 .... **38** E5
Regent Specl Sch B69 ...... **52** A1
Regent St Bedworth CV12 .. **78** C4
Bilston WV14 .... **40** D6
Birmingham, Hockley B1 .... **66** C4
Birmingham, Stirchley B30 ... **104** A7
Blackheath B64 .... **62** F2
Coventry CV1 .... **165** A2
Dudley DY1 .... **51** C6
Hinckley LE10 .... **75** D8
Nuneaton CV11 .... **73** D5
Royal Leamington Spa CV32 . **161** F8
Smethwick B66 .... **65** A6
Tipton DY4 .... **51** E8
Willenhall WV13 .... **27** A3
Regent Wlk B8 .... **68** B7
Regents Park Jun & Inf Sch
B10 .... **87** B8
Regents The B15 .... **85** D8
Regina Ave B44 .... **55** E8
Regina Cl B45 .... **101** E2
Regina Cres Coventry CV2 .. **115** A7
Wolverhampton WV6 .... **24** C4
Regina Dr Birmingham B42 ... **55** D3
Walsall WS4 .... **29** B4
Reginald Rd Birmingham B8 . **67** D4
Smethwick B67 .... **64** F2
Regis Beeches WV6 .... **24** C5
Regis Gdns B65 .... **63** C2
Regis Heath Rd B65 .... **63** E2
Regis Ho B68 .... **64** C2
Regis Rd Blackheath B65 ... **63** C2
Wolverhampton WV6 .... **24** C5
Regis Sch WV6 .... **24** B5
Regis Wlk CV2 .... **114** F7
Reid Ave WV12 .... **27** D6
Reid Rd B68 .... **64** D1

Reigate Ave B8 .... 68 B4
Reindeer Rd B78 .... 20 E1
Relay Dr B77 .... 36 C7
Reliance Trad Est WV14 .. 40 B5
Relko Dr B36 .... 68 C7
Relton Mews CV6 .... 113 F6
Rembrandt Cl Cannock
WS11 ◆ 2 D2
Coventry CV5 .... 112 C3
Remburn Gdns CV34 ...... 160 F8
Remembrance Rd
Coventry CV3 .... 134 D6
Wednesbury WS10 .... 42 C3
Remington Dr WS11 .... 4 F8
Remington Pl WS2 .... 28 C5
Remington Rd WS2 .... 28 B5
Rene Rd B77 .... 21 E5
Renfrew Cl CV12 .... 77 E1
Renfrew Gdns DY11 .... 116 C5
Renfrew Sq B35 .... 58 B4
Renfrew Wlk CV4 .... 132 A8
Renison Rd CV12 .... 77 E1
Rennie Gr B32 .... 84 D5
Rennison Dr WV5 .... 49 A6
Renown Cl DY5 .... 61 B7
Renton Gr WV10 .... 11 A1
Renton Rd WV10 .... 11 A1
Repington Rd N B77 .... 22 A5
Repington Rd S B77 .... 22 A5
Repington Way B75 .... 47 B5
Repton Ave WV6 .... 23 E3
Repton Cl WS11 .... 4 B8
Repton Dr CV6 .... 96 B2
Repton Gr B9 .... 68 B3
Repton Ho B23 .... 56 F6
Repton Rd B9 .... 68 B3
Reservoir Cl WS2 .... 42 B8
Reservoir Pas WS10 .... 41 F3
Reservoir Pl WS2 .... 42 B8
Reservoir Rd
Birmingham, Edgbaston B16 ... 65 F2
Birmingham, Rednall B45 ... 122 C3
Birmingham, Selly Oak B29 .. 85 C3
Birmingham,
Stockland Green B23 .... 56 E4
Blackheath B65 .... 63 D3
Cannock WS12 .... 2 D4
Kidderminster DY11 .... 116 C3
Oldbury B68 .... 64 C4
Solihull B92 .... 106 F8
Reservoir Retreat B16 ..... 65 F1
Reservoir St WS2 .... 42 B8
Retallack Cl B66 .... 65 B8
Retford Dr B76 .... 46 E4
Retford Gr B25 .... 88 C6
Retreat Gdns DY3 .... 50 E7
Retreat St
Astwood Bank B96 .... 158 E1
Wolverhampton WV3 ...... 163 A1
Retreat The B64 .... 82 E7
Revesby Wlk ◙ B7 .... 67 A4
Revival St WS3 .... 28 C8
Rex Cl CV4 .... 131 D8
Reyde Cl B97 .... 153 A2
Reynalds Cross Sch B92 .. 106 D7
Reynards Cl Dudley DY3 ... 51 A7
Redditch B97 .... 152 F3
Reynolds Cl WS13 .... 3 B2
Reynolds �10 B68 .... 84 B8
Reynolds Gr WV6 .... 24 A5
Reynolds Ho B19 .... 66 E7
Reynolds Rd Bedworth CV12 .. 78 A4
Birmingham B21 .... 65 E7
Reynolds Wlk WV11 .... 27 B8
Reynoldstown Rd B36 ...... 68 C8
Rhayader Rd B31 .... 102 E5
Rhodes Alms Hos The B21 .. 65 F7
Rhodes Cl DY3 .... 50 A4
Rhone Cl B11 .... 87 C3
Rhoose Croft B35 .... 58 B3
Rhuddlan Way DY10 .... 116 E1
Rhyl Rd CV11 .... 79 F6
Rhys Thomas Cl WV12 ...... 27 D4
Ribbesford Ave WV10 .... 25 B8
Ribbesford Cl B63 .... 82 D6
Ribbesford Cres WV14 ...... 40 D1
Ribble Cl CV12 .... 79 B2
Ribble Ct B73 .... 46 B5
Ribble Rd CV3 .... 113 F2
Ribble Wlk B36 .... 69 F8
Ribblesdale B77 .... 36 B7
Ribblesdale Ave LE10 .... 71 E3
Ribblesdale Rd B29,B30 .. 104 A8
Ribbonfields CV11 .... 73 D3
Rich Cl CV34 .... 161 B7
Richard Cooper Rd WS14 .... 17 F5
Richard Joy Cl CV6 .... 95 C2
Richard Lee Prim Sch
CV2 .... 114 E3
Richard Lighton Ho ◙ B1 .. 66 C3
Richard Pl WS5 .... 43 C8
Richard Rd WS5 .... 43 C8
Richard St Birmingham B7 ... 66 F5
West Bromwich B70 .... 53 B3
Richard St S B70 .... 53 C2
Richard St W B70 .... 53 C2
Richard Williams Rd WS10 .. 42 B2
Richards Cl Birmingham
B31 .... 122 F6
Blackheath B65 .... 63 E4
Kenilworth CV8 .... 147 F5
Richards Ct WS11 .... 5 F6
Richards Ho ◙ Oldbury B69 .. 63 E4
◙ Walsall WS2 .... 28 D3
Richards Rd DY4 .... 40 F1
Richards St WS10 .... 41 D7
Richardson Cl CV34 .... 155 F1
Richardson Dr DY8 .... 80 E8

Richardson Ho DY4 .... 52 C8
Richborough Dr DY1 .... 50 F4
Riches St WV6 .... 24 F3
Richford Gr B33 .... 69 D2
Richmere Ct WV6 .... 24 B3
Richmond Ave
Birmingham B12 .... 86 F5
Wolverhampton WV3 .... 24 F1
Richmond Cl Birmingham
B20 .... 55 A3
Cannock WS11 .... 2 A5
Tamworth B79 .... 21 A5
Richmond Croft B42 .... 54 F6
Richmond Ct
Birmingham B29 .... 103 C7
Halesowen B63 .... 82 E3
Oldbury B68 .... 64 C5
◙ Royal Leamington Spa
CV31 .... 162 B7
Stourbridge DY9 .... 81 B1
◙ Sutton Coldfield B72 .... 57 B7
Richmond Dr Lichfield WS14 .. 9 D7
Perton WV3 .... 24 A3
Wolverhampton WV3 .... 24 E1
Richmond Gdns
Stourbridge DY8 .... 80 F7
Wombourne WV5 .... 49 A5
Richmond Gr B68 .... 80 E8
Richmond Hill B68 .... 64 C5
Richmond Hill Gdns B15 .. 85 E7
Richmond Hill Rd B15 ...... 85 F6
Richmond Ho ◙ B37 .... 70 C1
Richmond Mews WV3 .... 25 A1
Richmond Pk DY6 .... 60 C8
Richmond Pl B14 .... 104 F8
Richmond Prim Sch LE10 .. 71 C3
Richmond Rd
Birmingham, Eachway B45 .. 121 E7
Birmingham, Hockley B18 .... 66 B6
Birmingham, Yardley B33 ... 68 D2
Dudley DY2 .... 62 C8
Hinckley LE10 .... 71 C3
Hollywood B47 .... 125 C7
Nuneaton CV11 .... 73 A4
Sedgley DY3 .... 50 E7
Smethwick B66 .... 65 A2
Solihull B92 .... 88 F2
Sutton Coldfield B73 .... 46 B6
Wolverhampton WV3 .... 24 E1
Richmond St Coventry CV2 .. 114 A3
Halesowen B63 .... 83 A4
Walsall WS1 .... 29 A1
West Bromwich,
Great Bridge B70 .... 52 F6
West Bromwich,
Ryders Green B70 .... 52 E5
Richmond St S B70 .... 52 E5
Richmond Way ◙ B37 ...... 70 C3
Rickard Cl B93 .... 127 E6
Rickman Dr B15 .... 86 D8
Rickyard Cl
Birmingham,
Northfield B29 .... 103 A6
Birmingham, Yardley B25 ... 88 D1
Rickyard La B98 .... 154 D5
Rickyard Piece B32 .... 84 E4
Riddfield Rd B36 .... 68 E8
Ridding La WS10 .... 41 F2
Riddings Cres WS3 .... 14 F4
Riddings The
Birmingham B33 .... 68 F4
Coventry CV5 .... 132 E7
Stourbridge DY9 .... 81 D2
Sutton Coldfield B76 .... 58 B8
Tamworth B77 .... 21 E5
Wolverhampton WV10 ...... 26 A7
Riddon Dr LE10 .... 75 B8
Ridgacre Ent Pk B71 .... 53 B6
Ridgacre La B32 .... 84 C6
Ridgacre Rd Birmingham
B32 .... 84 C6
West Bromwich B71 .... 53 B6
Ridgacre Rd W B32 .... 84 A6
Ridge Cl Birmingham B13 .. 105 C6
Willenhall WS2 .... 27 D3
Ridge Ct CV5 .... 112 A6
Ridge Gr DY9 .... 81 C5
Ridge La WV11 .... 26 D7
Ridge Prim Sch DY8 .... 80 C5
Ridge Rd DY6 .... 60 C5
Ridge St DY8 .... 80 C6
Ridge Way WS9 .... 30 B4
Ridgefield Rd B62 .... 83 C7
Ridgeley Cl CV34 .... 155 E2
Ridgemount Dr B38 .... 123 D8
Ridgethorpe CV3 .... 134 E6
Ridgewater Cl B45 .... 122 B6
Ridgeway Birmingham B17 .. 65 B2
Dudley DY3 .... 50 D6
Ridgeway Ave Coventry
CV3 .... 133 C6
Halesowen B62 .... 84 A6
Ridgeway Cl B80 .... 159 E2
Ridgeway Ct WS2 .... 27 F2
Ridgeway Dr WV4 .... 38 F3
Ridgeway Prim Sch WS7 .... 7 A5
Ridgeway The Stourbridge
DY8 .... 60 F2
◙ Tipton DY4 .... 52 A8
Ridgeway Specl Sch
CV34 .... 156 A1
Ridgeway The
Birmingham B23 .... 56 A5
Burntwood WS7 .... 7 A4
Hinckley LE10 .... 75 D6
Warwick CV34 .... 156 A1
Ridgewood B34 .... 69 B6
Ridgewood Ave DY8 .... 80 C7

Ridgewood Cl
Royal Leamington Spa
CV32 .... 156 C1
◙ Walsall WS1 .... 42 F8
Ridgewood Dr B75 .... 32 B1
Ridgewood Gdns B44 .... 55 F7
Ridgewood High Sch DY8 .. 80 C5
Ridgewood Rise B77 .... 22 A5
Ridgley Rd B33 .... 131 E8
Ridgmont Croft B32 .... 84 E5
Riding Cl B71 .... 53 F7
Riding Way WV12 .... 27 D6
Ridings Brook Dr WS11 ...... 2 A2
Ridings La B98 .... 154 B6
Ridley St B1 .... 164 A1
Ridpool Prim Sch B33 .... 69 B3
Ridpool Rd B33 .... 69 B3
Ridware Ho WS13 .... 3 E1
Rifle Range Rd DY11 ...... 116 B3
Rifle St WV14 .... 51 A8
Rigby Cl CV34 .... 161 D4
Rigby Dr WS11 .... 1 F4
Rigby Hall Sch B60 .... 151 E6
Rigby La B60 .... 151 C8
Rigby St WS10 .... 42 A1
Rigdale Cl CV2 .... 114 E2
Righton Ho B77 .... 21 D1
Riland Ave B75 .... 46 D5
Riland Ct ◙ B73 .... 57 C7
Riland Gr B75 .... 46 C5
Riland Ind Est B75 .... 46 D5
Riland Rd B75 .... 46 D5
Riley B77 .... 21 E3
Riley Cl CV8 .... 148 D4
Riley Cres WV3 .... 39 A6
Riley Dr B36 .... 59 A1
Riley Rd B14 .... 105 D3
Riley Sq CV2 .... 96 B1
Riley St WV13 .... 27 B2
Rills The LE10 .... 71 E2
Rilstone Rd B32 .... 84 F5
Rindleford Ave WV4 .... 38 C6
Ring Rd WS7 .... 6 E7
Ring Road St Andrews
WV1 .... 163 A3
Ring Road St Davids
WV1 .... 163 C3
Ring Road St Georges
WV2 .... 163 C2
Ring Road St Johns WV2 .. 163 B2
Ring Road St Marks WV3 .. 163 B1
Ring Road St Patricks
WV1 .... 163 C4
Ring Road St Peters WV1 . 163 B3
Ring The B25 .... 88 C8
Ringhills Rd WV8 .... 10 B2
Ringinglow Rd B44 .... 44 D2
Ringmere Ave B36 .... 69 B7
Ringswood Rd B92 .... 88 E4
Ringway WS11 .... 1 E1
Ringway Hill Cross CV1 .. 165 A3
Ringway Ind Est WS13 ...... 3 C3
Ringway Queens CV1 ..... 165 A2
Ringway Rudge CV1 .... 165 A2
Ringway St Johns CV1 .... 165 C2
Ringway St Nicholas CV1 . 165 B3
Ringway St Patricks CV1 . 165 B1
Ringway Swanswell CV1 .. 165 C3
Ringway The CV1 .... 116 F5
Ringway Whitefriars CV1 . 165 C3
Ringwood Ave WS9 .... 30 B5
Ringwood Dr B45 .... 102 A1
Ringwood Highway CV2 .... 96 E2
Ringwood Rd WV10 .... 11 D1
Rinhill Gr CV31 .... 162 D6
Ripley Cl B69 .... 62 F8
Ripley Gr B23 .... 56 B5
Riplingham ◙ CV32 .... 156 F2
Ripon Cl CV5 .... 112 B8
Ripon Dr B71 .... 42 D1
Ripon Rd Birmingham B14 . 105 D4
Walsall WS2 .... 28 B2
Wolverhampton WV10 ...... 25 C7
Rippingille Rd B43 .... 44 C4
Ripple Rd B30 .... 104 B7
Risborough Cl CV5 .... 112 C3
Rischale Way WS4 .... 29 D8
Risdale Cl CV32 .... 156 D2
Rise Ave B45 .... 122 A7
Rise The
Birmingham, Great Barr B42 .. 55 A8
Birmingham,
Marston Green B37 .... 90 A7
Hopwood B48 .... 123 B4
Kingswinford DY6 .... 60 E5
Riseley Cres B5 .... 86 D7
Rising Brook WV6 .... 24 B4
Rising La Chadwick End B93 .. 145 B5
Lapworth B94 .... 144 F5
Rising Rd B94 .... 144 C5
Rissington Ave B29 .... 104 A8
Ritchie Cl B13 .... 87 A1
Rivendell Gdns WV6 .... 24 B5
River Brook Dr B30 .... 104 B8
River Cl Bedworth CV12 ... 77 F1
Royal Leamington Spa
CV32 .... 161 D8
River Ct ◙ CV1 .... 113 B3
River Lee Rd B11 .... 87 E5
River St B5 .... 67 A2
River Wlk CV2 .... 96 C2
Riverbank Rd WV13 .... 27 D2
Riverdrive B77,B78 .... 21 D5
Riverfield Gr B77 .... 21 D5
Riverford Croft CV4 .... 132 D4
Rivermead CV11 .... 73 A4
Rivermead Pk B34 .... 69 A6
Riverside ◙ CV32 .... 161 E8

Riversdale Rd B14 .... 105 D3
Riverside B80 .... 159 F4
Riverside Cl Coventry CV3 . 134 A7
Lickey End B60 .... 137 C6
Riverside Cres B28 .... 105 D4
Riverside Ct
Birmingham B38 .... 103 D3
◙ Coleshill B46 .... 70 F7
Riverside Dr B91 .... 107 E2
Riverside Ind Est B78 .... 35 B8
Riverside Dr DY8 .... 80 E8
Riversleigh Dr DY8 .... 80 E8
Riversleigh Rd CV32 ...... 156 C1
Riversley Rd CV11 .... 73 C3
Riverway WS10 .... 42 B2
Rivington Cl DY8 .... 80 E4
Rivington Cres B44 .... 45 C1
Ro-Oak Rd CV6 .... 112 F5
Roach B77 .... 35 D6
Roach Cl Birmingham B37 . 70 C3
Brierley Hill DY5 .... 61 D5
Roach Cres WV11 .... 26 F8
Roach Pool Croft B16 .... 65 C2
Road No 1 DY10 .... 116 E2
Road No 2 DY10 .... 116 E2
Road No 3 DY10 .... 116 E2
Roanne Ringway CV11 ...... 73 B4
Robert Ave B23 .... 56 E6
Robert Cl Coventry CV3 .. 134 C4
Tamworth B79 .... 20 F7
Robert Cramb Ave CV4 .. 131 F8
Robert Ct ◙ B13 .... 87 B2
Robert Rd Bedworth CV7 .. 95 F8
Birmingham B20 .... 55 B1
Tipton DY4 .... 51 F6
Robert St DY3 .... 50 D4
Robert Wynd WV14 .... 40 A1
Roberts Ct B24 .... 57 C6
Roberts Green Rd DY4 ...... 50 E4
Roberts La DY9 .... 99 B8
Roberts Prim Sch DY3 ...... 50 D4
Roberts Rd Birmingham B27 . 88 D3
Walsall WS3 .... 28 F5
Wednesbury WS10 .... 42 E2
Robertson Knoll B36 .... 68 F7
Robertsons Gdns ◙ B7 .... 67 C7
Robeson Cl DY4 .... 51 D5
Robey's La B78 .... 22 D3
Robin Cl Birmingham B36 . 70 A8
Huntington WS12 .... 1 C7
Kingswinford DY6 .... 61 A6
Robin Ct DY10 .... 117 A2
Robin Gr WV11 .... 26 C7
Robin Hood Cres B28 ..... 105 E7
Robin Hood Croft B28 .... 105 F6
Robin Hood La B13,B28 .. 105 E7
Robin Hood Rd
Brierley Hill DY5 .... 61 F2
Coventry CV3 .... 134 C6
Robin Hood Sch B28 ..... 106 B6
Robin Rd B23 .... 56 E5
Robin Wlk WS2 .... 27 F3
Robin's Cl CV8 .... 81 A3
Robina Cl CV32 .... 157 B2
Robinfield Dr B31 .... 123 A7
Robins Bsns Pk B70 .... 52 E7
Robins Cl WS6 .... 4 D1
Robins Gr CV34 .... 160 C4
Robins Hill Dr B48 .... 139 B5
Robins Rd WS7 .... 6 E7
Robins Way B10 .... 72 A3
Robinson Rd Bedworth CV12 . 95 D8
Burntwood WS7 .... 6 F8
Robinson Way LE10 .... 75 F4
Robinson's End Mid Sch
CV10 .... 72 A3
Robinson's Way B76 .... 58 D5
Robottom Cl WS2 .... 28 B6
Robson Cl WS8 .... 15 F5
Rocester Ave WV11 .... 26 E7
Rochdale Wlk B10 .... 87 C7
Roche Rd WS3 .... 13 F1
Roche The WS13 .... 8 A8
Roche Way WS3 .... 13 F1
Rochester Ave WS7 .... 7 A7
Rochester Cl CV11 .... 73 B3
Rochester Croft WS2 .... 28 A4
Rochester Rd
Birmingham B31 .... 103 A4
Coventry CV5 .... 132 E8
Rochester Way WS12 .... 2 C1
Rochester Wlk DY10 .... 117 C5
Rochford Cl
Birmingham B45 .... 121 E7
Halesowen B63 .... 82 F2
Sutton Coldfield B76 .... 58 A8
◙ Walsall WS2 .... 42 C7
Rochford Ct
Royal Leamington Spa CV31 . 161 E7
Solihull B90 .... 127 A6
Rochford Gr WV4 .... 38 D5
Rock Ave B45 .... 122 C6
Rock Cl CV6 .... 96 B1
Rock Gr B92 .... 88 C3
Rock Hill Bromsgrove B61 . 150 D7
Weeford WS14, B78 .... 19 C4
Rock La CV7 .... 94 C7
Rock Mill La CV32 .... 161 C8
Rock Rd Sedgley WV14 ..... 50 F8
Solihull B92 .... 88 E3
Rock St DY3 .... 50 E5
Rock The WV6 .... 24 D5
Rocken End CV6 .... 113 D8
Rocket Pool Dr WV14 .... 41 A2
Rockford Cl B98 .... 158 F5
Rockford Rd B42 .... 55 A7

Rockingham Cl
Dorridge B93 .... 127 D2
Dudley DY3 .... 50 B3
◙ Walsall WS3 .... 14 B1
Rockingham Dr WV6 .... 23 F3
Rockingham Gdns B74 ..... 46 B6
Rockingham Hall Gdns DY9 . 99 D7
Rockingham Rd B25 .... 88 D8
Rockland Dr B33 .... 68 E4
Rockland Gdns WS13 ...... 40 F8
Rocklands Cres WS13 .... 3 D1
Rocklands Dr B75 .... 46 B8
Rocklands Specl Sch WS13 . 9 C8
Rockley Gr B45 .... 122 B7
Rockley Rd B65 .... 63 A6
Rockmead Ave B44 .... 44 F2
Rockmoor Cl B37 .... 69 E3
Rockrose Gdns WV10 .... 12 A7
Rockville Rd B8 .... 68 A4
Rockwell La B48 .... 139 E4
Rockwood Rd B27 .... 88 B4
Rocky La Birmingham B6 ... 67 A6
Birmingham B7 .... 67 B6
Birmingham, Great Barr B42 . 55 B5
Bournheath B61 .... 136 E7
Kenilworth CV8 .... 148 D2
Rodbaston Coll WS14 .... 19 A5
Rodborough Rd
Birmingham B26 .... 89 B7
Dorridge B93 .... 127 E3
Rodbourne Rd B17 .... 85 C3
Roddis Cl B23 .... 56 D8
Roden Ave DY10 .... 117 A7
Roderick Dr WV11 .... 26 D7
Roderick Rd B11 .... 87 C5
Rodhouse Cl CV4 .... 111 D1
Rodlington Ave B44 .... 44 F1
Rodman Cl B15 .... 85 D8
Rodney Cl Birmingham B16 . 66 A2
Hinckley LE10 .... 71 D4
Solihull B92 .... 89 B1
Rodney Rd B92 .... 89 B1
Rodway Cl Birmingham B19 . 66 E7
Brierley Hill DY5 .... 81 D7
Wolverhampton WV4 .... 39 D3
Rodway Dr CV5 .... 111 D4
Rodwell Gr B44 .... 56 A8
Roe Cl CV34 .... 160 F6
Roebuck Cl B34 .... 69 E5
Roebuck Glade WV12 .... 27 E4
Roebuck La Smethwick B66 . 64 F8
West Bromwich B70 .... 53 E1
Roebuck Pl WS3 .... 28 E6
Roebuck Rd WS3 .... 28 E6
Roebuck St B70 .... 53 F1
Roedean Cl B44 .... 56 B7
Roford Ct DY3 .... 50 E5
Rogerfield Rd B23 .... 57 A6
Rogers Cl WV11 .... 13 A2
Rogers Rd B8 .... 68 B5
Rogers Way CV34 .... 160 B4
Rogue's La LE10 .... 71 C6
Rokeby Cl B76 .... 46 E4
Rokeby Rd B43 .... 43 F2
Rokeby Wlk B34 .... 69 A6
Rokewood Cl DY6 .... 49 D1
Rokholt Cres WS11 .... 1 C1
Rolan Dr B90 .... 125 E8
Roland Ave CV6 .... 95 C3
Roland Gdns ◙ B19 .... 66 C8
Roland Gr ◙ B19 .... 66 C8
Roland Mount CV6 .... 95 C3
Roland Rd B19 .... 66 C8
Roland Terr ◙ B19 .... 66 C8
Rolfe St B66 .... 65 A6
Rollason Cl CV6 .... 113 C6
Rollason Rd Birmingham
B24 .... 57 A3
Coventry CV6 .... 113 B8
◙ Dudley DY2 .... 62 D8
Rollason's Yd CV6 .... 96 A3
Rollesby Dr WV13 .... 40 F8
Rolling Mill Cl B5 .... 86 E7
Rollingmill St WS2 .... 28 C1
Rollswood Dr B91 .... 107 A4
Rolvenden Cl WV13 .... 27 C2
Roma Rd B11 .... 87 E5
Roman Cl WS8 .... 6 E2
Roman Ct Birmingham B38 . 124 B8
Cannock WS11 .... 4 E5
Tamworth B77 .... 35 E7
Roman La B74 .... 31 B4
Roman Pk B74 .... 31 B4
Roman Rd Coventry CV2 . 114 B3
Little Aston B74 .... 31 C4
Roman Rd (Sandy La) DY8 . 80 C3
Roman View WS11 .... 4 F5
Roman Way Birmingham
B15 .... 85 D3
Blackheath B65 .... 63 C3
Bromsgrove B61 .... 137 B4
Coleshill B46 .... 59 F2
Coventry CV3 .... 133 D3
Lichfield WS14 .... 9 D7
Tamworth B79 .... 20 E7
Roman Way Fst Sch B98 . 154 E3
Romany Rd B45 .... 101 D1
Romany Way DY8 .... 80 C3
Romford Cl B26 .... 89 B6
Romford Rd CV6 .... 95 B2
Romilly Ave B20 .... 55 B3
Romilly Cl Lichfield WS14 ... 9 E7
Stourbridge DY8 .... 80 E6
Sutton Coldfield B76 .... 47 A4
Romney B77 .... 35 F8

Romney Cl Birmingham B28 105 F7
Hinckley LE10 71 A3
Romney House Ind Est WS10 41 B7
Romney Way B43 44 D4
Romsey Ave CV10 73 D8
Romsey Gr WV10 11 C3
Romsey Ho WS2 42 C7
Romsey Rd WV10 11 C3
Romsey Way WS3 13 F3
Romsley Cl Birmingham B45 121 E8
Halesowen B63 83 B2
Redditch B98 154 F3
Walsall WS4 15 C2
Romsley Ct 8 DY2 62 B8
Romsley Hill Grange B62 100 F1
Romsley Rd
Birmingham B32 102 B8
Oldbury B68 64 B2
Stourbridge DY9 81 C5
Romulus Cl B20 55 B3
Ronald Gr B36 58 D1
Ronald Pl B9 67 E2
Ronald Rd B9 67 D2
Rood End Prim Sch B68 64 C6
Rood End Rd B69 64 C7
Rooker Ave WV2 39 F6
Rooker Cres WV2 39 F6
Rookery Ave Brierley Hill DY5 61 A2
Wolverhampton WV4 40 A3
Rookery Cl B97 153 D1
Rookery Ct WS13 8 E7
Rookery La Aldridge WS9 30 B6
Coventry CV6 95 B4
Weeford B75, B78 19 C2
Wolverhampton WV2 39 B6
Rookery Par WS9 30 B6
Rookery Pk DY5 61 B5
Rookery Rd
Birmingham, Handsworth B21 54 E1
Birmingham, Selly Oak B29 85 F2
Wolverhampton WV14, WV4 40 A3
Wombourne WV5 49 B6
Rookery Rise WV5 49 B6
Rookery Road Jun & Inf Schs B21 54 E1
Rookery St WV11 26 C5
Rookery The B62 84 A2
Rooks Mdw DY9 99 B6
Rookwood Dr WV6 23 F2
Roosevelt Dr CV4 111 E2
Rooth St WS10 42 B4
Roper Way DY3 50 F6
Roper Wlk DY3 50 F6
Rosafield Ave B62 83 F6
Rosalind Ave DY1 51 B6
Rosalind Gr WV11 27 A5
Rosamond St WS1 42 D7
Rosary RC Prim Sch B8 67 E3
Rosary Rd B23 56 D3
Rosary Villas 1 B11 87 C5
Rosaville Cres CV5 112 A6
Rose Ave Alvechurch B48 139 A5
Coventry CV6 112 F5
Kingswinford DY6 60 F5
Oldbury B68 84 C7
Rose Bay Mdw WS11 2 C2
Rose Cl B66 65 C5
Rose Cottage Flats CV5 111 D5
Rose Cotts 6
Birmingham, Selly Oak B29 85 F2
Birmingham, Stirchley B30 104 A6
Rose Croft CV8 147 E6
Rose Ct CV7 130 B8
Rose Dr WS8 15 E5
Rose Hill Barnt Green B45 122 B4
Brierley Hill DY5 62 A1
Willenhall WV13 41 A8
Rose Hill Cl B36 69 B8
Rose Hill Gdns WV13 27 B1
Rose Hill Rd B21 66 A7
Rose La Burntwood WS7 7 C7
Nuneaton CV11 73 C3
Tipton B69 52 C2
Rose Rd Birmingham B17 85 D6
Coleshill B46 70 F8
Rose St WV14 40 F2
Rose Terr B45 138 D8
Rosebay Ave B38 123 F8
Roseberry Ave CV2 96 C1
Rosebery Rd Smethwick B66 65 C4
Tamworth B77 35 D4
Rosebery St Birmingham B18 66 A4
Wolverhampton WV3 25 B1
Rosecroft Rd B26 89 C6
Rosedale Ave
Birmingham B23 56 E3
Smethwick B66 65 C5
Rosedale CE Inf Sch WV12 27 D5
Rosedale Gr B25 88 C8
Rosedale Pl WV13 41 A8
Rosedale Rd B25 88 C8
Rosedale Wlk 5 DY6 60 E8
Rosedene Dr B20 54 F2
Rosefield Croft B6 66 F7
Rosefield Ct B67 65 A4
Rosefield Pl 14 CV32 161 F8
Rosefield Rd B67 65 A4
Rosefield St CV32 162 A8
Rosefield Wlk 13 CV32 161 F8
Rosegreen Cl CV3 133 E6
Rosehall Cl Redditch B98 158 E6
Solihull B91 106 F1
Rosehill WS12 2 A8
Rosehip Cl WS5 43 A3
Rosehip Dr CV2 114 B6
Roseland Ave DY2 51 F1
Roseland Rd CV8 147 F3
Roseland Way 7 B15 66 B1
Roselands Ave CV2 114 D8
Roseleigh Rd B45 122 B6
Rosemary Ave Bilston WV14 40 F6
Cheslyn Hay WS6 4 D3
Wolverhampton WV4 39 C6
Rosemary Cl Clayhanger WS8 15 D6
Coventry CV4 111 E3
Rosemary Cres Dudley DY1 51 A6
Wolverhampton WV4 39 C5
Rosemary Cres W WV4 39 B5
Rosemary Dr Huntington WS12 1 D5
Little Aston B74 31 C3
Stoke Prior B60 150 C1
Rosemary Hill CV8 147 F5
Rosemary Hill Rd B74 31 D4
Rosemary La DY8 80 D3
Rosemary Mews CV8 147 F5
Rosemary Nook B74 31 D5
Rosemary Rd
Birmingham B33 68 F2
Cheslyn Hay WS6 4 D4
Halesowen B63 82 E2
Kidderminster DY10 117 B7
Tamworth B77 21 F4
Tipton DY4 52 A6
Rosemary Way LE10 75 B7
Rosemoor Dr DY5 81 B7
Rosemount Birmingham B32 84 E5
Wolverhampton WV6 24 D5
Rosemount Cl CV2 114 E7
Rosemullion Cl CV7 96 B8
Rosetti Cl DY10 117 C6
Roseville Ct 4 WV14 51 C8
Roseville Gdns WV8 10 A4
Roseville Prec 5 WV14 51 C8
Rosewood CV11 73 F1
Rosewood Cl Hinckley LE10 75 F6
Tamworth B77 21 D4
Rosewood Cres CV32 157 B2
Rosewood Ct B77 21 D4
Rosewood Dr
Barnt Green B45 138 C7
Birmingham B23 56 D2
Willenhall WV12 27 B8
Rosewood Gdns WV11 13 B3
Rosewood Pk WS6 4 D2
Rosewood Rd DY1 51 B5
Rosewood Specl Sch DY1 50 E1
Roshven Rd B12 87 A4
Roslin Cl B60 137 B1
Roslin Gr B19 66 C6
Roslyn Cl B66 65 A6
Ross B65 63 B2
Ross Cl Coventry CV5 112 A5
Wolverhampton WV3 24 E2
Ross Dr DY6 60 C7
Ross Hts B65 63 B3
Ross Rd WS3 28 F6
Ross Way CV11 79 B7
Rosse Ct B92 107 F8
Rossendale Cl B63 82 D6
Rossendale Way CV10 72 E2
Rosslyn Ave CV6 112 E6
Rosslyn Rd B76 57 F6
Roston Dr LE10 71 A1
Rostrevor Rd B10 67 F1
Rosy Cross B79 21 B5
Rotary Ct 2 WV3 25 A1
Rothay B77 35 F8
Rothbury Gn WS12 2 E2
Rotherby Gr B37 90 B7
Rotherfield Cl CV31 162 B7
Rotherfield Rd B26 89 B8
Rotherham Rd CV6 95 C2
Rotherhams Oak La B94 142 F7
Rothesay Ave CV4 112 B2
Rothesay Cl CV10 73 A2
Rothesay Croft B32 102 B7
Rothesay Dr DY8 60 C3
Rothesay Way WV12 27 B6
Rothwell Dr B91 106 D4
Rothwell Rd CV34 155 C1
Rotten Row WS13 9 C7
Rotton Park Rd B16 65 D2
Rotton Park St B16 65 F3
Rough Coppice Wlk B35 58 A2
Rough Hay JMI Sch WS10 41 C7
Rough Hay Pl WS10 41 C7
Rough Hay Rd WS10 41 C7
Rough Hill Dr Blackheath B65 62 F6
Redditch B98 158 F6
Rough Hills Cl WV2 39 F6
Rough Hills Rd WV2 39 F6
Rough Rd B44 45 A3
Rough The B97 158 D8
Rough Wood Ctry Pk WV12 27 E6
Roughknowles Rd CV4 131 D6
Roughlea Ave B36 68 F7
Roughley Dr B75 32 C2
Rouncil Cl B92 107 D7
Rouncil La CV8 155 C8
Round Croft WV13 27 A2
Round Hill DY3 39 D2
Round Hill Ave DY9 81 C1
Round House Rd
Coventry CV3 134 B8
Dudley DY3 50 E4
Round Moor Wlk B35 58 A3
Round Oak Specl Sch CV32 157 A3
Round Rd B24 57 B2
Round Saw Croft B45 121 F8
Round St DY2 62 C6
Roundabout The B31 102 D1
Roundhill Cl B76 46 E4
Roundhill Terr B62 63 E1
Roundhill Way WS8 7 A2
Roundhills Rd B62 83 F8
Roundlea Cl WV12 27 B7
Roundlea Rd B31 102 E7
Rounds Green Prim Sch B69 63 E7
Rounds Green Rd B69 63 F7
Rounds Hill CV8 147 E2
Rounds Hill Rd WV14 51 D8
Rounds Rd WV14 40 D3
Roundway Down WV6 23 E3
Rousay Cl B45 101 F1
Rousdon Gr B43 54 D8
Rover Dr B36 58 F1
Rover Rd CV1 165 B2
Rovex Bsns Pk B11 87 F5
Row The CV7 97 D3
Rowallan Rd B75 32 D2
Rowan Cl Binley Woods CV3 135 D7
Bromsgrove B61 136 E2
Hollywood B47 125 B5
Lichfield WS13 9 D8
Rowan Cres Dudley WV14 40 B1
Redditch B97 153 A4
Wolverhampton WV3 38 E7
Rowan Ct Birmingham B30 104 A2
Oldbury B66 64 D8
Rowan Dr Birmingham B28 106 A5
Essington WV11 13 B3
6 Warwick CV34 160 F8
Rowan Gr Burntwood WS7 6 F7
Coventry CV2 96 E2
Rowan Rd Cannock WS11 1 C2
Nuneaton CV10 72 C6
Redditch B97 153 A4
Sedgley DY3 39 F1
Sutton Coldfield B72 46 C3
Walsall WS5 42 F4
Rowan Rise DY6 60 E6
Rowan Way
Birmingham, Chelmsley Wood B37 70 C1
Birmingham, Longbridge B31 122 F8
Rowans The CV12 77 E2
Rowantrees B45 122 B5
Roway La B69 52 F1
Rowbrook Cl B90 125 E8
Rowcroft Covert B14 104 C2
Rowcroft Rd CV2 115 A6
Rowdale Rd B42 55 C6
Rowden Dr Birmingham B23 57 A6
Solihull B91 106 E2
Rowena Gdns DY3 39 C2
Rowheath Ho B30 103 E5
Rowheath Rd B30 103 F4
Rowington Ave B65 63 D3
Rowington Cl CV6 112 D5
Rowington Gn CV35 144 F1
Rowington Rd B34 69 E6
Rowington Terr B25 88 B7
Rowland Ave B80 159 E3
Rowland Gdns WS2 28 C3
Rowland Hill Ave DY11 116 B5
Rowland Hill Ctr 9 DY10 116 E6
Rowland Hill Dr DY4 52 C5
Rowland St WS2 28 C3
Rowland Way (Road 1a) DY10 116 E1
Rowlands Ave Walsall WS2 27 E3
Wolverhampton WV1 26 B2
Rowlands Cl WS2 27 E4
Rowlands Cres B91 107 B8
Rowlands Rd B26 88 E7
Rowley Cl WS12 2 B8
Rowley Dr CV3 134 B4
Rowley Gr B33 69 D3
Rowley Hall Ave B65 63 C4
Rowley Hall Prim Sch B65 63 C4
Rowley La CV3 134 D3
Rowley Pl WS4 29 B7
Rowley Rd
Coventry CV3, CV8 134 B3
Whitnash CV31 162 A2
Rowley Regis Coll B65 63 A3
Rowley Regis Com Hospl B65 63 B2
Rowley Regis Sta B65 63 E2
Rowley St WS1 29 A2
Rowley View Bilston WV14 41 A3
Darlaston WS10 41 C4
West Bromwich B70 53 B3
Rowley Village B65 63 C3
Rowley's Green La CV6 95 E4
Rowleys Green Lane Ind Est CV6 95 E4
Rowney Croft B28 105 E4
Rowney Green La B48 139 F5
Rowood Dr B91 107 D7
Rowthorn Cl B74 45 A7
Rowthorn Dr B90 127 A6
Rowton Ave WV6 23 E3
Rowton Dr B74 44 F5
Roxall Cl DY10 98 C2
Roxburgh Croft CV32 157 C6
Roxburgh Gr B43 44 C4
Roxburgh Rd Nuneaton CV11 73 E1
Sutton Coldfield B73 46 A3
Roxby Gdns WV6 25 A5
Royal Brierley Glassworks DY5 61 C2
Royal Cl Blackheath B65 63 C5
Brierley Hill DY5 81 C8
Royal Cres CV3 134 C5
Royal Ct Hinckley LE10 75 D7
Sutton Coldfield B73 46 B2
Royal Doulton Glassworks DY8 80 F7
Royal Hospl WV2 163 C2
Royal Leamington Spa Rehabilitation Hospl CV34 161 E4
Royal Mail St B1 164 B2
Royal Oak La CV12 95 C7
Royal Oak Rd Blackheath B65 62 F5
Halesowen B62 83 F5
Royal Oak Yd CV12 78 B4
Royal Orthopaedic Hosp The Birmingham, Ladywood B16 66 B1
Birmingham, Northfield B31 103 B5
Royal Priors 9 CV32 161 F8
Royal Rd B72 46 C4
Royal Scot Gr WS1 42 D5
Royal Sq 6 B97 153 E3
Royal Sta The WV1 163 D2
Royal Star Cl B33 69 C2
Royal Way DY4 52 A2
Royal Wolverhampton Sch WV3 39 B7
Roydon Rd B27 106 C8
Roylesden Cres B73 45 C2
Royston Chase B74 31 A3
Royston Cl CV3 115 A3
Royston Croft B12 86 F6
Royston Ct 7 B13 87 B2
Royston Way DY3 50 C8
Rubens Cl Coventry CV5 112 C3
Dudley DY3 50 D5
Rubery Ct WS10 41 C7
Rubery Farm Gr B45 121 F7
Rubery La B45 102 A1
Rubery La S B45 121 F8
Rubery St WS10 41 D8
Ruckleigh Sch B91 107 C4
Ruckley Ave 4 B19 66 C7
Ruckley Rd B29 103 B8
Rudge Ave WV1 26 B3
Rudge Cl WV12 27 C4
Rudge Croft B33 69 A4
Rudge Rd CV1 165 A2
Rudge Wlk B18 66 A3
Rudgewick Croft 1 B6 66 F6
Rudyard Cl WV10 11 E4
Rudyard Gr B33 69 B3
Rudyngfield Dr B33 68 F4
Rufford B79 20 E6
Rufford Cl Birmingham B23 56 D8
Hinckley LE10 75 D3
Rufford Prim Sch DY9 81 C5
Rufford Rd DY9 81 C4
Rufford St DY9 81 D5
Rufford Way WS9 29 E7
Rugby Rd Binley Woods CV3 135 D8
Bulkington CV12 79 D2
Cubbington CV32 157 E6
Hinckley LE10 75 D6
Royal Leamington Spa CV32 156 D1
Stourbridge DY8 80 D7
Rugby St WV1 25 B4
Rugeley Ave WV12 27 D8
Rugeley Rd
Burntwood, Chase Terrace WS7 6 F8
Burntwood, Gorstey Ley WS7 7 C7
Cannock, Hazelslade WS12 2 F6
Cannock, Hednesford WS12 2 D7
Ruislip Cl B35 58 A4
Ruiton St DY3 50 D4
Rumbow B63 83 B4
Rumbow La B62 100 D3
Rumbush La B94 125 F3
Rumer Hill Bsns Est WS11 4 E7
Rumer Hill Rd WS11 4 F8
Runcorn Cl Birmingham B37 70 C4
Redditch B98 158 F8
Runcorn Rd B12 87 A5
Runcorn Wlk 10 CV2 115 A7
Runneymede Gdns CV10 72 F3
Runnymede Dr CV7 130 C5
Runnymede Rd B11 87 E3
Rupert Rd CV6 113 B8
Rupert St Birmingham B7 67 A4
Wolverhampton WV3 25 A2
Rush Gn B32 84 E2
Rush La Redditch B98 154 B6
Tamworth B77 35 D4
Rushall Cl Stourbridge DY8 80 E8
Walsall WS4 29 B4
Rushall Ct B43 54 E7
Rushall Manor Cl WS4 29 B4
Rushall Manor Rd WS4 29 B4
Rushall Prim Sch WS4 29 B7
Rushall Rd WV10 11 E2
Rushbrook Cl
Clayhanger WS8 15 D6
Solihull B92 88 E2
Rushbrook Gr B14 104 C4
Rushbrook La B94 141 D3
Rushbrooke Cl B13 86 F4
Rushbrooke Dr B73 45 C3
Rushbury Cl Bilston WV14 40 B5
Solihull B90 106 D4
Rushden Croft B44 44 F1
Rushey La B11 88 A5
Rushford Ave WV5 49 A6
Rushford Cl B90 127 A7
Rushlake Gn B34 69 B5
Rushleigh Rd B90 125 E8
Rushmead Gr B45 122 A7
Rushmere Rd DY4 52 A8
Rushmoor Cl B74 46 B6
Rushmoor Dr CV5 112 F3
Rushmore St CV31 162 B7
Rushmore Terr 9 CV31 162 B7
Rushock Cl B98 159 C7
Rushton Cl CV7 130 C7
Rushwick Croft B34 69 D6
Rushwick Gr B90 127 A6
Rushwood Cl WS4 29 A3
Rushy Piece B32 84 D3
Rusina Ct 2 CV31 161 F6
Ruskin Ave Blackheath B65 63 D2
Dudley DY3 50 A5
Kidderminster DY10 117 C6
Wolverhampton WV4 39 F2
Ruskin Cl Birmingham B6 66 F7
Coventry CV6 112 D6
Nuneaton CV10 72 A5
Ruskin Ct 5 B68 84 B8
Ruskin Gr B27 88 B2
Ruskin Rd WV10 12 A1
Ruskin St B71 53 C5
Russel Croft B60 151 A7
Russell Bank Rd B74 31 E4
Russell Cl Tipton, Moxley DY4 41 C1
Tipton, Tividale B69 52 D2
Wolverhampton WV11 12 F1
Russell Ct
12 Royal Leamington Spa CV31 162 A7
Sutton Coldfield B74 31 D3
Wolverhampton WV3 163 A2
Russell Ho WS10 41 F2
Russell Rd Bilston WV14 40 F7
Birmingham, Hall Green B28 87 E1
Birmingham, Moseley B13 86 D3
Kidderminster DY10 116 F4
Russell St Coventry CV1 165 C4
Dudley DY1 51 B1
Royal Leamington Spa CV32 156 F1
Wednesbury WS10 41 F2
Willenhall WV13 27 B2
Wolverhampton WV3 163 A2
Russell St N 2 CV1 165 C4
Russell Terr CV31 162 A7
Russell's Hall Rd DY1 50 E1
Russells Hall Hospl DY5 61 D7
Russells Hall Prim Sch DY1 50 E1
Russells The B13 86 D3
Russet Way B31 102 E6
Russet Wlk WV8 10 E1
Russett Cl Burntwood WS7 7 A6
Walsall WS5 43 D8
Russett Way DY5 61 B7
Ruston St B16 66 B1
Ruth Chamberlain Ct 3 DY11 116 D6
Ruth Cl DY4 41 C2
Ruthall Cl B29 103 C7
Rutherford Glen CV11 73 F1
Rutherford Rd
Birmingham B23 56 E7
Bromsgrove B60 151 B7
Walsall WS2 28 A5
Rutherglen Ave CV3 134 A6
Rutland B17 85 A6
Rutland Ave Hinckley LE10 75 C7
Nuneaton CV10 72 F4
Wolverhampton WV4 38 D4
Rutland Cres Aldridge WS9 16 B1
Bilston WV14 40 E7
Rutland Croft 3 CV3 134 F8
Rutland Dr Birmingham B26 88 E7
Bromsgrove B60 151 A8
Tamworth B78 21 A1
Rutland Pl DY8 80 D8
Rutland Rd Cannock WS12 2 E1
Smethwick B66 65 A1
Wednesbury WS10 42 D4
West Bromwich B71 53 C7
Rutland St WS3 28 E5
Rutland Terr 5 B18 66 A5
Rutley Gr B32 84 F4
Rutter St WS1 42 E8
Rutters Mdw B32 84 B4
Ryan Ave WV11 27 A7
Ryan Pl DY2 62 C6
Rycroft Gr B33 69 C2
Rydal B77 36 A7
Rydal Ave CV11 74 A6
Rydal Cl Aldridge B74 30 F2
Allesley CV5 112 B8
Cannock WS12 2 A8
Hinckley LE10 74 F7
Wolverhampton WV11 26 C7
Rydal Dr WV6 23 F4
Rydal Gn WV1 26 B1
Rydal Ho 6 B69 63 D5
Rydal Way B28 105 F7
Rydding La B71 53 B8
Rydding Sq B71 53 B8
Ryde Ave CV10 73 D7
Ryde Gr B27 88 A1
Ryde Park Rd B45 122 C7

Ryder Ho B70 ... 52 E3
Ryder St Birmingham B4 ... 164 C3
Stourbridge DY8 ... 60 D2
West Bromwich B70 ... 52 F5
Ryders Green Prim Sch
B70 ... 53 A4
Ryders Green Rd B70 ... 52 F4
Ryders Hayes Jun & Mix
Inf Sch WS4 ... 15 A5
Ryders Hayes La WS3 ... 15 B4
Ryders Hill Cres CV10 ... 72 C7
Rye Croft 8 Birmingham
B27 ... 88 C5
Hollywood B47 ... 125 A6
Stourbridge DY9 ... 81 E2
Rye Gr B11 ... 87 F4
Rye Grass Wlk B35 ... 58 B3
Rye Hill CV5 ... 112 A6
Rye Piece Ringway CV12 ... 78 C3
Ryebank Cl B30 ... 103 C5
Ryeclose Croft B37 ... 70 D3
Ryecroft Ave WV4 ... 39 B5
Ryecroft Cl DY3 ... 50 C8
Ryecroft Cotts WV4 ... 39 B5
Ryecroft Dr 3 WS7 ... 7 A8
Ryecroft Pk 1 WS2 ... 28 E3
Ryecroft Pl WS3 ... 28 F6
Ryecroft Sh Ctr 4 WS7 ... 7 A8
Ryecroft St 2 WS2 ... 28 E3
Ryefield WV8 ... 10 E1
Ryefield Cl Hagley DY9 ... 99 A4
Solihull B91 ... 106 E5
Ryefield La B76 ... 48 B2
Ryefields Rd B60 ... 150 C3
Ryegrass La B97 ... 158 C6
Ryemarket 2 DY8 ... 81 A5
Ryhope Cl CV12 ... 77 C1
Ryhope Wlk WV9 ... 11 A3
Ryknild Cl B74 ... 31 F6
Ryknild St WS14 ... 9 E6
Ryland Cl Halesowen B63 ... 82 E2
Royal Leamington Spa
CV31 ... 162 C6
Tipton DY4 ... 52 B5
Ryland Ho B19 ... 66 D5
Ryland Rd
Birmingham, Edgbaston B15 ... 86 C8
Birmingham, Gravelly Hill B24 ... 56 F1
Birmingham, Sparkhill B11 ... 87 D4
Ryland St B16 ... 66 B1
Rylands Dr WV4 ... 39 A4
Rylcroft WV4 ... 39 F4
Ryle St WS3 ... 14 D1
Rylstone Way 4 CV34 ... 155 E1
Rymond Rd B34 ... 68 E6
Ryton B77 ... 35 F8
Ryton Cl Coventry CV4 ... 132 B8
Redditch B98 ... 154 D1
Sutton Coldfield B73 ... 46 B5
Wolverhampton WV10 ... 26 A5
Ryton Gdns CV8 ... 135 C1
Ryton Gr B34 ... 69 D7

Sabell Rd B67 ... 64 F6
Sabrina Rd WV6 ... 23 E1
Sackville Ho 1 CV1 ... 165 D4
Sacred Heart RC Jun &
Inf Schs B20 ... 55 D1
Sacred Heart RC Prim
Sch
Coventry CV2 ... 114 A3
Tipton DY4 ... 52 A4
Saddington Rd CV3 ... 134 E8
Saddlers Cl LE10 ... 75 F6
Saddlers Court Ind Est
WS2 ... 28 A7
Saddlers Cl WS1 ... 28 E1
Saddlers Mews B91 ... 107 C1
Saddlestones The WV6 ... 23 D4
Saddleworth Rd WS3 ... 14 A4
Sadler Cres B11 ... 87 D4
Sadler Ho B19 ... 66 C6
Sadler Rd Brownhills WS8 ... 16 A8
Coventry CV6 ... 113 A4
Sutton Coldfield B75 ... 46 F7
Sadlers Ct WS2 ... 42 B7
Sadlers Mill WS8 ... 16 A7
Sadlers Wlk B16 ... 66 A1
Sadlerswell La B94 ... 143 B6
Saffron B77 ... 22 B4
Saffron Gdns WV4 ... 39 A4
Saffron Ho 2 B38 ... 123 E8
Sage Croft B31 ... 102 F5
Sagebury Dr B60 ... 150 C1
SS Peter & Paul RC
Prim Sch CV2 ... 114 F7
St Agatha's Rd
Birmingham B8 ... 68 B5
Coventry CV2 ... 114 A3
St Agnes Cl Birmingham
B13 ... 87 B2
Studley B80 ... 159 C4
St Agnes La CV1 ... 165 B3
St Agnes Rd B13 ... 87 B1
St Agnes Way CV11 ... 73 F4
St Aidan's Rd WS11 ... 1 E5
St Aidans Wlk B10 ... 87 C8
St Alban's Ave B70 ... 116 A7
St Alban's CE Prim Sch
WV1 ... 27 B8
St Alban's CE Sec Sch
B12 ... 86 F7
St Alban's RC Inf & Jun
Sch B14 ... 104 F4
St Alban's Rd B67 ... 64 E6

St Albans Cl
Royal Leamington Spa CV32 ... 156 C2
Smethwick B67 ... 64 E6
Wednesfield WV11 ... 27 A8
Wolverhampton WV11 ... 13 A1
St Albans Ct WV13 ... 26 E1
St Albans Ho B32 ... 84 F5
St Albans Rd B13 ... 87 A4
St Alphege CE Inf Sch
B91 ... 107 C3
St Alphege CE Jun Sch
B91 ... 107 C2
St Alphege Cl B91 ... 107 C3
St Ambrose Barlow RC &
Inf Sch B28 ... 106 A6
St Ambrose's Inf Sch
DY10 ... 116 F6
St Ambrose's RC Jun Sch
DY10 ... 116 F6
St Andrew's CE Fst Sch
B45 ... 138 D8
St Andrew's CE Inf Sch
CV5 ... 111 C3
St Andrew's Cl DY3 ... 50 A3
St Andrew's Gd
(Birmingham City FC)
B9 ... 67 C1
St Andrew's Inf & Jun Sch
B9 ... 67 B2
St Andrew's RC Prim Sch
B92 ... 89 B2
St Andrew's Rd
Birmingham B9 ... 67 B2
Coventry CV5 ... 132 F8
Royal Leamington Spa CV32 ... 157 B5
St Andrew's St
Birmingham B9 ... 67 B2
Dudley DY2 ... 62 C5
St Andrews St ... 22 B4
St Andrews Ave WS3 ... 15 B4
St Andrews CE Inf & Jun
Sch WV6 ... 24 F4
St Andrews Cl
Birmingham B32 ... 85 A3
Stourbridge DY8 ... 80 F2
Wolverhampton W6 ... 25 A4
St Andrews Ct 2 B10 ... 67 B1
St Andrews Dr
Nuneaton CV11 ... 74 B1
Perton WV6 ... 23 D5
Tipton B69 ... 63 B7
St Andrews Ho WV6 ... 25 B4
St Andrews Ind Est B9 ... 67 C2
St Andrews Rd B75 ... 46 D7
St Andrews Way B61 ... 150 D8
St Ann's Cl CV31 ... 162 C7
St Ann's Rd CV2 ... 114 A3
St Anne's Cl WS7 ... 6 E4
St Anne's Ct Birmingham
B13 ... 86 E4
Willenhall WV13 ... 27 B1
St Anne's RC Jun & Inf
Sch B12 ... 87 A8
St Anne's RC Prim Sch
Birmingham B37 ... 70 A2
Coventry CV3 ... 134 C6
Nuneaton CV10 ... 72 D7
St Anne's Rd Blackheath
B64 ... 62 C1
Willenhall WV13 ... 27 B3
Wolverhampton WV10 ... 11 B1
St Annes Cl B20 ... 54 F4
St Annes Ct B44 ... 56 A7
St Annes Gr B93 ... 128 A6
St Annes Ind Est WV13 ... 27 B3
St Annes Rd WS13 ... 3 B3
St Annes Way B44 ... 56 A7
St Anns RC Inf & Jun Sch
B74 ... 44 E8
St Anthony's RC Comb
Sch CV31 ... 162 C7
St Anthony's RC Prim Sch
WV10 ... 11 D3
St Anthonys Dr WS3 ... 15 B5
St Antony's RC Prim Sch
B37 ... 70 A5
St Asaphs Ave B80 ... 159 D4
St Athan Croft B35 ... 58 B3
St Audries Ct B91 ... 106 F2
St Augustine's Prim Sch
B91 ... 107 A2
St Augustine's RC Comb
Sch CV8 ... 147 E2
St Augustine's RC Prim
Sch Birmingham B21 ... 54 D2
Coventry CV6 ... 113 A7
St Augustine's RC Sch
B97 ... 158 C3
St Augustine's Rd B16 ... 65 D1
St Augustine's Wlk CV6 ... 113 A7
St Augustus Cl B70 ... 53 F2
St Austell Cl Nuneaton
CV11 ... 74 A5
Tamworth B79 ... 21 A6
St Austell Rd Coventry CV2 ... 114 E3
Walsall WS5 ... 43 E7
St Barnabas CE Jun &
Inf Sch B24 ... 57 A1
St Bartholemews Cl CV3 ... 115 A2
St Bartholomew Terr
3 WS10 ... 41 F3
St Bartholomew's CE
Prim Sch
Coventry B24 ... 134 C7
Nuneaton WV14 ... 38 E3
St Bede's Mid Sch B98 ... 154 A3
St Bede's RC Mid Sch
B98 ... 153 F3

St Benedict Biscop Prim
Sch WV5 ... 49 B7
St Benedict's Cl B70 ... 53 F2
St Benedict's Inf Sch B70 ... 87 F7
St Benedict's RC Prim Sch
CV1 ... 113 E4
St Benedict's Rd WS7 ... 7 B6
St Benedicts Rd
Birmingham B10 ... 87 F8
Wombourne WV5 ... 49 A6
St Bernadett's RC Prim Sch
B25 ... 88 B8
St Bernard RC Jun &
Mix Inf Sch WS8 ... 15 F8
St Bernard's Rd B92 ... 106 E7
St Bernards Rd Jun &
Inf Sch B13 ... 87 C1
St Bernards Rd B72 ... 46 C2
St Bernards Wlk CV3 ... 134 D6
St Blaise Ave B46 ... 59 C2
St Blaise Rd B75 ... 32 D3
St Brades Cl B69 ... 63 C7
St Bride's Cl 6 CV31 ... 162 C6
St Brides Cl DY3 ... 50 C8
St Brigid's RC Prim Sch
B31 ... 102 F3
St Caroline Cl B70 ... 53 F3
St Catharines Cl WS1 ... 43 A7
St Catherine's LE10 ... 75 F7
St Catherine's Cl CV3 ... 134 B8
St Catherine's Cres
Whitnash CV31 ... 161 F3
Wolverhampton WV4 ... 38 F4
St Catherine's Lodge 7 CV6 ... 113 A4
St Catherine's RC Inf &
Jun Sch B1 ... 66 D1
St Catherine's Rd B60 ... 138 A6
St Catherines Cl
Blackwell B60 ... 138 A5
Dudley DY2 ... 52 A1
Sutton Coldfield B75 ... 46 F7
St Catherines Rd WS13 ... 3 B3
St Cecilia Cl DY10 ... 116 E2
St Cecilia's WV11 ... 26 C5
St Chad's Cath B4 ... 164 B4
St Chad's Circus
Queensway B3 ... 164 B3
St Chad's Cl Cannock WS11 ... 2 A4
Dudley DY3 ... 50 B3
St Chad's Inf & Jun Sch
B19 ... 66 D5
St Chad's RC Sch DY3 ... 50 D7
St Chad's Rd Bilston WV14 ... 40 F7
Birmingham B45 ... 121 F7
Lichfield WS13 ... 3 C1
Sutton Coldfield B75 ... 46 F5
Wolverhampton WV10 ... 25 F8
St Chad's Stowe Prim Sch
WS13 ... 9 C8
St Chads Cl WS13 ... 3 B1
St Chads Ind Est B19 ... 66 E5
St Chads Mews B94 ... 144 D3
St Chads Queensway B4 ... 164 C4
St Chads Rd B80 ... 159 C4
St Christian's Croft CV3 ... 133 E8
St Christian's Rd CV3 ... 133 E8
St Christopher Cl B70 ... 53 E2
St Christopher Prim Sch
CV5 ... 112 D4
St Christopher's Cl CV34 ... 160 D8
St Christopher's Dr B77 ... 21 C1
St Christopher's RC Prim
Sch WV8 ... 10 A3
St Christophers B20 ... 54 F4
St Clare's RC Prim Sch
B20 ... 55 B1
St Clement's Ave WS3 ... 28 D7
St Clement's CE Inf &
Jun Sch B7 ... 67 C7
St Clement's La B71 ... 53 D4
St Clements Ct CV2 ... 114 D8
St Clements Ho 3 B71 ... 53 D4
St Clements Rd B7 ... 67 C6
St Columba's Cl CV1 ... 165 B4
St Columba's RC Prim
Sch B45 ... 122 D7
St Columbas Dr B45 ... 122 D7
St Cuthbert's Cl B70 ... 53 F2
St Cuthberts RC Jun &
Inf Sch B8 ... 68 C4
St David's Cl
Royal Leamington Spa
CV31 ... 162 C7
West Bromwich B70 ... 53 F2
St Davids Cl WS3 ... 15 B5
St Davids Dr B32 ... 84 B5
St Davids Gr B20 ... 54 F4
St Davids Orch CV3 ... 134 F7
St Davids Pl WS3 ... 14 D2
St. Davids Way CV10 ... 78 A6
St Denis Rd B29 ... 103 B7
St Dominic's Rd B24 ... 56 E1
St Dunstan's RC Inf &
Jun Sch B14 ... 104 F8
St Edburghs Rd B25 ... 68 E1
St Edith's Gn 2 CV34 ... 161 B8
St Edith's Ho 1 CV34 ... 161 B8
St Editha's Cl B79 ... 21 B5
St Editha's Hospl B79 ... 21 B7
St Edmund Campion RC
Lower Sch B24 ... 57 C6
St Edmund Campion RC
Sch B23 ... 57 B5
St Edmund's Cl
West Bromwich B70 ... 53 F2
Wolverhampton WV6 ... 24 F3

St Edmund's RC Inf & Jun Sch
B18 ... 66 A4
St Edmund's RC Sch WV3 ... 24 E3
St Edward's Rd B29 ... 85 F2
St Edward's Sch B29 ... 86 A1
St Edwards RC Jun &
Inf Sch B29 ... 86 B1
St Eleanor Cl B70 ... 53 F3
St Elizabeth's Prim Sch
B79 ... 20 F8
St Elizabeth's RC Prim
Sch CV6 ... 113 E7
St Elizabeth's Rd CV6 ... 113 E7
St Francis Ave B91 ... 106 E6
St Francis Cl WS3 ... 15 B5
St Francis Factory Est B70 ... 53 D2
St Francis Jun & Inf Sch
B30 ... 103 D6
St Francis of Assisi RC
Comp Sch WS9 ... 30 C5
St Francis RC Comb Sch
CV12 ... 78 C3
St Francis RC Inf & Jun
Sch B19 ... 66 B6
St Francis RC Prim Sch
WS4 ... 15 C1
St Francis Xavier RC Prim
Sch B69 ... 64 A8
St Gabriel's RC Prim Sch
B77 ... 21 E1
St George Dr B66 ... 65 A7
St George & St Teresa
RC Sch B93 ... 128 A4
St George's Ave LE10 ... 71 C1
St George's CE Fst Sch
B98 ... 153 F4
St George's CE Inf Sch
B19 ... 164 B5
St George's CE Jun & Inf
Sch B16 ... 65 F1
St George's CE Sch DY10 ... 116 F7
St George's Cl
Darlaston WS10 ... 41 D7
Sutton Coldfield B75 ... 46 F6
St George's Ct
Birmingham B30 ... 103 E7
Darlaston WS10 ... 41 D7
St George's Gdns 3 B98 ... 153 F4
St George's Par WV1 ... 163 C2
St George's Pl
Kidderminster DY10 ... 116 E7
4 Walsall WS1 ... 28 F2
St George's Rd
Coventry CV1 ... 113 F2
Royal Leamington Spa
CV31 ... 161 F6
Solihull B90 ... 126 D8
Stourbridge DY8 ... 80 D2
St George's Sixth Form
Campus B19 ... 164 B5
St George's St
Birmingham B19 ... 164 B4
Darlaston WS10 ... 41 D7
St George's Terr DY10 ... 116 F6
St George's Way B77 ... 21 F4
St Georges Ave B23 ... 57 A5
St Georges Cl B15 ... 86 A7
St Georges Ct
Sutton Coldfield B74 ... 31 E5
5 Walsall WS1 ... 28 F2
St Georges Pl B70 ... 53 C3
St Georges Rd Dudley DY2 ... 62 E6
Redditch B98 ... 153 F4
St Georges Way CV10 ... 78 B8
St Gerards RC Jun &
Inf Sch B35 ... 58 B4
St Gerards Rd B91 ... 106 E2
St Gerrards RC Jun &
Inf Sch B35 ... 58 B4
St Gile's Ct WV13 ... 27 B1
St Giles Ave B65 ... 63 B4
St Giles' CE Prim Sch
WV13 ... 27 B2
St Giles Cl B65 ... 63 C4
St Giles Cres CV1 ... 26 A2
St Giles Ct B65 ... 63 D3
St Giles Cty Mid Sch CV7 ... 95 F8
St Giles Rd Birmingham B33 ... 69 D2
Burntwood WS7 ... 7 B6
Coventry CV7 ... 95 D6
Willenhall WV13 ... 27 B1
Wolverhampton WV1 ... 26 A2
St Giles St DY2 ... 62 C5
St Godwald's Cres B60 ... 151 B8
St Godwald's Rd B60 ... 151 C7
St Govan's Cl 7 CV31 ... 162 C6
St Gregory's RC Prim Sch
Coventry CV2 ... 114 E3
Smethwick B67 ... 64 F2
St Helen's Rd
Royal Leamington Spa
CV31 ... 162 A5
Solihull B91 ... 107 A6
St Helen's Way CV5 ... 112 B8
St Helens Ave DY4 ... 52 C5
St Helens Pas B1 ... 66 C3
St Helens Rd WS3 ... 3 B3
St Heliers Rd B31 ... 102 F4
St Hubert's RC Prim Sch
B68 ... 84 C8
St Ives Cl B79 ... 21 B6
St Ives Rd Coventry CV2 ... 114 D7
Walsall WS5 ... 43 D7
St Ives Way CV11 ... 73 F5
St James Ave B65 ... 63 B4
St James CE Jun Sch B90 ... 106 B2
St James CE Mid Sch CV12 ... 79 C2

St James CE Prim Sch
Birmingham B21 ... 54 D1
Stourbridge DY8 ... 80 D7
St James Cl Walsall WS3 ... 15 B5
West Bromwich B70 ... 53 F2
St James Ct
Bromsgrove B60 ... 137 A3
Coventry CV3 ... 134 E6
St James Gdns CV12 ... 79 C2
St James' La CV3 ... 134 D6
St James Meadow Rd
CV32 ... 156 C2
St James' Pl B7 ... 67 A3
St James Pl B90 ... 106 B2
St James' Rd Jun & Inf
Sch B45 ... 122 A7
St James' Rd B21 ... 65 D8
St James Rd
Birmingham, Edgbaston B15 ... 86 B8
Cannock WS11 ... 1 C1
Norton Canes WS11 ... 6 B5
Oldbury B69 ... 63 E8
Sutton Coldfield B75 ... 32 C2
St James' St DY3 ... 50 D3
St James St
Wednesbury WS10 ... 41 E2
Wolverhampton WV1 ... 163 D3
St James Wlk WS8 ... 15 F7
St James's Cl LE10 ... 75 D5
St James's Rd DY1 ... 51 B2
St James's Terr DY1 ... 51 A2
St John Bosco RC Prim
Sch B71 ... 53 B7
St John Fisher RC Fst Sch
B98 ... 154 D6
St John Fisher RC Prim
Sch Birmingham B31 ... 123 B7
Coventry CV2 ... 114 D5
St John St Bromsgrove B61 ... 136 F2
Lichfield WS13 ... 9 B7
Tamworth B79 ... 21 B5
St John & St Monica RC
Jun Sch B13 ... 86 E4
St John the Baptist CE
Fst Sch CV31 ... 161 F2
St John the Baptist RC
Prim Sch B36 ... 70 B7
St John the Divine CE
Prim Sch CV3 ... 134 C5
St John Vianney RC Prim
Sch CV5 ... 112 B3
St John Wall RC Sch B21 ... 54 C2
St John's Arc WV1 ... 163 B2
St John's Ave
Kenilworth CV8 ... 148 A3
Kidderminster DY11 ... 116 B6
St John's CE Fst Sch
DY11 ... 116 B6
St John's CE Inf & Jun Sch
B16 ... 66 A2
St John's CE Jun & Inf Sch
B11 ... 87 C4
St John's CE Mid Sch
DY11 ... 116 B6
St John's CE Prim Sch
Coventry CV5 ... 112 C4
Essington WV11 ... 13 A4
Wednesbury WS10 ... 41 F2
St John's Cl Brownhills WS9 ... 15 F3
Cannock WS11 ... 4 D8
6 Kidderminster DY11 ... 116 C6
Lichfield WS13 ... 9 B6
West Bromwich B70 ... 53 F3
St John's Com Home Sch
B24 ... 56 E2
St John's Ct Cannock WS12 ... 2 E1
Walsall WS3 ... 14 B1
4 Warwick CV34 ... 160 F7
St John's Dr WS14 ... 17 F5
St John's Hill WS14 ... 17 F5
St John's Prep Sch CV3 ... 9 B7
St John's Rd Birmingham
B17 ... 85 D6
Cannock WS11 ... 4 E7
Darlaston WS10 ... 41 C5
Dudley DY2 ... 51 E1
Halesowen B63 ... 82 E4
Royal Leamington Spa CV31 ... 162 A6
Stourbridge DY8 ... 81 A5
Tipton DY4 ... 51 F8
St John's Sch B61 ... 136 F1
St John's Sq WV2 ... 163 B2
St John's St Coventry CV1 ... 165 C2
Dudley DY2 ... 62 C5
Kenilworth CV8 ... 148 A3
5 Kidderminster DY11 ... 116 C6
St John's Terr 10 CV31 ... 162 A6
St Johns Hinckley LE10 ... 71 E1
Warwick CV34 ... 160 F7
St Johns Ave B65 ... 63 B4
St Johns CE JMI Sch WS9 ... 16 A3
St Johns Cl B93 ... 128 B6
St Johns Ct 20 DY5 ... 61 D2
St Johns Gr B37 ... 69 F3
St Johns Ho
Sutton Coldfield B74 ... 31 E4
West Bromwich B70 ... 53 C2
St Johns Mid Sch CV8 ... 147 F2
St Johns Rd Birmingham B11 ... 87 C5
Brownhills WS8 ... 16 A5
Essington WV11 ... 13 A3
Oldbury B68 ... 64 C5
Walsall, Pelsall WS3 ... 15 B5
Walsall, Pleck WS2 ... 42 B8

St Johns Ret Pk WV2 ...... 163 B1
St Johns Way B93 .... 128 C6
St Johns Wlk B42 .... 55 D4
St Johns Wood B45 ...... 122 B5
St Joseph St **7** DY2 ...... 51 D1
St Joseph's Convent Prep
Sch
WV6 .... 24 E6
St Joseph's RC Comb Sch
CV31 .... 162 A3
St Joseph's RC Inf &
Jun Sch B7 .... 67 B6
St Joseph's RC Jun &
Inf Sch B30 .... 103 E4
St Joseph's RC Mid Sch
CV11 .... 73 C3
St Joseph's RC Prim Sch
Cannock WS12 .... 2 C4
Darlaston WS10 .... 41 D7
Dudley DY2 .... 51 E4
Lichfield WS14 .... 9 C7
Sutton Coldfield B75 ...... 46 C7
St Joseph's Sch CV8 ...... 148 B7
St Joseph's & St Theresa's
RC Prim Sch WS7 .... 6 F6
St Josephs Ave B31 ...... 103 B5
St Josephs Cl **6** WS3 .... 15 A4
St Josephs St WV4 .... 38 D6
St Josephs RC Prim Sch
Birmingham B30 .... 103 F5
Stourbridge DY8 .... 80 F2
St Josephs Rd B8 .... 68 C5
St Jude's CE Inf Sch WV6 .. 24 D7
St Jude's CE Jun Sch WV6 . 24 D7
St Jude's Cres CV3 ...... 134 D7
St Jude's Ct WV6 .... 24 D7
St Jude's Pas B5 .... 164 B1
St Jude's Rd WV6 .... 24 D7
St Jude's Rd W WV6 ...... 24 D7
St Judes Ave B80 .... 159 D4
St Judes Cl Birmingham
B14 .... 104 F2
Sutton Coldfield B75 ...... 46 F6
St Judes Ct B14 .... 104 F7
St Judes RC Inf & Jun Sch
B14 .... 104 F2
St Katherine's Rd B68 .... 64 B2
St Kenelm's CE Fst Sch
B62 .... 101 A4
St Kenelm's Cl B70 .... 53 F2
St Kenelm's Pass DY9 .... 100 A4
St Kenelm's Rd B62 ...... 100 E5
St Kenelms Ave B63 ...... 82 E1
St Kilda's Rd B8 .... 67 E5
St Laurence Ave CV34 .... 160 D5
St Laurence CE Inf Sch
B31 .... 103 B4
St Laurence CE Jun Sch
B31 .... 103 B4
St Laurence Cl B48 ...... 139 B6
St Laurence Rd B31 ...... 103 B5
St Laurence Cl B93 ...... 128 B5
St Lawrence Dr WS11 ...... 2 B2
St Lawrence Mews B31 .. 103 A3
St Lawrence Way WS10 .. 41 D6
St Lawrence's Rd CV6 .... 95 F1
St Leonard's CE Prim Sch
WV14 .... 40 B6
St Leonard's Wlk CV8 .... 135 A1
St Leonards Cl B37 .... 90 A7
St Leonards View B78 .... 36 F8
St Loye's Cl B62 .... 83 D8
St Luke's CE Fst Sch B97 . 153 D1
St Luke's CE Jun & Inf Sch
B15 .... 86 D8
St Luke's CE Jun Sch WV2 . 39 B7
St Luke's Cl WS11 .... 4 D8
St Luke's Cotts B97 ...... 153 D1
St Luke's Inf Sch WV2 .... 39 C7
St Luke's Rd Birmingham B5 . 86 E7
Burntwood WS7 .... 7 C6
Coventry CV6 .... 95 D3
Wednesbury WS10 .... 42 A3
St Luke's Terr DY1 .... 62 A8
St Lukes Cl B65 .... 63 B4
St Lukes St B64 .... 62 D1
St Margaret Mary RC
Jun & Inf Sch B23 .... 56 C6
St Margaret Rd CV1 ...... 113 F2
St Margaret's B74 .... 31 C3
St Margaret's CE Mid Sch
CV31 .... 162 B3
St Margaret's CE Prim Sch
Birmingham B43 .... 43 E4
Solihull B92 .... 88 F2
St Margaret's Ct **3** B92 .. 88 E1
St Margaret's Ho CV31 .. 162 B4
St Margaret's Hospl B43 .. 44 B3
St Margaret's Rd
Birmingham B43 .... 43 F2
Royal Leamington Spa CV31 . 162 B5
2 Solihull B92 .... 88 E1
Tamworth B79 .... 21 B7
St Margaret's Specl Sch
CV12 .... 78 B3
St Margarets Ave B8 ...... 68 B6
St Margarets Dr B63 ...... 82 F2
St Margarets Rd
Birmingham B8 .... 68 B6
2 Walsall WS3 .... 15 A4
Wolverhampton WS13 .... 3 B3
St Mark's Annexe
(Coventry&
WarwickshireHospl)
CV1 .... 165 C4

St Mark's CE Prim Sch DY5 . 61 C7
St Mark's Ct DY5 .... 61 D7
St Mark's Mews CV32 .... 156 E1
St Mark's RC Prim Sch B42 . 54 F6
St Mark's Rd Burntwood WS7 . 7 C6
Dudley DY2 .... 51 F1
Royal Leamington Spa
CV32 .... 156 D1
Smethwick B67 .... 64 D3
Stourbridge DY9 .... 81 D5
Tipton DY4 .... 52 A8
Wolverhampton WV3 .... 25 B1
St Mark's St WV3 .... 163 A2
St Marks Cres B1 .... 66 B3
St Marks Dr WV6 .... 4 F4
St Marks Rd Brownhills WS8 . 16 A5
Walsall WS3 .... 15 A4
St Marks St B1 .... 66 B3
St Martin's CE Prim Sch
WV14 .... 41 A2
St Martin's Circus
Queensway B5 .... 164 C2
St Martin's Cl
West Bromwich B70 .... 53 F2
Wolverhampton WV2 .... 39 E6
St Martin's Dr DY4 .... 52 A5
St Martin's Mkt B5 ...... 164 C1
St Martin's Rd CV8 ...... 133 C2
St Martin's St **6** B15 .... 66 B1
St Martin's Terr WV14 .... 40 E4
St Martins B91 .... 107 D3
St Martins Ave B80 ...... 159 D4
St Martins CE Prim Sch
DY4 .... 52 B5
St Martins RC Jun & Inf
Sch B13 .... 87 A3
St Martins Rd B75 .... 46 F5
St Mary Magdelene CE
Jun & Inf Sch B71 .... 53 D6
St Mary of the Angels RC
JMI Sch WS9 .... 30 B5
St Mary St CV1 .... 165 C2
St Mary & St John RC
Prim Sch B23 .... 56 E3
St Mary & St Margaret's
CE Prim Sch B36 .... 69 B8
St Mary's CE Jun & Inf Sch
B20 .... 55 B1
St Mary's CE Jun & Inf Sch
B29 .... 85 D1
St Mary's CE Jun Sch
B80 .... 159 E3
St Mary's CE Prim Sch
Kidderminster DY10 ...... 116 E8
Kingswinford DY6 .... 60 D7
St Mary's Cl Sedgley DY3 . 50 F8
Warwick CV34 .... 160 D8
St Mary's Cres CV31 .... 162 B7
St Mary's Ct Nuneaton CV11 . 73 B5
4 Willenhall WV13 ...... 27 A2
St Mary's Ho **4** B71 .... 53 D4
St Mary's La DY8 .... 81 B3
St Mary's of the Mount
Prim Sch WS1 .... 42 F8
St Mary's RC Jun & Inf Sch
B17 .... 85 C5
St Mary's RC Jun & Inf
Sch B80 .... 159 E4
St Mary's RC Prim Sch
DY5 .... 61 E2
St Mary's RC Prim Sch
WS11 .... 4 E8
St Mary's RC Prim Sch
Coventry CV1 .... 113 F3
Wednesbury WS10 .... 41 F4
St Mary's RC Sch WV10 .. 26 A7
St Mary's Rd Hinckley LE10 . 75 D8
Nuneaton CV11 .... 73 B5
Royal Leamington Spa
CV31 .... 162 B7
Smethwick B67 .... 64 F1
Wednesbury WS10 .... 41 F3
Wolverhampton WS13 .... 3 B3
St Mary's Row
Birmingham, Moseley B13 .. 86 F3
Birmingham,
New Town Row B4 .... 164 C3
St Mary's St WV1 .... 163 C3
St Mary's & St John's RC
Sch WV2 .... 163 C1
St Mary's Terr CV31 ...... 162 B7
St Mary's Way Aldridge WS9 . 30 B5
Tamworth B77 .... 21 E4
St Marys Cl B27 .... 88 B3
St Marys Ct **12** DY5 .... 61 D2
St Marys Rd B17 .... 85 C5
St Marys Ringway DY10 .. 116 E6
St Marys View B23 .... 56 D8
St Matthew St WV1 .... 25 F1
St Matthew's Ave WS7 .... 7 F7
St Matthew's CE Prim Sch
B66 .... 65 C5
St Matthew's Cl WS1 .... 28 F1
St Matthew's Rd WS7 ...... 7 F7
St Matthews CE Inf & Jun
Sch B7 .... 67 A4
St Matthews Cl WS3 ...... 15 B5
St Matthews Rd Oldbury
B68 .... 64 A2
Smethwick B66 .... 65 C5
St Mawes Rd WV6 .... 24 A3
St Mawgen Cl B35 .... 58 C4
St Michael Rd WS13 ...... 9 D8
St Michael St Walsall WS1 . 42 E8
West Bromwich B70 .... 53 C3
St Michaels Ct B70 .... 53 C3

St Michael's CE Jun & Inf Sch
B32 .... 102 C8
St Michael's CE Jun & Mixed Inf
Sch WS3 .... 14 F2
St Michael's CE Prim Sch
Blackheath B69 .... 63 C5
Lichfield WS14 .... 9 C7
Lichfield WS13 .... 9 C8
Walsall WS3 .... 15 A3
Wolverhampton WV6 ...... 24 E5
St Michael's Cl Walsall WS3 . 15 A2
Wood End CV9 .... 36 C1
St Michael's Cres B69 .... 64 A4
St Michael's Ct B68 ...... 64 A4
St Michael's Ct WV6 ...... 24 E5
St Michael's Gr B32 ...... 52 A1
St Michael's Hill B18 .... 66 A7
St Michael's Hospl
Lichfield WS13 .... 9 D8
Warwick CV34 .... 160 E8
St Michael's Mews B69 .. 52 A2
St Michael's RC Prim Sch
WV3 .... 38 D7
St Michael's Rd
Birmingham B18 .... 66 A7
Coventry CV2 .... 114 A3
Sutton Coldfield B73 ...... 56 F8
Warwick CV34 .... 160 D8
St Michael's Way CV10 .. 72 C4
St Michaels CE Inf & Jun
Sch
B21 .... 66 A7
St Michaels Dr WS12 ...... 2 F5
St Michaels Rd DY3 ...... 49 F5
St Michaels Way DY4 .... 52 A3
St Nicholas Ave CV8 .... 147 F3
St Nicholas CE Comb Sch
CV8 .... 147 F3
St Nicholas Church St
CV34 .... 160 F7
St Nicholas Cl Coventry
CV1 .... 113 C5
5 Walsall WS3 .... 15 A4
St Nicholas Ct
Coventry, Edgwick CV6 .. 113 F7
Coventry, Radford CV6 .. 113 B6
St Nicholas RC Prim Sch
B73 .... 45 F2
St Nicholas Rd CV31 .... 162 F5
St Nicholas St CV1 ...... 165 B4
St Nicholas Terr CV31 .. 162 E4
St Nicholas Wlk B76 ...... 59 B6
St Nicolas CE Fst Sch CV11 . 73 F6
St Nicolas Gdns B38 .... 103 F2
St Nicolas Park Dr CV11 . 73 F7
St Nicolas Rd CV11 ...... 73 D5
St Osburg RC Prim Sch
CV1 .... 165 A3
St Osburg's Rd CV2 ...... 114 A3
St Oswalds Cl DY10 ...... 116 F8
St Oswalds Rd B10 .... 87 E8
St Patrick's CE Prim Sch
B94 .... 126 C2
St Patrick's Ct DY11 .... 116 B1
St Patrick's RC JMI Sch
WS2 .... 28 E3
St Patrick's RC Jun & Inf
Schs
WV11 .... 26 C5
St Patrick's RC Prim Sch
Birmingham B37 .... 70 C2
Coventry CV2 .... 96 D1
St Patrick's Rd CV1 ...... 165 B1
St Patricks Cl B14 .... 104 E5
St Patricks RC Comb Sch
CV31 .... 161 F6
St Patricks RC Jun & Inf
Sch B18 .... 65 F4
St Paul's Ave
Birmingham B12 .... 87 A5
Kidderminster DY11 ...... 116 A6
St Paul's CE Comb Sch
CV32 .... 157 B1
St Paul's CE Comb Sch
(Annexe) CV32 .... 157 A1
St Paul's CE Fst Sch CV10 . 72 C3
St Paul's CE Prim Sch
WV9 .... 11 A4
St Paul's Cl Cannock WS11 .. 2 B1
Walsall WS1 .... 28 E2
Warwick CV34 .... 160 D6
St Paul's Convent Sch B75 . 46 C7
St Paul's Cres
5 Coleshill B46 .... 70 F7
West Bromwich B70 ...... 52 E7
St Paul's Ct B77 .... 35 C4
St Paul's Dr DY4 .... 52 B4
St Paul's RC Inf & Jun Sch
B38 .... 104 A1
St Paul's Rd Birmingham
B12 .... 87 A5
Burntwood WS7 .... 7 C6
Cannock WS12 .... 2 E3
Coventry CV6 .... 113 E6
Dudley DY2 .... 62 D5
Nuneaton CV10 .... 72 D3
Smethwick B66 .... 64 E7
Wednesbury WS10 .... 42 C5
St Paul's Sch for Girls B16 . 65 E1
St Paul's Sq Birmingham
B3 .... 164 A4
4 Royal Leamington Spa
CV32 .... 157 B1
St Paul's St WS1 .... 28 E2
St Paul's Sta B19 .... 164 B4
St Paul's Terr CV34 ...... 160 D6
St Pauls CE Sch DY4 ...... 51 F6
St Pauls Cres WS3 .... 15 B5

St Pauls Ct Blackheath B62 . 63 D1
Water Orton B46 .... 59 B3
St Pauls Dr B62 .... 63 D1
St Pauls Gdns LE10 .... 71 E1
St Pauls Terr B3 .... 164 A4
St Peter & Paul RC Jun &
Inf Sch B24 .... 57 C3
St Peter & St Paul RC Prim
Sch WS13 .... 3 B1
St Peter's CE Inf Sch B17 . 85 B4
St Peter's CE Jun Sch B17 . 85 B5
St Peter's CE Mid Sch
B98 .... 154 E2
St Peter's CE Prim Sch
WS12 .... 2 D4
St Peter's Cl Redditch B97 . 158 E5
Stonnall WS9 .... 16 E4
Tamworth B77 .... 21 D1
Water Orton B46 .... 59 B2
West Bromwich B71 ...... 52 D4
St Peter's Collegiate Sec
Sch WV3 .... 24 E3
St Peter's Croft B73 ...... 56 F8
St Peter's Ct Coventry CV1 . 165 D4
Walsall WS3 .... 14 B1
St Peter's RC Fst Sch
B60 .... 150 E8
St Peter's RC Sch
Hinckley LE10 .... 71 E1
Solihull B91 .... 107 B2
Walsall WS3 .... 14 B2
St Peter's Rd
Birmingham B20 .... 66 C8
Burntwood WS7 .... 7 C6
Cannock WS12 .... 2 D4
Dudley DY2 .... 62 D5
7 Royal Leamington Spa
CV32 .... 161 F8
Stourbridge DY9 .... 81 C1
St Peters Cl
Birmingham B28 .... 105 D6
Sutton Coldfield B72 ...... 46 B3
St Peters Dr WS3 .... 15 A4
St Peters La B92 .... 90 D1
St Peters RC Sch B32 .... 84 C1
St Peters Rd B17 .... 85 B5
St Peters Terr WS2 .... 28 E4
St Philip's Cath B2 ...... 164 B3
St Philip's Gr WV3 .... 38 F7
St Philip's Pl B2 .... 164 C3
St Philip's RC Prim Sch
B66 .... 65 B6
St Philip's Sixth Form Ctr
B16 .... 65 F1
St Philips Ave WV3 .... 38 F7
St Quentin St WS2 .... 42 C7
St Saviour's CE Prim Sch
B8 .... 67 D5
St Saviour's Cl WV2 ...... 39 F6
St Saviour's Rd B8 .... 67 D4
St Silas' Sq B19 .... 66 B7
St Simons Cl B75 .... 46 F6
St Stephen's Ave WV13 .. 26 F2
St Stephen's CE Fst Sch
B98 .... 153 F5
St Stephen's CE Mid Sch
B98 .... 153 F5
St Stephen's CE Sch WV10 . 25 F4
St Stephen's Ct WV13 .... 26 F1
St Stephen's Gdns
1 WV13 .... 27 A1
St Stephen's Rd WS7 ...... 7 C6
St Stephens Gdns B98 .. 153 F5
St Stephens Rd
Birmingham B29 .... 104 B8
West Bromwich B71 ...... 65 B8
St Stephens St B6 .... 66 E6
St Teresa's RC Prim Sch
WV4 .... 39 E5
St Teresa's RC Sch
(Jun & Inf) B20 .... 55 A3
St Thomas Aquinas RC
Sec Sch B30 .... 103 D3
St Thomas CE Com High
Sch B15 .... 86 C8
St Thomas CE Jun & Inf
Sch B15 .... 86 D8
St Thomas CE Prim Sch
WV11 .... 26 D7
St Thomas' Cl WS9 .... 16 B1
St Thomas Cl
Sutton Coldfield B75 ...... 46 F5
Walsall WS8 .... 28 E6
St Thomas More RC Comp
Sch WV14 .... 41 A7
St Thomas More RC Fst
Sch B98 .... 159 B7
St Thomas More RC Prim
Sch Coventry CV3 ...... 133 D5
Great Wyrley WS6 .... 5 A4
St Thomas More Sch
CV10 .... 73 A3
St Thomas More's RC
Jun & Inf Sch B26 .... 89 B5
St Thomas of Canterbury
RC Sch WS3 .... 28 F6
St Thomas' Rd
Birmingham B23 .... 56 D3
Coventry CV6 .... 96 A3
St Thomas Rd DY2 .... 62 C5
St Thomas's Ct **13** CV1 . 113 B2
St Thomas's Ho **12** CV1 . 113 B2
St Valentines Cl B70 ...... 53 F2
St Vincent Cres B70 ...... 52 F6
St Vincent St B16 .... 66 B2
St Vincent St W B16 ...... 66 A2

St Vincent's RC Inf & Jun
Sch B7 .... 67 B3
St Wilfrid's RC Jun & Inf
Sch B36 .... 68 F8
Saintbury Dr B91 .... 127 C8
Saints Way CV10 .... 73 D5
Saladin Ave B69 .... 63 E5
Salcombe Ave B26 .... 89 C5
Salcombe Cl Cannock WS11 .. 4 B7
Coventry CV3 .... 134 D6
Nuneaton CV10 .... 73 F5
Salcombe Dr DY5 .... 81 C7
Salcombe Gr WV14 .... 40 D1
Salcombe Rd **8** B66 .... 65 B5
Saldavian Ct WS2 .... 42 B6
Salem Rd LE10 .... 75 F5
Salem St DY4 .... 52 D5
Salford Cir B23 .... 56 D1
Salford Cl Coventry CV2 .. 114 A5
Redditch B98 .... 159 B6
Salford St B6 .... 67 C8
Salisbury Ave CV3 ...... 133 C6
Salisbury Cl Birmingham
B13 .... 86 E3
Dudley DY1 .... 50 F3
Lichfield WS13 .... 3 C3
Salisbury Dr Cannock WS12 .. 2 B1
Kidderminster DY11 ...... 116 A6
Nuneaton CV10 .... 72 B7
Water Orton B46 .... 59 C3
Salisbury Gr B72 .... 57 C7
Salisbury Ho
3 Birmingham B24 .... 56 F4
Hinckley LE10 .... 71 C4
Salisbury Pl WV3 .... 25 B1
Salisbury Prim Sch WS10 . 41 F7
Salisbury Rd
Birmingham, Lozells B19 .. 66 D8
Birmingham, Moseley B13 . 86 E3
Birmingham, Saltley B8 .. 67 E5
Hinckley LE10 .... 76 B7
Smethwick B66 .... 65 B4
West Bromwich B70 ...... 53 E1
Salisbury St Darlaston WS10 . 41 E7
Wolverhampton WV3 ...... 25 B1
Salisbury Tower B18 ...... 66 A3
Sally Ward Dr WS9 .... 16 A4
Salop Cl B71 .... 53 B6
Salop Dr Cannock WS11 .... 4 F8
Oldbury B68 .... 64 C2
Salop Rd Oldbury B68 .... 64 C2
Redditch B97 .... 153 D3
Salop St Bilston WV14 .... 40 E4
Birmingham B12 .... 86 F8
Dudley DY1 .... 51 B2
Oldbury B69 .... 52 E1
Wolverhampton WV3 .... 163 B2
Salstar Cl B6 .... 66 E6
Salt La CV1 .... 165 B2
Saltash Gr B25 .... 68 C1
Saltbrook Rd B63 .... 82 A7
Saltbrook Trad Est B63 .. 82 A7
Salter Rd DY4 .... 51 F7
Salter St B94 .... 126 C2
Salter's La Redditch B97 . 153 B5
Tamworth B79 .... 21 B6
West Bromwich B71 ...... 53 E4
Salter's Rd WS9 .... 16 A3
Salters Vale B70 .... 53 E1
Saltisford CV34 .... 160 D7
Saltisford Gdns CV34 .. 160 C8
Saltley Ind Ctr B8 .... 67 C3
Saltley Rd B7 .... 67 C5
Saltley Sch B8 .... 68 A3
Saltley Trad Est B8 .... 67 D6
Saltley Viaduct B8 .... 67 C5
Saltney Cl B24 .... 57 D5
Salts La B78 .... 34 E4
Saltwells La DY2 .... 62 B2
Saltwells Rd DY2 .... 62 C2
Salwarpe Gr B29 .... 84 F2
Salwarpe Rd B60 .... 150 F8
Sam Barber Ct WS12 ...... 2 E2
Sam Gault Cl CV3 .... 134 E7
Sam Spencer Ct DY10 .. 118 A1
Sambar Rd B78 .... 20 F1
Sambourn Cl B91 .... 107 E6
Sambourne Dr B34 .... 69 D7
Sambourne La
Astwood Bank B96 ...... 158 F1
Sambourne B96 .... 159 A1
Sambourne Park La B96 . 159 A1
Sambrook Rd WV10 ...... 26 A5
Sammons Way CV4 ...... 111 D1
Sampson Cl Birmingham B21 . 54 C1
Coventry CV2 .... 114 C8
Tipton B69 .... 63 C7
Sampson Rd B11 .... 87 B3
Sampson Rd N B11 ...... 87 B8
Sampson St WS10 .... 42 B3
Sams La B70 .... 53 C1
Samuel Cl WS13 .... 3 C2
Samuel Hayward Ho
5 CV2 .... 96 B1
Samuel St WS3 .... 14 B1
Samuel Vale Ho CV1 .... 165 B4
Samuels Rd B32 .... 84 A5
Sanby Cl CV12 .... 78 A4
Sand Bank WS3 .... 14 A1
Sand Pits B1 .... 66 B3
Sand St B70 .... 52 E4
Sanda Croft B36 .... 70 B6
Sandal Rise B91 .... 107 E3
Sandalls Cl B31 .... 102 D1
Sandals Rise B62 .... 83 D3
Sandalwood Cl WV12 .... 27 B6
Sandbarn Cl B90 .... 126 F6
Sandbeds Rd WV12 ...... 27 C4

Sandbourne Rd B8 .... 68 A4
Sanderling Cl WV10 .... 12 B7
Sanderling Ct DY10 .... 117 A1
Sanderling Rise
  Burntwood WS7 .... 7 B8
  Kingswinford DY6 .... 61 A6
Sanders Cl Dudley DY2 .... 62 E7
  Redditch B97 .... 153 B4
Sanders Ct CV34 .... 161 C8
Sanders Ind Est B61 ...... 136 E1
Sanders Rd Bedworth CV6 .... 96 B6
  Bromsgrove B61 .... 136 E1
Sanderson Ct DY11 .... 116 C5
Sandfield **1** B66 .... 64 E7
Sandfield Cl B90 .... 126 B8
Sandfield Gr DY3 .... 50 B2
Sandfield Rd Stourbridge
  DY8 .... 60 F2
  West Bromwich B71 .... 42 E2
Sandfields Ave B10 .... 87 B8
Sandfields Rd B68 .... 64 C2
Sandford Ave B65 .... 63 C3
Sandford Cl CV2 .... 96 E3
Sandford Ho
  B13 .... 87 A3
  Dudley DY1 .... 50 E1
Sandford Rise WV6 .... 24 E6
Sandford St WS13 .... 9 B7
Sandgate Cres CV2 .... 114 C2
Sandgate Rd
  Birmingham B28 .... 106 A4
  Tipton DY4 .... 52 A8
Sandhill Farm Cl **1** B19 .. 66 D7
Sandhill St WS3 .... 14 A1
Sandhills Cres B91 .... 127 B8
Sandhills Gn B48 .... 138 E7
Sandhills La B45 .... 138 D7
Sandhills Rd B45 .... 138 D8
Sandhurst Ave
  Birmingham B36 .... 68 D6
  Stourbridge DY9 .... 81 D2
Sandhurst Cl B98 .... 154 C6
Sandhurst Dr WV4 .... 39 A4
Sandhurst Gr Coventry
  CV6 .... 113 B5
  Stourbridge DY8 .... 60 E3
Sandhurst Ho B38 .... 104 B1
Sandhurst Rd
  Birmingham B13 .... 86 F2
  Kingswinford DY6 .... 61 A4
  Sutton Coldfield B74 ...... 31 F5
Sandicliffe Cl DY11 ...... 116 C8
Sandilands Cl CV2 .... 114 E4
Sandland Cl WV14 .... 40 F6
Sandland Rd WV12 .... 27 D8
Sandmartin Cl DY2 .... 62 D2
Sandmartin Way DY10 .... 117 A2
Sandmere Gr B14 .... 105 D3
Sandmere Rd B14 .... 105 D3
Sandmere Rise WV10 ...... 11 E1
Sandon Cl B98 .... 154 A3
Sandon Gr B24 .... 57 B4
Sandon Ho WV6 .... 24 E5
Sandon Rd Birmingham B17 .. 65 B1
  Nuneaton CV11 .... 73 B5
  Stourbridge DY9 .... 81 F4
  Wolverhampton WV10 ...... 11 C2
Sandown B77 .... 21 F5
Sandown Ave
  Cheslyn Hay WS6 .... 4 E3
  Coventry CV6 .... 95 F2
Sandown Cl CV32 .... 157 C4
Sandown Ct B29 .... 103 C7
Sandown Dr WV6 .... 23 F4
Sandown Fst Sch WV6 .... 23 F4
Sandown Rd B36 .... 68 D8
Sandown Tower **3** B31 .. 103 A1
Sandpiper B77 .... 36 A5
Sandpiper Cl Cannock
  WS12 .... 2 C7
  Kidderminster DY10 ...... 117 B2
  Stourbridge DY9 .... 81 F5
Sandpiper Gdns B38 ...... 123 F7
Sandpiper Rd CV2 .... 96 B3
Sandpit Cl WS10 .... 42 E2
Sandpits B76 .... 59 B6
Sandpits Ind Est **4** B1 .... 66 B3
Sandpits La CV6 .... 94 F2
Sandpits The CV12 .... 79 C2
Sandra Cl WS9 .... 30 B5
Sandringham Ave WV12 .... 27 B6
Sandringham Ct CV10 .... 72 F6
Sandringham Dr
  Aldridge WS9 .... 16 B1
  Blackheath B65 .... 63 C4
Sandringham Pl DY8 ...... 60 D1
Sandringham Rd
  Birmingham B42 .... 55 B6
  Halesowen B62 .... 83 B7
  Stourbridge DY8 .... 60 D1
  Wolverhampton WV4 .... 39 B4
Sandringham Way DY5 .... 81 C8
Sandstone Ave B45 ...... 122 A8
Sandstone Cl DY3 .... 50 D4
Sandway Gdns B8 .... 67 D6
Sandway Gr B13 .... 105 C7
Sandwell Ave WS10 .... 41 B5
Sandwell Bsns
  Development Ctr B66 .... 64 C7
Sandwell Bsns Pk B66 .... 64 C8
Sandwell Coll
  Wednesbury WS10 .... 42 F5
  West Bromwich B70 .... 53 C3
Sandwell Coll (Kendrick
  Campus) WS10 .... 42 A3
Sandwell Coll (Knowles
  Annexe) WS10 .... 42 A3

Sandwell Coll Oldbury
  Campus B68 .... 64 A3
Sandwell Coll Smethwick
  Campus B66 .... 65 A5
Sandwell Coll
  (Wednesbury Campus)
  WS10 .... 42 A1
Sandwell Ct B21 .... 65 D8
Sandwell Ctr B70 .... 53 D3
Sandwell District General
  Hospl B71 .... 53 D5
Sandwell & Dudley Sta
  B70 .... 53 A1
Sandwell Ho **1** WS1 ...... 42 F8
Sandwell Park Farm B71 .. 53 F3
Sandwell Pl WV12 .... 27 D7
Sandwell Rd Birmingham B21 .. 54 D1
  West Bromwich B71 .... 53 C4
  Wolverhampton WV10 ...... 11 B1
Sandwell Rd N B71 .... 53 D4
Sandwell Road Pas B70 .. 53 C4
Sandwell St WS1 .... 42 F8
Sandwell Valley Ctry Pk
  B71 .... 54 A5
Sandwell Valley Nature Ctr
  B43 .... 54 C6
Sandwell Wlk **8** WS1 .... 42 F8
Sandwick Cl CV3 .... 134 E8
Sandwood Dr B44 .... 55 F8
Sandy Cres Hinckley LE10 .. 71 C1
  Wednesfield WV11 .... 27 A8
Sandy Croft
  Birmingham B13 .... 105 C7
  Sutton Coldfield B72 ...... 46 C3
Sandy Hill Rd B90 .... 106 A4
Sandy Hill Rise B90 ...... 106 A4
Sandy Hollow WV6 .... 24 C2
Sandy La
  Birmingham, Aston B6 .... 67 B7
  Birmingham, Great Barr B42 .. 55 D8
  Blackdown CV32 .... 156 F6
  Blakedown DY10 .... 118 C7
  Cannock WS11 .... 1 B1
  Codsall WV8 .... 10 A4
  Coventry CV1 .... 113 C5
  Royal Leamington Spa
  CV32 .... 156 D4
  Wednesbury WS10 .... 42 F3
  Wildmoor B61, B62 .... 120 E5
  Wolverhampton,
  Bushbury WV10 .... 11 E1
  Wolverhampton,
  Tettenhall WV6 .... 24 E6
Sandy Lane Bsns Pk CV1 .. 113 C5
Sandy Mount WS7 .... 7 B6
Sandy Mount Rd WS1 .... 42 F8
Sandy Rd DY8 .... 80 D1
Sandy Way Birmingham B15 .. 66 B1
  Tamworth B77 .... 22 B3
Sandyacre Way DY8 .... 81 B5
Sandyfields Rd DY3 .... 50 B6
Sandygate Cl B97 .... 152 F2
Sandythorpe CV3 .... 134 E6
Sangwin Rd WV14 .... 51 C7
Sankey Rd WS11 .... 1 F3
Sankey's Cnr WS7 .... 6 F7
Sansome Rd B90 .... 105 F2
Sansome Rise B90 .... 105 F2
Sanstone Cl WS3 .... 14 C3
Sanstone Rd WS3 .... 14 C3
Sant Rd B31 .... 123 B7
Santolina Dr WS5 .... 43 A3
Santos Cl CV3 .... 134 F8
Santridge Ct B61 .... 137 A4
Santridge La B61 .... 137 A4
Sapcote Bsns Ctr B10 .... 87 E6
Sapcote Gr CV2 .... 96 B4
Sapcote Ind Est B64 ...... 62 F3
Sapcote Rd LE10 .... 76 B7
Saplings The B76 .... 58 A8
Sapphire Ct Birmingham
  B3 .... 164 A4
  3 Solihull B92 .... 88 F1
Sapphire Dr Cannock WS11 .. 2 C3
  Royal Leamington Spa CV31 .. 161 F5
Sapphire Gate CV2 ...... 114 C2
Sapphire Tower **2** B6 .... 66 F6
Sara Cl B74 .... 32 A3
Saracen Dr CV7 .... 129 E6
Sarah Cl WV14 .... 40 E1
Sarah Ct B73 .... 45 D1
Sarah Gdns WS5 .... 42 F4
Sarah Siddons Ho **2** WS13 .. 9 B7
Sarah St B9 .... 67 B2
Saredon Cl WS3 .... 15 A1
Saredon Rd WS6 .... 4 B3
Sarehole Mill Mus B13 .. 105 D8
Sarehole Rd B28 .... 87 E1
Sargeaunt St CV31 ...... 161 F7
Sargent Cl B43 .... 44 D4
Sargent Turner Trad Est
  DY9 .... 81 F6
Sark Dr B36 .... 70 B6
Satchwell Ct **11** CV32 .. 161 F8
Satchwell Wlk **10** CV32 .. 161 F8
Satellite Ind Pk WV11 .... 26 D4
Saturn Rd WS11 .... 2 A5
Saumur Way CV34 .... 161 C6
Saunders Ave CV12 .... 78 B2
Saunders Cl WS12 .... 2 F6
Saunders Ho **10** CV32 .. 156 F2
Saunderton Ho B31 ...... 102 E5
Saunton Cl CV5 .... 112 B8
Saunton Way B29 .... 85 C2
Saveker Dr B76 .... 46 E4
Savernake Cl B45 .... 102 A2
Saville Cl Birmingham B45 .. 122 B7
  Hinckley LE10 .... 71 E2

Saville Gr CV8 .... 148 C5
Savoy Bldgs DY2 .... 62 D5
Savoy Cl B32 .... 85 A5
Saw Mill Cl WS4 .... 28 E3
Saxelby Cl B14 .... 104 E2
Saxelby Ho B14 .... 104 E2
Saxon Bsns Pk B60 ...... 150 E2
Saxon Cl Binley Woods CV3 .. 135 D7
  Great Wyrley WS6 .... 5 A2
  Polesworth B78 .... 22 F1
  Studley B80 .... 159 E5
  Tamworth B77 .... 35 F6
Saxon Ct WS13 .... 8 E7
Saxon Dr B65 .... 63 C4
Saxon Hill Specl Sch WS14 .. 9 C6
Saxon Mdws CV32 .... 156 C2
Saxon Mill La B79 .... 21 C4
Saxon Rd CV2 .... 114 B4
Saxon Way B37 .... 69 F3
Saxon Wlk WS13 .... 8 E7
Saxon Wood Cl B31 ...... 103 A4
Saxon Wood Rd B90 .... 126 D5
Saxoncourt WV6 .... 24 C5
Saxondale Ave B26 .... 88 F6
Saxondrive B79 .... 21 C5
Saxonfields WV6 .... 24 C5
Saxons Way B14 .... 105 A2
Saxton Dr B74 .... 31 F6
Sayer Ho B19 .... 66 D6
Scafell Cl CV5 .... 112 A4
Scafell Dr Bilston WV14 .... 40 F7
  Birmingham B23 .... 56 C5
Scafell Rd DY8 .... 81 B6
Scaife Rd B60 .... 151 B7
Scammerton B77 .... 36 B8
Scampton Cl WV6 .... 23 E5
Scampton Way B79 .... 21 C8
Scar Bank WS14 .... 155 E1
Scarborough Cl **2** WS2 .. 42 B8
Scarborough Rd WS2 .... 42 B8
Scarborough Way CV4 .. 131 F7
Scarfield Hill B48 .... 138 E5
Scarsdale Rd B42 .... 55 D8
Schofield Ave B71 .... 53 B8
Schofield Rd B37 .... 70 A5
Scholars Gate
  Birmingham B33 .... 69 B2
  Burntwood WS7 .... 7 B6
Scholefield Tower B19 .. 66 D5
Scholfield Rd CV7 .... 95 A6
School Ave WS8 .... 15 F8
School Bell Mews CV8 .. 149 B6
School Cl Birmingham B37 .. 70 A6
  Burntwood WS7 .... 6 D8
  Codsall WV8 .... 10 A4
  Coventry CV3 .... 113 F2
  Hinckley LE10 .... 76 A6
  Norton Canes WS11 .... 6 B6
  Tipton B69 .... 63 C7
  Wolverhampton WV3 .... 38 B7
School Cotts CV35 ...... 145 F3
School Cres WS11 .... 6 A6
School Croft CV35 .... 146 C2
School Ct WS12 .... 2 C6
School Dr Bilston WV14 .... 41 A2
  Bromsgrove B60 .... 137 A3
  Dudley WV14 .... 40 C1
  Stourbridge DY8 .... 80 F8
  Wythall B47 .... 125 A3
School Dr The DY2 .... 62 D7
School Gn WV14 .... 40 C8
School Hill CV10 .... 72 A8
School Ho The WS7 .... 7 D7
School House La CV2 .... 115 A6
School La Alvechurch B48 .. 139 B5
  Bedworth CV7 .... 95 F7
  Birmingham,
  Buckland End B34 .... 69 B7
  Birmingham,
  Kitt's Green B33 .... 68 F1
  Brierley Hill DY5 .... 61 B4
  Burntwood WS7 .... 6 D8
  Hagley DY9 .... 99 D6
  Halesowen B63 .... 82 F2
  Hopwas B78 .... 20 B7
  Kenilworth CV8 .... 147 F5
  Lickey End B60 .... 137 B6
  Norton Canes WS3 .... 5 E2
  Radford Semele CV31 .... 162 E5
  Shuttington B79 .... 22 F7
  Solihull B91 .... 107 D4
  Tamworth B77 .... 35 D5
  Walsall WS3 .... 14 F4
  Weeford B78 .... 19 D2
  Wolverhampton WV10 ...... 11 E2
  Wroxall CV35 .... 145 E4
School of Art, Univ of
  Wolverhampton WV1 ...... 163 B4
School Rd
  Birmingham, Eachway B45 .. 121 C6
  Birmingham,
  Hall Green B28 .... 106 A8
  Birmingham, Moseley B13 .. 86 F1
  Birmingham,
  Yardley Wood B14 .... 105 C4
  Brierley Hill DY5 .... 62 A2
  Bulkington CV12 .... 79 C2
  Himley DY3 .... 49 B3
  Norton Canes WS11 .... 6 A6
  Solihull B90 .... 106 B2
  Tanworth-in-A B94 .... 143 B7
  Trysull WV5 .... 37 C1
  Wednesbury WS10 .... 42 D2
  Wolverhampton,
  New Cross WV11 .... 26 C6
  Wolverhampton,
  Tettenhall WV6 .... 24 B3
  Wombourne WV5 .... 49 B7

School St Blackheath B64 .. 62 D1
  Brierley Hill DY5 .... 61 D7
  Darlaston WV10 .... 41 E5
  Dudley, Eve Hill DY1 ...... 51 B1
  Dudley, Roseville WV14 .. 51 C8
  Sedgley DY3 .... 50 E8
  Stourbridge DY8 .... 80 F6
  Tamworth B77 .... 21 E4
  Walsall WS4 .... 15 D1
  Willenhall WV13 .... 26 F1
  Wolverhampton WV3 ...... 163 B2
School St W **2** WV14 .... 51 C8
School Terr **1** B29 ...... 85 F2
School Wlk Bilston WV14 .. 40 C8
  Burntwood WS7 .... 6 D8
  Nuneaton CV11 .... 73 E2
Schoolacre Rd B34 .... 69 B6
Schoolacre Rise B74 .... 30 E1
Schoolfields Rd WS14 .... 18 A5
Schoolgate Cl WS4 .... 15 D1
Schoolhouse Cl B38 .... 104 B2
Scimitar Cl B79 .... 20 E7
Scorers Cl B90 .... 106 B6
Scotch Orch WS13 .... 3 D1
Scotch Orchard Prim Sch
  WS13 .... 3 D1
Scotchill The CV6 .... 95 A1
Scotchings The B36 .... 68 E8
Scotia Rd WS11 .... 1 D3
Scotland La B32 .... 102 C7
Scotland St B1 .... 66 C3
Scots Cnr B14 .... 104 E8
Scots La CV6 .... 112 F6
Scott Arms Sh Ctr B43 .. 43 F1
Scott Ave Nuneaton CV10 .. 73 D8
  Wednesbury WS10 .... 42 B2
  Wolverhampton WV4 .... 38 E4
Scott Cl Lichfield WS14 ... 9 B6
  West Bromwich B71 .... 53 D5
Scott Gr B92 .... 88 E3
Scott Ho B43 .... 54 F7
Scott Rd Birmingham B43 .. 43 F2
  Kenilworth CV8 .... 147 E2
  Redditch B97 .... 158 C8
  Royal Leamington Spa
  CV31 .... 162 B6
  Solihull B92 .... 88 E2
  Tamworth B77 .... 21 E4
  Walsall WS5 .... 43 D6
Scott St B12 .... 2 F3
Scott's Green Cl DY1 ...... 62 A8
Scott's Rd DY8 .... 80 F6
Scotwell Cl B65 .... 63 B3
Scout Cl B33 .... 69 C2
Scribban Cl B66 .... 65 B4
Scribers La Birmingham
  B28 .... 105 D4
  Birmingham B28 .... 105 E4
Scrimshaw Ho **1** WS2 .. 42 C7
Sculthorpe Rd DY10 ...... 98 B2
Seacroft Ave B25 .... 68 E1
Seafield B77 .... 21 F5
Seafield Cl DY6 .... 60 E4
Seafield La Beoley B98 .. 141 A2
  Portway B48 .... 140 E4
Seaford Cl CV6 .... 96 B4
Seaforth Dr LE10 .... 71 A1
Seaforth Gr WV12 .... 13 B1
Seagar St B71 .... 53 E4
Seager's La DY5 .... 61 D2
Seagrave Rd CV1 .... 165 D1
Seal Cl B76 .... 46 E3
Sealand Dr CV12 .... 78 A3
Seals Gn B38 .... 123 D7
Sear Hills Cl CV7 .... 130 B6
Seaton B77 .... 35 F8
Seaton Cl Hinckley LE10 .. 76 B7
  Nuneaton CV11 .... 73 F5
  Wednesfield WV11 .... 26 F5
Seaton Gr B13 .... 86 D1
Seaton Pl WS11 .... 60 C2
Seaton Rd B66 .... 65 B5
Seaton Tower **2** B31 .. 102 C2
Sebastian Cl CV3 .... 134 B5
Seckham Rd WS13 .... 9 A8
Second Ave
  Birmingham,
  Bordesley Green B9 .... 67 F1
  Birmingham,
  Selly Oak B29 .... 86 B3
  Birmingham, Witton B6 .. 55 F3
  Brownhills WS8 .... 7 A1
  Coventry CV3 .... 114 C1
  Kingswinford,
  Barrow Hill DY6 .... 61 A7
  Kingswinford,
  Wall Heath DY6 .... 60 F8
  Wolverhampton WV10 ...... 25 E7
Second Exhibition Ave
  B40 .... 90 D4
Security Ho WV2 .... 163 B2
Sedge Ave B38 .... 103 F3
Sedgeberrow Covert
  3 B38 .... 123 E8
Sedgeberrow Rd B63 ...... 83 A2
Sedgefield Cl DY1 .... 50 E3
Sedgefield Gr WV6 .... 23 F4
Sedgeford Cl DY5 .... 81 D8
Sedgehill Ave B17 .... 85 B4
Sedgemere Gr
  Balsall Common CV7 ..... 130 C5
  Walsall WS4 .... 29 C8
Sedgemere Rd B26 .... 68 F1
Sedgemoor Ave WS7 .... 7 B5
Sedgemoor Rd CV3 ...... 134 B5
Sedgley B98 .... 153 F4
Sedgley Gr B20 .... 54 C8
Sedgley Hall Ave DY3 .... 50 C8

Sedgley Rd Dudley DY1 .. 51 B6
  Wombourne WV4 .... 38 F2
Sedgley Rd E DY4 .... 52 A3
Sedgley Rd W DY4 .... 51 D5
Sedgley St WV2 .... 39 C7
Seed Field Croft CV3 .... 133 E7
Seedhouse Ct B64 .... 83 B8
Seeds La WS8 .... 15 F8
Seekings The CV31 ...... 162 B3
Seeleys Rd B11 .... 87 E5
Seeswood Cl CV10 .... 72 C2
Sefton Dr B65 .... 62 F6
Sefton Gr DY4 .... 41 C2
Sefton Rd Birmingham B16 .. 65 F2
  Coventry CV4 .... 132 E6
  Tamworth B77 .... 35 D4
Segbourne Rd B45 .... 121 F8
Segundo Cl WS5 .... 42 F4
Segundo Rd WS5 .... 42 F4
Seisdon Rd WV5 .... 37 A1
Selba Dr DY11 .... 116 A6
Selborne Cl WS1 .... 29 A1
Selborne Gr B13 .... 105 C5
Selborne Rd Birmingham
  B20 .... 55 A2
  Dudley DY2 .... 62 D7
Selborne St WS1 .... 29 A1
Selbourne Cres WV1 ...... 26 B1
Selby Cl B26 .... 68 F1
Selby Gr B13 .... 105 C6
Selby Ho B69 .... 63 D6
Selby Way Nuneaton CV10 .. 72 B5
  Walsall WS3 .... 13 E2
Selcombe Way B38 ...... 123 F7
Selcroft Ave B32 .... 84 F5
Selecta Ave B44 .... 44 D2
Selina Dix Ho CV1 .... 165 C4
Selker Dr B77 .... 21 F5
Selkirk Cl B71 .... 53 C6
Selly Ave B29 .... 86 A2
Selly Cl B29 .... 86 B2
Selly Hall Croft B30 .... 104 A6
Selly Hill Rd B29 .... 85 F2
Selly Manor Mus B30 .. 103 F7
Selly Oak Hospl B29 ...... 85 F1
Selly Oak Ind Est B29 .... 85 E1
Selly Oak Rd B30 .... 103 E5
Selly Oak Specl Sch B29 .. 103 E8
Selly Oak Sta B29 .... 85 E2
Selly Park Girls Sec Sch
  B29 .... 86 B1
Selly Park Rd B29 .... 86 A2
Selly Wharf B29 .... 85 E2
Selly Wick Dr B29 .... 86 B2
Selly Wick Rd B29 .... 86 B2
Sellywood Rd B30 .... 103 E8
Selma Gr B14 .... 105 D5
Selman's Par WS3 .... 14 C2
Selmans Hill WS3 .... 14 C2
Selsdon Cl
  Kidderminster DY11 ..... 116 B5
  Wythall B47 .... 125 C5
Selsdon Rd WS3 .... 13 F3
Selsey Ave B66 .... 65 B5
Selsey Cl CV3 .... 134 C4
Selsey Rd B17 .... 65 B3
Selston Rd B6 .... 66 E7
Selvey Ave B43 .... 44 C3
Selworthy Rd
  Birmingham B36 .... 69 F8
  Coventry CV6 .... 95 E3
Selwyn Cl WV2 .... 39 C7
Selwyn Ho B37 .... 70 D3
Selwyn Rd Bilston WV14 .. 40 F7
  Birmingham B16 .... 65 D2
Semele Cl CV31 .... 162 E3
Seneschal Rd CV3 .... 133 E7
Senneleys Park Rd B31 .. 84 E1
Sennen Cl Nuneaton CV11 .. 74 A5
  Willenhall WV13 .... 26 F1
Sensall Rd DY9 .... 81 F3
Serin Cl DY10 .... 117 A1
Serpentine Rd
  Birmingham, Aston B6 .... 56 A1
  Birmingham, Harborne B17 .. 85 C6
  Birmingham, Selly Oak B29 .. 86 A2
Serpentine The DY11 .... 116 C4
Servite Ct B14 .... 105 A2
Servite Ho **2** Coleshill B46 .. 70 F7
  Kenilworth CV8 .... 147 F3
Seton Ho B74 .... 31 E2
Settle Ave B34 .... 68 F6
Settle Croft B37 .... 69 F1
Setton Dr DY3 .... 50 E7
Seven Acres WS9 .... 30 B5
Seven Acres La B98 .... 154 C5
Seven Acres Rd
  Birmingham B31 .... 103 C1
  Halesowen B62 .... 84 A5
Seven Star Rd B91 ...... 107 B5
Seven Stars Rd B69 ...... 64 A7
Severn Ave LE10 .... 75 A8
Severn Cl Birmingham B36 .. 69 F7
  Catshill B61 .... 137 A8
  Royal Leamington Spa CV32 .. 157 C3
  Tipton DY4 .... 51 F5
  Wednesfield WV12 .... 27 A4
Severn Ct Birmingham B23 .. 56 B3
  Sutton Coldfield B73 ...... 46 B5
Severn Dr Brierley Hill DY5 .. 61 B7
  Burntwood WS7 .... 7 D6
  Perton WV6 .... 23 E4
Severn Gr **6** Birmingham
  B19 .... 66 C7
  Kidderminster DY11 ..... 116 B3

Severn Ho **5** Dudley DY3 ..... 50 D3
4 Oldbury B68 ..... 84 B8
Severn Rd Brownhills WS8 ..... 6 C2
Bulkington CV12 ..... 79 A3
Coventry CV3 ..... 113 F1
Halesowen B63 ..... 82 B5
Stourbridge DY8 ..... 80 F3
Walsall WS3 ..... 14 E1
Severn St B1 ..... 164 B1
Severn Stars Ind Est CV3 .. 134 A7
Severn Tower B7 ..... 67 B5
Severn Way B47 ..... 124 E2
Severne Gr B27 ..... 88 C1
Severne Jun & Inf Sch
B27 ..... 106 C8
Severne Rd B27 ..... 106 C8
Sevington CI B91 ..... 127 C8
Sewall Ct CV6 ..... 114 A8
Sewall Highway CV2 ..... 114 B6
Seward CI WS14 ..... 9 D6
Seymour CI Birmingham B29 . 86 A2
Cheslyn Hay WS6 ..... 4 D1
Coventry CV3 ..... 134 C5
Seymour Dr B98 ..... 154 A5
Seymour Gdns B74 ..... 31 E3
Seymour Gr CV34 ..... 161 D6
Seymour Rd
Kidderminster DY11 ..... 116 B8
Nuneaton CV11 ..... 73 D3
Oldbury B69 ..... 64 C7
Stourbridge DY9 ..... 82 A6
Tipton DY4 ..... 41 C1
Seymour St B5 ..... 164 D3
Shackleton Dr WV6 ..... 23 E5
Shackleton Rd WS3 ..... 14 D2
Shadow Brook La B92 ..... 108 E7
Shadowbrook Rd CV6 ..... 113 A5
Shadwell Dr DY3 ..... 50 D3
Shadwell St B4 ..... 164 C4
Shady La B44 ..... 44 E2
Shadymoor Dr DY5 ..... 81 C8
Shaft La CV7 ..... 93 A4
Shaftesbury Ave
Keresley CV7 ..... 95 A7
Stourbridge DY9 ..... 81 C2
Shaftesbury CI B60 ..... 137 B2
Shaftesbury Dr WS12 ..... 2 C7
Shaftesbury Rd
Coventry CV5 ..... 132 F8
Wednesbury WS10 ..... 42 B2
Shaftesbury Sq B71 ..... 53 C5
Shaftesbury St B70 ..... 53 C4
Shaftmoor Ind Est B28 ..... 87 F2
Shaftmoor La B27, B28 ..... 87 F2
Shaftsbury Ave B63 ..... 82 B7
Shaftsbury CI WV14 ..... 40 F7
Shaftsbury Rd B26 ..... 89 C5
Shakespear Gr WS11 ..... 1 D4
Shakespeare Ave
Bedworth CV12 ..... 78 D2
Lichfield WS14 ..... 9 B6
Redditch B98 ..... 154 A2
Warwick CV34 ..... 160 C4
Shakespeare CI
Dudley WV14 ..... 40 D2
Tamworth B79 ..... 21 A6
Shakespeare Cres WS3 ..... 28 F7
Shakespeare Dr
Hinckley LE10 ..... 71 C1
Kidderminster DY10 ..... 117 B6
Nuneaton CV11 ..... 74 A1
Solihull B90 ..... 106 B1
Shakespeare Ho B31 ..... 123 A8
Shakespeare Pl WS3 ..... 28 F7
Shakespeare Rd
Birmingham B23 ..... 56 B3
Burntwood WS7 ..... 6 F8
Dudley DY3 ..... 50 A4
Smethwick B67 ..... 64 E4
Solihull B90 ..... 126 B6
Tipton DY4 ..... 52 A8
Shakespeare St
Birmingham B11 ..... 87 C5
Coventry CV2 ..... 114 B4
Wolverhampton WV1 ..... 163 D2
Shakleton Rd CV5 ..... 113 A2
Shale St WV14 ..... 40 C5
Shalford Rd B92 ..... 88 E4
Shallcross La DY3 ..... 50 D3
Shalnecote Gr B14 ..... 104 C5
Shambles **2** WS10 ..... 41 F2
Shandon CI B32 ..... 84 F3
Shanklin CI WS6 ..... 5 A3
Shanklin Dr CV10 ..... 73 D6
Shanklin Rd CV3 ..... 134 B4
Shannon B77 ..... 35 F8
Shannon Dr WS8 ..... 6 C2
Shannon Rd B38 ..... 123 E7
Shannon Wlk WS8 ..... 6 C2
Shannon's Mill B79 ..... 21 A5
Shanti Niketan WV2 ..... 39 D7
Shapinsay Dr B45 ..... 101 F1
Shard End Cres B34 ..... 69 C6
Shardlow Rd WV11 ..... 26 E8
Shardway The B34 ..... 69 C5
Sharesacre St WV13 ..... 27 B3
Sharington CI **3** DY2 ..... 62 E8
Sharman Rd WV10 ..... 25 E6
Sharmans Cross Jun Sch
B91 ..... 106 E4
Sharmans Cross Rd B91 ..... 106 F4
Sharnford Rd LE10 ..... 76 F6
Sharon CI WV4 ..... 39 E5
Sharon Ct B27 ..... 88 C3

Sharon Way WS12 ..... 2 D3
Sharp CI CV6 ..... 95 C2
Sharp St CV34 ..... 160 E8
Sharpe St B77 ..... 22 A5
Sharpless Rd LE10 ..... 75 F7
Sharpley Ct CV2 ..... 115 A8
Sharps CI B45 ..... 122 A7
Sharrat Field B75 ..... 32 D2
Sharratt Rd CV12 ..... 78 A2
Sharrocks St WV1 ..... 163 D2
Shaw Ave DY10 ..... 117 B6
Shaw Dr B33 ..... 68 E2
Shaw Hall La WV10 ..... 11 C7
Shaw Hill Gr B8 ..... 68 A4
Shaw Hill Inf & Jun Sch B8 .. 67 F4
Shaw Hill Rd B8 ..... 68 A4
Shaw La Lichfield WS13 ..... 9 A8
Stoke Prior B60 ..... 150 C4
Wolverhampton WV6 ..... 24 B3
Shaw Lane Ind Est B60 ..... 150 C2
Shaw Park Bsns Village
WS3 ..... 25 D6
Shaw Rd
Dudley, Hurst Hill WV14 ..... 40 B1
Dudley, Netherton DY2 ..... 62 C7
Tipton DY4 ..... 52 C4
Wolverhampton,
Blakenhall WV2 ..... 39 C6
Wolverhampton,
Dunstall Hill WV10 ..... 25 C6
Shaw St Walsall WS2 ..... 28 D2
West Bromwich B70 ..... 52 E7
Shaw's La WS6 ..... 5 A2
Shaw's Pas B5 ..... 164 D2
Shawbank Rd B98 ..... 154 B3
Shawberry Ave B35 ..... 58 B4
Shawberry Rd B37 ..... 69 F5
Shawbrook Gr **10** B14 ..... 105 A3
Shawbury Cl B98 ..... 154 E3
Shawbury Gr Birmingham
B12 ..... 86 F8
Perton WV6 ..... 23 E5
Shawbury Rd WV10 ..... 25 F5
Shawe Ave CV10 ..... 73 C7
Shawfield B47 ..... 125 A5
Shawhellier Ave DY5 ..... 61 E2
Shawhurst Croft B47 ..... 125 A7
Shawhurst La B47 ..... 125 A6
Shawley Croft B27 ..... 88 E4
Shaws CI B97 ..... 152 F2
Shawsdale Rd B36 ..... 68 F7
Shayler Gr WV2 ..... 39 D7
Sheaf La B26 ..... 89 B4
Sheapecoate Ho **1** B71 ..... 42 F1
Shearwater Dr
Birmingham B45 ..... 121 F6
Kidderminster DY10 ..... 117 B1
Shearwater Wlk B23 ..... 56 B7
Sheaves CV1 ..... 40 B3
Shedden St **4** DY2 ..... 62 D8
Sheddington Rd B23 ..... 56 D7
Sheen Ho CV2 ..... 114 D8
Sheen Rd B44 ..... 44 E4
Sheepclose Dr B37 ..... 70 A3
Sheepcote CI CV32 ..... 157 A1
Sheepcote Grange B61 ..... 136 F5
Sheepcote La B77 ..... 21 F4
Sheepcote St B16 ..... 66 B2
Sheepcroft CI B97 ..... 152 F2
Sheepfold CI B65 ..... 63 A4
Sheepmoor CI B17 ..... 84 F8
Sheepwash La DY4 ..... 52 D5
Sheerwater Dr DY5 ..... 81 D7
Sheffield Rd B73 ..... 57 A7
Sheffield St DY5 ..... 62 A1
Shefford Rd B6 ..... 66 F5
Sheila Ave WV11 ..... 26 E7
Shelah Rd B63 ..... 83 A6
Shelbourne CI B69 ..... 52 D2
Sheldon Ave WS10 ..... 42 A4
Sheldon CI WV14 ..... 40 D4
Sheldon Dr B31 ..... 102 D2
Sheldon Gr Birmingham B26 .. 89 B5
Warwick CV34 ..... 155 F2
Sheldon Hall Ave B33 ..... 69 D3
Sheldon Heath Rd B26 ..... 89 B8
Sheldon Heath Sch B33 ..... 89 C8
Sheldon Rd Redditch B98 ..... 159 A8
West Bromwich B71 ..... 53 E8
Wolverhampton WV10 ..... 11 A1
Sheldon Wlk B33 ..... 69 C1
Sheldonfield Rd B26 ..... 89 D5
Shelduck CI DY10 ..... 117 B3
Shelfield CI CV5 ..... 112 B3
Shelfield Com Sch WS4 ..... 15 C2
Shelfield Rd B14 ..... 104 C3
Shell Corner Trad Est B62 .. 83 D8
Shelley Ave
Kidderminster DY10 ..... 116 E7
Tipton DY4 ..... 52 B8
Warwick CV34 ..... 160 C4
Shelley CI Bedworth CV12 ..... 78 D1
Catshill B61 ..... 137 A8
Dudley DY3 ..... 50 A5
Redditch B97 ..... 158 C8
Stourbridge DY8 ..... 81 A8
Shelley Dr Birmingham B23 .. 56 B3
Sutton Coldfield B74 ..... 31 F6
Shelley Gdns LE10 ..... 71 E3
Shelley Ho Halesowen B63 .. 82 B5
1 Oldbury B68 ..... 64 C4
Shelley Rd **3** Burntwood WS7 7 A8
Cannock WS11 ..... 1 E5
Coventry CV2 ..... 114 C3
Tamworth B79 ..... 21 A7
Willenhall WV12 ..... 27 E7
Wolverhampton WV10 ..... 11 D2
Shellon CI CV3 ..... 134 F8

Shelly CI B37 ..... 69 F2
Shelly Cres B90 ..... 127 B6
Shelly Croft B33 ..... 69 A3
Shelly La B90 ..... 127 B6
Shelly Tower B31 ..... 103 C3
Shelsley Ave B69 ..... 63 D5
Shelsley Dr B13 ..... 87 B2
Shelsley Way B31 ..... 107 B1
Shelton CI WS10 ..... 42 C5
Shelton La B63 ..... 82 E5
Shelton Sq CV1 ..... 165 B2
Shelton St B77 ..... 35 F7
Sheltwood CI B97 ..... 153 A2
Sheltwood La B60 ..... 152 A3
Shelwick Gr B93 ..... 127 F4
Shenley Ave DY1 ..... 51 C6
Shenley Court Sch B31 ..... 102 F7
Shenley Fields Dr B31 ..... 102 F8
Shenley Fields Rd B29 ..... 103 B8
Shenley Gdns B29 ..... 103 A7
Shenley Gn B29 ..... 102 F6
Shenley Hill B31 ..... 102 F6
Shenley La B29 ..... 102 F7
Shenstone Ave
Halesowen B62 ..... 83 E5
Stourbridge DY8 ..... 80 D3
Shenstone CI
Bromsgrove B60 ..... 137 B3
Sutton Coldfield B74 ..... 31 E6
Shenstone Ct
Bromsgrove B60 ..... 137 B3
Solihull B90 ..... 105 D2
Shenstone Dr Aldridge WS9 .. 30 A8
Balsall Common CV7 ..... 130 A6
Shenstone Flats B63 ..... 83 F5
Shenstone Ho WS13 ..... 3 E1
Shenstone Lodge Specl
Sch WS14 ..... 18 A3
Shenstone Rd
Birmingham, Edgbaston B16 .. 65 C3
Birmingham, Great Barr B43 .. 54 E3
Birmingham,
Higher's Heath B14 ..... 105 A1
Shenstone Sta WS14 ..... 17 F6
Shenstone Trad Est B62 ..... 83 C4
Shenstone Valley Rd B62 .. 83 F6
Shenton Wlk B37 ..... 69 F5
Shepheard Rd B26 ..... 89 D5
Shepherd CI Coventry CV4 .. 111 F3
Lichfield WS13 ..... 3 C3
Shepherd Dr WV12 ..... 27 C5
Shepherds Brook Rd DY9 .. 81 D5
Shepherds Fold B65 ..... 63 B2
Shepherds Gdns **8** B15 ..... 66 B1
Shepherds Green Rd B24 .. 56 F1
Shepherds Pool Rd B75 ..... 32 E2
Shepherds Standing B34 .. 69 B6
Shepherds Way B23 ..... 56 C8
Shepherds Wlk
Bromsgrove B60 ..... 150 E7
Wolverhampton WV8 ..... 10 F2
Shepley Rd Barnt Green
B45 ..... 138 A7
Birmingham B45 ..... 122 B6
Shepperton Bsns Pk CV11 .. 73 C1
Shepperton Ct CV11 ..... 73 C1
Shepperton St CV11 ..... 73 C2
Sheppey Dr B36 ..... 70 B5
Shepwell Gdns WV10 ..... 12 C7
Shepwell Gn WV13 ..... 27 C1
Sherard Croft B36 ..... 70 B6
Sheraton CI Aldridge WS9 .. 30 B6
Cannock WS12 ..... 2 A1
Sheraton Dr DY10 ..... 117 B6
Sheraton Grange DY8 ..... 80 F2
Sherborne Ave CV11 ..... 73 F8
Sherborne CI B98 ..... 154 D2
Sherborne Cres CV5 ..... 112 E4
Sherborne Ct CV1 ..... 165 B1
Sherborne Dr B27 ..... 88 C4
Sherbourne Fields Sch
CV6 ..... 112 D5
Sherbourne Rd
Birmingham,
Acock's Green B27 ..... 88 C4
Birmingham,
Balsall Heath B12 ..... 86 F7
Blackheath B64 ..... 83 B8
Stourbridge DY8 ..... 81 A4
Sherbourne St CV1 ..... 113 A2
Sherbrook Rd WS11 ..... 1 C1
Sherbrooke Ave B77 ..... 35 F6
Sherdmore Croft B90 ..... 126 F6
Sheridan CI **2** WS2 ..... 42 B7
Sheridan Gdns DY3 ..... 49 F5
Sheridan St Walsall WS2 ..... 42 B7
West Bromwich B71 ..... 53 D4
Sheridan Wlk B35 ..... 58 A3
Sheriff Ave CV4 ..... 132 B7
Sheriff Dr DY5 ..... 61 F2
Sheriffs CI WS14 ..... 9 E6
Sheriffs Orch CV1 ..... 165 B2
Sherifoot La B75 ..... 32 B4
Sheringham B15 ..... 85 E8
Sheringham CI CV11 ..... 73 F2
Sheringham Rd B30 ..... 104 B3
Sherington Ave CV5 ..... 112 C4
Sherington Dr WV4 ..... 39 D5

Sherlock CI WV12 ..... 27 D5
Sherlock Rd CV5 ..... 112 D3
Sherlock St B5 ..... 86 E8
Sherrans Dell WV4 ..... 39 D3
Sherratt CI B76 ..... 57 F8
Sherringham Dr WV11 ..... 13 C1
Sherron Gdns B12 ..... 86 F5
Sherston Covert **11** B30 ..... 104 C2
Shervale CV4 ..... 39 A6
Sherwin Ave WV14 ..... 40 A2
Sherwood Ave DY4 ..... 51 F4
Sherwood CI
Birmingham B28 ..... 105 F5
Solihull B92 ..... 106 F7
Wood End CV9 ..... 36 C1
Sherwood Dr Brierley Hill
DY5 ..... 61 F2
Cannock WS11 ..... 2 A3
3 Kidderminster DY10 ..... 116 F6
Nuneaton CV10 ..... 72 D4
8 Stourbridge DY8 ..... 80 F5
Tipton DY4 ..... 51 E8
Walsall WS3 ..... 28 D1
Wednesbury WS10 ..... 41 E3
Willenhall WV12 ..... 27 C5
Wolverhampton WV1 ..... 163 C3
Sherwood Jones CI CV6 ..... 113 B6
Sherwood Mews B28 ..... 105 E6
Sherwood Rd
Birmingham B28 ..... 105 E7
Bromsgrove B60 ..... 151 A6
Smethwick B67 ..... 65 A1
Stourbridge DY8 ..... 80 E7
Sherwood St WV1 ..... 163 B4
Sherwood Wlk
Royal Leamington Spa
CV32 ..... 157 C4
Walsall WS9 ..... 29 E7
Shetland CI Birmingham B16 .. 65 F2
Coventry CV5 ..... 112 A4
Wolverhampton W6 ..... 25 B5
Shetland Dr Nuneaton CV10 .. 73 A1
Smethwick B66 ..... 64 D8
Shetland Wlk B36 ..... 70 B6
Shevlock Way CV6 ..... 114 A6
Shidas La B69 ..... 63 E7
Shifnal Wlk B31 ..... 122 F8
Shillcock Gr B19 ..... 66 E5
Shillingstone CI CV2 ..... 115 A4
Shilton & Ansty Fst Sch
CV7 ..... 97 E5
Shilton CI B90 ..... 126 F6
Shilton Gr B29 ..... 102 F8
Shilton Ind Est CV7 ..... 97 E7
Shilton La Barnacle CV2, CV7 . 97 B4
Bulkington CV12 ..... 79 D1
Coventry CV2 ..... 96 F3
Shilton CV7, CV12 ..... 97 D8
Shinwell Cres B69 ..... 52 D2
Shipbourne CV32 ..... 84 F5
Shipley Fields B24 ..... 57 A3
Shipley Gr B29 ..... 103 A8
Shipston Rd
Birmingham B31 ..... 103 B1
Coventry CV2 ..... 114 C6
Shipton CI DY1 ..... 50 F3
Shipton Rd B72 ..... 46 C3
Shipway Rd B25 ..... 88 A7
Shire Brook CI B6 ..... 66 E8
Shire Brook Ct **2** B19 ..... 66 D7
Shire CI Birmingham B16 ..... 65 F2
Coventry CV6 ..... 96 B1
Oldbury B68 ..... 64 B2
Shire Oak Com Sch WS9 .. 16 A5
Shire Ridge WS9 ..... 16 B4
Shirebrook CI CV2 ..... 96 D2
Shirehall Pl WS11 ..... 2 B2
Shirehampton CI B97 ..... 152 F2
Shireland Brook Gdns
1 B18 ..... 65 D4
Shireland CI B20 ..... 54 F3
Shireland Hall Prim Sch
B66 ..... 65 C3
Shireland High Sch
Smethwick B66 ..... 64 F3
Smethwick B66 ..... 65 B3
Shireland Rd B66 ..... 65 B3
Shirelea CI **4** WS7 ..... 7 B8
Shires Gate Ret Pk CV31 .. 161 E6
Shires Ret Pk CV34 ..... 161 D6
Shirestone Jun & Inf Sch
B33 ..... 69 D2
Shirestone Rd B33 ..... 69 E2
Shireview Gdns WS3 ..... 15 B4
Shireview Rd WS3 ..... 15 B4
Shirlett CI CV2 ..... 96 B4
Shirley Dr B72 ..... 46 C4
Shirley Heath Jun Sch
B90 ..... 106 C1
Shirley La CV7 ..... 111 A5
Shirley Park Rd B90 ..... 106 B2
Shirley Rd
Birmingham,
Hall Green B27, B28 ..... 106 A7
Birmingham,
King's Norton B30 ..... 104 A5
Coventry CV2 ..... 115 A7
Dudley DY2 ..... 62 E8
Oldbury B68 ..... 64 C6
Shirley Sta B90 ..... 105 F1
Shirley Trad Est B90 ..... 106 E1
Shirley Wlk B79 ..... 20 F7
Shirleydale **3** B90 ..... 126 C8
Shirral Gr B37 ..... 69 F5
Shirrall Dr B78 ..... 33 E4
Shoal Hill CI WS11 ..... 1 B2
Sholing CI WV8 ..... 10 F1
Shooters CI B5 ..... 86 D6
Shooters Hill B72 ..... 46 D2
Shop La Nurton WV6 ..... 23 A1
Trescott WV6 ..... 23 A1
Shopping Ctr The CV31 .. 162 B5
Shopping Prec The CV34 .. 156 A1
Shops The DY6 ..... 60 D4
Shopton Rd B34 ..... 69 A7
Shoreham CI WV13 ..... 26 D1

Shorncliffe Rd CV6 ..... 112 E6
Short Acre St WS2 ..... 28 D3
Short Heath Jun & Inf Sch
B23 ..... 56 D6
Short Heath Jun Sch WV12 .. 27 D5
Short Heath Rd B23 ..... 56 E6
Short La WS6 ..... 4 E3
Short Rd Smethwick B67 ..... 64 D3
Wolverhampton WV10 ..... 11 E1
Short St Bilston WV14 ..... 40 D6
Blackheath B65 ..... 63 C2
Brownhills WS8 ..... 15 F7
Cannock WS11 ..... 1 F3
Coventry CV1 ..... 165 C2
Darlaston WS10 ..... 41 F7
Dudley DY1 ..... 51 A2
Halesowen B63 ..... 82 F5
3 Kidderminster DY10 ..... 116 F6
Nuneaton CV10 ..... 72 D4
8 Stourbridge DY8 ..... 80 F5
Tipton DY4 ..... 51 E8
Walsall WS3 ..... 28 D1
Wednesbury WS10 ..... 41 E3
Willenhall WV12 ..... 27 C5
Wolverhampton WV1 ..... 163 C3
Shortbutts La WS14 ..... 9 B5
Shorters Ave B14 ..... 105 A4
Shortland CI B93 ..... 128 A7
Shortlands CV7 ..... 95 C6
Shortlands CI B30 ..... 104 A2
Shortlands La WS3 ..... 14 F3
Shortley Rd CV3 ..... 133 F8
Shorwell Pl DY5 ..... 61 B1
Shottery CI Coventry CV5 .. 112 B3
Sutton Coldfield B76 ..... 46 F1
Shottery Gr B76 ..... 46 F1
Shottery Rd B90 ..... 106 B1
Shotteswell Rd B90 ..... 126 B8
Showell Cir WV10 ..... 25 E7
Showell Green La B11 ..... 87 C3
Showell Ho **10** B69 ..... 64 A7
Showell La Meriden CV7 ..... 93 A1
Wombourne WV4 ..... 38 B3
Showell Rd WV10 ..... 25 D6
Showells Gdns B7 ..... 67 C2
Shrawley Ave DY11 ..... 116 B3
Shrawley CI
Birmingham B45 ..... 121 F7
Halesowen B63 ..... 83 A2
Shrawley Ho **6** B38 ..... 103 D2
Shrawley Rd B31 ..... 103 C2
Shrewley Cres B33 ..... 69 E1
Shrewsbury CI WS3 ..... 13 F1
Shrewsbury Rd DY11 ..... 116 A6
Shrewton Ave B14 ..... 104 D2
Shrub La B24 ..... 57 B4
Shrubberies The CV4 ..... 132 E4
Shrubbery Ave DY4 ..... 51 D5
Shrubbery CI B76 ..... 57 D6
Shrubbery Ct DY10 ..... 116 F7
Shrubbery Rd B61 ..... 136 E1
Shrubbery Sch The B76 ..... 57 F7
Shrubbery St DY10 ..... 116 F7
Shrubbery The B16 ..... 65 F3
Shrubland St CV31 ..... 162 A6
Shrubland Street Com
Prim Sch CV31 ..... 162 A6
Shrublands Ave B68 ..... 84 B7
Shuckburgh Gr **4** CV32 .. 157 A2
Shugborough Dr DY1 ..... 50 E2
Shugborough Way WS11 .. 2 C1
Shulman's Wlk CV2 ..... 114 D7
Shultern La CV4 ..... 132 D6
Shuna Croft CV2 ..... 115 B7
Shustoke La WS5 ..... 43 B4
Shustoke Rd Birmingham
B34 ..... 69 C6
Solihull B91 ..... 107 D5
Shut Mill La B62 ..... 100 D2
Shutlock La B13 ..... 86 D1
Shutt La B94 ..... 126 B1
Shuttington Rd B79 ..... 22 B6
Shuttle St CV6 ..... 114 B8
Shyltons Croft B16 ..... 66 A2
Sibdon Gr B31 ..... 123 A8
Sibree Rd CV3 ..... 134 B4
Sibton CI CV2 ..... 96 C1
Sidaway CI B65 ..... 63 C6
Sidaway St B64 ..... 62 E1
Sidbury Gr B93 ..... 127 E3
Sidcup CI WV14 ..... 40 B3
Sidcup Rd B44 ..... 45 A1
Siddeley Ave Coventry CV3 .. 114 A1
Kenilworth CV8 ..... 147 E3
Siddons Factory Est B70 .. 52 F8
Siddons Rd WV14 ..... 40 D2
Sidemoor Fst Sch B61 ..... 136 E3
Sidenhill CI B90 ..... 126 B8
Sidford Gdns B24 ..... 57 C3
Sidford Gr B23 ..... 56 E7
Sidings The Birmingham B20 . 66 C8
Cannock WS12 ..... 2 C7
Hagley DY9 ..... 99 A6
Sidlaw CI Halesowen B63 .. 82 D2
Wolverhampton WV10 ..... 25 C6
Sidmouth CI Coventry CV2 .. 114 C7
Nuneaton CV11 ..... 73 F5
Sidney St WV2 ..... 163 B1
Sidney Stringer Com
Tech Coll CV1 ..... 165 C3
Sidon Hill Way WS11 ..... 2 C2
Sidwick Cres WV2 ..... 40 B5
Sigmund CI WV1 ..... 26 B3
Signal Gr WS3 ..... 14 A1
Signal Hayes Rd B76 ..... 47 A2
Signal Wlk B77 ..... 22 A2
Silesbourne CI B36 ..... 69 C8
Silhill Hall Rd B91 ..... 107 A5

Silica Rd B77 ...... 22 B2
Silksby St CV3 ...... 133 D8
Sillins Ave B98 ...... 154 A3
Silva Ave DY6 ...... 60 F4
Silver Birch Ave CV12 ...... 77 E2
Silver Birch Coppice B74 ...... 31 D5
Silver Birch Dr
　Hollywood B47 ...... 125 B6
　Kidderminster DY10 ...... 117 C5
Silver Birch Gr CV31 ...... 161 F5
Silver Birch Rd Aldridge
　B74 ...... 30 F1
　Birmingham, Erdington B24 ...... 57 B6
　Birmingham, Kingshurst B37 ...... 69 F6
　Huntington WS12 ...... 1 D8
　Norton Canes WS11 ...... 6 B5
　Wolverhampton WV2 ...... 39 E7
Silver Birches Bsns Pk
　B60 ...... 150 F6
Silver Court Gdns WS8 ...... 15 F7
Silver Ct WS8 ...... 15 F7
Silver End Ind Est DY5 ...... 61 B1
Silver Fir Cl WS12 ...... 2 A8
Silver Innage B63 ...... 82 C7
Silver Link Rd B77 ...... 22 A1
Silver St Birmingham B14 ...... 104 E8
　Brierley Hill DY5 ...... 61 C1
　Brownhills WS8 ...... 15 F7
　Coventry CV1 ...... 165 B3
　Hollywood B38 ...... 124 E5
　Kidderminster DY10 ...... 116 E7
　Redditch B98 ...... 153 E4
　Tamworth B79 ...... 21 B5
Silver Trees Dr CV12 ...... 79 B4
Silver Wlk CV10 ...... 72 F3
Silver's Cl WS3 ...... 14 F4
Silverbirch Cl CV10 ...... 72 A7
Silverbirch Rd B24 ...... 57 B6
Silverbirch Rd B91 ...... 107 E3
Silvercroft Ave B21 ...... 54 D3
Silverdale B61 ...... 136 F4
Silverdale Cl CV2 ...... 96 B4
Silverdale Dr WV10 ...... 25 E5
Silverdale Gdns DY8 ...... 60 C3
Silverdale Rd B24 ...... 57 D5
Silverfield Cl B14 ...... 104 E8
Silverlands Ave B68 ...... 64 B3
Silverlands Cl B28 ...... 87 F1
Silvermead Rd B73 ...... 46 A1
Silvermere Rd B26 ...... 89 D6
Silverstone Ave DY11 ...... 116 D8
Silverstone Cl WS2 ...... 27 E3
Silverstone Dr Coventry CV6 ...... 95 C5
　Sutton Coldfield B74 ...... 44 F6
Silverthorne Ave DY4 ...... 51 D5
Silverthorne La B64 ...... 82 B8
Silverton Cres B13 ...... 87 D1
Silverton Hts B67 ...... 64 F6
Silverton Rd Coventry CV6 ...... 113 F7
　Smethwick B67 ...... 64 E6
Silverton Way WV11 ...... 26 F5
Silvester Ct B73 ...... 53 E3
Silvester Rd WV14 ...... 40 F7
Silvington Cl B29 ...... 103 C7
Simcox Gdns B32 ...... 84 D2
Simcox Rd WS10 ...... 41 F5
Simcox St WS12 ...... 2 D4
Simeon's Wlk DY5 ...... 81 F7
Simmonds Cl WS3 ...... 14 D3
Simmonds Pl WS10 ...... 41 F7
Simmonds Rd WS3 ...... 14 D3
Simmonds Way WS8 ...... 16 A6
Simmons Cl B78 ...... 34 B1
Simmons Dr B32 ...... 84 D4
Simmons Leasow B32 ...... 84 E2
Simmons Rd WV11 ...... 13 B1
Simms La Dudley DY2 ...... 62 C5
　Hollywood B47 ...... 125 A5
Simon Cl Nuneaton CV11 ...... 73 D2
　West Bromwich B71 ...... 42 E1
Simon Ct CV7 ...... 96 A8
Simon Rd B47 ...... 125 A7
Simon Stone St CV6 ...... 113 F8
Simons Rd B7 ...... 67 A4
Simpkins Cl WS9 ...... 16 A3
Simpson Gr WV10 ...... 25 E6
Simpson Rd Lichfield WS13 ...... 3 B2
　Sutton Coldfield B72 ...... 46 C1
　Walsall WS2 ...... 28 B5
　Wolverhampton WV10 ...... 25 E6
Simpson St B69 ...... 64 A8
Sinclair Cl B13 ...... 86 E4
Singer Cl CV6 ...... 114 B8
Singer Croft B36 ...... 58 F1
Singh Cl B21 ...... 54 E1
Sion Cl DY5 ...... 61 D3
Sir Alfreds Way B76 ...... 46 E3
Sir George's Mall
　6 DY10 ...... 116 E6
Sir Georges Ct 10 DY10 ...... 116 E6
Sir Harrys Rd B5 ...... 86 C6
Sir Henry Parkes Prim
　Sch CV4 ...... 132 C8
Sir Henry Parkes Rd
　CV5 ...... 132 D7
Sir Hilton's Rd B31 ...... 123 C7
Sir John's Rd B29 ...... 86 C3
Sir Richards Dr B17 ...... 84 F4
Sir Robert Peel Hospl B78 ...... 20 D1
Sir Theodore Pritchett
　Inf & Jun Sch B14 ...... 104 D2
Sir Thomas White's Rd
　CV5 ...... 112 F2
Sir Walter's Mall 8 DY10 ...... 116 E6
Sir Wilfred Martineau
　Upper & Lower Sch B33 ...... 69 D3
Sir William Lyons Rd
　CV4 ...... 132 C6

Sir Winston Churchill Pl
　CV3 ...... 135 C7
Sisefield Rd B38 ...... 104 A1
Siskin Cl WS7 ...... 7 D5
Siskin Dr Birmingham B12 ...... 86 E6
　Coventry CV3 ...... 134 C4
Siskin Parkway E CV3 ...... 134 C1
Siskin Parkway W CV3 ...... 134 C2
Siskin Rd DY9 ...... 81 C3
Siskin Way DY10 ...... 117 B1
Sisley Way LE10 ...... 71 A3
Sister Dora Bldgs 2 WS1 ...... 28 E1
Sister Dora Gdns 1 WS1 ...... 42 E8
Siviter St B63 ...... 83 B4
Siviter's Cl B65 ...... 63 B3
Siviter's La B65 ...... 63 B3
Six Acres B32 ...... 84 C4
Six Ways B23 ...... 56 F4
Six Ways Ho B23 ...... 56 F4
Sixth Ave B5 ...... 55 F4
Skelcher Rd B90 ...... 106 A3
Skelwith Rise CV11 ...... 74 A6
Skemp Cl WV14 ...... 40 D4
Sketchley Cl B66 ...... 65 A6
Sketchley Hall Gdns LE10 ...... 75 C5
Sketchley Hill Cty Prim
　Sch LE10 ...... 75 E5
Sketchley La LE10 ...... 75 C5
Sketchley La Ind Est LE10 ...... 75 D5
Sketchley Manor La LE10 ...... 75 D5
Sketchley Mdws LE10 ...... 75 C5
Sketchley Meadows
　Bsns Pk LE10 ...... 75 C4
Sketchley Old Village LE10 ...... 75 C5
Sketchley Rd LE10 ...... 75 E5
Skidmore Ave Tamworth
　B77 ...... 35 C5
　Wolverhampton WV3 ...... 38 F8
Skidmore Dr B70 ...... 53 A3
Skidmore Rd WV14 ...... 40 D2
Skilts Ave B98 ...... 153 F1
Skinner La B5 ...... 66 E1
Skinner St WV1 ...... 163 B3
Skip La WS5 ...... 43 E7
Skipness B77 ...... 21 F5
Skipton Gdns CV2 ...... 114 B6
Skipton Gn WV6 ...... 25 A5
Skipton Lodge CV2 ...... 114 B6
Skipton Pl WS11 ...... 4 B7
Skipton Rd B16 ...... 66 A1
Skipworth Rd CV3 ...... 115 A1
Skomer Cl B45 ...... 101 A1
Sky Blue Way CV1 ...... 113 E3
Skye Cl Birmingham B36 ...... 70 B6
　Nuneaton CV10 ...... 72 F2
Skye Wlk 4 B64 ...... 62 E1
Skylark Cl Brierley Hill DY5 ...... 56 F7
　Huntington WS12 ...... 1 C7
Skylark Way DY10 ...... 117 A2
Slack La B20 ...... 54 E2
Slacky La WS3 ...... 14 F1
Slade Ave WS7 ...... 7 A8
Slade Cl Nuneaton CV11 ...... 79 C8
　West Bromwich B71 ...... 42 F2
Slade Gdns WV8 ...... 10 A4
Slade Gr B93 ...... 127 F6
Slade Hill WV6 ...... 24 F3
Slade Jun & Inf Sch B23 ...... 56 D2
Slade La Birmingham B28 ...... 105 E3
　Sutton Coldfield B75 ...... 33 A3
　Tamworth B77 ...... 35 C4
Slade Lanker B34 ...... 69 A5
Slade Mdw CV31 ...... 162 E5
Slade Rd Birmingham B23 ...... 56 D3
　Halesowen B63 ...... 82 C6
　Sutton Coldfield B75 ...... 32 E3
　Wolverhampton WV10 ...... 11 C3
Sladefield Inf Sch B8 ...... 68 A5
Sladefield Rd B8 ...... 68 A5
Sladen CE Mid Sch DY10 ...... 116 F7
Sladepool Farm Rd B14 ...... 105 A2
Slaithwaite Rd B71 ...... 53 E4
Slaney Rd WS2 ...... 42 B6
Slatch House Rd B67 ...... 64 E2
Slateley Cres B90 ...... 126 F6
Slater Rd B93 ...... 127 F4
Slater St Bilston WV14 ...... 40 E3
　Darlaston WS10 ...... 41 D6
　Tipton, Dudley Port DY4 ...... 52 A4
　Tipton, Great Bridge DY4 ...... 52 D5
　Willenhall WV13 ...... 27 C3
Slaters La WS2 ...... 42 B7
Slaters Pl WS2 ...... 42 C7
Sleaford Gr B28 ...... 106 A7
Sleaford Rd B28 ...... 106 B7
Sleath's Yd CV12 ...... 78 B3
Sledmore Cl CV2 ...... 96 B3
Sledmore Prim Sch DY2 ...... 62 D6
Sledmore Rd DY2 ...... 62 E7
Sleets Yd CV12 ...... 78 A2
Slideslow Ave B60 ...... 137 B2
Slieve The B20 ...... 55 A3
Slim Ave WV14 ...... 40 E3
Slim Rd WS2 ...... 27 E2
Slimbridge Cl Redditch
　B97 ...... 158 E5
　2 Solihull B90 ...... 127 A6
Slims Gate B33 ...... 83 A4
Sling The Dudley DY2 ...... 62 C6
　Kidderminster DY10 ...... 116 E6
Slingfield Rd B31 ...... 103 C1
Slingsby B77 ...... 35 C7
Slingsby Cl CV11 ...... 73 F2
Slitting Mill Cl B21 ...... 65 C8
Sloane Ho 7 B1 ...... 66 C3
Sloane St B1 ...... 66 C3
Slough The B97 ...... 159 B4
Small Cl B67 ...... 64 D5

Small Heath Bridge B11 ...... 87 B8
Small Heath Bsns Pk B10 ...... 87 F7
Small Heath Highway B11 ...... 87 D6
Small Heath Lower Sch B10 ...... 87 D7
Small Heath Sta B10 ...... 87 D7
Small Heath Trad Est B11 ...... 87 D6
Small Heath Upper Sch
　B10 ...... 87 D8
Small La B94 ...... 141 E6
Small St Walsall WS1 ...... 42 E8
　West Bromwich B71 ...... 53 B5
Smallbrook La WV5 ...... 49 B7
Smallbrook Queensway
　B5 ...... 164 C1
Smalldale Rd B42 ...... 55 D7
Smalley Cl WS11 ...... 2 A5
Smalley Pl CV8 ...... 147 F4
Smallshire Way DY8 ...... 80 D8
Smallwood Almshouses
　B98 ...... 153 E3
Smallwood Arch 5 B98 ...... 153 E4
Smallwood Cl B76 ...... 46 E3
Smallwood Rd WV8 ...... 10 E2
Smallwood St B98 ...... 153 E3
Smarts Ave WS14 ...... 32 A4
Smarts Rd CV12 ...... 77 F1
Smeaton Cl B18 ...... 65 E4
Smedley Crooke Pl B48 ...... 123 C2
Smeed Gr B24 ...... 57 B3
Smercote Cl CV12 ...... 77 D1
Smestow Ho B68 ...... 64 B1
Smestow Sec Sch WV3 ...... 24 B1
Smestow St WV10 ...... 25 D4
Smethwick Galton Bridge
　Sta B66 ...... 64 E7
Smethwick Ho B68 ...... 64 C2
Smethwick Sta B66 ...... 65 A6
Smethwick West Sta B66 ...... 64 E7
Smillie Pl WS11 ...... 1 F3
Smirrells Rd B28 ...... 105 E5
Smith Ave WS10 ...... 41 D4
Smith Cl WV14 ...... 40 A1
Smith Ho WS3 ...... 14 C3
Smith Pl DY4 ...... 52 B4
Smith Rd Walsall WS2 ...... 42 C6
　Wednesbury WS10 ...... 41 F1
Smith St Bedworth CV12 ...... 77 E1
　Bilston WV14 ...... 40 D5
　Birmingham B19 ...... 66 C5
　Coventry CV6 ...... 113 F5
　Dudley DY2 ...... 62 D7
　3 Royal Leamington Spa
　CV31 ...... 161 F7
　Warwick CV34 ...... 160 F7
　Wood End CV9 ...... 36 C1
Smith's Cl WS7 ...... 6 D6
Smithfield Pas B5 ...... 164 C1
Smithfield Rd WS3 ...... 14 D1
Smithfield Rise WS13 ...... 9 C8
Smithford Way CV1 ...... 165 B3
Smithmoor Cres B71 ...... 53 F8
Smiths Cl B32 ...... 84 B1
Smiths La B93 ...... 127 E7
Smiths Way B46 ...... 59 A3
Smiths Wood Sch B36 ...... 70 A6
Smithy Dr 7 WS3 ...... 15 A4
Smithy La Aston Flamville
　LE9 ...... 76 C8
　Dudley DY5 ...... 50 B1
　Lichfield WS13 ...... 3 A1
　Tamworth B77 ...... 35 F7
Smithy The B26 ...... 89 C6
Smorrall La CV12 ...... 77 C2
Smout Cres WV14 ...... 39 F2
Smythe Gr CV34 ...... 155 E1
Snake La B48 ...... 139 A6
Snapdragon Dr WS5 ...... 43 A3
Snape Rd Coventry CV2 ...... 114 F5
　Wolverhampton WV11 ...... 13 B1
Sneyd Com Sch WS3 ...... 13 E2
Sneyd Hall Cl WS3 ...... 28 A8
Sneyd Hall Rd WS3 ...... 14 A1
Sneyd Ho WS3 ...... 13 F1
Sneyd La WV11 ...... 13 C1
Snipe Cl WV10 ...... 12 B7
Snow Hill WV2 ...... 163 C2
Snow Hill Queensway B4 ...... 164 C3
Snow Hill Sta B3 ...... 164 B3
Snowberry Dr DY5 ...... 50 C1
Snowberry Gdns 7 B27 ...... 88 C5
Snowdon Cl CV10 ...... 72 B3
Snowdon Gr B63 ...... 82 D1
Snowdon Rd Cannock WS11 ...... 1 E6
　1 Stourbridge DY8 ...... 81 B6
Snowdon Rise DY3 ...... 50 D6
Snowdon Way
　Willenhall WV12 ...... 13 B1
　Wolverhampton WV10 ...... 25 B6
Snowdrop Cl WS8 ...... 15 D6
Snowford Cl B90 ...... 105 F1
Snows Drive Hill B90 ...... 126 D5
Snowshill Cl Nuneaton CV11 ...... 78 F8
　Redditch B98 ...... 154 B6
Snowshill Gdns DY1 ...... 50 F4
Soar Way LE10 ...... 75 A8
Soberton Cl WV11 ...... 26 F7
Soden Cl CV3 ...... 134 D6
Soden's Ave CV8 ...... 135 A1
Soho Ave B18 ...... 66 A7
Soho, Benson Road B18 ...... 65 F6
Soho Cl B66 ...... 65 C6
Soho Hill B19 ...... 65 C6
Soho Ho B66 ...... 65 C6
Soho House Mus B18 ...... 66 A7
Soho Rd B21 ...... 65 F8
Soho St B66 ...... 65 C6
Soho Way B66 ...... 65 B6

Solari Cl DY4 ...... 52 C8
Solent Cl WV9 ...... 10 F2
Solent Ct B73 ...... 46 B5
Solent Dr CV2 ...... 96 F1
Solihull By-Pass B91 ...... 107 E4
Solihull Coll B91 ...... 107 A3
Solihull Coll Chelmsley
　Campus B37 ...... 70 C4
Solihull Coll Sharmans
　Cross Campus B90 ...... 106 D3
Solihull Hospl B91 ...... 107 C4
Solihull La B28 ...... 106 A6
Solihull Parkway B37 ...... 90 E8
Solihull Parkway Hospl
　B91 ...... 107 E5
Solihull Rd Birmingham
　B11 ...... 87 D3
　Hampton in A B92 ...... 108 E6
　Solihull B90 ...... 106 D3
Solihull Sch B91 ...... 107 D4
Solihull Sixth Form Coll
　B91 ...... 107 D2
Solihull Sta B91 ...... 107 A4
Solly Gr DY4 ...... 52 D7
Solway Cl
　Royal Leamington Spa
　CV31 ...... 162 C6
　Tamworth B79 ...... 21 A7
　Wednesbury WS10 ...... 42 C4
Somerby Dr B91 ...... 127 A8
Somercotes Rd B42 ...... 55 F5
Somerdale Rd B31 ...... 103 C4
Somerfield Cl WS4 ...... 15 C1
Somerfield Rd WS3 ...... 28 C7
Somerford Cl WS6 ...... 4 E1
Somerford Gdns WV10 ...... 11 E2
Somerford Pl WV13 ...... 26 F1
Somerford Rd B29 ...... 102 F8
Somerford Way WV14 ...... 51 B8
Somerland Rd B26 ...... 69 A1
Somerleyton Ave DY10 ...... 117 A5
Somerleyton Ct 3 DY10 ...... 117 A5
Somerly Cl CV3 ...... 134 F8
Somers Pl 8 CV32 ...... 161 E8
Somers Rd Halesowen B62 ...... 83 C5
　Keresley CV7 ...... 95 A6
　Meriden CV7 ...... 91 F1
　Walsall WS2 ...... 42 A7
Somerset Cl B78 ...... 21 A1
Somerset Cres WS10 ...... 42 D4
Somerset Dr
　Birmingham B31 ...... 122 F7
　Nuneaton CV10 ...... 72 E4
　Stourbridge DY8 ...... 80 D7
Somerset Ho B33 ...... 69 A2
Somerset Pl WS11 ...... 1 F3
Somerset Rd
　Birmingham, Edgbaston B15 ...... 85 F5
　Birmingham, Erdington B23 ...... 56 F6
　Birmingham,
　Handsworth B20 ...... 54 F2
　Coventry CV1 ...... 113 C5
　Walsall WS4 ...... 29 A4
　West Bromwich B71 ...... 53 D6
　Willenhall WV13 ...... 27 D2
Somerton Dr
　Birmingham, Erdington B23 ...... 57 A6
　Birmingham,
　Marston Green B37 ...... 90 B7
Somerville Ct 2 B73 ...... 46 A2
Somerville Ho B37 ...... 70 D3
Somerville Jun & Inf Sch
　B10 ...... 87 D8
Somerville Rd
　Birmingham B10 ...... 87 E8
　Sutton Coldfield B73 ...... 46 A3
Somery Rd Birmingham B29 ...... 85 A2
　Dudley DY1 ...... 51 C3
Sommerfield Rd B32 ...... 84 D3
Sommerville Dr B73 ...... 46 A4
Sommerville Rd CV2 ...... 114 C4
Sonning Dr WV9 ...... 10 F1
Sopwith Croft B35 ...... 58 A2
Sorbus B77 ...... 22 B4
Sorrel B77 ...... 22 B5
Sorrel Cl Coventry CV4 ...... 131 E8
　Featherstone WV10 ...... 12 B7
　Tipton B69 ...... 52 B2
Sorrel Dr Birmingham B27 ...... 88 B2
　Walsall WS5 ...... 43 A3
Sorrel Gr B24 ...... 57 D3
Sorrel Ho B24 ...... 57 D3
Sorrel Rd CV10 ...... 78 D8
Sorrel Wlk DY5 ...... 81 B6
Soudan B97 ...... 153 D2
Souters Ho B32 ...... 102 D8
South Ave Coventry CV2 ...... 114 A2
　Stourbridge DY8 ...... 80 F4
　Wolverhampton WV11 ...... 26 C5
South Bank Rd B64 ...... 82 E8
South Birmingham Coll
　Digbeth Ctr B5 ...... 66 F1
South Birmingham Coll
　(Hall Green Ctr) B28 ...... 105 E8
South Birmingham Coll
　(The Health & Social
　Care Ctr)
　B28 ...... 106 B6
South Birmingham Tech
　Ctr B29 ...... 87 F1
South Bromsgrove High
　Sch B60 ...... 150 F8
South Car Park Rd B40 ...... 90 E3
South Cl WS11 ...... 4 C8
South Cres Bromsgrove
　B60 ...... 137 A1
　Featherstone WV10 ...... 12 C6
South Dene B67 ...... 64 F5

South Dr Birmingham B5 ...... 86 C4
　Coleshill B46 ...... 70 E6
　Sutton Coldfield B75 ...... 46 C6
South Gn WV4 ...... 38 D5
South Gr
　Birmingham, Aston B6 ...... 66 D8
　Birmingham, Erdington B23 ...... 56 F5
　Birmingham, Lozells B19 ...... 66 B8
South Holme B9 ...... 67 C2
South Oval DY3 ...... 50 E5
South Par B72 ...... 46 C4
South Park Mews DY5 ...... 61 C2
South Range 4 B11 ...... 87 B6
South Rd
　Birmingham, Erdington B23 ...... 56 F4
　Birmingham, Hockley B18 ...... 66 A6
　Birmingham, King's Heath
　B14 ...... 104 E8
　Birmingham, Northfield B31 ...... 102 F2
　Birmingham, Sparkbrook B11 ...... 87 B7
　Bromsgrove B60 ...... 151 B7
　Hagley DY9 ...... 99 A4
　Smethwick B67 ...... 64 F5
　Stourbridge DY8 ...... 80 E4
　Tipton DY4 ...... 52 B8
South Ridge CV5 ...... 112 B4
South Road Ave B18 ...... 66 A6
South Roundhay B33 ...... 69 A3
South St Birmingham B17 ...... 85 D5
　Brierley Hill DY5 ...... 61 C2
　Coventry CV1 ...... 113 E3
　Redditch B98 ...... 153 E3
　Walsall WS1 ...... 42 D8
　Willenhall WV13 ...... 26 F1
　Wolverhampton WV10 ...... 25 C6
South Staffordshire Bsns Pk
　WS11 ...... 4 C4
South Street Gdns WS1 ...... 42 D8
South Terr CV31 ...... 162 B3
South View Birmingham B43 ...... 54 E7
　Warwick CV35 ...... 160 A6
South View Cl Codsall WV8 ...... 10 B2
　Featherstone WV10 ...... 12 B6
South View Rd
　Royal Leamington Spa CV32 ...... 157 C5
　Sedgley DY3 ...... 50 C8
South Way B40 ...... 90 F3
South Wlk B31 ...... 103 C1
Southacre Ave B5 ...... 86 E8
Southall Cres WV14 ...... 40 C1
Southall Rd WV11 ...... 27 A8
Southall's La DY1 ...... 51 B1
Southam Cl Birmingham
　B28 ...... 105 E8
　Coventry CV4 ...... 131 E7
Southam Dr B73 ...... 46 B1
Southam Ho B13 ...... 105 A7
Southam Rd
　Birmingham B28 ...... 105 E8
　Radford Semele CV31 ...... 162 E6
Southampton St WV1 ...... 163 C4
Southbank Rd Coventry
　CV6 ...... 112 E5
　Kenilworth CV8 ...... 147 F4
Southbank View DY6 ...... 60 E4
Southborough Terr
　1 CV31 ...... 162 A6
Southbourne Ave
　Birmingham B34 ...... 68 D6
　Walsall WS2 ...... 28 B1
Southbourne Cl B29 ...... 86 A2
Southbourne Pl WS11 ...... 1 D2
Southbourne Rd WV10 ...... 11 C3
Southcote Gr B38 ...... 103 D1
Southcott Ave DY5 ...... 81 D8
Southcott Way CV2 ...... 96 F1
Southcrest Gdns B97 ...... 153 D1
Southcrest Rd B98 ...... 154 A6
Southdown Ave B18 ...... 66 A6
Southern Cl DY6 ...... 60 F3
Southern Cross WS13 ...... 9 C7
Southern Rd B8 ...... 68 C6
Southern Way WS10 ...... 41 C3
Southernwood Rd DY3 ...... 50 B7
Southey Cl Solihull B91 ...... 127 B8
　Willenhall WV13 ...... 27 E8
Southfield Ave
　Birmingham,
　Castle Bromwich B36 ...... 69 B8
　Birmingham, Edgbaston B16 ...... 65 D3
Southfield Cl CV10 ...... 73 D5
Southfield Dr
　Birmingham B28 ...... 106 A5
　Kenilworth CV8 ...... 148 A6
Southfield Gr WV3 ...... 38 C7
Southfield Rd
　Birmingham B16 ...... 65 D3
　Hinckley LE10 ...... 75 F7
　Wednesfield WV11 ...... 26 F5
Southfield Way WS6 ...... 4 F2
Southfields CV32 ...... 157 A3
Southfields Rd B91 ...... 106 F1
Southgate Blackheath B64 ...... 82 D8
　Cannock WS11 ...... 4 B7
　Wolverhampton WV1 ...... 163 A3
Southgate Cl DY11 ...... 116 A4
Southgate End WS11 ...... 4 B7
Southgate Rd B44 ...... 44 E2
Southlands 8 CV31 ...... 162 B7
Southlands Rd B13 ...... 87 A1
Southlea Cl CV31 ...... 161 E6
Southleigh Ave CV5 ...... 132 F7
Southmead Cres B98 ...... 153 F3
Southmead Dr B60 ...... 137 B6

Southmead Gdns B80 .... 159 E3
Southminster Dr B14 .... 104 E6
Southport Cl CV3 .... 134 B5
Southville Bglws For Old
People B14 .... 105 B4
Southwark Cl WS13 .... 3 C3
Southway CV31 .... 162 A5
Southway Ct DY6 .... 60 F4
Southwick Pl WV14 .... 40 D7
Southwick Rd B62 .... 83 D8
Southwold Ave B30 .... 104 C3
Southwood Ave B34 .... 69 E2
Southwood Cl DY6 .... 60 E4
Southwood Covert B14 ...... 104 C2
Sovereign Cl CV8 .... 147 F1
Sovereign Ct **8** B1 .... 66 C3
Sovereign Dr DY1 .... 50 E2
Sovereign Rd
  Birmingham B30 .... 104 A4
  Coventry CV5 .... 113 A2
Sovereign Row CV1 .... 113 A2
Sovereign Way B13 .... 86 F4
Sovereign Wlk **7** WS1 .... 28 F2
Sovereign Works DY3 .... 50 E4
Sowe Valley Prim Sch
  CV3 .... 134 D7
Sowerby March B24 .... 57 D4
Sowers Cl WV12 .... 27 D5
Sowers Gdns WV12 .... 27 D5
Spa Cl LE10 .... 71 E1
Spa Gr B30 .... 104 C8
Spa La LE10 .... 71 E1
Spa View CV31 .... 162 A5
Spadesbourne Rd B60 .... 137 C6
Spark St B11 .... 87 A7
Sparkbrook St CV1 .... 113 F3
Sparkbrook Workshops
  CV1 .... 113 F3
Sparkhill Ctr B11 .... 87 C5
Sparrey Dr B30 .... 104 A8
Sparrow Cl WS10 .... 42 B5
Sparrow Cock La B93 .... 129 C1
Spartan Cl CV34 .... 161 E4
Spartan Ind Ctr B70 .... 52 E6
Spearhill WS14 .... 9 E8
Speed Rd DY4 .... 51 E7
Speedway La CV8 .... 135 F7
Speedwell Cl
  Aldridge WS9 .... 30 A5
  Birmingham B25 .... 88 A6
  Wednesfield WV11 .... 26 E5
Speedwell Dr CV7 .... 130 A6
Speedwell Gdns
  Brierley Hill DY5 .... 81 B6
  Featherstone WV10 .... 12 B8
Speedwell Ho B38 .... 104 A1
Speedwell Rd
  Birmingham,
  Balsall Heath B5 .... 86 D6
  Birmingham,
  Tyseley B25 .... 88 A6
Speedwell Trad Est B11 ...... 88 A6
Speedy Cl WS11 .... 1 E5
Spencer Ave Coventry CV5 .. 113 A1
  Dudley WV14 .... 51 C8
Spencer Cl Dudley DY3 .... 50 A4
  5 West Bromwich B71 .... 53 F8
Spencer Dr WS7 .... 6 E8
Spencer Rd Coventry CV5 ... 165 A1
  Lichfield WS14 .... 9 B6
Spencer St
  Birmingham B18 .... 66 C4
  Hinckley LE10 .... 71 D1
  Kidderminster DY11 .... 116 C4
  Royal Leamington Spa
  CV31 .... 161 F7
Spencer Yd CV31 .... 161 F7
Spencer's La CV7 .... 110 E1
Spennells Fst Sch DY10 ... 117 A2
Spennells Valley Rd
  DY10 .... 117 A3
Spenser Ave WV6 .... 23 F4
Spenser Cl B79 .... 21 A6
Spenser Wlk B61 .... 137 A8
Spernal Ash B49 .... 159 F1
Spernal La B49 .... 159 F1
Spernall Gr B29 .... 85 A1
Spetchley Cl B97 .... 158 C6
Spey Cl B5 .... 86 D6
Sphinx Dr CV3 .... 114 B1
Spiceland Rd B31 .... 102 F6
Spiers Cl B93 .... 128 A6
Spies Cl B62 .... 83 F6
Spies La B62 .... 83 F5
Spills Mdw DY3 .... 50 E5
Spilsbury Cl CV32 .... 156 E2
Spilsbury Croft B91 .... 127 A8
Spindle St CV1 .... 113 D6
Spindles The LE10 .... 75 F5
Spindlewood Cl WS12 .... 2 D1
Spinners End Ind Est B64 ... 82 D8
Spinney Cl
  Binley Woods CV3 .... 135 E7
  Birchmoor B78 .... 36 F8
  Birmingham B31 .... 103 B3
  Kidderminster DY11 .... 116 A7
  Norton Canes WS11 .... 5 F5
  Stourbridge DY8 .... 60 C3
  Walsall WS3 .... 15 A2
Spinney Dr B90 .... 126 D4
Spinney Farm Rd WS11 .... 4 B7
Spinney Hill CV34 .... 156 A1
Spinney La CV10 .... 72 C4
Spinney Mews B97 .... 153 C1
Spinney Rd LE10 .... 75 C6

Spinney The
  Birmingham,
  Brown's Green B20 .... 54 E4
  Birmingham,
  Edgbaston B15 .... 85 E5
  Coventry CV4 .... 132 D3
  Dudley DY3 .... 50 C2
  Little Aston B74 .... 31 B6
  Royal Leamington Spa
  CV32 .... 156 D1
  Wolverhampton WV3 .... 24 D1
  Wythall B47 .... 125 B4
Spinning School La B79 ...... 21 B5
Spiral Cl B62 .... 83 E8
Spiral Ct Birmingham B24 .... 56 E2
  3 Dudley DY3 .... 50 D3
  Stourbridge DY8 .... 81 A4
  Sutton Coldfield B76 .... 46 F3
  Wednesfield WV11 .... 26 E7
Spiral Gn B24 .... 57 C4
Spiral Mews B78 .... 35 A8
Spire View B61 .... 136 F3
Spirehouse La B60 .... 137 E5
Spires The Lichfield WS14 ..... 9 E6
  Nuneaton CV10 .... 72 C4
Spitfire Rd B24 .... 57 D2
Splash La WS11 .... 2 C3
Spode Pl WS11 .... 2 B2
Spon End CV1, CV5 .... 113 A3
Spon Gate Ho CV1 .... 113 A2
Spon Gate Prim Sch CV1 ... 113 A3
Spon La B70 .... 53 D1
  West Bromwich B70 .... 53 D1
Spon La S Oldbury B66 .... 64 D8
Spon Lane Ind Est B66 .... 64 D8
Spon Lane Trad Est B70 .... 53 D2
Spon St CV1 .... 165 A3
Spondon Gr B34 .... 69 C5
Spondon Rd WV11 .... 26 E8
Spoon Dr B38 .... 103 D2
Spooner Croft B5 .... 86 E8
Spooners Cl B92 .... 107 F7
Spout La WS1 .... 42 E7
Spouthouse La B43 .... 54 F7
Spreadbury Cl B17 .... 84 F8
Sprig Croft B36 .... 68 C8
Spring Ave B65 .... 63 D2
Spring Cl **6** Coventry CV1 .. 113 E3
  Hagley DY9 .... 98 F4
  Solihull B91 .... 106 F3
  Walsall WS4 .... 15 C2
Spring Coppice Dr B93 ...... 128 A3
Spring Cres B64 .... 82 F7
Spring Ct Walsall WS1 .... 43 A8
  West Bromwich B70 .... 53 D2
Spring Gdns Birmingham B21 65 F7
  5 Dudley DY2 .... 62 D8
  Smethwick B66 .... 65 B3
Spring Gr B19 .... 66 B6
Spring Grove Cres DY11 .... 116 B3
Spring Grove Gdns B18 ...... 65 F6
Spring Grove Rd DY11 ...... 116 B3
Spring Head WS10 .... 41 F2
Spring Hill
  Birmingham, Erdington B24 .. 56 F3
  Birmingham, Hockley B18 .... 66 A4
Spring Hill Ind Est B18 .... 66 A4
Spring Hill La WV4 .... 38 B4
Spring Hill Pas B18 .... 66 A3
Spring Hill Rd CV10 .... 72 C6
Spring La Birmingham B24 .... 57 A3
  Lapworth B94 .... 143 D3
  Radford Semele CV31 .... 162 E5
  Romsley B62 .... 100 D4
  Tanworth-in-A B94 .... 143 B5
  Walsall WS4 .... 15 C2
  Willenhall WV12 .... 27 C4
Spring Mdw
  3 Blackheath B64 .... 62 F1
  Cheslyn Hay WS6 .... 4 D1
  Halesowen B63 .... 82 F2
  Tipton DY4 .... 52 C6
Spring Meadow Rd DY2 .... 62 C2
Spring Parklands DY1 .... 62 A8
Spring Pool CV34 .... 160 E7
Spring Rd Barnacle CV7 .... 97 B6
  Birmingham,
  Balsall Heath B15 .... 86 D7
  Birmingham, Tyseley B11 ..... 87 F3
  Coventry CV6 .... 95 F1
  Dudley DY2 .... 62 D6
  Lichfield WS13 .... 3 D2
  Smethwick B66 .... 64 D8
  Walsall WS4 .... 15 D1
  Wolverhampton WV4 .... 40 A4
Spring Road Ind Est WV4 ..... 40 A4
Spring Road Sta B28 .... 88 A2
Spring St Birmingham B15 .... 86 D8
  Cannock WS11 .... 4 E8
  Halesowen B63 .... 82 D6
  Stourbridge DY9 .... 81 E4
  Tipton DY4 .... 52 C8
Spring Vale Cl WV14 .... 40 A1
Spring Vale Ind Pk WV14 ..... 40 C5
Spring Vale Island WV14 ..... 40 C4
Spring Vale Prim Sch
  WV4 .... 39 E4
Spring Vale Rd B65 .... 63 A5
Spring Wlk Halesowen B63 .. 82 D1
  Oldbury B69 .... 64 A5
  Walsall WS2 .... 28 B3
Springavon Croft B17 .... 85 B6
Springbank B19 .... 68 A3
Springbank Rd B15 .... 86 D7
Springbrook Cl B36 .... 58 D1
Springbrook La B94 .... 142 A7
Springcroft Rd B11 .... 87 F2
Springdale Coll B29 .... 85 C1

Springdale Jun & Inf Schs
  WV4 .... 38 D5
Springfield B23 .... 56 E3
Springfield Ave **6**
  Birmingham B12 .... 87 A6
  Bromsgrove B60 .... 151 A8
  Sedgley DY3 .... 39 E1
  Stourbridge DY9 .... 81 E4
Springfield Cl B65 .... 63 A5
Springfield Cres
  Bedworth CV12 .... 78 B2
  Dudley DY2 .... 62 F8
  Solihull B92 .... 89 C3
  Sutton Coldfield B76 .... 47 A4
  West Bromwich B70 .... 53 E1
Springfield Ct
  Birmingham B28 .... 105 F8
  Nuneaton CV11 .... 73 D3
  Sutton Coldfield B75 .... 47 C5
  Wolverhampton WV10 .... 11 D5
Springfield Dr B62 .... 83 D7
Springfield Gn DY3 .... 39 E1
Springfield Gr DY3 .... 39 D1
Springfield House Specl
  Sch B93 .... 129 A5
Springfield Ind Est B69 .... 64 B7
Springfield Jun & Inf Sch
  B13 .... 87 D2
Springfield Jun & Inf
  Schs B65 .... 63 A4
Springfield La
  Blackheath B65 .... 62 F5
  Kidderminster DY10 .... 116 F8
  Wolverhampton WV10 .... 11 D4
Springfield Mill Ct WS10 ..... 41 E6
Springfield Pk LE10 .... 71 A3
Springfield Pl CV1 .... 165 C4
Springfield Rd Bilston
  WV14 .... 40 E7
  Birmingham,
  Castle Bromwich B36 .... 69 D8
  Birmingham,
  King's Heath B14 .... 104 F8
  Birmingham, Moseley B13 ... 87 D2
  Coventry CV1 .... 165 C4
  Halesowen B62 .... 83 D7
  Hinckley LE10 .... 75 D7
  Nuneaton CV11 .... 73 E2
  Sutton Coldfield B76 .... 47 A4
  Tamworth B77 .... 35 D8
  Wolverhampton WV10 .... 25 E3
Springfield Rise WS12 .... 2 C6
Springfield St B18 .... 66 A3
Springfield Terr B65 .... 62 F5
Springfields Coleshill B46 .... 70 F5
  Walsall WS4 .... 29 C6
Springfields Rd
  Brierley Hill DY5 .... 61 B2
  Oldbury B68 .... 64 C4
Springhill CV10 .... 72 A8
Springhill Ave WV4 .... 38 C4
Springhill Cl Walsall WS4 ..... 15 D1
  Willenhall WV12 .... 27 D7
Springhill Ct **5** WS1 .... 42 F8
Springhill Gr WV4 .... 38 C4
Springhill Pk WV4 .... 38 B3
Springhill Prim Sch WS7 ...... 7 A6
Springhill Rd Brownhills
  WS8 .... 16 A7
  Burntwood WS7 .... 7 A6
  Walsall WS1 .... 28 F1
  Wednesfield WV11 .... 26 E7
Springmeadow Rd B19 ...... 66 D6
Springs Ave B61 .... 121 A1
Springs The B64 .... 63 A1
Springside B45 .... 159 C8
Springslade Dr B24 .... 57 D3
Springthorpe Gn B24 .... 57 C4
Springthorpe Rd B24 .... 57 D4
Springvale Ave WS5 .... 43 C7
Springvale Prim Sch WS11 ... 4 E8
Springvale Rd B97 .... 152 F2
Springvale St WV13 .... 27 B3
Springvale Way WV14 .... 40 C4
Springwell Rd CV31 .... 162 D6
Sproat Ave WS10 .... 41 C5
Spruce B77 .... 22 B4
Spruce Gr Birmingham B24 .. 57 B2
  Royal Leamington Spa
  CV31 .... 161 F5
Spruce Ho **4** B36 .... 57 F1
Spruce Rd **5** Coventry CV2 .. 96 B2
  Walsall WS5 .... 43 B3
Spruce Way WV3 .... 24 D1
Spur Tree Ave WV3 .... 24 A1
Squadron Cl B35 .... 58 C4
Square The Aldridge WS9 ..... 30 B6
  Alvechurch B48 .... 139 B6
  Birmingham B17 .... 85 B7
  3 Birmingham B17 .... 85 C5
  2 Birmingham,
  Ladywood B15 .... 66 B1
  Fazeley B78 .... 35 A8
  Kenilworth CV8 .... 147 F4
  Nuneaton CV11 .... 73 E2
  Solihull B91 .... 107 C3
  Tipton DY4 .... 52 D7
  Willenhall WV12 .... 27 D8
  Wolverhampton WV2 .... 163 C1
Squires Croft Coventry CV2 .. 96 F1
  Sutton Coldfield B76 .... 47 A2
Squires Gate WS7 .... 7 C8
Squires Gate Wlk B35 .... 58 A3
Squires Gn LE10 .... 75 F6
Squires Way CV4 .... 132 D6
Squirhill Pl **1** CV31 .... 162 B7

Squirrel Cl WS12 .... 2 D2
Squirrel Hollow B76 .... 47 A2
Squirrel Wlk Little Aston
  B74 .... 31 C5
  Wolverhampton WV4 .... 39 A5
Squirrels Hollow B68 .... 84 D7
Sring La CV8 .... 148 A5
Stable Croft B71 .... 53 F7
Stable Ct DY3 .... 50 E6
Stable Way B60 .... 150 E6
Stable Wlk CV11 .... 73 F2
Stableford Cl
  Birmingham B32 .... 84 F3
  Redditch B97 .... 158 D7
Stables The Berkswell
  CV7 .... 110 C4
  Birmingham B29 .... 86 B2
Stacey Cl B64 .... 62 E1
Stacey Dr B13 .... 105 A5
Stacey Grange Gdns B45 ... 122 A6
Stackhouse Cl WS9 .... 16 A4
Stackhouse Dr **3** WS3 ...... 15 A4
Stadium Cl Coventry CV6 ..... 95 D2
  Kidderminster DY10 .... 116 F4
  Willenhall WV13 .... 27 B3
Stafford Cl Bulkington CV12 .. 79 C2
  Walsall WS3 .... 14 B2
Stafford Ct Birmingham B43 .. 54 E7
  Wolverhampton WV10 .... 11 C5
Stafford Dr B71 .... 53 B6
Stafford Ho B33 .... 69 E2
Stafford La B92 .... 2 B5
Stafford Rd Birmingham
  B21 .... 65 F8
  Coven Heath WV10 .... 11 D4
  Darlaston WS10 .... 41 C6
  Huntington WS11, WS12 .... 1 C5
  Walsall WS3 .... 14 B3
  Wolverhampton WV10 .... 11 D4
Stafford St Bilston WV14 ...... 40 D5
  Birmingham B5 .... 164 D3
  Cannock WS12 .... 2 E1
  Dudley DY1 .... 51 B1
  Walsall WS2 .... 28 E3
  Wednesbury WS10 .... 41 F2
  Willenhall WV13 .... 27 A2
  Wolverhampton WV1 .... 163 C4
Stafford Way B43 .... 54 E7
Staffordshire Pool Cl
  2 B6 .... 55 F1
Stag Cres Norton Canes
  WS11 .... 6 A6
  Walsall WS3 .... 28 E6
Stag Hill Rd WS3 .... 28 E7
Stag Ind Est WV14 .... 40 F4
Stag Wlk B76 .... 57 D7
Stagborough Way WS12 .... 2 B4
Staines Cl CV11 .... 73 F7
Stainforth Cl CV11 .... 74 A2
Stainsby Ave B19 .... 66 C5
Stainsby Croft B90 .... 127 B5
Staircase La CV5 .... 112 C2
Stakenbridge La DY10 .... 98 D4
Staley Croft WS12 .... 1 C4
Stalling's La DY6 .... 60 D8
Stallings La DY9 .... 49 F1
Stambermill Cl DY9 .... 81 D5
Stambermill Ho DY9 .... 81 D5
Stamford Ave CV3 .... 133 C6
Stamford Cres WS7 .... 7 A8
Stamford Croft B91 .... 107 B2
Stamford Gdns CV32 .... 156 E1
Stamford Gr B20 .... 55 C1
Stamford Rd Birmingham
  B20 .... 55 C1
  Brierley Hill DY5 .... 81 C6
Stamford St DY8 .... 80 F7
Stamford Way WS9 .... 16 C1
Stanbrook Rd B90 .... 127 A5
Stanbury Ave WS10 .... 41 B6
Stanbury Rd B14 .... 105 B4
Stancroft Gr B26 .... 89 A8
Stand St CV1 .... 160 D6
Standard Ave CV4 .... 112 B1
Standard Way B24 .... 67 F8
Standbridge Way DY4 .... 52 A5
Standedge B77 .... 36 B7
Standhills Rd DY6 .... 60 E6
Standish Cl CV2 .... 114 C2
Standlake Ave B36 .... 68 D7
Standlake Ho B31 .... 102 E5
Standlake Mews
  17 CV31 .... 162 C6
Standleys Tower B23 .... 57 A6
Stanfield Rd
  Birmingham, Pheasey B43 ... 44 D5
  Birmingham, Quinton B32 ... 84 E6
Stanford Ave B42 .... 55 A7
Stanford Cl B97 .... 158 B6
Stanford Gr B63 .... 82 C1
Stanford Rd Blackheath
  B65 .... 63 B4
  Wolverhampton WV2 .... 39 C7
Stanford Way B69 .... 63 E4
Stanhoe Cl DY5 .... 81 D8
Stanhope Ho B79 .... 21 A4
Stanhope Rd B67 .... 64 F3
Stanhope St Birmingham
  B12 .... 86 F7
  Dudley DY2 .... 62 E4
  Wolverhampton WV3 .... 163 A2
Stanhope Way B43 .... 44 E4
Stanhurst Way B71 .... 43 A2
Stanier Ave CV1 .... 113 A4
Stanier Cl WS4 .... 29 B7
Stanier Gr B20 .... 55 B2
Staniforth St B4 .... 164 C4
Stanklyn La DY10 .... 117 C1

Stanley Ave Birmingham B32 . 84 E7
  Solihull B90 .... 106 B4
  Sutton Coldfield B75 .... 46 F4
Stanley Ct Birmingham B28 . 106 A5
  Redditch B98 .... 154 A5
  Wednesfield WV11 .... 26 F8
Stanley Ct
  9 Birmingham B13 .... 87 B2
  Perton WV6 .... 23 E4
  Royal Leamington Spa
  CV31 .... 162 C7
Stanley Gr **2** B11 .... 87 B6
Stanley Pl Bilston WV14 .... 40 B5
  Birmingham B13 .... 86 F3
  Walsall WS4 .... 29 B6
Stanley Rd
  Birmingham,
  King's Heath B14 .... 104 D7
  Birmingham, Nechells B7 ..... 67 C7
  Cannock WS12 .... 2 B6
  Coventry CV5 .... 132 F8
  Darlaston WS10 .... 41 D5
  Hinckley LE10 .... 71 C2
  Nuneaton CV11 .... 73 A5
  Oldbury B68 .... 84 C7
  Stourbridge DY8 .... 80 F3
  Walsall WS4 .... 29 B6
  West Bromwich B71 .... 53 E7
  Wolverhampton WV10 .... 11 D1
Stanley St WS3 .... 14 D1
Stanmore Gr B62 .... 84 A3
Stanmore Rd B16 .... 65 C1
Stansbury Ho **3** WS2 .... 42 C8
Stansfield Gr CV8 .... 148 D4
Stanton Ave DY1 .... 51 A6
Stanton Bridge Prim Sch
  CV6 .... 113 F6
Stanton Gr Birmingham B26 . 88 F8
  Solihull B90 .... 106 A4
Stanton Ho **2** B71 .... 42 F1
Stanton Rd Birmingham B43 . 54 D8
  14 Royal Leamington Spa
  CV31 .... 162 C6
  Solihull B90 .... 106 A4
  Wolverhampton WV1 .... 25 F2
Stanton Wlk CV34 .... 155 D1
Stanville Jun & Inf Sch
  B26 .... 89 C6
Stanville Rd B26 .... 89 C6
Stanway Gdns B71 .... 53 D6
Stanway Gr B44 .... 44 F3
Stanway Rd Coventry CV5 .. 133 A8
  Solihull B90 .... 106 C4
  West Bromwich B71 .... 53 D6
Stanwell Gr B23 .... 56 E6
Stanwick Ave B33 .... 69 E3
Stapenhall Rd B90 .... 127 A5
Staple Flat B60 .... 137 C8
Staple Hall Rd B31 .... 103 B2
Staple Lodge Rd B31 .... 103 C2
Stapleford Croft B14 .... 104 C2
Stapleford Gdns WS7 .... 7 D6
Stapleford Gr DY8 .... 60 C2
Staplehurst Rd B28 .... 105 F8
Staples Cl CV12 .... 79 C3
Stapleton Cl Redditch B98 .. 154 D3
  Studley B80 .... 159 D3
  Sutton Coldfield B76 .... 58 B6
Stapleton Dr B37 .... 70 A4
Stapleton La Barwell LE9 ..... 71 F8
  Hinckley CV13 .... 71 A8
Stapleton Rd Aldridge WS9 .. 29 F5
  Studley B80 .... 159 D4
Stapylton Ave B17 .... 85 B5
Stapylton Ct B17 .... 85 B5
Star Cl Tipton DY4 .... 52 C5
  Walsall WS2 .... 27 F4
Star Hill B15 .... 86 B8
Star Ind Pk CV2 .... 114 F1
Star St Stourbridge DY9 ...... 81 F5
  Wolverhampton WV3 .... 38 E8
Starbank Jun & Inf Sch
  B10 .... 88 A8
Starbank Jun & Inf Sch
  (Annex) B10 .... 68 B1
Starbank Rd B10 .... 88 A8
Starbold Cres B93 .... 128 B5
Starbold Ct B93 .... 128 A6
Starcross Cl CV2 .... 114 C7
Starcross Rd B27 .... 88 C2
Stare Gn CV4 .... 132 D5
Stareton Cl CV4 .... 132 F6
Starkey Croft B37 .... 70 D2
Starkie Dr B68 .... 64 C4
Starley Ct CV3 .... 135 A7
Starley Pk CV7 .... 96 B8
Starley Rd CV1 .... 165 A2
Starley Way B37 .... 90 C6
Startin Cl CV7 .... 95 F7
Startpoint Trad Est B11 ...... 87 D4
Statham Dr B16 .... 65 C2
Station App
  Barnt Green B45 .... 138 D8
  Dorridge B93 .... 127 F2
  Kidderminster DY10 .... 116 F5
  Royal Leamington Spa
  CV31 .... 161 F7
  Solihull B91 .... 107 A4
  Sutton Coldfield,
  Hill Hook B74 .... 31 F6
  Sutton Coldfield,
  Maney B73 .... 46 B2
Station Ave Birmingham
  B16 .... 65 C1
  Coventry CV4 .... 131 D8
  Warwick CV34 .... 160 F7
Station Bldgs B46 .... 59 B3
Station Cl WS3 .... 28 B8

Station Cotts B60 .... 138 A4
Station Dr Blakedown DY10 .. 98 C2
Brierley Hill,
Quarry Bank DY5 .... 61 E2
Brierley Hill,
Silver End DY5 .... 61 B1
Earlswood B94 .... 125 D1
Hagley DY9 .... 99 A6
Sutton Coldfield B74 .... 46 B8
Tipton DY4 .... 52 B4
Station La B94 .... 144 D3
Station Pl WS3 .... 28 B8
Station Rd Aldridge WS9 .... 30 A5
Alvechurch B48 .... 139 A5
Balsall Common CV7 ...... 130 B7
Bilston WV14 .... 40 E5
Birmingham,
Acock's Green B27 .... 88 C3
Birmingham, Aston B6 ...... 55 F1
Birmingham, Erdington B23 .. 56 F5
Birmingham,
Handsworth B21 .... 65 C8
Birmingham,
Harborne B17 .... 85 C6
Birmingham,
King's Heath B14 .... 86 E1
Birmingham,
King's Norton B30 .... 103 E4
Birmingham,
Marston Green B37 .... 90 A8
Birmingham,
Northfield B31 .... 103 A2
Birmingham, Stechford B33 .. 68 E3
Blackheath,
Haden Cross B64 .... 83 A8
Blackheath,
Rowley Regis B65 .... 63 D2
Blackwell B60 .... 138 A5
Brierley Hill DY5 .... 61 C3
Burntwood WS7 .... 7 E3
Cannock WS12 .... 2 C6
Coleshill B46 .... 59 F1
Great Wyrley WS6 .... 4 F4
Hagley DY9 .... 99 A6
Hampton in A B92 .... 109 B7
Hinckley LE10 .... 75 D8
Kenilworth CV8 .... 147 F4
Knowle B93 .... 128 B4
Lapworth B94 .... 144 D4
Lichfield WS13 .... 9 C7
Oldbury B69 .... 64 A5
Shenstone WS14 .... 17 F6
Solihull B91 .... 107 B4
Stourbridge DY9 .... 81 E6
Studley B80 .... 159 D4
Sutton Coldfield B73 .... 46 A1
Walsall, Pelsall WS3 .... 15 A3
Walsall, Rushall WS4 .... 29 A7
Warwick CV34 .... 160 F7
Wolverhampton WV10 ..... 25 F4
Wombourne WV5 .... 49 A8
Wythall B47 .... 125 B3
Station Road Ind Est B65 ... 63 D2
Station Sq CV1 .... 165 B1
Station St Birmingham B5 .. 164 B2
Blackheath B64 .... 82 C8
Bromsgrove B60 .... 136 F1
Cheslyn Hay WS6 .... 4 E3
Darlaston WS10 .... 41 E7
Sutton Coldfield B73 .... 46 C5
Tipton DY4 .... 52 B5
Walsall WS2 .... 28 E1
Walsall,
Blakenhall Heath WS3 .... 28 B8
Station St E CV6 .... 113 E7
Station St W CV6 .... 113 E7
Station Way Birmingham
B26 .... 90 D4
Redditch B97 .... 153 D3
Staulton Gn [5] B69 .... 63 E4
Staunton Rd
Royal Leamington Spa
CV31 .... 162 A5
Walsall WS3 .... 14 A3
Staveley Rd
Birmingham B14 .... 104 D6
Wolverhampton WV1 .... 25 C4
Staverton Cl CV5 .... 112 A3
Stead Cl Tipton DY4 .... 41 B1
Walsall WS2 .... 28 C5
Steadman Croft DY4 .... 52 D8
Stechford Jun & Inf Sch
B33 .... 68 D2
Stechford La B33 .... 68 D5
Stechford Rd B34 .... 68 E5
Stechford Sta B33 .... 68 D3
Stechford Trad Est B33 ..... 68 E3
Steel Bright Rd B66 .... 65 C6
Steel Dr WV10 .... 25 D8
Steel Gr B25 .... 88 C7
Steel Rd B31 .... 102 F2
Steel Rdbt WS10 .... 41 E2
Steelhouse La
Birmingham B4 .... 164 C3
Wolverhampton WV2 ..... 163 D2
Steene Gr B31 .... 102 F3
Steeplefield Rd CV6 .... 113 A5
Steeples The DY8 .... 81 B3
Steepwood Croft B30 ...... 103 D4
Steere Ave B79 .... 21 C7
Stella Croft B37 .... 70 C2
Stella Gr B43 .... 54 C8
Stella Rd DY4 .... 51 F6
Stenbury Cl WV10 .... 11 F4
Stencills Dr WS4 .... 29 B3
Stencills Rd WS4 .... 29 B4
Stennels Ave B62 .... 83 E4
Stennels Cres CV6 .... 112 F8

Stennels Cres B62 .... 83 E4
Stephens Cl WV11 .... 26 F8
Stephens Ind Est B11 .... 87 F4
Stephens Rd B76 .... 47 A4
Stephens Wlk WS13 .... 3 A2
Stephenson Ave WS2 .... 28 B5
Stephenson Cl
Royal Leamington Spa
CV32 .... 156 C1
Tamworth B77 .... 22 A2
Stephenson Dr
Birmingham B37 .... 70 B2
Perton WV6 .... 23 E5
Stephenson Pl B2 .... 164 C2
Stephenson Rd
Bedworth CV7 .... 96 C7
Hinckley LE10 .... 74 E7
Stephenson Sq WS2 .... 28 B5
Stephenson St
Birmingham B2 .... 164 B2
Wolverhampton WV3 ..... 163 A2
Stepney Rd CV2 .... 114 A4
Stepping Stone Cl WS2 .... 27 F4
Stepping Stones DY8 .... 81 B5
Stepping Stones Rd CV5 .. 112 F4
Steppingstone St DY1 ...... 51 B1
Sterling Pk DY5 .... 61 F4
Sterling Way CV11 .... 78 E8
Sterndale Rd B42 .... 55 C6
Steven Dr WV14 .... 40 E1
Stevenage Wlk [2] CV2 .... 115 A7
Stevens Ave B32 .... 84 D2
Stevens Dr WS12 .... 2 D6
Stevens Gate WV2 .... 163 B1
Stevens Ho CV1 .... 165 C4
Stevens Rd Halesowen B63 .. 82 B5
Stourbridge DY9 .... 81 D2
Stevenson Ave B46 .... 153 F3
Stevenson Rd Coventry
CV6 .... 113 A4
Tamworth B79 .... 21 A6
Stevenson Wlk WS14 .... 9 B6
Steward St B18 .... 66 A3
Stewart Cl CV4 .... 112 D2
Stewart Ct DY10 .... 116 E8
Stewart Rd Brownhills WS9 .. 16 A3
Kingswinford DY6 .... 60 D4
Stewart St Nuneaton CV11 .. 73 C3
Wolverhampton WV2 ..... 163 B1
Stewarts Rd B62 .... 83 D7
Stewkins DY8 .... 80 E8
Steyning Rd B26 .... 88 E5
Stickley La DY3 .... 50 C4
Stidfall Gr CV31 .... 162 D6
Stilehouse Cres B65 .... 63 C2
Stilthouse Gr B45 .... 122 A6
Stirchley Inf & Jun Sch
B30 .... 104 A6
Stirchley Trad Est B30 .... 104 B6
Stirling Ave Hinckley LE10 .. 71 A1
Royal Leamington Spa
CV32 .... 157 B6
Stirling Cl CV3 .... 134 F8
Stirling Cres WV12 .... 27 B6
Stirling Ct B16 .... 65 F1
Stirling Ho B75 .... 46 C5
Stirling Pl WS11 .... 4 B8
Stirling Rd Bilston WV14 ... 40 F2
Birmingham B16 .... 65 F1
Dudley DY2 .... 62 E6
Solihull B90 .... 126 E8
Sutton Coldfield B73 .... 45 E2
Stirrup Cl WS5 .... 42 F4
Stivichall Croft CV3 .... 133 B6
Stivichall Prim Sch CV3 ... 133 A6
Stockbridge Cl WV6 .... 23 F2
Stockdale Par DY4 .... 51 F5
Stockdale Pl B15 .... 85 D8
Stockfield Rd B25, B27 ..... 88 B5
Stockhay La WS7 .... 7 D5
Stockhill Dr B45 .... 121 F6
Stocking St DY9 .... 81 F5
Stockingford Fst & Mid
Sch
CV10 .... 72 D3
Stockland Ct B74 .... 44 F8
Stockland Green Sch B23 .. 56 F4
Stockland Rd B23 .... 56 D4
Stockmans Cl B38 .... 123 E8
Stockton Cl Birmingham B76 .. 58 C5
Knowle B93 .... 128 B4
Walsall WS2 .... 28 D4
Stockton Ct WV14 .... 51 B8
Stockton Gr Birmingham
B33 .... 69 D1
[2] Royal Leamington Spa
CV32 .... 157 A2
Stockton Rd CV1 .... 165 D4
Stockwell Ave DY5 .... 81 D8
Stockwell End WV6 .... 24 D6
Stockwell Head LE10 .... 71 D1
Stockwell Rd
Birmingham B21 .... 54 E2
Wolverhampton WV6 ...... 24 D5
Stockwell Rise B92 .... 107 D7
Stoke Cross B60 .... 151 E7
Stoke Gn CV3 .... 114 A2
Stoke Heath Prim Sch
CV2 .... 114 A6
Stoke La B46 .... 154 B7
Stoke Park Mews CV2 .... 114 A3
Stoke Park Sch & Com
Coll CV2 .... 114 B4
Stoke Pound La
Stoke Pound B60 .... 151 A4
Stoke Prior B60 .... 150 F3
Stoke Prim Sch CV2 .... 114 A4
Stoke Prior Fst Sch B60 .. 150 C3

Stoke Rd
Bromsgrove,
Aston Fields B60 .... 151 A7
Bromsgrove, Charford B60 .. 150 F7
Hinckley LE10 .... 71 B4
Stoke Row CV2 .... 114 A4
Stoke Way B15 .... 66 C1
Stoke's La WS11 .... 5 F7
Stokes Ave [7] Tipton DY4 .. 52 A8
Willenhall WV13 .... 40 F8
Stokes St WS3 .... 28 B8
Stokesay Ave WV6 .... 23 F3
Stokesay Cl
Kidderminster DY10 ...... 116 E2
Nuneaton CV11 .... 73 B3
Tipton B69 .... 63 A8
Stokesay Gr B31 .... 122 F8
Stokesay Ho [1] B23 .... 56 F6
Stom Rd WV14 .... 40 B5
Stone Ave B75 .... 47 A5
Stone CE Fst Sch DY10 ... 117 E2
Stone Cl B38 .... 103 F2
Stone Cotts B31 .... 103 A3
Stone Cross B46 .... 59 B3
Stone Hill DY10 .... 117 E2
Stone Pine Cl WS12 .... 1 F8
Stone Rd B15 .... 86 D7
Stone St Dudley DY1 .... 51 C1
Oldbury B69 .... 64 A7
Stone Yd Birmingham B12 .. 66 F1
Blackheath B64 .... 82 C8
Stoneacre Cl WV3 .... 24 A1
Stonebow Ave B91 .... 127 B8
Stonebridge Cres B37 ...... 69 F4
Stonebridge Highway
CV3 .... 133 E4
Stonebridge Rd Coleshill
B46 .... 70 F5
Little Packington B46 ...... 91 A7
Stonebridge Trad Est
CV3 .... 134 B4
Stonebrook Way
Birmingham B29 .... 84 F2
Coventry CV6 .... 95 F3
Stonebury B90 .... 85 D8
Stonebury Ave CV5 .... 111 E4
Stonechat Cl DY10 .... 117 B2
Stonechat Dr B23 .... 56 C2
Stonecroft Ave B45 .... 122 A7
Stonecrop Cl
Birmingham B38 .... 123 F8
Clayhanger WS8 .... 15 D6
Stonedown Cl WV14 .... 40 A3
Stonefield Cl CV2 .... 115 A8
Stonefield Dr DY5 .... 61 A7
Stonefield Prim Sch
WV14 .... 40 D4
Stonefield Rd WV14 .... 40 D5
Stoneford Rd B90 .... 106 A4
Stonehaven B77 .... 21 F5
Stonehaven Dr CV3 .... 133 C3
Stonehaven Gr B28 .... 106 B8
Stonehenge Croft B14 ... 104 D1
Stonehill Croft B90 .... 126 F6
Stonehill Wlk B77 .... 35 F6
Stonehouse Ave WV13 .... 26 F4
Stonehouse Cl
Redditch B97 .... 153 D1
Royal Leamington Spa
CV32 .... 157 D5
Stonehouse Cres WS10 .... 42 B2
Stonehouse Dr B74 .... 31 C4
Stonehouse Gr B32 .... 84 D2
Stonehouse Hill B29 .... 85 A3
Stonehouse La
Birmingham B32 .... 84 E2
Coventry CV3 .... 134 C4
Hopwood B48 .... 123 E2
Stonehouse Rd
Bromsgrove B60 .... 137 A1
Sutton Coldfield B73 ...... 45 F3
Stonelea WS9 .... 30 B5
Stonelea Cl B71 .... 53 E8
Stoneleigh Ave CV8 .... 148 A6
Stoneleigh Cl Redditch
B98 .... 158 F6
Stoneleigh CV8 .... 149 C6
Sutton Coldfield B74 .... 45 F8
Stoneleigh Ct CV11 .... 73 C3
Stoneleigh Gdns CV11 .... 73 C3
Stoneleigh Ho B32 .... 84 F5
Stoneleigh Rd
Birmingham B20 .... 55 E2
Blackdown CV32 .... 157 A7
Coventry CV4 .... 132 C2
Kenilworth CV8 .... 148 A6
Solihull B91 .... 106 E6
Stoneleigh CV8 .... 149 B3
Stoneleigh Way DY3 .... 50 D6
Stonepit B97 .... 21 C1
Stonepits La B97 .... 158 D4
Stonerwood Ave B28 ..... 105 E8
Stones Gn B23 .... 56 F6
Stoneton Cres CV7 .... 130 A6
Stoneton Gr B29 .... 103 A8
Stoneway Gr CV31 .... 162 D6
Stonewell Cres CV11 .... 79 B8
Stoney Cl B92 .... 107 E7
Stoney Croft WS11 .... 1 F1
Stoney Ct CV3 .... 135 A7
Stoney La
Birmingham,
Balsall Heath B12 .... 87 B5
Birmingham, Quinton B32 .. 84 B6
Birmingham,
Stechford B25 .... 68 E1
Blackwell B60 .... 138 C2

Stoney La continued
Churchill DY10 .... 98 E3
Dudley DY2 .... 62 C3
Kidderminster DY10 ...... 116 E8
Walsall WS3 .... 14 C3
Walsall WS3 .... 14 D3
West Bromwich B71 .... 53 D4
Stoney Lane Ind Est
DY10 .... 116 E8
Stoney Lea Rd WS11 .... 1 F1
Stoney Rd Coventry CV1 .. 165 B1
Nuneaton CV10, CV11 ..... 73 B6
Stoney Stanton Rd
CV1, CV6 .... 113 E5
Stoneycroft Tower [4] B36 .. 68 E8
Stoneydelph Inf Sch B77 .. 22 A1
Stoneydelph Jun Sch B77 .. 22 A1
Stoneyfields Cl WS11 .... 1 F2
Stoneyford Gr B14 .... 105 A4
Stoneygate Dr LE10 .... 71 F3
Stoneyhurst Rd B24 .... 56 F1
Stoneymoor Dr B36 .... 58 D1
Stoneythorpe Cl [2] B91 .. 107 B1
Stoneywood Rd CV2 ...... 114 A4
Stonleigh Ave CV5 .... 132 F7
Stonnal Gr B23 .... 57 A6
Stonnall Gate WS9 .... 30 C8
Stonnall Rd WS9 .... 30 C8
Stonor Park Rd B91 .... 106 F5
Stonor Rd B28 .... 106 A5
Stony La B67 .... 64 F5
Stony St B67 .... 64 F6
Stonydelph La B77 .... 36 A7
Stornoway Rd B35 .... 58 B4
Storrage La B48 .... 139 E3
Storrs Cl B9 .... 67 D1
Storrs Pl B10 .... 67 D1
Storrs Way The B32 .... 102 B7
Stot Fold Rd B14 .... 104 F2
Stour B77 .... 36 A5
Stour Cl Burntwood WS7 .... 7 D6
Halesowen B63 .... 82 E6
Stour Hill DY5 .... 82 A8
Stour Ho [2] B68 .... 84 B8
Stour St Birmingham B18 .. 66 A3
West Bromwich B70 .... 52 E3
Stour Vale [8] DY9 .... 81 F6
Stour Vale Road Ind Est
DY9 .... 81 F6
Stour Valley Cl DY5 .... 81 D7
Stourbridge Coll
Stourbridge,
Old Swinford DY8 .... 81 A4
Stourbridge, Wollaston DY8 .. 80 E5
Stourbridge Coll Annexe
DY8 .... 81 A4
Stourbridge Coll (Church
Street Ctr) DY8 .... 81 A5
Stourbridge Coll (Westhill
Ctr) DY8 .... 81 B4
Stourbridge Juntion Sta
DY8 .... 81 B3
Stourbridge Rd
Belbroughton DY9 .... 120 B7
Brierley Hill DY5, DY2 ...... 61 E6
Bromsgrove B60 .... 136 F7
Catshill B61 .... 120 D2
Churchill DY10 .... 98 A5
Dudley DY1 .... 62 A8
Hagley DY9 .... 99 C7
Halesowen B63 .... 82 F5
Harvington DY10 .... 118 C4
Kidderminster DY10 ...... 116 F8
Lower Clent DY9 .... 99 E3
Stourbridge DY9 .... 99 E3
Wombourne DY3, DY6, WV5 .. 49 B5
Stourbridge Town Sta DY8 .. 81 A6
Stourbridge Trad Est DY8 .. 81 A6
Stourdale Rd B64 .... 82 C8
Stourdell Rd B63 .... 82 E6
Stourminster Sch DY10 .. 117 B4
Stourmore Cl WV12 .... 27 D6
Stourport Rd DY11 .... 116 C2
Stourton Cl Knowle B93 .. 128 B7
Sutton Coldfield B76 .... 46 F4
Stourton Dr WV4 .... 38 C5
Stourton Rd B32 .... 84 B5
Stourvale Trad Est B63 .... 82 D6
Stow Dr DY5 .... 81 B6
Stow Gr B36 .... 68 E7
Stow Heath Jun & Inf Sch
WV13 .... 26 D1
Stow Heath La Bilston
WV1 .... 40 B8
Wolverhampton WV1 .... 26 C1
Stow Heath Pl [1] WV1 ..... 40 B7
Stowe Hill Gdns WS13 .... 3 C1
Stowe Pl CV4 .... 111 C1
Stowe Rd WS13 .... 9 B8
Stowe St Lichfield WS13 ..... 9 B8
Walsall WS3 .... 28 C7
Stowecroft WS13 .... 3 C2
Stowell Rd B44 .... 55 F8
Stowheath Ind Est & New
Ent Ctr WV1 .... 40 A8
Stowlawn Prim Sch
WV14 .... 40 C8
Stowmans Cl WV14 .... 40 B3
Strachey Ave CV32 .... 156 E2
Straight Rd WV12 .... 27 D6
Straits Gn DY3 .... 50 B4
Straits Prim Sch DY3 .... 50 B5
Straits Rd DY3 .... 50 B3
Strand The DY3 .... 50 A4
Strand The B61 .... 137 A3
Stratford Cl DY1 .... 50 E2
Stratford Ct B72 .... 46 B3
Stratford Dr WS9 .... 30 C8

Stratford Pl B12 .... 87 A8
Stratford Rd Birmingham
B11 .... 87 B6
Birmingham, Sparkhill B11 .. 87 D3
Bromsgrove B60 .... 137 A2
Dorridge B94 .... 127 B3
Solihull B90 .... 126 D7
Tanworth-in-A B94 .... 143 C5
Warwick CV34 .... 160 C3
Stratford St Birmingham
B11 .... 87 C5
Coventry CV2 .... 114 A4
Nuneaton CV11 .... 73 C4
Stratford St N B11 .... 87 A8
Stratford Way WS11 .... 1 F5
Stratford Wlk B36 .... 68 C8
Strathdene Gdns B29 .... 85 C1
Strathdene Rd B29 .... 85 C1
Strathearn Rd CV32 ...... 156 E1
Strathern Dr WV14 .... 40 A1
Strathfield Wlk WV4 .... 38 C6
Strathmore Ave CV1 ...... 113 E1
Strathmore Cres WV5 ...... 38 A1
Strathmore Pl WS11 .... 1 F2
Strathmore Rd Hinckley
LE10 .... 75 A7
Tipton DY4 .... 52 A8
Stratton St WV10 .... 25 E4
Strawberry Cl B69 .... 63 C7
Strawberry Fields CV7 ..... 92 B1
Strawberry La
Great Wyrley WS6 .... 13 C8
Willenhall WV13 .... 26 D3
Strawberry Lane Ind Est
WV13 .... 26 C2
Strawberry Wlk CV2 .... 96 D2
Stray The DY5 .... 61 C6
Stream Mdw WS4 .... 15 D1
Stream Pk DY6 .... 60 E4
Stream Rd DY6 .... 60 D4
Streamside Cl CV5 .... 112 A8
Streamside Way Solihull
B92 .... 89 D4
Walsall WS4 .... 29 D8
Streatham Gr B44 .... 45 A2
Streather Rd B75 .... 32 C2
Streetly Cres B74 .... 31 B3
Streetly Dr B74 .... 31 D3
Streetly La B74 .... 31 D2
Streetly Rd B23 .... 56 D5
Streetly Sch The B74 .... 45 A6
Streetly Wood B74 .... 31 A2
Streets Corner Gdns WS9 .. 16 A4
Streets La WS6 .... 4 E1
Streetsbrook Inf Sch B90 .. 106 C4
Streetsbrook Rd B91 ..... 106 D5
Streetway Rd WS14 .... 18 B7
Strensham Ct B13 .... 86 E4
Strensham Hill B13 .... 86 E4
Strensham Ho [4] B7 .... 67 A4
Strensham Rd B12 .... 86 E5
Stretton Ave B23 .... 134 C6
Stretton Cl LE10 .... 75 D6
Stretton Cres CV31 .... 162 B5
Stretton Ct Birmingham B24 .. 56 E2
Hinckley LE10 .... 75 D3
Stretton Dr B45 .... 122 A2
Stretton Gr [2]
Birmingham, Lozells B19 .. 66 C7
Birmingham,
Sparkbrook B11 .... 87 C6
Birmingham, Stechford B8 .. 68 C6
Stretton Ho B97 .... 153 A4
Stretton Pl Dudley DY2 ..... 62 D5
Wolverhampton WV14 ..... 40 A1
Stretton Rd
Kidderminster DY11 ...... 116 B3
Nuneaton CV10 .... 73 A3
Solihull B90 .... 126 B8
Willenhall WV12 .... 13 D1
Stretton St B77 .... 21 E3
Stringer Cl B75 .... 32 A4
Stringers Hill WS12 .... 2 D7
Stringes Cl WV13 .... 27 C3
Stringes La WV13 .... 27 B3
Strode Ho B79 .... 21 A4
Strode Rd WV2 .... 39 C6
Stroma Way WV10 .... 72 F2
Stronsay Cl B45 .... 101 F1
Stroud Ave WV12 .... 27 D5
Stroud Cl WV12 .... 27 C4
Stroud Rd B90 .... 105 F2
Strutt Cl B15 .... 85 D8
Strutt Rd LE10 .... 76 A5
Stuart Bathurst RC High
Sch WS10 .... 42 B5
Stuart Cl CV34 .... 160 D5
Stuart Cres DY2 .... 51 E2
Stuart Ct Coventry CV6 .. 114 A8
[7] Royal Leamington Spa
CV32 .... 156 E1
Stuart Rd Blackheath B65 .. 63 C4
Halesowen B62 .... 83 F5
Stuart St Birmingham B7 .. 67 C7
Walsall WS3 .... 28 B8
Stuart's Dr B33 .... 68 D1
Stuarts La DY9 .... 99 B8
Stuarts Rd B33 .... 68 D2
Stuarts Way B32 .... 102 B7
Stubbers Green Rd WS9 .. 29 E8
Stubbington Cl WV13 ...... 26 D1
Stubbs Cl CV12 .... 78 A4
Stubbs Gr CV2 .... 114 B5
Stubbs Rd WV3 .... 39 A6
Stubby La WV11 .... 27 A6

Stubley Dr WV10 .... 25 E6
Stud Farm Cotts B78 ...... 20 E2
Stud La B33 .... 68 F4
Studland Gn CV2 .... 115 A4
Studland Rd B28 .... 106 A8
Studley Croft B92 .... 89 D3
Studley Cty Inf Sch B80 .. 159 E4
Studley Dr DY5 .... 81 C8
Studley Gate DY8 .... 80 D5
Studley High Sch B80 .... 159 E3
Studley Rd Redditch B98 .. 154 A2
  Wolverhampton WV3 ..... 38 C8
Studley St B12 .... 87 B5
Studley Tower B12 .... 86 F7
Sturgeon's Hill WS14 .... 9 C7
Sturley Cl CV8 .... 148 B6
Sturman Dr B65 .... 63 C1
Sturminster Cl CV2 .... 115 A4
Stychbrook Gdns WS13 ...... 3 B2
Styles Cl CV31 .... 162 A7
Styvechale Ave CV5 .... 133 A8
Suckling Green La WV8 .... 10 A2
Sudbury Cl
  Royal Leamington Spa
  CV32 .... 157 C3
  Wednesfield WV11 .... 26 E7
Sudbury Gr B44 .... 45 B2
Sudeley B77 .... 35 C7
Sudeley Cl B36 .... 58 B1
Sudeley Rd CV10 .... 78 C8
Suffield Gr B23 .... 56 B5
Suffolk Cl Bedworth CV12 .. 78 A3
  Coventry CV5 .... 112 A4
  Nuneaton CV10 .... 72 E3
  Oldbury B68 .... 64 B4
  Wolverhampton WV11 .... 26 C6
Suffolk Dr DY5 .... 81 C7
Suffolk Gr WS9 .... 30 B8
Suffolk Pl Birmingham B5 .. 164 B1
  Walsall WS2 .... 28 D5
Suffolk Rd Dudley DY2 ...... 62 A7
  Wednesbury WS10 .... 42 C3
Suffolk St CV32 .... 157 A1
Suffolk Street
  Queensway B1 .... 164 B2
Suffolk Way B78 .... 21 A1
Suffrage St B66 .... 65 B4
Sugar Loaf La Iverley DY10 .. 98 B7
  Stourbridge DY7 .... 80 C1
Sugarbrook La B60 .... 151 A5
Sugarbrook Rd B60 .... 151 A7
Sugden Gr B5 .... 86 E8
Sulgrave Cl Coventry CV2 .. 114 E2
  Dudley DY1 .... 51 A3
Sullivan Ct CV6 .... 114 B7
Sullivan Rd CV6 .... 114 B7
Sullivan Way WS13 .... 3 C2
Sullivan Wlk WS13 .... 3 C2
Sumburgh Croft B35 ...... 58 A3
Summer Croft B19 .... 66 D6
Summer Dr DY3 .... 50 C3
Summer Gr WS13 .... 3 D2
Summer Hill **6**
  Halesowen B63 .... 83 B3
  Kingswinford DY6 .... 60 C6
Summer Hill Ind Pk **2** B1 .. 66 B3
Summer Hill Rd B1 .... 66 B3
Summer Hill St B1 .... 66 B3
Summer Hill Terr B1 .... 66 B3
Summer La Birmingham
  B19 .... 66 D5
  Dudley DY3 .... 50 D3
  Minworth B76 .... 58 D6
  Walsall WS4 .... 15 C2
Summer Pl DY11 .... 116 C3
Summer Rd
  Birmingham,
  Acock's Green B27 .... 88 A2
  Birmingham, Edgbaston B15 .. 86 C7
  Birmingham, Erdington B23 .. 56 F4
  Blackheath B65 .... 63 D3
  Dudley DY1 .... 51 A4
  Kidderminster DY11 .... 116 C3
Summer Row
  Birmingham B3 .... 164 A3
  Wolverhampton WV2 .... 163 B2
Summer St Kingswinford
  DY6 .... 60 C6
  Redditch B98 .... 153 E3
  Stourbridge DY9 .... 81 E5
  1 Stourbridge,
  Wollaston DY8 .... 80 F5
  West Bromwich B71 ...... 53 D4
  Willenhall WV13 .... 26 F2
Summercourt Dr DY6 ...... 60 C6
Summercourt Sq DY6 ...... 60 C5
Summerfield Ave
  Kingswinford DY6 .... 60 C7
  West Bromwich B70 ...... 53 C4
Summerfield Cres B16 ...... 65 E3
Summerfield Ct B15 .... 65 C1
Summerfield Dr B29 ...... 103 A1
Summerfield Gr **5** B18 .. 65 E4
Summerfield Hospl B18 .... 65 F4
Summerfield New Prim
  Sch B18 .... 65 E4
Summerfield Rd
  Birmingham B16 .... 65 E3
  Burntwood WS7 .... 7 A5
  Clent DY9 .... 99 E2
  Dudley DY2 .... 62 D7
  Solihull B92 .... 89 A1
  Tamworth B77 .... 21 D4
  Wolverhampton WV1 ...... 25 B2
Summerfields Ave B62 .... 83 F7

Summergate DY3 .... 50 C4
Summerhill Ave DY11 .... 116 A5
Summerhill Rd Dudley
  WV14 .... 40 D1
  Tipton DY4 .... 51 F7
Summerhill Sch DY6 .... 60 B6
Summerhouse Cl B97 .... 158 A6
Summerhouse Rd WV14 .. 40 A1
Summerlee Rd B24 .... 57 B2
Summerton Rd Oldbury
  B69 .... 52 D1
  Whitnash CV31 .... 162 A3
Summervale Cl DY9 .... 99 A5
Summervale Rd DY9 .... 99 A5
Summerville Terr **4** B17 .. 85 C5
Summit Cres B66 .... 64 E8
Summit Gdns B63 .... 82 F3
Summit Pl DY3 .... 50 B2
Summit The DY9 .... 81 D4
Sumner Rd B46 .... 70 F6
Sun St Brierley Hill DY5 .. 61 F1
  Walsall WS1 .... 42 E7
  Wolverhampton WV10 .. 163 D3
Sunbeam B77 .... 21 E3
Sunbeam Cl B36 .... 58 F1
Sunbeam Dr WS6 .... 4 F3
Sunbeam St WV2 .... 39 C7
Sunbeam Way B33 .... 69 C2
Sunbury Ave WS14 .... 9 E7
Sunbury Cl WV14 .... 40 D1
Sunbury Cotts B31 .... 103 A4
Sunbury Rd Birmingham
  B31 .... 122 F8
  Coventry CV3 .... 134 C5
  Halesowen B63 .... 82 F4
Suncliffe Dr CV8 .... 148 A2
Suncroft B32 .... 84 C5
Sunbury Rise B31 .... 103 B5
Sunderland Dr DY8 .... 81 A8
Sunderton Rd B14 .... 104 E4
Sundew Croft B36 .... 68 D8
Sundew St CV2 .... 96 D2
Sundial La B43 .... 43 F1
Sundorne Cl CV5 .... 112 A4
Sundour Cres WV11 .... 12 B1
Sundridge Jun & Inf Sch
  B44 .... 44 E4
Sundridge Rd B44 .... 44 E4
Sundridge Wlk WV4 .... 38 C6
Sunfield Gr B11 .... 87 E4
Sunfield Rd WS11 .... 1 B1
Sunleigh Gr B27 .... 88 E4
Sunley Dr WS12 .... 2 D7
Sunningdale
  Bromsgrove B60 .... 137 A1
  Halesowen B62 .... 83 E4
  Sutton Coldfield B73 .... 46 B1
  Tamworth B77 .... 22 C5
Sunningdale Ave
  Coventry CV6 .... 95 D2
  Kenilworth CV8 .... 148 B4
  Perton WV6 .... 23 D5
Sunningdale Cl
  Birmingham B20 .... 54 E4
  Nuneaton CV11 .... 74 A1
  Stourbridge DY8 .... 80 F2
  Sutton Coldfield B73 .... 46 A2
Sunningdale Dr B69 .... 63 A7
Sunningdale Rd
  Birmingham B11 .... 88 A3
  Bromsgrove B61 .... 150 D8
  Sedgley DY3 .... 39 B1
Sunningdale Way WS3 .... 14 A3
Sunny Ave B12 .... 87 A5
Sunny Bank Rd B68 .... 84 C7
Sunny Hill Cl WV5 .... 49 B6
Sunnybank Ave
  Birmingham B44 .... 56 B7
  Coventry CV3 .... 134 B5
Sunnybank Cl WS9 .... 30 E2
Sunnybank Rd Dudley DY3 .. 50 F5
  Sutton Coldfield B73 .... 57 A8
Sunnydale Cres LE10 ...... 75 A7
Sunnydale Rd LE10 .... 74 F7
Sunnydale Wlk B71 .... 53 C4
Sunnydene B8 .... 68 A5
Sunnyhill LE10 .... 75 F7
Sunnyhill S LE10 .... 75 F6
Sunnymead B60 .... 137 A1
Sunnymead Rd
  Birmingham B26 .... 88 F6
  1 Burntwood WS7 .... 7 A8
Sunnymead Way B74 ...... 44 F7
Sunnymede Rd CV6 .... 61 A4
Sunnyside Brownhills WS9 .. 16 A2
  Hinckley LE10 .... 71 D3
  Tipton B69 .... 63 B7
Sunnyside Ave B23 .... 56 E3
Sunnyside Cl
  Balsall Common CV7 ... 130 C7
  Coventry CV5 .... 112 A3
Sunnyside Ct CV10 .... 72 F3
Sunnyside Hospl LE10 .... 71 D5
Sunnyside Ind Est LE10 .. 71 D4
Sunnyside La CV7 .... 130 C7
Sunridge Ave
  Birmingham B19 .... 66 D6
  Wombourne WV5 .... 49 A7
Sunrise Hill WS12 .... 2 B6
Sunrise Wlk B68 .... 84 C5
Sunset Cl Great Wyrley WS6 .. 4 F3
  Tamworth B79 .... 21 A5
Sunset Pl WV4 .... 39 F3
Sunshine Cl CV8 .... 148 A2
Sunshine Inf Sch The
  WS3 .... 28 C8
Sunway Gr CV3 .... 133 B6
Surfeit Hill Rd B64 .... 82 D8

Surrey Cl Cannock WS11 .... 4 F8
  Hinckley LE10 .... 75 E4
  Nuneaton CV10 .... 72 E3
Surrey Cres B71 .... 53 A8
Surrey Ct CV34 .... 160 E8
Surrey Dr Kingswinford DY6 .. 60 F3
  Tamworth B78 .... 21 A1
  Wolverhampton WV3 .... 24 E1
Surrey Ho **2** DY8 .... 80 F8
Surrey Rd Birmingham B44 .. 44 F4
  Dudley DY2 .... 62 A7
Surrey Wlk WS9 .... 16 A1
Sussex Ave Aldridge WS9 .. 30 A8
  Wednesbury WS10 .... 42 D4
  West Bromwich B71 ...... 53 C6
Sussex Cl CV10 .... 72 E3
Sussex Ct Birmingham B29 .. 103 C7
  Warwick CV34 .... 160 E8
Sussex Dr Cannock WS12 .... 2 B5
  Wolverhampton WV3 .... 24 E1
Sussex Rd CV5 .... 112 F4
Sutherland Ave
  Coventry CV5 .... 112 A4
  Solihull B90 .... 106 C3
  Wolverhampton WV2 .... 40 A8
Sutherland Cl
  Birmingham B43 .... 44 D4
  Warwick CV34 .... 155 E1
Sutherland Dr
  Bedworth CV12 .... 78 A4
  Birmingham B13 .... 86 F4
  Wombourne WV5 .... 38 A1
Sutherland Gr WV6 .... 23 F4
Sutherland Ho WV1 .... 25 A3
Sutherland Pl WV2 .... 163 C2
Sutherland Rd
  Blackheath B64 .... 82 E8
  Cheslyn Hay WS6 .... 4 E2
  Wolverhampton WV4 .... 39 B5
Sutherland St B6 .... 67 B8
Sutton App B8 .... 68 A4
Sutton Ave Coventry CV5 .. 111 D4
  Tamworth B78 .... 21 A2
Sutton Cl Hinckley LE10 .. 71 F3
  Redditch B98 .... 154 D2
Sutton Coldfield Coll
  Design Ctr B72 .... 46 C4
Sutton Coldfield Coll
  Erdington Ctr B24 .... 57 A4
Sutton Coldfield Coll of
  F Ed B74 .... 46 C6
Sutton Coldfield Girls Sch
  B73 .... 46 B3
Sutton Coldfield Hospl
  B72 .... 46 B4
Sutton Coldfield Sta B73 .. 46 B5
Sutton Cres B70 .... 53 A3
Sutton Ct
  3 Birmingham,
  Erdington B24 .... 57 B6
  Birmingham, Hamstead B43 .. 54 E7
  Sutton Coldfield B75 .... 46 B7
  Wolverhampton WV4 .... 39 E2
Sutton Lodge DY11 .... 107 A3
Sutton New Rd B23 .... 56 F4
Sutton Oak Cnr B73 .... 45 A5
Sutton Oak Rd B73 .... 45 A5
Sutton Park Ct B73 .... 46 B2
Sutton Park Fst Sch DY11 .. 116 B4
Sutton Park Gr DY11 ..... 116 C3
Sutton Park Rd DY11 .... 116 B3
Sutton Park Rise DY11 .. 116 B3
Sutton Pk Nuneaton CV10 .. 72 B7
  Sutton Coldfield B74 .... 45 D6
Sutton Rd Aldridge WS9 .. 30 A1
  Birmingham B23 .... 57 A5
  Kidderminster DY11 .... 116 C4
  Mile Oak B78 .... 34 A7
  Walsall WS5 .... 43 C8
  Wednesbury WS10 .... 41 A4
Sutton Sch DY1 .... 61 F8
Sutton Sq B76 .... 58 E6
Sutton St Birmingham B1 .. 66 D1
  Birmingham, Aston B6 .. 66 F6
  Stourbridge B9 .... 60 F1
Sutton Stop CV6 .... 96 B5
Sutton's Dr Birmingham
  B43 .... 44 A4
  Walsall B43 .... 43 F4
Swadling St CV31 .... 161 F6
Swain Gdns CV31 .... 162 B6
Swains Gn LE10 .... 75 F6
Swains Gr B44 .... 44 F4
Swale Rd B76 .... 47 A1
Swaledale Cl B60 .... 150 E6
Swallow Ave B36 .... 70 A8
Swallow Cl Birmingham B12 .. 87 B5
  Dudley DY2 .... 62 D2
  Wednesbury WS10 .... 42 B4
Swallow Croft WS13 .... 3 A1
Swallow Ct CV12 .... 95 C8
Swallow Dr DY10 .... 117 A2
Swallow Rd CV6 .... 95 C1
Swallow St Birmingham B2 .. 164 B2
  West Bromwich B70 ...... 53 A4
Swallowdale Brownhills
  WS9 .... 16 B4
  Wolverhampton WV6 ..... 23 F2
Swallowdean Rd CV6 .... 112 E8
Swallowfall Ave DY8 .... 80 C4
Swallowfield B79 .... 20 E6
Swallowfields Dr WS12 .... 2 B3
Swallowfields Rd DY3 ..... 39 C2
Swallows Cl WS3 .... 15 A5
Swallows' Mdw B90 ...... 126 D8
Swallows Rise Bsns Pk
  DY5 .... 61 E3

Swan Ave B66 .... 64 E7
Swan Bank WV4 .... 38 F4
Swan Cl Blakedown DY10 .. 98 B1
  Cheslyn Hay WS6 .... 4 D2
Swan Copse B25 .... 88 C5
Swan Corner Sh Ctr WS7 .. 7 C6
Swan Cres B69 .... 63 F4
Swan Ctr The **7** DY10 .. 116 E6
Swan Ctyd B25 .... 88 D6
Swan Gdns B23 .... 56 F4
Swan La Coventry CV2 .... 113 F4
  Fairfield B61 .... 120 E3
  Stourbridge DY8 .... 61 A2
  Upton Warren B61 .... 150 A3
Swan Lane Ind Est B70 .. 53 A5
Swan Mews WS10 .... 9 A8
Swan Pool Gr WS4 .... 15 D1
Swan Rd WS13 .... 9 A7
Swan Rdbt B70 .... 52 F5
Swan St Alvechurch B48 .. 139 B5
  Brierley Hill DY5 .... 61 C6
  Dudley DY2 .... 62 C6
  Royal Leamington Spa
  CV32 .... 157 A1
  Stourbridge DY8 .... 80 E5
  Warwick CV34 .... 160 E6
  Wolverhampton WV1 .... 25 F2
Swan Village Ind Pk B70 .. 53 A5
Swanage Gn CV2 .... 115 A4
Swanage Rd B10 .... 87 D8
Swancote Dr WV4 .... 38 C6
Swancote Rd Birmingham
  B33 .... 68 F5
  Dudley DY1 .... 62 A8
Swancroft Rd Coventry
  CV2 .... 114 A5
  Tipton DY4 .... 51 F8
Swanfield Rd DY8 .... 61 A2
Swanfields WS7 .... 7 C6
Swanley Cl B62 .... 84 A3
Swanmore Cl WV3 .... 38 E8
Swanmote B77 .... 20 F5
Swann Rd WV14 .... 40 A3
Swans Length B48 .... 139 A4
Swansbrook Gdns
  4 B38 .... 104 C2
Swanshurst Girls Sch
  B13 .... 105 B7
Swanshurst La B13 ...... 105 C8
Swanswell Rd B92 .... 106 D7
Swanswell St CV1 .... 165 C4
Swanswood Gr **3** B37 .. 70 C3
Swarthmore Rd B29 ..... 103 B7
Sweetbriar La WV12 ...... 27 D5
Sweetbriar Rd WV2 .... 40 A7
Sweetbrier Dr DY8 .... 60 E1
Sweetman Pl WV6 .... 25 A3
Sweetman St WV6 .... 25 A3
Sweetmoor Cl B36 .... 69 C8
Sweetpool La DY9 .... 98 F5
Swift B77 .... 21 E3
Swift Cl Birmingham B36 .. 70 A8
  Bromsgrove B60 .... 150 E8
Swift Park Gr DY10 ...... 117 E8
Swift's Cnr CV3 .... 133 E8
Swillington Rd CV6 ...... 113 B5
Swinbrook Gr B44 .... 44 E1
Swinbrook Way B90 ..... 106 D4
Swinburne Ave CV2 ...... 114 D2
Swinburne Cl CV10 .... 72 A5
Swinburne Rd Hinckley
  LE10 .... 71 C1
  Redditch B97 .... 158 C7
Swincross Rd DY8 .... 81 B3
Swindale B77 .... 36 B7
Swindale Croft CV3 ...... 134 F8
Swindell Rd DY9 .... 81 C1
Swindon Rd Birmingham
  B17 .... 65 B2
  Kingswinford DY6 .... 60 B6
Swinfen Broun Rd WS13 .. 9 A8
Swinford Gr B93 .... 127 E3
Swinford Rd Birmingham
  B29 .... 85 B3
  Stourbridge DY8 .... 81 A3
  Wolverhampton WV10 .. 25 E5
Swinnerton Mid Sch
  CV11 .... 73 C2
Swiss Dr DY8 .... 60 F2
Swiss Lodge Dr B78 .... 34 F8
Swynnerton Dr WV11 ..... 12 F4
Sycamore B77 .... 35 E7
Sycamore Ave
  Birmingham B12 .... 87 A5
  Redditch B98 .... 153 E5
Sycamore Cl Hinckley LE10 .. 75 E5
  Kidderminster DY10 .... 116 F7
  Stourbridge DY8 .... 80 D2
  Walsall WS4 .... 29 B8
Sycamore Cres B37 .... 90 A8
Sycamore Ct B30 .... 103 C6
Sycamore Dr Hollywood
  B47 .... 125 B6
  Wolverhampton WV3 .... 24 D1
Sycamore Gn Cannock
  WS11 .... 1 E6
  Dudley DY1 .... 50 F5
Sycamore Gr CV34 .... 156 A1
Sycamore Green Prim Sch
  DY1 .... 50 F5
Sycamore Ho B13 .... 87 A3
Sycamore Ind & Trad Est
  B21 .... 65 D7
Sycamore Paddock
  1 DY8 .... 61 A1
Sycamore Pl Bilston WV14 .. 41 A3
  Smethwick B67 .... 64 F4

Sycamore Rd
  Birmingham, Aston B6 .. 67 A8
  Birmingham, Bournville B30 .. 103 F7
  Birmingham, Erdington B23 .. 56 F7
  Birmingham,
  Handsworth B21 .... 65 D7
  Burntwood WS7 .... 6 F7
  Cannock WS12 .... 2 F4
  Coventry CV2 .... 96 B2
  Kingswinford DY6 .... 60 E6
  Nuneaton CV10 .... 72 D6
  Oldbury B69 .... 64 A4
  Smethwick B66 .... 65 B3
  Tipton DY4 .... 51 F7
  Walsall, Shelfield WS4 .. 29 B8
  Walsall, The Delves WS5 .. 42 F5
  Wednesbury WS10 .... 42 A2
Sycamore Terr B14 ...... 104 C7
Sycamore Way
  1 Birmingham B27 .. 88 C5
  Huntington WS12 .... 1 D8
Sycamores The
  Bedworth CV12 .... 77 E2
  Lichfield WS14 .... 9 B5
  Sutton Coldfield B74 .... 31 F2
  Wolverhampton,
  Elston Hall WV10 .... 25 F8
  Wolverhampton,
  New Cross WV11 .... 26 B5
Sydenham Dr CV31 ...... 162 B6
Sydenham Ind Est CV31 .. 162 B6
Sydenham Prim Sch
  CV31 .... 162 C6
Sydenham Rd
  Birmingham B11 .... 87 C6
  Smethwick B66 .... 65 A7
  Wolverhampton WV1 .... 26 B2
Sydnall Cl B97 .... 152 F2
Sydnall Fields CV6 .... 95 F4
Sydnall Rd CV6 .... 95 F4
Sydney Cl B70 .... 53 A7
Sydney Ct **1** CV12 ...... 77 F2
Sydney Ho B34 .... 69 E6
Sydney Rd Birmingham B9 .. 67 C2
  Blackheath B64 .... 82 C8
  Bromsgrove B61 .... 136 E3
  Smethwick B67 .... 64 E2
Sykesmoor B77 .... 36 B7
Sylvan Ave B31 .... 102 F3
Sylvan Dr CV3 .... 132 F6
Sylvan Gn B62 .... 83 D5
Sylvan Gr B90 .... 106 B5
Sylvester Ho **2** B36 ..... 57 F1
Sylvia Ave B31 .... 123 B8
Symphony Ct B16 .... 66 B2
Synkere Cl CV7 .... 95 A6
Sytch La WV5 .... 49 A5

T P Riley Com Sch WS3 .. 14 C2
Tabbs Gdns DY10 .... 117 A6
Table Oak La CV8 .... 130 B1
Tachbrook Cl CV2 .... 96 C2
Tachbrook Park Dr CV34 .. 161 E5
Tachbrook Rd CV31 ..... 161 F4
Tachbrook St CV31 ...... 162 A6
Tack Farm Rd DY8 .... 60 D1
Tackford Cl B36 .... 58 D1
Tackford Rd CV6 .... 114 A8
Tackley Cl B90 .... 126 B8
Tadmore Cl WV14 .... 40 D5
Tadworth Cl WV1 .... 26 A2
Tainters Hill CV8 .... 148 A6
Tait Croft B92 .... 107 F8
Talaton Cl WV9 .... 11 A2
Talbot B77 .... 21 E3
Talbot Ave B74 .... 31 B3
Talbot Cl Birmingham B23 .. 56 D8
  Walsall WS2 .... 28 C5
Talbot Ct CV32 .... 157 A1
Talbot Ho **5** B24 .... 56 F4
Talbot Pl WV14 .... 40 C6
Talbot Rd Bromsgrove B60 .. 150 E7
  Dudley DY2 .... 62 B4
  Smethwick B66 .... 65 A3
  Wolverhampton WV2 .... 39 C6
Talbot St Birmingham B18 .. 65 F6
  Brierley Hill DY5 .... 61 D3
  Halesowen B63 .... 82 C6
  Kidderminster DY11 .... 116 C4
  Stourbridge, Lye DY9 .... 81 F5
  Stourbridge,
  Stambermill DY8 .... 81 A8
Talbot Way B10 .... 87 F7
Talbots La DY5 .... 61 F1
Talford St B6 .... 66 E6
Talfourd St B9 .... 67 D1
Talgarth Covert B38 ..... 123 E7
Talisman Cl CV8 .... 147 F3
Talisman Sq CV8 .... 147 F4
Talke Rd WS5 .... 42 F5
Tall Trees Cl Catshill B61 .. 136 F8
  Sutton Coldfield B74 .... 31 D4
  Willenhall WV12 .... 27 C6
Tall Trees Dr DY9 .... 81 D9
Talladale B32 .... 102 B7
Talland Ave Coventry CV6 .. 114 A6
  Tamworth B79 .... 21 F5
Tallants Cl CV6 .... 114 A8
Tallants Rd CV6 .... 114 A8
Tallington Rd B33 .... 89 D7
Talton Cl B90 .... 127 A5
Tamar Cl WS8 .... 6 C2
Tamar Dr Birmingham B36 .. 69 D8
  Dudley DY5 .... 50 F6
  Sutton Coldfield B76 .... 58 B2
Tamar Gr Perton WV6 .... 23 E4
  Willenhall WV13 .... 27 C2

Tamar Rd Bulkington CV12 ..... 79 B2
Tamworth B77 .... 36 A5
Tamar Rise DY8 .... 81 A8
Tamarisk Cl B29 .... 103 B8
Tame Ave Brntwood WS7 ..... 7 D6
Wednesbury WS10 .... 42 C4
Tame Bridge WS5 .... 42 F4
Tame Bridge Factory Est
WS5 .... 42 F4
Tame Bridge Sta B71 ...... 42 F2
Tame Cl WS1 .... 42 E6
Tame Cres B71 .... 53 C6
Tame Ct 5 Fazeley B78 .... 35 B8
Tamworth B79 .... 21 A5
Tame Dr WS3 .... 15 A1
Tame Gr WS11 .... 4 D8
Tame Rd Birmingham B6 .... 56 A1
Oldbury B68 .... 84 B8
Tipton DY4 .... 52 C5
Tame Rise B68 .... 84 B8
Tame Road Ind Est B6 ..... 56 B1
Tame St Bilston WV14 ..... 40 F5
Tamworth B77 .... 21 C3
Walsall WS1 .... 42 E6
West Bromwich B70 .... 52 F8
Tame St E WS1 .... 42 F6
Tame Valley Bsns Ctr B75 . 35 E6
Tame Valley Ind Est B77 ... 35 E7
Tame Valley Jun & Inf Sch
B36 .... 68 D8
Tame Way LE10 .... 75 A8
Tamebridge Ind Est B42 ... 55 E4
Tamedrive B79 .... 21 A4
Tamerton Rd B32 .... 84 D1
Tameside Dr
Birmingham,
Castle Bromwich B35 ..... 58 A1
Birmingham, Erdington B6 . 56 A3
Tameside Jun & Inf Schs
WS10 .... 42 C2
Tamworth Bsns Ctr B77 .... 22 B3
Tamworth Bsns Pk B77 ..... 22 B3
Tamworth Castle B79 ...... 21 B4
Tamworth Cl WS8 .... 6 F2
Tamworth Coll of F Ed
B79 .... 21 B6
Tamworth Rd Cliff B78 .... 35 C2
Keresley CV6, CV7 .... 94 D5
Lichfield WS14 .... 9 D5
Polesworth B78 .... 22 E1
Sutton Coldfield B75 ...... 32 F1
Tamworth B77 .... 35 D8
Wood End CV9 .... 36 C1
Tamworth Rd (Amington)
B77 .... 21 F5
Tamworth Rd (Dosthill)
B77 .... 35 C6
Tamworth St B79 .... 21 C5
Tamworth Sta B79 .... 21 C5
Tanacetum Dr WS5 .... 43 B3
Tandy Dr B14 .... 104 F3
Tandy's La DY10 .... 118 E4
Tanfield Cl WV6 .... 24 B3
Tanfield Rd Birmingham B33 68 F3
Dudley DY2 .... 62 B7
Tanford Rd B92 .... 89 C3
Tanglewood Cl
Birmingham,
Castle Bromwich B34 ..... 69 C5
Birmingham, Quinton B32 . 84 B4
Blackwell B60 .... 138 A5
Tanglewood Gr DY3 .... 39 C2
Tangmere Cl WV6 .... 23 E5
Tangmere Dr B35 .... 58 A3
Tanhill B77 .... 36 B7
Tanhouse Ave B43 .... 54 C7
Tanhouse Farm Rd B92 ... 89 C2
Tanhouse La Halesowen
B63 .... 82 C5
Redditch B98 .... 154 C6
Tanners Cl B75 .... 46 F7
Tanners Ct WS1 .... 42 E8
Tanners Green La B47 .... 125 B2
Tanners' La CV4, CV7 .... 111 B1
Tannery Cl WS2 .... 28 D3
Tannery Ct CV8 .... 147 F4
Tansey Ct DY5 .... 61 B7
Tansey Green Rd
Brierley Hill DY5 .... 61 B8
Kingswinford DY6 .... 50 A1
Tansley Cl B93 .... 127 F4
Tansley Gr B44 .... 44 F1
Tansley Hill Ave DY2 ..... 62 F8
Tansley Hill Rd DY2 ...... 62 E8
Tansley Rd B44 .... 55 F8
Tansley View WV2 .... 39 D7
Tansy B74 .... 31 F4
Tantallan Dr B32 .... 84 D1
Tantany La B71 .... 53 C4
Tantarra St Walsall WS1 .. 28 F1
Walsall, The Chuckery WS1 . 29 A1
Tanwood Cl Redditch B97 . 158 A6
Solihull B91 .... 127 B8
Tanwood Cross DY10 ..... 119 B1
Tanwood La DY10 .... 119 A2
Tanworth Gr B12 .... 86 F6
Tanworth La B90 .... 126 C5
Tanworth-in-Arden CE
Sch B94 .... 142 A2
Tanyard WS13 .... 9 C8
Tanyard Rd Alvechurch B48 139 B6
Coventry CV1 .... 111 D1
Tanyard La B48 .... 139 B6
Tanyards B27 .... 88 D3
Tapcon Way CV2 .... 114 F5
Tapestries Ave B70 .... 53 A4
Taplow Pl WS11 .... 1 F4
Tappinger Gr CV8 .... 148 C5

Tapster La B94 .... 143 F2
Tapton Cl WS3 .... 14 C3
Tardebigge CE Fst Sch
B60 .... 152 B7
Tardebigge Ho B60 ...... 137 B3
Tarlington Rd CV6 .... 112 E6
Tarmac Rd WV14 .... 40 B5
Tarn Cl CV12 .... 78 A2
Tarquin Cl CV3 .... 134 D7
Tarragon Cl CV2 .... 96 D1
Tarragon Gdns B31 ...... 102 C2
Tarrant B77 .... 35 F8
Tarrant Gr B32 .... 84 F5
Tarrant Wlk CV2 .... 115 A5
Tarrington Covert
6 B38 .... 123 E8
Tarry Hollow Rd DY5 ..... 61 B7
Tarry Rd B8 .... 67 E5
Tarvin Mews DY5 .... 61 D1
Taryn Dr WS10 .... 41 D7
Tasker St Walsall WS1 .... 42 D8
West Bromwich B70 .... 52 E4
Tasman Gr WV6 .... 23 E5
Tat Bank Rd B69 .... 64 B6
Tatchbrook Ct 5 CV31 .. 161 F6
Tatnall Gr CV34 .... 160 E8
Taunton Ave WV10 .... 11 D4
Taunton Rd B12 .... 87 B4
Taunton Tower 1 B31 ... 102 C2
Taunton Way CV6 .... 95 A2
Taverner's Gn B20 .... 54 F3
Taverners Ct WV12 .... 13 C1
Tavistock St B79 .... 21 C7
Tavistock Rd B27 .... 106 C8
Tavistock St CV32 .... 156 F1
Tavistock Way CV11 ...... 73 E5
Tavistock Wlk CV2 ...... 114 C7
Taw Cl B36 .... 69 F7
Tay Croft B37 .... 70 C4
Tay Gr Birmingham B38 .. 123 F8
Halesowen B62 .... 83 E8
Tay Rd Birmingham B45 . 102 B1
Coventry CV6 .... 113 B6
Taylor Ave
Royal Leamington Spa
CV32 .... 157 B2
Walsall WS3 .... 28 D8
Taylor Cl CV8 .... 148 B6
Taylor Ct CV34 .... 160 D7
Taylor Ho 4 WS2 .... 42 C7
Taylor Rd Birmingham
B13 .... 104 F5
Dudley DY2 .... 62 E2
Wolverhampton WV4 ...... 39 F5
Taylor St WV11 .... 26 D5
Taylor's La Smethwick B67 64 F5
West Bromwich B71 .... 53 D4
Taylors La B69 .... 63 E7
Taylors Orch B23 .... 56 B4
Taynton Covert 4 B30 .. 104 C3
Taysfield Rd B31 .... 102 E6
Taywood Dr B10 .... 87 C7
Tea Gdn The CV12 .... 95 E8
Teachers Cl CV6 .... 113 A5
Teal Bsns Ctr LE10 ...... 74 D7
Teal Cres DY10 .... 117 B3
Teal Dr B23 .... 56 B3
Teal Rd B80 .... 159 F4
Tealby Gr B29 .... 86 A1
Teall Ct B27 .... 88 C3
Teall Rd B8 .... 67 E5
Tean Cl Birmingham B11 . 88 A3
Burntwood WS7 .... 7 D6
Teasdale Way DY9 .... 81 D4
Teasel Gr WV10 .... 12 B7
Teasel Rd WV11 .... 26 F5
Teazel Ave B30 .... 103 D6
Tebworth Cl WV9 .... 10 F2
Ted Pitts La CV5 .... 94 B2
Tedbury Cres B23 .... 56 E6
Tedder Rd WS2 .... 27 F2
Teddesley Ct WS11 .... 1 E1
Teddesley Gr B33 .... 69 C4
Teddesley St WS4 .... 28 F4
Teddesley Way WS12 ...... 1 C6
Teddington Gr B42 .... 55 D3
Tedstone Rd B32 .... 84 E5
Tees Gr B38 .... 123 F8
Teesdale Ave B34 .... 68 F6
Teesdale Cl WV1 .... 26 A2
Teeswater Cl B60 .... 150 E6
Teign B77 .... 36 A5
Teign Bank Cl LE10 ...... 71 D2
Teign Bank Rd LE10 ...... 71 D2
Teignmouth Rd B29 ...... 86 A1
Telephone Rd CV3 .... 114 C2
Telfer Rd CV6 .... 113 B7
Telford Ave Great Wyrley
WS6 .... 4 F3
Royal Leamington Spa
CV32 .... 157 B5
Telford Cl Burntwood WS7 . 7 C8
Smethwick B67 .... 64 D1
Walsall WS2 .... 28 A5
West Bromwich B71 .... 53 A8
Telford Cty Fst &
Mid Schs CV32 .... 157 C5
Telford Gdns WV3 .... 38 D7
Telford Rd Bedworth CV7 . 96 C8
Tamworth B79 .... 20 F8
Walsall WS2 .... 28 A5
Telford Way B66 .... 64 F8
Teme Ave DY11 .... 116 B3
Teme Ct B23 .... 56 B3
Teme Gr WV13 .... 27 D2
Teme Rd Halesowen B63 .. 82 B5
Stourbridge DY8 .... 80 F3

Tempest St Tamworth B79 . 21 A5
Wolverhampton WV2 ..... 163 C2
Templar Ave CV4 .... 112 A1
Templar Ct CV11 .... 73 C2
Templars' Fields CV4 .... 132 B7
Templars Prim Sch CV4 . 112 A1
Templars The Oldbury B69 . 63 E5
Warwick CV34 .... 160 F5
Temple Ave
Balsall Common CV7 ..... 129 F6
Birmingham B28 .... 106 A6
Temple Bar WV13 .... 27 A2
Temple Cl B98 .... 153 F4
Temple Ct CV34 .... 160 D5
Temple La B93 .... 129 A4
Temple Meadow Prim Sch
B64 .... 63 A1
Temple Meadows Rd B71 . 53 E6
Temple Pas B2 .... 164 B2
Temple Rd Dorridge B93 . 128 A3
Willenhall WV13 .... 27 B3
Temple Row B2 .... 164 C3
Temple Row W B2 .... 164 B3
Temple St Bilston WV14 .. 40 E5
Birmingham B2 .... 164 B2
Dudley DY3 .... 50 D3
West Bromwich B70 ...... 53 C4
Wolverhampton WV2 ..... 163 B2
Temple Way Coleshill B46 . 59 F1
Tipton DY4 .... 52 D2
Templefield Gdns B9 ..... 67 C1
Templefield Sq B15 ...... 86 B7
Templefield St B9 .... 67 C1
Templemore Dr B43 ...... 54 E7
Templeton Cl B93 .... 128 A3
Templeton Rd B44 .... 44 F2
Ten Acres End B30 ...... 104 B8
Ten Acres Fst Sch B98 .. 154 F3
Ten Ashes La B45 .... 122 C4
Tenacre La DY3 .... 50 E6
Tenacres La B45 .... 154 F3
Tenbury Cl Aldridge WS9 . 30 C8
Redditch B98 .... 154 C6
Willenhall WS2 .... 27 C3
Tenbury Ct WV4 .... 38 D5
Tenbury Gdns WV4 .... 38 D5
Tenbury Ho Birmingham
B33 .... 69 A2
2 Halesowen B63 .... 83 A3
Tenbury Rd B14 .... 104 E6
Tenby Cl CV12 .... 77 C1
Tenby Ct 2 CV32 .... 161 E8
Tenby Rd B13 .... 87 D2
Tenby St B1 .... 66 B4
Tenby St N B1 .... 66 B4
Tenby Tower 2 B31 ..... 103 A1
Teneriffe Rd CV6 .... 95 F1
Tenlands Rd B63 .... 82 F3
Tenlons Rd CV10 .... 72 F2
Tennal Dr B32 .... 84 F6
Tennal Gr B32 .... 84 F6
Tennal La B32 .... 84 F6
Tennal Rd B32 .... 84 F6
Tennant St Birmingham B15 . 66 B1
Nuneaton CV11 .... 73 C3
Tennis Ct B30 .... 103 D4
Tennis Ct The B15 .... 86 A5
Tennscore Ave WS6 .... 4 E3
Tennyson Ave
Sutton Coldfield B74 ..... 31 F6
Tamworth B79 .... 21 A6
Warwick CV34 .... 160 C4
Tennyson Cl CV8 .... 148 C4
Tennyson Ho
Birmingham B31 .... 123 A8
3 Oldbury B63 .... 64 C4
Tennyson Rd Birmingham
B10 .... 87 E7
Coventry CV2 .... 114 C3
Dudley DY3 .... 50 A4
Hinckley LE10 .... 71 C1
Redditch B97 .... 158 C8
Walsall WS3 .... 28 E8
Willenhall WV12 .... 27 E8
Wolverhampton WV10 .... 12 A1
Tennyson St DY5 .... 61 D7
Tennyson Way DY10 ..... 117 C6
Tenter Ct B63 .... 83 B4
Tenter Dr B63 .... 83 C4
Tenterfields B63 .... 83 B4
Tenterfields Prim Sch
B62 .... 83 C4
Tern Cl WV4 .... 39 D3
Tern Gr B38 .... 103 E1
Ternhill Ho B35 .... 58 A2
Terrace Rd B19 .... 66 B7
Terrace St Blackheath B65 . 63 B1
Brierley Hill DY5 .... 61 E5
Wednesbury WS10 .... 42 A3
Terrace The Blackheath
B64 .... 82 E8
Wolverhampton WV3 ..... 24 C1
Terry Ave CV32 .... 156 C1
Terry Dr B76 .... 46 F2
Terry Rd CV1 .... 113 F1
Terry St DY2 .... 51 E1
Terrys Cl B98 .... 153 F5
Tessall La B31 .... 102 D2
Tetbury Gr B31 .... 102 D3
Tetley Ave WS4 .... 29 B4
Tetley Rd B11 .... 87 E3
Tetnall St DY2 .... 62 D8
Tettenhall Arc WV6 ...... 24 D5
Tettenhall Coll WV6 ..... 24 D4
Tettenhall Rd WV6, WV1 . 24 C4
Tettenhall Wood Sch
WV6 .... 24 B3

Teviot Gdns DY5 .... 61 B6
Teviot Gr B38 .... 123 F8
Teviot Tower B19 .... 66 C5
Tew Park Rd B21 .... 65 E7
Tewkesbury Dr
Bedworth CV12 .... 78 C3
Dudley DY2 .... 62 D3
Tewkesbury Rd
Birmingham B20 .... 55 E2
Walsall WS3 .... 13 E2
Thackeray Cl CV10 .... 72 A4
Thackeray Dr B79 .... 21 A7
Thackeray Rd B30 ...... 103 D5
Thackhall St CV2 .... 113 F4
Thame Ct B47 .... 124 E2
Thames Cl Brierley Hill
DY5 .... 61 B7
Bulkington CV12 .... 79 A3
Thames Ct B73 .... 46 B5
Thames Ho 6 DY3 .... 50 D3
Thames Rd WS3 .... 14 E1
Thames Tower B7 .... 67 B5
Thamley Rd CV6 .... 113 A4
Thanet Cl DY6 .... 60 C7
Thanet Gr B42 .... 55 C4
Thatchway Gdns B38 ... 123 E7
Thaxted Rd B33 .... 69 E3
Theatre App B5 .... 164 C1
Theatre Ct CV34 .... 160 D6
Theatre St CV34 .... 160 D7
Thebes Cl CV5 .... 111 B8
Theddingworth Cl CV3 .. 134 E8
Thelbridge Rd B31 ...... 122 E6
Thelma Rd DY4 .... 51 E5
Thelma St 1 WS1 .... 42 D7
Thelsford Way B92 ...... 107 D8
Theodore Cl Birmingham
B17 .... 85 D4
Oldbury B69 .... 52 E1
Theresa Rd B11 .... 87 B7
Thetford Cl DY4 .... 51 D5
Thetford Gdns WV11 .... 26 D6
Thetford Rd B42 .... 55 B7
Thetford Way WS5 .... 43 C3
Thickett Cl WS2 .... 42 B8
Thicknall Dr DY9 .... 81 C2
Thicknall La DY9 .... 99 B3
Thicknall Rise DY9 ...... 99 B4
Thickthorn Cl CV8 ...... 148 B2
Thickthorn Orchs CV8 .. 148 B2
Thimble End Rd B76 ..... 47 A1
Thimble Mill La B6, B7 .. 67 B7
Thimblemill Rd B67 ..... 64 E3
Thimbler Rd CV4 .... 132 C2
Third Ave
Birmingham,
Bordesley Green B9 ..... 67 F2
Birmingham,
Selly Oak B29 .... 86 C3
Birmingham,
Witton B6 .... 55 F3
Brownhills WS8 .... 7 A1
Kingswinford DY6 .... 60 F8
Wolverhampton WV10 .... 25 F7
Third Exhibition Ave B40 . 90 D4
Third Rd B61 .... 120 F4
Thirlestane Cl CV8 ...... 148 C6
Thirlmere Ave CV11 ...... 73 F6
Thirlmere Cl Cannock WS11 . 1 E1
Coventry CV4 .... 111 E3
Wolverhampton WV6 ..... 24 D8
Thirlmere Dr
Birmingham B13 .... 105 D8
Essington WV11 .... 13 A2
Thirlmere Gr WV6 .... 23 F4
Thirlmere Ho B15 .... 85 D3
Thirlmere Rd Bedworth
CV12 .... 78 A2
Hinckley LE10 .... 75 A7
Wolverhampton WV6 ..... 24 D8
Thirlmere Wlk DY5 .... 81 B7
Thirsk Croft B36 .... 68 C8
Thirsk Rd CV3 .... 133 C5
Thirston Cl WV11 .... 27 A5
Thisledown Wlk DY3 ..... 39 C1
Thistle Cl DY3 .... 50 F6
Thistle Croft WV11 ...... 26 D5
Thistle Down B74 .... 31 A2
Thistle Gn B38 .... 123 E7
Thistle Ho B36 .... 68 D8
Thistle La B2 .... 102 B7
Thistledown Ave WS7 ..... 7 A6
Thistledown Dr Cannock
WS12 .... 2 D1
Featherstone WV10 ...... 12 A7
Thistledown Rd B34 ..... 69 C2
Thistlegreen Cl B65 ..... 62 F5
Thistlegreen Rd DY2 .... 62 A2
Thistlewood Gr B93 ..... 145 B6
Thistley Field E CV6 .... 113 A4
Thistley Field N CV6 .... 113 A7
Thistley Field S CV6 .... 112 F6
Thistley Field W CV6 .... 112 F7
Thistley Nook WS13 .... 3 A1
Thomas Barnes Cty Prim
Sch B78 .... 20 B7
Thomas Cres 2 B66 ..... 65 C5
Thomas Greenway WS13 .. 3 A2
Thomas Guy Rd B70 ..... 52 F6
Thomas Hardy Ct B79 ... 21 A7
Thomas Ho WS3 .... 14 D3
Thomas King Ho 4 CV1 . 113 E4
Thomas Landsdail St
CV3 .... 133 D8
Thomas Lane St CV6 .... 96 A1
Thomas Mason Cl WV3 ... 26 D7
Thomas Naul Croft CV4 . 111 F3
Thomas Sharp St CV4 .. 132 A7

Thomas St Bedworth CV12 . 78 A2
Birmingham B6 .... 66 F6
Royal Leamington Spa
CV32 .... 157 A1
Smethwick B66 .... 65 B5
Tamworth B77 .... 21 D4
Walsall WS2 .... 28 D2
West Bromwich B70 ...... 53 D2
Wolverhampton WV2 .... 163 B1
Thompson Ave WV2 ...... 39 E6
Thompson Cl Dudley DY2 . 62 B2
Willenhall WV13 .... 27 A3
Thompson Dr B24 .... 67 F8
Thompson Gdns B67 ..... 64 F4
Thompson Ho DY4 .... 52 C8
Thompson Rd Oldbury B68 . 64 B5
Smethwick B67 .... 64 F4
Thompson St Bilston WV14 . 40 D5
Willenhall WV13 .... 27 A3
Thompson's Rd CV7 ..... 94 F6
Thomson Ave B38 .... 103 D1
Thor Cl WS11 .... 2 A5
Thoresby B79 .... 20 E6
Thorn Cl WS10 .... 41 F4
Thorn Rd B30 .... 103 E7
Thorn Stile Cl CV32 ..... 157 E6
Thornberry Dr DY1 .... 61 E8
Thornberry Wlk B7 .... 67 C6
Thornbridge Ave B42 .... 55 D7
Thornbrook Ct 1 WS4 ... 28 F3
Thornbury Ct WV6 .... 24 A3
Thornbury La B98 .... 154 C7
Thornbury Rd B20 .... 55 D2
Thornby Ave Kenilworth
CV8 .... 148 B3
Solihull B91 .... 107 B5
Tamworth B77 .... 35 E8
Thornby Rd B23 .... 56 C8
Thorncliffe Cl B97 ...... 158 A6
Thorncliffe Rd B44 ...... 44 E2
Thorncroft Way WS5 ..... 43 B4
Thorne Ave WV10 .... 25 E7
Thorne Rd WV13 .... 27 A4
Thorne St WV2 .... 40 A7
Thornes Croft WS9 ...... 16 E4
Thorney Rd Aldridge B74 . 30 F1
Coventry CV2 .... 114 B6
Thorneycroft La WV10 ... 26 A5
Thorneycroft Pl WV14 ... 41 B3
Thorneycroft Rd WV14 .. 41 B4
Thornfield Cres WS7 ...... 7 A8
Thornfield Croft DY3 .... 50 E7
Thornfield Rd B27 .... 88 D2
Thornfield Way LE10 ..... 75 E8
Thorngrove Ave 7 B91 . 127 C8
Thornham Way B14 .... 104 D1
Thornhill Dr CV11 .... 79 C8
Thornhill Gr B21 .... 65 F8
Thornhill Pk B74 .... 45 A8
Thornhill Rd
Birmingham,
Handsworth B21 .... 65 F8
Birmingham, Sparkhill B11 . 87 D3
Brierley Hill DY5 .... 81 B8
Cannock WS12 .... 1 F7
Coventry CV1 .... 113 D5
Dudley DY1 .... 51 C4
Halesowen B63 .... 82 E3
Redditch B98 .... 154 E6
Solihull B91 .... 107 C7
Sutton Coldfield B74 ..... 45 A7
Thornhurst Ave B32 ..... 84 E7
Thornleigh DY3 .... 50 D5
Thornleigh Trad Est DY2 . 62 A7
Thornley Cl Birmingham
B13 .... 87 A1
Radford Semele CV31 ... 162 F5
Wolverhampton WV11 .... 12 F1
Thornley Gr B76 .... 58 C6
Thornley Rd WV11 .... 12 F1
Thornley St WV1 .... 163 C3
Thorns Ave DY5 .... 61 E1
Thorns Cty Fst Sch CV8 . 148 B4
Thorns Prim Sch DY5 .... 81 E7
Thorns Rd DY5 .... 81 E7
Thorns Sch & Com Coll
DY5 .... 81 E8
Thornsett Gr B90 .... 106 B6
Thornthwaite Cl B45 ... 102 B2
Thornton Cl Coventry CV5 . 111 C4
Tipton B69 .... 52 C2
Warwick CV34 .... 155 F1
Thornton Dr DY5 .... 61 E1
Thornton Ho B35 .... 66 E5
Thornton Jun Sch B8 .... 68 B5
Thornton Rd Birmingham
B8 .... 68 B5
Solihull B90 .... 126 F6
Wolverhampton WV1 ..... 26 B1
Thorntons Way CV10 ..... 72 A3
Thornwood Cl B68 .... 64 C5
Thornycroft Rd LE10 ..... 75 E8
Thornyfield Cl B90 ..... 106 C3
Thornyfield Rd B90 .... 106 C3
Thornyhurst La WS14 .... 17 A6
Thorp B5 .... 164 B1
Thorpe Ave WS7 .... 6 D8
Thorpe Cl Burntwood WS7 . 6 D8
Sutton Coldfield B75 ..... 46 C7
Thorpe Rd WS1 .... 42 E7
Thorpe St WS7 .... 6 D8
Threadneedle St CV1 ... 113 D6
Three Corner Cl B90 ... 125 E8
Three Cornered Cl CV32 . 157 E6

Three Crowns Specl Sch
  WS5 .... 43 F8
Three Oaks Rd B47 .... 125 B4
Three Pots Rd LE10 .... 75 E4
Three Shires Jct CV6 .... 95 E1
Three Shires Oak Rd B67 ..... 64 F2
Three Spires Ave CV6 .... 113 A6
Three Spires Ind Est CV6 ..... 96 A5
Three Spires Sch CV5 .... 112 D6
Three Spires Sh Ctr
  7 WS13 .... 9 B7
Three Tuns La WV10 .... 11 D1
Three Tuns Par WV10 .... 11 C2
Threshers Dr WV12 .... 27 D6
Threshers Way WV12 .... 27 D6
Throckmorton Rd B98 .... 159 A8
Throne Cl B65 .... 63 D5
Throne Cres B65 .... 63 D4
Throne Rd B65 .... 63 D5
Thrush Rd B68 .... 63 F2
Thrushel Wlk WV11 .... 26 C5
Thruxton Cl Birmingham
  B14 .... 104 F3
  Redditch B98 .... 154 E3
Thurcroft Cl B8 .... 67 F4
Thuree Rd B67 .... 64 E2
Thurlby Ct WV1 .... 25 A3
Thurlestone Rd
  Birmingham B31 .... 122 E7
  Coventry CV6 .... 112 F8
Thurloe Cres B45 .... 101 E1
Thurlston Ave B69 .... 88 F4
Thurlstone Dr WV4 .... 38 F4
Thurlstone Rd WS3 .... 14 B3
Thurne B77 .... 35 F8
Thursfield Rd
  Royal Leamington Spa
  CV32 .... 157 B3
  Tipton DY4 .... 52 A6
  West Bromwich B71 .... 53 E7
Thurso B77 .... 21 E5
Thurston Ave B69 .... 63 F6
Thynne St B70 .... 53 E2
Tibbats Cl B32 .... 84 C3
Tibberton Cl Halesowen
  B63 .... 83 C4
  Solihull B91 .... 127 A8
  Wolverhampton WV3 .... 38 D7
Tibberton Ct B60 .... 150 E7
Tibbets La B17 .... 85 B4
Tibbington Rd DY4 .... 51 E7
Tibbington Terr DY4 .... 51 F7
Tibbits Ct **5** CV34 .... 160 E6
Tibbits Ho **1** WS2 .... 28 D3
Tiber Cl CV5 .... 111 F4
Tiberius Cl B46 .... 59 F1
Tibland Rd B27 .... 88 D2
Tidbury Cl B97 .... 158 C6
Tidbury Green Jun &
  Inf Sch B90 .... 125 E4
Tiddington Cl B36 .... 58 B1
Tideswell Cl CV3 .... 115 A1
Tideswell Rd B42 .... 55 C7
Tidmarsh Cl CV7 .... 130 A6
Tidmarsh Rd CV35 .... 156 A7
Tidworth Croft **2** B14 ...... 105 A3
Tierney Dr DY4 .... 52 C6
Tiffany La WV9 .... 10 F2
Tiffield Rd B25 .... 88 C5
Tigley Ave B32 .... 84 D1
Tilbury CI WV3 .... 38 A8
Tilbury Gr B13 .... 86 D1
Tildasley St B70 .... 53 B5
Tildesley Dr WV12 .... 27 B5
Tile Cross Rd B33 .... 69 E2
Tile Cross Trad Est B33 .... 69 F1
Tile Gr B37 .... 70 A5
Tile Hill Coll of FE CV4 ...... 111 F1
Tile Hill La
  Coventry,
  Allesley CV4, CV5 .... 112 D2
  Coventry, Tile Hill CV4 ... 112 B1
Tile Hill Sta CV4 .... 131 D8
Tile Hill Wood Sch CV4 ..... 111 D2
Tile Hurst Dr CV4 .... 111 D1
Tiled House La DY5 .... 61 B6
Tilehouse B97 .... 153 D2
Tilehouse Green La B93 ..... 127 F6
Tilehouse La B90 .... 125 E6
Tilesford Rd B90 .... 127 A6
Tilewood Ave CV5 .... 111 F4
Tilia Rd B77 .... 22 B5
Tilley St WS10 .... 41 E6
Tillington Cl B98 .... 154 E3
Tillyard Croft B29 .... 85 C1
Tilshead Cl B14 .... 104 E3
Tilsley Gr B23 .... 56 B5
Tilston Dr DY5 .... 61 D1
Tilton Rd Birmingham B9 ..... 67 C1
  Hinckley LE10 .... 75 E6
Timber Mill Ct B17 .... 85 B6
Timberdine Cl B63 .... 82 D6
Timberhonger La B61 .... 136 B2
Timberlake Cl B90 .... 127 B6
Timberley Jun & Inf Sch
  B34 .... 69 D6
Timberley La B34 .... 69 C6
Timbers Way
  Birmingham B11 .... 87 A6
  Sutton Coldfield B24 .... 57 F4
Timbertree Cres B64 .... 82 E7
Timbertree Prim Sch B64 ... 82 E7
Timbertree Rd B64 .... 82 F7
Times Square Ave DY5 .... 61 F2

Timmins Cl B91 .... 107 E6
Timmis Cl WV14 .... 40 B3
Timmis Rd DY9 .... 81 C6
Timothy Gr CV4 .... 112 B1
Timothy Rd B69 .... 63 D7
Tinacre Hill WV6 .... 23 F2
Tinchbourne St **1** DY1 ..... 51 C1
Tindal Jun & Inf Sch B12 ... 86 F5
Tindal St B12 .... 86 F5
Tink-A-Tank CV34 .... 160 E7
Tinkers Farm Gr B31 .... 102 E3
Tinkers Farm Rd B31 .... 102 E3
Tinkers Green Rd B77 .... 35 F6
Tinkers La Earlswood B94 .. 142 E7
  Lapworth B94 .... 143 E1
Tinmeadow Cres B45 .... 122 C7
Tinsley St B70 .... 52 E5
Tintagel Cl Coventry CV3 ... 134 D5
  Perton WV6 .... 23 F3
Tintagel Dr DY1 .... 50 E2
Tintagel Gr CV8 .... 148 B4
Tintagel Way CV11 .... 74 A5
Tintern Cl Bromsgrove
  B61 .... 136 E1
  Sutton Coldfield B74 .... 45 A7
Tintern Cres WS3 .... 13 F2
Tintern Ct WV6 .... 23 E4
Tintern Ho B32 .... 84 F5
Tintern Rd B20 .... 55 E1
Tintern Villas **4** B12 .... 87 B5
Tintern Way Bedworth
  CV12 .... 78 C3
  Walsall WS3 .... 13 F2
Tipper Trad Est DY9 .... 82 A5
Tipperary Cl B36 .... 68 E8
Tippett Cl CV11 .... 79 A7
Tipping's Hill B97 .... 158 C5
Tipps Stone Cl DY4 .... 51 E4
Tipton Coll Willingsworth
  Campus DY4 .... 41 B2
Tipton Green Jun Sch
  DY4 .... 51 F4
Tipton Owen Street
  Sta DY4 .... 51 F6
Tipton Rd
  Dudley, Tipton Green DY1 ... 51 E3
  Dudley, Woodsetton DY3 ... 50 F7
  Tipton B69 .... 52 C2
Tipton St DY3 .... 50 E7
Tipton Trad Est DY4 .... 51 D6
Tirley Rd B33 .... 69 A4
Tisdale Rise CV8 .... 148 B6
Titan Way WS14 .... 9 F8
Titania Cl B45 .... 102 A3
Titchfield Cl WV10 .... 11 E4
Titford Cl B69 .... 63 F4
Titford La B65 .... 63 E4
Titford Rd B69 .... 63 F4
Tithe Barn La B94 .... 142 C6
Tithe Croft WV10 .... 25 F3
Tithe Rd WV11 .... 26 D6
Titterstone Rd B31 .... 123 A8
Tiverton Cl DY6 .... 61 A3
Tiverton Dr CV11 .... 73 F5
Tiverton Gr Coventry CV2 .. 114 D5
  Smethwick B66 .... 64 F6
Tiverton Jun & Inf Sch
  B29 .... 85 F2
Tiverton Rd Birmingham
  B29 .... 85 F2
  Coventry CV2 .... 114 D5
  Smethwick B66 .... 65 B5
Tiverton Sch CV2 .... 112 D5
Tiveycourt Rd CV6 .... 96 A3
Tividale Comp Sch B69 ...... 52 C1
Tividale Ho B69 .... 63 E8
Tividale Prim Sch B69 .... 52 B2
Tividale Rd B69 .... 52 A2
Tividale St DY4 .... 52 A4
Tivoli The B26 .... 88 D6
Tixall Rd B28 .... 105 E5
Tobruk Wlk Brierley Hill
  DY5 .... 61 D3
  Willenhall WV13 .... 40 E8
Tocil Croft CV4 .... 132 D4
Toler Rd CV11 .... 73 B5
Toll End Rd DY4 .... 52 C7
Toll House Rd B45 .... 122 C7
Tollard Cl CV2 .... 114 F5
Tolley Rd DY11 .... 116 B1
Tollgate Cl B31 .... 122 F8
Tollgate Dr B20 .... 66 B7
Tollgate Prec B67 .... 64 F6
Tollhouse Rd B60 .... 150 E6
Tollhouse Way B66 .... 64 F6
Tolman Dr B77 .... 21 D3
Tolson Ave B78 .... 35 B8
Tolson Cl B77 .... 35 C5
Tolworth Gdns WV2 .... 39 E7
Tolworth Hall Rd B24 .... 57 B3
Tom Ellis Ct CV7 .... 96 A8
Tom Henderson Cl CV3 ..... 134 F7
Tom Hill B94 .... 142 B3
Tom Ward Cl CV34 .... 134 E7
Tomey Rd B11 .... 87 D5
Tomkinson Dr DY11 .... 116 B4
Tomkinson Rd CV10 .... 72 F4
Tomlan Rd B31 .... 123 C7
Tomlinson Rd B36 .... 58 D1
Tompstone Rd B71 .... 53 F8
Toms Town La B80 .... 159 E3
Tomson Ave CV6 .... 113 B4
Tonadine Cl WV11 .... 13 A1
Tonbridge Rd
  Birmingham B24 .... 57 A1
  Coventry CV3 .... 134 A6
Tong Ct **9** WV3 .... 25 C4
Tong St WS1 .... 29 A1

Top Croft Rd B23 .... 56 F7
Top Field Wlk B14 .... 104 D2
Top Rd Barnacle CV7 .... 97 B7
  Wildmoor B61 .... 121 A4
Topcliffe Jun & Inf Sch
  B35 .... 58 A3
Topfield Ho B14 .... 104 E1
Topland Gr B31 .... 102 C2
Topp's Dr CV12 .... 77 E1
Topp's Heath CV12 .... 77 E1
Topsham Croft B14 .... 104 D5
Topsham Rd B67 .... 64 E6
Tor Way WS3 .... 14 F3
Torbay B77 .... 21 F5
Torbay Rd CV5 .... 112 C4
Torc Ave B77 .... 21 E4
Torcastle Cl CV6 .... 113 F7
Torcross Ave CV2 .... 114 C6
Torfield WV8 .... 10 E2
Toronto Gdns B32 .... 84 E6
Torpoint Cl CV2 .... 114 C7
Torquoise Gr WS11 .... 2 C3
Torre Ave B31 .... 102 E2
Torrey Gr B8 .... 68 C4
Torridge B77 .... 36 A5
Torridge Dr WV11 .... 26 C5
Torridon Croft B13 .... 86 D3
Torridon Rd WV12 .... 13 B1
Torrington Ave CV4 .... 131 E8
Torrs Cl B97 .... 153 C2
Torside B77 .... 36 B7
Torvale Rd WV6 .... 24 A2
Torwood Cl CV4 .... 131 F6
Totnes Cl CV2 .... 114 C7
Totnes Gr **2** B29 .... 85 F2
Totnes Rd B67 .... 64 F6
Tottenham Cres B44 .... 45 B2
Touchwood Hall Cl B91 .... 107 C4
Towbury Cl B98 .... 158 F5
Towcester Croft B36 .... 68 D8
Tower Croft B37 .... 70 B4
Tower Hill B42 .... 55 A6
Tower Rd Bedworth CV12 ... 78 B2
  Birmingham B6 .... 66 F7
  Birmingham B6 .... 67 A7
  Sutton Coldfield B75 .... 32 B3
  Tipton B69 .... 63 C7
Tower Rise B69 .... 63 C7
Tower St Birmingham B19 . 164 B5
  Coventry CV1 .... 165 B3
  Dudley DY1 .... 51 C1
  5 Royal Leamington Spa
  CV31 .... 162 A7
  Sedgley DY3 .... 39 D1
  Walsall WS1 .... 28 E2
  Wolverhampton WV1 .... 163 C3
Tower View Cres CV10 .... 72 B3
Tower View Rd WS6 .... 13 F8
Towers Cl Kenilworth CV8 . 147 F2
  Kidderminster DY10 .... 117 B5
Town Feilds Cl CV5 .... 112 B7
Town Jun Sch B72 .... 46 C4
Townend St WS2 .... 28 E2
Townesend Cl CV34 .... 155 F1
Townfields WS13 .... 9 A7
Townfold WS3 .... 15 A4
Townley Gdns B6 .... 55 E1
Townsend Ave
  Bromsgrove B61 .... 137 B4
  Sedgley DY3 .... 50 D8
Townsend Croft CV3 .... 133 C7
Townsend Dr Nuneaton
  CV11 .... 73 F3
  Sutton Coldfield B76 .... 57 F7
Townsend Pl DY6 .... 60 D6
Townsend Rd CV3 .... 133 C8
Townsend Way **5** B1 .... 66 B3
Townsends Cl CV11 .... 75 A1
Townshend Gr B37 .... 69 F4
Townson Rd WV11 .... 27 A8
Townwell Fold WV1 .... 163 B3
Towpath Cl B9 .... 67 B2
Towyn Rd B13 .... 87 D2
Toys La B63 .... 82 C5
Tozer St DY4 .... 51 F7
Traceys Mdw B45 .... 122 A7
Tractor Spares Ind Est
  WV13 .... 26 D2
Trafalgar Cl WS12 .... 2 E4
Trafalgar Ct B69 .... 52 C1
Trafalgar Gr B25 .... 88 A6
Trafalgar Ho Birmingham
  B11 .... 87 B8
  3 Coventry CV1 .... 113 B2
Trafalgar Rd
  Birmingham, Erdington B24 ... 56 F3
  Birmingham,
  Handsworth B21 .... 65 E8
  Birmingham, Moseley B13 ... 86 F4
  Smethwick B66 .... 65 C4
  Tipton B69 .... 52 B1
Trafford Dr CV10 .... 72 C6
Trafford Lodge **4** CV31 ... 162 B7
Trafford Pk The B98 .... 153 F3
Trafford Rd LE10 .... 71 F2
Trajan Hill B46 .... 59 F1
Tram St DY10 .... 116 E5
Tram Way B66 .... 64 C7
Tramway Cl Bilston WV14 ... 41 A7
  Darlaston WS10 .... 41 E7
Tranter Ave B48 .... 139 A5
Tranter Cres WS11 .... 4 F3
Tranter Rd B8 .... 68 A5
Tranwell Cl WV9 .... 10 F2
Traquain Dr DY1 .... 51 A3
Travellers Cl WS7 .... 7 A5
Travellers Way B37 .... 70 D3

Treaford La B8 .... 68 C4
Treasure Cl B77 .... 21 E4
Treddles La B70 .... 53 D3
Tredington Cl
  Birmingham B29 .... 103 A7
  Redditch B98 .... 159 B7
Tredington Rd CV5 .... 111 F4
Tree Acre Gr B63 .... 82 C4
Treedale Cl CV4 .... 131 D8
Treeford Cl B91 .... 106 F1
Trees Rd WS1 .... 42 F6
Treeton Croft B33 .... 69 A2
Treetops Dr WV12 .... 27 E4
Trefoil B77 .... 22 B5
Trefoil Cl B29 .... 103 A7
Treforest Rd CV3 .... 134 C8
Tregarron Rd B63 .... 82 C5
Tregea Rise B43 .... 54 C7
Tregony Rise WS14 .... 9 D6
Tregorrick Rd CV7 .... 96 A8
Tregullan Rd CV7 .... 96 B8
Trehern Cl B93 .... 128 A5
Treherne Rd CV6 .... 113 B8
Trehernes Dr DY9 .... 81 B1
Trejon Rd B64 .... 82 E8
Trelawney Rd CV7 .... 96 A7
Tremaine Gdns WV10 .... 25 E4
Tremont Ho WV10 .... 25 E3
Tremont St WV10 .... 25 E3
Trenance Cl WS14 .... 9 D7
Trenance Rd CV7 .... 96 A8
Trenchard Cl B75 .... 46 F5
Treneere Rd CV7 .... 96 B8
Trensale Ave CV6 .... 112 F4
Trent Cl Burntwood WS7 ...... 7 D6
  Perton WV6 .... 23 E4
  Stourbridge DY8 .... 81 A4
Trent Cres B47 .... 124 E2
Trent Dr B36 .... 69 F8
Trent Ho Cannock WS12 ..... 2 C5
  9 Dudley DY5 .... 50 E3
Trent Pl WS3 .... 28 D8
Trent Rd Bulkington
  CV12 .... 79 A2
  Cannock WS11 .... 1 E5
  Hinckley LE10 .... 75 A8
  Nuneaton CV11 .... 73 D5
  Walsall WS3 .... 15 A1
Trent St B73 .... 45 B5
Trent Tower **7** B7 .... 67 A4
Trent Valley Cotts WS13 ...... 3 F1
Trent Valley Rd WS13 .... 9 D8
Trentham Ave WV12 .... 27 B5
Trentham Cl Cannock
  WS11 .... 2 B1
  Nuneaton CV11 .... 78 F8
Trentham Gdns CV8 .... 148 C5
Trentham Gr B26 .... 88 E5
Trentham Rd CV1 .... 113 F4
Trentham Rise WV2 .... 39 F7
Tresco Cl B45 .... 101 C1
Trescott Prim Sch B31 ..... 102 D3
Trescott Rd B31 .... 102 D4
Tresham Rd Birmingham
  B44 .... 44 F1
  Kingswinford DY6 .... 60 D8
Tresillian Rd CV7 .... 96 B8
Trevanie Ave B32 .... 84 C6
Trevelyan Ho **1** B37 .... 70 C1
Treville Cl B98 .... 154 E3
Treviscoe Cl CV7 .... 96 A7
Trevithick Cl WS7 .... 7 C8
Trevor Ave WS6 .... 5 A3
Trevor Cl CV4 .... 131 D8
Trevor Rd Hinckley LE10 ..... 71 F1
  Walsall WS3 .... 14 F4
Trevor St B7 .... 67 C6
Trevor St W B7 .... 67 C6
Trevorne Cl B12 .... 86 F6
Trevose Ave CV7 .... 96 B8
Trevose Cl WS3 .... 13 F3
Trevose Retreat B12 .... 86 F5
Trewint Cl CV7 .... 96 A8
Trewman Cl B76 .... 57 F8
Treyamon Rd WS5 .... 43 D7
Treynham Cl WV1 .... 26 C1
Triangle The Birmingham
  B18 .... 65 F6
  Coventry CV5 .... 112 B4
Trident Bsns Pk CV11 .... 73 D3
Trident Cl
  Sutton Coldfield,
  Walmley B76 .... 57 F7
  Sutton Coldfield,
  Wylde Green B23 .... 57 A7
Trident Ct B20 .... 55 A3
Trident Dr Oldbury B68 .... 64 B5
  Wednesbury WS10 .... 41 D3
Trident Ho B35 .... 58 B3
Trigo Croft B36 .... 68 E8
Trimpley Cl B93 .... 127 E3
Trimpley Dr WV11 .... 116 A7
Trimpley Gdns WV4 .... 38 E3
Trimpley Rd B32 .... 84 B1
Trinder Rd B67 .... 64 D2
Trindle Rd DY2 .... 51 D1
Tring Ct WV6 .... 24 F4
Trinity CE Prim Sch
  WV10 .... 25 H4
Trinity Churchyard CV1 .... 165 B3
Trinity Cl **1** Birmingham
  B19 .... 66 D8
  Cannock WS11 .... 4 E8
  Shenstone WS14 .... 17 F6
  Solihull B92 .... 89 B1
  Stourbridge DY8 .... 60 D2

Trinity Ct Birmingham B6 ... 55 D1
  3 Blackheath B64 .... 62 E1
  Bromsgrove B60 .... 151 B7
  1 Kidderminster DY10 . 116 F6
  Willenhall WV13 .... 26 E1
  Wolverhampton WV3 .... 25 A2
Trinity Field DY10 .... 116 F6
Trinity Gr WV2 .... 42 A3
Trinity Grange DY10 .... 116 F7
Trinity Hill B72 .... 46 C5
Trinity Ho B70 .... 53 E1
Trinity La Coventry CV1 .... 165 B3
  Hinckley LE10 .... 71 C1
Trinity RC Sch The
  Royal Leamington Spa
  CV32 .... 156 D2
  Warwick CV34 .... 161 C6
Trinity Rd Bilston WV14 ...... 40 F5
  Birmingham B6 .... 55 E1
  Dudley DY1 .... 51 C1
  Stourbridge DY8 .... 81 A8
  Sutton Coldfield B75 .... 32 C1
  Willenhall WV12 .... 27 D7
  Wood End B78 .... 36 B3
Trinity Rd N B70 .... 53 D2
Trinity Rd S B70 .... 53 E1
Trinity St Blackheath B64 ... 62 E1
  Brierley Hill DY5 .... 61 D3
  Coventry CV1 .... 165 B3
  Oldbury B69 .... 64 A6
  Royal Leamington Spa
  CV32 .... 156 F1
  Smethwick B67 .... 65 A6
  West Bromwich B70 .... 53 D2
Trinity Terr **3** B11 .... 87 A8
Trinity Vicarage Rd LE10 ... 75 C8
Trinity Way B70 .... 53 D2
Trinity Way Sta B70 .... 53 D1
Trinity Wlk CV11 .... 73 E3
Trippleton Ave B32 .... 102 B8
Tristram Ave B31 .... 103 B1
Triton Cl WS6 .... 4 F1
Trittiford Rd B13 .... 105 C6
Triumph B77 .... 21 E3
Triumph Cl CV2 .... 114 E3
Triumph Wlk B36 .... 59 A1
Trojan B77 .... 21 E3
Trojan Bsns Ctr CV34 .... 161 E4
Tromans Ind Est DY2 .... 62 D3
Troon B77 .... 22 C4
Troon Cl Sutton Coldfield
  B75 .... 46 D8
  Walsall WS3 .... 14 A3
Troon Ct WV6 .... 23 D5
Troon Pl DY8 .... 60 C3
Trossachs Rd CV5 .... 111 F3
Trotter's La B71 .... 53 A7
Troughton Cres CV6 .... 113 A5
Trouse La WS10 .... 41 F3
Troutbeck Ave CV32 .... 156 C2
Troutbeck Dr DY5 .... 81 B8
Troutbeck Rd CV5 .... 111 F4
Troy Gr B14 .... 104 D4
Troy Ind Est B96 .... 159 A3
Troyes Cl CV3 .... 133 E7
Truda St **2** WS1 .... 42 D7
Trueman Ct CV34 .... 160 E8
Truemans Heath La B47 ... 125 C7
Truggist La CV7 .... 130 E8
Truro Cl Blackheath B65 ..... 63 E4
  Hinckley LE10 .... 71 E4
  Nuneaton CV11 .... 73 F5
  Wolverhampton WV13 .... 3 B3
Truro Dr DY11 .... 116 A5
Truro Pl WS12 .... 5 C8
Truro Rd WS5 .... 43 D7
Truro Tower **6** B16 .... 66 A2
Truro Wlk B37 .... 70 B2
Trustin Cres B92 .... 107 E8
Tryan St B7 .... 67 C6
Tryon Pl WV14 .... 40 E6
Trysull Ave B26 .... 89 C4
Trysull Gdns WV3 .... 38 D7
Trysull Holloway WV5 .... 37 C3
Trysull Rd
  Wolverhampton WV3 .... 38 E7
  Wombourne WV5 .... 37 E1
Trysull Way DY2 .... 62 C4
Tudbury Rd B31 .... 102 E4
Tudman Cl B76 .... 58 A7
Tudor Ave CV5 .... 111 F4
Tudor Cl
  Balsall Common CV7 .... 130 A6
  Birmingham,
  Highter's Heath B14 .... 105 A2
  Birmingham,
  King's Heath B13 .... 104 F6
  Birmingham, Sparkbrook
  B10 .... 87 C8
  Burntwood WS7 .... 7 B6
  Cheslyn Hay WS6 .... 4 E3
  Lichfield WS14 .... 9 F6
Tudor Cres Tamworth B77 ... 21 F4
  Wolverhampton WV2 .... 39 B6
Tudor Croft B37 .... 69 F1
Tudor Ct Coventry CV7 .... 95 E7
  Essington WV11 .... 12 F4
  Sutton Coldfield B74 .... 32 A2
  Tipton DY4 .... 52 A4
  Warwick CV34 .... 160 D5
Tudor Eaves **2** B17 .... 85 C5
Tudor Gdns B23 .... 80 E5
Tudor Gr B74 .... 45 A8
Tudor Hill B73 .... 46 B6
Tudor Ho DY2 .... 61 F6
Tudor Park Ct B74 .... 31 E4
Tudor Pl DY3 .... 50 E6

Tudor Rd Bilston WV14 .... 41 B4
Birmingham B13 .... 86 F3
Blackheath B65 .... 63 C5
Burntwood WS7 .... 7 C6
Cannock WS12 .... 1 F8
Dudley DY3 .... 50 E6
Hinckley LE10 .... 71 C3
Nuneaton CV10 .... 72 C6
Oldbury B68 .... 64 C4
Sutton Coldfield B73 .... 46 B5
Wolverhampton WV10 .... 26 A4
Tudor Row **3** WS13 .... 9 B7
Tudor St Birmingham B18 .... 65 E4
Tipton DY4 .... 52 A4
Tudor Terr Birmingham B17 .... 85 C6
Dudley DY2 .... 51 E1
Tudor Vale DY3 .... 50 E6
Tudor Way WS6 .... 4 D1
Tufnell Gr B8 .... 68 B7
Tugford Rd B29 .... 103 C7
Tuisi Ctr B19 .... 164 A4
Tulip Tree Ave CV8 .... 148 B5
Tulip Tree Ct CV8 .... 148 B4
Tulip Wlk B37 .... 90 C8
Tulliver Cl CV12 .... 78 B3
Tulliver Rd CV10 .... 73 C1
Tulliver St CV6 .... 113 B5
Tulyar Cl B36 .... 68 C8
Tunnel Dr B98 .... 153 E2
Tunnel La Birmingham
B30 .... 104 B4
Birmingham B14 .... 104 C4
Tunnel Rd B70 .... 53 A7
Tunnel St WV14 .... 51 C8
Tunstall Rd DY6 .... 61 A5
Turchill Dr B76 .... 58 B8
Turf Cotts WV4 .... 38 F2
Turf Pitts La B75 .... 32 F4
Turfpits La B23 .... 56 D6
Turfton Gr B24 .... 57 D3
Turlands Cl CV2 .... 115 A7
Turley St DY1 .... 51 A6
Turls Hill Rd WV14 .... 50 F8
Turls St DY3 .... 50 E8
Turnberry B77 .... 22 C5
Turnberry Dr CV11 .... 79 C8
Turnberry Gr WV6 .... 23 D5
Turnberry Rd
Birmingham B42 .... 55 B8
Walsall WS3 .... 14 A4
Turner Ave WV14 .... 39 F2
Turner Cl Bedworth CV12 .... 78 A4
Cannock WS11 .... 2 D2
Warwick CV34 .... 160 B4
Turner Dr Brierley Hill DY5 .... 81 D7
Hinckley LE10 .... 71 A3
Turner Gr WV6 .... 24 A4
Turner Rd CV5 .... 112 D3
Turner St Birmingham B11 .... 87 A6
Dudley, Gornalwood DY3 .... 50 D3
2 Dudley, Old Dock DY2 .... 62 B8
Tipton DY4 .... 51 F7
West Bromwich B70 .... 53 A4
Turner's Gr DY3 .... 50 C4
Turner's Hill B65 .... 63 B6
Turner's Hill Rd DY3 .... 50 C4
Turner's La DY5 .... 61 D1
Turners Croft B71 .... 54 A8
Turney Rd DY8 .... 80 F6
Turnham Gn WV6 .... 23 E3
Turnhouse Rd B35 .... 58 B4
Turnley Rd B34 .... 69 C6
Turnpike Cl B11 .... 87 A6
Turnpike Dr B46 .... 59 C2
Turnstone Dr WV10 .... 12 B7
Turnstone Rd DY10 .... 117 A1
Turpin Ct CV31 .... 161 F6
Turton Cl WS3 .... 14 A4
Turton Rd Tipton DY4 .... 40 F1
West Bromwich B70 .... 53 B2
Turton St DY10 .... 117 A8
Turton Way CV8 .... 148 C4
Turtons Croft WV14 .... 40 B3
Turves Gn B31 .... 103 A1
Turves Green Boys' Sec
Sch B31 .... 123 A8
Turves Green Girls Sch
B31 .... 103 A1
Turves Green Prim Sch
B31 .... 103 A1
Turville Rd B20 .... 55 C1
Tustin St B27 .... 106 C8
Tutbury B77 .... 35 C7
Tutbury Ave Coventry CV4 .. 132 E6
Perton WV6 .... 24 A3
Tutbury Cl WS11 .... 2 C3
Tutehill B77 .... 36 B7
Tutnall Cl B60 .... 137 F1
Tutnall La Blackwell B60 .... 138 A1
Tutnall B60 .... 137 F1
Tuttle Hill CV10 .... 72 D6
Tuttle Hill Ind Est CV10 ...... 72 E7
Tuxford Cl WV10 .... 25 E4
Twatling Rd B45 .... 122 A2
Tweed Tower B20 .... 55 D2
Tweeds Well B32 .... 102 B7
Tweedside Cl LE10 .... 71 F3
Twickenham Ct DY8 .... 80 C7
Twickenham Prim Sch
B44 .... 45 C1
Twickenham Rd B44 .... 45 C1
Twiners Rd B98 .... 153 F1
Two Gates B63 .... 82 C5
Two Gates Cty Prim Sch
B77 .... 21 C1
Two Gates La B63 .... 82 C5
Two Locks DY5 .... 62 A4
Two Woods Ind Est DY5 ...... 61 E1

Two Woods La DY5 .... 61 E1
Two Woods Trad Est DY5 ...... 61 F1
Twycross B36 .... 68 D7
Twycross Rd LE10 .... 75 F6
Twycross Wlk CV34 .... 155 D1
Twydale Ave B69 .... 52 C2
Twyford Cl WS9 .... 30 B5
Twyford Gr WV11 .... 26 F7
Twyford Rd B8 .... 68 C5
Twyning Rd
Birmingham,
Edgbaston B16 .... 65 D3
Birmingham,
Stirchley B30 .... 104 B7
Tybalt Cl Coventry CV3 .... 134 C5
Royal Leamington Spa
CV34 .... 161 D4
Tyber Dr B20 .... 55 B3
Tyberry Cl B90 .... 106 A1
Tyburn Rd Birmingham
B24 .... 57 C2
Wolverhampton WV1 .... 26 C2
Tyburn Sq B24 .... 57 D3
Tyburn Trad Est B24 .... 57 D2
Tye Gdns DY9 .... 81 B1
Tyebeams B34 .... 69 C5
Tyler Ct B24 .... 56 F3
Tyler Gdns WV13 .... 27 B1
Tyler Gr B43 .... 44 A1
Tyler Rd WV13 .... 27 B1
Tylers Cl B38 .... 104 B1
Tylers Gr B90 .... 126 F6
Tylney Cl Birmingham B5 .... 86 D7
Coventry CV3 .... 115 B2
Tyndale Cres B43 .... 44 C3
Tyndall Wlk B32 .... 84 A2
Tyne Cl Birmingham B37 .... 70 C4
Brownhills WS8 .... 6 C2
Tyne Ct B73 .... 46 B5
Tyne Gr B25 .... 88 D8
Tyne Pl DY5 .... 61 F2
Tynedale Cres WV4 .... 39 E3
Tynedale Rd B11 .... 87 F3
Tynemouth Cl CV2 .... 96 D5
Tynes The B60 .... 150 E7
Tyning Cl WV9 .... 11 A2
Tyninghame Ave WV6 ...... 24 D6
Tynings La WS9 .... 30 A5
Tynsall Ave B97 .... 152 F2
Tynward Cl CV3 .... 133 B5
Tyrley Cl WV6 .... 24 B2
Tyrol Cl DY8 .... 80 D6
Tyseley Hill Rd B11 .... 88 A4
Tyseley Ind Est B11 .... 87 E5
Tyseley La B11 .... 88 A4
Tyseley Sta B11 .... 88 A5
Tysoe Cl Redditch B98 ...... 154 D2
Tanworth-in-A B94 .... 143 C6
Tysoe Croft CV3 .... 134 F8
Tysoe Dr B76 .... 46 F4
Tysoe Rd B44 .... 55 F7
Tythe Barn Cl B60 .... 150 D6
Tythebarn Dr DY6 .... 60 A7
Tythebarn La B90 .... 125 F6
Tyzack Cl DY5 .... 61 C2

Udall Rd WV14 .... 40 D3
Uffculme Rd B30 .... 104 D8
Uffculme Specl Sch B13 .... 86 E1
Uffmoor Est B63 .... 82 E2
Uffmoor La B62 .... 100 D7
Ufton Cl B90 .... 106 E3
Ufton Cres B90 .... 106 D3
Ufton Croft CV5 .... 112 A3
Ullapool Cl B97 .... 158 D5
Ullenhall Rd Knowle B93 .. 128 A6
Sutton Coldfield B76 .... 57 F8
Ullenwood B21 .... 65 D7
Ulleries Rd B92 .... 89 A2
Ullrik Gn B24 .... 56 F2
Ullswater B77 .... 36 B7
Ullswater Ave Nuneaton
CV11 .... 73 F6
Royal Leamington Spa
CV32 .... 156 C2
Ullswater Cl B32 .... 84 F2
Ullswater Gdns DY6 ...... 60 D6
Ullswater Ho **4** B69 .... 63 D5
Ullswater Pl WS11 .... 1 E1
Ullswater Rd Bedworth
CV12 .... 78 A2
Coventry CV3 .... 114 C1
Willenhall WV12 .... 13 B1
Ullswater Rise DY5 .... 61 E5
Ulster Cl WS11 .... 2 A3
Ulster Dr DY6 .... 60 E4
Ulverley Cres B92 .... 106 E8
Ulverley Green Rd B92 ...... 88 F1
Ulverley Jun & Inf Sch
B92 .... 89 B1
Ulverscroft Rd CV3 .... 133 D7
Ulwine Dr B31 .... 103 A4
Umberslade Rd
Birmingham B29 .... 104 A8
Earlswood B94 .... 142 C7
Tanworth-in-A B94 .... 142 C3
Underhill Cl Coventry CV3 .. 133 D3
Redditch B98 .... 158 F6
Underhill Jun & Inf Sch
WV10 .... 12 B1
Underhill La WV10 .... 12 A2
Underhill Rd Birmingham
B8 .... 67 F3
Tipton DY4 .... 52 C6
Underhill St B69 .... 64 A5
Underhill Wlk B69 .... 64 A5
Underley Cl DY6 .... 60 B7
Underpass The B40 .... 90 E4

Underwood Cl
Birmingham, Edgbaston B15 .. 85 D4
Birmingham, Stockland B23 ... 56 C4
Redditch B97 .... 158 A7
Underwood Rd B20 .... 54 E5
Underwood Specl Sch
B23 .... 57 A6
Unett Ct **9** B66 .... 65 C5
Unett St Birmingham B19 .... 66 C5
Smethwick B66 .... 65 C4
Unett Wlk B19 .... 66 C5
Unicorn Ave CV5 .... 111 E4
Unicorn Hill B97 .... 153 E4
Unicorn La CV5 .... 111 F4
Union Bldgs CV1 .... 165 B2
Union Ctr WS10 .... 41 F2
Union Dr B73 .... 45 F2
Union La WV5 .... 37 D2
Union Mill St WV1 .... 163 D3
Union Pas B2 .... 164 C2
Union Pl CV6 .... 95 F4
Union Rd Birmingham B6 .... 67 B8
Oldbury B69 .... 52 E2
Royal Leamington Spa
CV32 .... 156 E1
Solihull, Lode Heath B91 .... 107 C4
Solihull, Shirley B90 .... 106 C2
West Bromwich B70 .... 52 F2
Union Row B71 .... 65 F7
Union St Bilston WV14 .... 40 C5
Birmingham B2 .... 164 C2
Blackheath B65 .... 63 C1
Burntwood WS7 .... 6 E5
Cannock WS11 .... 4 E6
6 Dudley DY1 .... 51 C1
Kidderminster DY10 .... 116 E7
Redditch B98 .... 153 F3
Stourbridge, Lye DY9 .... 81 E5
Stourbridge,
Stambermill DY8 .... 81 A4
Tipton, Princes End DY1 .... 51 F8
Tipton, Tipton Green DY4 .... 51 F5
Walsall WS1 .... 42 F1
Wednesbury WS10 .... 41 F2
West Bromwich B70 .... 64 D8
Willenhall WV13 .... 27 A2
Wolverhampton WV1 .... 163 C3
Unisant Trad Est B64 .... 62 F2
Unity Ho CV1 .... 165 C4
Unity Pl **7** Birmingham B29 .. 85 F2
Oldbury B69 .... 64 A8
Univ of Aston B5 .... 164 D4
Univ of Birmingham B15 .... 85 F4
Univ of Birmingham The
(Halls of Residence) B15 . 66 C1
Univ of Central England
Birmingham, Edgbaston B15... 86 A8
Birmingham,
Handsworth B42 .... 55 D2
Univ of Warwick CV5 .... 132 C4
Univ of Warwick Science
Pk
CV4 .... 132 B6
Univ of Warwick
(Westwood) CV4 .... 132 B6
Univ of Wolverhampton
WV1 .... 163 B3
Univ of Wolverhampton
(Annexe) WV1 .... 163 C3
Univ of Wolverhampton
Compton Park Campus
WV3 .... 24 E2
Univ of Wolverhampton
(Dudley Campus) DY1 .... 51 B2
Univ of Wolverhampton
Walsall Campus WS1 .... 43 A7
University Sta B15 .... 85 E4
Unketts Rd B67 .... 64 E5
Unwin Cres DY8 .... 80 E5
Upavon Cl B35 .... 58 A4
Upfield Cotts WS7 .... 7 E1
Upland Gr B61 .... 137 A4
Upland Rd Birmingham B29 .. 86 B3
Bromsgrove B61 .... 137 B4
Uplands Coventry CV2 ...... 114 A5
Halesowen B63 .... 82 A5
Uplands Ave Blackheath
B65 .... 63 D3
Willenhall WV13 .... 26 D1
Wolverhampton WV3 .... 38 D8
Uplands Cl DY2 .... 62 E7
Uplands Dr Sedgley DY3 .... 50 D8
Wolverhampton WV3 .... 38 E8
Wombourne WV5 .... 49 A6
Uplands Gr WV13 .... 26 C1
Uplands Inf Sch B67 .... 64 F3
Uplands Jun Sch B67 .... 64 F3
Uplands Rd Birmingham
B21 .... 54 D2
Dudley DY2 .... 62 F7
Wolverhampton WV13 .... 26 C1
Uplands The B67 .... 64 F4
Upleadon Cl B97 .... 158 A6
Upper Abbey St CV11 .... 73 B5
Upper Ashley St B62 .... 63 C1
Upper Balsall Heath Rd
B12 .... 86 F6
Upper Bond St LE10 .... 71 D1
Upper Brook St WS2 .... 28 D1
Upper Cape CV34 .... 160 D8
Upper Chapel St B69 .... 52 B2
Upper Church La DY4 .... 52 A7
Upper Cl B32 .... 84 D3
Upper Clifton Rd B73 .... 46 B5
Upper Coneybere St
7 B12 .... 86 F7

Upper Crossgate Rd
B98 .... 159 C8
Upper Dean St B5 .... 164 C1
Upper Eastern Green La
CV5 .... 111 E5
Upper Ettingshall Rd
WV14 .... 51 B8
Upper Field Cl B98 .... 154 C6
Upper Forster St WS4 .... 28 F3
Upper Gambolds La B60 .... 151 C5
Upper Gn WV6 .... 24 D5
Upper Gough St B1 .... 164 B1
Upper Green La WS2 .... 28 C4
Upper Grosvenor Rd B20 .... 55 B2
Upper Grove St **8** CV32 .. 156 E1
Upper Gungate B79 .... 21 B6
Upper Hall Cl B98 .... 154 D1
Upper Hall La **5** WS1 ...... 28 E1
Upper Hattons Cotts WV9 .. 10 D5
Upper High St
Blackheath B64 .... 62 D1
Wednesbury WS10 .... 41 F3
Upper Highgate St B12 ...... 86 F7
Upper Hill St CV1 .... 165 A3
Upper Holland Rd B72 ...... 46 C4
Upper Holly Wlk CV32 ...... 157 A1
Upper Ladyes Hills CV8 .... 148 A6
Upper Landywood La
Cheslyn Hay WS6 .... 4 D1
Great Wyrley WS6 .... 13 D8
Upper Lichfield WS13 .... 27 A2
Upper Marshall St B1 .... 164 B1
Upper Meadow Rd B32 .... 84 C5
Upper Mill La B5 .... 164 C1
Upper Navigation St WS2 .. 28 D2
Upper Pk CV3 .... 134 D6
Upper Portland St B6 .... 67 A7
Upper Ride CV3 .... 134 D5
Upper Rosemary Hill
CV8 .... 147 F5
Upper Rushall St WS1 ...... 28 E1
Upper Russell St **1** WS10 .. 41 F2
Upper Short St WS2 .... 28 D1
Upper Sneyd Rd WV11 ...... 13 B2
Upper Spon St CV1 .... 113 A3
Upper Spring La CV8 .... 147 F7
Upper St WV6 .... 24 D5
Upper St John St WS14 ...... 9 B6
Upper St Mary's Rd B67 .... 64 F1
Upper Stone Cl B76 .... 46 E4
Upper Sutton St B6 .... 66 F7
Upper Thomas St B6 .... 66 F7
Upper Trinity St B9 .... 67 A1
Upper Vauxhall WV1 .... 25 A2
Upper Villiers St WV2 ...... 39 C6
Upper Well St CV1 .... 165 B3
Upper William St B1 .... 66 C1
Upper York St CV1 .... 113 B2
Upper Zoar St WV3 .... 163 A1
Upperfield Way CV3 .... 115 A1
Upton Cl B98 .... 154 F3
Upton Ct B23 .... 56 B3
Upton Gdns WV14 .... 40 C5
Upton Gr B33 .... 68 C1
Upton Rd B33 .... 68 C2
Upton St DY2 .... 62 C5
Upwey Ave B91 .... 107 A4
Usam Trad Est WV10 .... 11 D2
Usk Way B36 .... 69 F8
Usmere Rd DY10 .... 116 F8
Utrillo Cl CV5 .... 112 C3
Uttoxeter Cl W6 .... 25 B5
Uxbridge Ave CV3 .... 114 C2
Uxbridge Cl DY3 .... 50 D2
Uxbridge Ct Burntwood WS7 .. 6 E5
Cannock WS12 .... 2 C5
Kidderminster DY11 .... 116 D1
Uxbridge St Birmingham
B19 .... 66 D5
Cannock WS12 .... 2 C4

Valbourne Rd B14 .... 104 C4
Vale Ave Aldridge WS9 ...... 30 B3
Dudley DY3 .... 50 D6
Vale Cl Birmingham B32 .... 84 D3
Lichfield WS13 .... 3 B1
Vale Ct B64 .... 82 D7
Vale Head Dr WV6 .... 24 A2
Vale Ind Est DY11 .... 116 C1
Vale Rd DY2 .... 62 E4
Vale Row DY3 .... 50 D5
Vale St Dudley DY3 .... 50 D5
Stourbridge DY8 .... 81 A8
West Bromwich B71 .... 53 E6
Wolverhampton WV2 .... 40 A6
Vale The
Birmingham, Edgbaston B15... 86 A6
Birmingham, Moseley B11 ... 87 B2
Coventry,
Stoke Aldermoor
CV3 .... 134 C8
Vale View Aldridge WS9 .... 30 B4
Nuneaton CV10 .... 72 E4
Valencia Croft B35 .... 58 B4
Valentine Cl B74 .... 44 F7
Valentine Ct B14 .... 86 E1
Valentine Rd Birmingham
B14 .... 86 F1
Oldbury B68 .... 64 C2
Valepits Rd B33 .... 69 C1
Valerian B74 .... 31 F4
Valerie Gr B43 .... 54 C8
Vales Cl B76 .... 57 E7
Valiant Ho B36 .... 58 B5
Valiant Way B36 .... 58 D1
Valley Farm Rd B45 .... 122 A6
Valley Gn WS6 .... 4 E2
Valley Inf Sch B92 .... 89 D3

Valley La Lapworth B94 .... 144 E7
Lichfield WS13 .... 9 D8
Tamworth B77 .... 35 E7
Valley Park Nature
Reserve WV3 .... 24 D3
Valley Rd Brierley Hill WV6 .. 24 F5
Valley Rd Birmingham B43 .... 54 C7
Blackheath B64 .... 82 E7
Bournheath B61 .... 136 E7
Cannock WS12 .... 2 D6
Coventry CV2 .... 114 A6
Dudley DY3 .... 50 E6
Earlswood B94 .... 126 A1
Halesowen B62 .... 83 F8
Radford Semele CV31 .... 162 E4
Royal Leamington Spa
CV32 .... 157 C3
Smethwick B67 .... 64 F3
Solihull B92 .... 89 D4
Stourbridge DY9 .... 81 F6
Sutton Coldfield B74 .... 44 F7
Walsall WS3 .... 14 D1
Wolverhampton WV10 .... 25 F5
Valley Side WS3 .... 14 F2
Valley The Burntwood WS7 .... 6 D8
Radford Semele CV31 .... 162 E4
Valley View WS8 .... 16 A7
Vallian Croft B36 .... 68 F7
Vallord Ct WV1 .... 163 B4
Van Dyke Cl CV5 .... 112 C3
Van Gogh Cl WS11 .... 2 D2
Vanborough Wlk DY1 .... 51 A2
Vanbrugh Ct WV6 .... 23 E3
Vanguard B77 .... 35 D6
Vanguard Cl **1** B36 .... 68 E8
Vanguard Ho B35 .... 58 B2
Vann Cl B10 .... 87 C8
Varden Croft B5 .... 86 D7
Vardon Dr CV3 .... 133 C2
Vardon Way B38 .... 103 D1
Varley Rd B24 .... 57 D4
Varley Vale B24 .... 57 D4
Varlins Way B38 .... 123 D6
Varney Ave B70 .... 53 D2
Vaughan Cl B74 .... 31 F6
Vaughan Rd WV13 .... 26 E1
Vaughan Trad Est DY4 ...... 52 C3
Vaughton Dr B75 .... 46 E6
Vaughton Ho B15 .... 86 C7
Vaughton St B12 .... 86 F8
Vaughton St S B12 .... 86 E8
Vauxhall Ave **3** WV1 .... 25 A2
Vauxhall Cl **4** CV1 .... 113 E3
Vauxhall Cres B36 .... 58 F1
Vauxhall Gdns DY2 .... 62 E7
Vauxhall Gr B7 .... 67 B3
Vauxhall Ho **2** WV1 .... 25 A2
Vauxhall Pl B7 .... 67 A3
Vauxhall Rd Birmingham B7 .. 67 A3
Stourbridge DY8 .... 81 A5
Vauxhall St Coventry CV1 .... 113 E3
Dudley DY2 .... 62 B8
Vauxhall Trad Est B7 .... 67 B4
Vaynor Dr B97 .... 158 D8
Vaynor Fst Sch The B97 .... 158 C7
Veasey Cl CV11 .... 73 E3
Vecqueray St CV1 .... 113 E2
Vector Ind Pk B71 .... 53 C6
Velsheda Rd B90 .... 106 A2
Venetia Rd B9 .... 67 C2
Venice Ct **2** B13 .... 87 B2
Venning Gr B43 .... 54 D7
Ventnor Ave
Birmingham, Lozells B19 .... 66 D3
Birmingham,
Ward End B36 .... 68 D8
Ventnor Cl Coventry CV2 .... 114 E3
Oldbury B68 .... 84 C7
Ventnor Rd B92 .... 89 C3
Ventnor St CV10 .... 73 D6
Ventura Park Rd B78 .... 20 F3
Ventura Rd B78 .... 21 A3
Venture Ct LE10 .... 74 E8
Venture Way B7 .... 66 F4
Vera Rd B26 .... 88 E7
Verbena Cl Coventry CV2 .... 96 B1
Stoke Prior B60 .... 150 C1
Verbena Gdns B7 .... 67 A5
Verbena Rd B31 .... 102 F6
Vercourt B74 .... 31 B3
Verden Ave CV34 .... 160 B4
Verdi Ct WS13 .... 3 C2
Verdun Cl CV31 .... 162 B2
Verdun Cres DY2 .... 51 F2
Vere St B5 .... 86 D8
Verity Wlk DY8 .... 60 E1
Vermont Gn WS11 .... 2 A3
Vermont Gr CV31 .... 162 D6
Verney Ave B33 .... 89 D7
Vernier Ave DY6 .... 61 A5
Vernolds Croft B5 .... 86 E8
Vernon Ave Birmingham
B20 .... 54 F4
Brownhills WS8 .... 16 A8
Tipton DY4 .... 51 E4
Vernon Cl **5** Coventry
CV1 .... 113 E3
Essington WV11 .... 12 F4
Halesowen B62 .... 83 D8
Redditch B98 .... 154 A5
Royal Leamington Spa
CV32 .... 156 D3
Sutton Coldfield B74 .... 31 E5
Willenhall WV13 .... 26 E1

Vernon Ct 9 Coventry
CV1 .... 113 E4
2 Oldbury B68 .... 84 B7
Vernon Rd Bilston WV14 ...... 40 F6
Birmingham B16 .... 65 E1
Halesowen B62 .... 83 C8
Oldbury B68 .... 64 C6
Vernon St B70 .... 52 E3
Vernon Trad Est B62 .... 83 C8
Vernon Way WS3 .... 13 E1
Vernons Ct CV10 .... 72 F4
Vernons La CV10, CV11 ...... 72 F4
Verona Cl CV11 .... 74 A1
Veronica Ave WV4 .... 39 E5
Veronica Cl B29 .... 103 A6
Veronica Rd DY6 .... 61 A6
Verstone Croft B31 .... 103 A3
Verstone Rd B90 .... 106 C4
Verwood Cl WV13 .... 26 D1
Vesey Cl Sutton Coldfield
B74 .... 31 E1
Water Orton B46 .... 59 B2
Vesey Rd B73 .... 46 B1
Vesey St B4 .... 164 C4
Vestry Cl B64 .... 62 F1
Vestry Ct DY8 .... 80 E6
Viaduct Dr WV6 .... 25 B6
Viaduct St B7 .... 67 A3
Vibart Rd B26 .... 88 F8
Vicar St Dudley DY2 .... 62 C8
Kidderminster DY10 .... 116 E6
Sedgley DY3 .... 50 D8
Wednesbury WS10 .... 42 A3
Vicar's Cl WS13 .... 9 A8
Vicarage Cl
Birmingham,
Great Barr B42 .... 55 D7
Birmingham, Strichley B30 .. 104 C7
Brierley Hill DY5 .... 81 C8
Bromsgrove B60 .... 151 B8
Brownhills WS8 .... 16 A7
Dordon B78 .... 36 F5
Tipton DY4 .... 51 E5
Vicarage Cres
Kidderminster DY10 .... 116 F6
Redditch B97 .... 153 C3
Vicarage Field CV34 .... 161 B8
Vicarage Gdns
Halesowen B62 .... 63 D1
Sutton Coldfield B76 .... 57 F7
Vicarage Hill Middleton B78 .. 48 B8
Tanworth-In-A B94 .... 141 F3
Vicarage La Brierley Hill DY5 .. 61 D7
Coventry CV7 .... 95 D7
Warwick CV35 .... 160 A1
Water Orton B46 .... 59 B2
Vicarage Pl WS1 .... 28 E1
Vicarage Prospect DY1 ...... 51 B1
Vicarage Rd
Birmingham, Aston B6 .... 67 A7
Birmingham, Edgbaston B15 .. 85 F8
Birmingham,
Handsworth B18 .... 66 A7
Birmingham, Harborne B17 .... 85 B5
Birmingham,
King's Heath B14 .... 104 D7
Birmingham, Stechford B33 .. 68 E1
Brierley Hill DY5 .... 81 C7
Brownhills WS8 .... 16 A7
Cheswick Green B94 .... 126 C3
Dudley, West Coseley WV14 .. 51 C7
Dudley, Woodsetton DY3 ...... 50 F5
Halesowen B62 .... 63 C1
Oldbury B68 .... 64 C5
Royal Leamington Spa
CV32 .... 157 B3
Smethwick B67 .... 64 F5
Stone DY10 .... 117 C2
Stoneleigh CV8 .... 149 B6
Stourbridge, Lye DY9 .... 81 F5
Stourbridge, Wollaston DY8 .. 80 D7
Tanworth-in-A B94 .... 143 F7
Walsall WS3 .... 15 A2
Wednesbury WS10 .... 42 A4
West Bromwich B71 .... 53 D6
Wolverhampton,
Blakenhall WV2 .... 163 C1
Wolverhampton,
New Cross WV11 .... 26 B6
Wolverhampton, Penn WV4 .... 38 E3
Vicarage Rd W DY1 .... 51 C6
Vicarage St Nuneaton CV11 .. 73 C4
Oldbury B68 .... 64 B5
Vicarage Terr 1 WS2 .... 42 C8
Vicarage View B97 .... 153 D3
Vicarage Wlk 8 WS1 .... 28 E1
Vicars Wlk DY9 .... 81 E2
Viceroy Cl Birmingham B5 .. 86 C6
Kingswinford DY6 .... 61 A5
Victor Cl WV2 .... 40 B6
Victor Rd Birmingham B18 .... 65 E6
Solihull B92 .... 89 D3
Victor St
Walsall, Caldmore WS1 .... 42 E8
Walsall, Pelsall WS3 .... 15 A1
Victor Tower B7 .... 67 B6
Victoria Arc WV1 .... 163 B3
Victoria Ave Birmingham
B21 .... 65 E8
Halesowen B62 .... 83 F6
Smethwick B66 .... 65 A5
Walsall,
Blakenhall Heath WS3 .... 28 D8
Walsall,
Wallington Heath WS3 .... 14 C1

Victoria Bldgs B16 .... 65 E3
Victoria Bsns Ctr
11 CV31 .... 162 A7
Victoria Ct
2 Birmingham B13 .... 86 F4
Brierley Hill DY5 .... 61 D3
Coventry CV5 .... 112 D4
Kidderminster DY10 .... 116 F6
Smethwick B66 .... 83 F6
Victoria Dr Fazeley B78 ...... 35 A8
Tamworth B78 .... 21 A1
Victoria Fold WV1 .... 163 B2
Victoria Gdns WS13 .... 8 F7
Victoria Gr
1 Birmingham B18 .... 65 E4
Wombourne WV5 .... 49 A8
Victoria Ho Birmingham
B16 .... 66 B2
Darlaston WS10 .... 41 C6
2 Walsall WS3 .... 28 D8
Victoria Hospl WS13 .... 9 A8
Victoria Infs Sch DY4 .... 51 F5
Victoria Mews Coventry
CV3 .... 114 E2
Walsall WS4 .... 29 A3
Warwick CV34 .... 160 D7
Victoria Park Rd B66 .... 65 B5
Victoria Pas WV1 .... 163 B3
Victoria Pl DY11 .... 116 B2
Victoria Rd
Birmingham,
Acock's Green B27 .... 88 C2
Birmingham, Aston B6 .... 66 F7
Birmingham,
Handsworth B21 .... 65 E7
Birmingham, Harborne B17 .... 85 B5
Birmingham, Stechford B33 .... 68 E1
Birmingham, Strichley B30 .. 104 A7
Birmingham,
Stockland Green B23 .... 56 D3
Blackheath B64 .... 62 F2
Brierley Hill DY5 .... 62 A1
Bromsgrove B61 .... 137 A3
Darlaston WS10 .... 41 D6
Dodford B61 .... 136 A4
Halesowen B63 .... 83 D8
Hinckley LE10 .... 75 F5
Nuneaton CV10 .... 72 B8
Oldbury B68 .... 64 D6
Royal Leamington Spa
CV31 .... 161 E8
Sedgley DY3 .... 50 E8
Sutton Coldfield B72 .... 46 C5
Tamworth B79 .... 21 C5
Tipton DY4 .... 52 A4
Walsall WS3 .... 15 A3
Wolverhampton,
New Cross WV11 .... 26 B6
Wolverhampton,
Newbolds WV10 .... 25 F7
Wolverhampton,
Tettenhall WV6 .... 24 E5
Victoria Sh Arc B79 .... 21 B5
Victoria Specl Sch B31 .... 103 A5
Victoria Sq Birmingham
B3 .... 164 B2
Lichfield WS13 .... 9 B6
Wolverhampton WV1 .... 163 C3
Victoria St Birmingham B9 .. 67 D1
Brierley Hill, Barrow Hill
DY5 .... 61 C7
Brierley Hill, Merry Hill DY5 .. 61 D3
Cannock, Bridgtown WS11 ..... 1 E4
Cannock, Broomhill WS11 ...... 1 E4
Cannock, Hednesford WS12 .... 2 C6
Coventry CV1 .... 165 D4
Halesowen B63 .... 83 A4
Hinckley LE10 .... 71 D1
Kingswinford DY6 .... 49 B1
Nuneaton CV11 .... 73 C4
7 Redditch B98 .... 153 E4
Royal Leamington Spa
CV31 .... 161 E8
Stourbridge DY8 .... 81 A5
Warwick CV34 .... 160 D7
Wednesbury WS10 .... 41 E2
West Bromwich,
Lambert's End B70 .... 53 C3
West Bromwich,
Swan Village B70 .... 52 F5
Willenhall WV13 .... 27 B3
Wolverhampton WV1 .... 163 B3
Victoria Terr
1 Royal Leamington Spa
CV31 .... 161 F7
4 Walsall WS4 .... 28 F3
Victory Ave Burntwood WS7 .. 6 F7
Darlaston WS10 .... 41 C5
Victory Cl WS12 .... 2 F4
Victory La WS2 .... 28 A4
Victory Rd CV6 .... 95 E1
Victory Rise B71 .... 53 D5
Victory Terr 4 B78 .... 35 B8
Vienna Ho CV5 .... 112 E2
View Dr DY2 .... 62 E8
View St WS12 .... 1 F6
Viewfield Ave WS12 .... 1 F7
Viewfield Cres DY3 .... 50 D6
Viewlands Dr WV6 .... 24 A2
Vigo Cl WS9 .... 15 F2
Vigo Pl WS9 .... 30 A8
Vigo Rd WS9 .... 16 A2
Vigo Terr WS9 .... 15 F2
Viking Rise B65 .... 63 C4
Vilia Cl LE10 .... 75 F4
Villa Cl CV12 .... 79 C2

Villa Cotts B19 .... 66 B7
Villa Cres CV12 .... 79 C1
Villa Cross B20 .... 66 B7
Villa Park B6 .... 55 F1
Villa Rd Birmingham B19 ..... 66 B7
Coventry CV6 .... 113 B6
Villa St Birmingham B19 ..... 66 C6
Stourbridge DY8 .... 81 A8
Villa Wlk B19 .... 66 C6
Village Mews The WV6 ...... 24 C5
Village Rd B6 .... 56 A1
Village The DY6 .... 60 E7
Village Way WV14 .... 40 C5
Village Wlk WS10 .... 42 B3
Villette Gr B14 .... 105 C4
Villiers Ave WV14 .... 40 D7
Villiers Ho WV2 .... 39 C7
Villiers Ind Est WV2 .... 39 B7
Villiers Prim Sch WV14 .... 40 D7
Villiers Rd Bromsgrove
B60 .... 150 E7
Kenilworth CV8 .... 148 B5
Villiers Sq WV14 .... 40 D7
Villiers St Coventry CV2 .... 114 A3
Kidderminster DY10 .... 117 A5
Nuneaton CV11 .... 73 B3
Royal Leamington Spa
CV32 .... 157 A1
Walsall WS1 .... 42 E7
Willenhall WV13 .... 27 B2
Vimy Rd Birmingham B13 .. 105 B8
Wednesbury WS10 .... 42 A4
Vimy Terr WS10 .... 42 A4
Vince St B66 .... 65 A3
Vincent Cl B12 .... 86 F6
Vincent Dr B15 .... 85 E4
Vincent Par B12 .... 86 F6
Vincent Rd B75 .... 46 E7
Vincent St Birmingham B12 .. 86 F5
Coventry CV1 .... 113 B2
Royal Leamington Spa
CV32 .... 157 A1
Walsall WS1 .... 42 E7
Vincent Wyles Ho CV2 ...... 114 E3
Vinculum Way WV13 .... 41 B8
Vine Ave B12 .... 87 A5
Vine Cres B71 .... 53 D6
Vine Ct B64 .... 82 D8
Vine La Cannock WS11 .... 4 D5
Clent DY9 .... 99 F3
Halesowen B63 .... 83 B3
Warwick CV34 .... 160 F8
Vine St Birmingham B6 .... 67 B7
Brierley Hill DY5 .... 61 E5
Coventry CV1 .... 165 C3
Kidderminster DY10 .... 117 A8
Redditch B97 .... 153 D4
Stourbridge DY8 .... 60 E1
Vinecote Rd CV6 .... 95 F4
Vineries The B27 .... 88 E4
Vineyard Rd B31 .... 102 F5
Vinnall Gr B32 .... 102 B8
Vintage Cl B34 .... 69 A5
Vinyard Cl B18 .... 65 F7
Violet Cl CV2 .... 96 C3
Violet Croft DY4 .... 41 B1
Violet La DY9 .... 99 E4
Virginia Dr WV4 .... 38 F4
Virginia Pl CV10 .... 72 E3
Virginia Rd CV1 .... 113 E3
Viscount Cl Birmingham
B35 .... 58 A2
Royal Leamington Spa
CV31 .... 161 F6
Viscount Ho B35 .... 58 B2
Vista Gn B38 .... 104 B1
Vista The DY3 .... 39 D2
Vittle Dr CV34 .... 160 D7
Vittoria St Birmingham B1 .. 66 C4
Smethwick B66 .... 65 D6
Vivian Cl B17 .... 85 C5
Vivian Rd B17 .... 85 C5
Vixen Cl B76 .... 57 D7
Vodena Ct 5 CV32 .... 156 E1
Vogue Cl CV1 .... 165 D3
Voyager Dr WS11 .... 4 F6
Vulcan Ho B35 .... 58 C3
Vulcan House Ind Est
B91 .... 107 C6
Vulcan Ind Est WS2 .... 28 C6
Vulcan Rd Bilston WV14 ...... 40 F5
Lichfield WS13 .... 3 E1
Solihull B91 .... 107 C7
Vulcan Road Island WV14 .. 40 F5
Vyrnwy Gr B38 .... 123 E8
Vyse St Birmingham,
Aston B6 .... 67 B6
Birmingham, Hockley B18 ..... 66 C4

Wackrill Dr CV32 .... 157 C3
Wadbury Hill B97 .... 158 D4
Waddam's Pool DY2 .... 51 D1
Waddell Cl WV14 .... 39 F2
Waddens Brook La WV11 .... 26 E5
Waddington Ave B43 .... 43 E1
Wade Ave CV3 .... 133 B5
Wade Gr CV34 .... 155 E2
Wade St WS13 .... 9 B7
Wadebridge Dr CV11 .... 73 F5
Wadesmill Lawns WV10 ...... 11 E4
Wadham Cl B65 .... 63 C6
Wadham Ho B37 .... 70 D3
Wadhurst Rd B17 .... 65 B2
Wadleys Rd B91 .... 106 F6
Waen Cl DY4 .... 52 B8
Waggon La DY10 .... 98 A3
Waggon St B64 .... 62 F2
Waggon Wlk B38 .... 123 C8

Waggoner's La B78 .... 33 E7
Waggoners Cl B60 .... 150 E6
Wagon La B92 .... 88 F4
Wagoners Cl B8 .... 67 F6
Wagstaff Cl WV14 .... 51 D8
Wainbody Ave N CV3 .... 133 A6
Wainbody Ave S CV3 .... 132 F5
Wainbody Wood Sch
CV5 .... 132 D2
Waine Ho WS8 .... 16 A6
Wainrigg B77 .... 36 B7
Wainwright Cl DY6 .... 60 A7
Wainwright St B6 .... 67 A8
Waite Rd WV13 .... 40 E8
Wake Gr CV34 .... 160 B5
Wake Green Pk B13 .... 87 B2
Wake Green Rd
Birmingham B13 .... 87 A2
Tipton DY4 .... 41 A1
Wakefield Cl Coventry CV3 .. 134 F7
Sutton Coldfield B73 .... 46 A2
Wakefield Ct B13 .... 87 B2
Wakefield Gr B46 .... 59 B3
Wakeford Rd B31 .... 103 C1
Wakehurst Cl CV11 .... 78 F8
Wakelam Gdns B43 .... 43 D1
Wakelams Fold DY3 .... 50 C3
Wakeley Hill WV4 .... 38 F3
Wakelin Rd B90 .... 126 B7
Wakeman Gr B33 .... 89 D7
Wakes Cl WV13 .... 27 B1
Wakes Rd WS10 .... 42 A2
Walcot Cl B75 .... 32 B3
Walcot Dr B43 .... 54 F6
Walcot Gdns WV14 .... 40 B4
Walcot Gn B93 .... 128 A2
Walcote Cl LE10 .... 74 F8
Waldale Cl WV11 .... 13 C1
Walden Gdns WV4 .... 38 E6
Walden Rd B11 .... 88 A3
Waldeve Gr B92 .... 107 F8
Waldon Wlk B36 .... 69 F8
Waldron Ave DY5 .... 61 B2
Waldron Cl WS10 .... 41 F6
Waldrons Moor B14 .... 104 C5
Walford Ave WV3 .... 38 F8
Walford Dr B92 .... 89 D3
Walford Gn B32 .... 102 B7
Walford Gr CV34 .... 155 F1
Walford Rd B11 .... 87 C6
Walford St B69 .... 52 A2
Walford Wlk 7 B97 .... 153 E3
Walhouse CE Jun Sch
WS1 .... 1 C1
Walhouse Cl 6 WS1 .... 28 F2
Walhouse Rd WS1 .... 29 A2
Walk La WV5 .... 49 A6
Walk The DY3 .... 39 D1
Walker Ave Brierley Hill
DY5 .... 81 D7
Stourbridge DY9 .... 81 E3
Tipton B69 .... 63 C7
Wolverhampton WV10 .... 25 E8
Walker Dr B24 .... 67 E8
Walker Grange DY4 .... 51 F6
Walker Pl WS3 .... 28 E8
Walker Rd WS3 .... 28 E8
Walker St Dudley DY2 .... 62 C4
Tipton DY4 .... 52 C7
Walkers Croft WS13 .... 3 C2
Walkers Heath Rd B38 ...... 104 B1
Walkers Orch CV8 .... 149 B6
Walkers Rd B98 .... 154 E6
Walkers Rise WS12 .... 2 D8
Walkers Way CV12 .... 77 F1
Walkmill Bsns Pk WS11 .... 4 D5
Walkmill La WS11 .... 4 D5
Walkmill Way WS11 .... 4 D5
Walkwood CE Mid Sch
B97 .... 158 C8
Walkwood Cres B97 .... 158 C6
Walkwood Rd B97 .... 158 D6
Wall Ave B46 .... 70 F5
Wall Croft WS9 .... 30 B7
Wall Dr B74 .... 31 F4
Wall End Cl WS2 .... 28 A7
Wall Heath La WS9 .... 16 F5
Wall Hill Rd CV5, CV7 .... 94 B3
Wall La WS8 .... 8 E3
Wall St WV1 .... 26 B2
Wall Well B63 .... 82 F3
Wall Well La B63 .... 82 F3
Wall's Rd B60 .... 150 C3
Wallace Cl Norton Canes
WS11 .... 5 F5
Oldbury B69 .... 63 D6
Wallace Ct WS6 .... 4 D1
Wallace Ho 8 Oldbury B69 .. 63 D5
Warwick CV34 .... 160 D7
Wallace Rd Bilston WV14 .... 41 A2
Birmingham B29 .... 86 B2
Brownhills WS8 .... 15 E8
Coventry CV6 .... 113 A8
Oldbury B69 .... 63 D6
Wallace Rise B64 .... 82 E7
Wallbank Rd B8 .... 68 A6
Wallbrook Prim Sch
WV14 .... 51 E8
Wallbrook St WV14 .... 51 D8
Wallheath Cres WS9 .... 16 E5
Walling Croft WV14 .... 40 B4
Wallingford Ave CV11 .... 73 F7
Wallington Cl WS3 .... 14 B2
Wallington Heath WS3 .... 14 B2

Wallis Ct 1 B13 .... 87 B2
Wallows Ind Est The DY5 ... 61 D5
Wallows La WS1, WS2 .... 42 C5
Wallows Pl DY5 .... 61 C5
Wallows Rd DY5 .... 61 D5
Wallows Wood DY3 .... 50 A4
Wallwin Ct CV34 .... 160 D6
Walmead Croft B17 .... 84 F7
Walmer Gr B23 .... 56 B5
Walmer Mdw WS9 .... 30 B7
Walmer Way B37 .... 70 C3
Walmers The WS9 .... 30 B7
Walmers Wlk The B31 ...... 102 D1
Walmley Ash La B76 .... 58 C6
Walmley Ash Rd B76 .... 58 A7
Walmley Cl Halesowen B63 .. 82 B7
Sutton Coldfield B76 .... 57 F8
Walmley Jun & Inf Schs
B76 .... 58 A7
Walmley Rd B76 .... 46 F2
Walney Cl LE10 .... 71 B1
Walnut Cl WV8 .... 10 B3
Walnut Ct Birmingham B37 ... 70 B1
Cannock WS11 .... 1 F3
Nuneaton, Camp Hill CV10 .... 72 E6
Nuneaton, Hartshill CV10 ..... 72 A8
Stourbridge DY9 .... 81 B1
Walnut Dr Cannock WS11 ...... 1 F3
Royal Leamington Spa
CV32 .... 157 B3
5 Smethwick B66 .... 65 B5
Wolverhampton WV3 .... 24 D1
Walnut Gr WV14 .... 9 F7
Walnut La Finstall B60 ...... 151 D8
Wednesbury WS10 .... 42 A2
Walnut Rd WS5 .... 43 A4
Walnut St CV2 .... 96 B2
Walnut Tree Cl CV8 .... 148 A3
Walnut Way B31 .... 122 F8
Walpole St WV6 .... 25 A3
Walpole Wlk B70 .... 53 D1
Walsal End La B92 .... 108 F3
Walsall Coll of Arts &
Tech Walsall WS1 .... 28 E1
Walsall, The Chuckery WS1 ... 29 A1
Walsall Coll of Arts &
Tech (Birchills Campus)
WS2 .... 28 C3
Walsall Coll of Arts &
Tech Shelley Ctr Campus
WS2 .... 28 C1
Walsall New Firms Ctr
WS1 .... 42 D8
Walsall Rd Aldridge WS9 ..... 29 E4
Birmingham B42 .... 55 B6
Cannock WS11 .... 4 E7
Darlaston WS10 .... 41 E6
Great Wyrley WS6, WS11 ...... 5 C5
Lichfield WS13 .... 8 C5
Norton Canes WS11 .... 5 F4
Stonnall WS14 .... 16 E8
Sutton Coldfield B74 .... 31 D4
Walsall, Pelsall WS3 .... 15 A1
Walsall, The Delves WS5 ...... 42 F4
Walsall Wood WS9 .... 15 E2
Wednesbury
WS10, B71, WS5 .... 42 F2
West Bromwich B71 .... 53 E8
Willenhall WV13 .... 27 C2
Walsall St Bilston WV14 ...... 40 D6
Coventry CV4 .... 132 B2
Darlaston WS10 .... 41 D7
West Bromwich B70 .... 53 D3
Willenhall WV13 .... 27 B1
Wolverhampton WV1 .... 163 D2
Walsall Sta WS2 .... 28 D2
Walsall Wood JMI Sch
WS9 .... 16 A4
Walsall Wood Rd WS9 .... 30 B7
Walsgrave CE Prim Sch
CV3 .... 115 A6
Walsgrave Cl B92 .... 107 D6
Walsgrave Dr B92 .... 107 D6
Walsgrave Gdns
5 CV2 .... 115 A7
Walsgrave Rd CV2 .... 114 B3
Walsh Dr B76 .... 46 F4
Walsh Gr B23 .... 56 D8
Walsh La CV7 .... 92 E2
Walsham Croft B34 .... 69 C5
Walsingham Dr CV10 .... 78 A7
Walsingham St WS1 .... 29 A1
Walstead Cl WS5 .... 43 C5
Walstead Rd WS5 .... 43 B5
Walstead Rd W WS5 .... 42 E5
Waltdene Cl B43 .... 43 E3
Walter Burden Ho B66 .... 65 C3
Walter Cobb Dr B73 .... 46 A1
Walter Nash Rd E DY11 .... 116 B2
Walter Nash Rd W DY11 .... 116 A1
Walter Rd Bilston WV14 ...... 40 F3
Smethwick B67 .... 64 E6
Walter Scott Rd CV12 .... 78 C1
Walter St Birmingham B7 .... 67 B6
Walsall WS3 .... 15 A1
West Bromwich B70 .... 53 E2
Walters Cl B31 .... 122 F6
Walters Rd B68 .... 84 B6
Walters Row DY1 .... 51 A1
Waltham Cl B61 .... 136 C1
Waltham Cres CV10 .... 72 B5
Waltham Gr B44 .... 45 B2
Waltham Ho
Birmingham B38 .... 104 B1
West Bromwich B70 .... 53 D3
Walthamstow Ct DY5 .... 61 D1
Walton Ave B65 .... 83 B8

Walton Cl Blackheath B65 ...... 63 A4
　Coventry CV3 .... 134 E7
　Halesowen B63 .... 82 F2
　Kidderminster DY11 ...... 116 B2
　Nuneaton CV11 .... 79 A7
Walton Cres WV4 .... 39 E5
Walton Croft B91 .... 107 B1
Walton Ct B63 .... 82 F3
Walton Dr DY9 .... 81 C5
Walton Gr B30 .... 104 B2
Walton Heath WS3 .... 13 F3
Walton Pool La DY9 .... 99 F2
Walton Rd Aldridge WS9 ..... 16 A1
　Bromsgrove B61 .... 137 B4
　Oldbury B68 .... 64 C2
　Stourbridge DY8 .... 81 A6
　Wednesbury WS10 .... 42 C2
　Wolverhampton WV4 .... 39 F5
Walton Rise DY9 .... 100 A3
Walton St DY4 .... 51 F5
Wanderer Wlk B36 .... 57 E1
Wanderers Ave WV2 .... 39 C6
Wandle Gr B11 .... 88 A3
Wandsbeck B77 .... 35 E8
Wandsworth Rd B44 .... 44 F3
Wanley Rd CV3 .... 133 D6
Wannerton Rd DY10 .... 98 B1
Wansbeck Gr B38 .... 123 E8
Wansbeck Wlk DY3 .... 50 F6
Wansfell Cl CV4 .... 132 A7
Wanstead Gr B44 .... 45 A1
Wantage Rd B46 .... 59 E1
Wappenbury Cl CV2 .... 96 C2
Wappenbury Rd CV2 .... 96 D2
War La B17 .... 85 B5
Warbage La
　Belbroughton DY9 .... 119 F1
　Dodford B61 .... 136 A7
Warbank Cl B48 .... 139 A6
Warbler Pl DY10 .... 117 A2
Ward Cl B8 .... 68 A5
Ward End Hall Gr B8 .... 68 A6
Ward End Jun & Inf Sch
　B8 .... 68 B6
Ward End Park Rd B8 .... 67 F5
Ward Gr Warwick CV34 ... 161 C7
　Wolverhampton WV4 .... 39 F3
Ward Rd WV4 .... 39 D5
Ward St Bilston WV2 .... 40 B6
　Birmingham B19 .... 164 C5
　Cannock WS12 .... 1 F6
　Dudley WV14 .... 51 B8
　Walsall WS1 .... 28 F2
　Willenhall WV13 .... 27 B3
　Wolverhampton WV1 ...... 163 D3
Warden Ave B73 .... 45 F8
Warden Rd Coventry CV6 .. 113 B6
　Sutton Coldfield B73 .... 56 F8
Wardend Rd B8 .... 68 A6
Wardens Ave The CV5 ..... 112 B6
Wardens The CV8 .... 148 C5
Wardle Cl B75 .... 32 A4
Wardle Pl WS11 .... 1 A6
Wardle St B79 .... 21 A5
Wardles La WS6 .... 4 F2
Wardlow Cl WV4 .... 39 B6
Wardlow Rd B7 .... 67 B4
Wardour Dr B37 .... 70 C2
Wardour Gr B44 .... 56 C8
Wareham Cl WS3 .... 28 F5
Wareham Gn CV2 .... 115 A5
Wareham Ho B28 .... 105 E3
Wareham Rd B45 .... 102 B2
Wareing Dr B23 .... 56 D8
Warewell Cl WS1 [8] 28 F2
Warewell St [9] WS1 .... 28 F2
Waring Cl DY4 .... 51 E8
Waring Rd DY4 .... 52 A8
Warings Green Rd B94 .... 126 D1
Warley Croft B68 .... 84 E8
Warley Ct B68 .... 64 B2
Warley Hall Rd B68 .... 64 D1
Warley High Sch B68 .... 64 A2
Warley Ho B67 .... 64 F2
Warley Inf Sch B68 .... 64 C2
Warley Rd B68 .... 64 C5
Warmington Cl CV3 .... 134 E8
Warmington Dr B73 .... 46 B4
Warmington Gr CV34 ...... 160 B8
Warmington Rd
　Birmingham B26 .... 89 C5
　Hollywood B47 .... 125 A6
Warmley Cl Solihull B91 .. 107 D5
　Wolverhampton W6 .... 25 B5
Warmwell Cl CV2 .... 114 F4
Warneford Mews
[13] CV31 .... 162 A7
Warner Cl CV34 .... 155 D1
Warner Dr DY5 .... 61 D1
Warner Pl [1] WS3 .... 28 F6
Warner Rd Walsall WS3 ..... 29 A6
　Wednesbury WS10 .... 42 C2
Warner Row CV6 .... 113 F7
Warner St [2] B12 .... 87 A8
Warners Wlk B10 .... 87 C8
Warnford Wlk WV4 .... 38 C6
Warple Rd B32 .... 84 C5
Warren Ave Birmingham
　B13 .... 86 F2
　Wolverhampton WV10 ...... 25 F5
Warren Cl Lichfield WS14 ... 9 E7
　Royal Leamington Spa
　CV32 .... 157 A3
　Tipton DY4 .... 52 A7
Warren Dr Blackheath B65 .. 62 F5
　Dorridge B93 .... 128 A3
　Sedgley DY3 .... 39 C1

Warren Farm Jun & Inf
　Schs B44 .... 56 A8
Warren Farm Rd B44 .... 56 A8
Warren Field B44 .... 135 A1
Warren Gdns DY6 .... 60 C6
Warren Gn CV4 .... 131 F7
Warren Hill Rd B44 .... 56 A7
Warren La B45 .... 122 B3
Warren Pl WS8 .... 16 A7
Warren Rd
　Birmingham, Perry B44 ..... 56 A7
　Birmingham, Stirchley B30 .. 104 A6
　Birmingham,
　Washwood Heath B8 .... 67 E6
　Burntwood WS7 .... 7 A5
Warrens Croft WS5 .... 43 D5
Warrens End B38 .... 103 F1
Warrens Hall Rd DY2 .... 62 E7
Warrington Cl B76 .... 47 A1
Warrington Dr B23 .... 56 D7
Warsash Cl WV1 .... 40 B8
Warstock La B14 .... 105 A4
Warstock Rd B14 .... 105 A3
Warston Ave B32 .... 84 D3
Warstone Dr B71 .... 53 E4
Warstone La B66 .... 66 B4
Warstone Mews [2] B18 .... 66 C4
Warstone Par E B18 .... 66 B4
Warstone Rd WV11, WV10 .. 13 C7
Warstone Terr B21 .... 65 E8
Warstone Tower B36 .... 68 D8
Warstones Cres WV4 .... 38 D5
Warstones Dr WV4 .... 38 C6
Warstones Gdns WV4 ...... 38 C6
Warstones Prim Sch WV4 .. 38 E6
Warstones Rd WV4 .... 38 D5
Wartell Bank DY6 .... 60 D7
Wartell Bank Ind Est DY6 .. 60 D7
Warton Cl CV8 .... 148 C4
Warwards La B29 .... 104 A8
Warwell La B26 .... 88 D6
Warwick Ave
　Bromsgrove B60 .... 151 A8
　Coventry CV5 .... 133 A8
　Perton WV6 .... 23 F3
　Wednesbury WS10 .... 42 C4
　Willenhall WV13 .... 27 D2
Warwick By-Pass
　Warwick,
　Hampton Magna CV35 ... 160 A5
　Warwick, Heathcote CV34 ... 161 A1
Warwick Castle CV34 ...... 160 E6
Warwick Cl Cannock WS11 .. 4 F8
　Oldbury B68 .... 64 B2
　Studley B80 .... 159 D3
　West Bromwich B70 .... 52 E7
Warwick Crest B15 .... 86 B7
Warwick Ct
[1] Birmingham,
　Acock's Green B27 .... 88 C2
[5] Birmingham,
　Chelmsley Wood B37 .... 70 D2
　Birmingham, Moseley B13 .. 87 A2
　Coventry CV3 .... 165 B1
[1] Dudley DY3 .... 50 D3
　Solihull B91 .... 107 C3
　Solihull, Lode Heath B91 .. 107 B4
　Wolverhampton WV4 .... 39 F4
Warwick Gdns Hinckley
　LE10 .... 71 E3
　Nuneaton CV10 .... 72 E4
　Tipton B69 .... 52 C2
Warwick Gn CV12 .... 79 C1
Warwick Gr B92 .... 88 E1
Warwick Grange B91 ...... 106 F7
Warwick Hall Gdns B60 .. 151 A1
Warwick Highway B98 ... 154 C2
Warwick Ho
[6] Birmingham B24 .... 56 F4
　Sutton Coldfield B73 .... 46 A3
Warwick Hospl CV34 ...... 160 E8
Warwick La CV1 .... 165 B2
Warwick Mus CV34 .... 160 F7
Warwick New Rd CV32 .. 161 C8
Warwick Park Ct B92 ...... 106 F8
Warwick Pas B2 .... 164 C2
Warwick Pl CV32 .... 156 E1
Warwick Rd Birmingham
　B42 .... 55 E2
　Birmingham, Sparkhill B11 ... 87 D4
　Chadwick End B93 .... 145 A7
　Coventry CV3 .... 165 B1
　Dudley DY2 .... 62 E3
　Kenilworth CV8 .... 148 A1
　Knowle B93 .... 128 D3
　Leek Wootton CV35 .... 155 F7
　Oldbury B68 .... 84 D7
　Solihull B27, B91, B92 .. 106 F7
　Stourbridge DY8 .... 60 D1
　Tamworth B77 .... 21 E4
　Wolston CV8 .... 135 F3
Warwick Road Trad Est
　B11 .... 87 D4
Warwick Row CV1 .... 165 B2
Warwick Sch CV34 .... 161 A6
Warwick St Bilston WV14 .. 40 E5
　Birmingham B12 .... 67 A1
　Coventry CV5 .... 112 V1
　Royal Leamington Spa
　CV32 .... 156 F1
　Walsall WS4 .... 28 F3
　Wolverhampton WV1 ...... 163 D2
Warwick St Mary's RC
　Prim Sch CV34 .... 160 E8
Warwick Sta CV34 .... 161 A8
Warwick Tech Pk CV34 .. 161 B5
Warwick Terr CV32 .... 156 E1
Warwick Way WS9 .... 16 A1

Warwickshire Coll CV32 .. 161 D8
Warwickshire Coll of Ag
　CV11 .... 73 E6
Warwickshire Mus CV34 .. 160 E6
Warwickshire Nuffield
　Hospl The CV32 .... 156 E5
Wasdale Cl CV32 .... 156 C2
Wasdale Dr B6 .... 60 D6
Wasdale Rd Birmingham
　B31 .... 102 F4
　Clayhanger WS8 .... 15 D6
Waseley Hills Ctry Pk
　B45 .... 121 C8
Waseley Hills High Sch
　B45 .... 121 D7
Waseley Rd B45 .... 121 E8
Wash La B25 .... 88 C8
Washbourne Rd CV31 ...... 162 A2
Washbrook La Allesley CV5 .. 94 A1
　Norton Canes WS11 .... 5 D5
Washbrook Rd B8 .... 68 A6
Washford Dr B98 .... 159 D7
Washford Gr B25 .... 88 B8
Washford Ind Est B98 .... 159 E8
Washford La B98 .... 159 D8
Washington Ct WV3 .... 24 D1
Washington Ctr DY2 .... 62 D4
Washington Dr B20 .... 55 B3
Washington St
　Birmingham B1 .... 164 A1
　Dudley DY2 .... 62 D3
　Kidderminster DY11 ...... 116 C5
Washwood Heath Rd B8 ... 67 E6
Washwood Heath Sch B8 ... 68 C5
Wasperton Cl
　Birmingham B36 .... 69 B8
[6] Coventry CV3 .... 134 F8
Wassell Cl B63 .... 82 E2
Wassell Grove Rd
　Hagley DY9 .... 99 F8
　Halesowen B63 .... 82 A2
Wassell Rd Bilston WV14 .. 40 D7
　Halesowen B63 .... 82 E2
　Stourbridge DY9 .... 81 E2
Wast Hill Gr B38 .... 123 F7
Waste La
　Balsall Common CV7 ...... 130 F6
　Coventry CV6 .... 94 F1
Wasthill La B38, B48 ...... 123 D5
Wastwater Dr WV6 .... 23 F4
Watch Cl CV1 .... 165 A3
Watchbury Cl B36 .... 58 C1
Watchmaker Ct CV1 .... 165 A2
Watchman Ave DY5 .... 81 F7
Watcombe Rd CV2 .... 114 E8
Water Dale WV3 .... 24 E2
Water La B71 .... 53 F7
Water Mill Cl B29 .... 85 D3
Water Mill Prim Sch B29 ... 85 D3
Water Orton La B76 .... 58 E4
Water Orton Prim Sch
　B46 .... 59 B2
Water Orton Rd B36 .... 58 E1
Water Orton Sta B46 .... 59 A3
Water Rd DY3 .... 50 C2
Water Side Way WV9 .... 11 B3
Water St Birmingham B3 .. 164 B3
　Burntwood WS7 .... 6 E8
　Kingswinford DY6 .... 60 D7
　West Bromwich B70 .... 53 D2
　Wolverhampton WV10 .... 163 D4
Water Tower La CV8 .... 147 F6
Watercall Ave CV3 .... 133 C6
Waterdale B90 .... 126 D5
Waterfall Cl Meriden CV7 .. 92 C1
　Smethwick B66 .... 64 E7
Waterfall La B64 .... 63 A1
Waterfall Lane Ind Est
　B64 .... 63 A1
Waterfall Rd DY5 .... 81 D7
Waterfall Way LE9 .... 71 F5
Waterfield Cl DY4 .... 51 D5
Waterfield Gdns CV31 .... 162 C7
Waterfield Way LE10 .... 75 C5
Waterford Rd DY6 .... 60 D7
Waterfront Bsns Pk DY5 ... 61 E4
Waterfront E DY5 .... 61 E4
Waterfront W DY5 .... 61 E4
Waterfront Way DY5 .... 61 E4
Waterglade La WV13 .... 27 A1
Waterhaynes Cl B45 .... 122 A6
Waterhead Cl WV10 .... 12 A2
Waterhead Dr WV10 .... 12 B2
Waterlinks Bvd B6 .... 67 A7
Waterloo Ave B37 .... 70 B4
Waterloo Bvd WS12 .... 2 A7
Waterloo Cl CV34 .... 161 A8
Waterloo Ind Est B37 .... 70 B5
Waterloo Pl [5] CV32 ...... 156 F1
Waterloo Rd
　Birmingham,
　King's Heath B14 .... 104 E8
　Birmingham,
　South Yardley B25 .... 88 C6
　Hinckley LE10 .... 75 D8
　Smethwick B66 .... 65 A3
　Wolverhampton WV1 ...... 163 B4
Waterloo St Birmingham
　B2 .... 164 B2
[8] Coventry CV1 .... 113 E4
　Dudley DY2 .... 62 B8
　Kidderminster DY10 ...... 116 E6
　Royal Leamington Spa CV31 .. 162 B7
　Tipton DY4 .... 51 F5
Waterloo St E DY4 .... 51 F5
Waterloo Terr WV1 .... 163 A4
Waterman Rd CV6 .... 113 F6
Watermeadow Dr WS4 ..... 15 D1

Watermere WS4 .... 29 D8
Watermill Cl WV10 .... 11 D3
Watermint Cl WS12 .... 2 E4
Waters Dr B74 .... 31 D3
Waters Edge The B1 .... 66 C2
Waters View WS3 .... 15 B5
Watersbridge Gdns CV10 .. 73 C1
Waterside
　Birmingham, Egdbaston B15 .. 86 C8
　Birmingham, Hamstead B43 ... 54 E7
　Royal Leamington Spa
　CV31 .... 161 D7
Waterside Cl B24 .... 58 A5
Waterside Ct
　Royal Leamington Spa
　CV31 .... 162 B6
　Tamworth B77 .... 21 F5
Waterside Est DY2 .... 62 C3
Waterside Ind Est
　Blackheath B65 .... 62 F4
　Wolverhampton WV2 .... 40 A6
Waterside View
　Birmingham B18 .... 66 A5
　Brierley Hill DY5 .... 81 B8
Waterside Way WS8 .... 6 D2
Watersmead Cl WS12 .... 2 F4
Watersmeet Gr CV2 .... 114 B6
Watersmeet Ho B78 .... 35 B8
Watersmeet Rd CV2 .... 114 B6
Waterson Croft B37 .... 70 D3
Waterward Cl B17 .... 85 C5
Waterways Dr B69 .... 63 E8
Waterways Gdns DY8 .... 60 E1
Waterworks Dr B31 .... 102 D4
Waterworks Rd B16 .... 65 F1
Waterworks St B6 .... 67 B8
Watery La Alvechurch B48 .. 124 C1
　Belbroughton DY9 .... 118 F7
　Birmingham B62 .... 84 A3
　Cheswick Green B90 ...... 126 D4
　Codsall WV8 .... 10 A5
　Corley CV7 .... 93 D5
　Coventry CV6 .... 95 A4
　Hopwood B48 .... 123 F2
　Keresley CV7 .... 94 F4
　Knowle B93 .... 128 E4
　Lichfield WS13 .... 3 C4
　Portway B48 .... 140 D7
　Redditch B98 .... 154 B2
　Smethwick B67 .... 65 A5
　Stourbridge DY8 .... 60 E2
　Tipton DY4 .... 51 F5
　Walsall WS1 .... 42 E8
　Warwick CV35 .... 160 A1
　Willenhall WV13 .... 26 E3
Watery Lane Ind Est
　WV13 .... 26 E3
Watery Lane Middleway
　B9 .... 67 B2
Watford Gap WS14 .... 32 A7
Watford Gap Rd WS14 ...... 32 A7
Watford Rd B30 .... 103 F5
Wathan Ave WV14 .... 39 F1
Wathen Rd
　Royal Leamington Spa
　CV32 .... 157 A2
　Warwick CV34 .... 160 E8
Watkins Rd B31 .... 103 C4
Watkins Rd WV12 .... 27 C5
Watland Gn B34 .... 69 B5
Watling Cl LE10 .... 75 C4
Watling Ct CV11 .... 73 F3
Watling Dr LE10 .... 75 C4
Watling Rd CV8 .... 148 B6
Watling St Brownhills WS8 .. 7 B1
　Dordon B78 .... 36 B6
　Hinckley CV11, LE10 .... 74 C8
　Mile Oak B78 .... 20 D1
　Tamworth B77 .... 35 D8
Watling Street JMI Sch
　WS8 .... 6 E1
Watney Gr B44 .... 56 C8
Watson Cl
　Sutton Coldfield B72 .... 46 C2
[3] Warwick CV34 .... 155 E1
Watson Rd
　Birmingham, Nechells B24 .. 67 D8
　Birmingham, Saltley B8 ... 67 F5
　Coventry CV5 .... 112 D2
　Wednesbury WS10 .... 41 A5
　Wolverhampton,
　Lanesfield WV4 .... 39 F2
　Wolverhampton,
　Pendeford WV10 .... 11 B2
Watson's Green Fields
　DY2 .... 62 E8
Watson's Green Rd DY2 ... 51 E1
Watsons Cl DY2 .... 56 E4
Watt Rd Birmingham B23 ... 56 E4
　Tipton DY4 .... 52 B8
Watt St Birmingham B21 ... 65 D7
　Smethwick B66 .... 65 B6
Watt's Rd B10 .... 87 D8
Wattis Rd B67 .... 65 A2
Wattisham Sq B35 .... 58 A4
Wattle Rd B70 .... 53 A4
Watton Cl WV14 .... 40 A1
Watton Ct B6 .... 66 E8
Watton Gn B35 .... 58 A3
Watton La B46 .... 59 D2
Watton St B70 .... 53 D2
Watts Cl DY4 .... 51 D5
Watts Rd B80 .... 159 E6
Wattville Ave B21 .... 65 C8
Wattville Jun Sch B21 ...... 65 B8
Wattville Rd B21 .... 65 C8
Watwood Rd B28 .... 105 F3

Waugh Cl B37 .... 70 B2
Waveley Rd CV1 .... 113 A3
Wavell Rd Birmingham B8 ... 67 E5
　Brierley Hill DY5 .... 81 F7
　Walsall WS2 .... 27 E2
Wavendon Cl CV2 .... 96 F1
Waveney B77 .... 35 E8
Waveney Ave WV6 .... 23 E4
Waveney Cl LE10 .... 75 A8
Waveney Croft B36 .... 69 F8
Waveney Gr WS11 .... 1 B1
Wavenham Cl B74 .... 31 E5
Waverhill Rd B21 .... 65 F7
Waverley Ave
　Birmingham B43 .... 44 B4
　Nuneaton CV11 .... 73 F1
Waverley Cl DY10 .... 117 A8
Waverley Cres Romsley
　B62 .... 100 F4
　Wolverhampton,
　Lanesfield WV4 .... 39 F3
　Wolverhampton, Penn WV2 .. 39 B6
Waverley Gdns WV5 .... 49 B7
Waverley Gr B91 .... 106 F3
Waverley Rd Birmingham
　B10 .... 87 D7
　Darlaston WS10 .... 41 D6
　Kenilworth CV8 .... 148 A3
　Royal Leamington Spa
　CV31 .... 162 B6
　Walsall WS3 .... 13 F2
Waverley Sch B10 .... 88 A8
Waverley Sq CV11 .... 73 F1
Waverley St DY2 .... 62 A8
Waverley Wlk WS14 .... 9 B6
Waverton Mews [13] CV31 .. 162 C6
Wavytree Cl CV34 .... 160 D7
Waxland Rd B63 .... 83 B2
Wayfield Cl B90 .... 106 C3
Wayfield Rd B90 .... 106 C3
Wayford Dr B72 .... 57 D7
Wayford Glade WV13 .... 40 F8
Wayford Gr B8 .... 68 B4
Waynecroft Rd B43 .... 43 E2
Wayside Birmingham B37 .. 90 A8
　Wolverhampton WV8 .... 10 F2
Wayside Dr B74 .... 31 C3
Wayside Gdns WV12 .... 27 E5
Wayside Wlk WS2 .... 28 A3
Waystone La DY9 .... 119 D4
Wealden Hatch WV10 .... 11 E4
Wealdstone Dr DY3 .... 50 D2
Weale Gr CV34 .... 155 F2
Weaman St B4 .... 164 C3
Weather Oaks B17 .... 85 B6
Weatheroak Cl B97 .... 153 A1
Weatheroak Hill B48 ...... 124 B1
Weatheroak Rd B11 .... 87 C5
Weatheroaks Brownhills
　WS9 .... 16 B4
　Halesowen B62 .... 84 A7
Weaver Ave Birmingham
　B26 .... 89 B6
　Sutton Coldfield B76 .... 47 C5
Weaver Cl DY5 .... 61 B6
Weaver Gr WV13 .... 27 D2
Weavers Hill B97 .... 158 D4
Weavers Rise DY2 .... 62 D3
Weavers Wlk CV6 .... 114 B8
Weaving Gdns [2] WS11 ... 1 E1
Webb Ave WV6 .... 23 E5
Webb La B28 .... 105 E6
Webb Rd DY4 .... 52 C7
Webb St Dudley WV14 ...... 40 C1
　Nuneaton CV10 .... 72 D3
　Willenhall WV13 .... 26 F2
Webbcroft Rd B33 .... 68 F4
Webheath Fst Sch B97 ... 153 A2
Webley Row WV11 .... 11 F4
Webner Ind Est WV2 .... 40 A6
Webster Ave CV8 .... 148 B5
Webster Cl Birmingham B11 .. 87 B6
　Sutton Coldfield B72 .... 57 B7
Webster Rd Walsall WS2 ... 28 E5
　Willenhall WV13 .... 27 A3
Webster Steet CV6 .... 113 E7
Webster Way B76 .... 58 B8
Webster Wlk WS11 .... 2 A4
Weddell Wynd WV14 .... 40 F1
Weddington Fst Sch CV10 .. 73 D2
Weddington Rd CV10 .... 73 C7
Weddington Terr CV10 ..... 73 D5
Wedge St [10] WS1 .... 28 F2
Wedge-Woods CV5 .... 132 F8
Wedgewood Ave WS7 .... 7 C7
Wedgewood Ct WS4 .... 15 C1
Wedgewood Dr B20 .... 55 B2
Wedgewood Ho B37 .... 70 B4
Wedgewood Pl B70 .... 52 F7
Wedgewood Rd
　Birmingham B32 .... 84 D5
　West Bromwich B70 .... 52 F7
Wedgnock Gn CV34 .... 160 D8
Wedgnock Ind Est CV34 .. 155 C1
Wedgnock La CV34 .... 155 C1
Wedgwood Cl WV1 .... 26 A1
Wednesbury, Great
　Western Street Sta
　WS10 .... 41 D2
Wednesbury Oak Prim Sch
　DY4 .... 41 A1
Wednesbury Oak Rd DY4 .. 41 A1
Wednesbury Parkway Sta
　WS10 .... 41 D2
Wednesbury Rd WS1 .... 42 D7

Wednesbury Trad Est
  WS10 .... 41 E4
Wednesfield High Sch
  WV11 .... 26 E5
Wednesfield Rd
  Willenhall WV13 .... 27 A3
  Wolverhampton
  WV1,WV10 .... 163 D4
Wednesfield Village Prim
Sch
  WV11 .... 26 D5
Wednesfield Way WV11 ... 26 D4
Wedon Cl CV4 .... 131 E7
Weeford Dr B20 .... 54 F4
Weeford Rd B75 .... 32 F3
Weethley Ho B97 .... 153 A4
Weights La B97 .... 153 C7
Weirbrook Cl B29 .... 103 C7
Welbeck Ave Hinckley
  LE10 .... 75 D4
  Wolverhampton WV10 ... 25 D7
Welbeck Dr
  Kidderminster DY11 .... 116 B5
  Walsall WS4 .... 29 D7
Welbeck Gr B23 .... 56 B5
Welbury Gdns WV6 .... 24 F5
Welby Rd B28 .... 87 F1
Welches Cl B31 .... 103 B5
Welcombe Dr B76 .... 57 F7
Welcombe Gr B91 .... 106 F4
Welcome Dr B61 .... 121 A1
Welford Ave B26 .... 88 F8
Welford Cl B98 .... 158 F5
Welford Gr B74 .... 31 F3
Welford Inf & Jun Sch
  B20 .... 66 A8
Welford Pl CV6 .... 113 D7
Welford Rd Birmingham
  B20 .... 66 A8
  Solihull B90 .... 106 C4
  Sutton Coldfield B73 .... 45 E1
  Tamworth B77 .... 35 C5
Welgarth Ave CV6 .... 112 F6
Welham Croft B90 .... 127 A6
Well Cl Birmingham B36 ... 68 E8
  Redditch B97 .... 158 E5
Well La Birmingham B5 ..... 164 D2
  Great Wyrley WS6 .... 5 A1
  Hinckley LE10 .... 71 D1
  Tanworth-In-A B94 .... 142 A1
  Walsall WS3 .... 28 D7
  Walsall WS3 .... 28 E8
  Wolverhampton WV11 .... 26 C4
Well Mdw B45 .... 122 A6
Well Pl WS3 .... 28 E8
Well St
  Birmingham, Hockley B19 .. 66 C5
  Birmingham,
  Newtown B19 .... 66 D6
  Coventry CV1 .... 165 B3
  Darlaston WS10 .... 41 E6
Welland Cl B46 .... 59 B2
Welland Dr DY8 .... 81 A8
Welland Gr Birmingham
  B24 .... 57 D3
  Willenhall WV13 .... 27 C2
Welland Rd Coventry CV1 .. 113 F1
  Halesowen B63 .... 83 A2
Welland Way B76 .... 58 A7
Wellcroft Gr B64 .... 69 A7
Wellcroft St WS10 .... 41 F3
Wellesbourne B79 .... 21 C8
Wellesbourne Cl
  Redditch B98 .... 153 E4
  Wolverhampton WV3 .... 38 B8
Wellesbourne Dr WV14 .... 51 B7
Wellesbourne Rd
  Birmingham B20 .... 55 B1
  Coventry CV5 .... 112 A3
Wellesbourne Tower
  B5 .... 86 E8
Wellesley Dr DY4 .... 51 F5
Wellesley Gdns B13 .... 87 D1
Wellesley Rd B68 .... 64 B6
Wellfield Cl WS11 .... 4 B7
Wellfield Gdns DY2 .... 62 E6
Wellfield Rd Aldridge WS9 .. 30 B8
  Birmingham B28 .... 106 B6
Wellhead La B42 .... 55 E3
Wellhead Way B42 .... 55 F2
Wellington Ave WV3 .... 38 F7
Wellington Cl DY6 .... 60 E4
Wellington Cres B20 .... 55 B2
Wellington Ct
  Birmingham B20 .... 55 C2
  Blackheath B64 .... 62 F2
  Kidderminster DY11 .... 116 C5
Wellington Dr WS11 .... 4 B8
Wellington Gdns ■ CV1 ... 113 B2
Wellington Gr B91 .... 106 F6
Wellington Ho B32 .... 84 F4
Wellington Ind Est WV14 ... 51 C7
Wellington Pl WV13 .... 26 F3
Wellington Rd Bilston
  WV14 .... 40 D6
  Birmingham B20 .... 55 C2
  Birmingham,
  Edgbaston B15 .... 86 C7
  Bromsgrove B60 .... 151 A8
  Dudley DY1 .... 51 B1
  Royal Leamington Spa
  CV32 .... 157 C2
  Smethwick B67 .... 65 A3
  Tipton DY4 .... 52 A4
  Walsall WS5 .... 43 C6

Wellington St
  Birmingham B18 .... 65 E5
  Blackheath B64 .... 62 F2
  Coventry CV1 .... 165 D4
  Oldbury B69 .... 64 B6
  ■ Redditch B98 .... 153 E4
  Walsall WS2 .... 42 B7
  West Bromwich B71 .... 53 C4
Wellington St S B70 .... 53 C4
Wellington Terr
  ■ B19 .... 66 B7
Wellington Tower
  ■ B31 .... 103 A1
Wellman Croft B29 .... 85 D1
Wellman's Rd WV13 .... 27 C1
Wellmead Wlk B45 .... 121 F8
Wellmeadow Gr B92 .... 109 A7
Wells Ave WS10 .... 41 B6
Wells Cl Cannock WS11 .... 1 E6
  Kidderminster DY11 .... 116 A6
  Perton WV6 .... 23 D4
  Tipton DY4 .... 41 A1
  West Bromwich B71 .... 53 D8
Wells Ct Coventry CV3 ..... 133 F7
  Dudley DY2 .... 62 C5
Wells Green Rd B92 .... 89 A4
Wells Rd Bilston WV14 ..... 40 E3
  Blackheath B65 .... 63 E4
  Brierley Hill DY5 .... 61 B3
  Solihull B92 .... 89 C4
  Wolverhampton WV4 .... 38 F5
Wells Tower B16 .... 66 A2
Wells Wlk B37 .... 70 A1
Wellsford Ave B92 .... 89 B4
Welney Gdns WV9 .... 11 A3
Welsby Ave B43 .... 54 F7
Welsh Cl CV34 .... 155 E2
Welsh House Farm Prim
Sch B32 .... 84 F4
Welsh House Farm Rd
  B32 .... 84 F4
Welsh House Farm Sch
  B32 .... 84 F5
Welsh Rd Coventry CV2 .... 114 B4
  Cubbington CV33 .... 157 F2
Welshmans Hill B73 .... 45 C3
Welton Cl B76 .... 47 A2
Welton Rd CV34 .... 155 D1
Welwyn Rd LE10 .... 71 F1
Welwyndale Rd B72 .... 57 C6
Wem Gdns WV11 .... 26 D6
Wembley Gr B25 .... 88 C8
Wembrook Cl CV11 .... 73 D2
Wembrook Ho CV11 .... 73 E2
Wendell Crest WV10 .... 11 F4
Wendiburgh St CV4 .... 132 B7
Wendover Dr LE10 .... 71 E4
Wendover Rd
  Birmingham B23 .... 56 C7
  Blackheath B65 .... 63 A5
  Wolverhampton WV4 .... 39 F2
Wendover Rise CV5 .... 112 C4
Wendron Cl B60 .... 137 B2
Wendron Gr B14 .... 104 D4
Wenlock B77 .... 21 D3
Wenlock Ave WV3 .... 38 E8
Wenlock Cl Halesowen
  B63 .... 82 D2
  Sedgley DY3 .... 50 C7
Wenlock Dr B61 .... 137 A5
Wenlock Gdns WS3 .... 28 E5
Wenlock Gdns Birmingham
  B20 .... 55 F1
  ■ Stourbridge DY8 .... 81 B6
Wenlock Way WV10 .... 72 B3
Wenman St B12 .... 86 F6
Wensley Croft B90 .... 106 B6
Wensley Rd B26 .... 88 F6
Wensleydale Rd B42 .... 55 B6
Wensum Cl LE10 .... 75 B8
Wentbridge Rd WV1 .... 26 C1
Wentworth Ave B36 .... 69 B8
Wentworth Cl Burntwood
  WS7 .... 7 C7
  Hinckley LE10 .... 71 E3
Wentworth Ct
  Birmingham B24 .... 56 F2
  Sutton Coldfield B75 .... 32 B1
Wentworth Dr
  Blackwell B60 .... 138 A5
  Lichfield WS14 .... 9 D5
  Nuneaton CV11 .... 74 A1
  Tipton B69 .... 63 A7
Wentworth Gate B17 .... 85 B6
Wentworth Gr WV6 .... 23 D5
Wentworth Park Ave
  B17 .... 85 B6
Wentworth Rd
  Birmingham B17 .... 85 B6
  Royal Leamington Spa
  CV31 .... 162 D6
  Solihull B92 .... 88 F3
  Stourbridge DY8 .... 80 E7
  Sutton Coldfield B74 .... 46 A8
  Walsall WS3 .... 13 F3
  Wolverhampton WV11 ..... 11 F3
Wentworth Rise B62 .... 83 D3
Wentworth Way B32 .... 84 F3
Wenyon Cl DY4 .... 52 B4
Weoley Ave B29 .... 85 C2
Weoley Castle B29 .... 85 A2
Weoley Castle Rd B29 ...... 84 F1
Weoley Hill B29 .... 103 C8
Weoley Park Rd B29 .... 85 C1
Wergs Dr WV6 .... 24 A7
Wergs Hall Rd WV6, WV8 .. 24 A7
Wergs Rd WV6 .... 24 B6
Werneth Gr WS3 .... 14 A1

Wesley Ave Cheslyn Hay
  WS6 .... 4 D3
  Codsall WV8 .... 10 B2
  Halesowen B63 .... 82 B8
Wesley Ct ■ Blackheath
  B64 .... 82 F8
  ■ Cannock WS11 .... 1 E1
  Willenhall WV13 .... 26 E1
  Wolverhampton WV4 .... 39 F4
Wesley Gr WS10 .... 41 E3
Wesley Ho ■ WS2 .... 42 C7
Wesley Pl Cannock WS12 .. 2 C7
  Tipton DY4 .... 52 C7
Wesley Rd Birmingham B23 .. 56 F5
  Brierley Hill DY5 .... 61 B5
  Codsall WV8 .... 10 B2
  Willenhall WV12 .... 27 C6
Wesley St Bilston WV14 .... 40 E2
  Oldbury B69 .... 64 A8
  West Bromwich B70 .... 53 B3
  Wolverhampton WV2 .... 40 A6
Wesley Way B77 .... 21 F4
Wesley Wlk B60 .... 150 E7
Wesley's Fold WS10 .... 41 D6
Wessenden B77 .... 36 B7
Wessex Cl Bedworth CV12 .. 78 A4
  Brownhills WS8 .... 15 F7
Wessex Ct B79 .... 22 F7
Wessex Dr WS11 .... 1 F2
Wessex Rd WV2 .... 39 F6
Wesson Gdns B63 .... 83 A3
Wesson Rd WS10 .... 41 C8
West Acre WV13 .... 26 F1
West Ave Bedworth CV12 .. 78 D2
  Birmingham,
  Castle Bromwich B36 ...... 69 D8
  Birmingham,
  Handsworth B20 .... 55 A4
  Coventry CV2 .... 114 A2
  Redditch B98 .... 153 E3
  Tipton B69 .... 63 B7
  Wolverhampton WV11 ..... 26 C6
West Bromwich Central
Sta B70 .... 53 C2
West Bromwich Rd WS5 ... 42 F5
West Bromwich Ringway
  B70 .... 53 D2
West Bromwich St
  Oldbury B69 .... 52 F1
  Walsall WS1 .... 42 E7
West Bvd B32 .... 84 F4
West Cl LE10 .... 75 D7
West Coppice Rd WS8 ...... 15 C8
West Ct B60 .... 150 F6
West Dr
  Birmingham,
  Edgbaston B5 .... 86 C5
  Birmingham,
  Handsworth B20 .... 66 B8
  Fazeley B78 .... 20 E2
West End Ave B66 .... 64 D7
West End Ct CV34 .... 160 D6
West End Villas B38 .... 103 F2
West Gate B16 .... 65 E3
West Gn WV4 .... 38 C5
West Green Cl B15 .... 86 B8
West Heath Hospl B38 ..... 123 C8
West Heath Jun & Inf
Sch B38 .... 123 C8
West Heath Rd
  ■ Birmingham,
  Edgbaston B18 .... 65 D4
  Birmingham,
  Northfield B31 .... 103 B1
West Hill Ave WS12 .... 2 B6
West Hill Ct B44 .... 104 C4
West Hill Prim Sch WS12 .. 2 B6
West Holme B9 .... 67 C2
West House Sch B15 .... 86 C8
West Lodge WV1 .... 25 A3
West Mead Dr B14 .... 104 E6
West Mews B44 .... 44 D2
West Midlands Private
  Hospl B63 .... 82 D5
West Mill Croft B38 .... 123 E7
West Orchards Sh Ctr
  CV1 .... 165 B3
West Park Ave B31 .... 102 E2
West Park Ct WV1 .... 25 A2
West Park Hospl WV1 ...... 25 A2
West Park Inf Sch WV1 .... 163 A4
West Park Jun Sch WV1 ... 163 A4
West Park Rd B67 .... 64 D6
West Pathway B17 .... 85 C6
West Point B17 .... 85 C8
West Rd
  Birmingham,
  Hamstead B43 .... 54 E7
  Birmingham,
  Handsworth B42 .... 55 E2
  Bromsgrove B60 .... 137 A2
  Halesowen B63 .... 82 B6
  Tipton DY4 .... 52 B8
West Rd S B63 .... 82 B6
West Ridge CV5 .... 112 A5
West Rise B75 .... 46 C6
West Rock CV34 .... 160 D7
West Side Bsns Ctr CV4 ... 131 F8
West St Birmingham B7 .... 66 F4
  Blackheath B65 .... 63 C1
  Brierley Hill DY5 .... 81 F8
  Cannock WS11 .... 4 E6
  Coventry CV1 .... 113 E3
  Dudley DY1 .... 51 B2
  Redditch B98 .... 153 E4
  Royal Leamington Spa
  CV31 .... 162 A7
  Stourbridge DY8 .... 80 F5

West St continued
  Tamworth B79 .... 21 C5
  Tamworth, Kettlebrook B77 .. 21 C5
  Walsall WS3 .... 28 C7
  Warwick CV34 .... 160 D5
  Wolverhampton W6 .... 25 C5
West View B8 .... 68 C4
West View Dr DY6 .... 60 E5
West View Rd
  Royal Leamington Spa
  CV32 .... 157 C5
  Sutton Coldfield B75 .... 46 E6
West Way B44 .... 15 B2
Westacre Cres WV3 .... 24 C1
Westacre Dr DY5 .... 81 F8
Westacre Gdns B33 .... 68 F3
Westacre Inf Sch WV3 ..... 24 C1
Westbourne Ave
  Birmingham B34 .... 68 E6
  Cannock WS11 .... 1 D3
  Cheslyn Hay WS6 .... 4 E3
Westbourne Cl B61 .... 136 E1
Westbourne Cres
  Birmingham B15 .... 86 A8
  ■ Burntwood WS7 .... 7 B7
Westbourne Ct
  Darlaston WS10 .... 41 F7
  Walsall WS4 .... 29 A3
Westbourne Gdns B15 ..... 86 A7
Westbourne Gr B21 .... 65 F7
Westbourne Rd
  Birmingham B21 .... 54 D1
  Birmingham,
  Edgbaston B15 .... 86 A8
  Darlaston WS10 .... 41 F7
  Halesowen B62 .... 83 E7
  Solihull B92 .... 106 F8
  Walsall WS4 .... 28 F4
  West Bromwich B70 .... 53 B2
  Wolverhampton WV4 .... 39 A5
Westbourne St WS4 .... 28 F3
Westbourne Terr B61 .... 136 E1
Westbrook Ave WS9 .... 29 F5
Westbrook Ct CV5 .... 112 A4
Westbury Ave WS10 .... 41 F6
Westbury Ct ■ ....
  Coventry CV3 .... 114 A3
  Warwick CV34 .... 161 A7
Westbury Rd Coventry
  CV5 .... 112 D5
  Nuneaton CV10 .... 72 D3
  Smethwick B17 .... 65 B3
  Wednesbury WS10 .... 41 F6
Westbury St WV1 .... 163 C3
Westcliff Dr CV34 .... 155 E2
Westcliff Pl B31 .... 102 F4
Westcliffe Dr CV3 .... 133 B5
Westcombe Gr B32 .... 84 A1
Westcote Ave B31 .... 102 C2
Westcote Cl B92 .... 89 A2
Westcotes CV4 .... 112 B1
Westcott Cl DY6 .... 60 F3
Westcott Rd B26 .... 89 A8
Westcroft Ave WV10 .... 12 A1
Westcroft Gr B38 .... 103 D3
Westcroft Rd Sedgley
  DY3 .... 39 B2
  Wolverhampton WV6 .... 23 F6
Westcroft Sch WV10 .... 12 B2
Westcroft Way B14 .... 105 B1
Westdean Cl B62 .... 83 C4
Westerdale Cl DY3 .... 51 A7
Westerham Cl B93 .... 127 F6
Westeria Cl B36 .... 69 C8
Westeria Ho B36 .... 69 C8
Westering Parkway
  WV10 .... 11 F4
Westerings B20 .... 55 C2
Western Ave
  ■ Birmingham B19 .... 66 C7
  Brierley Hill DY5 .... 61 B2
  Halesowen B62 .... 83 E4
  Sedgley DY3 .... 50 B8
  Willenhall WV13 .... 27 D3
Western Bsns Pk
  Birmingham B18 .... 65 E6
  Halesowen B62 .... 83 B7
Western By-Pass WS13 .... 8 F8
Western Cl WS2 .... 27 D3
Western Hill Cl B96 .... 158 E1
Western Rd
  Birmingham,
  Edgbaston B18 .... 65 F4
  Birmingham,
  Erdington B24 .... 57 A3
  Blackheath B64 .... 82 E8
  Cannock WS12 .... 2 B6
  Hagley DY9 .... 99 B4
  Oldbury B69 .... 64 B5
  Stourbridge DY8 .... 80 F4
  Sutton Coldfield B73 .... 46 A1
Western Way
  Kidderminster DY11 .... 116 A5
  Wednesbury WS10 .... 41 C3
Westfield Ave B14 .... 105 B1
Westfield Cl Dorridge B93 .. 127 F2
  Nuneaton CV10 .... 73 D5
Westfield Ct LE10 .... 75 C7
Westfield Cty Jun & Inf
Schs
  LE10 .... 75 B7
Westfield Cty Prim Sch
  WV5 .... 49 A7
Westfield Gr WV3 .... 38 C8
Westfield Hall ■ B16 .... 65 D1
Westfield Ho B36 .... 70 A7
Westfield Manor B75 .... 32 A4

Westfield Rd Bilston WV14 .. 40 B7
  Birmingham,
  Acock's Green B27 .... 88 B3
  Birmingham, Edgbaston B15 .. 85 D7
  Birmingham, Moseley B14 .. 86 E1
  Brierley Hill DY5 .... 81 F8
  Dudley DY2 .... 62 D7
  Halesowen B62 .... 63 E1
  Hinckley LE10 .... 75 B7
  Sedgley DY3 .... 39 E1
  Smethwick B67 .... 64 F5
  Willenhall WV13 .... 40 E8
Westfields B61 .... 136 F8
Westford Gr B28 .... 105 E3
Westgate Aldridge WS9 .... 29 E6
  Cannock WS12 .... 2 F6
Westgate Cl Sedgley DY3 .. 50 E7
  Warwick CV34 .... 160 D6
Westgate Cty Prim Sch
  CV34 .... 160 D6
Westgate Ho ■ CV34 .... 160 E6
Westgate Trad Est WS9 .... 29 E6
Westgrove Ave ■ B90 ...... 127 A6
Westgrove Terr ■ CV32 ... 161 D8
Westham Ho B37 .... 70 B4
Westhaven Rd B72 .... 46 C5
Westhay Rd B28 .... 106 B7
Westhill ■ WV3 .... 24 C2
Westhill Cl B92 .... 106 E8
Westhill Coll B29 .... 103 D8
Westhill Rd Birmingham
  B38 .... 103 F3
  Blackdown CV32 .... 157 A6
  Coventry CV6 .... 112 F6
Westholme Croft B30 .... 103 E8
Westhouse Gr B14 .... 104 D4
Westland Ave WV3 .... 24 F2
Westland Cl B23 .... 56 F5
Westland Gdns
  Stourbridge DY8 .... 80 F7
  ■ Wolverhampton WV3 ... 25 A2
Westland Rd WV3 .... 24 F2
Westland Wlk B35 .... 57 F2
Westlands Rd
  Birmingham B13 .... 87 A1
  Sutton Coldfield B76 .... 57 F6
Westlea Rd CV31 .... 161 E6
Westleigh Ave CV5 .... 132 F7
Westley Cl B28 .... 106 B6
Westley Rd B27 .... 88 B3
Westley St Birmingham B9 .. 67 A2
  ■ Dudley DY2 .... 62 B8
Westmead Ave B80 .... 159 E4
Westmead Cres B24 .... 57 C4
Westmead Dr B68 .... 64 B4
Westmede Ctr CV5 .... 112 C4
Westminister Rd DY11 ..... 116 A6
Westminster Ave WV4 ..... 39 B5
Westminster Cl
  Bromsgrove B61 .... 136 D1
  Dudley DY1 .... 51 A2
Westminster Ct
  Birmingham,
  Handsworth B20 .... 55 C2
  Birmingham, Kingshurst B37 .. 69 F5
  ■ Bromsgrove B61 .... 137 A2
Westminster Dr
  Birmingham B14 .... 104 F4
  Hinckley LE10 .... 75 F4
  Nuneaton CV10 .... 72 B7
Westminster Ind Est DY2 .. 62 D2
Westminster Jun & Inf
  Schs B20 .... 55 C1
Westminster Rd
  Birmingham,
  Handsworth B20 .... 55 C1
  Birmingham, Stirchley B29 .. 104 A3
  Cannock WS11 .... 1 E6
  Coventry CV1 .... 165 A1
  Kidderminster DY11 .... 116 A6
  Stourbridge DY8 .... 60 D2
  Walsall WS4 .... 29 B7
  West Bromwich B71 .... 53 D8
Westmore Way WS10 .... 42 D5
Westmorland Ave CV10 .... 72 E4
Westmorland Ct B71 .... 53 D7
Westmorland Rd
  Coventry CV2 .... 114 F4
  West Bromwich B71 .... 53 D7
Weston Ave Birmingham
  B11 .... 87 C6
  Tipton B69 .... 52 B1
Weston Cl Cannock WS11 .. 2 C1
  Dorridge B93 .... 128 A2
  Hinckley LE10 .... 71 A1
  Royal Leamington Spa
  CV31 .... 162 C6
  Walsall WS1 .... 42 E6
  Warwick CV34 .... 160 F7
Weston Cres WS9 .... 30 B4
Weston Ct ■ WV3 .... 25 C4
Weston Dr Bilston WV14 ... 40 B5
  Great Wyrley WS6 .... 4 F1
  Tipton DY4 .... 41 C2
Weston Hall Stables CV12 .. 79 A3
Weston Ho Birmingham B19 .. 66 E6
  Wolverhampton WV6 .... 24 E5
Weston Ind Est B11 .... 87 E4
Weston La Birmingham B11 .. 87 E4
  Bulkington CV12 .... 79 B3
Weston Rd Birmingham B19 .. 66 B7
  Lichfield WS13 .... 3 A2
  Smethwick B67 .... 64 F2
Weston St Coventry CV1 ... 165 D4
  Walsall WS1 .... 42 E7
Weston Terr ■ B19 .... 66 D8

Westonbirt Cl CV8 148 C6
Westonhall Rd B60 150 D1
Westover Rd B20 54 E4
Westport Cres WV11 26 F5
Westray Cl B45 101 F1
Westray Dr LE10 71 C1
Westridge DY3 50 C8
Westridge Rd B13 105 C6
Westside Dr B32 84 D1
Westville Ave DY11 116 A5
Westville Rd WS2 28 A3
Westward Cl B44 55 F8
Westway Ho WS4 15 B1
Westwick Cl WS9 16 E4
Westwood Ave
Birmingham B11 87 D4
Stourbridge DY8 80 D3
Westwood Bsns Pk
Birmingham B6 56 B1
Coventry CV4 131 F6
Westwood Gr B91 106 F2
Westwood Heath Rd CV4 131 E6
Westwood Rd
Birmingham, Aston B6 56 A2
Birmingham, Kingstanding B73 45 A4
Coventry CV5 113 A1
Westwood St DY5 61 A1
Westwood View B24 57 C3
Westwood Way CV4 132 A6
Westwoods Hollow WS7 7 B8
Wetherby Cl Birmingham B36 68 D8
Wolverhampton WV10 11 D5
Wetherby Rd
Birmingham B27 88 C2
Walsall WS3 14 A4
Wetherfield Rd B11 88 A3
Wexford Cl DY1 50 F2
Wexford Rd CV2 96 D1
Weybourne Rd B44 44 E2
Weycroft Rd B23 56 B7
Weyhill Cl WV9 10 F2
Weymoor Rd B17 85 B3
Weymouth Cl CV3 134 D5
Weymouth Dr B74 31 F4
Weymouth Ho B79 21 B5
Whaley's Croft CV6 113 B8
Whar Hall Rd B92 107 E8
Wharf App WS9 29 F7
Wharf Cl WS14 9 C7
Wharf La Birmingham B18 66 A6
Burntwood WS8 6 F3
Lapworth B94 143 D4
Solihull B91 107 D6
Tardebigge B60 138 B1
Wharf Lodge CV31 161 D7
Wharf Rd
Birmingham, King's Norton B30 104 A2
Birmingham, Tyseley B11 88 B5
Coventry CV6 113 F5
Wharf St
Birmingham, Aston B6 67 A7
Birmingham, Hockley B18 66 A6
Walsall WS2 28 C1
Warwick CV34 161 A8
Wolverhampton WV1 163 D2
Wharf The B1 164 A2
Wharfdale Rd B11 88 A5
Wharfedale Cl DY6 60 B7
Wharfedale St WS10 42 A2
Wharfside B69 63 F7
Wharrington Cl B98 159 A8
Wharrington Hill B98 159 A8
Wharton Ave B92 107 E7
Wharton St B7 67 D8
Wharton St Ind Est B7 67 D8
Wharwell La WS6 5 A1
Whatcote Gn B92 107 D8
Whateley Ave WS3 28 F6
Whateley Cres B36 69 D8
Whateley Ct CV11 73 B4
Whateley Gn B74 46 A8
Whateley Hall Cl B93 128 C7
Whateley Hall Rd B93 128 B7
Whateley La B78 35 F4
Whateley Lodge Dr B36 69 C8
Whateley Pl WS3 28 F6
Whateley Rd Birmingham B21 65 E8
Walsall WS3 28 F6
Whateley Villas CV9 36 B2
Whateley's Dr CV8 148 A5
Wheat Hill WS5 43 E8
Wheat St CV11 73 D4
Wheatcroft Cl Burntwood WS7 7 A5
Halesowen B62 83 F8
Wheatcroft Dr B37 70 C1
Wheatcroft Gr DY2 51 F1
Wheatcroft Rd B33 68 F2
Wheate Croft CV4 111 F2
Wheaten Cl B37 70 D3
Wheatfield Cl B36 70 A7
Wheatfield View B31 102 D6
Wheatfield Way LE10 71 C4
Wheathill Cl
Royal Leamington Spa CV32 156 E2
Wolverhampton WV4 38 E3
Wheatlands Cl WS12 2 C1
Wheatlands Croft B33 69 E3
Wheatlands The WV6 23 D3
Wheatley Cl Oldbury B68 84 C8
Solihull B92 107 E8
Sutton Coldfield B75 32 C3
Wheatley Grange B46 70 F6
Wheatley Rd B68 84 D8
Wheatley St
West Bromwich B70 53 A3
Wolverhampton WV2 39 F6
Wheatmill Cl DY10 98 B2
Wheatmoor Rise B75 46 E6
Wheaton Cl WV10 25 C7
Wheaton Vale B20 54 E3
Wheatridge Cl DY6 60 A8
Wheatridge Rd B60 150 E6
Wheats Ave B17 85 B3
Wheatsheaf Rd
Birmingham B16 65 D2
Tipton B69 63 A8
Wolverhampton WV8 10 E1
Wheatstone Cl DY3 50 E6
Wheatstone Gr B33 68 F5
Wheeler Cl B93 145 B7
Wheeler Ho 12 B69 64 A7
Wheeler Rd WV11 26 C8
Wheeler St Birmingham B19 66 D7
Stourbridge DY8 80 F5
Wheeler Street Sh Ctr B19 66 D6
Wheeler's Fold WV1 163 C3
Wheeler's La B13 105 A7
Wheelers La B13 104 F7
Wheelers Lane Boys Sec Sch B13 104 F7
Wheelers Lane Inf Sch B13 104 F7
Wheelers Lane Jun Sch B13 104 F7
Wheelers Lane Jun Sch (Annexe) B13 105 A6
Wheeley Moor Rd B37 70 A5
Wheeley Rd Alvechurch B48 138 D5
Solihull B92 107 D7
Wheeley's La B15 66 C1
Wheeleys Rd B15 86 B8
Wheelock Cl B74 44 F7
Wheelwright Cl B60 150 E6
Wheelwright Ct 5 B24 56 E2
Wheelwright La CV6 95 C4
Wheelwright Lane Comb Sch CV7 95 D5
Wheelwright Rd B24 56 F1
Wheldrake Ave B34 69 C6
Wheler Rd CV3 134 A7
Whernside Dr WV6 25 A5
Wherretts Well La B91 107 E6
Whetstone Cl B15 85 F5
Whetstone Field JMI Sch WS9 30 B4
Whetstone Gr WV10 25 D8
Whetstone La WS9 30 B4
Whetstone Rd WV10 25 D8
Whetty La B45 121 F7
Whettybridge Rd B45 121 E6
Whichcote Ave CV7 92 C1
Whichford Cl B76 57 D6
Whichford Gr B9 68 C2
While Rd B72 46 B4
Whilmot Cl WV10 12 B6
Whimbrel Gr DY10 117 A1
Whinberry Rise DY5 50 C1
Whinchat Gr DY10 117 A2
Whinfield Rd B61 136 B6
Whinyates Rise WS11 4 F8
Whiston Ave WV11 27 A7
Whiston Gr B29 103 B8
Whiston Ho 9 WS1 28 F1
Whitacre La WS14 16 E7
Whitacre Rd Birmingham B9 67 F3
Knowle B93 128 B7
Nuneaton CV11 73 E4
3 Royal Leamington Spa CV32 157 A2
Whitacre Rd Ind Est CV11 73 F4
Whitaker Rd CV5 112 C3
Whitbourne Cl B12 87 B5
Whitburn Ave B42 55 A5
Whitburn Cl
Kidderminster DY11 116 B5
Wolverhampton WV9 11 A2
Whitburn Rd CV12 77 C1
Whitby Cl WS3 13 F3
Whitby Rd B12 87 A4
Whitby Way WS11 4 C8
Whitchurch Cl B98 158 F6
Whitchurch Way CV4 131 F8
Whitcot Gr B31 122 F8
White Bark Cl WS12 2 A8
White Beam Rd B37 90 D8
White City Rd DY5 62 A1
White Cl DY9 81 C2
White Falcon Ct B91 106 F2
White Farm Rd B74 31 E4
White Field Ave B17 85 A6
White Friars La CV1 165 C2
White Friars St CV1 165 C2
White Hart The 8 WS1 42 E8
White Hill B31 103 B6
White Ho B19 66 D6
White Horse Rd WS8 6 E2
White House Ave WV11 26 F7
White House Cl
Barnt Green B45 122 A2
Solihull B91 106 F3
White House Gn B91 106 F3
White House Way B91 107 A3
White Houses La
Featherstone WV10 12 A6
Wolverhampton WV10 12 B5
White Oak Dr
Kingswinford DY6 60 C6
Wolverhampton WV3 24 C1
White Rd
Birmingham, Quinton B32 84 D6
Birmingham, Sparkbrook B11 87 C7
Smethwick B67 64 F6
White Rose Ho 4 CV32 156 F2
White Row WV5 37 C1
White St Birmingham B12 87 A5
Coventry CV1 165 C3
Walsall WS1 42 E8
White's Dr DY3 50 E8
White's Rd B71 53 C6
Whitebeam Cl
Clayhanger WS8 15 E6
Coventry CV4 111 D1
Whitebeam Croft 3 B38 103 E1
Whitecrest B43 44 A2
Whitecrest Prim Sch B43 44 A2
Whitecroft Rd B26 89 D5
Whitefield Cl Codsall WV8 10 B2
Coventry CV4 131 D6
Whitefields Cres B91 107 B2
Whitefields Gate B91 107 A1
Whitefields Rd B91 107 A2
Whitefriars Dr B63 83 A4
Whitegate Dr DY11 116 A3
Whitegates Rd WV14 40 D2
Whitehall Ct WV3 38 F6
Whitehall Dr Dudley DY1 51 A2
Halesowen B63 83 B4
Whitehall Ind Pk DY4 52 E5
Whitehall Inf Sch WS1 42 E7
Whitehall Jun Sch WS1 42 F7
Whitehall Rd
Birmingham, Bordesley Green B9 67 E1
Birmingham, Handsworth B21 66 A8
Blackheath B64 82 C8
Halesowen B63 83 B4
Kingswinford DY6 60 C6
Stourbridge DY8 81 B2
Tipton DY4, B70 52 E4
2 Walsall WS1 42 E7
Wolverhampton WV4 39 B4
Whitehead Dr
Kenilworth CV8 148 C7
Minworth B76 58 D6
Whitehead Rd B6 66 E8
Whiteheads Ct 15 CV32 156 F1
Whiteheath CE Jun Sch B69 63 D5
Whiteheath Ct 6 B65 63 E4
Whitehill La B29 103 A5
Whitehill Rd DY11 116 A4
Whitehorn Dr CV32 157 B2
Whitehorse Cl CV6 96 B6
Whitehouse Ave
Darlaston WS10 41 B7
Wednesbury WS10 41 F3
Wolverhampton WV3 38 D8
Whitehouse Common Jun & Inf Schs B75 46 D7
Whitehouse Common Rd B75 46 E7
Whitehouse Cres
3 Burntwood WS7 7 B7
Nuneaton CV10 72 D3
Sutton Coldfield B75 46 E7
Wolverhampton WV11 12 F1
Whitehouse Ct B75 46 F6
Whitehouse La Codsall WV8 10 A6
Redditch B98 154 E4
Whitehouse Rd Dordon B78 36 F7
Kidderminster DY10 116 D4
Whitehouse St
Birmingham B6 66 F6
Dudley WV14 51 C8
Tipton DY4 52 A2
Walsall WS2 28 D3
Whitehouse Way WS9 29 F4
Whitelaw Cres CV5 112 C6
Whitemoor Dr B90 127 A7
Whitemoor Rd CV8 148 B5
Whitepits La B48 140 F4
Whites Row CV8 148 A3
Whites Wood WV5 49 A5
Whiteside Cl CV3 134 F8
Whiteslade Cl B93 128 A7
Whitesmith Cl DY3 50 D8
Whitesmith Croft B14 104 E8
Whitesmore Sec Sch B37 69 F1
Whitestitch La CV7 92 C3
Whitestone Fst Sch CV11 79 A8
Whitestone Rd
Halesowen B63 83 A6
Nuneaton CV11 79 B7
Whitethorn Cl WS12 2 A8
Whitethorn Cres B74 30 D1
Whitethorn Rd DY8 61 A1
Whitewood Glade WV12 27 E4
Whitfield Gr B15 86 D8
Whitfield Rd WS12 2 C7
Whitford Bridge Rd B60 151 A2
Whitford Cl B61 150 D8
Whitford Dr B90 127 C7
Whitford Hall Sch B61 136 D2
Whitford Rd B61 136 D2
Whitgreave Ave
Featherstone WV10 12 B7
Wolverhampton WV10 25 F8
Whitgreave Inf Sch WV10 25 E8
Whitgreave Jun Sch WV10 25 E8
Whitgreave Prim Sch WV10 12 B7
Whitgreave St B70 52 E3
Whiting B77 35 D7
Whitland Cl B45 122 B6
Whitland Dr B14 104 F3
Whitley Abbey Comp Sch CV3 133 F5
Whitley Abbey Prim Sch CV3 134 A6
Whitley Ave B77 21 E5
Whitley Cl WV6 24 B2
Whitley Court Rd B32 84 C6
Whitley Ct CV3 133 F7
Whitley Dr B74 45 A8
Whitley St WS10 41 E3
Whitley Village CV3 133 F7
Whitlock Gr B14 105 A3
Whitlock's End Halt B90 125 E7
Whitminster Ave B24 57 B3
Whitminster Cl WV12 27 C4
Whitmore Hill WV1 163 B3
Whitmore Ho W6 25 A4
Whitmore Park Prim Sch CV6 95 A1
Whitmore Park Rd CV6 95 D3
Whitmore Rd
Birmingham B10 87 C8
Stourbridge DY8 80 D5
Whitnash CV31 162 A3
Whitmore St Birmingham B18 66 B6
Walsall WS1 42 D7
Wolverhampton WV1 163 C3
Whitnash Cl CV7 130 A6
Whitnash Cty Comb Sch CV31 162 A4
Whitnash Gr CV2 114 D5
Whitnash Rd CV31 162 B4
Whitney Ave DY8 80 D6
Whittaker St WV2 39 E6
Whittall Dr E DY11 116 B1
Whittall Dr W DY11 116 A1
Whittall St B4 164 C3
Whittimere St WS1 28 F2
Whittingham Gr WV11 26 F6
Whittingham Rd B63 83 A5
Whittington Cl
Birmingham B14 104 E5
Warwick CV34 161 B8
West Bromwich B71 53 F8
Whittington Gr B33 68 F2
Whittington Hall La DY7 80 B3
Whittington Ho WS13 3 E1
Whittington Oval B33 69 A2
Whittington Oval Sch B33 68 F2
Whittington Rd DY8 80 E3
Whittle Cl CV3 134 F8
Whittle Croft B35 57 F3
Whittle Ct 9 CV32 157 A1
Whittle Rd LE10 74 E7
Whittleford Gr B36 58 C1
Whittleford Rd CV10 72 C4
Whitton St WS10 41 E6
Whitville Cl DY11 116 C7
Whitwell Dr B90 127 A6
Whitworth Ave CV3 114 B1
Whitworth Cl WS10 41 E7
Whitworth Dr B71 42 E1
Whitworth Ind Pk B9 67 C2
Whoberley Ave CV5 112 D2
Whoberley Hall Prim Sch CV5 112 C3
Whyley St B70 53 A4
Whyley Wlk B69 64 A5
Whynot St B63 82 B5
Wibert Cl B29 86 A1
Wichnor Rd B92 88 F5
Wickam Sq B70 53 B2
Wickets Tower B5 86 C5
Wickham Cl CV6 94 F2
Wickham Ct CV32 157 B3
Wickham Gdns WV11 26 A6
Wickham Ho 2 B7 67 A4
Wickham Rd B80 159 F4
Wicklow Cl B63 82 D1
Wiclif Way CV10 72 B3
Widdecombe Cl CV2 114 D7
Widdrington Rd CV1 113 C5
Wide Acres B45 101 F1
Wideacre Dr B44 55 E7
Widney Ave Aldridge WS9 16 B1
Birmingham B29 85 C1
Widney Cl B93 127 F5
Widney Jun Sch B91 106 F1
Widney La B91 127 B8
Widney Manor Rd B91 127 D7
Widney Manor Sta B91 127 C8
Widney Rd B93 127 F5
Wigeon Gr WV10 12 B7
Wigford Rd B77 35 C5
Wiggin Cotts 5 B17 85 C5
Wiggin Ho WS3 14 C3
Wiggin St B16 65 F3
Wiggin Tower 5 B19 66 D7
Wiggins Croft B76 46 F3
Wiggins Hill Rd B76 58 F7
Wigginsmill Rd WS10 41 D1
Wigginton Rd B79 21 B7
Wight Croft B36 70 B6
Wightman Cl WS14 9 E6
Wightwick Bank WV6 24 A2
Wightwick Cl 4 WS3 14 B1
Wightwick Ct WV6 24 A2
Wightwick Gr WV6 24 A2
Wightwick Hall Rd WV6 23 E1
Wightwick Hall Specl Sch WV6 23 E2
Wightwick Manor WV6 23 F1
Wigland Way B38 104 A1
Wigmore Gr B44 56 B8
Wigmore La B71 54 A8
Wigorn Ho B67 84 F8
Wigorn La DY9 99 B8
Wigorn Rd B67 64 F1
Wigston Rd CV2 96 F1
Wilberforce Way B92 107 F7
Wilbraham Rd WS2 28 C1
Wilcote Gr B27 106 C8
Wilcox Ave WS12 2 B7
Wild Goose La B98 159 D8
Wildacres DY8 80 C6
Wildcroft Rd CV5 112 C3
Wilde Cl B14 104 D4
Wilden Cl B31 102 C3
Wilden La DY10 116 E1
Wilderness La B43 43 D3
Wildey Rd CV12 77 D2
Wildfell Rd B27 88 D2
Wildmoor Cl CV2 96 B4
Wildmoor La B61 121 A3
Wildmoor Rd B90 106 B5
Wildtree Ave WV10 12 A2
Wiley Ave WS10 41 C5
Wiley Ave S WS10 41 C5
Wilford Gr Solihull B91 107 B2
Sutton Coldfield B76 58 D6
Wilford Rd B71 53 D6
Wilkes Ave WS2 27 F2
Wilkes Cl WS3 14 E3
Wilkes Croft DY3 50 D7
Wilkes Green Jun & Inf Sch B21 54 E1
Wilkes St West Bromwich B71 53 E7
Willenhall WV13 27 A1
Wilkin Rd WS8 6 C2
Wilkins Ho WS3 14 A1
Wilkins Rd WV14 40 D7
Wilkinson Ave WV14 40 E3
Wilkinson Cl
1 Burntwood WS7 7 B8
Sutton Coldfield B73 46 A2
Wilkinson Croft B8 68 C6
Wilkinson Prim Sch WV14 40 F3
Wilkinson Rd WS10 41 A4
Wilks Gn B21 54 D3
Willard Rd B25 88 C6
Willaston Rd B33 89 D7
Willclare Rd B26 89 A7
Willcock Rd WV2 39 E6
Willenhall Comp Sch WS2 27 E5
Willenhall Ind Est WV13 27 C3
Willenhall La Coventry CV3 134 F7
Walsall WS3 28 A8
Willenhall Lane Ind Est WS3 28 A8
Willenhall Rd Bilston WV14 40 F7
Darlaston WS10 41 D8
Wolverhampton WV1, WV13 26 C1
Willenhall St WS10 41 C7
Willenhall Trad Est WV13 27 A1
Willenhall Wood Prim Sch CV3 134 D6
Willerby Fold WV10 11 F4
Willersey Rd B13 105 D8
Willes Ct 2 CV31 162 B7
Willes Rd Birmingham B18 65 E6
Royal Leamington Spa CV31, CV32 162 A8
Willes Terr CV31 162 B8
Willett Ave WS7 6 E5
Willett Rd B71 53 E8
Willetts Dr B63 82 B4
Willetts Rd B31 103 A1
Willetts Way B64 62 F2
Willey Gr B24 57 B2
William Arnold Cl CV2 114 A4
William Batchelor Ho CV1 165 B4
William Baxter Specl Sch The WS12 2 A6
William Beesley Cres CV11 79 E6
William Bentley Ct WV11 26 C5
William Booth La B4 164 B4
William Bree Rd CV5 111 C5
William Bristow Rd CV3 133 E7
William Cook Rd B8 68 B5
William Cowper Inf & Jun Sch B19 66 E6
William Ct B16 65 E1
William Green Rd WS10 42 C3
William Groubb Cl CV3 134 D7
William Harper Rd WV13 27 B1
William Hawke Ind Est DY5 61 E1
William Henry St B7 67 A6
William Iliffe St LE10 75 B7
William Ker Rd DY4 52 C5
William Lunn's Homes
4 WS13 9 C8
William Macgregor Prim Sch
Tamworth B77 21 C3
Tamworth B77 21 D4
William Malcolm Ho CV2 114 E3
William McKee Cl CV3 134 E7
William Morris Gr WS11 1 E4
William Rd B67 64 D3
William Sheriden Ho CV2 114 E3

William St Bedworth CV12 ..... **78** D2
  Birmingham B15 .... **66** C1
  Brierley Hill DY5 .... **61** C3
  Nuneaton CV11 .... **73** E3
  Redditch B97 .... **153** E4
  Royal Leamington Spa
  CV32 .... **162** A8
  Walsall WS4 .... **28** F3
  West Bromwich B70 .... **52** E5
William St N B19 .... **164** B4
William St W B66 .... **65** B7
William Tarver Cl CV34 ..... **161** A7
William Thomson Ho
  2 CV1 .... **165** D4
William Wiggin Ave WS3 ... **14** B2
Williams Cl WV12 .... **27** C5
Williams Rd CV31 .... **162** E4
Williamson St WV3 .... **163** A2
Willingsworth High
  Sch DY4 .... **41** B2
Willingsworth Rd WS10 ..... **41** D1
Willington Rd B79 .... **21** B7
Willington St CV11 .... **73** B5
Willingworth Cl WV14 .... **40** A3
Willis Gr CV12 .... **78** C3
Willis Pearson Ave WV14 ... **41** A3
Willis St DY11 .... **116** C3
Willmore Gr B38 .... **123** F8
Willmore Rd B20 .... **55** D2
Willmott Cl B75 .... **32** D3
Willmott Rd B75 .... **32** D3
Willoughby Ave CV8 .... **147** E3
Willoughby Cl CV3 .... **134** E8
Willoughby Ct B76 .... **46** F2
Willoughby Dr B91 .... **107** B1
Willoughby Rd B29 .... **85** A1
Willoughby Rd B79 .... **20** E7
Willow Ave Birmingham B17 .. **65** A2
  Burntwood WS7 .... **7** C6
  Wednesbury WS10 .... **41** F4
  Wolverhampton WV11 ..... **26** B8
Willow Bank WV3 .... **24** C1
Willow Bank Rd B93 .... **127** F6
Willow Brook Rd B48 .... **139** A7
Willow Cl Bedworth CV12 ... **78** B5
  Blackheath B64 .... **62** E1
  Bromsgrove B61 .... **136** E2
  Hagley DY9 .... **98** F5
  Hinckley LE10 .... **75** E5
  Nuneaton CV10 .... **72** A7
Willow Coppice B32 .... **84** C1
Willow Ct Birmingham B13 ... **87** A3
  Bromsgrove B61 .... **136** E3
  Lichfield WS14 .... **9** C5
  Oldbury B66 .... **64** D8
  Smethwick B66 .... **65** A2
Willow Ctyd CV2 .... **114** D7
Willow Dr Birmingham B21 ... **54** C1
  Cheswick Green B90 .... **126** D4
  Codsall WV8 .... **10** B3
  Tipton B69 .... **63** C7
Willow End DY9 .... **81** D3
Willow Gdns Birmingham
  B16 .... **65** F4
  Bromsgrove B61 .... **136** E3
Willow Gr Coventry CV4 ..... **112** B2
  Essington WV11 .... **13** B3
Willow Ho Birmingham B7 ... **67** B4
  Walsall WS4 .... **15** D1
Willow Hts B64 .... **83** A8
Willow Meer CV8 .... **148** B5
Willow Mews B29 .... **85** B1
Willow Park Dr DY8 .... **81** B2
Willow Rd
  Birmingham,
  Bournville B30 .... **103** F8
  Birmingham, Great Barr B43 .. **44** A2
  Bromsgrove B61 .... **136** E3
  Dudley DY1 .... **51** A4
  Nuneaton CV10 .... **72** F5
  Solihull B91 .... **106** E2
  Wolverhampton WV3 ...... **38** D8
Willow Rise DY5 .... **61** C1
Willow Sheets Mdw
  CV32 .... **157** E6
Willow Tree Dr B45 .... **138** D8
Willow Way Birmingham
  B37 .... **70** B1
  Redditch B97 .... **153** B4
Willow Wlk WS12 .... **1** D8
Willowbank B78 .... **21** B1
Willowbank Rd LE10 .... **75** C4
Willowdale LE10 .... **75** A7
Willowdale Grange WV6 ... **24** E5
Willowfield Dr DY11 .... **116** C8
Willowfields Rd CV11 .... **74** A1
Willowherb Cl Cannock
  WS11 .... **2** C2
  5 Coventry CV3 .... **134** F8
  4 Walsall WS3 .... **43** A3
Willows Cres B12 .... **86** E5
Willows Prim Sch WS13 ..... **3** B2
Willows Rd Birmingham B12 .. **86** E5
  Walsall, Shelfield WS4 ..... **29** C8
  Walsall, The Chuckery WS1 .. **29** A1
Willows The Bedworth
  CV12 .... **77** E2
  Birmingham B27 .... **88** B2
  Cannock WS11 .... **1** C1
  Hollywood B47 .... **125** A6
  Sutton Coldfield,
  Streetly B74 .... **31** F2
  Sutton Coldfield,
  Walmley B76 .... **46** F2
  Wolverhampton WV11 ..... **26** B5

Willowsbrook Rd B62 .... **83** F8
Willowside WS4 .... **29** C8
Willowsmere Dr WS14 ...... **9** F7
Willowtree Cl WS13 .... **3** B2
Wills Ave B71 .... **53** B7
Wills Ho B70 .... **53** C2
Wills St B19 .... **66** C7
Wills Way B66 .... **65** C4
Willsbridge Covert
  8 B14 .... **104** C2
Wilson Croft B28 .... **105** D3
Wilmcote Cl B12 .... **86** E6
Wilmcote Ct B61 .... **150** D8
Wilmcote Dr B75 .... **32** B3
Wilmcote Gn CV5 .... **112** A3
Wilmcote Ho B97 .... **153** B4
Wilmcote Rd B61 .... **106** F6
Wilmcote Tower **6** B12 ... **86** F7
Wilmington Rd B32 .... **84** B6
Wilmore Ho B20 .... **55** D1
Wilmore La B47 .... **124** F4
Wilmot Ave B46 .... **70** F6
Wilmot Dr Birmingham B23 .. **57** A6
  Tipton DY4 .... **51** E6
Wilmot Gdns DY1 .... **51** A2
Wilmott Cl WS13 .... **9** A7
Wilnecote Gr
  Birmingham B42 .... **55** D4
  Royal Leamington Spa
  CV31 .... **162** B5
Wilnecote High Sch B77 ..... **35** E8
Wilnecote Jun Sch B77 ..... **35** F7
Wilnecote La B77 .... **21** D2
Wilnecote Sta B77 .... **35** D7
Wilner's View WS3 .... **14** F5
Wilsford Cl Birmingham
  B14 .... **104** D1
  Walsall WS4 .... **29** C8
Wilson Dr B75 .... **47** A5
Wilson Gn CV3 .... **114** F1
Wilson Gr Cannock WS11 ... **2** C2
  Kenilworth CV8 .... **148** C4
Wilson Ho B69 .... **63** C5
Wilson Rd Birmingham B19 .. **66** D8
  Brierley Hill DY5 .... **61** C4
  Dudley WV14 .... **51** C7
  Oldbury B68 .... **64** D1
  Smethwick B66 .... **65** B3
Wilson St Tipton DY4 .... **52** A5
  Wolverhampton WV1 ...... **163** C4
Wilson Stewart Sch B23 .... **56** C6
Wilson's La CV6 .... **95** F6
Wilsons La CV7 .... **96** A6
Wilsons Rd B93 .... **128** C6
Wiltell Rd WS14 .... **9** B6
Wilton Ave DY11 .... **116** B8
Wilton Cl DY3 .... **50** E7
Wilton Rd
  Balsall Common CV7 .... **130** B5
  Birmingham,
  Balsall Heath B11 .... **87** B5
  Birmingham, Erdington B23 .. **57** A5
  Birmingham,
  Handsworth B20 .... **55** B1
Wilton St B19 .... **66** D8
Wiltshire Cl Bedworth CV12 .. **78** A3
  Coventry CV5 .... **112** B3
  Walsall WS2 .... **28** D4
Wiltshire Dr B63 .... **82** B7
Wiltshire Ho **3** DY8 .... **80** F8
Wiltshire Way B71 .... **53** C7
Wimberger Ho **2** B71 ..... **53** D4
Wimblebury Rd
  Cannock, Heath Hayes WS12 .. **2** F2
  Cannock, Wimblebury WS12 .. **2** F2
Wimbledon Dr DY8 .... **81** B2
Wimborne Dr CV2 .... **115** A4
Wimborne Rd WV10 .... **26** A6
Wimbourne Cl CV10 .... **72** B5
Wimbourne Rd
  Birmingham B16 .... **65** D3
  Sutton Coldfield B76 ...... **47** A4
Wimperis Way B43 .... **44** C4
Wimpole Gr B44 .... **56** B7
Wimshurst Mdw WV10 ..... **11** F4
Wincanton Croft B36 .... **68** C8
Winceby Pl CV4 .... **111** D1
Winceby Rd WV6 .... **23** F3
Winchat Cl CV3 .... **114** F1
Winchcombe Cl Dudley
  DY1 .... **50** E3
  Solihull B92 .... **89** B2
Winchcombe Rd B92 .... **89** B2
Winchester Ave
  Kidderminster DY11 .... **116** A6
  Nuneaton CV10 .... **73** C7
Winchester Cl
  8 Blackheath B65 .... **63** E4
  Hagley DY9 .... **99** A6
  Lichfield WS13 .... **3** C3
  Sutton Coldfield B74 ...... **31** F2
Winchester Dr
  Birmingham B37 .... **70** A2
  Hinckley LE10 .... **76** B7
  Stourbridge DY8 .... **81** A3
Winchester Gdns B31 ...... **103** A3
Winchester Gr B21 .... **65** C8
Winchester Rd
  Birmingham B20 .... **55** D1
  Cannock WS11 .... **2** A4
  West Bromwich B71 .... **53** B8
  Wolverhampton WV10 ..... **11** C3
Winchester Rise DY1 .... **51** A2
Winchester St CV1 .... **113** E3
Winchfield Dr B17 .... **84** F7
Wincote Dr WV6 .... **24** C4
Wincrest Way B34 .... **69** C5
Windermere B77 .... **36** A7

Windermere Ave
  Coventry, Binley CV3 .... **114** E1
  Coventry, Upper Eastern Green
  CV5 .... **111** E4
  Nuneaton CV11 .... **73** F6
Windermere Dr Aldridge B74 .. **30** F3
  Kingswinford DY6 .... **60** D6
  Royal Leamington Spa CV32 .. **156** D2
Windermere Ho
  Kidderminster DY10 .... **116** E7
  11 Oldbury B69 .... **63** D5
Windermere Pl WS11 .... **1** E1
Windermere Rd
  Birmingham,
  Handsworth B21 .... **54** E2
  Birmingham, Moseley B13 ... **87** B1
  Wolverhampton WV6 ...... **24** D8
Windermre Ho B15 .... **85** D3
Winding Mill N DY5 .... **81** E7
Winding Mill S DY5 .... **81** E7
Windings The WS13 .... **3** A1
Windlass Croft B31 .... **102** F4
Windleaves Rd B36 .... **69** E8
Windley Ho B73 .... **45** C2
Windmill Ave
  Birmingham B45 .... **121** E8
  4 Coleshill B46 .... **70** F7
Windmill Bank WV5 .... **49** A7
Windmill Cl
  Birmingham B31 .... **103** C5
  Kenilworth CV8 .... **148** A6
  Lichfield WS13 .... **3** A2
  Tamworth B79 .... **21** A8
Windmill Cres
  Smethwick B66 .... **65** C5
  West Bromwich B71 .... **42** F1
  Wolverhampton WV3 ...... **24** A1
Windmill Croft CV32 .... **157** D5
Windmill Ct CV6 .... **96** A3
Windmill Dr B97 .... **158** C6
Windmill End DY2 .... **62** E5
Windmill Gr DY6 .... **60** B8
Windmill Hill
  Birmingham B31 .... **103** B5
  Halesowen B63 .... **82** D5
  Royal Leamington Spa
  CV32 .... **157** D5
Windmill Hill The CV5 ...... **112** A7
Windmill Ind Est CV5 .... **111** F7
Windmill La
  Balsall Common CV7 .... **130** D4
  Corley CV7 .... **93** D6
  Dorridge B93 .... **127** F1
  Lichfield WS13 .... **3** A2
  Smethwick B66 .... **65** B5
  Tanworth-in-A B94 .... **144** A8
  Wolverhampton WV3 ...... **38** A8
Windmill Prec B66 .... **65** C5
Windmill Rd Bedworth CV7 .. **96** A8
  Coventry CV6 .... **96** A3
  Nuneaton CV10 .... **72** D7
  Royal Leamington Spa CV31 .. **161** F5
  Solihull B90 .... **105** E2
Windmill St Birmingham
  B1 .... **164** B1
  Dudley, Eve Hill DY1 ...... **51** A2
  Dudley, Gornalwood DY3 ... **50** D5
  Walsall WS1 .... **42** F8
  Wednesbury WS10 .... **42** A3
Windmill Terr WS10 .... **42** A3
Windmill View DY1 .... **51** B7
Windridge Cl CV3 .... **134** C6
Windridge Cres B92 .... **107** F8
Windrow The WV6 .... **23** D4
Windrush Cl Redditch B97 .. **158** D6
  Solihull B92 .... **89** A2
Windrush Dr LE10 .... **75** A8
Windrush Gr B29 .... **104** A8
Windrush Ho B31 .... **102** E5
Windrush Rd Cannock WS11 .. **1** E6
  Hollywood B47 .... **125** B7
Winds Point DY9 .... **99** A6
Windsor Arc B2 .... **164** C3
Windsor Ave Oldbury B68 ... **64** A3
  Wolverhampton WV4 ...... **38** E6
Windsor Cl
  Birmingham,
  Coft Common B31 .... **123** A6
  Birmingham, Frankley B45 ... **102** A2
  Blackheath B65 .... **63** C4
  Dudley DY3 .... **50** B2
  Halesowen B63 .... **82** F3
  Tamworth B79 .... **21** C7
Windsor Cres CV2 .... **62** D6
Windsor Ct Birmingham
  B38 .... **103** F1
  Coventry CV4 .... **112** B2
  Hinckley LE10 .... **76** A5
  Lichfield WS14 .... **9** B6
  Nuneaton CV10 .... **72** E6
  2 Royal Leamington Spa
  CV32 .... **161** F8
Windsor Dr Birmingham
  B24 .... **57** C5
  Kidderminster DY10 .... **116** E7
  Solihull B92 .... **89** B2
Windsor Gate WV12 .... **27** C4
Windsor Gdns
  Bromsgrove B60 .... **137** A2
  Nuneaton CV10 .... **72** E4
  Wolverhampton WV3 ...... **38** A8
Windsor Gr Stourbridge
  DY8 .... **60** E1
  Walsall WS4 .... **15** C2
Windsor High Sch B63 ..... **82** F4
Windsor Ho
  3 Birmingham B23 .... **56** F6
  Dudley DY2 .... **61** F7

Windsor Ind Est B7 .... **67** A5
Windsor Lodge B92 .... **106** D8
Windsor Pl Birmingham B7 .. **67** A3
  8 Royal Leamington Spa
  CV32 .... **156** F1
Windsor Rd
  Birmingham,
  Castle Bromwich B36 ..... **69** F7
  Birmingham,
  New Oscott B73 .... **45** D1
  Birmingham, Stirchley B30 .. **104** B5
  Blackheath B65 .... **63** C5
  Cheslyn Hay WS6 .... **4** E4
  Halesowen B63 .... **82** F4
  Oldbury B68 .... **64** A3
  Redditch B97 .... **153** D5
  Stourbridge DY8 .... **80** E3
  Tipton DY4 .... **52** A8
  West Bromwich B71 .... **42** B1
  Wolverhampton WV4 ...... **39** F5
Windsor St Bilston WV14 ... **40** C6
  Birmingham B7 .... **67** A4
  Bromsgrove B60 .... **137** A2
  Coventry CV1 .... **113** B2
  Hinckley LE10 .... **76** A5
  Nuneaton CV11 .... **73** B4
  Redditch B97 .... **153** D4
  Royal Leamington Spa
  CV32 .... **161** F8
  Walsall WS1 .... **42** F7
Windsor St S B7 .... **67** A4
Windsor Terr **5** B16 ...... **65** F1
Windsor View B32 .... **102** B7
Windsor Way WS4 .... **29** D7
Windsor Wlk WS10 .... **41** D8
Windward Way B36 .... **70** B6
Windward Way Ind Est
  B36 .... **69** F8
Windy Arbor Prim Sch
  B37 .... **70** D2
Windy Arbour CV8 .... **148** B4
Windyridge Rd B76 .... **58** A6
Winfield Rd CV11 .... **73** B5
Winford Ave DY6 .... **60** E4
Winforton Cl B98 .... **154** E3
Wing Cl WS2 .... **27** F4
Wingate Cl B30 .... **103** F4
Wingate Ct B74 .... **31** E4
Wingate Rd WS2 .... **27** E2
Wingfield Cl B37 .... **69** F3
Wingfield Ho B37 .... **69** F5
Wingfield Rd
  Birmingham B42 .... **55** C7
  Coleshill B46 .... **70** F5
Wingfoot Way WV6 .... **95** A2
Wingfoot Ave WV10 .... **25** E8
Wingrave Cl CV5 .... **112** A6
Winifred Ave CV5 .... **113** A1
Winifride Ct B17 .... **85** B5
Winkle St B70 .... **53** B4
Winleigh Rd B20 .... **54** F2
Winn Ho **3** WS2 .... **28** D3
Winnall Cl WV14 .... **40** D2
Winnallthorpe CV3 .... **134** E6
Winnie Rd B29 .... **85** E1
Winnington Rd B8 .... **68** A7
Winnipeg Rd B38 .... **124** A8
Winscar Croft DY3 .... **50** D3
Winsford Ave CV5 .... **112** B4
Winsford Cl
  Balsall Common CV7 .... **130** A6
  Halesowen B63 .... **83** A6
  Sutton Coldfield B76 ...... **46** E3
Winsford Ct CV5 .... **112** C4
Winsham Gr B21 .... **65** E8
Winsham Wlk CV3 .... **133** D3
Winslow Ave B8 .... **68** B4
Winslow Dr Coventry CV5 ... **112** B3
  Redditch B98 .... **154** F1
  Royal Leamington Spa
  CV32 .... **156** C1
Winslow Dr WV6 .... **24** E4
Winslow Ho **11** CV1 ...... **113** B2
Winson Green,
  Outer Circle B21 .... **65** E7
Winson Green Rd B18 ..... **65** E5
Winson St B18 .... **65** D4
Winsor Ave WS12 .... **2** B6
Winspear Cl CV7 .... **92** B1
Winstanley Rd B33 .... **68** D2
Winster Ave B93 .... **127** E4
Winster Cl CV7 .... **95** A7
Winster Gr B44 .... **44** D2
Winster Grove Ind Est
  B44 .... **44** D2
Winster Rd Birmingham B43 .. **54** D8
  Wolverhampton WV1 ...... **26** B1
Winston Ave CV2 .... **114** D8
Winston Churchill Ct
  WV14 .... **40** C8
Winston Cl CV2 .... **114** D8
Winston Dr Birmingham B20 .. **55** B1
  Romsley B62 .... **101** A4
Winterbourne Croft B14 ... **104** C1
Winterbourne Rd B91 ..... **106** F4
Winterdene CV7 .... **130** B7
Winterfold Cl DY10 .... **117** B6
Winterley Gdns DY3 .... **50** E6
Winterley La WS4 .... **29** C6
Winterton Rd
  Birmingham B44 .... **44** F4
  Bulkington CV12 .... **79** C2
Winthorpe Dr B91 .... **127** C8
Wintney Cl B17 .... **85** A7
Winton Gr B76 .... **58** A6
Wintour Wlk B60 .... **150** E7

Winward Rd B98 .... **154** F1
Winwood Ct DY8 .... **80** F4
Winwood Heath Rd B62 ... **100** E2
Winwoods Gr B32 .... **102** A8
Winyate Hill B98 .... **154** A2
Winyates Crafts Ctr B98 ... **154** E3
Winyates Ctr B98 .... **154** E3
Winyates Way B98 .... **154** E4
Wirehill Dr B98 .... **153** F1
Wiremill Cl B44 .... **55** E6
Wirral Rd B31 .... **102** F6
Wise Gr CV34 .... **155** E2
Wise St CV31 .... **161** F7
Wise Terr CV31 .... **161** F7
Wiseacre Croft B90 .... **105** E2
Wiseman Gr B23 .... **45** D1
Wisemore WS2 .... **28** E2
Wishaw Cl Redditch B98 ... **159** A8
  Solihull B90 .... **105** E2
Wishaw Gr B37 .... **69** F5
Wishaw La Curdworth B76 ... **59** F1
  Middleton B78 .... **48** C6
  Minworth B76 .... **58** E7
Wisley Gr CV8 .... **148** C5
Wisley Way B32 .... **84** F5
Wissage Cres WS13 .... **9** D8
Wissage La WS13 .... **3** D1
Wissage Rd WS13 .... **9** D8
Wistaria Cl Birmingham
  B31 .... **103** A6
  2 Coventry CV2 .... **96** B2
Wisteria Gr B44 .... **44** E2
Wistwood Hayes WV10 ... **11** F4
Witham Croft B91 .... **107** C1
Withdean Cl B11 .... **87** D6
Witherford Cl B29 .... **103** C8
Witherford Croft B91 ...... **106** E2
Witherford Way B29 .... **103** C8
Withern Way DY3 .... **50** D3
Withers Rd WV8 .... **10** B3
Withers Way B71 .... **53** D4
Withington Covert B14 .... **104** D2
Withington Gr B93 .... **127** E4
Withum Cl B76 .... **47** A1
Withy Gr B37 .... **69** F5
Withy Hill Rd B75 .... **47** B8
Withy Rd WV14 .... **40** C3
Withy Road Ind Est WV14 ... **40** C3
Withybed Cl B48 .... **139** A6
Withybed La B48 .... **139** A6
Withybrook Cl CV2 .... **96** D2
Withybrook La CV7 .... **97** F5
Withybrook Rd
  Bulkington CV12 .... **79** D2
  Solihull B90 .... **126** B8
Withymoor Prim Sch DY5 ... **61** D1
Withymoor Rd Dudley DY2 ... **62** E4
  Stourbridge DY8 .... **81** A7
Withymore Ct WS2 .... **25** A1
Withywood Cl WV12 .... **13** C1
Witley Ave Halesowen B63 ... **82** E4
  Solihull B91 .... **107** C2
Witley Cl DY11 .... **116** B2
Witley Cres B69 .... **63** E5
Witley Farm Cl B91 .... **107** C2
Witley Rd **1** B31 .... **103** D2
Witney Dr B79 .... **20** F7
Witney Dr B37 .... **69** F2
Witney Gr WV10 .... **11** B3
Wittersham Ct WV13 ...... **27** B2
Witton Bank B62 .... **83** F7
Witton La Birmingham B6 ... **55** F1
  West Bromwich B71 .... **53** B8
Witton Lodge Rd B23 ..... **56** D7
Witton Rd Birmingham B6 ... **66** E8
  Wolverhampton WV4 ...... **39** A6
Witton St Birmingham B9 ... **67** B2
  Stourbridge DY8 .... **80** F4
Witton Sta B6 .... **55** F1
Wixford Gr B90 .... **106** D2
Wobaston Rd WV9, WV10 .. **11** B4
Woburn B77 .... **21** D3
Woburn Ave WV12 .... **27** B6
Woburn Cl Bromsgrove
  B61 .... **136** D1
  Hinckley LE10 .... **71** E3
  Royal Leamington Spa
  CV31 .... **162** C6
Woburn Cres B43 .... **43** D1
Woburn Dr Brierley Hill
  DY5 .... **81** B8
  Halesowen B62 .... **83** B7
  Nuneaton CV10 .... **73** A2
Woburn Gr B27 .... **88** C1
Woburn Ho B15 .... **86** C7
Wodehouse La DY3 .... **49** E8
Woden Ave WV11 .... **26** C6
Woden Cres WV11 .... **26** C6
Woden Rd WV10 .... **25** F4
Woden Rd E WS10 .... **42** B4
Woden Rd N WS10 .... **41** F5
Woden Rd S WS10 .... **42** A1
Woden Rd W WS10 .... **41** D4
Woden Sch WV10 .... **25** E4
Wodensborough High Sch
  WS10 .... **42** B2
Wodensfield Cty Inf &
  Jun Schs
  WV11 .... **26** B6
Wodensfield Twr WV11 .... **26** C5
Wold Wlk B13 .... **105** C6
Wolfe Rd CV4 .... **131** F8
Wolfsbane Dr WS5 .... **43** A3
Wolfson Dr B15 .... **85** E4
Wollaston Cres WV11 ..... **26** D6

Wollaston Ct Stourbridge
DY7 .... 80 C6
1 Walsall B23 .... 28 F2
Wollaston Rd
Stourbridge, Amblecote DY8 .. 80 F8
Stourbridge, Wollaston DY7 .. 80 C7
Wollerton Gr B75 .... 46 F6
Wollescote Dr B91 .... 107 B2
6 DY9 .... 81 F5
Wollescote Factory Ctr
6 DY9 .... 81 F5
Wollescote Prim Sch DY9 .. 81 F4
Wollescote Rd DY9 .... 81 D3
Wolmer Rd WV11 .... 13 A2
Wolseley B77 .... 21 F3
Wolseley Ave B27 .... 88 D4
Wolseley Bank WV10 .... 25 F7
Wolseley Cl Birmingham
B36 .... 59 A1
Wolverhampton WV10 ...... 25 F7
Wolseley Dr B8 .... 68 B7
Wolseley Gate WV10 .... 25 F7
Wolseley Rd Bilston WV14 ... 40 C7
West Bromwich B70 .... 52 F6
Wolseley St B9 .... 67 B2
Wolsey St CV3 .... 134 D6
Wolston Cl B90 .... 106 B5
Wolston La CV8 .... 135 C4
Wolverhampton Dudley &
Dist Inst for the Blind
The WV4 .... 39 D3
Wolverhampton Girls High
Sch WV6 .... 24 F3
Wolverhampton Gram Sch
WV3 .... 24 F2
Wolverhampton & Midland
Cties Eye Infmy WV3 ... 25 A2
Wolverhampton Rd
Cannock WS11 .... 4 D8
Cheslyn Hay WV10, WS6 .. 4 B2
Codsall WV8 .... 10 A3
Essington WV11 .... 13 A3
Kingswinford DY6 .... 60 C8
Nurton WV6 .... 23 A3
Oldbury B69 .... 63 F4
Sedgley DY3 .... 39 D2
Walsall, Birchills WS2 .... 28 B2
Walsall, Pelsall WS3 ...... 14 F3
Walsall,
Wallington Heath WS3 ... 14 B1
Wedges Mills WS11 .... 4 B5
Wolverhampton
WV10, WV11 .... 26 B4
Wolverhampton Rd E
WV4 .... 39 E5
Wolverhampton Rd S B32 .. 84 E7
Wolverhampton Rd W
WV13, WS2 .... 27 D2
Wolverhampton St
Bilston WV14 .... 40 C6
Darlaston WS10 .... 41 C6
Dudley DY1 .... 51 B1
Walsall WS2 .... 28 D2
Willenhall WV13 .... 27 A1
Wolverhampton St
George's Sta WV1 .... 163 C2
Wolverhampton Sta
(High Level) WV10 ...... 163 C3
Wolverley Ave
Stourbridge DY8 .... 80 C6
Wolverhampton WV4 ...... 38 D5
Wolverley Cres B69 ...... 63 E5
Wolverley Rd
Birmingham B32 .... 102 B8
Halesowen B63 .... 82 F2
Solihull B90 .... 89 D2
Wolverson Cl WV12 ...... 27 C4
Wolverson Rd WS9 .... 16 A4
Wolverton Cl B98 .... 154 E2
Wolverton Rd
Birmingham,
Marston Green B37 .... 90 B7
Birmingham, Rednall B45 ... 122 C6
Coventry CV5 .... 112 A3
Dudley DY2 .... 51 E1
Wolvey Rd Bulkington CV12 ... 79 E2
Hinckley LE10 .... 75 E4
Wombourne Cl B90 ...... 50 C8
Wombourne Pk WV5 .... 49 A4
Wood Ave Dudley DY3 .... 50 C4
Wednesfield WV11 .... 26 D6
Wood Bank Rd WV3 ...... 38 A8
Wood Cl B46 .... 70 F7
Wood Croft B47 .... 125 B6
Wood Ct Birmingham B20 ... 55 A2
Coventry CV2 .... 114 D7
Wood End Dr B45 .... 138 A8
Wood End Fst Sch CV9 .... 36 C1
Wood End Jun Sch CV2 .. 96 D1
Wood End La
Birmingham B24 .... 56 F3
Lichfield WS13 .... 3 F6
Tanworth-In-A B94 .... 141 F5
Wood End Prim Sch
WV11 .... 26 C7
Wood End Rd
Birmingham B24 .... 56 F3
Walsall WS5 .... 43 D8
Wednesfield WV11 .... 26 D7
Wood End Sta B94 .... 141 F4
Wood End Way WS9 ..... 16 B1
Wood Green High Sch
WS10 .... 42 B5
Wood Green Jun Sch WS10 .. 42 A4
Wood Green Rd
Birmingham B18 .... 65 D4
Wednesbury WS10 .... 42 A3
Wood Hayes Rd WV11 ... 12 C1
Wood Hill Rise CV6 ...... 95 D2

Wood Ho 1 WS1 .... 42 E7
Wood La Aldridge B74 .... 30 E2
Birmingham, Erdington B24 .. 57 C1
Birmingham,
Handsworth B20 .... 55 B2
Birmingham, Harborne B17 ... 85 A6
Birmingham,
Marston Green B37 .... 90 A8
Birmingham,
Woodgate B32 .... 84 A1
Cannock WS12 .... 2 D4
Earlswood B94 .... 125 E1
Fairfield B61 .... 120 C3
Hampton in A B92 .... 108 F2
Nuneaton CV10 .... 72 A8
Shenstone, WS14 .... 17 B2
Shilton CV7 .... 97 D5
Walsall WS3 .... 14 F4
Wedges Mills WS11 .... 4 A6
West Bromwich B70 ...... 53 A3
Willenhall WV12 .... 27 E7
Wolverhampton WV10 ... 11 D2
Wood Lane Cl WV12 ..... 27 E7
Wood Leasow B32 .... 84 D2
Wood Leigh Cl B63 ...... 83 A6
Wood Piece La B98 ...... 154 D7
Wood Rd Dudley DY3 ..... 50 C4
Wolverhampton WV6 ...... 24 C3
Wombourne WV5 .... 49 B7
Wood Ridings WS13 ...... 3 A1
Wood Side WV11 .... 27 A8
Wood St Bedworth CV12 .. 78 B5
Bilston WV14 .... 40 D5
Birmingham B16 .... 66 A2
Darlaston WS10 .... 41 F6
Dudley DY2 .... 61 F6
Hinckley LE10 .... 71 D1
Kidderminster DY11 .... 116 D5
Nuneaton CV10 .... 72 F4
Royal Leamington Spa
CV32 .... 162 A8
Stourbridge, Lye DY9 .... 81 F5
Stourbridge,
Wollaston DY8 .... 80 D6
Tipton DY4 .... 51 E5
Willenhall WV13 .... 27 B2
Wolverhampton,
Lanesfield WV4 .... 40 A3
Wolverhampton,
Park Village WV10 ...... 25 F5
Wood End CV9 .... 36 C1
Wood Street Cl LE10 .... 71 E1
Wood Terr B96 .... 159 B1
Woodacre Rd B24 .... 57 C4
Woodall Ho WS3 .... 28 C8
Woodall Rd B6 .... 55 F1
Woodall St Blackheath B64 ... 62 C1
Walsall WS3 .... 28 C8
Woodard Rd DY4 .... 52 C7
Woodbank LE10 .... 76 A7
Woodbank Dr B61 .... 136 F8
Woodbank Rd DY3 .... 50 C7
Woodberrow La B97 ..... 158 D6
Woodberry Dr B76 .... 47 A2
Woodberry Wlk B27 ..... 88 D3
Woodbine Ave B10 ...... 87 D8
Woodbine Cotts
4 CV32 .... 161 E8
Woodbine Croft B26 .... 89 A6
Woodbine St 3 CV32 .... 161 E8
Woodbine Wlk B37 ...... 70 D2
Woodbourne B15 .... 85 D8
Woodbourne Rd
Birmingham B15, B16 .... 85 C8
Smethwick B67 .... 64 E2
Woodbridge Cl
Walsall, High Heath WS4 ... 15 D1
Walsall,
Wallington Heath WS3 ... 14 A3
Woodbridge Rd B13 ..... 86 F3
Woodbrook Ho 9 B37 ... 70 B2
Woodbrooke Rd B30 .... 103 E7
Woodburn Cl CV5 .... 112 B4
Woodburn Rd B66 .... 65 D7
Woodbury Cl Brierley Hill
DY5 .... 61 E2
Halesowen B62 .... 83 F8
Redditch B97 .... 158 A6
Woodbury Gr 3 B91 ..... 107 B1
Woodbury Rd Halesowen
B62 .... 84 A8
Kidderminster DY11 .... 116 B4
Woodchester DY9 .... 99 B4
Woodchester Rd B93 .... 127 E2
Woodclose Ave CV6 ...... 112 F6
Woodclose Rd B37 ...... 69 F3
Woodcock Cl B94 .... 141 E3
Woodcock Gdns WV10 .. 12 B7
Woodcock Hill Prim Sch
B31 .... 102 E7
Woodcock La
Birmingham,
Acock's Green B27 .... 88 D3
Birmingham,
Northfield B31 .... 102 E8
Woodcock La N B27 ..... 88 D4
Woodcock St B7 .... 66 F4
Woodcombe Cl DY5 ...... 81 B7
Woodcote Ave
Kenilworth CV8 .... 147 D6
Nuneaton CV11 .... 73 F8
Woodcote Dr Birmingham
B8 .... 67 F5
Dorridge B93 .... 128 B2
Leek Wootton CV35 ...... 155 F7
Woodcote La
Belbroughton DY9 .... 119 E1
Leek Wootton CV35 ...... 155 F7

Woodcote Rd
Birmingham B24 .... 57 D5
Royal Leamington Spa CV32 .. 160 F8
Warwick CV34 .... 160 F8
Wolverhampton WV6 ..... 24 C4
Woodcote Way
Birmingham B18 .... 66 A4
Sutton Coldfield B74 ..... 44 F6
Woodcraft Cl CV4 .... 112 A2
Woodcroft Ave
Birmingham B20 .... 54 E3
Dudley DY4 .... 51 C4
Tamworth B79 .... 21 B6
Woodcroft Cl 3
Blackheath B64 .... 82 F8
Blackwell B60 .... 137 F5
Woodcross La WV14 ..... 40 A4
Woodcross St WV14 ..... 39 F2
Woodend B20 .... 54 E6
Woodend Cl B97 .... 153 B2
Woodend Croft CV4 ..... 131 E8
Woodend Pl WV6 .... 24 B4
Woodfall Ave B30 .... 103 F5
Woodfield DY9 .... 119 E7
Woodfield Ave
Blackheath B64 .... 82 D8
Brierley Hill DY5 .... 61 B7
Oldbury B69 .... 64 A4
Stourbridge DY9 .... 81 F2
Wolverhampton WV4 ..... 38 F6
Woodfield Cl
Norton Canes WS11 ...... 5 F7
Redditch B98 .... 154 A5
Sutton Coldfield B74 ..... 46 B8
Walsall WS5 .... 43 E5
Woodfield Cres
Birmingham B12 .... 87 A6
Kidderminster DY11 .... 116 D5
Woodfield Dr WS11 ...... 5 F7
Woodfield Ho WS3 .... 15 B3
Woodfield Hts WV6 ...... 24 D4
Woodfield Jun & Inf Schs
WV4 .... 38 F6
Woodfield La B62 .... 120 D8
Woodfield Rd
Birmingham,
Balsall Heath B12 .... 87 A6
Birmingham,
King's Heath B13 .... 104 F8
Coventry CV5 .... 132 E8
Dudley DY3 .... 50 C4
Hinckley LE10 .... 75 C6
Solihull B91 .... 107 B6
Woodfield St 4 DY11 .... 116 C6
Woodfields Dr WS14 .... 9 E5
Woodfold Croft WS9 .... 30 B7
Woodford Ave B36 ...... 69 B8
Woodford Cl Ash Green
CV7 .... 95 D5
Nuneaton CV10 .... 72 D4
Wolverhampton WV9 ..... 10 F2
Woodford Cres WS7 ..... 7 B7
Woodford End WS11 ..... 1 F4
Woodford Green Rd B28 .. 106 B8
Woodford Way WS12 .... 2 D1
Woodfort Rd B43 .... 54 E7
Woodgate Bsns Pk B32 .. 84 B2
Woodgate Dr B32 .... 84 A1
Woodgate Gdns B32 .... 84 A2
Woodgate Ho B97 .... 153 B4
Woodgate Jun & Inf Sch
B32 .... 84 B1
Woodgate La B32 .... 84 A2
Woodgate Rd Hinckley
LE10 .... 76 A8
Stoke Prior B60 .... 151 B1
Woodgate Valley Ctry Pk
B32 .... 84 D3
Woodgate Way DY9 ..... 119 E7
Woodglade Croft B38 ... 103 E2
Woodgreen WS11 .... 4 E5
Woodgreen Cl B97 .... 158 B7
Woodgreen Croft B68 ... 84 C7
Woodgreen Rd B68 ...... 84 C7
Woodhall Cl Nuneaton
CV11 .... 74 A2
Tipton DY4 .... 52 A8
Woodhall Croft B92 ..... 88 F3
Woodhall Rd WV4 .... 38 E5
Woodham Cl B45 .... 101 E1
Woodhams Rd CV3 ...... 134 C3
Woodhaven Walsall WS4 .. 15 D1
Wedges Mills WS11 .... 4 B5
Woodhouse Cl CV3 ...... 134 E8
Woodhouse High Sch B77 .. 21 F4
Woodhouse La B77 ...... 22 A5
Woodhouse Orch DY9 ... 119 E7
Woodhouse Prim Sch B32 .. 84 E6
Woodhouse Rd
Birmingham B32 .... 84 E5
Wolverhampton WV6 ..... 24 B4
Woodhouse Rd N WV6 .. 24 B4
Woodhouse St CV34 ..... 160 D6
Woodhouses La WS7 .... 7 F6
Woodhouses Rd WS7 .... 8 A7
Woodhurst Cl B77 .... 21 F5
Woodhurst Rd B13 ...... 87 A4
Wooding Cres DY4 ...... 41 B1
Woodington Fst Sch B75 .. 47 A5
Woodington Rd B75 ..... 47 B5
Woodland Ave
Brierley Hill DY5 .... 62 A1
Coventry CV5 .... 132 F7
Dudley DY1 .... 51 C3
Hagley DY9 .... 98 F5
Hinckley LE10 .... 76 A4
Kidderminster DY11 ...... 116 C7
Wolverhampton WV6 ..... 24 B3

Woodland Cl Cannock WS12 .. 2 B8
Stourbridge DY9 .... 81 D2
Willenhall WV12 .... 27 D6
Woodland Cres WV3 ..... 38 D7
Woodland Ct Cannock WS12 .. 1 C4
Shenstone WS14 .... 32 A7
Woodland Dr Cheslyn Hay
WS6 .... 4 E4
Smethwick B66 .... 64 E7
Woodland Gr
Birmingham B43 .... 43 E3
Dudley DY3 .... 50 B3
Woodland Rd
Birmingham,
Handsworth B21 .... 65 C8
Birmingham,
Northfield B31 .... 103 B3
Dodford B61 .... 136 A7
Halesowen B62 .... 83 D8
Hinckley LE10 .... 71 F1
Kenilworth CV8 .... 148 B7
Redditch B97 .... 153 B3
Tamworth B77 .... 22 A4
Wolverhampton WV3 ..... 38 D7
Woodland Rise
Blackheath B64 .... 82 F8
Sutton Coldfield B73 ..... 46 B4
Woodland Way
Birchmoor B78 .... 36 F8
Burntwood WS7 .... 7 A6
Woodlands Ave Walsall
WS5 .... 43 E5
Water Orton B46 .... 59 B2
Woodlands Cotts WV4 .. 38 F4
Woodlands Cres WS3 ... 14 F5
Woodlands Ct
Binley Woods CV3 .... 135 D7
Coventry CV5 .... 133 A8
Woodlands Farm Rd B24 .. 57 A4
Woodlands Inf Sch B90 .. 126 B8
Woodlands Jun & Inf Sch
B36 .... 70 B6
Woodlands La
Bedworth CV12 .... 77 E4
Solihull B90 .... 126 B8
Woodlands Paddock WV4 .. 38 E4
Woodlands Park Rd B30 .. 103 C5
Woodlands Prim Sch
Tamworth B77 .... 21 E4
Willenhall WV12 .... 27 D6
Woodlands Rd
Bedworth CV12 .... 77 F3
Binley Woods CV3 .... 135 D7
Birmingham, Moseley B11 ... 87 C2
Birmingham, Rubery B45 ... 121 D7
Birmingham, Saltley B8 .. 67 F3
Wombourne WV5 .... 49 A5
Woodlands Sch The CV4 .. 111 D3
Woodlands St B66 .... 65 C5
Woodlands The
Blackheath B64 .... 83 A7
Lichfield WS13 .... 9 D8
Nuneaton CV10 .... 72 A8
Stourbridge DY8 .... 81 A2
Wood End CV9 .... 36 C1
Woodlands Way B37 .... 70 D3
Woodlawn Gr DY6 .... 60 D5
Woodlea Dr Birmingham
B24 .... 56 F2
Solihull B91 .... 106 E4
Woodleaves B47 .... 124 F8
Woodleigh Ave B17 ..... 85 D4
Woodleigh Cl B38 .... 103 F1
Woodleigh Rd B72 ...... 46 C1
Woodleys The B14 ...... 105 B4
Woodloes Ave N CV34 .. 155 F1
Woodloes Ave S CV34 .. 155 F1
Woodloes Fst Sch CV34 .. 155 E1
Woodloes Mid Sch CV34 .. 155 E1
Woodloes Rd B90 .... 126 B7
Woodman Cl B63 .... 83 C3
Woodman La Cheslyn Hay
WS6 .... 4 E4
Clent DY9 .... 99 E4
Woodman Rd
Birmingham B14 .... 105 A1
Halesowen B63 .... 83 C3
Woodman Wlk B23 ...... 56 A5
Woodmeadow Rd B30 .. 104 B3
Woodnorton Dr B13 ..... 86 E2
Woodnorton Rd B65 ..... 63 F2
Woodpecker Gr
Birmingham B36 .... 70 A7
Kidderminster DY10 ...... 117 B2
Woodpecker Way WS11 .. 2 C3
Woodperry Ave B91 ..... 107 C5
Woodridge B6 .... 55 E1
Woodridge Ave
Birmingham B32 .... 84 B4
Coventry CV5 .... 112 A6
Woodridge Rd B63 ...... 83 A5
Woodrough Dr B13 ...... 86 F2
Woodrow Cl B61 .... 120 F1
Woodrow Cres B93 ...... 128 A5
Woodrow Ctr B98 .... 159 B8
Woodrow Dr B98 .... 159 B6
Woodrow Fst Sch B98 .... 159 B7
Woodrow La
Bluntington DY10 .... 118 C2
Catshill B61 .... 121 B2
Woodrow N B98 .... 159 A7
Woodrow S B98 .... 159 B7
Woodrow Wlk B98 .... 159 B7
Woodruff Way WS5 ..... 43 A3
Woodrush High Sch The
B47 .... 125 A6

Woods Bank Terr WS10 .. 41 C5
Woods Cres DY5 .... 62 A1
Woods Croft WS13 ...... 3 A1
Woods The B14 .... 82 C8
Brierley Hill DY5 .... 81 D7
Woods The B14 .... 86 F1
Woodsbank Ind Est The
WS10 .... 41 D4
Woodsetton Cl DY1 ...... 51 B6
Woodsetton Specl Sch
DY3 .... 50 F7
Woodshill Ave B45 ...... 122 A2
Woodshires Rd Coventry
CV6 .... 95 F5
Solihull B92 .... 106 E7
Woodside Birmingham B37 .. 69 E4
Sutton Coldfield B74 ..... 31 E2
Woodside Ave B97 .... 153 B2
Woodside Ave N CV3 .... 132 F6
Woodside Ave S CV3 .... 132 F5
Wood End CV9 .... 36 C1
Woodside Cres B93 ..... 128 B4
Woodside Dr
Barnt Green B45 .... 138 B8
Little Aston B74 .... 31 C5
Woodside Gr WV8 .... 10 B2
Woodside Pl WS11 ...... 1 E5
Woodside Rd
Birmingham B29 .... 86 A1
Dudley DY2 .... 61 F2
Walsall WS5 .... 43 E6
Woodside Way Aldridge
WS9 .... 30 B5
Birmingham B45 .... 102 E4
Solihull B91 .... 106 E5
Willenhall WV12 .... 27 E7
Woodsome Gr B23 ...... 56 C7
Woodsorrel Rd DY1 ..... 51 A4
Woodstile B34 .... 69 B6
Woodstile Cl B75 .... 32 D3
Woodstock Cl Dudley DY1 .. 62 A8
Hinckley LE10 .... 76 A5
Stourbridge DY8 .... 60 C1
2 Walsall WS5 .... 43 A3
Woodstock Cres B93 .... 127 F3
Woodstock Ct B13 ...... 87 B4
Woodstock Dr
Huntington WS12 .... 1 C7
Stourbridge DY8 .... 60 C2
Sutton Coldfield B74 ..... 31 D4
Woodstock Ho B13 ...... 105 A7
Woodstock Rd
Birmingham,
Handsworth B21 .... 65 F8
Birmingham, Moseley B13 .. 87 B3
Coventry CV3 .... 133 D7
Nuneaton CV11 .... 73 E1
Wolverhampton WV1 .... 26 B1
Woodston Gr B91 .... 127 C8
Woodthorne Cl DY3 ..... 50 D2
Woodthorne Inf & Jun
Schs WV6 .... 24 A4
Woodthorne Rd WV6 .... 24 A6
Woodthorne Rd S WV6 .. 24 A5
Woodthorne Wlk 4 DY6 .. 60 E8
Woodthorpe Dr DY9 ..... 81 D3
Woodthorpe Gdns B14 .. 104 E3
Woodthorpe Inf & Jun
Sch B14 .... 104 E5
Woodthorpe Rd B14 ..... 104 E5
Woodvale Dr B28 .... 105 E4
Woodvale Rd
Birmingham, Woodgate B32 .. 84 A2
Birmingham,
Yardley Wood B28 .... 105 E4
Woodview Dr B15 .... 86 C7
Woodville Ct 3 B23 ..... 56 E2
Woodville Gdns DY3 .... 39 F1
Woodville Rd
Birmingham, Harborne B17 .. 85 A6
Birmingham,
King's Heath B14 .... 104 F8
Warwick CV34 .... 160 E8
Woodward Cl CV31 ...... 162 A2
Woodward Pl DY9 .... 81 C4
Woodward Rd DY11 ..... 116 C4
Woodward St B71 .... 53 E4
Woodwards Cl WS2 ..... 42 B8
Woodwards Pl WS2 ..... 42 B8
Woodwards Rd WS2 .... 42 B8
Woodway B24 .... 57 C5
Woodway Cl CV2 .... 114 F8
Woodway La CV2 .... 96 F1
Woodway Park Sch &
Com Coll CV2 .... 96 F1
Woodway Wlk CV2 ...... 114 E8
Woodwells Rd B8 .... 68 B5
Woody Bank WS6 .... 4 E2
Woolacombe Lodge Rd
B29 .... 85 C2
Woolaston Rd B98 .... 159 C8
Woolgrove St CV6 .... 96 A3
Woolhope Cl B98 .... 154 F3
Woolmore Rd B23 .... 56 C5
Woolpack Cl B65 .... 63 A4
Woolpack St WV1 .... 163 B3
Woolwich Rd CV11 ...... 79 F6
Wooton Gr B44 .... 56 C8
Wootton Ave WV11 ..... 26 C9
Wootton Cl WS11 .... 2 B3
Wootton Ct Coventry CV2 .. 114 D7
6 Royal Leamington Spa CV32 .. 156 F2
Wootton Green La CV7 .. 130 A8

Wootton La B92 .... **109** E1
Wootton Rd
  Birmingham B31 .... **123** A6
  Wolverhampton WV3 ...... **38** D8
Wootton St CV12 .... **78** D3
Woottons Ct WS11 .... **1** F1
Worcester Cl Allesley
  CV5 .... **112** B7
  Cannock WS11 .... **4** F8
  Hagley DY9 .... **99** A5
  Sutton Coldfield B75 ...... **32** D3
  Wolverhampton WS13 ...... **3** B3
Worcester Cross
 3 DY10 .... **116** E5
Worcester Ct Coventry CV6 ... **96** B4
  Wolverhampton WV3 ...... **39** A6
Worcester Gn B71 .... **53** C7
Worcester Gr WV6 .... **23** D4
Worcester Ho
  Birmingham B36 .... **70** A8
 4 Halesowen B63 .... **83** A3
Worcester La
  Stourbridge DY9 .... **99** B7
  Sutton Coldfield B75 ...... **32** D4
Worcester Rd Birmingham
  B6 .... **55** F2
  Bromsgrove B61 .... **136** F1
  Dudley DY2 .... **62** E3
  Hagley DY9 .... **99** A5
  Kenilworth CV8 .... **148** B3
  Kidderminster DY10 ...... **116** E2
  Mustow Green DY10 ...... **117** F1
  Oldbury B68 .... **84** A8
  Stoke Heath B61 .... **150** B4
  Willenhall WV13 .... **27** D2
Worcester Rise B29 .... **86** B1
Worcester Sq **1** B98 .... **153** E4
Worcester St
  Kidderminster DY10 ...... **116** E6
  Stourbridge DY8 .... **81** A4
  Wolverhampton WV2 ...... **163** B2
Worcester Wlk B37 .... **70** A1
Word Hill B17 .... **84** F7
Wordsley Cl B98 .... **154** B7
Wordsley Ct DY8 .... **60** E3
Wordsley Green Sh Ctr
  DY8 .... **60** D2
Wordsley Hospl DY8 ...... **60** E4
Wordsworth Ave
  Redditch B97 .... **158** C8
  Tamworth B79 .... **21** A6
  Warwick CV34 .... **160** D5
  Wolverhampton WV4 ...... **39** F4
Wordsworth Cl Cannock
  WS11 .... **1** D4
  Lichfield WS14 .... **9** B5
  Tipton DY4 .... **52** A8
Wordsworth Cres DY10 ... **117** B6
Wordsworth Ct WV6 ...... **23** E4
Wordsworth Dr CV8 ...... **148** C4
Wordsworth Ho
  Birmingham B31 .... **123** A8
  Halesowen B63 .... **82** B5
 4 Oldbury B68 .... **64** C4
Wordsworth Rd
  Bedworth CV12 .... **78** D1
  Birmingham B10 .... **87** D7
 2 Burntwood WS7 .... **7** A8
  Coventry CV2 .... **114** C4
  Dudley DY3 .... **50** B5
  Walsall WS3 .... **28** E8
  Willenhall WV12 .... **27** E7
  Wolverhampton WV10 ... **26** A8
Wordsworth St B71 .... **53** C5
Worfield Cl WS4 .... **29** A4
Worfield Gdns WV3 ...... **38** F6
Workhouse La LE10 ...... **76** A4
Works Rd B26 .... **90** A3
World's End Ave B32 ...... **84** D6
World's End La B32 ...... **84** D5
Worlds End Jun Sch B32 ... **84** D5
Worlds End Rd B20 ...... **55** A3
Worleys Wharf Ave WS10 ... **42** E2
Worsdell Cl CV1 .... **113** B4
Worsey Dr DY4 .... **52** D6
Worsfold Cl CV5 .... **112** A7
Worthen Gr B31 .... **123** A8
Worthings The B30 ...... **104** B6
Worthy Down WV11 ...... **26** F5
Worthy Down Wlk B35 ... **58** B3
Wortley Ave WV10 ...... **25** E6
Worton Rd DY9 .... **81** F2
Wragby Cl WV11 .... **11** B3
Wrekin Cl Halesowen B63 ... **82** C1
  Kidderminster DY11 ...... **116** B2
Wrekin Ct B74 .... **31** F2

Wrekin Dr Bromsgrove
  B61 .... **137** A5
  Stourbridge DY9 .... **81** D4
  Wolverhampton,
  Penn WV3 .... **38** E8
  Wolverhampton,
  Tettenhall WV6 .... **24** A5
Wrekin La WV6 .... **24** A5
Wrekin Rd Birmingham B44 ... **56** A6
  Sutton Coldfield B73 ...... **46** A1
Wrekin View Brownhills
  WS8 .... **16** A5
  Huntington WS12 .... **1** C7
  Wolverhampton WV1 ...... **163** B3
Wrekin View Rd WV3 ...... **50** C8
Wren Ave WV6 .... **23** D3
Wren City Coventry CV2 ... **113** F3
  Dudley, Netherton DY2 ... **62** B5
  Dudley, Swan Village DY1 ... **51** C6
Wren's Nest Nature
  Reserve DY1 .... **51** B4
Wren's Nest Prim Sch
  DY1 .... **51** A4
Wren's Nest Rd DY1 ...... **51** A5
Wrenbury Dr CV6 .... **96** A4
Wrens Ave Dudley DY4 ... **51** D4
  Kingswinford DY6 .... **61** A4
Wrens Hill Rd DY1 .... **51** B5
Wrens Nest Pl DY1 ...... **51** A5
Wrens Nest Rd DY1 ...... **51** A4
Wrens Park Ave B76 ...... **57** E7
Wrentham St B5 .... **86** E8
Wretham Ct B19 .... **66** B7
Wretham Rd B19 .... **66** B6
Wrexham Ave WS2 .... **27** F1
Wright Ave WV11 .... **26** E7
Wright Rd B8 .... **67** E5
Wright St Bilston WV14 ... **40** E4
  Birmingham B10 .... **87** D8
  Coventry CV1 .... **113** D4
  Halesowen B63 .... **83** B4
  Wolverhampton WV10 ... **25** D4
Wright's Ave WS11 .... **1** F5
Wright's La B64 .... **63** A1
Wrighton Cl WV12 .... **27** C8
Wrighton Dr DY5 .... **50** C1
Wrigsham St CV3 .... **133** D8
Wrottesley Park Rd
  WV6, WV8 .... **23** D5
Wrottesley Rd
  Birmingham B43 .... **43** D1
  Wolverhampton WV6 ...... **24** B5
Wrottesley Rd W WV6 ... **24** A6
Wrottesley St B5 .... **164** C1
Wroxall Abbey (Sch)
  CV35 .... **145** E2
Wroxall CE Jun & Inf Sch
  CV35 .... **145** E3
Wroxall Cl DY5 .... **81** C8
Wroxall Dr CV3 .... **134** D5
Wroxall Gr B13 .... **105** A6
Wroxall Rd B91 .... **106** E6
Wroxham Glen WV13 ...... **40** F8
Wroxton St B26 .... **88** E8
Wulfrun Coll WV3 .... **24** E3
Wulfrun Coll Annexe,
  Newhampton Ctr WV1 ... **163** A4
Wulfrun Ctr WV1 .... **163** C2
Wulfrun Sq WV1 .... **163** C2
Wulfrun Trad Est W6 ...... **25** C5
Wulfruna Ct WV3 .... **163** A2
Wulfruna Gdns WV3 ...... **24** F1
Wulfruna St WV1 .... **163** B3
Wyatt Cl B5 .... **86** C5
Wyatt Ho CV2 .... **114** D7
Wyatt Rd B75 .... **47** B5
Wyatts Ct CV12 .... **78** B3
Wych Elm Dr DY1 .... **161** F5
Wych Elm Rd WS8 ...... **15** E5
Wychall Dr WV10 .... **11** E4
Wychall Farm Inf Sch
  B31 .... **103** C2
Wychall Farm Jun Sch
  B31 .... **103** C2
Wychall La B38 .... **103** E2
Wychall Park Gr B38 ...... **103** D2
Wychall Rd B31 .... **103** C3
Wychbold Cl Redditch
  B97 .... **158** A6
  Willenhall WV12 .... **13** D1
Wychbold Cres B33 ...... **69** C3
Wychbold Ct DY9 .... **99** C8
Wychbold Way WV11 ...... **13** D1
Wychbury B76 .... **47** A1
Wychbury Ct
 7 Dudley DY2 .... **62** B8
  Halesowen B63 .... **83** A3
Wychbury Dr DY9 .... **99** C7
Wychbury Grange DY9 ...... **81** C1

Wychbury Rd
  Birmingham B32 .... **102** B7
  Brierley Hill DY5 .... **81** E8
  Stourbridge DY9 .... **81** E2
  Wolverhampton WV3 ...... **38** C7
Wyche Ave B14 .... **104** D4
Wyche Cotts B60 .... **150** C1
Wychelm Farm Rd B14 ... **105** A1
Wychnor Gr B71 .... **42** E2
Wychwood Ave
  Coventry CV3 .... **133** C3
  Knowle B93 .... **128** B8
Wychwood Cres B26 ...... **89** A6
Wychwood Dr B97 .... **158** D6
Wyckham Cl B17 .... **85** A4
Wyckham Rd B36 .... **69** F8
Wycliffe Gr CV2 .... **114** B5
Wycliffe Rd W CV2 ...... **114** C5
Wycome Rd B28 .... **106** A7
Wye Bulkington CV12 ...... **79** B2
  Hinckley LE10 .... **75** A8
  Perton WV6 .... **23** F4
  Royal Leamington Spa
  CV32 .... **157** C3
  Sutton Coldfield B76 ...... **58** A7
Wye Cliff Rd B20 .... **66** B8
Wye Ho **4** DY3 .... **50** D3
Wye Rd WS3 .... **14** E1
Wyemanton Cl B43 .... **43** C1
Wyke Rd CV2 .... **114** C4
Wykeham Gr WV6 .... **23** D3
Wykeley Rd CV2 .... **114** C4
Wyken Ave CV2 .... **114** D5
Wyken Cl B93 .... **127** E2
Wyken Croft CV2 .... **114** D6
Wyken Croft Prim Sch
  CV2 .... **114** E5
Wyken Grange Rd CV2 ... **114** C5
Wyken Way CV2 .... **114** B5
Wykin Rd LE10 .... **71** A3
Wyld Cl B91 .... **53** B8
Wyld Ct CV5 .... **112** B5
Wylde Cres B65 .... **63** C4
Wylde Green Coll B72 ... **46** C1
Wylde Green Jun & Inf
  Sch B73 .... **57** B7
Wylde Green Rd B72, B76 ... **46** D1
Wylde Green Sta B73 ...... **46** B1
Wyley Rd CV6 .... **113** B5
Wymering Ave WV11 ...... **26** F7
Wyn-Griffith Dr DY4 ...... **52** A3
Wynall La DY9 .... **81** F3
Wynall La S DY9 .... **82** A3
Wynbrook Gr B90 .... **127** A6
Wynchcombe Ave WV4 ... **38** D4
Wyncote Cl CV8 .... **148** A4
Wynd The DY3 .... **39** D1
Wyndcliff Rd B9 .... **67** D1
Wyndcliffe Inf Sch B9 ... **67** D1
Wyndcliffe Jun Sch B9 ... **67** C1
Wyndham Gdns B30 ...... **103** D4
Wyndham Rd B16 .... **65** F1
Wyndhurst Ct B33 .... **68** E4
Wyndhurst Rd B33 .... **68** E5
Wyndley Dr B73 .... **46** B4
Wyndley L Ctr B73 ...... **46** A5
Wyndley La B73 .... **46** A4
Wyndmill Cres B71 ...... **42** F1
Wynds Covert B14 ...... **104** D2
Wynds Point B31 .... **103** B5
Wynfield Gdns B14 ...... **104** F5
Wynford Rd B27 .... **88** C5
Wynford Road Ind Est
  B27 .... **88** C5
Wynn Rd WV4 .... **38** F5
Wynn St B15 .... **86** D8
Wynne Cres WV4 .... **38** C3
Wynstead Covert **6** B14 ... **104** C2
Wyntor La B71 .... **53** B8
Wynyates B79 .... **20** E6
Wyre Cl Birmingham B45 ... **102** B1
  Brownhills WS9 .... **15** F4
Wyre Rd DY9 .... **80** E7
Wyrley Brook Pk WS11 ... **4** D5
Wyrley Cl Burntwood WS8 ... **6** F3
  Lichfield WS14 .... **9** A5
  Willenhall WV12 .... **27** D7
Wyrley Ho Birmingham B23 ... **56** C6
  Tipton DY4 .... **52** B3
Wyrley La WS3 .... **14** E8
Wyrley Rd Birmingham B6 ... **56** A2
  Sutton Coldfield B75 ...... **32** D1
  Wednesfield WV11 ...... **27** A6
Wyrley St WV10 .... **25** F2
Wyrley Way B23 .... **56** A6
Wythall Green Way B47 ... **124** E3
Wythall Rd B63 .... **83** A2
Wythall Sta B47 .... **125** C4
Wythwood Cl DY9 .... **81** D1

Wythwood Gr
  Hollywood B47 .... **125** C6
  Tipton DY4 .... **52** A8
Wythwood Rd B47 .... **125** C6
Wyver Cres CV2 .... **114** C3
Wyvern **1** F3
Wyvern Cl
  Sutton Coldfield B74 ...... **46** B7
  Wednesfield WV12 ...... **27** A7
Wyvern Gr Birmingham B29 ... **85** C2
  Cannock WS12 .... **2** A5
Wyvern Rd B74 .... **46** B7
Wyvis Cl WV3 .... **24** E2

Yale Dr WV11 .... **26** E5
Yardley Cl Oldbury B68 ... **64** B1
  Redditch B98 .... **154** E3
  Warwick CV34 .... **155** F2
Yardley Fields Rd B33 ... **68** E2
Yardley Green Hospl B10 ... **68** A1
Yardley Green Rd B9 ...... **68** A2
Yardley Inf Sch B26 ...... **88** D7
Yardley Jun Sch B26 ...... **88** D7
Yardley Rd B27 .... **88** C5
Yardley St Coventry CV1 ... **113** E4
  Darlaston WS10 .... **41** C7
  Stourbridge DY9 .... **81** C6
Yardley Wood Inf & Jun
  B13,B14 .... **105** D4
Yardley Wood Rd
  B13,B14 .... **105** B5
  Yardley Wood Sta B28 ... **105** D5
Yardleys Lower Sch B11 ... **87** E3
Yardleys Upper Sch B11 ... **87** F4
Yarmouth Gn CV4 .... **131** E8
Yarn Cl B47 .... **125** A5
Yarnborough Hill DY8 ... **81** A2
Yarnbury Cl B14 .... **104** E1
Yarner Cl DY1 .... **50** E2
Yarnfield Prim Sch B11 ... **88** A3
Yarnfield Rd B11 .... **88** A3
Yarningale Cl B98 .... **158** F6
Yarningale Rd
  Birmingham B14 .... **104** D5
  Coventry CV3 .... **134** D5
Yarningdale **7** B90 ...... **126** C8
Yarnold La Bournheath B61 ... **136** C8
Yarrow Cl Walsall WS3 ... **15** A5
  Wednesfield WV11 ...... **26** F5
Yarrow Dr B38 .... **123** F8
Yarwell Cl WV10 .... **163** C4
Yateley Ave B42 .... **55** A7
Yateley Cres B42 .... **55** A7
Yateley Rd B15 .... **85** E7
Yates Croft B74 .... **31** F6
Yates La B65 .... **63** F2
Yatesbury Ave B35 ...... **58** A3
Yeadon Cl B97 .... **153** A1
Yeadon Gdns WV3 ...... **38** D8
Yeames Cl B43 .... **44** C4
Yellowhammer Ct DY10 ... **117** A4
Yelverton Cl WS3 ...... **14** B4
Yelverton Dr B15 ...... **85** E8
Yelverton Rd CV6 ...... **113** D8
Yeman Rd B68 .... **64** D3
Yems Croft WS4 .... **29** A5
Yemscroft WS6 .... **14** A8
Yenton Cl B78 .... **21** A1
Yenton Gr B24 .... **57** C6
Yenton Jun & Inf Schs B24 ... **57** C6
Yeoman Cl DY10 .... **116** E3
Yeomanry Cl **12** CV34 ...... **160** F7
Yeomans Wlk B60 .... **150** E8
Yeovil Ct **15** DY5 ...... **61** D2
Yeovilton B79 .... **21** C8
Yerbury Gr B23 .... **56** B4
Yew Cl CV3 .... **114** C1
Yew Croft Ave B17 ...... **85** B6
Yew St WV3 .... **25** A1
Yew Tree Ave
  Belbroughton DY9 ...... **119** E8
  Birmingham B26 .... **88** E7
  Lichfield WS14 .... **9** E8
Yew Tree Cl Lapworth B94 ... **144** D3
  Norton Canes WS11 ...... **6** A5
  Redditch B97 .... **153** A4
Yew Tree Ct CV31 ...... **161** F5
Yew Tree Gdns WV8 ...... **10** A4
Yew Tree Hills DY2 ...... **62** C4
Yew Tree La
  Birmingham, Frankley B32 ... **101** E3
  Birmingham, Yardley B26 ... **88** E7
  Dudley WV14 .... **40** D1
  Fairfield B61 .... **120** D2
  Lapworth B94 .... **144** B1
  Solihull B91 .... **107** E5
  Wednesbury WS10 ...... **42** A2
  Wolverhampton WV6 ...... **24** A5

Yew Tree Pl Romsley B62 ... **101** A5
  Walsall WS3 .... **14** D3
Yew Tree Prim Sch
  Solihull B91 .... **107** E6
  Walsall WS5 .... **43** C4
Yew Tree Rd
  Birmingham,
  Castle Bromwich B36 ...... **69** C8
  Birmingham, Edgbaston B15 ... **86** C8
  Birmingham, Handsworth B6 ... **56** A1
  Birmingham, Moseley B13 ... **86** D2
  Dudley DY2 .... **62** C4
  Halesowen B63 .... **82** F3
  Kidderminster DY10 ...... **116** F5
  Smethwick B67 .... **64** E4
  Walsall, High Heath WS4 ... **15** B1
  Walsall, The Delves WS5 ... **43** A5
Yew Tree Rise B76 ...... **46** F3
Yew Tree Sch B6 .... **56** A1
Yew Tree Villas B73 ...... **57** A7
Yew Wlk B37 .... **70** B2
Yewdale B17 .... **85** C4
Yewdale Cres CV2 ...... **96** E1
Yewdale Ct CV2 .... **96** F1
Yewhurst Rd B91 .... **106** E4
Yews The CV12 .... **77** E2
Yewtree Dr B60 .... **137** B2
Yewtree La B65 .... **63** B2
Yewtree Rd
  Sutton Coldfield,
  Boldmere B73 .... **57** A7
  Sutton Coldfield,
  Streetly B74 .... **44** D8
Yockleton Rd B33 ...... **69** C3
York Ave Bedworth CV12 ... **78** D2
  Bromsgrove B61 .... **136** E4
  Walsall WS2 .... **28** B2
  Willenhall WV13 .... **27** D2
  Wolverhampton WV3 ...... **24** E1
York Cl Birmingham B30 ... **104** A6
  Bromsgrove B61 .... **136** E4
  Coventry CV3 .... **134** C5
  Lichfield WS13 .... **3** C3
  Studley B80 .... **159** C4
  Tipton DY4 .... **51** D4
York Cres Darlaston WS10 ... **41** D6
  Stourbridge DY8 .... **80** D7
  West Bromwich B70 ...... **53** A6
  Wolverhampton WV3 ...... **24** E1
York Dr B36 .... **68** B8
York Gdns WV3 .... **24** E1
York Rd Birmingham B23 ... **56** F4
  Birmingham, Edgbaston B16 ... **65** E1
  Birmingham,
  Handsworth B21 .... **65** F8
  Birmingham,
  King's Heath B14 .... **104** D8
  Birmingham, Tyseley B28 ... **87** F2
  Blackheath B65 .... **63** E3
  Bromsgrove B61 .... **136** F4
  Cannock WS11 .... **4** F7
  Dudley DY2 .... **62** E3
  Hinckley LE10 .... **71** D3
  Royal Leamington Spa
  CV31 .... **161** F8
  Walsall WS4 .... **29** D7
  Wolverhampton WV3 ...... **38** B8
York St Birmingham B17 ... **85** D6
  Coventry CV1 .... **113** B2
  Kidderminster DY10 ...... **116** E7
  Nuneaton CV11 .... **73** A4
  Wolverhampton WV1 ...... **163** D2
York Terr B18 .... **66** C5
Yorkbrooke Dr B26 ...... **89** B5
Yorkdale Cl DY3 .... **50** D3
Yorke Ave DY5 .... **61** A1
Yorklea Croft B37 ...... **69** F2
Yorkmead Jun & Inf Sch
  B28 .... **87** F2
Yorkminster Dr B37 ...... **70** D3
Yorks Wood Dr B37 ...... **69** E5
Yorksand Rd B78 .... **34** F8
Yorkswood Prim Sch B37 ... **69** F5
Young Cl CV34 .... **160** B5
Young St B70 .... **53** A3
Yoxall Gr B33 .... **69** A3
Yoxall Rd B90 .... **106** D2
Yule Rd CV2 .... **114** D5
Yvonne Rd B97 .... **158** D7

Zealand Cl LE10 .... **71** F3
Zion Cl WS6 .... **4** D3
Zion St WV3 .... **51** F8
Zions Cl B64 .... **62** F1
Zoar St Dudley DY3 ...... **50** C3
  Wolverhampton WV3 ...... **25** B1
Zorrina Cl CV10 .... **72** B5
Zouche Cl DY8 .... **80** E8

Name and Address	Telephone	Page	Grid Reference

Addresses

Name and Address	Telephone	Page	Grid Reference

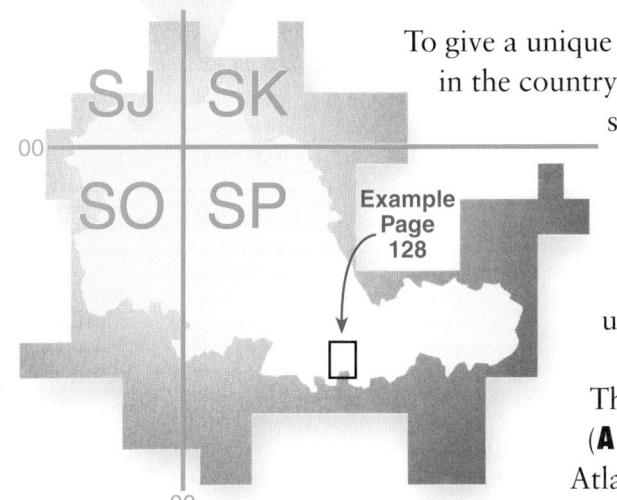

Any feature in this atlas can be given a unique reference to help you find the same feature on other Ordnance Survey maps of the area, or to help someone else locate you if they do not have a Street Atlas. The grid squares in this atlas match the Ordnance Survey National Grid and are at 500 metre intervals. The small figures at the bottom and sides of every other grid line are the National Grid kilometre values (**00** to **99** km) and are repeated across the country every 100 km (see left).

To give a unique National Grid reference you need to locate where in the country you are. The country is divided into 100 km squares with each square given a unique two-letter reference. The atlas in this example falls across the junction of four such squares. Start by working out on which two-letter square the page falls. The Key map and Administrative map are useful for this.

The bold letters and numbers between each grid line (**A** to **F**, **1** to **8**) are for use within a specific Street Atlas only, and when used with the page number, are a convenient way of referencing these grid squares.

Example   The railway bridge over DARLEY GREEN RD in grid square B1 on page 128

Step 1: Identify the two-letter reference, in this case page 128 is in **SP**

Step 2: Identify the 1 km square in which the railway bridge falls. Use the figures in the southwest corner of this square: Eastings **17**, Northings **74**. This gives a unique reference: **SP 17 74**, accurate to 1 km.

Step 3: To give a more precise reference accurate to 100 m you need to estimate how many tenths along and how many tenths up this 1 km square the feature is (to help with this the 1 km square is divided into four 500 m squares). This makes the bridge about **8** tenths along and about **1** tenth up from the southwest corner.

This gives a unique reference: **SP 178 741**, accurate to 100 m.

Eastings (read from left to right along the bottom) come before Northings (read from bottom to top). If you have trouble remembering say to yourself "Along the hall, THEN up the stairs"!

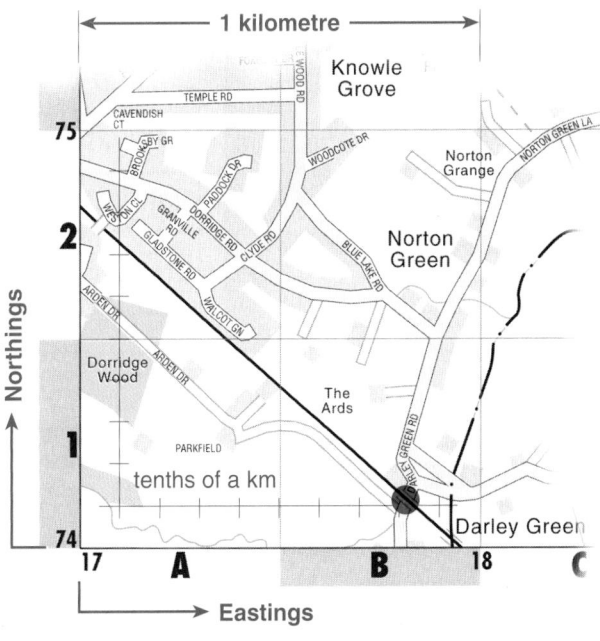

STREET ATLASES
ORDER FORM

The Street Atlases are available from all good bookshops or by mail order direct from the publisher. Orders can be made in the following ways. **By phone** Ring our special Credit Card Hotline on **01933 443863** during office hours (9am to 5pm) or leave a message on the answering machine, quoting your full credit card number plus expiry date and your full name and address. **By post or fax** Fill out the order form below (you may photocopy it) and post it to: **Philip's Direct, 27 Sanders Road, Wellingborough, Northants NN8 4NL** or fax it to: **01933 443849**. Before placing an order by post, by fax or on the answering machine, please telephone to check availability and prices.

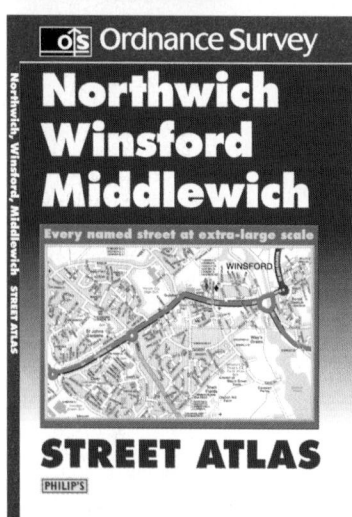

COLOUR LOCAL ATLASES

	PAPERBACK Quantity @ £3.50 each	£ Total
CANNOCK, LICHFIELD, RUGELEY	☐ 0 540 07625 2 ➤	☐
DERBY	☐ 0 540 07608 2 ➤	☐
NORTHWICH, WINSFORD, MIDDLEWICH	☐ 0 540 07589 2 ➤	☐
PEAK DISTRICT TOWNS	☐ 0 540 07609 0 ➤	☐
STAFFORD, STONE, UTTOXETER	☐ 0 540 07626 0 ➤	☐
WARRINGTON, WIDNES, RUNCORN	☐ 0 540 07588 4 ➤	☐

COLOUR REGIONAL ATLASES

	HARDBACK Quantity @ £10.99 each	SPIRAL Quantity @ £8.99 each	POCKET Quantity @ £4.99 each	£ Total
BERKSHIRE	☐ 0 540 06170 0	☐ 0 540 06172 7	☐ 0 540 06173 5 ➤	☐
MERSEYSIDE	☐ 0 540 06480 7	☐ 0 540 06481 5	☐ 0 540 06482 3 ➤	☐

	Quantity @ £12.99 each	Quantity @ £8.99 each	Quantity @ £4.99 each	£ Total
SURREY	☐ 0 540 06435 1	☐ 0 540 06436 X	☐ 0 540 06438 6 ➤	☐

	Quantity @ £12.99 each	Quantity @ £9.99 each	Quantity @ £4.99 each	£ Total
BUCKINGHAMSHIRE	☐ 0 540 07466 7	☐ 0 540 07467 5	☐ 0 540 07468 3 ➤	☐
DURHAM	☐ 0 540 06365 7	☐ 0 540 06366 5	☐ 0 540 06367 3 ➤	☐
HERTFORDSHIRE	☐ 0 540 06174 3	☐ 0 540 06175 1	☐ 0 540 06176 X ➤	☐
EAST KENT	☐ 0 540 07483 7	☐ 0 540 07276 1	☐ 0 540 07287 7 ➤	☐
WEST KENT	☐ 0 540 07366 0	☐ 0 540 07367 9	☐ 0 540 07369 5 ➤	☐
EAST SUSSEX	☐ 0 540 07306 7	☐ 0 540 07307 5	☐ 0 540 07312 1 ➤	☐
WEST SUSSEX	☐ 0 540 07319 9	☐ 0 540 07323 7	☐ 0 540 07327 X ➤	☐
TYNE AND WEAR	☐ 0 540 06370 3	☐ 0 540 06371 1	☐ 0 540 06372 X ➤	☐
SOUTH YORKSHIRE	☐ 0 540 06330 4	☐ 0 540 06331 2	☐ 0 540 06332 0 ➤	☐

	Quantity @ £12.99 each	Quantity @ £9.99 each	Quantity @ £5.50 each	£ Total
GREATER MANCHESTER	☐ 0 540 06485 8	☐ 0 540 06486 6	☐ 0 540 06487 4 ➤	☐

	Quantity @ £12.99 each	Quantity @ £9.99 each	Quantity @ £5.99 each	£ Total
BIRMINGHAM & WEST MIDLANDS	☐ 0 540 07603 1	☐ 0 540 07604 X	☐ 0 540 07605 8 ➤	☐

STREET ATLASES
ORDER FORM

COLOUR REGIONAL ATLASES

	HARDBACK	SPIRAL	POCKET	£ Total
	Quantity @ £12.99 each	Quantity @ £9.99 each	Quantity @ £5.99 each	
CHESHIRE	☐ 0 540 07507 8	☐ 0 540 07508 6	☐ 0 540 07509 4	➤ ☐
DERBYSHIRE	☐ 0 540 07531 0	☐ 0 540 07532 9	☐ 0 540 07533 7	➤ ☐
SOUTH HAMPSHIRE	☐ 0 540 07476 4	☐ 0 540 07477 2	☐ 0 540 07478 0	➤ ☐
NORTH HAMPSHIRE	☐ 0 540 07471 3	☐ 0 540 07472 1	☐ 0 540 07473 X	➤ ☐
OXFORDSHIRE	☐ 0 540 07512 4	☐ 0 540 07513 2	☐ 0 540 07514 0	➤ ☐
WEST YORKSHIRE	☐ 0 540 06329 0	☐ 0 540 06327 4	☐ 0 540 06328 2	➤ ☐
	Quantity @ £14.99 each	Quantity @ £9.99 each	Quantity @ £5.99 each	£ Total
LANCASHIRE	☐ 0 540 06440 8	☐ 0 540 06441 6	☐ 0 540 06443 2	➤ ☐
STAFFORDSHIRE	☐ 0 540 07549 3	☐ 0 540 07550 7	☐ 0 540 07551 5	➤ ☐

BLACK AND WHITE REGIONAL ATLASES

	HARDBACK	SOFTBACK	POCKET	£ Total
	Quantity @ £10.99 each			
WARWICKSHIRE	☐ 0 540 05642 1	—	—	➤ ☐
	Quantity @ £12.99 each	Quantity @ £9.99 each	Quantity @ £4.99 each	Total
BRISTOL AND AVON	☐ 0 540 06140 9	☐ 0 540 06141 7	☐ 0 540 06142 5	➤ ☐
CARDIFF, SWANSEA & GLAMORGAN	☐ 0 540 06186 7	☐ 0 540 06187 5	☐ 0 540 06207 3	➤ ☐
EDINBURGH & East Central Scotland	☐ 0 540 06180 8	☐ 0 540 06181 6	☐ 0 540 06182 4	➤ ☐
EAST ESSEX	☐ 0 540 05848 3	☐ 0 540 05866 1	☐ 0 540 05850 5	➤ ☐
WEST ESSEX	☐ 0 540 05849 1	☐ 0 540 05867 X	☐ 0 540 05851 3	➤ ☐
NOTTINGHAMSHIRE	—	☐ 0 540 05859 9	☐ 0 540 05860 2	➤ ☐
	Quantity @ £12.99 each	Quantity @ £9.99 each	Quantity @ £5.99 each	£ Total
GLASGOW & West Central Scotland	☐ 0 540 06183 2	☐ 0 540 06184 0	☐ 0 540 06185 9	➤ ☐

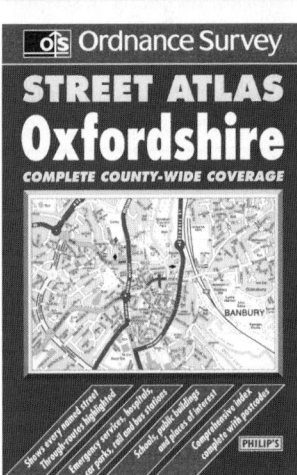

Post to: Philip's Direct, 27 Sanders Road, Wellingborough, Northants NN8 4NL

◆ Free postage and packing

◆ All available titles will normally be dispatched within 5 working days of receipt of order but please allow up to 28 days for delivery

☐ Please tick this box if you do not wish your name to be used by other carefully selected organisations that may wish to send you information about other products and services

Registered Office: 25 Victoria Street, London SW1H 0EX

Registered in England number: 3396524

I enclose a cheque / postal order, for a **total** of ☐ made payable to *Reed Book Services*, or please debit my

☐ Access ☐ American Express ☐ Visa ☐ Diners

account by ☐

Account no
☐☐☐☐ ☐☐☐☐ ☐☐☐☐ ☐☐☐☐

Expiry date ☐☐ ☐☐

Signature..

Name..

Address..

....

....

....POSTCODE